THE EDITORS

LeRoy P. Graf and Ralph W. Haskins are professors of history at The University of Tennessee.

THE PAPERS OF
Andrew Johnson

Sponsored by

The University of Tennessee

The National Historical Publications and Records Commission

The Tennessee Historical Commission

An engraving of Andrew Johnson during the early war years,
by B. B. Russell & Co., Boston.
Courtesy Library of Congress.

THE PAPERS OF
Andrew Johnson

Volume 5, 1861-1862

EDITORS

LEROY P. GRAF AND RALPH W. HASKINS

ASSOCIATE EDITOR, PATRICIA P. CLARK

1979

THE UNIVERSITY OF TENNESSEE PRESS
KNOXVILLE

Clothbound editions of University of Tennessee Press books
are printed on paper designed for an effective life of
at least 300 years, and binding materials are
chosen for strength and durability.

Library of Congress Cataloging in Publication Data (Revised)

Johnson, Andrew, Pres. United States, 1808-1875.
  The papers of Andrew Johnson.
  Includes bibliographical references and index.
  CONTENTS: v. 1. 1822-1851.—v.2. 1852-1857.—
v. 3. 1858-1860. [etc.]
  1. United States—Politics and government—1849-
1877—Sources. 2. Johnson, Andrew, Pres. U.S., 1808-
1875. 3. Presidents—United States—Correspondence.
I. Graf, LeRoy P. and Haskins, Ralph W., eds.
E415.6.J65 1967   973.8'1'0924 [B] 67-25733
ISBN 0-87049-273-x

Contents

1861

1862

Illustrations

Introduction

ANDREW JOHNSON: TRIBULATIONS OF A SOUTHERN UNIONIST, 1861-1862

During the dark winter of 1862, shortly after the victories at Henry and Donelson had cast a glow upon the Tennessee horizon, a friend wrote to Andrew Johnson inquiring whether "you spend your Sundays still in reading the lamentations of Job" and reminding him that "the war is not over yet."[1] The Johnson papers do not disclose the senator's reaction. Yet for one given to occasional sabbath-day reflections on the futility of life and the immanence of death,[2] recourse to Job would hardly have been surprising. Contrary to his hopes and expectations, the nation stood dissevered, caught up in the maelstrom of war; notwithstanding his oft-expressed conviction that the Volunteer State would stand steadfast as a rock, she had espoused the Confederate cause; despite his most frenetic efforts, succor for East Tennessee, his "adopted home," was not forthcoming. Save for Union successes in certain areas of the western theatre, the past was disheartening, the future uncertain. Indeed the manifold challenges of these twelve months from September, 1861, through August, 1862—a period marked by the conclusion of his Senate service, his assumption of the military governorship, and his experience with its multifarious problems—held a constant reminder that the struggle was not yet over. On the contrary, it was merely joined in dead earnest.

In the course of an often frustrating autumn, Johnson occupied himself with the same round of activities begun during the summer of 1861. Touring portions of Kentucky and Ohio, he undertook a small-scale "swing around the circle"—a technique which he would later essay in the national arena—delivering an occasional speech, conferring with state and local leaders, agitating schemes for the prosecution of the war. He played a significant role as morale-builder, comforting Tennessee refugees, stiffening the spines of Kentucky unionists, and alerting Ohioans against Confederate invasion. For this senator-in-exile, East Tennessee had long since become an emotion, its cause the epitome of the Union cause. Hence he did his utmost to redeem the homeland: trying to expedite Federal aid, encouraging plans for the raising of troops and the construction of military railroads, and—furious at what he considered an intolerable delay—joining briefly in November the Union columns inching south.

1. Letter from William S. Speer, February 19, [1862].
2. See Letter to Blackston McDannel, January 10, 1847, *Johnson Papers*, I, 368-70, and Johnson on Death, June 29, 1873, Johnson Papers, LC.

The surviving records do not indicate the number of speeches he made or all the locations at which he spoke. "Schedules," as announced in the press, were not always kept; nor were speeches generally reported in detail. Yet an examination of the addresses at Cincinnati in late August,[3] at Newport in early September, and at Columbus a month later, suggests that the content was basically the same: defense of the Union and arraignment of the "aristocratic" Confederacy; the necessity for unbending allegiance to the flag; the betrayal of Tennessee's loyal people by "King" Harris and his cohorts; and, withal, tales of treason and oppression most foul.

Kentucky, a significant military and ideological salient, had earlier proclaimed neutrality, solemnly warning the belligerents not to set foot on her "sacred soil." In late summer the state clung to a precarious "neutrality"; Johnson's campaign, like Lincoln's own policy, was designed to counter the influence of "the white flag or *Breech Clout* party"[4] and grapple Kentucky to the Union. Speaking at Newport the senator insisted that this was not Lincoln's war but the outcome of a southern conspiracy. Secession and its symbols took on biblical raiment: an insidious process originating in the garden of Eden "under the wiles of the arch serpent" had culminated in the birth of the Confederacy and Alabama's adoption of a rattlesnake flag. He decried compromise—a road open but not taken, inasmuch as Jefferson Davis and the "bogus southern aristocracy," who "could not brook the elevation of a man to the Presidential Chair because he rose from the ranks of the people," were unwilling to await redress at the polls.[5]

At Columbus the line of argument followed rather closely that laid down in his most recent Senate address;[6] however, this speech also contained odds and ends taken from his various public statements since December, 1860. Party strife heretofore, he declared, had been designed to promote, not destroy, the Union. Why inquire about political affiliations now? Again he traversed the labyrinth of conspiracy, recalling not only Jackson's thesis that nullification was a pretext for disunion but also his prophecy that slavery would provide the next excuse, and picturing in appropriate mortuary detail the Old Hero's reaction to the present crisis. Paying his respects to extremism North and South, he delighted his listeners with a syllogism: "an abolitionist is a disunionist; a disunionist is a secessionist; therefore, a secessionist is an abolitionist." For the edification of this particular audience Johnson delivered a brief essay on economics, denying that cotton was king and asserting that midwesterners could do without southern cotton much easier than southerners

3. See Speech at Cincinnati, August 31, 1861, *Johnson Papers*, IV, 700-705.
4. Letter from Richard Apperson, September 2, 1861.
5. Speech at Newport, Kentucky, September 2, 1861.
6. See Speech in Support of Presidential War Program, July 27, 1861, *Johnson Papers*, IV, 606-49.

could dispense with midwestern bread and meat. Once again he recited, this time in mournful numbers, the iniquities visited upon East Tennessee.[7]

The historian reads these declarations with due skepticism. The allegations of long-standing conspiracy, the ready assessment of responsibility for the abortion of compromise and the initiation of war, the facile equation of abolitionist with disunionist, are obvious oversimplifications. But which is more significant: historical hindsight or the views of contemporaries, translated into action? It is well to remember that such generalizations represent "the truth" as set forth by a fiery partisan. Nor can the historican discount the atmosphere of the day, heavy laden with plot and counterplot, cumbered with the haze of the battle between right and wrong. The northern public was victory-starved, standing desperately in need of any consolation which a staunch southern defender of the Union could offer, and quite receptive to the exaggerations of a propagandist.

For the senator himself, the tour must have provided some solace during these months of disappointment. It must have recalled memories of the Tennessee hustings—overflowing and volatile crowds, occasional exchanges with the audience, the warm greetings of old friends, and the making of new ones. In times past Andrew Johnson of "the deep, dark *Webster-like* orbs" had exorcised (or exercised) the demons of Whiggery; now, in the high drama of an American tragedy, what was more logical (or titillating) than bludgeoning the devils of disunion? And, in retrospect, how sharp the contrast between Senator Johnson's successful foray into Ohio during this fall of 1861 and President Johnson's disastrous invasion exactly five years later! Seen in a somewhat different way, these patriotic effusions in Kentucky and Ohio, like the public appearances elsewhere during his exile, represented a catharsis. While students of our own turbulent century have given much attention to the psychology of the displaced, the Civil War itself provides a fascinating realm for similar speculation. Indubitably figures like Andrew Johnson and Parson Brownlow suffered from the refugee syndrome—suffered, yes, but at the same time enjoyed, a certain gratifying martyrdom.

But there was something else that this campaign recalled to Johnson, something associated with his highest ambition. It is scarcely conceivable that the Tennessean, in thus advancing the Union cause, was unmindful of his own. Although the evidence remains sketchy, it would seem that this professional plebeian, leveller and sworn enemy of "the interests," advocate of the "white basis" and champion of the Homestead, had for some time enjoyed a following in the egalitarian Northwest.[8] His free-land panacea had become a part of the Republican program, his fight

7. Speech at Columbus, October 4, 1861.
8. See Patrick Riddleberger, *George Washington Julian, Radical Republican: A Study in Nineteenth-Century Politics and Reform* ([Indianapolis], 1966), 76-77.

for the Union their fight. Leaving aside the Wades and the Julians, it is not illogical to believe that for numerous northern Democrats turned Republican, a loyal southerner who demanded the relentless prosecution of the war and at the same time asserted the old democratic values offered considerable attraction. In this wise the swing 'round the circle in 1861 was part of a continuing climb toward the highest rung on Jacob's ladder.

Whatever the implications for the future, the efforts of Johnson and others to prosecute the border war fell short. In September Kentucky abandoned its neutralist stance and adhered to the Union; subsequently Federal forces entered the state. Yet during the fall and winter the situation deteriorated, not only for the area in general but for Johnson's family in particular. Confederate detachments invested parts of East Tennessee and secessionists scoured the countryside for recalcitrant unionists; meanwhile such officers as Sherman, Thomas, and Buell reiterated their desire, but pleaded their inability, to mount effective action. Johnson, in southern Kentucky with Thomas, is said to have become so intemperate after the failure to advance that the latter nearly ordered his arrest; and in mid-November General Albin Schoepf complained that the senator had "made himself very troublesome . . . using language calculated to incite the men and officers of my command to insubordination."[9] These difficulties with the generals foreshadowed one of Johnson's most perplexing problems as military governor.

The reins of Confederate control in East Tennessee, at first loosely drawn, were gradually tightened, and secessionist wrath boiled over after the sensational railroad "bridge-burning" engineered by loyalists on the night of November 7. In the weeks which followed, the senator's correspondents painted a picture of trial and tribulation "never witnessed in any civilised country": arrest and punishment upon the slightest suspicion, old men undergoing drumhead court for the mere expression of opinion, unionists "Striped of evry thing, they and their familis turned out upon the charities of *Rebel Devils*," the land ground under the "*Iron heel* of despotism."[10] It was a time to flee, to go into hiding, as hundreds streamed across the Kentucky border and others took to the mountains. The iron heel rested somewhat less heavily upon the Johnsons. In January Eliza and her sons were served with a writ of attachment and the family home eventually became a rebel hospital. Although Robert made his way to Kentucky, Charles came in "out of the Bresh" and took the Confederate oath of allegiance, while son-in-law David Patterson, twice arrested and released, negotiated an understanding which allowed him to retain his circuit judgeship under the charities

9. McKinney, *Education in Violence*, 118; Harry Williams, "Andrew Johnson as a Member of the Committee on the Conduct of the War," ETHS *Publications*, No. 12 (1940), 73n.

10. Letter from Robert L. Stanford, December 31, 1861.

of the rebel devils. In January Andrew Johnson himself officially became "an Alien Enemy" of the South.[11]

Amid such trying circumstances he repaired to Washington in December for the second session of the Thirty-Seventh Congress. His own state of mind comported well with the pall of gloom which hung over the capital and the pall of smoke which pervaded the Senate chamber.[12] To a public impatient for a major victory, the Union military achievements during the nearly nine months since Sumter appeared insignificant; in fact, the most recent memories were of the "disasters" at Bull Run and Ball's Bluff. While George B. McClellan trained and paraded a splendid aggregation of more than 100,000 men near Washington, the enemy blockaded the Potomac and interrupted the communications line of the Baltimore and Ohio Railroad to the west. The capital thus stood in a virtual state of siege, a circumstance exceedingly mortifying to the friends of the Union—"that disgrace to the nation," Johnson called it in February.[13] Neither Henry Halleck, commanding in the West with headquarters at St. Louis, nor Don Carlos Buell, whose Army of the Ohio was charged with the relief of East Tennessee, could muster a major offensive. "Tardy George" and his associates had seemingly gotten the slows.

In turn, the military stalemate worsened factionalism in the civil sphere. The Republican party was gripped by bitter strife between administration supporters and the "Radicals," men like Thaddeus Stevens, George Julian, Charles Sumner, Benjamin F. Wade, and Zachariah Chandler. Already discussing among themselves the question of emancipation, the Radicals were disappointed that Lincoln's primary objective was the preservation of the Union. Their irritation increased as they observed that the President had filled certain leading military posts with Democratic officers; they were aghast at the cloak of secrecy which commanders drew around their plans. What lay behind all this masterly inactivity? Was it merely incompetence, or something more sinister? Were McClellan and other army Democrats sympathetic to the Confederate cause? The search for answers to such intriguing questions brought the creation on December 19 of the Joint Committee on the Conduct of the War. Designed ostensibly as an investigative agency, it was in reality much more: a meddling, atrocity-collecting, propaganda-disseminating body which furthered the intentions of the Radical wing of the party.

That Andrew Johnson was appointed to the committee undoubtedly

11. Writ of Attachment, January 18, 1862; Letter from Michael L. Patterson, January 31, 1862.

12. The smoke came from the operation of the army bakeries in the basement. Solomon Foot of Vermont, speaking on February 3, deplored the fact that "the most costly and expensive building upon the American continent" had been "converted into a smoke-house and a bakery." *Cong. Globe*, 37 Cong., 2 Sess., 608.

13. *Report of the Joint Committee on the Conduct of the War, Senate Report* No. 108, 37 Cong., 3 Sess., I, 84.

reflected his growing prestige in northern circles. His courageous Union speech in December, 1860, had attracted some attention, while his more militant addresses of February and March had received widespread acclaim.[14] In July he had endorsed the presidential war program; and his various activities for the cause, as well as his earlier crusade for the Homestead, made him acceptable to Republican Radicals. Perhaps Ben Wade recalled the previous February, when this "lifelong Democrat" had identified the two as allies in defense of the Union and the Constitution.[15] Although Wade and Chandler dominated the proceedings, Johnson was hardly a passive observer. On the contrary, writes the historian of the Committee, he was the only Democrat who played a significant role during its existence.[16]

Impatient with the situation in the Kentucky-Tennessee area and hoping to use his membership as a lever to secure military relief for East Tennessee, he must have listened with keen interest to the interrogations concerning the impasse in the East. Not infrequently his own questions became acute observations. "Does not inactivity—remaining in quarters—have a tendency to demoralize troops?" And at another time, with Clausewitzian perception, he queried: "There is a political element connected with this war which must not be overlooked?"[17] In late December he turned grand strategist. Let a strong defensive force be retained around Washington and the naval blockade made complete from Baltimore to Galveston. Two armies would assault the Confederates at Manassas, while a third executed a movement from the coast, thus cutting off Richmond's railway connections with North Carolina. Finally, a fourth army would sweep through Kentucky and Tennessee with the objective of seizing parts of "that great railroad" from Richmond to Little Rock.[18] Plainly enough, he considered the Kentucky-Tennessee invasion critical; it would take the rebellion in the rear, and—properly coordinated with the other coils of the Andrew Johnson anaconda— "substantially bag the whole Confederacy."[19]

Nor did Johnson's connection with the committee end when he left the Senate: we are told that in March, 1863, as the members prepared their final report on McClellan's tenure with the Army of the Potomac, the military governor, then in the capital on official business, came to the committee rooms to lend his aid.[20] All in all, this was a brief and not

14. For a perspective on the relative impact of these speeches, see *Johnson Papers*, IV, xxvi-xxxii.

15. Speech on the Seceding States, February 5-6, 1861, *ibid.*, 239-40.

16. Williams, "Johnson as a Member of the Committee," 16, and *Lincoln and the Radicals* (Madison, 1941), 65. It should be pointed out that the Johnson papers provide no evidence of the senator's role.

17. *Report of the Joint Committee*, I, 226, 142.

18. *Ibid.*, 125.

19. *Ibid.*, 213.

20. Williams, "Johnson as a Member of the Committee," 80.

unpleasant association with the "Jacobins"; its implications are some-what more obscure. Doubtless it enhanced Johnson's standing among leading Union politicians; perhaps it played a role in his vice-presidential selection; unquestionably it encouraged Wade and his colleagues sub-sequently to believe that Lincoln's successor would follow a vindictive line toward the defeated South. The historian cannot but draw a parallel between Andrew Johnson's service with the Joint Committee on the Conduct of the War, an organization which bearded and harassed Lin-coln, and his own confrontation with the Joint Committee on Recon-struction, a body which dealt devastating blows at his own policies.

Johnson's participation in regular Senate business during these re-maining months was largely routine. Unsuccessful in obtaining approval for military railroads in portions of Kentucky, Tennessee, and North Carolina, he sponsored a resolution which provided for a reading of Washington's Farewell Address before a joint session on February 22. But his principal contribution came in January, during the protracted debate over the expulsion of Bright of Indiana. Emphasizing still further his thorough commitment to coercion, this last major disquisition in the Senate contained nothing novel. Mainly a withering denunciation of the South's adamant stand against compromise, it concluded with a thun-dering demand for the extirpation of the rebellion and its leaders. "You have got to subdue them; you have got to conquer them; and nothing but the sacrifice of life and blood will do it."[21] Perhaps the bitterness in Johnson's arraignment of Bright stemmed from his own personal feel-ings of anxiety and frustration. Nor is it impossible that this speech, affording the spectacle of a Democrat arrayed against a former party associate and coming only a month before his appointment as military governor, may have served as further reminder to Lincoln of a certain compatibility in war aims.

Notwithstanding Johnson's pessimism, conditions in the border re-gion were changing even before Zollicoffer's defeat at Mill Springs on January 19 augured better things for East Tennessee; and the victories at Henry and Donelson in February not only appeared to turn the tide in favor of the Union, but, of even greater import to the senator, held out the early prospect of restoring Federal authority in his home state. In late February, as Buell's army moved south from Bowling Green toward Nashville, rumor began to circulate that Andrew Johnson would be dispatched to Tennessee to "assist in organizing a Provisional Govern-ment."[22] The man who had given the rebels hell on the rostrum would shortly be in a position to "give 'em hell" as military governor.

Except for one bittersweet month in 1875, the winter of 1862 marked the close of Johnson's service as senator; it provides, therefore, an op-

21. Speech on Expulsion of Senator Bright, January 31, 1862.
22. Cincinnati *Enquirer*, February 20, 1862.

portunity to view that tenure in retrospect. That he contributed no legislation of major significance is obvious: his Homestead, vetoed by a Democratic President, was taken over by the Republicans; and none of the "andyjohnsonisms"—constitutional amendments designed to further the democratic process—received serious consideration. A watchdog of the treasury he remained, but the extraordinary expenditures associated with the crisis doomed these efforts to failure. Perhaps Johnson's greatest achievement as senator lay in the principles he *advocated*: the extension of democracy and the preservation of the Union.

Beyond his response to the extraordinary challenges of the day, those characteristics which had long ago stamped his public life remained unchanged. Several years later his old antagonist Jefferson Davis presented a shrewd assessment of the man with whom he had served in both House and Senate. Calling Johnson "an immense worker and student, but always in the practicalities of life; little in the graces of literature," Davis added that his habits were not only "marked by temperance, industry, courage and unswerving perseverance," but also by "inveterate prejudices or preconceptions." Although other senators were of the people by birth, the Tennessean "remained so by conviction"; his "was the pride of having no pride."[23] Anent Johnson's speaking, a congressman observed that "his elocution was more forcible than fine— more discursive than elegant."[24] These were salient traits of the man who left Washington early in March "to exchange the soft cushioned seat in the Senate for the jolting saddle of the war horse."[25]

What shall we say of his selection to the new assignment? Was he, as many of his contemporaries and most of his biographers would have us believe, the right man in the right place, a choice so logical as to be a foregone conclusion? What considerations moved Lincoln in creating this precedent-setting military governorship? And what qualifications did Johnson bring to his new assignment? If one were to judge by press comment alone, contemporaries accepted the choice without cavil. Apparently caught up in the wave of acclaim for the Tennessean, editors tended to be perfunctory and even laudatory, hailing his courage and devotion to his state, his experience as governor, and his personal fitness for the office.[26] Nor did the Senate itself debate the matter; instead, it merely confirmed Johnson as brigadier without reference to the military governorship.[27] All this, reported John Forney in the Philadelphia *Press*, "has been done by the Government, without the aid of Congress. And it is a significant evidence of the justice and expediency of this policy

23. John J. Craven, *Prison Life of Jefferson Davis* (New York, 1905), 262-64.
24. Samuel S. Cox, *Three Decades of Federal Legislation* (Providence, 1888), 71.
25. Letter from William Patton, March 4, 1862.
26. Typical comments appeared in the Washington *National Intelligencer*, March 4; Cleveland *Plain Dealer* and Philadelphia *Bulletin*, March 5; and the New York *Times* and Louisville *Journal*, March 6, 1862.
27. *Sen. Ex. Journal*, XII (1861-62), 147-48.

that no portion of the Representatives and Senators . . . are found to object to it."[28] Forney oversimplified the case. In reality, Congress was just beginning to consider this facet of the reconstruction process: the issue of provisional governments was already under discussion and several bills were pending; debate over the military governorship would come later.

Meanwhile, others associated with "the Government" were exploring some of the complexities accompanying the transition from military to civil authority. Although they addressed themselves specifically to the Tennessee situation, their arguments had implications for the larger problem of military government. General William Nelson, contending that a Union party existed throughout the state, urged that its leaders be allowed to take the initiative in establishing a provisional government and nominating their own officers. The President should not send a governor: "If Andy Johnson comes here clothed with authority, he will be a Govenor nominated at Washington and not at Nashville, and it will greatly retard the object in view." He added that "the time for talking *has just arrived* in Tennessee. Let the politicians have their way a little while . . . and when they do take a definite direction, it can be easily controlled . . . and we will have Tennessee back into the Union."[29] Nelson's apprehensions were shared by Buell, who wrote McClellan on March 6 that a provisional government for the state "would be injudicious at this time" and "may not be necessary at all."[30]

Undersecretary of War Thomas A. Scott, then in Nashville, also entertained reservations, but dealt more directly with the choice of Andrew Johnson as governor. Inasmuch as Tennessee was the first state to be reorganized, great care should be used, for "the people of the South . . . are very sensitive upon the subject of state rights." Noting that the senator was "a decided out and out Union man . . . opposed to everything concerning the Southern Confederacy," Scott remarked that a governor thus rigid in stance would be likely to provide the rebels with a convenient tyrant and to alienate from the Union cause many people of moderate view. In the past Johnson had controlled "a large share of the masses of Tennessee"; but many leading representatives of these same masses were now his enemies. Inasmuch as Buell was "managing matters with great prudence," there should be no hurry in appointing a military governor. Perhaps reflecting the preferences of Nashville unionists, he suggested former governor William B. Campbell; but in any case, neither Andrew Johnson nor any other national figure should be chosen, for "it would only serve to draw party lines and create fresh trouble."[31] Undoubtedly the generals were sensitive in matters of authority and would have

28. Quoted in Washington *National Intelligencer*, March 8, 1862.
29. William Nelson to Garrett Davis, March 5, 1862, Lincoln Papers, LC.
30. Quoted in Maslowski, *"Treason Must Be Made Odious,"* 78.
31. Thomas A. Scott to Edwin M. Stanton, March 3, 1862, Stanton Papers, LC.

carried a brief against any governor, let alone an Andrew Johnson with his established reputation as a troublemaker. Nonetheless, in the light of the next three years, Nelson and Scott appear as major prophets.

The objections seem to have come from Nashville rather than Washington, for the Lincoln papers are silent on the subject. Yet some considerations which faced the President are readily discernible. Since this was a Republican administration, why not take the party line? Why choose a Democrat over such Whigs as Campbell, Emerson Etheridge, or Horace Maynard? After all, Andrew Johnson, the President's own patronage referee, had set an example by filling state offices with Democrats rather than Whigs.[32] Yet it does not follow that the astute chief executive would necessarily look to his own party. Why not, instead, select the best man irrespective of political affiliation—especially one who, as James G. Blaine wrote later, "possessed the unbounding confidence of Mr. Lincoln."[33] Spread out before the President's eyes was Johnson's record: his admirable courage during the secession winter, his unceasing battle for the Union, his support of administration war policies. Certainly no Tennessean rivaled him in prestige; indeed he had attained national stature and was a key figure in Lincoln's border-state policies. That the two men shared the same misconceptions about the strength of southern unionism was undeniable. Moreover, the Republicans were engaged in a process of political syncretism, conferring upon themselves and their adherents the patriotic label of "the Union party." In these circumstances the selection of a War Democrat was logic itself. And not the least important consideration was his two terms as civil governor.

But there may have been another contingency less obvious, so much so that it can be offered here only as speculation. Can it be possible that Andrew Johnson *was* too prominent–not merely in Tennessee, as Scott contended, but in quite another and larger sense? Here was a Democrat sitting as a member of the Committee on the Conduct of the War, mingling with Republican Radicals. Here was a gadfly, rapidly becoming a nuisance with his criticism of the military and his importunities for East Tennessee. Here was a grass-roots politician who might well become an opposing candidate in 1864. Who knew how much inter-party support he would attract? Given these premises, why not accomplish two ends: send the right man to Tennessee and get him out of Washington? Such a move would put Johnson in his place. Yet this hypothesis, as yet unsubstantiated by evidence, may attribute to Lincoln a Machiavellianism unwarranted in the particular case.[34]

32. See J. Milton Henry, "The Revolution in Tennessee, February, 1861, to June, 1861," *Tenn. Hist. Quar.*, XVIII (1959), 109-14.

33. James G. Blaine, *Twenty Years of Congress* (2 vols., Norwich, Conn., 1884-86), I, 446.

The appointee brought to the new post certain characteristics which constituted both strengths and weaknesses. One was his unquestioned patriotism. In the vernacular of the day, he was a flaming unionist, tested and annealed in the crucible—hardened not only by the disruption of the nation but also by his own family experiences. The great crisis demanded leadership which would deal sternly with the rebellion; and Andrew Johnson, both in the Senate and out of it, had a reputation for a kind of old testament rectitude and judgment, an image which strongly reinforced northern confidence in him. To those who believed that treason must be crushed out and traitors punished, he stood as an avenging angel of retribution.

Enhancing his attractiveness in certain northern circles was a history of incessant strife against "the interests" and an abiding faith in "the people." His relationship with the Middle Tennessee Democracy of the Polks and the Browns, the Harrises and the Ewings, had never been close; now this clique had "sold out" the state, just as, in popular fancy above the Mason and Dixon line, "the chivalry" had disrupted the great American essay in freedom. Now the bottom rail was on top and the aristocracy was to receive its comeuppance. A Carolinian, who had known the youthful Andy Johnson of Raleigh days, perceived in the appointment a certain historical irony: "Did my old Grandfather when he sent his Coachman to whip him & his cousins, altogether known as 'Jesse Johnson's boys,' back to their cabin because they had a fancy to run naked on the road, ever think he would reach such a height as that? So we go."[35] On the other hand, Johnson enjoyed much popularity with the Tennessee rank and file who, according to contemporary folklore, were unionists through and through—an illusion in which many northerners, from Lincoln and Seward down, were fond of indulging themselves. Yet those things which made Johnson a driving force for unionism and democracy were also likely to prove a weakness in that they alienated people of middling view irrespective of economic and social status—men who had been reluctant secessionists and were now wavering in the face of altered circumstances. Anathemas pronounced upon traitors, thunderbolts hurled in the Senate or on the stump, did not necessarily qualify him for the intricacies of a position virtually without precedent in American history. Quite the contrary, they seemed rather to foreshadow a despotism.

Moreover, to an assignment which called for firmness tempered with

34. An interpretation advanced by Dr. William T. M. Riches, Ulster College, Northern Ireland, as an outgrowth of his research for The Commoners: Andrew Johnson and Abraham Lincoln to 1861 (Ph.D. dissertation, University of Tennessee, 1976).

35. Diary of Catherine Ann Edmondston, March 23, 1862, North Carolina Department of Cultural Resources, Division of Archives and History, Raleigh.

diplomacy, justice commingled with mercy, Johnson carried a number of unpromising personal traits. Intolerant of the views of others, he tended to translate disagreement into error. His own inspiring ascent in the political sphere doubtless strengthened a conviction that *his* principles were the *right* principles. Fundamentally, too, he was a lone wolf, a maverick who had strained mightily against the Democratic party harness and would view with exasperation the Byzantine maze of wartime organization. Perhaps as a reflection of his basic insecurity, of forever being on the defensive, he had great difficulty working with his peers. A politician with few intimates, Johnson displayed a rugged individualism which deprived him of much advice from which he might have profited. "Of the people" not only by birth but by principle, he displayed throughout his life a proclivity for drawing class lines, a tendency which became all too obvious during the military governorship. How could this "man of violent passions"[36] quell the raging conflict, bind up Tennessee's wounds?

History retains a grim stereotype of the Greeneville tailor, an image fashioned in his own day and by no means discarded by twentieth century interpreters. Such views were largely influenced by the ordeal of war and Reconstruction, but they were also shaped by internecine strife in antebellum Tennessee. To Oliver P. Temple, an old Whig rival writing near the turn of the century, Johnson's outstanding characteristic was a lust for power: "In all the wide universe, he worshipped no deity but that of ambition—the ambition to rise to become great, to have his name sounded abroad, and to bestride the world." The Johnson of *Notable Men* cherished hatreds: "Toward his enemies he was implacable and unforgiving."[37] That the Temple animus continues is demonstrated by a modern study of military reconstruction in Nashville. "What was needed," the author observes, "was a good deal of give and take and a deep understanding of and sympathy for humanity. Johnson was incapable of giving and loving. He could only take and detest."[38]

Stereotypes are amalgams of truth and falsehood, the one sometimes virtually indistinguishable from the other. The sharply etched portrait of a grim presence, ambitious, violent, unforgiving, is overdrawn; some of its lines need softening. That the Plebeian was inordinately ambitious is beyond cavil; that he could "take and detest" seems undeniable. One may agree that there was about him a vindictiveness which often went beyond reason; his treatment of the dissident Nashville divines and his imprisonment of A. O. P. Nicholson, a longtime friend and colleague, offer cases in point. Yet a closer examination of Johnson's career suggests that he was neither implacable and unforgiving nor incapable of giving and

36. Alexander McClure, *Recollections of Half a Century* (Salem, Mass., 1902), 300.
37. Temple, *Notable Men*, 456, 466.
38. Maslowski, *"Treason Must Be Made Odious,"* 55.

loving. Leaving aside his obvious devotion to his family, one detects in him a strong sense of leniency and a lifelong tendency to champion the underdog. During the military governorship these qualities were reflected in his concern for soldiers who had gone into the Confederate army and were now incarcerated in various Lincoln bastiles; their letters undoubtedly influenced his romantic view that the average Tennessean was a unionist and that those who wore the butternut had been inveigled or even coerced into the rebel ranks by wealthy and influential secessionists. Moreover, Johnson was always vulnerable to the feminine sex and particularly to the pleas of women in distress. Why, even those secesh ladies who insulted the Federal soldiery possessed the right instincts—but they had been seduced and corrupted by rebel parsons! He was highly susceptible to flattery, not only from the ladies but also from representatives of the upper class. A twentieth-century theorist views political ambition as "characterized by an intense and ungratified craving for deference."[39] Interpreted in this way the mechanic, denied a place among the aristocrats, not only hated, but likewise envied and even deferred to, that aristocracy. Such human frailties would appear to give the lie to the image of a despot without mercy; but again, seen from a purely objective point of view, they could be considered handicaps. It was a mixed cargo of assets and liabilities that Johnson carried back to Tennessee.

The governor reached the Kentucky shore on March 10, enroute to Nashville. "He left Tennessee a fugitive," remarked the Louisville *Journal*; "he returns in the pride of power."[40] It was not, however, a return attended with pomp and ceremony, for rumors of plots to kidnap or assassinate him were circulating. Rebel soldiers, it was said, had vowed to take his life; and, warned by friends and relatives concerned for his safety, he was further counselled by Buell "to enter without any display."[41] A telegrapher recalled Johnson's progress from Kentucky south on March 12: a special train constructed out of "the *debris* remaining at Bowling Green"; an engine "patched up from odds and ends," looking like "a snorting wreck on wheels"; and "a boxcar, in which sat the Hon. Andrew Johnson, Military Governor of Tennessee." There were noticeable difficulties in locomotion. "On a level track the engine was a success, but whenever an up grade was struck, every body but the Honorable Andrew got out and footed it, while the engine made running jumps to reach the top." When the party reached Nashville late that night, only one light was visible.[42] If this journey under wartime exigencies offered a

---

39. See Harold Lasswell, *Power and Personality* (New York, 1948), 38.
40. Louisville *Journal*, March 6, 1862.
41. "M. C." to "Dear Nan," March 24, 1862, Johnson Papers, LC; Letter from Don Carlos Buell, March 11, 1862.
42. William R. Plum, *The Military Telegraph during the War* (2 vols., Chicago, 1882), I, 204.

scenario which smacked of low-comedy burlesque, it was not devoid of symbols and portents: a patched-up engine and a makeshift government, trouble on the upgrade and multiplying challenges for the governor, a near stygian darkness and an opaque future.

The Nashville to which Johnson returned presented a striking contrast to the city he had quitted at the close of his civil governorship in 1857. A peacetime prosperity based upon its advantageous location, its importance as an agricultural market and commercial entrepôt, and its burgeoning industrial development, had been succeeded by a wartime boom in the manufacture of ordnance, munitions, and supplies. Earlier this "Athens of the South" had nourished hopes of becoming the permanent capital of the Confederacy; now its strategic location, together with its multifarious economic activities, made it a prime military objective. Singularly enough, Governor Harris and his advisors had neglected the city's defenses, relying largely upon Forts Henry and Donelson, hastily constructed bastions on the Tennessee and Cumberland rivers near the Kentucky line. Grant's land and water campaign, launched against the forts in early February, provoked a war of nerves in the capital. Henry fell on February 6 and ten days later, on "black Sunday," Nashvillians learned of the loss of Donelson; soon afterward, the harsh realities of the situation were brought home by the arrival of dejected Confederate troops retreating south. Shortly it became known that the military authorities, considering the city's position untenable, had decided to abandon it. Bull-Run time had come, and a great panic ensued. The Army of Tennessee retired to Murfreesboro and then toward Corinth, Mississippi, but not before its officers had destroyed the railroad and suspension bridges across the Cumberland—the latter structure "a glory in architecture and public estimation."[43] Governor Harris, taking with him the state archives and treasury, lost no time in removing to Memphis, the new capital of Confederate Tennessee; at his order the General Assembly abruptly adjourned and "advanced" in the same direction; and the citizenry, dreading "the Hessians," prepared to flee for points south and west. A southern woman remembered streets "filled with carriages, horses, buggies, wagons, drags, carts, everything which could carry a human being from the doomed city. Men, women, and children, the rich, the poor, white and black, mingled in one struggling mass."[44] For those, who stayed behind, the doomed city retained some compelling attractions, especially when it developed that a part of the huge store of supplies assembled for the Confederate army was to be abandoned. Now followed a stampede on the commissary, with people staggering under quantities of pork and bacon, while rowdies heaved barrels of flour and

43. Fitch, *Annals*, 630.
44. *The Private War of Lizzie Hardin*, C. Glenn Clift, ed. (Frankfort, Ky., 1963), 33.

meat into the river. Surrendering on February 25, Nashville became the first major Confederate city to fall to Union arms.[45]

During the spring great parts of Middle and West Tennessee were taken by the Federals as the "anaconda" scheme, tentative and indistinct during the earlier months of the conflict, now began to be implemented. As the Confederates abandoned their former line of defense in southern Kentucky, Union forces moved up the Tennessee toward the general region of Pittsburgh Landing and Corinth, menacing the Memphis-Chattanooga railway line. The sanguinary battle of Shiloh, fought April 6-7, was an important strategic victory for the North in that the Confederates had failed to prevent a concentration of Union forces. Meanwhile the movement of Federal power down the Mississippi presaged the investment of Memphis, which was surrendered June 6. Transferring its headquarters to Chattanooga, the Harris administration now literally became a government on the move. Thus in the middle and western portions of Tennessee, Union military power held the upper hand; but the area was by no means cleared of Confederate armies—to say nothing of guerrillas, "home guards," bushwhackers, and others, who remained a constant threat.

Similarly in East Tennessee, there was not only the formal military action in the Kentucky-Tennessee border area, but also the fratricidal strife characterized by the activities of organized militia companies, home guards, and guerrillas, as well as the transgressions and reprisals to be expected in a territory predominantly unionist but with strong Confederate sentiment. The overriding reality was that here, the rebel armies were in control. In military thinking, the section in southern hands represented a potential staging area for a Confederate movement into Kentucky and the North, just as Federal possession of East Tennessee would represent a Union salient into the Confederacy. In political terms, the redemption of an important pocket of southern unionism was a major goal for the Lincoln administration; for Johnson in particular, the investment of his homeland by traitors was a wound in the heart.

Upon his arrival in Nashville the governor, accompanied by Congressmen Maynard, Etheridge, and others, was conducted to the St. Cloud Hotel, his temporary living quarters. Serenaded the next evening by a military band, he responded with an hour's speech, the principal burden of which was that he came with the sole purpose of restoring the Constitution and the laws.[46] Although the Cincinnati *Enquirer*, in re-

---

45. For discussion of the fall of Nashville, see *ibid.*, 30ff; John M. McKee, "The Evacuation of Tennessee," *Annals of the Army of Tennessee*, I (1878), 219-29, 249-69; Stanley Horn, "Nashville during the Civil War," *Tenn. Hist. Quar.*, IV (1945), 3-22; Charles F. Bryan, Jr., "Nashville Under Federal Occupation," *Civil War Times Illustrated*, XIII (1975), 4-11, 40-47.

46. Louisville *Journal*, March 18, 1862.

porting Johnson's assignment to Tennessee, had announced that "The people there are panting for freedom and resumption of their connection with the Union,"[47] it is impossible to ascertain with any accuracy the prevailing opinion in Nashville and the midstate area. Was it fundamentally loyal, with the unionists' having been overslaughed by the wealthy and influential secessionists? Or was it a nest of traitors, with unionism no more than a thin veneer? Doubtless the truth lay in delicate shadings complicated by circumstances. The incoming Federals found Nashville business establishments closed and many houses shuttered; the city, according to one of the governor's correspondents, wore the appearance "of Sabbath in cholera times"; and Maynard, writing to Stanton in late March, reported that they had "found secesh very sultry and the Union men not well assured."[48] The rebels had by no means been driven from Middle Tennessee; they had merely evacuated Nashville and retired South. The presence of major Confederate commands at no great distance, the occasional raids conducted to the outskirts of Nashville itself by the intrepid cavalrymen Morgan and Forrest, and paramilitary operations in the countryside served as a reminder that the capital was a beleaguered city—both militarily and psychologically, and it would continue so for the succeeding two and one-half years. Patently there remained an air of uncertainty about Nashville, about the middle area, and by inference, the whole state. One of Johnson's immediate tasks was to convince Middle Tennesseans that the Federal government had power to put down the rebellion and retain control.

The warmest greetings accorded the governor did not come from representatives of his old party. Obviously not all the Democracy became rebels nor did all the Whigs remain loyal; yet in the great crisis Middle and West Tennessee Democrats by the thousands had "gone South," and to those who considered southern interests best served by secession, Johnson had long since become anathema. "Embalmed in hate and canonized in scorn," the Memphis *Avalanche* had said of him in March, 1861,[49] and a year later the epitaph seemed hardly less appropriate. Rejected and reviled by former friends and associates, he found his most enthusiastic welcome tendered by the Whigs, those unclean spirits of his antebellum stump wars. This liaison with the ancient foe was not solely a product of his recent appointment; instead it represented a continuance of that revolution in sentiment which had begun with his stand for the Union in December, 1860. Applauded then by many Whigs, he had worked closely during the ensuing months with such men as T. A. R. Nelson, Horace Maynard, and Emerson Etheridge. Now William B. Campbell became a friendly counsellor and shared the speaker's podium

.47. Cincinnati *Enquirer*, February 20, 1862.
48. Letter from Rees W. Porter, March 1, 1862; Horace Maynard to Edwin M. Stanton, March 24, 1862, Lets. Recd., Sec. of War, RG107, NA.
49. Memphis *Avalanche*, March 11, 1861.

with him, while "Brave John Lellyett" received the Nashville post-mastership, and Horace Maynard was appointed state attorney-general. Perhaps the counterpoint in his romance with Tennessee Whiggery occurred in April, when a redoubtable adversary of old visited him at the capitol. The governor—whom Editor Brownlow had identified as "a mountebank," "a living mass of *undulating* filth," and "one of the 'buttenders' of society"—and the Parson—whom Congressman Johnson had denominated "a hyena," "a brute in human form," and "a worse than Tom Paine infidel"—were overcome with emotion. According to Temple, they "rushed into each other's arms and wept like women."[50] It was a touching little skit which portrayed with fidelity the otherwise incongruous sodalities spawned by this cruel war. It was likewise an episode in a troubled honeymoon which had begun during the secession winter and would end during Reconstruction.

What can be said of this *volte-face* of '61? What are the implications to be drawn from Johnson's rupture with the Democrats and liaison with the Whigs? A reexamination of the past suggests that he had ridden into higher office on the crest of Jacksonian Democracy and that, although his real strength lay with the East Tennessee Democracy, he enjoyed a considerable following among the masses in Middle and West Tennessee. Now, through his unequivocal stand for the Union and demand for the extirpation of the rebellion, he had cut himself off from these erstwhile supporters. In this one sense at least, the exile was still an exile—a man without a party. For the time being, the Brownlows, the Johnsons, and the Maynards could cooperate in an uneasy *modus vivendi*, but the supreme struggle for the Union could not efface bitter memories of strife in bygone days. How valuable to this lifelong Democrat would his newfound bedfellows ultimately be? Only time would tell. For the nonce the governor, "now returning in the pride of power," would find that this marriage of convenience availed him but little for the task at hand—returning the state to the Union. In reality, he would find himself frequently falling between the two stools of Democratic animosity and Whig distrust.

Had the restoration of the democratic process in Tennessee been the sole end, it would have represented a major undertaking. But there were many other challenges associated with the military governorship: challenges so entangled, so vexing, so formidable, that they required all the courage, the initiative, the perseverance, and the unfailing dedication of an Andrew Johnson. The vaguely defined nature of his office raised a myriad of questions, some of them perhaps insoluble. What were the precise lines of authority between his civil and military functions? How would a civil governor who was also a brigadier general fare with

50. Temple, *Notable Men*, 316. The author got the story from Samuel A. Rodgers, later his law partner, who was not himself present, but "heard it at the time in such a reliable way as to leave no doubt of its truthfulness."

commanders whose authority, in an area where the armies continued to engage the enemy, took precedence? His difficulties with the military were to be compounded by its own overlapping jurisdictions. Responsible for the maintenance of Tennessee troops, the governor had not only to raise and equip units but also to mediate the quarrels among their officers; with that perennial problem he was already familiar. Significant as a military, political, and personal goal was the rescue of East Tennessee; hence Johnson perforce kept an eye on the border war which raged back and forth between that section and the dark and bloody ground of Kentucky. What measures should be taken to inculcate a loyal spirit in Tennessee? Conversely, what was to be done with the secessionists, whether diehards or "counterfeit coins?" The disposal of Tennessee soldiers languishing in northern prisons occupies a considerable portion of the Johnson correspondence for these years. Could some of these men in gray be redeemed and returned to their families, or even "galvanized" into blue? The protection of the loyal was a never-ending problem, as was the thorny question of trade; so, too, was the patronage, an issue which went much beyond the filling of offices. To such major questions must be added the nagging day-to-day perplexities. Upon the resolution of tasks great and small, and upon the fortunes of war, hinged the state's eventual return to civil government under the Constitution—and that, after all, was Johnson's paramount object. If the military governorship was to be "his finest hour,"[51] it would, to employ one of the Honorable Andrew's favorite clichés, require "a long pull, a strong pull, and a pull all together."

An examination of his official instructions emphasizes still further the tortuous path he trod. The official view was set forth in Stanton's commission, under date of March 3; Johnson's initial interpretation was expressed in his "Appeal to the People of Tennessee" some two weeks later. According to the secretary's instructions, he was to exercise all "the powers, duties and functions pertaining to the office of Military Governor (including the *power* to *establish all necessary offices and tribunals*, and *suspend* the *writ* of *Habeas Corpus*) . . . until the inhabitants should organize a civil government" in conformity with the Federal Constitution.[52] In the "Appeal," the governor saw himself commissioned "to preserve the public property of the State, to give the protection of law actively enforced to her citizens, and, as speedily as may be, to restore her government to the same condition as before the existing rebellion."[53] On the surface of things, he seemed to have been granted almost despotic authority designed to meet extraordinary conditions; but what were these "powers, duties and functions?" His was a broad but not plenary

51. Eric L. McKitrick, *Andrew Johnson and Reconstruction* (Chicago, 1960), 90.
52. Appointment as Military Governor, March 3, 1862.
53. Appeal to the People of Tennessee, March 18, 1862.

mandate, lacking detailed instructions as to how it was to be implemented. In part, policy would depend upon his own judgment; in part, specific orders would come from above as the need arose.

Apparently Johnson himself entertained, at least at the outset, grave misgivings. According to Christopher Andrews, a Union officer who visited him in April, the governor read the commission, remarking that there was no authority for it under the Constitution—precisely the point of view expressed by Thaddeus Stevens nearly a year later.[54] Clearly the old Andrew Johnson, constitutionalist, had surfaced once again; whereas the appointment had been made by Abraham Lincoln, perhaps the greatest of the latitudinarians. One can readily agree with the thesis that "no path had been blazed for him; he must wait for the difficulties to appear and then settle them as best he might."[55] It was a fearful responsibility.

Along with this civil charge, Johnson was commissioned a brigadier general—an appointment which seems, in retrospect, quite as controversial as the governorship itself. The underlying reasoning remains obscure. Perhaps he would be expected to administer large sections of conquered territory; possibly it was anticipated that the commission would give him greater standing among the army officers concerned: not merely with Buell but also with Halleck, commanding the Department of the West, and others. The commission would likewise allow Johnson to perform military functions and command military subordinates.

Yet there were a number of anomalies. For one thing, his own peculiar kind of "military rank" was unique even in a conflict which numbered many political generals. Other governing "generals" were expected to be military men *per se*: Benjamin F. Butler, in New Orleans, functioned as an army officer; but with Johnson, the vantage-point was different. It may be speculated whether he would not have been better off without the designation. Not least interesting of the paradoxes—or, better to say, ironies—associated with the commission was General Johnson's opinion of things military. In the past he had voiced strong convictions about officer castes, professional armies, and the resort to force. "A standing army is an incubus, a canker—a fungus on the body-politic," he told the Senate in 1858; "Rely on the citizen soldier—the man that loves his country."[56] In early 1861, anticipating the outbreak of hostilities, he had delivered himself of some homespun pacifism: "I would rather wear upon my garments the dinge of the shop and the dust of the field, as badges of

54. Christopher C. Andrews, *Recollections, 1829-1922*, Alice E. Andrews, ed. (Cleveland, 1928), 153. Stevens' observation came in January, 1863, during a House debate over an appropriation bill. See *Cong. Globe*, 37 Cong., 3 Sess., 240.

55. James W. Patton, *Unionism and Reconstruction in Tennessee, 1860-1869* (Chapel Hill, 1934), 31.

56. Speech on Maintaining Federal Authority in Utah, February 17, 1858, *Johnson Papers*, III, 23.

the pursuit of peace, than the gaudy epaulet upon my shoulder, or a sword dangling by my side, with its glittering scabbard, the insignia of strife, of war, of blood, of carnage."[57] So much for the jolting saddle of the war horse! The rider was to feel its chafings not upon the battlefield but in the council—in the contretemps with West Pointers like Buell and Rosecrans, in piddling quarrels with provost marshals, in securing protection for loyalists. Should this citizen soldier, now become brigadier general and military governor, bestraddle successfully his two mounts, no one could gainsay his horsemanship. T'would be a marvelous equestrian performance.

It was to the equivocal state of unionism in Middle Tennessee that Johnson turned his immediate attention. One of his basic tasks would be to foster the growth of loyalism: its progress would constitute one of the critical tests of his governorship. If his speeches and his other actions raise some lingering doubts, his early correspondence suggests that he continued to entertain great illusions about the strength of unionism and endeavored to strengthen such illusions in the minds of others. "There is a most decided reaction going on," he wrote Seward in mid-April, "and I feel well assured that Tennessee, always against secession by the voice of her people, will, when the rebel soldiery shall have been driven beyond her borders, wheel back into her old place in this glorious Union by a majority of tens of thousands."[58] But such an eventuality anticipated military victory and a civil canvass, neither of which appeared likely in the near future. In the meantime, how inculcate a loyal spirit? By imposing oaths of allegiance? By sending secesh preachers North? By manipulating the press? Not, most certainly, by requesting that every house in the capital display the stars and stripes on July 4.[59]

It might readily have been predicted that, for a redoutable stump speaker like Johnson, the public address would be one of the principal weapons for shoring up loyalty to the old flag. Beginning in Nashville, he expanded his efforts over the next several months to the periphery of Federal arms, holding forth not only in the capital but also at Murfreesboro, Shelbyville, and Columbia. Some of these speeches were prepared, others impromptu; some were directed to military units, others to unionist rallies; one was a formal statement as governor. Long accustomed to the makeshifts of the hustings, the governor spoke from a variety of platforms: "a couple of boards on the heads of barrels," atop a freight car, "upon a butcher's block—the stump of a huge oak tree."[60] In an area rent by dissension and dislocated by war, these discourses came in an extremely fluid power situation—a stark reality which must have provoked

57. Speech on the Seceding States, February 5-6, 1861, *ibid.*, IV, 222.
58. Letter to William H. Seward, April 19, 1862.
59. McGavock, *Pen and Sword*, 647.
60. Samuel R. Glenn Diary, May 24, June 2, 1862, in New York *Herald*, April 24, 1865.

mingled reactions from his listeners. Murfreesboro, a hotbed of secessionist sentiment, was to be captured and recaptured by Federal and Confederate; when he spoke in May before an audience said to be composed mostly of country people—"a queer mixture of blue coats and butternuts"—it was amid reports of the presence nearby of six hundred rebel cavalry, rumors of threats to capture him, doubts whether his train could return safely to the capital.[61] When he spoke at Nashville in mid-July, the occasion was a meeting hastily called to organize a force for home defense against enemy cavalry alleged to be advancing upon the city.

Although these speeches reiterated much that he had said previously, they also touched upon newer themes. Predictably he insisted that all other issues were subordinate to the question "Are you for the Union?" Inevitably he drew the sharpest of class lines in assessing loyalism, bestowing his blessings upon the people, "the true source of power"— the people, swayed, deceived, and even coerced by wealthy ultras—and the "uppertendom," in whom the secessionist disease was most virulent. Perhaps mindful that to some of his constituency he himself represented an alien presence, Johnson welcomed northern troops to the soil of Tennessee, and, endeavoring to allay fears of emancipation, denied that the North had come to set the Negro free. Moreover, he devoted some attention to the semantics of the day. Denying indignantly that Americans were "in the midst of a revolution," he asserted instead that they were "in the midst of a rebellion"—for the uprisings of 1776 and 1861 bore no analogy whatsoever, the one designed "to establish and perpetuate freedom," the other "to subvert and destroy it." He contended that, since Tennessee was still in the Union, the proper word to describe his task was not "Reconstruction," but "restoration to allegiance," a construction which foreshadowed his presidential view of the seceded states. Obviously the fervent appeal to loyalty constituted an important part of his message. Let those "deluded and erring Union men, who had by force or choice joined the rebel armies, return to their allegiance"; to all, except conscious traitors, he promised amnesty. By mid-July, however, he was obviously becoming disillusioned, calling on all "sincere, honest, true-hearted Union men—not these pseudo loyalists—these hermaphrodites—these counterfeit coins," to buckle on their armor and rally to the cause. Inevitably, too, the governor found himself obliged to defend some of his policies, particularly the treatment of those Protestant clergymen whom he described, in *double entendre*, as "rebel priests." Generally speaking, in his public statements during these early months Johnson was firm but conciliatory, holding out the olive branch and the Constitution.

How effective were these harangues? That they had an impact is

61. *Ibid.*

probable. That some listeners were uninformed and unsophisticated, and therefore, highly impressionable, was demonstrated by a Nashville audience which received "in mute astonishment" his revelations about those absentee secessionist congressmen who had defeated the Critten-den compromise.[62] A Williamson countian, deploring the persistence of disunionist sentiment there in late April, suggested that a Johnson speech at Franklin would provide a sovereign remedy; according to a northern reporter, at Murfreesboro "he seemed to know where and how to touch the hearts of Tennesseans and make them vibrate with patriotic emotions."[63] Whether such vibrations represented anything more per-manent than an old-time backwoods soul-saving is debatable. What would be more likely to impress a man: the oratory of Andrew Johnson one day or the presence of John Morgan the next? Notwithstanding the valiant forensic efforts of Johnson and former governors William B. Campbell and Neill S. Brown—the one a confirmed unionist and the other a converted "hermaphrodite"—it was sheer optimism to believe that Tennessee sentiment could be swayed decisively in so brief a period. Federal power must be firmly established, secesh officials weeded out from local governments, a loyal press created. The governor himself must employ a variety of techniques: a little wheedling and cajoling, a little intriguing and "speechifying," and, albeit judiciously, a resort to the mailed fist. In short, a sound unionism would be contingent upon the passage of time and the practice of statecraft.

Conditions in the capital epitomized the difficult problem of dealing with disloyalty in Tennessee. Whatever the nuances of opinion may have been, John G. Nicolay, Lincoln's secretary, reported soon after the occupation that "secessionist sentiment is still strongly predominant, and manifests itself continually in taunts and insults to Federal soldiers and officials."[64] A carpenter wrote that secessionists "tell the people to keep in good spirits that the rebel army will be back here by the first of june next," warning that "this sort of thing keeps the union people afraid to talk and emboldens the rebels."[65] Was there to be no surcease from the "pouters," those ladies who made mouths and pinched their "nasal protuberances," flaunted insolent skirts and furbelows, and cast vituperations from their pretty lips? Such females, remarked the govern-or, "unsexed themselves by a display of treason and ill breeding."[66] It is not mere coincidence that the Johnson papers contain a copy of Beast Butler's notorious "woman order," though no such policy was invoked in Tennessee.

But there were other overt evidences of disunionism. The local gov-

62. Speech at Nashville, May 12, 1862.
63. Letter from Alexander Moss, April 28, 1862; Glenn Diary, May 24, 1862.
64. Quoted in Maslowski, *"Treason Must Be Made Odious,"* 76.
65. Letter from Hugh C. Thompson, April 28, 1862.
66. Speech at Nashville, July 4, 1862.

ernment was shot through with disloyalty: Mayor Richard B. Cheatham and the council were secessionists almost to a man, and a number of other city employees apparently shared the same point of view. Nor had all the leading adherents of disunion fled the area; several representatives of that wealthy and influential class which Johnson considered most culpable remained. From time to time, there were allegations concerning others. An informer counselled investigation of a foundry operator who "has been making cannon, shell, shot, and torpedoes to kill the damb Yankees."[67] Still more difficult was the problem of those who played both sides. The governor was deeply concerned about clergymen who influenced others, not merely from the pulpit but also by way of the printed word; given his abiding respect for womanhood, he viewed as most heinous the spell these reverend traitors supposedly cast on some members of the feminine sex described by the Nashville *Union* as "demonized maniacs of the secession folly . . . the she-wolves of society."[68] And, most assuredly, the local journals must change their tune or be supplanted by a true-blue press. Overt actions aside, the beleaguered city was a hotbed of intrigue characterized by smuggling, espionage, and movement to and from the Confederate lines. Eradicating disloyalty would be a most formidable undertaking.

Recognizing the significant role played by officialdom and keeping in mind the object lesson to local governments elsewhere in the state, Johnson turned quickly to purifying the city government; on March 25 he requested the mayor and council, the police, and other officials to take an oath to support the Constitution of the United States. The city fathers demurred, pointing out that neither the Nashville charter nor the state and federal constitutions enjoined upon them such fealty; whereupon the governor issued a proclamation removing the nonjuring members and replacing them with another slate of officials. Meanwhile, he had ordered the arrest of Mayor Cheatham, charging him with uttering "treasonable and seditious language" as well as furnishing "counsel and extended comfort to the nation's enemies," among other things proposing "to invite to this City for a permanent official residence one Jefferson Davis."[69] A correspondent observed that "I see you are putting the *screws* to the City officers—it makes the boys *wince* a little, but I reckon they'll take it—"[70] Insofar as Nashville officialdom was concerned, Johnson's purge was successful. Cheatham, after wincing for some weeks, took the oath; the new council, attuned to current realities, even accorded the Yankee invaders a vote of thanks "for the unexampled kindness and courtesy extended to our fellow-citizens."[71]

67. Letter from "Observer," April 3, 1862.
68. Nashville *Union*, June 10, 1862.
69. Letter to Stanley Matthews, March 29, 1862.
70. Letter from Connally F. Trigg, April 1, 1862.
71. Nashville *Union*, April 15, 1862.

But what of individuals, particularly those disunionists who had not only been active in the secession movement but had also played a key role in raising troops for the Confederate armies? The governor's later requisitions for the relief of the Nashville poor would disclose in some detail the names of the culpable; but particularly prominent at this time were John Overton, said to have pledged his entire fortune of $5,000,000 to Isham G. Harris;[72] Washington Barrow, one of three men commissioned by the governor to enter into a civil and military league with the Confederacy; Judge Joseph C. Guild, a longtime Democrat who had been making incendiary statements from the bench itself; and General William G. Harding, proprietor of Belle Meade and an original secessionist.

The views expressed publicly and privately by Johnson prior to the governorship seemed to leave little doubt that short shrift would be given such disunionists. An acquaintance, writing in April, recalled his previous remark "that the moment a man became a secessionist he became a *Demon*"; back in January Horace Greeley, asserting that "rebels had no right to own anything," had explained that this was the Tennessee senator's opinion.[73] Johnson's convictions may have been reinforced by those of his correspondents: an incendiary letter from a gentle Quaker called for "a general *Confiscation* of all property both *real* and *personal*."[74] Thus in late April, when Mrs. Washington Barrow inquired of the governor by what right her riverfront property was being used, he allegedly replied, "By the right of conquerors."[75]

On April 1 the conqueror ordered Overton's arrest for treason, only to have the provost marshal report shortly that "The body of the within named ... has not been found."[76] Barrow, Guild, and Harding remained, but firmly refused the oath; apprehended and sent North, they became for the time being privileged political culprits and in the long run authentic historical figures, spending a "tranquil summer" at Fort Mackinac under the eyes of a Michigan unit detailed to guard the only prisoners that post entertained and nowadays preserved there in wax for the edification of the visitor.[77] Aside from such representatives of the uppertendom, there were others who excited Johnson's wrath. In a May election Turner S. Foster, lawyer and secessionist, defeated the governor's nominee for the circuit judgeship, only to be arrested shortly afterward and dispatched to a colder climate.

72. Nashville *Union and American*, April 21, 1861.

73. Letter from Dorus M. Fox, April 5, 1862; William B. Hesseltine, *Lincoln and the War Governors* (New York, 1948), 234.

74. Watson Newbolde to Andrew Johnson, February 1, 1862, Johnson Papers, LC.

75. Glenn Diary, April 30, 1862.

76. Letter to Stanley Matthews, April 1, 1862, with Matthews' endorsement.

77. Walter Havighurst, *Three Flags at the Straits: The Forts of Mackinac* (Englewood Cliffs, 1966), 185-86.

Beyond the proscribed were others whose stance was cloudy—those who were unionists and had temporarily "gone over," or perhaps were mild southern men. An outstanding case in point was former governor Neill S. Brown, at the onset of the crisis a unionist but when the state left the Union a cooperative secessionist. Arrested at Johnson's order in May, Brown recanted, and, to the disgust of southern men and women, became active in behalf of the Union, asserting that the Confederate cause was lost and urging Tennesseans to return to their former allegiance. Yet the governor remained wary, naming Brown in his July 4 arraignment of secessionist leaders and subsequently including him in his requisitions for the relief of the poor. Years later, in what was perhaps an unconscious bit of irony, Judge Guild would say of the erstwhile Whig: "in politics you can't hold him, he will slip through your hands."[78]

The governor's strongest feelings appear to have been reserved for certain Nashville ministers who had chosen the wrong side. Many years' later a Kentucky senator, eulogizing the departed Johnson, remarked that if he "belonged to any church, it must have been the church militant, for life with him was a warfare from beginning to end."[79] That he ever formed a denominational tie seems unlikely; indeed this affair with the secesh preachers may well have been his closest personal contact with men of the cloth. That he had long engaged in warfare against the vested interests was a commonplace; now it was a conflict with those who had "stolen the livery of Heaven to serve the devil in."[80] How reprehensible, to this member of the church militant, must have seemed the course of Samuel D. Baldwin, Collins D. Elliott, R. B. C. Howell, William H. Wharton, and other prominent divines who had not only bestowed their blessings on the disruption of the Union but also furthered by word and deed the progress of the rebellion, and who had evinced no change of heart since the fall of Nashville. Perhaps adhering to a "schedule" for oath-taking,[81] the governor delayed a showdown for more than two months. Conferences in June—at which Johnson, according to Howell, turned upon them with the "fury of an enraged tiger," but, according to a northerner, was "Perfectly composed"[82]—proved barren of result. For various reasons they declined the oath. Elliott denied having committed any act since Federal occupation which would require him to swear fealty, to which declaration the governor allegedly replied that "A visit to the North . . . may be of benefit to you."[83] The Reverend Doctor Howell,

78. Jo. C. Guild, *Old Times in Tennessee* (Nashville, 1878), 343.

79. *Cong. Record*, 44 Cong., 1 Sess., 339.

80. Speech at Nashville, July 4, 1862.

81. Howell wrote subsequently that Secretary of State Edward East told him Johnson had devised a sequence, beginning with bankers and insurance men, then ministers, doctors, and eventually the entire city. Rufus B. Spain, "R. B. C. Howell: Nashville Baptist Leader in the Civil War Period," *Tenn. Hist. Quar.*, XIV (1955), 335n.

82. *Ibid.*, 335; Glenn Diary, June 18, 1862.

83. *Ibid.*

who had earlier exhorted his congregation to expel the foe "by the ordinarily feeble hands of age, infancy, and womanhood" and later vowed that "We may be crushed, destroyed, annihilated, but conquered never," deemed it his "religious duty, to conform . . . strictly to the government under which I live," but asserted that "An oath would not increase my sense of obligation . . . nor the absence of an oath diminish it."[84] Wharton, who as penitentiary chaplain had recommended that selected inmates be released to join the rebel army, conceded that he owed his temporal loyalty first to Tennessee but announced that, as "*a citizen of Heaven*," he possessed a higher allegiance.[85] These and other ethereals were shortly committed to Nashville City Prison. In the course of a public tirade on July 4, Johnson declared that "I punish these men, not because they are priests, but because they are traitors and enemies of society, law and order."[86] Their confinement caused a wave of indignation and crowds of people, among them John Berrien Lindsley of Nashville University, came to express their sympathy. Recalling that some of these ministers had been outspoken sectarians before the war, he observed that "They now live in a continuous love feast."[87] Excluded from the fare by gubernatorial order were such expressions of sympathy as "ham, sweet pickle and other delicacies."[88] City Prison was the first stop on a conducted tour which took several of these nonjuring clergymen to the Louisville area and ultimately to Camp Chase in Ohio. Repentant or otherwise, some eventually took the oath and were paroled; others went South; "Alphabet" Howell, possessed by a fever, remained in Nashville gaol until released in August; and in the long run "Armageddon" Baldwin, who had once foreseen the triumph of "The Millennial Republic," became a Johnson supporter, lauding the newly-elected vice president as "the choice of providence."[89] Thus were silenced the dissenting voices from the pulpit, but the governor's solution became one of his most controversial acts.

Johnson could attend to the cases of refractory secessionists, but his running battle with the military admitted of no final solution. Inherent in the military governorship were tensions arising from his relationship with those who held responsibility for the conduct of the war in the West. These difficulties rested upon a combination of factors: the nature of his assignment, his distrust of things military, a fundamental difference in

84. Howell Memorial (microfilm), Tennessee State Library and Archives.
85. Nashville *Union*, June 29, 1862.
86. Speech at Nashville, July 4, 1862.
87. Quoted in Alfred Leland Crabb, "The Twilight of the Nashville Gods," *Tenn. Hist. Quar.*, XV (1956), 299.
88. Speech at Nashville, July 4, 1862.
89. See Samuel D. Baldwin, *Armageddon: or the Overthrow of Romanism and Monarchy* (Nashville, 1854); and Baldwin to Judge ———, January 8, 1865, in St. Louis *Republican*, November 2, 1865.

focus. They were exacerbated by Johnson's personality and, to a lesser extent, by the army's own organization. Virtually from the beginning of his tenure, the governor and his subordinates locked horns with the military, irrespective of level, in a more or less continuous battle. Sometimes it w.s a petty quarrel over the disposal of requisitioned property; not infrequently it was an emotional outburst, punctuated with a fusillade of dispatches, over Nashville's state of defense. Now and then it became a matter of procuring an assignment for a favorite officer; occasionally the governor presumed to instruct commanders in matters strategic. Often he went over the heads of the generals, appealing directly to Lincoln or Stanton.

Given the nature of Johnson's appointment, friction could not have been avoided. It was impossible to separate the civil and military functions. Neither could play an exclusive role: the governor must contribute to the waging of the war and the army must have a hand in civil as well as military administration. But the East Tennessean had neither the talent nor the inclination for sharing responsibility with others—the past afforded ample evidence that cooperation was not his forte. It may also be conjectured that Johnson's opinion of the military mind was not of the highest. He who scorned "the gaudy epaulet" had only recently been privy to the sessions of the Committee on the Conduct of the War; moreover, he was still smarting from the army's apparent indifference to the plight of East Tennessee.

Finally, behind these contretemps lay a profound difference in emphasis. For Halleck, Buell, Rosecrans, and others, who must perforce address themselves to a theatre which extended from the Appalachians to the Mississippi, Tennessee was but a single facet, albeit an exceedingly important one, of a larger problem. On the other hand, Johnson's horizon—both by virtue of his official position and his personal bias—was much narrower. Originally his attention had been centered upon East Tennessee and its recovery; now it became the security of the capital, the struggle with guerrillas, and the expulsion of Confederate forces from the entire state.

It was not long before the battle was joined. Shortly after Johnson's arrival in Nashville, the veneer of cooperation gave way to a curt exchange of ideas. A variety of troublesome issues presented themselves, ranging from the disposition of secessionist property to the disposition of troops—the former involving the governor in often unseemly disputes with provost marshals and the latter in continuing debates with the commanding general himself. As early as April 26 Johnson, attempting to get an Ohio regiment assigned to Nashville, was complaining to Lincoln that "Petty jealousies and contests between Generals wholly incompetent to discharge the duties assigned them have contributed more to the defeat and embarrassment of the Government than all other causes combined," and demanding "I want a reply from the President."[90] But this was only a beginning. Telegrams and letters to Maynard, Stanton, and Lincoln followed close upon each other until the President, confronted early in July with the governor's latest ultimatum regarding troop placement, patiently but incisively reminded him, "Do you not my good friend percieve that what you ask is simply to put you in Command in the west. I do not suppose you desire this. You only wish to Control in your own localities, but this you must know may derange all other parts."[91] Although Johnson acquiesced in this rebuke, he continued to quarrel with the field commanders and their subordinates.

It was a tension not difficult to explain. Indeed Nashville offers a case study of Johnson's difficulties with the military. Throughout these months the city's situation remained precarious, beset by resentful secessionists inside and outside, infested by guerrillas, menaced by Confederate forces. As the summer wore on, a garrison mentality inevitably emerged; Nashville, like East Tennessee, became for the governor an emotion. His everlasting bombardment of Washington with demands for troops to defend the capital would elicit from Halleck the pithy observation that "to accommodate Governor Johnson would be releasing our grasp on the enemy's throat in order to pare his toe-nails"; while Buell would castigate the governor's views on troop disposition as "absurd."[92] Notwithstanding the fact that the city remained in Union hands, it became increasingly isolated. Moreover, the governor's effort to bring Tennesseans back to their loyalty, a campaign inaugurated in early spring, was slowly being undermined. In June he had pointed out the liability which the insecurity of Nashville placed upon his efforts: its defenseless condition served to keep alive "a rebellious spirit that could otherwise have been put down by this time." In August a Union officer quoted him as arguing that "an evidence of *determination to hold* on our part at any cost would deter" an enemy attack.[93] Had he lived in our century, Johnson would have been a votary of psychological warfare. The continued weakness of Federal authority fueled secessionist promises or threats—depending upon the audience—of Confederate return to power in Middle Tennessee. Under such circumstances the spirit of intransigence was nurtured, thwarting the governor's efforts to win back to the flag his fellow Volunteers.

A not inconsiderable amount of Johnson's time was devoted to transmitting news and needs from the Tennessee front to Washington and to various military headquarters. As intelligence came in from the several

90. Telegram to Abraham Lincoln, April 26, 1862.
91. Telegram from Abraham Lincoln, July 11, 1862.
92. Halleck to Buell and Buell to Halleck, July 26, 1862, *OR*, Ser. 1, X, Pt. II, 128-29.
93. William H. Sidell to James B. Fry, August 1, 1862, Dept. of the Ohio, Misc. Lets. Recd. (1862-68), RG393, NA.

fronts—Murfreesboro, Cumberland Gap, Sparta, Clarksville, etc.—he dutifully passed it on, always highlighting those aspects which gave promise of bringing additional troops into Tennessee. At the same time he was busy responding to, and often refereeing, the needs of volunteer forces gradually being organized within the state or in nearby Kentucky. Especially voluminous were the communications from son Robert and several friends who brought to the governor's attention their griev-ances—as when, in a most unheroic catabasis, they were evacuated from Cumberland Gap to the mouth of the Kanawha with the prospect of service in western Virginia—as well as their personal disputes. And for Robert, by and large a disappointed youth, the goal of a cavalry regiment to replace his infantry became an obsession which his father strove mightily to gratify.

Yet the resolution of these military questions, though it occupied an inordinate amount of Johnson's time and contributed immensely to his *Sturm und Drang*, was not his major assignment. The instructions he received in March make it clear that the restoration of civil government was his chief mission; indeed he was the first military governor appointed for that specific purpose. In a sense, Johnson was a caretaker, charged with returning Tennessee expeditiously "to the same condition as before the existing rebellion."[94] But the establishment of a military gover-norship carried implications which went beyond the state itself. Tennes-see may well have been intended as an example not merely of the *process* of restoring a state to the Union, but also of Federal moderation, thereby holding out an inducement to southerners increasingly disillusioned by the continuing struggle and potentially receptive to embracing once more the national fold. In none of these respects was Johnson successful. Only after three long, frustrating years would a civil government emerge. Far from serving as an enticement to the irresolute and the undecided, the Tennessee experiment may have alienated more than it wooed. Whatever expectations the governor carried with him to Nash-ville, the response of Middle Tennessee during the first three or four months of his incumbency foreshadowed what would become a dismal failure. Writing to Buell in late July, General William Nelson presented a sobering view of Johnson's impact on the popular temper:

The hostility to the United States Government and the troops has increased 1,000 per cent. It seems settled into a fierce hatred to Governor Johnson, to him personally more than officially, for in questioning many people they cannot point to an act that he has not been warranted in doing by their own showing; but still, either in manner of doing it, or that it should be done by him, or from some undefinable course touching him their resentment is fierce and vindictive, and this country, from being neutral at least, as you left it, is now hostile and in arms, and what makes it bad for us it is in our rear.[95]

From the outset Nelson and others had been dubious about the

94. Appeal to the People of Tennessee, March 18, 1862.
95. Nelson to Buell, July 24, 1862, *OR*, Ser. 1, XVI, Pt. I, 816.

appointment of a military governor; beyond question, the generals were jealous of military prerogative. Had Middle Tennessee been "neutral" even in April? Still, with due allowance for skepticism, one detects in the "Bull's" convoluted prose a strong ring of truth. Apparently Tom Scott's reservations about the choice of the Plebeian to administer the delicate business of reconciliation were being borne out. Johnson the apostate had become Johnson the oppressor, symbol of a hated regime imposed by force of arms.

If the attitudes of Tennesseans toward the governor were hardening, so too was his own attitude toward the implementation of his task. While there had been abundant evidence of his impatience with conscious and affluent secessionists, nonetheless he had in the beginning displayed a judicious leniency to others. Sometimes it was a matter of assessing a case on its merits; more often it was a question of luring the erring and misguided back to the old flag. In suggesting that a militia general be given a conditional release rather than sent North, Johnson remarked that, insofar as "the public mind" was concerned, it would be preferable to keep such men at home. Examine some of "their cases before giving them so much importance," he cautioned the Nashville authorities.[96] The governor entertained high hopes of restoring the loyalty of Tennessee Confederate soldiers incarcerated in various northern prisons, adding that "their appearance among their friends and relatives will I doubt not exert a great moral influence in favor of the perpetuity of the Union."[97]

Yet as the months went by Johnson was slowly becoming disillusioned. Had he misjudged the public mind? Were Tennesseans, after all, predominantly secessionist and not unionists hoodwinked or coerced into forsaking the flag, ready to return to allegiance by the "tens of thousands?" To what extent did loyalty, particularly in Middle Tennessee, spring from pure calculation? Whatever the shadings of opinion, disloyalty continued to manifest itself in intransigent planters and businessmen as well as in "boys and silly women," to say nothing of counterfeit coins and hermaphrodites. Guerrillas and rebel cavalry—Johnson drew little distinction, calling Morgan's men "a mere band of freebooters" who "should not be admitted within the rules of civilizied warfare [sic]"[98]—added to the trauma. Over the embattled governor and his understrappers hung, like a sword of Damocles, the prospect of a Confederate assault on the capital. In midsummer the military situation appeared to be deteriorating. On July 13 Bedford Forrest took Murfreesboro, bagging the entire garrison in the process; two days later, Nashvillians girded themselves for a rumored attack which did not materialize. For the governor, the olive branch—"The erring and mis-

96. Letter to Stanley Matthews, April 22, 1862.
97. Letter to Edwin M. Stanton, April 17, 1862.
98. Letter to Horace Maynard, May 18, 1862.

guided will be welcomed on their return"[99]—was giving way to the sword. Perhaps the primordial, uncompromising Johnson had merely reasserted himself.

The new grimness showed itself in a variety of ways, but for the public at large it was displayed in a Fourth of July oration. In content, the speech revealed nothing with which Johnson's audiences over the past few months were unfamiliar; in tone and phraseology, it was harsher, even vindictive—an excursion into the semantics of irreconcilability, one might say. Invoking class lines and etching sharply the dichotomy between right and wrong, the speaker called the chivalry "the greatest robbers and enemies of the rights of the people, that the country has ever seen," and asked freemen whether they were incapable of acting for themselves. He contrasted the rebel hordes, spreading "horror and desolation," and the patriot hosts, "law-abiding and orderly." He pilloried the parsons and those women whose hands were "red with. . . . the blood of your own husbands, brothers and sons." He pronounced a *brutum fulmen* which he would repeat over and over again, repeat until the name Andrew Johnson became a symbol of unbending retribution: *"treason must be made odious and traitors impoverished."* Let the instigators of war be made to pay for their crimes: *"They* are the guilty ones. *They* are the real criminals."[100]

The governor was as good as his word. Although unable to secure from Stanton "an order similar to that of Gen Pope in Virginia in regard to subsisting, &c. on the Enemy,"[101] he condoned a policy which permitted the Federal soldiery more freely than ever to live off the land, unceremoniously taking from known rebels and giving receipts for subsequent redemption to those claiming to be unionists. Before year's end, he would levy monetary assessments upon more than eighty individuals and firms regarded as secessionist sympathizers, in order to provide assistance for Nashvillians "reduced to poverty and wretchedness in consequence of their husbands, sons and fathers having been forced into the armies of this unholy and nefarious rebellion."[102] Whatever was necessary to accomplish his mission, the governor would do: for, as he reminded his listeners on July 4, "I have enlisted for the war, and will not go back." Appropriately, the defensive works erected around the capitol were to be named in his honor; literally and emotionally, Nashville had become *fortress Andrew Johnson*.

But what shall be said of the man behind the barricades? Elsewhere in this volume appears a likeness executed sometime during the governorship.[103] Ostensibly the setting is the capitol. In artistic fidelity, it is

99. Appeal to the People of Tennessee, March 18, 1862.
100. Speech at Nashville, July 4, 1862.
101. Telegram to Edwin M. Stanton, July 26, 1862.
102. Circular Assessing Confederate Sympathizers, August 18, 1862; Assessment for Relief of the Poor, December 13, 1862, Johnson Papers, LC.
103. See page 588.

hardly memorable; yet in its symbolism, it captures the spirit of the times. Depicted is a taller and thinner Johnson than the "man of medium height and strong build" we are accustomed to viewing during these years—a Johnson become "pale and careworn" from the exactions of his grim mission. The visage is stern, "almost a scowl," a demeanor often affected by nineteenth century politicians, but one habitual with the Plebeian. In evidence is the panoply of wartime: a sealing device for the correspondence which poured from his pen; a bust of Washington, universal hero to a divided nation; and outside, a vista of troops drilling—a reminder of his military function. Excluded from this "state sitting," but part of the actual chamber's appointments, were a full-length portrait of Jackson and one of Johnson himself as civil governor.

Other contemporaries provide a less imaginative but more realistic picture of the governor's life. Essentially he lived alone, his wife spending no more than a month in Nashville during 1862. Lodging temporarily at the St. Cloud—his room "a plain affair, half filled by a bed"—he took his meals, as befitted a tribune of the people, in the public dining hall, wearing "No mark of his military honors."[104] In July he moved to a commodious brick house facing the capitol; owned by Lizinka Campbell Brown, an antebellum acquaintance gone South and soon to become the wife of Confederate General Richard S. Ewell, the dwelling had apparently been commandeered for Johnson's use.

During the course of a working day, which began in his office at 8:00 a.m. and ended in his room where he often sat "until midnight, reading and inditing dispatches by the tallow candles,"[105] the governor occupied himself with a bewildering variety of issues involving friend and foe, the city and the area, the state and nation. Rumors mingled indiscriminately with realities. Tennessee unionists wanted protection from guerrillas or compensation for property losses; Tennessee rebels languishing in northern prisons asked to be released, promising to return to the old allegiance. Those covetous of civil posts, military commissions, or merely small favors, solicited his aid; correspondents apprised him of disloyalty or evaluated the progress of unionism. His business with the army was well-nigh endless, his bickerings with its minions almost chronic. Hordes of petitioners—brokers, special pleaders, men and women in distress—crowded into his office, seeking relief. "For weeks we have not stepped into the Governor's room . . . without finding widows in tears, piteously entreating some assistance to save them from starvation," wrote a reporter.[106] Subsequently a clergyman would describe Johnson as "the most approachable public man I ever saw or read of . . . as accessible to the poor and lowly as to the proud and lordly."[107] The most approachable

104. Nashville *Union*, June 20, 1862.
105. *Ibid.*, June 1, 1862.
106. *Ibid.*
107. Baldwin to Judge ——, January 8, 1865.

public man! Surely this Nashville experience represented something of a dress rehearsal for the presidency.

And yet at times the harried governor must have been "marvelous ill-favoured," virtually unapproachable. Presiding over a city peopled by numerous hostiles and menaced by rebel armies from without—a city often cut off from communication with the Federals—he partook of its garrison psychology. Tales of his personal hazards were abroad. A Georgia paper, picturing him as "living in mortal terror," added that he "never ventures out, even to answer the calls of nature, without a guard of Federal soldiers tramping at his heels."[108] On one occasion it was reported, with some slight exaggeration, that he had been shot and killed by Neill Brown; on another, that he had been on the losing side of a fisticuff with Buell.[109] In August he received intelligence that some of Morgan's operatives had left Knoxville with the express purpose of assassinating him.[110] Nor was this precariousness of life soon to be alleviated. In a sense, Johnson's own danger epitomized the state of affairs in Tennessee. The perils that beset Nashville, the failure to redeem East Tennessee, the evidence that unionism was weak elsewhere in Tennessee, and the delay in inaugurating a loyal state government afforded ample cause for discouragement.

During these months of insecurity and frustration, he undoubtedly derived much personal comfort from the approving voices which followed his course as senator and governor. To a sycophantic clerk, Johnson's good opinion was like "apples of gold in pictures of silver"; to an ardent feminine admirer, he was "par excellence, a revolutionist."[111] Another correspondent called him "the representative man of the age," while an editor hailed him as "the Cromwell of his day, in his love of freedom, his intense scorn for a corrupt aristocracy, and his devotion to the glory and progress of his country."[112] How seriously the Cromwell of his day took such showers of blessing must remain a moot question; but the continuing approbation of Abraham Lincoln was something else. The chief executive, Maynard apprised him in June, was pleased that Johnson had not "let them raise any 'nigger' issues to bother him."[113] A month later Schuyler Colfax assured him that "the President has told me twice that, while he has had troublesome questions to settle from other Military Governors & officers ... 'Andy Johnson' had never embarrassed him in the slightest degree. You enjoy his fullest confidence as you

108. Rome (Ga.) *Tri-Weekly Courier*, May 29, 1862.

109. *Ibid.*, June 12, 1862.

110. Glenn Diary, August 17, 1862.

111. Letter from William Patton, March 4, 1862; Letter from Mrs. Rae Batten, December 20, 1861.

112. Letter from Francis U. Stitt, February 19, 1862; Nashville *Union*, June 7, 1862.

113. Letter from Horace Maynard, June 7, 1862.

so richly deserve."[114] Never embarrassed him! His fullest confidence! For the present, certainly, he could ask for no greater reward. Would not the future bring a brighter prospect?

And yet his countenance must have darkened perceptibly as he pondered the intricacies of his Eng-Chang mission in Tennessee and contemplated the sad state of the Union. Who could predict the outcome of the American tragedy? Undoubtedly the governor applauded—nay, possibly inspired and most certainly subsidized[115]—a grim August prophecy in the Nashville *Union*, conducted by Samuel Mercer, editor, propagandist, and sometime poet. Reminding his audience that "we are not only *making* history, but . . . *living* for history," he deplored the leniency accorded treason. But the world would see that "we arose at last and crushed the rebels to the dust, and ran the ploughshare of desolation over their homes and sewed them with salt."[116] Yes, indeed! Let this war of extirpation proceed—and meanwhile let Andrew Johnson, a modern Cato, have frequent recourse to Job's lamentations.

THIS VOLUME

Bridging Johnson's final six months in the Senate and his first six as military governor, these documents, all concerned with the sundered nation and its restoration, fall into two parts. Just as in March, 1862, Johnson moved physically from the national to the state capital, so must the reader transport himself psychologically from the banks of the Potomac to the banks of the Cumberland. Although the governor would continue his campaign to keep Tennessee's needs before the President and secretary of war, the emphasis and method change. Where the salvation of East Tennessee had long been his primary focus, the maintenance and expansion of a Federal presence in the mid-area became an all-consuming concern; where personal contacts, speeches, and occasional letters had been the tools, correspondence with cohorts in Washington and an avalanche of telegrams now became his implements. In a very concrete way, the epistolary voice of the man from Greeneville is louder than in previous volumes; yet this does not mean that more of Johnson and his inner self emerge. There are virtually no thoughtful, self-searching communications to family or intimates; the letters are what might be called "advocacy," rather than "reflective," correspondence. There is also a decided decline in gratuitous advice from friends and strangers which loomed so large in earlier volumes. And, polemical

114. Letter from Schuyler Colfax, July 5, 1862.
115. Numerous vouchers (in the possession of Mrs. Betsy Bachman Carrier, Bluff City, Tennessee) during 1862-63 attest to the fact that Editor Mercer and the *Union* were maintained by the governor's funds.
116. Nashville *Union*, August 28, 1862.

and repetitious though they may have been, the addresses of yore did reveal something of the man and his thought processes—an insight severely restricted in this period by the paucity of recorded speeches.

This volume also differs from its predecessors both in the number of documents and in the proportion of Johnson items *per se*. In consequence of the lack of extended speeches (a single senatorial effusion and only two among the remaining eight addresses preserved in any detail), nearly forty-three percent more individual documents appear here than in Volume IV. Further, there are significantly more letters, dispatches, and proclamations emanating from Johnson himself: 152, or twenty-five percent of the items printed.

The chronological distribution reveals something of the vagaries of documentary preservation. Little has survived from the autumn of 1861, probably a reflection of the senator's peripatetic life in Kentucky and Ohio as a hawker of East Tennessee rescue and Union restoration. Once returned to Washington in December he again received and retained a sizable correspondence. Nor is it surprising that the first six months of the governorship produced a flood of material, especially telegrams, which would be sharply reduced during early fall by the interruption of dependable communication with beleaguered Nashville.

If all periods are not proportionately represented, neither are all aspects of Johnson's life and experience equally well delineated. Notably lacking is evidence concerning his two months' service as a member of the Committee on the Conduct of the War. Those seeking insight into his rôle must perforce resort to the committee's official records and to other manuscript collections; the Johnson papers provide no assistance. Again, one could wish that the documents offered clues to the considerations which brought about his designation as military governor; once more, silence. And, as always, there is the scarcity of family correspondence—a dearth, if anything, worse than in earlier volumes when there were occasional revealing letters to or from one of the children, or, failing that, a comparable glimpse of the private man as revealed in exchanges with intimates. Rather, here is the man of affairs, rarely relaxed, much less unmasked. Evidences of emotion appear chiefly in expressions of anger and indignation found in telegrams, letters, and face-to-face exchanges with secessionists, as well as with military and political associates whose vigor in prosecuting the war or dealing with traitors does not conform to the governor's draconian standards.

But if these documents in some ways disappoint, they in many ways delight. Revealing the complexity and at the same time simplicity—the flaws as well as the virtues—of the East Tennessean, they contribute further to an understanding of the man who would one day occupy the White House. Here is abundant evidence of the manifold problems which came before him, both as senator and as governor. Especially in the latter capacity was he drawn into the maelstrom of pain and personal sacrifice brought on by the war—prisoners, North or South, and their grieving and oft starving families; Tennesseans, unionist or secessionist, caught up in the destructive currents of the conflict; women, obliged single-handedly to attempt to preserve life and property in the face of the ruthless depredations of both sides—in short, he shared vicariously and personally the impact of the contest on the rank and file, whether at home, in hiding, or in exile. Unfortunately, we are seldom able to discern firsthand Johnson's response to these conditions. Yet, all in all, the economic and social upheaval which accompanied our national tragedy is vividly portrayed in this record of a "man of the people."

ACKNOWLEDGMENTS

We owe much to numerous individuals and institutions without whose assistance an undertaking of this magnitude would have been exceedingly difficult if not altogether impossible. Among those who have contributed significantly are the following: Frank E. Burke, Executive Secretary of the National Historical Publications and Records Commission, and members of his staff, especially Sara Dunlap Jackson, Richard Shelton, Mary Giunta, and Anne Harris Henry; Robert Bassett, Olive Branch, Danuta A. Nitecki, and John Dobson of the University of Tennessee Library; Cleo Hughes and Jean Waggener of the Tennessee State Library and Archives; William J. MacArthur of the McClung Collection, Knoxville-Knox County Public Library, Knoxville; James R. Bentley of the Filson Club, Louisville; John L. Ferguson, Arkansas State Historian; and W. Neil Franklin, formerly of the National Archives.

A project such as this rests upon the foundation provided by the professionalism and devotion of able staff members. With Associate Editor Patricia Clark as the considerate yet efficient supervisor of the "tailor shop," many individuals have made a variety of contributions, all necessary to produce this volume: Richard Bland, National Historical Publications and Records Commission Fellow; Marion O. Smith and C. James Taylor, research assistants; Lynda Lasswell Crist and Kent Cave, graduate assistants; Gloria Bagby and Janet Hickman, secretaries; Frank Joseph Tighe and Curtis LeMay, work-study students; and Professors Carl A. Pierce and R. McDonald Gray of the University of Tennessee Law School.

We are most grateful to those repositories (see Editorial Method, Symbols List A) whose holdings are represented herein. To Mrs. Margaret Johnson Patterson Bartlett of Greeneville, Mrs. Betsy Bachman Carrier of Bluff City, Leonard Stern of Studio City, California, and the late Colonel Fay W. Brabson, USA, we are especially indebted for items from their private collections.

The three agencies most significantly involved in support of the

Andrew Johnson Papers are the University of Tennessee, Knoxville, which provides housing for the Project, released time for the editors, and the services of its Press; the National Historical Publications and Records Commission, which makes available generous annual grants and a supplementary sum for printing costs; and the Tennessee Historical Commission, which contributes annual subsidies, as well as publication assistance.

At the onset of the third decade with Andrew Johnson, we continue to marvel at our wives' patience and forbearance.

LeRoy P. Graf
Ralph W. Haskins

Knoxville, Tennessee
September 1, 1978

Editorial Method

By far the largest number of documents herein come from the Library of Congress and the National Archives, with comparatively few selections from other repositories, private collections, and newspapers. While the volume contains all significant correspondence and reported speeches, it omits, except for representative samples, routine material such as recommendations, petitions, invitations to speak, unsubstantiated or trivial military information, and letters of introduction or inquiry. For the first time in this series there is a significant incidence of multiple copies; in such cases, the sender's date and recipient's copy are used. As a rule, the sources of footnote data are indicated. The absence of annotation may mean that the subject is a matter of general knowledge, that the person has been previously identified (as reference to the Index will show), or that information is unavailable. Reference to extended identifications found in the first four volumes is provided in the footnotes. Most city and business directories are from the microform collection produced by New Haven Research Publications, Inc.

In transcribing, the editors have sought to combine fidelity to the original with consideration for the reader. Hence orthography is reproduced without change, except where confusion might occur; in such instances, bracketed letters and words or *sic* are employed to clarify the meaning. Where not otherwise cited, *Webster's Third International* is the authority for spelling, definition, and usage. For the sake of economy and uniformity, the placing of salutations, addresses, and complimentary closings has been modified; moreover, the "State of Tennessee" letterhead has been removed on most Military Governor items. Aside from the insertion of bracketed periods or question marks, the original punctuation is retained; repetitious words or phrases, obviously slips of the pen, have been eliminated. Although information added by the editors is normally bracketed, exceptions are made when a correspondent's location or the date of a document are beyond doubt. Normally cities and towns without a state designation are in Tennessee.

SYMBOLS

A. Repositories

CLU	University of California at Los Angeles
CSmH	Henry E. Huntington Library, San Marino, California
DLC	Library of Congress, Washington, D.C.
DNA	National Archives, Washington, D.C.

RECORD GROUPS USED

RG15   Records of the Veterans Administration

RG21   Records of District Courts of the United States

RG36   Records of the Bureau of Customs

RG45   Naval Records Collection of the Office of Naval Records and Library

RG56   General Records of the Department of the Treasury

RG59   General Records of the Department of State

RG92   Records of the Office of the Quartermaster General

RG94   Records of the Adjutant General's Office, 1780's-1917

RG107 Records of the Office of the Secretary of War

RG109 War Department Collection of Confederate Records

RG153 Records of the Office of the Judge Advocate General (Army)

RG249 Records of the Commissary General of Prisoners

RG366 Records of Civil War Special Agencies of the Treasury Department

RG393 Records of United States Army Continental Commands, 1821-1920

IHi	Illinois State Historical Library, Springfield
MH	Harvard University Library, Cambridge, Massachusetts
MHi	Massachusetts Historical Society, Boston
MiU-H	University of Michigan, Bentley Historical Library, Ann Arbor
NcD	Duke University, Durham, North Carolina
NHi	New-York Historical Society, New York
NN	New York Public Library, New York
NNC	Columbia University Library, New York, New York
NNPM	Pierpont Morgan Library, New York, New York
NRU	University of Rochester, Rochester, New York
OC1WHi	Western Reserve Historical Society, Cleveland, Ohio
PHi	Historical Society of Pennsylvania, Philadelphia
RPB	Brown University, Providence, Rhode Island
T	Tennessee State Library and Archives, Nashville
TKL	Knoxville-Knox County Public Library, Knoxville
TU	University of Tennessee, Knoxville
VtHi	Vermont Historical Society, Montpelier

B. Manuscripts

ALI	Autographed Letter Initialed
ALS	Autograph Letter Signed

Copy	Copy not by writer
D	Document
DS	Document Signed
L	Letter
L draft	Letter draft
LB copy	Letter Book copy
LS	Letter Signed
Mem	Memorial
PC	Printed Copy
Pet	Petition
PL	Printed Letter
Tel	Telegram
Tel draft	Telegram draft

ABBREVIATIONS

GENERAL

A.; App.	Appendix
Appl.	Application
b.	Born
c, ca.	About
Corres.	Correspondence
CSA	Confederate States of America
CSR	Compiled Service Records
Dist.	District
Div.	Division
Ex.	Executive
fl	Flourishing
Gen. Let. Bk.	General Letter Book
l, ll.	Line, lines
LC	Library of Congress
Lets. Recd.	Letters Received
Lets. Sent	Letters Sent
Mil. Gov's	Military Governor's
NA	National Archives
RR	Railroad
Recs. & Appts.	Recommendations and Appointments
Sec.	Secretary, section
Ser.	Series
Sess.	Session
St.	Stanza
Subdiv.	Subdivision
Supp., Supps.	Supplement, supplements
Tel., tels.	Telegram, telegraph, telegrams

Tels. Recd.	Telegrams received
v	Versus

MILITARY

Arty.	Artillery
Bde.	Brigade
Btn.	Battalion
Bty.	Battery
Capt.	Captain
Cav.	Cavalry
Cld.	Colored
Co.	Company
Col.	Colonel
CSA	Confederate States of America (Army)
Dept.	Department
Div.	Division
Gen.	General
Inf.	Infantry
Lgt.	Light [Lgt. Arty.]
Lt.	Lieutenant
Mid. Tenn.	Middle Tennessee
Mtd.	Mounted
Rgt.	Regiment
USA	United States of America (Army)
Vol.	Volunteer

SHORT TITLES

Acklen, *Tenn. Records*	Jeanette T. Acklen, comp., *Tennessee Records* (2 vols., Nashville, 1933).
American Annual Cyclopaedia	*American Annual Cyclopaedia and Register of Important Events* (42 vols. in 3 series, New York, 1862-1903).
Appleton's Cyclopaedia	James G. Wilson and John Fiske, eds., *Appleton's Cyclopaedia of American Biography* (6 vols., New York, 1887-89).
Bartlett, *Quotations*	John Bartlett, *Familiar Quotations*, Emily M. Beck, ed. (Boston, 1968).
Basler, *Works of Lincoln*	Roy P. Basler, ed., *The Collected Works of Abraham Lincoln* (9 vols., New Brunswick, N. J., 1953-55).

Battles and Leaders	Robert N. Johnson and Clarence C. Buel, comps., *Battles and Leaders of the Civil War* (4 vols., New York, 1956 [1887]).
BDAC	*Biographical Directory of the American Congress, 1774-1961* . . . (*House Document* No. 442, 85 Congress, 2 Session, Washington, 1961).
Boatner, *Civil War Diction-ary*	Mark M. Boatner, *The Civil War Dictionary* (New York, 1959).
Campbell, *Tenn. Attitudes*	Mary R. Campbell, *The Attitude of Tennesseans toward the Union, 1847-1861* (Knoxville, 1961).
1860 [1870, 1880] Census, Tenn., Greene [other states and counties]	U. S. Bureau of the Census, Eighth Census 1860, Population [state, county, post office, district or ward] (original schedules on microfilm).
1890 Special Census, Union Veterans and Widows	U. S. Bureau of the Census, Special Schedules of the Eleventh Census (1890) Enumerating Union Veterans and Widows of Union Veterans of the Civil War [state, county, post office, district or ward] (original schedules on microfilm).
Clayton, *Davidson County*	W. Woodford Clayton, *History of Davidson County, Tennessee* (Philadelphia, 1880).
Collins, *Kentucky*	Lewis and Richard H. Collins, *History of Kentucky* (2 vols., Covington, Ky., 1874).
Cong. Globe	U. S. Congress, *The Congressional Globe* (23 Congress to 42 Congress, Washington, 1834-73).
Connelly, *Army of the Heartland*	Thomas L. Connelly, *Army of the Heartland: The Army of Tennessee, 1861-1862* (Baton Rouge, 1967).
Coulter, *Civil War in Kentucky*	E. Merton Coulter, *The Civil War and Readjustment in Kentucky* (Chapel Hill, 1926).
DAB	Allen Johnson and Dumas Malone,

eds., *Dictionary of American Biography* (20 vols., supps., and index, New York, 1928-).

DNB
The Dictionary of National Biography (21 vols. and supps., London, 1938-).

ETHS *Publications*
East Tennessee Historical Society's *Publications*.

Ex. Record Book (1862-63)
Record Book, Executive Office, Nashville, Tennessee, 1862-1863, Johnson Papers, Series 4C, Library of Congress.

Filson Quarterly
Filson Club History Quarterly.

Fitch, *Annals*
John Fitch, *Annals of the Army of the Cumberland* (Philadelphia, 1864).

Futrell, Federal Trade
Robert F. Futrell, Federal Trade with the Confederate States, 1861-1865: A Study of Governmental Policy (Ph.D. dissertation, Vanderbilt University, 1950).

Garrett, *Confederate Soldiers*
Jill K. Garrett, ed., *Confederate Soldiers and Patriots of Maury County, Tennessee* (Columbia, 1970).

Garrett and Lightfoot, *Civil War in Maury County*
Jill K. Garrett and Marise P. Lightfoot, *The Civil War in Maury County, Tennessee* ([Columbia], 1966).

Goodspeed's East Tennessee
Goodspeed's Bedford [and other counties]
Goodspeed Publishing Company, *History of Tennessee, from the Earliest Time to the Present . . .* (Chicago, 1886-87).

Hall, *Military Governor*
Clifton R. Hall, *Andrew Johnson: Military Governor of Tennessee* (Princeton, 1916).

Heitman, *Register*
Francis B. Heitman, *Historical Register and Dictionary of the United States Army, from Its Organization, September 29, 1789, to March 2, 1903* (2 vols., Washington, 1903).

Hesseltine, *Civil War Prisons*
William B. Hesseltine, *Civil War Prisons: A Study in War Psychology* (New York, 1964 [1930]).

House Ex. Doc.
House Executive Document.

JP
Andrew Johnson Papers, Library of Congress. JP refers to the first

series only; JP2, etc., to succeeding series.

Johnson Papers	LeRoy P. Graf and Ralph W. Haskins, eds., *The Papers of Andrew Johnson* (4 vols., Knoxville, 1967-).
Johnson-Bartlett Col.	Andrew Johnson materials in possession of Mrs. Margaret Johnson Patterson Bartlett, Greeneville, Tennessee.
Lindsley, *Military Annals*	John B. Lindsley, ed., *Military Annals of Tennessee: Confederate . . .* (Nashville, 1886).
Long, *Civil War Almanac*	E. B. Long, with Barbara Long, *The Civil War Day by Day: An Almanac 1861-1865* (New York, 1971).
McBride and Robison, *Biographical Directory*	Robert M. McBride and Dan M. Robison, comps., *Biographical Directory of the Tennessee General Assembly* (1 vol., Nashville, 1975-).
McGavock, *Pen and Sword*	Randal W. McGavock, *Pen and Sword: The Life and Journals of Randal W. McGavock*, Herschel Gower and Jack Allen, eds. (Nashville, 1959).
McKinney, *Education in Violence*	Francis F. McKinney, *Education in Violence: The Life of George H. Thomas and the History of the Army of the Cumberland* (Detroit, 1961).
Maslowski, *"Treason Must Be Made Odious"*	Peter Maslowski, *"Treason Must Be Made Odious"*: Military Occupation and Wartime Reconstruction in Nashville, Tennessee, 1862-1865 (Ph.D. dissertation, Ohio State University, 1972).
Mathews, *Americanisms*	Mitford M. Mathews, ed., A *Dictionary of Americanisms on Historical Principles* (2 vols., Chicago, 1951).
Maury County Cousins	Maury County Historical Society, tr., *Maury County Cousins* (2 vols., Columbia, 1967-71).
Moore, *Rebellion Record*	Frank Moore, ed., *The Rebellion*

Record: A Diary of American
Events (11 vols. and supp., New
York, 1861-68).

Nashville Bus. Dir.   John P. Campbell, comp., Nashville
(1855-56)   City and Business Directory,
                              1855-56 (Nashville, 1855).

——— (1860-61)   L. P. Williams & Co., Nashville City
                              and Business Directory, 1860-61
                              (Nashville, 1860).

Nashville City Cemetery In-   Index to Interments in the Nashville
dex   City Cemetery, 1846-1962 (Nash-
                              ville, 1964).

NCAB   National Cyclopaedia of American
                              Biography . . . (54 vols., New
                              York, 1967-73 [1893-   ]).

OED   James A. H. Murray and others, eds.,
                              The Oxford English Dictionary (13
                              vols., Oxford, 1933).

Official Army Register: Adjutant General's Office, Official
Volunteers   Army Register of the Volunteer
                              Force of the United States Army for
                              the Years 1861, 1862, 1863, 1864,
                              1865 (8 vols., Washington, 1865-
                              67).

Official Army Register   Adjutant General's Office, Register of
(1863)   the Army of the United States for
                              1863 ([Washington, 1863]).

OR; OR-Atlas   War of the Rebellion: A Compilation of
                              the Official Records of the Union and
                              Confederate Armies (70 vols. in
                              128, Washington, 1880-1901).

OR-Navy   Official Records of the Union and Con-
                              federate Navies in the War of the
                              Rebellion (30 vols., Washington,
                              1894-1927).

Parson Brownlow's Book   William G. Brownlow, Sketches of the
                              Rise, Progress, and Decline of Se-
                              cession (Philadelphia, 1862).

Porch, 1850 Census, David-   Deane Porch, tr., Davidson County,
son   Tennessee, 1850 Census (Fort
                              Worth, 1969).

———, 1850 Census, Maury   Deane Porch, tr., 1850 Census,
                              Maury County, Tennessee
                              (Nashville, 1966).

————, *1850 Census, Nash-*
  ville

Powell, *Army List*

Robison, *Preliminary*
  Directory, Bedford [and
  other counties]

Savage, *Life of Johnson*

Senate Ex. Journal
Senate Misc. Doc.
Sistler, *1850 Tenn. Census*

Smith's Maury County

Speer, *Prominent Tennes-*
  seans

Stevenson, *Macmillan Book*
  of Proverbs

Temple, *East Tennessee*

————, *Notable Men*

Tenn. Acts, Extra Sess.,
  1861
Tenn. Adj. Gen. Report
  (1866)

Tenn. Hist. Mag.
Tenn. Hist. Quar.
Tenn. House Journal

Deane Porch, tr., *1850 Census of the
City of Nashville, Davidson
County, Tennessee* (Fort Worth,
1969).

William H. Powell, *List of Officers of
the United States from 1779 to 1900*
(Detroit, 1967 [1900]).

Dan M. Robison and Robert M.
McBride, comps., *Biographical Directory* (Preliminary) *of Tennessee
General Assembly* (Nashville,
1967-   ).

John Savage, *The Life and Public
Services of Andrew Johnson* (New
York, 1866).

Senate Executive Journal.
Senate Miscellaneous Document.
Byron and Barbara Sistler, trs., *1850
Census Tennessee* (8 vols.,
Evanston, Ill., 1974-76).

Maury County Historical Society,
*Frank H. Smith's History of Maury
County, Tennessee* ([Columbia],
1969).

William S. Speer, *Sketches of
Prominent Tennesseans* (Nashville,
1888).

Burton E. Stevenson, *The Macmillan
Book of Proverbs, Maxims and Famous Phrases* (New York, 1948).

Oliver P. Temple, *East Tennessee and
the Civil War* (Cincinnati, 1899).

Oliver P. Temple, *Notable Men of
Tennessee from 1833 to 1875* (New
York, 1912).

Acts of the State of Tennessee, Extra
Session, 1861.
*Report of the Adjutant General of the
State of Tennessee on the Military
Forces of the State from 1861 to
1866* (Nashville, 1866).

Tennessee Historical Magazine.
Tennessee Historical Quarterly.
Tennessee House Journal.

Tenn. Senate Journal	*Tennessee Senate Journal.*
Tenn. Official Manual (1890)	Charles A. Miller, comp., *The Official and Political Manual of the State of Tennessee* (Nashville, 1890).
Tennesseans in the Civil War	Civil War Centennial Commission, *Tennesseans in the Civil War: A Military History of Confederate and Union Units with Available Rosters of Personnel* (2 pts., Nashville, 1964).
Titus, *Picturesque Clarksville*	William P. Titus, ed., *Picturesque Clarksville, Past and Present* (Clarksville, 1887).
U. S. Official Register	*Register of the Officers and Agents, Civil, Military and Naval in the Service of the United States ...* (Washington, 1851-).
U. S. Statutes	*United States Statutes at Large.*
Warner, *Generals in Blue*	Ezra J. Warner, *Generals in Blue* (Baton Rouge, 1964).
———, *Generals in Gray*	Ezra J. Warner, *Generals in Gray* (Baton Rouge, 1959).
Webster's Third International	*Webster's Third New International Dictionary of the English Language, Unabridged* (Springfield, Mass., 1968).
West Point Register (1970)	The West Point Alumni Foundation, Inc., *Register of Graduates and Former Cadets of the United States Military Academy: Cullum Memorial Edition* (West Point, 1970).
West Tenn. Hist. Soc. *Papers*	West Tennessee Historical Society *Papers*.
White, *Messages*	Robert H. White, *Messages of the Governors of Tennessee, 1796-1907* (8 vols., Nashville, 1952-72).
Wooldridge, *Nashville*	John Wooldridge, ed., *History of Nashville* (Nashville, 1890).
WPA	U. S. Works Project Administration, Historical Records Survey (Nashville, 1936-41).

Chronology

1808, December 29	Born at Raleigh, North Carolina
1812, January 4	Death of father Jacob Johnson
1822, February 18	Bound as tailor's apprentice to James J. Selby, Raleigh
1826, September	Arrived in Greeneville, Tennessee
1827, May 17	Married Eliza McCardle
1828, October 25	Birth of daughter Martha
1829-35	Alderman, then mayor
1830, February 19	Birth of son Charles
1832, May 8	Birth of daughter Mary
1834, February 22	Birth of son Robert
1835-37, 1839-41	State representative
1841-43	State senator
1843-53	Congressman, first district
1852, August 5	Birth of son Andrew, Jr.
1853-57	Governor of Tennessee
1857, October 8	Elected to Senate
1860, May-June	Candidate for Democratic presidential nomination, Charleston
1860, December 18-19	Speech on Secession
1861, September-October	Speaking in Kentucky and Ohio
1861, November 27	Sequestration proceedings against Greeneville property
1861, December 5	Return to Senate
1861, December 19	Named to Joint Committee on Conduct of the War
1862, January 31	Speech on Expulsion of Senator Bright
1862, March 3	Appointed military governor
1862, March 12	Arrived in Nashville
1862, March 18	Appeal to the People of Tennessee
1862, March 22	Speech to Davidson County Citizens
1862, March-April	Purge of Nashville city government
1862, May 9	Proclamation re guerrillas
1862, May 12	Speech in Nashville
1862, May 24-early June	Speeches in Middle Tennessee area
1862, June-July	Controversy with Nashville clergymen

1862, July 4	Speech at Nashville
1862, August 18	Assessment of Confederate sympathizers
1864, November 8	Elected vice president
1865, April 15	President following Lincoln's assassination
1866, August 28-September 15	"Swing around the circle"
1868, February 24	Impeachment by House
1868, May 16, 26	Acquittal by Senate
1869, March	Returned to Greeneville
1869, October 22	Defeated for Senate
1872, November 5	Defeated for congressman-at-large
1875, January 26	Elected to Senate
1875, March 5-24	Served in extra session
1875, July 31	Died at Stover home in Carter County

THE PAPERS OF

Andrew Johnson

1861

Speech at Newport, Kentucky[1]

September 2, 1861

We are in the midst of a civil revolution, such as is unparalleled in the history of nations, but it is not my purpose to entertain you with a fine speech, but to speak to you of facts. I appeal not to your passions or prejudices, but to your understanding, in a plain, blunt manner.

Secession is the cause of the present woe of this nation. Secession commenced in the Garden of Eden, when Adam and Eve hid themselves from the presence of God, and it might be traced by its skulking characteristics down to the present time, all through the history of the world. Let me ask any one within sound of my voice what right they have lost under the folds of the Stars and Stripes? [Cries of none, none.] When and where have the traitors of the South shown any violation of their rights under the Constitution? They have not and cannot make such a showing.

I most heartily concur in the sentiments embodied in those resolutions,[2] and I say again with the distinguished President and patriot, Jackson, that the Union must and shall be maintained. [Cheers.] Not like the late President did Jackson do when danger threatened the Union, "By the Eternal," he "took the responsibility;" but Buchanan lay supinely upon his back while the Union was being frittered away by traitors before his eyes! Then South Carolina hauled down the glorious Stars and Stripes, and hoisted the Palmetto flag. Louisiana next put up hers, a Pelican, noted only for its great capacity for swallowing, and she was true to the genius of her banner in swallowing United States property, robbing arsenals and treasuries.[3] Next, Alabama hoisted her rattlesnake banner—what a charming one to rally under?—and the banner of freedom was trailed in the dust. Thus, Secession commenced in Eden, under the wiles of the arch serpent, and it ended with the rattlesnake of Alabama. But what is the consequence? Industry is paralyzed, and amid the general stagnation our very liberties are imperiled.

Slavery was made the pretext to break up our glorious Union. There was no right violated, nor never could be if the people would abide by the Constitution. But, thank God, the *people* of the United States did not, do not, sanction this unholy rebellion. The leaders of it tell you here in Kentucky that Slavery is in danger; but it is only a pretext to terrify you and draw you into the yawning gulf of Secession. I am a Southern man, sharing the prejudices of my section, and I am no abolitionist, but I tell you, my fellow countrymen, that Secession has done more harm today than all the abolitionists in the country put together since we were a nation. [Cheers.]

Men talk about their rights, will you go to the South to get them? Will you tell them in the South to come here and get them for you? [Cries of "no! no!"] Your distinguished representative in the United States Senate—I say distinguished, for I use terms of respect toward him as I would toward any other Secessionist—I labored hard for. I spent my money to print and circulate his speeches, and I stumped the State of Tennessee to elect him, but I stand here to-day to disavow those acts. I disown him. He deceived me. The fault was his; if he deceive me again the fault will be mine. I desire to express my mind here, which I cannot do in Tennessee, from which I am an exile, John C. Breckinridge was not representing Kentucky when he was sent to the Senate by her people. He was helping to break up the United States.[4] [Shouts of "down with the traitor!"] Now let us look at the eligibility of representatives to that Government to be erected upon their views. The Senator must be worth five hundred pounds sterling and ten negroes. I have asked in Kentucky if the Hon. John C. Breckinridge is eligible upon those conditions,[5] and I have been told no. Now I own but eight negroes, and not nearly the amount of money named,[6] yet the people of my State sent me to the Senate of the United States, and, I thank God, I was made welcome there. [Loud cheering.]

We are fighting for our Government! Government was made for man, and not man for Government. The old monarchical idea is just the reverse, and so it will be under Secession rule. Its leaders commenced by violence and force, and by those means they will sustain themselves. They have excluded the voice of the people; don't let them do so with you in Kentucky. Don't let them shut the doors of your Legislature. [Cries of "No!" "No!" "We'll tear down the doors first."]

I am not particularly for the Administration, but if Mr. Lincoln administer the laws according to the Constitution, I will sustain him, and so will you, my friends. If he does not, impeach him and hurl him from his seat. But he has done well thus far. What power had he when he assumed the reins of Government? None.[7] Despotism was out, and its march was from the South! Traitors cry out about Lincoln's war. Lincoln's war, forsooth! Who brought it on? Answer me *that*. Why, the South, and let her take the consequences! Let us see. Fort Sumter was garrisoned by 60 or 70 men under Buchanan, and Beauregard erected his batteries opposite its walls, but could not wait a few days until the inmates would be starved out. So he played his artillery upon that little band of brave men, and made them surrender. This is a fair sample of the whole course of Secession.

But where are their boasts of taking the Capital by a certain date, now long past, and all the other threats made thereabout? What have they done? Proclaimed war. Now whose war is it—Lincoln's? [Cries of "No!" "No!"]

The Secessionists' object now is to keep up excitement by which alone they can carry their point, which if carried, a rule with the iron rod will follow. But let us fight for the Government we have, and not be betrayed, deluded into advocating for a moment one untried, which is sure to lead to the devil. Oh! let us, my fellow-countrymen, fight for that Government founded and cemented by the noble blood of the sires and patriots of the Revolution.

Talk has been made about compromise! But there is no sincerity in these talkers about compromise. What, compromise with traitors armed and with cannon pointed at your Capital. Treat with them indeed! If we cannot live with them as we have lived, think you we can live peaceably under the treaty? Never. Never.

But fighting must be done; let us do it now and do it well. We must hand down to our children unsullied that national honor handed down to us and purchased by the blood of our fathers. What kind of a Government will you have framed by Jeff. Davis and his myrmidons, think you, if they should succeed in seizing the capital?[8] [Shouts of hang them.] I know him well, and his crew of traitors. They are worse traitors and more corrupt than was the Roman Senate with Catiline at its head. Disappointed ambition like a canker, has gnawed at their hearts[9] in which there is only bitterness and hate left to dictate their actions. They are a bogus aristocracy and could not brook the elevation of a man to the Presidential Chair because he rose from the ranks of the people. They could not wait four years, when in due course of things they might have taken their chance of power, but they made the election of Mr. Lincoln a mere excuse for their treason, and if they should succeed, a military despotism will inevitably take the place of this free, liberal and most glorious Government. If this Republic falls, it can never be succeeded by another, nor can an example be found in history to controvert my statement.

I am an exile—a fugitive, not from but for justice, and my crime is my feeble efforts to support the Constitution; but if the people of Tennessee could speak to-day, an overwhelming majority of her people would shout for the Union! We want Kentucky, who fought with us side by side, at New Orleans,[10] to come and do so again and under the same flag for the same cause—Liberty. If you give us your help, the Stars and Stripes will float over every Court House in the State in a very brief period. [Cries of "We will, we will."]

Let me ask you again, to be again assured are you Kentuckians willing to see the graves of Washington and Jackson and your own beloved Clay surrounded by accursed Secession bayonets? [Shouts of never, never.]

Then again I feel encouraged, and in the name of Tennessee I thank you, and I thank those fair women present who have come here to encourage, by their presence, their sons and brothers and fathers and lovers to fight the good fight. Long may they live to set a patriotic example not excelled in history, and long may we live to fight for our glorious privileges as a people and a nation, even if they are only to be continued at the cost of our heart's best blood.[11]

Cincinnati *Gazette*, September 3, 1861.

1. Fresh from his August 31 address in Cincinnati, Johnson reached Newport on September 2, drawing the largest crowd in the town's history. After a lengthy parade of home guards and unconditional Union men, the procession gathered at the Court House Square—"crowded with ladies"—to hear the "patriot exile from Tennessee." Following welcoming resolutions which depicted him as "torn and sundered" from his family "by wicked and traitorous hands" and which declared that Kentuckians would see him "returned to their arms," the patriot exile acknowledged with a bow the "deafening and enthusiastic cheers" and proceeded with his speech. Cincinnati *Gazette*, September 3, 1861.

2. Before Johnson spoke, Newport Mayor Edward W. Hawkins had read a list of nine resolutions which blamed the war on southern disunionists, endorsed Jackson's "Our Union must and by the eternal shall be preserved," and went on record in full support of the effort to restore the Union. *Ibid.; Williams' Cincinnati Directory* [Newport] (1866), 152.

3. A reference to the seizures by state troops on January 10 and 12 of Forts St. Philip and Jackson on the Mississippi River and the arsenal at Baton Rouge and to the $536,000 in the U. S. mint in New Orleans, appropriated by the state and turned over on March 14 to the Confederate government. *American Annual Cyclopaedia* (1861), 318-19; Long, *Civil War Almanac*, 24, 49.

4. During August and September, Breckinridge, still senator, canvassed Kentucky organizing "Peace Picnics" as a means of ensuring adherence to the legislature's policy of neutrality. He spoke at Lexington on August 29 and in Owen County on September 5. His recent visit in Newport was probably typical of his between-speech activity of meeting with friends in an effort to gain support. William C. Davis (editor, *Civil War Times Illustrated*) to Andrew Johnson Project, April 9, 1971. For Breckinridge, see *Johnson Papers*, II, 387n.

5. On the surface, Johnson seems to be describing senatorial qualifications for the Confederate Congress; actually he is presenting a garbled version of the conditions for sitting in the South Carolina house of representatives under that state's constitution of 1790, the model Johnson apparently assumed the Confederacy would adopt. The Confederate Constitution had no property requirements for either House or Senate. Had there been such a stipulation, the Kentuckian would not have met it, inasmuch as he had been obliged to sell his last slave and Lexington residence in 1857, in order to buy a home in Washington when he became vice president. *The Constitutions of the Several States of the Union and United States in the Year 1859* (New York, 1879), 268; William C. Davis, *Breckinridge: Statesman, Soldier, Symbol* (Baton Rouge, 1974), 172.

6. In 1860 Johnson held five slaves: one adult male, one adult female, and three children—two females and one male; he made no declaration of property. 1860 Census, Slave Population, Tenn., Greene, 14th Dist., 5.

7. As early as his speech of December 18-19, 1860, Johnson had invoked this argument, which presumed the unity of Democratic senators on all southern issues. His reasoning here was more fully elaborated by the *Enquirer*, whose correspondent reported him as saying, "Had there been no secession from the Capitol of members of Congress from the South, there would have been six of a majority against all of Lincoln's policy, and so far as making aggressions upon the South, the Administration would have been powerless." Speech on Secession, December 18-19, 1860, *Johnson Papers*, IV, 42; Cincinnati *Enquirer*, September 3, 1861.

8. "A h-ll of a Government," a voice replied—to which Johnson rejoined, "Yes, sir . . . and my friend, you'll have the devil for a ruler." *Ibid.*

9. Perhaps suggested by "Banish the canker of ambitious thoughts." Shakespeare, *Henry VI*, Part Two, Act I, sc. 2.

10. Kentucky and Tennessee soldiers made up the bulk of the forces under Jackson at New Orleans in 1814.

11. The speaker, who concluded "amid . . . loud and prolonged cheering," was followed by Marcellus Mundy, a Philadelphia attorney who would later command the 23rd Ky. Inf. in Tennessee and become one of Johnson's closest allies.

From Richard Apperson

September 2, 1861, Mount Sterling, Ky.; ALS, DLC-JP2.

Wants Johnson to come to Kentucky inasmuch as a "large majority of the Secession party . . . formerly belonged to the Democratic party— Hence there would be peculiar fitness in your addressing them"; observes that the "white flag or *Breech Clout* party" is untiring in its efforts "to inflame the public mind."

To John P. Wilson[1] [Olney, Ill.]

Cincinnati Ohio

Private   Sept 4th 1861.

J. P. Wilson Esqr
Dear Sir
     Your letter of the 4th inst[2] has just been recieved. I regret that I cannot give you the information desired in your letter— I have not recieved a letter from my own family Since I left home in June— I have heared from them occasionally by person who have come from Tennessee—
The last time I saw your father which was before I left home I think they were all well and doing as well as could be expected where secession bears sway[.] You cannot get letters into Tennessee now and it will be some time before you can— I hope though the time will come when the constitution and the Supremacy of the law will [be] restored, when Tennessee will again be what she once was—
If the Legislature of Ky will do what it ought to do,[3] there will be in a short time a force sufficient to go into Tennessee and brush secession out— There are five thousand troops now in Ky ready for the march[.] Some 1,500 of them are from E. Ten who have been run off from their homes and fled to Ky for protection— I start to dy for Camp Robinson where the troops are stationed—[4]
     Pardon this hurried and in coherent scrawel and accept assurances of my esteem[.]

Andrew Johnson

ALS, DLC-JP.

1. Although Johnson addressed the envelope to "James P. Wilson," the correspondent was John P. (b. *c*1832), a blacksmith in 1850 and a decade later an "Ambrotypist" in Olney, Illinois. His father, James C. (b. *c*1810), a farmer and carpenter, was elected chairman of the Greene County Court in 1864. 1850 Census, Tenn.,

Greene, 368; (1860) 10th Dist., 96; *ibid.*, Ill., Richland, Olney Township, 49; Carl N. Hayes, Neighbor Against Neighbor, Brother Against Brother: Greene County in the Civil War (typescript), University of Tennessee Library, Knoxville, 20.

2. Not extant.

3. Unionist-dominated after the August election, the legislature finally abandoned its neutrality policy on September 18, calling for the expulsion of Confederates occupying Columbus and placing Gen. Robert Anderson, of Sumter fame, in command of Kentucky volunteers; perhaps this was "what it ought to do." Coulter, *Civil War in Kentucky*, 97-98, 114.

4. For Tennessee exiles in Kentucky, see *Johnson Papers*, IV, 664-65, 671, 681-82.

From Amos A. Lawrence[1]

(near) Boston. Sept 13. 61.

Dear Sir

A person calling himself Carlyle Murray[2] of Adair Co Ky has been here with letters from yrself & Mr Emerson Etheridge[3] addressed to himself. He professed to be in the confidence of the Union men of the Border States & to be a member of a secret Union organizatn.

I fear that he is a secessionist & a spy, & that he is a member of the Union League,[4] if that extends thro. the Border States. There is reason to believe that his name is Parker H French a man noted in the S. West. He is very much of a gentleman, modest, & intelligt, & about 36 years old. He has lost his right arm, & has several scars on his person. By one name or the other, I think he draws a pension from Govt. When he left here ostensibly for Washn. I gave him $1000 wh. he was to hand over to you or to Mr Crittenden[5] after paying his own expenses incurred in a matter of buss <u>ss</u> for me with one of the Departments.

Please to inform me whether you know such a man, or have recieved or written letters to him.

At the same time please to inform me whether you have recd $200 wh. I sent you several weeks since for Mr Brownlow.[6]

I have ordered his arrest in Phil.[7] In order that this may not be made public before he is taken, it will be the safest course not to mention the matter at present.

Yrs Respy & truly

Amos A Lawrence

Hon. Andrew Johnson.

ALS, DLC-JP.

1. See *Johnson Papers*, IV, 61*n*.

2. For Parker H. French, alias Carlyle Murray, see *ibid.*, 563*n*.

3. See *ibid.*, III, 88*n*.

4. The reference to "Union League" is rather puzzling, inasmuch as the league's position ran counter to French's imputed disloyalty. The explanation may lie in Lawrence's growing awareness that French was recruiting for the Knights of the Golden Circle, an organization which sought to disguise its southern cast by a constitution and purpose couched in misleading verbiage, including many references to the Union. His confusion may also have arisen from the fact that both the Knights and the emerging Union League dealt heavily in secrecy, rituals, and passwords—symbols dear to the

hearts of mid-century Americans. Lafayette C. Baker, *History of the United States Secret Service* (Philadelphia, 1867), 97; Clement M. Silvestro, *Rally Round the Flag: The Union Leagues in the Civil War* ([Ann Arbor, 1966]), 4; George F. Milton, *Abraham Lincoln and the Fifth Column* (New York, 1942), 81.

5. For John J. Crittenden, Kentucky unionist senator, see *Johnson Papers*, II, 217n.

6. Lawrence seems to have forgotten Johnson's acknowledgment of the two hundred dollars he had received in August. See Letter to Amos A. Lawrence, August 14, 1861, *ibid.*, IV, 677; for William G. Brownlow, see *ibid.*, I, 130n.

7. In addition to collecting funds for East Tennessee from Lawrence and his friends, French had also involved the Boston philanthropist in a scheme to sell two steamers to the U. S. Navy—a swindle which led Lawrence to charge him with obtaining money under false pretenses. Temporarily taken into custody at Philadelphia in October, French was soon released, only to be apprehended in Branford, Connecticut, by Lafayette C. Baker, "the Superintendent of the Government detective police from Washington," and Benjamin Franklin, Philadelphia chief of police; under the alias of "Jackson," he had been organizing a lodge of the Knights. Incarcerated at Fort Warren until February, 1862, French was released after taking the oath of allegiance. Edward McGowan, *The Strange Eventful History of Parker H. French, with Introduction, Notes and Comments by Kenneth M. Johnson* (Los Angeles, 1958), 49; Washington *National Intelligencer*, November 9, 1861; *OR*, Ser. 2, II, 1275; Baker, *United States Secret Service*, 93-98; Boston *Daily Advertiser*, February 25, 1862.

From James W. Smith[1]

Cleveland, Ohio. Sept. 18th., 1861.

Hon. Andrew Johnson,
Dear Sir,

I would beg pardon for the liberty, and introduce myself as brother of the Adjt. 10th. Penna. Regiment, S. B. Smith,[2] who claims the honor of paying you a visit. I left Wilson Co., Tenn. about the first of June. Wholesale falsehood carried that county for secession; and that from Gen. Caruthers[3] and others in whom the people had confidence. Ex Gov. Campbell[4] was the only *true* man of influence there, and he did not dare to speak lest his property or family should be molested. I think that the K.G.C's[5] although comparatively limited in number gave most of the life and zest to the movement that carried the state into rebellion. "Bill" Stokes[6] talked in July of coming to Washington but being insulted went to his farm an anti-war semi-Union man. A large majority of the people in Wilson and adjoining counties would vote for the Union if the *true* issue was put befor them; but the probability is that the decided measures which the government will have to adopt on the slavery question will keep them deceived until an army carries intelligence to them.

But, Sir, I write to tell you that I am a Tennesseean in need. I left my property in Tenn., am just finishing my l[e]gal studies at the school here;[7] there is no business for a young lawyer to do now and I want some employment.

If you could procure me an office either in the civil or military state paying $75 or $100 per month, though I might never be able to repay, I would always acknowledge the favor. I am not drilled. I would volunteer as a private if it were not for the indolent and demoralizing habits such a life engenders. I can rely upon nothing but my candor and your sympathy to influence you to notice this. I could get a few men in Ohio to recommend me but could not ask them to do so. *This* is the most humiliating act I ever did. *My life* secession may *take but my integrity* it *can never shake*.

J. W. Smith
Box 2127. Cleveland. Ohio.

Hon. A Johnson,
Tenn.

ALS, DLC-JP.

1. James W. Smith (b. c1837) was a farm laborer with $300 in personal property. 1860 Census, Tenn., Wilson, 15th Dist., 218.

2. Sion B. Smith (b. c1836), first lieutenant and adjutant in the 10th Pa. Vols., USA, was promoted to major in 1862 and commanded companies at Mechanicsville, Gaines Mill, and Glendale in the Peninsular Campaign. 1850 Census, Tenn., Wilson, 10th Dist., 852; OR, Ser. 1, V, 479, 487; XI, Pt. II, 424.

3. Robert L. Caruthers (1800-1882), Tennessee legislator (1835-37), congressman (1841-43), and state supreme court judge (1852-61), was a member of the Confederate Provisional Congress. Elected in 1862 to succeed Harris as governor, he never assumed office; appointed brigadier in the state militia in 1864, he subsequently became professor of law at Cumberland University, Lebanon. BDAC, 669; Robison, *Preliminary Directory*, Wilson, 58-59.

4. For William Campbell, see *Johnson Papers*, I, 367n.

5. Originating in the South and spreading to the Midwest, the Knights of the Golden Circle, a secret order advocating the extension of slavery, eventually became the organization of the Peace Democrats who opposed the war. In 1863 its name was changed to the Order of American Knights; in 1864, to Sons of Liberty. Wood Gray, *The Hidden Civil War: The Story of the Copperheads* (New York, 1942), 70, 163, 166.

6. For Stokes, Tennessee congressman, see *Johnson Papers*, IV, 406n.

7. Probably the Ohio State and Union Law College, established at Poland in 1855, moved to Cleveland in 1857, and later, when operated by former congressman John Crowell, known as the Crowell Law School. James H. Kennedy, *The Bench and Bar of Cleveland* (Cleveland, 1889), 120-21; Virginia R. Hawley (Western Reserve Historical Society) to Andrew Johnson Project, March 19, 1974.

From William S. Speer[1]

Louisville Ky 29 Sept 1861

Gov. Johnson—
My Dear Sir—

I have had to leave Tennessee on account of my devotion to the Federal Union. Of course I left nearly all I owned behind. I write to offer you a fellow exile's regards and to request you to do me the favor (which I much need) to remind the President of my application for an office. My papers on file at the State Department will show that it was promised me. I asked for a Consulship, but will accept any position the President may assign me. I beg you to act promptly in this matter, as in case I can not get my appointment I must turn my attention to some business in this strange land for a support. My funds are low.

I came by private conveyance by way of Murfreesboro, Lebanon, Gallatin, Glasgow, Bardstown and Louisville.— Kentucky is arming—for both sides—but the enlistments for the Union are not so numerous rapid and hearty as to quell all my fears as to the result in this State.

In Middle Tennessee the feeling remains about what it was three months ago. But the numerous victories of the Confederate arms have made Union men despair, and many of them are going over "for the South." It will tickle your vanity a little to learn that your ancient brethren would give ten of the best regiments in the Southern service to have you in Nashville![2] But, my friend, the hearts of all good men are with you. I heard numbers of Kentuckians on my route say "Andrew Johnson shall be our next President." How zealously I would labor for such a consummation I need not again say to you.

Volunteering is "done for" in Tennessee.[3] The last requisitions for the "reserve" thirty thousand has not been responded to. Two fifths of the citizens refuse even to muster. And the Union men never will fight against their country even under a draft. Ah, how it pains one to hear cultivated men, noble men, once proud and happy freemen say—"We are slaves,—subjugated—let us still hope for deliverance."— Oh for the bugle blast of a Rhoderic Dhu[4] on the hills of Tennessee! It would not sound in vain. But the patriots are unarmed, and displays of bravery now would be fool hardiness. There is no mail—no press—by which to concentrate opinion or effort there.— Yesterday I sent a long letter to the Secretary of State[5] on the state of affairs South. Doubtless you can get to peruse it if you desire.—

Poor Tom Nelson got his tail bobbed and returned to East Tennessee advising every body to bob theirs![6] It is incredible and yet true. Brownlow is inching South![7] On the 16th seven prisoners went down on the cars to Nashville—Union soldiers of East Tennessee—"Traitors" to the State,—and John Bell, Neill Brown[8] would not raise a voice in their behalf! Damn such leaders to all eternity, say I! The very first to desert and betray the friends of the Union, and yet the champions par excellence of "the Union, the Constitution and the Enforcement of the laws!"[9] It makes my blood boil to think of it.—

It seems hard that I who have done and suffered so much for this administration have not the chance to take service under it in these times. A word and an hour of your time will secure me a place I am confident. I sent you several letters—but doubtless they never reached you—the Secession rascals having intercepted much of my correspondence, and used them to my detriment[.][10]

Let me hear from you *this week*.

Your faithful friend
Wm. S. Speer

ALS, DLC-JP.

1. See *Johnson Papers*, IV, 369n.

2. Speer, in his desperate need for place, may be forgiven for what would appear to be patent, nay errant, flattery in suggesting that Johnson's former Democratic associates, now so diametrically opposed to his unionist stand, would be willing to forgo such military might if they could but have the Senator in Nashville where he could be silenced. That they wished to remove him from the fray is clear; that they would make such a sacrifice is not documented.

3. An obvious reference to the raising of troops for the Confederacy. The military bill of May 6 had authorized the governor to call up 55,000 volunteers—25,000 for active service and 30,000 reservists. Since all males between eighteen and forty-five were technically enrolled in the state militia, some of which had already reported as units, there was considerable duplication of rolls which caused confusion whenever a call for volunteers or reserve militia was made. There is some doubt about the numbers Harris was actually able to enlist. Connelly, *Army of the Heartland*, 33-34.

4. A sixteenth-century Highland chieftain and outlaw who befriended the Douglases, bitter enemies of King James V, Roderick Dhu with his bugle summoned his clans to a gathering place in preparation for battle with the royal army. Frank N. Magill, ed., *Cyclopedia of Literary Characters* (New York, 1963), 588; Walter Scott, *The Lady of the Lake* (1810).

5. This letter to Seward has not been found.

6. Although refusing to identify himself with the Confederacy when captured and taken to Richmond early in August, Nelson drew up a statement promising to abide by Tennessee's recent decision. Released and allowed to return to his home in Knoxville, he wrote an explanation disavowing "any promise to Confederate authorities that he would use his influence for the Confederacy," but counseling his friends "to abstain from further opposition to the Confederate or Tennessee Government." Thomas B. Alexander, *Thomas A. R. Nelson of East Tennessee* (Nashville, 1956), 87-93; *OR*, Ser. 2, I, 826. For Nelson, see *Johnson Papers*, I, 159n.

7. Early in the month Brownlow had explained to his readers that reports of his adherence to the secessionist cause were inaccurate. Rather "I am not a candidate for martyrdom or imprisonment during the war and as I have been overpowered . . . I have determined to moderate in my tone, to cease the course of warfare I have waged and to yield to the neceseity upon us." Knoxville *Whig*, September 7, 1861.

8. For former Governor Brown, see *Johnson Papers*, IV, 302n.

9. The key phrase in the short platform of the Constitutional Union party—the political principle upon which the party of Bell and Brown stood. Donald B. Johnson and Kirk H. Porter, comps., *National Party Platforms, 1840-1972* (Urbana, 1973), 30.

10. There is no evidence that Johnson received any of Speer's letters after mid-March. On February 26 an anonymous letter, purported to have been written by Speer, appeared in the New York *Tribune* stating that three-fourths of the people of Bedford County "will vote for the total abolition of Slavery rather than have this Union dissolved." New York *Tribune*, February 26, 1861. See *Johnson Papers*, IV, 369n, 386n, and H. M. Majors to Johnson, March 6, 1861, Johnson Papers, LC.

To Gideon Welles,[1] Washington, D. C.

Cincinnati, Sept. 30, 1861

I have been principally in Ky Since leaving Washington, not losing one day. I have visited a large number of the Counties in State and can confidently state that Ky is now right and will settle down so.[2] The Clamor about Lincolns guns[3] and federal troops have all subsided, and the *Union* Sentiment or the feeling to sustain Govt. is now in the ascendant, and increasing daily. There are now two thousand fugitives from East Tennessee under Arms in Ky and impatient to march back upon their oppressors. Tennessee can be and must be redeemed, the people are for the Union. There are large numbers of Ky volunteering every day into the service of the U. S. I shall be a few days in Ohio for the purpose of aiding in keeping up the feeling of volunteering. . . .

Andrew Johnson

ALS, NN-Stan V. Henkels Catalog No. 1342, p. 38.

1. For Gideon Welles, secretary of the navy, see *Johnson Papers*, IV, 504n.

2. The senator's role in Kentucky was not exclusively that of morale builder among wavering Kentuckians and uprooted East Tennesseans. Under Secretary of War Cameron's directive, Johnson's endorsed approval was required on all vouchers issued by Alexander H. Adams, the treasury agent authorized to make disbursement under the Act of July 31, "providing for certain expenses for the protection of the loyal citizens of the States of which the inhabitants are or may be in rebellion against the Government of the United States." In fact, Adams was admonished that "In all matters relating to your Agency in which you shall not receive express instructions from this Department, you will follow the directions which may be given you by Mr. Johnson, who has my entire confidence." Cameron to Adams, August 26, 1861; Vouchers endorsed by Johnson, September-October, 1861, Mrs. Betsy Bachman Carrier, Bluff City, Tennessee.

3. Although Kentucky was officially neutral during the early months of the war, there was widespread unionist sentiment. Lt. William Nelson of the navy, eager to capitalize on this feeling, called on President Lincoln early in May and convinced him that the Kentucky unionists should be furnished arms immediately. The President approved an initial consignment of 5,000 muskets to be sent to Cincinnati from whence they were to be sent to home guard units in different parts of Kentucky. The first issue of guns was soon exhausted and on June 5th, 5,000 more were authorized. Disunionists sneeringly spoke of them as "Lincoln guns," commenting on "the atrocity of Lincoln in arming one class of men in Kentucky by the lawless instrumentality of clandestine agents." Coulter, *Civil War in Kentucky*, 88-90; Daniel Stevenson, "General Nelson, Kentucky, and the Lincoln Guns," *Magazine of American History*, X (August, 1883), 115, 119-28, 132.

Speech at Columbus[1]

October 4, 1861

Gov. Johnson said that, though he was himself an exile he nevertheless came among the people of Ohio as a friend and fellow-citizen, and bespoke their kind indulgence of his plain spoken manner and husky voice. I come to speak of the condition of our country, both as it was and now is; also to speak of the condition of political parties as they have been and now are.

Heretofore the condition of the country has been such that when we divided into parties we did it in the spirit of concord and amity. Our party strife then was mostly to demonstrate which was the most devoted to the Union of the States and the perpetuity of the Government. On occasions of our conventions all parties, whig, democratic, or republican, would place their flags upon their stands, and carry them at the head of processions; but they were always and everywhere the *same flag*,—the "Stars and stripes," emblematic of our National Union. So also the subjects and issues upon which we divided were various,—the tariff, the sub-Treasury, the Public Lands, Internal Improvements, &c., but in the advocacy and discussion of them all, the effort of each was, still, to show their policy best for promoting and strengthening the Union. Who ever heard, amid them all, measures advocated to destroy the Government? Never was such a measure admitted; but even the thought and tendency were discountenanced and disavowed. This was our course, and such our policy, my friends, in times past.

But now a new issue is made. The clear, naked question now made is—shall this Union of States be disrupted? Shall this Government, under which we have lived so long and done so well, and by which we have made progress in prosperity beyond any other nations on the globe, be overturned and destroyed?

In truth, only so long ago as the last autumn, during the canvass for the Presidential election, no party had avowed any different views from those of old. Mr. Lincoln, Mr. Bell, Mr. Breckenridge, and Mr. Douglas all advocated the Union of the States. In this canvass I had a part, and advocated the candidate of my choice because I deemed him the best to secure the Union for which all seemed to be contending. I come not here, my friends, to speak with a forked tongue: I have nothing to conceal. I have been all my life a Democrat,—a Democrat in the proper acceptation of that word, the central idea of which is *man's capability of self-government.* It is this fundamental principle that I have ever held as a cardinal tenet in my political creed as a Democrat. As far back as the year '33, when Gen. Jackson was President, with whom many differed as to policy, but whom all concede to have been, a Patriot, a Soldier, and a Statesman, when I was but a young man engaged in my shop, when the Old Hero's proclamation was issued in that struggle with Calhoun to put down the monster nullification, which was the parent of this greater monster, Secession, then my mind imbibed the doctrine of that proclamation. On that I took my stand as a Democrat; and have ever since to this day held the same doctrine in relation to the Union of the States.

During that struggle with nullification all the prominent statesmen of the nation, Webster, Clay and others, rallied to the support of Gen. Jackson, who did not hesitate to use both the army and the navy to put down that opening rebellion against the government. And shall we now continue divided? Shall we stop to ask whether the Administration or the President is a Whig, or a Republican, or a Democrat? Whosoever is for preserving this government as handed down to us from our fathers will rally to the support of the President now, as all patriotic statesmen of every party rallied to the support of the President in 1833. This is the only way to preserve this government. Let the government first be secured then we may again divide, in a friendly way, upon party issues as before. But now the question is how to maintain our Constitution and protect our country from overthrow.

Last fall, as I remarked, I engaged in the Presidential contest. As a democrat, my selection of candidates was between Douglas and Breckinridge. I advocated and labored for Mr. Breckinridge. I did so because I thought him the stronger man of the two, and best calculated to preserve our National government from disaster. I thought him the stronger man to preserve, not to destroy. And I had, what I deemed, good and sufficient reasons for that opinion, in Mr. Breckinridge's public acts and speeches; which I, as did thousands of others, accepted as the true exponent of his views. (Here Gov. Johnson read extracts from speeches of Breckinridge, breathing the most exalted devotion to the Union, and invoking anathemas upon all who would assail it!)

For these reasons, continued Gov. Johnson, I esteemed him to be altogether reliable in the cause of the Union; and my judgment led me to believe that we could best preserve the Union under him. Accordingly, on our Breckenridge tickets, in Tennessee, we had printed the following:—"NATIONAL DEMOCRATIC TICKET—INSTEAD OF DISSOLVEING THE UNION, WE INTEND TO LENGTHEN AND STRENGTHEN IT." (Applause.) But now how do we stand? Because Breckenridge has proved recreant, shall we Democrats follow him into the infamous bond of traitors? (No, no!) Now that he has proved false to all his own declarations, and joined Jeff. Davis and his accomplices, I ask you, as patriots and men who are governed by principle, can you, will you, *dare* you follow Breckenridge into this camp of treason and rebellion? (Cries of *No, never*! and great applause.) I sustained him in good faith, on the basis of his supposed fidelity to Democracy. I, like you, am mortal; I cannot see what is passing in the secret recesses of the human heart, any more than you can. I was deceived, as you might have been. I did not know that he was a traitor. I trusted him; and he deceived me. That was *his* fault. But let me assure you, my friends, that if ever John C. Breckenridge deceives me again, it will be *my* fault! (Cheers and laughter.) I mention this not from egotism, but to make known to you my true position. And standing now in this position, my eyes opened, my mind now undeceived, let me exhort all of you in Ohio to quit party issues and stand up with an undivided front for your flag and your country.— (Immense applause.)

But it is said that all this difficulty might have been compromised. Who brought this war upon the country? Not those who talk of compromise; but by those who scout all compromise. It is said that it could all have been arranged at the last Congress, if the right spirit had been shown? Those who speak thus talk as though this idea of Secession were a new thing; and therefore they use very prettily the dainty phrases of compromise, peace, &c. But when we examine this question we shall find that this idea is not of modern origin. When, then, did it begin? When was it started? Gov. Johnson here read from the Montgomery (Ala.) *Advertiser*—the great secession organ—which says: "Shall it be said that we have been precipitate? On the contrary, it has been done coolly and deliberately. It has been the subject of thought for *forty years, and for ten years the all absorbing theme in political circles from Maine to Mexico*.["]²

Thus you see, my friends, that this goes considerably beyond the last Congress, and we see the condition now. And even further back than this—as far back as 1833 this idea was nestling in the treacherous mind of South Carolina. I hold in my hand the manuscript letter of the Old Hero of the Hermitage, signed in his own peculiar, long, uncouth, but bold and unmistakable handwriting. It is the signature and sign manual of him whose bones are now environed by the base myrmidons of Secession, and is addressed to his friend, Hon. A. J. Crawford, of Georgia. (Gov. Johnson here read Gen. Jackson's well-known letter, in which he speaks of nullification as "dead," &c., speaking of this as but a "pretext" for disunion; and prophesying that *"negro slavery will be the next* PRETEXT."³

Continuing, Gov. J. said—Here my friends, you see the wise forecast of this remarkable man. Nothing in Daniel or Isaiah has been more literally fulfilled than this prediction of Andrew Jackson, written 28 years ago—this war of Secession is upon us, and the subject of Slavery is the "PRETEXT!" I feel, my friends, in thus reading from this letter now before me, a degree of awe, as though I were handling mystic things: here is the prophesy,—behold about us its *absolute fulfillment*! To my mind it seems as though through this a voice spoke from the tomb, and that I heard the coffin breaking, the shroud rustling; could see the long, skeleton finger of the departed shake menacingly at the traitorous horde, and a sepulchral voice exclaiming—"BY THE ETERNAL, THIS UNION MUST AND SHALL BE PRESERVED!"⁴ (*Thunders of applause.*)

You will notice, my friends, that Gen. Jackson used a peculiar and expressive word—*"pretext."* You know its meaning; it signifies a false appearance, an ostensable reason for covering up the real motive; and exactly such the slavery question is. With the Seceders it is but a "pretext." I was in the U. S. Senate at the time of the introduction of what are called the Crittenden Resolutions of Compromise. The members then present, who are now with the rebel forces some five or six in number, *refused to vote, for the purpose of having them voted down*. Then they forthwith telegraphed to every capital and county in the South— *"there is no hope of compromise!"*⁵ And at the same time, had they desired and voted for the compromise the resolutions would have been carried.

Compromise is a pleasant and pretty word to utter; it falls "trippling [*sic*] from the tongue."⁶ But, my friends, let me ask, what has the Government to compromise? If it is right, there is nothing to retract. Would you have justice compromise with crime? Shall truth compromise with falsehood?—right with wrong?—virtue with vice? I tell you, nay; for in all such compromises the wrong will advance upon the right; vice will encroach upon virtue; falsehood will infringe upon truth; and crime will trench upon justice. Satan himself, after setting up the standard of revolt in Heaven, would have been glad to gain a compromise; and, because it was refused him, he seceded, and established a separate confederacy in Pandemonium![7] (Laughter and applause.) Again, my friends, if you offer peace, can you get a compromise? Those arch traitors say, 'no—there can be no peace without a full recognition of their Confederacy'—and this is to admit the *right* of Secession. It is equivalent to admitting away the whole structure of our government, and resolving substance into shadow,—changing order into chaos.

I know that it is charged here in Ohio, as well as elsewhere, that if certain things had been done war would have been avoided. But I do not believe it. Remember, that in the phrase of General Jackson, they only wanted a "pretext;" and Lincoln's election was seized upon. I do not stand here as Mr. Lincoln's advocate. When right I will sustain him; if wrong I will condemn him, as I would "any other man." But what danger to Southern interests or institutions could arise from Mr. Lincoln? Even if his heart were fatally bent on mischief he would have been powerless. There was in the Senate, at his inauguration, a majority of ten against him, politically; and the changes in the Senate during his administration would not have left less than five or six of a political majority against him.[8] He had his Cabinet to appoint, but it remained with the Senate to confirm. If these rebel and run-away Senators had remained; as they should have done, Mr. Lincoln could not have appointed a Cabinet Officer, nor a foreign minister, nor a commercial consul, nor a commissioner, nor even a clerk, unless the appointees were suitable and satisfactory to the majority in the Senate. If he were to negotiate an unfavorable treaty we could reject it; he could not even draw his own salary for bread and cheese at the White House without the consent of the Senate. But those traitorous Senators would not stay to defend the Government against any danger, real or imaginary, that Mr. Lincoln's administration might cause. Nay, they only wanted a "pretext," and hence they ran away, to raise the standard of rebellion against the best government that the circling sun had ere looked down upon. And it is with these traitors, and others such as they, that you are asked to compromise while they stand with the bayonet at your bosom, and their swords at your throat! Are you ready? will you do it? (*A thundering–No!*)

Again, it was claimed by certain apologists for secession, that as the Free States were becoming so much greater in number, there would be danger of their obtaining an amendment to the constitution of such a character as to militate against the peculiar interests and institutions of the South. But what are the facts? Was any such proposal ever submitted, or even hinted at? On the contrary, your own distinguished citizen, Mr. Corwin, proposed an amendment to the constitution that should deprive Congress of the power of such hostile legislation, and proposed it in such form that the amendment should itself be unamendable.[9] The recusant

Senators and Representatives could have adopted this; and thus closed the door *forever* against the danger they pretended to fear. But, nay; they only sought a "pretext" for consummating this plan, that had been the "subject of their thoughts for *forty years*."

Much has been said about the wrongs of the South in regard to the territories. But what was done by the Free States in the last Congress? They passed three territorial bills, for Nevada, Dacotah, and Colorado; and these included every acre we have. And in all three of the Bills provision is made against any hostile legislation, and against "any legislation *impairing the right of private property*" of any kind.[10]

This then, my friends, leaves now nothing but the Negro—the "pretext." It is perfectly clear that the rebel States want no compromise. They stubbornly demand total separation and recognition of their Confederacy. And you see, furthermore, that it is nonsense to charge this war upon parties, as such. There is something beyond and behind all this. Mr. Lincoln, in his inaugural, took the true ground, in declaring that this is essentially the people's contest for the protection of the Union.[11]

I would not be personal, but an abolitionist is as much a secessionist as any to be found in South Carolina. Now as much as these disunionists of both classes abuse each other, they, nevertheless, both unite in laying violent hands upon the government that never harmed either. If I were an abolitionist I would break up the Union; for the disruption of the Union must inevitably destroy and obliterate slavery. Hence we are for the prosecution of this war to save the government as founded by our fathers; for restoring the Constitution as we received it, without regard to the peculiar institutions of any State. That a secessionist and an abolitionist are on a par, I can prove by a simple syllogism—an abolitionist is a disunionist; a disunionist is a secessionist; therefore, a secessionist is an abolitionist! (Cheers and laughter.) Let us then stand by the Country and the Constitution as they were. What better compromise than the Constitution is possible? Suppose we separate, and form a treaty: then we become aliens, and directly we become enemies. We cannot divide these rivers that go coursing through our land. A treaty would only be a source of unending wars. Not a day would pass without causes of difficulty and contests that would drench the border in blood. If we cannot live under the constitution, we certainly cannot be safe by a treaty, nor rest upon compromise.

Not only is it the aim of the seceders to break up this Government, but they aim to change its whole form and genius. They intend to revolutionize not only its forms, but also its character. Such is my deliberate opinion. To my personal knowledge there are many in the South who have lost all confidence in the capacity of man for self government. And there are these now in the U. S. who are laboring and striving to overturn this idea, on which the whole doctrine of Democracy must rest. In Richmond this is enunciated as a principle in the new dispensation. The demonstration is small, to be sure, but like the speck on the horizon it foretells the approaching cloud,—it indicates the end in view. And that end is a *monarchy*![12] (Here Gov. J. quoted from the Richmond *Examiner* and *Whig*, passages to this purport—declaring that "rather than submit to the rule of Lincoln, they would prefer the royal rule of the amiable Queen of Great Britain!") And, said the Speaker, Mr. Toombs' organ, a leading Georgia paper, declared that "*the experiment of self-government had failed*. What kind shall we now establish? We answer, *a Constitutional Monarchy*!" The speaker cited many other items of a like character going to show that they are systematically aiming to familiarize the minds of the people with the idea. It was even broached, said Governor J. that Isham G. Harris should be king of Tennessee, and Mcgoffin king of Kentucky! (hooting and derisive laughter!) I know this Isham G. Harris, king of Tennessee! He my king! so far from being my king, I would not have him for my slave! (*immense applause*.) I know that it has been claimed of old that the masses of mankind were born with saddle and bridle on, and a favored few born booted and spurred to ride them.[13] But the idea is a libel on the manhood of man. But such is the doctrine of Jeff. Davis and his followers, who have never gained power except by usurpation. Am I to call such men my brethren? who with sword and bayonet demand that I acknowledge their usurpations? No they are not my brothers— I am a Suthern man, but thank God, I am not a Suothern traitor. (Thunders of applause.)

Who is this Jeff. Davis? Do you know? In youth, without means, this government which he now seeks to destroy, took him, and educated him at West Point, paid him, and clothed him, and fed him. When he was through his education for war the country put a sword in his hands, and charged him to use it in her defense. He now turns it upon the bosom of the country who has given him all he has, and has made him all he is. Such is the man who leads in this monster sin of secession. Men prate about Lincoln's infraction of the constitution; but have they a word of condemnation for the violations of the constitution that secession involves? No,—of that they are silent. They call it "Lincoln's war!" But whose is it? Who began it? The guns of South Carolina opened it, in firing upon the flag of the Union, and on its starving soldiers. (The Governor then proceeded to give an eloquent and glowing synopsis of the drama at Charleston.)

Suppose then, Jeff. Davis should drive out the U.S. officers, take Washington, and putting his sacrilegious hand within our archives and tear thence our Constitution and trample upon it, what kind of a government would you have? Would not the sword be used to keep that power which the sword had usurped?

But we are told if you don't go for cotton you are all ruined! But, my friend, let me tell you that there is a king over cotton— That is a homely unpretending monarch they call bread and meat! And which can live longest think ye—they who live on cotton without bread and meat, or they who have bread and meat but no cotton? (*cheers and laughter.*)[14]

Speaking of cotton, let me tell you, my friends, that Cotton is no King at all. Those who live by raising Cotton cannot do without your bread and meat half as well as you can do without their cotton. Certainly it is true that South Carolina buys a great deal of your produce; but did you ever hear of her buying any that she didn't want? Was she ever known to buy your surplus for mere accommodation to you? Did you ever know her to spend her millions for your flour and bacon out of mere generosity? And must we bow down to her, and do her high and mighty bidding for fear of losing her market for our flour and beef, our corn and bacon? True, as I passed along up through Kentucky, I found that most all those stock raisers there, who had sold great numbers of their mules to South Carolinians on credit, were nearly all Secessionists.[15] Do you ask what connection there can be between raising mules and becoming Secessionists? I'll tell you,—'tis this: Those Kentuckians think that by following South Carolina out of the Union they will stand a good chance to get their pay. But I tell you, my friends, 'tis all a mistake: the best way to get your money back is to compel South Carolina to come back.— (Laughter and applause.)

The South may be a good customer for the products of your farms and factories; but after all you will find that the great bulk of your surplus food finds its way across the ocean.[16] And, in any event, it is certain that the whole matter of buying and selling, of raising and supplying, is governed, not by man's generosity, but by the laws of commerce, which secession can no more control than it can stop the sunshine. And there is a day of reckoning to come when the hundreds of millions that the South owes to the North, of her commercial debt, will have to be paid. Are they fool hardy enough to presume that that mountain of indebtedness is to be sunk and lost in this opening gulf of secession? They but deceive themselves if they cling to any such shadow: It will have to be paid, even to the uttermost farthing. Yet secession would promise them that all is to be wiped out with the achievement of "Southern independence!"

And such, my friends, is secession. It promises nothing, aims at nothing, but *pulling down*. Its great purpose is, disruption and destruction. It is entirely an element of dissolution and disintegration. It builds up nothing; it is but the universal dissolver of all that society holds sacred. It wages war upon humanity and civilization. It strikes at all the recognized and cherished organizations of the country, including the constitution and the laws. See its desolating effects in my own State. Only so long ago as last April we were a peaceful and a prosperous people. When our people were then called upon to come up to the polls, and express their minds upon the subject of secession from the old Union, they came; and they recorded a vote of 64,000 of a majority against secession.[17] The leaders of the secession party, who had sold themselves to the Southern Confederacy, finding themselves foiled by this loyal vote of the people, through the villainy of this same Isham G. Harris, the would-be king of Tennessee (!) at the dictation of South Carolina,[18] procured a meeting of the Legislature; and *in secret session*, in defiance of the popular will as expressed by this popular vote, made over the State of Tennessee, with all its people and interests, its forts, arms, and arsenals, with an army of 55,000 men, to the Southern Confederacy! Yes, my friends, *in secret session* was this great iniquity consummated. Our people were not consulted, were not even permitted to know the deep laid schemes of damning villainy that were taking them in its toils, and laying them and their State as a sacrifice upon this altar of unhallowed ambition.

And *after* they had done this, *after* the ordinance was passed by this secret and sinful conclave, then they graciously granted us permission to vote upon the matter in June following! And I would to God, my friends, that it were in the power of human tongue to depict before your minds the mockery of that June election. Think of it:—they had scattered the armies of the Confederacy through the State; Virginia soldiers were there; South Carolina troops were there; Alabamians were there; and all were permitted to vote![19] And while thus voting in mockery and derision themselves, they kept, by violence and outrage, and threats, our peaceable and order loving citizens from the polls. And yet whenever, we, the advocates of the Union, could go into such counties as we could reach, the vote against the ordinance of secession was almost unanimous,—at least four out of every five voted with us.[20] And this too in counties where we found ourselves threatened and outraged to such an extent that when we stood up to speak we had to announce to the bullies and bragadocios present that if there was any fighting to be done during the meeting we would prefer to attend to that first, and do the speaking afterwards.[21] (Cheers and shouts of "bully for you!")

But, *they voted us out*! And even afterwards we sent to them commissioners,[22] saying to them, Our people do not desire to separate from the Union and leave the Constitution of our fathers; if you insist upon going, act for yourselves, and go; but in God's name we ask of you to let us alone! To this, what was the reply? *Armed men*! We appealed to them yet again in like terms. What was the answer from Montgomery? *Their cavalry*![23] Yes; while yet beseeching them to act upon their own doctrine, and let us alone, the hoofs of their cavalry were indenting our plains, and the tramp of their troops was about our homes! And yet there are those who set up the puling cry—'Let there be no coercion!'[24] What! A secessionist declaring against coercion! Why, God bless you, friends, they never got anything except by coercion. They coerced Tennessee, Georgia, Alabama and Virginia out of the Union. They attempted it in Maryland—the Government stopped it:[25] they are now attempting it in

Kentucky, and there the *People* will stop it! (Cheers, "good, good!") Their whole career has been one of coercion, of outrage, insult, blasphemy and crime. Detachments of their myrmidons, who were sent, as they said, 'to protect us from the despotism of Abe Lincoln,' (?) would pass through our county, in Tennessee, on the railroad. As they went they saw the flag of our country, the glorious old Stripes and Stars, floating from the gable of an humble school house, where the little boys had placed it as an emblem of their pure and dawning love for the Union. What did those miscreants do? They stopped their train, and with hootings and ribaldry, with menaces, and execrations and blasphemy, they tore it from the children and trampled it in the mire! They would enter private houses, and under pretence of seeking for ammunition, would rummage drawers and desks, robbing the family of the money, and the females of their jewels and heir-looms.— They would order their meals and their lodging in tones of insolence and in terms of insult. They would feed their horses with wastefulness, and scatter the food recklessly on the ground. And after eating to the fill of their insatiate appetites, and rioting and rummaging, they would mount, and, with oaths and obscenity, would tell the family to charge it all to Jeff. Davis. And this, my friends, is Secession!

They came into my own county: they called at my house. Some of their number came forward and demanded of my family whether I was at home,—saying that if I was they had come to take me, and hang me! Pleasant intelligence this, for *gentlemen* (!) to communicate to wife and daughters! But my daughter, indignant at their conduct, said, 'No, my father is not at home; he is absent in another county where he is making a speech for the Union; and this I presume you knew, or your cowardly crew would not have dared to show themselves at this house!' (Thunders of applause!) They then sullenly withdrew. As they passed on through the neighborhood they came upon the house of a Union family: the husband was not at home; but his wife, a stout hearted woman, had her Union flag at the gate post.— They insolently commanded her to remove it—she would not. They attempted to seize it, and she seized it; they struggled for it, but she kept her flag. They then went into the woods, cut a hickory withe, and returning scourged her person with it![26] (Hisses and cries of "shame, shame!") This my friends is Secession, and these are the men you are to "compromise" with! Some of these same demons, five of them, fiends in human shape, stopped at the house of a man named Markham, who, seeing them approach, and fearing insult and outrage to himself, if he remained, and thinking that they would not be so likely to provoke a quarrel with the family if he were not present, took his rifle from its resting place, and retired unobserved by them into a little thicket hard by the house, in order to be at hand in case they offered any abuse to his family. He had an amiable wife, and two daughters, the youngest a girl of about twelve years, and the other just blosoming into womanhood, about sixteen, as beautiful as the morning and as pure as the dewdrop. The Secessionists entered and insolently demanded dinner for themselves and feed for their horses. The wife told them there was the crib and the fodder, and they would give them their dinner. They took the hay and the corn and scattered it about the ground, and ordered the ladies to hasten their dinner.

In due time the meal was prepared, and soon greedily devoured. After sating their appetites at the table they began to address rude remarks to the wife and daughters. One attempted to make love to the young lady, when her young sister, seizing the tin horn, or trumpet, which is kept in almost all rural home-steads to make a summons to diner or sound an alarm to the neighbors in case of any accident, sprang to the door and blew a blast. At this the hellish demon turned, drew a pistol from his girdle, fired its bullet through her brain; and with one wild shriek she fell in agonizing death at the feet of her screaming mother! That blast, the shot, the shriek and scream pierced the ear of the waiting father: he sprang from his retreat, he stood at his door—one glance revealed all; and, taking deliberate aim, he sent his rifle's bullet straight through the villian's heart! (*A suppressed voice*, '*Good, by God!*' followed by tremendous applause!) The other four alarmed at the trumpet blast, and knowing that the whole neighborhood would soon be upon them, mounted their horses and fled. The enraged father, finding them beyond his reach, turning to where the slayer of his little daughter lay, seized his ax and cut his brutal body into quarters and threw them out as only fit for the dogs to devour![27]

Such, my friends, is secession at home. It is robbery, rapine, and murder. And it is marching towards you, and will be upon you. You must arm for your own defence. I speak not to you in fables. These things occurred not in a remote country, but right over there in Tennessee. I seem even yet to hear the shriek that went up from that young and innocent heart, as it took leave of life, so wild, so clear, so agonizing, that even angelic spirits might come to listen and avenge![28] Will you not then, rush to the support of your government, and the rescue of your country from a reign of terror that has no parallel in the history of civilized man? We demand it of you as a right and not as an appeal to your sympathy. And if you would secure your own State of Ohio from the same ruthless aggression, you must arm and meet this monster iniquity without delay. And let me tell you, friends, that you do not best secure your safety by throwing up ditches and trifling entrenchments around Cincinnati. No—*the line of your defence is the Southern boundary line of Kentucky*![29] (Cheers, and "that's so.")— Kentucky is now open. She is ready and determined to fight *for* the Union and *in* the Union (Great applause.) She has heretofore fought *for* Ohio and Indiana in their infancy, she will now fight *with* them to repel from her own borders an invader not less ruthless than those who then invaded yours.[30]

But am I told that Kentucky is for neutrality? That was an idea of the politicians: not the people's idea. The *people* of Kentucky are right. And when the people are right, you cannot conceive, my friends, how quickly the politicians become right! (Cheers.) They have a most holy dread of minorities. (Laughter and applause.) Kentuckians have said to us of Tennessee—"you shall not only have arms, but also *regiments to carry them*, to liberate you from the tyranny of secession."[31] (Great applause.) And will you of Ohio not join hands with Kentucky in this crusade for the redemption of the land that holds the sepulchre of Andrew Jackson? (Shouts of 'yes, yes, we will!') Then, as I said before, your columns must advance to drive te invader from their contemplated winter quarters among the full granaries of Kentucky and Ohio, back through Tennessee, and thence into the Gulf of Mexico! (Cheers.) Yes, friends, let them be driven like the swine of old, who were likewise possessed of the devil, into the depths of the sea, and be overwhelmed in its waters![32] (Laughter and applause.)

As Tennessee, and Kentucky, and Ohio joined hand in hand to march through the swamps and lagoons round about New Orleans in 1815, so let them be united again. True we have lost battles. Lyon is slain, Mulligan surrendered,[33] and Manassas was lost. What of it? The *cause* nor the country is neither surrendered nor lost. And these mishaps of war should only serve, like the receding lava in the volcano, to send forth a still more fiery and engulphing torrent of vindicating power. (*Applause*.) Our course and our cause must then be onward; and we shall hope, with the aid of the mighty Northwest, to open our way through Kentucky, and into Tennessee, where there are 265,000 patriots and Union men—more than the whole white population of South Carolina[34]— waiting for the coming of your banners, and ready to take the van of your column when you come. (*Tremendous applause*.) We want not the rear nor the flank—give us the post of danger, and with your stalwart columns around which to rally, and we ask no favor of the defiant foe.

I had always given myself credit for some manhood. But, the other day, when I stood in the presence of TWO THOUSAND Tennesseeans,[35] exiled like myself from their homes of comfort and the families of their love, I found that my manhood and sternness of mind were all nothing, and that I was only a child. There they were, my friends and fellow citizens of my beloved State, gathered upon the friendly soil of Kentucky, from the tender stripling of sixteen to the gray-haired fathers of sixty, all mourning the evil that has befallen our land and our homes, but all seeking for arms wherewith to go back and drive the invader from our fields and hearth-stones. (Applause.) I essayed to speak to them words of counsel and encouragement. But speech was denied me. I stood before them as one who is dumb. If it be true that out of the fullness of the heart the mouth speaketh,[36] it is also true that the heart may be too full for the utterance of speech. And such were ours—two thousand of us exiled

Tennesseeans, and all silent! Silent as a city of the dead! But there was no torpor there. There were the bounding heart and throbbing brain, there were the burning cheek and the blazing eye, all more eloquent than ever were the utterings of human speech. (*Cheers*) Each of that throng of exiles, who had wandered among the mountains and hid in their caverns, who had slept in the forest and squeezed themselves, one by one, through the pickets of the invader, each was now offering comfort and pledging fidelity to the other. Youth and Age were banding together in a holy alliance that will never yield till our country and our flag, our government and our institutions are bathed in the sunlight of peace, and consecrated by the baptism of patriotic blood. (*Vociferous applause.*)

There were their homes, and there too is mine,—right over there. And yet we were homeless, exiled! And why? Was it for crime? Had we violated any law? Had we offended the majesty of our government or done wrong to any human being? Nay, none of these. Our fault, and our only fault, was loving our country too well to permit its betrayal. And for this the remorseless agents of that "sum of all villanies,"[37] Secession, drove us from our families and firesides, and made us exiles and wanderers. But the time shall soon come when we wanderers *will go home*! (Cheers.)— For depend upon it, my friends, this monstrous iniquity cannot long subsist. Some bolt of Heaven's righteous vengeance "red with uncommon wrath, will blast the traitors in their high estate."[38] But whatever they may do,—though they may ravage our State and make desolate our homes, though they convert the caves of our mountains into sepulchres and turn our vallies and plains into grave-yards, there is still one thing they *cannot do*—they never can, while God reigns, *make East Tennessee a land of slaves*!— (Tremendous and continued applause.)[39]

Ohio State Journal (Columbus), October 5, 7, 1861.

1. This Columbus appearance came in the midst of a nine-day tour during which the senator addressed "mass meetings of the friends of the Union and the Constitution" in eight cities of central and southeastern Ohio. Although Johnson was scheduled to speak at two o'clock on the east piazza of the capitol, the threat of rain caused an adjournment to the house chamber. The crowd filled "the ample Hall to its utmost capacity . . . a large number of ladies" standing in the galleries "throughout the whole of Gov. Johnson's three hour speech." The reporter observed that the senator looked "exceedingly well, though his voice was a little hoarse from previous speaking." It may be noted that the line of argument follows rather closely that laid down in Johnson's most recent Senate address. Cleveland *Plain Dealer*, September 24, 1861; *Ohio State Journal* (Columbus) October 5, 1861; see Speech in Support of Presidential War Program, July 27, 1861, *Johnson Papers*, IV, 606-42.

2. Although placed in quotation marks, this passage is derived from the presumably more accurate version found in *ibid.*, 617-18.

3. Jackson's letter of May 1, 1833, directed to the Rev. Andrew J. Crawford, register of the land office at Demopolis, Alabama, had been previously quoted by Sumner of Massachusetts in a Senate speech, December 10, 1860. John Spencer Bassett, ed., *Correspondence of Andrew Jackson* (6 vols., Washington, 1926-33), V, 71-72; *Cong. Globe*, 36 Cong., 2 Sess., 32.

4. An embellishment of the Old Hero's Jefferson birthday toast in 1830: "Our Union; it must be preserved!" Bassett, *Jackson Correspondence*, IV, 191n.

5. Johnson refers to the failure to vote, not on the compromise *per se*, but on Senator Clark's amendment, a substitute for the Crittenden resolutions, which passed, 25-23, on January 16, 1861. Southern senators abstaining were Johnson of Arkansas, Iverson of Georgia, Benjamin and Slidell of Louisiana, and Hemphill and Wigfall of Texas. Toombs of Georgia, and Hunter and Mason of Virginia were the originators of telegraphic dispatches advising their constitutents of the failure of compromise. *Cong. Globe*, 36 Cong., 2 Sess., 409; Allan Nevins, *The Emergence of Lincoln* (2 vols., New York, 1950), II, 402; see also *Johnson Papers*, IV, 176n, 644n.

6. Shakespeare, *Hamlet*, Act III, sc. 2.

7. Milton portrays Pandaemonium as Satan's capital. *Paradise Lost*, Bk. I, ll. 755-56; Bk. X, ll. 424-25.

8. For examples of Johnson's earlier discussion of the Democratic majority in the Senate, see *Johnson Papers*, IV, 42, 51n, 135, 151, 567.

9. Thomas Corwin, chairman of the House Committee of Thirty-three, had submitted on January 14 a series of five resolutions, the most significant of which declared that the Constitution could not in any way be altered or amended so as to interfere with the domestic institutions of a state. Passed on February 28 (133-65), the proposal was approved by the Senate on March 2 (24-12). Though nine of its Senate supporters were Republicans, all of the negative votes came from members of that party. Nevins, *Emergence of Lincoln*, II, 405, 409-10; *Senate Journal*, 36 Cong., 2 Sess., 383; see also *Johnson Papers*, II, 16n; IV, 573n, 614-15.

10. Quoting Section 6 of the acts establishing these territories, Johnson had made the same point in his latest Senate address. Speech in Support of Presidential War Program, July 27, 1861, *ibid.*, IV, 615-16.

11. The passage—"This is essentially a People's contest. On the side of the Union, it is a struggle for maintaining in the world, that form, and substance of government, whose leading object is, to elevate the condition of men"—appears in Lincoln's message to Congress, July 4, 1861, rather than in his inaugural address. Basler, *Works of Lincoln*, IV, 438.

12. The ensuing discussion of monarchial tendencies in the Confederacy repeats essentially the position taken in his July 27 speech. *Johnson Papers*, IV, 618-20. For Robert Toombs Georgia senator, and Beriah Magoffin, Kentucky governor, see *ibid.*, I, 612n; III, 416n.

13. Awaiting execution in 1685 for conspiracy to assassinate Charles II of England, Richard Rumbold remarked philosophically, "none comes into the world with a saddle upon his back, neither any booted and spurred to ride him." In a letter written shortly before his death, Jefferson made a similar observation. *DNB*, XVII, 397; Jefferson to Roger C. Weightman, June 24, 1826, in Paul L. Ford, ed., *The Writings of Thomas Jefferson* (10 vols., New York, 1892-98), X, 391-92.

14. At this point the October 5 report of the speech ends, to be resumed two days later.

15. According to the Louisville *Journal* of July 3, 1861, "some of the most rampant secessionists in the State are mule-traders who have large sums of money due them in the Confederate States."

16. Although adverse weather conditions in Europe and a series of bountiful harvests in the United States greatly increased grain exports in the early 1860's, Johnson was unduly optimistic about the prospect. Despite the fact that overseas shipments of corn and cornmeal increased in 1861 and 1862, the amount was less than what the South had customarily purchased. Paul W. Gates, *Agriculture and the Civil War* (New York, 1965), 224, 228.

17. In his speeches during the months following the February 9 (there was no Tennessee referendum in April) vote on whether to call a convention to consider the crisis of the Union, Johnson chose to ignore those figures which were less dramatic (69,387 against and 57,798 for convention) and regale his listeners with the somewhat more dubious statistics of the vote for delegates. These, as cited by pro-Union sources, gave a 64,114 or 67,054 majority for unionists out of a total vote of 116,552. That these figures were palpably unreliable is obvious from the fact that a purported analysis by sections found an overwhelming Union sentiment (24,091 to 9,344) in West Tennessee, a proportion but little less than that shown for the eastern and middle divisions of the state. *American Annual Cyclopaedia* (1861), 677-78; see also *Johnson Papers*, IV, 680n.

18. In this somewhat misleading assertion, the speaker is apparently using South Carolina as a surrogate for the Confederacy. In the wake of Sumter, Harris summoned the General Assembly into a second extraordinary session on April 25. After hearing the governor's message calling for Tennessee's affiliation with her sister states, the legislators conducted their deliberations in secrecy; five days later they were addressed by Confederate special agent Henry W. Hilliard of Alabama; and on May 1 they adopted a resolution providing for a military league with the Confederacy. In view of these developments the June 8 popular referendum on a state declaration of independence was in effect *ex post facto*. White, *Messages*, V, 279-89; *OR*, Ser. 1, LII, Pt. II, 70, 84, 88.

19. There is no proof that soldiers from other states voted in the election of June 8. However, in an effort to ensure a verdict favorable to separation and in order that Tennessee soldiers serving outside the state might participate, the legislature waived the constitutional requirement that each voter must cast his ballot in the county in which he had resided for six months. Estimates of this out-of-county vote vary from 2,711 to 6,241; a breakdown of the latter figure shows nearly 2,500 in service in Virginia or Florida. Temple, *East Tennessee*, 208-9; J. S. Hurlburt, *History of the Rebellion in Bradley County, East Tennessee* (Indianapolis, 1866), 49; White, *Messages*, VI, 303.

20. Although the vote in several East Tennessee counties was as one-sided as Johnson claims—Anderson (97 for separation, 1,278 for no separation), Campbell (59 to 1,000), Morgan (50 to 630), Sevier (60 to 1,528)—there is no clear evidence that these majorities resulted from the telling arguments of unionist speakers. Campbell, *Tenn. Attitudes*, 291.

21. During the second canvass for secession, Johnson found his safety threatened even in unionist East Tennessee. The danger of assassination forced him to avoid public conveyances, and he was warned that should he attempt to speak at Blountville, Rogersville, or Concord, his life would be in danger. Temple, *East Tennessee*, 197-98, 201.

22. The Greeneville Convention, which met June 17-20, 1861, appointed Oliver P. Temple of Knox County, John Netherland of Hawkins, and James P. McDowell of Greene as commissioners to petition the General Assembly to allow "East Tennessee and such counties in Middle Tennessee as desire to co-operate with them [to] form and erect a separate State." *OR*, Ser. 1, LII, Pt. I, 176.

23. Soon after General Zollicoffer's July 26 assignment to the Department of East Tennessee, he notified the Confederate authorities that he proposed to "form a chain of infantry posts" from Cumberland Gap to Livingston and, with the object of cutting off communication between Kentucky and Tennessee unionists, had six cavalry companies patrolling the mountain gaps. In early September he sent a cavalry company to assist the infantry operating in the Johnson-Carter County area. *OR*, Ser. 1, IV, 374, 382, 398.

24. The charge of Federal "coercion" had been one of the telling arguments among southerners both during and after the secession crisis.

25. Alabama and Georgia extremists, exerting strong pressure for immediate action in their secession conventions, triumphed over fairly sizable delegations of moderates and cooperationists. Neither convention called for a referendum. Although Virginia's convention and the Tennessee legislature called for a popular vote, both states were already aligned with the Confederacy before the ballots were cast. In Maryland secessionist hopes were dashed by Federal occupation after the Baltimore riot of April 19, 1861. Ralph A. Wooster, *The Secession Conventions of the South* (Princeton, 1962), 52-59, 81-91, 142-49, 181-88, 247-50; *Johnson Papers*, IV, 250; George L. P. Radcliffe, *Governor Thomas H. Hicks of Maryland and the Civil War* (Baltimore, 1901), 54-112 *passim*.

26. Documentation for this incident has not been found. However, there is some reason to think that Johnson's account may have provided the inspiration for a report subsequently circulated to the effect that a "band of rebels," failing to find Johnson at his home, "scourged" his wife with a "hickory withe." Louisville *Journal*, October 18, 1861.

27. Probably a variation of the story told many years later by Julia Marcum (*c*1845-*fl*1934), whose father, Hiram C. (b. *c*1813), a Scott County farmer with $4,000 in real estate and $1,500 in personal property, was a member of the home guard. According to Julia, a "score of rebels" came to the house, threatened to burn it and kill all the family. Although her father shot at the intruder, it was Julia, with axe in hand, who

slew him. There is no mention of a younger child's being murdered nor of the quartering of the Confederate soldier's body which was turned over to his conrades. Julia later taught school in Williamsburg, Kentucky. 1860 Census, Tenn., Scott, 6th Dist., 17; Esther Sharp Sanderson, *Scott County and Its Mountain Folk* (Huntsville, 1958), 188-89.

28. A very loose paraphrasing of a passage from Pope's "The Temple of Fame," this was one of the speaker's favorite poetic allusions. See *Johnson Papers*, I, 143; III, 348.

29. The legislature, having abandoned Kentucky's "neutrality" through the passage of resolutions demanding the withdrawal of Confederate troops and calling the citizenry to the defense of the state, had in reality made Kentucky the southern boundary of the Union—the line at which military thrusts from the Confederacy must be repelled. Coulter, *Civil War in Kentucky*, 114-15.

30. A reference to Kentucky assistance against the Indians north of the Ohio at the end of the eighteenth century. At first conducting small freebooting or filibustering raids, Kentuckians later made up a large portion of the expeditions of Generals Arthur St. Clair (1791) and Anthony Wayne (1794). Again in 1811, Kentuckians fought under William Henry Harrison at Tippecanoe, Indiana. Randolph C. Downes, *Council Fires on the Upper Ohio* (Pittsburgh, 1940), 311-13, 315-19, 324-26; Charles Freeman, *Old Tippecanoe: William Henry Harrison and His Time* (Port Washington, N.Y., 1969[1939]), 99, 103.

31. Hard upon its formal action of September 18 abandoning neutrality, the Kentucky legislature resolved shortly to place all available arms and equipment under Federal control; and on the last day of the month it passed legislation authorizing recruitment of 42,000 volunteers to be mustered into Federal service. Clearly, such resources, in addition to defending the state against its own secessionists and any Confederate reprisals, would be enlisted in the salvation of Tennessee. Coulter, *Civil War in Kentucky*, 114, 126.

32. Matt. 8:30-32.

33. Nathaniel Lyon (1818-1861), Connecticut native and West Point graduate (1841) who had served in the Mexican War, prevented Missouri troops from capturing the Federal arsenal at St. Louis on June 13; subsequently he drove secessionist forces to the southwestern part of the state, where he was defeated and slain at Wilson's Creek, near Springfield, on August 10. Flushed with victory, the Confederates proceeded to Lexington, an important post on the Missouri River, and besieged 2,600 Union troops under Col. James A. Mulligan who surrendered September 20. Mulligan (1830-1864), a New York-born Chicago lawyer and clerk in the department of the interior (1857-61), had organized the "Irish Brigade," the 23rd Ill. Captured in September, he was exchanged in November, and after briefly lecturing in the east and superintending Camp Douglas, he returned to the field in Virginia where he was mortally wounded at the battle of Winchester in July, 1864. *DAB*, XI, 534-35; *NCAB*, V, 329; John McElroy, *The Struggle for Missouri* (Washington, D.C., 1909), 171, 206-15.

34. Even if Johnson had used the 1850 census figures, he would have been incorrect, for South Carolina's white population at that time was 274,563; by 1860, it had risen to 291, 300. J.D.B. DeBow, *The Seventh Census of the United States: 1850* (Washington, D. C., 1853), 339; Joseph C. G. Kennedy, comp., *Population of the United States in 1860 . . . The Eighth Census* (Washington, 1864), 451.

35. According to the Louisville *Journal*, October 12, 1861, Johnson here refers to a recent speech at Camp Dick Robinson, near Lancaster.

36. Matt. 12:34.

37. It is interesting that this phrase, usually associated with slavery, should be employed to describe secession. An early application appears in John Wesley's *Journal* of February 12, 1772, in which he castigates the slave trade as "that execrable sum of all villanies." F. W. MacDonald, ed., *The Journal of the Rev. John Wesley, A.M.* (4 vols., New York, 1906), III, 461.

38. A free adaptation of another Johnson favorite: "Is there not some chosen curse, / Some hidden thunder in the stores of Heav'n, / Red with uncommon wrath, to blast the man / Who owes his greatness to his country's ruin?" Addison, *Cato*, Act I, sc. 1, l. 22; see also *Johnson Papers*, I, 507; III, 341.

39. The reporter concluded: "Gov. Johnson then made some beautiful and touching remarks to the ladies, who had honored the meeting with their presence; alluding to their influence in the support of patriotism, and their duty in the common defense of the common country."

To William T. Sherman[1] [Louisville, Ky.]

Private   Camp-Dick-Robinson
                                                        Oct 30th 1861—

Genl W. T. Sherman,
Dear Ser,

My intention was last night to have started this morig in Compay with Judge Adams[2] for Louisville for the purpose of Consultig with you in regard to the future movents of the Troops in this portion of your Dept— But this morig find that I will be compelled to go to London where a portion of the Regiments are now station— My opinion is, that if Zollicoffer[3] Could have been followed up at the time of his retreat, he would not have stopped until he reached Knoxville[.] If the present force Can be increased Some four or Six Regiments, prepard to take the field at once we Can have the E. Tennessee & Va Rail Road in our possession in less than three weeks with Sufficient force to hold it against the whole power of the S. confederacy which Can be brought to bar at this time— It is not necessey to make any great loss of men at Cumbrland Gap— There are other Gaps through which we can pass and turn his rear or Cut him off from all supplies— I hope that it will be both Convenient and in Conformity with your judgement to Send a force sufficient to penetrate E. Tennessee and take possession of the Road at two points— If ten or fifteen thousand men could enter E. Tennessee they could be doubled by recruits from the people in ten day's time— Hence the importance of send[ing] along in the rear of the invading Army some twenty thousand stand of arms to be placed in the hands of the new allies as they come to our standard— To remain in winter quarters on this Side of the mountain or in Ky *will* be *ruinous* to the *Union men* in the South and especially in Tennessee— The delay has already been so great, that dispare would now follow— If we invad Tennessee and place Arms in the hands of Union men they will in a very short time take charge of secession themselves and releive others from the trouble— I was *informed* at *Cincinnati that there were regimts which Could* be forwarded— I know of some my self who prefer coming to Ky & Tenn— Judge Adams will communicate all that I can write and much more intelligibly and will say no more until I see you which will be in a few dys—

Pardon the leberty I have taken in writing this note— You know the great anxity I have upon this subject—

Private

Camp-Dick-Robinson
Oct 30th 1861 —

Genl W. T. Sherman,
        Dear Sir,
                My intention
was last night to have started both
this moring in company with Judge
Adams for Louisville for the purpose
of consulting with you in regard to the
future movements of the Troops in this
portion of your Dept — But this moring
find that I will be compelled to go
to London where about
...

Please accept asserance of
my entire confidence and high
esteem
                Andrew Johnson

"Military suggestions" to General Sherman in *re* East Tennessee,
October 30, 1861
Courtesy Leonard Stern, Studio City, California.

Please accept assurance of my entire Confidence and high esteem[.]

Andrew Johnson

ALS, Leonard Stern, Studio City, California.

1. William T. Sherman (1820-1891), served in the Mexican War and resigned his commission to become a San Francisco banker (1853-57); he also practiced law in Kansas, and was from 1859-61 superintendent of the Louisiana State Seminary and Military Academy, forerunner of Louisiana State University. Reentering the army in May, 1861, he became brigadier general commanding volunteers in Kentucky and was later assigned to the Department of the Missouri under Maj. Gen. Henry W. Halleck. After service at Shiloh, Vicksburg, and Missionary Ridge, he succeeded Grant as supreme commander in the western theater. His celebrated "March to the Sea" and campaign northward, characterized by a "scorched earth" policy in Georgia and South Carolina, made his name a byword to future generations. Various postwar assignments culminated in his appointment as commanding general of the army (1869-84). Warner, *Generals in Blue*, 441-44; see also Earl S. Miers, *The General Who Marched to Hell: William Tecumseh Sherman and His March to Fame and Infamy* (New York, 1951).

2. For Green Adams, former Kentucky congressman (1847-49, 1859-61) and judge of the circuit court (1851-56), see *Johnson Papers*, IV, 525n.

3. For Gen. Felix Zollicoffer, see *ibid.*, 685n.

From George H. Thomas[1]

Hd. Qrs. Crab Orchard
Novr. 7th 1861

Gov Andrew Johnson
London Ky
Dear Sir

Your favor of the 6th inst is at hand.[2] I have done all in my power to get troops and transportation and means to advance into Tennessee[.] I believe *Genl. Sherman* has done the same. Up to this time we have been unsuccessful. Have you heard by authority that the troops at London were to fall back? because I have not, and shall not move any of them back unless ordered, because *if not interfered with*, I can have them subsisted there as well as here. I am inclined to think that the rumor has grown out of the feverish excitement which seems to exist in the minds of some of the Regiments that if we stop for a day, that no further advance is contemplated. I can only say I am doing the best I can. Our Commanding Genl is doing the same, and using all his influence to equip a force for the rescue of Tennessee.[3]

If the Tennesseans are not content and must go, then the risk of disaster will remain with them. Some of our troops are not yet clothed, and it seems impossible to get clothing[.]

For information respecting the organization of Regiments I enclose you General Order No. 70 from the War Department[.] If the Gentlemen you name can raise Regiments agreeable to the conditions & instructions contained in said order; the Government will accept them, and I hope will have arms to place in their hands, in the course of two or three months[.]

In conclusion I will add that I am here ready to obey orders, and earnestly hope that the troops at London will see the necessity of doing the same.[4]

Very Respectfuly and Truly Yours

G. H. Thomas

LB copy, DNA-RG94, Gens. Papers, G. H. Thomas; *OR*, Ser. 1, IV, 342-43.

1. George H. Thomas (1816-1870), a native Virginian and West Point graduate (1840), served in Florida, Texas, and the Mexican War, taught at West Point, and later served as a cavalry officer in Missouri and Texas. Remaining in the Federal army when the war came, he was made brigadier general of volunteers in August, 1861, assigned to duty in Kentucky, and in November placed in command of the 1st Division of the Army of the Ohio. Warner, *Generals in Blue*, 500-502; see also McKinney, *Education in Violence*.

2. The editor of the *Official Records* brackets "Not found."

3. As Thomas would learn the following day, he was mistaken about an early movement into East Tennessee. Sherman was convinced that the Confederates would not use the passes to the east, but would penetrate Kentucky in the vicinity of Somerset or Danville, aiming toward Louisville and Lexington. While not doubting the importance of an East Tennessee expedition, he had decided that there was neither force nor transportation sufficient for such a campaign and that wisdom dictated a concentration, rather than a dispersion, of effort. Sherman to Thomas, November 8, 14, 1861, *OR*, Ser. 1, IV, 347, 358.

4. Among Tennesseans encamped at London, Kentucky, discontent over delays in the liberation of East Tennessee had risen to such a pitch as to produce threats of advancing without waiting for orders. Behind Thomas' correct tone may be sensed a warning to Johnson and others who were chafing at the bit. On the same day, enclosing a copy to Gen. Albin Schoepf, commanding at London, Thomas commented: "It is time that discontented persons should be silenced both in and out of the service." Although sympathizing with the East Tennesseans, he pointed out that "to make the attempt to rescue them when we are not half prepared is culpable," especially since Gen. Simon Buckner "has an overwhelming force within striking distance whenever he can get us at a disadvantage." A clear clue to Thomas' intent is found in Schoepf's reply, approving of "the decided manner in which the case is laid down to Governor Johnson" and declaring, "this outside pressure has become intolerable and must be met with firmness, or the Army may as well be disbanded." Thomas to Schoepf, November 7, 1861; Schoepf to Thomas, November 8, 1861, *ibid.*, 343, 347.

From Horace Maynard[1]

Washington Nov. 13. 1861—

Dr. Sir,

Gen. Buell[2] left at 6 this morning & will reach his Head Quarters at Louisville tomorrow night.— Gen. Sherman going into Missouri.

I have done my best to impress upon him & Gen. McClellan,[3] that the operations between Louisville & Nashville, are quite distinct from ours. How well I have succeeded I cannot yet tell. I see that our people in E. Tennessee have begun active operations & have explained to Gen. McClellan that they must now be supported & protected, or they will be overpowered & crushed out under a most cruel & relentless tyranny. Knowing the influences which will be brought to bear upon Gén Buell at Louisville, & judging from the tone of a letter just recieved from Gen. Sherman,[4] I fear for our people. And I do not think it safe for me to leave here until affairs take a more decided turn in our direction. You know very well, how hard it is to get anything done here & then, it is only by close & assiduous & persevering attention. When our officials hear no complaint, they assume that all is going quite right & do not take the trouble to inquire.

The papers bring us a report of a brilliant victory in Eastern Ky.[5] This ought to & I suppose will leave Nelson's[6] force at liberty to operate in our behalf. Then with what we have: with the operations in western Ky, & the demonstration in front of Buckner,[7] & the destruction of the communications & the terror inspired by the blow from the Naval Expedition,[8] I should think might make a force sufficient for our purposes—

I have heard nothing from you since I left you at the camp fire near London[9] & very little indeed from the line of operations. I have looked anxiously for something, in reply to my own communications if no more.

Not seeing any good that I could do by returning just now, & thinking it likely to be important for us that some one should remain here, I will stay until I can hear from you.

Every body here seems encouraged by the improved condition of affairs.

I am very Truly Yrs
Horace Maynard

Hon. Andrew Johnson.

ALS, DLC-JP.

1. For Maynard, Tennessee unionist congressman, see *Johnson Papers*, III, 28n.

2. Don Carlos Buell (1818-1898), Ohio native, West Point graduate (1841), and Mexican War veteran, became a brigadier in 1861 and helped organize the Army of the Potomac. Transferred to the Army of the Ohio, replacing Sherman, he was promoted to major general in 1862 and participated in various Tennessee campaigns; during the fall, he undertook the defense of Kentucky against the invasion of Confederate armies under Braxton Bragg and Edmund Kirby Smith. Accused of dilatory tactics after the indecisive battle of Perryville, he was removed from command, investigated by a military commission which made no recommendations, and mustered out of the service in 1864. As the documents in this volume show, Johnson came to regard Buell as a *bête noire*, and in some quarters it was subsequently alleged that the general's downfall came as a result of a correspondence and newspaper campaign studiously mounted by the governor himself. Settling in Kentucky after the war, Buell engaged in coal mining and iron manufacturing. Warner, *Generals in Blue*, 51-52; Hall, *Military Governor*, 58-67; Maslowski, *"Treason Must Be Made Odious,"* 78-95 *passim*; see also James R. Chumney, Don Carlos Buell: Gentleman General (Ph.D. dissertation, Rice University, 1964).

3. George B. McClellan (1826-1885), West Point graduate (1846), veteran of the Mexican War, and a West Point instructor before resigning in 1857 to work with railroad interests, was appointed in May, 1861, as major general in charge of the western Virginia and Kentucky forces and promoted in November to general-in-chief of the armies. In 1864 he was the peace candidate on the Democratic ticket for President and after the war served as governor of New Jersey (1878-81). Warner, *Generals in Blue*, 290-92; see also Warren Hassler, Jr., *General George B. McClellan: Shield of the Union* (Baton Rouge, 1957).

4. A reference to the November 8 letter to Thomas: "Mr. Maynard still presses the East Tennessee expedition. I do not doubt its importance, but I know we have not force enough and transportation to undertake it. Instead of dispersing our efforts we should

concentrate; and as soon as possible our forces must be brought nearer together." *OR*, Ser. 1, IV, 347.

5. This "brilliant victory" was apparently a series of maneuvers in which Gen. William Nelson, commanding Ohio and Tennessee volunteers, forced Confederate Gen. John S. Williams from his position at Prestonburg on November 5, and from Piketon three days later, obliging him to retreat through Pound Gap into Virginia. *Ibid.*, 225-30; *Battles and Leaders*, I, 383-84; New York *Times*, November 5, 13, 1861.

6. For William Nelson, see *Johnson Papers*, IV, 549n.

7. For Simon B. Buckner, see *ibid.*, 689n.

8. All these events took place on or about November 7. The Federal forces under Grant conducted a "reconnaissance" at Belmont, Missouri, across the Mississippi from Columbus, Kentucky, using gunboats to attack Confederate batteries as a diversionary measure; the "demonstration" in the Bowling Green vicinity seemed to threaten either the disruption of Buckner's communications with Clarksville, Tennessee, or a direct attack upon his position; and the bridge-burning in East Tennessee also came on the seventh. Meanwhile, on that same day, a squadron under Flag-Officer Samuel Dupont steamed into Port Royal Sound on the South Carolina coast and captured Forts Beauregard and Walker, thereby giving the Union a strategic foothold in the area between Charleston and Savannah. *Battles and Leaders*, I, 360-67; Arndt M. Stickles, *Simon Bolivar Buckner: Borderland Knight* (Chapel Hill, 1940), 109; Washington *National Intelligencer*, November 9, 11, 1861; Long, *Civil War Almanac*, 136.

9. Maynard and Johnson had spent much of October and early November in Kentucky, the latter remaining at London with Thomas' advance units. McKinney, *Education in Violence*, 117-18.

From Joseph Powell

November 13, 1861, Sacramento, Calif.; ALS, DLC-JP.

Former "Brigr. Genl of Militia for four years," seeks army post assuring Johnson that the Tennessean has "thousands of devoted and enthusiastic friends in California," that he "could desire no position at the hands of our people that would be withheld," and that "Your defiant attitude in defence of the Union—amidst the ordeal through which you have been compelled to pass—is with us . . . the theme of daily converse and admiration."

From Lorenzo Sherwood[1]

New York November 26th 1861.

Hon. Andrew Johnson
In Senate Washington—
Dear Sir—

"What are the American Armies fighting about"—And, "what the purpose to be gained in the result of arms"—are grave questions now being agitated by all classes in Europe. "What are we fighting for"—is a question with many people at the north, who have drank in the impression that the *South* was composed of *nothing* but the *pro-Slavery* interest.

I will tell you in few words what I am fighting for. I am engaged in this contest as far as in me lies, in behalf of the non-Slave holding population of the Southern States. You know its character; and you know at the same time the disparagements under which that population, as an aggregate has labored ever since its birth. You also know the helpless, hopeless condition in which it would be placed by the Slave holding power in case it were permanently separated from its natural political Affinity with the north. You know enough of the plans of Secession to know its designs upon the mass of free labor, South; If you do not, please trace the pages of DeBow's Review[2] for the last ten years, and add what you observe cropping out in those pages, to what you must have listened to coming from individuals of high standing, and I think you will not be at a loss to discover the ultimate plan of half disfranchising the free labor of the South. It is true, this design has been covered with all but masonic Secresy; but, it has nevertheless been sufficiently disclosed, and continuously disclosed for the last ten years to convince me of its purposes.

The Slave holder of the South fears that the voting power of the South may become the governing power. In all my conversations with the intellectual politicians, I have observed this jealousy; this fear; and what has troubled the pro-Slavery Spirit most, has been the contemplated possibility of an affinity between the free labor north and South. When that transpires, it will prove the destruction of the Slave holding prestige, even in the South; and we shall hear no more of plans to break up the government, or to dismember the union.

I have grown to be sick and disgusted with the mawkish sensibility over the negro, when there is so much higher, and better, and more available ground to take in favor of the white man. Six & one half, or seven millions of white men; their disparaged condition, their fitness to be free men, and their right to disenthrallment from the prejudice which the pro-Slavery Spirit in politics has thrust upon them, affords to my mind a just basis for government consideration, in the prosecution of this war.

Allow me to tell you plainly, Sir, my Sympathies are enlisted in the great cause of white humanity in its Shirt Sleeves—the cause of that twenty six, or twenty seven millions of free American Citizens, who are bound to the eternal business of subsistence through their own industry. Their lot is, & ever must be, to toil—to toil on from generation to generation, and a pretty business it is, for less than one hundred thousand rebel Slave holders[3] to Set these toiling millions to cutting one another's throats.

What right, Sir, have we of the north to abandon our white non-Slaveholding brethren of the South to the hopeless tyrany of an Exclusive pro-Slavery policy? What right has Congress to forbear the bold and manly declaration in favor of this population, and to pledge all the adhering elements of the government to protect it, and to shelter it under the national Ensign?— Yea—if need be, to so far humble and subordinate the Slave holding spirit as to give encouragement in the right direction to the masses of the Southern white population?

It would be useless to say, that this non-Slave holding population cannot be reached. It can be reached, and can be enlisted on the side of its own protection. Let Congress, and all the governmental powers declare their Solicitude for it; and let us of the north hail it as a Brotherhood in political destiny and political right. Arms will remove the blockade to intelligence. We shall have the mass of this population with us if we take the bold, and Strong means to invite it.

It strikes me that you are the man to bring out this Subject through a congressional declaration.[4] Your Sympathies are known to be with the masses of the laboring white men, South. You are known and marked in every part of the union as their Friend. You have the moral courage to do just what your conscience tells you is best. Congresses & Conventions have been truckling to rebel Slave holders, and endeavoring to Salve over their antipathies to the Union. No effort has made them better, and nothing could make them worse. Suppose the effort Should now be made in the direction where the process of reason would naturally carry it. Nothing can be lost by making the attempt. A bold declaration would Strike more terror into the minds of the Slave holders than half a dozen Port Royal canonades—terrific as that affair appeared.[5] It would be worthy an American Congress, and Command the approval of the world. The question "what are *we* fighting for" would no longer be asked—[6]

Very Truly &c

Lorenzo Sherwood—

ALS, DLC-JP.

1. Lorenzo Sherwood (1808-1869), New York native, school principal, newspaper editor, and lawyer, was a member of the legislature's executive committee which revised the state constitution in 1846. Moving to Galveston three years later, he established a lucrative law practice and served in the Texas legislature (1855-56). As an ardent reformer and enemy of private interests, Sherwood worked in vain for the "State Plan," a state-controlled system of finance for railroads and banks; he was also a Free Soiler and antislavery advocate whose speeches prompted threats on his life, leading to his resignation from the legislature. During the war and afterward he practiced law in New York City, where he devoted "his pen and voice to the national cause." An active supporter of the Republican party, he represented Texas at a postwar convention of southern unionists and was also president of the National Cheap Freight Railroad League. New York *Times*, May 13, 1869; Earl W. Fornell, *The Galveston Era: The Texas Crescent on the Eve of Secession* (Austin, 1961), 159-78 *passim*.

2. Sherwood himself had been a contributor. See "Texas Rail-roads," *De Bow's Review*, XIII (1852), 523-25; "Agencies to be Depended upon in Constructing Internal Improvements," *ibid.*, XIX (1855), 81-88; "Agencies to be Depended on in the Construction of Internal Improvements, with Reference to Texas, by a Texan," *ibid.*, 201-5.

3. According to the 1860 census, there were 306,300 slaveholders in the states which later seceded; of these, only 95,585 owned ten or more slaves. Joseph G. Kennedy, comp., *Agriculture of the United States in 1860 . . . the Eighth Census* (Washington, 1864), 247.

4. An enclosed set of resolutions, apparently intended as a model for Johnson, declared that "the Southern rebellion has had its origin mainly in the Slave holders distrust of the political power and enfranchisement of the non-Slave holding population," and that the object of the revolt was to separate the white population of the South from their northern brothers with the view to "measurable disfranchisement." Comparing slave owners to the privileged classes in Europe who sought to control the

masses, the resolution concluded "That the wholesale murder of the white industrial class of the Union is a greater calamity upon our common country and its people, than would be the extirpation of every rebel Slavholder in the land."

5. According to contemporary accounts, the four-hour shelling of Forts Walker and Beauregard and the Confederate counterfire produced a din "distinctly heard at Fernandina [Florida], seventy miles away." Most of the defensive artillery was destroyed and the garrisons routed. *Battles and Leaders*, I, 682; *American Annual Cyclopaedia* (1861), 290.

6. Subsequent letters from Sherwood on November 28 and December 1 reiterate the same themes. Johnson Papers, LC.

Notice of Sequestration Proceedings[1]

November 27, 1861

TO Mrs. Johnson, wife of Andrew Johnson, David T. Patterson, Charles Johnson, Robert Johnson and Daniel Stover.

THIS IS TO NOTIFY YOU, that the petition[2] of which the annexed is a true copy, has this day been filed in the Clerk's office of the District Court of the CONFEDERATE STATES OF AMERICA, *for the Eastern Division of the* District of *Tennessee to be* held at *Knoxville on the 3d Monday of May 1862*, in pursuance of the provisions of the Act of the Provisional Congress of the said CONFEDERATE STATES, entitled "An Act for the Sequestration of the estates, property and effects of alien enemies, and for the indemnity of citizens of the CONFEDERATE STATES, and persons aiding the same in the existing war with the UNITED STATES." Approved August 30th, 1861.

WITNESS my hand, as *Clerk* of the said Court, this *27th* day of *November, 1861*.

Wm. G. McAdoo,[3] *Clerk*.

DS, DLC-JP18.   The original document is a printed form; the italicized material was inserted in longhand.

1. We are indebted to Professor Carl Pierce of the University of Tennessee Law College for assistance in interpreting this and subsequent (January 18, 1862) documents arising from legal actions against the exiled senator.

2. This petition, drafted by Landon C. Haynes, sequestration receiver for the Confederate States District Court at Knoxville, is not available. Pursuant to the Confederate Sequestration Act of August 30, 1861, Haynes had apparently requested the court to enjoin Eliza Johnson and others from disposing of her husband's Tennessee assets, pending his classification as an alien enemy. Moore, *Rebellion Record*, Supp. I, 19-23; for discussion of Confederate court transactions during these months relating to East Tennessee in general and Johnson in particular, see William M. Robinson, Jr., *Justice in Grey* (Cambridge, Mass., 1941), 268ff.

3. See *Johnson Papers*, II, 243n.

From Catherine M. Melville[1]

[Washington, D. C.]
441 11th St. Nov. 29th 61

Hon: Andrew Johnson,
Dear Sir,

We are exceedingly anxious to see you, or any one who can tell us the true state of things in East Tennessee.

Can we get Boxes sent to the E Ten: men who are in Kentucky? Mr. Maynard told us that *you* had got them clothing. We are constantly forwarding socks, shirts, drawers, &c. &c. to the regimental Hospitals or the needy in the troops around this place. We *would like to do some thing for the noble men of Tennessee* who have stood *firm* in the glorious cause. There are many ladies both in Penna. & N. Jersey, who would, I think, willingly help. Only let us know in what, & I assure you we have the wish to do all within the compass of our ability for the true-hearted—the brave & loyal Exiles of Tennessee. I do trust that the time is not far distant, when East Tennessee will be again as free as the breezes which fan her beautiful hills and valleys;—when *your home*, & the homes of all my beloved friends there, will again be sacred, & unpoluted by the tread of those who wear the chains of King Cotton, or cling to a supercilious & would be aristocracy.

Let us know if we can do any thing to show that we love Tennessee & honor the men who have stood unflinchingly in her defence[.]

Respectfully—   C. M. Melville[2]

ALS, DLC-JP.

1. Catherine M. Melville (*c*1810-1881), a native of Scotland, was for many years a teacher at various schools in eastern Tennessee, including the Jonesboro Female Academy in the 1830's, Greeneville, where she opened the Female Academy sometime before 1844, Bolivar Academy in Monroe County (1850-54), and the East Tennessee Female Institute in Knoxville (1855-56). Removing to Washington on the eve of the war, she sought government employment and by 1863 was a clerk in the quartermaster general's office. After the war she was a clerk in the treasury department. 1860 Census, Tenn., Greene, 10th Dist., 87; Melville to Edward C. Trigg, February 1, 1862, Johnson Papers, LC; P. H. Grisham to Oliver P. Temple, January 31, 1881 [1882], Oliver P. Temple Papers, University of Tennessee Library, Knoxville; *U. S. Official Register* (1863), 130; *Boyd's Washington and Georgetown Directory* (1864), 211; (1870), 267; Laura E. Luttrell, "One Hundred Years of a Female Academy: The Knoxville Female Academy, 1811-1846—The East Tennessee Female Institute, 1846-1911," ETHS *Publications*, No. 17 (1945), 80; Richard H. Doughty, *Greeneville–One Hundred Year Portrait, 1775-1875* (Greeneville, 1975), 187-88; see also *Johnson Papers*, I, 393*n*.

2. Three months earlier Miss Melville had thanked Johnson for "your very handsome and useful present," adding, that, when settled in her Washington residence, she would "always be glad to see you, or any of our true patriotic friends at our home." Melville to Johnson, August 26, 1861, Ser. 2, Johnson Papers, LC.

From Solomon Harrison[1]

Bloomington McLean County Illinois
Nove 30th 1861.

Gove A. Johnson (of Tennessee) Dear Sir having moved from Greene County Ten. Some fifteen months ago, and Settled down in McLean County Illinois. And all Correspondence is cut off between my old friends in Tenn. and my Self, by the Secessionists, who entercpts the mails about Cumberland Gap— Now Gove, I wish to have Some Correspondence with you. And by you I may gain all the Information required about the times in East Ten. As you are well posted on all the doings of the Secessionists of East Ten. I shall expect and Solisit a full Statement of what is going on in East Ten. and Kentucky.

The last letter I have got from East Tenn. was frome my old friend Christn Bible[2] of Warrensburg, (your old friend) in May last, (And as you) he was fore the Union, and So am I. And I hope to remain So as long as I live. For the following reasons: first the democrats had the Majority in Congress, if they had held on to it, and Could have ruled, and kept the president at bay. If he had a desire to do any thing Antagonistick to the interests of the South, he could not do it, As a Majority was against him. Therefore if the South had held on, and waited, to See what the President would recommend, and, if against the Intrest of the South, then vote it Down. I wish you to inform me if T. A. R Nelson and H Maynard are Still held as prisionors by the Secessionist at Richmond.[3] Tell me when we will have peace. let me know what prospects for peace if any. tell me if any Secession Army is Camped in Greene County Tenn. If So, where they are Stationed.

I Am living in a Settlement of Black Republicans. Some few Douglas Democrats but all for the union. Well Illinois is a fine, beautiful, level and rich Soil Country. Millions of Bushels of Corn and wheat are raised, hear with little labor. But at present grain bears very little price. Corn only 14 cts a bushel, wheat 50 cts[.] our winters are long and cold, pine Wood Scarce, and in the whole I do not like the Country as will as East Tenn.

Please write to me as Soon as you can. Direct to Solomon Harrison Bloomington McLean County Ill, and by So doing you will Confer much of a favor. My best Respects to your honour.

Solomon Harrison

P S. please Send me Some of your own Speeches, and other Documents as ocasion m[a]y Suit, and oblige[.]

S. H.—

ALS, DLC-JP.

1. Solomon Harrison (b. *c*1825) was a Tennessee-born blacksmith. 1850 Census, Tenn., Greene, 568.

2. Christian Bible (b. *c*1823), Greene County farmer, had $8,000 in real and $3,000 in personal property. *Ibid*. (1860), 8th Dist., 127.

3. Although rumors of their incarceration were rife, Nelson had been released August 14 and Maynard was never captured. Alexander, *T. A. R. Nelson*, 93.

From Leonidas C. Houk[1]

Camp Calvert Near London Ky
Dec 7th 1861

Hon Andrew Johnson:
Dear Sir,

I addressed you a letter the other day,[2] supposing you to be yet at Louisville, but for fear you do not get it, I now address you at Washington! I assure you it has been a dark time here, ever since you left.

The Soldiers have been quite impatient, and at times almost nothing would have created a general Stampede! Some of the Boys have gone home, and returned. One who went to See his folks brought back Seventeen men, to join the Service! I do not think, our men under any contingency, will turn Traitor. But, at the Same time, they are becoming Suspicious, and a great many are fearful the government is unable to Sustain itself! They are of the impression, that the government is either a failure, or it cares nothing for the East Tennesseeans. They think a demonstration Should have been made on this column ere now.

But, Just as we were getting up transportation to move to Summerset, the Acting Gen[3] received a dispatch from Gen Buell,[4] directing him to *hold on*, and we Should have a Battery, and Some Cavalry. This *Revived* the men greatly, as it Seems to indicate Something is to be done!

As to Gen Carter, the men as a general thing have nothing against him, further than they begin to Suspect he is under the Influence of Col JIM and Dr. Standford,[5] both of whom have managed to get the *ill will* of the vast majority of Soldiers as well as citizens, about this place. Col JIM is quite a man in his own opinion! Wants to rule every thing and every body! Talks Big and does nothing! He has come to the conclusion, judging from his way of doing, that he ought to have command of this Department! I have had to tell the Gentleman, that there were other men, equally as Great as him! He threatened to have me put under Guard, but I told him plainly he could not do any Such thing; that there were 800 East Tennesseeans who would rally around me, and die rather [than] See me imposed upon!

He did not attempt to carry out his threat!

You know, he is Col of a Regiment not a man of whom he was instrumental in bringing here!

I don't wish to be captious, nor to assume a Spirit of dictation, but the very best thing that could happen would be the throwing, of this important Col: and the Aristocratic, Standford, Skie-high!! They both, deserve to be cast from place, where they may not assume so much power!

I look upon them both as a curse to our Army. We hear from East Tennessee, every day, and from the news received, times are Squally indeed! The Bridge burning business,[6] has brought upon the people, the fiery vengeance of the Rebel horde! They are redoubling their diligence, in the work of Treason, and Tyrannical oppression! Arrests, and punishment, upon the Slightest Suspicion, have become common— the Secessionists are running to and fro, over the country! Brownlow, is part of his time in Blount, and part, in Sevier county![7] I don't think he has as many men around him as Report Says, but Hamp Tipton,[8] and him can render themselves Safe there, in the mountains for Some time to come! Will the government do nothing to emancipate Such *heroes*, and patriots, as the East Tennesseeans, have proved to be? Are they forsaken, by that government, for which *they* have contended, and looked upon as the greatest, and best upon earth? My good Sir, it does Seem cruel to leave those *Brave* people to the tender mercies of those who have proved to be Incarnate Devils, who possess none of the sympathies commonly entertained in the human heart?

Oh! my God, how long until East Tennessee will be redeemed?

As I write, I am informed Col Garrard,[9] is Striking his Tents to leave, for Barboursville[.]

Under what "Order" or from whom, I know not! I have *pressed* wagons, three different times, but just as I would get them in camps, an "Order" would be received to pay them, and turn them loose![10]

Bad management, Somewhere! The thing was reenacted this morning!

I am making out my Reports and as Soon as I get them completed, I intend to resign! I expect to have to visit Washington, and Louisville, in order to complete my Settlements.

There is too much responsibility attached to the Quarter Master's position; and too many to please who don't care what I may lose![11]

The Tennesseeans are coming rapidly, and if I was now ready to form a Regiment I could Soon do it, and that without much trouble!

I wish to trouble you enough to have that thing, at which we were at work when you left, attended to, if it can be done.

It Strikes me, that it would be better, to get old Simon to authorize me to raise a Regiment of East Tennesseeans.[12]

Then the captiousness, of Acting Brigadiers will not have to be consulted. I know you have a great deal to harass and perplex you, but as I will Soon be out of the Quarter-Master's buisness, as a matter of choice, I ask you to attend to getting this matter arranged! I know, it will not trouble you very much, as the Government wants men, and I can get them! If you will just Step to Simon, and Say to him you desire me to have authority to raise the Regiment, I know he will order it to be Granted! If you accomplish the matter, I wish Carpenter, Adgt of the 2d Regiment. and my Quarter master Sergeant, Will. R. McBath, and William Cross,[13] a private of Company H detailed or detached to aid me in organizing the Regiment.

Capt M. L. Phillips, and his father John Phillips[14] also wish to have authority to raise a Regiment, which I have no doubt they can easily do.

If I can make an arrangement to get Some money to advance to the men, I can get them Very fast, and that come to the Army! [sic] You may look for me in Washington in from five to ten days.

I will Send you an Instrument of Writing,[15] either with this, or in a few days which I wish you to Examine, and pass upon.

Write Soon, and give me Some Ideas, about things in general, and the prospect of getting home in particular!

Pardon this intrusion, and accept my highest regards: and come back to us as quick as you can, consistent with public duty!

Very Truly &c   L. C. Houk

To Hon A Johnson.

ALS, DLC-JP.

1. Leonidas C. Houk (1836-1891) of Clinton, at this time first lieutenant and quartermaster of the 1st Tenn. Rgt., was a cabinet-maker by trade and after 1859 a lawyer. On the outbreak of war, he enlisted as a private and was later colonel of the 3rd Tenn. Inf., USA, before resigning in April, 1863, because of ill health. Circuit court judge (1866-70) until he moved to Knoxville to practice law, he was elected to the legislature (1873-75), built a powerful political organization, and served as a Republican congressman (1879-91). *BDAC*, 1079; Temple, *Notable Men*, 128-36; *Tenn. Adj. Gen. Report* (1866), 15.

2. Not extant.

3. For acting Brig. Gen. Samuel P. Carter, see *Johnson Papers*, IV, 659n.

4. At General Schoepf's request, Buell had countermanded orders that reinforcements from Carter's regiment be sent to Somerset; the expected battery and cavalry had been ordered by Thomas. Buell to Thomas, Thomas to Buell, Carter to Thomas, December 6, and Schoepf to Thomas, December 7, 1861, *OR*, Ser. 1, VII, 477-81.

5. For Col. James P. T. Carter of the 2nd Tenn. and Robert L. Stanford, surgeon of the 1st Tenn., see *Johnson Papers*, IV, 518n, 603n.

6. Pursuant to a plan devised by the Reverend William B. Carter for crippling railroad service in East Tennessee, unionists attacked nine bridges on the night of November 8, destroying five. It was hoped that this action, coupled with a military expedition from Kentucky, would restore East Tennessee to the Union. In the absence of an invading army to accompany the "Bridge burning business," Confederate reprisal was swift; the former conciliatory policy was rescinded and martial law imposed. *OR*, Ser. 1, IV, 231, 359; Paul A. Whelan, Unconventional Warfare in East Tennessee, 1861-1865 (M.A. Thesis, University of Tennessee, 1963), 44-50; E. Merton Coulter, *William G. Brownlow: Fighting Parson of the Southern Highlands* (Chapel Hill, 1937), 170-75.

7. Although the last issue of the *Whig* appeared in October, Parson William G. Brownlow had not been arrested by Confederate authorities. Fearing for his safety, friends prevailed upon him to refugee among unionists in the mountain valleys. After the bridge coup, in which the Confederates firmly believed that the Parson was implicated, he and his friends alternated between Tuckaleechee Cove in Blount and Wear's Cove in Sevier, until they surrendered on December 4. *Ibid.*, 178-82, 187; *Parson Brownlow's Book*, 279-82.

8. Probably Jonathan Wade Hampton Tipton (1822-1894), called "Hamp" or "Hampton," a Blount countian and Mexican War veteran who named his son, born in 1863, William Brownlow Tipton. Olga J. Edwards and Izora W. Frizzell, *The "Connection" in East Tennessee* (Washington College, Tenn., 1969), 238.

9. For Theophilus T. Garrard, see *Johnson Papers*, IV, 536*n*.

10. Transportation for subsistence and ammunition was difficult to acquire. On several occasions during late November General Carter, commanding the Tennessee regiments at Camp Calvert, wrote Gen. George H. Thomas that he "had the whole country scoured for wagons" but was unable to obtain a sufficient number. "Six wagons (for which a requisition was made some time ago) are still wanting for the Second Regiment," of which Houk was quartermaster. On November 28, Carter still needed some "25 to 30 . . . in addition to those of the baggage train, to transport the stores and ammunition in case we have to move." Carter to Thomas, November 22, 24, 27, 28, 1861, *OR*, Ser. 1, VII, 445, 446-47, 454, 456.

11. Despite his current discouragement, Houk did not resign until sixteen months later, a delay which undoubtedly reflected the turn in his fortunes—promotion to colonel on January 15, 1862, and transfer to the 3rd Tenn. Inf., which he organized in February. *Tenn. Adj. Gen. Report* (1866), 57.

12. By the time Johnson arranged for the secretary of war to authorize Houk to raise a regiment and serve as its colonel, Simon Cameron had been replaced by Edwin M. Stanton. See Stanton to Houk, February 5, 1862, Lets. Sent, Vol. 47, RG107, NA; for Cameron, see *Johnson Papers*, I, 508*n*.

13. Only Cross was reassigned to the 3rd Inf. Rgt. Daniel A. Carpenter (1837-1918), Kentucky-born Clinton merchant and grocer, had joined the 2nd Tenn. Inf. in September as lieutenant and adjutant; promoted to major in November, 1862, he saw action in eastern Kentucky and Tennessee until captured near Rogersville a year later and sent first to Libby prison in Richmond and then to Macon, Georgia. Paroled in October, 1864, he resumed his business in Clinton, served as sheriff of Anderson County (1866), and was appointed by Johnson collector of internal revenue in 1867, at which time he moved to Knoxville, later becoming mayor (1876-77). In addition to holding several minor political posts, he experimented with grape culture on his Knox County farm. William R. McBath (b. *c*1838), who enrolled at Clinton as a sergeant in August, 1861, was promoted to captain the following March and to major, 2nd Cav., in August. After the war he was clerk of the Knox County circuit court (1866-70) and served in the legislature (1869-70). William Cross (b. *c*1839), Anderson County farmer, was mustered in at Barbourville, Kentucky, in August, 1861, in the 1st Rgt., became major of the 3rd in February, 1862, and was promoted to colonel in June, 1863, to replace Houk. 1860 Census, Tenn., Anderson, 75; *Tenn. Adj. Gen. Report* (1866), 33, 34, 41, 57, 330; Temple, *Notable Men*, 81-84; Mary U. Rothrock, *French Broad-Holston Country: A History of Knox County, Tennessee* (Knoxville, 1946), 192; *Tennesseans in the Civil War*, I, 380-81; Daniel A. Carpenter, CSR, RG94, NA; Pension Files, RG15, NA; Robison, *Preliminary Directory, Knox*, 74.

14. Milton L. Phillips (*c*1839-1863) enlisted in Co. B, 1st Tenn. Inf., at Jacksboro, in August, 1861, and was a lieutenant colonel at the time of his death. His father John (b. *c*1814) was a Campbell County farmer with $2,000 in real and $1,100 in personal property. *Tenn. Adj. Gen. Report* (1866), 15; *Tennesseans in the Civil War*, I, 375; 1860 Census, Tenn., Campbell, 1st Dist., 69; Sistler, *1850 Tenn. Census*, V, 118.

15. Not located.

To Don Carlos Buell, Louisville, Ky.

Washington, Dec 7 1861

To Gen'l D C Buell

We have just had interviews with the President & Gen'l McLellan & find they concur fully with us in respect to the East Tennessee Expedition[.] our people are oppressed & pusued as beasts of the forest[.] the

Government must come to their relief[.] we are looking to you with anxious solicitude to move in that direction[.]

Andrew Johnson
Horace Maynard

Tel, DNA-RG393, Dept. of the Ohio, Tels. Sent (Nov., 1861-Mar., 1862); *OR*, Ser. 1, VII, 480; Ser. 2, I, 897-98.

From Don Carlos Buell

Louisville Ky.
Dec. 8th 1861.

For Gov. Johnston and Hon Mr Maynard of Tennessee.
Washington D. C.

I have received your dispatch. I assure you I recognize no more imperative duty and crave no higher honor than that of receiving[1] our loyal friends in Tennessee whose sufferings and heroism I think I can appreciate.

I have seen Col Carter[2] and hope [he] is satisfied with this.

D. C. Buel
Brig Genl.

Tel, Johnson-Bartlett Col.; DNA-RG94, Gens. Papers, D. C. Buell; *OR*, Ser. 2, I, 898.
1. Sender's letterbook copy reads more accurately "rescuing."
2. Col. James P. T. Carter had left Camp Calvert for army headquarters at Louisville on December 4, to obtain arms for his regiment. Buell's postscript to General McClellan, January 13, 1862, probably alluded to a proposal made by Carter: "The plan of any colonel whoever he is for ending the war by entering East Tennessee with his 5,000 men light—that is with pack-mules and three batteries of artillery, &c.—while the rest of the armies look on though it has some sensible patent ideas is in the aggregate simply ridiculous." *OR*, Ser. 1, VII, 473; Ser. 2, I, 901.

From Montgomery C. Meigs[1]

Quarter-Master General's Office,
Washington City, 9th Dec 1861.

Hon Andrew Johnson
U S Senate
Dr Sir—

Col Vinton[2] informs me that he can send 2500 suits of clothing in 8 days & 5000 in 15 days from New York for Eastern Tennessee—

I have not yet heard from Phil. & Cincinnati—

By what route should these be forwarded.

Capt Gillem[3] A.Q.M. was ordered to Camp Dick Robinson to take charge of Affairs in S E Kentucky— Is Gen Thomas still in that region?

I presume that the whole 10000 suits could be started from Phil & N Y & Cincinnati within 20 days part of them Earlier—

But I must have some authorized Gvt officer to take charge of them.

Respy   Meigs Q M

ALS, DLC-JP.

1. For Quartermaster General Meigs, see *Johnson Papers*, III, 179n.

2. David H. Vinton (1803-1873), Rhode Islander and West Point graduate (1822), had been in the quartermaster corps since 1836, serving in Mexico and the western departments; during the Civil War, he was chief quartermaster in New York with the rank of lieutenant colonel. In September, 1861, Meigs had advised Vinton, then in charge of the clothing depot at New York, to employ two or three of the best established manufacturing firms to expedite the supply for the coming winter. *NCAB*, IV, 282; Erna Risch, *Quartermaster Support of the Army: A History of the Corps, 1775-1939* (Washington, 1962), 354.

3. For Alvan C. Gillem, see *Johnson Papers*, IV, 680n.

From John Orf[1]

Head Quarters *German Workingmen's Legion*
'Zach Taylor's Sharpshooters'
New York Dec'b 10, '1861.'

Hon A. Johnson!

Dear Sir:

Permit me Sir, to in form you that at last, I have been successfull, being allowed to organise at least, one Regt. as aluded to [in] the printed Circular[2] giving a Statement of the material [?] said Regt will be composed.

The Ministers' of several Religious Detominations as well as the Merchants of Newyork. Who desire to support our enterprive have advised me to have them printed and I have no doupt will meet the desired result.

The reason: I [am] informing you of our enterprive is indented to encuradge it. be on [beyond?] doupt, namley: If you should feel enclined to Speack in your Answer so faverable duarts my undertaking as you have donne duarts my suggestion in July last, when I desired you to Exept the Brigade Geterl Ship for East Tenn. and offeret my services du you in your Staff.[3] (If that hat been donne, ther would have been Rebell Camps, by this time neather in Kentucky, Tenn. nor North Carolin[.] I can not help, to clame that hat, my Plane send after warts to Post master General M. Blair ben onley partly consideret it, this [*sic*] 3 named States would be [with]out doupt, be free of all Rebell forcer by this time)[.] your closing part in said answer was,

"If however, I can serve you, consistently with other obligations, in any application you may desire to make I shall be most happy to do so. Yours & & & A. J. Johnson.["][4]

I ther fore have taken the liberty in making application for said favor as aforsaid stated believing it be consistent,

however if you should find it consistent to honer our Regt with the desired favor you may depent upon that such a act will be enderet [entered] in the Minute Book of every workingmens Association in every part of the U S A.

and should I comme back alife you may feel asured that [I] shall know the proper time to call attention to such a nobel estimation. exppecting a early replay I remain very respectfully your most obedient Servant

John: Orf

The Chosen Colonel

(lat Editor of Am. Patriot & Workers

address me 76 Ann St New York

ALS, DLC-JP.

1. See *Johnson Papers*, IV, 591n.

2. The enclosed undated circular, over Orf's signature, calls for raising a regiment composed of "a superior class of men . . . who have previously seen active service, and who can show evidence of good moral character." All who enlist are to bind a portion of their pay to dependents; for the "better promotion" of this requirement, Orf guarantees that no sutler will be permitted near the camp. He added in an accompanying note: "I do not desire to be undersbut [understood] by sending this list along, that it was indented to be used for raising a sartent summe for said enterprise[.] No, a faverble letter for the purpose to showed to my Collegue's of the press, will accomplish the same purpose wich I have no doupt you will send." Johnson Papers, LC.

3. Letter from John Orf, July 20, 1861, *Johnson Papers*, IV, 590-91.

4. Johnson's letter has not been found.

To Don Carlos Buell [*Louisville, Ky.*]

Washington Dec 10 1861

To Genl D. C. Buell

Comdg

Ten thousand stand of arms as you requested, have been forwarded to be used in East Tennessee. Clothing for ten thousand soldiers to be used in East Tennessee is deposited in Cincinnati. God give you success and to the oppressed people of East Tennessee a speedy deliverance[.]

Andrew Johnson

Horace Maynard

Tel, DNA-RG393, Dept. of the Ohio, Tels. Sent (Nov., 1861-Mar., 1862).

From Nelson J. Waterbury

December 11, 1861, New York, N. Y.; ALS, DLC-JP.

District attorney, believing that Lincoln, "threatened with the hostility of the abolition faction in Congress," should be sustained in his efforts to "restore and preserve the Union in its former harmony," invites Johnson to address a mass meeting at Tammany Hall. Claiming that "not ten thousand out of [New York City's] ninety thousand voters have the least sympathy with Sumner, Stevens and their coadjutors," Waterbury regards it as highly desirable "that those who opposed Mr. Lincoln's election, should now declare explicitly their unselfish determination to stand by him . . . forgetful of the past, faithfully and to the end."

From Leslie Combs

Frankfort Decr. 12/61

D Sir:

We consider the Military Rail road recommended by the President, most important now & hereafter—& our Legislature will, not only, pass Strong resolutions of approbation—but all necessary laws to give right of way &c &c for the road—

It so happens that my attention has been given to this great National work for more than 25 years[1]—and my last Engineer has prepared a connected plat of all the various surveys—made by McNeil & other Engineers[2]—connecting Knoxville with the present road in Kentucky as named by the President— I am also fully posted up as to the different routes & can give full information to any Committee of Congress to whom the matter may be refered—bringing with me the afsd map. My court is in Session[3] & it would be very inconvenient for me to leave home, but no private interest ought to stand in the way of such an enterprise— The construction of this short line will unite, thro central Kentucky, (the most productive region on earth, of food)—five thousand miles of finished R. Rd. *North* of the Ohio with a like amt resting on the South Atlantic & Gulf of Mexico; &, with the aid of the Surveys already made, could be commenced in 30 days—& speedily finished.

Please ascertain the Committee[4] & write me, when I could have a hearing before it— What is your present abode?[5] I should like to stop near you—

The Same folly which has heretofore ruled the Military of Kentucky, still prevails on our Eastern frontier & I expect daily to hear of a battle on or near Cumberland river—by a large Rebel force—agt only a part of Thomas' command—the remainder being scattered at Camp Dick Robinson & else where in the rear—beyond Supporting distance—

Very truly Yr M. O. S.

Leslie Combs[6]

Hon. A. Johnson

ALS, DLC-JP.

1. Combs's long-standing concern with this topic is attested by his chairmanship, as far back as 1833, of the Kentucky legislature's committee of internal improvements. Nearly a decade before this letter, he was described as devoting himself "to the work of arousing the public mind to the importance of railroad communication." "Life of General Leslie Combs," *American Whig Review*, XV (1852), 150, 155; see also *Johnson Papers*, IV, 531*n*.

2. William G. McNeill (1801-1853), West Point graduate (1817) and internationally recognized railroad engineer, had participated, as a member of the Army Engineering Corps, in building the Baltimore and Ohio Railroad (1827-30) and acted as chief engineer in the construction of the Baltimore and Susquehanna (1830-36). Resigning from the service in 1837, he was one of two engineers selected to plan the

route of the proposed Louisville, Cincinnati, and Charleston Railroad; with Captain William G. Williams, he made a "thorough survey" of the area involved, presenting a "detailed report" to the stockholders. *DAB*, XII, 152-53; Samuel M. Derrick, *Centennial History of the South Carolina Railroad* (Columbia, S. C., 1930), 161.

3. Combs was clerk of the Kentucky court of appeals.

4. On the same day that Combs wrote, Johnson moved that a Senate select committee be formed to consider "so much of the President's message as relates to the construction of a railroad from some point in Kentucky, to touch the railroad running through Eastern Tennessee, and thence to North Carolina." Appointed December 23, the committee (Johnson, John Sherman of Ohio, and Garrett Davis of Kentucky) brought in a bill (S. 179) on January 30, providing for the construction of a military railroad in Kentucky and Tennessee—a measure which received no further action. *Cong. Globe*, 37 Cong., 2 Sess., 71, 159, 555.

5. Johnson was in Washington, having returned to the Senate on December 5, three days after the session opened, and again staying at the St. Charles Hotel, Pennsylvania Avenue at Third Street. *Ibid.*, 16; *Boyd's Washington and Georgetown Directory* (1862), 106.

6. Two weeks later Combs presented Lincoln with a plan for a "National Military R. road," a project which, he averred, had been suggested by the President's annual message. Combs to Lincoln, December 26, 1861, Lincoln Papers, LC.

From Robert L. Stanford

Summerset Ky.
Dec. 13th /61

Senator Andrew Johnson Dear Sir:

I promised to write you at Cincinati. I had nothing at that time worth your attention.

I now can give you what has occurred recently. After I Saw you at Craborchard, We had orders to leave London for the Orchard[.] After our Sick were about Mount Vernon, an order came countermanding the one given two days before, and ordering us to remain at London. This you know was in keeping with what had occured, often, while you were at London, & upon the line of Gen. Thomas & Gen. Schoeffs[1] opperations. I will say nothing of the weather only that, it rained all the time of the above march, & Counter march, and you may judge the effect it had on the troops.

The march to Craborchard before the last disabled one Regiment of my Brigade totally, producing about six hundred cases of sickness. The Regiment will do no more service this winter. Gen. Bewell after this gave Gen. Carter a Brigade to march for Tennessee,   this Brigade consisted of 1st & 2nd Tennessee the 31st Ohio and Garretts regiment of Kentuckians[2] with a battery & a half Regiment of Cavaldry, and as I understood that he intended to give all the support necessary to push this column through the Gáp into E Tennessee. Gen. Carter on friday last gave marching orders to Garrett, and he proceeded on his way towards Barberville. Next morning orders came from Gen. Sheff to march with all Carters Brigade to Summersett with as much Speed as possible. Garrett was called back and we took up our line of march for this place, when, about half way from London, an order came from Gen. Schoeff to return Garrett, and to march with the other Regiments to this place with speed proportionate to the absolute dander [danger]. Dispach Stated that Zolicoffer was over the River & marching on Summerset with from eight to 12 thousand forces, and only three Regiments to meet him.[3]

Well we got here in two & a half days from London a distance of about fifty miles of bad road, our troops worn out, Some left on the way to be hawled up.

Will you believe me, that this was the cry of wolf, when, there was no wolf near here. When we arrived Gen. Schoeff could not tell where the enemy was, whether in this Side or the other of the river,   we have been here now 3½ days and no one knows where the enemy is posted, whether, in this county, or in Wayne Co. The crossing place of the River is fiften miles below here, and no one has been half way down there. There will be no fight at this place, judging from present indications.

Our plans for going to E. Tennessee from London by way of Barberville are all frustrated for the present. I know not what is to follow: but if I were to judge from the past, I would say that for the next month we will be marched and countermarch up and down Cumberland River. This may be all right But if our Commanders Could be made [to] see the terable Suffering of the loyal people of East Tennessee I am Satisfied they would lead us on to relieve them. The *Rebel Devils* Since the Bridge Burning are producing a State of Suffering altogether to Shocking to be discribed. Some 300 of the best men in Eastern Tennessee have been taken & carried off to Nashville.[4] They have striped the unionists of evry thing down to the negros Blankets and Clothing. I will not dwell on this picture,   we have men from there almost evry day, who, inform us that all the active men are lying out in the mountains, while thier families are striped of evry thing at home[.]   Your own son I understand from men who arrived yesterday has been Lying out for over three months; and will ly out until the Union forces cross the mountains, so, that he can reach them.[5] Oh! My God what is the Nation about! There is nothing to hinder us from going to the relief of our people: but an order to march, we have them to whip and we can do it, if permited.

In Gods name if it is in your power to do any thing to push us forward do it at once, or our loyal & beloved E. Tennessee is forever ruined; but I need not ast you to do any thing, for, I know you are exerting evry nerve, and will do all things in your power.

In concluding this letter, permit, me again to express my gratitude to you for your noble assistence you rendered me in obtaining my present position in the Army of the U. S.

My Dear Sir; you will always find me supporting you in all your laudable undertakings.

I pray God, you may have many days upon earth to enjoy the fruits of your patriotism, for verily I believe, if, you are permitted to live you will see this nation restored to peace & unity, and then, I firmly believe the people of this great nationality will elevate you to the highest honors within thier gift. I flater not, you know it is not my nature. I look to the past, the present is before me. I draw conclusions from both for the future. The nations eyes are upon you, and the nations best tallent will fall into your support, when the time comes, the time is not far distant.

Your humble Servt

R. L. Stanford   Brig. Surg.

U. S. Vols.

ALS, DLC-JP.

1. Albin F. Schoepf (1822-1886), born in Austrian Poland, educated at Vienna, and a captain in the imperial army, had defected during the Hungarian uprising in 1848, later migrating to the United States, where he worked in the patent office. Commissioned a brigadier in 1861, he participated in various Kentucky campaigns, including the battles of Mill Springs and Perryville; caught up in the wave of removals which followed Perryville, he served out the war as commandant of the Federal prison at Fort Delaware, and subsequently returned to the patent office. Warner, *Generals in Blue*, 424-25.

2. Evidently Theophilus T. Garrard was temporarily assigned to the 6th Ky. Rgt. which was in Carter's brigade. *OR*, Ser. 1, VII, 479.

3. In order to hold an effective blocking position, Zollicoffer shifted his forces westward through Jamestown, Tennessee, and thence northeast to Mill Springs, Kentucky, on the south bank of the Cumberland River and eighteen miles southwest of Somerset, by November 29. A few days later, December 5-8, he moved the bulk of his men across the river to Beech Grove and set up winter quarters; in so doing he committed a major tactical error, occupying a position which afforded no natural barrier between himself and the enemy and at the same time practically cutting off his line of communication and retreat. Peter F. Walker, "Holding the Tennessee Line: Winter, 1861-62," *Tenn. Hist. Quar.*, XVI (1957), 240-41; Clement Evans, ed., *Confederate Military History* (12 vols., Atlanta, 1899), IX, 53; *OR*, Ser. 1, VII, 12; Lowell H. Harrison, "Mill Springs, 'The Brilliant Victory,'" *Civil War Times Illustrated*, X (1972), 7.

4. Most of those apprehended were sent to Tuscaloosa, Alabama; although Temple claimed that ultimately 1,500 to 2,000 were incarcerated, the number generally cited is 400. *OR*, Ser. 2, I, 858; Thomas W. Humes, *The Loyal Mountaineers Of Tennessee* (Knoxville, 1888), 148-50; Temple, *East Tennessee*, 409.

5. Robert Johnson remained "in the brush" until the following February when he left Greene County for Kentucky by way of Hawkins and Hancock counties, Tennessee, and Lee County, Virginia, arriving on the thirteenth at the camp of the 49th Ind. Rgt. See Letter from Robert Johnson, February 13, 1862.

From Charles A. Stetson

December 13, 1861, [New York, N. Y.]; ALS, DLC-JP.

Hoping Johnson will accept the New England Society's invitation to attend its annual festival at the Astor House on January 23, writer declares that "The profound reverence we feel for your brave, noble course . . . has drawn so strongly upon our hearts that it will be a bitter disappointment if you do not find it in your heart to mingle your patriotism with ours."

From John G. Winter[1]

Liverpool Dec. 13, 1861.

Hon. Andrew Johnson
U S Senate

* * * * I do not see that John Bull has softened his bellowing one atom.[2] He has got a smell of blood, & it would seem as though nothing but a surfeit of the same article can abate his rage. The most prevalent opinion appears to be that he will vindicate his honor by acknowledging the Pirates & Robbers of the Sunny South as Independent & break the blockade, & leave it to us to declare the war. If this *be* his game, I hope he will meet with no other obstructions than the stone Fleet,[3] & that our government will not permit for the present anything to interfere with the one great object of crushing out the rebellion. One at a time is as much as we ought to *think* about; but after we dispose of the Rebellion & some of the Rebels, I vote for turning our attention to this gallant band, who are raging, for a fight with a cripple whom they dare not assault when *sound*.—

I have terrible forebodings of the consequences of a war with England at this time. It will create a fury at the North that will manifest itself I apprehend, by arming the slaves. *That* bids fair to be followed by a *war* of *races*, the southern white, against the Southen Black man. Should that War ever be inaugurated & spread to any extent, like a fire in the Prairie it will never cease until the whole shall have been destroyed. A Peace bathed in blood of for millions of unoffending Africans, is enough to sicken the heart to think of. It is one of the heart rending consequences which I dreaded before the War commenced, & I have seen nothing as yet to make the dread the less.

Excepting the difficulty with the British Cabinet, the prospects are very encouraging for an early termination of the conflict.

I see that Governor Milton of Florida has forbidden Florida soldiers to enlist in the service of other States, & orders the arrest of such Persons as attempt to enlist his subjects for service in other States.[4] This is *significant*. As he has but a handful of men all told, he is not able to defend himself. Other States after his proclamation will of course not allow their soldiers to defend him; ergo, he will not be able to resist the U S troops which will be sent there. It is plain therefore that he is fixing to have no more men than such a body as can without disgrace to their Commander in Chief, surrender to such a force as he knows the U S will shortly send into Florida. He is known to have Union proclivities, & is arranging to indulge them without discount. Whenever U.S. forces take Fernandina[5] with 20,000 men & Milton is called upon to surrender, to the Government, he is going to do it I think very promptly. Of course he will want to make terms, & I hope *'terms will be made to suit'*[.] Let one State come in bodily & the others will follow like a flock of sheep.

I see it suggested that our Government will send a military Governor to Florida.[6] I doubt whether this is the best plan. The Charter which made her a State, being violated deliberately, should be repealed & then a Governor appointed as usual; an election for Members of the Legislature ordered & held under the auspices of a Loyal Governor—she would then start straight. It would be better yet if Milton could be secured to the federal interest, & the legislature now in power unionized, which I think could be done through him if he would go into it. I think he & Yulee[7] could both be interested in restoring Florida to her allegiance—

I have been traveling about considerably & I am pained to acknowledge that the only Party in this Country whose voice is not for War is the John Bright's Party,[8] & that is comparatively very small. *All* the others want to have a Kick at the Dead Lion (as they think)[.] They have not had such a chance in many a day, & their desire to improve it is quite irrepressible & rampant.

In haste   John G. Winter

Copy, DLC-JP; also printed in LeRoy P. Graf and Ralph W. Haskins, eds., "The Letters of a Georgia Unionist: John G. Winter and Secession," *Georgia Historical Quarterly*, XLV (1961), 397-99.

1. Samuel W. Thomas, a New York "segar" merchant, forwarded this communication on December 31 with a note: "By request of Mr John G. Winter, I send you above copy of a letter we have just recieved from him." *Trow's New York City Directory* (1861), 847. For Winter, see *Johnson Papers*, IV, 319n.

2. An allusion to the furor occasioned by the *Trent* affair of November 8; "his bellowing" was undoubtedly the ultimatum demanding the release of Mason and Slidell and an apology to Her Majesty's government.

3. During November and December the Federal navy had begun to sink small sailing ships filled with stones at the entrance of several southern harbors, including Charleston and Ocracoke Inlet, North Carolina, in what proved to be an ineffectual effort to close channels to blockade runners. Boatner, *Civil War Dictionary*, 801.

4. Winter's general optimism—and, perhaps, wishful thinking—about the "Union proclivities" of John Milton (1807-1865), governor since early 1861, may reflect a previous acquaintance in Columbus, Georgia, where Milton had practiced law for a few years during the 1830's, or it may have arisen from the latter's dispute with the Florida secession convention over efforts to limit the governor's powers. Other southern governors, notably Joseph E. Brown of Georgia, also wrangled with Confederate authorities over control of troops; this same month Brown, after attempting to retain state troops, assented to a resolution of the legislature transferring volunteer forces to the Confederacy, providing they were used for the defense of Georgia and not transferred without their consent. *DAB*, XIII, 21; Charlton W. Tebeau, *A History of Florida* (Coral Gables, 1971), 222; T. Conn Bryan, *Confederate Georgia* (Athens, 1953), 82.

5. Although he believed in a strong state militia, Milton by no means withheld military support from the Confederate government. In March, 1862, when Federal forces invested nearly-abandoned Fernandina, most Florida soldiers fighting for the Confederacy were outside the state. Florida's surrender, however, did not occur until May, 1865, more than a month after Milton's suicide—the consequence, perhaps, of his failure to defend the state. Tebeau, *Florida*, 208-9, 217, 224.

6. During early December, 1861, both press and Congress expressed concern for the future of Florida, the most vulnerable Confederate state and a likely area for the resettlement of former slaves. Journalists, supporting the idea of military control of Florida, suggested, that if the contraband population must be segregated, Florida

offered the ideal refuge, possessing an inviting tropical climate, an almost negligible loyal white population, and lands which would permit the free blacks to remain under American sovereignty. On December 9, Congressman John A. Gurley introduced a bill (H.R. 121) containing sections calling for immediate military possession of Florida, confiscation of rebel property, and relocation there of liberated slaves from throughout the Confederacy; Florida would be governed by military law pending the return of sufficient loyal white inhabitants to reestablish a legitimate state government. New York *Tribune*, December 5, 1861; Chicago *Tribune*, December 11, 1861; House Bills, 37 Cong., 2 Sess., H.R. 121.

7. For David Yulee, former U. S. senator, see *Johnson Papers*, III, 430*n*.

8. English labor leader John Bright and the working class were generally favorable to the Union cause, remaining so even during the reaction to the *Trent* affair. Winter's assessment of the popular mood, in light of the intense public reaction to the crisis, may have been accurate. Leaders of both the Tory and Whig parties, however, sought to avoid war. Norman B. Ferris, *The Trent Affair: A Diplomatic Crisis* (Knoxville, 1977), 71-75, 142-43, 152-67.

From Samuel C. Hayes[1]

Philad Decr 14[?] 1861

Hon A. Johnson,
Dear Sir,

Some time last summer I received a letter from a highly respectable and responsible Gentle[man] at the South suggesting to me the propriety of visiting N. C., and borders of the adjoining states and without committing myself to either party endeavor to correct false impressions and prejudices which prevail at the South, against the Govt or rather against the North. His idea was that the people would be more apt to listen to one of their own people who had lived at the North for many years and whose intimate business relations with their merchants wold impart a certain amount of credit to his statements. My friend requested me to destroy his letter as soon as read[.] in it he especially spoke of Mr Seward[2] and requested me to call upon him but not to use his name. I wrote to Mr Seward giving him an outline of the letter[.] Mr. S. seemed favorably struck with the project[.] Subsequently I had an interview, I proposed the Gov. paying my expenses which Mr S. said could be done. I have now raised a suffiency to enable me to undertake the trip, at my own expense and if it be deemed advisable by the Goverment to give me a passpt and let me go. Have you any advice or council to give me *besides advising me to make my will before going*. I would enter N. C. and make for Greensboro on to Hillsboro, Lexington, Salisbury, Lincolnton, Statesville, Rutherford Morganton Ashville thence to your town Greenville Ten Knoxville, Jonesboro &c Abingdon, Va. thence across the country to Wilksboro N. C. Mt. Airy, Rockford &c[.] I have left Charlotte N. C. out of the list though I should certainly go there as I have many friends in that place. Whilst on this trip I would most certainly look after debts due me, I would not go for the ostensible purpose of collecting but as it seems almost Providential I have a deranged Brother who has wandered from Va. into N. C. whom I would be anxiously seeking. Please excuse this liberty in a stranger, and yet I am not altogether a stranger as I have more than once stood in the crowd and heard you from the stump. I think the last time was at Blountville (you and Gentry)[.]³ hardly standing room for acquaintanship you think— I have some doubts about myself. I am however

Very Respectfully Your Friend
S. C. Hayes.

ALS, DLC-JP.

1. Samuel C. Hayes (b. c1819), a Virginia-born "bookseller and stationer" at 439 Market Street, possessed real estate worth $7,000. A Confederate sympathizer, Hayes was evidently attempting to enlist Johnson's help in getting through the Federal lines. Leaving Philadelphia in March, 1862, he was by January, 1864, employed in the register's office at Richmond. 1860 Census, Pa., Philadelphia, 15th Ward, 12; *McElroy's Philadelphia Directory* (1861), 419; S.C. Hayes to Jefferson Davis, January 6, 1864, *OR*, Ser. 4, III, 4-6.

2. William H. Seward, secretary of state.

3. According to the list of proposed speaking engagements for the gubernatorial canvass, published in the Knoxville *Whig* of April 14, 1855, Johnson and his opponent, Meredith P. Gentry, were scheduled for July 14 at Blountville.

From John Orf

Head Quarter's German Workingmens Legion
'Zach Taylor's Sharp shooters'
Newyork December, 14. 1861.

Hon. Andrew Johnson:

Dear Sir!

at the fore part of this week, I tuke the Liberty informing you that I hat recived at last permission to raise a Regt.&c &c &c. I ask you at the time for a small inesend [innocent] favor, wich I have no doubt you will grant, me[.]   should how ever the desired answer by the arrival of this not been forwardet, (mailed) then I would sujest wrather to answer me to this, wich I think would be best to allow me to come and see you, and others interested on the subject. I now intent, to call your attention to considering the late arangement, orderet by the war Depart. to send all troops desiring to enlist to a Depot, of the State, and Keepe them ther for the purpose to feel up Regt's allready at the Seat of War, is by my estimation a very poor measure[.]¹   it my suid a few, but it will not, to the gread mass; particularly the actual Soldier, and allow me to ashoure you thir are large Numbers jet of that Kind at least of my Contrymen, Who all desire to be when enlisted employed as urley as posible. I ther fore make to you at this time the following sujestion: for instance you desire that the Goverment, should assist the People of East Tenn[.] Kenducky I andostand desires the same.

even the Prest in his massage² recomands it as a measure of gread importense to concet, the west parst of North Caroline, Eeast Tenn. with

Kentucky and I believe that eather one or the other Line, I have marked at the Lloyd's Mape[3] will be considering it by a strategic view the most practible one for the indented purpose. all that aquires military protection[.]

my Sujestion, for the porpos to meet, that, is that your selve with the Honls Emers Edrige [Etheridge], Maynott [Maynard], John J Crittenten, and others interested jointley request, the Prest. to allow a seperate force (to [illegible] volentarily enlist for the time entill peac'e is restored.) be raised.[4] That the Presitend will grant that, I have no doubt. and that the welthy People of Newyork, Philadelphia Boston &c &c &c, will donate large sum's for the purpose to arme said Corps with Extra wapons for instance the Bowy Knive Bayonet, and artilery, Pontoone Bridges, tulles [tools] for the Sappeer Corps.— I feel most convetent the will feel prout to do so.

such a measure would then give does desiring, or being compeled for wand of employ ment to enlist, a opetunity to juse to enlist eather in said force, or for the reserve remaining in the State's military Depot[.] However, for the purpose to enable me to expresse my selve corectley to make my selve usefull I desire to consuld you and all such Who feel a intrest in it, personely before you make any appelication to the Presit.

hopping to have at least by next Thursday a answer condening a invitation to come and see you, I remain very respectfully

your most Obt Humbl Servand,
John: Orf acting Colonel Commanding
76 Ann Street

N.B.: please Keep said Mape on till I come:

ALS, DLC-JP.

1. General Orders No. 105, dated December 3, 1861, provided for a new system of recruiting whereby small squads of recruits were assembled at depots manned by drill officers and, after some preparation, were forwarded to serve with units already in the field. *OR*, Ser. 3, I, 722-23.

‣ 2. Orf closely paraphrases Lincoln's comment in his recent (December 3) annual message: "I deem it of importance that the loyal regions of East Tennessee and Western North Carolina should be connected with Kentucky and other faithful parts of the Union by railroad." John G. Nicolay and John Hay, eds., *Abraham Lincoln: Complete Works* (2 vols., New York, 1920 [1894]), II, 94; *Cong. Globe*, 37 Cong., 2 Sess., App. 1.

3. *Lloyd's Official Map of the State of Kentucky* was published in 1862 by J. T. Lloyd of New York. Library of Congress, *A List of Maps of America in the Library of Congress* (Washington, 1901), 351.

4. In light of General Orders No. 105, Orf now feels that he will need special presidential permission to recruit his regiment to serve in Tennessee under Johnson; otherwise his men could be shipped off to fill vacancies in other New York units.

From Truman Smith[1]

New York City 49 Wall St
Private
Decr 14th 1861

Hon A Johnson
Dear Sir

I got back last night from Washington city and now address you briefly on the subject adverted to at our late interview. You have already seen enough to satisfy you that the majorety in the two houses of Congress are not likely to be content with the existing *State* of the slavery question and it seems to me that there is no small danger that measures may be carried alike impracticable & mischvious[.] To prevent this nothing in my judgment is wanting (at least so far as the Senate is concerned) but prompt energetic and persistent action so as to obtain a concentration of views & purposes on the part of the moderate & reasonable members of the body to which you belong whose primary object is the preservation of our glorious Union[.] It was with a view to the importance of that concentration that I addressed myself to you as I thought that from your position & energy of character you were much more likely to bring it about than any one else— It has been to me a source of regret that there should be in the Senate so much of what may properly be denominated *isolation*— Each Senator has seemed to me to act for himself & hence the conservatism of that body has not exhibited that strength which I believe it would otherwise possess. I have seen enough of Congressional life to satisfy me that little of good is really effected by mere speech making— I mean in the body itself, tho much may be done in that way by operating on public sentiment. The substance & details of all important measures should be arranged by private consultation among the members—particularly in this time of such a delicate and difficult subject as that of slavery— Hence I think you can in this way do much good but I can safely leave the matter in your hands to act as you may deem best. I will only add that I have kept the hints I gave you in the form of the bill[2] which I put into your hands a profound secret no one being aware of the step I took but mr Hinman,[3] There are obvious reasons why this should be so & hence I dismiss the entire subject[.] with sentiments of high respect I am most faithfully & truly your friend

Truman Smith

ALS, DLC-JP.

1. Truman Smith (1791-1884), a Connecticut lawyer, served in the state legislature (1831-32, 1834), as a Whig congressman (1839-43, 1845-49), and in the Senate (1849-54), resigning to practice in New York City. In the slavery controversy he took a middle position, refusing to identify with either the "Cotton Whigs" or the free soil faction. Lincoln appointed him judge (1862-70) of the court of arbitration in New York,

a court set up under an 1862 treaty with Great Britain for the suppression of the slave trade. *DAB*, XVII, 350; *BDAC*, 1624; see also *Johnson Papers*, I, 471n.

2. The Johnson papers do not contain a copy of this "bill," but the envelope's endorsement—"Truman Smith on confiscation of property"—gives a clue to its contents. Although a number of proposals on this topic were being brought to the Senate during these weeks, the senator from Tennessee was apparently not identified with any of them. *Cong. Globe*, 37 Cong., 2 Sess., 18, 178, 334.

3. Probably Royal R. Hinman (1785-1868) of New York City, a Yale graduate (1804) and lawyer who had served as Connecticut secretary of state (1835-42), postmaster at Roxbury, was judge and clerk of the probate court, and spent four sessions in the general assembly; he also published various historical, legal, and genealogical compilations. *NCAB*, XI, 357; see also Royal R. Hinman, *A Catalogue of Names of Early Puritan Settlers of the Colony of Connecticut* (Hartford, 1852-56), 854-56.

From Abner A. Steele[1]

Tamaroa Perry Co. Ill.
Dec. 14th. 1861.

Hon Andrew Johnson.

I am glad to hear of your getting safely back to Washington, and I congratulate you on the great public services you have rendered to the union cause in our State. I did hope that the army under Genl. Nelson and Schoept, after the action at Wild Cat[2]—would have passed the Cumberland Gap, and relieved the long oppressed and suffering union men of East Tenn. and destroyed the communication between Virginia and the cotton States. My hopes are now in Genl. Buell's Division moving south *via* Bowling Green to Nashville— The general opinion is that Columbus is shortly to be attacked.[3] It seems the rebels think so too, as they are strongly re-enforcing and fortifying it. Now when Buell moves on Bowling Green, if our gun boats and a land force from Cairo & Paducah, would move up the Cumberland to Clarksville & Nashville, it does seem to me that the rebel army in Southern Ky. could be defeated & captured, and then Columbus on the west & Zollicoffer in the East, would be flanked. So that in a short time, the rebels would be either compelled to evacuate their defences, or be Surrounded, beyond a hope of escape. I suppose that our gun boats could go up the Cumberland to Clarksville, if not now to Nashville—

If Tennessee is once under the control of the Union army, our oppressed union fellow citizens there can rise, and drive out or hang Harris & his confederate minions. With Tennessee under the control of the union men, I believe the rebels will have to yield soon, or be involved in irremediable ruin.

I have lately talked with several gentlemen who were forced to flee, from their homes in Middle and West Tenn— They tell me that union men are threatened with death if they refuse to join the rebel army—that Harris' drafting the militia,[4] causes great dissatisfaction and alarm—even among the rebels. that if the people dared to speak out they are tired and disgusted with the hopeless efforts of the rebellion—and that the union there are numerous in Etheridges' and Wrights Stokes' & Hatton's old districts[5]—patiently & anxiously awaiting the advance of the federal armies, to take up arms and put in motion a loyal state Government. The government should relieve Tennessee. That relief has been already too long delayed—when we take into account, the devotion of the true & patriotic men there, and expelled from the state—their trials—losses— sufferings for no other crime than love for the old flag and government of their fathers. For we union men to be called, and treated as "*traitors*", by those who are the *real* and *only* "*traitors*" in America—shows the hellish principles & feelings of the wicked rebellion— You are in a position to know what is best to be done for our State— and I doubt not you will press on government, the duty of relieving our friends from the tyranny and anarchy of the remorseless & unfeeling rule of the Cotton oligarchy. Thousands of men there have sacrificed home—property—friends—and some their lives—for loyalty to their country and that country will I trust come to their aid—

I left Tennessee last July— not heard from home Since— my relatives all there— I want to return— would have joined the army—but incapacity on account of Serious white swelling in right thigh and leg—making me an invalid for life—prevented— still if I was certain, that by going to Kentucky to the Tenn. troops—I would be allowed to go with them, I could at least *try* to be of some service, however humble and little it might be.

I am surprised and pained to see that my old friend George W. Jones, has at last yielded to Secession—and is now a member to the rebel Congress.[6]

out here we are pleased with Mr. Lincoln's message— I hope Congress will not get up serious divisions among union men by any action they may take on the slavery question. Slavery will be crippled if not entirely ruined, by the war, if it lasts long, without Congress taking any radical premature action on it. The rebels will destroy it, if they persist in rebellion— Rather let it be done that way, than for Congress to take Such action as may cause dissatisfaction among union men in the Border States. To Confiscate the property of armed rebels is just, but it will not do to emancipate the slaves to live among the whites[.]

But Sir, at last, if this government or Slavery has to perish, I say perish slavery, for it will end any how Sooner or later, and our government may be perpetual. The very idea of the noble white men of Ky, Tenn, Va etc. being governed by an oligharchy based on cotton & *niggers*, makes me believe they will repudiate it when reason & free discussion resume their Sway. I am astonished that so many non slaveholding whites take up arms, for the rebellion. Why can't they see that they are forging their own chains?

Gov. I would like to hear your views and what you think will be done for

Tennessee— What is the relative strength of the union men of East Tenn &c. &c—

Why don't the government, Send Some gun boats and troops up to Clarksville to capture or destroy the Pork packing there for the rebels. There is only one fort at Dover to Silence and I am reliably informed that there are but few troops much provisions at C.[7] I have seen the gun boats & floating batteries at Cairo & St Louis, and we are confident that they can stand any thing the rebels will shoot at them, from their batteries on the Mississippi river[.] Wishing a forward movement Soon, and victory to the federal armies, and navy,

I am Truly Yours
A. A. Steele.

ALS, DLC-JP.

1. Abner A. Steele (b. c1830), a Marshall County unionist, was a lawyer, justice of the peace, and member of the legislature (1853-55, 1865-66, 1869-71) who resigned from the Reconstruction house of representatives in February, 1866, because of dissatisfaction with the Brownlow administration. Johnson then nominated him assessor for the 4th Tennessee district, but the Senate failed to confirm. McBride and Robison, *Biographical Directory*, I, 695; 1870 Census, Tenn., Marshall, 15th Dist., 39; Steele to Johnson, July 19, 1866, Johnson Papers, LC.

2. On October 20, 1861, Gen. Felix Zollicoffer advanced on Wildcat, a Union camp at Rockcastle Heights north of London, established for mustering Kentuckians into service. Holding the stronger position, the Union forces under Schoepf repelled the attack the next day, with Zollicoffer retreating toward Cumberland Gap; instead of pursuing the enemy, Schoepf, a few days later was ordered by Gen. George H. Thomas to countermarch to Crab Orchard, Kentucky. There ensued the "Wildcat Stampede," a two-day flight toward Ohio, later described by Horace Greeley as "strewing the road with wrecked wagons, dead horses, baggage, etc., and leaving East Tennessee to her fate." Some Tennesseans threatened to mutiny and proceed into their own state. Stamper, Zollicoffer, 82-84; *OR*, Ser. 1, IV, 213, 321; Horace Greeley, *The American Conflict* (Hartford, 1864), 615-16; McKinney, *Education in Violence*, 119.

3. After Grant's early November raid on Belmont, Missouri, the Confederates feared for the safety of Columbus, Kentucky, where Gen. Leonidas Polk had his headquarters. In reality Buell was planning a demonstration on Columbus in order to hold Confederate troops there while the major Union thrust would be toward the forts on the Tennessee and Cumberland rivers and Nashville. For the time being the enemy was confused; Albert Sidney Johnston, expecting an attack on Bowling Green, appealed to Polk for reinforcements. By mid-December, however, the Confederates recognized the Union strategy. *OR*, Ser. 1, VII, 487-88, 742, 752, 758, 769, 773-74, 792-93, 794.

4. Urged to activate "every member of the militia that could be armed" and determined to "meet the despotic invader and his minions at the threshold," Harris issued a proclamation on November 19, stipulating that thirty thousand militiamen were to be called out immediately unless sufficient volunteers were forthcoming. *Goodspeed's History of Tennessee*, 541, 546; Nashville *Union and American*, November 19, 1861; Moore, *Rebellion Record*, III, Doc., 403-4.

5. Seven of the thirty-four counties comprising the districts of Congressmen Emerson Etheridge, John V. Wright, William B. Stokes, and Robert H. Hatton (9th, 7th, 4th, and 5th) had voted against separation in the June 8 election. In the late presidential canvass, fourteen had gone for Bell, one for Douglas, and the remaining nineteen for Breckinridge. Campbell, *Tenn. Attitudes*, 285-87, 292-94. For comment on some of these counties, see Letter from Emerson Etheridge, December 19, 1861.

6. Jones, Johnson's old friend and former colleague in the House (1843-59), served one term in the Confederate Congress (1862-64); he was not a candidate for reelection. See *Johnson Papers*, I, 20n.

7. At the outbreak of war a pork-packing plant at Clarksville, built in 1854 by J. K. Smith & Company, had been taken over by the Confederate government, which operated it until the fall of Donelson in February, 1862. As Steele suggests, the defenses of the town and the Cumberland River below were weak, with Col. William A. Quarles' regiment at Clarksville having only 317 guns—two-thirds of which could not fire—and a force of only about 600 at Donelson, on the river bluff just north of Dover. Connelly, *Army of the Heartland*, 39, 78-80, 91, 116, 124; Titus, *Picturesque Clarksville*, 349.

To Amos A. Lawrence

Washington City,
Decr. 14th, '61.

Private.

Hon. Amos A. Lawrence,
Boston, Mass.
Dr Sir

Your letter of 13th. Sept. last addressed to me at Washington, not having been forwarded, was not opened until my recent arrival here.

I must say that I am much surprised at its contents. In the correspondence we have had, consequent upon and with reference to the fraud attempted upon you by the forgery of my name, I find, by referring to your letters, that, under date of Augt. 9th last,[1] you state "Mr. Murray of Adair Co. Ky is here and I shall to-morrow put him in the way of collecting" &c. As the same mail brought me a letter from this socalled "Carlyle Murray" of the same date of yours, advising me of your action in transmitting a draft for $200" for the use of Rev W. G. Brownlow, I very naturally inferred that you were somewhat acquainted with his character and that, from your consulting with him, he was worthy of consideration.

The only knowledge I have of this "Carlyle Murray" is through some letters he has written to me, from Boston and now in my possession.[2] He represented himself as devoted to the Union, alleging that he was a native of Kentucky, and desirous of contributing such aid as his means would allow for the development of the Union sentiment in Tennessee. In connection therewith, I was requested to direct him as to the best manner of rendering the proffered assistance, and, in response, he was advised that any aid extended to the "Knoxville Whig", the leading Union paper in the State, altho' unsolicited by the editor Mr. Brownlow, would, in my opinion, be very acceptable to the Union men of that section, and serving well the cause.

Mr. Murray has never at any time either by letter, in person, or by deputy had any money transaction with me.

I regret exceedingly that you should have been made the special object of imposition through your well known devotion to the Union.

In reply to your inquiry as to whether the draft for $200" sent by you on the 9th. Augt. last was received, I have to state that the draft for $100" first sent, and that for $200" just referred to were received and duly acknowledged;[3] and that the same was confided to a proper person for delivery to Mr. Brownlow.

> With great respect,
> I remain, Your Obt. Sert
> Andrew Johnson.

L (in hand of Col. William A. Browning), MHi.
1. For Letter from Amos A. Lawrence, August 9, 1861, see *Johnson Papers*, IV, 674.
2. See Letters from Carlyle Murray, July 12, August 19, 23, 1861, *ibid.*, 562-63, 674-76, 684-85, 691-93.
3. See Letter to Amos A. Lawrence, August 14, 1861, *ibid.*, 677. The presence of this communication in Lawrence's files can only make one speculate about a memory which led him just a month later to inquire concerning receipt of the drafts.

From Jonathan D. Hale[1]

Somersett Decr 16th 1861

Honerable Andrew Johnson
Dear Sir

Our company is now Rapidly filling up & we have no arms except muskets[.] they are poor things for Scouts[.]

We learn by men from Overton & Fentress Cos men that the Tories are pressing every Union man they can catch into the Service & They are fleeing to us in considerable numbers[.]

I cant understand why we should not us[e] the negroes in the way the Tories do[2] if it is necessary[.]

Their gunners are negroes[.] at least I have seen several & was canonaded by some at the time Col Hoskins[3] Regiment was fired at neer Waitsboro[.][4]

Please try & do something about our army[.] we are now very near the enemy[.] Scouting is necessary nearly indispensable[.]

> Very Respectfuly   J D Hale

ALS, DLC-JP.
1. See *Johnson Papers*, IV, 581n.
2. Although the Confederate government did not take extensive steps to enlist Negroes into the military until March, 1865, individual states recruited free Negroes early in the war. In June, 1861, the Tennessee legislature authorized the use of all "free persons of color" between the ages of fifteen and fifty, but the act required that such persons be required to perform "menial service for the relief of the volunteers." During the autumn of 1861 reports of Negro artillerymen in Virginia served as an argument for those who favored the use of black soldiers in the Union army. Dudley Cornish, *The Sable Arm: Negro Troops in the Union Army, 1861-1865* (New York, 1956), 15-17; *Tenn. Acts*, Extra Sess., 1861, pp. 49-50.
3. William A. Hoskins (b. *c*1826), a native Kentuckian, enlisted on October 1, 1861, becoming colonel of the 12th Ky. Inf., which he organized. Resigning in April, 1864, he later built a coal railroad from the Cumberland River to the mines at Short Mountain and also served briefly as a member of the legislature from Boyle County (1871-73). Heitman, *Register*, II, 112; Collins, *Kentucky*, II, 85, 114; CSR, RG94, NA.
4. In late November, pickets attached to the 4th Ky. Inf., commanded by Colonel Hoskins, had a brief skirmish with Confederates at Mill Springs, twelve miles below

Camp Hoskins in Pulaski County. When Thomas reported to Buell on December 3 that "The enemy are opposite Somerset and have commenced cannonading Hoskins' camp," relief was dispatched to the beleaguered regiment. Waitsboro, a Pulaski County town, no longer exists. *OR*, Ser. 1, VII, 453, 471.

From Elisha Smith[1]

Mt. Vernon Ky

Decr. 17/61

D. Col: I am sorry I did not know when you passed here[.] I owe you for the many Speeches you sent me the last two years that I want to take you by the hand. I am told it is likely you will have a winter Campaign to E. Ten: It should have been pressed after Wild Cat. I hear Crittenden[2] has been reinforced by 12 thousand from Richmond by rail, and is looking for 7 thousand from Sandy and S. W. Va, then to march for Lexington.[3] Schoeff has but about 1600 effectives if that and no Artilery. If Crittenden comes without artillery he will have to give the road. The sec. of War[4] should ord[er] Buel to send one or two batteries, and three or four Regts! Surely they are overstocked in the South. If troops advance to E. Ten. the Gap[5] should be avoided. That point well fortified with a few thousand we would [be] defeated. The march should be by Whitly, C. H. through Walker's Gap[6] to Knoxville, the best & highest road. A Rigt. at the foot of Pine Mountain with a battery would hold in Check Crittenden. The march of our troops towards Knoxville would cause him to fall back to around Knoxville. Dont let Thomas command,[7] the troops have no confidence in him. I am not alone in the belief he is not in the *right place*. If you could git Rosecrans,[8] he is the man or Genl. Michel.[9] Buel may be a good officer, but Wool[10] ought to be in command of Ky, and the march (if it ever goes) down the river. His name and deeds in the filed are known to every Soldir in Camp. Like Old Rough and Ready[11] there would be but little reviewing, but fight. His presence and his name would give to the army the strengh of 10 thousand men in arms. It is to the interest of E. Ten he should be there. The people are impatient at the slow movements of M-Cleannan[12] and Buel. We want such a Genl. as Wool in Mo: I fear Halleck[13] will not meet the storm. We want a Genl. here in the place of Thomas. The inglorious retreat from London has rendered the 2nd Regt. useless. The mountains would feel proud if Garrard[14] was made a Brigadier Genl. not as head commander[.] He is a mountain boy and we feel proud of him.

Yrs truly,　　Elisha Smith

Occationaly send me a news paper with a good debate and any public Dockument of interest. The latest news no fighting at Somerset. Armies close together[.][15]

ALS, DLC-JP.

　1. Elisha Smith (b. *c* 1800), Mt. Vernon lawyer with real estate valued at $7,000 and personal property at $1,200, had been a legislator from Rockcastle County (1831-32,

1842-43, 1845). 1860 Census, Kentucky, Rockcastle, 126; Collins, *Kentucky*, II, 691; James R. Bentley (The Filson Club) to Andrew Johnson Project, December 2, 1970.

2. George B. Crittenden (1812-1880), oldest son of Senator John J. Crittenden and a West Point graduate (1832), fought in the war for Texas independence and the Mexican War, practicing law in his native state during the intervening years. Resigning from the army in 1861, he was appointed a Confederate brigadier in August and on November 9 became a major general commanding the district of East Tennessee. His strategy upon invading Kentucky in January, 1862, was called into question after Mill Springs, and, following an official censure, he was under arrest for several months. Subsequently he served without rank until 1864, when, recommissioned a colonel, he was put in charge of the Department of Western Virginia and East Tennessee. Following the war, he returned to Frankfort, where he served as state librarian (1867-71). Evans, *Confederate Military History*, IX, 232-34.

3. It is difficult to ascertain with any great degree of accuracy the forces available for Crittenden's invasion. Although he had visited Richmond in early December and had been promised ten regiments, and though Confederate Gen. William H. Carroll reported 11,000 men in East Tennessee on December 9, there was so much misinformation—"every form of rumor"—from both sides, that Gen. Jeremiah T. Boyle complained that "even the good Union people, circulate the most devilish lies in regard to the enemy, and our own scouts . . . are not reliable." *OR*, Ser. 1, VII, 40ff, 498, 706, 740, 745, 751.

4. Simon Cameron.

5. Cumberland Gap, which, though held by only a small Confederate force, could be further protected by Zollicoffer if a movement were made in that direction. *Ibid.*, 406, 705, 715, 843.

6. The route south from Mt. Vernon went through Whitley Court House and Walker Gap, down to Jacksboro in Campbell County.

7. George H. Thomas.

8. William S. Rosecrans (1819-1898), commanding the Department of West Virginia at this time, was an Ohio native and West Point graduate (1842), who had resigned the service in 1854 to work as a civil engineer and architect. Re-entering the army in 1861, he became commanding general of the Department of the Ohio and later (October, 1862) commander of the Army of the Cumberland, relieving Buell in Kentucky. During 1863, he participated in Tennessee campaigns, including Murfreesboro, until removed in October following Chickamauga, when he was assigned to the Department of the Missouri. After the war he served as minister to Mexico (1868-69), California congressman (1881-85), and register of the treasury (1885-93). Warner, *Generals in Blue*, 410-11; *DAB*, XVI, 163-64; see also William M. Lamers, *The Edge of Glory: A Biography of General William S. Rosecrans, U. S. A.* (New York, 1961).

9. Ormsby M. Mitchel (1810-1862), Kentucky native and West Pointer (1829), taught at the Academy and at Cincinnati College, practiced law, and wrote several books on astronomy. Named brigadier in August, 1861, and promoted to major general the following April, he commanded the 3rd division, Army of the Ohio (1861-62), before being transferred to the Department of the South and dying of yellow fever on October 30. Warner, *Generals in Blue*, 327; Boatner, *Civil War Dictionary*, 557.

10. John E. Wool (1784-1869), New York native, studied law, fought in the War of 1812, and in 1816 became inspector general, a position he held for a quarter of a century. Taking part in the Indian removal of 1836, he organized Kentucky and Tennessee volunteers into an efficient army during the Mexican War. Credited with saving Fortress Monroe with timely re-enforcements, he later served as commander of the Department of the East and of the Middle Department until his retirement in 1863. Warner, *Generals in Blue*, 573-74; *DAB*, XX, 513-14.

11. Zachary Taylor.

12. George B. McClellan was the commanding general directing Buell's projected invasion of East Tennessee, which never materialized. See *OR*, Ser. 1, VII, 468, 482-83, 487-89, 520-21.

13. Henry W. Halleck (1815-1872), a New Yorker and West Point graduate (1839), was the author and translator of several books, including *Elements of Military Art and Science* and *Vie Politique et Militaire de Napoleon*. After serving in the Mexican War, he was stationed in California until he resigned in 1854 to practice law, becoming president

of the Pacific and Atlantic Railroad, director of a quicksilver mining operation, and continuing to produce works on international law and mining. Returning as a major general, he was appointed chief of the Department of the Missouri in November, 1861, and in the following July was called to Washington as general-in-chief and military advisor to the President; in January, 1864, he became chief of staff. After the war Halleck was assigned to the military division of the Pacific and in 1869 was transferred to command the division of the South in Louisville, Kentucky. Warner, *Generals in Blue*, 195-97; see also Stephen E. Ambrose, *Halleck: Lincoln's Chief of Staff* (Baton Rouge, 1962).

14. Theophilus T. Garrard.

15. In a letter to Johnson and Maynard written later the same day, Smith reported that his first news about the return of Tennessee troops to London was in error, that they had remained at Somerset, and that Schoepf, expecting assistance from Lebanon, "thinks he can hold his position." At the same time a rumor was circulating that "Crittenden is advancing [toward Barbourville] from the [Cumberland] Gap." Johnson Papers, LC.

From Charles Leib[1]

Office of Assist Q Master
Clarksburg Va. Dec 18 1861

Senator

I learn that Senator Trumbull[2] is again making an effort to defeat my Confirmation by the Senate— It is a hard Case that an officer who is five hundred miles from the Capitol should be Struck down while in the discharge of his duty in spite of the voice of the General Commanding and the officers with whom he has served, merely to gratify the hatred of a few men[.]

I have had the most difficult post, the most trying time of any officer in my department in Western Virginia— I have discharged the duties of my office honestly and faithfully, so honestly and faithfully that I have made enemies among the men who tried to use my department and who *presented* me a hord of Claims that I could not and would not allow[.] When there was not a dollar of funds at this post, I borrowed over *eleven thousand dollars* to relieve the actual wants of the employees, many of whom Came into my office and Cried, declaring their families had nothing to eat and that they were almost naked, the evidence of which latter was before me, and then was charged with speculating with government funds because I paid them in Wheeling Money, the only Kind I could get— They did not Know that the General (Rosecrans) who knew all the facts endorsed my paper for $6,500 of it—

I will if I have an opportunity disprove every Charge that Can be brought against me and so far as my official action *want the most thorough investigation*[.]

You are a just man and I ask that my Case may not be acted on by the Military Committee until I can be heard through my friend *Col Carpenter*[3] who will be at Washington next week[.]

If you will take some interest for me in this matter that will place me under obligation to you whatever may be the result of this matter—[4]

Respectfully yr obed Sert
Chas Leib Capt U S A
&A. Q. M

Hon Andrew Johnson U S S
Washington City D C.

ALS, DLC-JP.

1. Charles Leib (c1826-1865), Pennsylvania-born physician and former clerk of the Illinois legislature, migrated to Kansas in 1854. A Kansas census-taker in 1855, he became involved in the secret society of "Danites," or anti-Douglas Democrats, an activity exposed in June, 1858, by Stephen A. Douglas, who called him a Republican agent, a charge Lyman Trumbull of Illinois denied. Moving to Chicago, Leib edited a Buchanan campaign paper, was appointed mail agent for Illinois, and, with the Republican victory of 1860, became "Cameron's leading confidant in Chicago." As the war began he received an appointment as first lieutenant in the 11th Ill. Inf. (May 21, 1861), only to be rejected by the Senate in August; his commission as captain and acting quartermaster of the regiment was likewise denied (February 19, 1862) because of charges in the fall of 1861 that he used the office to speculate with government funds. His service record contains these charges, along with "loud complaints" against him for malfeasance, drunkenness, and "the habit . . . to treat in a rude and insulting manner all who had business with him"; meanwhile, Rosecrans and others were recommending him highly. He was finally removed, April 1, 1862, and shortly after published his sensational *Nine Months in the Quarter-Master's Department; or, The Chances for Making a Million* (Cincinnati, 1862). *Senate Ex. Journal*, XI (1858-61), 458, 510, 538, 559; XII (1861-62), 129; Charles Leib, Consolidated File, RG92; Lets. Recd., 420-L-1861, RG94, NA; George Fort Milton, *The Eve of Conflict* (Cambridge, Mass., 1934), 295, 303-4; Erwin S. Bradley, *Simon Cameron, Lincoln's Secretary of War* (Philadelphia, 1966), 164; Roy F. Nichols, *The Disruption of American Democracy* (New York, 1948), 216-17.

2. For Lyman Trumbull, see *Johnson Papers*, III, 350n.

3. There is no service record for "Col." Richard B. Carpenter, Kentuckian and anti-Douglas Democrat, who went to Chicago in 1855 and was practicing law in 1860. For his campaigning in behalf of Buchanan he was named governmental disburser in the construction of the Chicago post office and courthouse. In 1867 Johnson nominated him associate justice of the Idaho territorial supreme court, but the Senate failed to confirm. Nichols, *Disruption of Democracy*, 216; Lillian Foster, *Wayside Glimpses, North and South* (New York, 1860), 215-16; *List of Offices to which Nominations were made and not Confirmed during the First Session of the Fortieth Congress*, Ser. 20, Johnson Papers, LC.

4. Six weeks later, Leib again importuned Johnson for assistance, claiming his "enemies" wanted "to Control" his department "for their own benefit . . . but I have pursued a straight forward Course and to day even they are Compelled to acknowledge that I am a faithful public officer." Leib to Johnson, February 1, 1862, Johnson Papers, LC.

From Emerson Etheridge

Paducah Decr. 19. 1861.

Dear Sir:

I have been here since Sunday. I found the place full of straggling Tennesseeans, who have fled from the despotism at home—the *drafting* process—which, because of the extreme excitement and resistance it produced, has been temporarily suspended—[1] The greatest resistance was in Weakley, Carroll, Henderson, McNairy and Hardin. Some of the Scroundels who voted for Secession—for the war—have fled, and if the Federal troops were in my old District for one week, it would put a full Brigade in the field— But the difficulty in getting to this place is very great. Two days since two men, from Hardin and McNairy arrived, leaving their armed squad of thirty two in the woods of Carroll— They came to ask, at what point on the State line, their comrades might hope to meet Federal aid— The[y] had to return heart-broken, without it. The people there are daily praying for an advance of the Union Army, and it seems hard that they should, so long endure the suspense and the disappointment.

Through these fugitives, I have been able to communicate with my friends in Tennessee. The Union sentiment is stronger than I had supposed it to be, and *increasing*. One Federal victory in Kentucky, will be the death knell of the Rebellion in Tennessee. Great complaint exists here, because of the lenient, do-nothing policy of Genl. Smith,[2] the Commandant at this post. A rigorous policy is absolutely necessary. This is a hell-hole of Treason—and every suspected villain ought to be put to work under a negro overseer— Until the rebels are made to suffer in the guts, they will be insolent, and act the part of spies.

I shall remain here some days longer, and until I can hear directly from those with whom I am anxious to communicate. It is but forty miles to the Tennessee line near which is a Rebel camp in this state—[3] It is this camp which makes the flight of the Tennesseans so hazardous.

Whenever the Federal army advances, those who have been drafted (on paper) will be ordered under arms, and then the Exodus will begin in earnest. One Entire district in my County refused to permit a draft, and were quieted only by an assurance that it would be suspended—[4]

"Contrabands"[5] are arriving daily from Burnetts[6] constituents who lost their rights under the Federal Government! Their apology for their pedestrian performances, is that their rebel masters were preparing to run them off to Dixie. Of course all Union men are glad to see them come, and not one of the traitors will ever be permitted to reclaim them— Why Should they be? The negroes are in all respects better and more respectable than *such* masters.

Now is the time for action. A counter current has set in—and a little energy will produce the best results.

If any one wishes to know when I will return, tell him not while I can do the thieves and Traitors in Rebeldom any harm—

Yours truly,   Em: Etheridge

Hon. A. Johnson U. S. S.
Washington D. C.

ALS, DLC-JP.
    1. Gov. Isham Harris' "draft" of November 19 had met with considerable resistance. In January a Paducah correspondent of the New York *Times* commented on the

unfavorable response from Weakley, Etheridge's own county, and reported that secessionist recruiters had withdrawn; similar information came from Carroll, Henderson, McNairy, Wayne, and Hardin. Nashville *Union and American*, November 19, 1861; New York *Times*, January 3, 1862.

2. Charles F. Smith (1807-1862), Pennsylvanian and West Point graduate (1825), taught at the Academy, served in the Mexican War, and in September, 1861, was named commander of the District of Western Kentucky. A subordinate of Grant, who had been a cadet when Smith was an instructor, he commanded the 2nd division, Army of the Tennessee, during the opening stages of the Shiloh campaign when he contracted a foot infection which claimed his life. During his command at Paducah, Smith acquired so objectionable a reputation for inactivity and for leniency toward the rebels that critics publicly questioned his loyalty. *DAB*, XVII, 247; Boatner, *Civil War Dictionary*, 769; *OR*, Ser. 1, VII, 67; Chicago *Tribune*, December 6, 1861.

3. Camp Beauregard, at Feliciana, immediately north of Fulton and the Tennessee line, on the New Orleans and Ohio Railroad.

4. Although it has not been possible to discover the district to which Etheridge refers, the strong unionist sentiment in Weakley and adjacent counties was acknowledged by contemporaries. See Nashville *Union and American*, May 12, 1861; Nashville *Republican Banner*, December 18, 1861.

5. That Etheridge employed quotation marks reminds us of the novel use of this word here. According to the standard sources, the term originated when Gen. Benjamin F. Butler, commanding at Fortress Monroe earlier in 1861, referred to three black refugees who sought sanctuary as "contraband of war." Boatner, *Civil War Dictionary*, 172; Mathews, *Americanisms*, I, 384.

6. Henry C. Burnett (1825-1866), a native Virginian, practiced law in Cadiz, Kentucky, and was elected to Congress (1855-61). Expelled by the House, he became a Confederate colonel, serving as president of the Kentucky Southern Conference in Russellville (October 29, 1861) and of the November 18 convention which passed a secession ordinance and established a "southern" government. A member of the Provisional Confederate Congress (1861-62), he later sat in the Senate (1862-65). *BDAC*, 632; *Appleton's Cyclopaedia*, I, 459.

From Robert R. Link[1]

Raleigh Saline Co. Illinois
Dec. 19th, 1861

Hon Andrew Johnson,
My dear Sir:
I have, according to request, been recently favored by you with two of your truly great Speeches.

I am truly obliged to you for the favors. Myself with many more Refugee Union Men, from Middle & West Tennessee, want to see every thing you say on this war question. Further the whole country here, in Southern Illinois indorses you unconditionally. Your view of the Subject Suits us exactly.

I Supported Bell in Tenn. last year—was County Elector in Wilson County; but am now ready and anxious, to throw away all old party affiliations, and unite with & support all the true friends of the Union North & South.

Sir, our glorious old State Tenn. was taken out [of] the Union against the wishes of her people. It was done by Isham G. Harris' Military despotism. Had you, Gov. W. B. Campbell, the two Stokes and Balie

Peyton,[2] and the noble Ethridge & Maynard, been permitted to have gone over Mid. & West Tenn. They would have Stood by gallant & patriotic East Tenn. God bless East Tenn!

I have not a doubt on the Subject[.] I know the Sentiments of the people. I know the people of Tenn were against the whole movement. They endeavored to buy the noble Campbell, by giving him the position of Maj. General in their Rebel army. But thank God! he was too patriotic to be thus bought. At last accounts he sent me word that he was more and more displeaed with the whole Conspiracy.

Several Union men have arrived within this Co. in last few days from West Tenn; they inform me that a regiment of Union men Could be had in Weakly County alone. The Secessionists are drafting[.] That makes the Unionists there more bold.

Every thing is all right on the war question in the great *West*[.]

The government can get any amount of troops in this State[.] Moreover the Union Democratic party have carried all the late elections[.][3] The people here were displeased with Cameron's Report, but were satisfied with the Presidents amendment[4] to it. Now Sir Please send me Some public documents accasionally, especially any speches that you or Maynard may make. Please excuse me for such a long Scroll.

I am your obt. Servant, Robt. R. Link

ALS, DLC-JP2.

1. Robert R. Link (b. *c* 1833) had been a Wilson County teacher with $1,800 worth of property. 1860 Census, Tenn., Wilson, 22nd Dist., 144.

2. Jordan and William B. Stokes. For Jordan Stokes and Balie Peyton, see *Johnson Papers*, IV, 159*n*; III, 443*n*.

3. The Illinois state and local elections, as well as the process of selecting delegates to the state constitutional convention, held November 5, were supposed to be nonpartisan, with all candidates adhering to the principle of union. When the final tally was taken, however, more Democrats than Republicans had been chosen; whereupon the losers accused the Democrats of ignoring the pledge. Chicago *Tribune*, November 13, 1861.

4. In submitting his annual report, the secretary of war had recommended arming slaves for use "in quelling the rebellion." This phraseology was altered by Lincoln before its transmittal to Congress, but not before the original had been made public by the press. The President's version suggested that retaining captured slaves, whose labor "may be useful to us," would "constitute a military resource," depriving the South not only of their employment "in producing supplies to sustain the rebellion," but of their possible use as soldiers "against us." Bradley, *Simon Cameron*, 202; New York *Herald*, December 2, 3, 1861; Edward McPherson, *The Political History of the United States of America, During the Great Rebellion* (Washington, 1865), 249; *OR*, Ser. 3, I, 708.

From George B. McClellan

Head-Quarters, Army of the Potomac,
Washington, Dec 19 1861.

My dear Senator
Your's with newspaper slip was duly received.[1]

More than a week ago I sent 10,000 good arms (rifled) & 10000 suits of uniform camp equipage etc. to Buell for *Eastern Tenn*—to be used for no other troops.

Buell writes in good spirits— his preparations are advancing with great rapidity & he will very soon be able to move decisively[.][2]

Sincerely yours

Geo B McClellan

Hon A Johnson

ALS, DLC-JP.

1. Undoubtedly, this "newspaper slip" was about East Tennessee. Such an article from the "Clipper, [Baltimore?] Dec. 19, 1861"—about the "Terrible State of Affairs" in East Tennessee—appears in the Johnson Papers. The senator may have had two copies, or McClellan may have returned the clipping in his note; both men were in Washington, so that the letters could have been hand delivered.

2. On December 10 Buell had assured McClellan that he was hastening "preparation with all energy and industry" he could "bring to bear" for the East Tennessee expedition, although he had less optimism for a planned attack into Middle Tennessee—a two-pronged movement he was then contemplating. *OR*, Ser. 1, VII, 487-88.

From John G. Winter

Liverpool Dec 19. 1861

My dear Sir— You may recollect me as one who wrote you several letters from Columbus Ga. last winter— Senator Latham[1] can tell you who & what I am—

We are now on the verge I fear of ruin, unless arrested by practical Patriots in the U. S. who will not allow ambitious unthinking men to plunge us into everlasting ruin— This Government has been spending untold millions in preparing her navy for a Conflict with Louis Napoleon—[2] She is well prepared for a Conflict of arms & the very Power which she has thus gathered togeth, *creates* a desire to pick a quarrel with somebody & she looks across the Atlantic for a subject upon whom to vent her warlike propensities— That she can make a crushing blow there can be no doubt— She can force us back from the Southern Ports & open the Confederate Ports— our army & ships will have to return to the North immediately, or be starved out by the supplies & transports being all cut off— our credit will be ruined & we shall lose ground in all the Loyal Nothern States & we shall have to abandon all idea of relieving our loyal friends in Tennessee— Let us get out of the scrape in the best way possible, but *get out*— our *Salvation* depends upon it— If they treat us badly, bottle up our wrath for a future & more favorable occasion, which is sure to offer— some of these days she & Napoleon will fall out— we can then pay her off as she is now trying to pay us off for the manifold snubs which she has had to endure at our hands—

mail closing—hastily Yr Obt St

John G. Winter

ALS, DLC-JP; also printed in LeRoy P. Graf and Ralph W. Haskins, eds., "The Letters of a Georgia Unionist: John G. Winter and Secession," *Georgia Historical Quarterly*, XLV (1961), 398-99.

1. Winter probably became acquainted with Milton Latham when the latter practiced law in Russell County, Alabama, just across the Chattahoochee from 'the writer's home in Columbus, Georgia. Latham had emigrated to California in 1850. For Latham, see *Johnson Papers*, IV, 48*n*.

2. To the alarm of the British, Napoleon III had begun an expansion of the French navy after the Crimean War, enlarging personnel beyond the number in British service, improving shore defenses on the channel, and developing armored steam vessels at a time when England was still relying on wooden sailing ships. The 1859 launching of *La Gloire*, a steam vessel made of wood but encased in iron, resulted in British construction of the *Warrior*, built entirely of iron, and in an order for eleven new ironclads. During this period the bellicosity of the press heightened tensions on both sides of the channel. J. Holland Rose and others, eds., *The Cambridge History of the British Empire* (8 vols., Cambridge, 1940), II, 556-57, 820-22.

From Rae Burr Batten[1]

Philada. Dec 20th, 1861

Hon Andrew Johnson
Valued Friend

The perusal of your ever welcome, and highly interesting letter, afforded me great pleasure, I assure you!—for we have been so anxious to learn of your health, and happiness, we are delighted to find you are again in Washington,   from accounts, we Sometimes feared, you would never reach there!—knowing you were engaged in so difficult and dangerous combat,   well may it be Said, the revolutionary annals of modern times have not produced a man so Singularly modelled in the readiness, accuracy, and adroitness of his perception, in the promptitude, firmness, and vigor of his action, and in the Moral force, Courage, and nerve of his resolution, for the task he has undertaken, as the chief of the East Tenne. Unionists, Andrew Johnson. He is par excellence, a revolutionist.
May a just God ever bless, and protect him, is the Prayer of many hearts—
Govenor! I fear you will never again visit us!—for we have been so often promised the pleasure of a visit from you, then Sadly disappointed, but you will come as Soon as you can; will you not?—   Cicile & Helen,[2] often, very often speak of you, and Send much love.   they have grown finely,   Cicile is quite a Lady in Size,   they are going to School, and enjoy excellent health,   Mother, Father, Sister, & brothers are well,   Sister Mrs. Fidler[3] is a widow,   her husband Mr. Fidler died in April last—   she is residing at No. 1002 Race St, quite near Mothers, which make it so pleasant for all—   she has a delightful house, and has five lovely children. She often speaks of you, and desires to be kindly remembered,   my husband is well and we are still with Mother, and are as happy as can be,   he is one of the very best of Men, and is a kind good husband.   we have our rooms nicely furnished & board with Mother, so

you See I have the comforts of a home, without having the charge and many cares of housekeeping.   Doctor desires to be remembered to You, and would like myself, be most happy to See you Soon.   the very first leisure time you must come See us.   Doctor promised me a visit to Washington, a place I have never been, but I have long desired to visit, Washington City, and hope ere long I may be allowed the plea-sure,   with a hope you will write often, and will come Soon, and make the long promised visit. I must bid you adieu, with Love from all, and with many wishes for your health & happiness

I Remain Truly
Mrs Rae Batten
811 Race St

A Merry Christmas & Happy New Year

ALS, DLC-JP.
  1. See *Johnson Papers*, III, 4*n*.
  2. Cecilia and Helen Morton, Rae's nieces. See *ibid*.
  3. After the death of James B. Fidler (*c*1822-*c*1861), New Jersey-born jeweler, his widow Helen [Hope?] E. (b. *c*1830), remained in Philadelphia; in 1867, she moved permanently into the home of her brother-in-law, Dr. A. Nelson Batten, at 811 Race Street. Philadelphia city directories (1864-69), *passim*; 1860 Census, Pa., Philadelphia, 20th Ward, 346; see also *Johnson Papers*, III, 308*n*; Letter from Rea Burr Batten, January 15, 1862; Batten to Johnson, February 4, 1862, Johnson Papers, LC.

From Samuel J. Pooley[1]

Liberty Corner Somerset County
New Jersey   Dec the 20, 1861

To Hon. Andrew Johnson
Washington
My dear sir:
   The all absorbing question, now Engageing the public attention, is the case of the Trent[2] & the views taken on the subject, by the leading public prints of England & of France. Of course it is Evident, that the views of the English government, on the question at issue, is in accord with the "London Post,"[3] at best. The point to be insisted on by said government, then, is this—"That as the arrests of Slidell Mason, & their "attaches" is against the letter of international Law, that the ship, if suspected of having countraband on board, should have been seized by the belligerent ship, & taken into port & to be tried before a prize Court on the charge, indicated, & if found guilty, both the ship, & those suspected of Treason be handed over to the government, the ship for confiscation & Messrs. Slidell & Mason for punishment." This I take it is the plain position which the government of England will set up, in the coming Negociation on the Subject. I did think that the case was not a new one, & that several analogous ones, could be found strictly in point, with the decisions of the British Courts, upon the Subject. Lord

Stowell's decisions[4] in particular, I thought were a case in point, & would bear out Wilkes,[5] fully & clearly in his action in the premises. It seems that the English Newspapers, takes a different view of the case. The government of England is no friend to us, in heart & in principle[.] a profitable trade, is the measure that has prompted & obliged her, to have kept the peace, toward us, for so long a time past. Yet I would [give protection?] to her, not in this case, solely for her interest, but in the interest of the general rights of the Family of Nations, in any case, when we may have, inadvertently committed an infraction against the law of Nations. However, I don't wish to be understood that my mind is wholly made up on this subject. Secretary Seward knows I may differ with him,[6] on some one, or more of his political crotchets, yet it must be admitted, that he is a very able statesman, & that his conduct of the State department, so far as its action has found publicity among us, is worthy of the highest commendation. This praise I could not resist from bestowing on the gentleman referred to, who I repeat in spirit, had no claims, on my support. That Mr S. will conduct this point in dispute, ably & honorably I make no doubt & that this unhappy difficulty, will be settled in the interests of peace & to the discomfiture of the purposes of Traitors, & demago[g]ues, "at home and abroad."

Please dont forget to send occasionly a pub document.

Yours Very Respectfully

Samuel James Pooley

ALS, DLC-JP.

1. See *Johnson Papers*, III, 563*n*.

2. James M. Mason and John Slidell, former U. S. senators but now Confederate commissioners to Europe, were aboard the British mail-steamer *Trent* when it was apprehended off the Bahamas on November 8, by an American warship commanded by Captain Charles Wilkes. The envoys and their attachés were removed and imprisoned at Fort Warren near Boston. To the North Wilkes became a hero; but the British reaction, coming at the end of November when the news reached England, was intense and the government, threatening armed reprisal, took steps to strengthen its military position in Canada. While this affront to the British flag and violation of international law could have led to war, England was appeased by the Lincoln administration's conciliatory attitude and by the release of the envoys. Allan Nevins, *The War for the Union* (2 vols., New York, 1959-60), I, 388-94; see also Ferris, *The* Trent *Affair*.

3. The London *Morning Post*, established in the late eighteenth century, was considered the organ of the Palmerston ministry, reflecting the official government viewpoint. Verbatim and paraphrased accounts of the *Trent* Affair from the *Post*, agreeing in tone and substance with Pooley's quotation, were currently appearing in the New York *Times*. Henry R. F. Bourne, *English Newspapers: Chapters in the History of Journalism* (2 vols., London, 1887), I, 220; II, 204-5; New York *Times*, December 14, 16, 1861.

4. Sir William Scott (Lord Stowell) declared that "you may stop the ambassador of your enemy on his passage"—a dictum based upon Vattel, who had limited seizure to the vessel of a belligerent, and not of a neutral. Scott (1745-1836), an eminent English jurist and an authority on maritime and international law, had been judge of the high court of admiralty (1798-1828). [Richard H. Dana], "The Trent Affair: An Aftermath," Massachusetts Historical Society *Proceedings*, XLV (1911-12), 510n; *Gentleman's Magazine*, CLIX (1836), 427-30.

5. Charles Wilkes (1798-1877), naval surveyor and author of numerous reports, including the five-volume *Narrative of the United States Exploring Expedition* (1844),

had been commander of the *San Jacinto* since May. In his report Wilkes informed the secretary of the navy that it had been his intention to capture the *Trent* and send her as a prize to Key West, but that the reduced number of his officers and crew, as well as the large number of Europe-bound passengers aboard the *San Jacinto*, impelled him to let the *Trent* proceed on her course. Commenting on "the notorious action [of the British] ... in doing everything to aid and abet the escape of [Mason and Slidell and their secretaries] and endeavoring to conceal their persons on board," he explained that those captured had no "passports or papers of any description" from the United States; for "this and other [obvious] reasons" he made them his prisoners. Following the *Trent* affair, Wilkes was soon placed in command of the Potomac flotilla. Court-martialed in 1864 for disobedience, disrespect, and insubordination, he was reprimanded and suspended. *DAB*, XX, 216-17; William W. Jeffries, "The Civil War Career of Charles Wilkes," *Journal of Southern History*, XI (1945), 324-48; Moore, *Rebellion Record*, III, Doc., 321-22.

6. Pooley, as was his wont, had obviously been providing Seward, just as he had Johnson, with disquisitions on the correct policy and procedures for handling the *Trent* affair.

From George A. Gowin[1]

Crab Orchard, Ky.
Decb. 21st, 1861

Dear Govenor,

I know you will excuse the liberty I take in writing you a few lines. You will remember becoming acquainted with me at Camp Dick Robinson. Since I saw you "I have been transferred to this place as Post Surgeon and Asst. Medical Purveyor."

Col. C. F. Trigg, I suppose, has given you all the news from Upper East Tennessee. Since he passed through here I have visited our friends of the two E. Tenn. Regts. at Somerset and saw a number of my acquaintances from Hamilton, Rhea, Bledsoe and Marion Counties. According to their reports (and they are reliable) no people were ever so crually treated as our union friends are in those Counties. Squads of Rebel Soldiery are literally SCOURING the Country. The union men have had to flee from their homes and hide among the fastnesses and caves of the Mountains, and the Rebels pursue and hunt them day and night like wild beasts. Thousands are trying to make their way to Kentucky, while hundreds despair of reaching here and still lie concealed in the mountains, freezing and starving. All that the Rebels can capture they hurry off to Tuscaloosa Ala or to the penitentiary at Nashville, or which is worse still, murder and leave them to rot in the mountains. They also destroy and steal all kinds of property—Horses, cattle, hogs, corn, bedding, furniture, clothing, cloth, etc. etc. And they report, *That it is getting worse every day*. Good Heavens! cannot, will not, the Goverment send help to them?"

Our friends blame a great deal of it on the Carters for having those bridges burned. The very name of Carter seams to be hated by almost all of them. They believe that the Carters don't care how much East Tenn. suffers so that they *can make money*. The question is very gravely asked, what became of all that money Carter took with him to pay for the burning of those bridges?[2] I saw several persons in Camp who said they were engaged in the bridge burning and were promised money, but it had never been paid to them. I think myself, it is well to enquire, what became of it. You and every other East Tennessean know that it did not require money to get those bridges burned. All that was necessary was to tell the Union party that the Federal Army was coming and we want those bridges burned, and it would have been done without promising one cent. The union party are too patriotic to require to be hired to do their duty and it is offering an insult to East Tennessee to take large sums of money there to pay for such work. But as the Government furnished the money and it was promised to them for doing the work, I think they ought to have it, although they say they care nothing about it and would have done what they did without pay. I was told by Trewhitt, Cleaveland[3] and others that the Carters were wanting to have more bridges burned. Now Govenor, for your sake stop that bridge burning if you can, for it won't do any good at this time, but much harm, because it will exasperate the Rebels that much more— See that there are no more large sums of money placed in the hands of designing money makers. The remarks that I have made about bridge burning apply to the lower portion of East. Tenn.

Since I came from Somerset, I have determined, if possible, to place myself in a position to be more actively engaged in the War in the future. I wish you (if you can conscientiously do so) to get me authority from the President to raise and organize a Regiment. If East Tennesseans continue to come over I can before long have a Regiment here— But if the Army goes to Tennessee soon I want to be authorized to organize a Regiment there. I will gladly resign my present position of Post Surgeon and Asst. Med. Purveyor, if I can get the position asked for. I am anxious to be actively engaged to relieve my countrymen in E. Tenn. and would be willing to go into the private ranks, but I know, I would not be able to make long marches on foot.

You will be glad, I know, to hear that our men are enjoying good health at present—very few cases of sickness in the two Regiments.

Will you be kind enough to let me hear from you immediately upon the subject named above?

My address is Crab Orchard, Ky.

Respectfully, Your Obt. Sevt.
G. A. Gowin.

Gov. Johnson
Washington, D.C—

P.S. If you are in possession of any information that would be calculated to render the Carters more agreable to the men, you would do much good by conveying that information to Trewhitt or Cleaveland. I have only stated facts learned while at Somerset, and feel sorry that there is such a feeling existing—whether that feeling exists with or without a just cause—

G. A. G---

ALS, DLC-JP.

1. George A. Gowin (c1827-fl1880), North Carolina native and Hamilton County school teacher, possessed $4,800 in real and personal property. At this time he was an "Assistant Surgeon" in the army. He subsequently served as a lieutenant colonel of the 6th Tenn. Mtd. Inf., USA (1864-65), and after the war as a Chattanooga physician. Before and during the war he edited *The Watchman* at Harrison and was founder and editor of the *Tennessee Weekly Republican* from 1876 into the eighties. 1860 Census, Tenn., Hamilton, 16th Dist., 238; (1870), 2nd Dist., 10; Zella Armstrong, *History of Hamilton County and Chattanooga, Tennessee* (2 vols., Chattanooga, 1940), II, 145, 148; *Tenn. Adj. Gen. Report* (1866), 264; Washington *National Intelligencer*, December 30, 1861.

2. According to a statement of the amount paid William B. Carter "by the War Dept for burning Bridges in E. Tenn.," $2,500 was remitted on October 9 and $17,800 on December 18 for a total of $20,300—of which only $11,041 seems to have been accounted for. Such recent historians as McKinney and Patton give the figure as $20,000, while Temple cites Carter as asserting that he received only $2,500 for the mission. McKinney, *Education in Violence*, 117; Patton, *Unionism and Reconstruction*, 60n; Temple, *East Tennessee*, 371; Memorandum of money sent into East Tennessee by Rev. W. B. Carter [August 13, 1861], Johnson Papers, LC.

3. Daniel C. Trewhitt and Eli Matthew Cleveland, both of Hamilton, had been delegates from that county to the Union conventions at Knoxville and Greeneville. Cleveland (b. c1822), a Hamilton County farmer with $25,000 in real and personal property, was elected to the legislature in 1861, but did not serve. Enlisting September 28, 1861, as a major on the staff of J. P. T. Carter's 2nd East Tenn. Rgt., he resigned early in 1862 because of poor health. 1860 Census, Tenn., Hamilton, 13th Dist., 59; *Tenn. Adj. Gen. Report* (1866), 41; *OR*, Ser. 1, LII, Pt. I, 150, 169; Cincinnati *Commercial*, February 20, 1862. For Trewhitt, lieutenant colonel of the 2nd Tenn. Inf., USA, see *Johnson Papers*, IV, 159n.

From Leonidas C. Houk

Cincinnati 23rd Dec 1861.

To Hon Andrew Johnson

Carters[1] have took up notion you & I are working against them[.] use me pretty rough[.] my resignation dates first January[.] Can I get the authority to raise Regt[?] Telegraph me what you have done. If necessary I will come to Washington[.]

L. C. Houk
Burnett House

Tel, DLC-JP.

1. Gen. Samuel Carter and brother, Col. James P. T. Carter.

From William S. Mitchell[1]

December 23, 1861

Gov Andrew Johnson

My dear Sir

It is very cold, & Peterson[2] cannot make a coat in less than a week's time. There may be some good coats already made at some of the Stores to fit, & if you will select any that may suit, please lay it aside, & I will call this afternoon, learn where it is, and get it. Please let it be the very best to be found as I desire it for a Christmas present— You have no friends, Gov, who's feelings follow you through your difficulties & trials more than mine, & your kindness in permitting me to do any little acts of friendship is most gratifying[.]

Yours truly Wm. S. Mitchell

Dec 23d, 1861

ALS, DLC-JP.

1. It is interesting to note that Mitchell, listed as a clerk in an 1860 Washington directory, was apparently planning to make Johnson a present of the coat referred to. Although conclusive evidence as to their prior relationship is lacking, he was apparently a friend of Robert and served both father and son as a purchasing agent for clothes, including the ordering and selection of suit, shirt, and stock for Johnson's swearing-in in 1865. Mitchell to Robert Johnson, April 7, 1862, and to Andrew Johnson, February 7, March 30, April 5, 1865, Johnson Papers, LC; *Boyd's Washington and Georgetown Directory* (1860), 114.

2. William Peterson was a Washington tailor located at 480½ Pennsylvania Avenue. *Ibid.*, 123.

From Thomas H. Wiley[1]

Capitol Hill— 24, Decem. 1861—

Gov. Johnson

Much Respected Sir

For more than three months past I have been Endeavouring to obtain Employment in the public service, in that capacity which would make my Experience and former acquaintance with the Southern people, most useful to our country, in the present war of violence and barbarism on the part of those in Rebellion.

Early in October last I sent a communication to the Secretary of the Navy[2]—urging the necessity and Expediency of Sending a small force to the coast of my native State (Georgia) to Secure the inlet to Darien, and the bays and inlets to St. Simons Sound—by far the best and most Extensive deep waters on the Southern coast.[3] Those waters were taken into possession, in the fall and winter of 1814—by Admiral Cockburn of the British navy[4] to the great annoyance and injury of the coast inhabitants. The Entrance into St. Simons Sound lies between the

Island of the same name & *Jakyl*, & being the main outlet of the Altamahaw river, is kept open by the regular flow of its current. Vessels drawing as much water as the old class of British friggates could pass the Sea bar at ordinary tide, as was the case with the flag-ship of Admiral Cockburn the *Lacedemonian* & other ships of the same class.[5] The Entrance there is deep and safe—the anchorage spacious & land locked, while St. Simons Sound & its connecting waters pass round nearly the Entire coast of Georgia & places it Entirely at the mercy of the power having possession of the Sounds & inlets of the Extensive Sea coast. Three months ago, one Single regiment could have taken possession of the islands and waters of Georgia lying to the west of Savannah— Say from the mouth of the Ogechee—to St Mayry's on the border of Florida. Now it may require a more Efficient force, as the attack on Hatteras inlet & Port Royal, harbour, has warned the Enemy of their danger.—[6] About the midde of October last I sent another letter to the President[7]—of similar import with that to Mr. Wells—but more in detail. Obtaining no acknowledgement from Either of them, I was induced to apply to the Hon. Joseph Holt—(Late Secretary of War) who obligingly undertook to lay a third communication on the same subject, *before the Cabinet.*[8] Some week or ten days afterwards I received from the Secretary of the Navy—an acknowledgement of the last communication—and thanking me for the patriotic Suggestions it contained.

Up to this time however, no further action has been had upon the Effort—I have been makeing, to give the Enemy Employment at home—which is and has been for months past, *his most vulnerable quarter*.

I do not think the Administration is fully aware of the necessity of occupying the inner bays and sounds on the coast of Georgia, and the many facilities it would give them to secure Rebel property and force the loyal men of the sea coast to lay down their arms & rally to the national standard. More could be done on the coast of Georgia than any of the Southern States—as there are still loyal men there and who sigh for an opportunity to shake off their bondage.

As to South Carolina I have no hopes of her returning sobriety.

Thirty years of lawless rule and despotism, has prepared her for Every state of violence, which an unscrupulous oligarchy could devise—and now rule or ruin seems in that State to be frantically invoked.

The foregoing remarks brings me to the conclusin, that I can be of service to the government in the present attitude of our affairs.

My life has been spent mostly among the Southern people & in the Cotton States. Without a man of Experience and knowledge of their caprices, their property on the Sea coast will soon be destroyed, without a sufficient Effort to guide them into a better method of using it.

I propose to go down South as a commissioner (in some of the public vessels) and without delay, procede to gather up property for the national government—and to prevent as far as possible any further destruction of rice—cotton and other valuable property which in South Carolina has been so wantonly destroyed.[9] The Southern mind has become warped into a state of phrenzy by what has long been regarded by its people, *an Encroachment upon their rights*.

Thirty years of Careful training under the tutors and other disciples of Mr. Calhoun has made many—many of his followers perfect Mahometans in faith & practice.[10] As we now behold them, it is useless for any one to confer with them who does not understand their prejudices and their method of doing business.

I propose to go down among these people (on the coast of Georgia) and save what property has not been destroyed—and cause as many as possible to abandon the Error of their ways and return to their allegiance. This however must be speedily done to save the property which is threatened—and done without flourish or noise, as the whole sea coast must now be on the alert, and the utmost circumspection called for to approach loyal men—who can only be induced to abandon the rebellion, from a knowledge of worse times and bitter suffering awaiting them.

I submit these views for the *fourth time*, in the hope they may be concured in by Gov. Johnson—Col. Maynard and other Southern men who see in them somthing Expedient for national consideration in this wide spread rebellion—which becoming more bitter as it advances, in some portions of our country has Even now made war upon the sleep of the cradle. At the age of sixty five I am admonished of the past, and that of the future, but little remains for my use. But whatever of use I can be to my country for the remainder of life is now cherfully offered to its service, and I hazzard nothing in the view here taken, that I could save much property on the southern coast, if properly Employed there, which must be seedily destroyed under the policy Enforced by Southern leaders, who seem to be moved by a wild and remorseless spirit of revenge.

Thomas H. Wiley

ALS, DLC-JP.

1. Thomas H. Wiley (c1793-1863), Georgia native, had lived during the 1850's in Knoxville where he was associated with railroad interests and maintained close ties with prominent East Tennessee Whigs. Currently residing in Philadelphia with a son who was a student there, he was promoting a new air springs invention for railroad cars. He was appointed a treasury department surveyor's aid in Nashville in 1863 shortly befo·e his death. *U. S. Official Register* (1863), 94; Thomas H. Wiley to O. P. Temple, June 3, 1858, June 13, 20, November 27, 1860; Moses Wiley to O. P. Temple, March 21, 1864, Temple Papers; *Nashville City Cemetery Index*, 85.

2. This letter to Gideon Welles has not been located.

3. The entrance to the Brunswick, Georgia, harbor, reputed to be the outstanding port on the South Atlantic coast, could accommodate an eighteen-foot draft at low tide. C. H. Wells, Jr., to Secretary of the Navy, November 15, 1861, *OR-Navy*, Ser. 1, XII, 345; New York *Times*, April 14, 1862; Robert Blanchford, *Sailing Directions for the Harbours of North America* (London, 1811), 52.

4. During the War of 1812 Sir George Cockburn (1772-1853), admiral of the British fleet, participated in skirmishes in the Chesapeake area, terrorizing Maryland and Virginia inhabitants. After an attack on Hampton, Virginia, in June, 1813,

Cockburn sailed south and raided the Carolina and Georgia coasts, returning to the Chesapeake the following year. *DNB*, IV, 640-42; Francis F. Beirne, *The War of 1812* (New York, 1949), 170-74, 264-68.

5. Wiley is inaccurate; Cockburn's flagship was the third-class *Marlborough*, 175 feet long with 74 guns. The *Lacedaemonian*, launched in December, 1812, was a fifth-class frigate, 150 feet long and 38 guns. J. J. Colledge, *Ships of the Royal Navy* (1 vol., New York, 1969-   ), I, 307, 347; Beirne, *The War of 1812*, 172.

6. On August 28, a naval squadron under Flag-Officer Silas H. Stringham attacked the defenses at Cape Hatteras, North Carolina, and by the next day had forced the abandonment of Forts Clark and Hatteras, as well as taking 670 prisoners; two months later on November 7, a fleet under Flag-Officer Samuel F. Dupont steamed into Port Royal Sound, South Carolina, and forced the Confederates to evacuate Forts Beauregard and Walker, thereby establishing a base for coaling and supplying blockaders. Long, *Civil War Almanac*, 136; Francis T. Miller, ed., *The Photographic History of The Civil War* (10 vols., New York, 1911), VI, 100; Boatner, *Civil War Dictionary*, 385.

7. This letter is not extant.

8. Although it was presented to the cabinet, this communication has not been located. Wiley to Holt, December 24, 1861, Gideon Welles Papers, LC; for Holt, see *Johnson Papers*, III, 430n.

9. On November 28 Federal authorities near Port Royal Sound were ordered to employ Negro slaves in the task of confiscating crops; the following day planters in the vicinity of Charleston and Savannah put the torch to their cotton to prevent its seizure. Long, *Civil War Almanac*, 144.

10. The implication of devout, uncritical disciples.

From Leslie Combs[1]

Washington Dcbr 26/61

Dr Sir

I have handed a Railroad map to Mr Davis,[2] which he will show you[.] I know the whole country from Lexington to Chatanooga right & left— I give you my deliberate opinions— The Engineer Regiments ought, at once to begin the work— *Now* or *never* is the word—

If there is any trouble as to route & terminus South—appoint Military *Engineers* to determine the matter & beware of thieving Contractors—

I have profiles of the whole route in Ky—accurately calculated—

Yours Truly   Leslie Combs[3]

Hon A. Johnson

		Miles
1st	Chatanooga to Knoxville	110
	To Lynchburgh Va	444
	" Richmond "	602
2d	To Stevenson Westward &tc	37
	" Memphis	309
	" New Orleans	680
3d	To Atlanta Georgia	138
	" Augusta	309
	" Charleston	446
	" Savannah	431

Note

I give these distances, but the connexion is complete also to Mobile, Pensacola &c &c.

I have hoisted the *Flag* at Beaufort[4]—*now* in our possession—half way between Charleston & Savannah.

ALS, DLC-JP.

1. Undoubtedly this communication was prompted by Johnson's December 23 appointment as chairman of a select committee to consider the construction of "a railroad to connect the loyal portions of Tennessee and North Carolina with Kentucky." *Cong. Globe*, 37 Cong., 2 Sess., 159.

2. Probably Garrett Davis, Kentucky senator. See *ibid.*, I, 347n.

3. A brief New York *Herald* article of December 25, 1861, enclosed with this letter, noted congressional consideration of a plan to connect Chattanooga with Louisville and Cincinnati by direct railroad; the idea, credited to Combs, was deemed practicable for both commercial and military purposes. In an appended note, he added with becoming modesty: "One mistake—Genl C. did *not* suggest this road to the President— It was his own patriotic project—worthy of the age & country & free institutions—"

4. Confederate forces at Forts Walker and Beauregard, near Beaufort, South Carolina, on Port Royal Sound, were ordered to retreat from their indefensible position on November 7. Occupied by Union troops two days later, Beaufort served as a supply base for blockaders during the remainder of the war. *OR*, Ser. 1, VI, 27-30; Long, *Civil War Almanac*, 135-36, 138.

From Salmon W. Wilder[1]

Fitchburg Massachusetts
Dec 27th 1861

Hon Andrew Johnson
My dear Sir

I am, and have been since 1853 a citizen of Tennessee. My residence was Chattanooga, Hamilton Co. My only apology for intruding upon your valuable time, and patience, for a few moments is my *extreme* anxiety to hear in a reliable way from my section of Tenn. I was formerly a citizen of the town and State where I am now writing, and am known by Hon G. F. Bailey[2] representative in Congress from the 9th District of this State. I left Chattanooga the 23d of August last. I was not driven away, but left sooner than I otherwise would had not a report been put in circulation that I had been influancing the Union men in the upper end of the county (Districts 11 & 12) where I have formerly resided to *rebellion*, and that I was the correspondent of the New York Herald.[3] Having been informed by a friend of the reports being circulated I left immediately without waiting to know their effect. Being a Northern man by birth, and known in community as a Union man I was *watched* and suspected. When I left there was a *determined* spirite manifested among the Union men of the County to resist the demands of the Confederate Government, and the *Despot* Gov Harris. William Crutchfield, and Benj Chandler,[4] of Chattanooga were outspoken Union men up to the time I left. Col William Clift[5] of Soddy and Abel. A. Pearson[6] of Sale

Creek were keeping the Union spirite up to a high pitch in that direction, and were about instituting a camp for the *drilling* and instruction of Union men in military exercises. Of those *brave*, *loyal*, men I have heard nothing since I left.[7] My interests, are all in Tenn. My sympathies are with her loyal Sons. I intend returning there soon, to share the fate of those who are loyal to their country. News Paper reports are so very unreliable and being so very anxious to know the true condition of things there I beg you to give me any information you may be able to in regard to the condition of things in Tenn, and her probable future.

I am Sir Yours Truly   S. W. Wilder

ALS, DLC-JP.

1. Probably Salmon W. Wilder (b. *c*1824), a Vermont-born paper manufacturer. 1850 Census, Mass., Worcester, Fitchburg, 344.

2. Goldsmith Fox Bailey (1823-1862) was a Massachusetts lawyer who served in the House from March, 1861, until his death. *BDAC*, 502.

3. His neighbors may have thought that Wilder was the "friend from Tennessee—a Union man," identified by the *Herald*'s Louisville correspondent in his August 2 dispatch as the source of his information about the large number of troops passing through Chattanooga en route to Virginia. New York *Herald*, August 12, 1861.

4. For William Crutchfield, see *Johnson Papers*, IV, 166*n*. Benjamin Chandler (b. *c*1814), a longtime resident of Chattanooga, was engaged in pork packing and possessed $15,000 in real and $5,000 in personal property. 1860 Census, Tenn., Hamilton, Chattanooga, 14th Dist., 89; Armstrong, *Hamilton County*, I, 135, 208.

5. The aged William Clift (*c*1794-1866), a prosperous Hamilton County landowner ($50,000 real and $13,000 personal property) and industrialist who had been an outspoken foe of disunion and a member of both East Tennessee unionist conventions, became the center of resistance to Confederate pressures in a predominantly secessionist area. When Clift and other unionists rendezvoused on Sale Creek in the northern part of Hamilton County during the early fall of 1861, a contretemps with several hundred Confederate sympathizers was averted by the "Crossroads Treaty," which maintained a precarious truce for the time being. Fleeing subsequently to Kentucky, he organized a band of partisans into what later became the 7th Tenn. Vol. Inf. Rgt. The divisions in Clift's own family illustrate dramatically this fratricidal conflict: two sons followed him into Union service, while two other sons and three sons-in-law served in the Confederate army. 1860 Census, Tenn., Hamilton, Dist. 1, 267; Temple, *Notable Men*, 94-100; Gilbert E. Govan and James W. Livingood, *The Chattanooga Country, 1540-1951: from Tomahawks to TVA* (New York, 1952), 185-89, 241; Clift Register, Tennessee State Library and Archives.

6. Abel A. Pearson (*c*1818-*fl*1890), Sale Creek postmaster (1856-66) and prominent farmer, with real estate worth $6,000 and personal property in the amount of $12,000, was a delegate to the East Tennessee unionist convention at Knoxville in May, 1861. Following the war, he served as Chattanooga police commissioner (1866), city recorder (1869), and state senator (1869-70). 1860 Census, Tenn., Hamilton, Dist. 11, 285; Robison, *Preliminary Directory*, Hamilton, 63; *Goodspeed's Hamilton*, 830, 898.

7. Late in November the pressure from Confederate troops obliged Clift and his men to abandon their encampment near Sale Creek, some fleeing directly to Kentucky, others returning to their homes, while a few joined Clift in the mountains before making their way into Union territory. *Tennesseans in the Civil War*, I, 390.

From Joseph Cable[1]

Van Wert, Ohio, Dec. 28th '61.

HON. ANDREW JOHNSON

Dear Sir: I have the honor to break that long silence which has been uninterrupted between us, by way of correspondence; and in view of your trials and the unhappy circumstances which surround your home, would offer the condolence of a pleasant New Year.

If your life and health be spared, I feel as though the long anticipated time, for your triumph over all, the political barriers, is rapidly approaching as set forth in my letter to you in 1854[?]. With a view of the then incipient stages of the present infernal rebellion, then inaugurated, I could not support the administration of Pierce. That offshoot from Democracy, by a party to which I was indebted, cost me all my pecuniary means.—rendered me poor and pennyless— I retired to the smallest populated county in the state,[2] "to raise calves and pigs." Then I became sick, and was afflicted with Chill-fever for fourteen months—became a wreck in system. So it was with my small family.

In the fall of 1856,—still feeble I was dragged from my retiracy by my friends, and took the stump for Fremont.[3] In 1859, I was induced to take the editorial department of a paper in this place, which I continued until the election of Lincoln, whose cause I advocated with all my energy. To sustain our beloved country as it was handed down to us, I knew it had become necessary to overthrow the new and demoralized democratic party in the free states. Hence, I acted as one of the vice presidents and one of the committee on resolutions of the first "REPUBLICAN" meeting ever held in Ohio—on the 16th of February 1854.[4] We there inaugurated the *old* Democratic, or Jeffersonian Republican principles, with the addition of the HOMESTEAD.[5] On these we went before the people of Ohio and have been successful ever since. This brief, explains to you my course. When Mr. Lincoln was elected, I ceased to edit, and while laboring to close my business here one year ago I was arested by Paralysis of the right side, caused by a serious fall on the left side of the head. I am now, thank Providence, recovered therefrom. I have a nice little property here, which, under present depression I cannot sell, hence, I feel like establishing a paper here in the spring, if possible.

One word further of explanation. In last fall's campaign in Ohio, certain leaders repudiated or ignored the Republican organization and went for a *Union Party*[6]—loseing as many as gained. Hence, another party cognomen will be advisable. With the foregoing you will be enabled to understand the local bearing of Politics in Ohio.

There will be—if southern DEMONOCRACY—*not* Democracy—be wiped out—an attempt will [be] made to inaugurate, under Mr. Lincoln, a CENTRALIZED CONSOLIDATED FORM OF GOVERNMENT, directly the opposite extreme of Secession, and equally as foreign to the spirit and design of the Constitution. This will be done by a portion of the Union press and politicians of doubtful virtue, and they will be joined by the sympathizers of this rebellion and broken down political hacks. Such, it will be necessary to meet.

You are the man to meet that issue when it shall come. And if I should succeed in getting up a paper in Ohio, I should like to write out at length, your BIOGRAPHY and publish it—you furnishing speeches, messages, *ect., ect.*

Will it be consistent with your views and feelings to get up our HOMESTEAD BILL as passed the House in May, 1852—make a speech thereon, giving a minute history of it in the House, with a passing notice of its original friends and their labors, with its defeat, from time to time, by the then plotters of the rebellion now upon us? I think this would be well. That bill should pass this session[.] The people in Ohio expect it; and you are the man to carry it through and receive the honors.

With the fervent hopes for the safety and comfort of yourself and family, I have the honor to be, etc.,

Joseph Cable

P.S. My son, Fielding S. Cable,[7] whom you may recollect of having seen in Washington, 1852, is Probate Judge at Center Paulding, Paulding county Ohio—an active friend of yours—

ALS, DLC-JP.

1. For Cable, longtime journalist and former Democratic congressional colleague of Johnson, see *Johnson Papers*, I, 633n.

2. Retiring from Congress (1853) to Paulding County, Cable became the spokesman of Free Soilers in northern Ohio through the establishment of newspapers in various northwestern communities. The Sandusky *Mirror* (1853), was followed by the Van Wert *American* (1857) and *Bulletin* (1860), the Wauseon *Republican* (1863), and subsequently the Paulding *Gazette*. Joseph P. Smith, ed., *History of the Republican Party in Ohio and Memoirs of its Representative Supporters* (2 vols., Chicago, 1898), I, 789; Eugene H. Roseboom, *The Civil War Era, 1850-1873* (Columbus, 1944), 281; J. D. B. DeBow, *Statistical View of the United States . . . Compendium of the Seventh Census* (Washington, 1854), 284, 290; Joseph G. Kennedy, *Population of the United States in 1860 . . . The Eighth Census* (Washington, 1864), 396-97.

3. John C. Frémont (1813-1890), a Georgia native, received an appointment in the army topographical engineers (1838) and before the Mexican War led several scientific expeditions through the West. A leading figure in the conquest of California, he resigned from the army in 1848 after a court martial. Elected to the Senate from California in 1850, he received the 1856 Republican presidential nomination. Although he was appointed major general and commanded the Department of the West from May to November, 1861, his military career was a disappointment and he resigned in 1864. Failing in business and never again achieving his former prominence, he was subsequently governor of Arizona Territory (1878-81). Warner, *Generals in Blue*, 160-61; *BDAC*, 916; see also Allan Nevins, *Frémont: the West's Greatest Adventurer* (2 vols., New York, 1928).

4. The first recorded meeting of Ohioans opposed to the Kansas-Nebraska Act was held at Columbus on February 14, 1854; there is no record of Cable's having attended. It can be assumed that other county meetings were held prior to the state convention of March 22, in Columbus, when Cable, then in Sandusky, was elected one of the vice presidents but not appointed to the committee on resolutions. Smith, *Republican Party*

in Ohio, I, 9, 11-13; *Ohio State Journal* (Columbus), February 15, March 22, 1854.

5. Resolutions adopted in the Columbus meeting of February 14 expressed firm opposition to the Kansas-Nebraska Act and the repeal of the Missouri Compromise, but did not mention the Homestead. Perhaps Cable was recalling later Republican endorsement of the Homestead. *Ibid.*, February 15, 1854.

6. Two factions had developed within the Republican party by the fall of 1861. The conservatives supported the Crittenden Resolution, insisting that the war be fought solely to preserve the Union; the radicals maintained that abolition was necessary to achieve this objective. This divisiveness became evident in the 1861 fall election. A Union convention called by the Republican state executive committee met at Columbus on September 5, and nominated War Democrat David Tod, who won by a decided majority. Delaware, New Jersey, and Pennsylvania followed Ohio's example, adopting a "Union" label to attract support from War Democrats. Porter, *Ohio Politics*, 86-91.

7. Fielding S. Cable (b. *c*1833), a lawyer, was associated with his father in the publication of the *Gazette* in Paulding (*c*1867-70). 1860 Census, Ohio, Paulding, Paulding Township, 6; Smith, *Republican Party in Ohio*, I, 789.

From James T. Shelley[1]

Camp near Somersett, Ky
Decr 28th 1861

Hon A Johnson
Dr Gov.
Sir,

We have not heard from you for some time and are exceedingly anxious to know your whereabouts, but suppose you are still battling for the cause of E Tennessee[.]

We are recieving new additions from E Tennessee every day[.] the *Bridge Burners* are coming in rapidly, and by the by that was the worst Step ever taken by our people in Tennessee for it has been ever since one Continual Step of oppression on our people by the Rebels. there has been several of the very best Citizens sent to the different State prisons, in the south[.][2] they never send any to the state prison of Tennessee[.] It is currently rumered here that *Col Carter* has had his Commission dated back beyond Col Byrds[3] and that his Regt is claimed as the 1st E Tenn Regt,[4] now Carters Comm bears date the 28th Sept 1861 and that of Col Byrds bears date the 1st day of Sept 1861. You know this yourself and how can he have his dated back[?] I wish you would see to this and not let them swindle us, for you know our *Col* has not energy enough to Contend, tho he may have written to you on the subject, before this.

please attend to this for me and further I wish you would use your influence in my favor for the appointment of Col of the 3d or 4th Regt. of Tenn Vols.[5] When we get over home, I think I could manage the business as well as *some* and if we had such a man as Col Spears[6] as Brigdr Genl things would go on quite different to what they do now. please have him appointed if you can.

The Boys are all doing tolerable well. Now I think we will leave here before long for Cumberland Gap or some other sea port. Genl Zolly is not going to fight us here[.]   his is only a foraging party, &c[.][7]

Accept my Kind Reguards Your Obtsvt

Jas T Shelley

If I Should be so fortunate get the appointment I would like to have Rifels[.]

J. T. S.

ALS, DNA-RG94, Volunteer Service, Lets. Recd., 1862, Jas. P. T. Carter.

1. James T. Shelley (c1829-fl1890), Alabama native, Roane County court clerk (1860-61), and clerk and master (1863-70), became a major in the 1st Tenn. Inf., USA, upon its organization at Camp Dick Robinson, Kentucky, on September 1, 1861, and a colonel in the 5th Rgt. in February, 1862. 1890 Special Census, Union Veterans and Widows, Tenn., Roane, Rockwood, 1; *Tennesseans in the Civil War*, I, 375; Emma M. Wells, *The History of Roane County, Tennessee, 1801-1870* (Chattanooga, 1927), 35, 285; William J. Fowler, History of Roane County, 1860-1870 (M.A. thesis, University of Tennessee, 1964), 13.

2. As a result of the bridge-burning episode, the Confederates began a wholesale roundup of East Tennessee unionists. Courts martial were ordered, but charges were reduced from treason to prisoner-of-war status, except for the bridge burners, several of whom were hanged. Most of these political prisoners were sent to Tuscaloosa, the total number so incarcerated ranging as high as 400, among them several legislators, including state senator Francis Samuel Pickens, and Levi Trewhitt, both of whom died in prison; however, at least a few were sent to Nashville and later political prisoners to Macon and Madison, Georgia, as well as to Tuscaloosa and Mobile. On January 7, 1862, Col. Danville M. Leadbetter reported that 130 were still held in Greeneville and that all those taken in arms had been removed to Tuscaloosa. More might have been transported had not the civilian courts, by the use of habeas corpus writs, impeded the military arrests. Humes, *Loyal Mountaineers*, 135-51; Temple, *East Tennessee*, 392-97, 403-8; *OR*, Ser. 1, VII, 701, 704-5, 759-60, 765, 778; *ibid.*, Ser. 2, I, 842-43, 852, 854, 869.

3. Robert K. Byrd (1823-1885), Roane County farmer and trader with $14,500 in real property and $17,700 in personal, had been a lieutenant in the Mexican War, county trustee (1860-61), and a delegate to the Knoxville Union Convention. Credited with taking two thousand Roane countians—more than three-fourths of the adult male population—to Kentucky to enlist, he organized the 1st Tenn. Inf. at Camp Dick Robinson and commanded the regiment until mustered out in 1864. According to a contemporary, Byrd was extremely popular with his men, some of whom had fought with him in Mexico. A prewar Whig, he later served as a Democrat in the state senate (1879-81). Fowler, Roane County, 11-12, 102; Robison, *Preliminary Directory, Roane*, 9-10; Harriman *Record*, October 5, 1961; Cincinnati *Enquirer*, October 12, 1861.

4. Charges brought against James P. T. Carter five weeks later included the allegation that he had requested and received a change in the date of his commission,'from September 28 to August 1, so that his appointment antedated that of Byrd of the 1st Tenn., formerly the senior officer. J. P. T. Carter, Volunteer Service, File J-2 (1862), RG94, NA.

5. In February, 1862, Shelley received his commission as colonel of the 5th Tenn., formed a month later. *Tennesseans in the Civil War*, I, 385.

6. James G. Spears (1816-1869), Bledsoe County lawyer, was clerk of the circuit court (1848) and a delegate to the Knoxville and Greeneville Union meetings. Commissioned a lieutenant colonel of the 1st Tenn. Inf., USA, in September, 1861, he was appointed brigadier the following March, fighting at Wild Cat, Mill Springs, Cumberland Gap, and on the Kanawha expedition. Spears was adamantly opposed to the Emancipation Proclamation, regarding it as unconstitutional and as depriving him of his slaves. Because of "the jealousy of some of his officers," according to a contemporary, his sentiments were reported to Lincoln, charges were filed against him, and he was dismissed from service in August, 1864, returning to his law practice. Warner, *Generals*

in *Blue*, 466-67; Temple, *Notable Men*, 186-90; CSR, RG94, NA; General Courts-Martial, RG153, NA.

7. During December "Genl Zolly" had moved his army into Kentucky for winter camp and was now relocated on the north side of the Cumberland at Beech Grove, within a dozen miles of the Union encampment. Stamper, Zollicoffer, 96-98; *OR*, Ser. 1, VII, 753, 797.

From Robert L. Stanford

Somerset
31st. Dec. 1861

Senitor A. Johnson Dear Sir:

I write again to inform you, that we are still in Statu quo at this place, nothing doing towards a forward movement to E. Tenn.

Zolicoffer takes his pleasure within ten miles of us. Since our movement to within three miles of his lines (of which I wrote you) and our return back to camp, he has Sent his pickets consisting of about one hundred Cavalry twice within a mile of our lines. The weather has never been milder & drier than for the last four weeks. Tennesseans come in nearly evry day. The 2nd. Regt. is nearly full. Such suffering as they portray brought by the *Iron heel* of despotism on our people has never before been witnessed in any civilised country. Old men of 70 or 80 years are tied and carried of to Knoxville,[1] and other points, to under go a drum head court-martial[2] for no crime, except, that of expressing thier opinions in favour of the government they have lived up through. Union men evry where are Striped of evry thing, they and thier familis turned out upon the charities of *Rebel Devils*, Unionists having nothing with which to relieve one another. Oh! My God, will the government never sympathise with loyalists in the *Border States*. Will she never go to thier support. This delay may be all right but it is hard so to think.

I am no General, have no power to move armies, and it may be rong in me to urge a forward movement, Rong to express an opinion unless it be favourable to those in power, an army may stand in Statu quo upon the Potomac for four dreadful months. This army may embrace three hundred thousand soldier, anothe stand in Statu quo upon the border of Ky. Another upon the borders of Missouri, until, the cost to the Nation is one thousand millions. Still no one who is not a West pointer dare to urge a forward movement. The loyalists in the border States may during this time all be crushed in spirit, in property, in evry thing they hold sacred and dear. What need then to send armies to their relief!

I will not dictate, but mearly suggest that if relief is not soon Sent into East Tennessee all that is worth saving there will be lost to the Government. Loyalists will be compelled to take up arms to mak a support for themselves and families. Oh! look at the disastrous effects already following delay, hundreds sent to prison, hundreds killed, and thousands lying out in the dead of Winter in the mountains with scarcely any clothing, without any thing to satisfy the cravings of hunger, only as it is procured by the stealthy tread of caution in the stillness of night, and then by beging from door to door of loyal women who remain at home. Oh! how long must these patriots thus suffer! Has the nation no bowells of compassion?[3] Has she no champion in her Legislative halls who is possessed of moral courage sufficient to lay bare the misconduct of military chieftains, or is the Nation afraid to chastise West pointers.

Governor our only hope is in you. Sturr up the military authorities and the nation will bless you, patriotism evry where will say amen[.] Not only this; but you will be serving your country in a way, that the wise and the good of all nations and climes will approbate now & through all time to come.

Governor not only Tennesseans here are looking to you, but the whole army, we have some of the first men of the State of Ohio, living for the time being, on the hope & prospect that you will pich in to the right man, in the right places. All know you have the ability all believe you will do your duty all are waiting with breathless anxiety to here from you. If men in high places under such a crisis as is now upon the country have not done thier duty, the Country should know it. Pardon me, for reverting again to the condition of union men in East Tennessee[.] From Adam to the present hour, there has never existed upon earth a people more devoted to thier government. They have sacrafized thier property, left thier wifes & little ones and traveled hundreds of miles in the night, (for they dare not travel in day light) to join the United States army, to aid the government of their fathers in puting down an unholy rebellion. These have come mostly from the counties bordering upon Kentucky, thousands in the interior and upon the border of North Carolina and Virginia, would come & join the army but cannot, because, they are hunted like the wolf in the forrest. These are they, who are now lying out in the mountains waiting the arrival of help, & among them Governor is your own son, and among the arrested is your soninlaw Judge Patterson.[4] Let an army go into East Tennessee, and the whole Union population capable of bearing arms will flee to it. then *Rebel devils* can be chastised— Then the thank of patriots will go up from the very spot disecrated for months by demons, to such extent, as no ear ever before witnessed in the holy mountains of East Tennessee. Then I immagine we will see women as well as men runing to the hill and mountain tops to plant once more the standard of thier country, that patriotic eyes may see once more the beautiful stars & stripes floating upon the breeze over the very spot where an husband, a son, or a father had poured out his life blood unassisted in defence of his country. With Sentiments of high respect. Ever mindful of your favours & your freindship I Subscribe myself your friend.[5]

R. L. Stanford Brig Surg. U.S.

ALS, DLC-JP.

1. Both before and after the bridge burnings in November, East Tennesseans suspected of Union sympathies were arrested and transported to Knoxville or sent to Tuscaloosa. Among those of advanced age were W. H. Duggan, a Methodist minister, Francis Samuel Pickens, a prominent Sevier County citizen, and Levi Trewhitt, a Bradley County lawyer. Temple, *East Tennessee*, 404-8, 416-20; Humes, *Loyal Mountaineers*, 144-45; *OR*, Ser. 1, IV, 250-51.

2. A "drum head court martial"—so called because a drum was used as a judge's table—was held in the field for offenses committed during military operations. Secretary of War Benjamin issued instructions to try by this means all who could be positively identified as bridge burners; if found guilty, they were to be hanged. All others arrested were to be "treated as prisoners of war," and sent to Tuscaloosa for the duration of the war. Stanley F. Horn, *Tennessee's War, 1861-1865: Described by Participants* (Nashville, 1965), 34; Temple, *East Tennessee*, 390-95; *OR*, Ser. 1, VII, 701.

3. 1 John 3:17. "But whoso hath this world's good, and seeth his brother have need, and shutteth up his bowels *of compassion* from him, how dwelleth the love of God in him?"

4. Apprehended by Confederate forces under Col. William B. Wood in November, 1861, and ordered to Tuscaloosa, David T. Patterson was paroled after taking the oath on December 16, 1861. *OR*, Ser. 1, IV, 250-51; VII, 701; *NCAB*, XII, 217; Lets. Recd., 8709-1861, RG109, NA.

5. In a second letter of the same date Stanford urged that the 1,500 Tennesseans, then serving in out-of-state regiments, be transferred to Tennessee units as early as possible. Johnson Papers, LC.

1862

From John G. Eve[1]

London Ky
January 1st 1862

Hon Andrew Johnson

Enclosed herewith I send you an extract from the "Louisville Journal" of the 31st Decr.,[2] in regard to the Rail Road. Will Congress pass a bill such as suggested in said Extract? Why should Chattanooga be connected *directly* with Louisville & Cincinnati to the exclusion of better routes?

It is about 125 or 130 miles from Lexington or Nicholasville to Cumberland Gap. It is then about 30 miles to Morristown. Here then is 155 or 160 miles of Rail Road to construct against 220 as stated in the *Extract*. At Cumberland Gap you would connect with a Rail Road in process of construction from that point to Bristol where you connect by Rail Road with, Lynchburg, Richmond and the Eastern portion of Va & N. C. You can connect from the Gap with Morristown on the East Tenn & Va R. R. Here it would connect with a Rail-Road in process of construction and nearly completed though Ashville N. C. into South Carolina[.] Besides this the connection at Morristown will have all the advantages of the connection at Chattanooga. Why then does the government not build the road to Cumberland Gap. I make these suggestions. You can amplify. Why the necessity of sending troops to Chattanooga & then on up the East Tenn & Va R R to Va when it might be done better otherwise[.] Let Hons. Horace Maynard, Green Adams & yourself co-operate in this matter[.]

Very Respectfully &c.
John G. Eve

ALS, DLC-JP.

1. See *Johnson Papers*, IV, 549n.

2. The article, virtually identical with one printed six days earlier in the New York *Herald*, described the route proposed by Gen. Leslie Combs in his plan for a "national military road across the States of Kentucky and Tennessee." See Letters from Leslie Combs, December 12, 26, 1861.

From Samuel J. Pooley

Liberty Corner Somerset County
New Jersey January the 2, 1862.

To Hon. Andrew Johnson
Washington
My dear sir,

In the event of you having a other copy of the correspondence had between Lyons & Seward, on the Trent Affair,[1] will you oblige me by sending it, to my address. The copy I have, is almost unintelligible, it is so blurred in the printing. It is a happy termination to what might have proved, a serious if not fatal obstacle to a restoration of the Union "as it was." The destructionists of our Union, both at home & abroad, will have broken, their "cherished" hope, foreign war, to consummate their traitorous purposes, against the best government in the world. Yancy Mason Slidell &Co, will now rapidly fall, into disgrace, & be held up by all good Union men South as their worst enemies. Altho a serious injury has been done to the South, & its best interests by those fanatics & others, yet it is not too late for our Southern brethren to come back to the fold of their Fathers. I doubt not: That by this time, many, very many, have found out in the South, that, the cry "That Cotton is King"[2] has proved a Syren cry, that it has led them if not to destruction, yet into a path of sorrow & of much misery. Oh God how it has, pained my heart, when I have contemplated both in the prospection & in the reality, the dread abyss, which intemperate persons, & a false estimate, of their true & best position, they have flung themselves[.] England & France, one the mother of abolition the other her ally & prototype, by their own folly brought to their very shores and to their own southern frontier, thus destroying all expansion, south, rendering a dead letter, of all that was, noble & grand in the prospective, as was embraced in the "Monroe doctrine[.]"[3] They say "that prosperity is the worst School, to learn wisdom in,"[4] & thus the south, is a sorry illustration, of this fact.

Yours Very Respectfully
Samuel James Pooley

ALS, DLC-JP.

1. The seizure of Mason and Slidell had drawn an immediate response from the Foreign Office. On December 19, Richard Lyons, British minister in Washington, personally delivered Foreign Secretary Russell's firm demand for their release. Seward, replying on December 27, assured the minister that the Confederates would be "given up, immediately and unconditionally." Nevins, *War for the Union*, I, 388-92; Ferris, *The Trent Affair*, 131-33, 182-84, 187-89; Washington *National Intelligencer*, December 28, 1862; New York *Times*, December 29, 1862.

2. Even before the war began there were intimations that cotton was not the potentate lauded by Hammond and others. As early as February, 1861, a pamphlet of anonymous authorship warned southerners that wheat and corn were more powerful—an argument which seemed stronger as the conflict progressed. Modern scholarship

suggests that this argument has been exaggerated. "Neither wheat nor cotton were princes enough to cause or prevent British intervention in American affairs." Nevins, *War for the Union*, I, 97; Robert H. Jones, "Long Live the King," *Agricultural History*, XXXVII (1963), 166-69.

3. Pooley alludes to European intervention in the internal affairs of the Confederacy's neighbor to the south. After the Mexican Congress suspended payment on all foreign debts in 1861, England, France, and Spain planned a joint armed expedition to recover the claims—a prospective intrusion which Americans considered a violation of the Monroe Doctrine. England had abolished slavery in 1832, the first western power to do so; France followed in 1848. Samuel F. Bemis, ed., *The American Secretaries of State and Their Diplomacy* (17 vols., New York, 1929-67), VII, 105-6; W. H. C. Smith, *Napoleon III* (London, 1972), 167-85.

4. Not found.

To William H. Seward

Senate Chamber
Jany 2-1861 [1862]—

Sir,

We have received Gen. Mc.Clellan's note of the 30th ult. addressed to you upon the subject of Gen. Lewis Wallaces[1] project of an Expedition into East Tennessee, & proposing to submit the paper to Gen. Buell.[2] As we have retained no copy of the original paper, we beg you to procure one for us; if it be inexpedient to return the original paper.

Very Respectfully—
Andrew Johnson
Horace Maynard

Hon. W. H. Seward
Secy of State—

LS, NRU.

1. Lewis Wallace (1827-1905), son of an Indiana governor, studied law, served in the Mexican War, and was elected to the state senate as a Democrat (1856). Commissioned colonel of the 11th Ind. Vols. in 1861, he took part in the capture of Fort Donelson, and, as a major general at Shiloh, incurred opprobrium for having lost himself and his division at a crucial point during the battle. Subsequently governor of New Mexico Territory (1878-81) and minister to Turkey (1881-85), he is best remembered for the novel *Ben Hur* (1880). Warner, *Generals in Blue*, 535-36; see also Lew Wallace, *An Autobiography* (2 vols., New York, 1906); Irving McKee, *"Ben-Hur" Wallace: the Life of General Lew Wallace* (Berkeley, 1947).

2. Lacking a copy of Wallace's "project," we can speculate that the Indianian, restless in the face of inactivity and routine assignments during the fall months of 1861, had drawn up a proposal for the relief of East Tennessee, an enterprise in which he would, of course, play a major rôle.

From Samuel R. Mott[1]

Camp Near Somerset
Jan 5th 1862

Hon Andrew Johnson
United States Senator From Tenesee

Dear Sir The only apology I have to make for takeing the liberty of addressing you is the acquaintance I made with you at Camp Dick Robinson[.] We are here at this point within about Eight miles from the Camp of Zolicoffer who is posted in the gorges of the Cumberland Mountains awaiting our attack. But when that event will take place God only knows I think. For it Seems we are under the Comand of Brig Gen Thomas who is as I think Something like McClelland never in a hurry.[2] We have been here three weeks with some 5000 of a force and verry willing to attack if we were permited But are not[.] There are forces at London that could aid us But by some strange cause here we are compelled to Remain idle Spectaters whilst Zolicoffer is Raveageing & laying waste the Country in the neighbourhood where he is encamped And if we are not allowed to procede any farther than we have done when we shall be able to Render any aid to the down troden Unionists of Your State it will be hard to tell. Our Regiment came into Kentucky Oct 2nd 1861, and in three months have advanced Forty miles & if we continue to advance in the same Ratio you may be able to tell when we will be able to Render material aid to Your immediate Neighbours and freinds But I cannot[.]

The object I have in writing to You is to ask of You in the name of our common country to use Your influence in trying to have some advance made somewhere to put down this *unholy* rebelion[.] If the Government is not paveing the way to Recognize the Southern confederacy By their blunders and truckling to the English Nation as they have done in the surender of Mason & Sidell Both of whoom were guilty of Treason & Refugees from Justice or contrabands of war as I think & should not have been surendered under no circumstances[.] And a few more such steps will show the Powers at Washington that the People constitute this Government And not the President and his Cabinet[.] I want You to pitch into all the comanders from Washington to Louisville and see if this masterly inactivity[3] cannot be Stoped & something done to save our Country from utter ruin[.]

I know your Duties are burthensome & will not ask You to answer this Scrall But wish You to try & do Something to get us to do Something[.]

Verry Truly Your Obedient Servt
S. R. Mott Captain of
Co. C. 31st Regt., O. V. U. S. A.

ALS, DLC-JP.

1. Samuel R. Mott (c1818-fl1893), Knox County, Ohio, lawyer, at this time a captain in the 31st Ohio Inf., later became colonel of the 118th, serving during 1863 in East Tennessee. Threatened with court martial for conduct unbecoming an officer (gambling), he resigned at Knoxville in February, 1864. CSR and Volunteer Service Branch, Doc. File 708-1878, RG94, NA; *Official Army Register: Volunteers*, V, 99, 214.

2. George B. McClellan, commander of the Army of the Potomac and also general-in-chief after November 1, 1861, had spent most of the summer and fall organizing, equipping, and drilling his forces until the phrase "all's quiet on the Potomac" became a derisive description of his campaigning. Thomas was the subject of similar criticism. Arriving at Camp Dick Robinson on September 15, 1861, he found an "unorganized mob" of about 6,000, lacking not only supplies, equipment, and transportation, but even food and shelter. He spent the greater part of the fall whipping these recruits into an army. He was currently moving his forces southward toward London and Zollicoffer, but at a snail's pace of five miles per day because of mud-clogged roads from recent heavy rains. The fact that Mott's regiment was serving in Carter's Tennessee division, where discontent with Thomas was rife, colors these observations. Warren W. Hassler, Jr., *General George B. McClellan* (Baton Rouge, 1957), 31-40; Kenneth P. Williams, *Lincoln Finds a General* (5 vols., New York, 1949-59), I, 131-32; McKinney, *Education in Violence*, 107-24; *OR*, Ser. 1, VII, 485-87, 495, 530-32, 548-49.

3. A phrase dating back to the strategy of the Roman general Quintus Fabius Maximus in the Punic Wars. First used in the United States by John Randolph in 1828 to advise the incoming Jacksonians "against premature action," and soon after by Calhoun in the nullification crisis, when he advised the Federal government that "the highest wisdom of a State [is] 'a wise and masterly inactivity,'" the expression was currently in vogue in consequence of the excessive caution ascribed to certain northern generals at this stage of the war. Hans Sperber and Travis Trittschuh, *American Political Terms: An Historical Dictionary* (Detroit, 1962), 262-63.

From A. H. Jackson

January 7, 1862, Dakota City, Neb. Territory; ALS, DLC-JP.

Land office receiver calls attention to bill amending preemption laws so as to empower local land officers to compel attendance of witnesses at hearings. "By giving your attintion and influance to some remedy for this defect . . . you will confer a favor upon hundreds of wronged settlers in the 'far west[.]' "

From Henry C. Tarrant

January 7, 1862, Harrisonville, Mo.; ALS, DLC-JP.

Former Cocke countian asks that Johnson give audience to H. W. Younger, concerning the treatment of Colonel R. A. Brown and other loyal Cass County, Missouri, slave owners: "if Govenment Winks at all this will it drive Hundreds of Men south that hapens to own a fiew slaves that othewise would Remain Withe the Union[.]"

To Lorenzo Thomas, Washington, D. C.[1]

Senate Chamber
Jany 9th 1861[1862]—

Hon L. Thomas (Adutant Genl)

Will Genl Thomas be kind enough to send me a copy of the letter addressed to Col Carter[2] of the 2d Regiment of Tennessee Vol in regard

to his appointment of Col— Hon Horace Maynard and my self Consuted you and the secretay of War on saturday last in reference to it &c—
I sent one of the pages with a letter to you on mondy last[3] for a Copy, but presume it has been overlooked or your answer misplaced. If convenient send the Copy by the bear and much oblge[.]

Andrew Johnson

ALS, Goodspeed's Book Shop.
   1. See *Johnson Papers*, IV, *523n*.
   2. Col. James P. T. Carter.
   3. Johnson to Thomas, January 7, 1861 [1862], in James P. T. Carter, Volunteer Service, File J-2 (1862), RG94, NA.

To James R. Langdon,[1] Washington, D. C.

Washington City
Jany 11th 1862

Mr Jas. R. Langdon
Your note was found on my table making inquiry as to openig a Correspondence with your Sister residing in E Tennessee—[2] I know of [no] way by which you can convey letters to her at this time— I have not the means of writing to my own family and do not expect to have any means of doing so until this nefarious rebellion is put down, until treason is crushed out and Traitors are punished which I hope is not distant—

I have the honor to be &c
Andrew Johnson

ALS, VtHi.
   1. James R. Langdon (1813-1895), a successful flour merchant, manufacturer, and railroad promoter of Montpelier, Vermont, served in the legislature (1868, 1869). At the time of this communication he was in Washington at Willard's Hotel. Abby M. Hemenway, ed., *Vermont Historical Gazetteer* (5 vols., Burlington, Vt., 1868-91), IV, 544; Charles T. Morrissey (Vermont Historical Society) to Andrew Johnson Project, March 8, 1974.
   2. According to Vermont records, Langdon had only one sister, Caira R. Langdon (1817-1897), who married Anastasius Nicholas, a Greek-born New York City resident; there is no evidence that Mrs. Nicholas was ever in East Tennessee. *Ibid.*

From Leonidas C. Houk

Somerset Ky, January 14th 1862.

Hon. Andrew Johnson:
Dear Sir,
   Pardon my intrusion upon you, in assuming to address you again.
   But times are such I cannot refrain from communicating to you, the condition of things here! They are bad enough indeed!! It does one good, to unbosom to a friend, and when looking at the way matters Stand, it has a tendency to remove the Sadness of heart, created by a contemplation of the realities that surround us, to correspond with those whom we know

sympathize for us! We are here with a little force of Seven Regiments, comprising about 5000 fightingmen! Over this force we have TWO Brigadier Gen'ls Schoepf!!! (who ever heard of Such a name before?) and Carter! Neither of these Gentlemen are remarkable for their Military exploits! Neither have very great control over the affections of the men of their commands.

There has been no time for the last four weeks, until within the past five or six days, but we could have cleaned the Rebels out nicely; but no move was made to draw Zollicoffer, from his entrenchments, while he was left to enjoy himself in his glory; (and our men dying daily;) until now the tables are turned, and Zollicoffer is a very great fool, if he does not Shell us out forthwith! He has been reinforced about 10,000, and he has now from 15 to 20,000, in his command. The news is, as I write, that, he is advancing upon us and it has credence! If this be true, which I can't doubt, we are in a *bad Box*.[1] I am in favor of giving them Hell, as long as we can hold out! But, God knows, his force is large enough to overwhelm us, unless we take some great *Strategetic* advantage! Now Govenor, why under Heaven is it, we are left here, in this helpless condition? Zollicoffer has from 1500, to 2000, cavalry, while we are without any—not even one whole company. This too, when the Secratary of War announces to the world, that we have more Cavalry, in the field, than the exigencies of the times demand, and must be gradually reduced![2] Would it not be a relief to this redundancy of the Secretary, to distribute Some of those cavalry in these parts?

Would it not, look better in the Secratary, and the commander-in-chief of our army, to Send us a few Cavalry, from the regions of the Potomac, than to publicly declare that, there are more in the field, than are needed, and at the Same time leave us here menanced with a far Superior force of Infantry, with a Super abundance of Cavalry, and without any upon our part!

Our men are much dissatisfied, and occasionally go home, and after seeing their folks return. The news from East Tennessee, is of the very worst character.

The people are absolutely frightened out of their wits! They don't know what to do. If they stay there, they must Suffer, and to come hear, they fear they can never more See their children, wives, and friends! They have in a great measure given us out, and fell into a State of desponding dispair!

I presume there is no question but Brownlow has been released, and it now remains to be Seen, whether they will murder him, or redeem the pledge of their Bogus government.[3] I have some hope he will get through Safe, yet!

The Carters are a Selfish Set! They don't want any one to do anything, that will give them any credit, but themselves!

I have said Something in regard to the want of Cavalry! If, I can get permission to raise some, I can have five hundred in the field in ten days. To meet with entire success, I wish it was so, they would be received for 12 months. There are now in Ky, along the line at least 200, who are exiled from Tenn, but can't be induced to enter the 3 years Service, but desire to *goin* [*sic*] for one.

I shall come to Washington in a few days, and hope to be able to Secure Arms for at least five hundred men.[4] If I can get them, I intend to harass the Damned Secessionists, along the border.

I will Kill some body, or be Killed, as certain as God lives! With five hundred men I can make a dash on the Rebels in Campbell and Anderson Counties, and capture their leaders, and bring them away! This would relieve our friends, upon the principle of fear.

But, of all these things I hope to be able to talk with you soon!

Mr Andrew Winters,[5] of Cleaveland got in, a few days ago, after being a prisoner, in Zolly's Camp, some few days, and Sends his warmest regards to you.

Yours Very Truly

L. C. Houk

ALS, DLC-JP.

1. A contemporary colloquialism signifying "to be in a bad predicament." Mathews, *Americanisms*, I, 60.

2. In his annual report (December 1, 1861), Simon Cameron advised that the cavalry had "reached a numerical strength more than adequate to the wants of the service" and at its present strength could "only be maintained at a great cost"; therefore, "measures [would] be taken for its gradual reduction." *Senate Ex. Doc.* No. 1, 37 Cong., 2 Sess., 4; *OR*, Ser. 3, I, 700.

3. Following negotiations with the Confederate government in late November and early December, Parson Brownlow received word from Gen. George B. Crittenden on the fourth that if he called at army headquarters in Knoxville within twenty-four hours he could get a pass through Confederate lines to Kentucky. However, two days later, as Brownlow was preparing to leave, local civil authorities, charging high treason, arrested him. Although the prosecution entered a *nolle prosequi* and the editor was released on December 27, he was immediately placed under house arrest where he remained until escorted to the Union lines, arriving on March 15. *DAB*, III, 177-78; Coulter, *Brownlow*, 180-88, 200-205; Temple, *Notable Men*, 311-15.

4. As a result of his visit to the capital, Houk was appointed colonel on February 5, and authorized by Stanton to raise a regiment of volunteer infantry in Tennessee, to be equipped by and placed under General Buell, commanding the Department of the Ohio. *OR*, Ser. 3, I, 882.

5. Andrew Winter (b. *c*1827), a South Carolina unionist, was briefly in Cleveland, Tennessee, before making his way to Kentucky, where he enlisted in the army, becoming first lieutenant, Co. F, 1st Tenn. Cav. Transferred to the Invalid Corps in 1863, he lived in Ohio after the war. *Tenn. Adj. Gen. Report* (1866), 315; CSR, RG94, NA; William R. Carter, *History of the First Regiment of Tennessee Volunteer Cavalry* (Knoxville, 1902), 298.

From John Lellyett[1]

Paducah, Jany 14, 1862.

Hon. Andrew Johnson
Washington D C

Sir,—I am still here. You will probably understand why I am here—but why here *so long* I cannot undertake to explain.

My special object in writing you to-day, is to refer to a matter personal to Brig. Gen. C. F. Smith, of this post. I do not propose to enter into an examination of the charges against him[2]—if indeed there can properly be said to be any *charges* against him. Some persons here became offended with his administration of the affairs of this post; and instead of first going to him and making their complaint, and that failing in its desired effect, preferring charges in a regular way, giving that officer an opportunity to defend himself,—the parties complaining ran right off in a tangent, and proceeded to pursue a course entirely improper. They have charged Gen. Smith through the press, *anonymously*, with disloyalty and mal-administration; and then have proceeded to pull all the political wires they could reach, to affect his removal. This wire-working was done without giving Gen. Smith an oppertunity to defend himself.

His removal had been almost affected in this way; and it is now supposed that a similar effort will be made to prevent his confirmation by the Senate.[3]

In my opinion these ex-parte representations should be treated as entitled to no attention. Gen. Smith, as I understand, demands that if he is to be subjected to punishment, either positively or negatively, he shall be given the benefit of an investigation.

In my opinion (after certainly giving the case a fair hearing on the part of the complainants) there need have been no serious misunderstanding between the complaining parties and the general, if the former had pursued any thing like a proper course. Gen. Smith is a thorough soldier of the regular school. I have had occasion to have frequent intercourse with him in connection with the public service; and I am thoroughly satisfied of his loyalty. And I furthermore believe that his accusers (who are clever men and my personal friends) are more to blame than the accused for what has been going on here.

I write this at the instance of a friend of Gen. Smith, to put you as a Senator, on your guard against the underground workings that are going on to injure an officer at whose door no regular charge has been laid.

We shall, I hope, have a movement before long, in earnest. I think the present is a feint. Of that, however, I would say nothing.

I neglected to say, further, in reference to Gen Smith, that Mr Etheridge will verify what I have stated above[.]⁴ He may reach Washington as soon as this letter.

Yours Respectfully
John Lellyett

ALS, DLC-JP.

1. For Lellyett (d.1893), see *Johnson Papers*, IV, 62*n*.

2. During the last months of 1861, a number of incidents of insubordination occurred within Gen. Charles F. Smith's command, and letters accusing him of inactivity, inefficiency, and even disloyalty were written to his superior, General Halleck, as well as to others. Halleck, firm in his loyalty to the veteran officer, nevertheless conducted an investigation which proved to his satisfaction that the accusations were completely false. Although deeply hurt, Smith informed Halleck that he would serve "in any capacity, under any commander" until the end of the war, at which time he would retire from the service. *OR*, Ser. 1, III, 299-304; VII, 929; Bruce Catton, *Grant Moves South* (Boston, 1960), 87-88.

3. Despite the opposition, Smith was confirmed, first as colonel in the regular army on February 3, as brigadier general of volunteers on February 14, and a month and a half later (March 24) as major general of volunteers. *Senate Ex. Journal*, XII (1861-62), 109, 119, 179.

4. Unless Etheridge had changed his mind during the preceding month, his opinion of Smith's effectiveness as a commandant was not as favorable as Lellyett suggests. See Letter from Emerson Etheridge, December 19, 1861.

From Andrew Winter

Sumerset Ky Jan 14th 1862

Hon Andrew Johnson
Dear Sir

having lately arrived from East Tenn I thought perhaps I might be able to give you some news from that much abused Section, though I must confess to picture the scenes that are dayly occuring there would be a work not easy accomplished. And I will therefore give a brief ou[t]line and pass on to a subject less painful in its character[.] Near all the union men of any note as far as I know in Bradley Meggs & Hamilton have been taken without any pretext except that they were union men and sent to different places to penitentiaries to be confined until the end of the war.¹ The people there have been looking and praying for help to assert their rights but they have looked in vain and now are on the brink of dispair[.] the old grey headed father sees with grief his last Son dragged from his long cherished and happy home to fight for a cause that both have looked upon as worst than suicide but there is no escape but to flee into Ky to the army[.] all cannot do this and even if they do are they sure of bettering their condition; the way is very dificult and when they get here what do they first See—a lot of officers dashing about the Streets on fine horses doing nothing, but Showing their brass buttons drinking whisky and gambling at night while the country is not talked of or thought of except to Speak of how the united States will manage to pay the expences of the war[.] There has not been a time in two months that the Southern Army here on the Cumberland river could not have been taken with ease until within a few days but now Zolicoffers army out-numbers the army here under this duchman[2] two to one or more and if old Zolly was any sort of a general he would take this whole force in three days[.] it is only 15 miles and a good road from one army to the other[.] If insted of men to talk of finantial Schemes we had military activity energy celerity and victory we would have men and means a plenty and all kinds of Supplies would be abundant. But continue the policy of waiting and waching a little longer and evey loyal man from the South will be driven by force or circumstances into the rebel army and instead of having their help we will have them to Shoot. Fighting is the best financereing. Then let us have a few Bonaparts and let us say as he did when told by his engineer that his plan of crossing the Alps was barely practicable.[3] We have all looked to you as our only hope to lay all our grievences before the goverment and the only one that has taken this monster by the throat and now if we can only have some officers that will concentrate the available force here in a few days march of Zolicoffer we may yet Save a portion of Tenn but if this is put off for a few months longer it will be a bootless undertaking as all will be against us who are not in prison or hung. Tennesseeans here have waited until they can wait no longer and the men are diserting daily and all are loosing confidence in this rebelion ever being put down. If it is within the range of possibility let us have cavalry and a force Sufficient for the work and above all let us have *officers* that will not turn their backs on the enemy. The force here is pehaps 6000 men in all fit for duty while the rebel army is not less than 16000 and being reinforced every day. I have had a fair chance to see the difference in the two armies as on my way here I was taken prisner and taken to the rebel camp. While we are lieing still the rebels are busy all the time laying plans how to do us injury[.] The fact is we have not got officers that feel any interest in our cause[.] if they have they have a lack of sense or courage one or both. I have no doubt I have wearried you in this but I can hardly stop talking on this subject— You will without doubt remember me[.] I Saw you at the Cleveland hotel last Spring when you spoke there[.][4] I am not a Tennesseean[.] I am from S. C. I am the only one I know of from S. C. who Stands firm in favor of the government and it has taken all I had in the world and exiled me from home perhaps for life[.] I said to you in cleveland when parting from you that my best wishes should ever be with you. I repeat that to day and add that I too will go with you to death or victory in the cause of the union the constitution and the enforcement of the laws[.]

I am with assurance of the highest regard yours very Truly

Andrew Winter

ALS, DLC-JP.
1. During the fall of 1861 Confederate forces were twice sent into Bradley and Hamilton counties to break up armed camps and incipient rebellion; immediately after

the bridge burning of November, some forty or fifty unionists were rounded up and sent to Tuscaloosa, among them Brownlow's brother-in-law, William Hunt. Temple, *East Tennessee*, 403, 406-7; Hurlburt, *Bradley County*, 67-77, 113-17; Govan and Livingood, *Chattanooga Country*, 185-89.

2. Brigadier General Albin F. Schoepf, a "duchman" of Austrian and Polish extraction, commanded the 1st Ky. Bde. with headquarters at Somerset. *OR*, Ser. 1, VII, 7-9.

3. This story was available in two books with which Winter may have been acquainted. As reported in *Napoleon: His Army and His Generals; Their Unexampled Military Career. By an American* (New York, 1855), 124-25, the First Consul and General Armand-Samuel Marescot, discussing in May, 1800, the prospect of a military passage through the Alps, had the following exchange: " 'Is the route practicable?' said Buonaparte,—'it is barely possible to pass,' replied the engineer. 'Let us set forward then,' said Napoleon, and the extraordinary march was commenced." The same ancedote appears in William Hazlitt, *The Life of Napoleon Buonaparte* (3 vols., Philadelphia, 1828-30), II, 179.

4. Johnson was in Cleveland on Friday, April 26, 1861. Knoxville *Whig*, April 27, 1861.

From Rae Burr Batten

[Philadelphia]
Jan 15., /62

Hon Andrew Johnson
Loved Friend

You must pardon me for tresspassing upon your valuable time, reading Rae's uninteresting letters but really I cannot refrain from writing you occasionally. I am always so happy to hear from you, and to learn that you are well, and happy. I wish we could have visited Washington this winter. I have long desired to visit Washington when Congress was in session. You will visit our City will you not?— Say Yes! we are all anxious to see you. Cicile, has grown to be quite a Lady for size, and in appearance quite like her dear Mother, the children are both going to School and I am happy to Say they enjoy excellent health. I think I made mention of the death of Mr. Fidler, his widow resides at 1002 Race St, she Sometimes talks of coming to Washington to reside, open a fashionable first class boarding house, what do you think of it Govenor?— she has good furnature, Silver ware and some means, and is a Splendid housekeeper. She thinks best to do some business, she has always had a plentiful home, every comfort for Mr Fidler was a first class business man, and if he had taken proper Care could have left her independant. she is liveing only two squares from us, in a lovely house, but is doing no business, altho' she would prefer to have three or four first class boarders but as Yet, has not fully made up her mind. She has five lovely children and is so Young to be left with sutch a Care, she enjoys health, and is one of the most amiable of woman[.] I think this winter she had better remain here, a few months may make a great change in affairs, and she may then know better how to decide[.] Govenor? when have you heard from home,? how is all your family?—and Robert & Charles, are they with you in Washington?—

how often I think of your arm: is it still painful?[1] I hope not:— take good Care of yourself— dont expose yourself this disagreeable unhealthy weather, and write us you are Soon Coming—

Doctor often speaks of you with a great deal of pride, and would love dearly to See you— *we all* would love to see you—very very Soon:— Write to me and to Doctor.[2] I always take great pleasure, in reading your ever welcome letters, with much Love, from all, I bid you adieu, adieu and remain Truly!

R. A. Batten
811 Race

ALS, DLC-JP.

1. For his broken right arm, see *Johnson Papers*, III, 4n.

2. Evidently Johnson did write, for three weeks later Rae, in a friendly, complimentary letter, took occasion to put in a good word for an acquaintance named "Steptracher" who had been importuning Dr. A. Nelson Batten, her husband, for a letter of introduction to Johnson "merely to have the honour of shaking an honest man's hand, the hand of Andrew Johnson . . . (he has no other object only to see you and shake your hand)" Rae Batten to Johnson, February 4, 1862, Johnson Papers, LC.

From J. Rutherford Worster[1]

[Washington, January 15? 1862][2]

Hon. Andrew Johnson
U. S. Senate
Dear Sir—

As your time would not permit you to hear me, on a subject of deep interest to us all, I beg to lay before you a few ideas in writing, relative to Mr. Wilson's Bill,[3] for the better regulation of the relations of sutler & soldier, and also, to the Resolution of December,[4] abolishing the lien, on the pay of the soldier of $4\frac{1}{3}$ per mo. which, at once destroyed all confidential relations between the sutler and soldier; leaving the former at the mercy of the latter, if he trusted him, besides the chances of active war added to the risk.

Mr. Wilsons Bill may be a good one, in many respects, but in its effect, in general, it will be productive of serious evil; of such a magnitude, as the author may not clearly comprehend.

It interdicts trade with the soldier, and curtails those indulgences, from which his position cuts him off, from any other quarter. It insures nothing to the sutler for a valuable consideration. The soldier desires credit, till pay-day,—equivalent to borrowing so much money, and is not unwilling to assure the lender, if the Law would allow him the privilege, the just and true way of dealing. The result of abolishing this Law will be productive of more mischief in the army and be the groundwork of a tumult and dissatisfaction, such as its author never dreamed of. It is folly to talk of the bleeding process, or as the sage Sanitory-Commn. has characterized it, "leeching", of the Sutlers &c in a report of theirs just out,[5] of all the abortions of the day, the same Sany. Commn. is one, paramount, & modesty should keep their mouths closed.— The soldiers in our army are well known to be, mainly intelligent men, and know what they want, buy or let it alone. The sutler carries to the soldier such articles as are not furnished by the Govt. and, "the value of a thing is what it will bring."[6] Prices of goods are no secret in the army or out, and soldiers are no more amenable to imposition than others, not soldiers.

Sutlers are not unlike out-door clerks: they usually act for the merchant, for a share of profits, in lieu of salary and commensurate with their exertion, will be their reward, and it is evident, under such contingences he ought to receive more wages than in-door-salesmen—

This Bill, in its provisions, embraces a sort of protectorate or espoinage, over sutler, soldier & merchant, equally insulting to each and ought not to be tolerated—[7]

Since the balance of trade has gone against us, by the stupidity of somebody, our currency has & must fluctuate, under the pressure of suspension of specie—which presents another serious burthen to the sutler & capitalist, which should not be lost sight of in this connection.

It will be impracticable to keep our paper circulation at par any length of time, as the finances of the country now stand,—and you will readily perceive, the less we legislate the better, at present, which will be the conclusion reached by every sensible mind. The Hon. genln. could not have taken a step, to generate anethemas on his own head, more effectively, than to meddle with this subject at the present time— Let soldier sutler & merchant muddle and do the best they can.

Whatever may be done in the premises, justice demands, if sutlers are allowed or required, the necessity of which cannot be doubted, that they should be protected in their interests, which can only be accomplished by restoring the lien, as it stood before, and allowing the soldier, all the indulgence possible, as there are abundant causes of discontent already—which the passage of this Bill will augment a hundred fold— Since writing the above—the news from N.Y. has reached me confirming my views of the currency.—[8] Here I would pause and say—you are the acknowledged honest advocate of right, in the Senate, and could do yourself great credit by severely handling the assumptions of Mr. Wilson.

If sutlers commit overt acts, let them be dealt with as other offenders:—either acknowledged under Martial or Civil Law—and not treated as barbarians; they are flesh and blood, like the men who make the law— Millions of property hangs on the Bill under consideration, embarked to supply the army, under the Law as it stood, and a more flagrant wrong, could not be done, to our people than to change the order, as contemplated in the Bill. The merchant embarked his property in good faith, and encountered all the embarrasments of transportation by the blockade of the Potomac & otherwise, with a greatly increased Tariff— If there had been any idea of removal of the lien, our army would have suffered for the necessaries, indispensible to their comfort. Is it fair, or is it honorable, for an enlightened Congress, to cut into the interests, of good and loyal men, by an ex-post facto-law,—for the repeal of the lien, is that, precisely—& nothing else—

Just remember, My dear Sir, that greater injustice could not be done, than to deceive the merchant, disappoint the soldier, and I will add, (confidently believing what I assert,) have a demoralising influence over the whole army & the country—to let the repeal of the sutlers lien, stand as it now does.

Trusting I may not have wearied your excellent patience

I remain ever & anon—

Your Obt. Sert.

J. Rutherford Worster

ALS, DLC-JP2.

1. J. Rutherford Worster, Washington physician and "medical electrician," was a steadfast admirer of Johnson "from the time I met you, twenty years ago, in your own little town." Apparently interested throughout the war in military supply, he wrote Lincoln in the spring of 1864, enclosing some leather "sandal socks" which he proposed to sell to the army. *Boyd's Washington and Georgetown Directory* (1860), 158; *Hutchinson's Washington and Georgetown Directory* (1863), 215; Worster to Johnson, March 6, 1861, Johnson Papers, LC; Worster to Abraham Lincoln, April 13, 1864, Lincoln Papers, LC.

2. Such internal evidence as the Sanitary Commission's report of January 9 and "the news from N. Y."—possibly the discussion in the New York *Times* (January 13) of a growing inclination to accept legal tender currency in place of gold—suggests that this letter was written in the middle of the month.

3. On January 2, Henry Wilson, chairman of the committee on military affairs, introduced a bill (S. 136) to regulate sutlers, those merchants who accompanied the army, furnishing the necessities and comforts not afforded by the commissary. Originally designed to abolish the sutler system altogether, the proposal was modified after Wilson became convinced it had some merit. On January 10 the bill was amended to prohibit credit exceeding one-fourth of a month's pay. The final bill, as enrolled March 19, included a list of articles and foodstuffs permitted for sale, specifically excluding whiskey, created a board to fix prices, and provided for one regimental sutler, selected by the officers, who could establish a lien of up to one-sixth of the soldier's monthly pay. Johnson supported the bill. *Cong. Globe*, 37 Cong., 2 Sess., 68-69, 182, 271-73, 1246; *Senate Journal*, 37 Cong., 2 Sess., 78, 290, 307-8, 326; *U. S. Statutes*, XII, 371-73; Francis A. Lord, *Civil War Sutlers and Their Wares* (New York, 1969), 39.

4. This measure, not a "resolution" but a substitute bill "to provide for Allotment Certificates among the Volunteer Forces," repealed a section of the act of June 12, 1858, "giving sutlers a lien upon the soldier's pay," and was reported by Wilson on December 17, 1861, becoming law a week later. *Cong Globe*, 37 Cong., 2 Sess., 114-15; *U. S. Statutes*, XII, 331; Lord, *Civil War Sutlers*, 34.

5. The report of Frederick Law Olmsted, secretary of the "Commission of Inquiry and Advice in respect of the Sanitary Interests of the United States Forces" (the U. S. Sanitary Commission), which appeared in the New York *Times*, January 9, 1862, did not use the word "leeching," but implied that there were "corrupt bargains" between sutlers and officers—the latter often being the recipients of gifts of wine. Olmsted also complained that the inducements offered by sutlers prevented soldiers from saving and forwarding to their families a portion of their pay. The commission, a private organization inspired by the example of the British Sanitary Commission, was established in June, 1861, by citizens concerned about soldiers' welfare and had inspected two

hundred camps during September and October. Seeking to gain recognition and influence during the early stage of the conflict, it was at war not only with sutlers but also with the army's quartermaster and medical divisions. Charles Stillé, *History of the United States Sanitary Commission* (Philadelphia, 1866), 27, 63; Lord, *Civil War Sutlers*, 25, 46, 65; William Q. Maxwell, *Lincoln's Fifth Wheel: the Political History of the United States Sanitary Commission* (New York, 1956), 4-10, 26.

6. A paraphrase of "For what is worth in anything / But so much money as 'twill bring?" Samuel Butler, *Hudibras*, Pt. II, canto I, l. 465; Bartlett, *Quotations*, 127.

7. That Wilson was not altogether disinterested in the relationship between soldier and sutler is suggested by a later note: "Senator (alias Col. Wilson) Mass 22d Vols. appointed a Sutler on condition that he should have half the profits. The Sutler who came out with the Regt. and the man who came along with him as Banker can testify— make the inquiry and you will learn this is Gods truth— Ask if the Senator has nothing to do with the Army shoe contract." The story circulated during the winter of 1861-62 that Wilson had a lucrative government contract for a "million pair of shoes." The senator denied this, and there is no indication that he ever profited on such a sale. Unsigned note in Worster's hand [February 26, 1862], Johnson Papers, Ser. 18, LC; Ernest McKay, *Henry Wilson: Practical Radical* (Port Washington, N.Y., 1971), 150.

8. One effect of the suspension of specie payment, announced by the New York banks on December 30, was a fluctuation in currency; on January 7, 1862, the *Times* reported a "bull" market characterized by a rise in the price of gold which pushed currency rates upward. Davis R. Dewey, *Financial History of the United States* (New York, 1928), 281-87; New York *Times*, December 30, 1861.

From Leonidas C. Houk

Somerset Ky.
January 17th/62

Hon Andrew Johnson.

My friend McFalls,[1] having determined to visit Washington, in advance of the time I will be able to do so, I venture to drop you another line. The two Tenn Regiments, are about full.

The East Tennesseeans are flocking in rapidly. There are a good number now here, and in the vicinity, who are holding on, in order to get into a Regiment with me! If, I was ready prepared to commence, I could have five hundred men in ten days. My policy will be to go into the mountains to recruit, and pick off their Scouts.

The Rebels, have their Scouts all through the country. They are *Scourging* the country, robing the citizens, and *pilliaging* everything they can find! One of our men dare not go into the country, without being picked up by some of their marauding bands! And Strange to Say, we not only have no orgaization to resist them, but no Cavalry, to prevent their Hellish purposes! Now, I am coming to Washington, and I want to make arrangements for at least 500 good Rifles, and some clothing, and I pledge myself to thin them out, in a very short time! I wish you to think upon this subject, and when I come, and lay my plans before you, I wish your assistance in arranging this matter!

The word failure don't belong *to my* vocabulary, in this concern[.]

I have the right men at work, and I know success is certain! I have spent over two hundred dollars of my own money, in preparing for this arrangement. Therefore I hope you will aid me in perfecting the thing! I can have a Regt in the field in a few days.

I prefer to organize a Regt of mounted Rangers!

Do what you can for me.

Nothing new hereabouts, futher than Thomas is in about 8 or 10 miles of Zollicoffer.

Yours Truly L. C. Houk

ALS, DLC-JP

1. Probably Francis M. McFall (c1837-1868), a Washington County bookkeeper who organized Co. A, 8th Tenn. Cav., USA, at Camp Nelson in June, 1863, and served as its captain. 1860 Census, Tenn., Washington, 3rd Dist., 47; *Tenn. Adj. Gen. Report* (1866), 488, 523; Mrs. Frank M. McFall to Johnson, September 3, 1868, Johnson Papers, LC.

Application to Amend Sequestration Petition[1]

[January 18, 1862]

To the Hon. West H. Humphreys, Judge of the District Court for the Confederate States of America for the District of Tennessee, holding Court at Knoxville.

The Confederate States of America by Landon C. Haynes,[2] Receiver for the Eastern District in said State, respectfully represents unto your Honor that they heretofore filed their petition in this Court for the Sequestration of the property and effects of Andrew Johnson. In addition to the facts therein stated, by way of amendment to said petition, the said States further represent by said Receiver upon his information and belief, that a debt due by Joseph Henderson[3] formerly to the said Andrew Johnson, amounting to about three thousand dollars, is still due by said Henderson; that the said Johnson failing to collect it, his son Charles Johnson procured the said Henderson to execute a new note for said debt to the said Charles Johnson in his own name; that the said Charles Johnson has caused suit to be brought in his own name in the Circuit Court of Greene County to recover the same, as said States are informed, and as said Receiver believes, for the use of the said Andrew Johnson, and that the said pretended gift of said debt by Andrew Johnson to the said Charles Johnson is fraudulent and void, and intended to cheat and defraud the said States out of the Sequestration of said sum and that Samuel Milligan[4] is the Attorney prosecuting the said Suit.

Said States further represent as they are informed and believe upon information coming to said Receiver which he believes, that the negroes mentioned in said petition belonging to the said Andrew Johnson, numbering as they now number 5 or 6, perhaps more or less, have been removed to Carter County to one Daniel Stover, as said Receiver is informed and believes, that the said Daniel is a son-in-law of the said

Andrew Johnson; that Mrs. Johnson, wife of Andrew, has also gone to the said Stovers from Greene County, to live, and that said negroes are under the supervision & control of the said Wife and son-in-law, or their agents.

Said States represent, that they, as the Receiver is informed and believes, are about to be removed from this State with a view to prevent their sequestration and defraud the said States. Said States represent that they have reason to fear that all his negroes may be transferred or removed as aforesaid, and that they ought to be attached. Said States hereby refer to the former Petition, to which this is an amendment, which said Receiver is informed and believes is true in its Statements as far as his knowledge extended.

The premises considered, said states pray by said Receiver, that the said Wife of Andrew Johnson whose name is unknown to them, Charles Johnson, David T. Patterson, Robert Johnson and Daniel Stover & Joseph Henderson be made parties defendant to this amended petition, and answer the same on oath; that writs of injunction & attachment issue to the Marshal & that all said property, debts, effects, negroes &c be attached & the said Charles Johnson and Samuel Milligan be enjoined and inhibited from farther prosecution of said suit against said Henderson, or in any manner attempting to dispose of or collect said debt, & that all said parties be enjoined & inhibited from disposing of or removing, or in any manner transferring said property, real & personal or mixed, or any other rights credits debts dues or demands owing to the said Andrew Johnson; that copies of this petition issue according to law; and that on final hearing everything be done in the premises required by the said Sequestration Act.

Landon C. Haynes,
Receiver.

State of Tennessee

Knox County   Personally appeared L. C. Haynes the Receiver &c. and made oath in due power of law, that the facts stated in the foregoing petition he believes to be true.   L. C. Haynes
Sworn to & subscribed before me in open Court this 18th. day of January 1862[.]

Henry Elliot, Dep Clk
District Court. C.S.A.

Copy, DLC-JP.

1. Landon C. Haynes, responsible for preserving Johnson's Tennessee assets for the Confederacy, evidently became alarmed that the Henderson debt of $3,000 might escape his receivership through transfer to Charles Johnson, who, remaining in Greeneville, had made his peace with the new regime, and that Johnson's slaves might be spirited out of the state. Since apparently neither debt nor slaves were adequately covered in the pending petition (see Notice of Sequestration Proceedings, November 27, 1861), he brought this amendment before the district court on January 16, 1862. The writ immediately following reveals his success. Although there is no clear evidence, it would appear that Haynes's suspicions were valid, inasmuch as Charles could have received the

money as his father's agent—a role he had often played in the past—without changing the terms of the indebtedness. Minute Book, Confederate Court Records, Eastern District of Tennessee, RG21, NA.

2. For Haynes, see *Johnson Papers*, I, 159n.

3. Henderson was a substantial landowner who deeded to Johnson in 1867, perhaps in payment of this debt, a 516-acre Greene County farm, which the latter gave to his daughter Martha five years later. Johnson v. Patterson, 13 *Tenn. Reports* (1884), 628-58; Deed of Gift, February 18, 1873, Johnson-Bartlett Collection, Greeneville.

4. For Milligan, see *Johnson Papers*, I, 114n.

Writ of Attachment[1]

January 18, 1862.

Confederate States of America

District Court of the Confederate States, for the Eastern Division of the District of Tennessee.

To the Marshal of the District of Tennessee; Greeting!

Whereas the Confederate States of America, by Landon C. Haynes Receiver filed their Petition and amended Petition in the District Court of the Confederate States of America setting forth that Andrew Johnson is an Alien Enemy, and that there is a debt amounting to about three thousand dollars due and owing to Andrew Johnson by Joseph Henderson, that a note therefor was fraudulently taken by Charles Johnson in his own name and sued on in the Circuit Court of Greene County, that five or six negroes the property of said Andrew Johnson had been removed to Carter County and the petitioners fearing that said negroes may be removed from the State to avoid their being sequestered (said negroes) numbering five or six more or less, and praying for writs of attachment and injunction, enjoining Mrs. Johnson, wife of Andrew Johnson, Charles Johnson, David T. Patterson, Daniel Stover, Samuel Milligan, (Attorney) & Joseph Henderson and inhibiting them from disposing of or removing or in any manner transferring any of said property real, personal or mixed, or other rights, credits, debts, dues or demands owing to the said Andrew Johnson; and that the said Charles Johnson and Samuel Milligan Attorney from the further prosecution of said suit against said Henderson, or in any manner attempting to dispose of or collect said debt, and a Judicial fiat having been granted for the same.

You are hereby Commanded to Attach said debt, of about three thousand dollars in the hands of said Henderson, and to make known to said Henderson, Charles Johnson, Robert Johnson, Mrs. Johnson the wife of Andrew Johnson, David T. Patterson, Daniel Stovers and Samuel Milligan the terms and tenor of this Writ.[2] Herein fail not and make due return of this writ, to the next term of this Court, to be held at the Court House in Knoxville on the 3d Monday of May next, and the manner in which you shall have executed the same.

Witness, Wm. G. McAdoo, clerk of said Court, at office in Knoxville the 2nd. Monday of January 1862[.]

Henry Elliot. Dep——

Copy, DLC-JP.

1. This writ represents the favorable response of Confederate States district court judge West H. Humphreys, Jr., to receiver Haynes's request that he be authorized to attach Johnson's property.

2. Evidently Haynes went beyond making known "the tenor of this Writ," for the slaves were seized and taken to Knoxville a few days afterward; they were, however, soon returned. See Letter from Robert Johnson, February 13, 1862.

From Robert Anderson[1]

5th Avenue Hotel. [New York]
January 20th, 1862.

Hon Andrew Johnson
U. S. Senate,
My dear Sir

When I had the pleasure of seeing you at Camp Dick Robinson, we left Lt Carter there, acting as Brig. Genl. in command of a Tennessee Brigade. His name had been favorably presented to the War Dept, in a letter forwarded, through me, by Brig Genl Thomas, backed by the recommendation of the Tennesseans then at Camp Robinson.[2]

Had that letter been addressed to me instead of to the Secy of War, and had it asked for his appointment to a Brigade serving in Kentucky, I think that, under the full Commission which I had from the President, I should have appointed him.

As it was, I could only forward it, as I did, to the War Dept. I told Lt. Carter that I would, on my arrival in Washington, speak to the Secy about him—but I found Mr Cameron, unfortunately absent from the City; and, not having been well enough since I reached here to attend to any matters of business, the case stands now, just as it did then.

Can you do any thing in this matter or will the President wait until our troops enter Tennessee and then confer commissions in that State? I was very much pleased with what I saw and heard of Lt Carter, and would be glad (unless you, who know more about it than I do, think otherwise), to see him rewarded for his devotion to the cause which both you and I have so much at heart.

I am afraid that it will be many long and tedious weeks before I will be permitted by my physician to report myself for duty.[3] I am writing, now, more than I ought, but could not well do less.

I am sorry that the newspaper scribblers are attacking Genl Sherman and myself for having "done nothing in Ky."— I pay no attention to such remarks, but Sherman, until his brain was too severely tasked,[4] did, I have no doubt, as well and as much as any other man could have done.

He had, as you know, very few troops in Ky., and they were just coming in about the time he applied to be relieved.

I am greatly in hopes that Genl Buill will soon feel that he is sufficiently strong to make an onward move into Tennessee. That he may succeed there, and raise our honored flag once more, never again to be lowered, in your beloved but suffering State, is the prayer of

Your Sincere friend,

Robert Anderson

P. S. Thank God for the glorious news we have from Ky this morning—[5]

R. A.

ALS, DLC-JP.

1. See *Johnson Papers*, IV, 113n.

2. Samuel P. Carter was nominated brigadier on March 20, 1862, and commissioned May 1. The letter and recommendations have not been found. C-48-1863, Commission Branch, RG94, NA; *Senate Ex. Journal*, XII (1861-62), 176, 273.

3. Given command, on August 15, 1861, of the Department of the Cumberland headquartered at Louisville, Anderson relinquished his post on October 8 because of failing health; his duties were limited until his final retirement from active service on October 27, 1863. *DAB*, I, 274-75; *OR*, Ser. 1, IV, 254, 273, 296-97.

4. Reluctantly assuming command of the department following Anderson's resignation, Sherman delayed his offensive, fearful of the enemy's possible strength and feeling the necessity of moulding raw recruits into a fighting force. In so doing he alienated the press, which published distorted accounts of his requests for troops and circulated rumors that he was suffering from a mental collapse. Whatever the facts may have been, it is interesting to note that Sherman obtained a twenty-day rest leave following his transfer to Halleck's command in Missouri. *Ibid.*, III, 548; IV, 297-316 *passim*, 340-41; LII, Pt. I, 198; William T. Sherman, *Memoirs* (2 vols., New York, 1875), I, 197-218; James M. Merrill, *William Tecumseh Sherman* (Chicago, 1971), 170-71, 174-79, 184-85.

5. In the battle of Mill Springs (Wayne County) fought on January 19, between Federal troops under General Thomas and Confederate forces commanded by Maj. Gen. George B. Crittenden, the Confederates were repulsed, forced to abandon their camp and equipment and to retreat beyond the Cumberland River. *OR*, Ser. 1, VII, 78-114.

From John M. Hay[1]

Executive Mansion,

Washington, Jan 20, 1862.

My Dear Sir

The President directs me to send you copy of dispatch just received from Baltimore:

"We have dispatch from Cincinnati announcing that Schoeff killed Zollicoffer and routed his army at Somerset on Saturday. Twelve hours fight. Heavy loss both[.]"[2]

John Hay

Hon Andrew Johnson

U S S

ALS, DLC-JP.

1. John M. Hay (1838-1905), writer, diplomat, and secretary of state, studied law in his uncle's Springfield office where he became acquainted with Lincoln. Following the

latter's nomination and election, Hay assisted his friend John G. Nicolay with the President-elect's correspondence and accompanied the Lincoln entourage to Washington. There being no provision for an assistant secretary to the President, Hay was first given a clerkship in the pension office, later commissioned a major, with the title assistant adjutant general, and assigned to the executive mansion. *DAB*, VIII, 430-36; Tyler Dennett, *John Hay: From Poetry to Politics* (New York, 1933), 32-35.

2. Gen. George H. Thomas reported 39 men killed and 207 wounded, as against 192 Confederates killed and 157 captured, of which 68 were wounded. Gen. George B. Crittenden's corresponding figures for southern casualties were 125 killed, 309 wounded, and 95 missing. *OR*, Ser. 1, VII, 81-82, 108.

From Fearless A. Armstrong[1]

Sandoval Marion Co. Ill.
Tuesday Jan. 21st, 1862.

Hon Andrew Johnson,
Dear Sir

I have watched with great interest the noble & decided stand you have taken from the beginning in relation to the unnatural & monstrous rebellion that is now desolating the land. To prevent similar scenes in the future is it not greatly desirable that ample provision should be made for the education of *all* the sons & daughters of the land. And now while the confiscation bill is under consideration will you not entrench yourself in the heart of millions & cause multitudes yet unborn to rise up & bless your memory if you throw your whole soul into the work of having that bill so modified that *at least 1/3 of all property Confiscated shall be devoted to common schools in the respective states, from which the Word of God shall not be excluded.*[2] Who can measure the good that would result from the compound influence of this & the Homestead law together. As a native of East Tennessee & intensely interested in whatever concerns its welfare in common with the rest of the land I feel assured you will excuse the liberty I take in calling your special attention to this point, although it may have before occupied your mind.

The Lord be with you & bless you in every struggle for the right is the prayer of

Your freind
F. A. Armstrong
Missy. A. H. M. S.[3]

ALS, DLC-JP.

1. Fearless A. Armstrong (b. *c*1819), a Knox County delegate to the East Tennessee Union Convention at Knoxville (May, 1861), was a farmer who had $1,000 in real and $200 in personal property. 1860 Census, Tenn., Knox, 8th Dist., 64; *OR*, Ser. 1, LII, Pt. I, 152.

2. Armstrong's suggestion was never considered during the debates on the second confiscation bill in the winter of 1862. Introduced by Lyman Trumbull on December 5, 1861, the bill, which made all Confederate property liable for confiscation, was designed to serve as an instrument for emancipation. It did not pass until July, 1862. Nevins, *War for the Union*, II, 146; *Cong. Globe*, 37 Cong., 2 Sess., 18.

3. The American Home Missionary Society was founded at New York in 1826 by members of the Congregational, Presbyterian, Lutheran, Dutch Reformed, and German Reformed churches. It helped to organize and support new churches, especially in the western states and territories. For two generations its members were a significant force in the educational, political, and cultural maturation of the West. Robert Baird, *Religion in the United States of America* (Glasgow, 1844), 311-12; Sydney Ahlstrom, *A Religious History of the American People* (New Haven, 1972), 423.

From Johnston H. Jordan[1]

Cincinnati O, Jan. 24/62

Thank the Lord! the signs begin to look a little more favorable for *East Tennessee!*

That was a glorious victory of Sunday last—And the result must have a very discouraging effect upon the balance of the rebels, both in Kentucky and Tennessee.

Shall it not be followed up—and the advantage improved? If Thomas and Shoepff will only now push *right on—straight to Knoxville*—with their 12 or 14,000 troops—(and they can do it *easily* enough) and *another column* of 10,000 or more *follows right* after them—with supplies, extra arms—and to serve as a *support* in case of need—All m[a]y soon be well (as well as *possible*) and East Tennessee yet saved—   O! the shame! the crime! the sin! the way that people have been deceived, abandoned & neglected by this Administration! There is a chance now to redeem *some* of the loss, and atone for *some* of the criminal neglect! *Will it be done?*

Can you not see to it, and *have it done*? Now is the time, before the rebels get over their *panic* and rally, to push right on to Knoxville—and take possession of that great Railroad—[2] and raise the Stars & Stripes, and rally the people around it!

The two Tennessee Regiments (the refugees) did not participate in the Action—or were not allowed to. This was right. I am glad of it. Though they *wanted* to be in the battle, bad enough, yet, poor fellows, if they had been in, no doubt many of them would have been *killed*—and many *wounded*, for they would not have been restrained, and would have exposed themselves more, probably, than any others—

No—I would have them *all* saved, to go *home* again, and ere long, triumphant and rejoicing!

Were I Commander of the Brigade or Division in which they are—I would not allow them to fight at all, in open engagement—unless it was as a *reserve*, and then only because absolutely necessary—

But enough. I have hope— the People have hope, now, since the incoming of the *new Secretary of War*.[3] I believe now—with the new and vigorous policy which I believe will *begin* with his administration—and be carried out henceforth—that *the Nation* is Saved!—

But *see to it*—that Gen Thomas *goes on* to Knoxville—and that Gen

Buell, or somebody else, sends right along after him a *supporting column* of 8 or 10,000 more—And rebellion will begin to experience and [*sic*] *earth-quake*!

Truely Yours,
Dr. J. H. Jordan

Hon. Andrew Johnson
Washington D C. U.S Senate

ALS, DLC-JP.
1. See *Johnson Papers*, IV, 384*n*.
2. The East Tennessee and Virginia.
3. Edwin M. Stanton (1814-1869), Buchanan's former attorney general (December, 1860-March, 1861), had just been appointed. An Ohio native and former antislavery Democrat who supported Breckinridge in 1860, Stanton had moved to Washington four years previously to practice before the Supreme Court. After Lincoln's assassination, Johnson retained Stanton until his intrigue with the radicals culminated in his removal and led to the President's impeachment for violation of the Tenure of Office Act. Nominated by Grant to the Supreme Court, Stanton died before taking his seat. *DAB*, XVII, 517-21; Benjamin P. Thomas and Harold M. Hyman, *Stanton: The Life and Times of Lincoln's Secretary of War* (New York, 1962).

From John F. Parr

January 24, 1862, Fort LaFayette, New York; ALS, DLC-JP.

Nashville coachmaker, arrested a half hour after his arrival in New York and held on unspecified charges, requests trial or offers bond until he proves his loyalty; protests that "my acts and purpose was to keep out of the war . . . I was here in the North for staying with my relatives."

From Roswell B. Darling

January 28, 1862, Annapolis, Md.; ALS, DLC-JP.

Greene countian in U. S. General Hospital asks for word from home—"Brother writes me from Ohio that he hears that my family are dead"—and for fifty dollars' fare so that he may return to East Tennessee on his furlough.

From Philadelphia Central Republican Club

January 29, 1862, Philadelphia, Pa.; ALS, DLC-JP.

John M. Butler and eight other members of the club's executive committee, inviting Johnson to speak in Philadelphia on the evening of February 22, in observance of Washington's birthday, assure him that the proceeds will go toward supporting "Volunteer Refreshment Saloons," providing meals, medical attention, and hospital accommodations for soldiers. "Your Character as a Statesman, your earnest advocacy of every principle of Constitutional liberty, your unflinching devotion to your country and to your country's flag in many situations of danger and trial, have endeared you to your fellow-countrymen of the North."

From Gideon Welles

January 29, 1862, Washington, D. C.; LB copy, DNA-RG45, Gen. Let. Bk., Vol. 67.

Replying to Johnson's intercession on behalf of John Wilson, Jr., for a job in the Philadelphia Navy Yard, the secretary of the navy observes that "subordinate appointments" at navy yards are the responsibility of "The Master Workmen . . . [who] are allowed to select the men to be employed under them, subject to the approval" of their superintendents and the commandant; adds that the department "has recommended the Virginia exiles to the consideration of the Commandants of the Navy Yards."

From Michael L. Patterson

Greensburg Indiana
January 31st 1862.

Friend Johnson
Dear Sir—

I having Just arrived at this place—Direct from home— I left home on the 15th Inst and have been some 2 weeks on the rout— I Run the lines of the Rebels— when I left home—Judge Patterson[1] Requested me to go (if I got through) and see you— But I am very unwell—and will be compelled to lay over a Day or two till I get Better— Mrs. Johnson is in Carter County with Mrs. Stover— Frank is with her— she was a little unwell—when I left.[2] Charles has come in out of the Bresh—and taken the oath— Robert is Still in the Bushes— Mr. Stover is also in the Bushes—or made his way to Ky—[3] Judge Patterson has been arrested twice. But released—[4] Mrs Patterson is well— your house is now a Rebel *hospital*[5] and the Rebels ar cuting up Generlly.

I shall come to Washington in a few days. so soon as I get a little Better of my cold—And then I will give you all of the particulars—as near as I can—

Please excuse—

Yours Respectfully
M. L. Patterson

P.S.

If there will be any Dificulty in getting into your City—please inform me what will be necessary and how I will have to proceed—&c &c—
Yours &c—M.L.P.

ALS, DLC-JP.

1. Michael L. and David T. Patterson, Johnson's son-in-law, were perhaps distantly related, one descending from a North Carolina family and the other from Virginians. See also *Johnson Papers*, III, 388n; I, 110n.
2. During these months Eliza Johnson and her nine-year-old son were staying in the

country with her daughter Mary Stover. As late as May, the Confederate deputy provost-marshal observed: "I have consulted with several physicians who state that Mrs. Johnson is consumptive and to remove her will probably cause her death." William W. Stringfield to William M. Churchwell, May 19, 1862, *OR*, Ser. 2, I, 889.

3. After the bridge-burning arrests, many unionists, including Charles Johnson, felt compelled to swear allegiance to the Confederacy in order to stay in East Tennessee; others, like Robert Johnson, and for a time Daniel Stover, remained "in the Bushes,"— the former preparing to leave for Kentucky on February 4 and the latter still "out on the Scouts," engaging in guerrilla activities. See William M. Churchwell to The Disaffected People of East Tennessee, April 23, 1862, *ibid.*, 884; Letter from Robert Johnson, February 13, 1862.

4. Taken into custody in November, 1861, along with others suspected of bridge-burning activities, David Patterson had been ordered sent as a prisoner of war to Tuscaloosa. He was finally released by orders from Richmond, "after going three times to the depot," paroled on his honor, and continued as judge of the 1st judicial circuit court, a position to which he was reelected in March, 1862, and which he filled until Federal troops occupied East Tennessee in September, 1863. William B. Wood to Judah P. Benjamin, November 20, 1861, *OR*, Ser. 1, IV, 250; Benjamin to Wood, November 25, 1861, *ibid.*, VII, 701; Samuel P. Carter to G. M. Bascom, June 21, 1864, *ibid.*, XXXIX, Pt. II, 133-34; David T. Patterson to Col. Danville Leadbetter, December 16, 1861, Lets. Recd., 8709-1861, RG109, NA; Speer, *Prominent Tennesseans*, 531.

5. Both Confederate and Union troops occupied Johnson's home. Moving his headquarters from Jonesboro to Greeneville in late November, 1861, Confederate Col. Danville Leadbetter acknowledged Martha Patterson's note that the house was ready "for the reception of your patients." Apparently offended by her terseness, he reminded her that the house had been "vacant and accommodations scanty," suggesting that had it "continued to shelter its owner, this military force would now have been elsewhere, and engaged in more congenial duties." Martha and family were also refugeeing with the Stovers, while the furniture and household goods had been stored with friends. *OR*, Ser. 1, VII, 712, 842; Leadbetter to Martha Patterson, November 29, 1861, Huntington Library; Ernest A. Connally, "The Andrew Johnson Homestead at Greeneville, Tennessee," ETHS *Publications*, No. 29 (1957), 129-30.

Speech on Expulsion of Senator Bright[1]

January 31, 1862

Mr. JOHNSON. Mr. President,[2] when this resolution for the expulsion of the Senator from Indiana was first presented to the consideration of the Senate, it was not my intention to say a single word upon it. Presuming that action would be had upon it at a very early day, I intended to content myself with casting a silent vote. But the question has assumed such a shape that, occupying the position I do, I cannot consent to record my vote without giving some of the reasons that influence my action.

I am no enemy of the Senator from Indiana. I have no personally unkind feelings towards him. I never had any, and have none now. So far as my action on this case is concerned, it will be controlled absolutely and exclusively by public considerations, and with no reference to partisan or personal feeling. I know that since the discussion commenced, an intimation has been thrown out, which I was pained to hear, that there was a disposition on the part of some to hound down the Senator from Indiana. Sir, I know that I have no disposition to "hound" any man. I would to God it were otherwise than necessary for me, as I think, to say a single word upon this question, or even to be compelled to cast a vote upon it. So far as I know, there has never been any unkind feeling between the Senator and myself from the time we made our advent into public life down to this moment. Although party and party associations and party considerations influence all of us more or less—and I do not pretend to be exonerated from the influence of party more than others—I know, if I know myself, that no such considerations influence me now. Not many years ago there was a contest before the Senate as to his admission as a Senator from the State of Indiana; we all remember the struggle that took place.[3] I will not say that the other side of the House were influenced by party considerations when the vote upon that question of admission took place; but if my memory serves me correctly, there was upon one side of the House a nearly strict party vote that he was not entitled to his seat, while on the other side his right was sustained entirely by a party vote. I was one of those who voted for the Senator's admission to a seat upon this floor under the circumstances. I voted to let him into the Senate, and I am constrained to say that, before his term has expired, I am compelled to vote to expel him from it. In saying this, I repeat that if I know myself, and I think I do as well as ordinary men know themselves, I cast this vote upon public considerations entirely, and not from party or personal feeling.

Mr. President, I hold that under the Constitution of the United States we clearly have the power to expel a member,[4] and that, too, without our assuming the character of a judicial body. It is not necessary to have articles of impeachment preferred by the other House; it is not necessary to organize ourselves into a court for the purpose of trial; but the principle is broad and clear, inherent in the very organization of the body itself, that we have the power and the right to expel any member from the Senate whenever we deem that the public interests are unsafe in his hands, and that he is unfit to be a member of the body. We all know, and the country understands, that provision of the Constitution which confers this power upon the Senate. Judge Story, in commenting upon the case of John Smith,[5] in connection with the provision of the Constitution to which I have referred, used the following language:

The precise ground of the failure of the motion does not appear; but it may be gathered, from the arguments of his counsel, that it did not turn upon any doubt that the power of the Senate extended to cases of misdemeanor not done in the presence or view of the body; but most probably it was decided upon some doubt as to the facts. It may be thought difficult to draw a clear line of distinction between the right to inflict the punishment of expulsion and any other punishment upon a member, founded on the time, place, or nature of the offense. The power to expel a member is not in the British House of Commons confined to offenses committed by the party as a member, or during the session of Parliament; but it extends to all cases where the offense is such as, in the judgment of the House, unfits him for parliamentary duties.—*Story's Commentaries on the Constitution*, sec. 836.

The rule in the House of Commons was undoubtedly in the view of the framers of our Constitution; and the question is, has the member unfitted himself, has he disqualified himself, in view of the extraordinary condition of the country, from discharging the duties of a Senator? Looking at his connection with the Executive; looking at the condition, and, probably, the destinies of the country, we are to decide—without prejudice, without passion, without excitement—can the nation and does the nation have confidence in committing its destinies to the Senator from Indiana, and others who are situated like him?

If we were disposed to bring to our aid, and were willing to rely upon, the public judgment, what should we find? When you pass through the country, the common inquiry is, "Why has not Senator Bright, and why have not others like him, been expelled from the Senate?" I have had this question asked me again and again. I do not intend, though, to predicate my action as a Senator upon what may be simply rumor and popular clamor or popular indignation; but still it is not often the case that, when there is a public judgment formed in reference to any great question before the country, that public judgment is not well founded, though it is true there are sometimes exceptions.

Having shown our power in the premises to be clear according to the general authority granted by the Constitution and the broad principle stated by Judge Story in its elucidation, I next turn my attention to the case itself. The Senator from Indiana is charged with having written a letter on the 1st of March last to the chief of the rebellion, which is the basis of this proceeding against him. What was the condition of the country at the time that letter was written? Did war then exist or not? for really that is the great point in the case. On that point, allow me to read an extract from the charge of Judge David A. Smalley,[6] to the grand jury of the United States district court for the southern district of New York, published in the National Intelligencer of January 21, 1861:

[In an effort to define "high treason," Smalley cites various actions, such as preventing the execution of the laws, levying war against the United States, furnishing arms and munitions to her enemies, and "inciting and encouraging others to engage in or aid the traitors in any way."]

In this view, even if we were sitting as a court, bound by the rules and technicalities of judicial proceedings, should we not be bound to hold that this case comes within this legal definition. "And it is immaterial," adds Judge Smalley, "whether such acts are induced by sympathy with the rebellion, hostility to the Government, or a design for gain."

In view of these authorities, let us look at the letter. It was written on the 1st of March, 1861. The opinion of Judge Smalley was published in the Intelligencer of the 21st of January, 1861, and must, of course, have been delivered before that time. It would be doing the Senator's intelligence great injustice to presume that he was not as well informed on the subject as the judge was who was charging the grand jury in reference to an act of Congress passed at an early day in the history of the Government. It would be doing him great injustice to suppose that he was not familiar with the statute. It would be doing him great injustice to suppose that he had not observed the fact that the attention of the country was being called by the courts to the treason that was rampant throughout the land. The letter complained of is as follows:

Washington, *March* 1, 1861.

My Dear Sir: Allow me to introduce to your acquaintance my friend Thomas B. Lincoln, of Texas. He visits your capital mainly to dispose of what he regards a great improvement in fire-arms. I recommend him to your favorable consideration as a gentleman of the first respectability, and reliable in every respect.

Very truly, yours,   JESSE D. BRIGHT.

To His Excellency Jefferson Davis,
President of the Confederation of States.

According to the charge of Judge Smalley, which I have already read, the flag of the United States had been fired upon before the 21st of January, 1861,[7] and war then did in fact exist. When the rebels were taking our forts; when they were taking possession of our post offices; when they were seizing our custom-houses; when they were taking possession of our mints and the depositories of the public money, can it be possible that the Senator from Indiana did not know that war existed, and that rebellion was going on? It is a fact that the ordinance of the convention of Texas seceding from the Union and attaching herself to the southern confederacy, was dated back as far as the 1st of February, 1861. Then, at the time the letter was written, Thomas B. Lincoln[8] was a citizen of a rebel State; a traitor and a rebel himself. He comes to the Senator asking him to do what? To write a letter by which he could be facilitated in his scheme of selling an improved fire-arm, an implement of war and of death. Can there be any mistake about it? He asks for a letter recommending an improved fire-arm to the president of the rebel States, who was then in actual war; the man who asked for this being himself from a State that was in open rebellion, and he himself a traitor.

Now, sir, if we were a court, how would the case be presented? I know the Constitution says that "no person shall be convicted of treason unless on the testimony of two witnesses to the same overt act, or on confession in open court."[9] Here is an overt act; it is shown clearly and plainly. We have the Senator's confession in open Senate that he did write the letter. Shall we with this discretion, in view of the protection of this body and the safety of the Government, decide the case upon special pleas or hunt up technicalities by which the Senator can escape, as you would quash an indictment in a criminal court? The case of John Smith has already been stated to the Senate. A true bill had been found against him for his connection with Burr's treason, but upon a technicality, the proof not being made out according to the Constitution, and Burr having been tried first and acquitted, the bill against Smith was quashed, as he was only an accomplice. He was, therefore, turned out of court; the proceedings against him were quashed upon a technicality; but John Smith was a Senator, and he came here to this body. He came again to take his seat in the Senate of the United States, and what did the Senate do? They took up his case; they investigated it. Mr. Adams made a report, able, full, complete. I may say he came well nigh exhausting the whole subject. The committee reported a resolution for his expulsion, and how did the vote stand? It is true that Mr. Smith was not expelled for the want of some little formality in this body, the vote standing 19 to 10. It only lacked one vote to put him out by a two-third majority according to the requirements of the nation? What was the judgment of the nation? It was that John Smith was an accomplice of Burr, and the Senate condemned him and almost expelled him, not narrowing itself down to those rules and technicalities that are resorted to in courts by which criminals escape. To show the grounds upon which the action in that case was based, I beg leave to read some extracts from Mr. John Quincy Adams's report in that case:

[In resounding periods, Adams set forth the argument that "the power of expelling a member must in its nature be discretionary, and in its exercise always more summary than the tardy process of judicial proceedings"—for "defective, indeed . . . that institution which should be impotent to discard from its bosom the contagion of such a member; which should have no remedy of amputation to apply until the poison had reached the heart."]

Mr. President, suppose Aaron Burr had been a Senator, and after his acquittal he had come back here to take his seat in the Senate, what would have been done? According to the doctrine avowed in this debate, that we must sit as a court and subject the individual to all the rules and technicalities of criminal proceedings, could he have been expelled? And yet is there a Senator here who would have voted to allow Aaron Burr to take a seat in the Senate after his acquittal by a court and jury? No; there is not a Senator here who would have done it. Aaron Burr was tried in court, and he was found not quilty; he was turned loose; but was the public judgment of his nation less satisfied of his guilt than if he had not been acquitted? What is the nation's judgment, settled and fixed? That Aaron Burr was guilty of treason notwithstanding he was acquitted by a court and jury.

It is said by some Senators that the Senator from Indiana wrote this letter simply as a letter of friendship. Sir, just think of it! A Senator of the United States was called upon to write a letter for a rebel, for a man from a rebel State, after the courts of the country had pronounced that civil war existed; after the judicial tribunals had defined what aiding and adhering to the enemies of the country was! Under such circumstances, what would have been the course of loyalty and patriotism? Suppose a man who had been your friend, sir, who had rendered you many acts of kindness, had come to you for such a letter. You would have asked where he was going with it. You would have said: "Here is a southern confederacy; there is a rebellion; my friend, you cannot ask me to write a letter to anybody there; they are at war with the United States; they are at war with my Government; I cannot write you a letter giving you aid and assistance in selling your improved fire-arm there." Why? "Because that fire-arm may be used against my own country and against my own fellow-citizens." Would not that have been the language of a man who was willing to recognize his obligations of duty to his country?

What was the object of writing the letter? It certainly was to aid, to facilitate the selling of his fire-arms, to inspire the rebel chief with confidence in the individual. It was saying substantially, "I know this man; I write to you because I know you have confidence in me; I send him to you because I know you need fire-arms; you need improved fire-arms; you need the most deadly and destructive weapons of warfare to overcome this great and this glorious country; I recommend him to you, and I recommend his fire-arms; he is a man in whom entire confidence may be placed." That, sir, is the letter. I have already shown the circumstances under which it was written. If such a letter had been written in the purest innocence of intention, with no treasonable design, with no desire to injure his own Government, yet, in view of all the circumstances, in view of the facts which had transpired, a Senator who would be so unthoughtful, and so negligent, and so regardless of his country's interests as to write such a letter, is not entitled to a seat on this floor. [Applause in the galleries.]

The PRESIDING OFFICER, (Mr. Sherman.) Order! Order!

Mr. JOHNSON. Then, Mr. President, what has been the bearing and the conduct of the Senator from Indiana since? I desire it to be understood that I refer to him in no unkindness, for God knows I bear him none; but my duty I will perform. "Duties are mine, consequences are God's."[10] What has been the Senator's bearing generally? Have you heard of his being in the field? Have you heard of his voice and his influence being raised for his bleeding and distracted country? Has his influence been brought to bear officially, socially, politically, or in any respect, for the suppression of the rebellion? If so, I am unaware of it. Where is the evidence of devotion to his country in his speeches and in his votes? Where the evidence of the disposition on his part to overthrow and put down the rebellion? I have been told, Mr. President, by honorable gentlemen, as an evidence of the Senator's devotion to his country and his great opposition to this southern movement, that they heard him, and perhaps with tears in his eyes, remonstrate with the leaders of the rebellion that they should not leave him here in the Senate, or that they should not persist in their course after the relations that had existed between them and him, and the other Democrats of the country; that he thought they were treating him badly. This was the kind of remonstrance he made. Be it so. I am willing to give the Senator credit for all he is entitled to, and I would to God I could credit him with more.

But do Senators remember that when this battle was being fought in the Senate I stood here on this side, solitary and alone, on the 19th day of December, 1860, and proclaimed that the Government was at an end if you denied it the power to enforce its laws? I declared then that a Government which had not the power to *coerce* obedience on the part of those who violated the law was no Government at all, and had failed to carry out the objects of its creation, and was, *ipso facto*, dissolved. When I stood on this floor and fought the battle for the supremacy of the Constitution and the enforcement of the laws, has the Senate forgotten that a bevy of conspirators gathered in from the other House,[11] and that those who were here crowded around, with frowns and scowls, and expressions of indignation and contempt toward me, because I dared to raise my feeble voice in vindication of the Constitution and the enforcement of the laws of the Union? Have you forgotten the taunts, the jeers, the derisive remarks, the contemptuous expressions that were indulged in? If you have, I have not. If the Senator felt such great reluctance at the departure from the Senate of the chiefs of the rebellion, I should have been glad to receive one encouraging smile from him when I was fighting the battles of the country. I did not receive one encouraging expression; I received not a single sustaining look. It would have been peculiarly encouraging to me, under the circumstances, to be greeted and encouraged by one of the Senator's talents and long standing in public life; but he was cold as an iceberg, and I stood solitary and alone amidst the gang of conspirators that had gathered around me. So much for the Senator's remonstrances and expressions of regret for the retirement of those gentlemen.

The bearing of the Senator since he wrote this letter has not been unobserved. I have not compared notes; I have not hunted up the record in reference to it; but I have a perfect recollection of it. Did we not see, during the last session of Congress, the line being drawn between those who were devoted to the Union and those who were not? Cannot we sometimes see a great deal more than is expressed? Does it require us to have a man's sentiments written down in burning and blazing characters, before we are able to judge what they are? Has it not been observable all through this history where the true Union heart has stood? What was the Senator's bearing at the last session of Congress? Do we not know that in the main he stood here opposed substantially to every measure which was necessary to sustain the Government in its trial and peril?[12] He may perhaps have voted for some measures that were collateral, remote, indirect in their bearing; but do we not know that his vote and his influence were cast against the measures which were absolutely necessary in order to sustain the Government in its hour of peril?

Some gentlemen have said, and well said, that we should not judge by party. I say so, too. I voted to let the Senator from Indiana into the body, and as a Democrat my bias and prejudice would rather be in his favor. I am a Democrat now; I have been one all my life; I expect to live and die one; and the corner-stone of my Democracy rests upon the enduring basis of the Union. Democrats may come and go, but they shall never divert me from the polar star by which I have ever been guided from early life—the great principles of Democracy upon which this Government rests, and which cannot be carried out without the preservation of the Union of these States. The pretense hitherto employed by many who are now in the traitors' camp has been, "we are for the Union; we are not for dissolution; but we are opposed to coercion." How long, Senators, have you heard that syren song sung? Where are now most of those who sang those syren tones to us? Look back to the last session, and inquire where now are the men who then were singing that song in our ears? Where is Trusten Polk, who then stood here so gently craving for peace? He is in the rebel camp. Where is John C. Breckinridge—a man for whose promotion to the Presidency I did what I could physically, mentally, and pecuniarily; but when he satisfied me that he was for breaking up this Government, and would ere long be a traitor to his country, I dropped him as I would the Senator from Indiana? He was here at the last session of Congress; and everybody could see then that he was on the road to the traitors' camp. Instead of sustaining the Government, he, too, was crying out for peace; but he was bitter against "Lincoln's Government." Sir, when I talk about preserving this great Government, I do not have its executive officer in my mind. The executive head of the Government comes in and goes out of office every four years. He is the mere creature of the people. I talk about the Government without regard to the particular executive officers who have charge of it. If they do well, we can continue them; if they do wrong, we can turn them out. Mr. Lincoln having come in according to the forms of law and the Constitution, I, loving my Government and the Union, felt it to be my duty to stand by the Government, and to stand by the Administration in all those measures that I believed to be necessary and proper for the preservation and perpetuation of the Union.

Mr. Polk has gone; Mr. Breckinridge has gone; my namesake, the late Senator from Missouri, has gone.[13] Did you not see the line of separation at the last session? Although Senators make speeches, in which they give utterance to disclaimers, we can see their bearing. It is visible now; and the obligations of truth and duty to my country require me to speak of it. I believe there are treasonable tendencies here now; and how long it will be before they will land in the traitors' camp, I shall not undertake to say. The great point with these gentlemen is, that they are opposed to coercion and to the enforcement of the laws. Without regard to the general bearing of the Senator from Indiana upon that point, let me quote the conclusion of his letter of the 7th of September, 1861, to J. Fitch.[14] I will read only the concluding portion of the letter, as it does him no injustice to omit the remainder:

And hence I have opposed, and so long as my present convictions last shall continue to oppose, the entire coercive policy of the Government. I hope this may be satisfactory to my friends. For my enemies I care not.[15]

Does not this correspond with the Senator's general bearing? Has he given his aid or countenance or influence, in any manner, towards the efforts of the Government to sustain itself? What has been his course? We know that great stress has been laid upon the word "coercion," and it has been played upon effectually for the purpose of prejudicing the southern mind, in connection with that other term, "subjugation of the States," which has been used so often. We may as well be honest and fair, and admit the truth of the great proposition, that a Government cannot exist—in other words, it is no Government if it is without the power to enforce its laws and coerce obedience to them. That is all there is of it; and the very instant you take that power from this Government, it is at an end; it is a mere rope of sand that will fall to pieces of its own weight. It is idle, utopian, chimerical, to talk about a Government existing without the power to enforce its laws. How is the Government to enforce its laws? The Constitution says that Congress shall have power "to provide for calling forth the militia to execute the laws of the Union, suppress insurrections, and repel invasions."[16] Let me ask the Senator from Indiana, with all his astuteness, how is rebellion to be put down, how is it to be resisted, unless there is some power in the Government to enforce its laws?

If there be a citizen who violates your post office laws, who counterfeits the coin of the United States, or who commits any other offense against the laws of the United States, you subject him to trial and punishment. Is not that coercion? Is that not enforcing the laws? How is rebellion to be put down without coercion, without enforcing the laws? Can it be done? The Constitution provides that,

The United States shall guaranty to every State in this Union a republican form of government, and shall protect each of them from invasion; and on application of the Legislature, or of the Executive, (when the Legislature cannot be convened,) against domestic violence.[17]

How is this Government to put down domestic violence in a State without coercion? How is the nation to be protected against insurrection without coercing the citizens to obedience? Can it be done? When the Senator says he is against the entire coercive policy of the Government, he is against the vital principle of all government. I look upon this as the most revolutionary and destructive doctrine that ever was preached. If this Government cannot call forth the militia, if it cannot repel invasion, if it cannot put down domestic violence, if it cannot suppress rebellion, I ask if the great objects of the Government are not at an end?

Look at my own State, by way of illustration. There is open rebellion there; there is domestic violence; there is insurrection. An attempt has been made to transfer that State to another power. Let me ask the

Senator from Indiana if the Constitution does not require you to guaranty us a republican form of government in that State? Is not that your sworn duty? We ask you to put down this unholy rebellion. What answer do you give us? We ask you to protect us against insurrection and domestic violence. What is the reply? "I am against your whole coercive policy; I am against the enforcement of the laws." I say that if that principle be acted on, your Government is at an end; it fails utterly to carry out the object of its creation. Such a principle leads to the destruction of the Government, for it must inevitably result in anarchy and confusion. "I am opposed to the entire coercive policy of the Government," says the Senator from Indiana. That cuckoo note has been reiterated to satiety; it is understood; men know the nature and character of their Government, and they also know that "coercion" and "subjugation" is mere *ad captandum*, idle and unmeaning slangwanging.[18]

Sir, I may be a little sensitive on this subject upon the one hand, while I know I want to do ample justice upon the other. I took an oath to support the Constitution of the United States. There is rebellion in the land; there is insurrection against the authority of this Government. Is the Senator from Indiana so unobservant or so obtuse that he does not know now that there has been a deliberate design for years to change the nature and character and genius of this Government? Do we not know that these schemers have been deliberately at work, and that there is a party in the South, with some associates in the North, and even in the West, that have become tired of free government, in which they have lost confidence? They raise an outcry against "coercion," that they may paralyze the Government, cripple the exercise of the great powers with which it was invested, finally to change its form and subject us to a southern despotism. Do we not know it to be so? Why disguise this great truth? Do we not know that they have been anxious for a change of Government for years? Since this rebellion commenced it has manifested itself in many quarters. How long is it since the organ of the government at Richmond, the Richmond Whig, declared that rather than live under the Government of the United States, they preferred to take the constitutional Queen of Great Britain as their protector; that they would make an alliance with Great Britain for the purpose of preventing the enforcement of the laws of the United States?[19] Do we not know this? Why then play "hide and go seek?" Why say, "oh, yes, I am for the Union," while every act, influence, conversation, vote is against it? What confidence can we have in one who takes such a course?

The people of my State, downtrodden and oppressed by the iron heel of southern despotism, appeal to you for protection. They ask you to protect them against domestic violence. They want you to help them to put down this unholy and damnable rebellion. They call upon this Government for the execution of its constitutional duty to guaranty to them a republican form of Government, and to protect them against the tyranny and despotism which is stalking abroad. What is the cold reply? "I am against the entire coercive policy; I am not for enforcing the laws." Upon such a doctrine Government crumbles to pieces, and anarchy and despotism reign throughout the land.

Indiana, God bless her, is as true to the Union as the needle is to the pole.[20] She has sent out her "columns;" she has sent her thousands into the field, for what? To sustain the Constitution, and to enforce the laws; and as they march with strong arms and brave hearts to relieve a suffering people, who have committed no offense save devotion to this glorious Union; as they march to the rescue of the Constitution and to extend its benefits again to a people who love it dearly, and who have been ruthlessly torn from under its protecting aegis, what does their Senator say to them? "I am against the entire policy of coercion." Do you ever hear a Senator who thus talks make any objection to the exercise of unconstitutional and tyrannical power by the so-called southern confederacy, or say a word against its practice of coercion? In all the speeches that have been delivered on that point, has one sentence against usurpation, against despotism, against the exercise of doubtful and unconstitutional powers by that confederacy, been uttered? Oh, no! Have you heard any objection to their practicing not only coercion but usurpation? Have they not usurped government? Have they not oppressed, and are they not now tyrannizing over the people? The people of my State are coerced, borne down, trodden beneath the iron heel of power. We appeal to you for protection. You stand by and see us coerced; you stand by and see tyranny triumphing, and no sympathy, no kindness, no helping hand can be extended to us. Your Government is paralyzed; your Government is powerless; that which you have called a Government is a dream, an idle thing. You thought you had a Government, but you have none. My people are appealing to you for protection under the Constitution. They are arrested by hundreds and by thousands; they are dragged away from their homes and incarcerated in dungeons. They ask you for protection. Why do you not give it? Some of them are lying chained in their lowly prison-house. The only response to their murmur is the rattling and clanking of the chains that bind their limbs. The only response to their appeals is the grating of the hinges of their dungeon. When we ask for help under the Constitution, we are told that the Government has no power to enforce the laws. Our people are oppressed and downtrodden, and you give them no remedy. They were taught to love and respect the Constitution of the United States. What is their condition to-day? They are hunted and pursued like the beasts of the forest by the secession and disunion hordes who are enforcing their doctrine of coercion. They are shot or hung for no crime save a desire to stand by the Constitution of the United States. Helpless children and innocent females are murdered in cold blood. Our men are hung and their bodies left upon the gibbet. They are shot and left lying in the gorges of the mountains, not even thrown into the caves there to lie, but are left exposed to pass through all the loathsome stages of decompositon, or to be devoured by the birds of prey. We appeal for protection, and are told by the Senator from Indiana and others, "we cannot enforce the laws; we are against the entire coercive policy." Do you not hear their groans? Do you not hear their cries? Do you not hear the shrieks of oppressed and downtrodden women and children? Sir, their tones ring out so loud and clear that even listening angels look from heaven in pity.[21]

I will not pursue this idea further, for I perceive that I am consuming more time than I intended to occupy. I think it is clear and conclusive, without going further into the discussion, that the Senator from Indiana has sympathized with the rebellion. The conclusion is fixed upon my mind that the Senator from Indiana has disqualified himself, has incapacitated himself to discharge the duties in this body of a loyal Senator. I think it is clear that, even if we were a court, we should be bound to convict him; but I do not narrow the case down to the close rules that would govern a court of justice.

But, sir, in the course of the discussion one palliating fact was submitted by the distinguished Senator from New Jersey, [Mr. Ten Eyck,][22] and he knows that I do not refer to him in any spirit of unkindness. There was more of legal learning and special pleading in his suggestion than solidity or sound argument. He suggested that there was no proof that this letter had ever been delivered to Jefferson Davis, and that therefore the Senator from Indiana ought not to be convicted. Well, sir, on the other hand, there is no proof that it was not delivered. It is true, the letter was found in Mr. Lincoln's possession; but who knows that Davis did not read the letter, and hand it back to Lincoln? It may have been that, being from his early friend, a man whom he respected, Lincoln desired to keep the letter and show it to somebody else. We have as much right to infer that the letter was delivered as that it was not; but be that as it may, does it lessen the culpability of the Senator from Indiana? He committed the act, and so far as he was concerned it was executed. It would be no palliation of his offense if the man did not deliver the letter to Davis. The intent and the act were just as complete as if it had been delivered.

During the war of the Revolution, in 1780, Major André, a British spy, held a conference with Benedict Arnold. Arnold prepared his letters, six in number, and they were handed over to Major André, who put them between the soles of his feet and his stockings, and he started on his way to join Sir Henry Clinton. Before he reached his destination, however, John Paulding and his two associates arrested Major André. They pulled off his boots and his stockings, and they got the papers; they kept them, and Major André was tried and hung as a spy. Arnold's papers were not delivered to Sir Henry Clinton; but is there anybody here who doubts that Arnold was a traitor? Has public opinion ever changed upon that subject? He was not convicted in a court, nor were the treasonable dispatches which were to expose the condition of West Point, and make the British attack upon it easy and successful, ever delivered to Sir Henry Clinton, and yet André was hung as a spy. Because Sir Henry Clinton did not receive the treasonable documents was the guilt of Benedict Arnold any the less? I do not intend to argue this question in a legal way; I simply mention this circumstance by way of illustration of the point which has been urged in the present case, and leave it for the public judgment to determine.

Sir, it has been said by the distinguished Senator from Delaware [Mr. Saulsbury][23] that the questions of controversy might all have been settled by compromise. He dealt rather extensively in the party aspect of the case, and seemingly desired to throw the *onus* of the present condition of affairs entirely on one side. He told us that if so and so had been done these questions could have been settled, and that now there would have been no war. He referred particularly to the resolution offered during the last Congress by the Senator from New Hampshire, [Mr. Clark,][24] and upon the vote on that he based his argument. I do not mean to be egotistical, but if he will give me his attention I intend to take the staple out of that speech, and show how much of it is left on that point.

The speech of the Senator from Delaware was a very fine one. I have not the power, as he has, to con over and get by rote, and memorize handsomely rounded periods, and make a great display of rhetoric. It is my misfortune that I am not so skilled. I have to seize on fugitive thoughts as they pass through my mind, make the best application of them I can, and express them in my own crude way. I am not one of those who prepare rounding, sounding, bounding rhetorical flourishes, read them over twenty times before I come into the Senate Chamber, make a great display, and have it said, "Oh, that is a fine speech!" I have heard many such fine speeches; but when I have had time to follow them up, I have found that it never took long to analyze them, and reduce them to their original elements; and that when they were reduced, there was not very much of them. [Laughter.]

The Senator told us that the adoption of the Clark amendment to the Crittenden resolutions defeated the settlement of the questions of controversy; and that, but for that vote, all could have been peace and prosperity now. We were told that the Clark amendment defeated the Crittenden compromise, and prevented a settlement of the controversy. On this point I will read a portion of the speech of my worthy and talented friend from California, [Mr. Latham;] and when I speak of him thus, I do it in no unmeaning sense. I intend that he, not I, shall answer the Senator from Delaware. I know that sometimes, when gentlemen are fixing up their pretty rhetorical flourishes, they do not take time to see all the sharp corners they may encounter. If they can make a readable sentence, and float on in a smooth, easy stream, all goes well, and they are satisfied. As I have said, the Senator from Delaware told us that the Clark amendment was the turning-point in the whole matter; that from it had flowed rebellion, revolution, war, the shooting and imprisonment of people in different States—perhaps he meant to include my own. This was the Pandora's box that has been opened, out of which all the evils that now afflict the land have flown. Thank God I still have hope that all will yet be saved. My worthy friend from California, [Mr. Latham,] during the last session of Congress, made one of the best speeches he ever made. I bought five thousand copies of it for distribution, but I had no constituents to send them to, [laughter;] and they have been lying in your document-room ever since, with the exception of a few, which I thought would do good in some quarters. In the course of that speech, upon this very point, he made use of these remarks:[25]

[Asserting that "it was a deliberate, willful design, on the part of some representatives of southern states, to seize upon the election of Mr. Lincoln merely as an excuse to precipitate this revolution," Latham pointed out that not only did South Carolina refuse to send her senators to Washington, but other southerners declined to vote for compromise measures, "for fear that the very propositions submitted to this body might have an influence in changing the opinions of their constituencies." In evidence he analyzed the vote on the Clark amendment.]

I sat right behind Mr. Benjamin,[26] and I am not sure that my worthy friend was not close by, when he refused to vote, and I said to him, "Mr. Benjamin, why do you not vote? Why not save this proposition and see if we cannot bring the country to it?" He gave me rather an abrupt answer, and said he would control his own action without consulting me or anybody else. Said I, "vote, and show yourself an honest man." As soon as the vote was taken, he and others telegraphed South, "We cannot get any compromise." Here were six southern men refusing to vote, when the amendment would have been rejected by four majority if they had voted.[27] Who, then, has brought these evils on the country? Was it Mr. Clark? He was acting out his own policy; but with the help we had from the other side of the Chamber, if all those on this side had been true to the Constitution and faithful to their constituents, and had acted with fidelity to the country, the amendment of the Senator from New Hampshire could have been voted down, the defeat of which the Senator from Delaware says would have saved the country. Whose fault was it? Who is responsible for it? I think that is not only getting the nail through, but clenching it on the other side, and the whole staple commodity is taken out of the speech. Who did it? Southern traitors, as was said in the speech of the Senator from California. They did it. They wanted no compromise. They accomplished their object by withholding their votes; and hence the country has been involved in the present difficulty. Let me read another extract from this speech of the Senator from California:

[Declaring that, had the departed southern senators been present for the March 2 reconsideration of the Crittenden amendments, these would have been endorsed by majority vote, Latham reiterated his conviction that "these gentlemen were acting in pursuance of a settled and fixed plan to break up and destroy this Government."]

When we had it in our power to vote down the amendment of the Senator from New Hampshire, and adopt the Crittenden resolutions, certain southern Senators prevented it; and yet, even at a late day of the session, after they had seceded, the Crittenden proposition was only lost by one vote.[28] If rebellion and bloodshed and murder have followed, to whose skirts does the responsibility attach? I summed up all these facts myself in a speech during the last session;[29] but I have preferred to read from the speech of the Senator from California, he being better authority, and having presented the facts better than I could.

What else was done at the very same session? The House of Representatives passed, and sent to this body, a proposition to amend the Constitution of the United States, so as to prohibit Congress from ever hereafter interfering with the institution of slavery in the States, making that restriction a part of the organic law of the land. That constitutional amendment came here after the Senators from seven States had seceded; and yet it was passed by a two-third vote in the Senate.[30] Have you ever heard of any one of the States which had then seceded, or which has since seceded, taking up that amendment to the Constitution, and saying they would ratify it, and make it a part of that instrument? No. Does not the whole history of this rebellion tell you that it was revolution that the leaders wanted, that they started for, that they intended to have? The facts to which I have referred show how the Crittenden proposition might have been carried; and when the Senators from the slave States were reduced to one fourth of the members of this body, the two Houses passed a proposition to amend the Constitution, so as to guaranty to the States perfect security in regard to the institution of slavery in all future time, and prohibiting Congress from legislating on the subject.

But what more was done? After southern Senators had treacherously abandoned the Constitution and deserted their posts here, Congress passed bills for the organization of three new Territories, Dakota, Nevada, and Colorado; and in the sixth section of each of those bills, after conferring, affirmatively, power on the Territorial Legislature, it went on to exclude certain powers by using a negative form of expression; and it provided, among other things, that the Legislature should have no power to legislate so as to impair the right to private property; that it should lay no tax discriminating against one description of property in favor of another; leaving the power on all these questions not in the Territorial Legislature, but in the people when they should come to form a State constitution.[31]

Now, I ask, taking the amendment to the Constitution, and taking the three territorial bills, embracing every square inch of territory in the possession of the United States, how much of the slavery question was left? What better compromise could have been made? Still we are told that matters might have been compromised, and that if we had agreed to compromise, bloody rebellion would not now be abroad in the land. Sir, southern Senators are responsible for it. They stood here with power to accomplish the result, and yet treacherously, and, I may say, tauntingly, they left this Chamber, and announced that they had dissolved their connection with the Government. Then, when we were left in the hands of those whom we had been taught to believe would encroach upon our rights, they gave us, in the constitutional amendment and in the three territorial bills, all that had ever been asked; and yet gentlemen talk about compromise. Why was not this taken and accepted? No; it was not compromise that the leaders wanted; they wanted power; they wanted to destroy this Government, so that they might have place and emolument for themselves. They had lost confidence in the intelligence and virtue and integrity of the people, and their capacity to govern themselves; and they intended to separate and form a government, the chief cornerstone of which should be slavery, disfranchising the great mass of the people, of which we have seen constant evidence, and merging the powers of government in the hands of the few. I know what I say. I know their feelings and their sentiments. I served in the Senate here with them. I know they were a close corporation,[32] that had no more confidence in or respect for the people than has the dey of Algiers. I fought that close corporation here. I knew that they were no friends of the people. I knew that Slidell and Mason and Benjamin and Iverson[33] and Toombs were the enemies of free government, and I know so now. I commenced the war upon them before a State seceded; and I intend to keep on fighting this great battle before the country for the perpetuity of free government. They seek to overthrow it, and to establish a despotism in its place. That is the great battle which is upon our hands. The great interests of civil liberty and free government call upon every patriot and every lover of popular rights to come forward and discharge his duty.

We see this great struggle; we see that the exercise of the vital principle of government itself is denied by those who desire our institutions to be overthrown and despotism established on their ruins. If we have not the physical and moral courage to exclude from our midst men whom we believe to be unsafe depositors of public power and public trust—men whose associates were rolling off honeyed accents against coercion, and are now in the traitor's camp—if we have not the courage to force these men from our midst, because we have known them, and have been personal friends with them for years, we are not entitled to sit here as Senators ourselves. Can you expect your brave men, your officers and soldiers that are now in "the tented field," subject to all the hardships and privations pertaining to a civil war like this, to have courage, and to march on with patriotism to crush treason on every battle-field, when you have not the courage to expel it from your midst? Set those brave men an example; say to them by your acts and voice that you evidence your intention to put down traitors in the field by ejecting them from your midst, without regard to former associations.

I do not say these things in unkindness. I say them in obedience to duty, a high constitutional duty that I owe to my country; yes, sir, that I owe to my wife and children. By your failure to exercise the powers of this Government, by your failure to enforce the laws of the Union, I am separated from those most dear to me. Pardon me, sir, for this personal allusion. My wife and children have been turned into the street, and my house has been turned into a barracks,[34] and for what? Because I stand by the Constitution and the institutions of the country that I have been raised to love, respect, and venerate. This is my offense. Where are my sons-in-law? One to-day is lying in prison; another is forced to fly to the mountains[35] to evade the pursuit of the hell-born and hell-bound conspiracy of disunion and secession; and when their cries come up here to you for protection, we are told, "No; I am against the entire coercive policy of the Government."

The speech of the Senator from California the other day had the effect in some degree, and seemed to be intended to give the question a party tinge. If I know myself—although, as I avowed before, I am a Democrat, and expect to live and die one—I know no party in this great struggle for the existence of my country. The argument presented by the Senator from California was, that we need not be in such hot pursuit of Mr. Bright, or those Senators who entertain his sentiments, who are still here, because we had been a little dilatory in expelling other traitorous Senators heretofore, and he referred us to the resolution of the Senator from Maine, [Mr. Fessenden,][36] which was introduced at the special session in March last, declaring that certain Senators having withdrawn, and their seats having thereby become vacant, the Secretary should omit their names from the roll of the Senate. I know there seemed to be a kind of timidity, a kind of fear, to make use of the word "expel" at that time; but the fact that we declared the seats vacant, and stopped there, did not preclude us from afterwards passing a vote of censure. The resolution, which was adopted in March, merely stated the fact that Senators had withdrawn, and left their seats vacant. At the next session a resolution was introduced to expel the other Senators from the seceded States who did not attend in the Senate;[37] and my friend [Mr. Latham] moved to strike out of that very resolution the word "expelled," and insert "vacated;" so that I do not think he ought to be much offended at it. I simply allude to it to show how easy it is for us to forget the surrounding circumstances that influenced our action at the time it took place. We know that a year ago there was a deep and abiding hope that the rebellion would not progress as it has done; that it would cease; and that there might be circumstances which, at one time, would to some extent justify us in allowing a wide margin which, at another period of time, would be wholly unjustifiable.

All this, however, amounts to nothing. We have a case now before us that requires our action, and we should act upon it conscientiously in view of the facts which are presented. Because we neglected to expel traitors before, and omitted to have them arrested, and permitted them to go away freely, and afterwards declared their seats vacant because they had gone, we are not now prevented from expelling a Senator who is not worthy to be in the Senate. I do not say that other traitors may not be punished yet. I trust in God the time will come, and that before long, when these traitors can be overtaken in the aggregate, and we may mete out to them condign punishment, such as their offense deserves. I know who was for arresting them. I know who declared their conduct to be treason. Here in their midst I told them it was treason, and they might make the best of it they could.

Sir, to sum up the argument, I think there is but little in the point presented by the Senator from New Jersey, of there being no proof of the reception of the letter; and I think I have extracted the staple commodity entirely out of the speech of the Senator from Delaware; and so far as the force of the argument based upon the Senate having at one session expelled certain members, while at the previous session it only vacated their seats, I think the Senator from California answers that himself. As to the polished and ingenious statement of the case made by the Senator from New York, [Mr. Harris,][38] I think I have answered that by putting the case upon a different basis from that presented by him, and which seems to control his action.

Mr. President, I have alluded to the talk about compromise. If I know myself, there is no one who desires the preservation of this Government more than I do; and I think I have given as much evidence as mortal man could give of my devotion to the Union. My property has been sacrificed; my wife and children have been turned out of doors; my sons have been imprisoned; my son-in-law has had to run to the mountains; I have sacrificed a large amount of bonds[39] in trying to give some evidence of my devotion to the Government under which I was raised. I have attempted to show you that on the part of the leaders of this rebellion there was no desire to compromise—compromise was not what they wanted; and now the great issue before the country is the perpetuation or the destruction of free Government. I have shown how the resolution of the venerable Senator from Kentucky [Mr. Crittenden] was defeated, and that southern men are responsible for that defeat—six sitting in their places and refusing to vote. His proposition was only lost by two votes; and in the end, when the seceders had gone, by only one. Well do I remember, as was described by the Senator from California, the sadness, the gloom, the anguish that played over his venerable face when the result was announced;[40] and I went across the Chamber, and told him that here were men refusing to vote, and that to me was administered a rebuke by one of them for speaking to him on the subject.[41]

Now, the Senator from Delaware tells us that if that compromise had been made, all these consequences would have been avoided. It is a mere pretense; it is false. Their object was to overturn the Government. If they could not get the control of this Government, they were willing to divide the country and govern a part of it. Talk not of compromise now. What, sir, compromise with traitors with arms in their hands! Talk about "our southern brethren" when they lay their swords at your throat and their bayonets at your bosoms! Is this a time to talk about compromise? Let me say, and I regret that I have to say it, that there is but one way to compromise this matter, and that is to crush the leaders of this rebellion and put down treason. You have got to subdue them; you have got to conquer them; and nothing but the sacrifice of life and blood will do it. The issue is made. The leaders of rebellion have decreed eternal separation between you and them. Those leaders must be conquered, and a new set of men brought forward who are to vitalize and develop the Union feeling in the South. You must show your courage here as Senators, and impart it to those who are in the field. If you were now to compromise they would believe that they could whip you one to five, and you could not live in peace six months, or even three months. Settle the question now; settle it well; settle it finally; crush out the rebellion and punish the traitors. I want to see peace, and I believe that is the shortest way to get it. Blood must be shed, life must be sacrificed, and you may as well begin at first as last. I only regret that the Government has been so tardy in its operations. I wish the issue had been met sooner. I believe that if we had seen as much in the beginning as we see to-day, this rebellion would have been wound up and peace restored to the land by this time.

But let us go on; let us encourage the Army and the Navy; let us vote the men and the means necessary to vitalize and to bring into requisition the enforcing and coercive power of the Government; let us crush out the rebellion, and anxiously look forward to the day—God grant it may come soon—when that baleful comet of fire and of blood that now hovers over this distracted people may be chased away by the benignant star of peace. Let us look forward to the time when we can take the flag, the glorious flag of our country, and nail it below the cross, and there let it wave as it waved in the olden time, and let us gather around it, and inscribe as our motto, "Liberty and Union, one and inseparable, now and forever."[42] Let us gather around it, and while it hangs floating beneath the cross, let us exclaim, "Christ first, our country next."[43] Oh, how gladly rejoiced I should be to see the dove returning to the ark with the fig leaf, indicating that land was found, and that the mighty waters had abated. I trust the time will soon come when we can do as they did in the olden times, when the stars sang together in the morning and all creation proclaimed the glory of God.[44] Then let us to our duty in the Senate and in the councils of the nation, and thereby stimulate our brave officers and soldiers to do theirs in the field.

Mr. President, I have occupied the attention of the Senate much longer than I intended. In view of the whole case, without personal unkind feeling towards the Senator from Indiana, I am of opinion that duty to myself, duty to my family, duty to the Constitution, duty to the country, obedience to the public judgment, require me to cast my vote to expel Mr. Bright from the Senate, and when the occasion arrives I shall so record my vote.[45]

Cong. Globe, 37 Cong., 2 Sess., 584-89.

1. On December 16, 1861, Morton S. Wilkinson of Minnesota introduced a resolution to expel Jesse D. Bright of Indiana. The latter had written Jefferson Davis on March 1 introducing Thomas B. Lincoln who, when arrested in Cincinnati during the summer on "suspicion of being in complicity with the southern rebellion," had in his possession Bright's letter. The resolution, referred to the judiciary committee which reported adversely, was called back to the floor where it was under discussion. *Cong. Globe*, 37 Cong., 2 Sess., 89. For Bright, see *Johnson Papers*, I, 491n.

2. Either Vice President Hannibal Hamlin or John Sherman of Ohio was in the chair. *Cong. Globe*, 37 Cong., 2 Sess., 583, 585.

3. The matter of seating Bright and Graham N. Fitch, whose election was protested by members of the Indiana legislature, had been referred on February 10, 1857, to the judiciary committee which reported favorably on May 24, 1858; the vote was taken on June 12, with Johnson among the ayes. It is interesting to recall that several months earlier Bright had officially introduced the Tennessean to the Senate. Only four of the twenty-three nays were Democrats; the others were Republicans or old-line Whigs. Every senator supporting Bright was at the time a Democrat, with the possible exception of John B. Thompson of Kentucky, whose party affiliation was somewhat uncertain. *Ibid.*, 34 Cong., 3 Sess., 633; 35 Cong., 1 Sess., 2353, 2981; *BDAC*, 166n and *passim*.

4. Art. I, Sec. 5.

5. Joseph Story (1779-1845), legal scholar and associate justice of the Supreme Court (1811-45). John Smith (1735-1816), Ohio senator (1803-08), had been an intimate friend of Aaron Burr. When the latter's activities were being investigated, Smith aided the government by contributing provisions for the Ohio militia and by going to New Orleans to assist James Wilkinson. There he learned of his own indictment, fled to West Florida, and later surrendered to American authorities. When Burr was acquitted, the indictment was dropped; the Senate then appointed a committee to investigate charges against Smith. The vote on the committee's recommendation of expulsion was 19 for and 10 against—one less than the two-thirds required by the Constitution. *BDAC*, 1618; *DAB*, XVII, 296-97; *Annals of Congress: Debates and Proceedings in the Congress of the United States, 1789-1824* (42 vols., Washington, 1834-56), 10 Cong., 1 Sess., 62, 323; Charles Francis Adams, ed., *Memoirs of John Quincy Adams* (12 vols., Philadelphia, 1874-77), I, 528.

6. David A. Smalley (1809-1875), Vermont lawyer assigned in 1857 to the circuit court of Vermont, was a delegate to the Democratic conventions of 1852 and 1856 and, as chairman of the party's executive committee, called to order the Charleston Convention. Lanman, *Biographical Annals*, 389; William B. Hesseltine, ed., *Three Against Lincoln: Murat Halstead Reports the Caucuses of 1860* (Baton Rouge, 1960), 11, 19, 31.

7. On January 9, the *Star of the West*, sent to reinforce Sumter, was fired on as it entered Charleston harbor and withdrew without returning the fire. *OR*, Ser. 1, I, 9-10, 134-37.

8. Thomas B. Lincoln, "a very genteel looking man, about forty-five years of age," was a Philadelphian who settled in Madison, Indiana, as a wholesale-retail merchant for about four years after 1837, turning during that time to Bright for legal counsel. Moving to Texas in the early 1840's, he had been associated with the Southern Pacific railroad and also engaged in land speculation in the South, and now considered himself "a Southern man, and in favor of 'Southern rights.'" Cincinnati *Gazette*, August 2, 1861; *Cong. Globe*, 37 Cong., 2 Sess., 651; Louisville *Journal*, August 20, 1861.

9. Art. III, sec. 3.

10. See Speech on Secession, December 18-19, 1860, *Johnson Papers*, IV, 48n.

11. Perhaps Johnson had in mind the circumstances accompanying a later speech; an examination of contemporary records fails to disclose the presence of any such "bevy."

12. On July 18, 1861, speaking to an amendment offered by Lazarus Powell of Kentucky which declared that the army should not be used to subjugate a sovereign state, Bright expressed himself as unwilling "to vote either men or money to invade States that have formally declared themselves out of the Union" until every effort to solve the existing crisis by peaceful means had been exhausted. *Cong. Globe*, 37 Cong., 1 Sess., 186, 193.

13. By unanimous vote, Trusten Polk and Waldo P. Johnson, both of Missouri, were expelled on January 10, for their secessionist sympathies; in like manner, Breckinridge had been voted out on December 4. Waldo P. Johnson (1817-1885), Virginia native, moved to Missouri in 1842 where he practiced law, served in the Mexican War, was a member of the legislature (1847), and became senator in 1861. Serving in the Confederate army and Senate, he returned to his legal practice after the war. *Ibid.*, 2 Sess., 9-10, 263-64; *BDAC*, 1130-31; for Polk, see *Johnson Papers*, III, 205n.

14. Jonathan Fitch (b. c1793), a native of Maryland, was a Madison, Indiana, pork merchant with $20,000 in real and $6,000 in personal property. 1860 Census, Indiana, Jefferson, Madison, 496.

15. A reply to Fitch's inquiry about Bright's endorsement of Thomas B. Lincoln, this letter is printed in *Cong. Globe*, 37 Cong., 2 Sess., 89.

16. Art. I, sec. 8.

17. Art. IV, sec. 4.

18. "The making, writing, or publishing of noisy, ranting, abusive harangues." Mathews, *Americanisms*, II, 1560.

19. Richmond *Whig*, May 17, 1861; see also Speech in Support of Presidential War Program, July 27, 1861, *Johnson Papers*, IV, 618-19.

20. "True as the needle to the pole, / Or as the dial to the sun." Barton Booth, *Song*; Bartlett, *Quotations*, 353.

21. One of his favorite allusions, most recently employed in the Speech at Columbus, October 4, 1861.

22. John C. Ten Eyck (1814-1879), New Jersey lawyer and Burlington County prosecuting attorney (1839-49), was elected as a Republican to the Senate (1859-65). *BDAC*, 1698-99.

23. For Willard Saulsbury, see *Johnson Papers*, III, 245n.

24. On January 9, 1861, Daniel Clark offered as a substitute for the Crittenden proposal, resolutions declaring the Constitution "ample for the preservation of the Union," and proposing a vigorous effort to enforce the laws and protect public property, as opposed to "concessions to unreasonable demands." A week later the Senate adopted Clark's resolutions by a vote of 25 to 23. *Cong. Globe*, 36 Cong., 2 Sess., 283, 409; for Clark, see *Johnson Papers*, III, 250n.

25. The ensuing passages came from Milton Latham's speech of July 20 on the resolution to "confirm certain acts of the President of the United States for suppressing insurrection and rebellion." *Cong. Globe*, 37 Cong., 1 Sess., App. 21-22.

26. For Judah P. Benjamin, see *Johnson Papers*, III, 245n.

27. Speech at Columbus, October 4, 1861, note 5.

28. Voting at dawn on March 4, 1861, the Senate defeated the Crittenden resolutions, 20-19; all opposing votes were Republican. *Cong. Globe*, 36 Cong., 2 Sess., 1405; *Senate Journal*, 36 Cong., 2 Sess., 387; Albert D. Kirwan, *John J. Crittenden: The Struggle for the Union* (Lexington, Ky., 1962), 421.

29. Speech in Support of Presidential War Program, July 27, 1861, *Johnson Papers*, IV, 606-49.

30. H. R. 80 received the approval of two-thirds of the senators voting—yeas 24, nays 12. *Cong. Globe*, 2 Sess., 1403; *Senate Journal*, 36 Cong., 2 Sess., 383. For fuller discussion, see Speech at Columbus, October 4, 1861, note 9.

31. The Colorado, Nevada, and Dakota territorial bills, signed by Buchanan on February 28 and March 2, 1861, prohibited the legislatures from passing any law "impairing the rights of private property" or discriminating in the taking of "different kinds of property." Although there is no explicit consignment of these powers to "the people" of a subsequent state, Johnson accurately describes the freedom of decision inherent in state sovereignty. *U. S. Statutes*, XII, 174, 211, 241.

32. In an effort to convey the tightness of the southern senatorial clique from which he was so rigorously excluded, Johnson resorts to a figure drawn from the world of

business, in which a close, or closed, corporation was "One in which all of the shares . . . are held by a relatively few persons, and are not for sale to the public." Donald T. Clark and Bert A. Gottfried, *Dictionary of Business and Finance* (New York, 1957), 96.

33. For Alfred S. Iverson and Robert Toombs, senators from Georgia, see *Johnson Papers*, III, 110*n*; I, 612*n*.

34. Evidences of Confederate occupancy, not necessarily as a barracks but certainly as a hospital, were uncovered during the 1956 restoration of the house and included names and inscriptions ranging from "Shame on Old Andy" to "The Man that may go to Hell Andrew Johnson the Old Traitor" and "Andy you had better skedaddle from Nashvill for Lovejoy[?] is after you and if he git you you are a gonner sartan." Ernest A. Connally, *Survey Report (Architectural Data) Restoration of the Andrew Johnson Homestead, Greeneville, Tennessee* (August 20, 1956), 29; Connally, "Johnson Homestead," 130-31.

35. Martha's husband David T. Patterson, who actually had only briefly been in jail, and Daniel Stover, Mary's spouse, who was out "in the bushes."

36. William P. Fessenden's resolution of March 14, 1861. *Cong. Globe*, 36 Cong., Special Sess., 1452-53. For Fessenden, see *Johnson Papers*, III, 211*n*.

37. On July 11 Clark reintroduced his resolution to expel Mason and Hunter of Virginia, Clingman and Bragg of North Carolina, Chesnut of South Carolina, Nicholson of Tennessee, Sebastian and Mitchel of Arkansas, and Hemphill and Wigfall of Texas. Latham proposed that it be amended to read "that their names be stricken from the roll, and their seats declared vacant." Johnson had supported Latham's amendment which was rejected 32 to 11; Clark's resolution was then adopted by a vote of 32 to 10, with Johnson among the dissenters. *Cong. Globe*, 37 Cong., 1 Sess., 62-64.

38. Ira Harris (1802-1875), an Albany lawyer, member of the state assembly (1845-46) and senate (1847), served as a state supreme court justice (1847-59), as a Republican in the U. S. Senate (1861-67), and as a law professor in Albany (1867-75). Speaking on January 24, Harris, a member of the judiciary committee, had urged that Bright's case be considered as a legal, not a political, question, arguing that the evidence presented was not conclusive for expulsion on the grounds of treason. *BDAC*, 1012; *Cong. Globe*, 37 Cong., 2 Sess., 473.

39. Presumably his investments in southern railroad bonds, which three years earlier had amounted to at least $14,000 and perhaps as much as $30,000. See Statement of Bonds, December 1, 1858, *Johnson Papers*, III, 197-99.

40. A palpable exaggeration of Latham's phraseology in his July 20 speech, at least insofar as it was reported in the *Globe*; the Californian spoke merely of "the sorrow manifested by the venerable Senator," who was at that time seventy-three. *Cong. Globe*, 37 Cong., 1 Sess., App. 22.

41. See previous reference in this speech to the reaction of Judah P. Benjamin.

42. Webster's reply to Hayne, January 27, 1830. *Register of Debates in Congress, 18th-25th Congresses* (14 vols., Washington, 1825-37), 21 Cong., 1 Sess., VI, 80.

43. Not located.

44. A variant on two familiar biblical passages: "When the morning stars sang together, and all the sons of God shouted for joy" (Job 38:7) and "The heavens declare the glory of God" (Ps. 19:1).

45. On February 5, Bright was expelled by a vote of 32-14. *Cong. Globe*, 37 Cong., 2 Sess., 655.

From Samuel J. Pooley

Liberty Corner Somerset Co
N. Jersey Feby the 3 1862.

To/-Hon Andrew Johnson
Washington
My good sir,

Doubtless the vote will have been taken on the "motion to expell Senator Bright from your body," before this note is put into your hands, I candidly confess to you, that Mr B's position long anterior & down to the state of our present troubles, has been of a very suspicious character to me, Douglas, came out manfully & truly patriotically when the issue turned into "Armed insurrection" & arrayed himself by the side of the government, in its just efforts to maintain the integrity of the Union, the Constitution & the laws. If Senator Bright was a faithful supporter of the late Senator (Douglas) why did he not stand by his policy, why did he not array himself along side of the government of his Country[?] "He that is not for the Country at this crisis, is against it"[1] Moreover—he is either wickedly or ignorantly lending his assistance to break up our Union, assisting to consummate the long desired wish of the Autocracy & Monarchy of Europe, to destroy our prosperity & Democratic republican liberty in the world. What American or adopted citizen among us, worthy of the name will put himself in this position. To give strentgth to the chains by Kings & aristocracies to oppress still further the bodies & minds of their fellow men,

That my southern brethern or any portion of them could, raise an hostile hand against the Union, & the Constitution of their Fathers, fills me with wonder, but to fawn, to cringe to humililate themselves at the feet of the British Crown surprises me beyond measure. "Judas betrayed his Master" let my southern brethern standing out in hostile array against the Union of their Fathers, take care they don't find a "Judas", in the government refered to.

Yours very Respectfully
Samuel James Pooley

ALS, DLC-JP.

1. Speaking in Chicago on May 1, 1861, Stephen A. Douglas had declared "There are only two sides to the question. Every man must be for the United States or against it. There can be no neutrals in this war; *only patriots—or traitors*." New York *Tribune*, June 13, 1861.

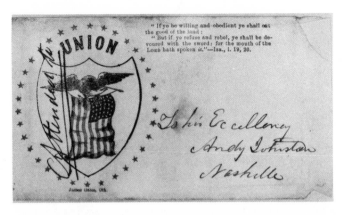

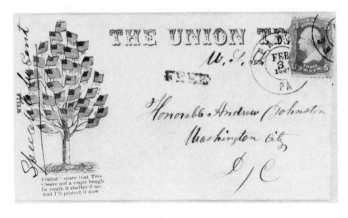

Patriotism by post!
Courtesy Library of Congress.

From Elisha Smith

Mt. Vernon Ky Feb 3/62

D. Col:

I see from the Daily Louisville Democratt of the 1st. that Thomas is makeing a road to reach Ten: on his way to Knoxville and will not reach there before the 20. Inst. If he is engaged makeing a road, you may take it for granted he will not git there (if at all) before the 1st. of Aprile. He lacks energey and self confidence, and he is not the man to reach Knoxville. Genl. Mc.Cook[1] is the man. Thomas is misibly slow. And so with Buel and Grant,[2] who marching up the hill and down again[3] recently from Caro. I see that Hunter[4] wants to command what is caled Laynes expidition.[5] If he goes it will be a failure. He was always behind time under Fremont. All our Gens. seem to hate the good weather of the winter, and give the rebels time to prepare. All seem to be quiet at Bowling-Green and Caro. A rigt. is at Boons-fork working the road well and to proseed to the Gap. If the object is to go to Knoxville, better not the road by Wheelers Gap. It is said several thousand troops will pass here by the 15 or 20. for London. It is said here Genl. Carter has gone back from Somerset to London. Garrard is there with a Battalion of horse.

Respectfully

E. Smith

Happy times on the Potomac. I see Burnside has gone to Hateras.[6] Had he of went to Orleans it would have counted worth something. I fear our troops at Caro and Bowling-Green will win no laurels. They want a Genl like Wood or Sigel.[7]

ALS, DLC-JP.

1. Robert L. McCook (1827-1862), one of the "Fighting McCooks of Ohio" and the popular leader of the 9th Ohio Inf., was promoted to brigadier general in March, 1862, for bravery at Mill Springs. Slain by Confederate guerillas on August 6, near New Market, Alabama, his body was sent to Nashville where, according to a newspaper report, "The Governor was visibly affected by the sight of the corpse of his late friend." *NCAB*, IV, 130; *Battles and Leaders*, III, 7n; Washington *National Intelligencer*, August 11, 1862.

2. In early January, Grant made an inconclusive foray into the vicinity of Columbus, Kentucky, withdrawing after a reconnoiter; subsequently, on the basis of information thus gained, he advanced on Fort Henry. Buell, despite Lincoln's and McClellan's urging that he advance south into East Tennessee, remained virtually inactive during the winter of 1861-62. John Y. Simon, ed., *The Papers of Ulysses S. Grant* (6 vols., Carbondale, 1967-   ), IV, xiii, xxi, xxii; Ulysses S. Grant, *Personal Memoirs* (2 vols., New York, 1885-86), I, 285-86; *OR*, Ser. 1, VII, 530-56, 656-71, 927-33, and *passim*; *Battles and Leaders*, I, 385-86.

3. An allusion to a popular nursery rhyme, originally French. One version went: "Oh, the brave old Duke of York, / He had ten thousand men; / He marched them up to the top of the hill, / And he marched them down again. . . . " Iona and Peter Opie, eds., *The Oxford Dictionary of Nursery Rhymes* (Oxford, 1952), 176, 442.

4. David Hunter (1802-1886), a West Point graduate (1822) who served as a

paymaster in the Mexican War, was stationed in Kansas when Lincoln called him to Washington in early 1861. Sent to serve under Frémont in Missouri, he and his fellow-general, John Pope, when ordered to advance against Confederate Gen. Sterling Price, both moved lethargically, complaining of a lack of preparation and supplies. Replacing Frémont as commander of the Department of the West on November 2, 1861, Hunter was soon appointed commander of the Department of the South (1862) and later served as president of the commission investigating Lincoln's assassination. Robert C. Schenck, "Major-General David Hunter," *Magazine of American History*, XVII (1887), 138-52; *DAB*, IX, 400-401; Nevins, *Frémont*, II, 601-13.

5. In January, 1862, when told that Kansas Senator James H. Lane had been authorized to raise troops for a western expedition, which would nonetheless be under Hunter's supervision, the latter issued orders advising that he, himself, would command "the expedition about to go south from this department, called in the newspapers 'General Lane's Expedition.' " The disagreement which ensued ultimately involved the President, the secretary of war, General McClellan, and the Senate. The "Lane expedition" never materialized. Lane (1814-1866), an Indianan who saw service in the Mexican War and in Congress (1853-55) before migrating to Kansas, was a "free-state" proponent and president of the Topeka constitutional convention. Elected to the Senate (1861), he served until his suicide. *DAB*, X, 576-78; *BDAC*, 1189; fragment of original letter, Lincoln to Hunter, October 24, 1861, Lincoln Papers, LC; *OR*, Ser. 1, VIII, 428-29, 525-76, 606, 829-31; *Cong. Globe*, 37 Cong., 2 Sess., 607, 619; New York *Times*, January 23, 30, 1862.

6. Ambrose E. Burnside (1824-1881), Indianan, West Point graduate (1847), and professional soldier (1847-53), had resigned from the army to manufacture his own invention, a breech-loading rifle, at Bristol, Rhode Island. In April, 1861, he organized the 1st R. I. Inf. Rgt., which participated in the battle of Bull Run. Commissioned a brigadier general in August, Burnside assembled at Annapolis a force for an amphibious campaign along the seaboard; on January 9, 1862, he embarked for Hatteras Inlet, capturing the forts on Roanoke Island, February 8, and proceeding down the coast occupied New Bern on March 14 and Beaufort on April 26. Warner, *Generals in Blue*, 57-58; Boatner, *Civil War Dictionary*, 107-8; see also Ben: Perley Poore, *The Life and Public Services of Ambrose E. Burnside, Soldier-Citizen-Statesman* (Providence, R.I., 1882).

7. Probably Thomas J. Wood and Franz Sigel. Wood (1823-1906), a West Pointer (1845), after serving as an engineer in the Mexican War, transferred to the cavalry, became a brigadier general of volunteers in October, 1861, under Gen. Robert L. McCook in the Army of the Ohio, and in the spring of 1862 was given command of the sixth division. Sigel (1824-1902) had been minister of war in Baden during the Revolution of 1848 before coming to New York in 1852. A resident of St. Louis upon the outbreak of war, he held a divisional command during the struggle to keep Missouri in the Union, playing an active but undistinguished role. The New York *Times* of February 3, 1862, printed a letter purportedly written by Sigel, proposing a "Great Western Campaign" south toward Columbus and Nashville, combined with a thrust toward Memphis, thereby throwing Confederate troops into confusion. Generally an inept officer who later fought in the Shenandoah Valley campaigns and commanded the Department of West Virginia, he nonetheless played a significant role in rallying the German element, with whom "I fights mit Sigel" became almost a password. *DAB*, XX, 474-75; Boatner, *Civil War Dictionary*, 761, 946-47; Warner, *Generals in Blue*, 447-48.

From James McMurtry

February 4, 1862, Carrollton, Mo.; ALS, DLC-JP.

Former journeyman cabinet-maker, who knew Johnson "while you were working at the Tayloring business," observes that "The falsehoods sent abroad by secessionists in the border states, did much mischief. Thousands supposed the government intended to liberate the slaves, though the rebel leaders certainly knew better. Even if this had been the mad intention . . . there was a bloodless—a constitutional mode of avoiding the evil. I am sure that neither you nor I would ever favor the liberation of the slaves—neither does the government aim at such a result." Inquires about the stand of old Greeneville acquaintances in the present crisis.

From William R. Tracy[1]

Camp on Barbourville road
Feb. 6th 1862

Hon Andy Johnson
Washington D. C.
Dear Sir

Another vile contemptible scheme of the Carters has been accomplished,—the removal of Mat. Cleveland Major of this Regt. They have been watching and waiting for an opportunity to get the advantage of him, and now they have got it and forced the Major to resign. it was done to day.

Major Cleveland is a noble son of East Tenn.; he is upright straightforward and *plain spoken*;—and it is chiefly for this last reason that he is to be sacrificed. Major Cleveland dared to say that East Tenn. ought to be redeemed, that the Government and Gov. hirelings were too slow in making the attempt to rescue the wives, and daughters of men who had thrown their whole confidence upon a power that had abused it. In fact because he dared to utter the same sentiments that you yourself frequently expressed at London, and on many occasions while with the Army.

The worst feature about it, and the thing most to be regretted is, that this step will render it impossible for Major Cleveland to raise a Regt. of his own in E. Tenn. Will it really disquallify him from so doing? Can there be no provision made to enable him so to do?

Its an ill wind that blows nobody good.[2] One thing brings on another.

The Charges against J. P. T. Carter have been made out tonight, and will be forwarded to Genl. (*Actg*) (God grant it may not be confirmed) Carter in the morning. They are preferred by John L. Snead Captain. Co. F. 2d Regt.[3] and a Court Martial immediately demanded.[4]

With kind regards for your good health I am

Yours Truly
Wm. R. Tracy

ALS, DLC-JP.

1. William R. Tracy (c 1839-1866), a native of Ohio and before the war a farmer near Chattanooga, enlisted in Co. G, 2nd Tenn. Inf., in November, 1861, as a private, and the next month was promoted to lieutenant. Resigning in June, 1862, because of difficulties with fellow officers, he was appointed major in the 1st Tenn. Cav. the following October. Later captain commissary of subsistence, he was at the time of his death commissioner of metropolitan police in Chattanooga. CSR, RG94, NA; *Tennesseans in the Civil War*, II, 594; Heitman, *Register*, I, 968-69; Nashville *Press and Times*, August 16, 1866; Chattanooga *Gazette*, August 23, 1864.

2. Virtually a folk proverb, this expression, appearing in the *Pickwick Papers* (ch. 32), is also found in Shakespeare (*Henry IV, Part Two*, Act V, sc. 3 and *Henry VI, Part Three*, Act II, sc. 5), as well as other sixteenth- and seventeenth-century writing. Stevenson, *Macmillan Book of Proverbs*, 2512.

3. John L. Sneed, captain of Co. F, 2nd East Tenn. Inf., died in February, 1863, of wounds received in the Stone River campaign. Wright, *Tennessee in the War*, 176; *Tennesseans in the Civil War*, II, 586; *OR*, Ser. 1, XX, 217.

4. No proceedings were initiated against Carter, who had incurred the enmity of certain Tennessee officers by obtaining, possibly through Johnson's aid, a colonelcy dated from August 1, 1861 (his original commission was dated September 1), so that he would outrank Col. Robert K. Byrd of the 1st Regiment. Upon investigation, the war department, determining that "injustice was done to the Colonel of the 1st Regiment of East Tennessee Volunteers," revoked Carter's latest commission. In February his brother and commanding officer, Gen. Samuel P. Carter, responded to Captain Sneed's "neglect of duty" charges, explaining that the colonel's absence was due to illness "consequent on exposure in camp," and that he was undergoing medical treatment. At the same time, the general blamed "malcontents" motivated by revenge. Samuel P. Carter to Capt. J. B. Fry, February 17, 1862; L. Thomas to J. P. T. Carter, January 6, 1862; Johnson to L. Thomas, January 7, 1862; J. P. T. Carter to Maj. J. A. Campbell, April 23, 1864; Carter file J-2 (V.S.) 1862, RG94, NA.

Resolution on Washington's Birthday Celebration[1]

February 11, 1862.

Mr. JOHNSON. I was not in the Chamber when the petitions were called for, but I ask leave now to present the memorial of the Mayor[2] and a very large number of citizens of Philadelphia, the most respectable persons in the city, and I hope it will be read to the Senate.

[Under date of January 31, the Philadelphia memorialists, citing their city's association with the patriotic events of the nation's beginnings, urge the occasion of Washington's impending birthday anniversary—"the first since the outbreak of the great rebellion"—as a time to read and publish in pamphlet form the Farewell Address.]

Mr. JOHNSON. I think the suggestions made by the memorialists are so appropriate that I have prepared a resolution to submit to the consideration of the Senate for the purpose of carrying out their prayer. In view of the perilous condition of the country, I think the time has arrived when we should recur back to the days, the times, and the doings of Washington and the patriots of the Revolution, who founded the Government under which we live, and under which we have prospered. I trust and hope that there will be no objection to this manner of celebrating the birthday of the Father of his Country. I submit the following resolution to carry out the prayer of the memorial:

Resolved, (the House of Representatives concurring,) That the two Houses will assemble in the Chamber of the House of Representatives on Saturday, the 22d of February instant, at twelve o'clock meridian, and that in the presence of the two Houses of Congress thus assembled, the Farewell Address of George Washington to the people of the United States shall be read; and that the President of the Senate and the Speaker of the House of Representatives be requested to invite the President of the United States, the heads of the several Departments, the judges of the Supreme Court, the representatives from all foreign Governments near this Government, and such officers of the Army and Navy and distinguished citizens as may then be at the seat of Government, to be present on that occasion.

Resolved, That the President of the United States, Commander-in-Chief of the Army and Navy, be requested to direct that orders be issued for the reading to the Army and Navy of the United States of the Farewell Address of George Washington, or such parts thereof as he may select, on the 22d day of February, instant.

Resolved, That _____ thousand copies of the proceedings of the two Houses of Congress, together with the Farewell Address of George Washington, be printed for distribution by the members of the two Houses of Congress to the people of the United States.

I hope the resolution will be adopted unanimously, and that it will be so entered on the Journal. I have nothing to say upon it. The memorial speaks for itself; the times speak for themselves; and it does seem to me that we ought to show a willingness to recur to those days which gave birth to the Republic.[3]

Cong. Globe, 37 Cong., 2 Sess., 738.

1. Several days earlier Johnson had received a letter from Benjamin Rush, grandson of the Revolutionary patriot, describing a memorial signed by many leading Philadelphians urging Congress to commemorate Washington's birthday with public reading of the Farewell Address, both in Congress and in military and naval installations throughout the country. "I suggested your name in the Senate, and that of Mr. Crittenden in the House, as most fit for every reason." Rush to Johnson, February 7, 1862, Johnson Papers, LC.

2. Alexander Henry (1823-1883), who served as mayor from 1858 to 1866, was a former Whig and Constitutional Unionist; a leader in the local "Peoples Party," he exhibited considerable skill in protecting order and freedom in the city during the war years. William Dusinberre, *Civil War Issues in Philadelphia, 1856-1865* (Philadelphia, 1965), 78, 85-87, 189; J. Thomas Scharf and Thompson Westcott, *The History of Philadelphia* (3 vols., Philadelphia, 1884), III, 1737.

3. Although Johnson was reluctant to specify the number of copies to be printed, Hamlin insisted that figure be set before the Senate took further action. When the Tennessean suggested "ten thousand," Hale of New Hampshire reiterated his strong disapproval of the whole idea; a more appropriate celebration, he averred, would be "to hang some public robber or shoot some cowardly officer of the Army who has occasioned our defeats"—the better "to show that there is vigor in the Government to deal with those that ought to be dealt with." Nevertheless, not wishing to be "ungracious . . . least of all to the Senator from Tennessee," Hale withdrew his objection and the resolution passed. On Saturday, February 22, the Senate, along with the President, Cabinet officials, Supreme Court justices, representatives of foreign governments, invited military officers, and other guests, met with the House for the observance. *Cong. Globe*, 37 Cong., 2 Sess., 738, 911.

From Robert Johnson

Camp Pogue[1]
Feby 13th 1862.

Dear Father,

I arrived here this evening, after many trials and troubles— I left home, or rather Greene County, on Tuesday night 4th inst— traveled by night, through Hawkins, Hancock & Lee Counties—[2] I am almost broke down, but will leave here in a day or two, and hope to meet you in Washington in good health— Mother is in Carter County— her health is very much improved— All the family are well— Stovers and Patterson family are well— Patterson was arrested, but finally released— Stover is out on the Scouts,[3] I tried to get him to come with me, but he declined— I have been out on the Scouts since 9th September— If they had arrested me, I have no doubt, but what they would have hung me. I have had a hard time, but through a kind Providence, I am permitted to reach a haven of safety— It is impossible to put on paper, the Scenes that have taken place in East Tennessee since you left— I will not attempt it now—but will give you full particulars on sight— I have been welcomed with enthusiasm here— In coming in to Camp I was arrested by the 49th Indiana Regiment, and taken to the Col's Camp,[4] who greeted me kindly & made me take supper with him— I am now writing this in Gen'l Carter's room, and have not time to write in full[.] I will write again to-morrow[.] Charles is at Stovers & is doing very well, attending to Stovers farm— Your Negroes were taken some three weeks since & taken to Knoxville, but finally Sent them all back— I do not think they will now confiscate them[.]

Your Son
Robt. Johnson

ALS, DLC-JP.

1. That is, Camp Cumberland, located in Knox County, Kentucky.

2. After the bridge burning and the ensuing proscription, Robert took to "the bushes," hiding out in the Greeneville area and making only two nocturnal visits to his home before starting north on February 4. Detouring around Cumberland Gap, heavily guarded by Confederates, he walked at night, stopping when he could during the day with friends and acquaintances. His route took him from Tennessee through Lee County, Virginia, into Kentucky; on February 28 he arrived in Washington, D.C. New York *Times*, March 2, 1862.

3. Stover had been rounding up unionists in Carter County for raids against the Confederate lines. This irregular force, having elected officers, among them Stover as lieutenant colonel, was attacked by Col. Danville Leadbetter and obliged to disband as an organized unit and flee into the mountains. Temple, *East Tennessee*, 385-86; Whelan, Unconventional Warfare, 47-48.

4. John W. Ray (1828-1906), Indiana lawyer and staunch Republican, having been a Lincoln elector in the late canvass, was colonel of the 49th, organized in November, 1861, at Jeffersonville. In June, 1862, Gen. George Morgan complained of the deplorable conditions in that regiment, with less than one-fourth of the men reporting for duty.

While not questioning the colonel's courage, Morgan described him as "totally unfit to command" and attributed his failure to congressional ambitions; Ray resigned in October. Subsequently he held several appointive offices, practiced law in Indianapolis, and became a banker. *OR*, Ser. 1, XVI, Pt. II, 7, 21; *Official Army Register: Volunteers*, VI, 108; Indianapolis *Star*, July, 28, 1906, from Kathleen Warner (Indiana State Library) to Andrew Johnson Project, June 14, 1974.

From Robert L. Stanford

Camp Cumberland
Feb. 14th. 1862

Hon. A Johnson Senitr U. S. Congress Dear Sir:

It has been some time since I wrote you. I Should have addressed you from Somerset; but every body was writing of the Fishing Creek victory[.][1] I knew that you would See as much in the papers about the fight there as you could take time to read,   this is my only apology for not writing from Somerset.

I wrote one article which was published in the Cincinati Commercial over the Signature of *Bonafida*.[2] I have some good news to write you from here[.] To day Col. Munday[3] was Sent out to See if any rebels were on the rout between this place (James Pogs)[4] and Cumberland gap. he found nine pickets about one mile from the gap and killed and wounded all of them except two which he took prisoners[.]

We will have a fight here in a few days or rather it will be at the gap.

With the reading of this you will have the great joy of the society of your son who bears it to you. You may be sure that when Robert came into camp and I heard of it that my heart was made leap within me[.] I had heard nothing from him for some time and feared he had fallen into the hands of the rebels and I knew that if they did get him he would fare badly. Bob is a hole-souled fellow and deserves a monument built to his memory for his firmness and patriotism[.]   I Shall love him to the end of my days[.]

Roads from the Big Hill to this place are bad beyond all description and are bad to the gap but we will Storm that place[.] I Saw it published in the northern papers that Genl. Schoepf was the principal actor in the fight at Fishing Creek. Governor that Genl. was not within 10 miles of the battlefield[.][5]

I hope you have noticed a letter written over the Signature of Felix.[6] He is of the 2nd Tennessee Regt. I think his most offensive article was published Cincinnati Commercial of 7th Feb. inst.   Such men ought to be drummed out of Service.

I hope the time is close at hand when we will get possession of our homes again[.]

Your Son will give you the News from East Tenn. better orally than I can write it. The health of my Brigade is very much improved, and the

Soldiers are anxious for a fight and are clammering for a movement over any and all opposition to E. Tenn.

Regts. are now on the march for Cumberland Ford[.]   the intention is doubtless to invest the gap. If we could get forces Sufficient we would take possession of the Rail Road from end to end in less than a month. Oh! do have 10 thousand troops Sent on here immediately[.]

I must close this hasty letter already too long, with the expression of my high Esteem for your kindness and favours[.]

I am now and Shall ever remain your Sincere friend

R. L. Stanford Brig. Surg
U S Vols

ALS, DLC-JP.
  1. This January 19 engagement, in which the Confederate advance was checked and Zollicoffer killed, is generally called the battle of Mill Springs or Logan's Cross Roads. Union forces pursuing the retreating Confederates were halted at the Cumberland, the enemy having burned the ferry boats. *Battles and Leaders*, I, 387-92.
  2. The *Commercial* of January 24, 1862, carried a description of the Battle of Fishing Creek by "BONA FIDE."
  3. Reuben Munday (b. c1810), was a Madison County, Kentucky, tanner and state senator, possessing a comfortable estate of $10,500 in real and $19,500 in personal property. At this time colonel of the 6th Ky. Cav., Munday had been out on reconnaissance; according to the official report, he killed five pickets, wounded two, and captured two, along with eight horses and some sidearms—all without loss in his own command. 1860 Census, Ky., Madison, 87; *OR*, Ser. 1, VII, 417.
  4. James H. Pogue, postmaster at Flat Lick, Knox County, Kentucky. *U. S. Official Register* (1863), 398.
  5. The first news of the encounter credited Gen. Albin Schoepf with the victory; later dispatches reported accurately that the Confederates had engaged Thomas before Schoepf could move from Somerset. The latter arrived in the evening after the battle. New York *Times*, January 21, 1861ff; New York *Herald*, January 21, 1861ff; *Battles and Leaders*, I, 387, 392.
  6. *Felix*, an irregular but frequent *Commercial* correspondent, was chafing at the inactivity of East Tennessee troops and casting aspersions upon the "powers-that-be," namely, General Thomas, for the lack of aggressive movement into Tennessee. In his column, dated February 3, and appearing four days later, he announced that the "1st and 2d Regiments East Tennessee Volunteers after a march of nine days from Somerset after the most approved style, that is *a la Thomas*, has come to this place [which he calls "Camp Swamp-O"] and encamped." Inasmuch as there is no forage nearby, "the only ostensible object" in stopping is to "guard this swamp and try to scare the tadpoles into subjection." The burden of the complaint is the uselessness of constant drill and the waste of time spent in preparing for combat. Cincinnati *Commercial*, February 7, 1862.

From Robert S. Northcott

February 17, 1862, Clarksburg, Va.; ALS, DLC-JP.

Former Murfreesboro *Telegraph* editor and onetime political opponent, now working for the Clarksburg *National Telegraph*, expresses hope that unionists— "oppressed with the tyranny of the usurper's government"—will prevail in Tennessee. "I sometimes reflect upon myself for not having stayed and suffered with them, but in my humble way, I did all I could, to check the monster, but when I saw my State . . . completely under the influence of the 'reign of terror' I concluded that my duty called me elsewhere."

From James M. Townsend[1]

New Haven, Ct., Feby 17th 1862

Hon. Andrew Johnson

Dear Sir

God Bless You! You glorious old Patriot, if you have no "Constituents" here you have thousands of friends, & those who love You. Now what I want is just as many of your speeches as you can send me, & if you have not any please have a lot printed for me & *I'll pay for them cheerfully*. Hon. J. E. English[2] the Rep. from this district will tell you who I am. Congratulating you upon the good news from Tennessee[3] I am very truly Your Obt. Servant

James M. Townsend

P. S. I have not gone to the War but I have done a little towards helping it on, I enclose a few extracts from our local paper of recent date.

ALS, DLC-JP.

1. James M. Townsend (1825-1901), New Hampshire-born, clerked in a New York City import house before becoming president and director of several banks and other business enterprises, including a railroad and a clock company, and organizing in 1854 the Seneca Oil Company, which furnished the capital for Edwin L. Drake's prospecting in Western Pennsylvania oil fields. During the war he helped raise, finance, and equip the "Townsend Rifles," one of the first regiments to land on the South Carolina coast in November, 1861. *NCAB*, IV, 196; Rollin G. Osterweis, *Three Centuries of New Haven, 1638-1838* (New Haven, 1953), 253, 306, 321.

2. James E. English (1812-1890), Democratic congressman (1861-65), served as a member of the state house (1855, 1872) and senate (1856-58) and as governor (1867-68, 1870-71), before being appointed U. S. senator (1875-76). *BDAC*, 862.

3. A reference to the fall of Forts Henry and Donelson, February 6 and 16.

From Leonidas C. Houk

Flat Lick [Ky.]
Feb 18th 1862.

Hon Andrew Johnson:

Dear Sir,

After much tribulation, I arrived here Thursday last! I found one company waiting for me, and there were all sorts of efforts made to *Swindle* me out of them, but I talked plain, and all went off right.

Col Spears,[1] has not yet decided what he will do in regard to the proposition I presented to him, in accordance with your Suggestion.[2]

Recruits are coming in, and I now have a company and a piece, and have no doubt, but I will soon be able to report the 3d Regt full.

If Spears will agree to accept the position, I Shall do Just as I told you, as I believe it will be an advantage in the end.

One Joseph A Cooper,[3] now Capt in the 1st Regt East Tennessee, is, I understand an applicant for a Colonelcy[.]

I think *candidly*, and I only speak what his neighbors, and acquaintances will bear witness to, that he is not *the man*! He is a *fidgety, meddelsome*, fellow, putting his nose into every body's buisness—infact he [is] a perfect Specimen of the human *fice*![4]

Maj Shelly, I understand wishes to be Col,[5] and any aid you may give him, will be duly appreciated, not only by me, but our East Tennesseeans generally.

Acting Brig. Gen Carter, I think concluded to throw his *great* weight against me, but has found he can't effect much.

Things I confess, are rather gloomy as respects our advance on the Gap! Where are those ten Regts?

Do us all the good posible!

Thomas I fear, has misinformed the authorities, at Head-Quarters, inadvertently though of course—in regard to the roads into Tennessee.[6]

We know an advance could have been made.

I congratulate you upon the Safe escape, and arrival of Bob. It did me good on your account. Write if you have time[.]

The boys are all anxious to See you. The continual inquiry on my arrival, was, "how is Gov Johnson? When will he be here?" Etc.

Col. Jim Carter, don't Stay any with his Regiment! He is Sick most all the time!!! He attempted to get my company, that was waiting for me! Some one did *Swindle me* out of Sixty odd men, by telling them that I would not be permitted to raise a Regt.

All these things I will remember.

This man Cooper, of whom I Spoke, is the *penny*, nay the *tesey*,[7] for Sam, and Jim![8] I have a copy of a letter written by him yesterday, which I expect to preserve!

I have no information that can be relied on, as to numbers at the Gap! Watch Maynard!

Trigg[9] is right!

Yours forever &c
L. C. Houk

P.S. E. C. Trigg[10] will see you in a few days, and tell you Several things.

ALS, DLC-JP.

1. James G. Spears.

2. Shortly after this, on March 5, 1862, Spears received the commission from the President promoting him to brigadier general. Perhaps this was the proposition that Houk carried from the capital.

3. Cooper received his appointment, dated February 27, 1862, as colonel of the 6th Tenn. Vol. Inf. *Tennesseans in the Civil War*, I, 387; *Tenn. Adj. Gen. Report* (1866), 119, 132; for Cooper, see *Johnson Papers*, IV, 663n.

4. In short, a dog of dubious ancestry, touchy and quarrelsome, looking for trouble. *Webster's Third International*.

5. James Shelley was promoted, February 27, 1862. *Tenn. Adj. Gen. Report* (1866), 15.

6. George H. Thomas, in dispatches to his superior, General Buell, repeatedly bemoaned the poor condition of the roads. *OR*, Ser. 1, VII, Pt. II, 500, 558, 563, 564, 567.

7. A penny-boy was one "who haunted cattle markets" in the hope of obtaining employment as a drover; "tesey" is probably a variant of "teaser"—one who stokes fires, or "an inferior stallion or ram used to excite mares or ewes." Eric Partridge, *A Dictionary of Slang and Unconventional English* (New York, 1961), 617; *OED*, XI, 134.

8. The Carter brothers.

9. Connally F. Trigg.

10. Edward C. Trigg (1834-1866), son of Connally and a sutler of the 2nd Rgt. East Tenn. Vols. WPA, Tenn. Knox County, Tombstone Records: Old Gray Cemetery, 136; Horace Maynard and Andrew Johnson to Wilson and Burns (Baltimore), January 3, 1861 [1862], Lincoln Memorial University, Harrogate, Tennessee.

From William R. Hurley[1]

Auditors Office of the Treasury
From [?] the P.O Department
Feb. 18 1862

Hon A Johnson—.

Dear Sir:

Permit me to congratulate you on the result of the great battle at Fort Donelson—.[2] All patriots should rejoice, at such a result, but to a Tenessean, it is a source of especial gratification. The prominent part *you* have been called upon to act[3] makes this result espeially cheering[.]

I am gratified to see that the people here appreciate the position of loyal Tenesseans. When the news reached this Department about fifty clerks assembled in the large Bookkeeprs room and sent for me & called on me for a speech. I declined but proposed three cheers for the Army and navy of the United States, which were given most heartily.

The way will soon be open for me to go home and I do not like a *clerkship*.[4] I propose to return at as early a day as possible. I will go at once to nashville, and will if I can make suitabe arrangements commence publishing a paper.[5] Will issue a Daily slip, which at the end of the week will make a weekly paper[.]   I desire to go as soon as the army reachs the City of nashville. To conduct a paper as I propose, I can attend to other business, it would require but little time or means. Besides I have private interests to look after[.] T.A.R. Nelson owes me $4000. for a home I sold him in Knoxville I suppose for his brother. Besides this I have sued for several thousand dollars on a farm in lower East Tennessee which might be paid in shin plasters,[6] in which event I would be without means. It is all important to me to be able to guard these interests. I am anxious to go, also on account of some debts, I owe, which must be met if possible to save my Press & Type.[7] I intend to meet secession as heretofore. May I ask you to furnish me with such documents from time to time as I will need?

Respectfully   W R Hurley

ALS, DLC-JP.

1. See *Johnson Papers*, IV, 75n.

2. In early February Grant moved down the Tennessee River to capture Fort Henry

on the sixth; ten days later he took Fort Donelson on the Cumberland, thereby exposing Middle Tennessee to invasion. *Battles and Leaders*, I, 398-429.

3. A reference to Johnson's pending appointment as military governor of Tennessee, news of which was beginning to circulate.

4. His clerkship in the 6th auditor's office paid $1,400 a year. *U. S. Official Register* (1861), 20.

5. There is no evidence that Hurley returned to Nashville.

6. Paper currency in small denominations, issued by both Union and Confederate governments in an effort to offset the shortage of small coins. Mathews, *Americanisms*, II, 1521.

7. On the eve of his flight from Tennessee, Hurley was threatened with a law suit filed by Anthony S. Camp and Company, publisher of the Nashville *Patriot*. Hurley and partner, being "non-residents of the State," were ordered to appear before the Davidson County court on June 27 or the case would be heard *ex parte*. There is no indication that the case came to trial on June 27. Nashville *Patriot*, May 24, 1861.

From William B. Carter

Bryantsville, Kentucky
19th. Feby, 1862

Dear Sir,

I congratulate you, with all my heart, on the glorious success with which our arms have been crowned. Do not the tyrants in Tennessee begin to quake and tremble? Have not the confiscators of our property, and the murderers of our friends and neighbors, already seen the "hand-writing on the wall?"

I was truly glad to meet with your son. My chief object in writing this note is to call your attention to our E. Tenn. union friends who are held as prisoners in Alabama. According to the order of Benjamin, the Rebel Secy. of War, they are held as "*prisoners of War*," and not as political prisoners.[1] Would it not be well for you to see whether they can be exchanged. I think it worth the effort, as we now have a super-abundance of gray, blue, & black devils in our possession—

Respy Yours   Wm. B. Carter.

ALS, DLC-JP.

1. Secretary of War Judah P. Benjamin had ordered the Confederate authorities to execute summarily upon proof of guilt, all those "identified as having been engaged in bridge-burning" and, as a lesson to others, to "leave their bodies hanging in the vicinity of the burned bridges." Men who had participated in or abetted the uprising were "to be treated as prisoners of war, and sent with an armed guard to Tuscaloosa, Ala.," and "In no case . . . to be released on any pledge or oath of allegiance" for the duration of the war; only those who surrendered voluntarily and took the oath were to be treated with leniency. Judah P. Benjamin to Col. William B. Wood, November 25, 1861, *OR*, Ser. 1, VII, 701.

From William S. Speer

Eastern Hotel, N. Y. Feb. 19. [1862]

Gov. Johnson—

Dr Sir—

On the 16th September last I went to Nashville on the Chattanooga R. Rd. and on the train with me there were nine East Tennessee Union soldiers prisoners. They were marched through Nashville under military guard and imprisoned as "traitors."[1] Though not mustered into the U. S. service I think the Federal Government should claim them as prisoners of war and demand their exchange.

I can give you no further particulars. Of the date I am positive. From what county they came I have forgotten. Doubtless there are hundreds of your brave East Tennesseans in the same condition.

If you can do any thing for them I know you will.

I again congratulate you on the recent victories in Tennessee.

Do you spend your Sundays still in reading the lamentations of Job? But the war is not over yet.

Faithfully Your friend,
Wm. S. Speer

ALS, DLC-JP.

1. On September 16, John Gray, John W. Smith, Joel W. Jarvis, and John W. Thornburgh, suspected "leaders in the rebellious movements in East Tennessee," arrived in Nashville as prisoners under escort. At a preliminary hearing in Knoxville, Judge West H. Humphreys ruling that they should stand trial for treason before the Confederate States district court, October term, sent them to Nashville because the Knox County sheriff had refused to take an oath to support the Confederacy. A fifth prisoner, Charles L. Barton, escaped from the train by jumping out of the window of the water closet. Thornburgh gained his release through the intervention of a friend with Jefferson Davis and returned to his home; Barton made his way to Camp Dick Robinson and joined Co. A, 1st Tenn. Cav., September 25, becoming its captain until his resignation on December 10; the others were probably not detained long in Nashville—Jarvis, for instance, joined Co. B, 1st Tenn. Cav., on March 16, dying of measles a few weeks later. Nashville *Union and American*, September 17, 1861; CSR, RG94, NA.; *Goodspeed's Jefferson*, 1190; *Tennesseans in the Civil War*, II, 465, 532.

From Francis U. Stitt[1]

Washington City Feb. 19/62.

Sir:—

A citizen of Tennessee greets the Senator. And that with a joy inspired by the certainty that soon the capital of our misguided State will receive (thankfully, I doubt not) the glorious old flag.

John Meigs[2] knows me personally. I am a citizen of Nashville, having lived there from boyhood. Will Senator Johnson read these few lines from a young man who has ambition to hope and strength of mind to attempt to make that hope a certainty?

Briefly, then, I was foreman of the "*Christian Advocate*"[3] in the Methodist Publishing House at Nashville, of which my elder brother was Superintendent.[4] I was the literary editor of the "*Gazette*"[5] for the past two years, and until that paper announced itself for Secession. I am well known to the people of Nashville, either personally or by reputation. I ranked among my personal friends, almost without exception, the clergy and editorial corps of that city. Doubtless Dr. Hurley knows me, although he was a newcomer in Nashville when he started the "Democrat."[6]

My wife and self, sacrificing our household go[o]ds, left Nashville about the first of September, the day before the passport system was inaugurated, and before Davis's thirty-days' notice had expired.[7]

After three months of idleness in the North, and after suffering all the pangs and rebuffs of an unsucessful search for work, the interest of Cornelius Wendell, Esq.,[8] of this city, procured for me a situation in the Government Printing Office. But this position is held by the frail tenure of Congressional printing, and at any time I may be discharged for want of work. The recent glorious achievements of the Union arms is about opening up the way to my old home. Knowing that your potent voice decides the fate of all applicants for office in Tennessee, I apply to you in regard to the postmastership of Nashville. If the criteria be, as I suppose it is, ability and Unionism, setting aside other claims, I am sure I possess the latter, and my friends both in Nashville, Philadelphia, and Washington will vouch for the former.

Mr. Senator Johnson, will you grant me an interview? I would have sought one, but knowing your many duties, and, being sensitive, not choosing to encounter even a cool reception, much less a real rebuff, I choose first to write you this note.

I can procure as many and strong recommendations as you may wish or desire. I want to stand upon none merit save my own. Will you be so kind a[s] to drop a single line to me at the Government Printing Office telling me when I can call upon you. I would have applied to Etheridge or Maynard; but one represents West the other East Tennessee. You represent the *whole* State, and I am proud of being Andrew Johnson's constituent.

That you are the coming man of the nation is clearly evident. The effete and corrupt politicians are dying their death. It becomes you, then, as the representative man of the age, to secure the personal veneration of the young men who on the death of the present shameful treason, will rise to take the reins of the government of our Union.

Will you oblige me, Mr. Johnson, with an interview?[9]

Respectfully, your obedient servant,
Frank Stitt,
Govt. Printing Office

Hon. Andrew Johnson
Senator

ALS, DLC-JP.

1. Francis U. Stitt (c1833-fl1891) was a Pennsylvania-born Nashville printer and compositor, temporarily employed in the government printing office. He became pardon clerk in the attorney general's division (1865), later returning to the printing office. 1860 Census, Tenn., Davidson, Nashville, 5th Ward, 152; *Nashville Bus. Dir.* (1855-56), 113; Stitt to Johnson, January 30, 1875, Johnson Papers, LC; *U. S. Official Register* (1879-93), *passim.*

2. John Meigs (b. c1835), the son of Return J. Meigs, was assistant state librarian in 1860. Porch, *1850 Census, Nashville,* 83; *Nashville Bus. Dir.* (1860-61), 220.

3. First published in 1834 as *The Western Methodist,* this journal, after various name changes and mergers, had by 1853 become the *Christian Advocate.* The Southern Methodist Publishing House, one of the city's largest printing establishments, utilizing eight power presses, issued several weekly, monthly, and quarterly religious publications. *Ibid.,* 99-101.

4. Alexander A. Stitt (b. c1822), native Pennsylvanian, was superintendent of the printing department of the Methodist Publishing House, with his residence at 106 North College Street. During the 1850's he started publication of *The Nashville Monthly Record of Medical and Physical Sciences* and was printer of *The Parlor Visitor.* *Ibid.,* 262; 1860 Census, Tenn., Davidson, Nashville, 2nd Ward, 60; Clayton, *Davidson County,* 234, 235.

5. Begun in 1844, the *Gazette* was the third Nashville paper of that name. Dallying with secession soon after the election of Lincoln, the *Gazette,* by the end of 1860, had fully embraced the cause of "complete and eternal separation." Editor James T. Bell, arrested on April 12, 1862, for "treasonable conduct," was released on $5,000 bail. The offices of the *Gazette,* along with those of the *Republican Banner, Union and American,* and the Southern Methodist Publishing House, were confiscated on May 24, 1862. Wooldridge, *Nashville,* 196, 347-48; Nashville *Gazette,* December 21, 1860; Linda Joyce Redden, A Historical Study and Content Analysis of Nashville Newspapers, 1860-1865 (M.S. thesis, University of Tennessee, 1975), 14; Nashville *Union,* April 16, 1862.

6. The Nashville *Democrat* was begun as a Douglas paper in July, 1860, during the presidential campaign. *Johnson Papers,* III, 667n; see also Letter from William R. Hurley, December 23, 1860.

7. In a proclamation issued August 14, 1861, Jefferson Davis had required all males fourteen years of age and older who did not acknowledge Confederate authority "to depart from the Confederate States within forty days." By order of Brig. Gen. R. C. Foster, III, on August 22, 1861, individuals were forbidden to travel north of Nashville "for the purpose of going out of the Confederate States, unless provided with a *passport,* to be furnished by a committee . . . whose office is in the Court House." *OR,* Ser. 2, II, 1367-70; Nashville *Patriot,* August 29, 1861.

8. Cornelius Wendell (c1812-1870), an Albany, New York, printer, moved to Washington, and was elected public printer in 1856. In the same year, he built the largest establishment in the capital, which the government purchased in 1861 to begin its own printing, after the Covode hearings revealed the graft engendered by subletting contracts. By 1860 Wendell had accumulated $125,000 in real estate and $75,000 in personal property. 1860 Census, Dist. of Columbia, Washington, 275; Nichols, *Disruption of Democracy,* 157-58, 285, 329, 468; Lanman, *Biographical Annals,* 456; New York *Times,* October 11, 1870.

9. The senator acquiesced and they met "at the old St. Charles Hotel, at third and the Avenue . . . by the light of the good old-fashioned log-fire on the hearth, your son Robert, (an old personal friend of mine) being present." During the interview Stitt, as he proudly recalled in 1875 when writing to congratulate Johnson on his recent election to the Senate, "predicted your accession to the Presidency." Stitt to Johnson, January 30, 1875, Johnson Papers, LC.

From Elisha Whittlesey

February 20, 1862, Washington, D. C.; ALS, DLC-JP.

First comptroller solicits Johnson's counsel on behalf of Mrs. Joseph Comegys, wife of the late Delaware senator and holder of Tennessee state bonds given her by her uncle, John M. Clayton. Having been offered forty-two to forty-three per cent of their value, she awaits advice "and I wrote to her, I would ascertain your opinion."

From John S. Craig[1]

Lebanon, Ind. Feb. 21, 1862.

Hon. A. Johnson, Dr. Sir:

I have been sometime thinking of writing to you, and making a statement of my difficulties and losses in getting to this country. The papers say, when Nashville is taken (which, from appearances, will not be long) you intend going to Ten. to assist in reorganizing her government, and, of course, to bring her into the Union as soon as possible. I left Maryville, Ten. on the 2nd. of last Sep. Took the cars at Concord, in Knox county on the 3rd., and reached this place on the 6th.— A confederate officer, armed, with other armed soldiers were on the cars with us from Nashville to the state line; and by threats, forced me to give up part of the money I had with me. He gave me no receipt or evidence of having obtained it. I had to leave my property—real estate—unsold. Perhaps they have confiscated it. At any rate, I am now short of means, and I want every cent that secession caused me to loose. I would rather any body or set of beings on earth would have my hard earned money than those abominable secessionists. Let me suggest that in the settling up of affairs in all the seceded states, provision be made that all losses sustained by loyal men be made up to them with good interest, from the property of the rebels. This I think the government owes to its loyal subjects. The rebels must be weakened more than will be done by conquering them. For if peace is made with the seceded states and all the rebels some of whom are now high in authority in their *bogus* government, exercising too a commanding influence from their wealth and position, are restored to citizenship, with all their means of evil and mischief untouched, it likely will not be 10 years before they may be attempting to create trouble again to our government. It would not be out of the way either to confiscate enough of their property to pay a large proportion of the expenses of the war, if not the whole of them.[2] If there be five hundred thousand active traitors in the South, heads of familes, and the expenses of the war be 500,000,000 dollars, it will but be, on the average $1,000. apiece. This would be but a small average, perhaps not nearly so much as their property is worth. They ought to be made to feel that there is a *strong* government—strong, because it is just and benefi-cent to its loyal citizens, but terrible to all its enemies, *especially* traitors. Humanity would say that the government ought, in its work of confiscat-ing rebels' property, to leave enough to support the wives and little children of the rebels, and not force them to be "wanderers upon the world's highway[.]"[3]   I am clear that the arch rebels—the Rhetts, Yan-cys, Toombs, Harrises, Davises, Slidells, Masons, and perhaps 20 to 50 out of every seceded state, and some out of the border states ought to be hung or banished farther than Napoleon was, their negroes set free and colonized in Africa or elsewhere, and much of their other property confiscated to remunerate Union men for their losses and to pay the expenses of the war. Then let other rebels remain in the government, if they will take the oath of allegiance; but set their negroes free and confiscate a portion of their property in like manner as that of the arch rebels, and in proportion to their zeal and ability shown in active efforts now put forth to establish their miserable, *bogus* confederacy. But never touch a hair of a Union man's head.

Maryville *was*, and no doubt *is*, a little contemptible hotbed of seces-sionists, with but few noble exceptions. Men who made pretensions to piety were among the foremost. But the county was largely for the Union—4 to 1 during last summer.[4] I learn from a refugee who left Blount county 15th of last Dec. of a few defections:—but these were rather weak kneed Union men. Those now for the Union are reliable[.] I should have stated perhaps that the authorities at the state line, not-withstanding they had stolen my money, examined my trunks; but found nothing contraband.   But by mistake, 2 of our trunks were put off at Cleveland, Ten., and have never been heard of since. The baggage master, when we came to the terminus of the road, Chattanooga, apologized for the mistake, and declared positively he would have them sent on. I suspect they were confiscated at the state line, not far from Clarksville. The value of the trunks with all that they contained was about 75 dollars. I would be much obliged to have your assistance in recovering all I have lost by this infernal rebellion, as you will no doubt try to recover your losses. Make what use of this you please. Please answer soon.

Yours Truly   John S. Craig

ALS, DLC-JP.

1. John S. Craig (c1814-1893), Tennessee native and Presbyterian minister, was professor of languages at Maryville College (1840-61). One of the last professors to leave when the school closed in 1861, he spent the remainder of his career as a minister in Anderson and Noblesville, Indiana. 1860 Census, Tenn., Blount, Maryville, 47; Ralph W. Lloyd, *Maryville College: A History of 150 Years, 1819-1969* (Maryville, 1969), 150; *Minutes of the General Assembly of the Presbyterian Church . . . U.S.A.* (New York and Philadelphia, 1862-93), *passim*.

2. The second session of the 37th Congress (December, 1861-July, 1862) was preoccupied with the issue of confiscation of private lands and other forms of property held by secessionists, the long debates in both houses culminating on July 17 in the

passage of the Second Confiscation Act. *Cong. Globe*, 37 Cong., 2 Sess., *passim*; App. 412-13.

3. Perhaps a free rendering of Hos. 9:17: "and they shall be wanderers among the nations."

4. In the June 8 referendum, Blount County cast only 418 votes for separation, 1,766 against. Campbell, *Tenn. Attitudes*, 291.

From Mary A. Stevenson[1]

Lexington Ky Feb 21st 1862.

Mr. Johnson

My Dear friend:

I feel that I can adress you as Such & one that will go as far as the next to Comply with the request of a *Lady*. I know you are aware that all of Daughters Property[2] as well as my own is in *Texas*[.] My Intention has been for some time to go there but found it impossible to get from Lousvill to Nashvill[.] I will request of you if you would Be so kind as to get me a *Permit* of Major General John A Dix of Baltm[3] & would you Be so kind as to send me a letter of Introduction to the Commandar[4] at Fortress Monroe, so that I Can pass from that point to Norfolk. I know It will be a long & tedious trip but I am ready & willing to undertake It provided: I Can pass the lines of the two armies. It [is] to my Interst & that of my Daughter that we should be there, in Texas as soon as possible & Can you & will you do this for me[?]   I know you are above Suspition & you know what is the base of my request. I hope you will excuse the Liberty I have taking in adresing you[.]   I will Close this huried & imperfect letter[.]   with much respect & high regard,

your Friend Mary A. Stevenson

P. S. please wit [write] soon & that me know what I [can] Depend apon.   M

ALS, DLC-JP.

1. Probably Mary A. Stevenson (b. *c*1834), Alabama-born wife of Samuel Stevenson, who was listed with no occupation in the 1860 census but possessing real estate in the amount of $12,000 and personal property of $1,000. 1860 Census, Ky., Fayette, Lexington, 371.

2. Daughter Virginia, aged seven, was born in Texas. *Ibid.*

3. Maj. Gen. John A. Dix assumed command of Fort McHenry at Baltimore on July 24, 1861, remaining there until he was transferred to Fort Monroe in Virginia in late May, 1862. Morgan Dix, comp., *Memoirs of John Adams Dix* (2 vols., New York, 1883), II, 25, 46; see also *Johnson Papers*, II, 104*n*.

4. Dix's predecessor at Fort Monroe was Maj. Gen. John E. Wool. *NCAB*, IV, 282.

From William A Gunn[1]

Lexington Ky. Feb 22/62

Dear sir

I send you today a map with the proposed R.Road to East Tennessee marked out on what appears to be the most feasible route; from the surveys which have been made.

I suppose all will agree that the road should be so located as to be most useful to Commerce as far as consistent with the military necessity which builds the road[.]

The trade of Ky is far greater with the more southerly country, than with the extreme corner of Tennessee, South west Virginia & North Carolina. Knoxville would therefore be the most desirable point to reach from here.

The Physical obstacles to overcome would be less on the line laid down than by way of Cumberland Gap, as there are three rivers between that point & Morristown with intervening mountains & all so close together and lying so directly across the route as to require heavy grades, Tunnells & very heavy work to pass them.

On the Knoxville line Powells & Clinch Rivers unite & pass through Clinch Mountain at Clinton & the R. Road at Knoxville is on the west side of Holston River.

I see also from Mr McLoed's report[2] of the survey from Lebanon to Knoxville that 10 miles of this line were finished a year ago & other work in progress to Clinton, so this would be that much the shortest route.

This line as laid down on the map strikes the Cumberland River about the mouth of Rockcastle River, connecting with the navigation of that stream, which is important & which cannot be done higher up.

Knoxville is the central point of East Tennessee, the terminus of the two R.Roads which run through that part of the state & I regard the location of the line there as a fair compromise for all the friends of the road, some of the warmest of whom are for running the line as far down as Chattanooga.

I have also marked out several projected lines of R.Road to connect with this line, of these one of the most important is from Greenville to Ashville N. C. & as it is short; it ought also to receive aid from the Government[.] The Lebanon Branch of this road ought to come to Danville so as to make that line an outlet for the eastern part of the state to Louisville & the southwest— I have written Mr Guthrie[3] on this subject.

Please show this map & letter to Hon. C. F. Trigg & to such others as you choose—

I should like to get the position of Engineer of this work if a civilian will stand any chance for it, and shall be greatly obliged for any assistance you can give me in that way. I have been connected with this enterprise for 10 years & know as much about it as anybody else & would refer you to Gen. Leslie Combs, Hon. Geo. Robertson,[4] M. C. Johnson[5] & any of the prominent citizens of this part of the state as to my qualifications— Hon. Garrett Davis[6] also[.] I congratulate you upon the success of our glorious cause in your state & hope you may be speedily restored to your home & friends—

Yours very truly
W. A. Gunn

Hon. Andrew Johnson

My father was a native of Caswell County North Carolina & was raised in Robertson Co. Tennessee & spent 35 years in Ky as a Methodist preacher.

I am a native of Shelby Co. Ky & have always lived in the state.

I think therefore I have as good claims as any body for the position which I seek—

I had the pleasure of meeting you here last summer as you may possibly remember & I take the liberty to ask your influence in my behalf—

W. A. G.

ALS, DLC-JP.

1. William A. Gunn (b. c1830), a native of Kentucky, was an engineer with $3,000 in real and $5,000 in personal property. 1860 Census, Ky., Fayette, Lexington, 107.

2. George MacLeod (*fl*1871), born in Scotland, had been a route agent and was subsequently chief engineer of the Louisville and Nashville Railroad (c1857-c1869). *U. S. Official Register* (1859), *429; *House Report* No. 34, 39 Cong., 2 Sess., 559, 691; Maury Klein, *History of the Louisville and Nashville Railroad* (New York, 1972), 51, 96.

3. For James Guthrie, president of the Louisville and Nashville Railroad, see *Johnson Papers*, III, 461n.

4. George Robertson (1790-1874), a native Kentuckian, was a congressman (1817-21), state legislator (1822-27, 1848, 1851-52), minister to Colombia (1824) and Peru (1828), chief justice of Kentucky court of appeals (1829-34), law professor at Transylvania University (1834-57), and judge of second district court of appeals (1864-71). *DAB*, XVI, 22-23; *BDAC*, 1528.

5. Madison C. Johnson (1807-*fl*1877), Fayette County lawyer and member of the legislature (1853-55, 1857-59), was law professor at Transylvania and president of the Northern Bank of Kentucky. Collins, *Kentucky*, II, 205.

6. Garrett Davis, former Whig congressman who had supported the Constitutional-Union ticket in 1860, was elected to fill the Senate vacancy caused by the expulsion of Breckinridge in 1861. *BDAC*, 782.

From George MacLeod

Hyattsville Maryland
February 22nd 1862

Hon. Andrew Johnson
Senate of the U.S.　　Sir,

In consequence of the Late Successes of the Federal Arms in Ky. & Tenn. I see it intimated that you will Soon proceed to the later State clothed with the Authority of Provisional Governor.　Presuming that, under

Such circumstances, Some change will be made in the management & control in the more Important Rail Roads in that State, I take occasion to offer my Services as Engineer or Superintendant upon Some one of them. A Service of many years in Public works in Ky. & Tenn., (during which Time I constructed the Louisville & Nashville R. Rd. and all its Branches & put the Same in operation) has acquainted me thoroughly with the Public works of those States, & will make me better qualified to manage their operations than any one not heretofor connected with them. I can refer you with regard to my Standing Professionally to Hon. Robert Mallory[1] of Ky. and Hon. James Guthrie. With the later gentleman I have long been closely associated on the L. & N. R. Rd.

Yours Respectfully
George MacLeod

ALS, DLC-JP.

1. Robert Mallory (1815-1885), Virginia-born Democratic congressman (1859-65), after graduating from the University of Virginia (1827), moved to Kentucky where he practiced law and "engaged in agricultural pursuits." In 1866 he was a delegate to the National Union Convention in Philadelphia. *BDAC*, 1257.

From William R. Hurley

Washington D. C.
Feb. 24th 1862

Hon A Johnson.
Dear Sir:

It is my opinion that you are under a misapprehension in regard to my position toward you[.] It has been suggested to me that the cause of it, was my *editorial* in relation to the appointment of McNish.[1] I did denounce the appointment as a *secession* appointment, and sent my paper out by Express most of the time after his appointment. *I knew* it *was* such at the time, but believed that either McNish or someone else had deceived you. And hence while my soul abhorred the appointment, it never caused me to doubt your loyalty, to the government. That appointment did the union cause more harm in nashville than any other one thing that occured in that city. I strove against the Current of secession as long as I could, and made a speech at the last union meeting that was held in that city, and did so under threats of assassination. On that occasion I read two letters addressed by men claiming to be my friends, warning me of my danger[.] I stood while Bell Ewing[2] & others fell—and refused to attend a union meeting & made speeches when scarce a man could be found in any part of Tennessee, who would dare to make a speech for the union in middle Tennessee though many were urged to do so as you doubtless know. Finally when I could do no more I wrote to my friends to arm themselves for defence & came to this city hoping to find you here

& through you to obtain arms & go back and arm my friends for the
conflict. I expected your countenance as a fellow laborer in the great
cause of the country. You saw how readily I forgave you for the support of
Breckenridge and did you ample justice through my paper. It rejoiced
my heart to find you battling manfully against the men you had sustained
because they had proved traitors. As long as you continue in the [good]
cause you will still find me a friend doing battle with you whatever course
you may choose to pursue towards me. As I stated before I expect to
return to my native and beloved Tennessee, and attempt to bring my
erring friends to their allegiance to the government, and feel sure that I
will be heard. I have numerous relatives in the state, my father[3] still
lives to grieve over the condition of the country. He lives where he has
lived in middle Tennessee for over fifty years[.] I can not be accused of
being a northern emisary—nor an abolitionst, as my father & all my
relatives are slave holders & cotton planters. You imagine that I am
spiteful towards you & would be disposed to take vengeance because you
have seemed to treat me coolly. If you think so you are greatly mistaken.
Although I would *regret* to find you persistently opposing me for some
unimaginable cause, yet while you do wright I *will sustain you—in the
right*. But when wrong—would *condemn the wrong*. I intend to conduct
an *independent* union organ. I write this letter merely to assure you that
[you] will always find me ready to cooperate, & not opposing any
measure that will conduce to the good of the country, and to ask you not
to interpose any obstacles in my way when I propose to do the same
thing. This is no time for such things. I want the Post Office because it
will afford me more means, & enable me to conduct my paper on a larger
scale than I could otherwise do— I hope you will appreciate the motive.
My friends from Nashville have asked the office for me[.] Judge Catron
Meigs[4] and all my neighbors now north, and I do hope you will not
oppose their wishes but will in the true spirit of old friendship join
them[.][5]

W R Hurley

ALS, DLC-JP.

1. The editorial which appeared in Hurley's paper, the Nashville *Democrat*, is not
extant.

2. For John Bell and Andrew Ewing, see *Johnson Papers*, I, 206n, 534n.

3. Amos Hurley (c1793-1876), a native of North Carolina, was a Lincoln County
farmer with $9,000 in real estate and an equal amount of personal property. 1860
Census, Tenn., Lincoln, 15th Dist., 138; Clayton, *Davidson*, 468.

4. For John Catron, U. S. Supreme Court justice, and Return J. Meigs, see *Johnson
Papers*, IV, 308n, 78n.

5. Hurley had written three days earlier requesting help in obtaining the Nashville
appointment. Postmaster General Blair had advised him to "*get Andrew Johnson to
recommend you and I will appoint you*." Hurley to Johnson, February 21, 1862, Johnson
Papers, LC.

From Robert S. Northcott[1]

Clarksburg Va. Feb. 24 1862

Hon. Andrew Johnson
My Dear Sir,

I am becoming fearful that our government will deal too mildly with the rebel leaders. You are aware that it will never do to turn these men loose, because if this should be done they will be continually stirring up strife and petty rebellions, and consequently the lives and property of loyal citizens would never be safe.

I believe that punishment by hanging until dead is the only safe method that can be pursued with the principal leaders.

There is a large class of men in Middle Tennessee and I suppose in other portions of the State as well as in the other so-called Confederate States, who though not fighting in the armies, have rendered great assistance to the rebellion by hiring and paying soldiers out of their private funds as well as subscribing liberally for this unholy purpose.[2] These men should not go "unwhipt" of justice.

I respectfully call these things to your mind, knowing that you are in a position in which you can exercise an influence in controlling the policy of the government in regard to these matters.

I do think that Some means should be devised to make the rebels pay the expenses of the war. That would be but a small atonement for the great wrong they have done.

I think that it would hardly be good policy to pass any general confiscation act, but to tax the people of the seceded States to pay the expenses of the war[.][3] I mean tax all that in any way, manner or form gave encouragement to the rebellion, and if the discrimination can be made, (I presume it can) let the property of loyal men be exempted. Some act of disability should also be passed[.] No man who has held office in the Confederate army should ever be permitted to hold any office of honor or profit either in their respective States or the united States. I would have none of these disabilities to extend to common soldiers. If there is any way of reaching them I would have all civil officers who took the oath of allegiance to the Confederate States disqualified from voting or holding office.

The class of men to which I have alluded who subscribed so liberally and hired men to fight the battles of the rebellion I think should have their property entirely confiscated and be disqualified from holding real estate or office, or from voting. The rebellion must be effectually killed. Nothing must be left to give the leaders a foundation upon which to base future insurrections. The snake must be killed and so effectually killed that the country will never be disturbed again by his rebellious hisses.

I think the yoke of oppression is about being lifted from the necks of the people of our State, and when they are again free, I want them to remain so.

Most Truly You Friend
R. S. Northcott.

ALS, DLC-JP.

1. Robert S. Northcott (1818-1906), native Tennessean, editor and publisher of the Whig Rutherford *Telegraph* (1855-60), was a member of the Constitutional Union Convention and a unionist candidate in the state February 9 referendum. When the war began, he suspended publication and removed to Clarksburg, West Virginia, establishing the *National Telegraph* in December and joining the 12th W. Va. Inf., in August, 1862. Captured the following June, he was sent to Libby prison. After the war he settled in Clarksburg, joining the Republican party and eventually becoming "a distinguished editor." Hesseltine, *Three Against Lincoln*, 292; *OR*, Ser. 2, VI, 977-78; Nashville *Union and American*, February 13, 1861; Charles H. Ambler, *West Virginia: the Mountain State* (New York, 1946), 346; Delf Norona and Charles Shetler, eds.,*West Virginia Imprints, 1790-1863* (Moundsville, W. Va., 1958), 220; William Hewitt, *History of the Twelfth West Virginia Volunteer Infantry* ([Steubenville, Ohio, 1892]), 44, 99.

2. Although the evidence is somewhat sketchy, it would appear that this charge is not without foundation. During the late spring of 1861, the Nashville press recorded various offers from prominent men like Byrd Douglas, John Overton, William G. Harding, John M. Lea, and Sterling M. Cockrill who "unreservedly tendered" to Governor Harris "their credit and cash, whenever he calls on them, to any amount they can command, to sustain the independence and sovereignty of their State." A Nashville paper reported on April 30 that "Our patriotic fellow-citizen, L. B. Fite, has, we learn, furnished the goods for uniforming a company of 100 men in Sumner County." At the same time several Knoxvillians, including William H. Sneed, John H. Crozier, James A. Mabry, and William G. Swan, pledged $18,500 for raising Confederate volunteers. Nashville *Union and American*, April 28, 1861; Nashville *Patriot*, April 30, 1861; Knoxville *Register*, May 2, 1861.

3. Two days later Northcott submitted for Johnson's consideration a proposed bill which, by confiscating the property "of all persons who have aided the rebellion by subscribing money for the purpose of prosecuting the war against the . . . United States or hiring soldiers to enlist in the armies of the rebellion by paying them monthly or yearly salaries, or supporting their families," would both punish those in rebellion and help finance the war, without interfering with "the status of slavery." Northcott to Johnson, February 26, 1862, Johnson Papers, LC.

From J. George Harris[1]

U. S. Frigate Sabine
Navy Yard, New York
Feb. 26th 1862.

My Dear Governor—

You know I have been attached to this ship, blockading the Coast of South Carolina, for the last six months.

When I took up the papers this morning and saw that the Old Flag was again hoisted over the Capitol of Tennessee I must confess to the weakness of weeping for joy. I resolved to write you.

Thanks for your noble course—a rich reward is at hand for you. The *unity* of this Government, as described by Washington, in his last address to the people he so dearly loved, will be maintained and forever established. It is time that the limits of legitimate State Rights under the constitution were *prescribed*— And this is about to be done. As for the *debt*, we can and will work it out, or, our children will cheerfully work out the balance we may leave. There was never so *mad* a project as that of Davis and his associates, of the Senate who; as I can bear personal witness treated you with so much scorn and contumely when you made your great Union Speech before them in the Senate a year ago. If their *ideas* were to prevail the *order* and *government* even of the Creator might be disturbed with *propriety* if possible.

Glorious old Tennessee! If she will only *speak out* and *act* according to her own high judgment at this moment she will be redeemed indeed.

I have a son of 18 and a daughter of 15 years at Nashville. Their and my property interests are there. It has been my home for a quarter of a century. I need not tell *you* this—for you know my career there. I have not heard from my children for nearly a year. I know they were brought up "in the way of righteousness and fed with the bread of wholesome doctrine."[2] My son (Joseph E.) delivered a most glowing Union Speech in the Representative Hall Feb 22, 1861, as the representative of his Society at the Nashville University[3]—and I have every reason to believe he is still devoted to the Union. My little daughter[4] is with her Aunt about 10 miles from Nashville.

Can I *write* to them? I have not heard from them for nearly a year. If I should write letters to them and send them to you would it be proper, and could *you* see that they are forwarded? You know what is a father's solicitude under the circumstances, I believe you will favor me with a reply to this.[5]

Most sincerely, as ever & always

Your Friend   J. Geo: Harris

Hon Ande Johnson
U. S. Senate Washington.

ALS, DLC-JP.

1. For Harris, onetime editor of the Nashville *Union*, who had become a navy disbursing officer (1845-71), see *Johnson Papers*, I, 28n.

2. The source of this quotation has not been found.

3. Joseph E. Harris (c1843-1865), who graduated from Nashville University and Yale, died in London at the age of twenty-two. The *Banner*, commenting on the university-sponsored celebration of Washington's birthday, reported that "The speeches were in excellent taste, and were delivered in fine style and with good effect. We were particularly struck with the remarks of the last speaker, Mr. Joseph E. Harris, a son of Jeremiah George Harris, Esq., of this city." Despite George Harris' protestation of loyalty, his son did serve the Confederacy as a third lieutenant in Rutledge's Tenn. Lgt. Arty. Bty., CSA. Speer, *Prominent Tennesseans*, 488; Clayton, *Davidson County*, 192; Nashville *Republican Banner*, February 24, 1861.

4. Lucie (or Lucy), once called "the most beautiful woman in Tennessee," was educated in Nashville, Philadelphia, and Boston, studying art in the latter city; in 1868 she married Dr. Van S. Lindsley, prominent Nashville surgeon and professor in the medical departments of Nashville and Vanderbilt universities. She was the founder and first president of the Nashville Reading Club, the city's first literary society. Speer, *Prominent Tennesseans*, 402, 488.

5. Evidently Johnson replied at once, assuring Harris that mail facilities to Nashville would probably soon be restored. In his response, written only three days after his original letter, Harris expressed enthusiasm over Johnson's accepting the military governorship. "If any man can bring order out of chaos in Tennessee it is yourself." Harris to Johnson, March 1, 1862, Johnson Papers, LC.

From Charles K. Smith

February 26, 1862, Hamilton, Ohio; ALS, DLC-JP.

Old-time Whig and more recent Douglas Democrat seeks aid in securing the promotion of his son Charles K. Smith, Jr., from regimental to brigade quarter-master. His only apology for troubling Johnson lies in the latter's being "a public man, a National man—regarding all sections, and all people alike—however setting (as I do) a higher value on the white man, than on the black race."

From Jacob Glasser

February 28, 1862, Pittsburgh, Pa.; ALS, DLC-JP.

Asks Johnson's influence with Secretary Chase in obtaining license "to trade in those parts of Tennessee occupied by Union men and also to convey Hospital supplies."

From George Pickering[1]

Lebanon, Ind. Feb. 28, 1862.

Hon A Johnson,   Dr. Sir:

Having lately escaped from rebeldom, I have concluded to address you a few lines in relation to the condition of our Union friends in E. Tenn. After the bridges were burned in E. Tenn. the 9th ulto. the secessionists were scared almost to death. If the government had then occupied the R. R say at Knoxville or some other point, the rebels would I believe, have caved. And this might have been effected by 1,000 men. It was, we think a great oversight or mistake in the government not to have sent sufficient force to hold the Road immediately after the battle of Wild Cat. I wish, through you, to say or suggest and urge upon the government, the importance of sending sufficient force now into that country to hold the road. This is the main artery through which the life blood of the rebellion has circulated. If our forces hold all W. Tenn. and still this road remains open, Richmond and Manassas can be reenforced, and their army in Virginia be supplied. You are doubtess aware, from what you know of the sufferings of your own family & friends, of what many of us have had to suffer. Lying out for weeks in the woods was, and perhaps is a common occurrence,—and that too by old, gray headed men in some cases. I have had to be absent from my helpless family more than 5 months because of the vile conduct of the infernal rebels. When they found that the Union forces were not coming to accomplish the work begun so boldly and patriotically by the bridge-burning, they became furious; and all Union men were under the hardest suspicion;—many were caught,—some were hung, and others were jailed. The Union men who burned the bridges, as doubtless they did, must certainly have had intimations of help, or they never would have undertaken so daring an act. If this be so, the deserting of them, under the circumstances, was too bad. *This will all come to light in time*.— Remember, we do not believe the force under the brave Gen. Carter is at all sufficient. We ought to have 15,000 to 20,000 men; and when he gets to the R. R., he ought to have arms sufficient for 20,000 more, for the Union men in E. Ten.— Further, I understand you made a speech on the subject perhaps in January.[2] Perhaps one also on Bright's case. I wish a few copies sent to me at Alto, Howard county, Ind. And one each to my friends as follows, viz. Rev. J. S. Craig, Andersontown, Ind. Wm. Zion, Lebanon, Ind. Ben. Pickering, Jno. Zion, J. W. Jay, B. Harris, all of Raysville, Ind. Elisha Pickering, Windfall, Tipton co. Ind. I was born in Greene co. Tenn.; but have been living in Blount co. Ten. for 9 years past.

Yours truly,

George Pickering.

ALS, DLC-JP.

1. George Pickering (b. *c*1826) was on the eve of the war a Blount County farmer with $2,500 in real and $1,250 in personal property. 1860 Census, Tenn., Blount, 6th Dist., 105.

2. It is possible that Johnson, in reporting from committee a bill for construction of a military railroad in Tennessee and Kentucky, may have alluded to the need for men and arms; but the *Globe* for January 30, 1862, does not print the accompanying comments, merely the action taken. *Cong. Globe*, 37 Cong., 2 Sess., 555.

From Nicholas A. Gray[1]

Cleveland Ohio March 1/62

Hon. Andy Johnson:—

Sir:—

I still say, as I said in person to you in the Senate chamber two years since; that "Next to Douglas   Andy Johnson was the idol of the North-west" and now as a sincere and ardent friend I ask you to say either openly or *confidentially* whether the enclosed from Forney,[2] which is just now floodding Ohio, is in consonance with your feelings, consistant with truth and whether you desire the election of Mr. Wade.[3]

I also enclose an editorial from this day's Plain Dealer[4] which gives my views[.]

Please address me at

Columbus Ohio where I shall be for 60 days[.]

Yours Truly

N. A. Gray

ALS, DLC-JP.

1. Nicholas A. Gray (1809-1877), older brother of Joseph W. Gray, editor of the Cleveland *Plain Dealer*, was connected with that paper as business representative, Washington and Columbus correspondent, and associate editor from 1845 until he joined the army in 1862. Subsequently, Grant appointed him to a superintendency in the post office department. Archer H. Shaw, *The Plain Dealer: One Hundred Years in Cleveland* (New York, 1942), 24-26, 41-42; *U. S. Official Register* (1873), 355.

2. Over the signature of John W. Forney, editor and publisher of the Philadelphia *Press* and secretary of the U. S. Senate (1861-68), a February 7 letter to "A Union Democrat," in support of Benjamin F. Wade's re-election was appearing in a number of midwest newspapers. Gray's inquiry was prompted by a recent article in the competing Cleveland newspaper which printed Forney's letter and quoted the Cincinnati *Gazette* as follows: "We happen to know that Wade and Johnson are warm personal and political friends; and we also feel at liberty to say that the re-election of the former to the United States Senate would be gratifying to the latter." Kenneth B. Shover, "Maverick at Bay: Ben Wade's Senate Re-election Campaign, 1862-1863," *Civil War History*, XII (1966), 29n; Cleveland *Morning Leader*, February 26, 1862.

3. With his second term due to expire in March, 1863, Wade had launched his reelection effort a year earlier. Despite the fact that he needed the support of Union Democrats in the legislature, he had alienated them by his attacks on McClellan. Consequently repeated caucuses failed to muster a majority vote, and the legislature adjourned in March, postponing the decision until the following winter, when Wade was successful. As to Gray's question, there is no evidence in the Johnson Papers that the senator overtly supported Wade's candidacy, although contemporary rumors were widespread. Hans L. Trefousse to Andrew Johnson Project, October 17, 1976; for Wade, see *Johnson Papers*, III, 485n.

4. The editorial, which Gray himself may have written, concerns Simon Cameron, Lincoln's former secretary of war, who had been appointed minister to Russia in January. Noting that the Baltimore and Ohio Railroad through Harper's Ferry had at last been occupied by Federal troops, the paper commented that had Cameron "continued as Secretary of War it would never have been done," inasmuch as the Pennsylvania Railroad, in which Cameron was a heavy stockholder, stood to benefit by continued disruption of the B. & O. Cameron is a "corrupt man, who knows no patriotism that don't pay him a handsome rate of interest," the editorial concluded: "if he goes to Russia it should be as an exile." Cleveland *Plain Dealer*, March 1, 1862.

From Henry S. Neal[1]

Senate Chamber
Columbus O. Mch 1, 1862

Hon Andrew Johnson
Dear Sir.

I take the liberty of asking your views in regard to the feeling of the *Earnest and patriotic men* of the Border slave states in regard to the reelection of Hon. B. F. Wade as United States Senator. I suppose it will be a very delicate matter upon your part to give an opinion, yet under existing circumstances, I feel as if you ought not to hesitate, because of the condition in which the country is in. The influence of a man occupying so high a position as U.S. Senator may exert very marked effects upon the future of this country either for weal or for woe. And it is therefore highly important that in the discharge of our duty we should select such a man as will faithfully labor for *the Union and the Constitution*, and that too without interfering in the domestic affairs of the States any farther than may be neccessary to crush out th rebellion and punish the Conspiraters— And I believe such to be the feeling of Every member of this legislature[.]

You will therefore confer a great favor upon me by giving me frankly your views—.

I refer you to Hons S. F. Vinton[2] J. J. Coombs[3] V. B. Horton[4] and C. A Trimble[5] with all of whom I am personally acquainted[.]

Yours Truly   Henry S. Neal
State Senator 9th Dist Ohio

ALS, DLC-JP2.

1. Henry S. Neal (1828-1906), Ironton, Ohio, lawyer, was a member of the state senate (1861-63), Republican congressman (1877-83), consul to Lisbon (1869), and solicitor of the treasury (1884-85). *BDAC*, 1379.

2. Samuel F. Vinton (1792-1862), Massachusetts-born attorney, graduated from Williams College (1814) and began the practice of law in Gallipolis in 1816. Whig congressman (1823-37, 1843-51), he was an unsuccessful candidate for governor (1851); Lincoln appointed him to appraise the slaves emancipated in the District of Columbia in 1862. *BDAC*, 1756.

3. Joseph J. Coombs (1810-*fl*1881), Ohio state senator (1845-47), lawyer, publisher associated with Weston & Coombs, and currently a chief examiner in the patent office, was appointed in May, 1863, to a District of Columbia Supreme Court committee "to prepare rules of practice in patent cases." Cincinnati *Enquirer*, October 26, 1846; *Boyd's Washington and Georgetown Directory* (1860), 58; (1881), 281; Washington *Evening Star*, May 7, 1861; Job Barnard, "Early Days of the Supreme Court in the District of Columbia," Columbia Historical Society *Records*, XXII (1919), 8.

4. Valentine B. Horton (1802-1888), a native of Vermont, studied law in Connecticut and practiced in Pennsylvania before moving to Ohio (1833) where he served in Congress as a Whig (1855-59) and later as a Republican (1861-63). In 1861 he was a member of the Washington Peace Conference. *BDAC*, 1077.

5. Carey A. Trimble (1813-1887), Ohio native and physician, served as a Republican congressman (1859-63). *Ibid.*, 1728.

From Samuel J. Paxson[1]

Buckingham, Bucks Co. Pa.
March 1. 1862—

Hon. Andrew Johnson

Dear Sir— Please accept my thanks for a pamphlet copy of your recent speech in the senate on the expulsion of Mr. Bright. I had an extract (nearly full) which I cut from an Illinois paper published by one of my apprentices, who is out there fighting his way among the Abolitionists and that did pretty well, but the pamphlet copy you sent is in much better shape. I have already read your pamphlet speech to audiences in the stores of two villages near me and all were much pleased with it. No rebel sympathizers live around me. All sustain the government and a vigorous prosecution of the war, with the exception of a few Abolitionists who are *against both*, unless the war is specially made a war for the extermination of slavery! Men in the Republican party who one year ago were strongly tinctured with *humanitarianism*, are skulking out of the Abolition boat and striking out for shore— I predict that in a year or two, our county will be on a firmer basis than it was before the war, and Abolition will be more unpopular than it was twenty years ago, when they used occasionally to amuse the Bostonians by parading Wm. Lloyd Garrison through the streets, in close proximity to a tar kettle and a bag of feathers.[2] I never want to see such a scene as that re-enacted, but would like to see his principles despised as they were then. The Democrats in this section are all in favor of crushing out this infernal rebellion with pouder and ball, and then crush out Abolition at the ballot box. Thus getting rid of Secessionists North as well as South, we will be about ready to elect you President in 1864—

yours truly
S. J. Paxson

P.S.—I clip a paragraph from the last number of the Abolition, nigger arming, Semi-Secession paper of this county.[3] If it is true, it looks as if you and myself were on different sides of the rebellion. This paper denounces every man as a secessionist who voted of [*sic*] "*Gen.*" Breckinridge. But never mind, it is an old grudge, for I published the *Doylestown* (Bucks Co. Pa.) *Democrat* for fourteen years, and during that time our majority ran from a minority to upwards of twelve hundred. The paper has lost a package of its subscribers by the publication of the article, for I have been President of all the union meetings held in my vicinity and an officer of most held in the county during the spring and summer. But like the other Democrats of this county with its population of 60,000, I refuse to unite with our enemies to form a ticket to elect Black Replicans to office. This last fall we elected our ticket by an average majority of 336. The fall before more than twice that number the other way.

S. J. P.

ALS, DLC-JP.

1. Samuel J. Paxson (1818-1864), editor and proprietor of the Doylestown *Democrat* (1845-58), was a Bucks County Democratic leader, whose only bid for elective office failed when he sought nomination for Congress in 1862. [Webster Grim], *Historical Sketch of the Doylestown Democrat, 1816-1916* (Doylestown, Pa., 1916), 78-88.

2. William Lloyd Garrison (1805-1879), leading New England abolitionist and editor of *The Liberator*, had narrowly escaped being dragged through the streets by a Boston mob in 1835. *DAB*, VII, 168-72; see also John L. Thomas, *The Liberator: William Lloyd Garrison* (Boston, 1963).

3. The most recent issue of the weekly *Bucks County Intelligencer* had opined: "—'Samuel Johnson Paxson of Buckingham,' who at present is considerably disturbed by the twitching of the office-worm, and who would like to occupy a cushioned seat in the lower House of Congress at an early day, professes to be a great admirer of Andy Johnson, of Tennessee, who, under certain circumstances, he thinks, might be an *available* Democratic candidate for the Presidency, in 1864. . . . He is truly a *loyal* man, and unless Mr. Paxson changes his course very considerably, and cuts the company of many of his old political associates, whose sympathies still run strongly with the enemies of the Government, he will not be able to claim much fellowship with such an unrelenting opponent of treason and rebellion and earnest, devoted friend of the Union." *Bucks County Intelligencer* (Doylestorn), February 25, 1862.

From Rees W. Porter[1]

Nashville March 1st. 1862

Hon A Johnson
Washington City
Dear Sir

Allow me to congratulate you upon our arrival back into the *United States*[.] I will not attempt to give the general history of the *event* (but enclose you two papers one of which will give you that information & the other the report of *His excellency* "Gid J Pillow *Brig Genl C. S. A.*"[2] which if you have not Seen will be amusing if not interesting) but will give Some of the miner events[.] Gov Harris V K Stevenson judge Baxter Andrew Ewing & Ed Ewing[3] and about half the City left as soon as they Saw the confederate troops coming from their "on to Louisville trip," and Such Scenes as were enacted in Nashville[4] will never be fully known in this world[.] it is estimated by competent judges that $5,000,000 worth of property was lossed to the City & C. S. A[.]   the Soldiers were So mad that they committed all excesses possible[.] Among other things they perfectly ruined that magnificent place of Andrew Ewings[.][5]   they even went So far as to feed their horses in his parlor using the Sofas for troughfs Saying Damn him he got us into the trouble and is now the first man (except the Gov) to run away[.] Such things are greatly to be regretted but Still they are Some what refreshing to a poor *Subjugated down trodden lover of the Union*[.]   Every Edditor left every Methodist Preacher left[.]   the City puts on the appearance to day of Sabbath in cholera times[.]   Not a house in the city open Not *one*[.]   Oh but the judgments of Heaven has fallen heavily upon Nashville and hundreds of men *who knew better* Gov, I doubt not are praying for rocks & mountains to fall on them & hide them from the face of a confiding but ruined People and if we had one man *even one* that had the nerve to tell the People the truth in an honest way the rebellion would be at an end here at least[.] It is Said & I hope truly that *you* will be here Soon[.]

In the organisation of the Postal arrangements of the Country I Suppose that the office of Mail agent in this newly *acquired* Territory will be a resposible office[.]   Should you think me the man to fill that position I would be pleased to have the appointment[.]   with my thorough knowledge of the men the feelings of the People I believe I could make myself useful to my country as I think it the interest of the Country to push the Post office along just as fast as circumstances will permit & let the People hear the other Side and if this is done judiciously I think it will be attended with happy results to the Country[.]   Should you feel disposed to do So and would call on M Etheridge no doubt He would assist you in getting me the appointment[.] I would not ask it if I did not think I was "*the* man for the place" as I would not like to hold an office unless I thought I could *excel* in the discharge of the duties of the Same.[6] I fear I trespass upon your time & patience in writing so lengthy[.]

very Respectfully
Rees W Porter

ALS, DLC-JP.

1. Rees W. Porter (b. *c*1810), Kentucky-born trader who a year earlier had been an applicant for Nashville postmaster, became a member of Tompkins & Co., U. S. claims agents and attorneys. 1860 Census, Tenn., Davidson, 18th Dist., 42; Porter to Johnson, January 24, 1861, Johnson Papers, LC; *King's Nashville City Directory* (1866), 261, 293.

2. Brig. Gen. Gideon J. Pillow, second in command to Gen. John B. Floyd at Fort Donelson, was reprimanded for his actions in the surrender, suspended, and never given another important post. Stressing poor selection of the site, inadequate arms and defenses, and the demoralized nature of the troops when he arrived on the scene, Pillow's official report described both his actions in strengthening his position and the heroics of his batteries in repulsing Federal gunboats on the Cumberland. As to the turn of events which resulted in defeat, Pillow emphasized the debilitating influence of the rain, sleet, and snow and the reinforcement of the enemy resulting in an estimated ratio of three or four to one. A Confederate prisoner observed, "Pillow's official report has been received and commented upon by the officers. It is all Pillow—and we are unanimously of the opinion that it is not a fair statement of facts and that President Davis did exactly right in suspending he and Floyd from their command." A modern historian stresses this complete breakdown in the Confederate command. *Johnson Papers*, II, 351*n*; *OR*, Ser. 1, VII, 278-85; Connelly, *Army of the Heartland*, 111-25; McGavock, *Pen and Sword*, 603.

3. Nathaniel Baxter (1812-1895), Tennessee native and a lawyer, was judge of the sixth circuit court (1852-58) and of the eighth (1870-78). Opposed to secession, he nevertheless acquiesced in separation and spent most of the war years refugeeing in the South, returning to Nashville in 1865. Wooldridge, *Nashville*, 577-78; William Waller, *Nashville in the 1890s* (Nashville, 1970), 310; *Tenn. Official Manual* (1890), 183. For Isham G. Harris, Vernon K. Stevenson, and Edwin H. Ewing, see *Johnson Papers*, II, 323*n*, 251*n*, 340*n*.

4. Harris' horseback ride through the main streets of Nashville announcing the fall of Fort Donelson set off a reign of panic and plunder prior to the arrival of Federal troops and permanent occupation by Union forces. The governor and legislature hastily departed for Memphis while civilians began raiding the sizable amounts of Confederate supplies stored in the strategic city. In an effort to save some of the government property, Nathan B. Forrest used cavalry to clear the streets and succeeded in salvaging approximately 250,000 pounds of bacon, 600 boxes of army clothing, 40 wagonloads of ammunition, and a vital rifling machine from the ordnance factory—in all only a fraction of the supplies of the Army of Tennessee. As a parting tactic the suspension bridge over the Cumberland, Nashville's pride for ten years, was destroyed, and railroad bridges and ordnance works were set on fire, before the Union advance guard arrived on February 24. Crabb, "Twilight of the Nashville Gods," *Tenn. Hist. Quar.*, XV (1956), 296-97; Stanley F. Horn, "Nashville During the Civil War," *ibid.*, IV (1945), 9-10; Connelly, *Army of the Heartland*, 136-37.

5. That Ewing's estate was severely damaged seems beyond question. "Trees were felled, fences torn down, windows broken entirely out, and several fine outbuildings destroyed." But who were the perpetrators? Porter's assessment of responsibility is at odds with the usual attribution of the mayhem to the Federal invaders, found in most accounts subsequently penned by pro-Confederate writers. Clayton, *Davidson County*, 121; Crabb, "Twilight of the Nashville Gods," 298; Elvira J. Power, *Hospital Pencillings* (Boston, 1866), 59.

6. It would appear that once again Porter was unsuccessful in his bid for a post office position.

From Officers of Tennessee Regiments[1]

Flat Lick Knox Co Ky.
March 2nd 1862

Hon Andrew Johnson:
Dear Sir,

We, the undersigned, officers of the Tennessee Regiments, would earnestly yet respectfully, appeal to you, and through you to the President and Secretary of war, to have Col. James. G. Spears, appointed Brig Gen'l!

We make this request from various considerations, many of which you already understand!

One great reason for so doing originates from the *merits of the man*, whose promotion we seek!

He is brave, noble and true, posessing as great an amount of patriotic chivalry, as the God of Liberty ever endowed any of his creation, with!

A pure type of the Roman Stateman, and Soldier embodying the courage of Cezar, and the unalloyed love of country of Cincinatus, with judgement and prudence unsurpassed by any modern character! He is eminently qualified for a commander. This he ex[em]plified in the fight near Somerset.[2] In the thickest of the contest he mingled.

In the commencement of the engagement, his Regiment having received "Orders" to occupy a position where but little firing was going on, he made himself useful by giving directions to the 10th Indiana, in the abscence of Col Manson,[3] who was Acting as Brig Gen. This Regiment, it will be remembered, were in the hotest of the fight! With a heroism, Scarcely equaled Since time began, Col Spears met, contended with, and conquered the enemy at various points during this engagement.—this warmly contested struggle!

He is a remarkable man in point of ability and courage! Segacious! Shrewed! cunning! Wise!

Nay, he is one of the extraordinary men of the times, posessing one of the best minds in America!

Trained to useful thinking, he looks at all sides of every question. Prudent as well as brave, he posesses daring with caution! Guided by the strong impulse of good common sense, he rarely commits an error in judgement. And a more honest man does not live. As to his gallantry displayed in the battle before alluded to, and his capture of the Rebel Lieut. Col Carter,[4] we enclose a communication copied from the Baltimore Clipper,[5] written by one who knew the facts as they were!

We enclose the statements therein contained as being Substantially true. You will eternally oblige us by urging upon the proper authorities, the importance nay the *almost military necessity*, of appointing Col

Spears, to the position we ask in his behalf! No! not his behalf, but the people's and country's behalf! Hoping our earnest pray, and heart's desire may be granted,[6] we remain,

Your obedient Servants.

Pet, DLC-JP2.

1. Petition signed by twenty-four individuals, twenty-two from the 1st and 3rd East Tenn. Vols. and two from Kentucky cavalry units.

2. This engagement of January 19, known as the battle of Mill Springs, Fishing Creek, or Logan's Cross Roads (Ky.), pitted poorly equipped and trained Confederate troops of Gen. Felix Zollicoffer against the Federal forces of Generals Thomas and Schoepf. The rôle of the Tennessee regiments and of Lieutenant Colonel Spears was devastatingly described by "Felix," the East Tennessee correspondent for the Cincinnati *Commercial*: "What were the East Tennesseans doing during all this engagement with this boasted bravery? The First Regiment I know but little about, except that it marched toward the edge of the woods in which the firing was going on and disappeared from sight. As a regiment they did not fire a gun, but Lieut-Col. Spears who is a whole team and a horse to let, some way got in ahead of his men . . . and [when he] turned around to see where his men were . . . he perceived an officer in between him and where his regiment ought to be, evidently trying to cut him off. But the officer—who turned out to be Lieut-Col. Carter—walked up the wrong passenger when he got after Spears, and the tables were turned; . . . the Colonel took him prisoner and brought him back into the regiment. The Second Tennessee went through various and sundry evolutions; they were marched and countermarched, right-obliqued and left-obliqued, right-faced and left-faced and brought up all standing in a brier patch. Well finally we were formed in a line of battle out of all harm's way and remained so until the firing was nearly all over, when we were double-quicked to the edge of the woods, and halted again, until the firing receded and died away entirely." *OR*, Ser. 1, VII, 96-98; Connelly, *Army of the Heartland*, 96-99; Cincinnati *Commercial*, January 24, 1862.

3. Mahlon D. Manson (1820-1895), Ohio native, moved to Indiana where he taught school, studied medicine, engaged in the retail drug business, and served as a Democrat in the state house of representatives (1851-52) and U. S. House (1871-73). His military career included service as a captain of volunteers in the Mexican War and advancement from captain to brigadier general in the Indiana Volunteer Infantry in the Civil War. Wounded and captured at Richmond, Kentucky, in August, 1862, he was later exchanged. Boatner, *Civil War Dictionary*, 508; *BDAC*, 1261.

4. Moscow B. Carter (1825-1913), Williamson County surveyor and Mexican War veteran, was lieutenant colonel of the 20th Tenn. Inf., CSA. Captured at Fishing Creek on January 19, and sent to Fort Warren, he was paroled and returned home to engage in farming and surveying. 1860 Census, Tenn., Williamson, 1st Dist., 106; biographical data, McRaven Papers, Tennessee State Library and Archives.

5. The attached correspondence from "Justice," originally in the Baltimore *Clipper* but here from an unidentified newspaper, reported in melodramatic detail far different from the mocking tone of the account offered in note 2 above, Spears's capture of Carter. Johnson Papers, LC.

6. Evidently Spears's virtues, so lyrically appreciated by his fellow-soldiers, were recognized by his military superiors, for he was promoted to brigadier general on March 5. Subsequently, as the upcoming documents reveal, there was considerable difficulty in accommodating the new general in the military organization.

From William Patton[1]

[Washington, D.C.], 2 Mar. 1862

Dear Governor

When I called on you last evening your manner seemed to be reserved towards me. I then attributed it to your mind being deeply absorbed in the subject of a paper which was lying before you. It had not occurred to me that I had said or done any thing to change our friendly relations. But on thinking the matter over, to day, it has flashed upon my mind that from the manner in which you replied to my question "whether you had asked Mr. Clark[2] for my statement" which you had so kindly agreed to do, in connection with your apparent reservedness of manner, that you are possibly laboring under a misapprehension in relation to *my manner* in parting from you the other morning—thursday I believe— and which I accordingly feel called upon to explain.

I am constitutionally tender hearted; and, since my removal from office, my feelings have been very much depressed. My pecuniary embarrassments, which you will find, when you come to read my statement, present the gloomy prospect of all I have in the world, being swept from me. With this feeling of depression that tender heartedness seems to have become more susceptible. On that occasion, when I left you and got to the head of the stairs and was about descending them, you followed me out of your room, to say to me that you would see Mr. Clark and get from him my statement. Your tone and manner were so kind and friendly that for the moment, in spite of myself, my grateful feelings quite overcame me; and, as I felt the warm unbidden tears coursing down my cheeks, I averted my face, to avoid an exposure of my frailty. You erroneously supposed, from my *apparent* indifference, that I did not hear you; and you then repeated the remark, in the same kindly tone, which added to the intensity of my overpowering emotions; and, to be candid, I found myself going down the stairs, crying like a child. In this embarrassing condition, I bowed acknowledgement of your kindness, so gratefully expressed, and in such generous contrast with most public men; and, in an inarticulate tone of choked utterance, scarcely audible, I said—"thank you Governor"—and, as I said it, I inclined my head towards you, as far as I dare, for I was ashamed to let you see my face. In the absence of an explanation, I can easily see how you may have construed the aversion of my face and muttering tone of voice, to be *disrespectful* to you. But, if you could have read my heart, you would have found that you are the last man, on God's earth, to whom I could be disrespectful in thought word or deed. Your associations in Tennessee your honest, faithful & patriotic career in Congress and the coincidences that have conjointly marked our respective histories, have all combined, strongly to endear you to me— politically and socially. Like you, I am, in a measure, self taught and the architect of my own fortune. My Father was an humble mechanic and only able to give but one of his children a collegiate education; and that was bestowed upon my younger brother (Judge Patton)[3] to whom I introduced you some time ago as the former recipient of Genl. Jackson's official favor—and, like yourself, all beyond the mere rudiments of a common english education, I have acquired by self-culture. In this parallel, however, you have been far my superior, in every thing, except in age and origin—in the one I am your senior and in the other only your equal. Your illustrious career is marked by the admiration of a grateful country and is a striking illustration of my favorite maxim, that "Honour and fame from no condition rise." "Act well your part and there the honor lies"[4] My more humble career has but the approbation of an honest conscience. Now, my dear friend, I am truly sorry, if I have been, even the, unintentional cause of unpleasant feelings to you; and I am sure you will forgive me, when I assure you that my heart was so overflowed with gratitude to you as to render me incapable of expressing its feelings, without a most mortifying exposure of a constitutional weakness, which was entirely beyond my control.

Sincerely your friend and obedt servt
W. Patton

P.S. May I ask the favor of you to drop me a line and leave it at the bar of your Hotel informing me whether the above explanation is satisfactory?

ALS, DLC-JP.

1. William Patton (c1805-fl1868) of Pennsylvania had been a Senate clerk from 1851 until the time of his dismissal. A few days earlier, describing himself as "the Washington correspondent of the [Harrisburg] *Patriot and Union*, the leading democratic paper [of] Pennsylvania," Patton, under the sobriquet "Solon," had extolled Johnson's wisdom, courage, and patriotism in articulating the Union sentiment of Tennessee. 1850 Census, Dist. of Columbia, Washington, 4th Ward, 432; *U. S. Official Register* (1851-59), *passim*; Patton to Johnson, March 3, 1862, March 17, 1868, Johnson Papers, LC; Harrisburg *Patriot and Union*, February 25, March 11, 1862.

2. Possibly Ambrose W. Clark (1810-1887), a New York publisher and political figure, currently a Republican in the House (1861-65). *BDAC*, 696.

3. Benjamin Patton (1810-1897), Pennsylvania native and Dickinson College graduate (1828), practiced law briefly in Nashville, was appointed U. S. district attorney for western Pennsylvania (1832) by Jackson, served as judge of the court of common pleas (1838), judge of the Allegheny County court (1839-50), clerk of the U. S. circuit court and U. S. commissioner (1858-70). Moving to Hicksville, Ohio, he served in the state legislature (1880-81). J. W. F. White, "The Judiciary of Allegheny County," *Pennsylvania Magazine of History and Biography*, VII (1883), 165-68; George L. Reed, ed., *Alumni Record, Dickinson College* (Carlisle, Pa., 1905), 84.

4. A slightly altered version of a line from Pope's *An Essay on Man* (1732), Epis. iv, l. 193. Stevenson, *Macmillan Book of Proverbs*, 1161.

From Thomas J. Burrin[1]

Cleveland March 3d, 1862.

Hon Andrew Johnson
Sir

Being urgently solicited to sign a petition to the Legislature of Ohio—asking that body to vote for the reelection of B. F. Wade to the Senate of the United States—now—Sir I being a Douglas Democrat—cannot be easily reconciled to the past political history of Mr. Wade but, it is asserted that he is and has been working faithfully with your self—for the common good of our country. If Sir, it be true will you be kind enough to address me a few lines confirming the fact, and give me your personal views on returning Mr. Wade to the Senate, in connection with the duty of a Democrat in the present State of the country— is it consistent to Support Mr Wade or any other man of his political ante- cedent— knowing Sir—and admiring your history and present politi- cal position so well I shall place much confidence in the views, with which you will be pleased to favor me[.]

Respectfully your
T. J. Burrin

Cleveland Ohio

ALS, DLC-JP.

1. Thomas J. Burrin (c1822-fl1873), a native of Canada, operated a block pump and spar factory at 15 Spruce Street in Cleveland and held property valued at $1,600 on the eve of the war. 1860 Census, Ohio, Cuyahoga, Cleveland, 10th Ward, 193; *Williston's Directory of Cleveland* (1859-60), 59; *W. S. Robinson's Cleveland Directory* (1872-73), 90.

From W. W. Farnum

March 3, 1862, Port Jervis, N. Y.; ALS, DLC-JP.

Asks Johnson for copies of speeches, observing, "We always admire your speeches much more than those of the other senators . . . and often suggest that we should make Mr Stanton and the Tennesseeian our next Union President should God spare their life— It is the man from Tenn who is the first & last loyal southern senator in our Congress."

From George Gould[1]

London Canada West
March 3d 1862

Hon Andrew Johnson,

Dear Sir. I know that your time is constantly occupied with public matters and I hope you will pardon me a seeming stranger intruding upon you and I will make this letter as brief as possible. I am a native of New York, but since 1854 a resident of Nashville. For something over two years I was partner in the firm of Allen & Co on Cherry Street just below the Theatre.

In 1860 I sold out and moved on a small farm I leased adjoining Andrew Ewings place just off the Murfreesboro pike. Being a strong Unionist and a Northern man to boot when the present rebellion brok out, I was one of the first driven away, and was compelled to fly with my family, on the day succeeding Dr Hurley.[2] I lost all I had the earnings of years, and arrived penniless in the North.

I have travelled this past year from place to place where I could get work to support my family, and am at present working at my trade in Canada. In todays Detroit Free Press I saw a telegram that you were about to return to Nashville as Provisional Governor, and a despatch tonight says the Cumberland & Tennessee rivers are to be thrown open to trade again. I want to return to Nashville, but that is impossible unless I can get something to do to earn a support.

It will be a number of months before business will revive so that I can get work again at my trade, so though a stranger personally to you I thought I would ask a favor at your hands. I would like to get a subordinate clerkship in the Post Office at Nashville, so that I can earn a living until I can fall back on my trade again. You will probably have the appointing, or at least nominating of the New Post Master, and if so a word from you would secure me a place under him.

I ask this favor merely as an opening to get back to my adopted state without which it would be impossible for me to return may be for years, while if I could get back now I might perhaps save some of my property.

For my character as a citizen, Mr. Burns[3] formerly one of the Directors of the Bank of Tennesee of your appointing can speak, having known me for years, so can John N. Ward[4] of the firm of Ward, Birmingham & Co. strong Unionists. I could give you hundreds of references, but know not how many of my old friends remain in Nashville. some I have met in poverty in the North[.]

If it is in your power to render me the assistance I ask, I would be under deeper obligations than my pen can express, and it would be a relief to my family & myself[.]

Please let me hear from you if possible, and wether you are able to help me[5] or not I shall alway remain

Yours Truly   George Gould

Care W & J McBride
London Canada West

ALS, DLC-JP.

1. George Gould (b. c1832), New York-born partner in the firm of Allen & Co., coach manufacturers, resided at 105 N. College Street in Nashville. 1860 Census, Tenn., Davidson, Nashville, 4th Ward, 122; *Nashville Bus. Dir.* (1860-61), 178.

2. William R. Hurley, physician and editor of the Nashville *Democrat*, went to Washington probably during May, 1861, inasmuch as the last issue of his newspaper appeared on March 30, and in early May he accepted a clerkship in the sixth auditor's office. Guy H. Stewart, History and Bibliography of Middle Tennessee Newspapers, 1799-1876 (Ph. D. dissertation, University of Michigan, 1957), 129; Washington *Evening Star*, May 15, 1862; Letter from William R. Hurley, February 18, 1862..

3. For Michael Burns, a close friend of Johnson, see *Johnson Papers*, III, 376n.

4. John N. Ward (b. c1820), a native of Washington, D. C., was a Nashville tailor. Porch, *1850 Census, Davidson*, 159.

5. There is no evidence that Gould received his clerkship or ever returned to Tennessee.

From William W. Peck[1]

New York Mch 3d 1862 .

Hon Andrew Johnson
U. S. Senator from Tennessee
Washington D. C.
Dear Sir

I have no correspondent in Tennessee, and in the present state of things there, I do not know how to get one for my present purpose. I therefore take the liberty of addressing you & hope you will find it convenient to favor me with a reply.

At the commencement of the Rebellion, a valuable *Saltpetre mine* in the vicinity of Nashville,[2] was being put into operation, by a gentleman residing here;[3] he was driven out by the rebellion, and, as he is informed privately by friends in the neighborhood the rebels have since then, been working the mine. The successes of the government have, or will, probably restore him to possession. The mine has quite likely been somewhat injured, and his valuable fixtures very much impaired; and it becomes necessary to obtain capital for resuming operations. The importance of the works is obvious, from the fact, that the Government, has been obliged to obtain Saltpetre from abroad during the past year; and that its supplies have in that quarter, been frequently interrupted. The Tennessee Code of '58 contains a general incorporating act,[4] the provisions of which, are too embarrassing to comply with conveniently, (as in requiring that the majority of the stock, shall be owned there,—the capital shall not exceed 200,000 Dollars—the Stockholders shall be individually liable, &c.). I cannot find any addition or alteration of the code. Has any been made on this subject and, in what particular? Can a foreign corporation do business within your State? Can it own lands and operate with them there? For instance a corporation formed within this state? Could such a corporation hold a lease of lands within your State? There is nothing in your Code upon the subject, & the matter depends upon your local dicisions. If you cannot conveniently reply will you be kind enough to refer me to some intelligent lawyer in Tennessee who is within reach of the Mails, and oblige

With Respects
Wm Ware Peck

ALS, DLC-JP.

1. William W. Peck (*c*1820-*fl*1880) was a partner with John Van Buren, the President's son, in a New York law firm. *Trow's New York City Directory* (1859-60), 669; (1880), 1190; 1860 Census, New York, N. Y., 1st Dist., 3rd Ward, Brooklyn, 145.

2. In all likelihood Big Bone Cave, about seventy-five miles southeast of Nashville. John G. Buxman to [S. D. Morgan, undated], Morgan Papers, Tennessee Historical Society Manuscripts, Tennessee State Library and Archives.

3. Probably John G. Buxman (*c*1827-*fl*1897), German-born mining engineer, liv-

ing in Warren County in 1860, who possessed $2,500 in real estate and $500 in personal property, and who a few years earlier had resided in White and Van Buren counties engaging in saltpeter operations. His name and the date September, 1856, have been found (by Marion O. Smith of the Andrew Johnson Project) on a wall of Cave Hill Saltpetre Pit #1, in White. Although a unionist, Buxman cooperated with Confederate state authorities until his escape north to New York City in the summer of 1861. Possibly due to Johnson's influence, he was appointed from Tennessee to a clerkship in the second auditor's office, where he remained until the early nineties when he became an auditor for the war department. 1860 Census, Tenn., Warren, McMinnville, 175; *U. S. Official Register* (1863-97), *passim*; Letter from John G. Buxman, August 1, 1861, *Johnson Papers*, IV, 657.

4. Art. II, "Corporations for Manufacturing, Quarrying, and Mining," sec. 1448, dealing with the residence of stockholders, merely states that a "majority of whom shall be citizens of this State." Return J. Meigs and William F. Cooper, comps. and eds., *Tennessee Code* (Nashville, 1858), 316.

From William Rowe

March 3, 1862, Jersey City, N. J.; ALS, DLC-JP.

The acting secretary of the National Land Reform Association, evidently unaware of Johnson's imminent departure from Washington, reminds him that the Homestead Bill passed the House on February 27 by "almost a unanimous vote"; he hopes Johnson will "make it your especial business to see to it that this important Bill is [not] overlooked or neglected[.] By so doing you will entitle yourself to the lasting gratitude of all good and Patriotic men and more especially to the gratitude [of the] Landless millions in our land."

Appointment as Military Governor[1]

War Department
March 3rd. 1862

To the Honorable Andrew Johnson
Sir:

You are hereby appointed Military Governor of the State of Tennessee, with authority to exercise and perform, *within the limits of that state*, all and singular, the powers, duties and functions pertaining to the office of Military Governor (including the *power* to *establish all necessary offices and tribunals*, and *suspend* the *writ of Habeas Corpus*) during the pleasure of the President, or until the loyal inhabitants of that state shall organize a civil government in conformity with the Constitution of the United States[.][2]

(Signed) Edwin M. Stanton
Secretary of State [*sic*]

Seal of the War Office

Copy, DLC-JP.

1. The phraseology of this document, the first designation of a military governor to preside over former Confederate territory, would become the pattern for subsequent appointments. The action was entirely executive, justified by the President's war powers, and involving the Senate only peripherally, insofar as that body the following day confirmed Johnson's nomination as brigadier general without discussion of his role as

governor. Congressional debate concerning that office came later in the year. *Senate Ex. Journal*, XII (1861-62), 147, 148; Edwin M. Stanton to Hannibal Hamlin, June 3, 1862; *OR*, Ser. 3, II, 106; *Cong. Globe*, 37 Cong., 2 Sess., 3140, 3141, 3145, 3146, 3149; 37 Cong., 3 Sess., 240.

2. Whereas later military governors would receive fuller instructions in an accompanying letter, none were given Johnson—perhaps because no one in Washington had any clear idea of the prospects in Tennessee and perhaps because the appointee was in the capital and had discussed his responsibilities informally with Stanton.

From James H. Cochran

March 4, 1862, Washington, D. C.; ALS, DLC-JP2.

Partner in firm of Cochran & Robertson congratulates Johnson on his appointment and requests marshalship for West Tennessee, inasmuch as "the reverses . . . occasioned by the late most odious rebellion, has so prostrated me in a pecuniary point. . . that my commercial business has suffered to the extent of not less than $200,000."

From John W. Forney[1]

Thirty Seventh Congress. Senate Chamber
Washington City, March 4 1862.

Dear Governor-General:—

Mr. Truman[2] goes to Tennessee as the Special Correspondent of my newspaper *The Press*. You will find him to be a loyal and reliable man, and I commend him to your consideration. Any facilities you may extend to him as the representative of *The Press* will be gratefully remembered by your friend[.]

Very truly   J. W. Forney.
Sec. Senate. U.S.

Hon. Andrew Johnson.
Governor-General of Tennessee.

LS, DLC-JP.

1. Forney, publisher of both the Philadelphia *Press*, established in 1857, and the Washington *Sunday Morning Chronicle*, begun four years later and soon to become a daily, had embraced the Republican cause in 1860. Possessed of "an unusually accurate instinct for winning causes," Forney, in a long career, and not without a degree of opportunism, had supported men as diverse as Buchanan, Douglas, and Lincoln. That Johnson was about to be added to the list may be sensed in an ingratiating salutation redolent of British imperial titles. *DAB*, VI, 527.

2. Benjamin C. Truman (1835-1916), a Rhode Islander who had been compositor and proofreader for the New York *Times* (1855-59), was employed by Forney on the Philadelphia *Press* (1859-61) and the Washington *Sunday Morning Chronicle* (1861). Becoming a war correspondent and aide to Johnson in March, 1862, he continued to report for the *Chronicle*, as well as serving from time to time on the staffs of Gen. James S. Negley and other officers. As confidential agent investigating affairs in the South during the summer and fall of 1865, Truman submitted his findings to President Johnson in April, 1866, and also testified before the Joint Committee on Reconstruction. Subsequently he traveled widely in the western United States and Asia, was correspondent for the New York *Times* and San Francisco *Bulletin*, editor of the Los Angeles *Evening*

Express, owner of the Los Angeles *Star*, and chief of the literary bureau of the Southern Pacific Railway. In his later years, he recalled nostalgically his relationship with Johnson. *Ibid.*, XIX, 6-7; see Truman, "Anecdotes of Andrew Johnson," *Century Magazine*, LXXXV (1913), 435-40.

From William R. Hurley

Washington D.C.
March 4th 1862

Hon A Johnson:

I was gratified to learn that you are appointed to *some* position in the army, whether a major general or a Brigadier. I fear however as a Brigadier you would not have discretionary power sufficient for what you would have before you in the state of Tenessee. I have not learned whether you have accepted the position or not and I write this to insist as a Tenesseean that you will do so. In the first place you have suffered enough to make you *feel* like punishing the fiendish acts of the rebels in Tenessee, and secondly your appeals to the misguided people will be heeded. If the government has not given you some considerable discretion, I hope you will ask for more. You should be *free* to act according to circumstances. Tenessee is capable of punishing her own traitors and will do it right if not prevented. Let me again insist that you go to Tenessee and go with pretty full discretion to act as you see best in the premises.

I expect to go home about the last of this month, whether I have any appointment or not.[1] If there is any thing I can do to advance your puposes, please inform me[.]

Very Respectfully Yours &c
W. R. Hurley

ALS, DLC-JP.

1. Hurley's bid for the Nashville postmastership was endorsed by eight Tennesseans, now resident in Washington, who had fled the state because of "the intolerence of the rebels then in power to all such loyal men." The petitioners stressed Hurley's unionism, exhibited publicly and privately, "at a time when *every newspaper* in Tennessee, except his own [Nashville *Democrat*] & Brownlow's was either dumb, or had begun to advocate treason." Nevertheless, the postmastership went to John Lellyett on March 20. Tennessee Citizens to Johnson, [March 4, 1862], Johnson Papers, LC; Wooldridge, *Nashville*, 130.

From William Patton

Washington City
4 March 1862

My dear Sir

My noted *frailty* was not impervious to the effect of your kind note of this morning, which opened afresh the avenue to those little gems of nature that occasionally chase each other down one's cheek—sometimes as messengers from the fountain of grief and sorrow and at other times, of gratitude and joy.

I am happy, however, to say that your letter[1] has caused them to flow from the latter; and has unwound the crooked thread of misunderstanding and woven it into the web of lengthened friendship. But—metaphors aside—my dear Govr. you dont know how happy your letter has made me feel. The opinion of men of low instincts, which too often characterize public men, I disregard; but the good opinion of natures noblemen[2]—a class to which I know *you* belong—is, to me, as precious as rubies; and I cherish it as "apples of gold in pictures of silver."[3]

I was not aware, til late last night, that you were going to exchange the soft cushioned seat in the Senate for the jolting saddle of the war horse. While I regret your absence from the Senate, my prayers will follow you through all the dangers to which you may be exposed; accompanied by the hope that you may acquire laurels as green and unfading, in the tented field,[4] as those you have achieved in the forum of the Senate.

Sincerely your friend & obedt. Servt.
W. Patton

Hon. Andw. Johnson
U. S. Senator from Tennessee

ALS, DLC-JP.
   1. Not available, but evidently a prompt response to Patton's distressed missive of March 2.
   2. A "Noble of Nature's own creating." James Thomson, *Coriolanus* (1749), Act III, sc. 3.
   3. "A word fitly spoken is like apples of gold in pictures of silver." Prov. 25:11.
   4. Shakespeare, *Othello*, Act I, sc. 3.

From Felix A. Reeve[1]

Treasury Department,
Washington, Mar. 4th, '62.

Sen. Johnson:—

It is with no ordinary pleasure I learn that one so perfectly qualified and well-suited as yourself, has been commissioned to form a Military Protectorate over our insulted and outraged state. There is a long list of accounts to settle there, particularly in *East* Tenn., and I hope to hear of justice—full, complete, unrelenting justice, having been Meted out to the traitors who have oppressed the noble loyal men of that section. *Let* DEATH, *and* CONFISCATION OF PROPERTY, *be the only compromise*!

I would esteem it a great favor if you would appoint my worthy friend, JOHN BELL BROWNLOW to some post of importance,[2] when you reach Tenn.

Having lived in Brownlow's family for a long while,[3] and knowing

John as intimately as is possible to know any room-mate, I take much pleasure in recommending him to your favorable notice, as fully worthy of any position of trust or honor that his modesty would allow him to accept.

I ask nothing for myself, however pleasant it were to return home, because I am a member of a large family (the Earnest)[4] who, being Whigs, never were supporters of yours; but I most earnestly and disinterestedly recommend my friend.

May God bless you in the performance of your duties.

In great haste,   Respectfully,

F. A. Reeve.

Hon. Andrew Johnson.

ALS, DLC-JP.

1. See *Johnson Papers*, IV, 391n.

2. It does not appear that Parson Brownlow's son received an appointment at this time. Accompanying his father on a tour of northern cities during much of 1862, he received authorization in May, 1863, to raise a regiment which became the 9th Tenn. Cav. For John B. Brownlow, see *ibid.*, 518n; *Tennesseans in the Civil War*, I, 342.

3. Reeve boarded at the Brownlow home in Knoxville for twelve months. John B. Brownlow to Andrew Johnson, August 30, 1862, Johnson Papers, LC.

4. Felix A. Reeve's mother, Rebecca Earnest Reeves (1811-1886), the wife of Thomas Jefferson Reeves (1812-1888), was the grandaughter of Henry Earnest (1732-1809), a Revolutionary War veteran and the founder of the Greene County Earnest clan. Contemporaries often employed the name Reeve rather than Reeves; Felix A. permanently adopted the shorter version. Robison, *Preliminary Directory, Greene*, 4; 1850 Census, Tenn., Greene, 9th Dist., 196; Reynolds, *Greene County Cemeteries*, 110-12; Felix A. Reeve, Pension File, RG15, NA.

From Edwin M. Stanton

War Department Washington City, D.C.

March 4 1862.

Hon Andrew Johnson
Military Governor of Tennessee
Sir

You are authorized to draw to the amount of $10,000 on the fund to aid in the organization of a Home Guard in the hands of the Assistant Treasurer of the United States at Cincinnati,[1] for the purpose of organizing a Home Guard of Union men in Tennessee loyal to the United States.[2]

Yours truly   Edwin M Stanton

Sec of War

ALS, DLC-JP.

1. Consequent to the Act of July 31, 1862, Appropriating Arms to Loyal Citizens, a measure introduced by Johnson, the treasury department had allocated a sum of $199,750 to be deposited at Cincinnati for use in behalf of the Union cause in Kentucky and Tennessee. As senator, the Tennessean had assisted in its disbursement during the preceding September and October; now, as military governor, he was being authorized to draw upon the same fund for a specific purpose. Certificate of deposit, A. H. Adams

with Enoch T. Carson, September 4, 1861, Mrs. Betsy Bachman Carrier.

2. During the ensuing months, the home guards, recruited for one-year enlistments, were both a source of support for Johnson's regime and of dispute with the regular military personnel. The men's preference for cavalry over infantry status, on the ground that the guerrillas could be pursued only with horses, created problems of supply and equipment, even when the animals of reputed secessionists were seized. Yet during the winter of 1863-64 the home guards, with all their shortcomings, were in many parts of the state the only protection available to civilians and, even more important, were invaluable in guarding the army's lines of communication. Hall, *Military Governor*, 178-81; *OR, passim*.

From Edwin M. Stanton

War Department Washington, D. C.

March 4 1862.

Hon Andrew Johnson

Sir

Your Compensation as Military Governor of Tennessee will be at the rate of Three Thousand dollars per annum, that being the rate of compensation for Governor in that State[.]

Your account will be settled in this Department[.]

Yours truly   Edwin M Stanton

Sec of War

ALS, DLC-JP.

From William W. Wick[1]

Indianapolis Feb. [March] 4, 1862[2]

Dear Sir

I have just read your speech upon the Bright expulsion question, kindly sent me from the Office of the Secretary of the Interior.[3] Had you known the culprit as well as I do, you would have put that Kid glove off your tongue, and suppressed a dozen civil disclaimers.[4] I am however glad that you voted to clear him out of the Senate; for he is the dirtiest of all "dirty dogs," interiorly[?], notwithstanding his plausible manner. I will not attempt to give you items concerning him, but for them refer you to our Senator Wright,[5] who knows all about him that I do except his effort, made at the West gate of the Capitol grounds, to induce me, with his aid, to supplant Whitcomb, who had been, in advance selected by public opinion as Brights colleague in the Senate.[6] His dying speech is in character—not a word of substance—all ad captandum plausibilitus.[7] Before a jury in a court of law, he would have been acquitted upon Teneyck's technicality.[8] Nay more, I presume he could have escaped by adducing proof that the Lincoln gun was worthless, and so could not "give the enemy aid, and comfort".[9] But, in the Senate he was on trial not for Treason, but for disloyalty; and if a man who does his d——dest to commit an overt act of Treason is not disloyal, I would like to know who is[.]

This proclivity of your's to touch lightly a northern man, and to bear down heavily upon Southern Senators named by you, and my proclivity to give our late Senator particular Hell, and to set up in my mind some sort of palliation for Southern misconduct puts me in mind that I noticed very plainly when at Washington that you watched Southern men closely, and detected their sinister purposes when I was unable to see them, while I had a red eye out for Giddings Brinkerhoff[10] and gentry of that Kind, and detected much wickedness in them, which you found excuses for. This difference I remember well. It reminds me of the time when a Presbyterian was reeling along, pretty well fuddled; and in that Condition was pointed out to a Methodist of strict temperance principles. Never mind (said he,) that man does not belong to my Church.

I know *now* that it was thus with me; for tho' I changed boarding houses two or three times to get among the fire eaters, in order to ascertain their drift I was unable to find but one (Yancey) whom I could make out a secessionist *per se*: While on the other hand my civil and kindly remonstrances to Mr. Giddings and more than a dozen others were met by a blunt and not very civil declaration of their purpose to tease the South into secession so as to get rid of Democratic ascendancy.[11]

I have made up my mind long ago that the Union restored, upon old line whig ideas will do. The active agent in the restoration—the Superintendant[12] has those ideas, and we must take his restoration just as he will give it to us. Sooth to say the more I think about it the more consequence I give to the Fact, and the less consequence do I give to the modus operandi.

But enough of such writing my feelings and thoughts. I look now pretty confidently upon the restoration of the same old undivided Union as the Country of my Children, as only a question of Time. *It must come.*

Mrs. W has been for the last week nursing a Ward of sick Southern prisoners—all Tennesseans, except one Mississippi boy of 16. Two of them died. Her nightly report, especially concerning one Tennessean who took her for his wife, called her "honey", and then apologized for his mistake on the score of mental wanderings, and told her of his two little girls at home, sent me to bed nightly in tears. Poor Tennessee died the night before last in great peace. His name was James Cameron.[13]

Truly & respectfully
W. W. Wick

[Note on back page]

Your development of the fact of six Senators failing to vote on the "Clark amendment" to the Crittenden proposition,[14] is new to me. How it escaped my notice I cannot say.

It *does* prove a Conspiracy. The blood of poor James Cameron and of thousands lie upon the heads of the conspirators. God will require it of them.

ALS, Johnson-Bartlett Col.

1. For Wick, lawyer and former Democratic congressman, see *Johnson Papers*, III, 421*n*.

2. The content and postmark make it obvious that this letter was written in March.

3. Caleb B. Smith, an Indiana Republican leader.

4. This observation from Johnson's onetime colleague is the keynote in a highly subjective letter; on the other hand, Bright, the object of the "Kid glove" speech, remarked that the Tennessean "has done me great injustice" with "these unfounded, absurd accusations." *Cong. Globe*, 37 Cong., 2 Sess., 653.

5. Joseph A. Wright, former congressman and governor, had just been elected to fill out Bright's term (February, 1862-January, 1863). See *Johnson Papers*, I, 146*n*.

6. James Whitcomb (1795-1852), Vermont native, Transylvania graduate, Bloomington lawyer, and prominent Democratic leader, served as Indiana state senator (1830-36), commissioner of the land office under Jackson, governor (1843-49), and U. S. senator (1849-52). In 1845 Bright, supported by the party leaders, had won election to the Senate over the far more popular Whitcomb but was unable, despite efforts to undermine his rival by injecting Wick into the race, to prevent the success of the Indiana farmers' favorite in 1849. *BDAC*, 1801; Roger H. Van Bolt, "The Hoosier Politician of the 1840's," *Indiana Magazine of History*, XLVIII (1952), 32.

7. Wick's derogatory comment is an unsubtle variant of *ad captandum vulgus*—to reach for popular favor. For Bright's farewell speech, see *Cong. Globe*, 37 Cong., 2 Sess., 651-54.

8. John C. Ten Eyck, New Jersey senator, had suggested that, inasmuch as Bright's letter to Jefferson Davis was dated March 1 and the war did not begin until April, the Indianan should not be accused of treason. *Ibid.*, 473-74.

9. The most telling argument for expelling Bright was that his letter introducing Thomas B. Lincoln to Davis constituted treason within the definition of the Constitution. However, as Wick suggests, one might well question the "aid and comfort" given by an inferior firearm. For more on Lincoln, his gun, and the letter, see Speech on Expulsion of Senator Bright, January 31, 1862.

10. Keeping a "red eye out" was a slang expression for being watchful and observant. Former Ohio congressman Joshua Giddings, previously a Whig, and Jacob Brinkerhoff, onetime Democrat, were ardent antislaveryites who had embraced Republicanism. Giddings, who advocated use of presidential power to free the slaves, was appointed consul-general to Canada in 1861; Brinkerhoff, often credited with the authorship of the Wilmot Proviso, was an Ohio supreme court justice (1856-71). William A. Craigie and James R. Hulbert, *A Dictionary of American English on Historical Principles* (4 vols., Chicago, 1940), IV, 1915; *DAB*, III, 49; VII, 260-61; see also *Johnson Papers*, I, 206*n*.

11. Apparently an allusion to boardinghouse conversations held during the forties when Yancey, Wick, and Giddings were in Washington; yet it is more likely an assessment based upon their congressional service, inasmuch as Yancey's term ended in 1846, only one year after Wick's four-year incumbency began, while Giddings remained until 1859. A gadfly critic of the South, Giddings was determined to see the Union disintegrate in order that the slave power's hold on Congress might be broken—an attitude which may well have been shared by other Republican leaders. One modern historian supports the thesis that radical Republicans goaded the South into secession, apparently believing that the threat, hurled so many times in the past, would never become reality. James B. Stewart, *Joshua Reed Giddings and the Tactics of Radical Politics* (Cleveland, 1970), 104-5, 111-13, 170-71, 274-75; David M. Potter, *Lincoln and his Party in the Secession Crisis* (New Haven, 1942), 9-14.

12. President Lincoln, a former Whig.

13. Pvt. James Cameron (c1838-1862), a Holmes County, Mississippi, laborer, was the only prisoner of that name to die at Camp Morton, Indianapolis, in March, 1862. His widow, Pamela, did not list dependents when applying for a pension later that year. Perhaps the confusion concerning the prisoner's home state may be attributed to his

having been captured with his 4th Miss. Inf., at Fort Donelson, while Cameron's reference to his two little girls may have been a consequence of his "mental wanderings." CSR, RG109, NA; 1860 Census, Miss., Holmes, 81.

14. Johnson's reference to the Clark amendment, one of his favorite propositions, had appeared most recently in his Speech on Expulsion of Senator Bright, January 31, 1862.

To Edwin M. Stanton and William H. Seward[1]

March 4. 1862.

Sirs:

As requested by you, we designate the following persons for the following places:

Marshals.

District of	West Tennessee—	William T. Wilson[2] Dresden
"	East Tennessee	(*no vacancy*)
" X	Middle Tennessee	_____

District Attorneys—

District of	West Tennessee—	Alvan Hawkins[3] Huntingdon
X District of	Middle Tennessee	M. M. Brien[4] Nashville
X District of	East Tennessee	_____

For U. S. Judge. Connally F. Trigg.

For the places marked thus X we will name suitable persons so soon as we reach Tennessee.

Very respectfully
Horace Maynard
Andrew Johson
Em: Etheridge

Hon E M. Stanton &
"   W. H. Seward.
Washington D. C.

LS, NRU. Letter written by Etheridge.

1. The three Tennesseans, evidently prompted by Seward and Stanton, sent on a copy of these recommendations to Attorney General Edward Bates on the same day, the preliminary paragraph being the only departure from the original—"Allow us to suggest the following persons as proper to be appointed to the following places, whenever it is deemed advisable to fill them." Maynard, Johnson, and Etheridge to Bates, March 4, 1862, Appointments of Judges, Marshals, and Attorneys, 1853-1901, RG60, NA.

2. William T. Wilson (b. *c*1815), a native Tennessean, was railroad tax collector (1860) and later Dresden postmaster (1869-70). His property, valued at $15,800 in 1860, was worth only $3,000 ten years later. 1860 Census, Tenn., Weakley, Dresden, 7th Dist., 142; (1870), 56; *U. S. Official Register* (1869), 666.

3. Alvin Hawkins (1821-1905), Kentucky native and Carroll County lawyer, served as Whig representative in the Tennessee legislature (1853-55), as elector on the Constitutional Union ticket (1860), and as a member of the state executive committee of the National Union party (1864) supporting Lincoln and Johnson. Later he was U. S. district attorney for West Tennessee (1864-65), state supreme court justice (1865-69), U. S. consul general to Havana (1869-70), and governor (1881-83). McBride and Robison, *Biographical Directory*, I, 346-47.

4. This entire line is crossed out in the letter to Bates. Manson M. Brien, Sr., (1811-1886), DeKalb County and Nashville lawyer who served in the legislature (1855-57) as a Whig, was a unionist during the war and later a Republican, serving as president of Nashville's board of aldermen (1862) and judge of the 9th judicial circuit (1864-68). *Ibid.*, 79; Nashville *Union*, June 12, 1862.

From J. Warren Bell

March 5, 1862, Benton Barracks, Mo.; ALS, DLC-JP2.

Former Tennessean, having raised "a splendid two Batn. Regiment of Cav." in Chicago, requests help in securing transfer: "I want you to ask of Genl *Halleck* of Saint Louis that I be ordered forthwith to report to you. . . . I *must be* in Tennessee. . . . I know the Topoghaphy of the state and I have travelled all its roads. I know its mountains, Rivers Valleys &c and can be more effective there than elsewhere. I also know the Country south of the state. My men have so much Confidance in me that the desire to go with *you* is universal[.]" Requests that Johnson "call to see Mrs Bell Cor 12th & G. St before you leave[.] She is the Warmest union woman in Washington[.]"

From Alexis Drashko

March 5, 1862, New Haven, Conn.; ALS, DLC-JP.

Russian-trained Moldavian professional soldier, a veteran of the Crimean conflict, "Having come to this Country for the sole object of offering my humble services . . . and having vainly applied to several Governors for a place," solicits Johnson's aid. Well "acquainted with American tactics, & speak the English fluently," he seeks "Any position at all, in which I can serve your country, & from whose income I may support my family."

From William P. Jones[1]

Nashville Mch 5th 1862

Hon Andrew Johnson
Dr Sr

You may possibly remember I wrote you a few lines about a year ago, expressive of my approbation, not to say admiration, of yr great speech in the Senate of the United States in reference to the Union & the means of preserving it.[2]

I am a Physician of this City and have been one of those who have not bowed the Knee to the South Carolina Calf, but have firmly breasted the storm which in its blackness spread over this state. But having suffered many things, of many men—indeed having been under the ban of Secessionists, so as to injure both my present & prospective usefulness in Nashville; it has occurred to me to say to you that I would like to have some position in the gift of the government sufficiently remunerative to support a family.

Though I am now Surgeon in charge of the "Academy Hospital"[3] I would prefer another position, and knowing yr well merited influence with the Administration I am induced to write you thus frankly. I am a native of Ky & am known to Col Grider[4] representative in Congress from the Bowling Green District[.] I am Verry Respectfully yr freind

W. P. Jones

Nashville breathes freely once again. Those, who wept when they remembered the United States, now joy & rejoice in its power and protection. God grant speedy deliverance to all the states.

Harris & his clan have fled to the Mountains— I think the Goverment forces will keep them moving[.]

In conclusion let me say I will appreciate any kindness you may find it convenient to bestow in my behalf[.]   Yrs truly

W P Jones

ALS, DLC-JP2.

1. William P. Jones (1819-1897), born in Adair County, Kentucky, and holding degrees from the Medical College of Ohio at Cincinnati and from the Memphis Medical College, practiced at Edmonton and Bowling Green, Kentucky, before moving to Nashville in 1849. From 1854 to 1857 he published the *Parlor Visitor*, an organ of the First Baptist Church of Nashville, and was a member of the editorial staff of the *Southern Journal of Medical and Physical Sciences*. One of the founders of the Shelby Medical College (1858), he was appointed by Johnson superintendent of the state hospital for the insane in Nashville (1862-69) and an inspector of the state penitentiary. During a term as state senator (1873-75), he promoted legislation to improve public education and to advance the lot of the insane. President of the city council (1862), Nashville's postmaster (1877-85), and a member of the state board of education, he became professor of psychological medicine at the University of Tennessee, serving for two decades as president of the faculty. *NCAB*, XI, 368; Speer, *Prominent Tennesseans*, 412-14; *Tenn. Senate Journal*, 1865, App. 41; *ibid.*, 1869-70, App. 295.

2. See Letter from William P. Jones, January 17, 1861, *Johnson Papers*, IV, 179.

3. The Academy Hospital—the converted Nashville Female Academy—situated on six acres of land with ample interior as well as exterior space, was one of the more pleasant hospitals in the city with all the rooms heated by steam and lighted by gas. In May, 1863, it had 350 iron cots, 191 patients, and a staff of five surgeons and ten Catholic Sisters of Charity who served as nurses. In addition there were twenty-six male nurses, two white male servants, and sixteen female and twenty-six male colored servants. Nashville *Dispatch*, May 7, 1863.

4. Henry Grider (1796-1866), a Bowling Green Whig lawyer, served in the Kentucky house of representatives (1827-31), the state senate (1833-37), and the U. S. House (1843-47, 1861-66). *BDAC*, 974.

From Jane H. Campbell[1]

Hamilton Ohio
March 6th 1862

Hon Andrew Johnson
Washington

Sir— We are all heartily rejoiced to learn that your beloved state is about to be relieved from the thraldom which has prevailed there, and that you are about to return to your home with merited honors conferred by the Government to which you have been so truly loyal.

I write to say that Mr. Campbell[2] has been absent for some two weeks with his regiment at Camp Chase Columbus Ohio. You may not know that his regiment have styled themselves the "Andy Johnson guard" and Mr. C and his men will be exceedingly anxious to go with you to Tennessee. I write in his absence to ask you to use your influence with the War Department to get an order for *Mr. C and his regiment to go with you to Tennessee.*

My daughter Kate[3] joins me in asking of you this favor[.]

Hoping that you may soon be again reunited with your family from whom you have been so long exiled and that an honorable peace may speedily be restored to our distracted Country I am Sir

Yours Respectfully
Jane H Campbell

Hon Andrew Johnston
U.S Senator Washington D C

ALS, DLC-JP.

1. Jane H. Reily Campbell (*c*1818-*fl*1882), member of a prominent Butler County, Ohio, pioneer family, married Lewis D. Campbell in 1835. The Campbells had been close friends of Johnson when both men were in Congress. 1860 Census, Ohio, Butler, Hamilton, 118; *DAB*, III, 461; *NCAB*, XIII, 279; Charles A. Isetts (Ohio Historical Society) to Andrew Johnson Project, February 11, 1976.

2. Lewis D. Campbell (1811-1882), Ohio native, was a printer for the Cincinnati *Gazette* (1828-31) and published the Hamilton *Intelligencer* (1831-35), before becoming a lawyer in 1835. Elected as a Whig to Congress (1849-58), he chaired the House committee of ways and means (1855-57), losing his seat (May, 1858) to Clement L. Vallandigham in a contested election. His brief military career as colonel, 69th Rgt., Ohio Vols., proved to be stormy; as Johnson's hand-picked provost marshal in Nashville, Campbell became a focal point in the feud between the governor and Major General Buell, commanding the Department of the Ohio, and resigned his commission in the summer of 1862. Appointed by Johnson envoy and minister to Mexico (1866-67), he broke with the Republican party, became a Democratic congressman (1871-73) and a member of the Ohio state constitutional convention, ending his career as a farmer near Hamilton. *DAB*, III, 461; *BDAC*, 655; Johnson to Lincoln, April 26, July 10, 1862, Lincoln Papers, LC.

3. Catherine Campbell (1841-*fl*1882), one of three daughters, later married Oscar Minor, an officer in the 75th Ohio; she admired Johnson greatly and closely followed his career. C. B. Galbreath, "James Edwin Campbell: In Memoriam," *Ohio Archaeological and Historical Quarterly*, XXXIV (1925), 13; *NCAB*, XIII, 279; Kate Campbell to Johnson, February 5, May 18, 1865; Lewis D. Campbell to Johnson, November 12, 1864, Johnson Papers, LC.

From David H. Creekmore

March 7, 1861 [1862], Somerset, Ky.; ALS DLC-JP.

A Tennessee veteran, living in exile with his family, inquires "if there will be any officers appointed to regulate & controle the conduct of our border Counties as they appear to be so out breaking & rude that I Do not wish to take my Family back home untell there is some provisions made to regulate the Citizans[.]" On three visits to Huntsville he has exhibited "the Stars & stripes floating in the Breases . . . unmolested as yet."

From William H. Mitchell[1]

Capitol Bakery,
Washington D. C. Mar. 7 1862.

Dear Sir:

I make what to you will seem a singular request, and what perhaps you cannot comply with yet so strong is my desire that I must beg you to pardon me for asking your attention to my letter.

I want to go to Tennessee with you, I do not care in what capacity, so that I *can only go*. I am now employed as Clerk in the bakery, and I can refer you to Hon. Daniel W. Gooch,[2] who is well acquainted with me as I am from his district; to Lieut Cate[3] in charge here, or to Senator Harlan[4] of Iowa as to my character &c. I do not care what position I go in if I can do any good; would go as a Clerk, as a messenger, or your servant if in any military capacity I can go and if you have any secret service, no matter what the consequences it would be just the thing to suit me.

Last winter I was a member of that treasonable association known as the "National Volunteers"[5] and was instrumental in exposing some of their treasonable designs, and that although dangerous at the time (as they were all armed and drilling as a military organization against the government) was just what suited me then. I am from the people and of the people, and as I have travelled much am a good judge of men.

Can you give me anything to do? if you will give me any position I care not in what capacity I will throw up my place here at once.[6]

Please consider my application and if possible grant me a chance to go with you, and you will not find a more devoted servant than—

Yours Respectfully,
Wm. H. Mitchell

P.S. I am 28 years of age and do not write this in any youthful fever[.][7]

W. H. M.

ALS, DLC-JP2.

1. Not identified.

2. Daniel W. Gooch (1820-1891), a Maine native and Boston lawyer, served in the Massachusetts house (1852), the state constitutional convention (1853), the U. S. House (1858-65, 1873-75), and as Navy agent for the port of Boston (1865-66) before Johnson removed him. *BDAC*, 954-55.

3. Thomas J. Cate (b. *c*1829), a New Hampshire-born brickmason, served as a lieutenant in the 6th Mass. Militia and the 16th U. S. Inf., before resigning in August, 1863; as superintendent of the capitol bakery he employed Mitchell and wrote Johnson highly recommending him. Cate later (April, 1864) reenlisted as an officer of the 36th U. S. Colored Inf., resigning in August, 1865. Heitman, *Register*, I, 290; Cate to Johnson, March 10, 1862, Johnson Papers, LC; 1860 Census, Mass., Essex, Lawrence, 3rd Ward, 218.

4. James Harlan (1820-1899), Illinois native, moved to Iowa in 1845 where he began the practice of law (1848) in Iowa City. He served as a Republican in the Senate (1857-65, 1867-73) and as Johnson's secretary of the interior (1865-66). Harlan

subsequently wrote Johnson on Mitchell's behalf. *BDAC*, 1008-9; Harlan to Johnson, March 14, 1862, Johnson Papers, LC.

5. It would appear that Mitchell was one of the men who, under the aegis of Col. Charles P. Stone, infiltrated the National Volunteers, a semi-political, southern-rights, militia-type organization which had appeared in Washington prior to the election of 1860 and which persisted during the following winter, threatening to cause trouble at Lincoln's inauguration. Margaret Leech, *Reveille in Washington* (New York, 1941), 28-29; *House Report* No. 79, 36 Cong., 2 Sess., 2.

6. Fearing that Johnson had forgotten his request, Mitchell wrote on April 12, "I see also there are many spies and enemies to yourself and the government which you represent in Nashville. Could you not employ me in secret service there or elsewhere in the State to frustrate some of their schemes?" Johnson Papers, LC.

7. Endorsed by Johnson: "This letter must be answered (soon)."

From Nathan T. Allman[1]

Camp Chase near Columbus, O
March 8th 1862

Hon" Andrew Johnson—
Washington City D.C.

Dear Sir. I write you to let you know that I am a Citizen of Stewart County Tennessee about Twenty miles below Clarksville and about Fifteen miles above Dover Stewart County Tennessee on the Cumberland River. I am a man advanced in age Forty Two years Old and in Verry Delecate Helth have bin Every Since the 15 last November. I am at this place a prisionor of War taken at Fort Donelson. Elected Capt of a Company, while at Home Sick. when I recoverd I went to the Fort and the Comander would not accept my resignation, but kept me in Camp Sick untell the Fort was Surrenderd[.] I have always bin your Supporter in all Elections, for Gov" and I see your late appointment as Gov" of Tennessee. I appeal to you and Hon Etheredge of West Tennessee to get me released. I am willing to take the Oath if that is not Satisfactory to you a Bond to bar true Alegians to the (US) Gov". and do all I can for its Support. I am not personally acquainted with you nor with (Hon" Etheredge). I can refur you to Mess Allison Anderson & Co. of Mess Gardner & Co W H Webb & Co Mess Fall & Cunningham of Nashville, J G Hornburger Esq[2] H S. Keeble Esq of Clarksville Dr Smith & Dr Williams, Hon Allen Shamwell of Dover Tennessee[.] the (US) has all the section of County in possession where I Reside, and will Soon have the State. I hope you will gave this your Imeddiate attention, and let me return Home to my Family and recover my helth. R E. Thomas[3] a Cozen would like to get released on the same termes. he is a near neighbor of mine[.] Your Imediate attention to the above will much oblige

Your Friend   N T. Allman
Capt 50th Regmt Tennessee Vol
Camp Chase near Columbus Ohio

I have Always bin Satisfide with the (US) Goverment and if I was kept a presioner for Twelve months it would not make me any truer to the (US) Govt than I am now[.] I Resede about Twelve miles from the Kentucky Line[.]

Yrs   N T Allman

ALS, DLC-JP.

1. Nathan T. Allman (b. c1821), native Tennessean, was a Bowling Green farmer with real estate valued at $2,500 and personal property at $12,000. Enlisting as 1st lieutenant, Co. B, 50th Tenn. Inf., CSA, September 19, 1861, he was elected captain January 1, 1862. On April 5, 1862, he was paroled from Camp Chase by order of Governor Tod on condition that he remain in Columbus for medical treatment, that he report to the governor at 10 a.m. every day when his health permitted, and that he not furnish aid or comfort to the enemies of the United States. 1860 Census, Tenn., Stewart, 71; CSR, RG109, NA.

2. Two months later Jacob G. Hornberger (1819-1871), a Clarksville lawyer and longtime friend, would assure Johnson that "any word, hand, or bond" that Allman—a "very high minded and honorable gentleman, with a handsome estate, the fruits of his own industry and energy"—might give would be "perfectly good and entirely reliable." He advised the governor that "a generous and magnamious action in cases like this will much relax the bitterness of the people towards the federal government. . . . The curse of inhumanity and the cruelty of the sword only make mankind bitter and determined enemies—they never yet have made a free people love their government." Hornberger subsequently served in the Tennessee lower house (1869-71). Hornberger to Johnson, May 6, 1862, Johnson Papers, LC; Robison, *Preliminary Directory, Montgomery*, 26.

3. Robert E. Thomas (b. c1840), native Tennessean and resident of Cumberland City, was a 2nd lieutenant in Co. B, 50th Tenn. Inf., CSA, when captured at Fort Donelson. 1860 Census, Tenn., Stewart, 66; *Tennesseans in the Civil War*, II, 399; Iris H. McClain, *A History of Stewart County, Tennessee* ([Columbia, Tenn.], 1965), 123.

From Joseph G. Oliver

March 8, 1862, Christiana, Del.; ALS, DLC-JP2.

Requests copies of Johnson's speech on the expulsion of Senator Bright because he and his friends are "so much pleased with it" and because "Both of our Senators from this state, are so notoriously opposed to the entire coercive policy of the Government, that we never can get any speeches, but those in favor of their policy."

From Robert M. Widmar[1]

St Louis, Mo., March 8th 62.

To his Excellency, Andy Johnson,
Prov. Gov. of Tennessee.
Nashville, Tenn.
Sir!

Having always taken a great interest in the welfare of your State, as my German Weekly: "the Mississippi Handels Zeitung" (Miss. Com. Gazette) published here, had a circulation of about 1,000 subscribers in Tennessee, I, hereby, offer you my services for the purpose of raising a German regiment of Riflemen for the war in your State.

I belive, that the Teutonic population of the South will be like their brethren in the North: "reliable and brave Companions to you in your noble and brave defence of our common country.

Governor H. R Gamble[2] of Missouri, issued me a Commssion: to raise a regiment of Riflemen for the service in Missouri, last fall, but having been very sick during the summer I was forced to decline the honor.

Having now recovered from my illness, I wish to contribute my share to the revival of our national happiness, and should especially feel happy to fight under so noble a Defender of our flag as you are.

Being perfectly familiar with the Militia System of my State (Missouri), I calculate to be of some service to you. The State of Missouri is now quiet as you know & the State thoroughly canvassed for soldiers; a commission, as above mentioned, would, therefore, be desirable to me, as my health now is recovered.

The formation of one or two German regiments in Tennessee would no doubt have such good effect, that it might induce many Germans to make their escape to Nashville, knowing that the chance to enlist in a regiment, with whose members they soon would feel themselves familiar, would keep them from starving.

Should your Excellency think proper to accept my offer: "to raise a regt. of Riflemen" for your brigade", I should respectfully ask you to furnish me likewise an order to headquarters of Genl Halleck for transportation of 15—20 officers, whom I should like to take along. Those officers are men who commanded, 3 months Volunteers at Carthage and Wilsons Creek, whose men went home after the time of enlisting expired.

An anwer by Telegraph or Express would be desirable as time is a too noble jewel to be lost, and I remain

Very Respectfully Your Obt Servt
Robt Widmar

Care of Col Robert Widmar
Editor "Gazette" St Louis, Mo.

ALS, DLC-JP.

1. Robert M. Widmar (b. *c* 1835), a native of Saxony, was associated with several St. Louis papers: business agent for the *Anzeiger des Westens* (1857), editor and proprietor of the *Mississippi Handels Zeitung*, a German language weekly begun in 1857, and later editor and proprietor of the *Journal of Commerce* (1864-69). 1860 Census, Mo., St. Louis, 1st Ward, 402; St. Louis city directories (1857-69), *passim*; William H. Taft, comp., *Missouri Newspapers: When and Where, 1808-1963* (Columbia, Mo., 1964), 157.

2. Hamilton R. Gamble (1798-1864), a Virginian who moved to the Missouri Territory in 1818, served in the state legislature (1846) and on the state supreme court (1850-54), and retired to Norristown, Pennsylvania, due to ill health. Returning to Missouri politics when secession appeared imminent, he became a leader of the triumphant Union faction and was elected provisional governor in 1861 when the state constitutional convention assumed governing powers and declared vacant secessionist-held administrative offices. *DAB*, VII, 120.

From James D. Johnston[1]

Detroit, Mich. 9 Mar 1862

Major General Andrew Johnson &c
General

It surely will not be displeasing to you for any body to offer you hearty congratulation that the Administration has placed you most judiciously as the Military head of a provisional Government for your loved State. May Almighty God grant you all the needful light and Sustaining power to enable you to restore it with established loyalty to its proper relations to the Federal Union.

Some vigorous and comprehensive efforts should now forthwith be employed, do you not think, to induce "*a Spring tide*" of white emigration both from Europe, the Northern States and the Canadas to settle in Virginia [which would flank Maryland &c] North Carolina, Tennessee and other States, now in a kind of interregnum of Slavery Ascendency— "*Now,* "*Now,* "*Now,*" *is, if at any time, as good a time as any*, and I am sure that with proper efforts, free Government land being offered to the settler, a large multitude of white vigorous & healthy agricultural laborers could be gathered in who would prove a great preponderating element of social and political strength against the debasing influences of the peculiar Institution, and would prove a source of incalculable wealth to those States, which, as a consequence of the War, are so desirably denuded of the Africans. It would be a good and paying policy for the provisional Governments of those States, aided by the Federal Government, to send active and hardworking emigrant agencies into the Countries of Europe, and into our own large Cities North, and into the British provinces *to induce* emigrants to move to those desirable and delightful regions which have been blighted by slavery.

I am on the wing myself from this city where I have lived during the last 12 years and where I have built me a nice home which I value at about $5 or 6000—and hope to be able to get away somewhere south (I have been favorably inclined to California or Oregon) before the month of October next. In the mean time I am not in any employment and would be glad to receive an appointment from the Government to work *zealously efficiently* and *discreetly* for my pay. Mr. Chandler[2] has been endorsing my application for Paymaster or Military Storekeeper, but I do not know whether I may succeed. If *your Staff* were not full I Should like to be near you in some capacity, and if you remember me and have me appointed to some office near you, I shall, you may be assured, render you *all the aid* in my power and carry out your wishes to the letter. This would give me an opportunity to look about for a Home in Tennessee which from its geographical position seems to be one of the most favored

States in the Nation. I am an old Military man having served 14 years in "Her Majestys Service", and I can find no difficulty in accommodating myself to almost any honorable adventure. Senator Zack Chander has seen my papers accounting for my earlier life until I came to Detroit in 1850, since when I presume I could get in this city 25000 adults to certify that I am "a decent man" and good citizen. I enclose you a long list of names I once appended to an application of mine[3] to Mr Buchanan, but having been a "Whig" *on the Tariff* question—while a "*democrat*" on other questions, I presume I was regarded as an *Unreliable* politician and altho' the old man sent me his "*kind regards*" I received no appointment, and never had a Dollar from any Government. You will not blame me for being the originator of the name "Republican"[4] for the party of the Government now in power.— — God Bless and preserve your useful life.

Trly & Res Yours

James Dale Johnston

I forward you a copy of our City Detroit Directory—and direct to Washington as they will know how to forward from the Genl Post Office.

J D Johnston

ALS, DLC-JP.

1. James D. Johnston (*c*1815-*fl*1881), Irish-born publisher of *Johnston's Detroit City Directory*, had $4,000 in real and $500 in personal property on the eve of the war. Leaving Detroit in the late 1860's, he settled in San Francisco where he was an officer in the California Silk Manufacturing Company (1871) and the California Cotton Growers' Association (1872-73), and subsequently a "general agent" (1875-81). 1860 Census, Mich., Detroit, 8th Ward, 78; Detroit city directories (1859-66), *passim*; San Francisco city directories (1871-81), *passim*.

2. For Senator Zachariah Chandler, see *Johnson Papers*, III, 439n.

3. Not found.

4. Historians have neither credited Johnston with, nor blamed him for, this achievement. "Spontaneously and almost simultaneously, numerous men and organizations" proposed the name for the party that appeared in the aftermath of the Kansas-Nebraska Bill. A New Yorker, Alvin E. Bovay, claimed the honor of first proposing the name in 1852, but by the summer of 1854 the use of the term was so prevalent and "inevitable" that it would be impossible to single out any one claimant. Allan Nevins, *Ordeal of the Union* (2 vols., New York, 1947), II, 322-23; Mathews, *Americanisms*, II, 1385.

From William M. Woolridge

March 10, 1862, Philadelphia, Pa.; ALS, DLC-JP2.

"By proffession an Architect and Civil Engineer," he requests position as engineer on Johnson's staff. "Owing to my Union sentiments I was obliged last June to leave my home in Nashville and come North. . . . I brought my family to Philada. almost penniless the secessionists not allowing us money or even the trunks containing my families clothing; all I possessed was left behind." His experience has included work "in connection with Mr. Isaih Rogers in building the new hotel (the Maxwell House) for Mr. John Overton at the corner of cherry and church Streets Nashville" and the captaincy of a corps of sappers and miners in the 71st Pa. brigade.

To Joseph G. Totten[1]

Cincinnati March 10th 1862

Col. Joseph. G. Totten
U. S. Army
Sir,

You are aware that Tennessee at this time is unrepresented in the way of Cadets at West Point[.]   you are also that there have not been Representatives in Congress from that State to make the nominations as required by law[.] I have therefore concluded in this Unsettled & irregular State of things to nominate J. M. Hughes[2] of Tennessee for one of the appointees at West Point from that State. I am advised that the young man is well qualified & of good moral character. I hope that the Secty of War will adopt Some rule by which Nominations can be made so that the State can be represented at the Military Academy until she can again elect & send Representatives to Congress which I hope will be before long[.]

Yours Obt   Andrew Johnson

L, DNA-RG94, U. S. Military Academy, Cadet Appl. File, 1862/141.

1. As chief of the corps of engineers and inspector of the military academy (1838-64), Totten held an intermediate position in the chain of command between the secretary of war and the superintendent. Not until 1866 was the engineer corps relieved of its control of West Point. Stephen E. Ambrose, *Duty, Honor, Country: A History of West Point* (Baltimore, 1966), 44; Russell F. Weigley, *History of the United States Army* (New York, 1967), 105-6, 272. For Totten, see *Johnson Papers*, I, 186n.

2. Probably James M. Hughes (b. c1843), son of a Nashville carpenter-architect. Found "deficient in 'orthography' by the Academic Board," Hughes was not admitted to West Point that year but did enter in July, 1863, following Johnson's request that he "be allowed a reexamination, he having failed to pass satisfactorily at the first," only to be discharged the following June for scholastic reasons. Porch, *1850 Census, Nashville*, 91; Cadet Register, 1863-64, Entry 238, RG94, NA; Totten to Johnson, July 2, 1862, Johnson Papers, LC; Johnson to Totten, June 2, 1863, Military Academy Letters, RG94, NA.

From Don Carlos Buell[1]

Headquarters, Nashville, March 11, 1862.

Gov. Andrew Johnston, Louisville:

I Have received your dispatch from Cincinnatti. I have seen and conversed somewhat frequently with the most prominent Union men in and around Nashville. They are true, but the mass are either inimical or overawed by the tyranny of opinion and power that has prevailed, or waiting to see how matters turn out. They will acquiesce when they see that there is to be stability. You must not expect to be received with enthusiasm but rather the reverse and I would suggest to you to enter without any display. I shall be happy to meet you when you land and escort you to my quarters until you can provide for yourself more satisfactorily. As for the route the river will be the most comfortable, the railroad the quickest[.] Perhaps time is of consequence. Please let me know when to expect you.

D. C. Buell

LB copy, DNA-RG393, Dept. of the Ohio, Tels. Sent (Feb.-Aug., 1862), Vol. 52; *OR*, Ser. 1, X, Pt. II, 612.

1. Johnson had telegraphed: "Any suggestion that Gen Buell may think proper to make in regard to the time or manner of my reaching Nashville will be thankfully received. I hope you have consulted with our Union friends. Answer to Louisville. I will be there tomorrow[.]" Johnson to Buell, March 10, 1862, Tels. Recd., Dept. of the Ohio, RG393, NA.

From James H. Embry[1]

Richmond Ky.
March 11th 1862

Hon. Andrew Johnson
Dr Sir.

I learn through the Newspapers that you are on your way to Tennessee to be the chief Agent in restoring her to the once proud position she held as one of the States of the American Union—

In the interior of Kentucky we hail with no little delight & joy the news that the "Old Flag" floats from the Dome of her Capitol—

I write chiefly to ask of you the position of Post Master at Nashville for my Brother in-Law—Joseph S. Fowler[2] formerly Professor of Mathematics in Franklin College Tennessee—

He has been living for several years past in Gallatin Tennessee and left there in September last with his family rather than take the Confederate Oath & became an exile in Springfield Illinois— In the Election last June upon which depended the Secession of Tennessee, out of 400 votes polled in the Gallatin District he & one other alone voted against Secession—[3]

When Tennessee left the Union he left her— His Unionism was severely tested, but he stood faithful to the Flag— If the Confederate Oath had not have been required he might have remained there & risked the chances of his life, but when he was required to take a vow to turn Traitor to his own government he could not stand it—but leaving friends & home & property he sought a refuge where the Stars & Stripes could still float over him—

It is unnecessary for me to say anything to you of his ability & fitness for the Office— He lived in Nashville sometime & is well acquainted there— Governor, if you can give him the post, which is doubtless in your power, you will find him a true man & one faithful in after life to the high obligation you would impose upon him—

My Father[4] has not been able to return to his home on the Mississippi River since you saw him in Mt. Sterling last Summer— He has been absent since May last— I saw my Aunt Mrs Barnes[5] in Mt. Sterling on yesterday & she wished to be kindly remembered to you—

I passed several days at Cumberland Ford last week & an order to march had been given, but the River was rising so rapidly & reliable news came that the Secesh had been re-enforced at the Gap & Gen Carter[6] ordered our forces back to their Camps— The two Tennessee, 16th Ohio, 49th Indiana, 7th Kentucky, Mundays Cavalry & a Battery of Artillery are there—

The Roads are in a terrible condition & it is to be hoped that a force will be sent from Nashville to drive them from the Gap so that our gallant little army can cross into Tennessee— I go to Washington on Thursday— With my best wishes for your health & happiness

I am   Very Truly Yours
James H. Embry

ALS, DLC-JP.
1. For Embry, a native Kentuckian who had been living in Nashville, see *Johnson Papers*, IV, 547*n*.
2. See *ibid.*, 323*n*.
3. Nashville *Union and American* (June 27, 1861) does not break down returns by districts but reports Sumner County as voting 6,465 for separation; 69, no separation.
4. For Bowling Embry, see *Johnson Papers*, IV, 547*n*.
5. Emily A. Barnes (1813-1865), the widow of Thomas C., a Mt. Sterling merchant and banker, and Louisa Embry (b. c 1811) were the daughters of George and Cassandra Howard of Mt. Sterling. Hazel Mason Boyd, *et al, Some Marriages in Montgomery County, Kentucky before 1864* (Lexington, Ky., 1961), 52; Porch, *1850 Census, Davidson*, 173; Montgomery County, Ky., County Court Wills, Book F, 158.
6. Samuel P. Carter.

To Don Carlos Buell, Nashville

Louisville March 11 1862

To Maj Genl. Buell

I will leave at seven oclock a.m. March twelfth (tomorrow). Mr Guthrie[1] will put us directly through without any detention on the way. I desire no demonstration of any kind whatever. Hon Horace Maynard & others will be in Company[.][2]

Andrew Johnson

Tel, RG94, Gens. Papers, D. C. Buell.
1. James Guthrie, currently president of the Louisville & Nashville Railroad.
2. Johnson, accompanied by his son Robert, William A. Browning, Horace Maynard, and Emerson Etheridge, left Washington the afternoon of March 7, and traveled by rail via Harrisburg and Pittsburgh to Cincinnati, arriving on the 9th. The next day they took a boat to Louisville and reached Nashville the night of the 12th. New York *Times*, March 8, 1862; Cincinnati *Commercial*, March 10, 1862; William P. Mellen to Salmon P. Chase, March 11, 1862, Special Agents' Reports, 1861-1915, RG36, NA; Horace Maynard to Jimmy Maynard, April 25, 1862, Horace Maynard Papers, University of Tennessee Library, Knoxville.

From John P. Heiss[1]

Chinendega Nicaragua
Mch. 12, 1862

"Private"
Dear Sir

I am in this half civilized country, seeking, if possible, better health than I have enjoyed for some years.

My present object in writing you, is, to ask your aid in securing the prompt ratification of the Treaty with Nicaragua.[2] I do assure you, that the property and even the lives of American Citizens resident here, may depend upon such a result. There is no knowing when a revolution may break out, and then no American can be safe as there are no ratified treaties in existence which secure them any rights whatever. The Govt. of the United States is in possession of a treaty which was ratified by the Govt. of Nicaragua near a year ago, and unless acted upon soon, the time limited for its ratification will have passed. In fact this may unfortunately be the case now. The Minister[3] sent here by the Govt. of the United States, I fear will not prove very efficient in behalf of American interests. Diplomacy I should judge, was entirely out of his line. He has had but little experience in matters except those appertaining to the purchase of, and fattening of cattle, ("critters as he calls them) for market. He is a very clever old gentleman, but, entirely incapacitated for the mission he has been sent upon.

My heart sickens at the news I recieve from home. It is well known that my sympathi[e]s have always been with the South and against Northeren aggression; but I never had much faith in the leaders who have brought things to their present unfortunate issue. South Carolina politics and politicians, I never had any respect for. Jefferson Davis, I regarded as a man of ability and integrity, but his messages, as the President of the Confederated States, bears evidence of his incapacity to become a great leader. He has done but little towards securing the Southeren States an independent Govt. The other prominent men connected with his administration of affairs, viz. Toombs, Benjamin, Cobb &c, &c, are much better calculated to break down a Government, than build up one.

Your course *in* the United Senate and out of it, will no doubt, eventually meet with general approval—even in the South. For years to come, you may have to contend against the influences of bitter and disappointed men, but you have proved in the past, and in the present, that you have the nerve and energy to face your opponents, let them come from what quarter they choose. I, myself, thought you should have left the Senate Chamber when your state seceeded, but I now think your remaining there was right, under the circumstances. To the course pursued by yourself, and such men as Mr. Holt[4] of Kentucky, and Mr. Stanton, the present Secy of War, the South may yet be indebted for the safety of her institution of slavery. No doubt such a course has moderated the policy of the administration, and made it more conservative than it otherwise would have been. I must admit, that the course of the Govt. has appeared to me, until recently, as very oppressive and tyrannical. Everything like liberty, and all constitutional guarantees, seemed to be trampled under foot. However, news and news papers are rarities here and therefore I may never have been enlightened upon the actual neccessities of such a line of policy. It may result for the best, which in Gods name I trust will be the case. I do not suppose for a moment that the people of the United States would long submit to a despotic and tyrannical Govt. When the war ends I trust everything like a *"strong Government"* will end with it.

The American Consul[5] for this district[6] leaves home by the Steamer which carries this letter. He has become disgusted with his Consulate and retires after filling the position but a few months. If I had not been such a bitter opponent of Messrs. Lincoln and Seward, and the Republican party in general, I would apply through you for the position. I know I could be of service to American Citizens resident here, as well as to the Government of the United States. My knowledge of the Spanish language, and my acquaintance with the leading men of the country would enable me to accomplish much more than might be possible, with a stranger. The salary is small—$2000 per year—which will about pay expenses. How[ev]er I presume it is a matter not to be thought of *so far as I am concerned*. With your reccommendation for the place I might get it, provided the President would overlook the past and ignore strict party doctrines regarding an appointment of this class. I claim Tennessee as my state, and if you think it advisable to present my name to the President for that small place, please do so, and accept the thanks of

Yours Truly
John P. Heiss.

Hon A. Johnson.

March 15, 1862

P.S.

A few days reflection has convinced me, that the subject referred to in the closing part of my letter,[7] *so far as I am concerned*, had better be "indefinitely" laid upon the table".... Although I have not directly, or indirectly, done anything to promote seccession since hostilities commenced, I really believe I was in favour of seccession previously, although not upon the South Carolina plan or of being led out of the Union by the politicians of that contemptable state. I *was* in favour of a convention of *all* of the Southeren States, for the purpose of demanding *unitedly* of the North their legitimate rights, under the Constitution, and if that was not conceeded, to go out of the Union in a body. The present rebellion was commenced under the lead of bad men, and I fear the results will be so disastrous to the South that the people will not recover from its effects for ages to come. So far as the Consulate for this district is concerned, there is an enterprising American here who would fill the place to the satisfaction of evey American in Nicaragua. He is a native of Massachusetts, and a man of more than ordinary intelligence. I refer to Mr. J. E. Russell.[8] He is a strong believer in the creed of the party which placed Mr. Lincoln in power, and would fill the office to the satisfaction of all concerned. Having lived here some years, he is well acquainted with the country, and speaks the Spansh language fluently. Mr. Russell will not, I presume, be an applicant, but if you will speak to the President regarding him, you will, in truth, be doing a service to the Govt of the U.S.

Mrs Heiss feels greatly alarmed regarding her family at home. She has a mother and sister residing in Clarksville Tenness, a son perhaps at Nashville and a brother at Memphis.[9] She has not heard a word from them since May last. Now that the Federal Army is moving in that direction, she is in a terrible state of suspense about their welfare.

Yours Truly   J. P. H

ALS, DLC-JP.

1. John P. Heiss (c1812-1865), Pennsylvania native, was an owner of the Nashville *Union* (1840-45) and later of the Washington *Union* (1845-48) and editor of the New Orleans *Delta* (1851-55). He first went to Nicaragua (1856) as a messenger for the state department; after briefly conducting the Washington *States* (c1857-58), he returned to Central America in 1860. While in Nicaragua Heiss grew cotton, acted as an agent of British bondholders, and was an associate of William Walker. St. George L. Sioussat, ed., "Papers of Major John P. Heiss of Nashville," *Tenn. Hist. Mag.*, II (1916), 137-47; New York *Herald*, August 24, 1865.

2. Because of numerous amendments and delays by both sides, a treaty of commerce and friendship between the United States and Nicaragua, signed March 16, 1859, failed of final ratification. *Senate Ex. Journal*, XII (1861-62), 238, 240, 283, 284.

3. Andrew B. "Bray" Dickinson (c1803-1873), a Steuben County, New York, cattleman, served in the state legislature (1839-43) and was twice United States minister to Nicaragua in the 1860's. 1860 Census, N.Y., Steuben, Hornby Township, 20; *NCAB*, XII, 477; DeAlva Stanwood Alexander, *A Political History of New York* (4 vols., New York, 1906-23), II, 399-401; W. W. Clayton, *History of Steuben County, New York* (Philadelphia, 1879), 314.

4. Joseph Holt, former secretary of war.

5. Thomas Howard of Pennsylvania, was nominated consul at San Juan del Sur in December, 1861, confirmed in February, 1862, and replaced in January, 1863. *Senate Ex. Journal*, XII (1861-62), 28, 129; XIII (1862-64), 25.

6. A marginal notation reads: "This consulate embraces the Ports of Releajo [Realejo] and San Juan del Sur."

7. Heiss crosshatched the final paragraph concerning the consulship in such a way as to leave it fully legible.

8. John E. Russell (1834-1903), born in Greenfield, Massachusetts, traveled extensively in South and Central America before returning to his native state where he engaged in agricultural and commercial pursuits. He served as a Democrat in the House of Representatives (1887-89) and ran unsuccessfully for governor (1893-94). *BDAC*, 1551.

9. Not identified.

From H. H. Adair

March 13, 1862, McConnelsville, Ohio; ALS, DLC-JP.

Asks "whether an establishment for . . . doing the *Official printing* will be created" in Tennessee; if so, requests that he be "connected therewith either as manager or employee" and offers credentials "evincing honesty, & integrity of character and devotion to our National flag."

To Edwin M. Stanton[1]

Louisville, Ky. March 13 1862

Sir,

The bearer, Gen. John B Rodgers[2] of Van Buren Co. Tennessee goes to Washington, in behalf of certain prisoners taken at Fort Donelson, & in our possession.

He will explain the circumstances of their enlistment, other effect likely to result from their discharge, discriminating between Officers & privates, in favor of the latter, & extending clemency to them upon their taking the oath of allegiance to the Government. Those in whose behalf he seeks to interfere were recruited in his own vicinage & are his neighbor's sons—

We have no hesitation in saying that a judicious & prudent interposition of the pardoning power, in behalf of young men introduced into the rebel armies by force or artifice & against those who have been active in elisting them into the service, will have a happy effect upon the popular mind in our state.

[Andrew Johnson]

[Horace Maynard]

Copy, DLC-JP.

1. An unsigned endorsement indicates that the letter was addressed to the secretary of war by Andrew Johnson and Horace Maynard.

2. John B. Rodgers (1799-1873), a Virginia-born lawyer, lived most of his life in Warren and White counties, Tennessee, serving in the state legislature (1843-45, 1867-69) and as postmaster at South Rock Island. Possessed of $31,000 in property at the outbreak of the war, he had engaged in numerous business ventures, including the operation of a tavern on the Kentucky-Alabama Road, a ferry and a forge, and "Bon Air," a White County summer resort which opened in 1842 and continued until burned by bushwhackers during the war. A longtime Whig, he attended the Republican convention in Chicago, returning home at some personal risk to espouse Lincoln's election. 1860 Census, Tenn., Van Buren, 37; *U. S. Official Register* (1863), 633; McBride and Robison, *Biographical Directory*, I, 637; Rogers to Lyman Trumbull, March 27, 1861, Johnson Papers, LC.

Speech in Nashville[1]

March 13, 1862

I deeply and truly appreciate this demonstration of respect and confidence. I am affected by the circumstances under which I return to you, which renders me all the more sensitive to, and grateful for this testimony from my fellow citizens. I return to you with no hostile purpose, with no new doctrine to avow, no strange teachings to inculcate. For what do I come? I come with the olive branch in one hand and the Constitution in the other, to render you whatever aid may be in my power, in re-erecting, upon her rightful domain of Tennessee, the Star Spangled Banner—that flag borne by him who was "first in war, first in peace, and first in the hearts of his countrymen;" borne by him also, whose sacred ashes repose almost within the sound of my voice, and borne also by many a thousand of our countrymen, when the blood spouted from their heel, and no covering sheltered them but the stormy, pitiless cloud; to aid you in re establishing the supremacy of this flag, so dear to your fathers and mine. I come to aid you in the upholding and defending of this the best Government that God ever spoke into existence! I have never deserted that Government. How could I? The exiled—my wife driven hither and thither, her servants stolen; my home a rebel hospital—how could I desert the glorious Government under which I had been so richly and abundantly [b]lessed, and under which so many of my fellow beings have enjoyed, and do enjoy, so bountifully the boon of liberty and security.

The Governor then passed to the inquiry for what purpose is the war, and pressed home with great zeal and force the answer, for the maintenance of the Constitution and Government. He then recurred to the wicked deception that had been practiced upon the people in the canvass of 1860. He referred to his town speech here at that time[2] in which he contended in all sincerity that the Breckinridge party was as much the party of the Union as any other. Bell, Breckinridge and Douglas men were all taught the doctrine of "the Union, the Constitution, and the Enforcement of the Laws." Breckinridge deceived him. He was a disunionist at the time. His was a disunion party.— Notwithstanding all the vieing with each other of these three parties for the palm of Unionism, every one of their several leaders in this State have become open rebels against the Government in the United States.

He then laid bare with scathing severity the real cause of the war against the Government, which he declared to be disappointed ambition, and not slavery. The latter was but a pretext, predicated by Jackson.— Look at the hyprocrite Yancey telling Great Britain now that slavery was not the cause of the war. These men pretended that they were protecting slavery by withdrawing from the Union, while it was clear to every candid mind that the only protection to slavery was in the Constitution of the United States.

Tennesseans, I have taken part in your politics since 1838[3]—have I ever deceived you? Is there a man within the sound of my voice, or a man, woman, or child in the State who can say that he or she has been deceived by Andrew Johnson? Why all this persecution against me and mine? Why am I exiled, driven from my home, and my hard-earnings taken from me? Simply because I adhere to my Government and yours, my flag and your flag, the Government and the flag of your fathers. Because I loved them too well. Because, having been born and bred under them, I have determined to die under them.

An eloquent tribute was then paid to the United States Government as the government of the people by the people.

He painted in telling terms the track of desolation that secession left. Bridges, crops, dwellings destroyed; brother arrayed against brother in deadly conflict; families torn asunder; widows broken-hearted, and orphans crying for bread. All such scenes as these are on the track of the Demon's tread. He pointed the eyes of secessionists present to this scene, and asked, were it not enough, had they not suffered enough at the hands of this accursed monster? Had they not been duped and deceived by such as Davis, Toombs and the like long enough? Would they not see their folly and crime and return to their allegiance? He searched them with the question, was there a man there who had lost a single right or been deprived of a single privilege under the Constitution? They were entreated to ponder and reflect upon their suicidal course; to remember that "the soul of liberty was the love of law;"[4] that there was no hope for us, but in reverence for the Constitution and laws of the country.

The Governor closed by a most affecting allusion to East Tennessee, where his desolate home was and his sick, sad wife. His voice rang out like a clarion through the silent city, calling upon his countrymen to come forward in the defense of his beloved section of the State; to show their hands, to fear not and speak out. He declared his willingness to share with them any and all dangers for the rescue of Tennessee from the jaws of the infernal monster.

Traitors should be punished and treason crushed. He came with no hostility or animosity in his heart; he came for the defense of the weak, the restoration of the erring, the punishment of the guilty, the re establishment of the Union and Constitution in Tennessee. Come, my countrymen, he exclaimed, let us gather around the old and lovely flag with one heart and soul, reading upon its folds the hallowed words of Webster: Liberty and Union, one and inseparable, now and forever.[5]

Cincinnati *Commercial*, March 19, 1862.

1. According to the reporter, this, the first Union speech on Tennessee soil since the Confederate take-over in May of the previous year, was made before a large crowd assembled in front of the St. Cloud Hotel to hear a serenade by one of the army bands. Johnson, in response to an "ovation," appeared on the balcony to speak for an hour,

followed by Etheridge and Maynard. Louisville *Journal*, March 18, 1862.

2. Johnson had last spoken in Nashville on September 27, 1860. *Johnson Papers*, III, 660n.

3. This date is inaccurate. The speaker was first elected to the state legislature in 1835 and again in 1839, having previously been alderman and mayor in Greeneville. *Ibid.*, I, xliii.

4. One of Johnson's treasured aphorisms which has thus far eluded discovery.

5. From Webster's Senate speech of January 26, 1830. Bartlett, *Quotations*, 547.

From John B. Logan[1]

Kirks X Roads, Clinton Co. Indiana
March 14, 1862.

Hon. Andrew Johnson,

Sir— Please excuse the liberty I take of addressing you at this time, inasmuch as I am to you a stranger personally. I first saw you at Moorsburg Ten. when Col Haynes & yourself were canvassing that Congressional district, in 1852 or 3 if I mistake not. Since then, I have frequently seen you, & heard you at Blountville Ten, & have kept pretty well posted in your political career. Never having been a strong political partizan myself, I have been somewhat competent to judge of men, and their *qualifications* for the suffrages of the people. And to this I have looked in voting, more than to party ties. Referring to past, or old, parties, I was a Whig. When the Democracy of Ten. cast you out of their ranks, because you refused to join them in their unholy crusade against the Constitution & Government of our Father's, I, with many others in E. Ten, stood with you in attachment, to the Union.

The churches that were under my care in Sullivan Co Ten, refused to sustain me longer, because of my Union Sentiments, and in July last (the 15) believing that there would be, sooner or later, a reign of terror in E. Ten, I removed my family to this State. It cost me all of property & means I possessed to get here, but I have not regretted the move. It is quiet here, and I have recently made arrangements to labour here as a Minister of the gospel, though on a very Small Salary.

I write this, Sir, to say to you, in addition to the above, that I Sincerely Sympathise with you, & others, loyal E. Tennesseeans, in your exile from home & family.

I wish also to say, Sir, and hope you will receive it in the kind spirit in which it is said, that, your course has won you, (I think I may safely say) thousands of warm friends in this great State, and also in all the Northern States. And more than one man has said months ago, that they would vote for you to succeed Mr Lincoln.

I am but a quiet man, but I have been around a good deal in the central part of this State, and have read the news of the day pretty closely since the troubles began, and at this early date allow me respectfully to ask, that you will let your name be run for the Presidency, for the next term, if Providence spares your life, & you are nominated, as I trust & believe you will be. This is no recent thought with me. I saw before I left Ten. that you would be the next President, if you was nominated and run.

A request, & I close. I have secured the likeness of one loyal E. Tennesseean, & I want some others. You will confer a great favour upon me, by sending me yours, either Daguerreotype or Photograph, by mail. I want the people here to see the likeness of the man they have learned to so highly respect for his loyalty to country.

I hope the day is not far distant, when you can return to the bosom of your family & find in E. Ten. that protection from your government, which used to be enjoyed there.

Please to write to me.

Very truly yours   John B. Logan

Reference
Hon. H. Maynard.

ALS, DLC-JP.
1. John B. Logan (c1818-1896), a Virginia native, was a Methodist minister before his admission to the Holston Presbytery in 1850. Pastor at Blountville for several years prior to the war, he later served churches in Indiana and Ohio. *Goodspeed's East Tennessee*, 916; J. E. Alexander, *A Brief History of the Synod of Tennessee, 1817 to 1887* (Philadelphia, 1890), 143; *Presbyterian Church, U.S.A., General Assembly Minutes* (1862-95), *passim*; (1896), 176.

To Edwin M. Stanton

Nashville Tenn. Mch 14 1862.

To Hon Edwin M Stanton
Secy of War
We see in the arrangement of military, Dept Tennessee west of Knoxville falls under Halleck east of Knoxville under Fremont[.] we entreat that the state be not divided[.] place it all under Halleck[.] this is most important[.] for Gods sake do not divide east Tennessee into two (2) Military Departments[.] We have suffered enough already from a conflict of Military authorities[.][1]

Andrew Johnson & Horace Maynard

Tel, DNA-RG107, Tels. Recd., Sec. of War, Vol. 6 (Mar. 12-24, 1862).
1. Stanton responded that Lincoln "regards the existing arrangement as a paramount necssity." Stanton to Johnson, March 22, 1862, Johnson Papers, LC.

From Return J. Meigs

15. Broadway, N.Y.
March. 15. 1862.

Hon. Andrew Johnson,
Dr Sir,
Most anxiously and earnestly hoping and expecting the success of your enterprise in Tennessee, and wishing, if possible, to contribute my mite

to secure it, I comply with your request and my own promise to put my ideas of your course upon paper.

When the loyal and disloyal masses in Tennessee were left free to express their sentiments on the proposal to secede, the majority of voices for the Union was overwhelming. But as soon as the disloyal mass had been made to organize 25.000 armed men to fight the government, and they had been placed under Confederate officers, and it became apparent to the people that this great army was acting in concert with the Executive of the State and the legislature, and that they had all the money of the state, all its arms, and that all its officers had sworn to support the Confederate Constitution, then the people either voted to secede, or quietly stayed at home, and permitted the agitators to carry them out of the Union.

Such is the difference between a compact, organized body, sustained by the machinery of government, armed and supported at the public expense, and a disorganized mass, without arms, a leader or means of support. The latter, though exceeding the former—a thousand to one in numbers, is easily reduced to passive submission. The mighty empire of Persia was conquered by Alexander with only 35.000 men.[1]

These observations show, what you must do, if you would succeed. You must place a Union man in every official position in the state, from the lowest to the highest; you must arm the Union men and disarm the disunionists; you must control the revenue of the State; you must have a disciplined army able to overawe the rebels; in a word the friends of the Union must be organized and combined, and must be made to see and feel their strength, and the other side must be reduced to their uncombined and disorganized elements. Then the state of things will be reversed, and you and the Union will stand in the very attitude which has till lately, been held by Harris and the Confederacy.

How is this transformation to be brought about? In answering this question, I take it for granted, that *every* office in the state is held either by an original Secessionist, or by some person who has become a Secessionist; and that every office holder has taken an Oath to support the Confederate Constitution. I assume again that every law passed since the Secession of the State is void, and every office is vacant,—because the laws have been passed and the offices are held, in defiance of the Constitution and laws of the United States, which are the supreme law. Now, then, the way is open for you. In the exercise of your authority as military governor, it seems to me you should conform as near as possible to the State Constitution and laws, as they were before the secession. All the offices which the Legislature has the right to fill, you will fill, as directed by the State Const. Art. 3. §14. Among these, are the Comptroller, Treasurer, Secretary of State, Librarian &c. As to the officers elected by the people, you will be compelled to fill them, as military governor, under the executive authority to take care that the laws be faithfully executed. As soon as it can be done safely writs of election to fill the vacant General Assembly should be issued. See Code. 173.174 178 And so of every other office, the filling of which belongs to the people, who, for the time being are to be regarded as refusing to exercise their authority to fill vacancies in accordance with the Constitutional laws of the State.

Truly   R. J. Meigs.

April 3, 1862. The foregoing is the substance of my letter to you of the 15th of March, which you inform me, by telegraph, has somehow disappeared. I beg to add, that Tennessee, since the 6th of May, 1861, has not enjoyed a "republican form of government." On that day, the conspirators, Isham G. Harris, Henry W. Hilliard, Gustavus A. Henry, A.O.W. Totten and Washington Barrow, subjected "the whole military force" of the State to "the control and direction of the President of the Confederate States."[2] In this gross transaction, the people of Tennessee have acquiesced. The men who had been chosen, at the election of August, 1859, to constitute of the Legislature of the State, subject to the Supreme Authority of the Constitution of the United States, assumed to pass, according to the forms of legislation, the act of May 6, 1861, entitled "An act to submit to a vote of the people a Declaration of Independence and for other purposes." The people of Tennessee acquisced in this usurpation; and, by an apparent majority, adopted this "Declaration of Independence." The men, who passed this act to submit said Declaration to the people, had no legal authority to pass it. The act was and is an absolute nullity, and the vote under it is void. But nevertheless, the people acquiesce; they will not exercise their lawful powers; but permit their will to be usurped by a handful of their fellow citizens. I suppose no one can say, that a government thus organized and conducted is a "republican form of government". If so, it follows, that the United States are bound to perform the duty assigned to them by their Constitution, Article IV Section IV, that is,—To guaranty to Tennessee a republican form of government, to protect it against invasion, and against domestic violence. And it is this duty, you have been commissioned to discharge. To enable you to perform it, you are clothed with military character and authority. For, it is in this character and by this authority only, that *invasion and domestic violence* can be repelled. The invaders, the men guilty of this violence are to be expelled from every cranny of the state. The civil authority must be organized, in every department, *great & small*, so that the people of Tennessee shall enjoy what they had always enjoyed till the 6th of May, 1861. The traitors, who assumed to sell the thews and sinews[3] of the people of Tennessee to the President of the Confederate States, must be driven from the country, or must be made to suffer the pe[n]alties of Treason. Every man, in office, who acts in the interest of the usurped government, whether his office be municipal, or State, must be declared illegally exercising his office, and be ejected from it. Till the regular election for all offices come round, these offices must be filled, under the authority of United States, and the United States will continue to guaranty to the people a legal and constitutional protection from invasion and domestic violence, until those disposed to invade the State and to commit violence, are brought to punishment or driven away.

R. J. Meigs.

You have a right to compel the aldermen and council men of Nashville to take an oath to support the Constitution of the U.S. But, if they take it, you must let them alone in their offices; whereas I think they ought to [be] ejected at once. In short my opinion is, you will have to resort to the salutary authority of military restraint.

ALS, DLC-JP.
  1. Alexander the Great invaded Asia in 334 B.C. with an army of about 35,000 men. *Encyclopaedia Britannica* (1973 ed.), I, 572.
  2. After an address on April 30 by Henry W. Hilliard of Alabama, Jefferson Davis' special agent to Tennessee, the legislature adopted a resolution requesting the governor to appoint three commissioners who would be authorized to unite the state in a military league with the Confederacy. Harris appointed Henry, Totten, and Barrow as commissioners to confer with Hilliard; these men drew up the "Convention Between the State of Tennessee and the Confederate States of America" which temporarily aligned the state with the Confederacy until a popular referendum could legitimize the union. White, *Messages*, V, 288-93.
  3. A figurative allusion to the strength and resources of the state.

From Farmar Burn

March 17, 1862, Philadelphia, Pa.; ALS, DLC-JP.

Requests information about nephew, Joseph Burn, a watchmaker in Bristol, Tennessee, who "left that place for Rodgersvill some 8 or 10 months ago, his parents are extreemly ancious to know what has become of him, wife & 2 children, as for myself if he has voluntarly connected himself with the Rebels let him go for what he is worth, as I never wish to hear of him again, hopeing that the first Triger he pulls on his Countrymen may be his last."

To Stanley Matthews, Nashville[1]

Executive Office,
Nashville March 17th. 1862

Colonel—

You are hereby directed to take immediate possession of the Building Fixtures and appurtenances in this City, Known as the Bank of Tennessee, and hold it and its contents securely until further orders.

You will also search for and, if found, bring to me at the Capitol the Records, files, papers and seals belonging to the Circuit and District Courts of the United States and of any pretended judicial tribunal professing to act under the jurisdiction and by the authority of the self styled Southern Confederacy.

Very Respectfully Your Obt. Sevt.

Andrew Johnson

Col. S. Matthews,
Provost Marshal &C

Ex. Record Book (1862-63), DLC-JP4C.
1. Stanley Matthews (1824-1889), Cincinnati lawyer and onetime editor of the *Morning Herald* (1846-47), served as lieutenant colonel of the 23rd Ohio Inf., and colonel of the 51st; as the latter he was provost marshal of Nashville. Resigning from the army, he was elected judge of the Cincinnati Superior Court (1863), became United States senator (1877-79), and spent his last years as an associate justice of the Supreme Court (1881-89). Charles T. Greve, *Centennial History of Cincinnati* (2 vols., Chicago, 1904), I, 766-67; *History of Cincinnati and Hamilton County* (Cincinnati, 1894), 191-92; *DAB*, XII, 418-20.

Appeal to the People of Tennessee[1]

March 18, 1862

Fellow-Citizens:

Tennessee assumed the form of a body politic, as one of the United States of America, in the year seventeen hundred and ninety-six, at once entitled to all the privileges of the Federal Constitution, and bound by all its obligations. For nearly sixty-five years she continued in the enjoyment of all her rights, and in the performance of all her duties, one of the most loyal and devoted of the sisterhood of States. She had been honored by the elevation of two of her citizens to the highest place in the gift of the American people, and a third[2] had been nominated for the same high office, who received a liberal though ineffective support. Her population had rapidly and largely increased, and their moral and material interests correspondingly advanced. Never was a people more prosperous, contented and happy than the people of Tennessee under the Government of the United States, and none less burdened for the support of the authority by which they were protected. They felt their Government only in the conscious enjoyment of the benefits it conferred and the blessings it bestowed.

Such was our enviable condition until within the year just past, when, under what baneful influences it is not my purpose now to inquire, the authority of the Government was set at defiance, and the Constitution and Laws contemned, by a rebellious, armed force. Men who, in addition to the ordinary privileges and duties of the citizen, had enjoyed largely the bounty and official patronage of the Government, and had, by repeated oaths, obligated themselves to its support, with sudden ingratitude for the bounty and disregard of their solemn obligation, engaged, deliberately and ostentatiously, in the accomplishment of its overthrow.

Many, accustomed to defer to their opinions and to accept their guidance, and others, carried away by excitement or overawed by seditious clamor, arrayed themselves under their banners, thus organizing a treasonable power, which, for the time being, stifled and suppressed the authority of the Federal Government.

In this condition of affairs it devolved upon the President, bound by his official oath to preserve, protect and defend the Constitution, and charged by the law with the duty of suppressing insurrection and domestic violence, to resist and repel this rebellious force by the military arm of the Government, and thus to re-establish the Federal authority. Congress, assembling at an early day, found him engaged in the active discharge of this momentous and responsible trust. That body came promptly to his aid, and while supplying him with treasure and arms to an extent that would previously have been considered fabulous, they, at the same time, with almost absolute unanimity declared "that this war is not waged on their part in any spirit of oppression, nor for any purpose of conquest or subjugation, nor purpose of overthrowing or interfering with the rights or established institutions of these States, but to defend and maintain the supremacy of the Constitution and to preserve the Union with all the dignity, equality and rights of the several States unimpaired; and that as soon as these objects are accomplished, the war ought to cease."[3] In this spirit, and by such co-operation, has the President conducted this mighty contest, until, as Commander-in-chief of the Army, he has caused the national flag again to float undisputed over the Capitol of our State. Meanwhile the State government has disappeared. The Executive has abdicated; the Legislature has dissolved; the Judiciary is in abeyance. The great ship of state, freighted with its precious cargo of human interests and human hopes, its sails all set, and its glorious old flag unfurled, has been suddenly abandoned by its officers and mutinous crew, and left to float at the mercy of the winds, and to be plundered by every rover upon the deep. Indeed the work of plunder has already commenced. The archives have been desecrated; the public property stolen and destroyed; the vaults of the State Bank violated, and its treasures robbed, including the funds carefully gathered and consecrated for all time to the instruction of our children.[4]

In such a lamentable crisis, the Government of the United States could not be unmindful of its high Constitutional obligation to guarantee to every State in this Union a republican form of government,[5] an obligation which every State has a direct and immediate interest in having observed towards every other State; and from which, by no action on the part of the people in any State, can the Federal Government be absolved. A republican form of government, in consonance with the Constitution of the United States, is one of the fundamental conditions of our political existence, by which every part of the country is alike bound, and from which no part can escape. This obligation the national government is now attempting to discharge. I have been appointed, in the absence of the regular and established State authorities, as Military Governor for the time being, to preserve the public property of the State, to give the protection of law actively enforced to her citizens, and, as speedily as may be, to restore her government to the same condition as before the existing rebellion.

In this grateful but arduous undertaking, I shall avail myself of all the aid that may be afforded by my fellow-citizens. And for this purpose, I respectfully, but earnestly invite all the people of Tennessee, desirous or willing to see a restoration of her ancient government, without distinction of party-affiliations or past political opinions or action to unite with me, by counsel and co-operative agency, to accomplish this great end. I find most, if not all of the offices both State and Federal vacated either by actual abandonment, or by the action of the incumbents in attempting to subordinate their functions to a power in hostility to the fundamental law of the State, and subversive of her National allegiance. These offices must be filled temporarily, until the State shall be restored so far to its accustomed quiet, that the people can peaceably assemble at the ballot box and select agents of their own choice. Otherwise anarchy would prevail, and no man's life or property would be safe from the desperate and unprincipled.

I shall, therefore, as early as practicable, designate for various positions under the State and County governments, from among my fellow citizens, persons of probity and intelligence, and bearing true allegiance to the Constitution and Government of the United States, who will execute the functions of their respective offices, until their places can be filled by the action of the people. Their authority, when their appointments shall have been made, will be accordingly respected and observed.[6]

To the people themselves, the protection of the Government is extended. All their rights will be duly respected, and their wrongs redressed when made known. Those who through the dark and weary night of the rebellion have maintained their allegiance to the Federal Government will be honored. The erring and misguided will be welcomed on their return. And while it may become necessary, in vindicating the violated majesty of the law, and in re-asserting its imperial sway, to punish intelligent and conscious treason in high places, no merely retaliatory or vindictive policy will be adopted. To those, especially, who in a private, unofficial capacity have assumed an attitude of hostility to the Government, a full and complete amnesty for all past acts and declarations is offered, upon the one condition of their again yielding themselves peaceful citizens to the just supremacy of the laws. This I advise them to do for their own good, and for the peace and welfare of our beloved State,[7] endeared to me by the associations of long and active years, and by the enjoyment of her highest honors.

And appealing to my fellow-citizens of Tennessee, I point you[8] to my long public life, as a pledge for the sincerity of my motives, and an earnest for the performance of my present and future duties.

Andrew Johnson.

Executive Office
Nashville, March 18th, 1862.

Printed broadside; DLC-JP.

1. Reportedly written and printed before Johnson left Washington, and delivered six days after his arrival in Nashville, this address, "intended for the eyes of the Tennesseans." was designed to be conciliatory and to present the military government as an instrument for the restoration of Tennessee to its proper place in the Union. Philadelphia *Evening Bulletin*, March 8, 1862; Hall, *Military Governor*, 38-41.

2. John Bell was the Constitutional Union party nominee for President in 1860.

3. See Remarks on War Aims Resolution, July 25, 1861, *Johnson Papers*, IV, 598.

4. The Bank of Tennessee, the agency charged with handling the state school fund since 1838, was removed by the Confederates from Nashville to Chattanooga after the fall of Fort Donelson (1862) and subsequently to several locations in Georgia before the Federal army seized its assets in Augusta (1865). Though the 1866 law which liquidated the bank attempted to recover the school fund, the state supreme court ruled that, since the fund constituted a portion of the bank's capital stock, it was liable to creditors' claims. Robert H. White, *Development of the Tennessee State Educational Organization, 1796-1926* (Kingsport, Tenn., 1929), 80, 188-89.

5. Art. IV, sec. 4.

6. The autograph draft of this sentence, in the hand of W. A. Browning, read: "Their authority, within their official limits will be respected and observed, during such its continuance by the people of the State, when their appointments shall have been made."

7. The draft: "for the peace and welfare of our proud old State. . . ."

8. The draft: "I point them. . . ."

From William H. Adams[1]

March the 19, 1862
Camp Chase, Ohio.

Gov. Johson,
Dear Sir.

Excuse this Claim on your time. I am a prisoner at Camp Chase was Chaplin of the 42 Ten. Reg. But never took up arms did nothing but preach to and instruct the soulders Religiously, at their request thinking it no offence to any one. My Father has always been a warm friend & supporter of yours, & voted for Mr Dog——s,[2] the last Election. My wife's family is Democratic also & have alwas been your friends[.] I am on the same side but have taken no part in war, but preach[.] in fact I have been oposed to the war[.] I took no oath to S.C.—— ——

I learn that my wife is dangerously ill & desires me to come to her & I desire to go home & stay there[.] if I have done wrong in this I ask forgivness[.] I am all right, & that I am, I am willing to pledge my life property & sacrid honor. If they make me take the oath of alg——when I go home, my life, & family, would be perhape Destroyed. If I ever was consdered a citizine of the U. S, I am yet[.] I would be glad if you can obtain my release you will confer a grat favor on my family & self. I would be glad to mett you soon at nashville on my way home. Jim a free black boy also wants go withe me to his family[.]   let me hear from you soon[.]

your Respectfuly   W. H. Adams

ALS, DLC-JP.
1. William H. Adams of Alabama enlisted in November, 1861, as a private at Camp Cheatham and was chosen chaplain the same month. Captured at Fort Donelson and held at Camp Chase until his transfer to Johnson's Island in May, he was released and paroled in August. CSR, RG109, NA.
2. Stephen A. Douglas.

From Don Carlos Buell

Headquarters Army of the Ohio,
Nashville, March 19, 1862.

Brig. Gen. Andrew Johnson,
Military Governor:

Sir: I have the honor to acknowledge the receipt of your communication of this date, inquiring–

Upon whom and to what extent you can rely for the military force necessary to execute such order or orders as you in the discharge of your duties may deem expedient, prudent, and proper to make.[1]

The troops under my command will be instructed to comply with the requisitions which you may in my absence make upon them for the enforcement of your authority as Military Governor within their respective limits.

For this city, your requisitions made directly to the provost-marshal will be executed by him without further reference. This, no doubt, will cover all the objects you will have in view, and therefore it may be unnecessary to add that any requisitions which would involve the movement of troops must of course be dependent on the plan of military operations against the enemy.

Very respectfully, your obedient servant,
D. C. Buell,
Brigadier-General, Commanding.

OR, Ser. 1, X, Pt. II, 47.
1. Johnson to Buell, March 19, 1862, Johnson Papers, LC.

From James G. Spears

Louisville Ky.
March 19th 1862.

Governor Johnson
Sir,

I have received and accepted a commission from the President of the United States appointing me a Brigadier Genl. of United States volun-

Brothers-in-law Robert Johnson (*above*) *from William R. Carter,* History of the First Regiment of Tennessee Volunteer Cavalry in the Great War of the Rebellion *(Knoxville, 1902), between pages 16 and 17;* and Daniel Stover (*below*), *courtesy Mrs. Betsy Bachman Carrier.*

teers[.] I have forwarded from this place my acceptance &c thereof to the office of the adjutant Genl at Washington City as required[.] I arrived here last night enroute to Nashville to confer with you and with Genl. Buell, but oweing to casualties or incendiarism on the R.Road[1] shall return to Cumberland Tenn and await orders from proper officers.

I desire immediately my Brigade assigned me and field of operations designated.

I deem it proper to inform you that recently the Rebels have as it is believed reinforced at Cumberland Gap to the amount of at least 4000, they are well fortified and entrenched—and have between as it is believed from best information between 15 & 20 pieces of artillery calibre ranging from 12 to 64 pounders. Our force at present is 49th Indiana, 16th Ohio 7th Ky. 1st & 2d Tenn. Mundys Cavalry and Hewetts battery.— Many are sick in the Regiments, Cavalry horses, worn out & much cut up not more than 250 or 300 can perform duty.— Most of the important artillery men sick but in the last 15 days about 1500 East Tennesseeans have come over and gone into the service.— Col Shelly's Regiment is over 800 strong, the others are divided into Cols. Houks, Coopers & Col Robert Johnsons Regiments—but these are all unclothed and provided for as soldiers—

Under all the circumstances, I wish & desire and urge the assignment of at least 10 000—more men on the Cumberland Gap line, out of which Mundys Cavalry should be filled out to a full Regiment, and an other Battallion of Cavalry of 1000 men organized. I take the privilege of making these suggestions before entering upon the duties which will devolve on me for perhaps afterwards Military rules would not allow me so much latitude in expression. On Friday last 20 wagons loaded with Tennessee Rifles passed towards the Gap through Barbourville—but no amunition is there for them and none on the way.— I talked to Capt Brown[2] quarter master &c on the subject yesterday and he knows nothing of any, but will forward it on as soon as he has power to do so. I hope something will be done without delay.— There is a Battery of 4 guns at Lexington for 12th Brigade as Capt. Brown says & for the East Tenn. Vols. which ought to be moved and up with the Troops,—and as I think no less than 18 Cannons or 3 batteries should accompany one division, that is the Division or Brigade assigned to Cumberland Gap.

If I can have the force and of the character suggested above, and Provisions cothing &c. for the soldiers, notwithstanding the Roads are verry bad indeed, you shall in a very short time have the satisfaction of knowing they will triumphantly march through the Gap into to East Tennessee.— The men and stock shall not suffer for Forage or subsistence. I would be verry Glad indeed to see you, but under the circumstances cannot without being a way from the army too long. Write to me immediately fully, as soon as you can,—and cause my Brigade &c assigned me, that I may go actively to work. D. C. Trewhitt has sent up his resignation as Lt. Col. in 2d Regt. Is now aiding Col. R. Johnson in raising a Regt. (4th)   He will take a position in my Staff. Hopeing for an early reply

I am your obt servt.

James G. Spears

P.S. Please give my respects to Col. Maynard and say to him Edward[3] is well & in fine spirits and is rapidly raising his Regiment. Col R. Johnson is well pressing forward and doing well & in a short time no doubt [will] raise his Regiment.

James G. Spears

ALS, DLC-JP.

1. On March 16 at Gallatin, Confederate raiders commanded by Capt. John H. Morgan destroyed two bridges, a water tank, a construction train, and two locomotives belonging to the L & N Railroad. Louisville *Journal*, March 29, 1862; *OR*, Ser. 1, X, Pt. I, 31-32.

2. Simon B. Brown (*c*1817-*fl*1887), Vermont native who resided in Illinois when appointed captain and assistant quartermaster in 1861, was currently stationed at Lexington, Kentucky. Placed in charge of all railroad service, freight and passenger, around Nashville during 1864, he was two years later mustered out, remaining in Tennessee to establish a claims and real estate office with his son, before returning to Chicago. 1880 Census, Ill., Cook, Chicago, 4th Ward, 45; Powell, *Army List*, 777; *U. S. Official Register* (1863), 180; (1865), 169; (1887), I, 93; *OR*, Ser. 1, XVI, Pt. II, 382; LII, Pt. I, 688-89; Nashville city directories (1866-68), *passim*; Chicago city directories (1873-81), *passim*; Brown to Johnson, October 29, 1866, Johnson Papers, LC.

3. Edward Maynard (1843-1868), oldest son of Horace Maynard, enlisted in the 1st Tenn. Inf., USA, in August, 1861, and served as adjutant until promoted to lieutenant colonel of the 6th Tenn. Inf. (April, 1862-65). After the war he worked briefly in the Tennessee secretary of state's office before becoming U. S. consul to Turks Island, West Indies, where he died of yellow fever. WPA, Tenn., Knox: Old Gray Cemetery, 3; *Tenn. Adj. Gen. Report* (1866), 15, 119; *NCAB*, IX, 286-87; Edward Maynard to "Pick" Maynard, September 28, 1865; Mrs. Horace Maynard to Mr. and Mrs. Harper, February 10, 1868, Maynard Papers.

From Reuben F. Bernard[1]

Fort Union N M
March 20th 1862

Hon. Andy Jonson
of Tennessee

Should thair bee volentors called for, for the union from Tenn. i shoudd Like very well to git som position with Troops of my one [*sic*] state[.]

I have served over seven years in the Regular army of the U.S.A[.]

I wer Borned and raised in Hawkins Co. Tennessee[.]

Enlisted at Knoxvill Tennessee February 19th/55[.]

Reimlisted 40 miles Nort Tuson N Mexico Dec" 19th 1859[.]

I wer apointed to the position of 2nd Lt 1st Cavly January 5th 1862[.]

This i give to you to Let you know who i am and what i have benn Doing.

I was at the Batle of val verda[2] wher we wer Badly whiped on the 21st Feburay 1862[.]

I wrote to you on the 18th Inst to Wn but see since that you ar at Nashvill[.] i write this as i would Like to do somthing for my country with Troops of my one state[.]

I give you my position and name asking you to do somthing for me if you can as thair is but few of my state that have remained in the Union[.] New Mexico is a place of slow operations and is Filled with Traitors and Cowards[.]

I will move in one Hower agains the Enemy under a Drunken comander.[3] Such is the Management of this Department[.]

Cal canby is at Fort craig to.[4] will move for this place Soone[.]

The confedrats ocupy Alburqurqu and Santa Fe[.] We air placed in a very bad position at presant tho it may all come right yet if we git our Troops all together which will be a scratch if we do it[.]

Do somthing for me if you can[.]

Very Respectifuly your obedient Servant
R. F. Bernard
2nd Lt. 1st Cavly

ALS, DLC-JP.

1. Reuben F. Bernard (c1832-1903), a Hawkins County native, enlisted in 1855 and remained in service until 1896. Receiving a commission as second lieutenant in the regular army (1862), he rose to brevet brigadier general (1890). 1850 Census, Tenn., Hawkins, 883; Powell, *Army List*, 192-93; New York *Times*, November 18, 1903.

2. In an effort to cut off Edward R. S. Canby's communication line to Fort Craig, Henry H. Sibley's Confederate Army of New Mexico moved north and at the ensuing Battle of Valverde routed the Federals and captured a battery. Boatner, *Civil War Dictionary*, 865; *OR*, Ser. 1, IX, 487-506 *passim*.

3. Probably John P. Slough (1829-1867), a Cincinnati lawyer and state legislator (1850), until expelled for striking another member, who moved to Kansas in the early 1850's and to Denver in 1860. After raising a company in June, 1861, he assumed command of the 1st Colo. Vols. and was ordered to the relief of Fort Union, then threatened by General Sibley's Confederates. Superseding the fort's commander after a disagreement over orders, Slough with his regiment and some regulars, including Bernard's unit, moved out on March 23 to intercept the enemy. He was later promoted brigadier general and transferred to Virginia where he served as military governor of Alexandria (1863-65). Appointed by Johnson chief justice of New Mexico, Slough served until he was shot and killed by a state senator whom he had challenged for sponsoring malfeasance resolutions against him, which included "public assault and cursing of important territorial officials, and drunkenness." *Appleton's Cyclopaedia*, V, 552; David Westphall, "The Battle of Glorieta Pass: Its Importance in the Civil War," *New Mexico Historical Review*, XLIV (1969), 143-48, *passim*; *OR*, Ser. 1, IX, 530-35, 651-58; Jane C. Sanchez, "Agitated, Personal and Unsound . . .," *New Mexico Historical Review*, XLI (1966), 220.

4. Having retreated to Fort Craig after the Confederate victory at Valverde, Col. Edward R. S. Canby did not leave until April 1, when he marched north to unite his forces with those at Fort Union. Canby (1817-1873), Kentucky-born West Point graduate (1839) and Mexican War veteran, commanded the Department of New Mexico (1861-62), before his promotion to brigadier and transfer to New York, where he performed staff duties for eighteen months. As commander of the Division of West Mississippi, he captured Mobile in April, 1865, and in June accepted the final surrender of Confederate forces under Gen. Kirby Smith. *Ibid.*; Westphall, "Battle of Glorieta Pass," 150; Warner, *Generals in Blue*, 67-68; *DAB*, III, 468-69.

From James L. Bottles

March 20, 1862, Camp Chase, Ohio; ALS, DLC-JP.

Incarcerated in "Prison No 1." at Camp Chase, Bottles, a Greene countian, is concerned about his wife, child, and elderly father, "who always worshiped" Johnson. "I hope you will assist me in getting back home again. *Once there*, I purpose remaining there." Hopes that Talbot Greene, an ill sergeant of his regiment, will be allowed to accompany him.

From Merrill Thomas & Co.

March 20, 1862, Baltimore, Md.; ALS, DLC-JP.

Sending Johnson "one of our breech loading carbines with accoutrements complete"; if he gives it a trial, he "will be satisfied of its being the most effective arm for Cavalry service yet produced[.]" Generals Dix and Stoneman have used it and believe it to be superior.

To David Tod[1]

Executive Office
Nashville March 20th 1862

Gov David Tod
Columbus, Ohio   Sir;

I have received your telegram of the 12th ins't,[2] advising that I should send an agent to confer with you in regard to the Tennessee prisoners of war at Camp Chase, together with the list of said prisoners subsequently transmitted. The object appears just, and the request reasonable. Accordingly I have appointed Connally F. Trigg Esq a well known and esteemed citizen of Tennessee as a Commissioner, to proceed to Columbus and to confer with you touching the treatment and disposal of the Confederate prisoners under your charge.

I have furnished him instructions, by which to guide his action. These I have directed him to submit to your inspection, with the fullest confidence that both you and he will cooperate, in effecting what is the great object of our National Government, to bring back to their allegiance, as many as possible of the misguided and erring[.]

I am, Sir, Very Truly, Your Obt. Sevt.
Andrew Johnson

Ex. Record Book (1862-63), DLC-JP4C.

1. David Tod (1805-1868), Warren, Ohio, postmaster (1830-38) and Democratic state senator (1838-40), served as minister to Brazil (1847-51). During the 1850's his dominant interests were the development of the coal and iron business and the presidency of the Cleveland and Mahoning Valley Railroad (1859-68). During his governorship (1862-64), Ohio faced many complex problems—draft evasion and resistance, the activities of the anti-war Democrats, and the arrest of Clement Vallandigham—as

well as the military operations against Cincinnati of Kirby Smith (1862) and Morgan (1863). Failing of renomination, Tod refused Lincoln's offer to be secretary of the treasury (1864). *DAB*, XVIII, 567-68; Richard H. Abbott, *Ohio's War Governors* (Columbus, 1962), 21-37; George B. Wright, "Hon. David Tod: Biography and Personal Recollections," *Ohio Archaeological and Historical Publications*, VIII (1900), 107-31.

2. Tod had reported that over five hundred Tennessee prisoners, mostly officers, were being held in Columbus—"they are all doing well & advise that you send a reliable agent to confer with me as to their future[.]" Tod to Johnson, March 12, 1862, Johnson Papers, LC.

To Connally F. Trigg

Nashville March 20, 1862

Sir: Being officially informed that there are confined in Camp Chase near Columbus Ohio many prisononers of war taken in arms against the Federal Government a large portion of whom are citizens of Tennessee, I hereby appoint you a Commissioner to interpose in their behalf. You will with as little delay as possible proceed to Columbus and call upon his Excellency Governor Tod to whom I hand you a letter. He will furnish you with proper facilities for visiting the prisons and conferring with their inmates. Should you be intrusted by their friends with letters or money or other articles of value and comfort not inconsistent with their condition as prisoners of war you will see the same promptly and carefully delivered.[1] In your intercourse with them, bear in mind rather their present unfortunate situation than any previous misconduct.

Necessarily you will exercise a large discretion to be governed by the circumstances of particular cases. Should you have an opportunity and think proper it may not be amiss to address them publicly. And should any or all of them desire a private conference with you do not fail to grant it. You will make copious notes of the results of such interviews being careful to designate all who express a willingness to take the oath of allegiance and resume their duties to the Government. Respecting all such cases make as full enquiries as the circumstances will permit with a view to ascertain whom and upon what conditions it would be sound policy to discharge.

When you shall have concluded your conferences which you will not unduly prolong, you will prepare a report of such cases as in your judgment, upon conference with Governor Tod, will require or justify the merciful interposition of the Government and proceeding at once to Washington present it to the Secretary of War for his official action.[2]

Andrew Johnson
Military Governor

Connally F. Trigg Esq.

Ex. Record Book (1862-63), DLC-JP4C.

1. This sentence was part of a "Public notice to the friends of prisoners of war at Camp Chase Ohio" inserted in the press the same day. Ex. Record Book (1862-63), Ser.

4C, Johnson Papers, LC.
    2. The following day, the governor, having discovered that additional Tennesseans were confined at Chicago and Indianapolis, gave Trigg similar responsibilities for them. Johnson to Trigg, March 21, 1862, Johnson Papers, LC.

To Edwin M. Stanton

Nashville Mch 21st 1862.

To Hon Edwin M. Stanton
Secy of War

I desire to be informed upon whom & to what extent I can rely for the military forces necessary to execute such order or orders as in the discharge of my official duties I may deem expedient prudent & proper to make[.] I am putting the state machinery in motion as fast as possible[.] all is working well[.] a great reaction is going on[.] the state will be overwhelmingly union as soon as rebel soldiers are driven beyond her border. Please answer immediately.

Andrew Johnson

Tel, DNA-RG107, Tels. Recd., Sec. of War, Vol. 6 (Mar. 12-18, 1862).

From Worthington G. Snethen[1]

Mar. 22, 1862

Dear Governor

I am an applicant for the office of "Commissioner of Internal Revenue," now on the anvil in Congress.[2] Can I for "Auld lang syne," ask you for your cooperation in getting it? I had hoped to have been sent either to Russia or Austria, as minister on the incoming of the present Administration, having devoted a life time to qualifying myself for representing my country, at one of those Courts, extending to the acquisition of the Russian and German and other European languages, but the President decided otherwise, and I retired to wait for another Administration, if perchance it might be of my party and I should live so long, for it had been a cherished ambition with me to fill one of those posts, if the political wheel should ever permit. Last fall, I sought to enter the field at the head of a division of 15,000 men, whom I proposed to raise in Maryland exclusively, for the war, but the President could not see his way clear to act independently of the State authorities, which was necessary to my success. I believe, I could have raised that force before the close of the year, if I had been allowed.

Office at home was then fortunately not necessary to me. I had enough to worry along with, but the opening of the present year brought the storm to my heartheland, swept away my little all, and the wolf stands at my door, to be driven back, as best I may. My profession is *nil* to me here, owing to my openly expressed Unionism and the press no longer affords a living to the pen of the journalist, or I should much prefer to use it, to any official post at home. So I am driven to office for a livelihood, if I can get it. In looking around for a place, there is no one better suited to my tastes, studies, pursuits &c. than the one I have applied for, for I have written largely in money matters, taxation &c. in the public press. Blair,[3] Bates,[4] and our new Senator, Reverdy Johnson,[5] have pledged me their hearty support, and if I can add yours to theirs, I shall feel the President will hardly be able to resist such influence, even if he desired to do so, which I have reason to believe he does not. As you are absent in a field of duty, that will keep you away from the Capitol, till long after this office is disposed of, if I should be so fortunate as to gain your favor, I will be obliged to you for a letter to the President in my behalf, at your earliest convenience, as the Bill will probably soon become a law, and I should like to be fortified before hand. Awaiting your answer,

 I am, Dear Governor, Most Truly Your's In this Common Cause.
W. G. Snethen
190 Hoffman St Baltimore
22 Mar '62

Hon Andrew Johnson
Govr of Tennessee
Nashville Tenn
P.S. I congratulate you with all my heart, that you stand once more on the soil of Tennessee, but this time as a conqueror of rebels. May your brave right hand bring order out of chaos, and reestablish a Tennessee, that shall never again raise her arm against the Union!
W. G. S.

Iterum. I forgot to say, that if I get the post I am asking for, I design, in conjunction with other earnest men here, to establish an Administration journal worthy the name of one, which I can easily do, with my twenty odd years' experience as a journalist, when once in position. I shall then be able to do justice to such true men as yourself and others, who have resisted the madness of the hour.
W. G. S.

ALS, DLC-JP.

 1. Worthington G. Snethen (c1805-fl1866), Maryland-born attorney and journalist, published the New Orleans *Morning Advertiser* (1842), edited the Baltimore *Patriot* (1859-60), and served as a New York *Tribune* correspondent. Compiler of *The Black Code of the District of Columbia* (1848), he practiced law in Washington, New York, and Baltimore for more than two decades. 1850 Census, Washington, D.C., 5th Ward, 44; *Pitts & Clarke's New Orleans Directory* (1842), 377; Snethen to Alexander G. Penn, April 19, 1844, James K. Polk Papers, LC; *Hunter's Washington and Georgetown Directory* (1853), 94; *Trow's New York City Directory* (1854-55), 693; (1856-57), 774; Baltimore city directories (1858-66), *passim.*

 2. First introduced in the House on March 3, the bill which created this office was reported to the Senate on April 10, extensively debated in both houses as H.R. 312, overwhelmingly approved, and signed into law on July 1. No internal tax had been collected in the United States between 1817 and the passage of an 1861 measure which provided for a direct tax, an income tax, and an increase in import duties. The 1862 bill

was even more extensive, forming the basis of the modern internal revenue service in terms of objects taxed and organization for collection. George S. Boutwell, later a House manager in the impeachment proceedings against Johnson, was named first commissioner (1862-63). *Cong. Globe*, 37 Cong., 2 Sess., 1040, 1603, 2611, 2891; Laurence F. Schmeckebier and Francis X. A. Eble, *The Bureau of Internal Revenue: Its History, Activities and Organization* (Baltimore, 1923), 6-8.

3. Montgomery Blair (1813-1883), Kentucky-born son of Francis Preston Blair and a West Point graduate (1835), resigned his commission to study law at Transylvania College. In St. Louis, as Thomas Hart Benton's protégé, he practiced law, served as mayor (1842-43), and was judge of the court of common pleas (1845-49). Moving to Maryland in 1853, he was appointed first solicitor for the U.S. court of claims (1855). A lifelong Democrat turned Republican, he served as Dred Scott's attorney and helped to prepare John Brown's defense after Harper's Ferry. A vigorous Lincoln supporter, he became postmaster general (1861-64), and served as a moderate advisor to both Lincoln and Johnson. After the war he drifted back into the Democratic party, running unsuccessfully for Congress in 1882. *DAB*, II, 339-40; see also Rita Lloyd Maroney, *Montgomery Blair: Postmaster General* (Washington, 1963).

4. Edward Bates (1793-1869), Virginia-born Missouri lawyer, was a Whig congressman (1827-29) and Lincoln's first attorney general (1861-64). A moderate Republican, he resigned because of differences with Seward, Chase, and Stanton and returned to Missouri to fight the Radicals who had gained control of the state. *DAB*, II, 48-49; see also Marvin R. Cain, *Lincoln's Attorney General: Edward Bates of Missouri* (Columbia, [1965]).

5. Reverdy Johnson (1796-1876), Baltimore attorney, and state senator (1821-29, 1860-61), served in the U. S. Senate as a Whig (1845-49) and a Union Democrat (1863-68). Johnson appointed him minister to Great Britain (1868-69). *DAB*, X, 112-14; *BDAC*, 1129.

From Edwin M. Stanton

War Dept Washington March 22d 1862

To Hon Andrew Johnson
Gov of Tenn.

Instructions have been given genl Halleck to place an adequate military force under your command and to communicate with you in respect to military aid[.][1] the department would be glad to have frequent & full reports of your operations & prospects by mail and will afford promptly any aid you may desire[.]

Edward M Stanton
Secy of war

Tel, DLC-JP; DNA-RG107, Tels. Sent, Sec. of War, Vol. 8 (Mar. 13-Apr. 22, 1862); *OR*, Ser. 1, X, Pt. II, 58.

1. Stanton to Halleck, March 22, 1862, *OR*, Ser. 1, X, Pt. II, 57-58.

Speech to Davidson County Citizens[1]

March 22, 1862

LADIES AND FELLOW-CITIZENS: I appear before you to-day under extraordinary circumstances, which, I presume, is understood by all. I am not in the habit of making a long exordium; but, in my crude way, I desire to address you in the spirit of one who feels a deep interest in your destinies. What I have to say I will begin by calling your attention to the time when I made my valedictory address as Chief Executive of your State.[2] When I made that address, I feel sure my fellow-citizens will testify to the truth that the affairs of the gubernatorial office had been faithfully administered, and that I yielded its honors in a state of undisturbed repose upon the bosom of Peace.

How have matters of State been disposed of since that period? I surrendered all the powers of the Executive, and laid them down, unimpaired, at your feet. Peace, with all its attendant happiness, pervaded the Commonwealth then. How is it now?

I have returned to address you, and ask your attention to the perilous and extraordinary condition of things now. When I quitted the gubernatorial chair, prosperity reigned throughout your State. What condition do we find the country in now? Look out, and see what is to be found. When you extend your vision over the vast boundary of this beloved country, what do you find? You see men armed in all the appointments of war; you look upon battle-fields, and see fellow-countrymen bleeding. Why all this? And may I not inquire what it has been for? Why is it that fathers are disconsolate, that mothers and sisters bear the impress of grief and sorrow?[3] Why is this disgrace brought upon a contented and happy people? Why is our beautiful land—the asylum of the oppressed of every clime—bathed in human blood? I hope you will keep up the inquiry. Why all this?

Four years ago I left my beloved State quiet and happy, her free sons and lovely daughters had not a dream of disorder. I return to-day in the midst of civil war and the camp—in the sound of cannon roar and in the view of glittering bayonets. Again I ask, why all this? Sisters, mothers, fathers—I intend to ask you something, and call upon you to hold the guilty responsible for shedding innocent blood.

You know that it has been said, and said to me, that this is an unjust war—that the United States is unjustifiably prosecuting war against the South. It is said the South is carrying on the war for rights—Southern rights. Who ever sought to abridge their rights? The Government has never ceased to respect and foster its national structure. Our pride knows no East, no West, no North, no South—it is purely national in its character.

The inquiry runs along, and what is the conclusion reached? They complain of lost rights; say they have been deprived of just and constitutional rights in the Territories; and for their restitution they have gone to war. Permit me to make an inquiry—in no offensive sense, but simply that I may be understood—another inquiry of mothers, whose hearts are bleeding for the slaughter of a dear son; of sisters, who pass their days in comfortless solitude, because a fond brother sleeps far away upon the battle plain. It is this. What right of the South has been denied? What privilege withheld? What prerogative lost, under the Constitution and laws of the United States? What one? Can you tell? Can you point it out? Can you take the Constitution, and call attention to any right there guaranteed which you have lost? Can you see it—smell it—taste it—feel it? You may tax all your faculties, and cannot tell what right has been lost.

What excuse, then, is there for all this turmoil of war? What has the South lost, under the Constitution, that palladium of our liberties, framed by the patriot fathers of another century? Slavery is the reply. Where has the institution of Slavery been invaded? Can any one tell? In what I have to say, I shall be pointed; address myself to your brains and hearts, to your judgment and patriotism. I can boast of no power of speech; but when I feel that truth and right are on my side, I am emboldened to speak with confidence. In this connection, permit me to remark that since this excitement in reference to Slavery, because I and others have determined to stand firm to our faith in self-government, we have been denominated as traitors. We declared faithfully to support the Constitution, and because we stood by that sacred instrument, we have been denounced as traitors. The Constitution defines treason to be, levying war against the Government—adhering to the enemy in time of war. I was the sworn representative of the people; had registered an oath in Heaven[4] to support the Constitution and see the laws faithfully executed. Because we stand for the Constitution, advocate and maintain the integrity of the Government of our fathers, for which the purest and best men shed their blood; because we use our energies in subserving the great and unshaken principles of the American Constitution, conceived by men who united in their characters the soul of honor, wisdom and prudence, with WASHINGTON at their head; because we work for the preservation in the [four words illegible] of those patriots and soldiers who bravely met privations and death—sleeping under inclement skies, and rising with the morning to push on their standards, braving every peril and sacrifice—to achieve our independence; because we dare stand by them, because we have espoused their deathless principles, we are denounced as traitors. If it be treason to stand by one's country, I am here to-day a traitor in your presence.

I was making the inquiry, "Why all this?" I direct your attention to some facts in our history. In the fall of 1860, you remember the memorable contest for the Presidency. Three candidates were put before the people—BELL, BRECKINRIDGE, DOUGLAS. A fourth was nominated—Mr. LINCOLN. What position did he take? I ask of Mr. BELL's friends, What position did he occupy? "The Union, the Constitution and the enforcement of the Laws." What did Douglas men propose? How did BRECKINRIDGE stand? If there is a Bell, Breckinridge or Douglas man present, let me ask him for a sincere and frank confession of his doubts, under the unprecedented aspect of things, as presented in the disunited ranks of all parties at this period. I was a Breckinridge Democrat. You remember I made a speech on Broad-street.[5] I did not take ultra grounds, many of my friends were displeased. My belief was that BRECKINRIDGE was a more eligible man than BELL; that, from his well-known position in the eyes of the nation, he could defeat and put down secession. He was, consequently, a stronger man in the South than DOUGLAS, while it was agreed that DOUGLAS was stronger at the North. We had reason to hope that a combination of their strength would overthrow LINCOLN. I took the ground, notwithstanding, that, should Mr. BELL be elected, the country would be reconciled. The election passed by, and Mr. LINCOLN was chosen to fill the Presidency. I resolved to acquiesce in the election of Mr. LINCOLN. If his Administration should prove good and satisfactory, there would be no need of dissatisfaction; if bad, disparaging to any part of the Government, turn him out. This would be our remedy, and the most effectual. I was not for breaking up this Government because, forsooth, the aims of any set of politicians had miscarried. If we are to have revolution upon such a pitiful pretext, what stability of Government do we possess? To yield to the displeasure of a certain set or party, so far as to partition a political structure of such grandeur as ours, would be to follow in the footsteps of distracted Mexico.[6] I told my countrymen to give LINCOLN a fair chance; if he sought to invade their rights or compress their freedom, elect another—the ballot-box, and not the sword was the instrument to wield.

In the support of BRECKINRIDGE for the Presidency, I had labored through a fatiguing canvass, exposing myself to all the unpleasantness of travel, and the exhaustion of declamation.[7] I was enlisted in his fortunes for the sake of my country. I believed him to be the safest for the crisis; and I can produce evidence from many sources to justify the belief. Threats were boldly made to destroy the country if BRECKINRIDGE should not be elected. To avoid the calamity, I would make the sacrifice of my health—nay, my life, my all.

Bell men, how can you justify yourselves for the part you are enacting in this bloody drama? Let me ask Douglas supporters, How could you go off into the Disunion camp? I was a witness of the reign of terror which followed the defeat of BELL, BRECKINRIDGE and DOUGLAS,[8] and when the election was over I repaired to Washington. It was there that BRECKINRIDGE showed the cloven foot. South Carolina was basely and adroitly attempting to dissolve the Union. I saw BRECKINRIDGE, and conversed with him; told him the people were all disappointed; that we had all been caught in a snap;[9] Secessionists would break up the Union. Said he, "Would you coerce a State?" I replied, "It is our duty to save the Government." "Will you coerce?" he demanded.[10] "Don't repeat the observation," I rejoined. "We are obliged to sustain the laws when disregarded, they should be enforced. If South Carolina would defy the power of the Government, and attempt to extend the defection to other States, duty compelled us to assert the majesty of the law, and enforce its provisions. Whether it is to operate upon one man or a State, enforce the law.[11] If the Government does not possess the power to protect its laws from wanton violation, it is no Government at all. The first thing impressed upon my mind when a boy, was the sacredness, the inviolableness of my country's laws. The soul of liberty is the love of law. If this be so, and you have no authority to enforce, you have no law to protect the weak and defy the strong.

What rights have been wrested from you? Has your family been interfered with? What does it amount to? Remember that families make communities, communities make counties, and counties make States. Preserve the whole; carefully guard its important unity. Commit no encroachments upon its interests, lest the fabric tumble, like a rope of sand, into ruins.

My interview with BRECKINRIDGE—it was like an iceburg in my bosom. To Mr. BRECKINRIDGE, I said: Sir, your strength has failed to satisfy the country. Said he: "I am disappointed in my calculations; I firmly believed myself capable of carrying the Border States."[12] Are you willing to disunite the States because of Mr. LINCOLN's success, and because discontented South Carolina agitates the subject? To this question BRECKINRIDGE replied in *ad captandum* slang about subjugation and the horrors of a civil conflict, convincing me that he had gone into the arms of disunion.[13] We separated. I turned back on him and said: You deceived me then—that was your fault; but when you deceive me again, it will be mine. [Laughter.]

Let me ask Bell, Breckinridge and Douglas men what was left for them to do? There was but one duty unperformed. What rights have you not been protected in? I entreated them to be prepared now to come forward as a band of brothers, gather around the altar of our country, with the Constitution, and swear that all shall sink, but preserve the Government.

In returning to my native State, I offer the olive branch in one hand, and the Constitution in the other. With and for it I have come to perish; if needs be; to pour out my blood a free libation[14] for its preservation. The Federal Government is made responsible for this war by the men who have entailed its horrors upon the country by crying out that their pretended rights are gone. Let us forget all prejudices, and see the question as it is.

The Slavery question is a mere pretext for the present state of the country. Knowing that fifteen States are interested in the institution, the ambitious and disappointed partisans of the South have thought by this means to irritate the people, and promote their own selfish machinations.

What pledge have I ever made and not fulfilled—what obligations have I broke, that I deserve to be denounced and persecuted? It is you, who have countenanced this rebellion, that are in the wrong. I merit not your anger for lifting my voice for the perpetuity of our Government. I have not deserted the old principles that underlie our Constitution. You are at fault. I have never deviated from the beaten track.

In 1832 I remember to have read the proclamation of President JACKSON;[15] felt that it contained the only doctrine to secure the preservation of the Government. It was sustained by those master statesmen, WEBSTER, CLAY and JACKSON. I stand now as they stood in the first storm of State; and for this I am persecuted. Do not be angry, but come up, show your manhood, acknowledge the error of your purpose and resolve to support the United States Government—the greatest and best fabrication of God and man.

In 1832—the year of nullification—JACKSON wrote a letter to Mr. CRAWFORD, of Georgia.[16] I invite your attention to it. What did he say? There existed an effort to break up the Government. It is now twenty-nine years; and, were it possible, many of you differed with him then; none can differ now. Were it possible for Old Hickory to return among us, what would be his treatment of Southern traitors, is illustrated in the answer of an old man who knew and loved him well. "If the 'stars and bars' should be planted over the General's grave, what would he say?" I would expect to see the old man jump from his grave, and order the last traitor to be ignominiously hung![17]

I was going to say, that if what is now transpiring could be made known to the slumbering hero and statesman—his sensitiveness so acute, his love of justice so uncontrollable—he would rise from the tomb and, in thunder tones, declare the "Union must and shall be preserved."

I hold in my hand the original manuscript letter. He tells CRAWFORD that if he had had time, he would have put nullification down. Tariff was the pretext then. He shows that the tariff embraced principles only in consonance with the Constitution. He proves the real object to have been disunion.

As the tariff was a pretext in 1842 [sic], the Slavery or negro question is the pretext now. How do the facts stand? When we come to examine, look at the proceedings of the last Congress. What was the true phase of the times? A compromise, you remember—the Crittenden proposition—was introduced. The Southern Senators, including BENJAMIN, TOOMBS, IVERSON,[18] and a list of others, pretended that if the measure passed, the South would not be satisfied. They desired everything else but compromise. Senator CLARK[19] offered an amendment which he believed would be acceptable to the South. I had critically kept pace with these pretenders. Their protest was only to disguise their real intentions, when the vote was put on CLARK's Amendment—mark well—only fifty-five ballots were recorded. The amendment was adopted by two votes, thus defeating the original compromise. Who is responsible for this work of destruction? Six Southern Senators refusing to record their votes.[20] If the Crittenden compromise had been adopted, they would have been deprived of a pretext for their treason. JUDITH [*sic*] BENJAMIN, a sneaking, Jewish, unconscionable traitor, was seated at my side when the vote was being taken. I told him it was his duty to come to the relief of the country by voting upon this important proposition. He sneeringly answered that "when he wanted my advice he would make the request." I said, you are a Senator, and I demand that your vote be recorded. With six others, he contrived to defeat the measure by slipping out.[21] They wanted no compromise. This, then, has caused the present difficulties? These six Senators destroyed the compromise, upon which they based revolution. Let us examine ourselves, gentlemen, and females, too, that we may arraign the guilty ones at the shrine of public suffering. Did LINCOLN dissolve the Union? Did Republicans distract and divide our nation? No. Who, then are to blame? Men, who in themselves were capable of averting the storm, and yet cried there was no hope for the South—no escape from subjugation!

You know the clamor has been raised that the nonslaveholding States would amend the Constitution, so as to legislate upon the subject of Slavery. On the 20th of December South Carolina passed an ordinance of secession—took Fort Moultrie—revolution commenced. Soon after South Carolina went out, seven other States followed. Their argument was, that the Free States would interfere with their peculiar institution by legislation.

By the withdrawal of these States, the power was conferred upon Congress so to legislate. Having the power, did they amend the Constitution? No. While they had the power, and fourteen Southern Senators were not there to say three-fourths does so and so, instead of legislating, what do they do? I ask for letting justice be done, though the Heavens fall. They come forward with an amendment *forbidding* any interference with Slavery where it exists.[22] The amendment was passed by a vote of two-thirds. Why did not you Tennesseeans take it up, instead of being governed by a petty tyrant?[23]

I wish to pay my respects to gentlemen who have been deprived of their rights in the Territories. We have had some clamorous harangues about rights; the most of them have proceeded from noisy dissolutionists, who never owned a negro; they have been terribly disturbed. I myself owned a few—only seven—and I expect they cost me more labor than those who owned a hundred.

During the last session of Congress three Territorial bills were passed, and afterward an amendment was adopted taking the power away from Congress to legislate upon the subject of Slavery. The three bills organizing the Territories of Dacotah, Nevada and Colorado provide that the Legislature shall have no power to interfere with the private property of citizens; defines slaves to be private property; that no tax shall be laid on him (the citizen) to drive him out of the Territories.[24]

How much of the question is left for Secessionists? Their Senators defeated a proposition, offered in a spirit of fairness and cordiality, and which, if accepted, would have restored the Government, and no blood would have flowed upon our consecrated soil.

What rights have they lost? Can they tell? I point them to the Territorial bills and amendment.[25] There is a party in existence who want dissolution and a Southern Confederacy. Slavery is the hobby. SUMNER wants the Government broke.[26] Abolitionists hold that if Slavery survives the Union cannot endure. Secessionists argue that if the Union continues, Slavery is lost. Abolitionists want no compromise; but they regard peaceable secession as a humbug. The two occupy the same ground. Why? Abolition is dissolution; dissolution is secession; one is the other. Both are striving to accomplish the same object. One thinks it will destroy, the other save Slavery.

If the Southern Senators were sincere, all their apprehensions about LINCOLN showed a wonderful lack of sagacity. When Mr. LINCOLN came into power on the 4th of March, he had six of a majority against him. He was powerless for evil. He could not form his Cabinet without our approval; he could not send a Minister to a foreign Court—we had the power to reject treaties entered into by Envoys; he could not send a Consul abroad. LINCOLN could not buy bread and meat without our cooperation. Where was the danger, then? Why not remain and control his action? Hence, all pretext for the crime of secession is unreasonable and silly.

In this connection, I must be permitted to repeat that, after establishing the truth, that negroes have been the excuse for all the scenes of domestic butchery and the confused scenes of war which have darkened the history of 1861-62 the authors of this commotion had in view some startling conspiracy.

Something underlies their conduct, showing Slavery to be nothing more than a pretext. I was taught, in my earliest days, to believe the United States capable of self-government; but a certain portion of the North and South repudiate that doctrine. The great boast of the Secessionists was, if the Government would [not] permit them to separate peaceably, after the prostration, demoralization, and combined horrors of a vigorous war, the country would submit, and let them revel in the elegance of their stolen treasures.[27]

Who is JEFF. DAVIS? How long has it been since he so scurrilously impugned the courage of those gallant, never-yielding sons of Tennessee, who sought the palm of victory or a soldier's grave on the distant plains of Mexico?[28] Why, you, the fathers, mothers, sons and brothers of those brave spirits, have been taught to believe their calumniator is the very essence of all that is great, glorious and wise. JEFF. DAVIS is the ungrateful beneficiary of the United States. He was taken by the Government, educated for the service and honor of the country. He was taught the military science, and was sent forth with the sword of his country to vindicate her cause. Now, when installed as the chief of an ungodly rebellion, we find him lifting, with sacrilegious hands, the same glittering sword. Are you prepared to make him your leader? Are you willing to bow your necks to the heel of usurpation of JEFF. DAVIS, a traitor to his country and his God, engaged in the most diabolical purpose that ever disgraced the life of man?

What kind of a Government do they want to establish? The organs of secession are boldly taking ground for a protectorate. They wish to become the subjects of Great Britain. I love woman—contemn the wretch who does not; but my love for woman would never permit me, or the good people of this State, to become the slaves of Queen VICTORIA. There are ten thousand women in the United States, all her equals, but not superiors. Her Majesty deserves our love, but we cannot tolerate foreign administration. They talk loudly, too, of a Dictator. The Press is industriously laboring in this behalf. The Richmond *Examiner* and Augusta *Chronicle*, which I hold in my hand, are its strongest advocates.[29] They are wasting ammunition on dead ducks. [Laughter.]

Would you like to live under the dictatorship of ISHAM G. HARRIS? The Memphis *Bulletin* supports this preposterous idea.[30] HARRIS, King! Great God! ISHAM G. HARRIS! I think I know the man. [Laughter.] He brought upon Tennessee all the anarchy and confusion now surging over our commonwealth. And yet, the people exclaim, let us have HARRIS for our King! Think of it! ISHAM G. HARRIS to be your master—the King, Dictator of Tennessee! Where is this self-constituted despot? On the first tramp of loyal soldiers upon this soil, he fled from the State and people.[31] Think of it! I-S-H-A-M G. HARRIS your master—my master! He should not be my slave! [Laughter.]

The time will speedily come when the justly indignant people will hurl this band of traitors from their tottering eminence, and turn them over to the right tribunal of justice.

What more do we find? When the Provisional Congress was in session at Montgomery, SPRATT, of South Carolina, sent in a protest to that clause in their Constitution, inhibiting the African Slave-trade.[32] SPRATT presented, as his basis and theory of Government for the South, the formation of a slave Republic. He said this was the only true basis of Government, that we should have no man interested unless he owns slaves; if it is right to exclude States, let the nonslaveholding be rejected. Hence, we see where we are swinging. Can slave-owners take better care of Government than those who own none? Why change the Government?

Turn to the South Carolina Legislature. What do we find in the organic law of that State? No man is eligible to a seat in the Legislature unless he owns ten negroes and a corresponding amount of land.[33] This is a law of the State looked upon as the great leader in the whole affair. No man, it matter not how gifted with the attributes of a legislator, is entitled to a seat unless he happens to be the owner of ten slaves and their value in land. See where we are traveling. Those of you who don't own any slave property are starting down there to get your rights! They say I couldn't look in! I own seven slaves—less than the required number. [Laughter.] Is this the plan? I have made the experiment, and have learned to love self-government.

I believe that slaves should be in subordination, and will live and die so believing. What constitutes a State?—the political body; not the most stately and magnificent public edifices—not the grandest scenery or the most luxurious fields; but men, high-minded, honorable men, who know their rights, and knowing, dare maintain them. So believing, I expect ever to stand—so, too, the people of Tennessee will stand. An infatuation has swept over the land as a poisonous epidemic—a frightful delusion; the senses of the people have been turned, and they find themselves in open resistance to the mandates of liberty. But Heaven has willed that the light of morning shall return, and before its effulgent splendor all delusive phantoms will disappear, and reason will once more resume her queenly empire.[34]

Having made the inquiry, What rights have you lost? Go and look upon the battlefields, and there, in the midst of bleaching bones and crimsoned sod, ask yourselves, Who are responsible? I have a few words to address to those who are responsible for this war. I have shown that there is no cause. What is secession? It may be traced to the creation of the world, and found to be the origination of sin. Yes, secession crept into the world in the Garden of Eden. The serpent's wiles there deceived and beguiled our first parents. It introduced the poison of secession into the minds of our mother and father. When the act was done, they seceded, and hid themselves. Secession, then, made its appearance with the advent of the world. South Carolina went out, and ran up, in lieu of the revered banner of freedom, the Palmetto flag, or rag, Louisiana seceded, and joined in with—what? the Pelican, (said to have a great capacity for swallowing—like the Southern Government.) [Laughter.] Alabama followed, hauled down the old flag, and displayed a banner adorned with a serpent.[35] Here we see that Secession was introduced by the serpent, and the serpent is at its end. The hideous monster, thanks to the giant strength of our cause, is about to be crushed out.

Who commenced the war? On the 20th of December it was commenced by the secession of South Carolina. Did the United States make the attack? Had the iron-willed JACKSON been at the helm instead of the impotent, truckling old man of Wheatland, BUCHANAN, he would have kept South Carolina.

But BUCHANAN let the flame go on—permitted the stream to widen, and stood by with folded arms and silent tongue, without an effort to arrest the evil. South Carolina went out, and what did she do? Maj. ANDERSON retired to Fort Sumter—a pen in the ocean. Rebel troops were mustered, and Castle Pickney and Fort Moultrie were garrisoned by them. They erected several batteries and breastworks, and commenced the siege of Sumter. An unarmed vessel, the *Star of the West*, was dispatched with provisions to the relief of the starving defenders of Sumter. She was fired into by the rebel guns, and driven from the harbor. Who commenced the war? Did the United States begin the war? The ladies will give the answer to this question. BEAUREGARD[36] was called to South Carolina to take command of her levied troops, and erected works to reduce the fort, to which Maj. ANDERSON had removed his men.

On the 11th of April, BEAUREGARD held a consultation with Major ANDERSON, and demanded the surrender of the fort. Major ANDERSON, who had the honor of his Government in his keeping, and feeling the [four words illegible] in him replied that he would not accede to the summons; that his supplies would soon give out, and he would be forced to starve or capitulate. This did not satisfy BEAUREGARD; PRYOR, of Virginia, was not satisfied. The Virginia Legislature was in session; PRYOR dispatched a member of that body that "in one hour by the Shrewsbury clock, Fort Sumter will be ours."[37] On the 12th, they opened their batteries on the starving garrison of Fort Sumter. The fort was soon in flames, and the men had to fall upon their faces to prevent suffocation. Major ANDERSON surrendered.

Who began the war? Is the Union responsible for it? On the 12th a dispatch was sent to Montgomery, announcing the fall of Sumter. A serenade to President DAVIS was gotton up. He was called on for a speech, but pleaded unwell. But the people were addressed by prominent fire-eaters, who excited their hearers to a pitch of fatal enthusiasm. Glowing pictures of conquest and glory were painted in all the attractive characters of speech. "By the first of May," said they, "the Confederate flag will wave over the Capitol at Washington."[38] On the 2d of March the Provisional Congress passed an act, calling for more men to invade the Capitol.[39]

After all this, President LINCOLN, on the 15th of April, issued his proclamation for 75,000 men, declaring his purpose of retaking the forts, and ordering the rebels to disperse. For this, the capital was to be invaded. In compliance with his duty as the head of the nation, he called for men to rally to the support of the laws. You are asked to join the Southern Confederacy, and to offer the blood of your sons upon the polluted altar of treason. Your Government is called upon to get back by war that which belongs to the nation in common, and which the treasure of all sections has contributed to purchase.[40]

We begin to see where the responsibility rests. I have seen regiments pass through my own county delirious with the idea of fighting the Yankees, and exclaiming, "O, we'll have the Capital in a week, sure."

[Laughter.] You are called on to do what? Join a band of rebels—to engage in the height of wickedness, the most diabolical scheme that ever had conception. Yet, it is LINCOLN's war—an Abolition war. In justice to the Free States, let me tell you that they are prosecuting this war upon no other principle than the maintenance of the Constitution, and the preservation of the Union. I know what I speak—have been in the Free States. They wish you to submit to law. They come in the name of the Constitution, and when obedience is yielded, war will be at an end. When this is so, I welcome the Union hosts as patriots and saviors. I know what they come for, [no] other purpose than to reestablish the authority of the Government, and to reinstate the glorious symbol of Liberty beneath which our fathers marched to battle, that we might have a Government worth maintaining.

It is very easy to talk about Lincolnites. I have shown you who they are. Go through their regiments, and your inquiries will be answered so as to set at rest all doubt. I have repeatedly asked them if the war was being directed to the institution of Slavery. Their reply has always been, "We've got more niggers at home than we want; d—n the niggers. When we have established the rightful power of the Government, we mean to return to our homes and our avocations." This contrivance to overthrow the Constitution will fail. The Government is about to be preserved. Justice is about to overtake traitors who have destroyed bridges, burned houses, torn up railroads, and left sad evidences of their presence throughout the States. Because they have not succeeded, you must suffer. In despair they call upon you to destroy your property. Will you do it?

Let me say to a large proportion of those who have been engaged in this bloody and disgraceful business, through the deception of others, that I welcome them back to loyalty. But treason must be punished. Their enormous offence is indelibly written upon the heart of this country, and when they are punished the Government will rest on a more enduring basis.

These brave officers and men come in our midst to help us in the work of restoration. I have heard it said: "Look at the legions they are pouring down upon us. They are coming down in almost countless legions. This Government cannot be destroyed; it was spoke into existence by the voice of the people, which is the voice of God. They will come.

> Hark to the trump and drum,
> And the mournful sound of the barbarous horn,
> And the flap of the banners that hit as they're borne,
> And the neigh of the steed, and the multitude's hum,
> And the clash and the shout, "they come; they come!"[41]

I love to hear our National airs—"Hail Columbia!" the Star-spangled Banner," and "Yankee Doodle." They are consecrated by the remembrance of our fathers, and inspire feelings of patriotism and love of country.

Again I ask, what is all this for? Do we not see who are in the wrong? Their castles will fall. We must triumph. The Government will succeed. It is my honest conviction that the only security for the institution of Slavery is in preserving the Constitution. If you want to enjoy your slave property unmolested, seek to restore the protection of the Government. You have seen who commenced the war. You have heard of the slaughter of sons and brothers, who have been beguiled by the serpent of secession. Can the Southern Confederacy bring back your dead sons? Who will bring them back?

Secession alone is responsible for the bloodshed by which, fathers and sons have been torn forever from the affectionate bosoms of their families. Will you not again introduce the Government under which you have shared so many blessings and lived on happily? The sooner you get right the better.

This is Secession! Our beautiful, God-favored land drenched in brother's blood, homes desolated, and anarchy extant, secession and nullification are one, and when, nineteen years ago,[42] the Government failed to crush the traitors, seeds were sown which brought forth the monstrous crimes of this revolution. Will we have more bloodshed? Call your sons back. Let the leaders be punished with the severity which their offense deserves.[43] I have no intention of speaking harshly. I have spoken in earnest. It is a part of my nature, and when the passions speak rudely, allowance should be made for the provocative [sic], as in this instance it is unparalleled.

Look beyond the mountains—the proud-created mountains of East Tennessee. I know you have had a hard time, a troublesome time, here in the middle division, where secession had its origin. But go with me beyond the mountains. When the State was voted out by four to one, the people up there, who knew the wickedness of disruption, held a Convention, and appealed to be let alone in the enjoyment of their honest political opinions. What was the response? The threatening hoof of the cavalry. This request was repeated over and over again. The dastardly reply was the bayonets of a myriad of infantry. What followed? Columns of riotous soldiery pressed along the railroads, committing every offence in the catalogue—insulting our wives and daughters, plundering our dwellings, scattering haystacks, pillaging the drawers of poor and honest laborers, without a shade of respect for their wants and sufferings. We were to be subjugated and coerced. In violation of our sacred bill of rights, which guarantees to all the privilege of bearing arms, our arms were taken away. We were left at the mercy of an intoxicated rabble, who knew not the feelings of humanity. They came to my own little village, during my absence in Washington. My wife, with her young child, being there, and unprotected, was turned into the street, and my house converted into a hospital.

What wrongs have we committed? We have shown our faithfulness to the flag of our country—have upheld its imperishable laws, and protested against rebellion. This is our crime, the cause of our proscription and suffering. After my wife, with her child, had fled to the protecting roof of a neighbor, and while confined to a bed of sickness, the act of sequestration was enforced to wrest her dwelling, leaving her houseless and the unguarded victim of insult. Even her two servants, who ministered to her wants while helplessly ill, were stolen from her![44] This is secession. Great God! can it go on unarrested in its career of violence and shame? Is there no justice to reach and crush it? Will not some bolt of wrath descend from heaven to avenge the wrongs of innocent men, women and children?

Where are we drifting? Where are we going? Though they endured all the aggravating curses and abuses of their enemies, the unoffending people of East Tennessee were driven from the shelter of their homes. Many of them are rejoiced that the army of the United States has come. We are looking forward to the time soon to arrive when they can claim the protecting aegis of the Star-Spangled Banner, and once more live under the wholesome laws of their old Government. Are you not willing, men of Davidson County, to return to the Government which loves you, and which will give you the same protection as when secession was unknown. They may burn our houses, sack our fields, convert our plains into graveyards, and our mountains into sepulchres, but never—no, never, can they eradicate our affection for the Government of our fathers. [Applause.]

When we turn to the mountains, and contemplate the rugged beauty of their scenery, and weep over the painful treatment of their steadfast, loyal inhabitants, we intend that some one shall march to the top of the loftiest summit, and plant there the glorious Stars and Stripes of America, as evidence of the reclaimed abiding-place of the Goddess of Liberty. [Applause.]

One other fact presents itself to blast the deceptive wiles of secession. They have made the Slavery question the sole pretext for their rebellious acts. Do you know what their Commissioners, Yancey, Rost and Mann,[45] have done? They sent an address, signed in London, to Lord John Russell,[46] saying that secession was not brought about by any apprehension of interference, on the part of the United States Government, with the institution of Slavery. How does this appear, after the great hubaboo about Slavery? This Administration will support the Constitution. I have no hesitancy in assuring you that Slavery can only be preserved by adherence to the United States and obedience to its laws. What else do we find? In a Paris paper, these Commissioners published a letter, setting forth three propositions to secure the recognition of their independence—the first, free trade; the second, emancipation of all slaves; and the third, a limited monarchy.[47]

Negroes do not constitute the question. They are willing to sacrifice the negroes for the sake of consummating their aristocratic purposes. They say Congress passed resolutions declaring the war to be prosecuted for the protection of Slavery! That the Senate and House concurred in their passage! And yet their plea for beginning this infamous war was that Slavery was to be abolished—their peculiar institution was to perish by Republican legislation.

I call upon you to lay aside all prejudices, and meet the question in its real phase. Let me ask the intelligent mass before me to look at the question in its true light. You can arrive at but one decision. Come around the altar of your country, and again stand by the flag of freedom, beneath which your institutions have ever reposed securely—echo and re-echo the living words of one of our illustrious founders, "Liberty and Union, one and inseparable, now and forever."[48] Let us be our masters—gather around the shrine of America, with the undying sentiment, "The Cross first—our Country next."[49] Go still further. Take the flag of your country, and bathe it in the blood of those who assail its honor, to preserve the Union, and perpetuate its dignity as a great and unsurpassed nationality.

I have spoken much longer than was my intention. But I wish to add a word to the ladies. Woman is deeply interested in the issue of this rebellion. Their influence is powerful. It is instinctive to love woman, and therefore her privileges are most certain to be protected. She possesses power and strength to soften the passions of man. Why should she not love Union? In ancient times, when countries were invaded and cities besieged, historians tell us woman came forward and stripped her person of jewelry, and offered up their all to aid the cause of the country; their silken tresses were woven into bow-strings to send the deadly shafts of the archers into the bosoms of their foe. The war is not over yet, but soon will be. Woman can aid us with a powerful influence.

Rather should the Government fail than to prosecute its work without the countenance of woman. Let them devote themselves to their country; say to their husbands who hesitate, your country needs your strong arms. Remember the Grecian mother, who placed a sword in the hands of her only boy, and bade him go forth to repel the enemies of his soil. The youth, taking the weapon in his fingers and holding it by the hilt and point of the blade, said to his mother, "The sword is too short." "Never mind that, my son, if the blade is short take one step forward, and it will be long enough!"[50] [Applause] Let us have the smiles, the heroism of woman, that we may exclaim, as in times gone by, "This is our country—our united and free country!"[51] [Applause.]

Congress and all say it is the purpose to restore that Government, of which we have made a fair experiment and found to meet every expectation of freemen. The power vested in me as the Acting Governor of your State will be exercised temperately. But I shall leave no stone unturned. I shall call around me, to fill the Executive offices, gentlemen of undoubted ability and loyalty. When the people of Tennessee have the opportunity of choosing, at the ballot-box, men of their preference for the administration of the State Government, I shall give up my authority, as on a former occasion. The law must be enforced; the Constitution must be preserved. Are you so weak-minded as to suppose that the Government will not mete out punishment to those who have trifled with its power? They must suffer. You who have brought death and destruction upon the victims of this unrighteous outbreak, shall take care of their suffering children, if the power lies in me. [Sensation.]

A word about the guerrillas infesting our State. If their depredations are not stopped, they shall be held to a terrible accountability. How has the war been conducted by secession? They say the people of East Tennessee have burned bridges and resorted to other acts of violence, to drive Secessionists out of there. Benjamin instructs the military to catch and hang all who dispute their authority, and leave their bodies to rot in the sun! This is secession. Is there any outrage half so revolting in its magnitude? Union men are apprehended, a mock trial is had, and they are condemned to die upon the tree nearest the railroad, that the passing soldiery may hoot at them, and thrust their bodies with bayonets and sticks![52] And such fiends talk of clemency! Heaven could not forgive their audacity.[53]

While visiting the military prison houses of the North, I received many entreaties to intercede for the unfortunate inmates, who had been torn from the endearing scenes of home, and the embraces of loving families.[54] Direct your efforts to the prisons of Alabama, where men, innocent of any crime but devotion to the Union, are incarcerated, suffering all the miseries of a neglected military jail.[55] Unite in procuring the release of these sufferers, and your own firesides will be gladdened by the presence of long-absent sons and fathers.

Did I hear some one hiss? [A Voice—"Yes."] Well, I believe there are but two animate things in the world, besides man, that ever hiss, the serpent in his venom, the goose in his simplicity. [Laughter.]

When a man hisses a speaker, it is owing to the absence of brains!

Ladies and gentlemen, I will not detain you longer. Permit me to return my kind thanks for the attention you have given me throughout. I thank you sincerely.[56]

New York *Times*, April 1, 1862.

1. Johnson's first formal address as military governor was delivered shortly before noon to a capacity crowd in the state house of representatives. According to one

observer, "The blue overcoats of the soldiers were surrounded and almost hid by the brown jeans of the farmer. Broadbrims preponderated, and there was but a sprinkling of blue caps. The audience was native and to the manor [sic] born." City folk were conspicuous by their relative scarcity. Johnson spoke for nearly three hours after a military band played "several old-time favorite airs" and "Hail Columbia." Cincinnati *Commercial*, March 28, 29, 1862.

2. See Valedictory Address, November 3, 1857, *Johnson Papers*, II, 511-12.

3. At this point another version quotes Johnson as asking: "Why is the matron clothed in black and bathed in tears?"—a phrase less rhetorical than descriptive, according to a local reporter. "About forty or fifty ladies sat near the speaker—most of them in black, with their veils down." Philadelphia *Inquirer*, April 1, 1862; Nashville *Banner*, March 24, quoted in Cincinnati *Commercial*, March 28, 1862.

4. A paraphrase of Lincoln's first inaugural: "*You* have no oath registered in Heaven to destroy the government, while *I* shall have the most solemn one to 'preserve, protect and defend' it." Basler, *Works of Lincoln*, IV, 271.

5. Probably a reference to his Nashville address of September 27, 1860. See *Johnson Papers*, III, 660n.

6. The instability of the Mexican government was notorious. Following her achievement of independence in 1821, Mexico was the scene of rebellion, revolution, uprising, and disobedience; treason became an almost respectable mode of conduct. Frank Tannenbaum, *Peace by Revolution* (New York, 1933), 75-76.

7. Johnson was wont to exaggerate his labors in behalf of his Kentucky neighbor. For a more realistic appraisal, see *Johnson Papers*, III, xxvi-xxvii; IV, 257n.

8. Not only after the election but during the entire preceding year mob violence markedly increased throughout the South. In the summer of 1860 stories of insurrection, arson, and murder, mostly unfounded, produced such a wave of hysteria that the mere appearance of a stranger in town brought out a lynching party. By the election the martial spirit had intensified; militarism and terrorism reached such a peak that unionists feared to raise their voices. In at least one partisan account the southern agitation was compared with the French reign of terror in 1794. Nevins, *Emergence of Lincoln*, II, 306-8; John S. C. Abbott, *The History of the Civil War in America* (2 vols., Springfield, Mass., 1863-66), I, 71-75.

9. A synonym for trap, deception, or trick. Craigie and Hulbert, *Dictionary of American English*, IV, 2161.

10. The vice president's attitude toward coercion—the use of force to maintain federal authority in a state—was an important issue during the 1860 campaign and one which he evaded, to the displeasure of many prospective supporters. His most recent biographer notes that as early as September 5, Breckinridge admitted the right of secession, thereby denying the validity of coercion; he was willing to countenance disruption of the Union to maintain peace. Davis, *Breckinridge*, 240, 260.

11. The *Inquirer* quoted the speaker as saying: "If one man in South Carolina should rob the mint, counterfeit money, or commit any other crime against the laws of the United States, he would be punished; and it matters not whether the law was broken by one man, or twenty, or a hundred, or even by the State itself, the Government must be vindicated." Philadelphia *Inquirer*, April 1, 1862.

12. According to the *Inquirer*, Johnson declared, "I was deceived in him, and discovered that Breckinridge had no hope of being elected, no hope but for Kentucky and the Southern States." *Ibid*.

13. Here the speaker charged that "As he could not be President of all the States, he was willing to divide them and become President of part of them." *Ibid*.

14. " 'Tis the last libation liberty draws / From the heart that bleeds and breaks in the cause." Thomas Moore, *Lalla Rookh, Paradise and the Peri*, st. 11.

15. In the version which appeared in the Philadelphia *Inquirer* of April 1, he is quoted as saying: "I well remember to have heard read [the proclamation of December 10, 1832], by a man named RUSSELL, while seated on my shop board." Threatening but conciliatory, Jackson insisted that the sovereignty of the national government must prevail. Asserting that South Carolinians had been deluded by their leaders into believing that treason was honorable, he stirred the patriotism of the nation; even Carolinians indicated a willingness to respond in moderation. In this speech the military governor

was attempting to make a similar appeal to the citizens of Tennessee. Robert V. Remini, *Andrew Jackson* (New York, 1966), 134-35.

16. This communication to the Rev. Andrew J. Crawford was dated May 1, 1833, not 1832. See Speech at Columbus, October 4, 1861, note 3.

17. Here, according to the reporter, Johnson "made some beautiful allusions to the illustrious dead."

18. Judah P. Benjamin, Robert Toombs, and Alfred Iverson.

19. Daniel C. Clark of New Hampshire.

20. The six southern senators abstaining from the vote on the Clark resolution were Benjamin and Iverson, John Hemphill, Robert W. Johnson, John Slidell, and Louis T. Wigfall. *Cong. Globe*, 36 Cong., 2 Sess., 409; *Seventh Brigade* (Columbia, Tenn.), April 15, 1862.

21. Whether they slipped out or abstained is a matter of conjecture. Benjamin's biographer asserts that they remained in their seats, refusing to vote; however, the *Globe* reporter is silent on the subject. Robert D. Meade, *Judah P. Benjamin: Confederate Statesman* (New York, 1943), 152; *Cong. Globe*, 36 Cong., 2 Sess., 409.

22. The Corwin amendment, arising out of the deliberations of the House Committee of Thirty-three and submitted in February, 1861, provided that "no amendment shall be made to the Constitution which will authorize or give to Congress the power to abolish, or interfere, within any State, with the domestic institutions thereof, including that of persons held to service or labor by the laws of said State." Approved by a two-thirds vote in both houses, the measure was never ratified. See *Johnson Papers*, IV, 569, 614-15.

23. Isham G. Harris, who had led Tennessee out of the Union.

24. See *ibid.*, 573n.

25. According to the *Inquirer*'s version, the speaker asked: "Who wants to take negroes into the territories, and is unable to do so? Who has lost any rights under the Constitution?"

26. Charles Sumner (1811-1874), Boston lawyer and longtime senator (1851-74)—first as a Free-Soiler, then as a Republican—asserted, in resolutions introduced on February 11, 1862, that the southern states had committed suicide under the Constitution and should be treated as conquered provinces. Johnson's comment was his interpretation of this theory, which critics insisted would spur the secessionists to greater sacrifice, prolong the conflict, and increase the likelihood of permanent separation. *DAB*, XVIII, 208-14; *BDAC*, 1676; *Cong. Globe*, 37 Cong., 2 Sess., 736; see also David Donald, *Charles Sumner and the Rights of Man* (New York, 1970).

27. Secession was accompanied by the seizure of Federal properties throughout the South. In his Senate speech of July 27, 1861, Johnson listed the installations that had fallen into Confederate hands between December 27, 1860, and the following January 11, placing the total value of these "stolen treasures" at $5,947,000, and the loss in arms at $6,513,000. *Johnson Papers*, IV, 209, 625.

28. During the capture of the fort at Monterrey in 1846, Mississippians led by Jefferson Davis and the 1st Tenn. Vol. Rgt. directed by William B. Campbell both participated. In response to Campbell's claim that the Tennesseans carried the day and were instrumental in defeating the Mexicans, Davis insisted that his regiment entered the fort first and that Campbell's unit played merely a supporting role. Dunbar Rowland, ed., *Jefferson Davis, Constitutionalist: His Letters, Papers and Speeches* (10 vols., Jackson, Miss., 1923), I, 61-63.

29. See *Johnson Papers*, IV, 618, 619.

30. In his July 27 speech, Johnson had declared that the Memphis *Bulletin* wanted Isham G. Harris for king and Memphis mayor Richard D. Baugh as despot; here he shifts the blame to the Memphis *Avalanche*. Inasmuch as the *Bulletin* supported William Polk in the 1861 governor's race, it probably did not suggest that his opponent receive a crown. On the other hand, the *Avalanche* had endorsed the incumbent and claimed Harris would do anything for his state, even take a crown—a claim made not because the editors wanted a kingdom but rather to demonstrate the candidate's patriotism and devotion to his state. *Ibid.*, IV, 620; Memphis *Avalanche*, July 3, 1861.

31. Upon the advice of Confederate commander Gen. Albert Sidney Johnston, who insisted that Nashville could not successfully be defended, Harris convened the legisla-

ture on February 16 and at once adjourned it to Memphis where the legislators assembled on February 20. Johnson's criticism of the governor's behavior may be justified. When word of the approaching enemy set off a panic among Nashvillians, Harris did nothing to calm the people or help prepare for the transition; his own hasty retreat through the streets may have fueled further disruption. MacMillan Smylie Watson, *Nashville During the Civil War* (M.A. thesis, Vanderbilt University, 1926), 37-38; Crabb, "Twilight of the Nashville Gods," 296; Horn, *Tennessee's War*, 60-62.

32. Although the Confederate Constitution, Art. I, Sec. 9, did not prohibit the slave trade, it restricted the importation of slaves from all places except the Confederate states and slave states and territories of the United States. Charles R. Lee, *The Confederate Constitutions* (Chapel Hill, 1963), 181. For Spratt's protest, see *Johnson Papers*, IV, 622-23.

33. Constitution of South Carolina, Art. I, Sec. 6. See also Speech in Support of Presidential War Program, *Johnson Papers*, IV, 621; also Speech at Newport, Kentucky, September 2, 1861, note 4.

34. Not found.

35. When the Alabama convention adopted the secession ordinance, the women of Montgomery presented the members with a new flag on one side of which appeared a rattlesnake coiled at the base of a cotton plant with the motto *Noli me Tangere* (touch me not). Clarence P. Denman, *The Secession Movement in Alabama* (Montgomery, 1933), 146.

36. In another version of this speech Johnson at this point allegedly referred to Gen. Pierre G. T. Beauregard as the "sometimes styled Noregard," a sobriquet apparently favored by the Tennessean. Philadelphia *Inquirer*, April 1, 1862; *Johnson Papers*, IV, 506.

37. For earlier reference to Pryor's action, see *ibid.*, 626. "A long hour by Shrewsbury clock," is found in Shakespeare, *King Henry IV*, *Part One*, Act V, sc. 4.

38. For Johnson's earlier allusion to the boast made by Secretary of War Leroy Pope Walker, see *Johnson Papers*, IV, 627.

39. This legislation, initiated four days earlier and passed March 6, 1861, authorized Davis to call up "any number of volunteers, not exceeding 100,000 who may offer their services . . . for twelve months." *OR*, Ser. 4, I, 126.

40. The unclear references in the above paragraph are not found in the *Inquirer* version which asserts that "DAVIS commenced the war, and you were called upon to assist the Southern Confederacy, to join them and take back Washington, which already belongs to you. You are called upon to join a band of robbers and disunionists, to get back what already belongs to you!"

41. Not found.

42. Obviously, either the speaker or the reporter was ten years in error in calculating the time since the South Carolina nullification crisis.

43. In general, the tone of the *Times* version used here is restrained—a reportage not inconsistent with the conciliatory approach which the governor employed during the first two months—but, according to a local version, Johnson, alluding to the role played by leading Nashvillians in enlisting soldiers for the Confederacy, pointed to individuals in the audience and exclaimed "here I tell you . . . and you, and you, make your calculations, for I tell you plainly, you have got to pay the bill. . . . The poor and destitute widows and orphans who have been made so by this war, must be cared for, and your wealthy leaders shall do it." Noting the source of the enthusiastic response, marked by cries of "That's right" and "make 'em pay up," the reporter observed that "The broadbrims and jeans clothing did the business." Nashville *Banner*, March 24, quoted in Cincinnati *Commercial*, March 29, 1862.

44. Evidently Johnson was not above suppressing the truth in the interest of high drama. Although his Negroes, including Eliza's personal servants, had been seized and taken to Knoxville during January, they were soon returned; the governor, before he left Washington, had been assured by his son Robert that he did "not think they will confiscate them." Meantime, Mrs. Johnson's health was "very much improved." Letter from Robert Johnson, February 13, 1862.

45. William L. Yancey, Pierre A. Rost, and Ambrose D. Mann, the Confederacy's first foreign emissaries, sailed for Europe in March, 1861, on a mission approved by the

Montgomery convention in February. Yancey was named head of the mission. Rost (1797-1868), French-born and educated, had been an ardent Napoleonist, emigrating to New Orleans (1816) after the emperor's final defeat. Admitted to the Louisiana bar, he became a state senator (1822) before being elevated to the state supreme court (1846). Rost had been selected for his French background, but unfortunately, his New Orleans accent and lack of knowledge concerning contemporary affairs in France made him a poor choice. Mann (1801-1889), a Virginia-born lawyer, had several diplomatic appointments (1842-53) in the German states, Hungary, and Switzerland, served as Franklin Pierce's private secretary (1853-56), and had written in *DeBow's Review* a series of articles calling for the commercial independence of the South. David P. Crook, *The North, the South, and the Powers, 1861-1865* (New York, 1974), 27-28; *NCAB*, XI, 468; XXV, 371-72; for Yancey, see *Johnson Papers*, I, 185n.

46. For Yancey, Rost, and Mann to Russell, August 14, 1861, see *OR*, Ser. 2, III, 238-46. Lord John Russell (1792-1878), son of the sixth Duke of Bedford and educated at the University of Edinburgh, held a seat in Parliament from 1813 until his death. Raised to the peerage in July, 1861, he held numerous cabinet positions including that of foreign secretary under Lord Palmerston (1859-65), before himself becoming Prime Minister (1865-66). During the Civil War his was an important voice influencing Britain's neutrality. *DNB*, XVII, 454-63.

47. Not found.

48. These were the final words in Daniel Webster's January 27, 1830, speech during the famous Webster-Hayne debate. *Debates in Congress*, VI, 21 Cong., 1 Sess., 80.

49. Not found.

50. Not found.

51. Probably of the speaker's own devising.

52. In a letter of November 25, 1861, Confederate Secretary of War Judah P. Benjamin informed John C. Ramsey, district attorney at Knoxville, that he wished to have the burners hanged near the bridges they had destroyed. After a hasty trial, Jacob M. Hensie and Henry Fry, accused of burning the Lick Creek bridge, were hanged near the Greeneville railroad depot. According to Parson Brownlow, who records this event as having occurred December 9, 1861 (although another report gives November 30 as the date), the officer in charge "ordered these two men to hang four days and nights, and the trains to pass by them slowly, so that the passengers could see, and kick, and strike with canes their dead bodies, from the front and rear platforms of the cars, as they passed,—which was actually done." Temple, *East Tennessee*, 391-94; *Parson Brownlow's Book*, 311.

53. Elaborating on the "terrible accountability" theme, the *Banner* reporter asserted: "Governor Johnson intimated that he should pursue the same line of policy, and guerrillas might expect when caught, to share the fate of robbers and murderers. This part of the speech met with hearty and universal applause." Cincinnati *Commercial*, March 29, 1862.

54. Johnson refers to Tennessee prisoners taken at Fort Donelson and incarcerated at Camp Chase in Columbus, Ohio, where Johnson had visited some two weeks previously. Philadelphia *Inquirer*, April 1, 1862.

55. Most of the approximately four hundred East Tennesseans imprisoned during this period were sent to a new Confederate prison at Tuscaloosa, Alabama. Created from an abandoned papermill, the dilapidated building, situated on low, damp ground and without cooking facilities, was particularly ill-suited for prisoners of war. To make matters worse, the camp was under the charge of Henry Wirz, of later Andersonville notoriety. Hesseltine, *Civil War Prisons*, 63.

56. While the band rendered the "Star Spangled Banner" and ladies congratulated the governor, a reporter noted some reactions registered by elderly men standing nearby. One was "glad that the rich leaders had to pay up," while another expressed hope that Johnson would carry out his plans to hang guerrillas. A third applauded the governor's intent to "reign mildly," while a fourth opined that Tennessee "would be readily brought back into the Union." At this point these "interesting remarks" were drowned out by shouts for Maynard, and the latter responded with a brief speech. Cincinnati *Commercial*, March 29, 1862.

From James F. Dudley[1]

Charlott March 24, 1862

Govnr Andw Johnson

I tak this privlige of righting you this fulins [few lines] hoping that the liberty of Spech may be once more granted to the union men of this state and conty. Thare is a larg proportion of this conty union men ovr one half and have bin so all the time but have bin forsed to tak sids the other way for fear of beeing mis treted and punished by the *Sechesh* hoo rased a company at the comensment of the rebelion and wich company is in the eleventh rigment and this company aged [egged] on by some of the leding *Sechesh* of this conty wich ar hear and, I will give you thar names, perscuted some union men till thay had to flee thare homs for life for only speeking in your faver and in the far [favor?] of the union. Thes same Secesionist ar talking too much and ar tring to git the volinteers that ware at home sick & that excaped from Fort Dolenson to return to the armey. thes men ware forced to goo in the firs place & ware detaled men that could not help them selvs, & ware detaled at the call mad in Novmbr last. Thes men swore that they nevr will fit a nother day on the side of *Secesh*, but thes leders ar tring to force them aught [out]. I am in hops that the day is not far of wen thay will have to shut thare mouths[.] The name of the leders[2] that ar talking is Robert McNeley lat Post Mastr at this place. Thoms Morris conty cort clirk E E Larkins Registr of the conty Thomas Overton R Revs J C Collier Jams Mathis & John Ew- banks lat membr of the ligislatur The lat Senater of this conty Thomas Mcnely[.] I will let [you] hear from him direckly. I am in hops that you at your plesure will ishue aproclamation that may mak the persons a bove named hush talking or confine them at some place as priseners, and this conty will bee all right for the union and more lik it was in Feby 1861[3] but thes vilans ar dooing all they can to push fored the strenth of the Secesh movement and thar is a man by the Name of Ben Roberson[4] that has a son & a son in law that was taking priseners at Fort Dolenson. This man is weathy & livs on harpr [Harpeth River] & wiped the men last somr for expresing thar apions. This man is aking as aspy and went to Genrel Buell or some othr General acting at Nashvll on[ly] last week and tried or asked for transportation to goo to see his son wich is a pris- ner[.] this man is a *Rebel* and avilan of the darkest dy. The lat Senatr Thomas Mcnely this vilan and trator to his cunty & the union left Nashvll the sundy after the surender of Fort Dolenson & The busting up of *Harris* & witthorns[5] rebel legislator & walked home skeard to deth & bleving that the north cant be wiped out in too months as he used to say[6] stay at home a fudays and left with ought [out] the peopel nowing ware he had goan and remand that way till a fudays a goo wen he turned up in bells[7] acting in the chape [shape] of a nigro, and wen fond sed that he belonged to bells estate wen thay thashed him severley so as to lay the trater Mcnely up, and is reported that he is in a camp in Bells coliny and that Dr Slaten[8] is treeting his case. I will be at Nashvll in a short time and will come to see you and shak hands like wee used to doo in other days wen you canvessd this state wich I am in hops you wil doo a gin in a short time[.] I wod send my name but fear that Som tratr mit git holt of it[.] I wll see you in a fudays[.]

A union man

PS March 27 1862 This vilan and tratar Thomas Mcnely arived at home this evning and he ses he is jest from memphis ware he has bin at tending the legislator war wich he is a membr of the senet[.] I under stand that Thomas Mcnely & Thomas Ovrton ar gooing to git up a cav company to drive all the unian men aught of the conty[.] I am in hops that the tine is not fare distance wen we will have the right of spech. I am in hops that you will ishue a procamatin to mak them hush or tak some of this vilans up and thene wee wod have a good time and tak the union though with aught eny trubel[.]

Your Fried &c
James Dudly

ALS, DLC-JP2.
    1. James F. Dudley (b. c1810), a South Carolina native, was a Dickson County farmer and wagoner with property worth $3,600 on the eve of the war. Deane Porch, tr., *Dickson County, 1850 Census* (Nashville, 1970), 139; 1860 Census, Tenn., Dickson, 57.
    2. Robert McNeilly (1807-1885), Dickson lawyer, farmer, and millowner, served in the legislature (1837-39) and was circuit court clerk (1842-62). Imprisoned briefly in Nashville for sending supplies to his sons in the Confederate army, he was released by Johnson upon taking "a modified oath of allegiance." Thomas C. Morris (1833-*fl*1886), Charlotte lawyer and "an outstanding Democratic leader," was county court clerk (1859-65) and represented Dickson at the 1870 constitutional convention. Ebenezer E. Larkins (b. c1813), Tennessee-born farmer, teacher and principal at Tracy Academy, and county register (1848-56, 1860-74), held property worth $22,595 in 1860. Thomas Overton (b. c1802), a Virginia native with an estate valued at $52,130, was a Dickson farmer and merchant. R. A. Reaves (b. c1809), born in Tennessee, was a farmer whose assets were worth $3,300. John C. Collier (c1790-1869), a Virginia-born attorney and farmer with $15,500 in property, was a Whig leader who had been circuit court clerk (1836-42) and clerk and master (1842-53). "Mathis" is probably James Mathis (b. c1815), native Virginian and Charlotte tavernkeeper whose 1860 holdings were valued at $13,137. John Eubank (1804-1891), farmer and tailor, had been presiding officer of the county court for some time before 1861 and was a state legislator (1839-49, 1861-63). Thomas McNeilly (1809-1887), onetime tavernkeeper, county clerk (1843-59), and currently state senator (1859-63), was associated with his brother Robert in a Charlotte law practice. Porch, *1850 Census, Dickson*, 27, 57; 1860 Census, Tenn., Dickson, 177, 179, 180, 181; McBride and Robison, *Biographical Directory*, I, 237, 486-87; Robert E. Corlew, *A History of Dickson County, Tennessee* ([Nashville], 1956), 90, 97, 131, 155, 227, 228, 230; *Goodspeed's Dickson*, 1332, 1345-46; WPA, Tenn., Dickson County Marriage Records, 1838-48, p. 47.
    3. A restoration to the status quo of February 9, 1861, would not necessarily guarantee a unionist preponderance. While the Dickson delegate vote was a clear victory for unionist as against secessionist candidates (813 to 278), the equally revealing vote on calling a convention was defeated by a narrow 9 out of 989 cast. Corlew, *Dickson County*, 101.

4. Benjamin C. Robertson (1809-1864), a Dickson farmer, had property valued at $155,895 in 1860. His eldest son, Christopher W. (c1839-1863), a recent graduate of the law school at Lebanon and major of the 50th Tenn. Inf., CSA, was imprisoned at Fort Warren; he subsequently saw active service in Louisiana, Mississippi, and Tennessee before his death at Chickamauga. 1860 Census, Tenn., Dickson, 149; Sarah F. Kelley, *Children of Nashville: Lineages of James Robertson* (Nashville, 1973), 428; Nashville *Press*, January 23, 1864; *Tennesseans in the Civil War*, I, 285-87; *OR*, Ser. 2, III, 641; Lindsley, *Military Annals*, 561-62.

5. For Washington C. Whitthorne, speaker of the Tennessee house (1859-61) and former state senator representing Dickson (1853-57), see *Johnson Papers*, III, 384n.

6. Arriving just ahead of Gen. Nathan B. Forrest's troops, McNeilly reported that Nashville had surely fallen and that Union forces had been sent to capture the retreating Confederates. Forrest, finding the inhabitants of Charlotte "in a state of wild alarm and agitation" as a result of the rumor, threatened the legislator with "summary punishment for the circulation of a 'false intelligence,' " and calmed the townspeople before moving on toward the capital. Thomas Jordan and J. P. Pryor, *The Campaigns of Lieut.-Gen. N. B. Forrest, and of Forrest's Cavalry* (New Orleans, 1868), 99-100.

7. Probably a reference to the estate of Montgomery Bell (1769-1855), whose holdings included numerous slaves and extensive property, mostly in iron furnaces. Corlew, *Dickson County*, 23-28, 37.

8. C. Slayden (b. c1827), a native Tennessee physician, had $2,500 in real and $3,197 in personal property. 1860 Census, Tenn., Dickson, 102.

From Albert Freerson

March 24, 1862, Camp Chase, Columbus, Ohio; ALS, DLC-JP.

Forage master of the 41st Tenn. Vols., CSA, asks Johnson's help in being released from Camp Chase. As a unionist, he had "withstood every entreaty" to enlist when a Confederate regiment was formed in his home town, Shelbyville, but "After the company was formed, ready for leaving, all of my intimate friends having enlisted, cowardly epithets were hurled upon me, and I was branded with *Treachery* to the *South*—At a moment, when such insulting taunts were uttered, my decision of character gave way, and public sentiment forced me to enlist."

To Nashville City Council[1]

Secretary's Office,
Nashville, Tenn., March 25, 1862.
To the Mayor,[2] Members of the Common Council, Police, and other Officials of the City of Nashville:

Gentlemen—In pursuance of the first section of the 10th article of the Constitution of the State of Tennessee,[3] each of you are required to take and subscribe the oath herewith enclosed;[4] and said oath, when so taken and subscribed, you'll return to this office by Friday next.[5]

Yours, etc.
Andrew Johnson, Gov.
Edward H. East,[6] Sec'y of State.

Cincinnati *Commercial*, April 2, 1862; Ex. Record Book (1862-63), DLC-JP4C.

1. Under special legislative decree of 1858, the corporation was governed by two separate boards, consisting of one alderman and two councilmen from each of the city's wards. Meeting in joint session with the mayor as the "City Council" to transact business, the two boards also convened separately; ordinances had to be approved by

both. The present council which had held office since October, 1861, may be found in the executive order naming the Nashville City Council, April 7, 1862. *Tenn. Acts*, 1857-58, Ch. LXIX, Secs. 12-17; Wooldridge, *Nashville*, 123.

2. Elected by the voters, the mayor was Richard B. Cheatham (1824-1877), a merchant who served in the legislature (1859-61, 1869-71), as Nashville alderman (1858-59, 1865-66, 1873), and as mayor (1860-62). Arrested under Johnson's order of March 29, Cheatham took the oath May 12. After the war he was a wholesale dealer in liquor, tobacco, and groceries. McBride and Robison, *Biographical Directory*, I, 139; Cheatham to Johnson, May 12, 1862, Johnson Papers, LC; Ex. Record Book (1862-63), Ser. 4C, Johnson Papers, LC.

3. A blanket stipulation that all officeholders were obliged to "take an oath to support the Constitution of this State, and of the United States, and an oath of office."

4. The attached was the oath of allegiance which, according to an act of August 6, 1861, was to be required of "every officer, clerk, or employe" in the Federal government. *Ibid.*; *U. S. Statutes*, XII, 326-27.

5. In the council meeting held on March 27 to consider the governor's directive, the discussion revolved about the limited time for deliberation, inasmuch as the deadline was the following day, and around the constitutional basis for the oath. The council's interpretation, embodied in a letter drafted by B. S. Rhea, president of the board of aldermen, and approved sixteen to one for transmission to the governor, argued that the required oaths applied to state and county, not municipal, officers. See From Nashville City Council, March 27, 1862.

6. Edward H. East (1830-1904), secretary of state (1862-64) and acting governor until Brownlow's inauguration, was later chancery court judge (1869-72) and unsuccessful Prohibition candidate for governor in 1892. McBride and Robison, *Biographical Directory*, I, 226-27; see also *Johnson Papers*, III, 410n.

From Abner S. Boone

March 26, 1862, Camp Chase, Columbus, Ohio; ALS, DLC-JP.

On behalf of his fellow officers—many of whom "have been your admirers & personal friends & political associates in former Struggles for political ascendency"—the captain of Co. F, 41st Tenn. Inf., CSA, appeals "for help amid the darkest day of their deep distress."

From Erwin P. Jett

March 26, 1862, Camp Chase, Columbus, Ohio; ALS, DLC-JP.

Having learned of Johnson's power to pardon all Tennessee Confederate noncommissioned officers and privates willing to lay down their arms, Jett pleads to be released. "I did not enlist in the Southern cause until the 4th of Nov last, and would not have done so then, had not Harris called for 30000 Vols and I saw that I had to enlist or be drafted."

To Silas R. J. Noble[1]

Nashville Tennessee
March 26. 1862.

Sir:

Mr Etheridge,[2] the bearer of this will communicate with you freely in relation to the condition of affairs in Weakley County, Tennessee.

If it is in your power, consistently with your duties at Paducah and the Military force at your Command, to afford the people of that Section of the State a Military force adequate to their protection; and also to supply them with arms and amunition I will be thankful.

Very respectfully   Your Obt. Servt.

Col Noble   Comdt. Post.
Paducah Ky.

L, DLC-JP.

1. Silas R. J. Noble (1808-c1871), Massachusetts native, moved to Dixon, Illinois, in 1841, engaged in business, and served as a Whig member of the legislature (1846-48), register of the Dixon land office (1851), and colonel of the 2nd Ill. Vol. Cav. until discharged in 1863. *History of Lee County* (Chicago, 1881), 183; John Clayton, *The Illinois Fact Book and Historical Almanac, 1873-1968* (Carbondale, 1970), 214; *U. S. Official Register* (1851), 140; *Official Army Register: Volunteers*, VI, 178; Basler, *Works of Lincoln*, I, 474n.
2. Emerson Etheridge.

From William H. Cherry[1]

Savannah Tenn.   March 27/62

Genl Andrew Johnson.
Nashville Tenn.

Dear Sir— I feel truly gratified that I can again have the pleasure of corresponding with you and other Loyal true men; and rejoice at the prospect of again seeing our state freed and disintraled from the blighting curse of Disunionism,   I should be glad to have a chance to visit Nashville and Confer with the friends of the Country—   I hope you will take a firm and decided policy and not allow too much of the Leaven of disunionism to steal in on you under the profession of coming to their senses—espicially careful not to place them in positions of trusts until well tried—   Our County (Hardin) has all the time been loyal[2] and we are ready to Cooperate with you in anyway to restore the State to its wonted Loyalty and true position in the union, and I think if you want to raise a force for the protection of our State this and the adjoining County Wayne will furnish a Considerable force—   Some of us have suffered in Person & property bourne insult and forced off as refugees—yet we are still willing to bear all for the Cause of truth and justice.   as you are no doubt aware we are now under the protection of the Union Army— Any information you may want as to this Section of Country I will take pleasure in furnishing you[.]   the last letters I was allowed to write to Nashville in favor of the Union were to John Lellyett & J. S. Brien[.][3]   I hope both have remained true to the Cause—   let us have as speedy a reorganization of the State Government as possible keeping in view the public safety—and put none but those well tried in power—and I think where it can possibly be done let those who have breasted the Storm, share the Sweets of the Calm—   Will you please write me or Some other friend here as to your policy what is expected of us &c &c—

very respectfully
W. H. Cherry

ALS, DLC-JP.

1. William H. Cherry (c1823-c1885) was a wealthy unionist merchant and farmer of Savannah with $47,500 real and $62,500 personal property; his mansion overlooking the Tennessee River was Grant's headquarters just prior to the battle at Shiloh (April 6-7, 1862). After the war he was associated with the Nashville firm of Cherry, O'Conner & Co. (later Cherry, Morrow & Co.), lessees of the state penitentiary in the manufacture of wagons. 1860 Census, Tenn., Hardin, 4th Dist., 55; Catton, *Grant Moves South*, 222; Wooldridge, *Nashville*, 228; *Nashville City Directory* (1881), 162; Cleo A. Hughes (director, Archives Section, Tennessee State Library and Archives) to Andrew Johnson Project, June 9, 1975.

2. In the June 8, 1861, referendum, Hardin County had voted decisively against secession—1,051 to 498—and at least six Federal companies were raised from within its borders. Campbell, *Tenn. Attitudes*, 292; *Tennesseans in the Civil War*, I, 426.

3. For Lellyett, who became Nashville's postmaster under Federal occupation, see *Johnson Papers*, IV, 62n. John S. Brien (1807-1867), a Nashville Whig lawyer, legislator (1838-39, 1865-66), and judge of chancery (1851-53) and Davidson circuit (1858-61) courts, opposed both secession by the South and coercion by the North, and hesitantly but firmly supported the Union. Temple, *East Tennessee*, 122, 219-20, 229-30; Nashville *Republican Banner*, November 7, 8, 1867; McBride and Robison, *Biographical Directory*, I, 78-79.

From Nashville City Council

City Hall, Nashville,
March 27, 1862.

Gen. Andrew Johnson,
Military Governor of the State of Tennessee:

Sir: Your communication of the 25th inst., requiring the Mayor,[1] Members of the City Council, Police and other City Officials, to take an oath to support the Constitution of the United States, pursuant to the first section of the tenth article of the Constitution of the State of Tennessee, has been received and duly considered.

We respectfully beg leave to submit the following facts for your Excellency's consideration.

Since we have had any connection with the City Government, which, in some cases, has been for several years, we have never before been required to take any other oath than the simple oath of office, to discharge our respective duties faithfully; and upon a reference to the records of the City, running back for twenty-five or thirty years, we find that no former Mayor nor Alderman has taken any oath to support either the Constitution of the State of Tennessee or the United States; but the understanding seems to have been that the provisions of the Constitution referred to, applied only to State and County and not Corporation Officers.

We have also consulted some of our ablest lawyers upon the subject, and the majority of them are of opinion that we, as Municipal Officers, do not come within the purview and meaning of said section of the Constitution, but that the same applies alone to State and County Officials.

Under the foregoing facts and circumstances, and we having taken the only oath ever taken by or required of any of our predecessors, and never having been required to take any oath inimical to our allegiance to the United States or the State Government, we respectfully ask to be excused from taking the oath sent us, honestly believing that, under the Constitution and our Charter, we are not properly subject to such requirement, and believing that the same was made of us under a mis-apprehension of what had been required of us heretofore.

A true copy,

C. M. Hays[2]
Recorder

Copy, DLC-JP.

1. Richard B. Cheatham.

2. Charles M. Hays (c 1824-fl 1881), a native Tennessean and farmer, served as agent of the state penitentiary (1852-54), acting city assessor (1861), city recorder (October, 1861-April 14, 1862), and was later a clerk, merchant, oil company executive, and salesman. Porch, *1850 Census, Davidson*, 48; *Tenn. Senate Journal*, 1853-54, App. 3; *Johnson Papers*, II, 218n; Hays to Johnson, March 13, 1861, Johnson Papers, LC; Clayton, *Davidson County*, 199; Nashville *Dispatch*, April 15, 1862; Nashville city directories (1865-81), *passim*.

To Pitcairn Morrison[1]

Executive office
Nashville,
March 27th, 1862

Col Morrison, Comdr. Post,
Camp Butler.
Sir:

Messrs John H. Duer, S. Hermans, L. Mussay, and John Edwards of this state, representing themselves to be good Union men, desire to visit their relatives and acquaintances, held as prisoners of war in your camp.[2]

As their object is to confer with them with the view of having them renew their allegiance to the Government of the United States and become good and loyal citizens, I hope you will afford them the necessary facilities for that purpose[.]

Very Respy, Your Obt. Sevt.
Andrew Johnson.

Copy, DNA-RG94, General Information Index, A. Johnson.

1. Pitcairn Morrison (c1794-1887), native New Yorker and so-called " 'grandfather of the U. S. Army,' the oldest and longest on the payroll of any officer," became 2nd lieutenant in 1820, was a captain by the Mexican War, and colonel, 8th U. S. Inf., by 1861. Commanding Camp Butler near Springfield, Illinois, in early 1862, he later that

year was the chief mustering and disbursing officer for that state. After his retirement, he commanded Benton Barracks in St. Louis (1864-65). Heitman, *Register*, I, 729; *OR*, Ser. 1, XLI, Pt. II, 974; XLVIII, Pt. I, 1033; Ser. 2, III, 363; Ser. 3, II, 435; Alzire K. H. Blow, "Olden Times in Carondelet," Missouri Historical Society *Bulletin*, XXI (1965), 113.

2. Those concerned with men captured at Donelson were John H. Duer, or Doer (c1822-fl1880), Robertson County farmer with $5,790 real and $5,720 personal property, father of Charles L. Duer; Sylvanus Herman (b. c1817), Sumner County farmer and merchant worth $12,300 and father of John C.; and John Edwards (b. c1826), also of Sumner, the older brother of Drew, or Drueseph. The Mussey mentioned may have been L. D. Mussey (b. c1839), a Macon County blacksmith. 1860 Census, Tenn., Robertson, 2nd Dist., 64; (1880), 2; (1860), Sumner, 19th Dist., 196; Macon, LaFayette, 91; Sistler, *1850 Tenn. Census*, II, 204; for young Duer, Herman, and Edwards, see also Letter from Joseph S. Fowler, April 6, 1862, notes 2 and 3.

From Robert G. Bails[1]

Camp Douglas Near Chicago
Mch 28/62

Gov. Andw. Johnson

My Old Friend—as I suppose you will suffer me to so call you—I am here at this place a prisoner of war so called.

Well "Old Crook"[2] I will take on myself to Suppose that the how and the way I and most, if not all, of my Regmt. came to be here will not prove altogether uninteresting.

Well Sir I was and am a Union Man and refused to join Davis &c as I promised you in my letter acknowledging the reception of your Speech in reply to them I would do.—[3] They elected me a Captain of a Co, which degatii[?] I declined[.] I was then arrested three times denounced as a "spy" "Traitor" "Blk Republican" "Abolitionist" etc[.] finally Harris & Co issued a ukase for 30,000 men. We were then told that go we must. No deception or artifice was left untried to get us in the ranks— it was the only "Short and Sure way of putting and end to the war"— if we turned out promptly the thing would be over before spring[.] It was publicly said that those of us that failed to comply with the mandate would have their property confiscated. No papers were allowed but Such as they choose to have us read— I was actually arrested for having a copy of the Louvle [Louisville] Jourl in my pocket. But it is useless to tell you who has Seen and Suffered so much as you have[.] I must not for get to say that I am one of the "Brown Jack"[4] and therefore took the liberty to address you as "Old Crook"[.]

Well here we are at Camp Douglas[.] We, I speak of Tennesseans, all want to go home to our families are perfectly willing to take the Oath of Allegiance to the U S A—nay are anxious to do so. Can you do anything for us. We have noticed in the papers that you have allowed a friend with a cheering word to go to Camp Chase[.][5] Could you "Speak a word" for us to the President? I am sure as I am of my existence that 19/20 of us are really true & loyal men to the Government of our Ancestors. Why keep us here when those who stand in Such want of our support, I mean our families—need us so much[.] There was a talk of Sending us home but I see that idea is abandoned[.] I repeat our men are Union Men to the Core, and are politically your friends & Supporters[.]

Will you let us know if you think there is anything to be done for us— Dont for a moment infer that our treatment is bad[.] it is good I might say, even kind but most of us having families dependent on us for Support are of Course extremely uneasy about them knowing well that a parents position is never filled well by a Substitute[.]

Our Regmt—48th—is composed of citizens of Maury Hickman Lawrence & Lewis.

You and your son "Bob" have Shown me in times gone by some kindness for which I sincerely thank you both.

It is perhaps useless to say that I have always been one of your most feeble but most earnest supporters— for that I ask nothing as God knows I acted from a Sense of duty to my Country. I believed then & yet believe had you been at the head of affairs treason would have been nipped in the bud—but enough[.] Please Sir write us if it be not asking too much of you and let us know if there is any chance of us getting to our families any way soon[.]

Adress Rob G Bails Prisoner   48th Regmt Co F Tenn Infty Camp Douglas Chicago Ill.

R G Bails

ALS, DLC-JP.

1. Robert G. Bails of Hickman County was first sergeant, Co. F[I?], 48th (Voorhies') Inf., when captured at Donelson. Taking the oath in 1864, he was listed on CSA records as a deserter who remained "North of the Ohio River during the war." CSR, RG109, NA; *Tennesseans in the Civil War*, II, 23.

2. A drinking companion. See *Johnson Papers*, IV, 305n.

3. Not extant.

4. Apparently a group of drinking associates.

5. The following "Public notice [March 20, 1862] to the friends of prisoners of war at Camp Chase" appeared in the press: "Having been officially notified by Governor Tod of Ohio, that many of my misguided fellow-citizens of Tennessee are now confined as prisoners of war at Camp Chase, I have appointed Connally F. Trigg, Esq. as a Commissioner to interpose in their behalf. I have instructed him, should he be entrusted by their friends with letters or money, or other articles of value or comfort, not inconsistent with their condition as prisoners of war to see the same promptly and carefully delivered. Andrew Johnson, Military Governor." Ex. Record Book, Ser. 4C, Johnson Papers, LC.

To Edwin M. Stanton

Nashville March 28th 1862.

To Hon E M Stanton
Secy of War

It is very important that Brigadier Genl Jas. G. Spears should be at once placed in command of a brigade at Cumberland ford. He is there &

identified with the forces[.] I have this day mailed letters upon the subject[.]¹

Andrew Johnson

Tel, DNA-RG107, Tels. Recd., Sec. of War, Vol. 7 (Mar. 25-Apr. 2, 1862).

1. Adj. Gen. Lorenzo Thomas replied that Spears "could not be properly placed" at Cumberland Ford and that he "has been ordered to report to Genl. Halleck for assignment." Thomas to Johnson, April 17, 1862, Johnson Papers, LC.

From Edward Everett¹

Boston 29 March 1862.

Hon. A. Johnson.

My dear Sir,

Permit me, though personally a stranger, to express to you the heartfelt approbation, with which, in common with all good citizens in this part of the country, I regard the course pursued by yourself and your patriotic associates, now engaged with you in restoring the noble state of Tennessee to the Union. I cannot doubt that the well-considered appeal which you have made to the understandings and the loyalty of your fellow citizens will dispel the gross delusions, of which so many of them have been the victims. It cannot be that, without one real grievance, the state which holds the ashes of Andrew Jackson will long countenance this unrighteous rebellion against the most beneficent government known in human history; a rebellion originating in that state and that school of politics, which, while he lived, General Jackson visited with the sternest displeasure and indignation.

My more immediate purpose, after tendering you this assurance of respectful sympathy is, to ask your acceptance of the accompanying pamphlet,² and to say that, if in your judgment, the gratuitous circulation of a hundred or two copies of it, in Tennessee, would tend, in any degree, to promote the good cause, in which you are laboring, they shall be sent to Nashville, free of expense, as soon as Adams & Co's Express resumes its operations, which will no doubt be before long.

Praying my best respects to my friend Maynard,³ if still with you to Mr. Etheridge, though I have not the pleasure of his personal acquaintance, I remain, my Dear Sir, with the highest respect, faithfully yours,

LB copy, MHi-Edward Everett Papers.

1. See *Johnson Papers*, IV, 479n.

2. Probably his July 4, 1861, speech on "The Questions of the Day; An Address Delivered in the Academy of Music in New York," published by G. P. Putnam; yet there is the possibility that it might have been an address on "The Causes and Conduct of the War," which, according to a biographer, "he delivered sixty times in all, beginning at Boston in 1861, and reaching as far west as Dubuque in 1862." However, no evidence has been found of the latter's having been printed in pamphlet form. Paul R. Frothingham, *Edward Everett: Orator and Statesman* (Boston, 1925), 425.

3. Congressman Horace Maynard had accompanied Johnson to Nashville, leaving Washington on March 7 and returning on April 20.

From James E. Yeatman[1]

St. Louis March 29th/62

Gov Andrew Johnson
Dear Sir

Your despatch of this date arrived to Mr. Hazzard Secretary of Sanitary Comn. is recd—and I responded to same by Telegraph[.]

> Prisoners here are sick in Hospital. Two Thousand Dollars would be ample to transport all such back to Tennessee but it would require a large amount to Transport all the Tennessee Prisoners at other points[.] Hope the goverment will agree to transport all prisoners[.][2]

The above is the purport of the despatch sent you. When Mr. Hazzard wrote to you Genl Halleck had stated that Govemt had made no provision for transporting discharged Prisoners—which is manifestly an oversight and would be unjust to throw so large a number of persons on the Community without friends or money— I have since seen Col Cutts[3] one of the Commissioners appointed by Genl Halleck to receive and report upon applications from Prisoners. he informs me that between Seven and Eight Thousand have already made applications to take the oath of allegiance—. he will report in favor of all privates within our lines being permitted to do so and that the goverment will furnish transportation & subsistance to Clarksville or Nashville— if this is done it will not be necessary to call upon you for aid—but I would recommend that a small sum be placed in our hands (The Western Sanitary Comn) to enable those in our Hospitals to return as they are able to do so prior to the general action of the government— I think we can procure the release of all such as may take the oath in our Hospitals— All that have proposed to take the oath have done so voluntarilly and usually acompanied with expressions of deep regret at the part they have taken against the general Goverment. I am glad to see that they are beginning to see the error of their ways and trust that it will not be long before Tennessee my native state will be fully restored to the Union— If I can serve you or the Cause, or the State in any way I am prepared to do it—

Very respectfully   James E Yeatman
Prest   Western Sanitary Commission

List of Prisoners belonging to Tennessee Regiments and where located—.

At Chicago	Camp Butler
Tennessee 3rd	Springfield
10th	18th Tennessee
42	30
48	32
49	41
50	57[4]

All others at Indianapolis[.]   Company officers at Columbus
Regimental & Field Fort Warren

ALS, DLC-JP.
1. James E. Yeatman (1818-1901), a Tennessean, spent most of his life in St. Louis,
where he was a founder and longtime president of the Merchants' National Bank
(1860-95) and an incorporator of the Missouri Pacific Railroad. Active in many educational and philanthropic enterprises, he devoted most of his time during the war to
working with Dorothea L. Dix on the Western Sanitary Commission, which organized
hospitals, soldiers' and orphans' homes, and distributed sanitary supplies. *DAB*, XX,
606-7.
2. This passage offers the substance but not the exact wording of Yeatman's telegram. Johnson Papers, LC.
3. Richard D. Cutts (1817-1883), a Washington native, son of Congressman Richard Cutts of Maine and nephew of James Madison, became an engineer employed
by the United States Coast Survey both before and after the war. Serving as Halleck's
aide-de-camp during the war, he was breveted brigadier in 1865 and placed in charge of
the captured Confederate archives. Boatner, *Civil War Dictionary*, 217; Ralph Ketcham,
James Madison (New York, 1971), 618; *Boyd's Washington Directory* (1860), 61;
(1866-81), *passim*; *U. S. Official Register* (1859), 23; (1867-83), *passim*; Dallas Irvine,
"The Archives Office of the War Department: Repository of Captured Confederate
Archives, 1865-1881," *Military Affairs*, X (1946), 96.
4. Probably 51st; there was no 57th Tenn.

To Stanley Matthews

March 29, 1862
State of Tennessee,

To Col Stanley Matthews, Provost Marshal &c

It being made known to me by Richard B. Cheatham, Mayor of the
City of Nashville, that he refuses to take the oath of allegiance to the
United States, and to acknowledge his loyalty and fidelity to the government thereof; and it further appearing that since he has held the said
office, he has uttered treasonable and seditious language against the
authority thereof, and that he has given counsel and furnished aid and
extended comfort to the enemies thereof, in this, among other things,
that he has proposed to invite to this City for a permanent official
residence one Jefferson Davis, engaged as the acknowledged head of an
organized rebellion and laboring for the overthrow of the government
thereof:

You are hereby commanded and empowered to arrest the body of him
the said Richard B. Cheatham, and the same to hold in custody until he
shall be discharged by proper authority.

Given under the hand and seal of Andrew Johnson Military Governor
of the State of Tennessee this twenty-ninth day of March A.D. 1862[.]

Andrew Johnson
Military Governor.[1]

Edward H. East.   Secretary of State.
by Wm. A. Browning   Acting Secretary.[2]

DS, DLC-JP.
1. Attached endorsements indicate that Cheatham was arrested the following day
and delivered to Matthews.

2. For William A. Browning, see *Johnson Papers*, IV, 422*n*.

To Edwin M. Stanton

Nashville, March 29th 1862.

Hon. E. M. Stanton,
Secy of War

This place as I conceive has almost been left defenceless by Gen'l Buell—[1] There are a few Regiments left in detached positions without one single piece of artillery— There are one or two regiments at Camp Chase Ohio and one at Lexington Ky that might be forwarded to this point— In addition to the forces here there should be one brigade complete— In this opinion Brig Genl Dumont[2] left in command most fully concurs—[3]

Andrew Johnson

Tel (in cipher), DNA-RG107, Tels. Recd., Sec. of War, Vol. 7 (Mar. 25-Apr. 2, 1862); DLC-JP; *OR*, Ser. 1, X, Pt. II, 76.

1. Buell, commanding the Army of the Ohio, had been ordered to advance with much of his force to Savannah on the Tennessee River near where the battle of Shiloh would be fought on April 6-7. *OR*, Ser. 1, LII, Pt. I, 20-21, 226.

2. Ebenezer Dumont (1814-1871), who commanded various units in the Army of the Cumberland, had previously been active in Indiana politics; serving later in Congress (1863-67), he was appointed governor of Idaho Territory but did not live to begin his term. *BDAC*, 834; Boatner, *Civil War Dictionary*, 251.

3. Stanton replied: "immediate measures will be taken to correct the evil[.]" Stanton to Johnson, March 30, 1862, Johnson Papers, LC.

Re Tennessee Prisoners in St. Louis

March 29, 1862

St. Louis, Mo., March 19, 1862

Hon. Andrew Johnson, Brig. General and
Military Governor, Nashville, Tenn.
Dear Sir:

There are daily discharged from our hospitals, citizens of Tennessee, formerly belonging to the rebel army, who have become convalescent and have taken the oath of allegiance to the U. S. Government. They are in our streets without the means of living, or of returning to their homes. The Commanding General can render them no assistance; it is not within the province of this commission nor are our means adequate to the object; and private generosity has been so long and so severely taxed that it ought not to be relied on.

Cannot your State furnish transportation and subsistence for them promptly to return home.

Very respectfully, for
Western Sanitary Com'n
R. R. Hazard, Jr[1]
Sec'y pro tem

In view of the foregoing statement, I feel called upon to appeal, not only to the charitable, but especially to those who have been instrumental in reducing their misguided fellow citizens to this sad degree of suffering, and who have been co-laborers in the unholy work in which they were engaged, to come forward and contribute to their relief.

Any monies so contributed and deposited with the Secretary of State will be promptly applied to that purpose.[2]

Andrew Johnson

Executive Office
Nashville, March 29, 1862.

Nashville *Union*, April 16, 1862; ALS, DLC-JP [for Hazard's letter].

1. Rowland R. Hazard, Jr. (b. *c* 1831), Virginia native and partner in the Newport, Rhode Island, firm of Hazard & Caswell, wholesale and retail druggists, had been a delegate to the Chicago convention (1860) and served as secretary of the Western Sanitary Commission. Hazard to Abraham Lincoln, July 15, 1861, Lincoln Papers, LC; Hesseltine, *Three Against Lincoln*, 299.

2. According to the editor of the *Union*, the "Nashville Secesh," as of two weeks after this notice, had contributed "NOT A SINGLE DOLLAR" for "these poor unfortunate discharged soldiers," although a year earlier a number of men had offered money and professional services in support of the Confederate effort. Nashville *Union*, April 16, 1862.

From James H. Conner[1]

Camp Chaise, Ohio March 30th 1862

To Gov Andrew Johnson of the State of Tennessee Excuse a stranger and a Citizen prisoner taken at fort Donelson at the Surrender, I was thear a non combattent and only on buisiness and to see a relative who was sick[.] I arrived thear on friday night preceeding the Battle on saturday with the intention of Leaving on that evening but was not allowed as was others debard from it by the powers that then ruled at that place then, I am a citizen of Giles County Tensse, and have always been a good union man, I supported William H Polk for Govener Against Isan. G. Harris because the sentiments of the former suited me, I can refer you to Attorney. J. Walker[2] of Pulaski as regards my Sentiments and others[.] I wish you would extend your clemency to affect my release as I never have been other than a union man and always opposed to disunion from principle,   You would confer a Lasting favour on me as Long as I Live never to be forgotten[.] I am feble and have Been in delicate health for 10 years[.] pleas get me released as soon as you can and I will ever remain Your true friend,

J. H. Conner

ALS, DLC-JP.

1. James H. Conner (b. *c* 1827), a Giles County farmer with $30,000 in real property and $27,000 in personal, was in Confederate service as 2nd lieutenant, Co. G, 53rd Tenn. Inf., and as an assistant quartermaster at Fort Donelson from January, 1862, until he was taken prisoner February 16. Obviously, he was concealing these facts from the governor, who refused his request; he was not released until September 20, 1862, when his regiment obtained a parole. CSR, RG109, NA; 1860 Census, Tenn., Giles, S. Subdiv., 16.

2. John C. Walker (b. *c* 1821) had $12,000 in real estate and $18,000 in personal property. *Ibid.*, N. Subdiv., 196.

From Joseph C. G. Kennedy[1]

Census Office, Department of the Interior,
Washington, 30 March 1862

Dear Govr.

I was most happy to learn of your selection for the important post of Mily Govr of the State of Ten.— it was taking the "right man for the right place"[.][2] I wish what I know [that] you will deserve every success in your trying position— If Cullum (Late Clerk HR)[3] professes loyalty he will doubtless "try to make his Jack"[4] out of the gov't— give him a wide berth—[5] in my opinion, the interests of the public cannot be in any way be promoted by such men—

Nab DeBow if he comes in your way[.] he has not the courage to enter the army while he has been as instrumental as the worst in bringing about the present lamentable state of affairs—[6] Do not over tax your energies but take care of yourself— the country will before long I hope have work for you in a more enlarged sphere— McClellan goes to day to Fortress Monroe whither I believe the largest portion of his army have gone. I regretted not to see yr son when he was here— please present my compt's to Maynard & Ethridge—

With unaffected esteem
Your friend Jos C G Kennedy

Honble. Andw Johnson   Gov Tene

ALS, DLC-JP.

1. See *Johnson Papers*, III, 615n.

2. An aphorism, attributed by John B. McMaster to Jefferson. Stevenson, *Macmillan Book of Proverbs*, 1517.

3. Kennedy may have feared that, in view of alleged irregularities in the handling of public funds when William Cullom was clerk of the House of Representatives, the latter would now try to enrich himself at the public expense. See *Johnson Papers*, III, 285n.

4. A slang expression for money.

5. A nautical term meaning "to keep well away from, steer clear of." *OED*, I, 813.

6. James D. B. De Bow (1820-1867) became editor of the *Southern Quarterly Review* soon after graduation from the College of Charleston (1843). For nearly two decades his *Commercial Review of the South and Southwest*, founded in 1846 and known popularly as *De Bow's Review*, was the leading southern magazine, preaching the gospel of self-sufficiency and advocating secession. De Bow also held the chair of political economy at the University of Louisiana and served as superintendent of the seventh (1850) U. S. census. During the war, he was chief Confederate agent for the purchase and sale of cotton. *DAB*, V, 180-82; see also Ottis C. Skipper, *J. D. B. De Bow: Magazinist of the Old South* (Athens, Georgia, 1958).

From Ormsby M. Mitchel

Head Quarters 3 Division
Camp Van Buren[1]
March 30 1862.

Governor.

I have your note of yesterday and will direct that the cotton be sent forward to Nashville, as early as the Road is opened and sold for acct of who ever may be the rightful owner, which I do not undertake to decide—

I wish you could come to this place and address the Citizens while we are here— We are doing what we can to bring them round to their allegiance— At Shellbyville there prevails an Extensive union feeling[2] and our troops were received with every demonstration of pleasure— Union Flags were displayed and shouts & waving of handkerchiefs came from every quarter—

In great haste.
Very truly & Respy.   Your. obt. sert.
O. M. Mitchel Br. Gen

Gov. Johnston

ALS, DLC-JP.

1. Near Murfreesboro.
2. Allowing for some exaggeration, there is evidence to suggest that Mitchel's assessment was not unrealistic. Voting two to one against convention (and therefore for adherence to the Union) in February, 1861, and only two to one for separation in June (a restrained secessionism for a Middle Tennessee county), Bedford harbored a goodly number of prominent men of unionist persuasion, among them William S. Speer, the Cooper brothers, Henry and Edmund, Harvey Watterson, and William H. Wisener. The county contributed eleven companies to the Federal army. According to *Goodspeed's History of Tennessee* (1886), Shelbyville had so many citizens who were loyal to the Union cause that the town earned the name "Little Boston." Charles R. Gunter, Jr., Bedford County during the Civil War (M. A. thesis, University of Tennessee, 1963), 21, 28; McBride and Robison, *Biographical Directory*, I, 164-65, 767, 813; *Tennesseans in the Civil War*, I, 417; *Goodspeed's Bedford*, 872.

From Isaac T. Reneau[1]

Tompkinsville, Ky., March 31, 1862.

Gov. A. Johnson:—

Hon. Sir, the object of this communication, is, the dection of rebellion and the punishment of *wilful* and *wicked murderers*.

There is a man, supposed to be some where in Tenn., by the name of Champ Ferguson.[2] This man was born and raised in Cumberland co., Ky., now *Clinton*, and is not far from 35 years old, common size, rather slender, sandy hair and beard, rather yellow sandy, *small* head and a scar on one side of his head, *while blue* eyes and *smiling* countenance, and *seems* to be friendly disposed. He shot a man by the name of Frogg,[3] who was on his own bed, and quite *sick*, he first shot him in the *mouth*, and then through the *brain*, the last shot, Ferguson said, was to make him *die easy*. This was done in Clinton co., Ky., some time in Sept. 1861, *without cause!* On the 2d day of October, the same Champ Ferguson rode up to the gate of Reuben B. Wood,[4] a member of the Cumberland Presbyterian Church, and innocent, useful, and popular citizen of Clinton co., and without any assignable cause, only that Wood *had been once to Camp Robeson*, shot him [in] the region of the bowels. Mr. Wood died on the 4th of Oct., leaving a widowed *mother* 86 years of age, a *wife*, seven children, and some grand children, to mourn his untimely death. Mr. Wood was, on his mother's sid, a descendant of the *Bayless* family of East Tenn. Ferguson has been engaged in horse stealling on a *large* scale ever since the great rebellion began, and, it is supposed, has stolen *thousands* of dollars' worth of property. He is now supposed to be united in company with another murderous rouge, of Jackson co., Tennessee, by the name of Oliver Hamilton,[5] who is commanding a small company of marauders in Jackson co. Hamilton is of ordinary height, fair complexion, and rather heavy—about 35 years of age, brisk walk, and quite self important. He also talks a great deal about "*State rights*." This man, with a company of 9 or 10, came over into Monroe co., Ky., on Friday last, shot James Syms, Alexander Atterberry, and Thomas Denham.[6] Denham was shot through the *head*, and of course fell dead, Syms, through the *stomach*, and Atterberry, through the *neck* and *hips*—these both died at 11 O'clock on Sat. night, and in the *same half minute*. These two young men both left families, I do not know whether Denham left a family or not. They were all peacable cleaver men— Their *sin* against the murderer Hamilton, was, that they were *Union* men. Hamilton [said] to Atterberry's *mother* when he killed her son, that he "*would kill* every *union* man that he could find, and, if he could not find the *men*, he would *kill* all the *boys* that were large enough to *plough* in that neighborhood." He did *kill* that day, and *try* to kill, every union man that he saw, and shot at one small boy! These are facts known to hundreds.

Can *you*, Honored Sir, have these brought to *justice*, by *reward*, or otherwise?[7] If you can, you will warm up the heart of many a weeping *mother*, sister, daughter, and wife.

You, I suppose, should know *who* I am. Well, I am a *preacher of* the Gospel, and am a desendant of the Tiptons and Reneaus of East Tennessee, and my own name is   Isaac T. Reneau, but so far as my *name* is conserned, I request you by all that binds loyal man to loyal man, gentleman to gentleman, Christian to Christian, *never* to let human being know my name, for my *life* would have to be sacrifised on the alter of Hamilton and Ferguson's ambition.

P.S. Please send me any proclamation or other document relating to your official course. We cannot learn much concerning affairs at Nashville.

Yours truly, I. T. R.

ALS, T-Mil. Gov's Papers, 1862-65.

1. Isaac T. Reneau (1805-1885), a Tennessee native, studied medicine in Overton County and taught school (1830-31) at Clear Fork (later Clinton County, Kentucky) before becoming a minister in the Church of Christ (1835). He preached in Kentucky and Tennessee and is credited with the organization of numerous churches. 1860 Census, Ky., Monroe, Tompkinsville, 57; Joseph W. Wells, *History of Cumberland County [Ky.]* (Louisville, 1947), 403-4; *Goodspeed's Macon*, 840; H. Leo Boles, *Biographical Sketches of Gospel Preachers* (Nashville, 1932), 115-19.

2. Champion Ferguson (1821-1865), born in Kentucky, was farming in Clinton County when the war began. A private in Willis Scott Bledsoe's partisan cavalry unit (1861-62), he was commissioned Confederate captain in 1862, raised his own company, and conducted raids along the Kentucky-Tennessee border, as well as into Virginia and Alabama, serving at times with Morgan, Wheeler, and Forrest. Indicted for the murders of fifty-three persons, Ferguson was tried, convicted, and executed by Federal authorities soon after the end of war. Thurman Sensing, *Champ Ferguson: Confederate Guerilla* (Nashville, 1942); *Tennesseans in the Civil War*, I, 15-16; John S. Daniel, Jr., Special Warfare in Middle Tennessee and Surrounding Areas, 1861-62 (M.A. thesis, University of Tennessee, 1971), 41-44; see also Letter from L. S. Clements, April 9, 1862.

3. William P. Frogg (c1838-1861), a Kentucky-born farmer who had known Ferguson before the war, was a private or corporal in Co. D, 12th Ky. Inf., USA. The murder occurred on November 1, 1861, not in September. In 1865 Ferguson testified that he shot Frogg because the latter had threatened to kill him. 1860 Census, Ky., Clinton, 17; Nashville *Press and Times*, August 3, October 22, 1865; Hester A. Bandy, Pension Application, RG15, NA.

4. Reuben B. Wood (1805-1861), Reneau's brother-in-law and longtime friend of Ferguson before the war, was shot on December 2, 1861, and died two days later. Ferguson later declared that he believed Wood had intended to kill him. Wells, *Cumberland County*, 431; Nashville *Press and Times*, August 5, 7, October 22, 1865.

5. Oliver P. Hamilton (c1829-1864), a Tennessean and Jackson County farmer with an estate valued at $4,300 in 1860, organized in December, 1861, a Confederate cavalry company later attached to Shaw's battalion in the Army of Tennessee. Promoted by 1863 to lieutenant colonel, Hamilton was captured at Celina (March, 1864) and killed by a guard while awaiting trial for his guerrilla activities. 1860 Census, Tenn., Jackson, 6th Dist., 3; Daniel, Special Warfare, 73-75; *Tennesseans in the Civil War*, II, 186; *OR*, Ser. 1, XXXI, Pt. II, 663.

6. All of these Monroe County farmers were native Tennesseans. In 1860 Sims (c1838-1862) had a wife and four children, with an estate of $400; Atterberry (c1838-1862) possessed personal property valued at $400; Denham (c1827-1862), a farm laborer with $100 in personal estate, was married and had six children. 1860 Census, Ky., Monroe, Tompkinsville, 14, 18, 24.

7. Johnson's endorsement reads "Reward to be offered for man"; another script adds "named Champ Ferguson."

From William P. Sharp[1]

Lamonte Po Pettis County Mo.
March the 31—1862

To the honorable A. Johnson   I write you a fiew lines to let you know that I am yet alive and allright & my family & to let you know that you & your famly has abiding place in my Memory also to Congratulate you to your Return as Cheif Executive of the state that I was Borned and Raised in, Andrew I live 10 miles West of George town & a boute the same Distance from the End of the Paciffick Railroad, and to discribe the distress & devastation of this Cuntry will take a abler man then my Selfe. When Cecesh Broak out here me and my Boys[2] had to leave our house and hide our selves in the weedes and grass to save our lives for No other Cause then we was independant a noughf to advocate the Cause of our national flag and the american Constitution. Andrew the cecesh for Several days & weeks was a round my house Either day or night hooping and hollowing like demonds and seemed to thirst for my blood like a Woolf woold the sheepe[.] they had Soldiers quarterd in one mile and a half of my house and I had to keepe myselfe hid until the Govement sent troops to our Rescue[.] then we Crawled from our hiding places and I tel you that we paid them Back With Compound intrust. the union men had twist to flee the tract here when cecesh first Broke out here & at the Surrender of lexington. Robert Craig Sam Craig[3] & Boys all cecesh & Robert in prices[4] Armey 2 of sam Craiges Boys also samuel McKeehan[5] & boys all cecesh one of Samuel McKeehan sons helped to murder and Rob a man in five miles of me By the name of Joseph Robertson[6] for the some of 50 cts. and has maid his Esscape as yet. Andrew it seemes as the Will of our fore fathers is going through a firey trial But I am in hopes to god that the will not Be broken nor the land deveded, But all of old george Washingtons lawful & law a Biding heirs shall sheer a like East West north and south in one Common Cuntry. & it dos seeme to me that thoes Basterd heirs that is trying to Brake the will should not shere Equal with the lawful & law a biding heirs[.] Andrew I know that time is pressues with you & your Burthen heavy But i am in hopes that you will have a fiew minuts to answer your humble survents letter and let me know whare Charley & Robert Johnsons is also D. T. Patterson and family & Mrs Johnson whare she is as I saw a peace in a nues paper stating that cecesh had Exiled your Wife and your house a hospettle[.] if you know whare my Brother John Sharp[7] is & what he & what has Become of Josh lane[8] & old george Jones[9] in this scramble[.] I still Remain your

Umble servent & true friend
Wm. P. Sharp

I was a very strong John Bell man for president but was Deceived in him for he is a trater[.]

ALS, DLC-JP.

1. William P. Sharp (c 1804-1866), a native Tennessean and Greene County farmer who had moved with his family to Missouri in the mid-1850's, owned an estate of $5,427 in 1860. 1850 Census, Tenn., Greene, 10th Dist., 593; I. MacDonald Demuth, *History of Pettis County, Missouri* (n.p., 1892), 899; 1860 Census, Mo., Pettis, Elkfork, 190.

2. Sharp's substantial family of ten children included at this time four sons, aged 30, 16, 15, and 12. *Ibid.*

3. Possibly Robert and Samuel Craig, sons of Pennsylvania-born Samuel Craig, Revolutionary War veteran, who died in Greene County in 1807; Johnson had helped

obtain widow Jane Craig's pension. Robert is probably the Greeneville alderman (1832-33) who served with Johnson on the council and in "Captain Andrew Johnson's" security force (Greeneville had no police), and who appears to have left the town after 1834. The Craig "Boys" have not been found. Lucy W. Bates, comp., *Roster of Soldiers and Patriots of the American Revolution Buried in Tennessee* (n.p., 1974), 102; Doughty, *Greeneville*, 62, 63; see also *Johnson Papers*, I, 411.

4. Sterling Price (1809-1867), Virginia-born Missouri legislator (1836-38, 1840-44), Democratic congressman (1845-46), resigning to serve in the Mexican War, and governor (1853-57), was in command of Missouri troops. Failing to secure the secession of Missouri in 1861, he became a Confederate major general, commanding in several trans-Mississippi battles. After the war he refugeed in Mexico before returning to his home state. Warner *Generals in Gray*, 246-47; *BDAC*, 1482; see also Albert Castel, *General Sterling Price and the Civil War in the West* (Baton Rouge, 1968).

5. Either Samuel McKeehan (b. *c*1807), Tennessee native with sons Elbert (b. *c*1831) and George W. (b. *c*1836), all of whom lived in Washington County in 1850, or the Samuel McKeehan, living in Greene in 1830, who was in his thirties and had four sons—one under 5, one between 5 and 10, and two others under 15. Sistler, *1850 Tenn. Census*, IV, 232; Byron Sistler, tr., *1830 Census East Tennessee* (Evanston, Ill., 1971), 170.

6. Probably Joseph Robison (*c*1812-*c*1862), a Kentucky-born farmer with real and personal property valued at $15,000. 1860 Census, Mo., Pettis, Elkfork, 1812.

7. Possibly the John Sharp (b. *c*1815) who resided in Greene in 1850. Sistler, *1850 Tenn. Census*, VI, 47.

8. Probably J[oseph] G. [C.?] Lane (b. 1820), native Tennessean and saddler who was Johnson's neighbor. 1860 Census, Tenn., Greene, 10th Dist., 92; Buford Reynolds, *Greene County Cemeteries* ([Greeneville, Tenn.], 1971), 165.

9. George Jones, Greeneville merchant and saddler at the time he served as alderman with Johnson in 1831, was a unionist during the war. *Johnson Papers*, I, 275n.

To Stanley Matthews

March 31, 1862, [Nashville]; Tel draft, DLC-JP.

Orders provost marshal to arrest Washington Barrow, one of the Tennessee commissioners who had signed the military agreement with the Confederacy, and who is "now at large in the City of Nashville, offering treasonable language and exerting his influence against and expressing himself as inimical to the Government of the United States."

Interview with Rebel Ladies[1]

[April] 1862

A very entertaining dialogue occurred some days ago in the Governor's office, between Governor Johnson and two rebel ladies of this city, who had come to complain of the occupation of a residence belonging to the rebel husband of one of the ladies, by a Federal officer. The conversation was substantially as follows:

Lady. I think It is too dreadful for a woman in my lonesome condition to have her property exposed to injury and destruction.

Governor. Well, Madam, I will inquire into the matter, and if any injustice has been done, will try to have it corrected. But your husband, you admit, has gone off with the rebels, and you abandoned your dwelling.

Lady.   My husband went off South because it was to his interest to do so. You mustn't find fault with anybody for taking care of himself these times. You know, Governor, that all things are justifiable in war.

Governor.   Well, Madam, it appears to me that this broad rule of yours will justify taking possession of your house. Acording to your maxim, I don't see any reason for helping you out of your difficulty.

Lady.   Oh! but I didn't mean it that way.

Governor.   No, Madam, I suppose not. I will try to be more generous to you than your own rule would make me. I do not believe in your rule that "all things are justifiable in time of war." But that is just what you rebels insist upon. It is perfectly right and proper for you to violate the laws, to destroy this Government, but it is all wrong for us to execute the laws to maintain the Government.

The rebel ladies looked around in various directions, and seemed to think that they had opened a knotty argument on a dangerous subject, with a very hard adversary. Heaving a long sigh, they retired, to become, we earnestly hope, "wiser and better *men*."

Nashville *Union*, April 18, 1862.

1. Both lack of substantiating evidence and the platitudinous tone of the report suggest that it was part of a propaganda campaign waged by the sycophant *Union* to build the image of the new military governor. Three days earlier a column had dilated on Johnson's frequent interviews with "poor women of the city, wives of soldiers in the rebel army" who were seeking shelter. Nashville *Union*, April 15, 1862.

From Samuel D. McCullough[1]

Lexington Ky. April 1. 1862.

Hon. Andw. Johnson
Nashville Tenn.
Sir,

You may perhaps recollect me, by having met you frequently in this place, & having traveled once from "Camp Dick"[2] to Lex. each one in his separate vehicle. My Wife has two Nephews now prisoners of war, one, a Lieut in the Rebel service, at Camp Chase, Columbus O. (named Joseph Anderson)[3] the other, his Cousin, a youth of about 20 years of age at Indianapolis; named Wm J. A. Willcox,[4] the only son of his widowed Mother.— The poor deluded boy has written to me, & expresses himself that he will frankly, freely, & in good faith, take the Oath of Allegiance to our Govt. if permitted to do so.— He says *his heart was never in the matter*,— & from all I can learn, was induced to lift up arms, only from the taunts of his school mates & associates casting imputations on his courage. He got into the current of treason and rebellion without a wish to to do, & asks the help of myself *"his loyal Uncle"* to get him away from his confinement. If necessary, he will report himself to me in Lexington, where I shall keep him, until the rebellion is crushed, or until ordered to report elsewhere. May I ask your kind offices for a poor erring, delicate boy, whose Mother's heart yearns over her only son.— God will bless you for that act too, as well as for all your other labors in the cause of our beloved Country.— My own loyalty can be easily attested by all in Lexington.— Judge Geo. Robertson, my neighbor, has known me for many years,— Dr Robt. J. Breckinridge[5] is also an old & intimate acquaintance. Let me beg to refer you to them or all others.

The other young man was a officer in the bogus Confederacy; a Lieut.— older than his Cousin Willcox. He desires a release on his parole.— I can say of him, that I know him so well, that should that parole be accepted, & himself discharged under it, he will strictly comply with the terms imposed.

May God bless you in your noble efforts to relieve our Country from the Curse of treason, with all its horrors.

Very respectfully   Your Obt St—

Saml. D. McCullough.

I can also refer you to Genl. and Col. Carter,[6] the brothers now near Cumberland Gap.— They have frequently made my humble residence their stopping place, when in Lexington. Col S. D. Bruce,[7] & Col S. W. Price[8] now in your City, can also vouch for my loyalty.

Both Joseph Anderson & Wm J. A. Willcox are from Tennessee: the former from Marshall, & the latter from Maury Co's.

ALS, DLC-JP.

1. Samuel D. McCullough (1803-1873) was a Lexington educator, the processor of "Burrow's Lexington Mustard," and author of several works on astronomy. W. R. Jillson, ed., "Samuel D. McCullough's Reminiscences of Lexington," Kentucky Historical Society *Register*, XXVII (1929), 411-32.

2. Camp Dick Robinson.

3. Joseph Anderson (c1835-fl1880), Tennessee-born lawyer and 2nd lieutenant, Co. E, 53rd Tenn. Inf., entered the Confederate army January 7, 1862, and was captured at Donelson February 16. Exchanged at Vicksburg September 1, and honorably discharged a month later, he returned to his home at Lewisburg, Marshall County, where he subsequently became a farmer. 1860 Census, Tenn., Marshall, 12th Dist., 11; (1880), 13; CSR, RG109, NA.

4. William J. A. Wilcox (1841-fl1922) of Maury County enlisted as a private and was later appointed quartermaster sergeant in the 53rd Tenn. Inf., CSA. Imprisoned at Indianapolis for more than seven months after Donelson, Wilcox subsequently saw active service in Mississippi, Louisiana, and Georgia. Confederate pension application no. 15710, Tennessee State Library and Archives.

5. Robert J. Breckinridge, Sr. (1800-1871), son of John Breckinridge, practiced law and served in the state legislature during the 1820's. Entering the Presbyterian ministry (1832), he occupied pulpits in Lexington and Baltimore, was president of Jefferson College in Pennsylvania and of Danville Theological Seminary in Kentucky. Breckinridge reformed Kentucky's schools during his tenure as superintendent of public instruction (1847-51). Long opposed to slavery, he stood staunchly with the Union during the war. *DAB*, III, 10-11; Will D. Gilliam, "Robert J. Breckinridge: Kentucky Unionist," Kentucky Historical Society *Register*, LXIX (1971), 362-85.

6. Gen. Samuel P. Carter and Col. James P. T. Carter.

7. For Sanders D. Bruce, see *Johnson Papers*, IV, 531n.

8. Samuel W. Price (1828-1918), a Kentucky-born portrait painter, served as colonel of the 21st Ky. Vol. Inf. until wounded at Kennesaw Mountain (1864) and thereafter as post commandant in Lexington. He acted as postmaster at Lexington (1869-76),

moving to Louisville in 1878 where, in spite of blindness brought on by war injuries, he published several historical works. J. Winston Coleman, Jr., "Samuel Woodson Price, Kentucky Portrait Painter," *Filson Quarterly*, XXIII (1949), 5-24.

From Connally F. Trigg

Columbus Apl. 1 1862

Gov. Andw. Johnson
Nashville.
Dear Sir—

When I came to Cincinnatti and found that my delay there would necessarily throw until some time in the day on Saturday before I could reach this place, I concluded to remain there until Sunday night, prefering to pass an idle day in Cincinnatti, to doing so here. Consequently I *did* not reach this City until near 4. o'clock on Monday morning. Soon after breakfast I called on Gov. Tod and presented your letter— He received me very cordially & tendered me every facility in promoting the object of my mission.[1] In the afternoon Qr. Mas. Genl. Wright[2] took me in his buggy and we drove out to the Camp— The officer in charge Major Ballard[3] accompanied us in our visit to the prisons and sought out the different messes among whom there were prisoners for whom I had letters. There are three prisons (extensive plank inclosures with suitable cabins or huts to accommodate 18 prisoners) containing some twelve hundred prisoners; and the Tennesseeans are pretty much divided between the three—

The prisoners were delighted to receive the letters, and seemed not less pleased to see me, having heard that I was to be among them— I talked with very many of them and stated briefly the object of my visit, with which many seemed evidently pleased. I am satisfied that quite a number of them will gladly take the oath, ground their arms and become loyal citizens. Many of them, and perhaps the greater number, will stand upon what they conceive to be a "point of honor," having, as they say, taken an oath to support the So. Confederacy, if they now take the oath of Allegiance to the genl. government, it would be "cross-swearing."

The former class are anxious to be wholly released, and the latter would like very much to be *paroled*— That is, they would like to have their *liberty and go home*, but with the privilege of remaining *harmless rebels*, until exchanged as they might possibly be. It strikes me that all such would be about as *harmless* within the prisons of Ft. Chase, as they could be, or would likely be upon their parol— Unless otherwise instructed by you, I shall only interpose with the Department for those who are loyally disposed and willing to attest it by the sanction of their oaths—

Gov. Tod and I were to have gone out to the Camp to day, but the rain prevented our doing so. I find that it will be an almost endless job to hold private interviews with those who desire, and at the suggestion of the governor, I have concluded to address the Tennesseans in their respective prisons, explaining the purpose of my visit and requesting any that may desire my good offices with the Government, to write me a note to that effect and set forth their feelings towards the Government, and the grounds upon which they ask a release.

In this way I can get each man's views, & their own letters will be better for my purposes than any notes I could take of the disclosures made to me privately. Gov. Tod has handed me quite a bundle of letters from Tennesseeans to him, many of which bear the internal evidence of *attachment* to the old government and flag— I fear I am wearying you— I am not prepared now to guess how long I shall have to remain here—perhaps early in next week I may be off—

I dined with the Gov. to day—had a pleasant time—going to-morrow night to the Theatre *with his daughter*—[4] I see you are putting the *screws* to the City officers[5]—it makes the boys *wince* a little, but I reckon they'll take it—

Kind regards to Mr Maynard & other friends—

Very Respectfully—   Connally F. Trigg.

ALS, DLS-JP.

1. Johnson had sent Trigg to confer with the Tennesseans, preliminary to interceding with the government on their behalf. Tod displayed a special concern for the welfare of the prisoners at Camp Chase, visiting them once a week. Hall, *Military Governor*, 194; George B. Wright, "Hon. David Tod: Biography and Personal Recollections," *Ohio Archaeological and Historical Publications*, VIII (1900), 123.

2. George B. Wright (1815-1903), an Ohio University graduate, attorney, and railroad executive (1857-61, 1871-80), was a Whig and Republican who served as state quartermaster general (1861-64), colonel of the 106th Ohio Inf. (1864), and U.S. ordnance officer at Columbus (1863-64); after the war he became the first state commissioner of railroads and telegraphs (1867-71). "Editorialana," *ibid.*, XII (1903), 441-44; Wright, "David Tod," 117; Heitman, *Register*, I, 1062.

3. Alexander S. Ballard (b. *c*1821), Adams County trader before the war and commissioned major of the 74th Ohio, was appointed permanent superintendent of prisoners of war at Camp Chase on March 6, 1862, resigning his commission in November, 1862. CSR, RG94, NA; *OR*, Ser. 2, III, 357; Ser. 1, XVI, Pt. I, 1171; Ira S. Owens, *Greene County Soldiers in the Late War* (Dayton, 1884), 188.

4. Probably Tod's oldest daughter, Charlotte, who married Gen. August V. Kautz in 1866; she died two years later. Wright, "David Tod," 109.

5. Johnson had arrested Mayor Richard Cheatham for refusing to take the oath and had replaced virtually all the council and aldermen.

To Stanley Matthews

April 1, 1862, Nashville; L, DLC-JP.

Orders arrest of John Overton for treason, under charges of having furnished money for "arms, uniforms and camp equipage" to those waging war against the United States and having spoken and acted so as to give aid and comfort to its enemies. [In an accompanying endorsement Matthews reports that "The body of the within named John Overton has not been found."]

From "Observer"[1]

Nashville April 3rd 62

Genl Johnson

I hope you will not think me troublesome in writing so often, but I would like to inform you of Such things as passes under my observation, that may benifit Uncle Sam.

I hope you will make enquires about Noble Ellis[2] a Foundryman on Market St a Rabid Secesh and one that has been making cannon, shell, shot, and torpedoes to kill the damb Yankees as he expressed himself and I think it would be but Justice to over haul all such as he is for the work that he has done may cause many a Widow and Orphan to be left alone in this uncharitable world[.]

Respectfully   Observer

ALS, DLC-JP.

1. Not identified.

2. Noble Ellis (b. c1821), Ohio native, Nashville machinist, and former alderman (1849) possessing $13,000 in real and $30,000 in personal property, was a partner in Ellis' and Moore's Foundry and Machine Shop. A firm of "long standing" which employed "about sixty hands," Ellis and Moore made engines, mills, machinery, gearing, and castings, and boasted the "most extensive boiler yard" in the city. 1860 Census, Tenn., Davidson, 13th Dist., 134; Wooldridge, *Nashville*, 122; *Nashville Bus. Dir.* (1860-61), 67.

From Rufus S. Bassett[1]

April 4, 1862

Hon. Andre Johnson.

Dear Sir.

Senator James H Lane, Owes me $375, obtaining it, by promising, on His Word, and Honor, and pledging himself Masonically, that He would pay me the next Week,   Part of the above Sum, He got, when Starting to go, to Topeka, to be Elected Senator, When He could not get half Doller anywhere, promising me that He would pay me, as soon as He got His Mileage, and also to get me an office as Indian Agent. I refer you to Msrs Pomroy,[2] and Conway,[3] of the Senate, and House, as to my Standing and Veracity. You will place me under lasting obligation, in urging Lane to pay me now. I resort to this method, as the ownly one to collect my pay, as Lanes property is covered up, if He has any[.]

Most respectfully
R S Bassett

Lawrence Kansas   Apr 4 1862

ALS, DLC-JP.

1. Rufus S. Bassett, a Lawrence businessman who settled in Kansas in 1855 and testified in James H. Lane's support when the latter was embroiled in an 1860 land claim

contest. *Herald of Freedom* (Lawrence), July 30, 1859; William E. Connelley, "The Lane-Jenkins Claim Contest," *Kansas State Historical Society Collections*, XVI (1923-25), 91, 97; Joseph W. Snell (Kansas State Historical Society) to the Andrew Johnson Project, June 23, 1976.

2. Samuel C. Pomeroy (1816-1891), born in Southampton, Massachusetts, was a member of the legislature (1852-53) before moving to Kansas in 1854 as an organizer and financial agent of the New England Emigrant Aid Company. Elected mayor of Atchison (1858-59) and selected one of the state's first senators (1861), Pomeroy was accused in 1872 of attempting to purchase a Kansas legislator's ballot in the senatorial election. Despite being exonerated by a Senate investigation, he was commonly believed guilty, and his political career, to all intents and purposes, came to an end, although he received the American Prohibitionist party's nomination for President in 1884. *BDAC*, 1469; Albert R. Kitzhaben, "Götterdämmerung in Topeka: The Downfall of Senator Pomeroy," *Kansas Historical Quarterly*, XVIII (1950), 243-78.

3. Martin F. Conway (1827-1882), printer and lawyer, left his native Maryland for Kansas in 1853. Agent for the Massachusetts Abolition Society and an organizer of the Kansas Free State government, Conway became a Republican member of the House of Representatives (1861-63), later receiving from President Johnson the consulship at Marseilles. *BDAC*, 732.

From Salmon P. Chase

Treasury Department
April 4, 1862.

Sir.

I have the honor to transmit herewith copy of a telegram[1] sent this day to Wm. P. Mellen, Special Agent of the Treasury Department;[2] also copy of the Modifications of Rules and Regulations concerning Commercial Intercourse, from which you will be able [to] inform yourself of the views and policy of this Department on that subject.

The telegrams sent by you submitting the name of a proper person for Surveyor of the port of Nashville, were received, but the name was so different in each, that official action could not be taken upon them. On receipt of a letter, giving the name of the person in full he will be duly appointed.[3]

With great Respect,   S. P. Chase,
Secretary of the Treasury.

Hon. Andrew Johnson,
Military Governor of Tennessee

LB copy, DNA-RG56, Sec. of Treasury Corres., Lets. Sent, Restricted Commercial Intercourse, BE Ser., Vol. 2 (Feb.-Dec., 1862).

1. The wire read: "Your suggestions are approved. Let Permits to trade in Tennessee be restricted to persons authorized by Gov Johnson or Committees appointed by him, to receive and dispose of the goods. As he is Military Governor of Tennessee, the sole authority to appoint such Committees [boards of trade] belongs, necessarily to him." April 4, 1862, Restricted Commercial Intercourse, Lets. Sent, RG56, NA.

2. William P. Mellen (*c*1813-1873), a New York native, had read law with Chase and engaged in coal mining in Appalachia. Appointed on March 22 a special agent of the treasury stationed in Cincinnati, he was "one of the Secretary's most efficient political supporters." Subsequently he resided in New York and Colorado. Futrell, *Federal Trade*, 6-7; *American Annual Cyclopaedia* (1873), 585.

3. The previous day Chase had wired "Send name of person to be appointed sur-

veyor[.]" Evidently, in the transmission of several earlier telegrams, the last dated April 1, the name of Johnson's nominee "Mr. Quincy C. DeGrove 2nd," of Nashville, had been garbled. The governor responded, clarifying the name and requesting "that Mr. De-Grove be at once appointed, the public interest requiring prompt action in this respect." Chase to Johnson, April 3, 1862, Johnson Papers, LC; Johnson to Chase, April 4, 1862, Box 15, Recs. & Appts., RG56, NA.

From James G. Spears

April 4, 1862, Barbourville, Ky.; L, DLC-JP.

Having "recd no answer as yet from any quarter" to his request that he be assigned a brigade, he urgently asks to be sent to "East Tennessee, in order as speedily as possible to redeem the oppressed people there," inasmuch as "The rebels are all over East. Tenn. murdering and Robing & stealing among the union men & families."

To Don Carlos Buell, Columbia

Nashville April 4th 61[1862]

Gen D C Buell

My information satisfies me that a small force of Cavalry, not less then one nor more then (3) Companies should be sent to a point one hundred miles from here, on the Kentucky line for an excursion of several days. Woolfords Cavalry[1] is at Glasgow Ky, and was largely recruited in the region mentioned— I request that you order Genl Dumont to detail from his Regiment a proper force for this service. Answer immediately[.]

Andrew Johnson

LB copy, DNA-RG393, Dept. of the Ohio, Tels. Recd. (Jan.-Aug., 1862); DLC-JP.

1. Frank L. Wolford (1817-1895), a Liberty, Kentucky, criminal lawyer, Mexican War veteran, and commander of the 1st Ky. Cav., USA, was dishonorably discharged in the spring of 1864 for criticizing Lincoln in a public address. A Democratic presidential elector in 1864 and 1868, he served in the Kentucky legislature (1865-66), as state adjutant general (1867-68), and as congressman (1882-86). Hambleton Tapp, "Incidents in the Life of Frank Wolford, Colonel of the First Kentucky Cavalry," *Filson Quarterly*, X (1936), 83-84; *BDAC*, 1842.

From Dorus M. Fox[1]

Head Quarters 9th Regt Mich Vol
Murfreesboro April 5th 1862

To His Excellency
Gov A. Johnson   Nashville
Sir—

Yesterday our pickits brought into camp a Man from beyond our lines upon whose person we found over one hundred letters (secreted) written by officers and others in the rebel army to their friends in the North part of the state—: Among them was the one enclosed in which you are refered to as likely to be "assasinated"[2]—and the same thing is alluded to in several letters— I presume Gov you have been made aware of these threats—but yet I thought best to call your attention to it again—for I believe this desire may be more *general* in the ranks of the infuriated rebels than you are aware of[.]

I well recollect a remark you made to me in (Louisville in November last—"that the moment a man became a secessionist he became a *Demon*"— Therefore be vigilant Gov—and excuse this liberty— You will perhaps recollect me as calling upon you the Sunday I passed through Nashville three weeks since— I should be glad to hear from you— think my Regt will remain here two weeks—

I Am Very Respectfully
Your Obt Servt   Dorus. M. Fox
Lt Col 9th Regt Mich Vol

ALS, DLC-JP.
1. Dorus M. Fox (b. *c*1818), New York native who in 1841 became a produce dealer in Lyons, Michigan, was associated briefly with the Democratic *Herald* (1856) and the *Present Age* (1868). Later becoming colonel, 27th Mich. Inf. (October, 1862), he was wounded at Petersburg and resigned from the army in October, 1864. 1860 Census, Mich., Ionia, Lyons Township, 108; Elam E. Branch, ed., *History of Ionia County, Michigan* (2 vols., Indianapolis, 1916), I, 132, 382-83; John Robertson, comp., *Michigan in the War* (Lansing, 1882), 830.
2. Threats on the governor's life became almost commonplace, his mail often warning of alleged assassination plots. The example forwarded by Fox was not preserved with the letter. Lately Thomas, *The First President Johnson* (New York, 1968), 228, 233.

From Ormsby M. Mitchel

Shelbyville April 5 1862
To Gov Johnston
Am I to permit the County & Circuit Court to meet & transact business here on Monday without requiring the officers to take the oath of allegiance[?]

Answer quick[.][1]

O. M. Mitchell Brig Genl

Tel, DLC-JP.
1. Johnson's endorsement reads "Telegraphed 'Yes' in reply."

From Daniel C. Trewhitt

Barbourville Ky April 5th 1862.
Gov. Johnson
Dear sir,

I write you a few lines this morning to request of you if you, have it in your power to give some position to a friend of mine from Hamilton County, John D. Haws.[1] He possesses fine business qualities & is a good pens man; easy and affable, a true Union man, and had to leave in August last and has been with us ever since. He wishes some position not *merely* to make money, but simply that he may be honorably employed and realize enough to support himself & family, consisting of himself & wife & child. I think on trial you would be pleased with him. He is 26 years of age. I would be very glad in deed if you could find some business for him to do.

The appointment of Col. Spears Brigadier General[2] gives almost universal satisfaction & *joy* to the Tennesseans. No difference what Doct Stanford & a few others may say otherwise—[3]   He & one or two other pliant tools are a little noisy—for some unproper purpose. All Spears wants is power and assignment of forces to go a head & redeem our down troden people. With him & all of us this is not a "Brass button war"

I have resigned in the 2d Regt. Tenn. vols. and will take the position of Assistant adjutant Genl, on Genl Spears Staff—[4]   the 2d Regt. is not doing well—   James P. T. Carter is obnoxious to them.[5] Many want Transfers to go into other Regiments but he refuses any as I am told.   he has appointed a Lt. Col. obnoxious to the Regiment.[6] Their universal choice almost is Mitchell Millsaps[7] Lt. of Co. B. but his claims have been overlooked over a unanimous petition of officers with one or two exceptions. He has refused the right of 2d Lt. of Co. A. D. Kittrell[8] to be promoted to 1st Lieut. when the position was vacant and put over him a 2nd or 3rd Sergeant, all as the boys say because Kittrell would not bow in worship to the Carter dynasty. Justice ought to be done. Kittrell has been *the* officer of the Co. for the last six months, and never off of duty. I regret to mention to, or trouble you with these matters, but the Regt. is in danger of disorganization, and they being dear to me, one of the finest Regiments in the Brigade, and pressing it on me I could not refuse to call your attention to it.

If Jim Carter is not commissioned a Col. one should be—   He is out of place,—and not qualified—in any one respect, for the position. Grave charges have been prefered against him near two months ago by Capt. John L. Sneed[9] of Co. F, 2d Regt. but they have never been heard from since.—   Why—   We little men must not inquire.

All our men want is a Gentleman & honest man & one who will fight to lead them on: Cols. Shelbys & Houks Regiments have their minimum—   Cols. Johnson & Cooper will soon have theirs.   we want more force and orders to move forward.

Your obt. Sevt.
D. C. Trewhitt.

Hon. Andrew Johnson
Military Gov. of Tenn.

ALS, DLC-JP.
   1. Possibly John F. Haws, a private in the 1st Tenn. Cav. who died of measles in January, 1863, at Louisville, Kentucky. John W. Gore to Robert Johnson, January 17, 1863, Johnson Papers, LC.
   2. Spears, lieutenant colonel, 1st Tenn. Inf., was promoted March 5, 1862.

3. Robert L. Stanford, ally of the Carters and surgeon with the 1st Tenn. Inf.

4. Lieutenant colonel, 2nd Tenn. Inf., USA, Trewhitt had resigned on March 14, ostensibly because of poor health. CSR, RG94, NA.

5. Col. James P. T. Carter was unpopular with a sizable portion of his command, some members feeling that the regiment was "nearly disorganized" and that he was at fault. By late January a petition signed by some of the junior officers asked Carter to resign, warning that if he refused, a court-martial charging incompetency would be initiated. This petition was lost in a trunk when a ferryboat sank in the Rockcastle River. William R. Tracy to Johnson, January 16, February 3, 1862, Johnson Papers, LC; for more of Carter's personal difficulties, see Letters from William R. Tracy, February 6, and Leonidas C. Houk, February 18, 1862.

6. The "obnoxious" officer was John W. Bowman, appointed April 1. Bowman (1831-1913), a Roane County farmer originally captain of Co. A, resigned in October, 1862, because of "protracted and continued ill health." In later years he was sometime chairman of the county court and served a term in the state senate (1895-97). *Tenn. Adj. Gen. Report* (1866), 41; *Official Army Register: Volunteers*, IV, 1198; Robison, *Preliminary Directory*, Roane, 3-4.

7. Mitchell R. Millsaps (1828-1889), Fentress County farmer and logger, in active military service from 1861 until he and his command were captured in Hawkins County (1863), was promoted to captain at this time, subsequently serving in the state legislature (1869-71) and as a county judge (1886-89). *Ibid.*, Fentress, 7.

8. Doctor F. Kittrell (b. *c*1830), a Tennessee native and shoemaker by trade, was mustered out of service, still a second lieutenant, in December, 1864. 1860 Census, Tenn., Roane, 9th Dist., 171; *Official Army Register: Volunteers*, IV, 1198.

9. Among the allegations against Carter was "neglect of duty." On February 17 his brother, Gen. Samuel P. Carter, defended him in a letter to Buell's chief of staff, James B. Fry, averring that the colonel had been "confined to the house & been under medical treatment for some time, for a disease consequent on exposure in camp." CSR, RG94, NA; *OR*, Ser. 1, X, Pt. I, 296; for Sneed and the charges against Carter, see Letter from William R. Tracy, February 6, 1862.

From Joseph S. Fowler

Springfield April 6th 1862.

Gov. A. Johnson:

Dr. Sir.

I have just written to E. H. East on several subjects. One of which I desire to bring before you. It is true you have been consulted and written favorably but an urgent application would do much if made at Washington where it ought to be made. Whilst I cannot reccommend an immediate release of all the prisoners under existing circumstances and under their particular impressions, there are some that ought at once be admitted to take the oath and come home or be removed to some place where they could have the attention of friends.

C.L. Duer[1] the son of John Duer of Robertson County was forced; under the baneful influence of bad men who urged the rebellion forward, to enlist in the Confederate Army. His father has stood firm amid the faithless & has one Sone in the army of the Union. He wishes to get his boy away who is now true to his country and has always believed his cause a bad one. Thos P. Shute Alex Stark R. H. Elam John Hermans (his father has ever been true) C. Muny Drew Edwards.[2] These boys are all sick excep Hermans some of them very low and need the best attention. I written full to Mr East about a Physician. He will consult with you on my suggestion.

I feel anxious that you would urge the department at once on the subject and in a special manner. It is a matter of no personal interest to me. I feel deeply for the misguided sons of my old neighbors and the citizens of a state I hope soon to See restored to her true position in the Union. I know you will labor for the release of all the meritorious prisoners who will return to their faith, but at this peculiar juncture it is neither the design of the war department nor is it policy to release all. Where there are objects of especial merit it is both right & plitic to effect the release. If your judgement approves the Course I have reccommended you would confer a favor on the boys and parents by urging the department to relese them. I shall be in Nashville in Ten days at farthest.

Yours respectfully
Jos. S. Fowler.

N.B. Write me what Course you think best to take. I have filed the application with Gen Halleck & have the recommendation of Gov. Yates,[3] Auditor & Treasurer of Illinois. I have interested myself with the poor victims of bad men from sympathy for their misfortune. I lived through the revolution[4] and know how much true men had to endure. Those poor boys are totally ignorant of their crime[.]   they fought for a vague idea of *a South*. This wicked device of a South & a North has been fraught with crime in this one whole Repubic of ours.

ALS, DLC-JP.

1. Charles L. Duer (1841-*fl*1910), born in Robertson County, served as corporal, Co. B, 30th Tenn. Inf., CSA. In ill health when captured at Fort Donelson, Duer took the oath of allegiance at Camp Butler, Springfield, Illinois, in October, 1862, and returned to Portland, Tennessee, where he later made a living by "operating [a] candy stand and selling spectacles." Confederate pension application no. 11672, Tennessee State Library and Archives.

2. Relief came too late for Sgt. Thomas P. Shute (b. *c*1842), Pvt. Alexander J. Starke (b. *c*1839), Pvt. Robert H. Elam (b. *c*1834), and Pvt. Drew [Druseph] Edwards (b. *c*1840), all of whom had enlisted during October and November, 1861, for one year in the Co. F, 30th Tenn. Inf. Captured at Donelson, they died at Camp Butler between April 7 and June 5, 1862. John Herman (b. *c*1843), a private in Co. I, 30th Tenn. Inf., was the son of Sylvanius Herman of Sumner County, and Muny was probably Caswell M. Mooney (b. *c*1843), a private in Co. K, 48th (Voorhies) Inf. According to the regiment's major, J. J. Turner, the privates were all sent to Butler; company officers to Camp Chase, later to Johnson's Island; and field and staff officers to Fort Warren. Unfortunately, said Turner, "treatment of the company officers and privates was the reverse of our treatment at Fort Warren. Their rations were just enough to barely sustain life, and many acts of tyranny and brutality were inflicted upon them." Lindsley, *Military Annals*, 445-46; CSR, RG109, NA; Sistler, *1850 Tenn. Census*, III, 167; see also Telegram to Pitcairn Morrison, March 27, 1862.

3. Richard Yates (1818-1873), Illinois lawyer and at this time governor (1861-65), had served in the legislature (1842-45, 1848, 1849) and as congressman (1851-55); later he became senator (1865-71). *BDAC*, 1856.

4. Probably a figurative allusion to the era of secessionist Tennessee, between May, 1861, and the arrival of the Federal military in March, 1862.

From B[erry] J. R[eneau][1]

[Olympus] April 6 1862.

Hon Andrew Johnson,

Sir permit me to inform you that, there is a band of Rebels at Livingston Overton County Tenn of about 600, and they dashed in to Clinton County Kentucky and killed Several men without mercy. Alvin Cullom[2] and James W. McHenry[3] are the leading men engaged in it, the union men would be glad, If you would Send a Suffishent force to kill all of them and let that be your orde.

Yours inhast   B. J. R

ALS, DLC-JP.

1. Possibly Berry J. Reneau, or Renow (b. *c*1827), Kentucky-born Overton County farmer. Sistler, *1850 Tenn. Census*, V, 193; 1860 Census, Tenn., Overton, 12th Dist., 72.

2. Alvan Cullom (1797-1877), Kentucky native and former Democratic colleague of Johnson in the House of Representatives (1843-47), had begun law practice in Overton County in 1823 and served as state legislator (1835-37), circuit judge (1850-52), and delegate to the Washington Peace Conference of 1861. A Confederate sympathizer by the summer of 1861, Cullom was said to have encouraged the guerrilla foray into Clinton County in April, 1862. *BDAC*, 762; McBride and Robison, *Biographical Directory*, I, 181; Sensing, *Champ Ferguson*, 95; Albert W. Shroeder, Jr., ed., "Writings of a Tennessee Unionist," *Tenn. Hist. Quar.*, IX (1950), 248.

3. James McHenry (b. *c*1833), a prosperous Kentucky-born attorney, was a secessionist orator, adjutant general of the state militia (1861), and organizer of the "Brown Rangers" (later a company in the 4th [Murray's] Cav.), which took part in guerrilla raids on the Kentucky border (1861-62). After the war, he "moved to Nashville to secure a wider field for his talents, and was rapidly entering upon a paying practice when he died." 1860 Census, Tenn., Overton, Livingston, 7; *OR*, Ser. 1, IV, 442; *Tennesseans in the Civil War*, I, 59-60; II, 276; Albert V. and W. H. Goodpasture, *Life of Jefferson Dillard Goodpasture* (Nashville, 1897), 87.

From James G. Spears

April 6, 1862, Barbourville, Ky.; L, DLC-JP.

Recently promoted brigadier, requesting prompt assignment to command, asks for sizable reinforcements: "ten thousand men at least, with two more Batteries of Artillery and some Cavalry," inasmuch as "the forces now here are vulnerable from Pound Gap to Jamestown a distance of 300[*sic*] miles, to an attack from the Secession Army on its retreat from Virginia."

From Elisha Harris

April 7, 1862, Washington, D.C.; ALS, DLC-JP.

Sanitary Commission physician introduces James Donaghe, of New York, visiting Nashville "on business relating to property invested in your State. A true &

loyal son of Virginia, & for thirty years a resident in New England," Donaghe "has watched & joined in the present great life-struggle of our Nation with the fervor of a patriot." On request of the medical bureau, Harris has sent six young New York surgeons to serve in the field or hospitals; "if more are needed. . . they can be had."

From Samuel Hays

April 7, 1862, Paducah, Ky.; ALS, DLC-JP.

Upon the Federal occupation of Memphis, intends to begin "a *vigorous* unconditional Union Daily paper"; desires Memphis postmastership to sustain the enterprise.

From John B. Rodgers

Norwalk Ct. 7 April 1862

Gov. Johnson
Dear Sir.

I have taken every pains to present the case of the drafted volunteers, before the President & secretary of war properly[1] and as I have been informed it is, they are favorably disposed towards a liberation of the prisoners in the event it meets your approbation.

The Secretary of war said he would immediately communicate with you, whose letter[2] I delivered to him on the subject,   part of the officers are at Camp Chase,   the soldiers I did not find where they were—   The secretary desires to give you all the strength he can & give you the credit of their release.   this I desire you should have, for I know full well you will have a hard undertaking in Ten and will need all the aid possible, and that you will have without Stint or denial from all the Union men of the State, I hope. There is a lot of Tennessee prisoners I have no sympathy for, who entered the Confederate army early willingly & indeed eagerly abusing every body they left behind. I say let them sweat; not so with the eleventh hour men who were beged, threatened and at last drafted and decemated before they would volunteer,   other would have gon also (three of whom were my nephews & possibly one son) if I had not have taken upon myself the responsibility of saying to them, I would take on my individual self the responsibility of defending them for the refusal & produced such a disaffection in my county with others, that they did positively refuse to go and King Harris could not force them into the service, untill he had to run away himself[.] But for which in fact I had to follow the glorious example set me by my illustrious King Governor,[3] and so I runaway myself at your Service—   better I thought to assume the responsibility—of leaving at the hour of midnight and in a hard Shower of rain better than to visit the confines of a southern prison. So I am up here in the midst of the best Union sentiments I ever saw, all breathing prayers for your success in Tennessee, all your ardent personal friends—

If you will send me authority, I will go & search out all the drafted volunteers, will fully satisfy them with you, attach them to the Union cause, & deputising them with their leaders—some of whom will remember my early advise, There is a particular way to manage them in my opinion—& you may find, a stranger to them cannot do it. but to give me the oppertunity of doing a service to them, gives me the ability to aid you and the Union cause generally & thereby making my home secure.

If you are pleased to address me you will find me at this place.

Respectfully
John B. Rodgers.

P.S. Some of the officers wept when I met & parted with them—a favorable indication I thought of repentance.

R.

Gov. Andrew Johnson
Nashville Tenn

ALS, DLC-JP.
1. Evidently Rodgers made an impression on Lincoln in this or subsequent interviews, for in July, responding to a petition from some Tennesseans and Kentuckians urging that Rodgers be sent to arrange the release of all loyal soldiers confined as prisoners of war, the President expressed concern that those wishing to renew their loyalty not be turned back to enemy hands and observed, "if any agent shall be deemed necessary, to make such discrimination and apply it, I doubt not Mr. Rodgers would be a suitable person for such Agency." Endorsement, July 18, 1862, on undated petition, Basler, *Works of Lincoln*, V, 333.
2. Not found.
3. A cryptic statement which might possibly refer to Johnson's own forced departure from Tennessee in the summer of 1861, but which is more likely directed to Isham G. Harris' precipitate exit as the Federal army approached Nashville in February, 1862.

From Connally F. Trigg

Columbus April 7. 1862.

Gov. Andrew Johnson
Nashville Ten—
Dear Sir—

My labors here are about terminated, and I have concluded to leave for the City of Washington on tomorrow night— After having visited the different prisons at the Camp, and conversed with quite a number of the prisoners, and finding that almost every one wanted a private interview, which I found it would be impracticable to afford, without extending my visit for many weeks, at the suggestion of Gov. Tod, I determined to address the Tennesseans, and receive their communications in writing— This mode I believed would afford each prisoner an opportunity of expressing his sentiments as *privately*, as he could do to me alone, and the suggestion was apparently very well received by them. Accordingly on Thursday last I addressed the prisoners confined in prison No. 3, and on the next day, those confined in Nos. 1 & 2— It was arranged to have all the Tennesseans brought together at one place to hear me in the afternoon of Thursday, but the Col. commanding the post, on reflection thought that separating the Tennesseeans from the others, might create some confusion, & told me when I went out, that he prefered that I should speak at the respective prisons— He said that the other prisoners, besides the Tennesseeans, would like to hear me, and thought my speech might have a good effect upon them. Of course I yielded to the suggestion, and spoke that evening to one, and on the next day to the others.

The general purport of my remarks, was to convince the prisoners that there never had been, and was not now any cause for the rebellion in which they had been engaged—that they had been deceived and misled by false representations, as to the purposes of the general Government, in relation to the slaves in the Southern States, &c &c and explaining the character and object of my mission— My remarks seemed to be well received by the prisoners generally, and I am gratified to state that Col. Campbell[1] and other intelligent gentlemen in the army, complimented me upon the good taste, both in manner and matter, which I had displayed— Of course it was very gratifying to me, that I should receive the commendation of such gentlemen, in the discharge of a public official duty, which was new to me.

Since my addresses, I have recd. written communications from between five and six hundred Tennessee prisoners, and I should think near two hundred from those of other States. Many of the letters were signed by quite a number together, and who sympathised in their views & feelings— But I have had an immense deal of reading to do, and not by any means a small job to endorse briefly upon the back of each communication, the character of its contents. The quarter master Genl. of this State, Genl. Wright,[2] says he will tomorrow detail a Clerk, from his office, to assist me in classifying the letters, and preparing an alphabetical list of the names of the prisoners— This is certainly very kind, but it is only one of the very many manifestations of kindness which have been tendered me by the Governor and his subordinate officers, to say nothing of others of the good people about Columbus—

I am not able now to say how many of the Tennessee prisoners are willing to take the *oath* & become *loyal* citizens, but there is quite a number; though I would guess that the larger proportion of them are anxious to be released upon their *parole of honor*— I am gratified to state that the feeling here among the citizens, so far as I have been able to gather it, is favorable to the release of such of the prisoners, as are willing to take the oath, and return to their loyalty—

I see from some of the papers that you have appointed Commissioners[3] to visit the other camps, and I therefore take it for granted that it will be unnecessary for me to go to the camps at Indianapolis & Chicago. But I hardly think it necessary to do so any how, for if the department lends a favorable ear to those who are *loyally* disposed in this camp, and liberates *them*, I cannot doubt, but that it will speedily take steps to liberate the *privates* of like disposition, who may be confined at other places. The work of *ascertaining* those who are loyal, and *discharging* them, might be performed by the same Comr. or agent of the department—

I fear I have written more than you will like to read, but I pray you excuse me. Edward[4] is with me to night. He comes with a petition from the officers of the Ten. Regts. in Ky, asking that Col. John Williams[5] be commissioned a Col. in the Fed. army, to raise a Regt. and Edward made Lieut Col. I hope you may find it agreeable to yourself, in some form, to promote the suggestion with the Secretary.[6] I learn from Edward that John Williams with some of his own boys, and probably my son Lilburn,[7] is now somewhere in the Smoky Mountain. I hope he may succeed in avoiding the villians, and eventually make *his* way into Kentucky, unless our army shall soon make *its* way to Knoxville. According to the information they have at our Camp opposite the Gap, there are at that place now, not over 2500— A Mississippi & Georgia Regiment whose time of enlistment had expired, threw down their arms, left the Gap, and swore that Jeff Davis and his government had played out, and they didnt intend to *re*enlist to be butchered—[8] These Regiments were from the northern part of their respective states— The man who tells it is a Kentuckian, who came over from Claiborne County, with his family, and old Davy Cottrell,[9] whom you know, says that he is to be relied on— There are four additional regiments of East Tennesseeans being organized in Kentucky. They range from something over 200, to 800 men; and will thus far average about 500 to a Regiment if they were divided out among them.

Robert was quite well and had some two hundred & twenty odd men.[10] Ed Maynard came over to Cincinnati with Edward, and was to return to Lexington Ky this morning—

I have mentioned to Col. Campbell the matter of his going to Nashville— He is anxious to go, and told me last night that he would write to Mr Stanton by me— I hope you will get a brigade at Nashville— It would exert a happy influence upon the public sentiment of that Country— The people here manifest great interest for your success in the restoration of our good old State to its legitimate status—

I am *sure* you will complain of this letter, but I couldnt help *spinning* it out.   With Kind regards to all friends I bid you good night!

Very Respectfully   Your Obt. Servt.

Connally F. Trigg.

ALS, DLC-JP.

1. Probably Lewis D. Campbell of Ohio.

2. George B. Wright.

3. It is possible that Trigg had read or heard about Johnson's letter of March 27 to Col. James A. Mulligan at Camp Douglas introducing Dr. Glover and B. J. Hurt who were visiting prisoners at that site. Johnson to Mulligan, March 27, 1862, Chicago Historical Society.

4. The writer's son, Edward C. Trigg.

5. For Williams, credited with recruiting a number of Union soldiers, see *Johnson Papers*, II, 317n; McBride and Robison, *Biographical Directory*, I, 795.

6. Two weeks later, the younger Trigg, writing from Lancaster, Kentucky, asked Johnson for his recommendation, observing that his father had reported "that everything connected with such appointments, for Tennessee, had been referred to you and that your recommendation would be necessary to obtain a commission." Edward C. Trigg to Johnson, April 28, 1862, Johnson Papers, LC.

7. Trigg's younger son Lilburn H. (1842-1870) served as deputy U. S. marshal in Knoxville before his suicide in 1870. WPA, Tenn., Knox: Old Gray Cemetery, 136; Knoxville *Chronicle*, September 15, 1870; *Helm's Knoxville City Directory* (1869), 110.

8. A reference to the 2nd Mississippi and the 5th Georgia regiments, which according to the northern press, upon their refusal "to reenlist, had their arms taken from them," and when they "applied for transportation home and that was refused . . . they marched off in a body, disgusted with the service." Cincinnati *Commercial*, April 12, 1862; see also, Edmund Kirby Smith to Samuel Cooper, March 31, 1862, *OR*, Ser. 1, X, Pt. II, 376.

9. For Cottrell, see *Johnson Papers*, IV, 595n.

10. Robert Johnson's success in raising a Tennessee volunteer regiment was reflected in the organization of the 4th Tenn. Inf. in April, 1862.

Proclamation re Nashville City Council

April 7, 1862

WHEREAS, At an election held in the city of Nashville on the last Saturday of September, 1861, for the purpose of electing a Mayor, Aldermen and Common Council for said city, the following officers were elected to the respective offices, to-wit:

Richard B. Cheatham, Mayor.

For Alderman of the First Ward—Jno. E. Newman.

For Councilman of the First Ward—John Coltart and John Hooper.

For Alderman of the Second Ward—James T. Bell.

For Councilmen of the Second Ward—Geo. S. Kinnie and Charles S. Thomas.

For Alderman of the Third Ward—Peyton S. Woodward.

For Councilmen of the Third Ward—L. F. Beech and Wm. Shane.

For Alderman of the Fourth Ward—James M. Hinton.

For Councilmen of the Fourth Ward—Chas. E. H. Martin and W. R. Demonbreun.

For Alderman of the Fifth Ward—Wm. S. Cheatham.

For Councilmen of the Fifth Ward—Jordan P. Coleman and W. H. Clemons.

For Alderman of the Sixth Ward—B. S. Rhea.

For Councilmen of the Sixth Ward—John J. McCann and James Haynie.

For Alderman of the Seventh Ward—A. H. Hurley.

For Councilmen of the Seventh Ward—Isaac Paul and F. O. Hurt.

For Alderman of the Eighth Ward—C. K. Winston.

For Councilmen of the Eighth Ward—John E. Hatcher and C. A. Brodie.

And, Whereas, The following persons of the afore-named, to-wit: R. B. Cheatham, Mayor, James T. Bell, P. S. Woodward, James M. Hinton, B. S. Rhea, A. H. Hurley, C. K. Winston, John Coltart, John Hooper, Geo. S. Kinney, Chas. S. Thomas, L. F. Beech, Chas. E. H. Martin, William R. Demonbreun, Jordan P. Coleman, W. H. Clemens, John J. McCann, James Haynie, Isaac Paul, F. O. Hurt, John E. Hatcher and C. A. Brodie have heretofore failed, and now refuse to come forward and be qualified according to law, by taking the oath prescribed in the 10th Article, Section 1st, of the Constitution of the State of Tennessee, and therein have manifested such disloyalty and enmity to the Government of the United States, as renders it unsafe for the public good that they should exercise the functions of the offices aforesaid.[1] Now, therefore, I, Andrew Johnson, Governor of the State of Tennessee, by virtue of the power and authority in me vested, do declare the aforesaid offices vacant, and said persons above mentioned are hereby enjoined from exercising the functions of said offices, or performing any of the duties thereof, or receiving the emoluments of the same, from this day.

And the following-named persons are hereby appointed and commissioned, after being duly qualified, to perform the duties of said offices, as required by law, and receive the profits and emoluments thereof until their successors are elected, respectively as follows, to-wit:

Councilman for First Ward—Wm. Roberts.

Alderman for Second Ward—John Hu. Smith.

Councilman for Second Ward—Chas. Walker.

Alderman for Third Ward—G. A. J. Mayfield.

Councilman for Third Ward—K. J. Morris.

Alderman for Fourth Ward—M. M. Monahan.

Councilmen for Fourth Ward—Lewis Hough and M. Burns.

Councilmen for Fifth Ward—Joseph B. Knowles and W. P. Jones.

Alderman for Sixth Ward—M. M. Brien.

Councilmen for Sixth Ward—T. J. Yarbrough and Wm. Driver.

Alderman for Seventh Ward—M. G. L. Claiborne.

Councilman for Seventh Ward—Wm. Stewart.

Alderman for Eighth Ward—Jos. C. Smith.

Councilman for Eighth Ward—James Cavert.

By order of Governor,
ANDREW JOHNSON.

Edward H. East, Secretary of State.
Nashville, April 7th, 1862.

Ex. Record Book (1862-63), DLC-JP4C; *Singleton's Nashville Business Directory* (1865), 112-13.

1. A comparison of the two preceding lists reveals that Aldermen John E. Newman and William S. Cheatham and Councilman William Shane were the only members of the council to take the prescribed oath. Confirmation is to be found in the subsequent roster of appointments which includes none for the first- and fifth-ward aldermen and only one third-ward councilman.

From Charles B. Cotton[1]

Louisville Ky Apr 8 1862.

Sir

I this day shipped to Morris & Stratan[2] subject to your order 20 Doz Cotton Cards[3] for Byers & Co Druggist[4] in that City.

I doubted the proprity and hence my action[.]   There will have to be some regulation there to prevent goods getting into disloyal hands, and I think the arrangement will be consummated in a few days. I understand the policy adopted will be for you to appoint a Committee who will act upon such cases there.

At present I am at a loss to know what to do with reference to shipment of goods there. I desire to act intelligibly and hence must have some one there upon whom I can rely. I have had to size [seize] several lots of goods presented there upon misrepresentation.

Besides I have sized some 294 Tierces lard—here—sent from Nashville—and libelled it.[5] It is Confederate property[.]

Some one should look after such things being shipped from Nashville;

Resply   Chas B Cotton
Surveyor

To Gov Johnson   Nashville

ALS, DLC-JP.

1. For Cotton, surveyor of the port of Louisville, see *Johnson Papers*, IV, 698n.
2. Kindred J. Morris & Thomas E. Stratton were wholesale grocers and commission agents. *Nashville Bus. Dir.* (1860-61), 133; Wooldridge, *Nashville*, 118, 253.
3. Wire-teethed instruments for cleaning and disentangling cotton fibers preparatory to spinning. *Webster's Third International*.
4. Byers & Bros., druggist, was located near the Public Square in Clarksville. George Newton Byers (b. *c*1836), a Virginia native, was proprietor. *King's Nashville City Directory* [Clarksville] (1869), 334; (1870), 354; 1880 Census, Tenn., Montgomery, 13th Dist., Clarksville, 54.
5. "Libel" here means to institute legal proceedings against the goods.

From Robert Johnson

Head Quarters 4th Reg't
Camp Garber
April 8th 1862

Dear Father—

I have been very unwell for the last few days, and am scarcely able to go about this morning, but I am in hopes all will be right in a few days—   I

have had everything to attend to so far in the organization of my Regiment and it has taken my whole time, but I now have a most excellent
Quarter Master and Adjutant,[1] which will take a greate deal of labor off
of my hands— As yet I have appointed no Lt Col. or Major, but will
leave these questions open for the present. Ed Trigg[2] became very much
offended because I would not confer upon him the appointment of Lt
Col— he is about as suitable for the position, as I am to translate
Chinese— I intend to have a man that understands his business in a
military sense, for that position— I could have had a full Regiment by
this time, if I had commenced an organization when I first came here, but
agreed with Col Shelley[3] to waite until he made up his Regiment— if
he had carried out his agreement, or if what he had stated had been true, I
would have been much farther advanced, but I held up two or three
weeks, and still he had not his Reg't full—and is not full yet— I then
went to work & have done fine under the circumstances— Howk's
Regiment is not near full, and I must say he is a great *Scoundrel*,[4] which I
will write more about in a few days— he has done every thing against
me that he possibly could, *lying* &c. I have five Companies under
organization and hope to fill out the Battalion before I cross the mountain—

I would like to have an order from the Commanding Gen'l, that when
we cross the mountains, my Regiment, which is the 4th, may locate at or
near Greeneville in order to recruit and Drill, and would like for you to
attend to it for me—
There are not many Tennesseeans coming over now— the mountains
are closely blockaded and it is almost impossible for them to get
over— I am though looking for a Company from Greene & Hawkins
every day[.]

I have heard nothing from home lately, not since, what Patterson
wrote you—[5]

If you could spare it, I would like to have a check for One hundred
Dollars (100$) as I am compelled to use money for some of the men that
are˘ sick.

Tell Browning[6] to write to me[.]

My respects to Ed East[.]

Your Son   Robert Johnson

Address me at
Barbourville Knox Co Ky

ALS, DLC-JP.
1. Robert J. Howell (c1836-1862), formerly of the 16th Ohio Vols., was appointed
regimental quartermaster, serving until his accidental death in late 1862. James O.
Berry (b. c1835), adjutant of the 1st Tenn. Cav., USA, was promoted to major on May
15, 1862. Resigning in January, 1863, because of poor health, he later settled in
Denton, Texas. Carter, *First Tenn. Cavalry*, 270, 273; CSR, RG94, NA.
2. Edward C. Trigg.
3. James T. Shelley.
4. Of Leonidas C. Houk's recruiting, Edward Maynard wrote his father: "I was in

hope Houk never would succeed in his undertaking as he uses mean low down means to get men such as $1.00 per man to his officers, and some others to [sic] mean to mention." Edward Maynard to Horace Maynard, March 24, 1862, Horace Maynard Papers.

    5. Possibly a reference to the Letter from Michael L. Patterson, January 31, 1862.
    6. William A. Browning.

From Jesse Hartley Strickland[1]

Phila April 8th. 1862

The Honl Andrew Johnson
Dear Sir

I wrote you at Washington but I suppose you did not receive the letter.[2] I have been very badly treated by the Field Officers of the Regt of which I held the post of Captain of Co H— after giving 4 months time in Recruiting a company—I was supirseded by a man who payed well in cash for my Place[.][3] I do think it one of the most contemptable things I ever heard of[.] I brought the best of Reccomendations for the Post as to capacity and other requirements but *Money* stood high with my Col. he did not care if a man were fit or not so as he had the *needfull* so I was dropped *Sans*—ceremony[.] well Sir I am now—I might say in a strange place— I am very anxious to do something for my self and the Country[.] I do think If I were allowed a chance that I could make a mark— I am well posted in Artillery Tacticts—both Field and seige Batterys— I am well drilled in Infantry movements. All I ask of you is to give me a Command as a Captain and I will prove to you that your previous good opinion of me shall be restored[.] I will exert all my energy and give up life for the Union Cause[.] Dear Sir if you can give me a position I will be thankful indeed— I will come to Tenn and raise a Regt. if Possible of [or] if you will authorise me I will try it in the North[.] all I want is a chance—for my Profession is that of a soldier and I pretend to know my business— I would be very glad if you can spare enough of your valuable time to write me[.] I shall feel greatful[.] let me know if you can now give me a Commission and I will come to Tenn and raise a Regt and if you like command it—*any thing*—can be done if we persevere. I am anxious to take part with my union friends— I will await your answer[.] hopeing you will give me a position I will conclude[.]

I am sir Very Respectfully Yours—
J. H. Strickland

I think I could raise a Regt in and about Louisville Ky—or Indianappolis Ind—to be equipped by the U. S.

J. H. S.

ALS, DLC-JP.
    1. Jesse Hartley Strickland (c1826-1899), younger son of the architect William, had sought Johnson's help on earlier occasions. Although frustrated at this time in his efforts to obtain a commission, he was later permitted in January, 1863, to raise a cavalry

regiment in East Tennessee, an authorization withdrawn in October by virtue of his "having been seen drunk in cars with a number of soldiers." Dismissed for being absent without leave, he subsequently appealed to General Burnside, explaining that he had been ill at Camp Nelson when his regiment, the 8th Tenn. Cav., moved to the front. Settling in Washington after the war, he was employed by the U. S. Post Office. CSR, RG94, NA; *Official Army Register: Volunteers*, IV, 1183; Agnes A. Gilchrist, *William Strickland: Architect and Engineer, 1788-1854* (New York, 1969), 138; see also *Johnson Papers*, II, 447n.

2. A month earlier, Strickland had requested an appointment on Johnson's staff. Strickland to Johnson, March 4, 1862, Johnson Papers, LC.

3. It has not been possible to determine the accuracy of this charge.

From Felix H. Torbett

April 8, 1862, Fort Larned, Kans.; ALS, DLC-JP.

Disenchanted with the "development of perfidy in the extreme Southern leaders & some of their constituencies," a Tennessean, friend of Robert and now a sergeant in the regular army, offers to assist Johnson as he organizes Tennessee troops. "I have seen Lincoln cast off negrophilists and appoint Douglas Democrats. I therefore think it more honourable to continue in the service than to pursue a passive course[.] Indeed a rigid enforcement of the Constitution & the Laws is all that will save the Country from Mobocracy & petty Tyranny[.]" On the local scene, "We have discouraging news from New Mexico. . . . We have five warlike Indian tribes camped within thirty miles of the post, but they are friendly with us, and a little huffed with Maj Gen. Hunter because he would not muster them into the U. S. service. Jay hawking Kansas is just what it has been for years—"

From Tyler Davidson & Co.[1]

Cincinnati O. 8th April 1862

Hon. Andrew Johnson
Nashville, Tenn
Dear Sir.

Enclosed invoice for pistol & case[2] sent this day pr "Adams Express Co" in accordance with yr esteemed favor of 3d inst. recd two days since: this day being the *first* trip of the Express to your City.

Whenever we can be useful to you, or any of your friends, for any thing obtainable in this City or elswhere, do not hesitate to command our services. We shall promise conscientiously to execute yr orders at the lowest possible prices, and promptly forward the goods as directed. We have during the past 9 months supplied the U. S. Government with immense supplies of "Colts" and "Remingtons" Cavalry pistols, Axes, Spades, Shovels, Mule and Horse shoes, Horse Shoe nails, Iron, Steel, Travelling forges, Setts of farriers tools, Curry Combs, Horse Brushes, Wagon Chains, Manilla picket rope, Pick-axes, Handled falling axes, Handled Hatchets, &c, &c, &c,—

The Quarter-Masters departments here, at Louisville, and St Louis, have, and are now, buying largely from us, and to them we can refer for our faithfulness in supplying first rate articles at uniformly low prices.

Your friends & obt svts
Tyler Davidson & Co.

ALS, DLC-JP.

1. Founded in 1834 by Tyler Davidson (*c*1810-1865), this company, "Importers & Jobbers of Hardware, Cutlery and Metals," was by 1846 the largest hardware concern in Cincinnati. S. B. Nelson and J. M. Runk, *History of Cincinnati and Hamilton County, Ohio* (Cincinnati, 1894), 498-99; New York *Times*, January 20, 1866, October 30, 1902.

2. The accompanying invoice shows that Johnson purchased for $45.00 a variation of the six-shot, double-action "Tranter's Patent" army revolver, produced at William Tranter's Birmingham, England, factory. A. B. Griswold & Co. and Messrs. Hyde & Goodrich, both of New Orleans, were the major American importers of Tranter's revolvers, which were used by both armies, but were especially popular in the South. A. W. F. Taylerson, *The Revolver, 1865-1888* (New York, 1966), 256-57; Taylerson, *Revolving Arms* (New York, 1967), 21-22.

From Peter M. Wilson[1]

Danbury Conn Apr 8/62

To Hon Andrew Johnson

Dear Sir

Will you accept a few lines from a young *sprout* of Andrew Jackson. if you should want any help to manage some of your large Foundrys in this trouble. Pleas let me know[.] I am with you[.] I will sell out my Foundry & come there. I served my time at West Point Foundry, with Robt P Parrott,[2] & made the most importent castings on the Rebble steamer Merrimack[.] if you should want me with you I can refer you to some of our best men in this state Hon R. Averel,[3] of Danbury Ct Hon E. S. Tweedy[4] & Robt P. Parrott of West Point Foundry, & plenty of others[.] if wished any of these will tell you that I am a pretty fare kind of a man[.] if you should not want any of this kind dont trouble your self about it, as I liked your docktrin &c, & for the good of our Country. I thought there was no hurt to offer this much to you as it is my business to over see Foundrys. if you should not want [to?] bleave you have a young hickeory Friend here in Danbury & *there is lots of them* here to.

If I could be any way useful there Pleas write in return mail[.]

From a *Friend* to our Country

Peter. M. Wilson

To Hon Andrew Johnson

ALS, DLC-JP.

1. Peter M. Wilson (b. *c*1831), a New York native, operated a Danbury iron foundry and on the eve of the war owned $1,500 in personal property. 1860 Census, Conn., Danbury, 14.

2. Robert P. Parrott (1804-1877), West Point graduate (1824) and inventor of the Parrott gun and projectile, served as artillery-ordnance officer (1824-36) and as superintendent of the West Point Iron and Cannon Foundry (1836-67). *DAB*, XIV, 260-61; Boatner, *Civil War Dictionary*, 621.

General Johnson (*above*), *courtesy Library of Congress;* and his Tranter double action (*below*), *from Claude Blair*, PISTOLS OF THE WORLD (*New York, 1968*), *illus. 650.*

3. Roger Averill (1809-1883), Connecticut-born attorney and graduate of Union College (1832), had been a schoolteacher before his admission to the bar in 1836. Serving in the state legislature (1843, 1868), he was probate court judge for two years (some time after 1849) and Republican lieutenant governor (1862-66). D. Hamilton Hurd, *History of Fairfield County, Connecticut* (Philadelphia, 1881), 264; "Rolls of Membership," *New-England Historical and Genealogical Register*, XLV (1891), App. 41.

4. Edgar S. Tweedy (c1807-fl1881), Danbury businessman, was a state legislator (1845) and delegate to the 1860 Republican convention. 1860 Census, Conn., Danbury, 57; Hurd, *Fairfield County*, 205-48 *passim*; J. Robert Lane, *A Political History of Connecticut during the Civil War* (Washington, 1941), 129.

From Leroy S. Clements[1]

Scottsville Ky Apl 9th 1862

Hon Andrew Johnson Gov
    Dear Sir

you will pardon me for taking the liberty of addressing you these lines they being on business in which many person in Tennessee are interested[.] I being a Tennessean myself having had to leave the State in the last few days on the account of several meraurdering bands of Cecessionists that are creating desperate havoc in many counties along the line[.] Unless there can be something done for Macon Jackson Overton Fentress in Tennessee and Wayne Clinton Cumberland Monroe and Allen in Kentucky they will be impoverished and finally ruined[.] the above named Counties turned out a large number of Soldiers for the Federal Army leaving many large Families at home which must be fed and protected and that protection must come from the Army or then many a poor Soldiers Family is bound to Suffer if not Starve[.] the bands under Oliver Hamilton Jams Eaton Champ Fergueson and Bledsoe[2] must be met and Infantry will do no good[.] they are all mounted men and this is a hilly country and would require Cavalry to do any good[.] the Soldiers Families seems to be one of the great objects to vent their Spleen on[.] a Sick or wounded Soldier has no Security[.] at home there came a band in but a few days ago and took out some 25 or 30 head of fine horses and bed clothing[.][3] the Rebels Say that Union men shall make nothing in all the Loyal portion of Tennessee along the line being a distance of about 100 miles unprotected[.] I would have written to my Brother[4] at Washington to interceded & Send some Cavalry but knowing that you was much nigher' & thinking that there might be four or five Companies or a Regiment of Cavalry in or about Nashville that could be Spared to hold the Rebels in check and Stop their depredations until a Regiment could be raised and Armed to protect this Country[.] there must be and armed force as a neuclus of Strength to hold them at bay until the men is raised and armed or they will be cut off[.] as soon as a few gets together you will by arranging and sending a few Companies into macon Jackson and Overton Save a large number of as loyal people as lives in this Government and unless it is done in a few days it will be too late as they will get to plant nothing and thus necessarially starve[.] many of the Citizens implored me to drop you this note of our troubles and implore you to send men if possible immediately to our assistance in doing which you will receive the greatful thanks of many hu[n]dred Loyal people[.] have men Stationed Some where in the Section[.]

Respectfully your Obt. Servt
L. S. Clements

ALS, DLC-JP.

1. Leroy S. Clements (b. c1824), Tennessee-born attorney. 1850 Census, Tenn., Jackson, 5th Dist., 450.

2. James Eaton (b. c1830), Tennessee native and a clerk living in Jackson County in 1860, was a first lieutenant in Hamilton's company, Shaw's cavalry. Willis S. Bledsoe (b. c1836), a Kentuckian practicing law in Jamestown in 1861, organized an independent cavalry company which took part in guerrilla activities in Kentucky and Tennessee in 1861-62. Commissioned major, 4th Tenn. Cav., CSA (1862), he was by the end of the war regimental commander. *Ibid.*, Fentress, 3rd Dist., 823; (1860), 1st Dist., 87; *Tennesseans in the Civil War*, II, 141; George B. Guild, *A Brief Narrative of the Fourth Tennessee Cavalry Regiment* (Nashville, 1913), 125, 183-84.

3. Led by Ferguson, Hamilton, Bledsoe, and James W. McHenry in late March and early April, 1862, these raids into Kentucky, mounted in retaliation for a Union guerrilla foray into Tennessee while McHenry's and Bledsoe's companies were in Alabama, resulted in the killing of some fifteen persons, many believed to be Federal soldiers on leave or members of home guards, and the seizure of horses and other personal property here cited. Pursued by Kentucky cavalry, the "lawless marauding band of ruffians from Tennessee" retreated unscathed to their camp at Livingston. See Letters from Isaac T. Reneau, March 31, 1862, and from [Berry J. Reneau], April 6, 1862; Sensing, *Champ Ferguson*, 29-30, 89, 94-98; Nashville *Union*, April 19, 1862; Schroeder, "Writings of a Tennessee Unionist," 256-57.

4. Andrew J. Clements (1832-1913), Tennessee-born physician, practiced at Lafayette before being elected as a unionist to the U. S. Congress (August, 1861). Fearing a secessionist plot to seize him, he fled the state, and served as assistant surgeon, 9th Ky. Inf., before taking his seat in the House (January, 1862). Later he served as surgeon, 1st Tenn. Mtd. Inf., USA, and in the state legislature (1866-67) before returning to his profession. *BDAC*, 176n, 706; Robison, *Preliminary Directory, Macon*, 2-3; Cincinnati *Gazette*, September 5, 1861; Louisville *Journal*, November 27, 1861.

From Thomas C. James[1]

Head Quarters
Clarksville Ten April 9 1862

Hon Andrew Johnson
Governor of Ten   Nashville Ten
Sir

I have the honour to repeat to you that your Telegraphic despatch of 6th. inst was duly rec'd—[2] on Monday 7th. inst the negro Boy "Anselm"[3] was tried by a jury of 12 Citizens before the Recorder & Magistrates of this City— After a fair & impartial trial, counsel having been appointed to defend him, he was convicted & condemned to be hung on

Friday 18 April— I was present at the time & saw that everything was fair— The boy has confessed his crime—

There was no excitement during the trial which was conducted in a very orderly manner— herewith I Send you a full report of the pro- ceedings—[4] the course pursued has given great satisfaction to the Citizens—[5]

I have the honour to be with much Respect

Yr obt Servt   Thomas C. James
Lt. Col 9th Regt Pa Cav. Comdg Post

ALS, DLC-JP.

1. Thomas C. James (c1812-1863), a Philadelphia merchant, commanded the First City Troop, of which he had long been captain, for three months early in the war. Subsequently he became lieutenant colonel of the 9th Pa. Cav. upon its organization and shortly before his death became its colonel. Frank H. Taylor, *Philadelphia in the Civil War, 1861-1865* (Philadelphia, 1913), 168; *McElroy's Philadelphia Directory* (1860), 480; Philadelphia *Evening Bulletin*, January 13, 14, 1863.

2. Although no telegram has been found, an endorsement, evidently written by one of Johnson's aides, on an envelope enclosing James's original message about Anselm reads "Answered by telegraph that he [James] pursued the proper course in delivering the slave over to State Authority[.]" James to J. M. Blain, [April] 5, 1862, Johnson Papers, LC.

3. Texas-born Anselm (Anslim, Ansolam, Ansalin, Auslom) D. Brown (b. c1844), a black servant accused of poisoning the family of his master Joshua Brown with arsenic, was arrested by city police, tried April 7 in a citizens' court—presided over by two justices of the peace and with an ad hoc jury—convicted, and sentenced to be hanged. Pending appeal to the state supreme court, the army held Brown for safekeeping until Johnson requested his transfer to the Nashville penitentiary in late December, 1863. Earlier that month the prisoner had enrolled in Co. C, 16th U. S. Cld. Inf. but seems to have spent the first six months of 1864 in custody, appearing as present on the company rolls only on July 20. Demoted in late October, after two months as a corporal, he deserted early in November, returning eventually to duty and being mustered out in April, 1866. For Brown's vicissitudes, see *ibid.*; Clarksville, Tenn., Citizens to Johnson, April 8, 1862 (including report of civil hearing at Clarksville courthouse, April 7); Frank T. D. Ketcham to Johnson, January 7, 1864; Johnson to Ulysses S. Grant, January 13, 1864, Johnson Papers, LC; CSR, RG94, NA.

4. The attached account of the April 7 proceedings, dated the following day, in- cludes the names of the "jurors," and is signed by W. T. Shackelford.

5. For a contrary view of the case, see Letter from Ebenezer Dumont, April 10, 1862.

From Salmon Skinner

April 9, 1862, New York, N.Y.; ALS-DLC-JP.

An associate of "W. M. E. Hartly in supplying army goods" asks Johnson to convey a letter to his daughter and son-in-law, J. T. E. McLean, who should now be in Nashville. Commends the governor's course in Tennessee: "your proclama- tion & speeches are read with much satisfaction; a little anxiety is felt that you may be too lenient with old friends." Wishes southerners "could understand the true sentiment of the North. We love them too well, to let them go out of the Union—or to violate the Constitution or the laws—or Commit any other suicidal act."

To Abraham Lincoln

Nashville Tenn. Apl 9th 1862

His Excellency Abraham Lincoln

Several prominent Disunionists have been arrested. It would exert a decided influence to send them beyond the limits of the State[.] where shall I send them.[1] All is working well beyond my most sanguine expectations[.]

Andrew Johnson

Tel, DLC-Lincoln Papers; RG107, Tels. Recd., Sec. of War, Vol. 8 (April 3-10, 1862); *OR*, Ser. 2, III, 435.
    1. Two days earlier Johnson had sent a similar message to Secretary of War Stanton; the latter directed the governor to "send them to Detroit under Guard with directions to take [turn] them over to Captain [Alfred] Gibbs," commanding. "They will be sent from there to Fort Macinaw on Lake Huron." *OR*, Ser. 2, III, 438; Johnson to Stanton, April 7, 1862, RG107, NA; Stanton to Johnson, April 10, 1862, Johnson Papers, LC; see also Order to Stanley Matthews, April 16, 1862.

From William T. Bailey

April 10, 1862, Milwaukee, Wis.; ALS, DLC-JP.

Bricklayer-plasterer asks "for a situasion as *Detecttive* on cecrit Police," because "by working a little at my trade I should not be Suspected."

From Ebenezer Dumont

Head Quarters U. S. Forces
Nashville April 10th 1862

Gov Johnson

I have looked at the papers forwarded you, by Lt Col James[1] Commanding at Clarksville, in regard to the trial with condemnation to death of the boy, Ansalin for poisoning the family of Brown. It dont appear that any of the family died, it dont appear that any of them were very sick, it dont appear that the substance supposed to be poison was analyzed by any one capable of making an analysis, it dont appear that a single witness was cross examined, the confession of the boy may have been obtained properly and may not, such confessions are to be considered with great caution. But aside from all this he was tried by a self constituted body, styling themselves a jury, and that is enough for me, without inquiring into the guilt or innocence of the accused. If he is guilty he can be tried by a legally constituted tribunal, and punished. If he is not, he ought not to be murdered. I am for crushing out the mob spirit, before which the innocent & guilty have alike suffered, and this case presents a fit opportunity.

If there was no law it would be another thing. I would then feel like inquiring with care, into the justice or injustice of the judgment of this "*town meeting*" but as it is, I will not take time to do it, the negro shall not be murdered if I can help it.

I felt glad at our former interview that our sentiments were harmonious, as to the propriety of giving the boy a fair trial by a legally constituted tribunal. After reading the documents my opinion is not changed[.] Murder cant be dignified in my estimation by any such mock solemnity and pretended circumspection. It is in my opinion a cool piece of impudence to send a Governor, who is bound to enforce the law, such a document with the hope that it will meet his approbation. Supposing that you forwarded the letter & documents to me with a view of eliciting my opinion. I have given it freely, And have the honor to be

Your obt Svt
E Dumont

ALS, DLC-JP.
1. James had included copies of his April 5 letter to J. M. Blain and of the April 7 proceedings in the Brown case.

To Edwin M. Stanton

Nashville, Apl 11 [10] 1862.

Hon. Edwin M. Stanton
Secy War—

I forwarded some time since a statement of Brig Genl Spears in regard to military operations at Cumberland Ford—

I hope the Secy will place Genl Spears at once in command of Tennessee Troops at that place[.]   this ought to be done[.] Leut Carter of the Navy has been acting as general as I conseive without proper authority—   The Tennesseans there and others on the way wish to return under the lead of Genl Spears—

Will the Secy telegh me his action—   Things are moving on right in Tennessee[.]

Andrew Johnson

Tel, DNA-RG107, Tels. Recd., Sec. of War, Vol. 9 (Apr. 11-17, 1862); DLC-JP; *OR*, Ser. 1, X, Pt. II, 101.

From Don Carlos Buell

Pittsburgh Landing Apl 11th 1862

To Brig Genl Andrew Johnson

With the pressing demand for troops in other quarters it will not be possible at present to spare troops for the service you suggest[.]¹ I hope to be able to send them before long.

D C Buell Maj-Genl

Tel, DLC-JP.

1. Probably a reference to Johnson's April 4 request for Buell to send a small cavalry force to the Kentucky line "for an excursion of several days."

From Harriet N. Henshaw¹

Washington Apr. 11th 1862

My dear friend

You will be surprised at receiving another line from me so soon, but I have to say that I am at last appointed a situation in the noteroom of the Treasury Department thanks to the kindness of Mr Bailey² who stated to Sec. Chase your wishes in regard to it and he immediately attended to it. I was taken by surprise as it was entirely unsolicited on my part.

I do not think I can write much that will interest you unless it be that your Proclamation and speech in the State House are winning golden opinions³ for you. I dare not tell you all I hear as I am fearful it might make you vain. Please write me how long you expect to remain in Tennessee and if you will come back before next winter.

Mrs Muldaur has just received a letter from Alonzo,⁴ he is sorrowing greatly that he has no opportunity of distinguishing himself. he is cruising on the coast of Florida, and doing very little indeed.

I am still at the St. Charles⁵ but am not decided how long I am to remain.

I sent you the Philadelphia Inquirer containing your speech and the editorial respecting it,⁶ also some extracts from other papers for your Scrap Book, did you receive them? Thus you see that I have not forgotten you entirely.

Your time is undoubtedly very much occupied and I will not trouble you with the reading of very long letters[.] I will therefore close by wishing you much pleasure in your grateful but arduous undertaking while I remain as ever your friend

Harriet

ALS, DLC-JP.

1. Harriet N. Henshaw (*fl* 1873), a Massachusetts native who had operated a school in Washington in 1860, was at this time one of several "females temporarily employed" in the treasury department at a salary of $600 per year; she continued as clerk after the war. *U. S. Official Register* (1863), 31; *Boyd's Washington and Georgetown Directory* (1860), 86; (1873), 238.

2. Probably Goldsmith Fox Bailey, Massachusetts congressman.

3. The Washington *National Intelligencer* of March 26, printing the text of Johnson's March 18 Appeal to the People of Tennessee, observed that the "excellent address" set forth a policy which conformed to that of Lincoln—"cautious but decided, conciliatory but firm."

4. Alonzo W. Muldaur (*c*1839-1870), born in Massachusetts, had been a Washington clerk and draftsman before becoming acting master on the U. S. S. *Santiago de Cuba* in October, 1861. In due time, despite Alonzo's pessimism, he received promotions, ultimately becoming a lieutenant commander in December, 1868, just thirteen months before he was lost on board the U. S. S. *Oneida* at Yokohama, Japan. In 1860 he and his mother Mary (b. *c*1820) were living in Seth Lamb's Washington boarding house. 1860 Census, Washington, D. C., 5th Ward, 1; *Boyd's Washington and Georgetown Directory* (1860), 116; (1869), 360; Thomas H. S. Hamersly, ed., *General Register of the United States Navy and Marine Corps . . . 1782-1882* (Washington, 1882), 516.

5. It is probable that Johnson had become acquainted with the Muldaurs through Harriet Henshaw while residing at the St. Charles during his last years in the Senate.

6. Printing the address in its entirety, the *Inquirer* of April 1 urged its audience "to read this strong and fervent speech of a true man and a fearless—a sterling patriot . . . 'tried in the furnace, and *not* found wanting.' "

From Thomas C. James

Head Quarters
Clarksville Ten   April 11, 1862

Hon Andrew Johnson
Governor of Ten. Nashville
Dear Sir

I had this honour [to present you?] a day or two since with a copy of the proceedings of the Committee who tried the boy Anslem for Poisoning his master—

Last night I recd your telegraph[1] & that of Genl Dumont—   I did not intend to allow the Execution of the boy without your authority for it— I have requested the Mayor to call the leading Citizens to gether & will show them your despatch—   the boy is in jail closely confined & the Mayor[2] promises me he shall not be meddled with—   When the order is made known I am afraid there will be much excitement & dissatisfaction—   Will you be good enough to tell me how soon there is a likelyhood of a Criminal Court being held here—   it is necessary that the negros of this town & County should know that punishment will follow such offences as this boy has been quilty of[.]

I have the honour to be   Yr obt Servt
Thomas C. James
Lt Col Comdg Post

ALS, DLC-JP.

1. Johnson had telegraphed: "An application in writing, to any Judge of Circuit or Criminal Courts, certified by the oath of at least five creditable persons, that they believe the negro did as is charged, then the Judge shall forthwith proceed to try him." Citing applicable Tennessee laws, he concluded that "The Criminal Judge will act on call of citizens at any hour." Johnson to James, [April 10, 1862], Johnson Papers, LC.

2. George Smith (*c*1799-1864) moved from his native Virginia to Wilson County before settling in Montgomery County in 1831, where he became involved in merchandising. In 1854 he took charge of the Franklin House in Clarksville, serving four years as mayor (1859-62), and two terms as county trustee. 1860 Census, Tenn., Montgomery, Clarksville, 4; Titus, *Picturesque Clarksville*, 152-53.

From "Observer"

Nashville Apl 11. 62

To His Ex Gov Genl Andrew Johnson

I think you would do well to appoint a new set of Firemen, for if one of the Federal Comissaries was to get on fire the firemen in South Nashville would do their best to let it burn up[.] Their Hall is a regular Secesh meeting house[.] They meet to talk treason daily[.] yesterday when the report got out that Morgan & Scotts Cavelry[1] with the Texans were in a few hours ride of hear some of them became verry bold[.] one in particular James Davis[2] a kind of a Captain among them when Old Deshields[3] is not there went so far as to say that he had severl union men spotted and was going to make them get up and rush as soon as The Southerners got here.

A great many console themselves with the Idea that some day Morgan with 4 or 500 Cavalry will come and arrest you and Secretary East and a No of Officers and make their escape— I hope you will take precautions against surprise[.]

Respectfully   *Observer*

ALS, DLC-JP.

1. John Hunt Morgan (1825-1864), Alabama-born Confederate cavalry leader, attended Transylvania College (1842-44), served in the Mexican War, and until 1861 manufactured hemp and engaged in merchandising in Lexington. Organizer in 1857 of the Lexington Rifles, a militia company, he led it "south" to join the Confederate force at Bowling Green in September, 1861. Promoted to colonel of the 2nd Ky. Cav. the following April, he was commissioned brigadier in December. Captured during a July, 1863, raid into Ohio, he escaped in November and had returned to active duty as commander of the Department of Southwestern Virginia, when he was surprised and killed at Greeneville, Tennessee. John S. Scott (c1826-fl1872), a wealthy planter of Pointe Coupee Parish, commanded the 1st La. Cav., active in Tennessee, Kentucky, and northern Alabama from 1861 to 1863. Resigning as colonel in October, 1863, he returned to Louisiana where he led "three well-equipped and well-armed regiments," operating from Clinton and Morganza. After the war he was a New Orleans cotton factor and commission merchant. *DAB*, XIII, 174-75; Cecil F. Holland, *Morgan and His Raiders: A Biography of the Confederate General* (New York, 1942); Howell Carter, *A Cavalryman's Reminiscences of the Civil War* (New Orleans, [1900]), 9-12, 18-33 *passim*, 50, 52, 96, 104-5, 134; 1860 Census, La., Pointe Coupee, Waterloo, 3; John D. Winters, *The Civil War in Louisiana* (Baton Rouge, 1963), 396-97, 412; *Edwards' New Orleans Directory* (1872), 367.

2. Possibly James M. Davis (b. c1834), a Tennessee-born shoemaker. 1860 Census, Tenn., Davidson, Nashville, 8th Ward, 43.

3. John S. Dashiell (c1808-fl1881), Maryland native, was a steamboat captain with $500 in personal property. First chief of the Nashville fire department (1860), he was later a clerk and bookkeeper. *Ibid.*, 5th Ward, 182; Clayton, *Davidson County*, 210; Nashville city directories (1866-81), *passim*.

From John H. Purnell[1]

Bardstown Ky Apl 11th 62

Brig Genl Andrew Johnson
Govr Tenn.
Dear Genl

I see in List of city officials whom you have ejected from office the name of L. F. Beech,[2] which I suppose is Lafayette Beech a tall handsome man with black whiskers, who was engaged last summer very extensively in the Smuggling business between Louisville and Nashville.

Furthermore if I am correct in my supposition, He is one among twenty five or thirty men who detached the Engine from the northern bound train to Louisville and came as far as Lebanon Junction aided in destroying my office there and stealing the instruments and the same night about mid night this same party of which He was *one*, burned the bridge over the Rolling Fork one mile South of the Lebanon Junction[.][3]

Very Respectfully Yours &C
John H. Purnell
of the Military Telegraphs.

L F Beech & Powers[4] a Jew & clothing merchant of this city boasted last Summer that [they] had done the things charged in the foregoing letter[.]

ALS, T-Mil. Gov's Papers, 1862-65.

1. John H. Purnell (c1839-fl1916), a Maysville, Kentucky, native employed in the telegraphic service by several railroads, including the L & N (1861-62), worked as an operator for the Union army. Moving from Louisville to Opelika, Alabama, in 1866, he continued as a railroad telegrapher until he accepted a position with the Western Union Company five years later. He unsuccessfully sought Federal employment during the Johnson and Cleveland administrations. Purnell to Johnson, February 22, 1866, Johnson Papers, LC; Purnell to Cleveland, May 14, 1886, Grover Cleveland Papers, LC; Purnell to Wilson, March 6, 1916, Woodrow Wilson Papers, LC.

2. Lafayette F. Beech (b. c1828), a Tennessean and former Franklin dry goods merchant with $50,000 real and $15,000 personal property, had by 1860 established a similar business in Nashville where he served as a councilman from the 3rd ward. In 1870 he was city tax assessor. Goodspeed's Williamson, 803; 1860 Census, Tenn., Davidson, Nashville, 3rd Dist., 67; Nashville Bus. Dir. (1860-61), 127; King's Nashville City Directory (1870), 87.

3. During the course of these incidents which occurred September 18, 1861, Purnell himself was apparently captured by the raiders but "escaped by walking to Bardstown Junction." Rebuilding on the strategically important Rolling Fork bridge, some thirty miles south of Louisville, was completed and railroad service restored by October 2. Louisville Journal, September 19, 21, 23, 27, October 4, 1861.

4. Probably one of the three Powers brothers, Michael (1821-1881), Louis (b. c1824?), and Samuel (1814-1875), English-born Jewish clothing merchants doing business in Nashville during the 1850's; the latter two were known to be Confederate sympathizers. Porch, 1850 Census, Nashville, 40, 144; Nashville Union and American, June 8, 1875; Fedora S. Frank, Five Families and Eight Young Men: Nashville and Her Jewry, 1850-1861 (Nashville, 1962), 56-57; Frank, Beginnings on Market Street: Nashville and Her Jewry (Nashville, 1976), 33, 42, 113, 139.

To David R. Haggard, Gallatin

April 11, 1862, Nashville; L draft, DLC-JP.

Orders the provost marshal at Gallatin to arrest Joseph C. Guild for uttering "treasonable language" and using "his influence against . . . the Government of the United States." [An April 15 letter from Thomas J. Jordan (Johnson Papers, LC) advises that the writ has been carried out.]

From Gilbert C. Breed[1]

Clarksville April 12th 1862.

Hon Andrew Johnson
Sir

A few weeks ago I wrote you concerning our Road, suggesting that as it had failed twice in the payment of the interest on its bonds, it by the law of Tennessee had passed virtually into the hands of the State. Since that time I have written Mr Guthrie[2] Prest of Louisville and Nashville R. Road (in answer to a telegram of his inquiring what this road was doing in the matter of building up its bridges, or what it was willing to do.) I represented to Mr Guthrie the exact financial condition of the Road, and stating to him the apathy—and secession sympathy of the Directors of the Road— I have a reply by telegraph from him to day saying that they could not help this road in its rebuilding of Bridges &c &c, but wanting to make an arrangement to run our road as far as the Bridge burnt near our town. Since writing to him however and previous to getting his dispatch, I have been discharged from the Superintendency of the Road by the President[3]—and am satisfied that it is from the same cause, that I was discharged on a former occasion from the Road—except that I was then discharged from a subordinate position on account of *supposed* Union proclivites, but now from my proclamation of them. I write this that you may weigh the matter whether the State should not take charge of its own for the benefit of the people—rather than that loud mouthed secessionists should still longer oppress those who would like to open the channels of business, and those who were the laborers and Employees on this and other connecting roads. I am satisfied that a large Union sentiment would be developed, which is now latent, if the legal rights of the State were immediately enforced, at the same time that the Federal Government is enforcing its power— I would like to have you give me a conference in regard to this matter—and if so will you telegraph me at your earliest convenience, when I can see you and hear your views on this subject. I have also a plan or rather an idea connected with the runing of the portion of this road that is uninjured with the Edgefield

& Kentucky Road which is also uninjured and which is now and has been for some time in the hands of the State.[4]

Yours Very Respy   G. C. Breed

Late Supt M.C. & L.R.R.

ALS, DLC-JP.

1. Gilbert C. Breed (b. *c*1830), Connecticut-born superintendent of the Louisville and Nashville Railroad, was later Montgomery County circuit court clerk (1865), unionist delegate to a Columbia convention (June, 1865), and general freight agent on the Memphis, Clarksville, and Louisville Railroad (1871). He also served briefly as a federal tax assessor (1866-67). 1870 Census, Tenn., Montgomery, 12th Dist., 81; Titus, *Picturesque Clarksville*, 353; *Goodspeed's Montgomery*, 771, 773; *Senate Ex. Journal*, XV (1866-67), Pt. I, 86, 239-40.

2. James Guthrie.

3. For Robert W. Humphreys, president of the Memphis, Clarksville, and Louisville Railroad, see *Johnson Papers*, IV, 382*n*.

4. The Edgefield and Kentucky, incorporated February 13, 1852, by the state of Tennessee, extended from Guthrie, Kentucky, to Nashville. Beginning operation about 1859, the road went into receivership the following year when it defaulted on interest payments to the state for bonds issued under the Internal Improvement Act of 1852. Breed's plan entailing state operation of the road was adopted. *Report of General J. T. Boyle to Gov. William G. Brownlow on the Condition of the Railroads in Tennessee* (Nashville, 1867), 5-7.

From Robert Johnson

Camp Garber Ky

April 12th 1862

Dear Father

I am succeeding very well in the organization of my Regiment and from all reports, if true, I will have a Regiment before we cross the mountain, unless Gen'l Morgan, who arrived here this morning and has assumed command, makes some movement in a very few days, which I do not believe he will do— I understand that there will be some 200 men from Claiborne County over by Tuesday or Wednesday who will join my Regiment and there are some 400 to 600 from Knox that I have no doubt, if they get this high up, but what will join me— at all events I will organize a Battalion before I cross the mountain and then I will have no difficulty in filling out the Regiment— I have not as yet appointed a Lt Col or Major, but will have to appoint a Lt Col as soon as I organize my Battalion—and I have no man, as yet, from East Tennessee that is qualified for the position— the Lt Colonel has almost the entire charge of the drilling of the Regiment and it requires a military man for the place— I am offered the services of the best military man in this Brigade,[1] if I will accept him— he is an affable, polite, genleman, but one of the finest disciplinarians in the service and I believe he would be of more advantage to me than any man I could possibly get— He is now the *Major* of the 16th Ohio Regiment stationed just above here, and that Regiment has the character of being the *best drilled* and orderly Regiment in the Brigade and he has done it all— he has always been a strong Democrat and continues in the faith— I have not yet appointed him but will hold the matter up for the present— I intend to appoint *James A. Galbraith*,[2] *Major*, as soon as we cross the mountain— Young Maynard is Col Cooper's Lt Colonel, which accounts for *some things*—[3] I can unfold a tale of *Treachery* when I see you, that you never dreamed of— Col Cooper is very near the character that Col Hawk[4] wrote you, although Hawk is as great a Scoundrel as ever lived and if I had the disposition could break up his Regiment tomorrow— he only has about 500 men, 200 of them have sent their officers to me, to know if I would receive them into my Regiment— I told them that I would not—that I would not interfere with Col Hawks Regiment or any other Reg't.— If I cannot make up a Regiment fairly and upon right principles I wont have it— If I would, I could fill my Regiment before 48 hours out of Col's Shelly & Hawks Reg't—but I wont do it—although *they* and especially Hawk take every advantage they can— I can get my Regiment without resorting to any such means[.]

I enclose a letter to you tonight that was enclosed to me by Judge Catron[5] to Mrs Ann Maria Brown,[6] which I hope you will have sent to her— It was sent to me to Nashville & remailed to me to Barbourville & I received it this morning—

Since I wrote you last my health has very much improved— I have been out to the Camp to day seeing to matters and things generally— I have received a new lot of Tents and had them pitched & had some Cabins built & the boys are getting along very comfortable— I will move to camp myself as soon as I get perfectly sound— I have *two Splendid New Wall Tents* and I will pitch them and try a Soldiers life the balance of the Season—

My Camp is about seven miles, on Cumberland Gap Road, from Barbarvourville & 1 mile from Flat Lick— I call it "Camp Garber," from Major Garber[7] the U. S. Quarter Master, at this point— he has shown great Kindness to me, furnished me waggons &c when he absolutely needed them himself— he has supplied me with all clothing, camp equipage &c & has even stopped his own work to accommodate me— I therefore in honor of him, called my Camp "Garber"[.]

Capt Matt. Adams,[8] the Commissary, has been very Kind to me and has shown me many favors— all here are my friends, *except a few*, of whom I will give you a history at no distant day— If from all I can learn, I will organize my Regiment before I cross the mountain, I will see you before I go over and talk in full upon some subjects— Gen'l Morgan[9] I understand to be a perfect gentleman and a man of energy— I will go and see him to morrow— Gen'l Spears & myself.

Before I close this rather long letter, I wish to make an inquiry. The Fund that was placed to your credit at Cincinnatti, for the benefit of East Tenn. Volunteers, cannot I get some of that fund for the organization of my Regiment— I am necessarily compelled to have money & must go on my own purse, which is now *broke*— If I could draw some two thousand Dollars of that fund it would afford a great relief— Our people come over entirely destitute and I am compelled to supply their wants— A great many get down sick— I have no sugeon, cannot appoint one until he goes to Louisville and is examined by the Medical Board—have to in the meantime do the best I can, get what physician I can find—buy medicine, for it wont do to let the boys die without some attention. I will spend every thing I have got & go in Debt before I will do it— I have already spent what little money I had, and I have but about 3 Dollars in my pocket to night— I do not feel able to do every thing, and I do think that if this fund was appropriated for the benefit of East Tennessians, that I and my Reg't is entitled to at least 2000 $ of it—to help us along in organization— If you think as I do, I would like to have some four or five checks for the amount— If I am mistaken about the object of the fund, all right— at all events I would lik to have some money for myself, for as I am into the thing I will carry it through or die in the attempt, and would like to have some money, if possible, Some way or other— If you send me any, send a check—

We heard to-day of the taking of Island No 10 and the Battle near Pittsburg Landing,[10] were greatly rejoiced at the result—

Sam is still working at Bob Carters[11] where I left him—
Mother is in Carter— Charles was at Greeneville—not drinking[.] Patterson at last accounts was holding his Courts[.]

If Trigg's' appointment[12] has not been confirmed or sent in, it would in my opinion be advisable to hold it up for the present—

Give my respects to Ed East— I was glad to see you had appointed him secretary of state— Tell him to write to me—also Browning[.][13]

Direct your letters to Barbourville Ky[.]

Your Son
Robert Johnson

ALS, DLC-JP.

1. Philip Kershner (*c*1833-*fl*1897), Springfield, Ohio, carpenter, and major in the 16th Ohio Inf., was recommended to Robert as a "good drill officer as well as disciplinarian." Kershner, as lieutenant colonel, remained with the 16th Ohio until wounded and captured at Vicksburg in December, 1862. Discharged from the service in October, 1864, he resided in Detroit after the war. 1860 Census, Ohio, Clark, Springfield, 2nd Ward, 70; *Williams' springfield & Urbana Directory* (1859-60), 17, 54; CSR, RG94, NA;S. P. Carter to Robert Johnson, April 14, 1862, Johnson Papers, LC.

2. James A. Galbraith (b. *c*1829), Greeneville depot agent prior to the war with property worth $2,500, seems not to have become a major. In June, 1863, he was refugeeing in Cincinnati, where he remained six months before returning to East Tennessee to engage in recruiting for the army during the fall of 1864. Following the war he was a Greeneville alderman and a pallbearer at Johnson's funeral. 1860 Census, Tenn., Greene, 10th Dist., 82; Doughty, *Greeneville*, 246, 261; Galbraith to Johnson, June 24, 1863, January 9, October 25, 1864, Johnson Papers, LC.

3. Perhaps Robert is suggesting that in his dispute with Joseph Cooper over the transfer of thirty to forty men from Cooper's to Johnson's regiment, the former has

some advantages by virtue of having the political influence within the army hierarchy stemming from having Congressman Maynard's son on his staff. S. P. Carter to Robert Johnson, April 10, 14, 1862, *ibid.*

4. See Letter from Leonidas Houk, February 18, 1862.

5. John Catron, U. S. Supreme Court justice.

6. Ann Maria Childress Brown (b.1810), wife of Judge Morgan W. Brown of Nashville, was the sister of Matilda (Mrs. John) Catron. Porch, *1850 Census, Nashville*, 80; Jane H. Thomas, *Old Days in Tennessee: Reminiscences* (Nashville, 1897), 21, 116; Kelly, *Children of Nashville*, 429.

7. Michael C. Garber, Sr. (1813-1881), a native Virginian, was a merchant and trader in Pennsylvania before moving to Madison, Indiana, in 1846. Owner and editor (1850-81) of the Democratic *Daily Courier* and enemy of Senator Jesse Bright, Garber became a staunch Republican in the late 1850's. Serving as quartermaster, U. S. Vols. (1861-66), he participated in campaigns in Kentucky, Mississippi, and Texas, and accompanied Sherman on the march through Georgia. Frank S. Baker, "Michael C. Garber, Sr., and the Early Years of the Madison, Indiana, *Daily Courier*," *Indiana Magazine of History*, XLVIII (1952), 397-408; Michael C. Garber, Jr., "Reminiscences of the Burning of Columbia, South Carolina," *ibid.*, XI (1915), 286, 299-300.

8. For George M. Adams, see *Johnson Papers*, IV, 556n.

9. George W. Morgan (1820-1893), a Pennsylvanian who served in the Texas revolution and Mexican War, farmed and practiced law in Ohio until appointed consul to Marseilles (1856-58) and minister to Portugal (1858-61). Commissioned brigadier general of volunteers in November, 1861, Morgan had just been assigned on March 28 to the 7th Division, Army of the Ohio. He was a central figure in the expulsion of the Confederate forces from Cumberland Gap in 1862, resigning from the army the following year to enter Ohio politics. Defeated for governor (1865), he later served in Congress (1867-68, 1869-73). *DAB*, XIII, 170-71; *BDAC*, 1356; *OR*, Ser. 1, X, Pt. I, 51.

10. Federal movements against Island No. 10 in the Mississippi near New Madrid, Missouri, beginning in late February, culminated in Gen. John Pope's capture of the garrison on April 7. The same day marked the end of the battle at Pittsburg Landing (Shiloh). Long, *Civil War Almanac*, 176, 195-96.

11. For Sam, one of Johnson's slaves, see *Johnson Papers*, III, 405n. Probably Robert C. Carter (1824-1907), a Greeneville farmer and former captain in the Mexican War. Carter had kept Robert Johnson "secreted at his house . . . for four months, after he had been proclaimed an outlaw by the infernal edicts of the bogus confederacy." Fleeing from East Tennessee and joining Daniel Stover's 4th Tenn. Inf. in December, 1862, as second lieutenant and rising to captain of Co. C, Carter was captured and paroled at McMinnville in October, 1863, to serve on detached duty collecting paroled men until he resigned in April, 1864. Reynolds, *Greene County Cemeteries*, 244; 1860 Census, Tenn., Greene, 12th Dist., 63; CSR, RG94, NA; Washington *Morning Chronicle*, December 11, 1862.

12. Edward C. Trigg's appointment as a lieutenant-colonel to raise a regiment. Trigg to Andrew Johnson, April 28, 1862, Johnson Papers, LC.

13. William A. Browning.

From Joseph Ramsay[1]

Shelbyville April 12th 1862

To his Excellency Andrew Johnston
Dear Sir

permit me a gain to Inform you that on yesterday morning that our troops was Taken By surprise & attacked whilst in their Tents asleep by a parcel of Cavalry Including as I understand the princpal portion to Be Citizens or at Least wer in Citizen Dress[.] this was near Wartrac Depot about 8 Miles From shelbyvlle[.]   the Rebels Killed some 4 of our men and wounded several more[.] they had several Killed Like-wise[.] I understand General Mitchl[2] Took possession of Huntsville Alabama day Before yesterday and Captured 15 Engins and about 200 prison[ers] and will soon have Stephenson & I presume De-catur[.] that will Be quite a Relif To our Friends in what is Called Seqatchie vally (IE) Marion & Bledsoe Counties as a gret many of the union Citizens has had to flee to this and other places for Refuge[.] our County is Right side up and as Long as you Continue to place such men as Henry Cooper on guard Every thing will Be kept safe[.] If you know of the where about of Frend Brownlow[3] pleas send me Word[.] all quet to day[.] let us have mail as Early as possable so that we can get the Louisvile Journal[.] Both Banner & patriott give Dis-cordant notes kind of Ashdod Language[.][4] I Regard them Both as un-reliable sentinels and not to Be Trusted[.]

some in fact many of your old political Friends are now your Worst Enemies Frequntly useing such Languge as this that you are a Traitor and ought to Be Hung particular the Breckenridge democracy[.] as I said Before in a note I sent you[5] Stephen A Douglass was the man for me. any way that I Can serve the union & Constitution of the Country By Giving information Either from this Waren Coffee or Cannon in which Countes I am Intimatly With their men[.]

Your &c   Joseph Ramsay

PS   I refer you Judge Cooper & Ed Cooper[6] or any other good union man in this plac or County for my antecedents & presentz[.]

J R

ALS, DLC-JP.

1. Joseph Ramsay (b. c1805), Bedford County farmer and Tennessee native, pos-sessed $3,000 in real and $5,000 in personal property. 1860 Census, Tenn., Bedford, 4th Dist., 79.

2. Ormsby M. Mitchel's forces had captured Huntsville the preceding day.

3. William G. Brownlow, exiled to the North, was currently on a speaking tour of Ohio, Indiana, and Pennsylvania. Washington *Evening Star*, April 3, 7, 1862; *Parson Brownlow's Book*, 425-41.

4. The writer's observations evidently refer to the equivocal stance of these journals under northern occupation. Suspended when Federal troops took over the city, both papers had been permitted to resume publication during March. By now the *Patriot* evidently had suspended activity, and on this very day the *Banner* editor, George Baber, was arrested for treasonable utterances. "Ashdod Language" apparently stems from Nehemiah 13:24, concerning mixed marriages between Jews and the women of that city: "And their children spake half in the speech of Ashdod, and could not speak in the Jews' language, but according to the language of each people"—in short, "double-talk." Linda Joyce Redden, A Historical Study and Content Analysis of Nash-ville Newspapers, 1860-1865 (M. A. thesis, University of Tennessee, 1975); *American Annual Cyclopaedia* (1862), 764, 766.

5. Not extant.

6. Brothers Henry and Edmund Cooper. Henry (1827-1884), Shelbyville lawyer, was a Whig and Know Nothing member of the legislature (1853-55, 1857-59) and judge of the 7th judicial circuit (1862-66). After the war he served on the law faculty of Cumberland University (1866-68), practiced in Nashville with his brother William F., and was a Conservative in the state senate (1869-71) and a Democrat in the U. S. Senate (1871-77). Visiting Mexico in connection with mining investments, he was killed by a

robber in February, 1884. McBride and Robison, *Biographical Directory*, I, 165; for Edmund Cooper, see *Johnson Papers*, IV, 270n.

To Abraham Lincoln

Nashville Tenn Apl 12th [1862]

His Excellency Abraham Lincoln
President

I hope the President will place Brigadier Genl James. G. Spears in command of the Tennessee forces at Cumberland Gap— They want to enter the State under his lead. Carter a Lieutenant in the navie has been acting as Brig Genl, as I think without authority— Let this be attended to at once and it will give great satisfaction to Tennessee troops. Will the President answer me at this point[?] there is a Messenger now waiting for a response. Send Col Lewis D. Campbells sixty ninth (69th) Ohio Regiment from Columbus to Nashville or the Cumberland Gap. I helped to raise the Regiment[1]—it bears my name and is very anxious to enter Tennessee service[.] There ought to be a complete Brigade at this point for a short time at least with the understanding that it could be moved to any part of the State— It would exert a powerful moral influence and would have a tendency to keep the rebels down without being moved[.] This place is almost defenceless now[2] and tends to keep alive the rebellious spirit— As soon as the rebel soldiers are driven from the State she will stand overwhelming for the union. East Tennesseeans are being pressed into the rebel service by thousands and no means of resistance[.] I will write fully in a short time giving you full account of matters here— They are working better than any one could have expected—

Andrew Johnson

Tel, DNA-RG107, Tels. Recd., U.S. Mil. Tel., Vol. 6 (Apr. 12-23, 1862).

1. Johnson and Campbell had shared a speaking tour of Ohio from September 30 to October 7, 1861, as the 69th Ohio, nicknamed the "Andy Johnson Guard," was being recruited. Cincinnati *Enquirer*, September 20, 1861; Letter to Gideon Welles, September 30, 1861; Letter from Jane H. Campbell, March 6, 1862; *Official Army Register: Volunteers*, V, 161.

2. Buell's departure for the Shiloh campaign drastically reduced the number of troops in the Nashville area, so much so as to alarm Johnson and to persuade him that Buell was intentionally undermining his position. In an effort to prevent further removal of troops, he telegraphed Buell, Stanton, Lincoln, and others in protest. Maslowski, *"Treason Must Be Made Odious,"* 81-84.

From Robert B. Ellis and Others[1]

[Camp Douglas] April 13, 1862

Hon. Andrew Johnson,—Sir,—

Permit me to introduce myself to you. I am a Tennesseean and, like many others, I am now confined in the barracks at Chicago. I will now state my case to you. I live fifty miles from Nashville. There is myself, R. B. Ellis, Franklin Gifford, Haley Russell and James Wiley. We all have large families at home, and they are suffering. Ellis has six children, Gifford has eight children, Russell has six children, Wiley has seven children. We are poor men and just made enough to barely live when we were there, and now they are suffering. And now I pray God to help you to help me to get home to my family once more, and the name of Andrew Johnson never will be forgotten. I want you to write to me quick if you please, and the terms of our release. We are willing to take the oath of allegiance and go home and there be contented. The rich men promised us to take good care of our families, but they have suffered ever since we left home.[2] Now, our friend, if you will help us back, I will never forget the name of you, our friend. If the Tennessee boys can get off from here on the oath or in any way, and at the same time know they were released by you, Mr. Johnson, the shouts when they get to Nashville you never heard the like.

I now sir, subscribe myself to you, yours truly. But give me an answer quick if you please. I dont sleep thinking of my poor wife and children. Help, help, help, oh, help suffering humanity! We are all from forty-five to sixty years old.[3] God help us!

> R. B. Ellis,
> Franklin Gifford,
> James Wiley,
> Haley Russell.

Nashville *Union*, April 22, 1862.

1. This "Affecting Appeal" came from Maury countians Robert B. Ellis, Franklin Gifford, and Haley W. Russell of Co. E, 3rd (Clack's) Tenn. Inf. and James H. Wiley of Co. B, 9th Tenn. Cav. Btn. who were captured at Donelson. Ellis (b. *c*1824) had been an overseer before the war; Tennessee-born Gifford (b. *c*1832), a farm laborer; Russell (*c*1812-1875), a brick mason; and North Carolina-born Wiley (b. *c*1821), a farmer with real estate valued at $80. All but Ellis were exchanged at Vicksburg in September, 1862. Wiley was discharged the following March. Porch, *1850 Census, Maury*, 364; 1860 Census, Tenn., Maury, 6th Dist., 80; 9th Dist., 64; 7th Dist., 10; CSR, RG109, NA; Garrett, *Confederate Soldiers*, 301.

2. Assurances, common during the spring of 1861, of money, free housing, food, and medical services to the families of volunteers, apparently were not carried out; within a matter of months the Nashville *Union and American* reported that wives and children were sorely in need of the basic necessities of life. The failure of wealthy secessionists to care for the dependents of Middle Tennessee soldiers required the enactment of both county and state legislation levying taxes "for the relief of families of indigent soldiers." Nashville *Union and American*, April 22, September 18, 1861; Nashville *Union*, April 16, 18, 19, May 21, 1862; *Goodspeed's Maury*, 785; *Tenn. Acts*, 1861-62, Chs. VIII, LII.

3. It would appear that the supplicants were making a calculated bid for the governor's sympathy. Only one of them, Wiley, was of this "advanced age"; the remainder were between thirty and forty-one.

From Henry Frazier[1]

State Prison Nashville Tenn
Aprl 16th 1862

Gov Johnson

Sir— I hope you will not look upon this as an obtrusive note but will give me a fair hearing[.]

I am confined here as a prisoner of war verry unjustly I think— Knowing you to be a kind hearted man and a Tennesseean I write this hoping you will look at it as favorably as you can and if you can do any thing for me consistant with the duties of your office I hope you will do so— I will make you a full statment of all[.]

In Oct last we were all satisfied that the malitia would be called out and we would be compelled to go whether we wanted to or not— I was placed so I could not leave as all the means I had was out in hands where I could not get it— I was induc[t]ed into the army on the 23d Oct. have been sick at home most of the time— Have spent all the means I had to get well[.]

When the Army passed through here I was compelled in a feeble state of health to go along[.]

Shortly after I Saw your proclamation[2] inviting home the Citizens of Nashville under the promise of protection— was down sick at the time[.] as soon as was able I sent in my Resignation and came home to stay— On my arrival was told by my old friends that I would be arrested and having held a Lieutenancy in the Army it would go verry hard with me— I concluded to go away[.] I could not go north and feel safe— After consultation I desided to go to Dr McDonalds[3] in North Ala wher I could Stay until I could come home safely— In the mean time I could have my wife come to me— My health is verry poor and my means are verry nearly gone— If I had my liberty I could no more than make a support for my wife— If I am kept in confinment She will be left on the charity of Nashville— *She* is a Northern woman and a union one consequently but little Sympathy from a large portion of Nashville[.]

Has had her feelings wounded a thousand times on account of her views being in favor of the Union[.]

I was sent here on the 9th Inst and have had no chance to do any thing— Was missunderstood by the Marshall and can get no chance to make it right[.]

My crime if any consists in first going into the army and second by trying to keep from arrest[.]

I have not been in any Battle nor did I wish to be— Have not been paid by the Confederacy and was glad when you invited us home—

Have not been treated as I expected when I came— I left the Army for good— Have no connection with it— Came Home to Remain a Citizen of this City— I am willing to tell you all and do what is right if you will give me a chance— If not and my crime is irepairable let me know it and I will try and make arrangment to send my wife home to Ohio among her people— Now Governor I know you can do me this favor as it was under your proclamation I came home— Now I ask your protection— I have no doubt but my arrest was cause by a personal enemy who has no kind feelings for you nor the Union— I think I have found him out— If I am right he is now secretly doing all he can against you and guilty of things I would Scorn— Please let me hear from you in some way[.]

Yours Respectfully

Henry Frazier

ALS,DLC-JP.

1. Perhaps Henry Frazier (b. *c*1824), a Tennessean married to a native of New York, and a patent medicine dealer with $1,000 in personal property in 1860. Transferred to Camp Chase as a political prisoner, he was paroled there in November, 1862. 1860 Census, Tenn., Davidson, Edgefield, 7; Parole bond, November 18, 1862, Johnson Papers, LC; see also Letter from Peter Zinn, November 18, 1862.

2. See Appeal to the People of Tennessee, March 18, 1862, in which Johnson assures "The erring and misguided" a welcome "on their return" with "complete amnesty . . . upon the one condition of their again yielding themselves peaceful citizens to the just supremacy of the laws."

3. Probably Dr. Jonathan McDonald (b. *c*1807), a Kentucky-born physician practicing in Athens, Alabama, and a prominent and wealthy planter ($50,000 real, $19,419 personal property), whose son Sterling married the niece of former Senator Ephraim Foster of Tennessee. A graduate of Jefferson Medical College in Philadelphia, McDonald was also a railroad promoter during the 1850's and served as a director of the Tennessee and Alabama which linked Athens to Nashville and is now part of the L & N. 1860 Census, Ala., Limestone, 1st Div., 61; Marie Bankhead Owen, *The Story of Alabama: A History of the State* (5 vols., New York, [1949]), IV, 27.

Order to Stanley Matthews

April 16, 1862, Nashville; L draft, DLC-JP.

Directs provost marshal to send Washington Barrow, William G. Harding, and Joseph C. Guild to Detroit for transferral to Fort Mackinac.

From William Crowell[1]

Freeport, Ill. April 17 1862

Hon. Andrew Johnson:

Sir: You are doubtless cognizant of the existence of an individual named J. R. Graves,[2] for many years the editor of a paper in Nashville called the "*Tennessee Baptist.*" The proofs of his open advocacy of treason, in his scandalous sheet, & by preaching are abundant & notorious. I see it reported in the news papers, that he has suspended the issues of his paper, & fled, announcing his intention to raise a legion of pikemen of which he proposes to become the leader, to help on this infamous rebellion.

Now, Sir, it has devolved on you to deal with rebellion in Tennessee, & lest you should feel some scruple in dealing with a clerical rebel with the same stern justice, as with others, let me tell you that I know something of this Graves, his course as an editor, his character as a man, & the estimation in which he is held by the body of Christians among whom he claims to have ecclesiastical affiliation. He has his admirers & partizans, & this rebellion shows who they are, but by the Baptist body generally, who are of any account in the religious world, he is held to be one of the most pestilent nuisances that ever afflicted a religious community. He is as violent & wrong headed in religion as in politics, ever fomenting strifes & divisions.

He has a publishing house in Nashville, though his residence is in Edgefield. Such men deserve the severest punishment for the miseries which they cause. The man who makes use of the influence which he acquires as a professed minister of the Prince of Peace & stirs up rebellion, & murder, deserves the severest penalties of the law. If this war shall be the occasion of putting down such nuisances as Graves' late sheet, as well as Mc Ferrin,[3] it will not be quite in vain.

I heartily wish you success in restoring the reign of peace & loyalty in Tennessee.

With much respect, I am Dear Sir,

Your obt Servant   Wm. Crowell

Late Ed. "Western Watchman" in St Louis, Mo.

ALS, DLC-JP.

1. William Crowell (1806-1871), Massachusetts-born Baptist minister and author, who had edited the *Christian Watchman* (1838-48), New England's leading Baptist paper, and the St. Louis *Western Watchman* (1850's), was a minister in central Illinois during the war. *Appleton's Cyclopaedia*, II, 22.

2. James R. Graves (1820-1893), Vermont-born preacher, editor, author, and publisher, came to Nashville in 1845, associating himself with the *Tennessee Baptist* (1846-62) and the Southwestern Publishing House. The primary leader of the Landmark movement among Southern Baptists during the 1850's, he conducted a literary warfare upon all who failed to entertain his view. In 1857-58 he openly feuded with the Reverend Dr. R. B. C. Howell, resulting in his own expulsion from Nashville's First Baptist Church, and the establishment of a splinter group. A strong disunionist, he had proposed that the South secede as a unit, with each state appointing delegates to a convention and presenting the Union with three demands: enforce the Fugitive Slave Law, protect property in the territories, and amend the Constitution to guarantee slavery where it existed. Moving to Memphis about 1870, he continued his career as a polemicist and publisher and a dealer in religious books. *DAB*, VII, 507-8; James J. Burnett, *Sketches of Tennessee's Pioneer Baptist Preachers* (2 vols., Nashville, 1919), I, 184-200; W. Harrison Daniel, "Southern Baptists," *Civil War History*, VI (1960), 390; W. Fred Kendall, *A History of the Tennessee Baptist Convention* (Brentwood, Tenn., 1974), 114-24.

3. John B. McFerrin (1807-1887), Methodist clergyman, businessman, and author, began preaching in 1825 as a circuit rider, served as a missionary to the Cherokee (1827-29), and edited the *South-Western Christian Advocate* (1840-58). A member of the convention which organized the Methodist Episcopal Church, South (1845), McFerrin, as book agent, directed the new denomination's publishing interests (1858-66) and during the war was in charge of Methodist missionary work in the Army of Tennessee. Subsequently he engaged in mission board activities (1866-78), wrote *History of Methodism in Tennessee* (3 vols., Nashville, 1875-79), and resumed his post as book agent. *DAB*, XII, 44-45; Oscar P. Fitzgerald, *John B. McFerrin: A Biography* (Nashville, 1888), 267-71.

From William L. Kelly

April 17, 1862, Louisville, Ky.; ALS, DLC-JP.

Assistant postmaster decries the lack of mail facilities, which prevents delivery of letters written by war prisoners, especially since "in many instances they are doubtless of a character tending to dis-abuse the Southern mind in regard to our Government & people"; suggests that the mail be "forwarded, by Flag of Truce or otherwise."

From William L. Putman[1]

Johnsons island
April the 17./62

to your Exlcency Andrew Johnson Gov of Tennessee your pertisener is a tennessean & has Been caut in a Bad scrape[.] I withe the rest of my people I held to the old union as long as I dar to[.] our congressmen returnd home [w]ho was Mr R. Hatten[2] & he perclamd that thar was nothen left for the people to do But to fite— I Roat to you then our Senetor to send me your vews & you sent me your last speach you maid in the Senett on the subjet[.] Now I am a prisner of war taken at dolerson [Donelson.]   my helth is a given a way her[.] I don't think I can stand the strong cool Breases with weak longs[.] I ask you to get me aparol until the 22 of may if no longer[.]   my time exp[i]res on that day[.] I taken the oath to serpoart Tennessee and I her learn she wil return to the old union a gane[.]   if so I am with her hart & hand[.] I roat you to use sum effert for me noing as I do that yowar a plain man or I shuld not dard to hav ad drest you with this letter with its meney defisiencys[.] answer your unbel & politickl friend

Wm. L Putman Capt of Comp (I)
18 Tenesse Rig vol.

ALS, DLC-JP.

1. William L. Putman (b. *c*1821), Tennessee native and Mexican War veteran, was a Woodbury saddler with an estate of $6,000 in 1860. Captain of Co. I, 18th Tenn. Inf., CSA, Putman was captured at Fort Donelson and imprisoned at Johnson's Island until his release in September, 1862. He did not reenlist when his regiment was reorganized in October. 1860 Census, Tenn., Cannon, Woodbury, 87; Dixon Merritt, ed., *The History of Wilson County* (Lebanon, 1961), 312; CSR, RG109, NA.

2. For Robert H. Hatton, see *Johnson Papers*, II, 474*n*.

From Edwin M. Stanton

Washington, April 17, 1862.

General Andrew Johnson,
Governor of Tennessee:

The President having delivered to me your telegram of the 12th to be answered, I would state that the troops at Cumberland Gap, being within General Halleck's department, it is not deemed proper for the War Department to change the command, which is now held by General Morgan.

Carter has been nominated and is now before the Senate for confirmation as brigadier.

Campbell's regiment has been ordered to Nashville to report to you.

Very respectfully, your obedient servant,
Edwin M. Stanton, Secretary of War.

Tel, DLC-JP; DNA-RG107, Tels. Sent, Sec. War, Vol. 8 (Mar. 13-Apr. 22, 1862); *OR*, Ser. 1, X, Pt. II, 110.

To Don Carlos Buell, Pittsburg Landing

Nashville April 17, 1862[1]

Maj Genl Buell

You will remember that Genl Spears was made a Brigadier General prior to my leaving Washington for the purpose of being placed in Command of a Brigade at Cumberland Ford embracing the Tennessee Regiments[.] as yet he has been assigned no command[.] Lieut Carter of the Navy has been acting as Brigadier as you are aware— Spears contributed more to raising the Tennessee troops than any other man[.] he is a Brave man a patriot & a Soldier & should have the honor of heading a Brigade of Tenneseeans upon their advent into East Tennessee— This will not come in conflict with the command of any General who may be assigned to the command of the Expedition— I hope that Genl Buell will find it convenient at once to assign Genl Spears the command of a Brigade[.] There is a Messenger here who will await your Reply[.]

Andrew Johnson

Copy, DNA-RG94, Gens. Papers, D. C. Buell; DLC-JP.

1. This is sender's date, although recipient's copy, dated April 22, is printed here.

To Edwin M. Stanton

Nashville, Tenn., April 17, 1862.

Hon. E. M. Stanton, Secretary of War,
Washington, D. C.

Sir: Inclosed herewith I send a petition from certain members of Tennessee regiments at Camp Douglas[1] in which they express a strong desire to renew their allegiance to the Government and become true and loyal citizens.

I will only state in presenting this petition for the consideration of the War Department that whenever circumstances shall justify the discharge of prisoners of war from this State entertaining such views and feelings as are set forth by these petitioners their appearance among their friends and relatives will I doubt not exert a great moral influence in favor of the perpetuity of the Union.[2]

With great respect, your obedient servant,

Andrew Johnson.

OR, Ser. 2, III, 457.

1. Members of the 42nd, 48th, 49th, and 50th Tenn. regiments captured at Donelson and held at Camp Douglas had requested that Johnson use his influence to secure their release. They expressed their willingness to take an oath of allegiance and a desire "to return to our homes and families in our native State as true and loyal citizens of the Union." Petitioners to Johnson, April 10, 1862, OR, Ser. 2, III, 457-58.

2. When Lincoln asked Johnson in June, 1862, if he wanted complete control over Tennessee prisoners, the governor replied that he did, in order "to exert a powerful influence throughout the state in our favor." Given authority in early August to control the release and exchange of Tennessee prisoners, he appointed William B. Campbell "to visit northern prisons and determine which prisoners should be released and the terms of release." Letter from Abraham Lincoln, June 4, 1862; Letter to Lincoln, June 5, 1862; Maslowski, "Treason Must Be Made Odious," 159.

To Lorenzo Thomas, Washington, D. C.

Nashville April 17th 1862.

Lorenzo Thomas A.G.

Your despatch[1] has been rec'd[.]   a line running north & south through Knoxville which is as I understand according to the orders recently made by the war dept is the western boundary of Gen Fremonts Dept.[2] Cumberland gap & the forces in that vicinity were east of that line & I supposed the disposition of the forces would be under his control or that of the War Dept[.] The intention was simply to give Genl Spears the command of a brigade embracing the Tenn regiments without reference to who should command all the forces constituting the expedition into East Tenn.   this would not interfere with the command of Genl Morgan or any Genl command.   the whole force there has been [under] an acting Brigadier Genl by the name of Carter who is a Lieutenant in the navy and was sent to that region of country upon Special duty. Spears was made a Br Genl in fact & contributed more men in the first instance to the organization of Tenn troops than any other man & ought to have the command of them as Brigadier upon their advance into Tennessee. The regts desire it should be so. Justice demands it[.] He is a brave & patriotic man & will lead them successfully[.] the acting Genl Carter has been in the way from the beginning & it would be much better for him to return to the naval service than to remain where he is. We need no more Br Genls present and there should be no more made especially for the east Tenn expedition[.] Genl Morgan & Spears are sufficient[.] More will be in the way[.] for fear I am mistaken I have telegraphed to the Gen Halleck on this subject. Hope Gen Thomas will at once bring this subject before the sec'y of war & forward to me an immediate reply[.] this matter should be at once attended to. All is working well in this part of Tenn. beyond my most sanguine expectations[.] as soon as we drive the rebel troops beyond the border of the state Tenn will be for the Union 70,000 votes.

Andw Johnson.

Tel, DNA-RG107, Tels. Recd., Sec. of War, Vol. 10 (April 18-29, 1862); DLC-JP; *OR*, Ser. 1, X, Pt. II, 110-11.

1. Thomas to Johnson, April 17, 1862, Johnson Papers, LC.
2. Gen. John C. Frémont had recently taken command of the newly-created Mountain Department in western Virginia and West Virginia with the ill-fated objective of crossing the mountains to seize the railroad at Knoxville, thus relieving East Tennessee's unionists. Nevins, *Frémont*, II, 635-36.

From Charles B. Cotton

Louisville Ky Apr 18 1862.

Gov Johnson
Nashville Tennessee.
Sir.

Mr J B McFerrin of your City has applied here for a permit to ship goods to Nashville including Salt &c.

I refused his application—unless you and your Committee would recommend him as a loyal man and law abiding man.

I do this from information and in justice to myself—himself & the Government.

To my knowledge and within my recollection I never gave him a permit for goods—and last fall he—in some way managed to receive and handle more goods at and from Bowling green Ky—than any other man.

He violated the rules & regulations of this office—and the laws restricting trade between the states of Tenn—& Ky. or loyal states—continually. This could be proven if necessary—by V C Durham[1] & others.

If he can clear himself—let him do it and I will be glad of it.

Resply   Chas. B Cotton   Sur—

ALS, T-Mil. Gov's Papers, 1862-65.

1. Vic C. Durham (b. *c*1808), Kentucky-born blacksmith and "Agency Aid" for U. S. customs on the Louisville & Nashville at Bowling Green, possessed $10,500 real and $600 personal property on the eve of the war. 1860 Census, Ky., Warren, 2nd Dist., 1; William D. Gallagher to Durham and to Salmon P. Chase, March 25, 1864, Lincoln Papers, LC.

From Daniel K. Boswell[1]

Washington D. C.
April 19th 1862

Hon. Andrew Johnson
Nashvill Tenn.

Dear Sir

In Gods name let me ask you to instruct the Commanding Genrl. Near Corinth,[2] to look to the safety of my family. I am endeavouring to get off that I may be with the advance. I may not succeed in time. In which case I have no other reliance for the safety of my family but that of our commanders, who if properly notified will act accordingly. I have written to Genrls Grant, Wallace, & Smith,[3] some time since.

If the Army has not a sufficient and reliable Guide I could render valueable service, in that way. I am well acquainted with both the general and Special Topography of the Country from the Tennessee to the Miss River. If needed I would be glad to serve on being notified.

My family I left in Corinth. God only knows where they may have been driven to ere this. Though I trust they are yet in Corinth. Sir no man knows better than yourself how to feel for & sympathise with my great anxiety. I therefore freely address you in full confidence.

Very truly   Your Humble Servant
D. K. Boswell
National Hotel

ALS, DLC-JP.

1. Daniel K. Boswell (b. *c*1810), a native of North Carolina and a resident of Mississippi, possessed $500 real and $500 personal property on the eve of the war. Claiming to have been opposed to secession since 1850, Boswell organized a group of unconditional Union men in northern Mississippi soon after Lincoln's inauguration, "the better to sustain the Administration . . . and retard the progress of the rebllion." As early as October, 1861, he "commenced a series of reconnaisances" involving Forts Pillow and Randolph and later Fort Henry and other Confederate installations in West Tennessee. Entering the Union lines at Paducah in December, he "brought to us valuable information, which was fuller than we had heretofore received." 1860 Census, Miss., Tishomingo, Corinth, 465; Boswell to Aaron Harding and others [1862], and John Lellyett to Johnson, March 5, 1862, Lincoln Papers, LC.

2. Maj. Gen. Henry W. Halleck, commander of the Department of the Mississippi, assumed field command of the Army of the Tennessee at Pittsburg Landing, April 11, and personally directed the operations against Corinth. Simon, *Grant Papers*, V, xxii.

3. Lew Wallace and Charles F. Smith.

From Curran Pope[1]

Fayetteville April 19" 1862

Hon Andrew Johnson
Dear Sir

I deem it not out of the way to inform you, that at the election held in this place last March Wm. Moffatt was elected Sheriff—David Whittington county court clerk—Miles Ramsey Sr register—Silvertooth tax collector—and that these officers[2] have not qualified— Moreover that Robert Farquaharson[3] chancey clerk is a prisoner at Camp Chase being a rebel colonel captured at Fort Donelson—that the offices of County court, Circuit court & chancey court clerk are closed and the records have been removed to adjoining conties or the state of Alabama. I have caused the families of these officers to be notified that they had better return with the official records to their offices but as yet without effect—

This regiment was raised in the vicinity of Louisville and the deportment of the soldiers of it at Bowling Green, at Shelbyville Tenn & here has been such always as to conciliate the Citizens[.] This county I understand has been noted as the most bitter disunion county in the state yet I can testify that a great change is going on in the minds of the people and I do not hesitate to express the Conviction that if the US Arms Suffer no future reverses mild yet firm measures in the course of two or three months will bring the people back to their allegiance— Very plainly the rich in this county and I suppose elsewhere who stimulated volunteering are not true to the lavish promises they made in regard to the families of the Soldier, and here to my mind is a fruitful As Cause for future prejudice and disaffection—if wisely used as I have every assurance it will be by you—

I suppose James B. Lamb[4] has exercised much influence over the people of this region. He has very recently returned & I suppose he is advising his friends that the rebellion is hopeless— I infer from his conversation today that he is still a warm admirer of yours and still acknowledging himself indebted to you for past policial favors—

You will excuse the freedom with which an entire stranger writes to you yet as these opinions have been formed by me whilst in the discharge of functions resting upon me as Col of 15" Ky Reg. & Provost Marshal of this place you will receive them I am sure in the same spirit with which they are written.

Having devotedly at heart the interests of the great Union which you have Served So truly I am

Very respectfully Yr obt Servt.
Curran Pope

ALS, DLC-JP.

1. Curran Pope (*c*1814-1862), wealthy Louisville lawyer ($220,000 real and $10,000 personal property) and West Point graduate (1834), had been clerk of Jefferson County court (1838-61) and city councilman (1858-59). Having raised the 15th Ky. Vols., he was commanding the 17th Bde., Army of the Ohio, when he died in November of wounds received at Perryville on October 8. 1860 Census, Ky., Jefferson, Louisville, 3rd Ward, 103; *Louisville City Directory* (1858-59), 310; Collins, *Kentucky*, I, 162; William E. Connelley and E. Merton Coulter, *History of Kentucky*, Charles Kerr, ed. (5 vols., Chicago, 1922), IV, 310; Ludie J. Kinkead and Katherine G. Healy, "Calendar of Division Book No. 1, Jefferson County Court, 1797-1850," *Filson Quarterly*, VIII (1934), 44.

2. Probably William Moffet (b. *c*1820), Tennessee native who was an overseer in 1850. Daniel J. Whittington (b. *c*1816), a North Carolina native who had $3,000 in real and $1,500 in personal property in 1860, served as Lincoln County register (1852-60) and county court clerk (1858-64). Miles Ramsey (b. *c*1826), also from North Carolina, was a wool carder. John A. Silvertooth (1818-1892), Lynchburg (Lincoln County) farmer with property worth $2,000, became Moore County's trustee upon its formation (1872-73) and was also tax collector (1876-82). Deane Porch, tr., *1850 Census, Lincoln County, Tennessee* (Nashville, 1970), 201, 396; 1860 Census, Tenn., Lincoln, 8th Dist., 225; 1st Dist., 1; *Goodspeed's Lincoln*, 771; *Goodspeed's Moore*, 810; Wright W. Frost, *The Frosts and Related Families of Bedford County, Tennessee* (Knoxville, 1962), 254-56.

3. Robert Farquharson (1813-1869), a Scot who came to the United States about 1827 and settled in Fayetteville, was clerk and master of chancery court (1848, 1854-61, 1864-69), justice of the peace, chairman of the Lincoln County court, alderman and mayor of Fayetteville, and served several terms in the state legislature (1839-41, 1843-45, 1851-55), where, during the early forties he was a close friend of Andrew Johnson. An officer in the Tennessee militia, Farquharson had been a major in the Mexican War and in 1861 became colonel of the 41st Tenn. Inf., CSA; captured at Donelson, he returned to his regiment after being exchanged five months later. McBride and Robison, *Biographical Directory*, I, 241-42; *Goodspeed's Lincoln*, 771; see *Johnson Papers*, I, 112.

4. For Lamb, see *ibid.*, II, 271n. A member of the Tennessee house during Johnson's first gubernatorial term (1853-55), Lamb had been a delegate to the 1860 Democratic convention at Charleston.

From Oliver D. Williams[1]

Alexandria, DeKalb Co. Tenn.
April, 19th, 1862.

Gov. Johnson,
Dear Sir:

Although I have but a very slight personal acquaintance with you, I must nevertheless, take the liberty of occupying a portion of your valuable time. Indeed, the only personal acquaintance with you that I can claim, is an introduction to you, at the Capitol, by the Hon. Wm B. Stokes, about two weeks ago, but being engaged with you in a common cause, (though only as a private citizen on my part,) I feel free to address you, on some topics of public importance. The first thing that I call your attention to, is to request you to consider the propriety of having troops stationed in this section of country.

The importance of that measure to my mind arises from the following considerations: The country around here, for some miles, has a large Union element in it—consequently is exposed to the devasting raids, (Morgan & Guerrilla) that may chance to come through it. In the next place, it would keep down the danger (always liable) of a collision between our own citizens, who are much divided in political sentiment. Again this road through here, has been much used as a highway for rebels, troops and privates, going South, since the way by Murfreesborough was cut off. It is not much used in that way now, though it is to some extent. A parcel of troops stationed here, under as good discipline as those at Lebanon, would have a good moral effect, alike upon secessionists and union men—restraining the former, encouraging the latter.

This place is 18 miles East of Lebanon, on the Sparta turnpike, and about the same distance from Smithville. There is also a turnpike from here North, by way of Carthage to Red Sulphur Springs, in Macon County. There is also a pike from Murfreesboro. which comes into our main pike between here and Liberty, 5 miles from this place. This is a heathy location. The village has a population of about 500 when they are all at home. There are now some good houses vacant.

The next subject deemed by me worthy of presentation to you, is the propriety of organizing home guards, over the State, in all places where there are loyal citizens sufficient to form them. They should be for permant use. We will be compelled to keep some thing of the kind for years, or to retain a portion of the army. Indeed, secessionists are already making their brags about what they will do, when their "boys" come back. And in regard to the latter class, I will passingly suggest, the propriety of arresting all that may return, (even if they have been discharged) and compelling them to take the oath or to be held prisoners of war. They should also be disarmed, (I suppose some of them at least will have pistols,) and bound over to keep the peace. All these matters must be sternly met. There are many persons who would doubtless, be willing to engage as home guards, under State authority, that would not, at all, engage in the regular service of the Federal armies. It may be that the United States håve, or will soon have, a sufficiency of small arms to spare, with which to arm all companies of loyal Home Guards, that may be formed in the Southern States. If there is any thing of the kind done, in order to be efficient, it must be systematic, and will have to emenate from head quarters. Mere voluntary effort made at random, without system or cooperation will not answer the purpose.

You will please excuse this intrusion and believe me, in the cause of the Union, the Constitution, and the Enforcement of the Laws, your Excellency's

         Obt Servt, O. D. Williams.

P.S.

I will probably send this down, by Mr David Dinwiddie,[2] my friend and neighbor, who goes to Nashville. I am informed as a juryman of the Federal court.

                O. D. W.

ALS, DLC-JP.
    1. Oliver D. Williams (b. *c*1817), a Dekalb County farmer with $7,000 in real estate and $10,000 in personal property, was later postmaster at Alexandria (*c*1863-65). Sistler, *1850 Tenn. Census*, VII, 80; 1860 Census, Tenn., DeKalb, 1st Dist., 7; *U. S. Official Register* (1863), 623; (1865), 340*.
    2. David Dinwiddie (b. *c*1820), a Kentucky native and DeKalb farmer, had $2,000 real and $9,000 personal property. 1860 Census, Tenn., DeKalb, 1st Dist., 3.

To William H. Seward

Nashville Ap'l 19th, 1862

My dear Sir,

    The Nashville Union,[1] a decidedly loyal newspaper, and zealous in its labors for the restoration of the Union, has been established here within the past ten days. Owing to the want of mail facilities its circulation South of this place must necessarily be limited, and it is very desirable that it should receive such patronage in the way of publishing the laws, etc, as the Federal Government may have to give. A sound union paper at this point cannot fail to exert great influence for good in Tennessee and indeed in states south of us.

    I therefore hope that the "Union" will be selected as one of the journals for the publication of the laws of the United States.[2]

    I am meeting with much greater success than I had expected. The union sentiment is rapidly being developed. The great difficulty at first was that the idea of the return of A. Sidney Johnston's Army to this City extensively prevailed. This, the leaders kept constantly before them, and the fear of the consequences to themselves, should such be the case, kept back that strong union feeling which, freed from all restraint, is daily being manifested.

    There is a most decided reaction going on, and I feel well assured that Tennessee, always against secession by the voice of her people, will, when the rebel soldiery shall have been driven beyond her borders, wheel back into her old place in this glorious Union by a majority of tens of thousands.

    Accept assurances of my high esteem & believe me

Yours Truly, Andrew Johnson

Hon Wm. H. Seward,
Secretary of State,
Washington City.

L, NRU.
    1. Initially published by "An Association of Printers" and later by William Cameron and Company, the Nashville *Daily Union*, edited by Samuel C. Mercer, first appeared on April 10. The following day the governor made the first of a series of payments to Mercer, "on account of services as Editor of . . . a paper started for the purpose of sustaining the Union, and in opposition to the Secession organs in the State." A subsequent receipt left no doubt whatsoever of the relationship: "such services being under direction of the Government." The subsidies varied from two to three hundred dollars a month.

Stewart, *Middle Tennessee Newspapers*, 188-89; Receipts from S. C. Mercer, April, 1862-August, 1863, Mrs. Betsy Bachman Carrier.

2. Seward acted upon Johnson's recommendation, and by September 30, 1863, the *Union* had received over $800 in patronage. Seward to Johnson, April 28, 1862, Johnson Papers, LC; *U. S. Official Register* (1863), 15, 16; Clayton, *Davidson County*, 241.

From Allen A. Hall[1]

Nashville, April 21st, 1861 [1862]

Hon. Andrew Johnson:

Sir:

In explanation of my refusal some time since to grant a permit for the shipment of a lot of books from the Methodist Book Concern[2] of this place, I beg leave to say:

From the beginning of the rebellion, that Concern has persistently and energetically used its vast influence to overthrow the Government. It has been a nest of traitors, possessing great powers for mischief, which were used without scruple. Foremost of these, is the Rev. John B. McFerrin,[3] the Manager of the Book Concern. If he had his deserts, instead of receiving permits to ship his books to loyal States, he would be in prison. In view of these facts, you will not be surprised to learn, that, when a permit was asked of me for the shipment of a lot of books, the bill of which bore the name of John B. McFerrin, I declined to grant it. I declined in language entirely civil, stating distinctly to the person who applied for the permit, my reason for doing so—that I could not, consistently with my sense of duty, grant permits for Mr McFerrin or that Concern. If the bill had not be[en] made out in the name of McFerrin, but in some other name, I should have been constrained by my sense of duty to decline granting a permit for the shipment of any books of that Concern, if I had known that the books belonged to the Concern. You will no doubt recollect the conversations we had in Washington on the subject of that Concern as well as the other printing establishments in the City, and that I entertained and expressed the opinion that they were all subject to confiscation under the act of the 6th of August, 1861.[4] Such is my opinion now. I believe the whole of the Methodist Book Concern is liable to confiscation under that Act. I am sure that sound policy would dictate the withholding from it of all favors, and that, so long as any restrictions exist on trade, those restrictions in all their rigor should be laid upon the Methodist Book Concern, of Nashville.

I will add, that almost every day I am embarrassed more or less by questions arising out of this duty of granting permits. As it was of great public importance that the produce of the country, particularly the Cotton and Tobacco, should go forward, I have generally in cases that I esteemed doubtful given a liberal interpretation to what I understand to be my instructions. I *do know* that *no person entitled to a permit has ever failed to receive it promptly when application has been made in the proper form.*

Very respectfully Your obdt. sert.

Allen A. Hall.

DNA-RG366, Fifth Special Agency, Port Royal Corres., Civil War, Vol. 19.

1. See *Johnson Papers*, IV, 461n. Appointed in February special treasury agent for abandoned property in Tennessee with authorization to sell, Hall reached Nashville March 2—a few days before trade was declared open to Louisville—and began issuing permits for the sale and transshipment of goods. Futrell, *Federal Trade*, 51-52, 59-60.

2. The Methodist Publishing House, established in 1854, was located on the northeast corner of the Public Square. There, in a pressroom containing twelve presses, every process of book printing was conducted, "embracing type setting, stereotyping, press work, and binding." Upon the occupation of Nashville, the quartermaster department took possession of the "Book Concern" and converted it into a government printing office for "official bulletins, orders, and army blanks." In October, 1865, the establishment was returned to the Methodist book agent, John B. McFerrin. *Nashville Bus. Dir.* (1860-61), 88, 100; Clayton, *Davidson County*, 241.

3. Referring to McFerrin and his assistants, Thomas O. Summers, L. D. Huston, and Holland N. McTyeire, one Louisville correspondent averred that "all early became traitors and omitted no opportunity to preach treason." When Nashville fell, all fled South, McFerrin taking his family to Cornersville in Giles County before continuing to Georgia and Alabama. Louisville *Journal*, April 28, 1862; Fitzgerald, *John B. McFerrin*, 267-71.

4. "An Act to confiscate Property used for Insurrectionary Purposes," introduced by Lyman Trumbull, provided "That if, during the present or any future insurrection against the Government of the United States . . . any person or persons, his, her, or their agent, attorney, or employé, shall purchase or acquire, sell or give, any property of whatsoever kind or description, with intent to use or employ the same . . . in aiding, abetting, or promoting such insurrection . . . all such property is hereby declared to be lawful subject of prize and capture wherever found; and it shall be the duty of the President of the United States to cause the same to be seized, confiscated, and condemned." *U. S. Statutes*, XII, 319; *Cong. Globe*, 37 Cong., 1 Sess., 120, 219, 455.

From Curran Pope

Fayetteville Tennessee

April 21. 1862

Hon Andrew Johnson
Nashville Tenn.
Dear Sir,

Will you please give me instructions, about granting passes to persons to go to Nashville to get passes to visit their families at Camp Morton & at Camp Chase. There are persons applying for passes to go thither to carry such articles of clothing and comfort as may be necessary for their friends and families in prison. Please let me hear from you on this subject at your earliest convenience.

Very Respectfully Your obt Servt   Curran Pope

Col 15 Reg Ky Vols & Provost Marshall Fayetteville

L, DLC-JP.

To John Hugh Smith[1]

Executive Office
Nashville, April 21st, 1862

John Hugh Smith, Esq.
Mayor of Nashville
Dear Sir—

I send you, accompanying this note, the flag of our country—the emblem of Union and Free Government—which was made and presented to me by an aged and patriotic lady of this city,[2] with the request that it be placed upon, and unfurled from, some one of the Public Buildings.

Knowing your devotion to the Union, I commit the flag to your care, with the confident hope that you will gratify the request made by her, by causing it to be raised over some one of the Public Buildings, under the control of the city authorities. I trust and hope that this patriotic example will soon be followed by many others as indicative of the Union sentiment of the people of Nashville and Davidson county.[3]

Very respectfully, Your obedient servant,
Andrew Johnson

Nashville *Union*, April 24, 1862.

1. John Hugh Smith (1819-1870), a Nashville lawyer, mayor (1845, 1850-52), and state legislator (1853-54), had just been elected mayor and would serve until 1865. Subsequently he was a city councilman and Davidson County criminal judge (1867-70). Nashville *Republican Banner*, July 8, 1870.

2. The flag had been made by Mrs. Winifred McFarland (1793-1863), widow of R. P. McFarland. See Mrs. Winnie McFarland to Johnson, April 18, 1862, Nashville *Union*, April 24, 1862; Acklen, *Tenn. Records*, II, 261.

3. Replying that the flag was too small for the purpose intended, Smith wrote that he had "placed it out of one of the windows of the Mayor's office, where it may now be seen fluttering in the breeze," and added that the city council was making arrangements to unfurl the "Stars and Stripes" from all public buildings. Smith to Johnson, April 21, 1862, Nashville *Union*, April 24, 1862.

From Emerson Etheridge

Washington D. C. Apl 22. 1862.

Dear Sir:

I have been here a week, and during that period have thought, daily, I would write. First: Let me thank you for the arrests which the newspapers inform us you have made— It is, in my judgement, the true policy, and I hope ere long, Fort Warren[1] will have a full representation from our state. *That* is the proper place for them. Morehead of Kentucky would never have come to terms,[2] if he had been left in prison in that state to have been lionized by his colleagues in Treason. 'Twould do me good to hear that all such as Wash Barrow and Neil Brown were *en route* for

Fort Lafayette.[3] I like the brief words which the Secretary of War spoke to you— "put it through"—and I like the news I hear that you have begun to beard the lion in his den—

At Cairo I saw a Regiment of prisoners taken at No 10 which had been mostly gotten up, in Henry County—[4] Nearly all the *pimps* of Harris and Atkins[5] were officers— W. T. Avery,[6] late M.C. from Memphis, was also in durance vile— He looked as if the Whiskey had given out a month before the Surrender— They were all out of money, and all but the professional office beggars seemed very penitent— The case of the Tennessee prisoners from Robertson—, represented by Mr Villines,[7] is before the President. He concurs in your view, that Stanton is reluctant to consent, because of the message of Jeff. Davis in regard to the release of the prisoners taken at Roanoke, from their parole.[8] What the issue will be I Know not.

Remember me Kindly to Maynard, Browning and Myers.[9]

Vy truly yours,   Em: Etheridge

Hon And. Johnson
Nashville Tenn

ALS, DLC-JP.

1. Designated a prison in 1861, Fort Warren, on George's Island in Boston Harbor, housed both state and war prisoners. Minor H. McLain, "The Military Prison at Fort Warren," *Civil War History*, VIII (1962), 136-38.

2. Charles S. Morehead (1802-1868), several-time Kentucky legislator, was for nearly six years state attorney general before serving as congressman (1847-51) and governor (1855-59). Criticism of the Lincoln administration, especially of Seward, brought his arrest on September 19, 1861, and incarceration at Forts Warren and Lafayette. Subsequent to his release in early January, 1862, he fled the country upon learning that he would be arrested again because of his refusal to take the oath of allegiance. After the war he lived in Mississippi. *DAB*, XIII, 157-58; Mrs. Chapman Coleman, *The Life of John J. Crittenden* (2 vols., Philadelphia, 1871), II, 348.

3. Washington Barrow, arrested following Johnson's order of March 31 for "having uttered treasonable and seditious language" and engaged in treasonable activities, was sent to Mackinac Island on April 16. Former governor Neill S. Brown, arrested May 14, was paroled within a few days after taking the oath. Fort Lafayette, at the entrance to New York harbor, was garrisoned from 1822 until 1868; during the war both political and military prisoners were confined there. Ex. Record Book (1862-63), Ser. 4C, Johnson Papers, LC; *American Annual Cyclopaedia* (1862), 765; Francis P. Prucha, *A Guide to the Military Posts of the United States, 1789-1895* (Madison, Wis., 1964), 84; *OR*, Ser. 2, II-VIII *passim*. For Brown and Barrow, see *Johnson Papers*, II, 325n; IV, 302n.

4. The 46th Tenn. Inf., CSA, organized at Paris November 29, 1861, and captured at Tiptonville the following April 8. *Tennesseans in the Civil War*, I, 275-76.

5. Isham G. Harris and John D. C. Atkins, Henry County's two most prominent secessionists. For Atkins, see *Johnson Papers*, III, 88n.

6. William T. Avery, lieutenant colonel, 39th (Avery's) Inf., CSA, captured at Island No. 10 on April 8, was first confined at Johnson's Island, transferred to Fort Warren in June, and exchanged in September. *Tennesseans in the Civil War*, I, 259; *OR*, Ser. 2, IV, 51, 434-35; see also *Johnson Papers*, III, 457n.

7. William Villines (1804-1876), a North Carolina native who came to Robertson County in 1830, operated a saw and grist mill on the Red River, and traded in slaves. Although "bitterly opposed" to the war, he "visited many of the hospitals and did all he could to alleviate the sufferings of his friends, and spent many thousand dollars in this way." After the war he ran a mill near Cross Plains. *Goodspeed's Robertson*, 1196.

8. It may be assumed that Villines sought the President's intercession with Stanton to release the captured Robertson countians from their paroles. The secretary of war's reluctance was prompted by Jefferson Davis's March 18 message recommending that Confederate prisoners taken at Roanoke Island be released from their paroles in order that they might resume fighting on behalf of the southern cause. *American Annual Cyclopaedia* (1862), 711.

9. William A. Browning, Johnson's private secretary. Henry R. Myer, resident of California prior to the war and currently on the governor's staff, was probably the "major" who helped recruit the 10th Tenn. Inf., Governor's Guard, in spring, 1862, who arrested Gen. William G. Harding and Judge Joseph Guild, and who attempted to recruit the 9th Tenn. Inf., Governor's Guard in Marion County and environs during the summer of 1862. Nashville *Union*, April 17, May 9, 1862; Letter from Henry R. Myer, August 18, 1862.

From Adrian V. S. Lindsley[1]

Nashville April 22, 1862

Hon Andrew Johnson
Governor of Tennessee
Dr Sir

As you well know I have remained here during the whole progress of the rebellion— With astonishment I witnessed its rise & progress, and have often thought over the causes that led to its success in Tennessee— After the vote in February 1861 I regarded the question as settled and that the Loyalty of Tennessee could not under any circumstances be mistaken. In this I was sadly & sorely disappointed and as you are aware a variety of causes combined to place our state in the false position she assumed,

I am clearly of opinion that no one lever that the Confederates used was as powerful or had as much effect as the Methodist Book Concern of Nashville. The Methodist denomination is a numerous & powerful body both in Tennessee & throughout the South. Its head quarters were at Nashville, its organ was the Nashville Christain Advocate, & press was the Methodist Publishing House of this City— The Reverend dignitaries who presided over it & controlled all its movements were the most noisy secessionists & the most active, inveterate & working rebels that we had in our midst.

They were active, in season & out of season; in the pulpit & out of it, in the chapel, family alter, in their religious paper, in their intercourse with their congregations, with their country parsons, with all over whom they had any influence or control,[2] their sole main object seemed to be to instil into them, not the doctrine of the Bible & of the Christian religion, but those of secession, rebellion & hatred of the General Goverment. The Book concern at Nashville I believe printed & published Hardees Tactics & pirated a number of School Books, copied verbatim from Northern Books, & palmed them off as strictly Southern simply substituting a new title & the name of some Southern Methodist Secession rebel preacher as Editor & Proprietor—[3] Last summer all the printers who were loyal left it and were treated with great injustice and harshness by the Revd Dignataries who had control over the concern—

I wish our friend Brownlow was present as he could shew up these Reverend Scoundrels in a more truthful light than I could possibly do. I will however take it upon me to say that we have had no more active leaders of this great rebellion than those who congregated about & presided over the Methodist Book concern at Nashville. They were the Revd Dr J. B. McFerrin, head devil, & the master spirit of all the wicked who gathered around this fountain head. During the week preceding *the ever to be remembered & never to be forgotten Sunday* (16 Feby. 1862) He marched about with the Pike Cos. & made most abusive speeches against the government, the Union Men &c. The Rev Dr Somers, Revd Dr McTyere Dr Houston, & A L P. Green[4] (that would be Brigadier General) & others of the same character centered & clustered around McFerrin & through the Methodist Publishing House scattered the seeds of rebellion far & wide over this once happy land.

I know of nothing in the State of Tennessee that is as objectionable to the Loyal men of Tennessee as the Methodist Book Concern & Publi[shing] House— All the Revd D.D.s above mentioned run away before the Advent of the Federals—

It is the prayer of all the good Union men of Tennessee that they will forever stay away, & that the Governor of Tennessee, or the proper authorities whoever they may be, will see that the Book Concern shall never more be the engine of treason & disloyalty that it has been heretofore[.]

Respectfully Yours

A. V. S. Lindsley

ALS, DNA-RG366, Fifth Special Agency, Port Royal Corres., Vol. 19; enclosed in E. H. East to S. P. Chase, April 22, 1862.

1. Adrian Van Sinderen Lindsley (1814-1885), a New Jersey native who moved to Nashville in 1824, served as president of the Mt. Olivet Cemetery Company and of the Nashville and Lebanon Turnpike Company, as Nashville postmaster (1862-67), and state senator (1868-69). A. V. S. and John Berrien were graduates of the University of Nashville and sons of Philip Lindsley, its president (1824-50). McGavock, *Pen and Sword*, 642n; Clayton, *Davidson County*, 199; Wooldridge, *Nashville*, 387-99 *passim*, 617; *Tenn. Senate Journal* (1868-69), 3, 267.

2. According to "H," special correspondent of the Philadelphia *Press*, the Nashville secessionist clergy had the ladies particularly under their influence and rebel pronouncements appeared not only in their sermons, but also in their prayers, doxologies, and benedictions. Philadelphia *Press*, July 7, 1862.

3. The accusation of pirating is not unfounded. An 1862 edition of Warren Colburn's *Intellectual Arithmetic*, supposedly "revised and adapted to the use of schools in the Confederate states" by Thomas O. Summers, reveals little that would distinguish the Nashville edition from its northern prototype.

4. Thomas O. Summers, Holland N. McTyeire, Lorenzo D. Huston, and Alexander L. P. Green were Methodist clergymen. Summers (1812-1882) emigrated from England in 1830 and entered the ministry five years later. Moving to Nashville in 1850, he served as the denomination's book editor, as well as editing the *Sunday School Visitor* (1851-56), *Quarterly Reveiw of the Methodist Church, South* (1858-61), and later the *Christian Advocate* (1868-78). In 1878 he became dean and professor of systematic

theology at the new Vanderbilt University. On the eve of the war he possessed $5,000 in real and $1,500 in personal property. McTyeire (1824-1889), native South Carolinian, educated at a manual labor school in Georgia and at Randolph-Macon College, was admitted to the Virginia conference in 1845 and later preached in Alabama, Mississippi, and Louisiana. He edited the New Orleans *Christian Advocate* from 1851 to 1858 when he moved to Nashville to guide that city's *Advocate* into the war years. Refugeeing in southern Alabama, where he became pastor of Montgomery's Clay Street Methodist Church in 1863, he returned to Nashville four years later and subsequently served as the first president of Vanderbilt (1873-89). Huston (b. *c*1820), an Ohio native with $4,000 real and $6,000 personal property in 1860, was editor of the monthly periodical, *Home Circle*. According to McFerrin, he was expelled from the church for immorality. Green (1806-1874), Sevier County native licensed to preach at eighteen, removed to Nashville in 1829. For six years pastor of McKendree Church, several times over a thirty-year period presiding elder of the Nashville district, and the person most influential in establishing the Publishing House, he was also a community promoter—stockholder, and frequently trustee, in railroads, academies, universities, and the Nashville Gas-Light Company. Fitzgerald, *John B. McFerrin*, 244-45, 247; McGavock, *Pen and Sword*, 535n; Speer, *Prominent Tennesseans*, 407-9; *NCAB*, VIII, 226; John J. Tigert, IV, *Bishop Holland Nimmons McTyeire* (Nashville, 1955), 124-25, 133; 1860 Census, Tenn., Davidson, 10th Dist., 68; Edgefield, 3, 13; Wooldridge, *Nashville*, 603-5; Clayton, *Davidson County*, 257, 293, 326, 385.

To Stanley Matthews, Nashville

Nashville, Tenn., April 22, 1862.

Colonel Matthews.

Dear Sir: From all that I can learn in connection with General Murray's arrest I am thoroughly satisfied that it would be the better policy to release him upon condition of his renewing his allegiance to the Government and entering into security for a reasonable amount for the faithful observance thereof. I should not hesitate in taking this course if I had caused the arrest to be made. His release will accomplish far more than sending him away.[1] He is a mere militia general, elected by the people, authorized by the militia law and commissioned by the Governor. He was never in the Confederate service as I understand. There are several others I understand who are to be sent away. I think it would be better to make some examination of their cases before giving them so much importance. It is much better to keep some here so far as affecting the public mind than to send them away. Many of these men are not known beyond their immediate neighborhood, and can exert no influence whatever upon the State or beyond its limits. I think that you or some other person ought to be authorized to make a partial examination at least of these cases before they are dignified with a trip North or any other point beyond the limits of the State.

Very respectfully, your obedient servant,

Andrew Johnson.

P.S.–I hope that you will submit this letter to Captain Greene[2] as I understand he has control of these cases. If he has not such control then to General Dumont.[3]

A. J.

OR, Ser. 2, III, 470.

1. Probably Zebulon Montgomery Pike Maury (*c*1816-1862), youngest son of Abram Maury, for whom the county was named. A farmer who had supported Johnson politically during the decade before the war, he subsequently appealed to the governor for his release from Camp Chase early in May, before being sent as "a state political prisoner," to Johnson's Island, where he died of pneumonia before the end of the month. 1860 Census, Tenn., Warren, McMinnville, 3; Prison Records, RG109, NA; Nashville *Dispatch*, May 2, June 6, 1862; Maury to Johnson, May 8, 1862, Johnson Papers, LC.

2. Oliver D. Greene (*c*1833-1904), New York native and West Point graduate (1854) and currently assistant adjutant general on Buell's staff, had a long career as an artillery officer, retiring in 1897. Powell, *Army List*, 341; *West Point Register* (1970), 248.

3. Ebenezer Dumont.

From William B. Campbell and Jordan Stokes

Lebanon Ten. April 23d 1862

Govr. Andrew Johnson

Dear Sir

Col Marc Munday[1] commanding the federal troops here has conducted himself and commanded his troops in such a manner as to give great satisfaction here and by his judicious course has strengthened the union sentiment here and softened the asperities of the secessionists. He is a gentleman of excellent sense & judgment and in his position can do much to bring about harmony & a union sentiment. We think it very important that he and his regiment should be continued here & throughout the counties east of this place. We hear that there is some probability that he will be soon ordered away and doubtless he is anxious himself to go to the main army, yet we think that he can be of more service here than elsewhere. Some troops will be obliged to be kept in this region for a while & particularly when the soldiers from the Confederate army, (whose term of service will be soon expiring) will be coming home. We now understand Col Mundays manner of getting along with our people, and we fear that any successor of his might not be able to get along so well with the people in this region. We must do all we can to bring back our erring Citizens to their true allegiance, and it is very desirable to accomplish it in as mild a manner as possible. Can you not manage to have him continued at this post? Our people are yet deluded with the idea of the return very shortly of the Confederate army and while east Tennessee & west Tennessee are in the possession of the Confedrates we can make but little impression upon those who have been deluded & who have sons or relatives in the confederate army. As soon as Ten. shall be cleared of the Rebel Army, we think a powerful change will come over our entire population. We will both visit nashville as soon as we can safely leave the sick beds of our wives.

If Col Munday could be supplied with one or two additional companies of cavalry, it would have a most beneficial effect upon the counties in the mountain District and even might extend his movement to the

Sequatchee valley. Protection should be given if possible to the Union men of the two last named regions of country, and We believe that it can be done by Col Munday with a small additional force. There are yet some Rebel troops in Overton county, who ought to be driven out. The number is small but they overawe & depredate upon the whole union population, and have made forays into Kentucky. We have our reasons for desiring this *letter* to be *considered* as *private* which we will explain when we see you[.]

truly yours   W B Campbell
Jordan Stokes

ALS (Campbell), DLC-JP.

1. Marcellus Mundy (1830-1901), Kentucky-born Philadelphia attorney with $10,000 real and $20,000 personal property, served as colonel of the 23rd Ky. Inf., USA, until his resignation due to poor health, December 31, 1863. Post commandant at Louisville until the close of the war, he remained in that city to practice law. James R. Bentley (The Filson Club) to Andrew Johnson Project, January 28, 1975; 1860 Census, Pa., Philadelphia, 5th Ward, 383; *Official Army Register: Volunteers*, IV, 1277; *Edwards' Louisville Directory* (1867-68), 320; (1881), 528; Louisville *Courier-Journal*, February 23, 1901.

From William H. Cherry

Savannah Tenn. April 23 1862

Gov Andrew Johnson
Nashville Tenn.

Dear Sir.   Your very kind letter of the Inst is to hand and contents duly noted. I am very anxious to visit Nashville but the presence of so large an Army and the necessary attendant excitement in our immediate vicinity prevents me from leaving home at this time.   the Battle of Pittsburgh landing was only 8 miles from our village[.]   I was present both days[.]   it was a very hard Contested and desperate Contest, but I assure you there never was the great danger of the Union Army being overwhelmed and beaten as represented by Newspaper Correspondents. Nor was the bad Generalship so much Condemned as much so as represented.   the only fault was in feeling too secure, and letting the Rebels get the Start of them.

Our friends here are frequently enquiring if there will be any organization of the Militia under your authority or whether if union Companies are formed for the protection of their homes they can get arms? when where and upon what terms? There are now within the Federal lines here hundreds of Citizens from adjoining Counties who are afraid to return to or stay at their homes as the Confederate Cavalry are scouring the Country— Many of them say if they Could get arms they would organize and defend themselves. Can or will any thing be done to meet such Cases?

I trust you will be able to reorganize the State Government in a short time and a Convention fresh from the people will undo so far as it Can be done the ruin and shameful disgrace brought upon us Contrary to the real wish of the people. Allow me to trouble you with an enquiry as it interest many others beside me. What will be the probable Condition of our Banks in Tennessee. will any of them Sustain themselves? and how low will they depreciate if they fail?

I hope to be at Nashville before a great while as I trust the Federal Army will be able to advance shortly and relieve us of the pressure of anxiety resting upon us at this time[.] I feel every Confidence that success will attend them as they advance.

I wish to ask your aid in a matter that is new to me. I have never sought office or appointment, but now the Confederate troops have burned Several thousand dollars worth of cotton of mine, And the Federal Army on account of the Situation of my Farm have ruined it for the present at least by trapping the land burning my fences, killing my Stock &C—that I have concluded if I Could serve the State or General Government in Some way that would also pay me I would be glad to do so—

Any information or assistance I Can render you will be cheerfully given at anytime.

Very respectfully   W. H. Cherry

P.S.

will you please have one of your best Triweekly Papers sent me[.] I will remit subscription on receipt—

W. H. C.

ALS, DLC-JP.

From Horace Maynard

Washington, April 23. 1862.

Dr. Sir.

I have just returned here having stopped over night in Baltimore, otherwise coming directly through. I find they are at work at the Confiscation Bill.[1] I am inclined to go for it, but cannot tell until I see more about it. I have seen no one yet, except Calvert[2] of Md. whom I met on the cars. Trigg is very sick I learn, but have not seen him. I will see the Prest. to-night & write to-morrow.

Very Truly Yours
Horace Maynard

Hon. A. Johnson

I have, since writing the within, seen Mr Trigg.[3] He is sick but is getting some better. Today he called on Mr. Stanton, for the first time, but nothing was done. I will write again to-morrow.

ALS, DLC-JP.

1. The Second Confiscation Act, discussions of which occupied considerable time during 1862 until its passage in July, made treason punishable by death or fine and

imprisonment and "rebellion or insurrection" by fine, imprisonment, and the liberation of slaves. Property of officers of the Confederate government was subject to forfeiture without warning, while property of others engaged in "rebellion" was also subject to seizure with sixty days' notice. Nevins, *War for the Union*, II, 145-46, 204; *U.S. Statutes*, XII, 589-92.

2. Charles B. Calvert (1808-1864), Maryland farmer and stock-breeder, founder of the first agricultural research college in the United States (1856) and early advocate of a national department of agriculture, served as a Union Whig congressman (1861-63). *BDAC*, 651.

3. Connally Trigg had recently been appointed commissioner to visit Tennessee prisoners of war.

From Marcellus Mundy

Lebanon, Tennessee
Hd. Qrs. Detacht. 23rd Brigade
April 23rd. 1862.

Gen: Johnson
Mil. Governor of Tenn.
Dear Sir

I had the honor to receive today per Mr. Haley,[1] your letter of 21st. Inst. with writ for the arrest of Jefferson J. Ford[2] and others— Following the prudent suggestion contained in your letter I had a conference with Ex Governor Campbell and Jordan Stokes Esq. whereupon we determined that the interposition of military authority (which would naturally create panic in the minds of people already terribly exorcised with apprehensions) for the proper punishment of that class of small political offenders who can be so readily reached and dealt with by the civil authorities so son as your court shall be organized, would be impolitic and therefore unwise— Whatsoever may be the antecedents of the persons named, having learned from Mr. Haley and William B. Stokes Esq. that at present they are pursuing their legitimate business quietly, we deem it most prudent to let investigation wait upon the due process of law, and so instructed Mr. Haley, who has the natural anxiety of the wronged to see retribution dealt out. I have already had Mr. William Floyd[3] and Mr. Alfred Bone[4] before me having been arrested by one of my scouting parties upon information obtained from their neighbors. After investigation I discharged Bone from military arrest without administering the oath to him— And Floyd, who informed me that upon taking his seat as Legislator he had taken an oath of allegiance to the Southern Confederacy I required to renounce such allegiance and take the oath of allegiance to the Federal Government, which he did most willingly and I discharged him. When I came here with my command I found the people full of apprehensions of outraged and unknown evils caused by the foul misrepresentations of our army industriously circulated by the rebel leaders, which I attempted to relieve by publicly stating to them, that while I was at war with rebels in arms and would arrest all such found—non beligerents had nothing to fear—as rather than molest them in person or property, in all legitimate pursuits I would protect them, and my aim has been to keep that promise. While the enmity incident with and inseparable from the accursed insanity of rebellion remains in the hearts of many—all of their apprehensions have long since vanished and business is beginning again to seek its proper channels. Seeing that the policy adopted and pursued by me is working to the reclamation of many misguided men in this community—I would be the more unwilling, unless specially urged, to arouse new apprehensions by exercising military power needlessly.

As you kindly left the matter to my discretion after conference with Messrs Campbell & Stokes I have taken the liberty of stating to you in brief the reasons which influence my non-action in the premises until further advised by you.

I would take great pleasure in obeying any order from you or in adapting any suggestion you may be kind enough to give for the benefit of the great cause in which we are engaged[.]

> I have the Honor to be
> Your Obedt. Sert.   M Mundy
> Col. Commanding Post.—

P.S. I have just received orders to move to Murfreesboro with my Command— Some other force should be sent to this Post immediately—

> Respectfully   M. Mundy.

ALS, DLC-JP.

1. Perhaps John T. Haley (b. c1821), a Virginia-born Wilson County farmer whose estate was valued at $5,144. 1860 Census, Tenn., Wilson, 16th Dist., 130.

2. Joshua Jefferson Ford (1822-fl1879), DeKalb County blacksmith-turned-lawyer who declared $1,500 in real and $9,100 in personal property in 1860, served in the state legislature (1859-61, 1877-79). Ibid., DeKalb, 1st Dist., 13; McBride and Robison, Biographical Directory, I, 255.

3. William Floyd (b. c1803), Tennessee native and Mexican War veteran, was a merchant and tanner who served as postmaster at Alexandria during the 1850's and as a Confederate state legislator. Robison, Preliminary Directory, DeKalb, 35.

4. Probably Alfred Bone (b. c1822), a DeKalb County clerk and farmer with $9,000 in real and $25,000 in personal property on the eve of the war. Joyce Lindstrom, Population Schedule of the United States Census of 1850 (Seventh Census) for DeKalb County (Provo, Utah, 1965), 1; 1860 Census, Tenn., DeKalb, 1st Dist., 1.

To Edwin M. Stanton[1]

Nashville, Apl 23d 1862

Hon Edwin M. Stanton
Secy of War

There are two (2) Tennessee Regiments complete & in service at Cumberland ford[.] Four others nearly complete[.] There is one being formed at that place and rapidly filling up Contrary to the Expecta-

tions of everybody[.]   as soon as order can be received [restored][2] there
will be a Report made to the Dep't[.][3]   Col Campbell's Regiment has
just reached here[.] decided reaction is going on in the public mind[.]
All will come out right[.]

Andrew Johnson

Tel, DNA-RG107, Tels. Recd., Sec. of War, Vol. 10 (Apr. 18-29, 1862); DLC-JP.

1. The day before Stanton had telegraphed: "How soon may this dept expect the
return of troops from your state[?]" An earlier circular of April 14 had asked for a "full &
accurate statement of all the troops from your state which are now in the service of the
Genl. government together with a seperate list of all not mustered into the service & all
used as home guards & c. . . . the object of this is to arrive at the entire number of men
armed & employed in the military service in any capacity in order to provide for adequate
appropriations." Stanton to Johnson, April 23[14], 22, 1862, Johnson Papers, LC.

2. Sender's copy reads "restored." *Ibid.*

3. Evidently this reply was unsatisfactory to the secretary of war who telegraphed
three days later: "Governor I have not rec'd your return of troops[.] when may I Expect
it." *Ibid.*

Remarks to Third Minnesota Regiment[1]

April 23, 1862

Governor Johnson said that, recognizing the men before him as the
defenders of the Law, the Constitution and the Union, he welcomed
them heartily to the State of Tennessee. He recognized in this great
contest no sectional line, but the broad and noble one of Union. He
believed the men, the citizen soldiers, who stood before him had come
not as subjugators and invaders, but as protectors and defenders of all
who were loyal and true. This was a momentous struggle which involved
the existence of free government itself. It was a battle between despotism
and democracy for supremacy. He knew the leaders of this rebellion well
and intimately, both personally and politically, and he declared it was the
firm determination of the rebel leaders to overthrow popular government, if they should succeed, and establish a despotism instead of our
present liberal institutions. Mr. Clayton,[2] the Assistant Secretary of
Hon. Howell Cobb, declared to him on one occasion that the people of
the South, as well as many at the North, were fully determined to submit
to the election of no President who had sprung from the common people,
as Abe Lincoln had. Andrew Jackson had foreseen this attempt to revolutionize the Government twenty-eight years ago, and had foretold that
the aristocrats in the next struggle would make slavery their pretext.
The prophecy is now in its fulfilment, and the leaders of this infamous
rebellion were trying to trample down all popular government and
establish a despotism, based not on man's inherent rights of self-government, not on the intelligence of the people, not on the sublime truths of
democracy, but solely on the institution of slavery, thus wresting government from the hands of the people where God had placed it, and
giving it to a mere institution. There was nothing noble or exalted in the
rebel movement. He knew the demon of secession to be an ignoble one.

It was a diabolical, hell-born concern. It was conceived and born in sin, and would end in Hell. And he was glad to see all over the land an instinctive rally around the flag of the Union by the people. All differences of birth and of former party associations are forgotten in this battle for the right of man. He hailed the men of Minnesota as the citizen soldiers of the Union, who had come not to infringe upon one right, but rather to protect us in the enjoyment of all. Yes, he spoke almost in sight of the tomb of the Sage and Soldier of the Hermitage, and if that noble old man could know what was going on to-day in Tennessee, it seemed to him that he would burst the cerements of his tomb, and walking forth in all his former majesty, would raise his hand and exclaim to the soldiers of the Union, "The Federal Union must be preserved" and then cry to the embattled host, "On to the conflict!" It had been charged by the apostles of treason that the North had come here to set negroes free. He knew the North—had travelled among her people, and he repelled the charge with scorn. There were Abolition fanatics there, it was true—sectionalists, traitors—brothers of Southern Secessionists—but these creatures constituted but a fraction of the great body of the North. The voice of the overwhelming mass of the North, as well as of nine men out of ten who stood before him was: "We care nothing for your negroes; manage them as best suits yourselves, but the Union shall be preserved, and you must obey the laws! (This sentiment was confirmed and endorsed by the soldiers with deafening shouts of applause and cries of "That's so.")

Yes, this Union must be preserved. He was in during the war, for its preservation, and if necessary would pour out his heart's blood as a free libation on the altar of freedom, in order that the blessings of free government might be transmitted down to generations in that remote future, whose grandeur no living man can estimate.[3]

Nashville *Union*, April 24, 1862.

1. Invited by Capt. Christopher C. Andrews to visit the regiment's camp about two miles south of Nashville, Johnson viewed a dress parade and then was introduced by Secretary of State Edward East. Nashville *Union*, April 24, 1862; Andrews, *Recollections*, 152.

2. Philip Clayton (1815-1877), a Georgia native, protégé of Howell Cobb and according to the New York *Times* "a roystering Secessionist when Cobb only whispered his treasonable intent into the ears of his friends," served as second auditor (1849-57) and assistant secretary of the treasury (1857-61), holding the latter post in the Confederacy from 1861 until 1863. Appointed consul at Callao, Peru, in 1874, he continued there until he succumbed to yellow fever. Jon L. Wakelyn, *Biographical Dictionary of the Confederacy* (Westport, Conn., 1977), 138-39; New York *Times*, January 23, 1861; see also *Johnson Papers*, II, 21.

3. Captain Andrews sent his version of the hour-and-a-half speech to the Boston *Post* where it appeared May 2. His text included the following paragraph on a topic ignored by the *Union* reporter: "In the last presidential canvas there were three candidates for the Presidency voted for in Tennessee,—Douglas, Bell and Breckenridge. Each, by his supporters, was claimed to be the best Union man. Strange as it might seem to them, he supported Breckenridge as the best Union man. He canvassed the State, spent money and printed documents to secure his election. But he told the people everywhere that if Lincoln should be elected, it was their duty to give him a fair trial—to support his measures if they were fair and just, and if they were not, to wait till his four years were up, and then elect some one in his place." Andrews, *Recollections*, 152n-53n.

From Horace Maynard

Washington, April 24, 1862

Dr. Sir.

The kindness with which I have been welcomed back, & the earnest enquiries made after you & the success of your administration, by men of all parties, illustrates, better than any thing else, the intense earnestness with which the public eye is directed towards our state.

Last night I had a very satisfactory interview with the President & at his suggestion, another equally satisfactory with the Secretary of War, this morning. Without elaborating or going too much into details, I will state as the result of these conferences.—

1. Gen. Dumont will be ordered to join Gen. Halleck, leaving the troops in the region of Nashville, subject to your orders.

2. No Tennessee prisoners of war will be exchanged or paroled. You will be authorized to discharge all such as you shall be satisfied are now & will continue to be loyal. There are reasons for postponing action in this matter for a little time; that appear feasible & are probably sufficient.

3. On the subject of Senators, I continued the matter to Senators Cowan[1] & Collamer.[2] The former declared at once against your power to appoint, the latter said he had thought nothing about the matter & had no opinion. The Prest. was in favor of the power being exercised: that it existed he expressed no doubt. The Secretary of War with his usual practical turn, not only asserted the power, but developed the mode of its exercise; to wit: that you should be invited informally by the Senators to fill the existing vaccancy.[3]

4. The promises for East Tennessee are such that I should be overjoyed if none had ever been made before.

5. Some additional Ohio troops, Campbell's regiment among others, have been sent to Nashville.

The confiscation question is before both Houses. Judge Collamer privately suggested a plan that strikes me favorably. It is, in brief, to reach rebel property by fines imposed.[4] Mr. Trigg still improves.

I am very Truly Yours
Horace Maynard

His Excy Andrew Johnson.

ALS, DLC-JP.

1. Edgar Cowan (1815-1885), Pennsylvania lawyer and Republican senator (1861-67), failed of reelection because of his Johnsonian stand on Reconstruction; in 1867 the Senate refused to confirm his appointment as minister to Austria. *BDAC*, 743.

2. For Jacob Collamer, see *Johnson Papers*, I, 324n.

3. Neither at this time, nor subsequently, did Johnson attempt to make an appointment; in fact, Tennessee remained without senators until 1866.

4. Evidently Collamer had discussed his proposed substitute for S. 151, a confiscation act, which had been presented January 15 by Lyman Trumbull of Illinois on behalf of the judiciary committee. Collamer's measure, offered the day this letter was written,

provided for a fine of not less than $10,000 on the property of those who had committed
an act of treason; this provision survived in the final joint resolution (H. R. 110—"An
Act to Suppress Insurrection . . . and confiscate the Property of Rebels"), signed into
law on July 17. *Cong. Globe*, 37 Cong., 2 Sess., 334, 1808-14, 1895; *U. S. Statutes*,
XII, 589-92

To Don Carlos Buell, Pittsburg Landing

Nashville Apl 24 [1862]

Genl Buell

I do hope that you will not withdraw the Minnesota Regiment from
this place, Col Munday's Regiment from Lebanon and the forces from
Murfreesboro[.] its influence will operate greatly against the Reaction
in favor of the Union throughout the Middle part of The State— It will
destroy confidence in the Union men and inspire on the part of Rebels
insolence and arrogance[.] In fine I hope Genl Duffields Brigade[1] will be
left where it is[.]

Adrew Johnson

Tel, DNA-RG94, Gens. Papers, D. C. Buell; DLC-JP.
    1. William W. Duffield (1823-1907), Pennsylvania-born Columbia graduate (1841)
and civil engineer, had served with the 2nd Tennessee in the Mexican War. Having
previously commanded two Michigan units, he was at this time leading the 23rd Bde.,
Army of the Ohio, just prior to assuming command of Federal troops in Kentucky (May,
1862). Wounded at Murfreesboro in July, Duffield resigned the following year, resumed his profession, and subsequently served in the Michigan legislature (1879-80)
and as superintendent of the coast and geodetic survey (1894-98). *Appleton's Cyclopaedia*, II, 248; Milton H. Thomas, *Columbia University Officers and Alumni, 1754-
1857* (New York, 1936), 157; *OR*, Ser. 1, XVI, Pt. I, 803.

From Don Carlos Buell

Camp near Pittsburg
Apl 24 1862

To Gov. Johnson

I do not intend to withdraw the force from nashville unless for the
defence of nashville and middle Tennessee in a more advanced position.
The regiments mentioned are first to be replaced by others that are
coming in. It will not do to let the Enemy close around your city before
we begin to drive him away.

D. C. Buell Maj Genl

Tel, DLC-JP.

To John A. Kasson[1]

Nashville, Tenn
Ap'l 24th 1862

Hon John A. Kasson,
1st Assistant Post Master Genl.
Washington City.

I am daily pressed to have Post offices opened at places within our lines. It is important they should be opened at once. It will exert great influence in our favor. Please send me blank commissions, bonds and oaths and I will see that good union and reliable men only are put in offices which can be opened with advantage to the Government. I have written you upon the subject[.]

Andrew Johnson.

Tel draft, DLC-JP.
1. John A. Kasson (1822-1910), a Vermont native who practiced law in St. Louis and Des Moines, served as assistant postmaster general (1861-62), Iowa congressman (1863-67, 1873-77, 1881-84), and minister to Austria-Hungary (1877-81) and Germany (1884). *BDAC*, 1144.

To Horace Maynard, Washington, D. C.

Nashville Tenn April 24th 1862

To Hon Horace Maynard.

I have this moment been advised that the 3d Minnesota Reg't stationed here & the forces at Murfreesboro & Lebanon have been ordered south by Buell. This is substantially surrendering the country to the rebels. My understanding was that I was sent here to accomplish a certain purpose. If the means are withheld it is better to desist from any further efforts. You are well aware of Genl Buell's course in regard to Tennessee from the beginning to the present moment. These forces ought to be detained where they are. I hope you will see the Sec'y of War at once.[1] The effect of removing the troops is visible in the face of every secessionist. Secession was cooling down & great reaction in favor of the Union was taking place.

Andrew Johnson

Tel, DNA-RG94, Gens. Papers, D. C. Buell; DNA-RG107, Tels. Sent, Sec. of War, Vol. 9 (Apr. 23-May 27, 1862).
1. Maynard referred this telegram to Stanton who forwarded it to General Halleck, asking him to acknowledge receipt and to "state what order, if any" was issued. Halleck's reply, sent also to Buell, assured Stanton "that we require every available man on this line, and . . . to send troops back to Nashville to accommodate Governor Johnson would be releasing our grasp on the enemy's throat in order to pare his toe-nails." Buell, agreeing that the movement was "absolutely necessary" for the defense of Middle

Tennessee and for the support of General Mitchel, considered "this a matter of far greater moment than the gratification of Governor Johnson, whose views upon the matter are absurd." Stanton to Halleck, April 25, 1862, Tels. Sent, Sec. of War, Vol. 9 (Apr. 23-May 27, 1862), RG107, NA; Halleck to Buell and to Stanton, Buell to Halleck, April 26, 1862, *OR*, Ser. 1, X, Pt. II, 128-29.

From Horace Maynard

Washington, April 25, 1862—

Dr. Sir,

Your dispatch came last night & was referred at once to the Secretary of War who sent it immediately to the President. They telegraphed to Halleck for the facts connected with the order, & as soon as they get a reply will act. They are both disposed to sustain you fully. The Secretary gave me some further information about the "cotters",[1] that I will reserve for another occasion.

Respecting Tennessee Volunteers, the Secretary says you have full authority to raise them; but *says he wishes you would send to the Department the names of all Tennessee Officers whom you propose to have commissioned*, so that proper records can be kept here. This you will doubtless very gladly do.

Mr. Trigg desires that I shall state that various persons wish John Williams as Col. & Edward Trigg as Lt Col. to have authority to raise a regiment & that the latter shall be permitted to commence at once, prior to our getting in to Tennessee.

Trigg is growing some better. He went with me to the War Department this morning. I think he will go to Nashville as soon as he is able to travel.

I find that John Trimble's[2] recommendation, though reported by the Judiciary Committee has not been acted upon by the Senate. I will try & have it got through as soon as possible.

How will old man Robert H. McEwen[3] do for Pension Agent? Please write me so that this place can be filled by somebody.

I am very Truly Yours
Horace Maynard

His Excy Andrew Johnson.

ALS, DLC-JP.

1. Employing a derisive Yankee spelling, Maynard appears to be promising further information, which he delivered the following day, about William B. Carter's efforts to procure a brigadier-generalship for his brother Sam.

2. Maynard was unduly alarmed; Lincoln had nominated Trimble as U. S. attorney for the middle district of Tennessee on April 9, and the Senate confirmed the nomination the day this letter was written. *Senate Ex. Journal*, XII (1861-62), 225, 258; for Trimble, see *Johnson Papers*, III, 409n.

3. Robert H. McEwen, Sr. (1790-1868), Trimble's father-in-law, was a prominent Nashville collection agent and attorney. No record of his becoming a pension agent was found. 1860 Census, Tenn., Nashville, 5th Ward, 181; McBride and Robison, *Biographical Directory*, I, 738; Acklen, *Tenn. Records*, I, 94; *Singleton's Nashville Directory* (1865), 211.

To Don Carlos Buell, Pittsburg Landing

Nashville Apr 25 [1862]

Maj Genl Buell

Glad to know that these places are not to be left defenceless.[1] Telegrams from Lexington Unionists at these points have been receivd praying that they might not be left to the mercy of the Rebels & they will rejoice at your determination not to leave them unprotected[.] reaction is rapidly progressing[.]

Andrew Johnson

Tel, DNA-RG94, Gens. Papers, D. C. Buell; DLC-JP.
1. A reference to Buell's reassurance of the preceding day.

To Don Carlos Buell

Nashville
Apr 25 [1862?]

Maj. Genl Buell

I have just learned that Campbells 69th Ohio Regiment has been ordered away from Nashville— In reply to a request of mine sec'y Stanton & Adjt General Thomas telegraphed me on the 17th that this Regiment had been ordered to Report to me.— I am anxious that Campbells Regiment should remaine here for reasons of a personal Consideration. The Regiment was raised in my name and I aided personally in its formation.— Please send an early Reply[.]

Andrew Johnson

Tel, DNA-RG94, Gens. Papers, D. C. Buell; DLC-JP.

To William Y. Elliott[1] and Others

Nashville Ap'l 25th

W. Y. Elliott G. W. Ashburn,[2]
E. D. Wheeler[3] & others, Murfreesboro, Tenn

General Buell just telegraphed me that forces will not be withdrawn unless for the defense of Nashville & Middle Tennessee in a more advanced position and that the forces are *first* to be replaced by others now coming in—

All officers should be required to take an oath to support Constitution of United States, as required by Constitution of this State. I send form of oath by·mail.[4]

The Government must pass into hands of its friends.

Andrew Johnson

Tel draft, DLC-JP.

1. William Y. Elliott (1827-1893), Murfreesboro businessman, prewar Whig, wartime Unionist, and postwar Republican, served in the state legislature (1865-69), as a delegate to Republican national conventions (1868-80), and as U. S. pension agent (1873-77). Robison *Preliminary Directory, Rutherford*, 19-20.

2. George W. Ashburn (*c*1812-1868), North Carolina native and Columbus, Georgia, cotton broker, in March, 1861, refugeed to his summer residence on Lookout Mountain and subsequently to Murfreesboro, where he volunteered as an aide or scout for the Department of the Cumberland and raised a regiment of southern loyalists. Returning to Columbus after the war, he served as a delegate to the state constitutional convention (1867-68), before his murder in April, 1868, by "unknown parties" produced an army investigation. 1860 Census, Ga., Muscogee, Columbus, 38; *NCAB*, IV, 399; Ashburn to Lincoln, June 18, 1864, Lincoln Papers, LC.

3. E. D. Wheeler (b. *c*1824), Kentucky native, Murfreesboro physician and dentist, declared $4,000 in personal property on the eve of the war. 1860 Census, Tenn., Rutherford, 13th Dist., 173; Carlton C. Sims, ed., *A History of Rutherford County* (Murfreesboro, Tenn., 1947), 138.

4. See Letter to Nashville City Council, March 25, 1862, note 4.

To Edwin M. Stanton

Nashville Apl 25 1862

Hon E M Stanton

Col Lewis D Campbell regt the sixty ninth 69th Ohio had hardly landed here before Gen Buell ordered it away[.] Your dispatch of the seventeenth 17 said they were ordered to report to me[.] I have before pressed the propriety of a brigade in addition to the forces at this place & do most earnestly hope that Campbells regt will be permitted to remain at this place[.] Please send an immediate reply as the regt is ordered to leave tomorrow[.]

Andrew Johnson

Tel, DNA-RG107, Tels. Recd., Sec. of War, Vol. 10 (Apr. 18-29, 1862); DLC-JP; DLC, Lincoln Papers.

From Don Carlos Buell

April 26th 1862
Camp near Pittsburg

To Gov Johnson

I am anxious to gratify you but you will see the propriety of making all other considerations yield to that disposition of the troops which is necessary for the security of nashville & will [*sic*] & middle tennessee[.]

D. C. Buell Maj Genl

Tel, DLC-JP; *OR*, Ser. 1, X, Pt. II, 621.

From Camp Morton Prisoners

April 26, 1862, Indianapolis, Ind.; ALS, DLC-JP.

Ambrose B. Coleman, Joseph D. Collier, and others of the 1st Tenn. Inf. Btn.—"Jenerley men of but little means" whose families suffer in their absence—petition Johnson for their release by parole, exchange, or oath of allegiance. Supporters of Johnson in the past, they had "voted for the union and the constitution as free men but the time had come when we had to lay our mouths in the dust and dared not Speak our sentiments." When "we was informed that we was going to be drafted and to keep out of the drawing . . . as well as to save or honor and personaly property we volunteered . . . and left home the 2nd day of January 1862[.]"

From Horace Maynard

Washington, April 26, 1862

Dr. Sir.

I have had another interview today with the Secretary of War. He told me he had received another dispatch from you, that is, another than that sent to me: & that he had referred it to Gen. Halleck. He remarked that he could not take the responsibility of interfering with, much less controlling military operations at a point so remote & in the presence of such an enemy. So I suppose it will be [too] much[?] to depend upon Gen. Halleck, who will think of but one thing until after the battle which seems to be impending.[1] Do you know whether the bridge across the Tennessee at Bridgeport has been destroyed?

I learned at the Post Office this morning that Mr. Lindsley[2] would be appointed Post Office Agent.

I also learned, what we had heard of before, that soon after we had left this city for Nashville, Rev. Wm. B. Carter came here, & by some assistance presented the renomination of his brother as Brigadier General.[3] I do not learn that the renomination has been confirmed.

I have this morning written to Gen. Frémont giving, at his request, such information & suggestions touching East Tennessee as seemed proper. I have not telegraphed you simply because I had nothing important enough to send in that way— And I know you have no wish simply to hear every running "from Banks's Column."[4]

Mr. Trigg still improves: but goes out very little.

Remember me kindly to the boys.

I am very Truly Yours
Horace Maynard

The Secretary promised to communicate with you by telegraph.

His Excy. Andrew Johnson.

ALS, DLC-JP.

1. Halleck was about to begin his advance on Corinth, Mississippi, an operation which he accomplished during May and early June. Boatner, *Civil War Dictionary*, 176.

2. Subsequently nominated as Nashville postmaster on June 11, Adrian V. S. Lindsley was confirmed the following day and served until 1867. *Senate Ex. Journal*, XII (1861-62), 337, 345.

3. Samuel P. Carter, nominated on March 20, was confirmed by the Senate, May 1. *Ibid.*, 176, 273; C-48-1863, Commission Branch, RG94, NA.

4. An allusion to the frequent appearance during April in the Washington press of reports headed "From Gen. Banks's Column"—despatches concerning the skirmishes of the V Corps as it alternately stalked Stonewall Jackson and withdrew to protect the capital. Nathaniel Banks (1816-1894), a Massachusetts native, served in the legislature (1849-52), the House of Representatives (1853-57), and as governor (1858-61) before his appointment as major general of volunteers. As a field commander, he was largely unsuccessful, inasmuch as his forces were twice defeated by Jackson in 1862—in the Shenandoah Valley and at Cedar Mountain—and suffered heavy losses at Port Hudson (1863) and during the Red River campaign (1864). Returning to Congress as a Republican (1865-73, 1875-79, 1889-91), he was elected to the state senate in 1874 and served as U. S. marshal (1879-88). Washington *National Intelligencer*, April 7, 15, 19, 21, 23, 1862; *BDAC*, 512; Warner, *Generals in Blue*, 17-18; see also Fred H. Harrington, *Fighting Politician: Major General N. P. Banks* (Philadelphia, 1948).

From Edward C. Williams

April 26, 1862, Camp Hetzel, Springfield; ALS, DLC-JP.

Colonel commanding Lochiel Cavalry acknowledges receipt of Buell's Special Orders No. 12. Springfield area citizens are "very civil" and he knows "of no one at present who should be arrested." Assures the governor of his "co-operation in restoring law and order—in crushing out this unholy rebellion and in assisting to bring back to these deluded people the protection of the Constitution and laws of the United States—"

To Abraham Lincoln

Nashville Tenn.
Apl 26th, 1862.

His Exc'y A. Lincoln
President.

A few days since I despatched to you some of the reasons why I desired the sixty ninth Ohio volunteers Col Campbell commanding should be transferred to this place. I received a reply from Sec'y Stanton stating that it had been done. immediately upon arrival of that regiment here it was ordered to another point where it is not needed. I hope you will send an order at once being the commander in chief that the regiment remain at this place. Petty jealousies and contests between Generals wholly incompetent to discharge the duties assigned them have contributed more to the defeat and embarrassment of the Government than all other causes combined. If I can be sustained in carrying out the object of the administration in restoring Tennessee to her former status in the Union and in not being dependent upon staff officers and Brigadier Generals—

it can be accomplished in less than three months. I want a reply from the President. I hope that you will send for Mr Maynerd and consult with him as to how matters have been managed since I reached this place in connection with the military.

Andw Johnson.

Tel, DLC-Lincoln Papers; DNA-RG107, Tels. Recd., Sec. of War, Vol. 10 (Apr. 18-29, 1862); DLC-JP; *OR*, Ser. 1, X, Pt. II, 129.

From Alvan C. Gillem

Assistant Quartermaster's Office.
Field of Shiloh Apl 27 1862.

Governor:

I have understood that you are organizing troops. I have never sought any preferment since my entry into the military service Eleven years ago, I should be highly gratified to have the command of a Regt. I do not pretend to have any particular claim to such distinction. I do not consider that there was any merit in remaining loyal, to my flag, & look upon it merely as my good fortune to have been present at the two hardest fought battles of the Rebellion Millsprings & Shiloh or as it is improperly called Pittsburgh Landing.

I could have probably obtained the command of Regts. from other States. My friend Genl. Boyle[1] endeavored to obtain the consent of the War Dept. for me to command a Kentucky Regt. but it was refused. *I* did not ask it.

Should it please you to confer the command of a Regt. on me I shall endeavor to justify the confidence reposed in me.

Our troops are organizing as rapidly as possible. Genl. Buells army is in fi[eld] condition. Genl Popes is said to also, but it will require sometime for Genl Grants army to recover from its defeat. of the 6th inst. its loss was very great especially in *captured*, four thousand seven hundred of his army are said to be missing.

The Union feeling is very strong from Waynesburg to Savanah. I am convinced that the Union feeling is stronger & more *Sincere* in Tenn. than Kentucky.

Excuse me for tresspassing on your valuable time, & allow me in conclusion to thank you for your kind attention to my family, and your endeavors to Shield my wife from the insults which my course in this rebellion & her devotion to me have drawn upon her.

I am Governor very respectfully yr obt servt.
Alvan C. Gillem

ALS, DLC-JP.

1. Jeremiah T. Boyle (1818-1871), a Kentucky lawyer, was appointed brigadier general of volunteers in November, 1861, and seven months later became military commander of Kentucky, with his headquarters at Louisville. Generally inept at con-

tending with the Confederate cavalry and guerrilla raids within the state, and alienating with his civilian policies all but the most determined Union sympathizers, he was relieved in January, 1864, and resigned shortly afterwards. After the war he amassed a fortune in the railroad business and land speculation. *DAB*, II, 532; Warner, *Generals in Blue*, 40.

From William Johnson

April 27, 1862; Nashville, ALS, DLC-JP.

A journeyman shoemaker, serving a one-year sentence in the state penitentiary on a "trivial charge," asks "executive Clemency." Arrested while intoxicated in Maury County, ostensibly for "taking a pair of brogan uppers valued at $1—and pawning them for a pint of Whiskey," Johnson may actually have been jailed on suspicion of being "a Spy—prowling round with the intention to burn the bridge at Duck River[.]" He attributes his plight to a continued refusal to join the Confederate army. Asserting that he had behaved "in an unexceptionable manner" while in prison and that he could "produce a good character from my former employers," the prisoner requests the governor's consideration.

From Abraham Lincoln

Washington April 27 1862

To Gov Andrew Johnson

Your dispatch of yesterday just rec'd as also in due course was your former one[.]¹   the former one was sent to Genl. Halleck & we have his answer by which I have no doubt he (Genl. Halleck) is in communication with you before this[.] Genl Halleck understands better than we can here & he must be allowed to control in that quarter[.]   if you are not in communication with Halleck telegraph him at once freely & frankly.

A Lincoln

Tel, DLC-JP; *OR*, Ser. 1, X, Pt. II, 131.
   1. Presumably Letter to Horace Maynard, April 24, 1862.

From John Sherman¹

(Private & Confidential)²

Senate Chamber
Washington City April 27 1862

Dear Sir

The telegraph about Carter was rec'd—³ I have thus far kept off his confirmation but unless you are heard from as to particular objections I think he will be confirmed—

You have warm friends here (of whom I sincerely am one) who desire your success in Tennessee—*above all things*— If Tennessee can be restored and loyalised other States will be likewise. The old Union and Constitution with such punishment to Traitors as will deter Treason hereafter is all we want— And I want you to do it— The honest People of this Country want somebody to rally about— The waste— fraud folly—weakness mingled with cruelty—jokes mixed with tragedy of many high in power sicken me[.][4] I want Honesty—Nerve—& fidelity to friends in a new leader not already stained with a disgraceful record. I therefore earnestly hope you may accomplish the task you have on hand—and then keep as clear as possible from all connexion with this Administration[.] I know in this I am speaking the general sentiment of the Young—active zealous Republicans who have a future before them— If it was not for the cohesive influence of the war the Administration would be Tylerised[5] in three days— But now a generous self sacrifycing patriotism keeps many quiet who would not for a moment share the disgrace that is brought upon the Party and the Country—[6]

Very truly Yours

John Sherman

Hon Andrew Johnson—

ALS, DLC-JP; DLC-Lincoln Papers.

1. John Sherman (1823-1900), younger brother of William Tecumseh, was a native Ohioan, a lawyer, businessman, and former Whig who served in the House (1855-61) and Senate (1861-77, 1881-97) and as secretary of treasury (1877-81) and state (1897-98). Noted for his expertise in fiscal affairs, Sherman helped plan the national banking system (1863), for ten years (1867-77) was chairman of the Senate finance committee, and is immortalized in the Sherman Anti-trust Act. *DAB*, XVII, 84-88; *BDAC*, 1593; *John Sherman's Recollections of Forty Years in the House, Senate and Cabinet: An Autobiography* (2 vols., Chicago, 1895).

2. This letter would appear to have been anything but "Private & Confidential." An endorsement on the original in the Johnson Papers reads: "Opened in mistake at Nashville Ohio by a Young, Active Zealous Union man[.] Andrew Johnston[.] N. B. I will divulge no secrets[.]" The communication found its way into the Lincoln Papers with the notation: "This is a copy of a Copy taken by Our Andrew Johnson [the Ohioan] & I have no doubt it is correct." "Zealous" Johnston (b. *c* 1836) was a native Ohioan who in 1860 was a schoolteacher with $1,150 in real and personal property. 1860 Census, Ohio, Holmes, Monroe Township, 71.

3. Not found.

4. Sherman was among those who found Lincoln's homespun, on occasion earthy, humor and wit objectionable—inappropriate to the dignity of the office and offensive in time of national travail.

5. Sherman was using the term to describe the falling away of support from Lincoln, even as earlier from Tyler, of those who felt themselves politically betrayed by the President's behavior.

6. The Ohio senator criticized the President personally and as an administrator in 1861-62, largely because of the state of the national economy, the slowness of Union enlistments, and some of Lincoln's Ohio appointees. Criticism of his brother's behavior at Shiloh probably aggravated Sherman's general unhappiness with the war effort. His opinions linked him with the "Unconditionals" in Congress and led to the circulation— under Sherman's frank—of an anti-Lincoln pamphlet in February, 1864. Friendly to Johnson in the early 1860's, he later aligned himself with the Radical Republicans and voted for Johnson's conviction in 1868. Sherman, *Recollections*, I, 262-81, 364-65, 427-29; Theodore E. Burton, *John Sherman* (New York, 1972[1906]), 84-85, 155-58; Rachel S. Thorndike, ed., *The Sherman Letters: Correspondence between General and Senator Sherman from 1837 to 1891* (New York, 1971 [1894]), 142, 147; William F. Zornow, *Lincoln & the Party Divided* (Norman, 1965), 49-51.

To Henry W. Halleck

Nashville, Tenn.
April 27th 1862

Maj Genl. Halleck,
Commanding Forces,
Near Pittsburg Landing, Tenn.

I have just received a despatch from President Lincoln in answer to a despatch in which I pressed the importance of a force at this point sufficient to exert not only a military but a moral power throughout Tennessee, which would be most salutary upon the public mind. I also pressed the propriety of the 69th Ohio Volunteers Col Campbell being located at this place, and which was ordered by the Secretary of War. There were many reasons given for this request.

The President informs me that the substance of this despatch has been transmitted to you, and that by this time it is expected you would be in communication with me. If the despatch has been received, I hope and trust that Genl. Halleck will find it consistent with the public service to grant the request made in regard to the amount of force to remain at this point to be disposed of as circumstances may require. I especially ask that at least Col Campbell's 69th Ohio Regiment may remain here, not only for reasons of public consideration but for reasons peculiar to myself. Please favor me with an early reply. I wish you complete success in the coming contest.

Accept assurances of my high esteem and respect[.]

Andrew Johnson.

Tel draft, DLC-JP; *OR*, Ser. 1, X, Pt. II, 132.

From Horace Maynard

Washington, April 28. 1862

Dr. Sir.

I having nothing especially new to communicate. Every body is excited with the report of the capture of New Orleans[1] & the inquiry goes every where, Can it be true. The disclosures made by the Nashville Union from the secret archives are attracting a good deal of attention.[2] I hope more such exposures will be made. The Intelligencer this morning has a leading editorial[3] upon them.

I have received no copy of the paper & have seen none since I left Nashville. It would gratify me to receive it. I saw a man this morning who left Knoxville three weeks ago, & came through by Cumberland Gap. He gave me some intelligence from my family, but nothing of general interest. He was a Pennsylvanian, & had been captured at Harper's Ferry.

We are having a good deal of talk about confiscation. Some bill will be passed. I have seen nothing that the Federal Court at Nashville has done.

I am very Truly Yours,
Horace Maynard.

His Excy. Andrew Johnson.

ALS, DLC-JP.

1. David G. Farragut had taken New Orleans three days earlier. Boatner, *Civil War Dictionary*, 592.

2. The *Union* editors, "culling from the State Archives," had been publishing the correspondence of such prominent Kentucky and Tennessee secessionists as Louisville *Courier* editor Robert B. McKee, Confederate agent George N. Sanders, Knoxville postmaster Charles W. Charlton, and Gen. Benjamin F. Cheatham. Letters captured earlier from Gen. Felix Zollicoffer's camp were also included. Nashville *Union*, April 19, 20, 22, 25, 1862.

3. The *National Intelligencer* of April 28 reprinted a *Union* article of the seventeenth, to illustrate Confederate stifling of free speech and subversion of the popular will.

From James A. Moore[1]

Columbus, O., April 28, 1861[1862].

Governor A. Johnson:

Dear Sir:

Pardon an humble rebel for again[2] assuming the liberty of addressing you. But then this a land of liberty, although I have enjoyed but very little of it since the reign of secession. Besides, a man must look to his friends for aid in time of need. I don't mean to insinuate that you are a friend to rebellion. But I believe you are a friend to the oppressed, and I think when you hear the history of my connection with the rebellion, you will set me down as one of your friends. And you will be mine. I was at Lebanon at the law school at the time of the fall of Fort Sumter, and I went immediately home and took the stump against Secession. I told my friends that Secession was a remedy for no evil—that it would destroy our Government, and bring upon us anarchy and ruin. I continued to plead with them and kept all from going into the Rebellion that I could, until in November, 1861, King Harris called for thirty thousand of militia from our division of the State. Then it was that we saw we had to go into the infernal Rebellion, willing or unwilling, either as volunteers or drafted men, and of course we preferred going as volunteers. We had too much pride to be drafted, and the consequence is, we are GENTLEMEN OF LEISURE up here in Ohio. Oh, Governor, you cannot imagine the feelings of a man who loves the Union and the land of his fathers, to be confined in prison, away from his home and business, whilst the leaders of Secession are rolling in luxury and ease at home. But you know what it is to be a Union man and be an exile from home. But your case was different from mine. I have been found in arms against the Union and the flag I love; whilst you have never deserted it. But you know the force of circumstances that drove myself and thousands of loyal Tennesseans to leave our homes to grow up in weeds, and go forth to aid in this unholy cause. Thank God! the sunlight of liberty is about to dawn, rebellion crushed and the Union preserved. I long to see the day when this rebellion will be forever crushed; and when the brave sons of East Tennessee will again be free, and be permitted to see their oppressors punished for the traitorous deeds they have inflicted upon them. Oh! just to think what the quiet, unassuming citizens of East Tennessee have suffered for the mere entertaining of opinion. But there is a just God who will avenge their wrongs. When I read your speech[3] the tears involuntarily trickled down my cheeks, to think of your being an exile, and your helpless and sick wife and children driven from their home? Great God! did we think our country would ever come to that? Did we think one portion of our countrymen would ever become border ruffians? None but traitors and cowards would be guilty of such a deed. But your brightest day is ahead. For you the future will give a silver lining to the darkest cloud that has overshadowed you in the past. I came out as a private in Capt. Logan's company,[4] the 26th of November, 1861, and served in that capacity until the 31st of December, 1861, when Capt. Logan resigned, and I was elected Captain, and served as Captain until the 16th of February, 1862, when my commission played out, and here I am. Now, Governor, if you can do anything for an unfortunate Tennessean who fought secession as long as it was in his power—yes, I it was who met the vigilance committee at the risk of my heart's blood, and rescued an aged minister (Parson Jenkins)[5] from the gallows for the mere entertaining of Union sentiments. This proof you can get from Edmond Cooper, Esq., of Shelbyville, Tenn., and all the Union men of Bedford county. They will all testify that I have ever been an unswerving Union man. You can get all the proof you wish from the citizens of Shelbyville, Tenn., and Bedford county. If you can do anything for me, there is nothing that I can ever do for you but I will take the greatest pleasure in doing. And you never have failed in any undertaking yet. I do not wish to be exchanged, for I never intend to be placed subject to rebel rule again. I will die first. I want to take the oath of allegiance to the Federal Government. If the authorities at Washington are afraid to let me take the oath and go home, I am willing to take the oath to the Federal Government and give any kind of bond they may require to remain in Columbus, Ohio, until the war is over. But I know if I was at home, I could do a great deal for the Union that I cannot do here. I will pledge my life—my all—to do everything I can to crush rebellion and restore the Union. I have been very low with pneumonia for six weeks. I am now on parole in Columbus, Ohio. All the prisoners are being sent to Sandusky.[6] My health is very bad; my lungs are badly affected, and the doctor says I will have to remain where I can get pure air and moderate exercise (a thing I cannot get in prison) or I cannot get well.

Governor Johnson, I wish you would telegraph to Governor Tod to let me remain here on parole until you can obtain my release. I would not go back to prison for the world. It is the next thing to hell to go to prison with those rabid secessionists. They call me a traitor. Some one who saw the letter that I first wrote you from Nashville, to one of the the Cincinnati papers,[7] stating that I had written to you asking my release. They saw a notice of it in the papers, and they would halloo out in prison, "Oh, yes! James A. Moore is the man who wants to see the damned traitor Andrew Johnson." I would not be put in prison amongst them again for the world. If you please telegraph to Governor Tod as soon as you get this to retain me here. If you will do this you will never regret it. Please attend to this soon, or I will be sent off in a few days.[8]

Governor, please do all you can for me; if you do I will released; then I will feel that I can never repay you.— Let me ask you again, in the name of humanity to grant my request, and remember me ever your friend,

James A. Moore

Nashville *Union*, May 8, 1862.

1. James A. Moore (1835-1872), Tennessee-born farmer and graduate of Cumberland Law School (1859) with personal property valued at $250 in 1860, served as 2nd lieutenant and later captain of Co. K, 41st Tenn. Inf., CSA. Taken prisoner at Donelson and paroled to Columbus, Ohio, on March 31, 1862, he was reported by Confederate authorities as a deserter in August. He practiced law in Shelbyville after the war. 1860 Census, Tenn., Bedford, W. Div., 10th Dist., 130; (1870), Shelbyville, 7th Dist., 6; CSR, RG109, NA; biographical data from James M. Gifford, Cullowhee, North Carolina.

2. Moore had written on March 10, begging to be allowed to take the oath of allegiance, since "that releases me from the power of the depraved leaders of secession forever"; the same day he asked Governor David Tod to intercede in his behalf. A week later Johnson addressed Stanton, requesting Moore's release because his father [John A. Moore] "is a clever and respectable gentleman [who] entertains union sentiments" and because the son himself "certainly evinces the right feeling and spirit." Moore to Johnson, and to Tod, March 10, 1862, Letters Received, 1862, RG107, NA; Johnson to Stanton, March 18, 1862, Frederick M. Dearborn Collection, Harvard University.

3. See Speech to Davidson County Citizens, March 22, 1862.

4. Littleberry Logan (1827-1908), native Tennessee farmer with $9,000 real and $700 personal property, was the first captain (November-December, 1861) of Co. K, 41st Tenn. Inf., CSA. 1860 Census, Tenn., Bedford, 22nd Dist., 196; Frost, *Frosts and Related Families*, 147, 174-75, 286; *Tennesseans in the Civil War*, I, 263.

5. William Jenkins (c1803-fl1870), a Maryland native and Bedford County minister, held $7,000 in real and personal property in 1860, and some $16,300 ten years later. 1860 Census, Tenn., Bedford, 25th Dist., 115; (1870), 25.

6. The Union army's first "special camp for the confinement of prisoners of war," opened on Johnson's Island near Sandusky in late February, 1862, was intended to relieve overcrowded conditions in older Federal facilities and in the more recently created makeshift prisons of the midwest. After the fall of Island No. 10, the increased congestion of Camp Chase led to Secretary Stanton's April 13 decision that all officers be removed to Johnson's Island which then became a compound for officers only. Hesseltine, *Civil War Prisons*, 37-40, 47; *OR*, Ser. 2, III, 448.

7. The Cincinnati *Enquirer* of March 28 carried a purported extract of a letter which corresponds in sentiments to those expressed in Moore's March 10 letter, written not from Nashville, but from Camp Chase.

8. Still on parole in Columbus as late as May 23, Moore again wrote Johnson begging to be released and returned to Tennessee. Johnson Papers, LC.

From Alexander W. Moss[1]

Franklin April 28th 1862

Gov. Andrew Johnson
Honorable Sir

In reply to your request for suggestions[2] I am at a loss where to commense. So many interest [*sic*] to civilized man have been and still are going wrong: the heart sickens to contemplate: however a short sketch of our condition may furnish you some data for a prescription[.]

Our Sherriff and cunstables[3] who are nearly all rebels are not doing anything that I know of. Our County Court clirk[4] who was sworn to suport the constitution of the United States has been an active agent of rebellion— The Recorder[5] acting under the same oath, I think, was the real Editor of the Secession News paper published at this place till after the fall of Fort Donaldson. Our circuit court clirk[6] has kept himself aloof from the rebellion and I think is a concientious man and loves his country. Our lawyers are all overboard. Our Bank has secession directors[7] which has been a source of much mischief[.]

The remedies necessary for this complicated disease of the body politic is the question. The course which seems best to me is this For you and Judge Brian,[8] or one of you, to come out here and make a speech: when those less contaminated with the secession spirit may recommit themselves to the Union cause, and from this class select the most suitable persons to fill offices[.]

The union men at heart form a majority in this State I think but being passive or negative and ignorant of the indivisibility of all good governments they suffered themselves deceived coaxed and browbeat by their devlish aggressive leaders— the Secession disease being in the *thin* upper Stratum of society. Now that the head way of the "my rights" and "Southern brother" party is checked by recent defeats on the battle field I do hope that you may be able to get laborers from the *now* upper stratum of society to carry on the machinery of Government, whose righs are not so numerous and hard to define[.]

I am not a negative union man nor an office seeker. I have been successfully engaged in business for twelve years. I am now in business and have much unsettled business but I will under the circumstances accept almost any position that I may be able to fill. I only proposed to act as Post Master to get it Started—as others refused to serve—but now that a loyalist—whose citizenship here is questionable proposes to serve if acceptable—I will still accept that or any thing else most compatable with the Government service or decline all if it will be as compatable.

You and I sprung from different political stocks, and therefore I have voted against you evry time I had an opportunity but now we are on the same platform and I most heartily hope that you may be blessed with helh and strength of body and mind to perform the arduous duties incumbent upon you[.]

> yours verry respectfully
> A. W. Moss

N.B. I am unable to mention the name of a suitable man to fill the office held by W. H. Crouch yet[.][9]

I am of opinion that the vacancies could soon be filled by better men if the present incumbents were turned out— would not such a course do? I would be glad to converse with and give you a better and more general idea of our condition than I can give by letter—not being in the habit of writing on such subjects[.] yours &c

> A. W. Moss

ALS, DLC-JP.

1. Alexander (or Abner) W. Moss (c1821-fl1880), Virginia-born merchant tailor worth $18,000, was for a time during the war Franklin postmaster (appointed in May) and afterward a member of the legislature (1865-66). Robison, *Preliminary Directory, Williamson*, 34; 1860 Census, Tenn., Williamson, E. Subdiv., 2; (1880), 9th Dist., 3; *U. S. Official Register* (1863), 627; (1865), 344; Nashville *Union*, May 10, 1862.

2. Lacking the tangible evidence of a letter or wire inviting Moss's "suggestions," we can speculate that a personal encounter, perhaps during a visit of the Franklin tailor to Nashville, or on the occasion of the governor's inspection trip to the Federal outpost, may have prompted this letter.

3. Moss refers to Williamson County sheriff Hezekiah Hill (b. c1800). He later recommended Simeon Shy (b. c1794), a former Kentucky law officer and "a most uncompromising union man," as a replacement for Hill. Frank M. Lavender (1823-1879) and John L. Burch (b. c1822) were town constables in 1860 and later Confederate soldiers, Lavender serving as lieutenant colonel, 20th Tenn. Inf., and Burch as sergeant, Co. D, 32nd Tenn. Inf. Subsequently Lavender was elected sheriff (1870) and served in the legislature (1877-79). 1860 Census, Tenn., Williamson, 1st Dist., 31, 32, 105; *Goodspeed's Williamson*, 796; Letter from Moss, May 28, 1862; *Tennesseans in the Civil War*, I, 217-18; II, 66, 244; Robison, *Preliminary Directory, Williamson*, 26-27; CSR (Lavender and Burch), RG109, NA.

4. William Cummins (b. c1818), a native Tennessean, possessed $2,000 real and $7,000 personal property. 1860 Census, Tenn., Williamson, 1st Dist., 23.

5. Not identified.

6. Mark L. Andrews (1796-1878), Kentucky-born Methodist preacher possessing on the eve of the war $11,500 in real and $9,000 in personal property, was longtime Williamson County circuit court clerk (1840-74). *Ibid.*, 64; *Goodspeed's Williamson*, 965.

7. Not identified.

8. Probably John S. Brien.

9. William H. Crouch (1804-1874) was a Virginia-born shoemaker and merchant of considerable means ($5,000 real and $22,500 personal property), whose son William H. (1835-fl1886), also a merchant and businessman ($8,000 personal property), served in the 4th Tenn. Cav., CSA (1862-63) and was later postmaster. On March 1 Crouch had been elected county trustee over James A. M. E. Stewart but could not assume the post because he was sworn to uphold the Confederate constitution. *Ibid.*, 977; 1860 Census, Tenn., Williamson, 1st Dist., 22; E. Subdiv., 2; CSR, RG109, NA; Louise G. Lynch, comp., *Bible Records of Williamson County, Tennessee* ([Franklin, Tenn.], 1970), 80; see also Letter from Alexander W. Moss, May 3, 1862.

From Hugh C. Thompson[1]

[Nashville] Aprile 28th/62

to the Honorable Andrew Johnson
Governor of Tennessee

My Dear sir permit me to give you a short acount of my locality. I am a native of east tennessee thank God— I have been liveing here in this neighborhood ever since 1849 have always been and am stil an uncompromising union man and am a poor man too[.] well just before the war broke out I entered into a contract with W. W. Berry[2] of Nashville to build him a house on the franklin turnpike about three miles south of Nashville for which he was to pay me twenty one dollars and fifty cts per week— all went on very well untill the memorable 8th of june at which time I voted the union ticket a coppy of which I enclose with this— mine was the only union vote polled in my district which is the 21st district of davidson county— there were 41 votes polled in all so you see I have 40 against one but here— well I was told that all the union mens votes were marked and that they would be required to take the oath of alegiance to the confederacy or leave the state[.] so I went to Berry and told him that I considered it my duty to him and myself to tel him that if I was required to take the oath or leave that I would be sure to leave—for that I was for ever and eternally opposed to sesession and the so called confederacy— he advised me to keep on at work on his house and not say any thing about political matters and he did not think I would be pestered[.] so I took his advice kept silent and was at work for him up to the fall of fort donaldson— I had a hard time of it but it was the best I could do as I am poor and have a family or at least a wife to care for— now my object in writeing to you is this—my neighborhood is almost entirely Reble and they dont get any better[.] if they did I would not have written to you— but the safety of myself and friends has indused me to write— I am sorry to say that myself and two or three more are all the friends you have here that I know of— I understand that one of the magistrates of this (21) district says he will have his neck streached as long as a clothes line before he will take the oath which was taken by the city officers—and I understand that the man who was elected constable[3] for this district at the last election says that if his nephew who is in Col Bates[4] regement is killed he will kill six union men in his place— and the second time I went to the city after the union troops got here I passed a squad of my used to be friends and one of them asked me how I liked the federals[.] I told him I liked them pretty well[.] he said you dont do yo and I said yes, he then said very well old fellow we will jerk you off the ground when they go away from here[.] and there are men going to and returning from the rebel army all the time at least they say they have been there and seen the boys— and they tell the people to keep in good spirits that the rebel army will be back here by the first of june next— now sir this sort of thing keeps the union people afraid to talk and emboldens the rebels.   there are some ten or a dozen of Bates men throughout this section of country—

I may be pardoned for asking how long are we to suffer. how long before the county officers will be made [to] take the oath[.] I have not voted since the 8th of june and will not til things get right— I may be wrong[.] if I am I hope you will excuse me—

I am forever yours in the union the constitution and the enforcement of the laws[.]

H. C. Thompson

ALS, DLC-JP.
1. Hugh C. Thompson (b. *c*1825), a Nashville carpenter with real estate valued at $500 in 1860, became the architect for the McKendree Methodist Church (1876). 1860 Census, Tenn., Davidson, 21st Dist., 105; Clayton, *Davidson County*, 326.
2. William W. Berry (1813-1878), a Baltimore native, for many years engaged in the wholesale drug business in Nashville, was a director of the Planters' Bank (1854-62) as well as president of the Third National Bank (1865-76) and Equitable Insurance Company. Having purchased the estate called Elmwood, he was in process of erecting a mansion designed by Adolphus Heiman, when work was interrupted in 1862. The property, occupied by Buell's army and other military units, sustained considerable damage before work was resumed in 1866. *Ibid.*, 412; "Elmwood," in May W. Caldwell, *Beautiful and Historical Homes In and Near Nashville* (Nashville, 1911), unpaged; Nashville *American*, June 23, 1878.
3. Kin Ray (b. *c*1820), possessed of $5,000 in property, had been elected in March, 1860. 1860 Census, Tenn., Davidson, 21st Dist., 110.
4. William B. Bate was at this time colonel of the 2nd (Bate's) Tenn. Inf., CSA. Warner, *Generals in Gray*, 19; see also *Johnson Papers*, III, 316*n*.

From Montgomery Blair

Washington, D. C. Apr 29/62

Dear Govr.

˙I am glad to hear that you are getting on well with your great charge. I think the common sense of our people will soon restore the old flag when the great armies of Jeff Davis are beaten & disbanded[.] Till that occurs the people will be acquiescent & non committal probably— There is one fact that you ought to let the Union men know viz: that Sumner & his class of politicians deny that there is any union sentiment at the South— These men want to disfranchize the South because they hope nothing presidentially from the South, & therefore they wish to impress the belief that there are no union men there, and that there is no way of Governing the country save as a conquest & by the territorial Forms— The fact that the abolitionists want the people of the South to be disloyal if known to them would help I think to make them loyal especially when they can in no way so effectually thwart them. It must begin to be obvious to them that the Secessionists have done more for

Abolition than any body else & unless the people of the South mean to suit their conduct to the purposes of these men they will Shortly change it.

I have no doubt this line of thought has often presented itself to you but I was so impressed with a conversation which has just been reported to me between Charles Sumner & Dr Hooper of Mass[1] that I thought it might be useful to write to you—

The eyes of the nation are upon you & its warmest feelings follow you— A paragraph from the N O Crescent advising your assassination[2] sent a thrill of horror through the nation as there is no crime which the Secessionists have not committed. But I have no fears for you. I have faith that God who has protected you so far for your countrys sake will yet shield you[.]

Yr friend truly   M Blair
Wash Apr 29. 62

His Excy Andrew Johnson
Nashville Tenn.

ALS, DLC-JP.
1. Samuel Hooper (1808-1875), close friend and associate of Charles Sumner, was a Massachusetts businessman who served as state legislator (1851-53, 1858) and Republican congressman (1861-75). *BDAC*, 1073; Edward L. Pierce, *Memoir and Letters of Charles Sumner* (4 vols., Boston, 1893), IV, 96.
2. Although the issue "advising" Johnson's assassination has not been found, the New York *Herald* of April 27 quotes from the *Crescent* [April 4]: "A rumor prevailed in Memphis last Monday that Andrew Johnson had been shot and instantly killed in Nashville, and that the man who killed him had made good his escape. If not true now, probably it will be, some of these days."

From Horace Maynard

Washington April 29, 1862

Dr. Sir,

I have seen the President this morning again. He is reluctant still to interfere with his commanding Generals while in the field & before the enemy; & expressed a wish that you should be put in communication with Genl Halleck. He showed me a dispatch from Genl. Mitchell, to the effect that he was about to take possession of Stephenson with his force. If so, all you will have to do, in all probability, will be to protect yourself against marauding parties.

I do not see the "Union", though I occasionally see extracts from it— I am very anxious to see its disclosures. I had a letter yesterday from Brownlow, who wrote me that he was preparing a book.[1] In reply, I suggested that he ought to examine some correspondence, which we have seen lately. Any exposition of public events in our part of the country would be very incomplete without an examination of these documents.

I hear at the Atto. Genl's Office, that the commission of Mr. Trimble[2] is sent forward to-day. I cannot explain why it has not been sent sooner, except what you know very well, the interminable delays incident to all departmental business.

I have had no communication from you since I left except two despatches. I am beginning [to] be a little anxious to know what is going on there—

I am very Truly Yours
Horace Maynard—

His Excy Andrew Johnson.

ALS, DLC-JP.

1. *Sketches of the Rise, Progress, and Decline of Secession; with a Narrative of Personal Adventures Among the Rebels*, more commonly known as *Parson Brownlow's Book*, was commissioned by George W. Childs of Philadelphia. Completed in May, 1862, and published that summer, the work indicted the South for provoking the war and depicted conditions in loyal East Tennessee under Confederate occupation. Coulter, *Brownlow*, 235-40.

2. For John Trimble's appointment as U. S. attorney, see Letter from Horace Maynard, April 25, 1862.

To James S. Negley[1]

Nashville Ap'l 29th.

Brig Genl. Negley Commanding Officer
Columbia, Tenn.

Please arrest Joseph C. Rye[2] a Cashier of branch Bank of Tennessee and send him under guard to Provost Marshal of Nashville.

Consult with Wm. H. Polk[3] and other Union men, and if in your opinion public interest requires it you will take charge of the bank and its contents and keep the same in your custody until properly disposed of.

Yours Truly   Andrew Johnson
Military Governor

Tel draft, DLC-JP.

1. James S. Negley (1826-1901), a Pennsylvania native and Mexican War veteran, served primarily in the western theatre, rising to the rank of major general in 1862 and participating in such major battles as Stone's River and Chickamauga. Charged with cowardice and desertion at Chickamauga, he was relieved of his command and, though subsequently cleared, did not receive another field assignment. After the war, Negley served several terms in the House of Representatives and was associated with various business interests in the New York area. Warner, *Generals in Blue*, 341-42; *BDAC*, 1380.

2. Joseph C. Rye (b. *c*1826), a Tennessee native and former merchant with real property valued at $14,100 and personal estate at $7,500 in 1860, was cashier of the Columbia branch of the Bank of Tennessee. Arrested the next day [April 30], Rye took the oath and was released, as he appeared in Chattanooga on bank business in June. Porch, *1850 Census, Maury*, 221; 1860 Census, Tenn., Maury, 9th Dist., 73; Ex. Record Book (1862-63), Ser. 4C, Johnson Papers, LC; Nashville *Union*, July 13, 1862; see H. B. Titcomb to Johnson, June 24, 1862, Johnson Papers, LC.

3. Polk, brother of the President, had written the governor on the previous day: "I think it would be well to make Mr Rice [*sic*] give an account of the disposition made of

the effects of the bank. It is said that he has been receiving confederate notes in payment of bank debts[.]" Polk to Johnson, April 28, 1862, Johnson Papers, LC; for Polk, see *Johnson Papers*, II, 229*n*.

From James S. Negley

Columbia April 29 1862

To Gov Andrew Johnson

Your request will be immediately complied with[.][1] Is it not advisable to include F. C. Dunnington President.[2] His course has been very prejudicial to the growth of union feeling[.]

James S Negley Brig Genl

Tel, DLC-JP.

1. Pursuant to Johnson's order, Negley arrested Joseph Rye the following day and dispatched him to the capital. Ex. Record Book (1862-63), Ser. 4C, Johnson Papers, LC; Nashville *Union*, May 3, 1862.

2. Two days later Negley telegraphed that Francis C. Dunnington had "fled in terror. The wicked flee when no man pursueth," and added that "The effict of Ryes arrest & Dunningtons flight has a more benefical influence than anticipated[.]" Negley to Johnson, May 1, 1861 [1862], Johnson Papers, LC; for Dunnington, a former Johnson supporter and later political enemy, see *Johnson Papers*, III, 8*n*.

To Salmon P. Chase

Nashville April 29 [1862]

Hon S. P. Chase
Secy. Treasy.

A letter from you to Mr Hall[1] announced the abrogation of the permit system from portions of insurrectionary states[.]   practically the system has work well & is doing much good & ought to be continued[.] The requiring of all persons appling for permits for export as well as import to take an oath of loyalty & allegiance to the U S. is having the finest effect[.][2]

Andrew Johnson

Tel, DNA-RG107, Tels. Recd., Sec. of War, Vol. 7 (Apr. 24-May 8, 1862).

1. In a letter of April 24, relieving Allen A. Hall of his duties—a step apparently prompted by the recurrence of an old drinking problem—Chase's opaque language led Johnson to the erroneous conclusion, reflected in this letter, that "all restrictions upon shipments from Tennessee are removed." Futrell, Federal Trade, 64-66.

2. Actually, Chase agreed with Johnson that trade should be restricted to those with permits attesting to present loyalty, a position clarified on May 19 when it was announced that trade from Tennessee would remain under the control of the governor and treasury agents. *Ibid.*, 66.

From John E. Cary[1]

On Board Hospital Steamer
City of Memphis
Louisville Ky Apl 30 1862

Hon A Johnson
Gov of Tenn.
My Dr Sir

Will you permit me to call your attention to a wounded union boy now lying in the Hospital (Marine) at Evansville Ind.

This boy was wounded at Pittsburgh Landing and is only 17 years of age. His name is William Hayne or Haynye of Red [Boiling] Springs Macon Co Tenn.[2] The circumstances connected with his wound are these as certified to by Col L F Ross[3] 17th Illinois Lewiston Fulton Co Ill. His thigh was severely fractured by a minee ball received from the Captain of his company because he would not fire on the union troops, having loaded his musket to the musle was discovered & in attempting to escape received the wound. He & many of his company attest the fact that he was pressed in the Rebel service and belonged to Co K 23d Tenn Rifles. The name of the Col & Captain are both forgotten.[4] The ball was extracted by Surg John Murray[5] of this Boat on the 17th Apl inst. and when he left at Evansville was fast recovering.

Dr Murray says, he was a boy of remarkable pluck & good sense, bearing the operation of extracting the bullet without a murmur.

I take the liberty to write you, because I feel assured you will feel an interest in caring for the little sufferer; and will know just how to reach his friends.

I reside in Cleveland Ohio, & am now on my return home from two weeks labor in assisting the sick & wounded from our section of the State.

Be assured Honored Sir, I would be happy to hear from you relative to the subject of this letter.

I am with great respect Your obt St & fellow laborer for the integrity of the Union[.]

John E Cary

ALS, DLC-JP.

1. John E. Cary (1821-1874), born in Canada, was for thirty years a Cleveland lawyer, specializing in admiralty cases. 1870 Census, Ohio, Cuyahoga, Cleveland, 4th Ward, 240; Cleveland *Plain Dealer*, December 31, 1874, January 2, 1875.

2. William C. Haynie (c1844-1862), private in Co. K, 23rd Tenn. Inf., CSA, had died the previous day. CSR, RG109, NA.

3. Leonard F. Ross (1823-1901), Illinois-born lawyer and Mexican War veteran, had served as Fulton County probate judge and county clerk (c1849-53). Elected colonel of the 17th Ill. Inf. (1861), he later became brigadier general of volunteers (1862), resigning his commission in July, 1863. A collector of internal revenue (1867-69), he twice ran unsuccessfully for Congress (1868, 1874) before moving to Iowa

(1882). Warner, *Generals in Blue*, 411-12; "General Leonard F. Ross," *Iowa Historical Record*, IV (1888), 145-83.

4. The colonel was James F. Neill (b. *c*1833), who had raised the Bell Buckle Co. K (later E), 23rd Tenn. Inf., CSA, in 1861 and was subsequently elected lieutenant colonel. He commanded the regiment at Shiloh where he was severely wounded; after his recovery he returned to active duty as a staff officer. The captain of Co. K at Shiloh was James A. Ridley (b. *c*1823), who, after being discharged from the regiment following a reorganization in May, 1862, later served as a private in the 23rd. *Tennesseans in the Civil War*, I, 222-23; Porch, *1850 Census*, Bedford, 6; *OR*, Ser. 1, X, Pt. I, 590; XXX, Pt. II, 477, 487; CSR, RG109, NA.

5. John Murray, English-born Dobbville, Illinois, physician who served with the 7th Mo. Cav., contracted for service as a surgeon on the hospital steamer, *City of Memphis*, from April 12 to May 13, 1862. He later was assigned to hospitals in Virginia and Philadelphia. Nashville *Union*, April 29, 1862; Medical Officers, RG94, NA.

From Horace Maynard

Washington, April 30, 1862—

Dr Sir,

My wife & family, & Mrs. Brownlow & her family, arrived here at noon today, having been ordered to leave, by Bill Churchwell,[1] Provost Marshall of Knoxville— They came by the way of Norfolk & a flag of truce to Fortress Monroe—

They bring most gloomy & distressing accounts of affairs in East Tennessee— And of the saddest pictures of their distress is that they are cursing Johnson & Maynard for having so utterly neglected them— O Heavens, if they only knew what we know, they would curse but not us. Perhaps it is better that they should blame us than their government. They have ordered your family away, but Mrs. Johnson was too unwell to leave.—[2] They say that the Confederate authorities have issued a proclamation to the effect that if the East Tennesseeans in Ky. do not within thirty days return & take the oath of allegiance to the Southern Confederacy, their families shall all be driven out into Ky—[3]

I have a copy of the Union of the 24th, from which I infer you are getting along pretty well—[4] The fall of New Orleans is a most disheartening affair for Secesh— Please keep me advised of what goes on with you—& use all your influence for the relief of our people at home—

I am very Truly Yours
Horace Maynard

His Excy Andrew Johnson—

ALS, DLC-JP.

1. For William M. Churchwell, see *Johnson Papers*, I, 622*n*. For the expulsion of Mrs. Maynard and Mrs. Brownlow, see Letter from William G. Brownlow, May 3, 1862.

2. On April 21, Churchwell, by General Kirby Smith's authority, had ordered Mrs. Johnson and family to "pass beyond the C. S. line." Unable to comply, despite an extension of thirty-six hours, she wrote General Smith on April 28, "In my present state of health, I know I can not undergo the fatigues of such a journey; my health is quite feeble, a greater portion of the time being unable to leave my bed." The order was held in

abeyance for several months; finally, on September 19, informing the authorities that her health had been "*comparatively* restored," she asked for passports to the Federal lines. *OR*, Ser. 2, I, 883, 885; Thomas, *The First President Johnson*, 230; Eliza M. Johnson to Kirby Smith, April 28, and to John P. McCown, September 19, 1862, Fay Brabson Papers, University of Tennessee Library, Knoxville.

3. Kirby Smith had announced on April 18, "That no person . . . who comes forward . . . and takes the oath to support the constitution of the State and of the Confederate States shall be molested or punished on account of past acts or words," including persons who, having joined the enemy "shall return within thirty days of the date of this proclamation." Five days later Churchwell called attention to the general's offer of amnesty and protection to those returning to their homes and becoming loyal citizens. After the expiration of the thirty-day period the families of recalcitrants would be sent to their care in Kentucky or somewhere beyond Confederate lines; similarly, those who subsequently left their homes would have their families "sent immediately after them." *OR*, Ser. 2, I, 882, 884; Joseph H. Parks, *General Edmund Kirby Smith* (Baton Rouge, 1954), 173.

4. This issue contained news of Johnson's warm reception at the camp of the 3rd Minnesota, where he viewed a military parade and made a speech, reported at some length, and his exchange of letters with John Hugh Smith over the hanging of Mrs. Winifred McFarland's flag from a public building. Nashville *Union*, April 24, 1862.

From George W. Morgan

Cumberland Ford April 30 1862

To His Excellency
Andrew Johnson, Gov.

Govenor on yesterday I received another telegram from the head quarters of Major General Buell instructing me to assign Brig Genl Spears to a brigade[.] I have already had the honor of informing you that on the fourteenth (14) ins't I had given him the command of the Twenty fifth (25) brigade composed of four (4) Regiments of Tennesseeans[.] I have 24 Tennessee Regiments or one (1) Brigade & a half[.] yet I have two (2) Brigade commanded by citizens of your state while Kentucky has four (4) good Regiments of infantary a battalion of cavalry without a brigade commander & acting like good soldiers & disinterested patriots[.] the Commander of these Regiments have uttered no complaints. I cannot sacrifice the interest of the public service to gratify the restless ambition of any officer[.]   At an early day I hope to receive arms for the Twenty fifth (25) Brigade & have used every effort to do so as division records prove[.] at present Genl. Spears commands two (2) of his Regiments at Boston two (2) being retained here until the arrival of their arms[.] in a very short time I hope to concentrate the entire brigade & you may rest assured that it shall have an honorable part assigned to it in the coming struggle. I remain Governor, very Respectfully

Geo W Morgan
Brig Genl Vols Comdg

Tel, DLC-JP.

From Curran Pope

Fayetteville April 30 [1862]

Gov Johnston

I have heretofore called your attention to the fact that the offices of jailer, Chy Clerk, Circuit Clk, County Clk, Sheriff register and trustee for this County are vacant by the abandonment of the incumbents or the failure of the officers elect to qualify, and that the persons heretofore holding them have left this place and in some cases as for the most part have removed the public records— My opinion is, if I may be excused for expressing it, that the cause of the union and the welfare of the state would be promoted by filling these offices with good union men— There are such here and there will be many more when they shall be entirely satisfied of the protection of the Govt— In justice to the following gentlemen whom I consider to be such and to whom I am indebted for help in the discharge of my duties and by way of assistance to the authorities I deem it not out of the way to annex a list of their names

    William French

    Chas A French who was acting as postmaster until the rebellion

    L. D. Akin

    Jas H Castleman

    Dr M. Perkins

    Joseph Scott

    Jno Washburn

    Abraham Washburn

    Wm. Wyatt[1]

There are others whom I regard in their hearts & from enlightened views of their own interest to be for the Union but I do not name them now.

              Very Respectfully   Yr. obt Servt

                             Curran Pope

                          Col. 15. R Ky Vol

ALS, DLC-JP.

1. William French (b. c1812) was a Maryland-born shoemaker; his brother, Charles A. (c1814-fl1886), who held $1,000 in real and $1,000 in personal property, was a printer who had been a proprietor and editor of the Fayetteville *Lincoln Journal*. L. D. Akin (b. c1816), with $7,500 in real and $3,500 in personal property, was a Kentucky-born saddler. James H. Castleman (b. c1823), Tennessee farmer, possessed $2,800 in real and $2,000 in personal property. Doctor M. Perkins (b. c1806), a North Carolina native and farmer, had $48,000 in real and $40,270 in personal property. Joseph Scott (b. c1810), Virginia-born cabinetmaker, claimed $2,500 each in real and personal property. John Washburn (b. c1816), Tennessean, was a merchant who owned $30,000 worth of real estate and $7,780 in personalty in 1860; described subsequently as "An enterprising citizen," he operated a distillery on Norris Creek during the war, selling his product to both Union and Confederate armies. His brother Abraham (1817-1894), a carpenter, held personal property valued at $50. William Wyatt (1802-1880), a South Carolina native, taught school, farmed, and later served in the state

legislature (1867-69). Apparently none of these men filled any Lincoln County offices during the war. *Goodspeed's Lincoln*, 769; 1860 Census, Tenn., Lincoln, 8th Dist., 203, 205, 211, 213, 217, 226; 9th Dist., 167; 10th Dist., 174; *Lincoln County Tennessee Pioneers*, I (1970), 8; Mabel A. Tucker and Jane W. Waller, comps., *Lincoln County, Tennessee Bible Records* (3 vols., Batavia, Ill., 1971-72), II, 9, 10; Robison, *Preliminary Directory, Lincoln*, 52-53; Stewart, Middle Tennessee Newspapers, 86.

From Robert Emmet Thompson[1]

[Nashville April 30, 1862]

Gov Johnson

Dear Sir

I notice that the Nashville Union of this morning quoting from a circular of mine from memory has done me injustice[.][2] I did not use the language attributed to me in the connection understood by the editor— I had reference to the outrages said to have been committed by the Federal troops in Virginia, ravishing women &c[.] I may be wrong, but I feel that I am the victim of malice and revenge[.] Col Bill and Jordan Stokes have been my bitter enemies ever since your canvass with Gentry[.][3] I denounced them both and spat on one of them in a public crowd and the bad feeling has existed ever since[.] I have not spoken to either of them since, until yesterday. Col Bill Stokes assures me that he is not actuated by his bad feelings towards me, but it is a remarkable fact that he did not attempt to arrest any one except myself when there were several soldiers and member of the legislature and divers of noisy partizans in town[.][4] I shall take it as a very kind favour if you will write to Dr Donoho W Z Neal[5] editor of the Lebanon Herald, and Giles H Glenn[6] Postmaster at Lebanon, and enquire of them relative to my conduct as a citizen[.] I determined to have nothing to do with this war and with the exception of the speeches which I made in the canvass I have not uttered one word for or against it. I have lost my hearing and consequently have determined to retire from the world and live to my self[.] I am inclined by my knowledge of your character to write you this rather strange letter[.] I believe that you are a man of your own head and will do what you believe to be right though the world opposes you[.] I have a very sick family and would like to be paroled, if thought to deserve it[.]

Yours with Respect

R E Thompson

ALS, DLC-JP.

1. Robert Emmet Thompson (1822-1897), Nashville native and Cumberland University graduate, served in the state house (1851-55, 1881-83) and senate (1877-79, 1883-85, 1887-89). A Lebanon lawyer and mayor (1866-71, 1876-78), he was a Whig before, and a Democrat after, the war. Jailed by Johnson "several" times during the war, he reputedly was saved from hanging by the intervention of Jordan Stokes. McBride and Robison, *Biographical Directory*, I, 720-21; Merritt, *Wilson County*, 145, 354; Acklen, *Tenn. Records*, I, 294.

2. A reference to a statement made in September, 1861, when Thompson was a candidate for the Confederate Congress, printed in the Nashville *Union and American*,

September 27. Declaring that he was "a Southern man, heart and soul," he had vowed to "vote the last dollar and the last man, if necessary, for I had rather see the Omnipotent wave the hand of desolation and utter woe over our happy land, and sink it beneath lakes of devouring flame, than to see its sacred soil desecrated by the foul tread of the corrupting Hessians of the North." In the excerpt reprinted by the Nashville *Union*, April 30, 1862, "woe" is rendered "war."

3. For Meredith P. Gentry, Johnson's opponent for the governorship in 1855, see *Johnson Papers*, I, 366n.

4. Not found.

5. Edward Donoho (b. *c*1827) was a native Tennessee physician and former Rutherford County resident, with $6,000 real and $26,155 personal property. William Z. Neal (b. *c*1831), editor of the Lebanon *Herald* with $3,000 real and $2,445 personal property, returned after the war to conduct a "lively" journal. 1850 Census, Tenn., Rutherford, Milton Dist., 530; (1860), Wilson, 10th Dist., 175, 190; Merritt, *Wilson County*, 217.

6. Possibly Giles H. Glenn, Sr. (*c*1800-*c*1881), but more likely his son Giles H., Jr. (b. *c*1828). The elder Glenn was a North Carolina native, Wilson County farmer, and register of deeds (1839-44), while the younger was a substantial farmer with $25,600 in real and $20,250 in personal property. One of them was Lebanon's postmaster (*c*1861-*c*1865) and served in the state legislature after the war (1869-71). Robison, *Preliminary Directory*, Wilson, 72-73; *U. S. Official Register* (1863), 629; (1865), *346.

To Curran Pope

Nashville, Tenn.,
April 30th, 1862

Col Curran Pope, Provost Marshal
Fayetteville, Tenn:

Dear Sir: Your favor of the 19th inst., relative to the affairs of state under your supervision, has been received, and I return you my sincere thanks for the information conveyed, and the interest you manifest in the restoration of Tennessee to her former position in the Union. Should my exertions in accomplishing this great work be seconded as heartily in all other places as they have been by yourself in the district under your command, I have no fears of its perfect completion.

You have pursued, in my judgment, the course calculated to have the happiest effect upon the people who have been so grossly deceived and betrayed by the unscrupulous leaders of the rebellion.

In regard to officers recently elected I will state that all of them will be required to take the oath of allegiance to the government before exercising any of the functions of their respective offices.

In reply to yours of the 21st inst., I would recommend that you permit such persons to visit Nashville as in your judgment is justified by due consideration of the public safety and the advancement of the Union cause.

I shall be glad to receive from you from time to time any suggestion you may think proper to make, either in relation to arresting prominent citizen rebels or any matter connected with the furtherance of our cause.

With sentiments of high regard I remain, very respectfully, your obedient servant,

Andrew Johnson,
Military Governor of Tennessee.

Louisville *Journal*, May 16, 1862.

To Edmund Cooper

Nashville May 1st. 1862

Edmund Cooper Esq
Columbia Tenn

Look to the interest of the State by making some arrangements to have the notes and bills in the Bank *protested*[.]¹

Andrew Johnson

Tel draft, DLC-JP.
1. The Columbia Bank, since 1838 a branch of the Bank of Tennessee, was authorized to receive and disburse Confederate treasury notes and bonds, continuing to do so after Donelson and the flight of the Nashville bank directors to Chattanooga. Johnson suggested that a formal protest be published announcing the bank's suspension of payment of bills and notes. No record of such a protest has been found, but the branch shortly ceased to function. Claude A. Campbell, *The Development of Banking in Tennessee* (Nashville, 1932), 160-62; *Century Review, 1805-1905, Maury County, Tennessee* (Columbia, 1905), 51.

From William G. Brownlow

Bordentown, N. J. May [?] 3, 1862.

Gov. Johnson:

Dear Sir: My wife and children arrived in Philadelphia yesterday, *via* Fortress Monroe, under a flag of truce, together with Maynards wife and children. Mine are here, where they will remain comfortable for a time. They had to leave upon 36 hours notice, given them by E. Kirby Smith,¹ through his Provost Marshall, *Bill Churchwell*, the Bank defaulter!² The result is, that they got off with their wearing apparel, but left my house and furniture, which were to be used for hospital purposes.

They are driving the Union families out of the country by scores, and are murdering and shooting them down on all occasions. They arrested 400 Union men before my family left—drove them through the street, starving for water and something to eat, and sent them to Atlanta to work on fortifications.— my son John says that they shot down fifty of these before they started them to Georgia. Such work was never heard of before.³ The *Sepoys of India*,⁴ are Christians beside these devils!

My John saw and red a notice in the hands of an officer on the train, as he was leaving, to be served on your wife, giving her 36 hours in which to get out of the Confederacy!

They had *twenty spies* belonging to Rains' Regiment,[5] constantly visiting Nashville, and coming every day over to Knoxville. They boasted of their regular line of spies, and of their keeping up with the news at Nashville. A foreigner named *Swabb*, a Knoxville liquor dealer,[6] is a regular Spy, and visits Nashville. They contemplate, as they say, the re-capture of Nashville. I only write these items to post you up.

Give my respects to Mr. Browning. If Dr. Hunt, my brother-in-law[7] is about your room, let him see this letter, as it will serve as an answer to one I received from him on yesterday. His family are well. His wife was up at Knoxville, and assisted in helping mine to pack up for the trip.

Col. Trigg, I learn, is very ill at Washington, and fears are entertained as to his recovery. I hope he may survive the spell.

I am, &C, &C,

W. G. Brownlow

ALS, DLC-JP.

1. Edmund Kirby Smith (1824-1893), Florida native and West Point graduate (1845), served in the Mexican War, on the frontier, and as a mathematics professor at his alma mater. Joining the Confederacy (1861), he was wounded at First Manassas. In September, 1862, while in command of the department which embraced eastern Tennessee and adjacent territory, Kirby Smith occupied Lexington, Kentucky, and returned in October to control Cumberland Gap; as commander of the Trans-Mississippi Department, he surrendered the last remnants of Confederate troops in May, 1865. Engaging briefly in business at war's end, he was subsequently chancellor of the University of Nashville (1870-75) and on the faculty of the University of the South. Warner, *Generals in Gray*, 279-80; Parks, *Kirby Smith*, 218, 241; Arthur H. Noll, *General Kirby-Smith* (Sewanee, 1907), 280.

2. When the Bank of East Tennessee suspended operations in 1856, Brownlow had made charges, none of which were proven, that William M. Churchwell, the president, had profited from his depositors' losses. As provost marshal, Churchwell on April 23 issued an order that families of East Tennesseans who failed to return from the North would be "sent to their care in Kentucky, or beyond the Confederate States lines, at their own expense." Two days earlier he had written Mrs. Brownlow that, although she and the children were "not held as hostages for the good behavior of your husband, as represented by him in a speech at Cincinnati recently," they would be "*required* to pass beyond the Confederate States line in thirty-six hours from this date." Upon her request for additional time, Churchwell complied with an extension until "Thursday next" and assured her that an escort, charged with her safety, would be provided. On Friday, April 25, Churchwell issued passports and the Brownlows were joined by Mrs. Maynard and family. Ruth O. Turner, The Public Career of William Montgomery Churchwell (M.A. thesis, University of Tennessee, 1954), 48-60; *Parson Brownlow's Book*, 446-52.

3. Brownlow reiterated these charges of excessive cruelty in the book which he was currently writing. The truth would appear to be that sometime in April, between four and five hundred young men who left Jefferson County to go north were intercepted and arrested by Confederate cavalry, marched forty miles to Knoxville on a hot day, and crowded into the already overflowing jail and adjacent yard. Although they were soon sent south as political prisoners, there is no evidence that any of them, much less fifty, were shot. *Ibid.*, 453; Temple, *East Tennessee*, 424.

4. Native Indian troops in the British army commanded by British officers, the sepoys during their 1857 revolt seemed to westerners to have been fiends incarnate. *Encyclopedia Americana* (1976 ed.), XXIV, 564.

5. The 11th Tenn. Inf., CSA, commanded by James E. Rains, was in East Tennessee from July, 1861, until the fall of 1862. Rains (1833-1862), a Nashville lawyer and onetime associate editor of the *Banner*, was commissioned colonel of the 11th Inf. in May, 1861. During the winter of 1861-62, he occupied Cumberland Gap, before being

dislodged by Gen. George Morgan in June. Promoted brigadier, he was killed during the battle of Murfreesboro. Warner, *Generals in Gray*, 250-51.

6. Abraham S. Shwab (b. *c*1818), a native of France, was a partner with his brother-in-law, Henry Dreyfous, in A. Shwab & Co. of Knoxville, importers, wholesalers, and retailers of liquors and wines. Shwab's son-in-law, Meier Salzkotter, of Nashville, allegedly engaged in smuggling since the war began, was convicted later in the year and sent to Alton, Illinois, for illegally conveying "medicines and other goods through the lines" in false-bottomed carriages. 1860 Census, Tenn., Knox, 1st Dist., 82; *Williams' Knoxville Directory* (1859-60), 75; Fitch, *Annals*, 491-97.

7. William Hunt (1810-1882), a Washington County physician who moved to Knoxville in 1850 and subsequently to Cleveland, served as surgeon in the 8th Tenn. Inf., USA, until his resignation in October, 1863, in the face of charges of incompetence and inattention to official business. He and Brownlow had married Sarah and Eliza O'Brien. Samuel J. Platt and Mary L. Ogden, *Medical Men and Institutions of Knox County, Tennessee, 1789-1959* (Knoxville, 1969), 281; CSR, RG94, NA; WPA, Tenn., Knox, Old Gray Cemetery, 224; Genealogical tables (Gaines, Strother, Pendleton), MS300, University of Tennessee Library, Knoxville.

From James Guthrie

Office Louisville and Nashville Railroad Company.
Louisville, May 3 1862.

Gov. And Johnson
Nashville Tenn   Dear Sir

Some of the Stockholders of the Memphis, Clarksville & Louisville R. R. Co have solicited a proposition from the L & N R R to operate that part of their road between the State Line & Red River, in consequence of which this Co sent their Supt A Fink[1] to examine the road to Red River with authority to make a proposition to operate the same subject to the confirmation of the Board of Directors of this Co— Enclosed please find a copy of the proposition & the action of our Board—[2] We have sent a copy to C. G. Smith[3] the Secty, also a copy to Dr Cobb[4] of Clarksville who is a large Stockholder, & was the first President of the Compy & send you a copy because we understand the Company have not paid their interest for a year & that the road is liable to be taken possession of by the State Authorities, for which reason this Compy do not wish to operate that part of the road without the consent of the authorities—

If the Company shall consent to our proposition for the operation it will require that we make immediate arrangements to put in a Turntable & a temporary Depot at some convenient point north of Red River— We understand the terminus would be about three or four miles north of Clarksville where there is an outlet by Turnpike until the Red River bridge shall be repaired & the operation extended to Clarksville—

Mr G C Breed who had something to do with the road informed us he had communicated with you upon the subject[.]

Very Resply
James Guthrie President

LS, DLC-JP.
1. Albert Fink (1827-1897), emigrating from his native Hesse-Darmstadt, worked for the Baltimore and Ohio Railroad (1849-57) before joining the Louisville and Nashville as a construction engineer, sucessively becoming chief engineer (1859), general superintendent (1865) and vice president (1869-75). A pioneer in studies of railroad economics, he served as commissioner of the Southern Railway & Steamship Association (1875-77) and of the Trunk Line Association (1877-89). *DAB*, VI, 387-88.
2. The accompanying "Copy from the Record Book" of the L & N R. R. over the signature of Willis Ramsey, secretary, indicated that the board had on April 28 authorized operation of the Memphis, Clarksville and Louisville road in Tennessee "from State Line to Red River," in accordance with the proposition which Superintendent Fink had made to the latter road on April 25. Report of Louisville and Nashville Railroad, May 2, 1862, Johnson Papers, LC.
3. Charles G. Smith (1834-1890), Clarksville lawyer and businessman, also held a variety of public offices including city recorder (1858-59), mayor (1859-62), chancellor of the 7th division of chancery court (1869-75), and state legislator (1877-79). Robison, *Preliminary Directory, Montgomery*, 55.
4. Joshua Cobb (1809-1879), Kentucky-born West Point graduate (1835), was for a time resident physician at the Cumberland Iron Works in Stewart County, Tennessee. Organizer of the Rough and Ready Furnace Company (c1844) and active for many years in the iron business, he moved to Clarksville in 1851, serving several times as mayor and later as Montgomery County magistrate (c1866). Titus, *Picturesque Clarksville*, 266-68.

From Alexander W. Moss

Franklin Tenn. May 3rd 1862

Gov. Johnson
Respected Sir

J. M. E. Stewart[1] the old Trustee of this county who was beaten for that office by W. H. Crouch, refuses to pay the funds belonging to the county over to Crouch. I had a conversation with Mr Stewart this morning and think that he should be suffered to hold the office until his successor is elected—Esqr Crouch not being eligible without he will take the oath prescribed by the Constitution of the State of Tenn. to wit. To suport the Constitution of the U. S. States—and he has as stated in a former letter[2] taken the sesesh oath[.]

An order from you to J. M. E. Stewart not to pay over, or to Crouch that he will not be permitted to hold office while he claims to be a citizen of an other Government will I think settle the matter right[.]

yours respectfully
A. W. Moss

N.B. Union men are getting bolder— From what Mr Stewart said to me this morning about oaths and constitutions I think he has the old fasion regart for them and will do to risk much better than Croch especially as he was accused of being a union man by the friends of Croch[.]

Yours   A. W. M.

ALS, DLC-JP.

1. James A. M. E. Stewart (b. *c*1788), a Virginia native, had been county clerk (1836) and was longtime county trustee. Williamson County Historical Society, tr., *1850 Census of Williamson County, Tennessee* (Franklin, 1970), 76; 1860 Census, Tenn., Williamson, 1st Dist., 22; *Williamson County Historical Journal*, No. 3 (1971-72), 86.

2. See Letter from Moss, April 28, 1862.

From George W. Morgan

H qrs Cumbd. Ford May 4 1862

To Gov Andrew Johnson

Two scouts who came in last night report that the enemy is in force at Big Creek Gap under Genls Reynolds & Barton[1] that Kirby Smith is at knoxville with a considerable force and that Cumberland Gap has been reinforced within the last month. The works at the Gap have been greatly strengthened. This morning I have recd. a letter from near Clinton, which confirms the intelligence of the scouts.

The enemy has not yet heard of the advance upon Chattanooga. To attack Cumbd. Gap in front would now be murderous in the extreme & I have determined to pass the mountains midway between Cumberland & Big Creek Gaps but to give me any reasonable hope of success there must be a real & not a feigned attack by Genl Negley. My effective force for the field will be six thousand five hundred baynets two hundred & fifty sabres & three hundred & fifty artillerists while the enemy has more than three times that strength.

One brigade is half way on the route to the Valley and the heavy guns have gone forward today.

Please keep me advised as to the operations of Negley and especially as to his strength.

Geo W. Morgan Brig Genl Comdg

Tel (in cipher), DLC-JP.

1. Alexander W. Reynolds (1817-1876), a West Pointer (1838) who had served in Florida and on the western frontier, became a Confederate colonel and in 1862 commanded the 50th Va. Inf. under Kirby Smith in East Tennessee. Captured at Vicksburg the following year, he was promoted to brigadier upon his exchange; subsequently he held various posts in the Egyptian army (1869-76). Like Reynolds, Seth M. Barton (1829-1900) was a West Point graduate (1849), also serving on the frontier before he resigned to join the Confederate army in 1861. One of Kirby Smith's brigadiers in East Tennessee, he was captured at Vicksburg and, after being exchanged, commanded brigades at the Wilderness and Richmond; captured again at Sayler's Creek, Barton was released from Fort Warren in July, 1865. After the war he was a civil and mining engineer at Fredericksburg, Virginia. Warner, *Generals in Gray*, 254-55, 18-19; 1880 Census, Va., Spotsylvania, Fredericksburg, 23.

From John B. Rodgers

Norwalk Ct. 4 May 1862.

Gov Johnson—

Dear Sir I will send a small box of Sharps rifles—or rather Carbines to Nashvill by Adams & Co. express—and have taken the liberty of sending to your address— please care for them untill my arival which may be a month or more yet, if the Govt. cannot I think I will aid in putting down some things in my region of our state.[1] many prayers are offered up for your success— when I go home I will aid you all I can.

very truly yours—
John B. Rodgers.

P.S. I should like to get the arms into the country without it going to the knowledge of the Seseshs. please do not mention my having them[.] I have invisted my individual means to obtain them. & I want them to pay back in equivalent services[.]

R.

Gov. Andrew Johnson
Nashville Tenn.

ALS, DLC-JP.

1. A cryptic observation for which precise evidence is lacking. Inasmuch as Rodgers seems to have spent some time refugeeing in the North, he may have been thinking in larger terms—that is, of conditions in Middle Tennessee as a whole, rather than in Warren and White counties, his particular "region." Although there were no major guerrilla operations in the vicinity at this time, he may have been alluding to the threat posed by Champ Ferguson, who had already begun bushwhacking in the Middle Tennessee counties adjacent to Kentucky. Again, Rodgers perhaps merely had in mind the activities of local secessionists and the other vicissitudes attendant upon the war itself.

From John Spence[1]

Snow Hill, Maryland—
May 4th 1862—

Hon. Andrew Johnson—
Sir—

Tho'. personally unacquainted your official position must pardon this intrusion upon the time devoted no doubt to subjects of importance to you.

About two years since I wrote to Hon. Neill S. Brown about the business of this communication but have received no intelligence of the issue.

Be pleased to deliver to the ablest Attorney of Nashville this letter and request him to give me a reply at his earliest convenience. My client is A. P. Swisher,[2] a citizen of Bastrop Co. Texas— I am an Attorney of seven years practice. A reference to Hon: J. A. Pearce or Hon. J. W. Crisfield[3] of this State—or to any Attorney of any Standing west of Brazos River in Texas will tell you my antecedents—

Memoranda.

Sinar Boyd[4] died about the year 1831, leaving as heirs my client A. P. Swisher then about two years of age—H. H. Swisher,[5] who died without marrying in Washington Co. Texas in 1845— and Nancy A. Swisher who married Rev. Ed. Fontaine[6] in 1839 or 40 and died in Texas in 1855 leaving three children, Lamar, Henry & Edward— Rev. E. Fontaine's address is Jackson, Miss— James Boyd died leaving certain negro property to Sinar Boyd his daughter & the Admin. has never paid over the legacies. Abner Boyd[7] in Boyd Co. Ky. or the adjoining Co. Tenn. was Administrator or Executor. The questions raised are these. In case some of the increase of negro property left by James Boyd has passed into the hands of innocent purchasers, under the Laws of Tennessee can we sue for the property or is our recourse upon the Adm. alone?

2ndly Is there in Tenn. any limitation to bar a Legatee under a will or an heir in regular descent? Yerger[8] says there is no such law and cites one case of thirty years standing—[9]

Please reply to this immediately—

Jno. Spence—

Att. for A. P. Swisher—

Hon. And. Johnson— will please reply to this so that I may know that it is received—

Jno. Spence.

Snow Hill, Md.

ALS, T-Mil. Gov's Papers, 1862-65.

1. John Spence (b. c1832), Maryland-born lawyer with $25,000 real and $2,000 personal property, lived in Bastrop, Texas, prior to the war. 1860 Census, Tex., Bastrop, Town of Bastrop, 9.

2. A. P. Swisher (b. c1829) was the son of Henry H. and Sina Boyd Swisher of Henry County, Tennessee.

3. James A. Pearce (1804-1862), Virginia native and Princeton graduate (1822), after a brief period as a planter in Louisiana (1825-28), returned to Maryland where he served in the state legislature (1831), the House of Representatives (1835-39, 1841-43), and the Senate (1843-62). John W. Crisfield (1806-1897), a Maryland lawyer, served in the state legislature (1836), the House of Representatives (1847-49, 1861-63), and as a delegate to the state constitutional convention (1866). Founder of the town of Crisfield (1866), he was president of the Eastern Shore Railroad. *BDAC*, 754, 1437.

4. A search of records shows that Spence's genealogical data concerning the Boyd-Swisher family is essentially correct. Elsie Alune Ray, The Life and Times of Edward Fontaine, a Mississippi Leonardo (M. A. thesis, Mississippi State University, 1951), *passim*.

5. Harvey H. Swisher, older son of Henry H. and Sina Boyd Swisher, went to Texas in 1833 and served as 1st lieutenant, Co. H, 1st Rgt. under Col. Edward Burleson at San Jacinto. Robert F. Karsch, "Tennessee's Interest in the Texas Revolution, 1835-1836," *Tenn. Hist. Mag.*, Ser. 2, III (1937), 235, 238.

6. Edward S. Fontaine (1814-1884), Virginia native, attended West Point (1830-32), studied medicine, was admitted to the bar (1835), served as Mirabeau B. Lamar's private secretary (1841), and taught school in Texas before his ordination (1848) as an Episcopal priest. Moving to Mississippi in 1859 he served as chief of ordnance for state

troops during the war. Walter P. Webb, ed., *The Handbook of Texas* (2 vols., Austin, 1952), I, 615; see also Ray, Edward Fontaine.

7. Son of James Boyd and brother of Sina Boyd Swisher.

8. George S. Yerger (1801-1860), Pennsylvania-born attorney, was reared in Lebanon, Tennessee, where he first practiced law. By 1825 he had settled in Nashville and as first state attorney general (1831-38) edited ten volumes of supreme court decisions (*Tennessee Reports*, vols. 9-18). Moving to Vicksburg in 1839 and five years later to Jackson, Mississippi, he was a successful lawyer, businessman, and editor of an Episcopal journal. James T. McIntosh, ed., *The Papers of Jefferson Davis* (2 vols., Baton Rouge, 1971-), II, 160-61; Merritt, *Wilson County*, 140.

9. Probably McDonald v. McDonald, 16 *Tenn. Reports* 145 (1835) in which a widow sued the co-executors of her husband's will to claim her legacy of Negro property which had never been paid, although her husband had been dead ten years. Commenting on the defense of the statute of limitations, the court declared, "an executor cannot be protected by the statute of limitations against a legatee." R. McDonald Gray (University of Tennessee College of Law) to Andrew Johnson Project, February 2, 1977.

To David Tod

May 5, 1862, Nashville; L, DNA-RG249, Lets. Recd. (1862-67).

Introduces W. M. Cook, Nashville merchant desirous of visiting his son, a prisoner at Johnson's Island. "I think if Mr. Cook is allowed to see his son and the other young men in confinement with him he will exert a good influence over them in inducing them to consent to become loyal citizens in the event of their release[.]"

From Richard M. Edwards[1]

Somerset Ky. May 6th 62

Gov Johnston.

Dear Friend.

I have just arrived at this point with my little squad, all dreadful tired and worn out. We staid near the Fishing Creek Battle ground last night and looked over it this morning; and I think afterwards our boys are keener than ever to get into a fight.

I learn here that Gen Spears is at Pine Ridge on the Big Creek Gap road preparing to go through and that they will start at an *early day*. This to us is joyful news. If he goes through we will go with him in some capacity or other.

I therefore have to request you to send my commission if it comes to the care of Brig Gen Spears. I know no better direction to give you unless Dr Hunt[2] will come on and go with us. We hope to go home soon.

Very truly Your friend
R. M. Edwards

ALS, DLC-JP.

1. For "Mitch" Edwards, currently recruiting East Tennessee refugees, see *Johnson Papers*, IV, 120*n*.

2. Dr. William Hunt.

From John A. Kasson

Unofficial

P. O. Dept. 6. May 1862

Dear Governor:

I wrote you officially[1] in reply to your late letter to me. But there was one thing suggested to which I did not reply. You spoke of a probable mistake in appointing Lellyett P. M. To that the P M G.[2] desires me to say that he takes your voice above all others in Tennessee matters, & when you say a change must be made, he will make it, and will appoint the man you name.

I was rejoiced to hear of your confidant hopes of Tennessee. I gave Blair your letter to present your appeal to the President for help to East Tennessee[.] The evacuation of Yorktown has stimulated the highest expectations, & I suspect McDowell[3] moves his corps to day toward Richmond from Fredricksburg. We look anxiously for news from Corinth.

I remain faithfully Yr friend.

John A. Kasson

Hon: Andrew Johnson &c &c &c
Nashville

ALS, DLC-JP.
   1. Not found.
   2. Montgomery Blair.
   3. Irvin McDowell (1818-1885), West Point graduate who taught at the academy (1841-45), served in the Mexican War and as adjutant general until 1861. In command of Federal troops at the first battle of Bull Run, he was succeeded by McClellan and as major general was assigned a corps of the Army of the Potomac. Failing to distinguish himself in the second battle of Bull Run, he spent the remainder of the war in relative inactivity, continuing in the army until his retirement in 1882. Warner, *Generals in Blue*, 297-99; *DAB*, XII, 29-30.

To Edwin M. Stanton

Nashville May 6 1862.

Hon Edwin M Stanton
Secy War

I feel well assured it is not by your authority that the Tennessee prisoners Barrow Harding & Guild[1] whom I desired should be sent to some place of confinement are permitted to go at large in Detroit & to receive the attention & sympathy of all persons with disunion proclivities & govt officers to act as their attendants[.][2] If this course is allowed & pursued in regard to Tennessee prisoners sent north while so large a number of Tennesseans are confined in southern dungeons for no offence save being for the union It could be better to discharge these men & send them back here[.] The manner in which these prisoners have been treated by the govt has increased rather than diminished secession sentiments & on the other hand has aroused the resentment of union men[.] I hope the Secy will have this at once corrected[.] There are other prisoners that should be sent but I will await your answer[.][3]

Andrew Johnson

Tel, DNA-RG107, Tels. Recd., Sec. of War, Vol. 11 (Apr. 30-May 1, 1862); DLC-E. M. Stanton Papers, Vol. 6.

1. For Washington Barrow and Josephus C. Guild, see *Johnson Papers*, II, 325*n*, IV, 581*n*. William G. Harding (1808-1886), prominent horse breeder and master of the 3,500-acre Belle Meade plantation, had been a general in the state militia before the war. Appointed by Harris to the military and financial board, Harding had contributed substantially to the arming of state Confederate troops. Arrested at Nashville in April, 1862, he was detained first in the state penitentiary and later in the Federal prison at Mackinac Island before being released in September. Herschel Gower, "Belle Meade: Queen of Tennessee Plantations," *Tenn. Hist. Quar.*, XXII (1963), 203, 207-15; *Tennesseans in the Civil War*, I, 9; Order for the arrest of William G. Harding, April 2, 1862, Johnson Papers, LC.

2. The Nashville *Union* of May 6, quoting from the Detroit *Advertiser*, reported the several-day sojourn of "three men—high in position in the South," who "have been feasted at one of our first hotels [Michigan Exchange], have paraded our streets, with an officer of the United States service for their lackey, and for aught we know to the contrary, have visited places of amusement, and been in communication with prominent secessionists in our midst." Elsewhere in the same issue, the *Union*, with the *Free Press* as its authority, reported that the three talked "freely with many of the prominent men of both political parties." Capt. C. H. Wood, the officer in charge of the prisoners indignantly denied the allegations. Not only were the Tennesseans kept closely under guard, but, far from "feasting at Uncle Sams *expence*," they also paid for any amenities and their interviews with local citizens were carefully monitored. Irrespective of the privileges which may have been extended them, their stay in the city was due to a combination of factors: not only must facilities at Fort Mackinac be prepared and a suitable guard assigned, but the weather must also moderate so as to allow navigation of Lake Huron. Nashville *Union*, May 6, 24, 1862; Chicago *Tribune*, April 26, 1862; C. H. Wood to Stanley Matthews, May 7, 1862, Johnson Papers, LC; *OR*, Ser. 2, III, 438, 451, 463.

3. Stanton replied: "The prisoners of state referred to in your dispatch have been ordered into close custody[.]" On the same date, the secretary notified the "Commanding Officer" at Detroit that the prisoners were not "to go at large. . . . This was not designed, and the evil must be corrected immediately." By May 15 they were at Fort Mackinac. Stanton to Johnson, May 6, 1862, Johnson Papers, LC; *OR*, Ser. 2, III, 521, 537.

From George Harrington[1]

Treasury Department.
May 7. 1862.

Sir.

I herewith enclose the copy of a letter from the Secretary of the Treasury to Jesse Thomas[2] Esq Surveyor of the Customs at Nashville dated 30. Jan 1855 enclosing 66 bonds of the State of Tennessee described in the power of Attorney accompanying them,—a copy of which is also enclosed, together with the copy of a letter to Cave Johnson Esq President of the Bank of Tennessee, which explains the circumstances under which these Bonds were placed by this Department in charge of the Surveyor of the Customs.[3]

They are not the property of the United States, but belong to the trust-fund placed by treaty in the charge of the Secretary of the Treasury for the benefit of the Chickasaw Indians.[4] It appears that the interest thereon was regularly received by the Surveyor and carried into the Treasury to the credit of the trust, until about a year since when it is understood that these Bonds were seized by certain individuals claiming authority under the State of Tennessee.

It being the duty of this Department to take all proper measures to preserve and secure the property belonging to this trust, I have to ask the favor of you to recover possession of these Bonds in behalf of this Department. If Mr Thomas and Mr Cave Johnson are still at Nashville they will probably be able and willing to furnish you with such details in regard to the seizure and present custody of these bonds as will facilitate their recovery.

It is not proposed, in case these bonds are recovered by you for this Department, to impose on you the responsibility of their custody. You will be pleased at once to enclose them by mail to Enoch T. Carson[5] Esq. Depository at Cincinnati, with a request that he hold them subject to the order of the Secretary of the Treasury or deliver them to Wm P. Mellen Esq the special agent of this Department and advise this Department of your doings in the premises.

Should you be able to communicate any information in regard to the payment of interest accrued and unpaid on these bonds, you will place this Department under further obligations.[6]

Very respectfully Your obt sevt.

Geo Harrington

Acting Secretary of the Treasury

His Excellency, Andrew Johnson
Military Governor of Tennessee. Nashville.

LS, DLC-JP; DNA-RG56, Lets. Sent re. Stocks and Bonds for Indian Tribes ("S Ser."), Vol. 2; RG366, Records of the Special Agent, Lets. Recd. from Sec. of War.

1. George Harrington (1815-1892), a native of Boston, received a clerkship in the treasury department from Polk, rose to chief clerk and assistant secretary (1861), and ended his government career as minister to Switzerland (1865-69). *NCAB*, XII, 337.

2. Jesse Thomas (*c*1809-*fl*1880), a Tennessee native with $7,500 in real and $2,000 in personal property, was surveyor of the port of Nashville (1846-60) and a Confederate treasury officer in Nashville and Chattanooga (1861-62). 1860 Census, Tenn., Davidson, 13th Dist., 154; (1880), 18; *Treasury Department Collection of Confederate Records* (*National Archives Preliminary Inventory 169*, Washington, 1967), App. I, 55, 56; *Senate Ex. Journal*, VII (1845-48), 114, 140.

3. For these letters from Secretary James Guthrie to Thomas and Johnson, both dated January 30, 1855, and the power of attorney, see Johnson Papers, LC; for Cave Johnson, see *Johnson Papers*, I, 170*n*.

4. Upon removal of the Chickasaw Nation to Indian Territory, the Federal government sold its land, located mostly in Mississippi. Proceeds of the sales were held in trust and invested by the government, much of it in state bonds. Arrell M. Gibson, *The Chickasaws* (Norman, Okla., 1971), 164.

5. Enoch T. Carson (1822-1899), customs surveyor and collector at Cincinnati, was a native of Hamilton County, Ohio. Serving as county deputy sheriff (1848-50, 1851-60), and subsequently holding various local public offices, he was a partner in a gas fixture business (1858-68) and later in an insurance agency. His extensive Shakespearean library ultimately became the property of the University of Cincinnati. 1860 Census, Ohio, Hamilton, Cincinnati, 6th Ward, 95; Greve, *History of Cincinnati*, II, 613-15; Cincinnati city directories (1849-70), *passim*.

6. A year and a half later the assistant secretary of the treasury wired, "Can you give information concerning Bonds of State of Tennessee, amounting to $66,666.66, sent to Surveyor of Customs in 1855, referred to in a letter to you May 7, 1862, to which no reply was received." Maunsell B. Field to Johnson, November 28, 1863, Vol. 2, Lets. Sent (XA Ser.), RG56, NA.

From "Observer"

Nashville May 8. 62

To His Excelency Gov Johnson

I was verry glad to learn that the great Southern detective had been picted up by the Federal Authorities. The Sharp detective Meacham[1] that hates the dambed Yankeys so bitterly and has been one of the Officers in bringing flying Unionists to Justice[.]   he arrested a Dr from East Tenn but I do not recolect his name, and sent him back a prisenor.[2] he was so valueble to the Vigilance Committee[3] that they presented him with a beautiful Sorrel Horse which he named Vigilance[.]   he has been trying this week to Sell Powder which he said he could get through by a Union Man's assistance[.]   he thought that he was so Sharp that No one could find Out any thing on him, but I hope the Federals will keep him in Custodey for he I think was one that was Selected to arrest you if you come this way in leaving East Tenn[.]   I think he deserves the sell in Some prison for you and Secty East would have both went to such a place if he could have caught you[.]

Yours Truly
Observer

ALS, DLC-JP.

1. Probably William F. Meacham (1826-1882), Virginia-born carpenter and a former assistant marshal, who was chief detective on the Nashville police force (1859-60); after the war he was a lawyer and justice of the peace. 1850 Census, Tenn., Davidson, S. Nashville, 481; (1870), 6th Ward, 23; *Nashville City Cemetery Index*, 54; Clayton, *Davidson County*, 90, 91; Nashville *Patriot*, June 29, 1861.

2. Possibly Dr. John Clark who was arrested in August, 1861, while employed as a teacher in Cumberland County, sent to Nashville, and charged with treason for organizing a military company "to make war against the Confederate States." Nashville *Republican Banner*, August 30, 1861.

3. The Davidson County Committee of Vigilance and Safety, organized late in April, 1861, sought to assist legal authorities in locating and removing subversive, i.e., unionist, elements from the community. Meeting as frequently as twice a week during the summer, the organization does not appear in the press after August, 1861. Wooldridge, *Nashville*, 191-92; Nashville *Union and American*, May 30, 1861; Nashville *Patriot*, July 7, 1861.

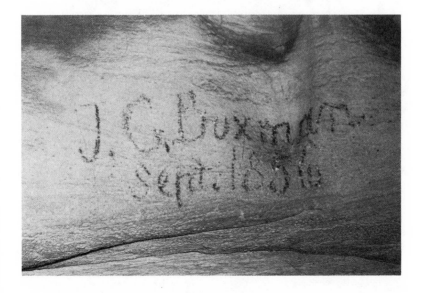

PROCLAMATION
BY
ANDREW JOHNSON,
GOVERNOR OF THE STATE OF TENNESSEE.

To all who shall see these Presents—Greeting:

WHEREAS, it has been made known to me that a certain THOMAS PARISH, charged with having committed a foul and atrocious murder on the 23d day of December, 1861, upon the body of JAMES GOODWIN, late of our County of Davidson, has fled from justice, and is now running at large.

Now, therefore, I, ANDREW JOHNSON, Governor as aforesaid, by virtue of the power and authority in me vested, do hereby offer a reward of TWO HUNDRED AND FIFTY DOLLARS, to any person or persons who may apprehend the said Thomas Parish and deliver him to the Sheriff or Jailor of our County of Davidson, in order that justice, in that behalf, may be had and executed.

{ L. S. } In testimony whereof, I have hereunto set my hand and caused the great seal of said State to be affixed at Nashville, the 16th day of August, 1862.

By the Governor: ANDREW JOHNSON.
EDWARD H. EAST, Secretary of State.

aug17–d1w

To catch a murderer (*above*), *from the Nashville Union, August 19, 1862.* Prima facie speleological evidence! (*below*), *courtesy Marion O. Smith, Knoxville.* (*See page 177n.*)

From William B. Stokes and William B. Campbell

Lebanon, May 8th,1862.

Gov. A. Johnson.

My Dear Friend:

W. L. Waters[1] will hand you this. We are in great distress. Our people are in great danger, from Morgan & Starns[2] Cavalry. They are all over Smith & DeKalb, in Small Squads. Cant you Send us Two or three Comp's of Cavalry. The force here is not Sufficient to give us aid.

Send us help if you Can on the spot. Can you let us have arms. I Can raise 500 men in 48 hours to defend our homes.

Mr Waters is true & all right, and what he tells you is true.

I made a narrow escape. have been exposed to the open woods, in the mountains. Since Saturday night. made my escape here last night. & Cannot return until I get help. For Gods Sake Send the assistance Soon. In haste.

yours Truley

W. B. Stokes

Govenor Johnson. I fear that the intercourse with Nashville by rebels is doing much harm, by their free ingress & egress into the city & their purchase of arms and amunition. I have heard of some cases who have gone there & bought arms, which ought not to be allowed, & it certainly is of the highest importance that we should have more troops in the Country above here. The Rebels are designing to overawe the union sentiment & to keep down any expression of opinion by union men, and armed soldiers of the Confederate army are permitted to go home, with their arms no doubt for the purpose of intimidating the rise of the unionists— they will be and are now being scattered through the country armed to over awe & attack honest union men. They came nigh getting many of your friends here & may yet get some of them. I only make these suggestions that you may do, as I know you will whatever you can to relieve the country— your friend

W B Campbell

ALS, DLC-JP.

1. Wilson L. Waters (1818-1903), Wilson County merchant, farmer, and industrialist, who freed his slaves before 1860, attended the Republican national conventions of 1856 and 1860, served in the state legislature (1865-69), and ran unsuccessfully for Congress (1865). Robison, *Preliminary Directory, Wilson*, 110-11.

2. James W. Starnes (1817-1863), a wealthy North Carolina-born physician and farmer, with combined property valued at $273,630, organized the "Williamson County Cavalry" in October, 1861, became colonel of the 8th Tenn. Cav. Btn., CSA, upon its organization two months later, and remained in command after it became the 3rd, then 4th, Tenn. Cav. Rgt. (May, 1862). Engaged in guerrilla activities in Tennessee during that summer, Starnes commanded a brigade under Forrest during the months preceding his death in June, 1863. 1860 Census, Tenn., Williamson, E. Subdiv., 101; Louise G.

Lynch and Volenia W. Hays, comps., *Cemetery Records of Williamson County* (Franklin, Tenn., 1969), 27; *Tennesseans in the Civil War*, I, 62-63; Chattanooga *Rebel*, July 2, 1863.

From L. S. Bond[1]

Johnsons Island Sandusky May 9th 1862

Genl. Johnson

Sir I have waited on the return of mr. Trigg ontill I have become satusfied that he is not coming here Any more[.] I think that he has treated us with great contempt[.]   he told me that he wanted me to speak my sentiments to him which I did and told him how it was that I come to Be in the army and then he asked me whare my family was[.] I told him that they ware 7 miles Below fort henry on the Bank of Tennee river[.] I also told him that general grant told me that I could take the oath and he said that was his Bisiness to see us A-Bout that and all of us resolved to go home and go with our state for wee ware sertain that she would return to her loyalty again and I would like to know what his object was in coming here and adviseing us what to do and then leaving us in suspense so long[.] I wish you to answer this immediately, and let me know owr doome[.]   when A man wishes to protect his own state and canot have the privilige of doing it of course it is not his fawlt[.]   your humble servant

L. S. Bond

ALS, DLC-JP.
1. L. S. Bonds (according to prison records), a first lieutenant in Forrest's Cavalry, was captured at Donelson in February and imprisoned on Johnson's Island until exchanged at Vicksburg in September, 1862. Prison Records, RG109, NA.

From Citizens of Madrid Bend

Madrid Bend
Tenn. May 9th 1862.

Brig Genl Johnson
Military Governor of Ten
Sir

We the undersigned citizens of Madrid Bend—who are and have been non combatants throughout the struggle now distracting our country do herein appeal to you as the executive authority of our once happy state for protection for our lives, property, and rights.

What we complain of is the action of the 15th Wisconsin regiment U. S. A. stationed at Island No 10. We charge the commander[1] and his forces with direct and gross violation of Order No 3 of Maj Genl Halleck.[2] And state that the order is not only violated but, that the soldiery have daily and nightly been allowed to prowl around the country persuading and in many Instances forcing off our slaves, especially the women and children, Secreting them in camp and upon the Island and sending off upon transports large numbers. Nearly all of the citizens have been subject to this loss, some to the number of 10 or 15 and some all they possessed[.] In many Instances, the negroes have earnestly desired to return and when seen by their masters they the owners are driven insulted &c from the camp.— Again the soldiers have visited the houses at night not sparing the lone widow and carry off the negro girls. In one Instance Lt. Col Robinson[3] of the 47th Indiana stationed at Tiptonville went with a lady and had released her maid. They went a few nights afterwards and again carried her off. The commanding officer of said Regt. Col Heg. keeps two negroes belonging to peaceable citizens to wait upon him. We do not wish to believe this policy the policy of the Goverment. And believing you to be willing to restore peace and prosperity and to protect us who have done no deed of Treason we appeal to you. We refer To the Col. of the 47th Indiana, Col Slack,[4] To Lt Col Robison, To Capt. Robison[5] and others of the 47th Indiana who (we are pleased to say keep the law) know of negroes in large numbers in Col Hegs Camp. Earnestly praying Governor that you cause our grievances redressed and protect us in our rights in peacable pursuit of our ordinary avocatins we are

With respect Yr Ot Sts[6]

H M Darnall	E. W. Neville
Willis Jones	Dan Watson
Sandy Hindes	Charles Riley
Milton Donaldson	

Pet, DLC-JP.

1. Hans C. Heg (1829-1863), Norwegian-born farmer and merchant, held several civil posts in Racine County, Wisconsin, before becoming state prison commissioner (1859-61). Commissioned colonel of the 15th Wis. Inf. early in the war, he was commanding a brigade when he died at Chickamauga. *Appleton's Cyclopaedia*, III, 158; Theodore C. Blegen, "Colonel Hans Christian Heg," *Wisconsin Magazine of History*, IV (1920), 140-65; Blegen, ed., *The Civil War Letters of Colonel Hans Christian Heg* (Northfield, Minn., 1936).

2. Asserting that fugitive slaves served as channels of information to the enemy, the original order, issued November 20, 1861, excluded them from "any camp or . . . forces on the march." A month later Halleck elaborated: "The object . . . is to prevent any person in the Army from acting in the capacity of negro-catcher or negro-stealer." *OR*, Ser. 1, VIII, 370, 465.

3. Milton S. Robinson (1832-1892), Anderson, Indiana, lawyer and Republican presidential elector (1856), advanced from lieutenant colonel to brevet brigadier general, returning to his law practice at war's end. A state senator (1866-70), delegate to the 1872 Republican national convention, and congressman (1875-79), he ended his career on the state appellate court (1891). *BDAC*, 1531-32.

4. James R. Slack (1818-1881), Pennsylvania-born lawyer and Indiana Democratic state senator in the 1850's, became colonel of the 47th Ind. Inf. (December, 1861), and subsequently commanded successively several divisions. Promoted to brigadier general of volunteers (1864), Slack was brevet major general when mustered out in 1866. Subsequently he served as judge of the twenty-eighth judicial circuit of Indiana. Warner, *Generals in Blue*, 449-50.

5. John T. Robinson (b. *c*1829), of Hamilton County, Indiana, enlisting in October, 1861, as captain of Co. G, 47th Ind. Vols., served until February, 1863, when he resigned. Reenlisting two years later as a private in Co. F, 147th Ind. Vols., he was mustered out in August, 1865. CSR, RG94, NA.

6. Henry M. Darnall (1808-1880), South Carolina native, farmer, and land speculator, who rose to brigadier general in the Tennessee militia, was a unionist who refused commissions from both sides during the Civil War. Tennessee-born Willis Jones (b. *c*1829) was a laborer in 1860 with no property. Sandy Hines (1802-1879), a Virginia-born farmer, lost much of his $7,200 real and $10,000 personal property during the war. Milton Donaldson (*c*1813-1881), a Tennessee-born farmer with $18,500 in real and $15,000 in personal property, was remembered as the "largest capitalist of Lake County." Charles H. Riley (b. *c*1835) was a Kentucky-born farmer with $47,500 in real and $20,000 in personal property. Neither E. W. Neville nor Dan Watson was located. 1860 Census, Tenn., Obion, 2nd Dist., 240; 4th Dist., 21, 23; 10th Dist., 59; (1870), Lake, 2nd Dist., 11; *Goodspeed's Lake*, 1075-76, 1078, 1081.

From Horace Maynard

Washington May 9, 1862—

Dr. Sir,

Your dispatch came about bedtime last night. I find that Col. Matthews[1] has been nominated as Brigadier General, but not confirmed—
As to Carter the facts appear to be, that directly after we left here, his brother came on & with the aid of Judge Adams[2] & of some other Kentuckians who appear to think very well of him, procured a nomination; which I find is confirmed[.] When, I do not know. I have not been consulted in the matter & have ascertained these facts, from a letter of Edward Trigg to his father while at Nashville, a casual conversation with Judge Adams on my return & the debate in the Senate day before yesterday— I shall hand your dispatch[3] to some one of the Senate Military Committee.

I have been here now more than two weeks, & excepting these despatches from you, & an occasional number of the Union, I have heard nothing from Tennessee besides what gets into the papers. Many persons question me about our affairs, & I sometimes regret not being able to answer more fully—

We have from rebel sources an account of a repulse of our troops before Cumberland Gap— Nothing, however, has reached us from our side, tho Morgan's maraudings in Middle Tennessee & Dumont's fight with him at Lebanon have been telegraphed— These are matters that we feel a great deal of interest in—

It does seem that our forces at Cumberland Gap have done about as little as it has been possible for men to do— Two months have elapsed since Spears was made Brig. Genl. & one month since Morgan assumed command, yet they seem very slow to put themselves on the other side of the mountain.

Our forces are pushing forward towards Richmond, & I should not be surprised to hear that it is in our possession before Saturday night.

Secesh is fast going to the Wall. The news has just come from our side of the taking of New Orleans, or rather the passing of the forts— The fighting was terrific—

I see with much justification, the unanimous call for a meeting next Monday.[4] I hope such steps will be taken as will affect not only the whole state, but the whole country— Col. Segar[5] was admitted to a seat as a representative from the first district of virginia, this week— I hope you will order Congressional elections, as soon as it can be prudently done—

I am very Truly Yours
Horace Maynard

His Excy. Andrew Johnson—

ALS, DLC-JP.

1. Stanley Matthews.
2. The nominated Carter was Samuel P. and the brother who "came on" was William B. For the judge, Green Adams, former Kentucky circuit judge, see *Johnson Papers*, IV, 525*n*.
3. Not found.
4. The Union meeting, to be held at the capitol on May 12.
5. Joseph E. Segar (1804-1880), Virginia-born lawyer who had served in the state legislature (1836-38, 1848-52, 1855-61), had presented his credentials in February as a unionist member of the 37th Congress, but was refused a seat; again elected to the same Congress, he was seated May 6 and completed the term, only to be denied seats in both the 38th and 41st Houses and in the Senate (1865). Unsuccessful in a race for a House seat in 1876, he was appointed U. S. arbitrator under the Spanish-American claims convention of 1877. *BDAC*, 176*n*, 1579; *Appleton's Cyclopaedia*, V, 453.

Proclamation Concerning Guerrilla Raids

Executive Office,
Nashville, Tenn., May 9, 1862.

WHEREAS, Certain persons, unfriendly and hostile to the Government of the United States, have banded themselves together, and are now going at large through many of the counties in this State, arresting, maltreating and plundering Union citizens wherever found;

Now, therefore, I, ANDREW JOHNSON, Governor of the State of Tennessee, by virtue of the power and authority in me vested, do hereby proclaim that in every instance in which a Union man is arrested and maltreated by the marauding bands aforesaid, five or more rebels from the most prominent in the immediate neighborhood shall be arrested, imprisoned, and otherwise dealt with as the nature of the case may require; And further, in all cases in which the property of citizens loyal to the Government of the United States is taken or destroyed, full and ample remuneration shall be made to them out of the property of such rebels in the vicinity as have sympathized with, and given aid, comfort, information or encouragement to the parties committing such depredations.

This order will be executed in letter and spirit. All citizens are hereby warned under heavy penalties from entertaining, receiving or encouraging such persons so banded together or in any wise connected therewith.

By the Governor:

ANDREW JOHNSON

Edward H. East,
Secretary of State.

PC, DLC-JP; also in Additional Speeches, 1851-1874, JP5.

From Solomon R. Burford[1]

May 11, 1862

Gov. Andrew Johnson

Sir— When I left home I thought probable I would visit Nashville. But oweing to the prospects of a speedy opening of the Mississippi River I wish to make my way down the river as far as Memphis as soon as praticable.

I was born in Lawrence county Alabama and have lived twenty four years (I am 29 years of age) in DeSoto county Mississippi. I left my home in the latter place the 21st of last month, came through on horseback, contending with but little or no difficulty in the way of Rebel pickets.

I have been a Union man from the beginning. I have never by word act or deed countenanced the present rebellion. These I have no doubt will appear strange assertions hailing as I do from Miss.

Every word can I prove & even more establishing my Union principles.

Union men in Miss are scarce nevertheless there are a few. There would be more were not life & property jeopardized by an expression of such sentiment. The fundamental principles upon which our great & good government was established are not respected by the Davis usurpers: the liberty of speech the liberty of the press, & the right of trial by jury are in effect obsolete and have no practical existence in "Dixie."

When I left home I parted with a Union cousin John B. Burford[2] who I fear may be pressed into the Rebel army. If so he will desert and apply to you to find my whereabots. He is about 22 years old, light hair & eyes tolerably large, & more particularly distinguished by being reeled[3] or crooked in his left foot. If he should call upon you for assistance, or information please bestow it upon him with the positive assurance that he is a Union man. Any pecuniary assistence you may bestow upon him will be immediately repaid upon application to A P Burditt & Co[4] Memphis Tenn (a union house).

As to myself I can give you no reference this side of Memphis. I was at

the University of Va. in 1852 & 3 & 4 & if I had a cataloge I might refer you to some acquaintance this side of "Dixie[.]"
May 11th, 1862

Respectfully   S. R. Burford
DeSoto County Miss

ALS, DLC-JP.

1. Solomon R. Burford (c1833-fl1921), a farmer with $11,000 in personal property, had attended the University of Virginia (1852-55); sometime after the war he moved to California and practiced law. 1860 Census, Miss., De Soto, 136; Robert E. Seifert (University of Virginia Library) to Andrew Johnson Project, January 26, 1977.

2. Not found.

3. Clubfooted.

4. A. P. Burditt Co., composed of Augustus P. Burditt, Angus Campbell, and James H. Smith, were wholesale grocers and cotton factors at 308 Front Street. *Memphis City Directory* (1866), 94.

From Prentice, Henderson & Osborne

May 11, 1862, Louisville, Ky.; ALS, DLC-JP.

Proprietors of the Louisville *Journal* [George D. Prentice, Isham Henderson, John D. Osborne] advise Johnson that "One of our correspondants W. C. Carroll aid of Genl Logan" and "thorough-union man," is on his way to Pittsburg Landing; "we suggested his telegraphing you, when anything occured of importance." They promise to send "all the news, at noon & at night up to the latest hours your opperators will receive a message."

From Henry Williard, Jr.[1]

Cin. O. May 11. [1862]
Hon A. Johnson:

Your singular misrepresentation of the union sentement in Te. as well as the attempted tricks of your Parson Brownlow,[2] have horrified honest men of the free states; and led them to conclude that your drift is money[.] Mr Lincoln has been warned against you[3] and will no doubt be on the alert for your wily pranks.

In the above I have reflected the opinions of as many as I have heard express themselves on the subject.

With respect,
Henry Williard jr.

ALS, DLC-JP.

1. Possibly Henry [H.?] Williard, Ohio native who was a clerk for A. J. Mackay, quartermaster in Nashville in 1865. *U. S. Official Register* (1865), 173; *King's Nashville City Directory* (1866), 305.

2. Perhaps a reference to Brownlow's current northern speaking tour during which he was asking for money to relieve East Tennessee.

3. If the President was indeed "warned," it must have been by word of mouth, for the Lincoln Papers provide no evidence.

To John G. Parkhurst[1]

Nashville May 11 [1862]

Col Parkhurst
Commanding officer,
Murfreesboro, Tenn.

I have just had consultation with E. L. Jordon,[2] G. W. Ashburn and E. D. Wheeler prominent citizens of Murfreesboro in regard to the shooting which took place last night.[3] There was some statement made to them just on starting which induced the belief that some development would be made throwing more light upon the affair. Has any thing of the kind transpired since they left. If not and no steps be taken satisfactory to you you will at once arrest as many persons as you in your judgment may believe will have proper effect upon spirit of insubordination [which] seems to prevail in that community. Transactions of this kind must be met and dealt with as the public interest requires. Act out your judgment & you shall be sustained[.]

I omitted to send back list of names for arrest leaving it to you to consult with mayor.

If you desire a list of names telegraph back immediately.

Teach them a lesson that they will not forget.

Andrew Johnson

Tel draft, DLC-JP.

1. John G. Parkhurst (1824-1906), New York native and Coldwater, Michigan, lawyer (1849-61), served as lieutenant colonel and later colonel (1863) of the 9th Mich. Inf. and was captured at Murfreesboro; upon exchange he became provost marshal of the XIV Army Corps. Briefly a Nashville lawyer at the end of the war, Parkhurst was nominated by Johnson to be marshal for the eastern district of Michigan (1866), but did not receive the appointment; subsequently he was a treasury agent (1867-69) and minister to Belgium (1888-89). *NCAB*, VII, 482-83; New York *Times*, May 8, 1906.

2. Edward L. Jordan (1817-1899), Murfreesboro merchant and banker, was "a nonparticipant, but strongly maintained his position in favor of the preservation of the Union." Deane Porch, comp., *Tombstone Inscriptions of Evergreen Cemetery* (Murfreesboro, Tenn., 1965), 98; *Goodspeed's Rutherford*, 1044-45.

3. About 10 P. M. on May 10, as Parkhurst and Provost Marshal O. C. Rounds were returning to camp from the courthouse, a shot was fired at them "by one of two citizens who were concealed by a fence." Parkhurst gave chase but "both of the would be assassins escaped." A similar episode occurred in the same vicinity the next evening, both incidents following an attempt on the life of a Federal sentinel "some weeks since." On May 12 Parkhurst, having no clues about the shooting, requested a list of "persons to be arrested"; he also reported that a search of the town revealed "*over two hundred pieces heavily loaded*," presumably to be used in support of Confederate general John Morgan. Johnson responded immediately with the names of twelve men, some or all of whom were to be arrested. Seized promptly and held "as hostages for the good behavior of the Citizens of Murfreesboro," they were sent to the penitentiary at Nashville on the 13th, while several others were detained at Murfreesboro. Parkhurst to Johnson and Johnson to Parkhurst, May 12, Parkhurst to H.M. Duffield, May 13, 1862, Johnson Papers, LC; Nashville *Union*, May 15, 1862; Nashville *Dispatch*, May 15, 1862; see also Letters from John G. Parkhurst, May 13, and from Rutherford County Citizens, May 22, 1862.

To Edwin M. Stanton

Nashville, May 11th 1862.

Hon Edwn. M Stanton

I am compelled to repeat and call the attention of the Secy of war to my former despatches[1] in regard to amount of military force which should have been left in and about this place to be disposed of as circumstances might require. The very fact of the forces being withdrawn from this locality has inspired secession with insolence & confidence & Union men with distrust as to the power & intention of the Govt to protect and defend them. They have not arms. Secessionists have. If there had been a military force left at this place sufficient to meet & suppress any uprising of disunionists combined with returning troops from Corinth & other points in streets & that fact being well known & understood through the whole country there would have been no further difficulty & trouble in Tennessee. The whole moral power has been lost and in fact we are here now almost in a helpless condition. Had my request been complied with there would have been no Morgan raids through Middle Tennessee & Kentucky no battles at Lebanon. This evening we hear of the capture of a train at Cave City Ky.[2] If these things had [not] occurred, on tomorrow we would have one of the largest union meetings ever held in the state[.]   as it is I think there will be a very decided demonstration which will do much good[.] The people are in a condition when they are satisfied the Govt will sustain them in their efforts to restore their former position in the Union. We are doing all we can & think we have done much. May God crown your efforts to save the country with success.

Andw. Johnson

Tel, DNA-RG107, Tels. Recd. Sec. of War, Vol. 12 (May 10-21,1862); *OR*, Ser. 1, X, Pt. II, 180-81.

1. On March 29 Johnson had complained to Stanton that Buell had left Nashville "defenceless," and on April 25 noted that Col. Lewis Campbell's 69th Ohio Inf. had hardly arrived in Nashville when the general ordered it away. See Telegrams to Stanton, March 29, April 25, 1862.

2. Morgan, under the impression that men from his command who had been captured at Lebanon were being sent north by train, moved toward the Louisville and Nashville Railroad to intercept them. The information proved to be false and he had to content himself with seizing at Woodland, on May 11, a southbound train from Louisville. Taking the train two miles on to Cave City, his men allegedly destroyed from 45 to 48 freight cars, 2 to 4 passenger cars, and 1 locomotive, in addition to taking $3,000 to $10,000 from the express agent. One locomotive, one passenger car, and the express car were permitted to return to Louisville. Nashville *Dispatch*, May 13, 1862; *OR*, Ser. 1, X, Pt. I, 891; Holland, *Morgan and His Raiders*, 104-6.

From Richard B. Cheatham[1]

Nashville. May 12th 1862.

Gov Andrew Johnson.

I do hereby Solemnly declare, that I will not aid or encourage the cause of the Rebellion by act word or deed, but on the Contrary, that I will use what influence I possess at Such times and on Such occasions as may appear to me discreet and profitable for the purpose of restoring the people of Tennessee in their loyalty to the Government of the United States—

Richard. B. Cheatham

If required I am prepared to give any bond for the faithful execution of the above—or will make oath to the Same, and would most respectfully ask to be released—but will hold my Self in readiness at all times to Answer any charges which may be preferred.

Very Respectfully   R. B. Cheatham.

ALS, DLC-JP.
1. This declaration, subscribed to by the former Nashville mayor, provides an example of the loyalty oath required of erstwhile Confederates.

From James G. Spears and Daniel C. Trewhitt

May 12, 1862, Barbourville, Ky.; ALS, DLC-JP.

Tennessee officers request the governor's aid in raising a regiment of East Tennessee refugees not presently in service to cope with rebel guerrillas whose "predatory incursions" on loyal districts encourage the "hopes of their friends" and injure loyalists from whom they steal horses and forage and whose "celerity" enables them to elude Federal infantry. Recommend commission for Richard M. Edwards.

Speech at Nashville[1]

May 12, 1862

He took the stand, and said he had not intended to speak; he wanted the people here assembled to proclaim it as their meeting, and merely the initiative one, to be followed by others, which he trusted would result in the triumphant restoration of the former relations of Tennessee to the Federal Union. As he had been called, however, he would make some allusion to former party relations. The people of Tennessee had been divided into two great parties, denominated Whig and Democrat, which had their distinctive measures; one favored a bank, tariff, and the distribution of the public lands; the other, an independent treasury and a revenue tariff, &c. These issues were discussed before the public, each party had its processions, mass meetings, and other collections, with music, colors, and banners, and each approached the stands under the folds of the self same national flag, and to the music of the same national airs, Hail Columbia, Yankee Doodle, and Star-Spangled Banner. These were respected by all parties then, even though the political contests were fierce and bitter, but all were under the stars and stripes and for the Union. What parties have we now? He answered that question by turning to ex-Governor Campbell, the Chairman, and saying, this is the proudest moment of my life to stand here with you, despite our past differences on party issues, contending for the preservation of the Union, and standing under the stars and stripes. Let me take you by the hand and let us together pledge lasting devotion in efforts to preserve the Federal government. If it goes down let us not survive it, but let us be buried beneath the ruins of the Union upon the field of battle and wrapped in the proud old flag of our country. Let us make no inquiry into the political antecedents of those who rally under that banner with us, but let our only question be "Are you for the Union?" Let us all clasp hands and swear that the last drop of our hearts' blood shall be poured out upon its altar as our last libation for its preservation. Let us remember that one great question underlies all others. Slavery and abolition may appear as jarring antagonistical elements on the surface; but he said what he knew, and spoke as he felt, when he declared that the great principle of free popular government, based upon man's capability to govern himself, was the vital question to be solved. This Union, founded on popular judgment and a written Constitution, must survive or perish. All other issues were mere pretexts; and when the Southern extremists found that their particular class could not secure the administration and carry on the government, through disappointed ambition they determined to break it up. Where is the man of understanding who does not see that their great object is to change the character and genius of our government, and to make it either a monarchy or an aristocracy? This cannot be disguised. South Carolina led the van in this unholy, nefarious, diabolical, infamous, and damnable revolution, she was always opposed to popular government as far back as the revolution, she was under the control of the tory party, which was willing and prepared to capitulate and leave the destiny of the State to the mercy of Great Britain. The leading inducement, the stimulating hope, and the main reliance of the rebel leaders were succor, recognition, and help from Great Britain and France. The authority of Great Britain had been destroyed by the revolution, and yet South Carolina was willing to bring about separation even at the alternative of accepting recognition from Great Britain. And if that recognition deprived the State of her position as one of the United States, whose independence was acknowledged in 1784 [sic], she could not but sink back into her colonial condition and under the rule of Victoria. This was the great stimulant in the struggle. Are we so blind and deaf as to stultify ourselves and not see these things, and, above all, the great, senseless clamor concerning Southern rights, the North against the South, the South against the North, and all similar clap trap? Because Davis, Toombs, Iverson, Benjamin, Wigfall, and other men, who are dangerous and inimical to civil liberty, have therefore conspired to ruin our Republican Government and lead us as vassals and subjects to Great Britain or other foreign governments, shall we be led astray and forget that we are the sons of sires who fought seven years for independence, and endured privations to secure for us those blessings of constitutional liberty, the ark of which we should now guard as the holy of holies? Are we the lineal descendants of such men, or has our blood grown thin and pale, to bow before treason and rebel marauders and traitors to the country and the country's constitution? Are you willing to quail and acknowledge their supremacy and surrender the best Government the world ever saw? He knew they would not do this. Though the sun of freedom has been eclipsed and rebellion has run rampant over the people, he saw the redeeming spirit of popular indignation aroused and a returning sense of justice pervading the hearts of a great majority of the people of Tennessee, which, like the lava flow from Vesuvius, will sweep away and devour in its fury the enemies of civil and religious liberty. Yes, this redeeming spirit is being vitalised. You who live in the forests, or have been in them when boys, understand how the roaring and moaning in the trees indicate the approaching storm; so from the hills and valleys of the State we hear the coming tempest, nearer and nearer, which foretells that an injured people are coming forth in the majesty of their power to crush treason and punish traitors. Treason must be crushed out and traitors must be punished. We mean by this that intelligent and conscious traitors must pay the penalty of their crimes and not the great mass of our deceived and deluded brethren, who were forced away by conscription, by a reign of terror, and by taunts of cowardice; for them we would plead; to them we would say, acknowledge your allegiance to the Government, return to the old flag, and support the stars and stripes. But to the leading traitors, who have drenched the land in blood, we extend no terms of compromise. Look around your streets and see the habiliments of woe, mothers and sisters draped in black. Who is responsible for this? There is a fearful responsibility somewhere, and let us ask who hurried off husbands and brothers and sons to acts of treachery, and involved them in riot and strife, plunder, bloodshed and contention? He feared that some mothers and sisters were responsible for the blood of their sons and brothers. To all such, who contributed so fearfully to our disasters, he would say, be ready to repent in sackcloth and ashes,[2] and ask pardon and forgiveness for the crime, wickedness, and sin they have brought upon the land. Theirs is a fearful responsibility, and instead of dancing over the graves of those who have died in defence of the Union, and insulting their toombs, they should bow their heads in shame. Are

we a civilized people, and do we live in a Christian land? Is our civilization relapsing into cannabalism and worse than savage barbarity? Why
should we heap opprobrium and disgrace upon the Union? He would
ask whom it had ever injured? Has anyone, male or female, ever been
deprived of one single right or privilege under our Union? Is there such a
one that he can put his finger upon? If so he would like him to speak, and
tell what right has been lost or what great principle given up. What sense
of injustice has any one? Is there any sense which we can touch, taste,
smell, or hear? If there is any, speak. There is no single right lost or
endangered. But the clamor is that Southern rights are invaded and our
rights in the Territories imperilled. The most clamorous brawlers for
those rights in Tennessee never owned a negro, never will own one, and
if they did, could not own him long. And yet this class of men are
exceedingly distressed about their rights in the Territories, where they
never intend to go, and if they did they have no negroes to take with
them. What did such men engage in such a contest for?[3]

[Johnson's remarks concerning the failure of southern senators to support the
Crittenden Compromise, "which would have satisfied the South," are omitted by
the reporter as being "well known to our readers, but . . . not to a large portion of
Gov. J's auditors, who received in mute astonishment his exposition of the
insincerity of Southern Congressmen."]

He showed that the defection of the cotton States Congressmen gave the
Republicans the majority in both Houses and that while that party voted
to protect Southern rights in the States, the secession sympathizers stood
aloof. He referred to the Corwin amendment[4] and other concessions of
the North, and yet while these things were passing the South was
secretly transferred to Jeff Davis and his minions. He asked, are we free
men or slaves that when these things stare us in the face we can be
mistaken or deceived? He made an energetic and eloquent call on all the
descendants of noble sires to save the best government in the world from
the spoliation of cruel men who were seeking to overthrow civil and
religious liberty. All our troubles originate from disappointed ambition
on the part of the Jeff Davisites. What confidence can we repose in them?
How long is it since they tried to tarnish the fair fame of Tennessee and
her loyal sons and insult your name?[5] And yet disloyal Tennesseeans
have dragged the State out of the Union in secret session, and those who
dared to lift their voices against the usurpation of the hermaphrodite,
hybrid Confederate Government, have had their mouths forcibly closed;
their personal liberty has been violated, and they are now in Mobile,
Montgomery, and other places confined in dark, loathsome dungeons,
covered with vermin, fed on rotten meat and decaying bones, their
patriotic limbs confined in iron bonds, and no response to their sufferings
but the clangor of chains! Is this the entertainment to which you were
invited? What crime, what wrong, what sin rests upon their heads? What
have they done? Their sole offence is that they loved their country and

were devoted to the flag of their fathers. Are you not prepared, with all the noble instincts of your fathers, to buckle on your armor and take up the line of march and break the tyrant's rod which is resting upon the necks of your countrymen in Alabama? And all this infamy is covered up under the pretext of Southern rights. Are you familiar with the Constitution of South Carolina, and have you read Spratt's address?[6] They are the foreshadowings of the monarchy which the hot brains of that State would impose upon us. Why, there a man is not eligible to the Legislature unless he owns ten negroes and his landed estate is worth £500. These are the Southern rights which the Senators of that State led the van in inviting you to fight for. The Governor said under these restrictions he would not be eligible to a seat in the lower branch of Legislature, for he owned but nine negroes, and they had been taken away from him by the rebellion. He had seen how Southern rights were protected by these fiends in his own town; his wife, with her sick boy, had been tumbled by the conspirators into the streets, and the house which he had built with the labor of his own hands had been occupied as a hospital and barracks.[7] His daughter, too, had her slaves taken from her protection.[8] If such are State rights, may God deliver me and mine from them! It is easy to clamor about rights and at the same time by usurpation take them all away and destroy the last vestige of popular rights. This has been the game of the rebellion. Some say they were for the Union until Sumpter fell, and that then the South was invaded and the war commenced by the administration. He proceeded to show how patient and enduring the Government had been; how its forts and arsenals had been stolen, how the bombardment of Fort Sumpter was precipitated from fear it should succumb from starvation, and how they wanted to precipitate the war by attacking it; how Walker, the rebel Secretary of War, boasted that the stars and bars would float on the Federal Capitol, and contended that the President had never done anything but his duty in efforts to faithfully execute the laws. He had but one objection to Lincoln's course, and this was that instead of 75,000 men he did not call out more to enforce the laws and put the rebellion down. What is Tennessee now called upon to do? One State has as much right to withdraw from the Union without the consent of all the States as a man has to apply the torch to his own house in a block of buildings without the consent of his neighbors, for he would endanger the surrounding property. There is no such right as secession, which in like manner would bring upon the country war, pestilence, and famine. His theory was that no State could withdraw without the consent of all the rest, and therefore Tennessee is not out of this Union. Reconstruction is not the proper term to apply to our work, for the State is still an integral part of the great national unit and it is restoration to allegiance that we are striving for. If he were to go out, he would not imitate the example of the 8th June,[9] or of King Harris's magnificent display of the courage of the friends of Southern rights and representatives of chivalry in their dastardly and precipitate flight from Nashville. If he were forced into rebellion, and had to retire, he would at least cover a decent retreat. If he were reduced to that degrading and humiliating situation, he would make one effort before he left the soil of Tennessee; he would dispute every inch of ground, burn the last blade of grass, and let the last intrenchment of liberty be his grave.[10] Before the separation Tennessee was part of the Union; this capitol was yours and its records and archives yours. What, then, is the sensible, sound, and philosophical principle presented to you? You are asked to give up what belongs to you, to take away from their places of deposit your annals and records,[11] and then go to war, join the Confederacy, and shed oceans of blood to get them back again! And all this in obedience to the behests of King Cotton! He thought cotton good enough in its way, and so were flax, wool, silk, and *hemp*. But he believed that bread and meat ruled the throne; and when the supplies of these, furnished by Tennessee and Kentucky, were cut off king cotton would be found impotent and weak.[12] If cotton were lost to the world, as it was for thousands of years practically until within the present century, we would get along as well without it; the world would not stop; its arrangements are pretty extensive and controlled by a master hand, and bread and meat is the real king, and cotton a mere servant. Many articles have had their day of supremacy and dwindled into insignificance, and cotton may be one of them. The production of a little more flax, wool, hemp, and silk will supersede its use entirely. But the South does not raise cotton independent of the great agricultural States. If we take all the mules and hay and hogs and sheep and beeves from this State that make their way into every bale of cotton, we actually raise more cotton than they do. Without the bread and meat of the great Northwest, and the mules and bacon of Kentucky, cotton could not be produced. And yet cotton is King! There is a great deal in familiarising the people to what may be obnoxious. If the flag of the Cross of St. George[13] had been raised in our streets a few years ago, and fealty asked to any flag but our own, inevitable death would have been the consequence; but cotton was first called King, and when the term has become euphonious and familiar, they then propose that foreign monarchies shall be called upon to protect it. Slow, cautiously, and insidiously does treason work. We must meet it firmly. Let traitors know that rebellion's banners are to be put down, treason crushed, and traitors hung. We have a great work before us. Differing as we have heretofore done in politics, he believed he could say without egotism he had fought his battles in open day and never deceived any man; his doctrines were inscribed upon his banner. Then standing here to-day, side by side with old political adversaries, he felt it the proudest day of his life to be associated with them in the great cause of saving the country. Let us go on and expel the rebels, elect a Legislature, Governor, Congressmen, members of the United States Senate, and Judges, and bring our civil affairs back into their old course.

The State government cannot be trusted with its enemies; it must pass into the custody of its friends. The people, the true source of power, must rise in their might and majesty; they "who know their rights, and knowing, dare maintain,"[14] are the true constituents of a State; they will put out its destroyers and reinstate its saviours. Come up like men as you are, and don't depend on those who trust to the grapevine and clothesline despatches,[15] waiting, like Micauber for "something to turn up;"[16] or for the fabrication of tales to inspire hopes with all the reality of belief. The time has come when the Union must manifest and exercise its power. The tyrant's rod must be broken, and "who would be free, themselves must strike the blow."[17] Come then to the work; you have a great and noble government engaged in putting down rebellion. It has the power and the capacity to put it down and will put it down, and the stars and stripes once more will wave over every city, village, and cross-road of Tennessee. Are you willing to engage in the glorious work or will you be ensconced and shrink from it because some swell-head secessionist sees danger in it. Nail your flag on the outer wall[18] though tattered by wild and merciless faction; wave it on high as your fathers upheld it. Will you give it up without an effort, or will you stand around the altars of your common country and with a long pull a strong pull and a pull altogether[19] cause Tennessee, in the language of Curran, to be "redeemed, regenerate and disenthraled!"[20] All his impulses were for the South, but it beats also for the North, the East, and the West—for the whole nation, and its flag, and beneath it he was willing to peril all and sacrifice all for its support and preservation. Gov. J. closed by a strong appeal to the loyalty of those ladies who were present on the occasion, and a severe rebuke to those who intermeddled in baneful political disquisitions.[21]

Louisville *Journal*, May 16, 1862.

1. In an effort to rally those Tennesseans "who are in favor of the restoration of the former relations of this state to the Federal Union," a public meeting was held in the hall of the house of representatives. Although Johnson spoke for three hours, he was but one of several speakers—William B. Campbell, William H. Wisener, Edmund Cooper, William B. Stokes, Russell Houston—of varying political antecedents. Nashville *Dispatch*, May 13, 1862; [T. B. Peterson, comp.], *Life, Speeches and Services of Andrew Johnson* (Philadelphia, 1865), 95.

2. Since biblical times wearing a garment of the coarsest possible texture and having ashes sprinkled on the head was a token of abject poverty, lamentation, or penitence. *OED*, IX, 11.

3. A rather cryptic observation, perhaps to be explained by the shibboleth "southern rights"—the right to the common American public domain, the right to ownership of private property, and the prerogative of being left undisturbed in the enjoyment of all such rights. In sum, it would appear to reflect the southern sensitivity of several decades' standing.

4. See Speech at Columbus, October 4, 1861, note 9.

5. For this allusion to the dispute between Davis and W. B. Campbell over credit for capture of Monterrey, see Speech at Nashville, March 22, 1862, note 23.

6. See Speech in Support of Presidential War Program, July 27, 1861, *Johnson Papers*, IV, 621-24, 645-46n. Much of what follows appeared not only in the above document, but also in the Speech at Nashville, March 22, 1862.

7. Among the preceding assertions—several of them found in earlier speeches—at least three are open to question. Nearly two months before, he was quoted as owning

seven slaves, rather than nine, while the 1860 census shows only five. Nor is there reason to attribute to "the labor of his own hands" the construction of the dwelling which he bought from James Brannan in 1851; although, according to family tradition, Johnson completed the house, an architectural historian suggests that the work was "very likely confined to interior details." And, while Eliza and Frank were evicted so that the building could be used as a hospital, it would appear that the speaker overdramatized the circumstances. See Speech on Expulsion of Senator Bright, January 31, 1862, note 29; Speech at Nashville, March 22, 1862; Ernest A. Connally, "The Andrew Johnson Homestead at Greeneville, Tennessee," ETHS *Pubilcations*, No. 29 (1957), 121-22; Letter from Michael L. Patterson, January 31, 1862.

8. These were probably the two slaves which, according to the census record, were the property of Martha Johnson and her husband David Patterson. 1860 Census, Slave Schedule, Tenn., Greene, 14th Dist., 5.

9. On June 8, 1861, Middle and West Tennessee, under pressure from the Harris regime, had gone overwhelmingly for "separation," while East Tennessee voted to remain in the Union. See *Johnson Papers*, IV, 487n.

10. For previous use of Irish patriot Robert Emmet's ringing declaration, see *ibid.*, 45-46, 51n.

11. When word came of the defeat at Fort Donelson, wrote a contemporary, "the archives were packed up and shipped in a special train during the afternoon of Sunday [February 16] to Memphis, whither they were accompanied by the Governor and heads of departments." Harris told Tennesseans in a proclamation of February 19: "It was a duty I conceived I owed you to remove, whilst it could be done in perfect safety, the archives of the state." John M. McKee, "The Evacuation of Nashville," *Annals of the Army of Tennessee*, I (1878), 226; Memphis *Appeal*, February 23, 1862.

12. During the prewar decades much of the deep South's food and livestock came from the upper South. Planters, aiming at self-sufficiency, succeeded to a large extent, but the lure of a money crop inhibited agricultural diversification. Middle and East Tennessee and central Kentucky were major livestock suppliers, as well as "important food source areas," for the cotton states where shortages frequently occurred. Soon after the war began, Confederate authorities vainly urged farmers and planters to replace staple crops with corn and vegetables, ultimately resorting as early as March, 1862, to legislation limiting cotton production. Sam B. Hilliard, *Hog Meat and Hoecake: Food Supply in the Old South, 1840-1860* (Carbondale, Ill., 1972), 127, 160, 193, 199, 214, 222, 231; Robert E. Gallman, "Self-Sufficiency in the Cotton Economy of the Antebellum South," in William N. Parker, ed., *The Structure of the Cotton Economy of the Antebellum South* (Washington, 1970), 22-23; Gates, *Agriculture and the Civil War*, 6-9, 15-18.

13. The central portion of the British flag consists of a plain red cross on a white field, symbolic of the patron saint of England.

14. From William Jones, *An Ode in Imitation of Alcaeus* (1781). Stevenson, *Macmillan Book of Proverbs*, 1993.

15. During these first months of Federal occupation a veritable rumor factory flourished in the city. According to the Louisville *Journal's* Nashville correspondent, the "office of the 'grape vine' telegraph, corner of the square and Cedar street," was the source from whence the throng of "eager and interested listeners" fanned out to spread the "teeming despatches . . . till all circles were permeated." The exaggeration of Confederate military success in Middle Tennessee and the imminence of Federal expulsion were the staples of these "despatches." Louisville *Journal*, April 28, 1862.

16. Wilkins Micawber, the shiftless but incurable optimist in Charles Dickens' currently popular *David Copperfield*, had become a byword for the well-intentioned planner of business schemes which came to naught. William R. Benét, ed., *The Reader's Encyclopedia* (New York, 1948), 719.

17. "Hereditary bondsmen! Know ye not / Who would be free themselves must strike the blow?" Byron, *Childe Harold*, c. II, lxxvi.

18. A corruption of "Hang out our banners on the outward walls." Shakespeare, *Macbeth*, Act V, sc. 5.

19. Quoted by Mr. Omer in *David Copperfield*, this expression was used earlier by "old Tom," a disabled seaman, in Frederick Marryat's *Jacob Faithful* (1834). Bartlett, *Quotations*, 497; Stevenson, *Macmillan Book of Proverbs*, 1915.

20. "The Trial of Archibald Hamilton Rowan [1793]," in *Sketches of Trials in Ireland, Including the Speeches of Mr. Curran* (Baltimore, 1805), 31. John Philpot Curran (1750-1817), County Cork native, studied law at Middle Temple and was admitted to the bar (1775) and the Irish House of Commons (1783) where he gained fame as a patriotic orator and defender of Irish Catholics. *DNB*, V, 332-40.

21. Johnson's remarks "to the female portion of the secession population" were reported at some length in another version of this address: "when a woman shall unsex herself she must be met in the character she assumes. . . . He believed that by women's influence many men have been induced to join the Confederates. . . . [He] paid a beautiful and eloquent tribute to woman in her natural and appropriate sphere." An admiring contemporary noted that after the speech, many Nashville rebels were calmer "and even the ladies of that persuasion were induced to cease torturing their pretty mouths into an 'ugly pout' whenever they met Unionists"! Peterson, *Life of Johnson*, 98; Savage, *Life of Johnson*, 263.

From John G. Parkhurst

Murfreesboro May 13 1862

To Gov A Johnson

I have arrested all of the persons named.[1] Shall I send them to nashville or hold them here. If sent to nashville I hope they will not be released on bonds. Bonds wont preserve life nor stop this rebellion. I also hope the two old Heads[2] you now have from this city will be forwarded to a Colder Climate[.]

J. G. Parkhurst

Tel, DLC-JP.

1. In his communication of the previous day, the governor listed a dozen men, any or all of whom might be arrested and held as hostages: G. T. Henderson, John E. Dromgoole, John A. Crockett, William A. Ransom, L. M. Maney, John Childress, Dr. King, F. C. Mosby, Dr. R. S. Wendel, James M. Avent, Dr. William T. Baskette, and Thomas Robinson. Johnson to Parkhurst, May 12, 1862, Johnson Papers, LC.

2. Probably former Congressman Charles Ready and Murfreesboro banker William Ledbetter, both of whom were taken to the state penitentiary on May 1; it was rumored that Ledbetter would be sent to Mackinac. Ready (1802-1878), born at Readyville in present Cannon County, graduated from Greeneville College, and practiced law at Murfreesboro where he served as mayor (1832, 1849-53, 1867), represented Rutherford in the legislature (1835-37) and Middle Tennessee as a Whig in Congress (1853-59). Two other prominent Murfreesboro citizens—LeGrand H. Carney (1808-1884), a wealthy North Carolina-born merchant, and David D. Wendel (1811-1873), Rutherford criminal and circuit court clerk—were arrested but by May 11, had been released. Nashville *Dispatch*, May 2, 11, 1862; Nashville *Union*, May 3, 1862; McBride and Robison, *Biographical Directory*, I, 610-11; *BDAC*, 1502; 1860 Census, Tenn., Rutherford, Murfreesboro, 5; 9th Dist., 21; Porch, *Evergreen Cemetery*, 104, 121; *Goodspeed's Rutherford*, 818; for Ledbetter, see *Johnson Papers*, II, 160n.

From A Private Soldier

Nashville Tenn May 13/62

To hon. A Johnson

noble Sir

as the governor of Tennessee i take the liberty to address you[.] I was present at the State Capitol yesterday and listend with deep enthusastic interest to the loyal, well toned, and Soul inspireing Sentiments of the heart uttered by yourself and the Several Self Sacrafiseing noble minded men of you Respective State and i Can assure you that i never heard anything in my life that gave me Such infinite pleasure as the orations delivered by you and your noble Statesmen of [May] 12; and now noble Sir believe me when i tell you that as far as i Can See your evry Sentiment was literaly true inasmuch as the majority of the Citizens of Nashville are most Generaly insolent and overbearing and to [do] not refain from takeing the advantage of the union Soldiers in any respect wherein they Can accomplish thier most diabolical designs wherein they Can decieve or betray the virtues of loyal Soldiers and Citazens[.]   for instance a man liveing not far from the fair Ground in a large brick house[1] an influential and wealthy Citizen upon whom many no doubt look with Confidence had the audacity to draw up in line a number of dupes to assist the outlaw morgan if he Came which was Generaly believed he would on the night of the 5th or thereabouts and oure Convalescent men Such as Could armed themeselves as no doupt you know and Stood ready to meet the maurauders[.]   but what Could we have done with an enemy befor and behind us[.]   the one had asumed the habilment of Soldiers and the other that of a Sneaking Cowardly treacherous Snake in the grass[.] it makes my blood boil to think that our milatary officers in Comand here do not take measures to repel Such Secret and hostile movements and punish the offenders[.]   i Can Say one thing and five hundred voices will repeat the echo that not much longer will this and that be Submited to and if it must Come they will throw aside all restraint and punish the offenders according to thier deserts[.]

but while i Speak thus dont for an instant think that i or any one that is prst [present] in the chamber have any thing to reprove you for for if man ever deserved the aprobation of a true hearted and loyal man it is you most exelent Sir and in peruseing this humble epistle i trust you will excuse the Corespondent for not Signing his name inasmuch as he is Conected with the union army[.]

yours truly may Success attend you is my ernest prayer[.]

private Soldier

ALS, DLC-JP.
    1. Not identified.

From Edmund T. Bainbridge[1]

Louisville May 14 1862

Gov. Andrew Johnson
Nashville Tenn.
Dear Sir.

I have always admired you as much as an old line whig could admire a Democrat who He believed to be an honest and talented patriot. Your recent proclamation[2] however has destroyed at once the confidence I had in your wisdom as a Statesman. In that proclamation you undertake to make laws— This Sir is subversive of Civil Government, and all who undertake it, whether Generals or Governors must ultimately fail—and go down. I do most deeply regret your having fallen into this error, for sir I had hoped, that much good would have resulted from your administration in Tennessee, would Sir that I could impress upon your mind the all important fact that the Constitution as it is and the laws as they are, can only save our beloved Country— I am respectfully

E. T. Bainbridge

ALS, DLC-JP.

1. Edmund T. Bainbridge (1798-1879), Virginia-born partner of Bainbridge & Matthews, hatters, was a longtime Louisville merchant who had built "Bainbridge's Row," a group of stylish townhouses on Jefferson Street in 1834; by 1860 he held real and personal property valued at $121,000. Moving from Louisville c1867, he lived the last years of his life in Morristown, New Jersey, and Baltimore. 1860 Census, Ky., Jefferson, Louisville, 5th Ward, 143; *Tanner's Louisville Directory* (1861), 24; George E. McCracken (editor, *The American Genealogist*) to Andrew Johnson Project, March 11, 1976.

2. Proclamation Concerning Guerrilla Raids, May 9, 1862.

From Neill S. Brown

Nashville May 14th 1862

Sir:

I have just been arrested on your warrant[1] & am in the hands of the Provost Marshall— The arrest found me engaged in the business of the Chancery Court & I would be glad on account of the interests of others in my hands, if I could be put on my parole until the last of the week as it would enable me to arrange my business to some extent— And if it is consistent with your sense of duty for that purpose & with a view to a fuller elucidation of my case, I would be glad to have an interview with you before I am committed[.] Such an interview I meditated on this day[.]

Respectfully   Neill S. Brown

His Excellency Andrew Johnson
Governor &c

ALS, DLC-JP.

1. Although the order for former Governor Brown's arrest was issued April 21, he was not taken into custody until May 14; immediately afterward he was released on parole. Originally opposed to secession, Brown had reluctantly followed Tennessee out of the Union, acting as a member of Governor Harris' military and financial board. Despite the fact that two sons and a brother were serving in the rebel army, he began—in the face of numerous Union victories in the state—to lose confidence in the Confederate cause. Within three weeks of his apprehension, while sharing the rostrum at Columbia with Johnson on June 2, Brown publicly denounced secession and the war and advocated a return to the Union. Ex. Record Book (1862-63), Ser. 4C, Johnson Papers, LC; Nashville *Dispatch*, May 16, 1862; Nashville *Union*, June 4, 1862.

From Alvan C. Gillem

Camp before Corinth Miss
May 14. 1862

Gov. Andrew Johnson.

Governor

I received your Telegraph of the 8th inst. on the 11. & immediately telegraphed you that I would accept the command of the Regt known as the "Governors Guard."[1] I am anxious to serve my own state. Since the rebellion began I have done all in my [power] to oppose it, before the liberation of Tennessee I was indifferent as to where I served, but now I desire to go to the aid of those Tennesseans who have suffered more than any, or all other people from the tyrany of the traitors[.] among the oppressed are my father & brother.[2]

I feel highly complimented by your request to take the Regt. bearing your name, & shall do all in my power to justify the confidence you repose in me, not only as commander of the Regt. but any other duty which you may assign me.

I will consider it not only a duty, but a very great pleasure to assist you, in organizing & drilling any of the troops raised in the state, & the happiest day of my life will be the one, on which I witness the *long delayed* liberation of East Tennessee.

It will be necessary for me to have authority from the War Department to be absent from the Regular Army— will you confer the additional favor, of asking the Secretary of War to give me leave of absence for the purpose of commanding a Tennessee Regiment.[3] The Secretary nor the President could refuse you nothing, no man has labored so faithfully, & sacrificed so much as yourself— If the Secretary of War will not grant me the same indulgence he has to so many other officers, there will be but one thing left me, & that is to surrender my commission in the Regular Army—a thing that would pain me beyond expression. I am devoted to the service but I am devoted also to the people to whose assistance I desire to go.

I think there will be a battle here to-morrow or the next day,[4] the enemies works can only be reached through dense swamps[.] these we are now cutting roads through, these will be finished to-morrow, & it is my opinion that our troops will be attacked as they debouch from the swamp. We have above one hundred thousand men, in good health & disciplined. I do not think a greater number could be employed to advantage, as from the nature of the county it will be impossible to form lines of battle of any length. I believe it will result in a number of minor battles & the evacuation of Corinth—

The Rebel troops are very dissatisfied by the "Conscript law"[5] making a soldier of *all* men from 18 to 35. years.   a deserter reports one of the

Tenn. Regts under guard for insubordination—also that Col. Sidney Stanton[6] says he will march his Regt. out on the expiration of their years service—

There is scarcely a man left in this region who was able to do military duty—most of them were Union men & forced to take arms. Shall these men be treated when captured with the same harshness as traitors *deserve* to be? I hope not. It is said these union men were put in front at the recent battle of Shiloh, and that the "Regular Confederate troops" were ordered to shoot all who fell back.[7] And yet we are expected to treat these villians as "prisoners of war."

The rebels are not to be conquered by kindness[.] they must be made to feel that they are *suddered*,[8] and that every offence will be speedily punished— Excuse me Governor but I often say more than necessary when I speak on this subject.

Allow me again to thank you for your kindness to me.

Believe me yours Sincerely
Alvan C. Gillem

ALS, DLC-JP

1. Johnson's telegram has not been found. Gillem's acceptance was dated May 12; the governor, responding on the thirteenth, asked that Gillem "report to me at the earliest date practical." Although original orders issued to all military governors included provision for a governor's guard—a brigade or less to be used in strengthening his authority—it would be another year (April, 1863) before Johnson succeeded, over General Rosecrans' protest, in detaching from the regular army the Tenth Tennessee Regiment as a nucleus for such a guard. He then appointed Gillem commander. Johnson Papers, LC; Stanton to Edward Stanly, May 20, 1863, *OR*, Ser. 1, IX, 397; Hall, *Military Governor*, 42, 83, 176, 179.

2. His father, Samuel J. Gillem (Gillum) (b. c1800), North Carolina native and Jackson County farmer, had two sons, Luke (b. c1834) and John (b. c1836), living with him in 1850. 1850 Census, Tenn., Jackson, 14th Dist., 553.

3. Johnson made the request on May 16; three days later Stanton approved and Adj. Gen. Lorenzo Thomas issued orders for Gillem "to take command of the Governor's Guard at Nashville Tenn." Johnson to Stanton, May 17; Stanton to Johnson, May 19; "Special Orders 111," May 19, 1862, Johnson Papers, LC.

4. No battle developed, but skirmishes continued, including one on May 17 at "Russell's house" near Corinth, in which over twenty Union and Confederate soldiers died. *OR*, Ser. 1, X, Pt. I, 839-43.

5. By a law of April 16, 1862, all white males between eighteen and thirty-five, except those specifically exempted, were liable for three years' military service. Forty-five became the upper limit in September, and in 1864 the ages were eventually stretched to seventeen and fifty. Boatner, *Civil War Dictionary*, 172.

6. Sidney S. Stanton (c1829-1864), a Jackson and Smith County lawyer, state legislator (1857-61), and Constitutional Union elector, who declared $1,500 in real and $2,000 in personal property in 1860, became colonel of the 25th Tenn. Inf. upon its organization in August, 1861. Resigning the following July because of a disciplinary dispute with Gen. John S. Marmaduke, he promptly raised the 84th Tenn. Inf. and commanded it until its merger with the 28th Tenn. Inf., which he led until killed in battle in May, 1864. 1860 Census, Tenn., Smith, 1st Dist., 7; McBride and Robison, *Biographical Directory*, I, 693-94; *Tennesseans in the Civil War*, I, 225-26, 232-33, 307-8.

7. That certain Tennessee troops were reluctant soldiers at Shiloh and that General Bragg lacked confidence in their dependability would appear to be true. Advised by his wife to "Put the Tennesseans where your batteries can *fire* upon them if they attempt to run," the general replied that he was scattering them "among better men" in the

corps—"I never realized the full correctness of your appreciation of them till now." For their part, the Tennesseans, according to one member of "Co. Aytch," cordially disliked and feared Bragg, in part because "When we were drawn up in line of battle, a detail of one-tenth of the army was placed in our rear to shoot us down if we ran." Grady McWhiney, *Braxton Bragg and Confederate Defeat: Field Command* (New York, 1969), 217-18; Sam R. Watkins, "*Co. Aytch*," *Maury Grays, First Tennessee Regiment* (Jackson, Tenn., 1952 [1882]), 71-72.

8. Perhaps "sudded" an archaic expression conveying the idea of being overwhelmed or inundated. James O. Halliwell, *A Dictionary of Archaic and Provincial Words* (2 vols., London, 1872), II, 825.

From Horace Maynard

Washington, May 14, 1862.

Dr. Sir.

Why in Heaven's name do not some of you write to me— Except three short despatches, a letter from R. M. Edwards & an occasional number of the Union, I have heard nothing of your doings, aside from what little I can skim off of the current of rumors floating through the newspapers— I wish you would put your aid de camp or your private secretary, up to sending me a letter of details—

Trigg is still here, slowly recovering his health. Nothing has yet been done by the War Department, that I can learn either about the prisoners, or about troops— They are trying to relieve from the sting of hackle tooth[1] that pricks hardest, believing that you will be able to hold your own, until some other points are made a little more secure—

I hear nothing from our troops near Cumberland Gap. Mr. Barton, of the firm of Cowan & Dickinson[2] passed through there some two weeks ago. He found Spears with a brigade near Boston, a place close to the Tennessee line, on the road from Williamsburgh to Big Creek Gap— Morgan & Carter were in front of Cumberland Gap— I received a letter from our multitudiness correspondent at Mt. Vernon, E. Smith,[3] written on the 7th which is not long & of such a character that I will copy it entire.

One of Monday's Cavalry just reached town from the Ford.[4] He brings bad news. A short time since Genl Morgan detached four regts. of Tennesseeans to Big Creek Gap— Just before he left the Ford, news reached that they were cut off, & that Genl. Morgan had ordered the troops to be ready for a march in twenty minutes, to what point he did not know. If the report (he said it was reliable) be true, no doubt he believes the force went from the Gap, & he intends to free that point before they return.

There is just enough of this to create some uneasiness, without absolutely conveying any information whatever.

The regiments with Spears were those recently formed &, of course, undisciplined—

Events are hurrying forward in this region with great rapidity. Every body is hopeful but anxious. I am asked many times a day, how goes the work in Tennessee. The eyes of the whole country are turned in that direction. We are all in suspense to hear from last Monday's meeting in Nashville.[5]

I am very Truly Yours
Horace Maynard

Please send me a copy of Judge Humphreys' charge to the Grand Jury, April Term 1861—[6]

His Excy. Andrew Johnson—

ALS, DLC-JP.

1. Probably a reference to the hackberry, a type of huckleberry bush with serrated, i.e., sawtoothed leaves. John K. Smith, *Flora of the Southeast United States* (New York, 1913), 364, 892.

2. Alvin Barton (1831-1885) was a Mississippi-born junior partner in the Knoxville firm of Cowan, Dickinson & Co., wholesale dry goods merchants, established in 1832. WPA, Tenn., Knox: Old Gray Cemetery, 170; *Williams' Knoxville Directory* (1859-60), 35; Rothrock, *French Broad-Holston Country*, 401-2, 411.

3. Elisha Smith

4. Cumberland Ford.

5. The May 12 gathering of unionist citizens in which Johnson and others spoke and pro-Union resolutions were adopted was held at the capitol. Nashville *Dispatch*, May 13, 1862; Nashville *Union*, May 14, 1862.

6. For West H. Humphreys, see *Johnson Papers*, II, 387n. Refusing to call the April, 1861, term of the Federal court in Nashville, Judge West H. Humphreys had nonetheless summoned the grand jury and, without formally impanelling it, taken the occasion to reply to Lincoln's April 15 proclamation and to define the nature of treason. As reported in the press, "In his charge to the grand jury, the judge maintained the ground that Lincoln's proclamation was unconstitutional; that the Governor [Harris] should disregard his requisition upon this State for volunteers to coerce the seceded States, and that the jury should find no true bills for treason. He also maintained the ground that in the present collision between the North and the South there is no such thing as treason, and that parties taken on the one or the other side should be held as prisoners and not as traitors." Maynard, having as early as January, 1862, initiated an investigation into Humphreys' behavior, was now seeking evidence for the impeachment resolution, favorably reported out of committee on May 6. As the result of his secessionist statements during 1860-61 and his recent appointment (March 29, 1862) as Confederate district judge, Humphreys, in a one-day trial late in June, 1862, was impeached, removed from office, and disqualified from holding future U. S. office. Nashville *Union and American*, April 17, 1861; Kermit L. Hall, "West Humphreys and the Crisis of the Union," *Tenn. Hist. Quar.*, XXXIV (1975), 48-69; *House Report* No. 44, 37 Cong., 2 Sess., 8-9.

From Michael L. Patterson

Barbourville Ky.
May 14th 1862.

Friend Gov. Johnson

I Should have written to you ere, this, But circumstances have been Such, that it has been next to impossible, I Rushed here on thursday after I left Nashville, next day I went to see Robt and handed over the Package sent by me to him; Robt told me that he had informed you that all was right— On the next day I went down below Boston Whitley County, to Gen Spears' Brigade[.] Finding him without a Commissary—and by his Solicitations, I concluded to act as Brigade Commissary until he could get Some one to take the place—And have been acting in that Capacity until the last day or so—When I quit for Reasons which I will give you at Some time— When the Gen. got Mitch Edwards[1] to take the position, and he is acting now—

To give you Some Idea how this Brigade is getting along, I will give you an item or two— Since the Brigade was formed they have not drawn a pound of Coffee, Sugar or anything else from the Commissary post of this division—and the way they have been living is this, On Corn Bread and Bacon, by sustaining themselves[.] the Bacon has been bought in lots from Citizens from 20-pounds upward and packed to Some convenient place for a wagon to haul from; then Corn meal has been Ground at little mills around—also there has not been a Brigade team assigned over as yet, or until yesterday when 5 teams was turned over—from the division—But few of the Boys have haversacks— On last Monday orders was given to march to Cumberland Ford, all the Regimental teams was called in—and before the two Regts 5th & 6th could move they had to go out and press Ox teams some 25 in number—and we come to this place got here on Friday evening—and on yesterday orders was given to go back to Big Creek Gap immediately, and for want of Transportation the Boys had to go out and press ox teams to move them again— you will See from the foregoing items that thing in this locality are going on with a vengence— I could write a good many thing which looks very curious to me; but will defer for the present—

I understand that Robert, has a company 400 men—or there abouts— that a part of his men are stationed at or near Judge Buttons[2] on the London road and part at London; I suppose he is placed at those points to keep Col John Morgan with his cavalry from cutting of the communication between those troops and the Ohio River— Gen Morgan seems to be a fraid of that being done—

Gen. Morgan who is commanding at the Ford has for the last few days created a good deal of excitement by expressing some fears of the communication being cut of in his rear—and has caused wire to be put up on the Old Road North of this place Some 6 miles and one line through Barbourville, the object is if one Line is Cut, then he will have the other—

No late news from Greeneville, rumors Say, there is only 3.000 at the Gap, while other rumors say there are 5 or 7. 9. 12 and 15.000[.] I dont think anyone believes the latter—

Gov. I am here and out of Buisness, and am ready and awaiting for any thing that may come up.

Yours Respectfully
Mike L. Patterson

ALS, DLC-JP.
    1. Richard M. Edwards.
    2. Not identified.

Petition from Isaac H. Poinier[1]

May [14?] 1862

To the Governor of the State of Tennessee

The undersigned, I. H. Poinere, a citizen of the state of Ky. respectfully states, that he is a loyal citizen of the United States & has never has been otherwise—, that he is fully able to show that he is a "union man"—in the language of yr recent Proclamation, & therefore comprehended by its terms. About the 29th April last he opened a little dry goods store in Pulaski in this state with the permission of the surveyor of the Port of Louisville[2] in the state of Ky—and of Allen A. Hall agent of the Government at Washington & Col. Stanley Mathews Provost Marshall of the City of Nashville— The nett Cost of the stock of goods delivered at Pulaski was twelve hundred and fifty nine dollars ninety six cents ($1259.96), but he thinks the goods, after their arrival there worth at least twice that sum— He had been in business but a few days & had sold about $200.00 worth of goods, when John Morgan[3] with several hundred men purporting to act as soldiers of the Southern Army, but really acting as plunderers, came into his store and took what money he had in his house and also his entire stock of goods, and appropriated them to their own use. They sold what they could not use to men in Pulaski, who bought them knowing them to be his, your petitioner's property— a portion of the goods was returned to him by one of the purchasers and one of them paid him in money, and if he were to be paid only for the nett cost of the goods at Pulaski, his a/c would stand as follows to wit.

Nett cost of goods & c		$1259.96
Deduct goods & money returned	246.08	
Proceeds & sale of goods	150 00	396.08
		$863.88

He will explain the item of $150.00 in this way— He had sold about $200.00 worth of goods—had paid $150.00 of it out to creditors or for purchases & lost $50.00 as he thinks by Morgan & his men. This would leave him loses $863.88 on the idea that his goods are to be estimated at their cost and not at their true value. This will not pay him his real loss by $500 or $600. He files his invoice of his goods, except some cottonades[4] worth about $175. He also files letters endorsing his character & loyalty[.] He now asks your Excellency to contitute a Military Commission or such other tribunal as may seem to you best, for the investigation of the facts of his case & the adjudication of his rights, with power to decree to him against the disloyal citizens of Pulaski, such compensation for his losses as may appear just and proper. There are as he is informed & believes, a great number of wealthy citizens of Pulaski who are secessionists & disloyal to the Government of the United States. He is ready to verify these statements by his oath and can produce testimony of others in addition & asks for such relief only as may be fair & in accordance with your recent Proclamation[.]

I. H. Poinier

Pulaski May 21st, 1862

I certify that these papers are a true copy of those in the case of I. H. Poinier and now in my possession[.]

Chas. B. Gillespie[5]
Provost Marshall

Copy, DLC-JP.

1. Isaac H. Poinier (b. c1836), an Ohio native, was a Louisville produce and commission merchant (1861-71) who had opened a dry goods store in Pulaski only a few days before Morgan's raid. 1860 Census, Ky., Jefferson, Louisville, 5th Ward, 132; *Tanner's Louisville Directory* (1861), 196; *Caron's Louisville Directory* (1871), 376.

2. Charles B. Cotton.

3. Morgan's report of May 2 mentions a skirmish at Pulaski and his capture of 268 men, with arms, wagons, and teams, as well as several wagonloads of cotton en route to Nashville, which he destroyed. *OR*, Ser. 1, X, Pt. I, 876.

4. Coarse cotton material used in work clothes. *Webster's Third International*.

5. Charles B. Gillespie (c1821-fl1894), physician of Freeport, Pennsylvania, with $300 personal property, was captain, Co. F, 78th Pa. Inf. (1861-64). 1860 Census, Pa., Armstrong, Freeport, 29; Robert Walter Smith, *History of Armstrong County, Pennsylvania* (Chicago, 1883), 70, 79, 419; J. T. Gibson, ed., *History of Seventy-Eighth Pennsylvania Volunteer Infantry* (Pittsburgh, 1905), 167.

To George W. Morgan

Nashville May 14th [1862]

Brig Genl. Morgan,
Commanding Forces,
Cumberlan Ford, Ky
Via Barboureville.

I have just received letter from Paymaster Larned[1] stating that Paymaster is at Lexington & will proceed without delay to pay your troops up to May 1st—

What is the prospect of entering East Tennessee—and driving the rebels from their midst. God grant that it may be soon, and that your mission may be triumphant. Is there anything I can do that will give you aid. If so, please tell me.[2]

Yours Sincerely,
Andrew Johnson.

Tel draft, DLC-JP.

1. Benjamin F. Larned (1794-1862), born in Massachusetts, entered the army in 1813 and was brevetted captain for gallantry at Fort Erie; appointed regimental paymaster in 1815, he succeeded to the paymaster generalship with the rank of colonel in 1854. *Appleton's Cyclopaedia*, III, 619.

2. In response, Morgan expressed his apprehension that the "Government" was

inadequately concerned about the Confederate threat to his supply line, concluding: "Should my supplies from Lexington be cut off, I will trust to East Tennessee[.] My troops are full of hope and full of courage. You need not fear for them[.]" Morgan to Johnson, May 14, 1862, Johnson Papers, LC.

From Robert Johnson

London May 15th 1862

To Gov. Andrew Johnson
Nashville Tenn

Your dispatch of the fourteenth (14th) recd a few hours Since[.] my regiment is now Stationed at Camp E. M. Stanton widow Colyars[1] twelve (12) miles from this place[.] I have been up on the road for four (4) days and nights and have not had time to write or dispatch you[.] no news from Tenn. no hope of relief to our people Soon. I have not been to bed for four (4) nights and have come here to dispatch you[.] Send dispatches to London.

Robert Johnson
Col 4th Regt Tenn vols

Tel, DLC-JP.
1. Olivia J. Colyer (b. c1829), a Kentucky native, was the widow of Stephen T. Colyer, a tavern keeper who in 1860 claimed $16,000 in real and $5,000 in personal property. Mrs. Colyer, who continued to operate the tavern after her husband's death, received $25.25 from Robert in payment for board and services supplied to members of the 4th Regt. Tenn. Vols. 1860 Census, Ky., Knox, Lynncamp Dist., 52; Account with Olivia J. Colyer, May 19, 1862, Johnson Papers, LC.

To John M. Lea[1]

Nashville Tenn
May 15th. 1862

John M. Lea Esq
Nashville, Tenn.
Dear Sir:

In consideration of the position and standing of Mr. John Overton,[2] his connection with the militia of the State, and in the capacity of Colonel detailing men to go into the Confederate Service, tendering his fortune to the cause of the rebellion[3] and giving his entire influence social and political to that cause I cannot consistently with the interest of the Government consent that Mr.Overton should return unless upon the strictest terms that the Government imposes in such cases, of oath, bond, and active co-operation with the Authorities in the restoration of harmony and Federal Authority,.

The permission to return, however, granted on a ready compliance with the conditions above indicated shall not in any manner be considered an amnesty or palliation in any proceedings which may be had in any courts of justice[.]

Copy, DLC-JP.

1. John M. Lea (1818-1903), wealthy Nashville lawyer ($800,000 real and $30,800 personal property in 1860) and University of Nashville graduate (1837), served as U. S. district attorney (1842-45), mayor of Nashville (1850), circuit court judge of Davidson County (1865-66), and state legislator (1875). On the preceding day, Lea had submitted a proposal which would permit his brother-in-law, John Overton, to come back to Nashville without taking the oath of allegiance, since he had "never born arms against the United States nor taken any oath to support the Confederate States." If allowed to return under these terms, he "will not only acquiesce . . . but he will use his influence to stop all resistance" to Federal authority and will be bound to the laws "as if the oath of allegiance had been administered to him." As this document reveals, the governor was not impressed. 1860 Census, Tenn., Davidson, Nashville, 5th Ward, 162; *NCAB*, X, 449; Clayton, *Davidson County*, 302-3; Mrs. John Trotwood Moore, "The Tennessee Historical Society, 1849-1918," *Tenn. Hist. Quar.*, III (1944), 221; John M. Lea, Statement in the Matter of John Overton, May 14, 1862, Johnson Papers, LC.

2. John Overton, Jr. (1821-1898), Davidson County "farmer" with $1,060,750 real and $361,690 personal property, had inherited the plantation "Travellers' Rest" from his father, Andrew Jackson's close friend. "One of the original secessionists" who devoted his treasure to the Confederacy, Overton had fled to avoid arrest in April, and his estate was occupied by Federal troops who laid waste his fields and woods. Spending the war years in aiding the Lost Cause behind Confederate lines, he subsequently resumed farming and served one term in the legislature (1877-79). 1860 Census, Tenn., Davidson, 8th Dist., 136; Henry Lee Swint, "Travellers' Rest: Home of Judge John Overton," *Tenn. Hist. Quar.*, XXVI (1967), 131-33; Nashville *Banner*, December 13, 1898; Fitch, *Annals*, 634, 667-69.

3. See Letter to Stanley Matthews, April 1, 1862.

To John G. Parkhurst, Murfreesboro

Nashville, Tenn.
May 15th 1862

Col Parkhurst;
Dr Sir,

I have to state that Col Childress[1] has been released on parole for a short time, for reasons of a satisfactory character made known to me.

Col Childress is a gentleman for whom I always entertained a very high regard and one who has the respect of his friends and acquaintances wherever found.

I hope that you will, on the return of Col Childress to his home, have a free and full conference with him in regard to the late affair at Murfreesboro.[2] Any statement that Col C. may make can be implicitly relied upon, and any bond or other agreement you and he may fix upon, in reference to the subject of his arrest, will be made by him in good faith and will be so regarded.

I sincerely hope that the interview proposed may prove highly satisfactory to yourself and Col Childress, and result in the removal of some of the unpleasant feelings and apprehensions connected with the recent affair at Murfreesboro.

Very Truly Yours &c
Andrew Johnson.

L, MiU-H.

1. For John W. Childress, president of the Planters' Bank and brother of Mrs. James K. Polk, see *Johnson Papers*, III, 393n.

2. Childress had been among those arrested and sent to Nashville following a shooting incident in Murfreesboro, May 10. See Letter to John G. Parkhurst, May 11, 1862, note 3; Johnson to Parkhurst, May 12, 1862, Johnson Papers, LC.

To Edwin M. Stanton

Nashville, Tenn,
May 15th 1862

Hon E M Stanton,
Secretary of War,
Sir:

Please permit me to introduce to your favorable notice Major James Given.[1]

Maj Given was captured by Capt. John Morgan, of the Rebel service, at Lebanon, Tenn, a short time since, and released by him on parole. The Major is exceedingly desirous of being exchanged, and I hope you will be pleased to grant every facility in your power to effect an exchange in his case.

He is a worthy officer, has rendered efficient service, and is ready and anxious to renew his efforts to put down this infernal rebellion. Capt. John Morgan and his marauding Cavalry ought not to be embraced within the rules and regulations of civilized warfare, and the whole number of those war prisoners at Lebanon should be dealt with as mere robbers and Free-booters, and the Government should wholly disregard paroles given by the leaders of such bands.[2]

Accept assurances of my high esteem &c &c
Andrew Johnson.

L, DNA-RG107, Lets. Recd., File J229(103).

1. James Givin (c1834-1880) of West Chester, Pennsylvania, enlisted in April, 1861, became major of the 7th Pa. Cav. in December, and after his capture on May 5, 1862, was released on his parole not to bear arms until regularly exchanged. Still on parole in December, 1862, he was medically discharged the following March soon after his exchange. He reenlisted in September, 1864, as lieutenant colonel of the 127th U. S. Cld. Inf., serving until October, 1865. Samuel P. Bates, *History of Pennsylvania Volunteers* (5 vols., Harrisburg, 1869-71), V, 1125; CSR, RG94, NA; Mary Price (James Givin) Pension File, RG15, NA.

2. The validity of paroles arising out of guerrilla warfare was a much debated subject during these months. Many, like Johnson, argued that Federal soldiers were under no obligation to observe paroles given following capture by guerrillas; at the same time they declared that captured guerrillas should be denied parole status and treated as common criminals. An effort to clarify the situation was made in General Orders No. 49, issued by Lorenzo Thomas, February 28, 1863, which forbade the giving of paroles to guerrilla commanders. Before this, paroles had generally been recognized as binding by both parties. *OR*, Ser. 2, IV, 86-87, 247, 306-7, 394; Hesseltine, *Civil War Prisons*, 92.

From Cave Johnson

Clarksville 16th May 1862.

Dear Sir,

I notice in the procedings at Nashville on Monday,[1] that an effort is being made to obtain a release of the Prisoners of this state taken in the recent battle by Federal troops— having recently spent two days in Camp Douglass I think I understand their wishes & feelings upon the subject and having expressed as well as a general interest in their welfare will be an apology for addressing you upon the subject— A large majority of them from their anxiety to return to their friends and families would willingly take any oath that might be presented, even the one prepared by Genl Halleck for the citizens of Missouri,[2] whilst a large number of the most intelligent and respectable would regard any oath of allegiance to the U.S. as a direct & palpable violation of the oath taken when they entered the service, to support the Constitution of the Confederate States and would under any circumstances refuse to take the oath, so long as the confederate Government had an existence— such conscientious scruples ought to be respected and regarded as strong evidence that they would be faithful citizens to whatever Government may be finally established— Such a violation of their oaths would be regarded in sections of country where the Confederate Government had been established as a want of moral firmness & of principles and degrade them in the estimation of many good men and destroy their future hopes & prospects— many of the young-men from this section belong to our best families, whose zeal to defend the State, withdrew them from their schools at ages between Sixteen & twenty one[.] whatever we may think of the inducements holden out to them, or truer motives, for entering the service, a liberal & generous nation ought not to desire to involve young men in such a dilemma, who may be made by kind treatment the best of citizens in any well regulated Government and much more reliable than the class who would take any oath and excuse themselves upon the plea of necessity and the illegality of the authority demanding it[.]

It seems to me, that the ends of the Government would be best promoted by having them discharged upon parol, entering into obligation, with security if thought advisable, not to serve again during the war unless regularly exchanged— Such a liberal course would impose upon them an honorary obligation more binding & more likely to control their conduct than any oath that might be prescribed.

I trouble you with these suggestions, because it is generally understood among the citizens here as well as among the prisoners, that the

President will submit the question of their release to your judgment[.]
I am very respectfully your obdt. servt
C. Johnson.

Hon. Andrew Johnson
Nashville

ALS, DLC-JP.
1. The Union meeting of May 12.
2. As commander of the Department of the Missouri (November, 1861-March, 1862), Halleck ordered that a loyalty oath be taken by "all city officials, business and educational leaders, attorneys, jurors and railroad officers." Initially required by the provisional government for those who had served with Sterling Price, the test oaths and performance bonds were employed later to determine political allegiance; failure to take the oath "usually led to arrest with subsequent imprisonment or banishment." William E. Parrish, *A History of Missouri* (3 vols., Columbia, Mo., 1973), III, 45, 67-68.

From Alexander W. Moss

Franklin Tenn May 17/62

Gov. Johnson
Sir

Judge P. G. S. Perkins[1] who was arrested by Col. Campbell[2] and forwarded to your city a few days ago deserves strict treatment. He is prety badly diseased morally as well as politically. I am informed that he stated in a confectionary in this place in regard to the oath of allegiance that he expected we would all have to take it but that he would not consider it binding atall[.] Not withstanding such remarks have been verry common in Rebeldom in the last twelve or fifteen months I trust that no man holding a responsible position will be permited to pass at par *into* the United States who entertains such views[.]
Yours respectfully   A. W. Moss

ALS, DLC-JP.
1. Philip G. S. Perkins (1818-1882), Williamson County farmer and lawyer, was a state representative (1849-51), county judge (1859-62), and unsuccessful candidate for the Confederate Congress (1863). He spent his last years in Nashville practicing law (1868-81). McBride and Robison, *Biographical Directory*, I, 581-82.
2. Lewis D. Campbell, Union commander at Franklin.

From Sarah C. Polk

May 17, 1862, Columbia; ALS, DLC-JP.

The former first lady asks Johnson to release or parole J. M. Avent of Murfreesboro so "that he may go home to his distressed family"—"his wife & children, who are in the midst of an encampment, which reaches to his door."

From John Lellyett

Post Office May 18, 1862

Hon Andrew Johnson
Governor of Tennessee

Sir,—An earnest desire to avoid any personal issue which might embarrass the public interests in this state, impelled me to seek an interview with you this morning. By that interview I was made to understand distinctly that you decline to withdraw, modify, or explain, the threat you so publicly made of my removal from office.[1]

As Military Governor and Brigadier General, I acknowledge and am ready both to *obey* and *support* your authority; but if I hold my office simply upon your personal pleasure, I have requested the authorities at Washington to appoint my successor[.]

Very Respectfully   John Lellyett

ALS, DLC-JP.

1. "This threat," wrote Lellyett to John A. Kasson, assistant postmaster general, "was made in front of the Post Office, and in hearing of a small but quite promiscuous crowd of persons. His manner was extraordinary and his excitement seemed strange." The encounter apparently occured sometime before May 9 when Lellyett first complained about the governor's "offensive manner to me" and of his "interference with the mails." Lellyett to Kasson, May 18, 1862, Johnson Papers, LC.

To John Lellyett, Nashville

May 18, 1862

John Lellyett Esq.

I have this moment received your note of this date in which you inform me, (after alluding to other matters,) that you had addressed a letter in regard to your continuance as Post Master at this place (to the Post Master General.)[1]

As you have notified me of the writing of such letter I desire you to furnish me at once with a copy thereof.

The assumption in your letter as to threats made by me is untrue and I so told you to-day. I further stated that I had no explanation to make in regard to what was said in connection with your permitting the mail of the United States to be carried in a stage named after one of the Generals in the Confederate Army.[2] I deemed it an outrage one that should not be tolerated—and told you that it would be as well to carry the mail under the "stars and bars" the flag of the Southern Confederacy, as to carry it under the name of a General then in the Army waging war against the United States.

Very Respectfully,
Andrew Johnson.

Copy, DLC-JP.

1. A reference to Lellyett's communication to John A. Kasson, of this same date. Johnson Papers, LC.

2. It has not been possible to determine the precise secessionist vehicle, whether coach or boat, to which Johnson alludes. Perhaps Lellyett was guilty of shipping mail by the steamer bearing the name of Confederate General Samuel R. Anderson. Nashville *Dispatch*, May 16, 18, June 20, 1862; Byrd Douglas, *Steamboatin' on the Cumberland* (New York, 1961), 332.

To Abraham Lincoln

Nashville May 18th 1862

His Excellency Abm Lincoln
President.

I hope you will make no nomination of Judge for Tennessee for the present.[1] There is ample time & we must have the right man, one who will meet present requirements. All is working as well as could be expected notwithstanding the impediments thrown in the way to which I have referred before. You have probably seen proceedings of great Union meeting here in which you and the policy of your administration were fully sustained and endorsed. That meeting has exerted a powerful influence. Reaction is rapidly going on and in less than three months Tennessee will be looking to you for protection instead of considering you the invader of their rights. For God's sake let the column at Cumberland ford move into East Tennessee and relieve that people from their unparalelled oppression. Nothing has saved them but their endurance and devotion to the union. Please show this to my friend Montgomery Blair and say that I want all the help he can give me.

May God crown all your efforts for the suppression of this rebellion with success.

Andrew Johnson

Tel, DLC-Lincoln Papers; DNA-RG107, Tels. Recd., U.S. Mil. Tel., Vol. 8 (May 8-19, 1862).

1. Although Judge West Humphreys' removal would not be accomplished until June 26, Johnson was evidently so confident of its imminence that he considered appropriate this warning about a hasty replacement. In due time, Connally F. Trigg was appointed and confirmed on July 17. *Senate Ex. Journal*, XII (1861-62), 416, 436.

To Horace Maynard

Nashville May 18 1862.

To Hon Horace Maynard. M. C.

Woods should be put in close confinement in some common jail[.][1] Capt Harris of Bloodhound notoriety with him[.][2] they should both be tried by a drum-head court martial & hung at once[.] Morgan and his marauding gang should not be admitted within the rules of civilizied warefare & that portion of his forces taken at Lebanon should not be held as prisoners of War— I hope you will call attention of Secty Stanton to the fact of their being a mere band of freebooters— all is moving on here as well as could possibly be expected[.] I hope the Secty of War will give the disposition of the prisoners from Tenn to the Governor & sec'ty of State or such person as he may deem proper to indicate.

Andrew Johnson

L, DNA-RG107, Lets. Recd., Sec. of War, File M646 (104); DLC-JP; *OR*, Ser. 2, III, 551.

1. At this time Robert C. Wood, Jr. (1832-1900), a grandson of Zachary Taylor and nephew of Jefferson Davis, a West Point cadet (1850-53), and sometime adjutant general and chief of staff for Braxton Bragg, was in jail at Nashville following his capture with some of Morgan's raiders at Lebanon on May 5. Later confined at Camp Chase and on Johnson's Island (May-September, 1862), he was subsequently a Louisiana sugar planter, president of the Gatling Gun Company of Buffalo, and compiler of the *Confederate Handbook* (New Orleans, 1900). *Confederate Veteran*, IX (1901), 132-33; Heitman, *Register*, I, 1055; Nashville *Union*, May 9, 1862.

2. William Hooper Harris (1835-1908), likewise captured at Lebanon, was an Alabama-born Nashville grocer before the war, who enlisted in May, 1861, and two months later was commissioned captain of Co. A, 1st (McNairy's) Cav., CSA. Incarcerated at Johnson's Island and subsequently exchanged, he became after the war head of a New York merchandising firm before moving back to Nashville to engage in the cotton business; by the end of the 1870's he was a Sumner County farmer. Within the past month, the local administration organ had reprinted an advertisement, which originally appeared in the Nashville *Gazette* during the preceding December, in which Harris and Frank N. McNairy offered "five dollars per pair for fifty pairs of well bred hounds, and fifty dollars for one pair of thoroughbred bloodhounds . . . to chase the infernal cowardly Lincoln bushwhackers of East Tennessee and Kentucky." 1860 Census, Tenn., Davidson, 6th Ward, 142; (1880), Sumner, 5th Dist., 1; CSR, RG109, NA; *Confederate Veteran*, XVI (1908), 468; Nashville *Union*, April 15, May 11, 1862.

From John Lellyett

Post Office May 19, 1862

Hon. Andrew Johnson
Governor &c

Sir,—I inclose you, as you request, a copy of my letter to the 1st As't P M General.[1] You will oblige me if, in return, you will furnish me with a copy of your letter to the authorities on the subject, should you write one.

As to the fact of your making the threat in question, and in the manner described, it can doubtless be established by competent testimony; and I did not understand you as disavowing it yesterday. If I had I should have had nothing more to say or do upon the subject. I did not ask any explanation or make any complaint as to the other matter, but offered an explanation to you.

The letter to Mr Kasson on the 9th, did not, as I remember, contain any important point not embraced in this. I have no copy of that note.

My duty requires me promptly to report to the Department all failures to send or receive the mails at the regular times, with the reasons

&c[.]   The doing of this necessarily opened the subject. You can doubtless obtain a copy of that letter from Mr Kasson.

Respectfully
John Lellyett

ALS, DLC-JP.

1. In this letter Lellyett recounted the episode which occurred in front of the
postoffice, denied any neglect of duty, and, searching for the cause of the governor's
antipathy, found it in the latter's conviction that Lellyett had been the instigator of
criticism which followed Johnson's recommendation of William McNish, "a man who
had voted an open secession ticket in February," as Nashville postmaster the preceding
spring. Declaring that he could not continue to hold the post "in a manner compromising my own self-respect," he asked that the matter be referred to the President and the
postmaster general. Lellyett to John A. Kasson, May 18, 1862, Johnson Papers, LC.

From Horace Maynard

Washington May 19, 1862

Dr. Sir

The matter of the enclosed scrap, cut from the Intelligencer of this
morning,[1] first attracted my attention, in a dispatch from Louisville. I at
once called on the Secretary of War, who directed me to read the dispatch
of the 17th to send the party to Fort Lafayette. Your reply came yesterday
& early this morning I communicated it to the Secretary of War, who
requested me to submit it to the Prest. This I have done. Whether, I
should succeed in preventing this marauder[2] from being turned loose
upon you again I cannot tell.

We are delighted with the proceedings at the Union meeting in
Nashville,[3] last Monday. Every thing betokens an early restoration of
our devoted state.

Mr. Stanton directed me to say to you in respect to Col. Wood & Capt.
Harris, to dispose of them as you thought proper,[4]—leaving the matter
entirely to your judgment & discretion.

As to our prisoners he is waiting the result of the expected battle at
Corinth before acting—then he will adopt your policy—

The report I sent you from Cumberland Gap, turns out to be unfounded. Still they seem to be delayed a long time there, to very little
purpose.

I am requested to ask permission for Capt. Vincent Myers,[5] Compy C.
1st Regt. E. Tenn. Vols. to raise a regiment, on the condition that if he
succeeds, he has a commission as Col; if he fails, nothing. You recollect he
was elected last August, to the Senate from the counties of Grainger,
Union, Claiborne, Campbell & Anderson; & directly after the election
went to Ky— He thinks that he in connection with one of the Huddle-
ston boys,[6] could raise a regt. & he is probably right. If you accede to his
request, a letter would reach him at Barbourville.

Edward Trigg writes & joins in asking my interposition in his behalf.—that is a Col's commission to John Williams, to himself a Lt. Colonel's. Williams would make a fine officer,[7] I am sure, & you are well acquainted with young Trigg.

Mr. Trigg (C. F.) is still here convalescing slowly— He receives frequent letters from the Tennessee prisoners, invoking his kind offices.

I wish you would call Mr East's attention to the Impeachment against Judge Humphrey's & ask him to furnish me, the names of witnesses & documentary evidence. Let him send the charges to Grand Jury, at the April term 1861.

I am very Truly Yours
Horace Maynard

His Excy Andrew Johnson.

ALS, DLC-JP.

1. Although the "enclosed scrap" does not appear in the Johnson Papers, it can be deduced that it was the notice concerning the arrival in Washington of Maj. William A. Coffey who had been captured by John Morgan and, according to the Louisville *Journal*, would be exchanged for Lt. Col. Robert C. Wood, of Morgan's regiment. Washington *National Intelligencer*, May 19, 1862.

2. Robert C. Wood was by now at Camp Chase.

3. Held May 12.

4. Both were later released, Wood by September 21, 1862, and W. Hooper Harris sometime before August, 1863.

5. Vincent Meyers (*c*1823-*fl*1880), a Tennessee-born Tazewell farmer and lawyer who had attended the 1861 Greeneville Convention, was captain, Co. C, 1st Tenn. Inf., USA, from August, 1861, until February, 1863, when he was authorized by Johnson to recruit an infantry regiment. A militia colonel before the war, Meyers had already organized a regiment "at his own expense," leaving them when he enlisted in the 1st Tenn. The last eighteen months of the war he served as captain, Co. C, 1st Tenn. Lgt. Arty. Btn. 1870 Census, Tenn., Claiborne, 11th Dist., 2; (1880), 13; *OR*, Ser. 1, LII, Pt. I, 169; *Tenn. Adj. Gen. Report* (1866), 21, 655, 658; Camp Cumberland, Ky., Officers to Johnson and Maynard, February 27, 1862, Johnson Papers, LC; CSR, RG94, NA.

6. Not identified.

7. Williams was never commissioned.

To Horace Maynard

Nashville, Tenn.
May 19th 1862.

Hon. Horace Maynard, M. C.
Washington City, D C

Please go to the Post Master General and say to him that A. V. S. Lindsley ought to be appointed Post Master at this place at once. It is not necessary for me to give you or Post Master General reasons why the present incumbent[1] should be removed. They are well known to you and you will communicate them to the Post Master General. The appointment ought never to have been made. Leaving all prior objections out of view, there has been recent cause sufficient for his discontinuance. He has become worse and worse, until it has reached that point at which it is no longer tolerable.

You will remember that Mr. Etheridge promised again and again that if we were dissatisfied with Lellyett he would make him resign. Maynard—he will not do, and let the appointment of Lindsley be made without delay. All is going on well here. The Union meeting is having a fine influence.

Mr. Lindsley as you are aware has been recently appointed mail agent for the P. O. Department. If he is now appointed Post Master we can get along without an agent for the present as he will discharge the duties of both. Acknowledge the receipt hereof[.]

Andrew Johnson

Tel draft, DLC-JP.
  1. John Lellyett was replaced in early June by Lindsley.

From J. B. Williams[1]

Cheatham Co May 20th 62

To his Excellency Andrew Johnson
Governor of Tenessee
Sir

We are indeed loth to chide your course, yet we feel it incummbent on us as supporters of the cause to which you profess such unbounded devotion to offer a protest against the measures you have seen proper to inculcate and encourage amongst us[.]

The union feeling has ever been good in this county[2] and the disclaimants of same have looked forward to your advent, and administration with an abiding faith; which to our utter dismay seems all in vain, for you must have ascertained ere this, of the organization of secret clans wherewith our property is destroyed or taken from us and devoted to the rebel cause, you are not unaware of the fact that there is a large amount of Confederate property in the county; you are not ignorant of the transportation of soldiers from our vicinity to the rebel army; you must certainly know that there is conspiracy in process against you and your government and which if not checked will prove disastrously to our cause[.]

Here, in our midst, you are tolerating things which the rebel leaders would punish as a high crime if committed by union men[.]

Here, our young men are paid inormous sums by the wealthy rebel to go in their army. Here our poor widows deprived of the sheer protection of a fifteen year old boy, by the temptation, held by rebels.

All this is carried on under the nose of our long wished for Andrew Johnson[.]

Now we wish to know if there is no alleviation from such a condition; why not send out a body of soldiers and arrest these rebels together with their property, leaving a competency for their families but hold the other in reserve for the indemnity of loyal citizens[.]

These are suggestions for your better judgement which I sincerely hope will prove beneficial, and I am confident you can find men to lead an expedition through this country and conduct it in such a manner as to be of great advantage to our cause without deleterious effect on the people[.]

There are no mails or I would ask you to write me your views on the subject,   However I will endeavour to come over as soon as I can leave without exciting suspicion,   being a union man I have to stay close in order to avoid suspicion and perhaps cruel assassination[.]

Respectfully
J. B. Williams

ALS, DLC-JP.

1. Although correspondent's signature is clearly "J. B.," the Williams has not been positively identified. There are two possibilities. The first is J. B. Williams, aged fifty, with real property of $1,656 and personalty of $700, including nine slaves, and living in Montgomery County "N & E of Cumberland River." The second is James H. Williams, a fifty-six-year-old Cheatham County farmer with $50,000 real and $48,700 personal property, including thirty-seven slaves; he was a former postmaster at Onecho, located on the border between Cheatham and Montgomery. Each presents problems: J. B.'s location in Montgomery, whereas the writer is clearly identified with Cheatham; James H., not only because of his initials but also, given his personal wealth, the pejorative remarks about "wealthy rebel." Perhaps the clue lies in a disparity in handwriting between the flourished "J. B." and the pedestrian "Williams"—the latter conforming more nearly to the body of the letter. It may be that Williams, because of the grave personal danger involved, wrote only his last name and the initials were erroneously added later. 1860 Census, Tenn., Montgomery, N & E of Cumberland River, 42; *ibid.*, Slave Schedule, 44; Cheatham, 7th Dist., 77; *ibid.*, Slave Schedule, 13; *U. S. Official Register* (1859), 360*.

2. The available records would seem to demonstrate otherwise. While there may have been strong sentiment during the early months of 1861 for defending southern rights within the Union, by June opinion was overwhelmingly for severing ties with the Federal government and joining the Confederacy. Moreover, no Union military units were organized in the county. Nashville *Patriot*, February 6, June 4, 1861; *Goodspeed's Cheatham*, 956, 960-63.

Decision in Poinier Case

May 20, 1862, [Pulaski]; Copy, DLC-JP.

Three officers of 11th Mich. Inf. [Col. William L. Stoughton, Capt. Henry N. Spencer, and Capt. Nelson Chamberlain], having been appointed by Johnson an investigatory commission, award Isaac H. Poinier the sum of $1,263.88, the value of goods and money seized by John Morgan and associates on May 2, "and order that the same be paid by the Mayor and Alderman of Pulaski or the disloyal citizens thereof."

From Charles B. Gillespie

May 21, 1862, Pulaski; Tel, DLC-JP.

Provost marshal at Pulaski transmits findings of the military commission in the Poinier case; ordered to collect the damages assessed, he has deferred action, inasmuch as "the Mayer & councilmen requested me to put off the execution of the writ until they could see you."

To Martha R. Nicholls,[1] Nashville

Nashville May 21 [1862?]

Miss M. R. Nicholls

Your note has just been received[.]　You desire permission to remove the family portraits of Mrs. Brown[.][2] In reply I have to state that every article of furniture connected with the house when you took possession must remain[.]

There will be a schedule made of all the articles, and their condition when you leave the property, and good care will be taken of them And a strict accountability rendered to the proper Authority[.]

Respectfully
Andrew Johnson

L, DLC-George Washington Campbell Papers.

1. Martha R. Nicholls (b. *c*1842), Washington, D. C., native and the daughter of Isaac Nichol[l]s (b. *c*1790), was employed as a clerk in the 2nd comptroller's office in Washington after the war. 1860 Census, Tenn., Davidson, 5th Ward, 152; *U. S. Official Register* (1867), 29.

2. When Lizinka C. Brown, an old friend of Johnson's, left Nashville in February, 1862, to escape the Federal occupation, she left her property in the hands of Misses Martha and Mary Nicholls, known unionists. Johnson requisitioned the house soon after his arrival. Lizinka C. Brown to General Buell, Grant, or Sherman, February 16, 1862, Campbell Papers, LC; Harriot S. Turner, "Recollections of Andrew Johnson," *Harper's Monthly Magazine*, CXX (1909-10), 172; see also *Johnson Papers*, III, 372*n*.

From Edmund Cooper

Shelbyville Ten.　May 22 1862

Govnr Andrew Johnson.
Dear Sir.

We have in our community a few active talking secessionists, between the ages of 20—and 40—that never have been in the war, and have a "holy horror" of fighting— In other words—they are all "gass", and no "deeds". They are too insignificant to be arrested and sent to Nashville—and yet as carriers of Grape vine telegraphs, they do some harm—

Now, what think you of this suggestion— Have about three or four of them arrested, who are liable to the "conscription act" of the so called confederate states—and send them down to "Dixie"—for the purpose of giving them a chance to act treason amongst their friends—instead of talking it here. They are all cowards—would not fight if they can help it—and yet are always talking.

We could not be charged with tyranny in sending them amongst *their* *friends*—and yet we would get rid of them?

The idea I think is a good one—and will be the most efficient way of breaking up the squad.

One or two of them, that I would select have actualy come here to avoid the "Conscription"—

We are moving along very quietly here, and the cause of the Government is rapidly gaining ground with us.

Hope to meet you at Murfreesboro.[1]

Very Truly Yr friend
Edmund Cooper

ALS, DLC-JP.
   1. The governor was scheduled to speak there two days later.

From Drury W. Parker

May 22, 1862, Camp Pine Knot, Campbell County; ALS, DLC-JP.

Adjutant of the 6th Tenn. Inf., "without imployment about a year on acount of this unholly war" and prohibited from practicing law because he "would not take the oath to suporte the S. C. A. [*sic*] so called," requests a commission to raise troops in East Tennessee.

From Rutherford County Citizens[1]

Nashville Tenn May 22d 1862.

To His Excellency Andrew Johnson
Military Governor of Tennessee

The undersigned citizens of Rutherford County Tennessee, having been arrested by the Military authorities of the United States, and being now held as *hostages*, to secure the safety of Murfreesboro, and as a measure to guard against the repetition of unlawful acts, said to have been committed, by residents of our town, against officers and soldiers of the Federal army stationed at Murfreesboro, and desiring to return home to our families, do hereby pledge our honor, to demean ourselves as peaceable and orderly citizens by yielding obedience to the Constitution and laws of the United States. We will give no aid to, nor sympathize with men who would attempt to waylay and shoot others, but will use our best efforts to discover such offenders, be they friends or foes, and bring them to just punishment— We also express our disapproval of all irregular warfare, carried on in the country by lawless bands, detrimental to the interests of the country, peculiarly annoying to the people, and very destructive of life and property— We further pledge ourselves to use our exertions in favor of these our sentiments, among our fellow citizens, and by the best means in our power, to obtain the co-operation of our countrymen in the suppression of wrongs by individuals, or by bands of disorderly men against the Federal Army, its officers or any portion of our citizens—[2]

D, DLC-JP.

1. The signatories were: G. T. Henderson, John W. Childress, Jno. N. King, Wm. T. Baskette, J. E. Dromgoole, H. S. Robertson, F. C. Mosby, Robt. S. Wendel, Lewis M. Maney, Wm. A. Ransom, Jn. A. Crockett, and Jas. M. Avent.

2. Upon acknowledging themselves "indebted to Andrew Johnson, Military Governor of Tennessee, in the sum of Ten Thousand Dollars," and subscribing to the various other assurances of actions supportive of the Union and order embodied in their petition, the twelve were released. Bond and Statement of Rutherford County Citizens, May 22; Johnson to Stanley Matthews, May 22, 1862, Johnson Papers, LC.

To Abraham Lincoln

Nashville Tenn May 22d 1862.

His Excellency Abraham Lincoln
Washington D. C.

I thank you for your proclamation[.][1] It gives great satisfaction here. The morning[2] Shadowed forth is in good time. Union Sentiment is being rapidly improved here. I hope you will have Richmond & Davis before this reaches you.

Andrew Johnson

Tel, DLC-Lincoln Papers; Johnson-Bartlett Col.

1. This proclamation, dated May 19, concerned David Hunter's General Orders No. 11 (May 9) which placed Georgia, Florida, and South Carolina under martial law and freed the slaves in those states. Declaring the order "altogether void" regarding emancipation and reserving that power to himself, Lincoln further urged citizens to consider a program of gradual abolition: "The change it contemplates would come gently as the dews of heaven, not rending or wrecking anything." Nashville *Union*, May 21, 1862; Basler, *Works of Lincoln*, V, 222-23.

2. In the process of telegraphing, the word "warning" became altered to "morning." See draft of Johnson to Lincoln, May 22, 1862, Johnson-Bartlett Collection, Greeneville, Tennessee.

To William H. Polk

Nashville May 22nd

Col William H. Polk
Columbia, Tenn.

I cannot recognize the election which will be held to day in any manner, and therefore must decline the appointment of any sheriff or Judge for that purpose.[1] In a short time all the vacancies in the various offices will be filled by appointment and elections ordered—that is— when the Rebel Army is expelled and the jurisdiction of the State can be extended. No disloyal person who may be elected for any office in this State can be commissioned or hold his office.

Andrew Johnson   Military Governor.

Tel draft, DLC-JP.

1. "Owing to the absence of the county court which has not held a session for some months," the sheriff-elect of Maury had not been qualified. Polk had requested that William H. Pillow be named "Special Sheriff" to conduct an "important election" which "is by law to be held today" for chancellor and circuit court judge. Polk to Johnson, May 22, 1862, Johnson Papers, LC.

From Daniel F. Carter and John Herriford[1]

Nashville May 23, 1862—

To his Excellency Gov. A. Johnson.

Dear Sir

The undersigned would represent to your Excellency that since an interview held by one of us with you on yesterday, we are satisfyed that you are laboring under a missapprenhension in regard to the courtesy with which you have been treated by the undersigned.

We, therefore, now disclaim any intention of treating your Honor with any disrespect whatever. We understood from the Officer who served the notice upon us, to take the Oath required by the Constitution of Tennessee, that an *immediate answer was* demanded, and in our estimation it was politely given. The Bearer of this note will explain to you the resons why as Bankers, we cannot take the oath required.

We trust that this brief explanation will justify you in placing us in the same category with the other Bankers of this City.[2]

Yours Truly   D. F. Carter

John Heriford

ALS (Carter), DLC-JP.

1. Daniel F. Carter (c1809-c1874), Virginia native with an estate valued at $327,000, had been a Nashville stage contractor before becoming president of the Bank of the Union (1857-62). John Herriford (c1808-fl1881), Tennessee-born stage agent, bank cashier, and later livery stable owner (1875), possessed $11,600 in real and $20,000 in personal property. 1860 Census, Tenn., Davidson, Nashville, 4th Ward, 118; 5th Ward, 161; Nashville city directories (1855-81), *passim*.

2. On Tuesday, May 20, Johnson had sent blank oaths of allegiance to the presidents, cashiers, tellers, and employees of the major Nashville banks. The next day Herriford and Carter "peremptorily refused to take the oath, and were subsequently arrested." Their noncompliance was probably based on an argument used by officials of the Union and Traders' banks; that the specie and assets of the banks, being within Confederate territory, would be confiscated if the officers took the oath. By May 28, however, the two bank officers, reconsidering their position, indicated a willingness to cooperate with Federal authorities. Ex. Record Book (1862-63), Ser. 4C, Johnson Papers, LC; Louisville *Journal*, May 28, 1862; Nashville *Dispatch*, May 22, 1862; New York *Herald*, May 28, 1862; see Letter from Carter and Herriford, May 28, 1862.

Petition from Pulaski Officials[1]

May [23?], 1862.

To the Hon' Andrew Johnson, Gov &c

The undersigned the Mayor & Aldermen of the town of Pulaski, would respectfully represent and show unto your Honor that on the ___[2] day of May 1862 they understand one J. H. Poinier filed before your Excellency, as Military Governor of Tennessee, his Petition setting forth among other things, that he was a good loyal Citizen, of the United States, and as such had brought a stock of goods to the town of Pulaski, where he had rented a store-house, and was selling the same at retail, (when Col John H. Morgan made a raid, into said town, and he & his associates, destroyed the same,) and claiming damages, from said Corporation, for the destruction of said goods,—whereupon a Commission was issued by your Excellency, appointing Col. W. S. Stoughter, Captains Spence & Chamberlain[3] Officers of the United States army, who on the 20th day of May 1862, served a notice upon the undersigned as Mayor & Aldermen, of said Corporation, to appear at the court house in the Town of Pulaski, and defend said proceeding—

The undersigned accordingly appeared and now file a coppy, of said proceedings,[4] duly certified which they now ask your Excellency to revise, having prayed an appeal from the decission of sd Commissioners, which they denied granting, alledging they had no power to grant the same,—

Your Petitioners would ask respectfully to point out and show to your Excellency the Errors of said award and decission,—

1st—Said award purports to be based upon a Military Order, or Proclamation issued by your Excellency as Military Governor of Tennessee, when said order or proclamation leaves date on the 9th of May, 1862, and the destruction of said goods, as shown by the proof, in said proceeding, occurred on the 1st of May 1862,— Said order could not constitusionally have a retrospective effect upon them as a corporate body,—

2nd—Said Petitioner obtained no licence from the Corporation but retailed said goods in violation of its charter, and Ordinances, as will appear by reference to the same, a coppy of which is herewith exhibited.—

3rd—The proof shows the destruction of the goods was by a Military Band, over which they had no control, and too powerful for them to resist, that neither the officers of the Corporation or the Citizens of the Town, had any agency in brining said Military District into Town, or knew any-thing of their approach, until they had entered its Limits—nor did they countenance or aid in the destruction of said goods, and would have opposed and prevented the same if they had had the power to do so.—

Your Petitioners would also state that no Martial Law had been proclaimed in their Town, and they are advised that all civil remedies are & were in full force, in which said Petitioner had clear and ample, and unembarrassed, remedies for redress, if the Corporation had been in any manner liable, and in which forum they are ready and willing at all times to answer,— They would respectfully point your Excellency to the 5th Article of the Amended Constitution of the United States, and to the 8th Section, Article 1st in the Bill of rights of the state of Tennessee,—

For these reasons your Petitioners would insist that they are not liable, and they ask your Excellency to revise and reverse said proceedings, and discharce them from said award,—

Your Petitioners for themselves, and the citizens of said Corporation, would beg leave to represent and show unto your Excellency their peculiar Situation,—

They have no army & no force at their command and living near where the hostile armies are arrayed in civil war against each other, and it being utterly out of their power to prevent the entrance, of either army into the limits of the Corporation, or prevent them when having entered from destroying private or public property, it would be ruinous and oppressive to hold said Corporation, or its citizens liable for the destruction of said property by either army.—

That shortly after, Col Morgan and his Battalion retired, the Federal army entered, and destroyed several thousand dollars worth of property.— Your Petitioners therefore ask that protection which is due to them, as peaceable, citizens, not connected with either army in any manner, or ever having had any connection with the same, They would also call your Excellency to the amount, of said award being Speculative damages or profits,—

Very respectfully submitted

C. C. Abernathy, Recorder

E. Edmondson   Mayor
M. McNairy
James A. Sumpter
J. L. Jones
Samuel Nickolson
John P. Ezell

Pet, DLC-JP.

1. The document is signed by the mayor, five councilmen, and the recorder. Mayor Elihu Edmondson (c1823-fl1886) was a South Carolina-born farmer and druggist with $22,000 in real and $30,000 in personal property; Mark McNairy (1833-fl1886), a Giles County farmer and merchant; James A. Sumpter (c1832-1885), a Kentucky-born physician who possessed $4,500 real estate and $7,000 personalty; James "Lew" Jones (1824-fl1886), a Mexican War veteran, deputy court clerk (1848-55), magistrate (1865), assistant assessor of internal revenue (1865-69), and county judge (1873-c1886); Samuel Nickolson (b. c1814), a Massachusetts-born manufacturer, possessing a personal estate of $12,500; John P. Ezell (b. c1819), South Carolina-born merchant with wealth of $4,000 real and $21,350 personal property. Charles C. Abernathy (c1827-fl1886), the recorder and a physician with $3,900 in personalty, in December, 1862, joined the Confederate ranks as a surgeon, serving until his capture, exchange,

and recapture in the fall of 1864. 1860 Census, Tenn., Giles, N. Subdiv., 180, 188, 193; S. Subdiv., 38, 39; (1880), Pulaski, 24; *Goodspeed's Giles*, 846, 858, 862; Charles C. Abernathy, CSR, RG109, NA.

2. "1st" was originally written and then crossed out, as the scrivener recalled that the incident occurred on the first and the complaint was prepared on some later unspecified date; we have calculated that it may well have been the 14th. See Petition of Isaac H. Poinier, May [14?], 1862.

3. The three men, commissioned by the governor on May 17, were officers of the 11th Mich. Inf. Lt. Col. William L. Stoughton (1827-1888), New York native and Michigan lawyer, promoted colonel after the battle at Stone's River, was wounded at Marietta (July 4, 1864). After the war he served in Congress (1869-73). Capt. Henry N. Spencer (b. *c*1818), a New York native and Three Rivers, Michigan, carpenter, resigned because of physical disabilities in November, 1862. Capt. Nelson Chamberlain (b. *c*1824), a Vermont-born marble cutter and Mexican War veteran, resigned in February, 1863, also for medical reasons. Unsigned commission, May 17, 1862, Johnson Papers, LC; *NCAB*, XI, 399; *BDAC*, 1665; 1860 Census, Mich., St. Joseph, Lockport Township, 197; Monroe, Monroe City, 2nd Ward, 65; Spencer and Chamberlain, CSR, RG94, NA.

4. The proceedings, including the testimony and cross-examination of Miles Goldsmith, nineteen-year-old clerk in Poinier's store, and Booker Shapard, longtime Pulaski merchant, concluded with the three-man commission's decision upholding Poinier's claim "against the Mayor and Aldermen of Pulaski, Tennessee, for compensation for injuries sustained by the depradations of John Morgan and his associates in ther raid into Pulaski on the 1st May 1862" in the amount of $1,263.88, and ordering that "the same be paid by Mayor and Alderman of Pulaski or the disloyal citizens thereof[.]" Poinier Hearing and Military Commission Decision, May 20, 1862, Johnson Papers, LC.

From George W. Morgan

Head quarters 7th Div Army of the Ohio
Cumberland Ford [May] 24, 1862

Gov A Johnson

Cumberland Gap has been reinforced by a Brigade of four Regiments of Infantry one battery of Artillery and four hundred Cavalry and a Brigade has just arrived at Big Creek Gap from Knoxville— Kirby Smith is again at the former Gap—the defences and which have been increased[.] since our last armed reconnoisance two Regiments from Virginia probably forced back by the advance of Cox[1] have reached Knoxville and the Enemy has withdrawn the bulk of his forces from the neighborhood of Chattanooga and Cleveland— I have taken steps to organize a partizan Regiment under Colonel Clift[2] commissioned by the Secretary of War in Scott and Morgan Counties Tennessee in order to annoy the Enemies rear— during the past three weeks there has been rumors of the intended invasion of Kentucky by Smith[.] some of our friends in East Tennessee attack consequence to these reports[.] three of my Brigades threaten the Enemy front[.]

George W Morgan
Brig Genl Vols Comdg

Tel, DLC-JP.

1. Jacob D. Cox (1828-1900), Ohio lawyer and state senator when the war began, became a brigadier general (May 17, 1861) and major general of volunteers (October 6,

1862), serving in West Virginia, Virginia, Maryland, Ohio, Tennessee, Georgia, and North Carolina before his resignation January 1, 1866. He was subsequently governor of Ohio (1866-68), secretary of the interior (1869-70), president of the Wabash Railroad (1873-78), congressman (1877-79), and president of the University of Cincinnati (1885-89). Cox also wrote a number of military volumes, most notably *Military Reminiscences of the Civil War* (1900). At the time of this letter he was operating near Lewisburg in western Virginia. Warner, *Generals in Blue*, 97-98; *DAB*, IV, 476-78; *OR*, Ser. 1, XII, Pt. III, 228.

2. William Clift began recruiting the 7th East Tenn. Inf., USA, in Scott County in early June, 1862. *Tennesseans in the Civil War*, I, 390.

From William S. Pierson

May 24, 1862, Sandusky, Ohio; ALS, DLC-JP.

The commander of the prisoner depot at Johnson's Island requests that the governor not issue "general letters of Introduction, except you state, that an Interview cannot be had"; interviews are allowed only "in cases of humanity, or where for the interest of the Government—"

Speech at Murfreesboro[1]

May 24, 1862

Fellow citizens of Rutherford . . .

In appearing before you to-day, by invitation, to address you on the important crisis in which the country is now involved, I appear, as on former occasions, to speak to you in a plain, frank manner, in the language of soberness and truth. Even as I did in times of party warfare, I will address your brains and hearts, and not your passions or impulses. We are now in the midst of a revolution. But I intend to call things by their proper names. We are now in the midst of a rebellion. He explained the difference between the revolution of their forefathers against Great Britain and the present rebellion against the government of their own selection, and graphically depicted the sufferings of the early heroes and founders of the Union. The audience could not resist some of the eloquent speaker's allusions in this connection, and, as they drew nearer and nearer toward him, they evinced the devoted interest they felt in what he had to say. He reiterated some of the forcible remarks he made in Nashville on the 12th of May, about the love he bore the soil of Tennessee, the adoration he had for the Stars and Stripes, and the fact that while parties differed in former times, they all assembled to discuss their differences under the same flag and to the same music—the flag and the music of the Union. Here there were among the audience a mingling of silent admiration with smiles of satisfaction and nods of approval. As he proceeded, recalling the familiar Union doctrines of the democratic party as enunciated by Jackson, the people became more and more earnest in their attention; and when he declared, in his usual emphatic manner, that the soul of liberty was the love of law, that there could be no liberty without law, and that there could be no law without a constitutional government, an impression was made which seemed to strike at the sense and understanding of his hearers. He declared that since the secessionists sprang up they seemed to think there was no law. They arrogate to themselves their convictions of the law as to the rights of property, and trample under foot the rights of others. Governor Johnson enchained the attention of the assemblage as he passed over and through the history of the political events which preceded the breaking out of the rebellion. He went for Breckinridge because he thought him a better Union man than either Bell or Douglas or Abe Lincoln, and read extracts from Breckinridge's Union speeches in support of his position. He now declared that Breckinridge had proved a traitor. He had deceived him once. That was not his fault. If he deceived him again it would be. He made the same remark with regard to Isham G. Harris.

Governor Johnson read an autograph letter from Gen. Jackson to A. J. Crawford, of Georgia, dated May 22, 1833, in which the old hero prophetically referred to the present condition of things, and placed its occurrence to the doctrines entertained and promulgated by John C. Calhoun for a dissolution of the Union, based upon any cause—tariff, negro slavery, or anything else. The Governor defended the Union soldiers from charges made against them, that they had come here for rapine and plunder and to steal their negroes.[2] He declared that the North and West did not want their negroes; that they had plenty of them already, and wanted no more. In emphatic words he urged the deluded and erring Union men, who had by force or choice joined the rebel armies, to return to their allegiance, and to all, except to the "intelligent and conscious traitors," would amnesty be granted.[3]

New York *Herald*, June 4, 1862.

1. The success of the Union meeting in Nashville, May 12, encouraged Johnson and others to plan speaking engagements nearby, of which this was the first. Appearing in front of the courthouse on a makeshift platform—"a couple of boards on the heads of barrels"—before a "queer mixture of blue coats and butternuts," the governor followed William Spence and Edmund Cooper, and according to a reporter, for approximately three hours, "Over the whole field of local—and a great proportion of national—politics did this inflexible and indefatigable exponent and defender of the constitution and the Union . . . enlist the attention of his auditors." New York *Herald*, June 4, 1862; Savage, *Life of Johnson*, 263.

2. Rumors of Negro stealing by Union officers, abroad as early as January, had become more prevalent by March and April. McClernand's men at Pittsburg Landing were accused of taking "a number of Negroes" belonging to residents of Savannah, and officers of the 7th Illinois at Clarksville were charged with carrying off fugitives. The Memphis *Appeal* in April expressed concern over "numerous outrages having been perpetrated by the Federal forces" at Huntsville: "A number of dwellings are reported to have been burned by the lawless soldiery, and all the cotton in the vicinity . . . has been seized. Large numbers of Negroes are in the Federal lines, most of whom have been forced to leave their masters and homes." Simon, *Grant Papers*, IV, 382-83, 437-38; Memphis *Appeal*, April 25, 1862.

3. Following the speaking, Johnson spent the night at William Spence's, where a guard was provided by the 3rd Minnesota, inasmuch as there were rumors of threats to capture him; it was reported that "some six hundred cavalry, supposed to be Morgan's men, were within six miles at sunset." Savage, *Life of Johnson*, 264.

From Horace Maynard

Washington, May 25, 1862

Dr. Sir,

I received your dispatch touching the Post office & filed it with Mr. Kasson. He will probably offer the P. M. an oportunity to resign & take the route agency between Nashville & Louisville. I mentioned the subject to Etheridge. He said he would have nothing to do in the matter—

The news from Banks Division at last has some thing in it of importance; but unfortunately of a most unfavorable character.

He has retreated across the Potomac, making, as he says, a march of thirty five miles in one day.[1] Pretty good time truly!

The Sergt. at Arms of the Senate[2] goes to Nashville, in the matter of Judge Humphreys. I hope you & our friends there will aid him in the general purpose of his trip.

We have some rather unfavorable news from your city touching the late elections.[3] I hope some of you will write me fully.

I am very Truly Yours
Horace Maynard

His Excy Andrew Johnson

ALS, DLC-JP.

1. During May Nathaniel Banks had been obliged to withdraw up the Shenandoah Valley in the face of pressure from Stonewall Jackson. As Maynard wrote, the Union commander was in full retreat north from Winchester. According to Long, *Civil War Almanac*, 853, Banks did not cross the Potomac until May 27.

2. George T. Brown (*c*1820-1880), a Scotsman who had settled in Alton, Illinois, in the 1830's, was a lawyer, mayor (1846-47), and secretary of the state senate (1855). In 1852 he established the Alton *Daily Morning Courier*, described as "the best and most influential daily in the state outside of Chicago"; after the paper failed in 1859, because it was "too large for the size of the town," he became Senate sergeant at arms (1861-69). Wilker T. Norton, ed. and comp., *Centennial History of Madison County, Illinois, and Its People, 1812-1912* (2 vols., Chicago, 1912), I, 113-14; *U. S. Official Register* (1867), 327; Winifred Gregory, comp., *American Newspapers, 1821-1936: A Union List of Newspapers* (New York, 1936), 115.

3. In an election for circuit judge, held May 22, Turner S. Foster, the Secessionist candidate, had outpolled Manson M. Brien, the Union candidate, in Nashville by a vote of 706 to 570, an outcome, according to Union sympathizers, to be explained by the fact that unionists generally declined to vote, "as they regarded the election invalid." New York *Herald*, May 24, 1862; Nashville *Union*, May 20, 1862.

To George W. Morgan

[May 25][1] 1862

Gen'l Morgan
Commanding Forces at Cumberland Ford, Ky

Both of your dispatches received for which accept my thanks. The enemy has no idea of invading Ky from Tennessee—that is thrown out no doubt for effect. If we had a force to move right upon Chattanooga, it would at once no doubt divert a large portion of their force from the Gap. I hope you will constantly keep me informed of movements towards East Tennessee. My own opinion is that whenever you enter the Country, there will be a general scattering of the rebel forces.

Andrew Johnson

Tel draft, DLC-JP.

1. Although the reverse of this draft bears the date "July 62," its contents suggest that it is more likely to have been dispatched in response to the alarm expressed in Morgan's telegram of May 24. It is possible that the second dispatch to which Johnson refers may have been lost.

From James S. Negley

Hq Columbia May 26th 1862

To Gov Andrew Johnson

Sir—William Biffle[1] of Hampshire one of the nest of noisy traitors in that place now my prisoner admits that he said to the crowd that Andy Johnson should be hung for holding secesh property liable for that of union men[.] shall I send him to you by this three Pm train[?]

Jas S Negley Brig Genl

Tel, DLC-JP.

1. William Biffle (1803-1885), North Carolina-born, Maury County farmer with $22,550 in real estate and $26,818 in personal property, was active in local Democratic affairs before the war. Four of his sons served in the Confederate army. Arrested again by Federal soldiers in November, 1863, and threatened with hanging "as an object lesson, as he was [a] great rebel," Biffle was released through the intercession of Hampshire citizens. 1860 Census, Tenn., Maury, 16th Dist., 229; Jill K. Garrett, comp., *Maury County, Tennessee, Newspapers (Abstracts), 1846-50* (Columbia, Tenn., 1965), 34, 67; Garrett, *Confederate Soldiers*, 26-27; *Maury County Cousins*, I, 658; Maury County Historical Society, *Frank H. Smith's History of Maury County, Tennessee* ([Columbia, Tenn.], 1969), 204.

From Curran Pope

Camp Taylor Huntsville Ala.
May 26 1862

Hon Andrew Johnson
Military Governor of Tennessee
Dear Sir.

I have recd. several letters from you which it has not been in my power to answer, because I have been engaged in so many expeditions over the Country. I requested Dr Talbott[1] our chaplain going to Nashville to deliver to you a list of names I could recommend to you for appointment in Lincoln Co. I furnished to Genl Mitchell and also to Col Jones[2] who relieved me at Fayetteville the intelligence of the escape from the hospital at Lafayette of the person residing in Lincoln requesting their particular attention to it[.]   I trust that Dr Talbott related these facts to you and returned to you personally my heartfelt thanks for the kind and generous terms in which you were pleased to speak of my regiment and myself.

You must believe that I could not receive a compliment from a more distinguished source; and that my friends at home receiving the letter in which you so kindly conveyed it, could not deny to them selves the pleasure of publishing it—[3]

Praying for your success in the great work in which you are engaged, and expressing again my admiration for the invincible spirit that animates you

I am Very Respectfully
Yr obt Servt   Curran Pope
Col 15th Ky Vol

ALS, DLC-JP.

1. Jeremiah J. Talbott (c1835-1876), Indiana native and chaplain of the 15th Ky. Inf., resigned his commission August 7, 1862. Returning to Louisville, where he served as rector of Calvary and St. John's Episcopal churches (1862-67), he eventually settled in Indiana and just prior to his death in Elkhart had established a temperance paper, the *Advance Guard*. CSR, RG94, NA; *Edwards' Louisville Directory* (1866-67), 81; Louisville *Courier-Journal*, September 3, 1876.

2. Ormsby M. Mitchel and James G. Jones. Jones (c1814-1872), lawyer, served as first mayor of Evansville and as state attorney general (1859-61), before becoming colonel of the 42nd Ind. Inf. (October, 1861) and later acting assistant provost marshal general of Indiana (1863-64). At the conclusion of the war, he resumed law practice and served as judge of the 15th judicial circuit. *Ibid.*; James G. Jones (Roseanna Jones), Pension file, RG15, NA; Spillard F. Horrall, *History of the Forty-second Indiana Volunteer Infantry* (Chicago, 1892), 24, 239; John E. Inglehart, "The Coming of the English to Indiana in 1817 and Their Hoosier Neighbors," *Indiana Magazine of History*, XV (1919), 122.

3. See Letter to Curran Pope, April 30, 1862, which had been published in the May 16 issue of the Louisville *Journal*.

From John B. Rodgers

Boston 26 May 1862

Dear Sir

A remark was made in my hearing, a few days since, that led me to the conclusion that it was no more or less than a threat against your life. I drop these lines to post you, look towards Augusta Geo. for it, if another opportunity presents. I intend to know further, & if necessary will advise you,

Yours.   J. B. Rodgers

Gov. Johnson
Nashville Tena.

ALS, DLC-JP.

1. Rodgers apparently was in New England to purchase arms for a battalion he was planning to raise to protect the unionists of the Fentress County area. See Letter from Rodgers, May 4, 1862.

To Pulaski Mayor and Aldermen[1]

Nashville, Tenn
May 26th 1862

To Mayor & Aldermen
of Pulaski, Tenn.
Gentlemen,

I have to acknowledge the receipt of your communication in relation to the claim of I. H. Poinier, and in which you set forth at length the reasons which induce you to ask for the revisal and reversal of the action of the Military commission organized under direction of this office to investigate said claim and make such award thereon as, after hearing all the testimony that might be presented on either side, to them seemed just and proper.

Your communication has received my careful consideration, and I shall briefly reply to the main points presented.

As to your first statement, that the award of the commission purports to be based upon my Proclamation of the 9th May, 1862, while the destruction of property, for which compensation is claimed, occurred on the 1st May 1862 and "therefore could have no retrospective effect upon them [you][2] as a Corporate body," I have to say that the action of said Commission was in no manner confined to cases arising subsequent to the date of said Proclamation, but said Commission was directed and authorized to investigate the case of I. H. Poinier and such other cases of a similar character as might be presented. The issuance of said Proclamation was not intended to operate as a waiver of the right then existing to indemnify Union men, for losses sustained in consequence of depredations on their property by armed bands of marauders, out of the property of secession sympathisers and aiders and abettors in the depredations aforesaid.

The Proclamation of the 9th May simply gave public notice that the course, which had been previously determined on in the case of I. H. Poinier, would be pursued and faithfully executed in all similar cases that might arise.

In regard to your second statement that the petitioner, I H. Poinier, obtained no license from the Corporation, but retailed his goods in violation of its Charter and Ordinances, it does not appear to me, admitting the fact to be as stated, that it in the least affects the award made in this case. For such violation of your ordinances he was legally responsible to the proper authorities, and the neglect, of those whose duty it was to see that the laws were executed, cannot be successfully urged in opposition to such a claim as is in this case presented.

In reply to your representation that the citizens of Pulaski had no knowledge of the intended raid of John Morgan and his marauding band, and were in no manner connected therewith, I have to state that it has been repeatedly urged on the other [hand] that, according to the sworn testimony presented to said Commission, many of the citizens of Pulaski welcomed the marauders with shouts and other manifestations of joy, and some of the merchants of said town actually attended the sale of the goods of said Poinier and bid off the goods so sold.[3] I fail to discover anywhere in the record an attempt to prove that any citizen of the town of Pulaski interceded in behalf of Mr. Poinier and against the destruction of his property, or as a community warned the marauders from its midst, or gave notice to the Federal Authorities of the facts, or manifested in any manner a disapproval of the acts of said marauders.

It cannot be expected nor can it be hoped, that the Government will, in every instance, lay hands upon the marauders committing such depredations upon loyal and unoffending citizens; but it is well known that such bands only go and remain in places when they have sympathisers, who entertain them in their houses, guide them through roads over which they can pass in safety, point out loyal citizens and their property, with the view of having said citizens subjected to depredations and bid for the latter when exposed by them for sale. Such disloyal citizens have brought about and are now, by acts of disloyalty, contributing to the organization and support of these bands. Although they may not personally be present at the origin of said bands, they yet participate in feeling with the object pursued and the results to be attained by them, and many of them openly espouse their cause.

It is regarded as eminently just and proper, both with the view of protecting the private property of loyal citizens and of preventing these raids of marauders, that the communities approving and thus sustaining such depredations upon the property of loyal citizens, as in the case of I. H. Poinier occurred, shall be required in all cases to remunerate to the fullest extent the parties so sustaining loss.

In reply to your last statement in relation to damages done to private property by the Federal forces upon their entrance into Pulaski after Morgan and his band had disappeared therefrom, I have to state that in all cases when the property of loyal citizens has been wantonly injured or destroyed by the Federal troops and the same shall be established by proof, the Government will promptly and amply remunerate the parties so sustaining loss.

The proceedings of said Commission appear to have been in all respects regular, and every opportunity was afforded to you to offer such testimony touching the matter at issue as you should think proper to produce. In fact no irregularity of proceeding or other complaint as to mode of procedure is alleged by you against said Board.

In view of all the facts in the case as presented in the report of the Military Commission, and in your communication, I can see no controlling reason for a reversal of the action of said Military Commission, and therefore must decline to interfere with the execution of the order made in connection with the award of said Commission.

Very Respectfully, Andrew Johnson

Military Governor.

L, DLC-JP.

1. Mayor Elihu Edmondson and Aldermen Mark McNairy, James A. Sumpter, James L. Jones, Samuel Nickolson, John P. Ezell, and Recorder Charles C. Abernathy.

2. Brackets in the original.

3. During the inquiry Poinier's clerk stated "when this cavalry came into town I heard some shouting on the part of some of the citizens in the town"; one of Morgan's officers recalled later that they were welcomed enthusiastically—"the men were wild with excitement, and the women were in tears." According to the testimony of Poinier himself—corroborated by the clerk and local merchant—Morgan and his men seized Poinier's stock and "sold what they could not use to men in Pulaski, who bought them knowing them to be his [Poinier's] . . . property." Poinier Hearing and Military Commission Decision, May 20, and Poinier to Johnson, May 21, 1862, Johnson Papers, LC; Basil W. Duke, *History of Morgan's Cavalry* (Cincinnati, 1867), 158.

From Francis H. Gordon[1]

Jennings' Fork. Smith Co Te.

May 27, 1862.

Gov Johnson

Dear Sir. Your position makes it necessary that you shall be kept well informed as to popular sentiment and movements in all parts of the State. I therefore write you in regard to this section.

Your recent proclamation[2] ruffles the temper of many a busy secesh talker, but it is already showing its influence. The hot rebels, begin to be more guarded, and I think will soon have an eye single to taking care of themselves. *Predictions* that union men will be arrested & hung, which were so common, & were meant as *threats*, have become less frequent since the proclamation. But more is done *secretly* to sustain the rebellion.

On the 13th ult a secret meeting[3] was held at night by leading rebels of the vicinity, at Cragwell's School house near Watertown of Wilson Co. They had a conference with Hardin George,[4] a volunteer of Starns'[5] Regiment, who met them there, returned at once to his regiment.

There are rebel volunteers returning home every day. Perhaps half of those who went from this section are now at home. About half of them express themselves as done with the war. Some speak of returning whenever they can, or may be required. Fully one third of those returned are not willing to take the oath of allegiance to the U S Government, & will not till forced. Most of those returned keep away from public roads & company. They travel by paths & mostly at night. Some keep themselves in hiding places. About one third still have their arms. The neighboring rebel residents, are doing all they can to drive these boys back to the army, or to hold them in readiness to join any marauding bands who may invade the country. Many rebel citizens would give every possible aid to such marauders as John Morgan, but they will do it secretly. No doubt proof could be got, that many rebel citizens aided Morgan's band in making their escape from Lebanon. Many of them do not seem to know, that robing, stealing & arresting or murdering unarmed citizens is unlawful warfare. They do not regard their aid to such bands as being any worse than aiding their sons in the rebel army. They do not regard their aid as treason against the U States. Could you reach every returned volunteer & every resident rebel with a plain talk—showing that all who lay down their arms will be welcomed as friends & protected, while all who join marauding bands will be treated as outlaws, and those who aid them will be treated the same way, such a proclamation would cause the returned volunters to hold up their heads and rally by hundreds to the standard of the Union, while all aiders of the rebellion would turn pale with fear.

Since writing the foregoing, several of my neighbors have come to tell me what is going on among the rebels. The facts they have collected, prove plainly, that terrible & general attack is being secretly planned against the Union men in Tenn. In several localities, bodies of men, from 10 to 30 are concealed in the bushes & fed daily by the rebel neighbors. At one place they swore vengeance against you for your recent proclamation & resolved to resist its execution. At another, they planed to capture Wm B Stokes & myself. At a third they swore to kill one of my neighbors who piloted the cavalry of Lebanon to capture a rebel volunteer who has been acting as a spy. These bands lie in the bushes by day, & are visited at night by numerous rebel citizens. The bands consist of some of Morgan's men, and returned volunteers of various regiments. They are evidently waiting for some general move of the confederate forces. They *predict* (a threat) that Nashville will be burnt, and union men generally will be hung & their property taken or destroyed. They breathe vengeance against you & all union men, declaring that they will not live under U S authority. Two days ago, I learn from a union man of White Co that, several hundred union men of White & Putnam are now hiding out to save themselves, & can not cultivate their crops. I think we ought to organize battallions of cavalry at once for home defence. If this is not speedily done, we shall not make enough to feed our people, and besides many persons will be killed.

Respectfully   F H Gordon

P S.   I think it imperious that a military force be stationed in Smith till we can organize a home force. Many of the secret plotters could be & ought to be arrested, & [run in.]

ALS, DLC-JP.

1. Francis H. Gordon (b. *c*1805), Tennessee-born physician, a founder of and instructor at Clinton College (1833-50's) in Smith County, and a Whig before the war, was a unionist who supported Johnson in the 1860's. 1870 Census, Tenn., Smith, 13th

Dist., 13; *Goodspeed's Smith*, 823, 833; Gordon to Johnson, February 27, 1866, February 4, 1869, Johnson Papers, LC.

2. See Proclamation Concerning Guerrilla Raids, May 9, 1862.

3. Contemporary records yield no information about this gathering.

4. Possibly William H[ardin] George (c1826-fl1880), a Tennessee native and Wilson County stonemason who claimed property worth $4,495 in 1860 and was a private in Co. C, 4th (Starnes'-McLemore's) Tenn. Cav., CSA. 1860 Census, Tenn., Wilson, 12th Dist., 137; (1880), 1; CSR, RG109, NA.

5. James W. Starnes.

From Thomas C. James

Hdqrs Clarkville
May 27 1862

To Hon Adrw Johnson

Judge Turner[1] is here, & proposes to hold a criminal court tomorrow[.] is this all right[?]   the matters I spoke of to you are in train & will be completed by tomorrow or next day.[2] This afternoon I found & took twenty three new double Barreled guns secreted in this place & belonging [to] the confederate Gov't[.]

Thomas C James
Col 9th Regt Pa Cav

Tel, DLC-JP.

1. William K. Turner (c1804-1871), North Carolina-born Clarksville lawyer, was attorney general for the 7th and 10th judicial districts (1829-39), state representative (1839-41), and criminal court judge for Davidson, Montgomery, and Rutherford counties (1848-62). Replaced in 1862, he built a lucrative criminal law practice in Nashville before serving as Davidson County court judge (1870-71). McBride and Robison, *Biographical Directory*, I, 743; Nashville *Union and American*, August 11, 1871.

2. Johnson's reply asked James to send Turner a copy of the oath which the governor had previously supplied. James did so and reported that Turner took the oath, which he was sending to the governor. Johnson to James, May 27, and James to Johnson, May 28, 1862, Johnson Papers, LC.

From Marcellus Mundy

Department of the Ohio
Pulaski May 27 1862

To Brig Genl Johnson
Mil Govr. Tenn.

If the award of the military commission in Poinier Case should be set aside by executive clemency[1] or even have its execution retarded, the wise policy inaugurated by you in such cases will have its essence[.]   This single case if promptly executed will stay further outrages & save future trials[.]   Cotton, merchants & others receive passes to this point upon simple pledge of honor not to give information to the enemy, the oath in their passes being erased. I have instructed the Provost Marshal here not to countersign such passes. If a man cant swear he ought to stay at home &

harpies following upon the very heels of our army for speculation, gain above all others should be sworn[.]   Merchants & others trading in cotton are also bringing in quantities of salt here for rebels who still denounce our Govt.   this in my opinion is wrong & in no case should cotton buyers be permitted to deal in salt[.][2]

Respectfully   M. Mundy
Col. Comdg

Tel, DLC-JP.
    1. Johnson replied that he would not "interfere with the action of [the] Military Commission"; he also concurred in Mundy's opinion regarding the permit system. Johnson to Mundy, May 27, 1862, Johnson Papers, LC.
    2. Salt, smuggled or traded in considerable quantities, had gone to supply Confederates in McMinnville. General Halleck, however, concerned about the civilian population, considered the exchange of cotton for provisions and salt a necessity and on June 21 opened the Tennessee River to all trade except contraband. Futrell, Federal Trade, 67, 76.

From Daniel F. Carter and John Herriford

Nashville May 28th 1862

To His Excellency Govr Andrew Johnson
Dr. Sir

The undersigned would respectfully represent to your Honor, that for some time we have been engaged in private Banking in this City. Since the suspinsion of specie payments by the Banks in Tennessee, we have done no business, save in taking steps to redeem our Circulation, and pay Depositors[.]   Our Circulation is now small. The assetts of our Banks is some what scattered. The Bonds, belonging to the Bank, being in the Bank of Tennessee (53) South[.][1]

Since the advent of the Federal Army we have regarded ourselves under the Federal laws, and have done nothing to prejudice the arms or Government of the United States. We are anxious to remain here with our Families and willing at present to forego the privelege of Banking except to wind up by redeeming the Circulation in the hands of the Community, and in the mean time we are willing to enter into an obligation to obey the laws and Government of the United States with security for the faithful performance of the same[.]

Very Respectfully   D F Carter
John Herriford

ALS (Carter), DLC-JP.
    1. Monetary distress, largely a result of the panic of 1857 and the failure of the Bank of Tennessee to provide adequate services to private citizens, continued in spite of banking reforms enacted by the 1859-60 General Assembly. For example, the suspension of specie payments without penalty until July 1, 1862, was allowed by an 1860 act. In the 1861-62 preparations for war, the payment of Confederate war taxes led to large issues of state bonds. When private subscriptions were not forthcoming, Governor Harris, under threat of closure or receivership, forced the privately-owned Union and Planters' banks to join the Bank of Tennessee in the first bond issues. After the fall of

Donelson, the assets of the Bank of Tennessee were moved first to Columbia, then to Chattanooga, and subsequently (1863) to Georgia, an action permitted by a March 15, 1862, statute which provided that "should any Bank of this State apprehend an attack upon the town or city where they are located . . . the said Bank shall have the privilege and right to make such removal, and shall have full power to conduct their business at the point to which they may have removed." Campbell, *Banking in Tennessee*, 152-62; *Singleton's Nashville Directory* (1865), 101; *Tenn. Acts*, 1861-62, Ch. LI.

From Alexander W. Moss

May 28, 1862, Franklin; ALS, DLC-JP.

Invites Johnson to speak at Franklin and recommends Simeon Shy, "a most uncompromising union man notwithstanding . . . having three Sons in the rebel army," for sheriff.

From Edwin D. Phillips[1]

Savannah May 28 1862

To Gov Johnson Nashville

Sir

You will commission three (3) men to Officer Company to guard and patrol *Menarey* [McNairy] Henderson and east part of Harden Counties[.] the people are suffering very much by oppression of rebel people[.] they have offered to furnish horses Waggons and Forage for one hundred Union men if they will guard their property and fight the rebels back[.] there is large amount Cotton in Secesh hands and Union mens cotton been burned[.]

I can get Guns ammunition here at Arsenal[.] Commander of Post says will issue them on my receipt providing I get permission from you to do work[.] if you will do this the men will enlist for three (3) years or during the war[.] all we ask is three (3) months to act as Scouts in those counties and then they will go into Infantry[.] they will want [to] draw pay from the date they Organized into company and mustered as such[.] answer quick.

Capt Phillips

Tel, DLC-JP.

1. Edwin D. Phillips (1827-1864), a New York native and currently captain, 1st U. S. Inf., was a West Point graduate (1852) who had seen frontier duty in Texas (1853-61). Captured at Matagorda Bay in April, 1861, he wrote a book on his experiences—*Texas, and Its Late Military Occupation and Evacuation* (1862). Briefly an instructor at West Point (1861-62), he was engaged in action at Corinth and Vicksburg before his death at New Orleans. George W. Cullum, *Biographical Register of the Officers and Graduates of the U. S. Military Academy* (2 vols., New York, 1868), II, 332.

From Jordan Stokes

Lebanon May 28th 1862.

Gov. Andrew Johnson.

Dear Sir:

I am informed that Captain Bass & Lieutenant Hamilton[1] have been arrested and are now in custody in the city of Nashville. I understand that they are willing to take the oath of allegiance & give bond for their faithful compliance with the terms of the oath. I feel more than an ordinary interest in the two cases taking this course. I had succeeded with the assistance of others in making an arrangment for quite a number of Captain Bass' company to come before Maj. Jordan[2] in command at this place & comply with the requirements of the Government, and the fulfillment of the arrangement has been delayed in consequence of the absence of Maj. Jordan. Our Union friends here were greatly delighted at the prospect of making so many loyal citizens from this Company. It was confidently expected by me that Capt. Bass & all his affairs would take the same course. I was much surprised to hear of the arrest— Dr. Knight & Mr. Cox[3] who go to Nashville as friends & neighbors of Bass & Hamilton, will explain to you the purpose of Bass & Hamilton in visit to the South, & I think you may rely fully on the truthfulness of their statments. I fear it will do the Union cause serious harm in this county if Bass & Hamilton are not released on taking the oath & giving bond. It may and will no doubt drive other returned soldiers from the county back into the rebel army, & prevent many from coming home who now intend to do so on the first good chance they have to make their escape.

I hope you will concur in my view of the two cases and use your influence in getting Bass & Hamilton discharged in the condition mentioned.

Yours truly: Jordan Stokes

ALS, DLC-JP.

1. Robert C. Bass (b. c1829) and Sumner C. Hamilton (c1821-fl1880), captain and 2nd lieutenant of Co. B, 2nd Tenn. (Smith's) Cav., CSA, were native Tennesseans and Wilson County farmers with property valued at $6,700 and $6,705 respectively. 1860 Census, Tenn., Wilson, 14th Dist., 233; 17th Dist., 67; (1880), 14th Dist., 24; CSR, RG109, NA.

2. Thomas J. Jordan (c1821-1895), Pennsylvania lawyer mustered in as major, 9th Pa. Cav., in August, 1861, was brevetted brigadier of volunteers in February, 1865. Ordered to pursue the Confederate raiders after Morgan took Cave City, Kentucky (May 11, 1862), Jordan was captured by Morgan at Tompkinsville on July 9 and imprisoned for five months. Returning to active duty, he later commanded a cavalry brigade under Sherman. After the war he was variously employed as an assessor and lumber merchant in Harrisburg and at the Philadelphia post and mint offices. CSR, RG94, NA; Boatner, *Civil War Dictionary*, 446; *OR*, Ser. 1, X, Pt. I, 914; Ser. 2, IV, 915; John W. Rowell, *Yankee Cavalrymen: Through the Civil War with the Ninth Pennsylvania Cavalry* (Knoxville, 1971), 21, 67, 221, 260; *Harrisburg City Directory* (1867-68), 89.

3. Sampson Knight (b. c1811) was a Tennessee-born physician possessing $3,925 in real and $9,505 in personal property. It has not been possible to determine which of the twelve adult Coxes in Wilson County accompanied Knight. 1860 Census, Tenn., Wilson, 13th Dist., 199.

From James S. Negley

Columbia Tenn May 29 1862

To Gov Andrew Johnson

I beg leave to respectfully intimate to you that I am fearful of the success of your union meeting here on Monday[.][1]   the Secessionists are flushed with the apparent success of their troops in Virginia[2] are very active in intimedating the Union men[.] public mind is in deep suspence relative to approaching conflict[.] many false reported have been lately circulated in the country to prevent the country people coming to town[.] the presence of a considerable scattered force of rebel Cavalry in the lower counties will effect these there[.] further a large portion of my command will be absent following up a reported large force near Winchester[.] with this information I hope you will be able to dictate the best policy & advise me[.] I leave tonight[.]

Jas S Negley Brig Genl

Tel, DLC-JP.

1. This meeting, held the following Monday, June 2, had few Columbia townspeople in attendance, the crowd consisting mainly of residents of the surrounding rural area and thirteen carloads down from Nashville. Johnson spoke for about two hours; former Governor Neill S. Brown declared that the rebellion, which he had earlier supported, had failed. Nashville *Union*, June 3, 1862.

2. "Stonewall" Jackson had recently defeated Nathaniel P. Banks in the Shenandoah Valley.

From Thomas C. James

Clarksville Tenn.
May 31, 1862

Hon Andrew Johnson
Governor of Tennessee
Dear Sir

I wrote you that I had arrested those persons accused of aiding the Rebel officer to Burn the R Road Bridge over the Cumberland River—[1]   To day I have rec'd orders to move to Bowling Green Ky & take command of that post with four companies of cavalry & shall leave immediately— The prisoners I have turned over to Col. R. Mason[2] 71 Regt Ohio Vols. to be sent to you whenever wanted— Enclosed I send depositions of O. M Blackman, G. C. Breed, T. W. Holte—[3] Messers Dortch & Martin have handed me the enclosed statements which they desired me to send to you with the other depositions—[4] Mr Blackman states that he can when wanted bring forward other important witnesses— I have requested Col Mason to arrest Phillip A V Johnson[5] so soon as he returns from Memphis where he has gone as requested to look for a negro that was carried off by the Rebels[.]

I am sorry to leave this department where I think so much good work is to be done & hope I shall ere long get back to it— Mr Shackleford[6] a prominent Lawyer here in a conversation of some length told me that he had been very much through this & the adjoining counties & that he had seen a decided & growing feeling particularly among the farmers in favour of a return to allegiance to the government of the United States or a reconstruction—that they are tired of the war[.]

I have within the two last weeks noticed the same feeling[.]

With my best wishes for your welfare & for a speedy restoration of the Union I am

Very Respectfully Yr Mo obt Servt

Thomas C. James

Lt Col 9th Regt Pa. Cav

ALS, DLC-JP.

1. Acting on orders from Albert Sidney Johnston and John B. Floyd, a Confederate officer with several of his men and some local sympathizers set fire to the railroad bridges over the Cumberland and Red rivers near Clarksville on February 19-20 just after the arrival of Union gunboats on their way to Nashville. Part of one span of the Cumberland bridge was damaged; the bridge over the Red River was destroyed. *OR-Navy*, Ser. 1, XXII, 619-20; Memphis *Appeal*, March 2, 1862; affidavit of O. M. Blackman, May 29, and George D. Martin to Thomas C. James, May 31, 1862, Johnson Papers, LC.

2. Rodney Mason (b. *c*1824), a Springfield lawyer, became colonel, 71st Ohio Inf., before two incidents forced him from the service. At Shiloh on April 6, claiming that his troops suffered from newness in the field, he had retired with his entire regiment; on August 18, he surrendered Clarksville to Confederate guerrillas without a shot being exchanged. Cashiered August 22, because of conduct described by the governor as "not only humiliating, but disgraceful in the extreme," he later persuaded President Johnson to reverse the order, March 22, 1866. *OR*, Ser. 1, X, Pt. I, 261-62; XVI, Pt. II, 388; Whitelaw Reid, *Ohio in the War: Her Statesmen, Her Generals, and Soldiers* (2 vols., Cincinnati, 1868), II, 407; 1860 Census, Ohio, Clark, Springfield, 4th Ward, 157.

3. O. M. Blackman (*c*1820-*fl*1880), an Ohio-born Clarksville merchant, farmer, and real estate agent, T. W. Holte (b. *c*1823), a Tennessean and mechanic, and Gilbert C. Breed, superintendent of the railroad at Clarksville, all testified that they had protested the bridge-burning on the grounds that it would serve no military purpose. Transportation already had been disrupted on the Memphis branch line through the destruction of another key bridge; moreover, on February 16 a few days before the bridges were burned, Clarksville had been abandoned by the Confederates. 1860 Census, Tenn., Montgomery, Clarksville, 29, 56; (1880), 12th Dist., 10; affidavits of Holte, Blackman, and Breed, May 28, 29, 30, 1862, Johnson Papers, LC; Memphis *Appeal*, March 2, 1862.

4. Accused by Blackman, Breed, and Holte of complicity in the bridge-burning, William T. Dortch and George D. Martin denied any involvement, proclaiming their "strict neutrality" in the matter. Dortch (*c*1833-*fl*1911), a Clarksville merchant, mill owner, and real estate agent with $31,000 worth of property, and Martin (b. *c*1834), a farmer who possessed wealth of $56,300, had been active in the local State Rights party in 1861. James arrested them two days after this letter for "supporting the Rebel officer in burning [the] Cumberland river bridge." 1860 Census, Tenn., Montgomery, Clarksville, 83, 116; *Who's Who in Tennessee* (Memphis, 1911), 75; Titus, *Picturesque Clarksville*, 98-99; Dortch and Martin to Thomas C. James, May 31, and James to Johnson, June 2, 1862, Johnson Papers, LC.

5. Phillip A. V. Johnson (b. *c*1822), a Tennessee-born farmer with nearly $44,000 in real and personal property, was implicated directly in the episode by Blackman's statement, corroborated by Holte and Breed. 1860 Census, Tenn., Montgomery, Clarksville, 43; affidavits of Holte, Blackman, and Breed, May 28, 29, 30, 1862, Johnson Papers, LC.

6. James O. Shackelford (1809-1880), a Nashville native, reared in Missouri and educated at Transylvania College, began his law practice in Tennessee at Dover. Settling in Clarksville in the late 1830's, he was a political foe of Johnson before the war. Although he opposed secession, Shackelford, according to one source, "rendered valuable service at home" to the Confederate cause. Appointed by Brownlow to the supreme court (1865-69), he subsequently practiced law in Nashville until his retirement (1875) to Denver. John W. Green, *Lives of the Judges of the Supreme Court, 1796-1947* (Knoxville, 1947), 158-62; Shackelford to Johnson, December 23, 1860, Johnson Papers, LC.

From John B. Rodgers

Norwalk Ct. 31 May 1862

Gov. Johnson

Sir. I have concluded (after the conduct of certain citizens in the mountain region contiguous to my residence) to say to the Sec. of War that if he will authorise me to organise a home troop of men say some 300—that I will aid you in Setting things right and keep it so in the region round about my residence—Say from Lebanon to the Cumberland mountains, & from McMinnville to the Ky State line. I am not able to take the command and expose my-Self as I would have to do—but if no better can be done, I will take the Command as a Col. & if I do not stop some things that are going on in that region I will give up the Ship— if you think such step advisable—write me to this point & I will forthwith procure Sharps Carbines & forward by express to you[.] I have some here of which I previously notifyed you & which I will forward in due time to meet me on my return— I can procure Colts Navy pistols. I have notifyed the government that I will purchase arms for 300 mounted men if it will pay & subsist the command[.] I mean I will arm & equip 300 men at my own private expense, if the government will pay & subsist the command[.] let me know without delay, what you think of it. private letters from that section of our State, suggest the necessity of some such organization. I know the men & can raise them very quick[.] I go to West Point in the morning as one of the visitors in the Military Accademy[1] & should like to hear from you, on my return to Washington City to the care of Maynard or Clemins— please do not delay—nor do you mention it till I can organise— & I should like some Military force could protect us 'till we organise— regard this as private and confidential for the present.

God speed you on in the good work. I would help you if I could— if I have to go into it I can find 300 men equal to Morgans command I think. I would like to Marion[2] them out of the country. I mean write me two letters one to this point & one to Washing city to the care as before stated of Maynard or Clemins—as also, one to the Secy of war. Let me select the Lieut. Col. I want the man for the place—& I have not got him in my mind & would want a Major also. this would give one field officer to each 100 men. all I would want. I am told there is a certain set of men preaching treason, which has been tolerated long enough. Many personal threats toward me as well as yourself. I want to stop such & can do it, with your aid [to] me[.]

Yours   J. B. Rodgers

ALS, DLC-JP.
  1. On this occasion Rodgers acted as secretary of the board of visitors. *House Ex. Doc.* No. 21, 37 Cong., 3 Sess., 6.
  2. Probably an allusion to Francis Marion's guerrilla tactics against South Carolina Tories and the British during the Revolution.

To Robert Johnson

Nashville May 31st 1862

To Col Robt Johnson
If your Mother & Charles get through telegraph me immediately[.][1]

Andrew Johnson

Tel draft, DLC-JP.
  1. Johnson assumed that his wife, recently ordered out of Greeneville by the Confederate authorities, would make her way into Kentucky with her oldest son.

To James S. Negley

Nashville June 1, 1862

General J. S. Negley,
Fayetteville, Tenn
via Shelbyville Tenn
I thank you for your despatch[.][1]   I have just sent it to Genl. Morgan. I hope he can make a corresponding move. If he can, the whole rebel force in East Tennessee can be cut off & bagged. God grant you success in contributing to the redemption of that oppressed and too long neglected people[.]

There is a decided reaction going on here in favor of the union[.]   East Tennessee once redeemed, the State will be overwhelmingly for the Union. Keep me informed of your movements as [soon?] as you can safely.

Andrew Johnson.

Tel draft, DLC-JP.
  1. Negley had informed the governor that he expected to join George Morgan in Chattanooga on June 5, querying whether such a move would be advantageous to the latter. Johnson telegraphed Morgan that Negley's command would march on June 2 "by

two important routes which will relieve for the time the Eastern portion of the State," to which Morgan replied, "My supplies will not be ready before the seventh or eighth inst." Negley to Johnson, June 1; Johnson to Morgan and Morgan to Johnson, June 3, 1862, Johnson Papers, LC.

From Lewis D. Campbell

Head Quarters 69th Rgt O Vols
Franklin, June 2, 1862

Governor—

I find it impossible to go back with you to Nashville to-day.[1] I think I shall be up to morrow evening.

I have some matters here (official) which require my presence.

When I go up to N. I will endeavor to stay a day, and should like to talk with you in regard to the *general* condition of things here, as well as some matters of interest to my regiment and myself[.]

For the present allow me simply to say that I think both my regiment and myself have not been well treated[2] since we came to Tennessee. Of course I do not blame you. On the contrary I am profoundly grateful for your kindness[.]

Very truly Yours &c
Lewis Campbell

ALS, DLC-JP.
1. Johnson, speaking in Columbia the same day, would probably be returning to the capital by way of Franklin. For Johnson's tour, see Samuel P. Glenn's diary in Savage, *Life of Johnson*, 265-68.
2. Arriving in Nashville in mid-April, Campbell and his 69th Ohio were almost immediately ordered south, distributed along a forty-mile line with the colonel headquartered in Franklin. In late June Campbell replaced Col. Stanley Matthews and the 51st Ohio as provost guard. *OR*, Ser. 1, XVI, Pt. I, 76; Pt. II, 72.

From John Francis

June 2, 1862, Nashville; ALS, TKL.

Addresses an impassioned plea on behalf of his niece, the mother of five little children, her husband having been inveigled into the Confederate army by several wealthy secessionists who promised to provide for his family. Not only have they "refused her evrey thing & Eney thing" for support and "accused her of receiveing stolen property from their Negroes," but have also made "threats of hanging & other violence." She seeks protection and "the nesisary aid of sustaining the life of her self & children[.]"

From James Haggard[1]

Burksville [Ky.] June 2nd 1862

Dear Sir

At the request of Mr Jo Ferkin[2] of this County I address you— You will see by the enclosed letter, that his son J W Ferkin[3] is in prisin—and desires to be released. Mr Jo Ferkin is a good union man as there is in Ky— his son marr[i]ed here and moved to your state and was persuaded to join the rebill army—

I must ask the favour of you to get him released as others are released daily[.] dont fail if you please[.] he is verry poor and his family needs his help[.] on last Friday Ferguson and his gang was in Albany 20 miles from here and killed a Mr Story[.][4] Mr Long[5] of this place saw him killed[.] cant we get some help[?] If my brother Col D R Haggard[6] is in your city show him this letter[.]

Please answer this letter, from your unseen friend,
Jas. Haggard

ALS, DLC-JP.

1. James Haggard (1811-1882), Virginia native, was a Kentucky state legislator (1839-41), Cumberland County court clerk (1851-58), and judge (1858-62). 1860 Census, Ky., Cumberland, 2nd Dist., 75; Wells, *Cumberland County*, 110, 115, 118, 194.

2. Joseph B. Firquin (also Ferquin) (1818-1887) was a native Kentuckian and Burkesville farmer with property valued at $2,900. 1860 Census, Ky., Cumberland, 2nd Dist., 76; Wells, *Cumberland County*, 193.

3. James W. Ferkin (Perkins in census) (b. c1839), Kentucky-born Clarksville painter and a private in Co. A, 49th Tenn. Inf., CSA, had been captured at Donelson and incarcerated at Camp Douglas. Exchanged at Vicksburg in September, he was detailed in mid-1863 as sergeant of the guard at the Officers' Hospital, Lauderdale Springs, Mississippi. Captured again at Franklin in November, 1864, he was back in Camp Douglas until May of the following year. In the accompanying letter Ferkin asserted that he had enlisted to avoid the draft and would like "to take [the] Oath and go home." In February, 1865, during his second incarceration, he made a similar claim. 1860 Census, Tenn., Montgomery, Clarksville, 157; Ferkin to "My Dear Brother," May 18, 1862, Johnson Papers, LC; CSR, RG109, NA.

4. Possibly Joseph W. Stover who had been a private in the 5th Ky. Cav., USA, before deserting in February, 1862, and who, as a member of the home guard, was shot by Ferguson in April in the vicinity of Rome's Mill, Kentucky. Nashville *Press and Times*, September 6-8, 1865; CSR, RG94, NA.

5. Possibly John Long (b. c1824), an Alabama-born farmer who on the eve of the war claimed $200 real and $100 personal property. 1860 Census, Ky., Cumberland, 2nd Dist., 14.

6. David R. Haggard (c1817-fl1875), Kentucky native, was a physician and farmer with $14,000 in real and personal property in 1860. A state legislator (1844-47, 1871-75), Haggard commanded a cavalry regiment, formally organized as the 5th Ky. on March 31, 1862, and currently serving under James S. Negley in Marion County. Haggard was discharged as colonel on March 24, 1863. 1850 Census, Ky., Cumberland, unpaged; (1860), 2nd Dist., 77; Collins, *Kentucky*, II, 151, 774; *U. S. Official Register: Volunteers*, IV, 1222; *OR*, Ser. 1, IV, 324; X, Pt. I, 904.

To George W. Morgan, Cumberland Ford, Ky.

Nashville Tennessee June 2d 62

To Genl. G. W. Morgan—

General J. S. Negley Telegraphs from Fayetteville Lincoln County Tennessee that he will be at Chattanooga on the fifth of June Thursday next if he Succeeds & he Speaks Confidently it will be gaining a very important position & will enable you to bag the whole Rebel force in East

Tennessee.[1] There is a decided reaction going on here in favour of the Union— The Rebel Army once driven from East Tennessee the State will be overwhelmingly for the Union— God grant you Success— Keep me informed of your movements—

Andrew Johnson

Copy, OClWHi.

1. Morgan replied the following day that his "supplies will not be ready before the seventh 7 or eighth 8 inst[.]" Morgan to Johnson, June 3, 1862, Johnson Papers, LC.

From James S. Negley

Winchester June 3 - 1862

To Gov Andrew Johnson.

The advance of my command Maj Wynkoops[1] battallion of Pa Cavalry dashed into Winchester this morning scattering Col Starnes[2] rebel cavalry in all directions and are now pursuing them, through the mountains. We surprised & captured Capt A D Trimble[3] the fighting Baptist preacher & four of his Company. It is reliably reported that a considerable reinforcement of the Enemy are near Jasper Expecting to join Starnes regt & attack us. We shall march forward to meet them at once. You will please forward this dispatch to Sec'y of War and oblige[.]

James S. Negley Brig Gen Comdg

Tel, DLC-JP.

1. John E. Wynkoop (c1825-1901), native Pennsylvania contractor living at Pottsville, was mustered in as a major in November, 1861, becoming colonel of the 181st Pa. Rgt. in July, 1863. 1860 Census, Pa., Schuylkill, Butler Township, 84; William B. Sipes, *The Seventh Pennsylvania Veteran Volunteer Cavalry* (Pottsville, Pa. [c1910]), Roster 2.

2. James W. Starnes.

3. A. D. Trimble (c1827-fl1870), Kentucky native and founding minister of the Missionary Baptist Church of Winchester, in 1860 possessed $7,000 in real and $8,000 in personal property. After service with the 8th Co., Tenn. Provisional Arty., and his capture and release, he returned to Winchester. Thomas F. Rhoton, A Brief History of Franklin County, Tennessee (M. A. thesis, University of Tennessee, 1941), 76; 1860 Census, Tenn., Franklin, 1st Dist., 4; (1870), 49; *Tennesseans in the Civil War*, II, 406.

From O. P. Weigart[1]

In Haste   Paducah Ky June 3d, 1862

To Hon. Andrew Johnson
Nashville Tenn
Dear Sir:

On yesterday I dispatched to you an abridged statement of the disturbed condition of affairs in the North Western Portion of Tennessee,[2] and at the sametime desired to be informed on some Points in relation to the Power vested in you as Brig.-Gen. and Prov-Gov- of the State. Not being able to communicate to you by Telegraph all that I desired, I have taken the liberty of writing you this letter, in which I hope to give you a more unabridged statement. Hoping that you will excuse me for my boldness I will Proceed to inform you that the Counties of Henry, Carrol, Gibson, Weakley, Obion &C are now infested with *marauding bands* of Rebel Cavelry very much to the annoyance of Loyal citizens— These bands are mostly made up of Soldiers whose time of service expired under the late Conscript law & Could they be removed or captured this Portion of the State in a very short time would return to its Original Loyalty. The Union cause is gaining ground here though the Loyal men at this time are greatly harrassed. The Federal lines having been extended many miles South of us, which to speak plainly are now in North Ala & Miss, yet behind them we find these lawless bands as well as a Portion of The Rebel Cavelry still *lirk* to disturb the quiet of the country— now as there is not a sufficient force of Federals at this Post (*Paducah*) Hickman, Columbus or Fort Hindman to Protect the before named Counties: We wish to know of you, this,? as Gov of the State, have you not the Power to call upon the Loyal men in this Portion of the State to Rendesvous at some convenient Point—and Organise themselves into Companies & Reg—say for three, six, or Twelve, months for the Purpose of aiding the Federal Troops to dispurse such bands and bring the guilty to Justice so that Peace and quietude may again be restored in this now distracted land—

In this Place (*Paducah*) & Vicinity there are several hundred Tennesseeans who are ready at a moments warning to take up arms and defend their homes from these ruthless Outlaws, Provided they can be clothed with the Proper authority— there are hundreds yes! I may say thousands of Loyal Men in the before named Counties who are now hiding about their farms, in the swamps &c to keep out of the way of these Lawless bands as well as out of the hands of those who Propose to be Regular Rebel Cavelry who frequently Pass through the counties before named in small squads, for the Purpose of running off all the Provision they can & arresting men for their Loyalty to the Old Govn. Some of whom a few days ago were sent to Corinth and shot & Others now confined in Prison awaiting the same sad end. These men will almost to a man respond to a call to Put this thing down, but at the Present time are not willing to inlist in the Federal army for 3 years or during the war, unless they can have Posative assurance that they will be sent into some of those counties to establish a camp before being sent any other direction, so that they may be able to Put these bands down, and thereby relieve their Families from the embarrasments which now surround them. A large number of these men left their Homes in great haste & their families Poorely Provided for[.] They make their living be the sweat of their Brow that is a large Proportion of them—therefore they are in a very critical condition having been run from home about the middle of seedtime & it [is] now about *Harvest* and still away from their

homes— *Kept* from their homes by an Organised band of Two Thousand Confederates in conjunction With a few marauders—Who could be
run out of the country by Twenty five Hundred men—or Captured—
which when done would free the Western District from the Ky line to a
line along the Memphis & Charleston R.R. now in Pos.—of the Fed—
giving us free access to all the Rail Roads and opening a way, for us to
market—

At a meeting of the Tennesseeans at Presant encamped near this Place it
was unanimouly requested that I should communicate to you Our condition and get your advice as to the best course to be pursued by us and at
the same time say to you that (they We were willing to Organise
them(our)selves into *Cos*. to defend their (our) homes, asking of you to
authorise Some One to call them (us) together at some suitable Place of
rendesvous to take command of them (us) for the term of___months as
you think proper or untill the confederates are drivn from the state—   If
the Power is not vested in you to call them (us)[3] out as above named—We
as Loyal men ask of you to use your Influence to have a Federal camp or
two established in some of the before named Counties so that we may be
Protected while Organising Union Citz in Obion & Humbolt in Gibson
Co would be good locations.

To Organise as State Troops or Home Gards we think it would be best to
be mounted on Horseback[.]   the men Propose to furnish their own
Horses,   all we want is arms & amunition and to be Clothed with the
Proper authority to act.

Shudering at the very Idea of forming Co. & acting without legal
Power—

Col. Noble[4] the Com. of this Post (Paducah) says he can furnish us with
guns & amunition such as are used by Infantry—but we wish to be
equiped as Cavely, at least for a while untill we can get the Rebels run out
of the state—

If our country was clear of this Cavelry force we would not ask to be
received as state troops but would Join the service for 3 years if called
upon which a large majority of the Loyal citizens in West Tenn will do as
soon as Fed. Camps can be established—for them to organise in safty[.]
In the condition we are now in I think to call out the Militia or Troops as
before named would be for the best—   Excuse me for (boring) your Pas.
[patience] so long but my Countrymen required it at my hands. Hoping
that your name will ever live in the Harts of the American People I with
much respect subscribe my name as, Friend & Odt Servt—

                                                        O. P. Weigart

Address me at Paducah Ky

ALS, DLC-JP.
    1. O. P. Weigart (b. *c*1832), was a Dedham merchant and farmer. 1860 Census,
Tenn., Weakley, 8th Dist., 213; (1870), 18.
    2. This communication has not been preserved.

3. The preceding parenthesized first-person pronouns appear above the line in the original text.

4. Silas R. J. Noble.

Disposition of Southern Sympathizers

State of Tennessee,
Executive Department,
Nashville, June 3d, 1862.

Col. Stanley Matthews, Provost Marshal.

Dear Sir: Mr. _____, is hereby remanded to your custody, there to remain until arrangements can be made for his transportation South (in connection with such others as may be ready and are required to be sent beyond the Federal lines, there to be left with the distinct understanding that if he recrosses and comes again within said lines during the existing rebellion he shall be considered a spy and dealt with accordingly.

Very Respectfully,
Andrew Johnson.
Military Governor.

P.S.   If Mr. _____, before he is remanded to prison, determines to take the oath of allegiance and give bond in the sum of $1000 for its faithful observance, he will be released on so doing.

Andrew Johnson.

Nashville *Union*, June 4, 1862.

From William B. Campbell

At Home near Lebanon Ten
June 4th 1862

Govr. Andrew Johnson
Dear Sir

The moment of my leaving nashville to day, Mr Hall[1] informed me that you had telegraphed to Washington City, asking an appointment of Brigadier General for myself.[2] with my thanks for your kindness & the honor intended. I must ask you to telegraph to have action on the case suspended at least for the present and until I see you & have consultation on the subject. I am not prepaired to say that I will accept the place, & it ought not to be tendered to me, if I should feel obliged to decline it.— I will certainly decline it unless I shall be better satisfied of the propiety of my accepting it than I am now. I am not satisfied that I could render as much service to the U. S. Government or to our state in that place as in the private station. There are other objections which I would communicate to you on sight—and it shall not be long until I see you. Had the matter been mentioned to me this morning by you or Mr Hall, I am very sure I could have satisfied you of the propriety of at least a short post-ponment of the application,—going on the ground that I could serve our country. But I am opposed to any thing like an application on my behalf being made to the Government at Washington,—for *I am sure* that unless my reputation would justify an appointment without *my friends* asking it for me,—I certainly ought not to be appointed. But I do not desire that or any other place, unless I shall be convinced of my ability to serve the Government & the State effectively in such position, which does not appear to my mind now. I certainly feel deeply obliged by your & Mr Halls kindness & high appreciation of me, but the thing must be stoped for further consideration or I shall be obliged to decline it—which ought not to be imposed upon me, by the application of my friends[.]

sincerely your friend

W B Campbell

L draft, NcD-William B. Campbell Papers.
1. Allen A. Hall.
2. Telegram to Horace Maynard, June 4, 1862.

From Abraham Lincoln

Washington D C

4th May [June] 1862

To Hon Andrew Johnson Govr &C.

Do you really wish to have Control of the question of releasing rebel prisoners? So far as they may be Tennesseeans[?]

If you do please tell us so distinctly.[1]

Your Answer not to be made public.

A. Lincoln

Tel (in cipher), DLC-JP; RPB.
1. Apparently the President, having for some time received indirectly, through Maynard and Stanton, intimations of Johnson's views concerning captured rebels, had decided that it was time to clarify responsibility on this question.

From Littleton W. Palmer[1]

Dresden Jun 4/62

His Exclency Andrew Johnson

Dr Sir— —

Whereas, the so called *Confederate* Army has taken & murdered the young & brave Farris,[2] a citizen of ours for no other crime, than that, of a *nobel* devotion to the Union & the Constitution of his Country I therefore appeal to you in behalf of his bereaved & distressed family to aveng his death, by arresting & hanging Mclanahan the U. S. Marshall of West Tennessee[3] who has bin Clamoring, & threatening to hav union me[n] shot, hung or murdered in some way or other[.]

The arrest & hanging of this infamous murrelite[4] would be a very Conselicating thing to the Loyal one of this section, I assure you[.] This man Mclanhan now lives near Parris where the gallant Farris was born & raised &, where his broken-hearted wife & kind old mother now lives[.] He is the dog who done all the dirty work in his section, for that *Low flung* pusilanimus brainless up-start I. G. Harris who by accident sneaked in-to the Chair so nobely filled by your Exlency[.]

I repeat the hanging of this infamus scamp would be moust agreable[.]

Resp   L W Palmer

ALS, DLC-JP.

1. Probably Littleton W. Palmer (b. *c*1806), South Carolina-born farmer with $1,150 real and $860 personal property. 1860 Census, Tenn., Henry, 8th Dist., 119.

2. John A. Farris (b. *c*1833), a native Tennessean employed as an overseer at the beginning of the war, had guided Federal troops through Paris on March 11. For this he was seized and hanged by southern sympathizers, leaving his wife Frances A. (b. *c*1838), at least one child, and his mother Elizabeth H. (b. *c*1806), a seamstress. *Ibid.*, 1st Dist., 18; 19th Dist., 323; Roger R. Van Dyke, A History of Henry County, Tennessee, through 1865 (M.A. thesis, University of Tennessee, 1966), 104.

3. Hampden McClanahan (b. *c*1830), a native Tennessean with $7,000 real and $10,000 personal property, was appointed in 1857; he had been replaced by Thomas J. Gardner in March, 1861. 1860 Census, Tenn., Madison, Jackson, 35; *U. S. Official Register* (1859), 170; *Senate Ex. Journal*, X (1855-58), 240; XI (1858-61), 352.

4. "Murrellite" was a pejorative household word, having its origin in the activities of John A. Murrell, a notorious outlaw. See *Johnson Papers*, I, 275*n*.

To Robert Johnson [Cumberland Ford]

Nashville Tenn   June 4th 1862

Col. R. Johnson

Henry R. Myers who came from Washington with us left for Cumberland Ford with authority, but not commissioned to raise a Regiment— I have no idea he can raise one, but I had no further use for him & did that to be releieved from further connection with him. You will therefore not be committed to him or permit him to form any obligations upon you. In fine have nothing to do with him farther than civility. He wont do to lie at as an Equal or make an associate of. A word to the wise is Sufficient. Do you hear any thing further from Home[?]

Andrew Johnson

Tel draft, DLC-JP.

To Horace Maynard

Nashville June 4th 1862.

To Hon Horace Maynard
House Reps

I have just returned from Columbia[.][1]   had a good meeting at which Neal S. Brown came out in a long speech took strong ground for

Union.[2] Union sentiment is gaining ground and had it not been for impediments which you are perfectly familiar with everything would have been right in Middle Tenn before this time— I want you to go to the President and ask him for me to nominate Wm. B. Campbell for Brig. General[.] it will exert a powerful influence in the military feeling of the whole state and especially right here[.] you can give the President his character and state the importance of its being done[.] what has become of the appointment of Post Master— Please answer immediately upon your interview with the President. Maynard have Campbell appointed at once[.]

Andrew Johnson

Tel, DLC-Lincoln Papers.
    1. There is no report available of Johnson's Columbia speech of June 2.
    2. According to diarist Samuel Glenn, this was the first Union appearance of Neill Brown, former Whig governor, whom Johnson had pardoned. Savage, *Life of Johnson*, 266.

From Edmund Cooper

Shelbyville June 5 1862

To Gov A Johnson

We look for you tomorrow evening— we have rumors of Col Starnes Cavalry assisted by Col Morgan have crossed the Mountains at the Head of Hickory Creek & are loitering about McMinnville & Winchester probably with the intention of striking at the train as you come up to our Meeting or as you Return— We do not fear anything here[.] we are safe & confident but we suggest to you that you have good guard on the train as you come up and as you return[.] We have advised Col Barnes[1] at Wartrace and Col Lester[2] at Murfreesboro to picket the Road— We will advise you if anything additional turns up— Col Wheat[3] now in command coinsided with me.

Edward Cooper

Tel, DLC-JP.
    1. Sidney M. Barnes (b. c1821), Kentucky lawyer, member of the state house (1848) and senate (1851-53), and owner of Estill Springs near Irvine, made numerous Union speeches in August, 1861, before enlisting in the 8th Ky. Inf., USA. Resigning early in 1864, he moved to Arkansas after the war, serving as a Greeley elector from that state in 1872. 1860 Census, Ky., Estill, 134; *Official Army Register: Volunteers*, IV, 1254; Thomas J. Wright, *History of the Eighth Regiment, Kentucky Volunteer Infantry* (St. Joseph, Mo., 1880), 17; Collins, *Kentucky*, II, 167, 774; Nashville *Union and American*, July 21, 1872.
    2. Henry C. Lester (1831-1902), colonel of the 3rd Minn. Inf., was a native of New York, an 1850 graduate of Hamilton College, and an attorney who settled in Winona, Minnesota, in 1857, where he became district court clerk the following year. Described in a contemporary report as "stupid with fear" and "cowardly" when he surrendered his command at Murfreesboro on July 13, he was cashiered in December. Afterward Lester returned to New York where he worked as a lawyer, civil engineer, "search clerk," and teacher. *OR*, Ser. 1, XVI, Pt. I, 807-9; Walter H. Trenerry, "Lester's Surrender at Murfreesboro," *Minnesota History*, XXXIX (1965), 194-95.

3. Basil A. Wheat (c1813-1863), lieutenant colonel, 21st Ky. Inf., USA, resigned effective October 26, 1862, dying of typhoid fever in Hart County, Kentucky, the next May. CSR, RG94, NA; Pension Record, RG15, NA.

To Henry W. Halleck

Nashville, June 5th, 1862.

Genl. Halleck,
Corinth, Miss.

Your dispatch[1] received, and will be immediately attended to[.]
There are many refugees from the Confederate Army all through this part of the State.

Large numbers of them are coming forward voluntarily & renewing their allegiance, and seem gratified of the opportunity of doing so.

There is a great reaction taking place here in favor of the Union & the restoration of the State. If poor East Tennessee could be relieved, it would produce a thrill throughout the nation. They are being treated worse than beasts of the forest and are appealing to the Government for relief & protection. God grant that it may be in your power ere long to extend it to them. If there could have been more forces left in the middle part of the State it would have convinced the Rebels that there was no chance of a successful rising up and by this time the Disunionists would have been put completely down, and the forces could have entered East Tennessee by way of Chattanooga, while general Morgan would have entered by way of Cumberland Gap, and the whole army in East Tennessee would have been bagged & the people relieved.

God grant that all your efforts in the noble work in which you are engaged may be crowned with success; and the hearts of the people made glad.

Andrew Johnson.

Tel draft, DLC-JP; *OR*, Ser. 2, III, 643.

1. Reporting that two hundred Tennessee refugees encamped near Paducah, Kentucky, desired to organize a Tennessee regiment, Halleck suggested that Johnson authorize them to do so, for "from their local knowledge they will be exceedingly useful." Halleck to Johnson, June 5, 1862, Johnson Papers, LC.

From Henry W. Halleck

Corinth June 5, 1862

To Gov Johnson
East Tennessee will very soon be attended to[.]   we drive off the main body of the enemy before we can attack his other Corps[.]   the head must be attended to first & the toe nails afterwards[.][1] Everything is working well & in few weeks I hope there will be no armed rebel in Tennessee[.]

H. W. Halleck

Tel, DLC-JP; DNA-RG393, Dept. of the Missouri, Tels. Sent and Recd., H. W. Halleck (Apr. 15-July 16, 1862).

1. This figure seems to have intrigued Halleck; over a month earlier, in refusing to detach troops from this army to send "back to Nashville to accommodate Gov. Johnson," he had declared that it "would be releasing our grasp on the enemy's throat in order to pare his toe-nails." By June, East Tennessee has replaced Nashville as the "toe-nails" of Halleck's simile; in each case, it might be noted, it was an arena of paramount concern to the governor. Halleck to Don Carlos Buell, April 26, 1862, Generals' Papers, D. C. Buell, RG94, NA.

From B. R. Peart[1]

Clarksville Tennessee June 5th 1862

Honorable Andrew Johnson Governor of Tennessee.

I do not deem it necessary to make any excuse for the liberty that I take in troubling you with those lines. Read them and if they Contain any matter worthy of your attention consider it, if not Table it, the writer will be satisfied.

The writer has resided here for Several years past, and is acquainted with many of the Residents of this Citty. Humble individual as I am, it has been my fortune (or rather misfortune) to remain here an unwilling observer of Passing events, unwilling, becaus they were not in unision with my views and feelings on Political matters, yet being alone or So nearly alone, that it was not in my power to help myself, or do anything to help others[.] enough of this for the present time[.]

My purpose in addressing those lines to your Excelency is to make a few Statements of things as they now exist as viewed by myself[.]

This Citty and its surroundings for several miles have been intensely Southern-Rights-Men, many of them went in to Military service some of whom were Captured at Fort Donaldson and are now Prisioners, others are yet in service, probably in Virginia;

Citizens that Remained at Home are many of them avowed and bitter Secesh, others say they are Tired of the War and wish it was ended, they scarcely cair how, so it is ended. Others frequently give intimations of Loyal feelings yet they seem to be a fraid to express such sentiments unless they had a better guarrantee of security against Maurauding Bands and Rampant Secesh at Home. The first Class swear loudly that they never will return to thir former allegeance. They also do all they Can to keep up an excitement that there by they may prevent others from doing so[.]

The second Class might and would most probably resume thier Allegiance if the first Class were rendered harmless by silence or removal from among the other two classes[.] The third class are not verry numorous though they would take the Oath of allegiance freely if they were satisfied of safety and Protection at all times[.]

In view of the above facts would it not be Right and proper to Require the Mayor, Aldermen, and all City Officers to take an Oath of Loyalty to the

Government of the United States and in the event they refuse to do so let the Government of the City pass in to other hands. if loyal Men who are Citizens will accept of the vacated places, if not then place the City in the hands of the Militairy. Follow the same Course in relation to County & State Officers and adhere to the present sistem in regard to shipments &c[.]

In order to Carry out the above suggestions it would probably be nessary to have a few more Troops conveniant to this point Ready for action in Case of necessity[.] Such are my views in relation to the present state of affairs in our City & vicinity and now is most probably a good Season for such action as they all [are] wearing quite long Faces,   Those are my own views huredly pened and poorly expressed[.] if they are worth anything well if nothing verry well. All of it is Submitted to your Judgement[.]

pr Chance I may take the liberty of sending a few lines at some other time when more at Leisure[.]

                                        Yours Truly   B. R. Peart

ALS, DLC-JP.
    1. B. R. Peart (c1813-1866), Kentucky-born unionist, was a Montgomery County stonemason with $8,500 real and $3,500 personal property. In May he had represented his county at a Union meeting in Nashville where he was described as an "estimable old gentleman who, when almost every one else grew faint-hearted, stood boldly up and declared his fidelity to the Union," a reference, perhaps, to his having walked out on a violent secession sermon early in the war. When the Federals captured Clarksville, they found, according to a newspaper reporter, "but one loyal Union man. . . . His name is Peart." Subsequently he was elected to the state senate (1865-66). 1860 Census, Tenn., Montgomery, Clarksville, 47; Robison, *Preliminary Directory, Montgomery*, 43-44; Nashville *Union*, May 20, 1862; Louisville *Journal*, March 3, 1862.

From Thomas W. Spivey[1]

                                        Franklin Tenn June 5th 1862
Governor Genl Andrew Johnson Dear Sir I wish to communicate some facts to you which I think my duty to do[.] on yesterday Thursday morning quite early I was siting on a corner of the public Square when I heard William Ewing Bullying James White[2] for having swallowed the word[.] he soon left there in company with Philip Eelbeck[3] and came to where I was and came very near & commenced saying to me that I was a damed raschal[.] I told him his saying so did not make it so[.] he said I had a son[4] in the army a friend of his to which I made no reply[.] he said I [was] a damed Scoundrel[.] I again told him that his say so did not make it so[.] he said he wanted to whip me to which I made no reply but I happened to take my Eye off of his & immediately he dealt me a severe Blow near my left Eye[.] it is quite a bad looking place[.] I raised to my feet & returnd the blow which brought him to the Bricks[.] his friends carryed him off[.] that's all of the fight which is certainly [a] Small matter but I wish to say something about this man William

Ewing[.] he was a member of the Legislature that Voted Tennessee out of the union[.] he left there I think before the ajournment came home & made up a company of horse[.] this Philip Eelbeck was one of his privates[.] my son also Joined them[.] Ewing was elected Captain[.] he returned home Just before the Battle of Fishing Creek[5] & has been here ever since[.] I think he risigned to avoid being Court marshalld[.] he is quite intemperate and I look upon him as a dangerous man[.] he generally carries his arms and when drunk has no discretion at all[.] I am quite uneasy[.] I know nothing about the use of fire arms & am too old to learn it[.] I think Eelbeck knew what he inte[n]ded to do & secretly abeted[.] he beged me not to notice him but [I] made no effort to carry him along[.] I think or it seems to me that such men ought to give some securitey[.] they are a terror to timed men[.] he has nothing against me except that from the beginning of this rebellion I have adhered to the union and am hated and dispised and I say to you now Governor that union men can not live her again while the aristcrats are allowed to keep negroe[s] or the army will have to be kept up every whare[.]

T. W. Spivey

ALS, DLC-JP.

1. Thomas W. Spivey (c1807-fl1872), North Carolina-born cabinet maker, plied his trade in Nashville after the war. 1860 Census, Tenn., Williamson, 1st Dist., 25; (1870), Davidson, 7th Ward, 34; Nashville city directories (1867-72), *passim*.

2. William Ewing (1823-1863), son of Dr. Andrew B. Ewing, served in the 33rd General Assembly (1859-61), and was Captain, Co. C, 1st (McNairy's) Cav. Btn., CSA. It has not been possible to determine which of the several Williamson County Whites was involved. McBride and Robison, *Biographical Directory*, I, 239; *Tennesseans in the Civil War*, II, 148.

3. Philoman (Philip) H. Eelbeck (Elbeck) (b. c1842), a native Tennessean and son of Henry Elbeck, was a lieutenant, Co. H, 20th Tenn. Inf., CSA, resigning at the beginning of 1862. 1860 Census, Tenn., Williamson, E. Subdiv., 1; CSR, RG109, NA; W. J. McMurray, *History of the Twentieth Tennessee Volunteer Infantry, CSA* (Nashville, 1904), 164-65.

4. Richard Spivey (b. c1826), Tennessee-born lawyer, enlisted as a private, Co. C, 1st (McNairy's) Cav. Btn., CSA, in May, 1861. 1860 Census, Tenn., Williamson, 1st Dist., 25; CSR, RG109, NA.

5. Fishing Creek, also known as the battle of Mill Springs, was fought January 19, 1862.

To Abraham Lincoln

Nashville June 5th 1862.

His Exclley Abraham Lincoln
Pres

There are seventy east Tennesseeans now lying in prison at Mobile[1] [many][2] of them the most respectable & valuable citizens of this section[.] They are there simply for being union men[.] They are treated with more cruetly than wild beast[s] of the forest[.] I have taken this day steps to arrest seventy 70 vile secessionists in this vicinity & offer them in exchange & if they refuse to exchange I will at once send them south at their own expense & leave them beyond our lines with the distinct understanding that if they recross or come again within said lines during the existing rebellion they shall be treated as spies and with death[3] accordingly[.][4]

Does this meet your approval[?][5] It is no punishment now to send secessionist north[.] in most instances they would rather go to the Infernal regions than to be sent south at this time[.] Everything is moving on well. We are having large union meetings[6] which are doing the work of restoration with fine effect[.]

Andrew Johnson

Tel, DLC-Lincoln Papers; DLC-JP; DNA-RG107, Tels. Recd., Sec. of War, Vol. 15 (June 6-16, 1862).
   1. While most of the East Tennesseans originally were incarcerated in Tuscaloosa, some had been transferred to Mobile. Hurlburt, *Bradley County*, 115.
   2. Found in Johnson's draft, but omitted in the several telegraphic versions.
   3. "With death" represents a telegrapher's error; the sender's version reads "dealt with."
   4. Several days later Johnson sent a similar wire to Halleck, asking him to "make some arrangement through Beauregard to have them [the Tennesseans] all released," advising him that he had "arrested a number of traitors here who will be released or handed over in exchange for them," and reiterating, "Traitors in this region would now rather be sent to the infernal regions than to be sent South." Johnson to Halleck, June 9, 1862, Johnson Papers, LC.
   5. The President replied, "I certainly do not disapprove the proposition[.]" Lincoln to Johnson, May [June] 9, 1862, *ibid*.
   6. The governor was in the midst of speaking at Union rallies in Middle Tennessee.

To Abraham Lincoln

Nashville June 5 1862.

To His Excellency Abraham Lincoln
Prest.

In reply to your dispatch asking if I desired the Control of the Question of releasing rebel Tennessee prisoners & requesting a distinct answer I have to state that I do believe we can prescribe such terms of release & so dispose of the question as to exert a powerful influence throughout the state in our favor & to a great extent make secessionits dependant upon Union influence though it would impose great labor & trouble upon me & friends I answer distinctly that I do desire the disposition of the question of releasing the Tennessee prisoners— I will add that there are many cases that ought to be well considered before releasing them— Many of them should be dealt with severity while others should be treated with great leniency.

Andrew Johnson

Tel, DLC-Lincoln Papers; DLC-JP; DNA-RG107, Tels. Recd., Sec. of War, Vol. 15 (June 6-16, 1862).

From John A. Campbell[1]

Columbia Maury co Tenn June 6th 1862

Gov Andrew Johnson

Dear Sir   yours with respects[.] I now take the opportunity of writing a few lines to you in my drole maner not being a lawer or a Minister of the Gospil but a mear cobler[2] of a blacksmith and by and by the best Union Man in the County of Maury[.] I have been threatin to be hanged and notice to leave the county[.]   the more they talk about hanging me the harder I cursed the Secesson Movement[.] I all soe Suggest to you a gentleman by the nam of Wm H Pillow[3] as being Sutable for Sherif of Maury county[.] he is a good wan [one] in any posion you place him[.] ther is offersers wanted in our county mity bad that will tend to bisness[.] ther is one parson Cline[4] in the town that is a buseing Every Solger that comes oup and exnoledg his errer and has a bused the Members of his one [own] church for askin genrel Negly to take te [tea] with them and ther is a good ma[n]y more of the Same grad[.] ther is one Y S Pickard[5] which you no very well I Guesss which youst to think that when he died he would goe to you cut in [cutting] oup very largly and ther is many others that is Still talking very larg[.] I allways difered with you in old polltics isues untill you mad your Speeches in the Sinet of the United States a gainst South Carolina[.] I then Stradle the fence with you and lade down all old prejuce satisfied that the Constitution and the union and the inforsment of the lawes was your Moto[.] I refur you to william H Polk to testafey what sort of a man I am[.] I waunt you to excuse my drole way of writing to you[.] I have dun this to let you no how sum thing is goin on her[.] I dount waunt you to call my nam at presant[.] you can find out by Send to Columba[.] they threting me evry fu days So I under stand but I dount ask them any odds[.]   yours respectfully

John A Campbell

ALS, DLC-JP.

1. Possibly the John A. Campbell (b. *c*1817), with $1,200 in personal property, whom the census listed as a farmer. 1860 Census, Tenn., Maury, 4th Dist., 100.

2. One who does clumsy or coarse work.

3. William H. Pillow (1809-1864), a money speculator with $15,000 in real and $40,000 in personal property, was sometime Columbia constable and Maury County deputy sheriff. *Ibid.*, 9th Dist., 2; *Maury County Cousins*, I, 536; *Goodspeed's Maury*, 948.

4. Abram L. Kline (1815-1881), a New Jersey native, licensed in the Charleston, South Carolina, Presbytery (1856) and ordained at Tuscumbia, Alabama, had churches in Alabama, Tennessee, and Mississippi; he served the Columbia church from 1862 to 1866. E. C. Scott, comp., *Ministerial Directory of the Presbyterian Church, U. S., 1861-1941* (Austin, Tex., 1942), 380.

5. Young S. Pickard (*c*1798-*fl*1870), a North-Carolina-born "Gentleman" with $10,000 in real and $60,000 in personal property, was soon after this arrested by General Negley. Subsequently he was a clerk in a warehouse. 1860 Census, Tenn., Maury, 9th Dist., 61; (1870), Columbia, 3rd Ward, 8; see Letter from James Negley, June 23, 1862.

From Stanley Matthews

Nashville Tenn June 6 1862

Governor:

In compliance with your request of this morning I proceed to state the military dispositions which in my opinion are immediately indispensable to the successful progress of your mission as Military Governor, in restoring the authority of the Federal Government and the sway of its Constitution and Laws over Middle Tennessee. This general purpose embraces several results, which may be briefly stated as follows:

1. The dispersion of the armed forces of the enemy, particularly bands of marauding cavalry, and the suppression of all such incipient organizations.

2. The full and complete protection of all Union Men, in every neighborhood, in the free expression of their sentiments and in all steps they may see fit to take, for giving them legitimate, practical operation. This involves the arrest and punishment of those, who not actually in arms, are still continuing to adhere to the Confederate Government and keeping alive hostility to the Government of the United States.

3. The rigid execution of orders regulating trade between the portions of the State under control of the military authority of the United States, and those beyond the lines of the US. forces.

Successfully and promptly to accomplish these results, I would advise, as essential, the following military dispositions:

1. The posting of a large force at Nashville, to consist of not less than a brigade, with a large proportion of cavalry.

This is necessary, 1. To protect the large amount of public stores, necessarily concentrated here, 2. To give assurances of the stability of the authority of the Government at the Capital of the State, & 3. As a reserve, from which detachments can be sent to other threatened points.

2. The posting of a brigade on the frontier between Middle and East Tennessee, with its Head Quarters at McMinnville, extending its defences from Sparta to Tullahoma. This would furnish the opportunity for opening and operating the railway communication with Nashville, and would cover the whole District of Middle Tennessee, from the guerillas that are now infesting and disturbing that mountain region, and disquieting the whole central portion of the state. A glance at the map with a slight knowledge of the country, I think, will abundantly sustain the value of this suggestion.

Respectfully   Stanley Matthews
Col & Provost Marshal

Brig Gen Andrew Johnson
Military Governor

ALS, DLC-JP.

From George W. Morgan

Camp Cumberland Ford, June 6, 1862.

His Excellency Andrew Johnson,
Military Governor, Nashville, Tenn.:

Munday's cavalry, one regiment of infanty, and a siege train of four pieces have gone forward this morning. The brigades of De Courcy,[1] Baird,[2] and Carter, with three batteries, march on the 7th, 8th, and 9th instant. The Pine Mountains are abrupt and steep, and the advance will be slow. My force being too small to divide, and Cumberland Gap having been made too strong to attack in front with less than 20,000 men, I will leave it on my left flank and pierce Powell's Valley midway between Cumberland and Big Creek Gaps. I hope to attack the enemy before he concentrates his forces. I have just received a letter from Clinton giving the enemy's strength at Big Creek Gap at 8,000; at Cumberland Gap, 6,000; at Clinton, one regiment, and at Knoxville 2,000 men. The information is reliable. My force being too small to divide, I have ordered the end of Pine Mountain to be blown into this valley to protect my line of supplies. The route will be obliterated, and every passage threatening my flank will be blockaded.[3]

George W. Morgan,
Brigadier-General of Volunteers, Commanding.

OR, Ser. 1, LII, Pt. I, 254; cipher tel (misdated May 6), DLC-JP.

1. John F. DeCourcy (b. c1821), a British army major who had commanded a Turkish regiment during the Crimean War, became colonel of the 16th Ohio Inf. (November, 1861) and later commanded a brigade at Cumberland Gap and in Mississippi (1862-63). After his resignation (March, 1864) he boarded briefly at the Phoenix Hotel, Lexington, Kentucky. OR, Ser. 1, XVI, Pt. I, 694; CSR, RG94, NA; Ella Lonn, Foreigners in the Union Army and Navy (Baton Rouge, 1951), 283; Williams' Lexington City Directory (1864-65), 43.

2. Absalom Baird (1824-1905), Pennsylvania native and West Point graduate (1849), became brigadier general (April, 1862) and saw action in command of various units, remaining in the regular army as brigadier until 1888. Boatner, Civil War Dictionary, 38-39; Warner, Generals in Blue, 15-16.

3. Morgan later reported that while he had even gone so far with the plan as to have mines constructed, "they were never sprung." Morgan to J. B. Fry, June 22, 1862, OR, Ser. 1, X, Pt. I, 58.

From James S. Negley

Four Miles East of Jasper
June 6. 1862

To Gov Andrew Johnson

Sir. I have the honor to transmit you the following particulars of our engagement with the enemy.[1] I have relived a number of poor union families by imposing a tax for that purpose upon their rich oppressors[2]

and at the same time shall bring you several violent secission repre-
sentions[.]

Jas S Negley Brig Genl Comdg

Tel, DLC-JP.

1. The skirmish at Jasper, June 4. *OR*, Ser. 1, X, Pt. I, 904-5.

2. Negley subsequently reported the capture of several prominent Jasper rebels
whom he fined $200 each with a view to providing a fund to be allocated to Union
families needing relief. New York *Herald*, June 20, 1862.

From Lucy Williams[1]

June 6 [1862]

STate of Tennessee Stward Cty fifth destrick

Mr Ander Jonson Govner of the State of tenn

I want to rite you a fue lines to lete you no of my trobles[.] the lord hath
give me my sone and now he is takin a way a prisner at Chichargo[.] he
was a union boy[.] he took no part in goin to ther Speakins nor where
they beat for volinters for he sayd he never would fite a gainst the
union[.] We can prove that he was a good union boy by owre nabors if
nessary[.] he never went out tel the malisha was calld and was compeld
to go[.]

Geovner I Wish you grate Suckcess in gaining the union as it Wonce has
ben[.] I am as much for the union as you are and So was my litle
Son[.] he was forced to go be cause he was for the union and he never
fird a gun at the fourt durn the batle[.] govner I am goin to beg you for
my Son as I am in hops that it is in your power[.] he is my baby 18 years
old[.] i am trobled all but to death about him[.] if you have got any
Children make a Self Case of it[.] I want you to have him brawt to you
and then send him home if you please and he never shall rase armes
against the north no more let times be as tha will and [illegible] Six more
respectable Citizens belonge to the Sam famly that Says they will go his
Secourity and they are all union men and they Saye they will be nothing
out of your favor if you only will Send him home[.] I begd govner haris
for him but he headed not to the cries of the pore trobled mother and he
may crie yet and not be herd[.] I want you to Simpathise with me and if
you have any Wife you and her converse about this troble and make a Self
case of it[.] I never nowd what troble was tel latly[.] I feel Some times
like I can't live and I can't die tel it is god will[.] if Stward county
belongs to the north why not let my child come home to his own
county[.] govner I Shall depend on you to do the best you can for me for
I dont no what other Sorce to looke too but you[.] if you no of any thing
els that I can do let me no it if please for I dont[.] if I could redeem my
child with money I would do So but I am pore[.] I can do nothin but
beg and the lord loves a beger that truly begs in deed[.]

I will give you my Son s name [Meavenows?] R Williams[.]² he belongs to the fiftyath Tennessee rigment[.]   he is a prisner at Chichargo[.]   if you have a mind to Send me a fue lines direct it to cumberland city to Lucy Williams[.]   no more at present[.]

remains a trobled Mother[.]

ALS, DLC-JP.
    1. Lucy Williams (b. c1815) was the wife of North Carolina native Henry Williams (b. c1804) who possessed $1,000 real and $400 personal property. 1860 Census, Tenn., Stewart, 5th Dist., 85.
    2. Mannius[?] R. Williams (b. c1843), Tennessee-born farm laborer who served as a private, Co. I, 50th Tenn. Inf., CSA, was captured at Fort Donelson, exchanged at Vicksburg, September, 1862, and "lost on retreat from Holly Springs." *Ibid.*; CSR, RG94, NA.

From Alexander Doran[1]

Savanna June 7 1862

To Gov Johnson
Can a citizen who has been an officer in the Southern army Hold a County office[?]   He offers to take the oath of allegiance[.]²

Alexander Doran
Chairman Co Court

Tel, DLC-JP.
    1. Alexander Doran (b. c1802), a Hardin County farmer and Tennessee native, possessed $12,850 in personal and $6,000 in real property. 1860 Census, Tenn., Hardin, 4th Dist., 63.
    2. Johnson endorsed the letter: "Any man who is a loyal Citizen of the United States can hold office. No other can."

From Horace Maynard

Washington June 7, 1862

Dr. Sir,
    Two weeks ago or more the P.O. Dep. sent to the Prest. a communication, in compliance with your wish. He had overlooked it until, I called his attention to it, last night.
    I handed him your despatches asking a Brig. Genl's Commission for Gov. Campbell, with such words as I regarded proper. I presume it will be granted.
    He showed me your two despatches relating to hostages & to the Tennessee prisoners. I am not pleased nor satisfied with the actions or rather nonaction of the Secretary of War touching our prisoners. I think it will come round right, now however. You know how slow our machine works here.

About the other matter, I think the Prest. will direct you, that in administrative details of this kind, you must act according to your own discretion & best judgment. He expresses himself gratified in the highest degree that you do not let them raise any "nigger" issues to bother him.[1] Indeed, with the possible exception of a few extreme men, I think your administration so far has commanded the approval, I might add the admiration, of the whole country. It is destined to place you in very highest rank of practical statesmen.

Now upon another topic, the case of Judge Humphreys. I am desirous to have evidence to make it out, if possible, as strong in proof as it is in fact. Tell me by whom can be proved his action[.]

1. In respect to the property of yourself, Judge Catron, or other Union men

2. In respect, to the whole secession movement, his public speeches, private talks on the street corners & elsewhere, efforts to stir up volunteering & the like.

I wish you would take a little pains in this matter & telegraph me. Do not neglect it, please—[2]

It is fast "going," "going" & will soon be "gone" with Secesh.

How about East Tennessee? I see but little hope. A letter from Edward Maynard to his mother,[3] a few days ago, written from his camp in Campbell Co. Tenn. above Big Creek Gap, gives a gloomy picture of affairs there.

McClellan has telegraphed to know if Chattanooga & Dalton cannot be seized! That would help us some.

Please keep me posted,

I am very Truly Yours
Horace Maynard

His Excy Andrew Johnson.

ALS, DLC-JP.

1. Probably a reference to Governor Edward Stanly's policy in regard to Negroes in North Carolina. A former Whig congressman and a unionist who was also a slaveholder, Stanly had been appointed in May to restore a loyal civil government in North Carolina. He immediately became involved in controversy with northerners who followed the army to set up schools for Negro children. Reports of his closing of the schools evoked a congressional inquiry into the nature of his orders as military governor. Although sustained by General Burnside, and ultimately by Lincoln, Stanly resigned in January, 1863, in disagreement with the emancipation policy. *DAB*, XVII, 515-16; *OR*, Ser. l, IX, 395-98; see also Norman D. Brown, *Edward Stanly: Whiggery's Tarheel "Conqueror"* (University, Ala., 1974).

2. Unless he actively cooperated with the Senate's sergeant-at-arms when that worthy visited Nashville to prepare for the impeachment of West Humphreys, Johnson seems to have been unresponsive to Maynard's pleas for assistance in building the case against the judge. There is no extant communication indicating a response to this, nor yet to Maynard's earlier (May 14, 19, 25) requests. John A. Bingham to Johnson, June 12, 1862, Johnson Papers, LC.

3. Not found.

From Edwin M. Stanton

Washington, June 7, 1862.

To Gov Johnson

The President has received your two despatches of the 5th[.] He approves your proceeding of reprisal against the secessionists[.]   in regard to the release of the Rebel prisoners he holds the question [as] to the time when executive clemency shall be Exercised under consideration[.]   it has always been the design of the Government [to] leave the Exercise of that clemency to your judgement & discretion whenever the period arrives that it can properly be Exercised.

Edwin M Stanton
Secy War

Tel, DLC-JP; *OR*, Ser. 2, III, 659.

Petition from Citizens of Stewart and Other Counties[1]

[June 7, 1862]

To his Excillency A Johnson provisional Governor of Tennessee,

The undersigned Citizens of Stewart County and others would most respectfully represent to your Excellency that N T. Allman, A. A. Willson and R. E. Thomas[2] prisioners belonging to the 50th Regt of Tennessee Volunteers C. S. A. and at present confined at Camp Chase near Columbus Ohio, are prisioners to the united States government, are willing to take the Oath of Alegiance to the Federal Government of the United States and give bond in any amount which may be deemed sufficient with ample securities for the faithful performance of said Oath to secure their release from further confinement and restoration to their friends and families. One of said parties N. T. Allman has past the meredian of life being 42 years of age and is in such feeble health as to render further confinement in prision almost certainly fatal to life[.]   he was Elected Capt of a company in the Confederate Army while at home on sick parole from said Company and confined to his bed[.]   Just before the engagement at fort Donelson he recovered sufficiently to go down to said Fort and tender his resignation which was refused by his commanding Officer[.] he remained in the fort during the engagement but took no part in it only lying in the trenches to protect himself from shells not being allowed to leave——and the said Willson (chaplain) is also in verry critical health having together with said Allman been in delicate health for some time previous to the fall of Fort Donelson, and the last of the above named prisioners R E Thomas is a verry young inexperienced person Just recently married to an amiable young Lady to whom he is devotedly attached and who now languishes in solitary bereavement at his absence and pines for his return home and who is willing to mak almost any sacrifice of opinion to return to the bosom of his family, and all three of said parties having signified their willingness to take the oath and enter into the bonds required, the undersigned would therefore most respectfully petition your Excellency to interest yourself with the war department of the united States to procure their release on these terms. they look upon their cases as rather exceptional, and as the counties from which their Regt. was formed are now all in the hands of the U S. Army to wit Robertson Stewart Montgomery Dickson and Humphreys counties, and as in duty bound will ever petition &c[.][3]

Pet, DLC-JP.

1. Apparently penned by T. B. Rowland, this document carried a total of eighty-five signatures.

2. For Allman and Robert E. Thomas, see Letter from Nathan T. Allman, March 8, 1862. Alexander A. Willson (b. c1821), Tennessee-born farmer and minister, held property valued at $8,869 in 1860. Captain, and later chaplain, Co. K, 50th Tenn. Inf., CSA, he was captured at Donelson and imprisoned at Camp Chase and Johnson's Island until "released by order War Department" on August 3, 1862. 1860 Census, Tenn., Humphreys, 3rd Dist., 73; CSR, RG109, NA; *Tennesseans in the Civil War*, I, 286.

3. An endorsement in another hand reads: "N. T. Allmon is on Parole in the city of Columbus Ohio—A A Willson & R. E. Thomas have been removed to Johnson's Iland Near Sandusky Ohio[.] June 9th 1862"

From Absalom B. Barner and William Odle[1]

Camp near Columbia Maury Co Tenn
June 8th. 1862.

Governor. Andrew Johnson.

Dear Sir   we arrived here the 29th day of may, and was here the day that you addressed the Citizens of this County at this place,[2] though I failed in geting a chance to speak to you, which I very much wished to do, as I wanted to know, of you if I could not, (in some way), get a transfer from this Regiment, (Col Wolfords Cav) & to some Tennessee, Regiment, or so I could make me a company of my own, which I can do if I was at Cumberland ford. I am not very well pleased with things as they are in this Regt. and being a Tennesseean I am generaly overlooked when there is a vacancy to fill in the way of appointing Officers, and in the Company that I belong to (Capt. Burress')[3] there is'nt but two men that can write their names. I am called upon even to make out a report though the Orderly should do that you know. And now sir if you can, do any thing to get me out of this I would be much obliged[.]   you know me perhaps. I saw you at Camp Dick Roberson, soon after I enlisted[.]   I know that you have'nt forgotten my Father who lived at Surgoinsville Hawkins Co Tenn though he now lives at Sneedville Hancock County Tenn. Where I have lived for the last five years or until I was forced to leave last summer.

My Father's name is Lewis C. Barner.[4] my friend Odle who is from the same County wishes to get a transfer too[.] we belong to the same Company, Captain N. D. Burress, Col Wolfords Regiment, 1st. Ky Cavalry.) please let me hear from you on the subject[.]

I am Sir your's most obediently

Absalom B. Barner.
Wm. Odle.

P.S. This Wm. Odle is the man that was taken with T. A. R. Nelson[5] last sumer by the Rebels. The Union sentiment is gaining strength here every day[.]

ALS (Barner), DLC-JP.

1. Absalom B. Barner (b. *c*1834), Tennessee-born Sneedville mechanic, was a sergeant, Co. K, 1st Ky. Cav., USA, before becoming captain, Co. B, 1st Tenn. Cav., in January, 1863; he resigned the following November because of poor health. William Odle (b. *c*1832), a Hancock County "land renter" who claimed $150 in personal property, later served as captain, Co. G, 2nd Tenn. Cav., USA. 1860 Census, Tenn., Hancock, Sneedville, 1; 6th Dist., 8; Absalom B. Barner, CSR, RG94, NA; *Tennesseans in the Civil War*, II, 464.

2. Johnson spoke in Columbia on June 2, 1862.

3. Nelson D. Burress (*c*1829-*fl*1894), a miller from Madison County, Kentucky, served as captain, Co. K, 1st Ky. Cav., USA, from September, 1861, until he resigned November 13, 1862. *Official Army Register: Volunteers*, IV, 1215; 1860 Census, Ky., Madison, W. Subdiv. No. 2, p.64; CSR, RG94, NA.

4. Lewis C. Barner (b. *c*1796) was a Prussian-born Sneedville mechanic who possessed $400 in real and $200 in personal property. 1860 Census, Tenn., Hancock, Sneedville, I.

5. In August, 1861, Nelson ran for Congress in the first district. Learning of a possible warrant for his arrest to take effect if he won, he set out to await the result in Barbourville, Kentucky. Leaving Rogersville at nightfall, Nelson's party, including his sixteen-year-old son David and Odle, a hired guide, was captured in western Virginia by a band of thirty Confederates. Alexander, *T. A. R. Nelson*, 87-89.

From Henry W. Halleck

Corinth June 8 1862

To Gov Johnson

Repot of Evacution of Fort Pillow Randolph & Memphis fully confirmed[.] our flotilla at Memphis & Miss River open Expect [except] possibly Vicksburg[.] Gueralla bands scattered through country burning Everything belonging to Union men[.] Our troops have cleaned them out as far west as Grand Junction & Bolivar & as far North as Jackson[.]

H W Halleck Maj Genl

Tel, DLC-JP.

From George W. Morgan

June 8th 1862
Hqrs Cumberland Ford

To His Excellency A. Johnson

Bairds Brig marches this morning & Carter will close up the rear tomorrow— It has become necessary to station the forty ninth (49) Ind with two pieces of Artillery at Barboursville[.] on yesterday a spy pretending to be a deserter was brought into Camp. He left Cumberland Gap on day before yesterday at ten 10 o clock a m. He represents the enemeys force at over five thousand (5000) men at Big Creek Gap. There are eight thousand (8000) with troops at Knoxville & Clinton[.] should these forces concentrate the enemy will out number me nearly three to one[.] what is Genl Negly doing. Please answer at once as I start at noon to go to the Head of the Column— I send copy [of] this to Secretary War & Genl Buell [.]

George W. Morgan
Brig Genl Vols Comdg

Tel, DLC-JP.

From Marcellus Mundy

Head Quarters 23d Ky. Volunteers, U. S. A.
Pulaski Tennessee June 8th 1862.

Genl A. Johnson
Mil. Govr of Tennessee.
General

Your kind reception of suggestions heretofore made by me, emboldens me to make others, which, from a careful study of the people of this section and patient analization of their sentiments, impress me as vitally important. A state of facts exists here which retards, if it does not absolutely check the revival of loyalty, and I deem it a part of my duty to report to you. The masses of the people who have heretofore, from custom, quickly yielded to the influence of political and other speakers, without searching for truth beyond the record they have presented to them, have learned from actual demonstration wherein they have been basely and wickedly deceived by the designing; they would now most willingly return to their loyalty, but, wanting the necessary confidence and energy to throw off the tramels which have shackled them, and the influence which has so long dictated to them, they stand like paralized men, fearing to arouse the enmity of their former leaders, half doubting demonstrated truth and dreading prophetic evil hissed continually into their ears, covertly, by that class of impudent and hardened rebels who are allowed to run at large professing, publicly, a desire for a restoration of the Federal relations between your State and the Government.

General, men go at large in this community who publicly contributed their means and influence to fill the ranks of the rebel army: more than that, men who acted officially with the rebellion and assisted to legislate your state into the vortex, fresh from Richmond where they occupied seats in the Molochian Council,[1] carry in their pockets, guarantees of personal safety and a license to roam at large, signed by those holding Federal authority in Tennessee.[2] I know that I entertain no malice or vindictiveness towards these men who are scarcely known to me personally:[3] but actuated as I am by an overwhelming desire to further the restoration of the Union, convinced by the closest investigation of the evil that these men are working, I would advise that every one of them be arrested and removed from this community until a healthy tone can be reestablished among the people.

Many have said to me in private that they wish to renew their oath of Allegiance and claim the protection of our Government; but they fear that such and such men who are rich and influential would work against them, mark them for future punishment, and frown upon them as neighbors. Others from whom I exact the oath, as I do from all who have been in the Southern Army, complain that they have done no worse than Mr So and So, who gave his money to help raise and maintain the rebel army, furnished his negroes to work on fortifications, publicly persuaded Citizens to join the Army and upbraided and scoffed at those who refused; and yet these men, because they are rich have immunity.

General, these complaints are well founded and suggest to my mind the adoption of a different policy. All men should be treated alike.

If the rule of punishment must vary, penalties should be incurred in proportion to a man's means, inclination and practice of evil, and all hinderances to returning loyalty should be promptly removed by those in power, without favor or affection, for we have a mighty and extremely delicate work before us.

The arrest and removal of these wicked men would have a two-fold effect. First, it would convince the masses that justice was blind and did not discriminate between men or classes, and secondly, the timid and hesitating would be convinced of our power and gather assurance for themselves. What little faith I may have had in the assurances of the men to whom I allude, of their desire to see the Government reestablished has been entirely swept away; first, by their hesitation to receive from the Government the benefit of the Post Office, unless it should be restored upon a basis that would leave them free to say they did not solicit it; and secondly, by their influence exerted to prevent Governor Niel S. Brown from speaking publicly here to enlighten the masses. They knew that his voice would carry conviction to the hearts of many, and while they did not oppose with force, yet quite as effectually they withheld an invitation to him which I urged upon them, and which I knew he was willing and anxious to accept; lamely pretending that they thought it would be premature.

Governor, I have attempted to give you my convictions calmly and deliberately formed for reasons I have enumerated, and I repeat, in order to remedy this great evil speedily, that the bad rich men must feel our power, and the masses must be disenthralled.

I have the Honor to be Your obedt. Servt.

M. Mundy.   Col. Com'dg Post.—

P.S. If you approve my suggestion a telegram from you saying "execute according to your Judgment." will be my cue to act.   for "if 'twere done then when 'tis done 'twere well 'twere done quickly[.]"[4]

Very respectfully   M M.

ALS, DLC-JP.

1. An allusion to the Confederate Congress. Moloch was the god of the Ammonites, for whom children "were made to pass through fire" in sacrifice; hence, any influence which demands from us the sacrifice of what we hold most dear. 2 Kings 23:10; Benet, *Reader's Encyclopedia*, 733.

2. Probably a reference to Thomas M. Jones, member of the Provisional Confederate Congress, who had returned to his home in Pulaski; he was assured by Gen. James S. Negley and others that he would be protected. See Letters from Jones, June 14 and Mundy, June 15, 1862.

3. Three weeks later, Mundy named those whom he was castigating for their secessionist loyalties. See Letter from Mundy, June 29, 1862.

4. Shakespeare, *Macbeth*, Act I, sc. 7.

To George W. Morgan

Nashville June 8th [1862]

General Morgan Commanding Forces
Cumberland Ford, Ky.

General Negley dispatched that his forces were four miles East of Jasper Marion County on the sixth instant. Forts Randolph, & Pillow and Memphis have been evacuated and are now in our possession. Mississippi river open. Our Gunboats in front of Richmond. Give that boy of mine Robert Johnson all the encouragement you can. I hope he will do his duty. I am hourly expecting a despatch from Genl. Negley. It will be sent to you as soon as received. May the Gods be propitious & your success complete.

Andrew Johnson

Tel draft, DLC-JP.

From Emerson Etheridge

Washington June 9, 1862

My Dear Sir:

You will remember that at the interview we had with the Secretary of War, just before we went to Nashville, he took the names of John A. Rogers[1] and William T. Wilson as persons in West Tennessee to whom he would give the necessary authority to raise Regiments— Rogers is in Kentucky, near the State line, and is well advanced with his Regiment— Last week Wilson's papers were sent to him and he will commence recruiting his regiment, immediately. They will be directed at the proper time to report to *you*, and I write you now to say that, when the Regiments are complete I hope *one* will be left in my portion of the State— I know you will consent to it, if consistent with your views of the public good. I think it will not be asking too much to leave one of these regiments in the vicinity where they may be recruited. Of course, I shall be satisfied with any arrangement which may be considered best. I have advised Wilson that he might make his headquarters for recruiting at Dresden, with safety, since the evacuation of Memphis— This, too, I hope will have your approval.

I expect to go to West Tennessee the first of July to remain until Fall— While there, I shall exert myself to co-operate with you; and will be glad to receive from you any suggestions you may think proper to make, as to the best course to be pursued— All my information from home is of the most cheering kind. I congratulate you upon your success in dealing with Rebeldom— Gov. Brown has proved that, 'tis better to throw stones than grass.[2]

Yours truly—Em: Etheridge.

Hon. And. Johnson.
Nashville, T.

ALS, DLC-JP.

1. John A. Rogers (*c*1824-*fl*1890), a North Carolina-born Weakley County lawyer, served as colonel of the 7th Tenn. Inf., USA. At Humboldt on December 20, Rogers disobeyed an order by "abandoning the fort and camping his regiment in the safest part of the town," an action for which he was arrested two days later. Released by Gen. Jeremiah C. Sullivan, he tendered his resignation in mid-January, 1863, becoming after the war a circuit court judge with total property valued at $22,000. 1860 Census, Tenn., Weakley, 7th Dist., 167; (1870), 65; 1890 Special Census, Union Veterans and Widows, Tenn., Weakley, 7th Dist., 3; *OR*, Ser. 1, XVII, Pt. I, 564-65; CSR, RG94, NA.

2. Brown had only recently returned to his Union loyalty, giving public evidence thereof when he joined Johnson to speak at Columbia earlier in the month.

From Henry W. Halleck

Corinth Miss 9th June 1862

To Gov Johnson

It is difficult to have any communication with the Enemy on his retreat— he is greatly in want of provisions and robs the Country people of everything they have— many Women and Children are in a starving condition— he released our prisoners taken at Pittsburg because he could not feed them[.][1] he will probably for the same reason release the Civil prisoners— whole Regiments have deserted saying they have very little to eat[.]

H W Halleck Maj Genl

Tel, DLC-JP; DNA-RG393, Dept. of the Missouri, Tels. Sent & Recd., H. W. Halleck (Apr. 15-July 16, 1862).

1. Although it has not been categorically established that the burden of feeding prisoners caused Beauregard to release them, it was probably a factor, since the Confederacy during these months was experiencing difficulty in providing food for prisoners at other places, notably Lynchburg, Virginia. The Union prisoners taken at Shiloh in early April were generally shipped to Memphis and then to Mobile, where privates and officers were separated and sent to different prisons. By mid-May the majority of privates had been released on parole; officers were not sent North until October and November. Stanley F. Horn, *The Army of Tennessee* (Indianapolis, 1941), 149; Hesseltine, *Civil War Prisons*, 67-68; *OR*, Ser. 1, X, Pt. I, 669; II, 196; Byron Plympton Zuver [Mildred Throne, ed.], "Iowans in Southern Prisons, 1862," *Iowa Journal of History*, LIV (1956), 67, 77-81.

From A. G. W. Thomas[1]

Mt Plesant June 9th /62

To his Excelncy Andrew Johnston
At Nashville

Dear sir sessession is growing stronger evry day in this community[.] there are some persons in this community if there is not something done with them we cannot stand their insults much longer[.] we will be compelled in self defence to take the law into our own hands and inflict such punishment as we think their deeds merits[.] soon after I arrived home from Corrinth an old friend (a good union man)[2] came to my house to see me[.] the next day he was attacked in publick by Jas Wortham[.][3] he said to mr Chapman that birds of a feather would flock together and accused him of gross falsehoods & drew his Pistoll on mr Chapman[.] said Chapman is one of the peaciblest men in this whole Town[.]

I enformed Col Starkwether[4] of the fact and he sent to have said Wortham arested and he got the news and left. When Col Starkwether left he sent to Gen Negly at Columbia to have said Wortham arested[.] the order was given after he returned but Gen Negly has gon off

and Jas Wortham was arrested and taken before Capt Hill[5] Acting in Gen Neglys place[.]   Wortham reports that they had no charges against him and he was turned loose the same day[.]   he has come back and is insulting mr Chapman and myself where ever he can see us in any crowd & he's in open defiance of the constituted authorities of this State[.]   Said Wortham was a Lieutenant in the Confederate Army and is a verry Lawless man has but little regard for truth or any thing else and he is set on by a great many Sessessionist in this town & Community and if there is not something done with him & many others a good Loyial men cannot stay at home in piece[.]   when the soldiers are about our sesesh are all for piece but let them be by themselves then they holler for Jef Davis and the Southern Confederacy[.] I think that it would be a good thing to have a good many of them arrested & take the oath and give bond and security for their good behavior[.]   with-out security it is not worth one cent for they do not regard the oath binding at all and will not stick by its provisions with out their purse is at stake[.]   any information that I can give you is at your service[.]   if you should wish it you can write to me or I will be in Nashville in a few weeks but I do think that sessession has reigned here long enough[.]   I long to see the day when that Old flag shall float over evry house top in this whole Land and Country and Traitors hung and treason punished[.]   If you wish the names of the prominent sessessionist in this Community I can give you them[.]   there was not any of this Community went to Columbia except T. A. Haris[6] and myself and Wife to our Union meeting on the 2nd of June[.]
I will now coles by subscribing myself your sincere friend &c

A. G. W. Thomas

ALS, DLC-JP.
1. Probably A. G. Thomas (b. c1822), a New York-born merchant with $31,000 real and $7,000 personal property. 1860 Census, Tenn., Maury, 12th Dist., 263.
2. Possibly John Chapman (b. c1815), an Alabama native and Maury County farmer who served in the 12th district homeguards. Ibid., 47; Garrett, Confederate Soldiers, 54.
3. James J. Wortham (c1822-fl1870), a North Carolina-born farmer and merchant with $207 real and $150 personal property in 1860, served as a 2nd lieutenant, Co. B, 48th (Voorhies') Tenn. Inf., CSA, resigning early in 1862. 1860 Census, Tenn., Maury, 11th Dist., 29; (1870), 12th Dist., 2; CSR, RG109, NA; Tennesseans in the Civil War, II, 445.
4. John C. Starkweather (1830-1890), a New Yorker who moved to Wisconsin and practiced law (1857-61), was colonel, 1st Wis. Inf. (1861-63). Promoted to brigadier in July, 1863, he fought at Chattanooga and was in command at Pulaski from May, 1864, until Nathan B. Forrest captured or dispersed a large part of his troops during the autumn of that year. After the war he was a Washington, D.C., attorney. NCAB, XII, 70; Warner, Generals in Blue, 472.
5. Probably Robert Hill (b. c1837), captain, Co. C, 1st Wis. Inf. and General Negley's acting assistant adjutant general until his resignation in August, 1862. CSR, RG94, NA.
6. Thomas A. Harris (1820-fl1886), born in Halifax County, Virginia, served as an escort of Sam Houston from West Tennessee to Texas in 1839 and was a private in the Mexican War. Settling as a farmer in Maury County, he accumulated $5,300 of real and $9,350 of personal property. Second lieutenant of state militia for three months of the Civil War, he resigned when his company was transferred to the Confederacy and became an active unionist, participating in a restoration meeting in Columbia, Febru-

ary 1, 1864, and serving as a delegate to the Union convention in Nashville early in 1865. Harris was present in Ford's Theatre at the time of Lincoln's assassination. 1860 Census, Tenn., Maury, 12th Dist., 49; *Goodspeed's Maury*, 926; Jill K. Garrett, *Maury County, Tennessee, Historical Sketches* (Columbia, Tenn., 1967), 153, 262; Garrett and Lightfoot, *Civil War in Maury County*, 157.

From Edmund Cooper

June 10, 1862, Shelbyville; ALS, DLC-JP.

Writes on behalf of John W. Burton, a relative by marriage and friend, lately arrested and sent to the penitentiary. Assured by Burton's family "that he has never been connected with the *Army* of the Confederate States," Cooper asks that "the same leniency be extended to him, that was shown to" the "political prisoners from Murfreesboro." Observes "your speech did great good—and many of your old friends are turning from the error of their ways[.]"

From Lewis C. Norvell[1]

Memphis June 10 1862

Hon Andrew Johnson
Nashville Tenn
Dr Sir

I thank God and the union army that I am once more permitted to Express and write my feelings freely upon all subjects whatever—

The Stars & Stripes now float over our city and never will I under any circumstances live under any other flag again[.]

I have often thought of you since we last met which was at the white house on the 5th Apl 1861 and I have prayed for the approach of the union army more fervently than I have ever done for the salvation of my own soul—

My prayer have at last been answered and now Treason gives way to Justice and truth—

the Rebellion I think will soon be crushed then the Guilty must be punished and the Inocent must be free[.]

Our Government must be sustained[.] the union shall be restored that the world may know that we have a country sustained by the people[.]

last fall and winter I purchased over 600 Bales Cotton and two hundred hhds sugar knowing that both articles were low and knowing that our currency would be no account—

My Cotton has all been burned[.] My sugar confiscated for the use and benefit of the Confederate army and sent to Miss from the fact that I was a Union man and given Expression to union sentiments[.]

Such oppression and tyriny the world has never known but Thank God we have been deliverd from their hands and can now stand once more like honest men and speak the truth[.]

they have left the Country In smoking ruins[.]   they have sacked the towns & cities from the fact as they say they are ruined themselves and they would ruin all that did not go with them south[.]

But let all this Go and go cherfully to save the Country and hand it down to our children as it was given to us— all this burning and distruction will only the more Effectually put down the Rebellion for as they pass over the Country the people rejoice and will rise up to a man to keep them out of it again— there will be no more armies raised to fight the Union again nor no more contributions[.] this burning process has done more to strengthen the union than all the bills that has been passed and its effects will last forever[.]

If I did not know that you had no time to read long letters I could write you a hundred pages but for the present I must conclude by wishing you a long life of usefulness and prosperity and that our beloved Country may reward your labors and fidelity to the union by placeing you in the highest office in the Gift of the people and above all that peace and happiness may be in you and yours forever hereafter—

Your frind   L C Norvell

ALS, DLC-JP.

1. Lewis C. Norvell (in census Charles Norvell) (*c*1837-*fl*1869), North Carolina-born partner in the Memphis firm of Norvell, Boone and Co., grocers, cotton factors, and commission merchants, possessed $8,000 personal and $6,000 real property on the eve of the war. He had earlier sought appointment as a consul to a European port "for the purpose of increasing my business in Memphis," and would subsequently be an applicant for a collectorship in New York. Secretary of a Memphis Union meeting in November, 1862, he later moved about, residing for a time in New York City. 1860 Census, Tenn., Shelby, 8th Ward, 162; Norvell to Johnson, March 25, 1861, November 25, 1865, Johnson Papers, LC; Memphis *Bulletin*, November 28, 1862; *Trow's New York City Directory* (1867), 760.

From Wright L. Rives

June 10, 1862, Bethel; ALS, DLC-JP.

Recent West Point graduate and son of Washington editor John C. Rives, dissatisfied with present position on McClernand's staff, where he has "nothing to do, and all what I have done so far could be done, by a child in two hours," reminds Johnson that the governor had earlier offered him a position on his staff, and asks if it is still available. "We took possession of Jackson three days ago and captured a quanity of rolling Stock[.] Your dominions are increasing daily in territory and members. The people of Jackson were at first very bitter as it contains many ladies wifes of Confederate Officers but even they now come out freely and admit that our troops are better looking dressed and behaved than their own[.] Every one is taking the oath of Allegiance and we are compelled to protect the Secessionists from the Union men for their animosity is so bitter. Our troops are very healthy."

From Emerson Etheridge

Washington, June 11, 1862.

Govr. Andrew Johnson—
Nashville, T.
Dear Sir:

Judge Trimble[1] of Paducah, the President of the New Orleans and Ohio Rail Road goes to Nashville on business concerning this Road. It begins at Paducah and connects in Tennessee with the Nashville and North Western Road in Weakley County. This communication, as you will see by reference to the map, puts the Ohio river, at Paducah, in direct communication with all the Rail Roads in West Tennessee. Trimble needs the iron for only *ten* miles; and I trust you will be able to comply with his wishes, especially as he will give all necessary security.

He will explain to you very fully the whole matter.

He further proposes, by your consent, to take charge of the Nashville & North Western Rail road from Hickman Ky. to McKenzie junction on the Memphis & Ohio Road and to put it in running order imme- diately— In this last proposal the people of my section are much interested, and I trust you will converse with him in his view about allowing him to take charge of the Road.

Very truly yours,
Em: Etheridge

ALS, DLC-JP.

1. Lawrence S. Trimble (1825-1904), president of the New Orleans and Ohio Railroad (1860-65), was a native of Flemingsburg, Kentucky, who began law practice at Paducah in 1847. His career included a term in the state house (1851-52), a criminal judgeship of the first judicial district (1856-60), service as a Douglas elector (1860), and membership in Congress (1865-71). He returned to the law after his removal to Albuquerque in 1879. *BDAC*, 1728; H. Levin, ed., *The Lawyers and Lawmakers of Kentucky* (Chicago, 1897), 413.

From Horace Maynard

Washington, June 11, 1862

D. Sir,

The President sent for me yesterday to say he thought he saw the light breaking in on East Tennessee. Morgan expects a movement, & Halleck telegraphs that he will send a column there. The whole state as well as all of Kentucky is now assigned to Hallecks department. Would not a word from you to Gen. Halleck have a good effect?

He told me he was just on the point of nominating Gov. Campbell when he received a dispatch from you requesting him not to do so. What does it mean?[1]

The post master's nomination was sent in on yesterday;[2] & Judge Collamer, to whom I spoke about it, says he will give it early attention.[3]

Judge Humphrey's case is postponed until the 26th when the trial will come off.

I wish you could find time for a letter; if not please request Mr Browning[4] to write.

I am very Truly Yours
Horace Maynard

His Excy Andrew Johnson

ALS, DLC-JP.

1. Reflecting his receipt of Campbell's June 4 letter, Johnson had four days earlier wired: "In the matter of the appointment of Wm B. Campbell, Brig Genl withhold any action for the present." Subsequently the governor urged prompt commissioning of Campbell but made no effort either to deny or explain the telegram. Johnson to Lincoln, June 7, 1862, Tels. Recd., Sec. of War, Vol. 15 (June 6-16, 1862), RG107, NA; see Telegram to Abraham Lincoln, June 14, 1862.

2. Probably Adrian V. S. Lindsley's nomination for Nashville postmaster; he was appointed the next day. Wooldridge, *Nashville*, 130.

3. Jacob Collamer of Vermont was chairman of the Senate post office and roads committee.

4. William A. Browning, Johnson's military secretary.

Petition of Michael Shyer[1]

June 11, 1862

To His Excellency, Governor Andrew Johnson.

Your Petitioner would show to your Excellency, that on Sunday, May 25th 1862, he was stopping, with his wagon, and a lot of goods, specified in the permit obtained from Mr. A.V. S. Lindsley & Col Mathews, which is hereunto appended, and made a part hereof—worth about $900—at the house of a certain _____ Gray [2] near Santa Fe, a little village in Maury County, about twelve miles west of Columbia. Petitioner was peddling said goods lawfully through the County. He is a poor man with a family, & the wagon & stock of goods aforesaid constituted his whole Capital and property.

During the above day a certain _____ Cooke,[3] residing in Santa Fe, came into Gray's house, &, in conversation with Gray, designed for Petitioner's hearing, said: 'One thing is settled. We are going to tolerate no more Yankee pedlars in this community.' After Cooke left, Gray advised Petitioner to quit the neighborhood as quickly as possible. He said, Cooke had not come to his house for nothing. That he was one of "The Blue Hen's Chickens,"[4] an appellation which your Petitioner understands to import a gang of marauders, banded together to prey upon Union men traveling with goods to Sell through the County, especially if of Supposed Northern extraction: and that he had undoubtedly come to look after Petitioner. Gray further said, that there was a plot on foot among some twenty five or thirty men in the neighborhood to plunder Union Men, & that this gang had their eyes on Petitioner, whom they regarded as a Lincolnite, and that he was in danger both of *life* & *property*. Petitioner replied that his wagon was out of repair, but that on the morrow, just so soon as he could get it fixed, he would take his departure. Accordingly on Monday he went to a blacksmith's shop, about a half a mile from Santa Fe, to see about having his wagon repaired. The blacksmith, a colored man, acquainted with Petitioner, expressed surprise at seeing him, and said if he had known it was he who was at Gray's, he would have come down on Sunday and told him something. That he had heard two pedlars much talked about, who were said to be stopping at Gray's, and that there was to his knowledge a plot on foot in the neighborhood to seize the property of Petitioner because he was a Lincolnite. That an attempt had been made to procure a Negro to steal a box of shoes from Petitioner's room, but that the negro had refused to do the job. Petitioner then went back to Gray's. It was now Monday afternoon. Gray reiterated his warning to Petitioner to leave the Neighborhood immediately. He said that John Johnson,[5] his wifes brother had been to his house during petitioner's absence, and told him that every road was guarded, to prevent Petitioner from leaving with his wagon. Gray further said, he had information that five men had agreed to watch every wagon-load, not only to seize Petitioner's wagon & goods, but also to kill Petitioner. Gray proposed to your Petitioner to sell him (Gray) his wagon & stock of goods, in order to save them, and urged him with great earnestness to be off right away, as his life was in imminent danger, and he ought to be in a great hurry. He offered to send two men with your petitioner to guide him by a bridle-path to a point of safety on the 'pike to Columbia. Petitioner, however, declined this proposition, and then proposed to Gray to accompany him & his wagon & goods, with two other honest men selected by Gray, whom, together with Gray, he would pay whatever was reasonable for this Service. Gray at first assented to this, but afterwards declined, saying that, if he should do as requested, he would be looked on himself as a Lincolnite. Finally, Gray advised Petitioner to leave his wagon & goods with him, and too get away as soon as he could, promising, for the compensation of ten dollars, to deliver said wagon & goods in a few days at Spring Hill, and saying that he would be responsible for such safe delivery. Seeing nothing else that was feasible, Petitioner assented to this. Accordingly, leaving said wagon & goods with Gray, he set out on Tuesday morning with Gray & reached the Columbia 'pike in safety. Petitioner now proceeded to Columbia & laid his case before Gen. Negley, but that officer was not able to afford him any assistance at that time.[6] On Wednesday, Petitioner proceeded to Spring Hill, and, thinking that possibly Gray might fulfil his engagement, waited there until Saturday, on which day two men, one named William Younker,[7] & the other _____ Cooke, the 'Blue Hen's Chicken" aforesaid, came into the town to seek Petitioner. They expressed much gratification at meeting with him, and said they would have gone all the way to Nashville to find him, in order to tell him how he had really been treated by Gray. They said Gray had scared him off—That the thing was a disgrace to the whole Community: that as soon as they heard of it they went to Gray's & examined him. Gray said that Wednesday night six men came to his house, and took all the goods of Petitioner, left there, down to the fence, & then divided them among themselves. Four of said men were dressed in Soldier's clothes, & two in Citizens' garb. Gray said he did not know any of said men, but his wife said she thought she could point out one, & another woman living with Gray said she could point out two.— Cooke & Younker however, professed to disbelieve Gray's statements. How this may be petitioner knows not. He has suffered from the spoliation of men hostile to him, partially because ill affected towards the Government of which he is a loyal citizen. He is disposed to believe that his goods were appropriated by marauders, banded together for the general purpose of plundering Union men. The premises considered, Petitioner, being advised that his case comes within the scope of Your Excellency's Proclamation, providing relief for Union Men despoiled by gangs of marauders hostile to the Government of the United States, respectfully prays for whatever relief your Excellency may see fit to accord under said Proclamation— Petition hereby makes oath that the above representations are true.[8]

Michel Shyer

Sworn to & subscribed before me this 11th June 1862.
George M Southgate Justice of the Peace
for Davidson County, Tennessee.

Pet, DLC-JP.

1. Michael Shyer (1825-1902), native of Hesse Darmstadt, Germany, was a Nashville confectioner. After the war he alternately operated a rag warehouse, produce market, and junk business, the latter in partnership with Nathan Rosenthal. 1860 Census, Tenn., Davidson, 1st Ward, 24; (1870), 2nd Ward, 23; *Nashville Bus. Dir.* (1860-61), 256; Nashville city directories (1866-74), *passim*; Frank, *Beginnings on Market Street*, 132.

2. Amos T. Gray (b. *c*1800) was a Virginia-born physician and farmer, with $6,400 real and $24,600 personal property, whose wife was Mary S. (Polly) Johnson Gray (b. *c*1808). His son Pinckney C. Gray (1830-1905), a farmer with $700 personal property, who served in the home guards, 18th District, and Co. E, 19th Tenn. (Forrest's) Cav., CSA, had married Mary P. Cook (*c*1829-1912), daughter of Enos and Priscilla Caughron Cook in February, 1852. 1860 Census, Tenn., Maury, 17th Dist., 165; *Maury County Cousins*, I, 580; *Century Review Maury County*, 272.

3. Probably William King Cook (1833-1915), Kentucky-born farmer and brother-in-law of Gray's son Pinckney, who resided at or near Santa Fe and had $3,630 real and $1,392 personal property. 1860 Census, Tenn., Maury, 18th Dist., 134; Garrett, *Confederate Soldiers*, 66.

4. Originally the nickname of a company of the 1st Del. Rgt. during the Revolutionary War, the designation "The Blue Hen's Chickens" arose from the practice of the men's carrying two game chickens of the brood of a blue hen celebrated for their fighting abilities; subsequently the term came to refer to all Delawareans. Probably its use in Maury County reflected the influence of young Cook's father, Enos, a native of Delaware. Walter A. Powell, *A History of Delaware* (2 pts., Boston, 1928), I, 155; Jill K. Garrett, ed., *War of 1812 Soldiers of Maury County, Tennessee* (Columbia, [1976]), 35.

5. Probably John Johnson (b. *c*1816), a Virginia-born farmer with $470 in personal property on the eve of the war. Porch, *1850 Census Maury*, 98; 1860 Census, Tenn., Maury, 18th Dist., 141.

6. Although unable to persuade Negley to act in May, Shyer was more successful in July when the general arrested Gray and sent him, accompanied by "the aggrieved parties," to Nashville "to answer the charge of aiding and abetting the parties who robbed the Pedlars while at his house about a month ago—" James S. Negley to Johnson, July 9, 1862, Johnson Papers, LC.

7. Probably William Younger (b. *c*1808), a native North Carolina farmer with $10,000 real and $18,500 personal property in 1860. Porch, *1850 Census Maury*, 97; 1860 Census, Tenn., Maury, 18th Dist., 131.

8. In a statement, dated Nashville, June 4, 1862, Nicholas Hewlett, H. Hewlett, David Yates, H. Campbell, and J. M. Seebury attested that they were well acquainted with Shyer and knew him "to have been at all times, and to be at present, a loyal citizen of the United States of America." Johnson Papers, LC.

From James A. Willson[1]

Columbia June 11th 1862

To Your Excel Gov Johnson
Dear Sir
We the original union men but few in number of old Maury, cheerfully, recommend W L Begley[2] to your consideration,   Gov you know but little of the heart felt intrest that he took since you first run for Govenor, Especially in the gentry canvass, & when taken up at Spring Hill by Scots Cavalry[3] & taken to head quarters, when all the hordes of secessionist was there to hear the result,

Col—question, Are you a Lincolnite

B—Answer, not so much as you might suppose

Col—q then you are for Jeff

B—no never

Col—then what are you for

B—for the constitution & the Union stars & stripes & Andrew
   Johnson, weal or wo[.]

He Astonished the Col so much that he told him to go Scot free, and also added that he thought more of B than he did of the informer. in reference to these facts I give you the names of the undersigned

John. A. Cambell[4]
John Nesbit[5]
A Little[6]
James. A. Haley[7]
I am, dear Sir Very truly yours
J. A. Willson

ALS, DLC-JP.

1. James A. Willson (*c*1822-*fl*1870), a native North Carolinian and house painter, possessed personal property worth $300. 1860 Census, Tenn., Maury, 9th Dist., 35; (1870), 10.

2. W. L. Bagley (b. *c*1827), was an Irish-born harness-maker with $100 in personal property. *Ibid.* (1860), 22nd Dist., 104.

3. John S. Scott's lst La. Cav., CSA.

4. Probably John A. Campbell (c1820-1895), a farmer and sawmiller with $200 in real and $6,000 personal property. *Ibid.*, 160; (1870), 4; Garrett, *Confederate Soldiers*, 48.

5. John D. Nesbit (b. c1825), a constable possessing $600 personal property, was a member of the home guard in district 22, and occasionally guided Federal soldiers. *Ibid.*, 257; *Smith's Maury County*, 205; 1860 Census, Tenn., Maury, 22nd Dist., 108.

6. Andrew Little (c1822-fl1870), Pennsylvania-born coach painter with $200 personal property, was Bagley's neighbor who moved to Nashville after the war. *Ibid.*, 104; (1870), Davidson, Nashville, 9th Ward, 11.

7. Probably James Haley (b. c1815), a North Carolina-born overseer with $500 personal property on the eve of the war. *Ibid.* (1860), Maury, 8th Dist., 22.

To John A. Kasson

Nashville, June 11th 1862

Hon John A. Kasson,
1st Ass't P. M. General
Washington City.

I hope the appointment of Post Master has been made for this place. If not, it should be done without delay. Either accept Lellyett's Resignation or remove him at once and appoint Lindsley. Things are moving on well here. If a few impediments which have been and still are in the way of a speedy restoration could be removed—Tennessee could be put right by 50,000 majority (fifty thousand) in 3. months. In a few days I shall write the Post Master General in full in regard to the difficulties I have had to contend with, I shall expect his assistance as heretofore[.] I think our forces will this day enter Tennessee at Cumberland Gap. Our information is that Cumberland & Big Creek Gaps have been evacuated by the rebels. If so General Morgan marches at once on Knoxville.[1]

Andrew Johnson

Tel draft, DLC-JP.
1. A line has been drawn through the final sentence, "God grant that it be soon."

From James S. Negley

Shelbyville June 12 1862

To Gov Andrew Johnson
Our Expedition into East Tennessee has proved successful. We are returning with eighty prisoners including a number of prominent officers[.] also captured a drove of cattle and a large quantity of stores intendereded for the rebel army[.] The defeat of Gen Adams[1] rebel forces in Sweedens Cove was more complete than reported, He escaped without sword hat or horse.[2] We silenced the Enemys batteries at Chattanooga on the evening of the seventh, after a firerce cannonading of three hours. We opened fire on the 8th at nine a. m. & continued six hour upon the town and rifle pits driving the enemy out forcing him to abandon his

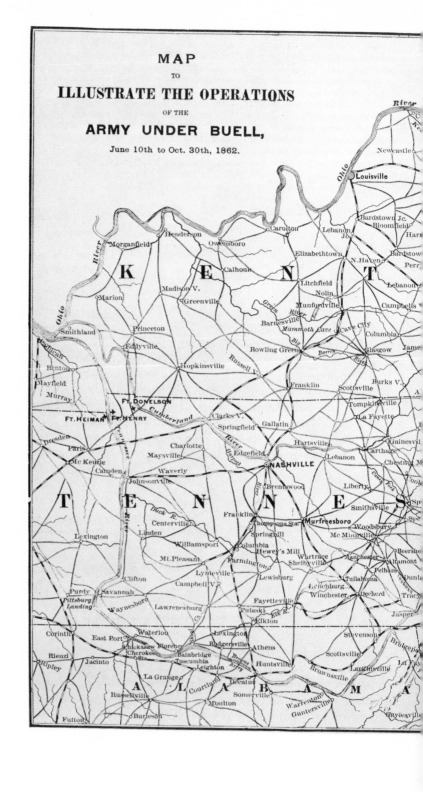

MAP
TO
ILLUSTRATE THE OPERATIONS
OF THE
ARMY UNDER BUELL,
June 10th to Oct. 30th, 1862.

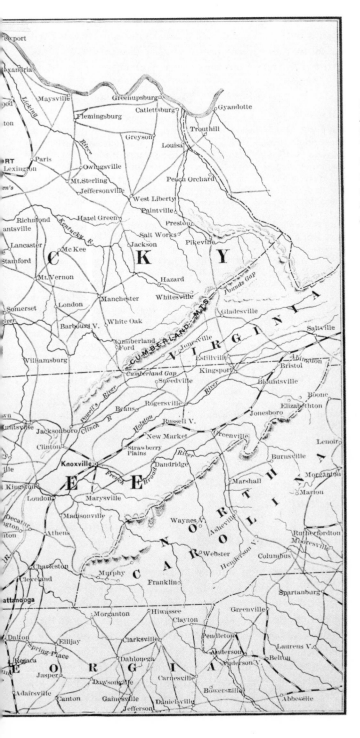

Scene of the action.
From James B. Fry,
OPERATIONS OF THE ARMY
UNDER BUELL, from June 10th
to October 30th, 1862, and
the "BUELL COMMISSION"
(New York, 1884),
between pages 200
and 201.

works and evacuate the city. They burnt several rail road bridges to prevent pursuit[.] The Union people in East Tennessee are wild with joy. They met us along the roads by hundreds. I shall send you a number of their principal perscurters from Sequachee Valley.[3]

Yours Very Truly

James S. Negley[4] Brig Genl

Tel, DLC-JP.

1. John Adams (1825-1864), Nashville-born of Irish ancestry, grew up in Pulaski, graduated from West Point (1846), served in the Mexican War, and saw duty on the frontier during the 1850's. Resigning in May, 1861, he returned to Tennessee, was appointed to command at Memphis as a captain of cavalry, and by May, 1862, was a colonel and acting brigadier commanding a force operating near Huntsville, Alabama. Assigned a brigade under Gen. Joseph E. Johnston in Mississippi (May, 1863), he fought in the Atlanta campaign and was killed in the holocaust at Franklin. *DAB*, I, 82-83; Warner, *Generals in Gray*, 2.

2. At 3 P.M., June 4, Negley's command surprised Adams' cavalry in Sweden's Cove, west of Battle Creek, Marion County. After a brief skirmish Adams' men turned in wild flight toward Jasper, leaving their ammunition and commissary wagons in Union hands. At Jasper, Adams tried unsuccessfully to rally his men, but they did not stop until they reached Chattanooga. *OR*, Ser. 1, X, Pt. I, 903-5; J. Leonard Raulston and James W. Livingood, *Sequatchie: A Story of the Southern Cumberlands* (Knoxville, 1974), 141.

3. During the following weeks, Negley captured a number of civilians, both in the Sequatchie Valley and in the vicinity of Chattanooga, and sent them, along with prisoners of war, to Nashville. He also arrested and fined several prominent rebels in Jasper, applying the funds so raised to the relief of those Union families who had suffered at rebel hands. New York *Herald*, June 20, 1862; Nashville *Union*, July 4, 1862.

4. Replying at once, Johnson asked, "Is Chattanooga in our possession? and what force is left there. Have the enemy fallen back on Georgia," to which Negley responded, "No troops were left at Chattanoogo for special reasons[.] it was first intended to only make a demonstration against that point but as the enemy made a stand there I took advantage of it to chastise him well—Genl Smith claims to have there now twelve thousand (12,000) but up to yesterday morning he did not know I had withdrawn my forces— Genl Mitchel and myself are actively engaged in preparations for a more decisive blow[.]" Johnson to Negley, and Negley to Johnson, June 12, 1862, Johnson Papers, LC.

Petition of Samuel E. Ogden[1]

[Columbus, Ohio], June 12, 1862

To Andrew Johnson Governor of the

State of Tennessee.

The undersigned respectfully states that Hawks Miller &Co a firm composed of W. B. Hawks, William Miller & S. E. Ogden[2] all citizens of Columbus in the State of Ohio & all loyal citizens of the United States, were lately the owners of twenty three bales of bagging & twenty three coils of rope worth as he believes $735. in the City of Nashville— that they got a regular permit from E. H. East & A. V. S. Lindsley[3] to ship said rope & bagging to Huntsville Alabama—that they started with it & passed through Fayetteville in this state with said property & about eight miles beyond Fayetteville in Lincoln County as he believes, some marauding band of Guerillas or persons engaged in the attempt to destroy the Government, or claiming to be Confederate Soldiers on the 28th day of May 1862 seized said property & destroyed it by fire or otherwise so injured it as to render it of no value[.] He is not fully advised as to the persons who were engaged in this outrage, but if able, he will show by the proof. The County of Lincoln & including Fayetteville especially, is strong secession as he is informed. The rope & bagging was worth a good deal more where it was consumed than in Nashville. They had bought cotton in Huntsville & was to furnish their own rope & bagging & this loss throws upon them a good deal of additional cost & trouble & perhaps the loss of the cotton itself. Their actual loss is more than double the value of the rope & bagging in this City.

He therefore, on behalf of the said firm of which he is a member, prays your Excellency to take such course in this behalf as will enable them to be paid for their loss by the persons who did this wrong, if they can be ascertained & if not, then by the disloyal citizens of Lincoln County, in the manner, you may see proper to direct.

S. E. Ogden

Subscribed and sworn to before me this 12th day of June 1862[.]
George M Southgate (Seal) Justice of the Peace

Pet, DLC-JP.

1. Samuel E. Ogden (b. *c*1825), New Jersey native, owned a "RR Eating House and Coffee Saloon" at the depot in Columbus prior to the war. During 1860-61 he was a member of the city council and part of the committee selected to welcome President-elect Lincoln in February, 1861. 1860 Census, Ohio, Franklin, Columbus, 1st Ward, 30; Daniel J. Ryan, "Lincoln and Ohio," *Ohio Archaelogical and Historical Society Quarterly*, XXXII (1923), 147; *Williams' Columbus Directory* (1856-57), 163; *Lathrop's Columbus Directory* (1860-62), 67, 126.

2. The "firm" would appear to have been a wartime creation to take advantage of speculative opportunities in the troubled South. None of its partners brought to the venture experience in cotton brokering. For many years William B. Hawkes (b. *c*1814), a Massachusetts native, operated a hack service and an omnibus line "running the entire length of High-st every half hour; fare each way, 5 cts." In 1860 he claimed $21,000 real and $38,000 personal property, each of which had increased to $100,000 by 1870 when he was a mail contractor. Possibly William Miller (b. *c*1824), a native Pennsylvanian who was listed in the 1870 census as a "Retired Merchant" with $56,000 real and $25,000 personal property. *Ibid.*, 134; 1860 Census, Ohio, Franklin, Columbus, 2nd Ward, 192; (1870), 5; 3rd Ward, 16.

3. Edward H. East, as the governor's secretary of state, and Adrian V. S. Lindsley, as a treasury agent, were authorized to issue trade permits. Nashville *Union*, May 4, 1862.

To Marcellus Mundy

Nashville, June 12th 1862

Col M. Mundy Com'dg Post
Pulaski, Tenn.

Your letter has been received. You are hereby authorized to make such arrests as you may deem proper & expedient in suppressing & putting down the Rebellion. I would select a few of the most important cases first, and see the effect, and then act as your best judgment dictates.

Things are going on well here. A decided reaction has taken place.

Andrew Johnson
Mil Governor

Tel draft, DLC-JP.

From Thomas M. Jones [1]

Pulaski Tenn
June 14th 1862.

Hon Andrew Johnson
Dear Sir

Sometime in the month of April last I addressed a communication, through Mr Hughes,[2] to Gen'l Negley, then in Command of the Post at Columbia, Stating to him frankly, that I had been a Member of the Provisional Congress of the Confederate States, but had declined a reelection after the expiration of that Government by its own limitation—And that I had returned to my home in Tennessee where I had determined to remain and abide the destiny of my State—That in a short time thereafter, the Federal Army entered the Capitol of the State, from which place Gen'l Buell, the Commander in Chief, had issued his proclamation, that the rights and property of all peaceable Citizens Should be respected and urging them to remain at home pursuing their usual vocations— Relying upon the good faith of this Proclamation, I not only determined myself to remain at home, but urged upon all of my fellow Citizens in public speeches & private Conversations to do So— that it was their duty to Submit to whatever Government might be extended over them—that I had no doubt a Military Governor would be appointed, who in his Administrative policy, would carry out in good faith, the proclamations of the Commanding General— In a short time after the forces had reached the Town of Columbia, I learned that an effort had been made to arrest my Colleague, the Hon. James H. Thomas,[3] when it was deemed prudent by myself & friends to keep beyond the lines of the Federal Army—That I had left my wife & little children wholly unprotected, and two Sons prisoners of War, one at Fort Warren & one at Chicago[4]—that my Situation was extremely painful and unhappy, and that I felt a great anxiety to return home to render Such protection to my family as I could and make such provisions for my Captive children as might be in my power—

I stated in my letter that owing to the large vote given by the State of Tennessee to dissolve its Connection with the Federal Government, and there was now pending as to whether that dissolution Shall be permanent, or its Federal relations again restored, I could not consistent with my Sense of Honor, and without forfeiting the respect of my fellow citizens take any oath of allegiance to the Federal Government, until the State of Tennessee through its constituted authorities should reverse its actions, or such Military possession should be taken of the entire state, as to render it a duty which all good Citizens owed to their families and friends, to move as a Community, for the restoration of peace and Civil Government, and in either event I would Cheerfully Cooperate—. I received a very prompt reply from Gen'l Negley assuring me that I might return home upon my Parole—that I should not be molested & might rely upon that protection to my person & property which was due to all peaceable Citizens— About the same time I saw a letter from Mr Cooke[5] addressed to Mr Thomas, Stating that he was authorized by you to give like assurances—. Upon these assurances I returned home, where I have remained ever Since exerting whatever influence I have to induce the Citizens to yeild obedience to the Military Government over them—. I have received through Dr Carter[6] & others, Citizens of this County, your messages to me to remain at home, and I have written Some two or three letters to Judge Brien[7] the Contents of which I presume have been Communicated, Stating my determination to do so, and whatever should be my fate, to abide the destiny of Tennessee—. I Should have done so, and intended to avail myself of the earliest opportunity to visit you at Nashville, had it not been for an order issued by the Commander of this Post, which places it out of my power—And which I feel it due to our past relations, to Communicate in explanation of again leaving my home and State—.

Col Mundey, in his administrative policy, feels it to be his duty, in order to hasten the restoration of the Federal relations of the State, to require of some of the prominent Citizens (among whom he has been pleased to designate me) now to take the oath of Allegiance, that our example may influence others, or to leave the State So that our presence may not exert a prejudicial influence—.

For reasons already Stated, as well as the Consciousness that by taking the oath at this time, I would be degraded in the estimation of the Community, and whatever influence I have wholly lost, and the additional Consideration that my children, and the children of my neighbours are prisoners of War and in the service of the Confederate Army, I feel that no other alternative is left me as an Honorable man, but again to leave my home and family although it is the most painful trial of my life—. In doing so, however I may differ with the policy of the Colonel, I desire to say to you, as I will say to him, that I do not go away with any feeling of resentment, or for the purpose, or with the view of connecting myself in any manner with the Confederate Army, or with the Confederate Government, but simply to Seek Some quiet place, and then await patiently and anxiously the development of Such a State of affairs, or such a change in the policy of the Officers in Command, as will permit me

Conscientiusly and Cordially to Cooperate with all who desire the restoration of Peace, And Order, and Civil Government—for which I would
willingly yeild my life, if that Sacrifice Could Secure it—. I feel, without any arrogance I trust (and in which I believe evey Union Man in the
County will concur), that I have done as much, if not more, and could
have done more (if I had been permitted to remain without taking any
oath) to prepare the public mind for the accomplishment of that object,
which the Colonel has in view; than any one who will remain—. I do not
say this in any Complaining spirit—far from it. When I came home &
found a Military Government over me, I determined to yeild it
obedience[.] I could not do otherwise if I was so disposed[.]

If my going into exile can bring peace, and repose, & protection to a
Community in which I have been raised, and to which I am indebted for
so many acts of Kindness, I Shall go without a murmur—let the pain be
as Keen as it may—.

All I desire to be understood, is that I do not go as *enemy*, nor Shall *fate*
or *Circumstances* ever force me to be *one* to my State—.[8]

Yours Respectfully
Thomas M. Jones

ALS, DLC-JP.

1. Thomas M. Jones (1816-1892), North Carolina native and Giles County lawyer
and businessman, served in the Seminole and Mexican wars, as state legislator (1845-
49), repeatedly as mayor of Pulaski, member of the Provisional Confederate Congress
(1861-62), and judge of the criminal court (1872-73), as well as delegate to the national
Democratic conventions (1856, 1860) and state constitutional convention (1870). He
was also a founder of the Ku Klux Klan. McBride and Robison, *Biographical Directory*, I,
417-18; Ezra J. Warner and W. Buck Yearns, *Biographical Register of the Confederate
Congress* (Baton Rouge, 1975), 139-40.

2. Archelaus M. Hughes (1811-1898), Maury County attorney and early in the war
a member of the district 9 home guard, later became a unionist, a member of the Maury
County committee for restoration (1864), and circuit court judge (1867-70). *Goodspeed's Maury*, 765; Garrett and Lightfoot, *Civil War in Maury County*, 157-59; Garrett, *Confederate Soldiers*, 175.

3. See *Johnson Papers*, IV, 271n.

4. Marietta Perkins (*c*1821-1872) of Williamson County and Thomas M. Jones
were married in 1838 and had nine children, eight of them born before 1862: Calvin,
Charles P. (1842), Thomas W., Hume F. (1848), Harriet (1852), Edward S. (1853),
Lucy A. (1855), and Lee W. (1857), all of whom except Calvin were still alive in 1888.
The three oldest served in the Confederate army and all were captured, although Charles
was not taken until Petersburg. Calvin Jones (1839-1872), a graduate of Nashville
University, served as adjutant, Co. E, 32nd Tenn. Inf., CSA, organized during October,
1861. After the 32nd surrendered at Donelson, he was imprisoned at Fort Warren,
remaining there until exchanged at Vicksburg, September 7, 1862. Returning to his
unit, he participated in the battle at Chickamauga and served in Macon, Georgia, before
resuming private life as a Giles County lawyer and planter. Thomas W. Jones (1845-
1923), the third son, enlisted as a private, Co. C, 3rd Tenn. Inf., CSA, in 1861; also
captured at Donelson, he was sent to Camp Douglas before being exchanged at Vicksburg in September. Discharged the following March as "under age and disabled," he
subsequently was assistant secretary at the 1870 state constitutional convention, engaged in the cattle business in Colorado, served in the Tennessee legislature (1893-95),
and practiced law in New Orleans and Mobile. 1860 Census, Tenn., Giles, N. Subdiv.,
186; Speer, *Prominent Tennesseans*, 475; *OR*, Ser. 1, VII, 356; Ser. 2, III, 640; Robison,
Preliminary Directory, Giles, 31.

5. Possibly James M. Cook (b. *c*1826), who was a Giles County constable on the eve of the war. 1860 Census, Tenn., Giles, N. Subdiv., 115.

6. Benjamin Carter (1792-1865), South Carolina native, studied medicine in Philadelphia and began practice at Elkton in Giles County about 1817, moving to Pulaski in 1829; subsequently turning to business, he became a wealthy merchant and farmer ($67,300 estate in 1860). *Ibid.*, 179; Deane Porch, tr., *1850 Census of Giles County, Tennessee* (Nashville, 1971), 41; James McCallum, *A Brief Sketch of the Settlement and Early History of Giles County* (Pulaski, 1928), 96.

7. John S. Brien, chancery court judge (1851-53).

8. Soon after the Federal troops occupied Pulaski, Jones was seized and sent to Nashville where on July 1, Johnson paroled him "on condition that he would not communicate with the Confederate Congress or the Confederate commanders while Pulaski was surrounded by the Federal forces." Subsequently "he went south, and . . . remained with the army till the close of the war. After the war he resumed his law practice." Speer, *Prominent Tennesseans*, 474; Nashville *Union*, June 28, 1862; Jones to Johnson, July 29, 1862, Johnson Papers, LC.

To Abraham Lincoln

Nashville June 14. 1862

To His Excellency
Abraham Lincoln President U S.

I have just learned that during my absence at Shelbyville on last saturday where I addressed a large Union meeting there was sent to you a dispatch requesting the postponement of the nomination of Ex. Gov. Wm. B. Campbell for Brig-Genl. I hope you will make this nomination at once[.]   It will be of great service to us & exert powerful influence on the public mind here at present even though in the future he should not act as such[.][1] I think I understand the posture of the public mind here and I hope you will have no hesitancy in making this nomination— It is to you that I look for help & if you will give it as heretofore you will be sustained & the state redeemed[.]

Andrew Johnson

Tel, DLC-Lincoln Papers; DLC-JP; RG107, Tels. Recd., Sec. of War, Vol. 15 (June 6-16, 1862).

1. Four days later, in urging Campbell's appointment upon Senator John Sherman, Johnson again sounded this note of expediency: "His connection with the Military in this State will be of immense service in the re-action that is now going on in the public mind." At the end of the month, after the governor had once more prodded the senator, reminding him that Campbell "is Very important to us especially now," Sherman wired the good news of Campbell's confirmation. Johnson to Sherman, June 18, 28, and Sherman to Johnson, June 30, 1862, Johnson Papers, LC.

From Edwin M. Stanton

Washington June 14 1862

To Gov Johnson
The appointment of Wm B Campbell as Brig Genl was made on the receipt of your telegram[1]—was countermanded the next day upon the receipt of another telegraph purporting to be from you asking its post-

ponement[.]² the appointment will be made on Monday as requested in your telegram to the President of this date[.]³

Edwin M Stanton Secy War

Tel, DLC-JP; DNA-RG107, Tels. Sent, Sec. of War, Vol. 10 (May 28-June 18, 1862).
    1. Probably a reference to Johnson's June 4 telegram to Maynard directing him to ask Lincoln to nominate Campbell.
    2. Johnson to Lincoln, June 7, 1862, Tels. Recd., Sec. of War, Vol. 15 (June 6-16, 1862), RG107, NA.
    3. The governor also wired Senator Wilson of Massachusetts urging his vote for confirmation—"It is right and will do us much good at this time. Please let it go right through." Johnson to Henry Wilson, June 15, [1862], Johnson Papers, LC.

From Andrew J. Hall¹

(Confidential)

Shellbyville June 15th 1862

Gov. Andrew Johnson
Sir

I have just learned of some facts connected with the Gurilla warfare of the *Sesesh* in the county of White Putnam & Overton which I hope you will take prompt action in suppressing if you have the authority to act in the premises. A soldier from Corinth is now at my house who has taken the Oath of alligiance and was a Union man at the first, & whom I have known all his life says that he learned from men who came to Corinth from Sparta that there was private parties in white who banded together and visited Overton & the Kentucky counties on the border and killed Union men and plundered them of property, then laid aside their weapons and claimed to be citizens. I know they have never been soldiers, the whole bands are my acquaintances and they are rich and influential in white and always was tyranical. I also learn that E L Gardenhire² is raising a band for some purpose[.] whilst I respect the Judge as a man I am down on his acts. if your Excellency thinks It proper to take some steps to suppress those rebels I will be at your command to give whatever aid I can. I wish to accompany the troops should any go, as I know every path in the whole country night or day & all the citizens. I wish to make a Speech to the citizens & raise the old Flag of our country once more in my native county. as a Democrat I have a great influence in that part of the country. as a soldier I am well posted, in the art of war; as to who I am, I cannot fully show by the good citizens of this place as my acquaintance is limited here. I am here as a refugee from White Co. being a Union man I thought It more safe to leave my Native Co. one more thing I will state as I received It. two men from white visited the camp of Lt Col G. G. Dibrell³ of the 25th Tenn vol. and in a confidential manner told Dibrell that Sam Turney⁴ had offered the Notorious Capt Forguson of Overton (who killed Ples Armstrong⁵ of Old Monroe,) that he would give him one thousand dollars if he would kill Andrew Johnson. my informant secretly over heard the whole conversation and he is a reliable man.   the men who told It stand high in white[.] I know them well.   one is the son of old Leftwich the merchant there.[6] now It will be but a short job to clean out all these bandittas if a thousand men could be sent on horseback and be properly guided.   they can subsist on the wealthy Gurillas in that county[.]   they have plenty.   whilst I have always loved the south, if I could not do justice to my conscience or country, and not give this information, and if I had been the worst of secessionists, I would revolt at this mode of establishing Its independence; I am poor but whatever I have I will spend In relivering my Native county of those murderers if I can have an opportunity. I can take my family to Nashville whilst I go up there. Now Gov confer with the proper authorities as to the expedency of this thing and if you wish to see me, summon me to Nashville & I will be there promptly when I can tell you more than I can write. I send this letter by Dr A Matson[7] who has known me some time partially, and can tell you of my courage as a man to accomplish what I undertake, or my knowlidge of the people and country. I remain yours with

High respect   Andrew. J. Hall

ALS, DLC-JP.

1. Andrew J. Hall (b. c1825) was a Vermont-born lawyer. 1860 Census, Tenn., White, Sparta, 1.

2. For Erasmus L. Gardenhire, Confederate congressman, see Johnson Papers, III, 499n.

3. George G. Dibrell (1822-1888), former Whig and Sparta merchant worth $44,000 on the eve of the conflict, had been county court clerk (1846-60) and for three weeks in October, 1861, a member of the 34th (Confederate) General Assembly; as an officer (1861-65) under Nathan B. Forrest, he rose to the rank of brigadier general (1864). At this time he was no longer lieutenant colonel, having failed of reelection when that unit was reorganized, but was engaged in recruiting a regiment of cavalry called "partisan rangers." Active in promoting industrial, railroad, and mining enterprises after the war, he served in the state constitutional convention (1870) and in the House of Representatives (1875-85). 1860 Census, Tenn., White, Sparta, 6; DAB, V, 286; BDAC, 807; Robison, Preliminary Directory, White, 62-63.

4. For Sam Turney, longtime state legislator, see Johnson Papers, I, 112n.

5. Although clearly writing "Ples," Hall must have been confused, since Pleasant Armstrong of Livingston in Overton was a rabid secessionist. On the other hand, both Thomas M. and Landon Armstrong of Monroe, a post office in the county, were loyal unionists, harrassed by Champ Ferguson during these months; however, neither was murdered. Nashville Press and Times, October, 1865, passim; Albert W. Schroeder, Jr., ed., "Writings of a Tennessee Unionist," Tenn. Hist. Quar., IX (1950), 251-52, 267-68.

6. Wayman Leftwich (b. c1798), a Virginia native whose business career at Sparta spanned four decades, was Dibrell's father-in-law and subsequently his partner. Leftwich's son Jefferson (b. c1836), who later served as captain under Dibrell in Co. D, 13th Tenn. Cav., CSA, was visiting his brother-in-law when he conveyed "in a confidential manner" the information about the threat to Johnson. 1860 Census, Tenn., White, Sparta, 4, 8; 8th Dist., 160; Byron Sistler, tr., 1830 Census Middle Tennessee (Evanston, Ill., 1971), 172; Goodspeed's White, 807, 810, 866.

7. Alpheus Matson (fl1876) was a Memphis dentist in the sixties and seventies. Memphis city directories (1867-76), passim.

From Marcellus Mundy

Head Quarters U.S. Forces
Pulaski, Tenn. June 15, 1862.

Brig. Genl. A. Johnson
Mil. Govr. of Tennessee.
General,

In pursuance of the policy I have marked out, and for which I have your kind permission, I have notified some ten of the most prominent rebels of this place, that they must decide by Tuesday morning next, whether they will take the Oath of Allegiance and become active workers for the restoration of the Federal Union, or "quit their country, for their Country's good." I tell them that if their hearts and sympathies are still with the so called Southern Confederacy they are not in their proper places here; that the Southern Confederacy needs in its Army all Sympathisers in this hour of its extremest peril; and that the Federal Government does not need and will not brook traitors under her Flag. I have therefore in short determined that all Traitors here, whether passive or active, shall abjure treason, or travel into the Southern Confederacy.

I was shown a letter by Major Jones,[1] this morning, which I have permitted him to send to you, and I will, in a few brief Sentences, answer. First, the good of this community, of Tennessee and of the whole conservative element of the Government requires that your state should be speedily restored to her Federal relations. Second, the men who have assisted to work the evil to Tennessee, which, hurling her into the Vortex of rebellion, certainly has done, are in *honor* bound to work as actively and energetically in drawing her out of her present evil and future ruin. After doing the evil, they cannot fold their hands and look on with their noses turned up, while other men, at greater sacrifices are tugging at the oar to remoor her to the Federal Wharf of Safety. Honor dictates that he who counsels or works evil, when satisfied that the good of his community requires it undone, should lend an active aid to that end.

Major Jones helped to hurl Tennessee into the vortex[.] he countenanced if he did not persuade his sons and the sons of his neighbors in taking up rebellious arms.

The high spirited sons of Major Jones are now Captives and his neighbors' sons who are not Captives, are exiles from their homes in a rebellious army by the fortunes of War.

Major Jones' State's destiny is now fixed with the Federal Government, and his sons and his neighbors' sons must remain Captives and exiles, unless they submit to the power which rules their homes and State. And therefore Major Jones as an *honorable* man is bound to set the example for good, as he set the example for evil. Major Jones as a Father, is called upon to set that virtuous example, which followed, will release his misguided Captive sons. Major Jones as a good Citizen and Patriot, considering the best interest of his fellow Citizens, should surmount his prejudice and take the lead in assisting to restore his State to her Federal rights. Major Jones, being satisfied, that the cause in which he embarked and in which he countenanced the embarkation of his young and inexperienced sons and neighbors, is a failure (which he now admits) should as an *honorable* man have the courage to make that declaration, publicly, in order that his opinions might influence their misguided minds, and further, he should first do, what they must do in this dilema.

Now as to a few facts I have discovered existing here.

Many of those who bore Arms and had fallen into my hands here, to whom I have administered the Oath, as I am compelled to do in discharging my duty, complain, that while Major Jones and others did much more evil than they, Major Jones has immunity from molestation, and is permitted to enjoy comfort and ease under his own Vine and fig tree, within sight of the Federal flag which he has sworn to desecrate. Many citizens of this County, who have only been hypocritical rebels, professing what their hearts contradicted; say, they are anxious to take the Oath and be fully restored to their Allegiance, but they fear that such men as Major Jones and others with whom I am now dealing, will mark them for future injury.

And General, these reasons appeal to me powerfully, and have dictated the policy I am now pursuing.

If you tear the bandage from the eyes of Justice and permit her to discriminate between rich and poor, favorites and others, that moment you kindle a mine under the Temple in which she dwells. If the policy I have inaugerated be checked, rebellion will go at a premium in this Country. And, much more important for the interests of all conservative men; time, which is now doubly precious to them will be wasted. Our good old Federal Ship of State is drifting upon Shoals and breakers.

There are wreckers, whose interests require that she should strike, handling the tiller-rope and steering her to destruction; We need more true men to set the Sails and rescue the helm, if we would save the ship, and we have not time to wait while men shall compromise with their prejudices. General, every hour now has the importance of an Age in our Country's peril, which threatens not so much from Armed rebels, as from perversion of the Constitution; and men must be made to help, save, or quit our Government, to make place for those who will. I have duly respected the arrangement with Major Jones.

I have given him time to prepare to go in search of his *Southern rights*, and will escort him with honor to the line which now limits the country of his choice—Dixey.

And he has nothing to complain of on the Score of justice, for I give him his Country and take proper care of mine by the same act. I take it for granted, if I were in his Country, I would get notice to quit, as a dangerous man and by parity of reasoning in obedience to a Christian precept, "I do unto him as I would be done by." If I am permitted to pursue my policy, I will undertake to have this part of your State healthy in Twenty days. But I need your concurrence and assurance. I have advertised a County meeting for Tuesday next, which is only preliminary to a Mass meeting I shall advertize for Saturday next, at which I must have you and H'ble. Niel S. Brown. I would suggest other Speakers of influence in this part of the State if you have any. I have the Cooperation of some good Union men here, and you must trust to my judgement and honor my demand for your Services on that occasion.

I enclose herewith Copy of Posters I have had put up over the Town and Country for Tuesday's meeting and will send you advertisement for Mass meeting next Saturday. Please have inserted in "Nashville Union".[2]—I mean the advertisement, not this letter.

I have the Honor to be   Your Obedt. Servt.—

M. Mundy. Col. Com'dg Post

ALS, DLC-JP.

1. See Letter from Thomas M. Jones, June 14.

2. In reporting the Union meeting held at Pulaski on Tuesday, June 17, the Nashville *Union* added: "Arrangements were made to hold a mass meeting on Saturday next, when Gov. JOHNSON and NEIL S. BROWN, with many others, will be present to address the citizens of Giles on the momentous issue of the day. All good citizens, who have the welfare of their State at heart, are earnestly invited to attend." Nashville *Union*, June 20, 1862.

From James M. Thomas[1]

Smith county Ten. June 15th 1862

Gov. Andrew Johnson

The undersigned, in deep distress, humbly presents this his petition to you, and represents. That he is now & always has been a loyal citizen of the United States—that he is a poor man. His oldest son William[2] is in the rebel army late of Corinth— He was induced to join it by fraud & falsehood, as were many of the sons of my neighbours. Now I am anxious to have my son out of the army, & I know he would leave if he could. There are three young men, sons of my neighbours, by the name of Stewart,[3] that I should like to see relieved[.] There are four men in the community who have been noisy all the time, & being men of property, they have had influence in causeing men to enlist. They are still noisy, exerting themselves to drive returned soldiers back to the rebel army, threatening them with disgrace and even violence should they not return. In fact manifesting the bitterest & most unscrupelous malignity towards union men & returned soldiers, and constantly uttering the foulest slanders upon the federal authorties. There names are P. Gold, T. H. Gold, W. R. Betty & H. C. Betty,[4] all living near Gordonsville Smith County Tennessee. The undersigned therefore respectfully requests, that you have P. Gold arrested & offered in exchange for his son, now in the rebel army against his convictions, & much by the influence of the man Gold. And that you would have the other three arrested & offered in exchange for the three young Stewarts mentioned above. No act of yours could more gratify a majority of the citezens of this community. I am most respectfully

Your distressed fellow citezen

James M. Thomas

ALS, DLC-JP.

1. Probably James Thomas (c1812-fl1880), Virginia-born tenant farmer with $1,500 in personal property. 1860 Census, Tenn., Smith, 15th Dist., 39; (1880), 14.

2. William Thomas (c1841-fl1870), native Tennessee laborer, joined Co. F, 24th Tenn. Inf., CSA, at Camp Trousdale in August, 1861; captured at Nashville in December, 1864, he was released from Camp Chase in April, 1865, becoming a farmer after the war. Ibid. (1860), 15th Dist., 39; (1870), 20th Dist., 13; CSR, RG109, NA.

3. James Stewart (b. c1796), was a North Carolina-born farmer, whose three sons, John W. (c1834-1863), Alexander (b. c1840), and Andrew (b. c1842) all enrolled August 24, 1861, at Camp Trousdale in Co. F, 24th Inf., CSA. John, elected corporal, was killed at Chickamauga; the two younger brothers, wounded and captured in October, 1862, were exchanged at Vicksburg in December. Both returned to service only to be recaptured—Alexander in 1863 and Andrew in 1864. Ibid.; Sistler, 1850 Tenn. Census, VI, 149; 1860 Census, Tenn., Smith, 15th Dist., 38, 39, 40, 41.

4. The Gold brothers, Pleasant (1806-1876), a farmer, and Thomas H. (b. c1807), were Virginia natives who had a mercantile partnership from 1856 to 1870. On the eve of the war, the former possessed $13,000 in real and $16,000 in personal property; the latter, $5,000 in personalty. The Bettys, father and son, were farmers: William R. (c1807-fl1880), a North Carolina native with property worth $14,300 in 1860 and H. C. (b. c1829), Tennessee-born with $26,400. Ibid., 36, 38; (1880), 1; Goodspeed's Smith, 943.

To Rodney Mason

Nashville June 16th [1862]

Commanding Officer,

Clarksville, Tenn.

I have received the following despatch Clarksville— Certain parties here have got Iron Rods from the wreck of the Nashville R. R. Bridge & want pay for saving it. We have possession of say 5000 pounds. Please instruct as what to do or it will be sold & scattered. Whitfield, Bradley & Co.[1]

You will please examine into this, and hold the iron as Govt. property, until we can know the nature of the case from your examination[.]

Andrew Johnson,

Military Governor.

Tel draft, DLC-JP.

1. Whitfield, Bradley, & Company, located in Clarksville, manufactured steam engines and tobacco screws until 1861, when they began production of six- and nine-pound cannon, together with ball, canister, and grapeshot. John P. Y. Whitfield (1827-fl1887), Philadelphia-born and educated, went to Tennessee in 1850 as a journeyman for the Nashville Manufacturing Company, working in South Carolina, Pennsylvania,

and Kentucky before settling in Clarksville four years later. In 1857 he bought the
Clarksville Foundry, operating it as Whitfield & Company until joined in partnership
(1860) by Larkin Bradley (b. *c*1817), a wealthy Kentucky-born "tobacconist." 1860
Census, Tenn., Montgomery, Clarksville, 60, 116; *Williams' Clarksville Directory*
(1859-60), 41, 70, 74; Ursula S. Beach, *Along the Warioto: A History of Montgomery
County* (Nashville, 1964), 179; Titus, *Picturesque Clarksville*, 429-31.

From Horace Maynard

Washington, June 17, 1862

Dr Sir,

I have received & attended to your several dispatches: The nomination
of Gov. Campbell has been sent to the Senate & will I do not doubt be
speedily confirmed.

We are all from the Prest. down very anxious to hear from East
Tennessee. He told me yesterday, that he was more hopeful of affairs
there just now than at any other point, that he understood Halleck was
advancing upon it with a large force. He inquired very particularly about
the details & especially the future policy of your administration. Warner
L. Underwood,[1] whom you saw one night at your room in Nashville, &
who lives you will remember at Bowling Green, was present with me, &
spoke in terms of very high appreciation of your govt.

In this connection, it occurs to me to say that I have prepared a speech
for publication, nominally upon the confiscation bills,[2] of which as they
have passed the House I think very poorly; but really upon the relation of
the seceded states to the Federal Govt. You know we have often inter-
changed views on this subject & concurred in opinion. I took advantage
of an extreme speech made by Mr. Sedgewick,[3] a prominent member
from New York of the Sumner style, to contrast your views & policy—
Of course, I have an eye to our own people & I hope I have, at least, done
no harm. I will send you an early copy—

Bouligny, presently the member of the House from New Orleans,[4] the
only one in the last Congress who did not secede—is here & wants to be
appointed Collector. He is very desirous of having a letter from you to the
Prest & Secty of the Treasury— When local appointees can be had I am
sure it is desirable.

The trial of Humphreys comes off next week. I will look with some
interest for our friends from Nashville, as I do for all intelligence from
them. I do not know whether you have extended your jurisdiction over
Memphis.

I have seen Brownlow's book, & am pleased with it, far more than I
expected to be. It will do good. Of course it is full of his idiosyncracies. I
wish he could have had access to Caswell's correspondence,[5] at Nashville. That, as well as all other writings of the Secesh, should be preserved. We should read them sometime. Besides they furnish the
material to write our history with.

Brownlow goes to Cincinnati to live with his family until he can return to East Tennessee.

I am very Truly Yours
Horace Maynard—

His Excy Andrew Johnson.

ALS, DLC-JP.

1. Warner L. Underwood (1808-1872), a Virginia native, began law practice in Bowling Green, Kentucky, in 1830, lived in Texas (1834-40), and served in the Kentucky legislature (1848-53), the House of Representatives (1855-59), and as consul at Glasgow (1862-64). *BDAC*, 1740.

2. For Maynard's speech on confiscation of rebel property, May 23, 1862, see *Cong. Globe*, 37 Cong., 2 Sess., App. 273-77.

3. Charles B. Sedgwick (1815-1883), Syracuse lawyer, served in the House of Representatives (1859-63) and as a "codifier" for the navy department (1863-65). *BDAC*, 1578.

4. For John E. Bouligny, who did not receive the collectorship, see *Johnson Papers*, IV, 269*n*.

5. William R. Caswell (1809-1862), East Tennessee lawyer who had served in the Mexican War as captain, Co. K, 1st Tenn. Mtd. Inf., in 1861 was appointed by Governor Harris brigadier general in the provisional army of Tennessee, commanding the forces gathered at Knoxville until they were turned over to the Confederate government. He was murdered near his home six miles east of Knoxville, August 6, 1862. The Nashville *Union* of April 20, printing part of a June 25, 1861, letter from Charles W. Charlton to Caswell calling for more troops to keep loyal East Tennesseans from turning that section over to the unionists, had observed that this and other letters "would have enhanced the study by Brownlow." Chattanooga *Rebel*, August 9, 1862; *OR*, Ser. 4, I, 174; Nashville *Union*, April 20, 1862; 1850 Census, Tenn., Jefferson, 13th Dist., 62; WPA, Tenn., Knox: Old Gray Cemetery, 91; William Richard Caswell Papers, Knoxville-Knox County Public Library.

To Henry W. Halleck

Nashville June 17th 1862

To Maj Genl Halleck
Corinth, Miss

There is much I would like to say in reference to the management of affairs in Tennessee since I reached the State. I left my position in the Senate not for the purpose of obtaining place and emolument but to give whatever aid I could in restoring my adopted state to her former position in the Union.

This has been my sole object. In accepting my present position I was assured by the President of the United States and the Secretary of War that I should be sustained in my efforts to do so and I was authorized to call upon you for adequate force to carry out all measures deemed necessary and expedient. This I have not done for the reason that I did not wish to be importunate or to manifest a desire to exercise power. I will say this much. This place has been left to a very great extent in a defenceless condition, thereby keeping alive a rebellious spirit that could otherwise have been put down by this time. Since I have been here, there has been a constant struggle between Staff Officers, Provost Marshals and Brigadier Generals left in command, which has paralyzed all the efforts of union men in bringing about a healthy and sound reaction of public sentiment.

I have now to ask of General Halleck, without going into detail or specifications that he will remove some of these impediments. Captain O. D. Greene,[1] a staff officer who has been assuming more much more than either you or Genl. Buell would have done or even allow should be ordered elsewhere and I earnestly hope that there will be a change of Provost Marshal of this place, & one appointed who is not in direct complicity with the secessionists of this City and a sympathizer with the master spirits engaged in this Rebellion.

General, if it were left to me, I could suggest the arrangements that ought to be made for Tennessee, and which would aid as I believe in successfully carrying out the designs of the administration and yourself. In claiming to understand the peculiar posture of affairs in Tennessee, I do not wish to be considered vain or egotistical, but I am willing to place my reputation and all that is sacred upon the part I am called to act.

I therefore ask you, Genl., to sustain me in these requests, and in taking the action I recommend, rest assured that any orders or demands you may think proper to make will be implicitly obeyed and carried out.

The demonstrations which have been made upon lower East Tennessee,[2] causing the people to manifest their Union feeling & sentiments and then to be abandoned, have been crushing and ruinous to thousands. I trust in God that when another advance is made upon that section of the State, our position may be maintained, at least until arms can be placed in the hands of the people to defend themselves against their relentless oppressors.

I hope General Thomas[3] and his Division may be sent in that direction. Genl. Thomas I believe to be truly brave & patriotic and his sympathies and feelings are for that people[.]

Please let me hear from you at the earliest moment practicable.

I earnestly hope that you will concur with me in the views I take and be pleased to give me the solicited aid[.]

Very Truly   Andrew Johnson
Military Governor.

Tel draft, DLC-JP; *OR*, Ser. 1, XVI, Pt. II, 30-37.

1. Oliver D. Greene, acting adjutant general on Buell's staff, detailed in Nashville, remained until mid-July; Col. Stanley Matthews was replaced as provost marshal by Col. Lewis Campbell, Johnson's own choice, on June 29. For fuller discussion, see Maslowski, *"Treason Must Be Made Odious,"* 88-92; James B. Fry to O. D. Greene, June 29, 1862, *OR*, Ser. 1, XVI, Pt. II, 72.

2. Probably a reference to the movements of portions of Buell's army under General Negley before Chattanooga, June 7-8, at the conclusion of which they withdrew to Shelbyville. *Ibid.*, X, Pt. I, 904-5, 919-20; Hall, *Military Governor*, 54.

3. George H. Thomas.

To Rodney Mason[1]

Nashville June 17. [1862]

Col. R. Mason,
Commanding at Clarksville, Tenn

The plea of Garnishment by the so called Southern Confederacy is inadmissable as to non-payment of debts, and the party who persists in alleging such garnishment as a reason for non payment and refuses on that account to pay will be at once arrested and held in custody until there is some satisfactory action on his part in respect to the debt and until he takes the oath of allegiance[.]

Andrew Johnson
Mil. Gov'r.

Tel draft, DLC-JP.
1. Mason had asked whether men who sought relief on such grounds should not be "arrested as asserting their allegiance to the rebel Government[.]" Mason to Johnson, June 17, 1862, Johnson Papers, LC.

To John Sherman

Nashville June 18th, 1862.

Hon. John Sherman
U. S. Senate Washington City.
Confidential.

I see that Col Stanley Matthews of Ohio, now Provost Marshal of this place, has been nominated as Brigadier General. Who is he? Does Ohio need his services as a Brigadier? We have had as much of him here as Provost Marshal as we desire. My deliberate opinion is that he is in complicity with the secessionists of this place and that his sympathies are with the leaders of the Rebellion. This is my opinion deliberately formed.   Accept assurances of my esteem.[1]

Andrew Johnson.

Tel, DLC-John Sherman Papers; DLC-JP.
1. Sherman responded: "After consulting Wade we agree with you as to Stanley Matthews & will attend to his case." Sherman to Johnson, June 18, 1862, Johnson Papers, LC.

Interview with Secesh Clergy[1]

June 18, 1862

[Gov. Johnson—] Well, gentlemen, what is your desire?

Rev. Mr. Sehon[2]—I speak but for myself, Governor; I do not know what the other gentlemen wish. My request is that I may have a few days to consider the subject of signing the paper. I wish to gather my family together and talk over the subject.

Gov. Johnson—How long a time will you require?

Rev. Mr. Sehon—My wife is at some distance, and my family having recently labored under a severe domestic affliction, I would, if you have no objection, Governor, have fourteen days allowed me for the purpose of gathering my family together.

Rev. Mr. Ford[3]—That is not to be understood to be the request of all of us.

Rev. Mr. Sehon—Oh, no, Governor. We have been conversing on the subject, and I did not know but that it would be desirable to have a mutual consultation before we again met.

Rev. Mr. Howell[4]—I did not so understand the brother.

Rev. Mr. Kendrick[5]—Nor I. We can come as well singly as together.

Rev. Mr. Saurie[6]—I did not so understand the proposition.

Rev. Mr. Sehon—It was a bare suggestion, and the object might have been misapprehended by the brethren.

Gov. Johnson—It seems to me that there should be but little hesitation among you, gentlemen, about this matter. All that is required of you is to sign the oath of allegiance. If you are loyal citizens you can have no reason to refuse to do so. If you are disloyal, and working to obstruct the operations of the government, it is my duty, as the representative of that government, to see that you are placed in a position so that the least possible harm can result from your proceedings. You certainly cannot reasonably refuse to renew your allegiance to the government that is now protecting you and your families and property.

Rev. Mr. Elliott[7]—As a non-combatant, Governor, I considered that under the stipulations of the surrender of this city I should be no further annoyed. As a non-combatant, I do not know that I have committed an act, since the federals occupied the city, that would require time [me?] to take the oath required.

Gov. Johnson—I believe, Mr. Elliott, you have two brothers in Ohio.

Mr. Elliott—Yes, Governor, I have two noble brothers there.[8] I have seen them but on occasional visits for thirty-four years. They have been good friends to me. They did not agree with me in the course I pursued in regard to secession. But I have lived in Tennessee so many years that I have considered the State my home, and am willing to follow her fortunes. Tennessee is a good State.

Gov. Johnson—I know Tennessee is a good State; and I believe the best way to improve her fortunes is to remove those from her borders who prove disloyal and traitors to her interests, as they are traitors to the government that has fostered and protected them. I think, Mr. Elliott, a visit to your brothers in Ohio will prove of service to you.

Rev. Mr. Elliott—I do not know whenever I have been proven disloyal. I am no politician, and never attended but one political meeting, and never but once perpetrated a political joke.

Gov. Johnson—Perhaps not, sir. But by your inflammatory remarks and conversation, and by your disloyal behavior in weaning the young under your charge from their allegiance to the government established by their fathers, you have won a name that will never be placed on the roll of patriots. A visit to the North, I repeat, may be of benefit to you. (Sensation.)

Rev. Mr. Kendrick—(after reading the oath)—I would like a few days' time before I sign this paper, Governor.

Gov. Johnson—How long do you require?

Rev. Mr. Kendrick—Just as you please, Governor. One, two or three days, or a week.

Gov. Johnson—A week from to-day?

Rev. Mr. Kendrick—Yes, Governor, say a week.[9]

Nashville *Union*, July 5, 1862; New York *Herald*, April 24, 1865.

1. Nashville's clergy, predominantly secessionist, were summoned to appear before the governor and take the oath. This interview, recorded by Samuel Glenn, the " 'religious' correspondent of the New York *Herald*," appeared in the Nashville *Union* July 5, and was part of an extended printing of Glenn's report offered readers of the *Herald* in April, 1865, nine days after Johnson became President.

2. Edmund W. Sehon (1808-1876), Virginia-born Methodist minister, lived for a time in Ohio, and by the late 1840's had moved to Louisville, Kentucky, where he served on the Louisville committee appointed to work with the Nashville *Christian Advocate* (1851); moving to Nashville where he became secretary of the Methodist Missionary Society in 1855, he possessed $40,000 in assets on the eve of the war. He seems to have gone South, his family joining him in January, 1863; for that spring, in Macon, he helped devise a plan for Confederate army missions. During the 1870 Methodist Conference in Memphis, he was one of six ministers appointed to aid the colored people in setting up a separate church organization. 1860 Census, Tenn., Davidson, Nashville, 5th Ward, 178; W. Harrison Daniel, "A Brief Account of the Methodist Episcopal Church, South, in the Confederacy," *Methodist History*, VI (1968), 33; Clayton, *Davidson County*, 236, 335; *Louisville City Directory* (1848), 183; *Nashville Bus. Dir.* (1855-56), 104; Nashville *Dispatch*, February 4, 1863.

3. Reuben Ford (c1813-1870), native Virginian and pastor of the Cherry Street Baptist Church, was imprisoned first in Louisville, later at Camp Chase, and was paroled October 23, 1862. 1860 Census, Tenn., Davidson, 8th Ward, 27; Clayton, *Davidson County*, 320; see also Parole Order for Reuben Ford, October 9, 1862; Ford to Mrs. L. A. Ford, August 31, 1862, Johnson Papers, LC.

4. Robert B. C. Howell (1801-1868), North Carolina-born preacher, editor, author, and denominational leader educated at Columbian College (1824-26), Washington, D. C., moved in 1834 to Nashville, where he served the First Baptist Church, except for a sojourn at the Second Baptist Church of Richmond, Virginia (1850-57). Influential in the development of the Baptist Church in prewar Tennessee, he supported the State Rights theory and when the war began expressed his sentiments publicly. Too ill to be sent North, he was released from prison on August 18; and although still under military surveillance, resumed his pastoral duties as his health improved, remaining, however, a confirmed Confederate throughout the war. Rufus B. Spain, "R. B. C. Howell: Virginia Baptist Tradition Comes to the Old Southwest," *Tenn. Hist. Quar.*, XIV (1955), 99-119, 195-206, 323-40.

5. Probably John T. Hendrick (1815-c1897), Kentucky-born Presbyterian minister serving in Kentucky (1835-45) and in Clarksville (1845-58, 1886-92), who was in Nashville as supply minister for the First Presbyterian Church. In 1863, he returned to

Paducah as pastor (1858-85). Scott, *Ministerial Directory*, 307-8; Titus, *Pictur-esque Clarksville*, 378; *The First Presbyterian Church, Nashville, Tennessee* (Nashville, 1915), 61.

6. William D. F. Sawrie (1812-1884), North Carolina native, had filled pulpits in Clarksville and Nashville and when arrested was pastor at Andrew Church, later serving as superintendent of Methodist city missions (1865-68), minister at Claiborne Chapel (1869-76), and presiding elder of the Murfreesboro and Nashville districts (1877-81). Sent to Camp Chase, he was paroled on October 23, 1862. 1870 Census, Tenn., Davidson, Nashville, 6th Ward, 85; *Minutes of the Annual Conferences of the Methodist Episcopal Church, South, for the Year, 1859* (Nashville, 1860), 120; *ibid., 1865* (Nashville, 1870), 548; Nashville city directories (1867-81), *passim*; Parole Order for William Sawrie, October 9, 1862, Johnson Papers, LC; Jean B. Waggener (Tennessee State Library and Archives) to Andrew Johnson Project, August 31, 1977.

7. Collins D. Elliott (1810-1899), Ohio-born minister and teacher, came to La-Grange College, Alabama, in 1831 as a language professor. Licensed to preach in 1835, he became president of the Nashville Female Academy in 1839, and in 1861 took a firm southern position for himself and the school, courting his arrest by Johnson. Sent from the Nashville penitentiary to Camp Chase, he was paroled on November 18, following the intercession of Mrs. James K. Polk, and later served as a Confederate chaplain. He was unable to continue his school after the war when a civil suit brought against him by stockholders was decided in the latter's favor. Governor William B. Bate appointed him chaplain of the state penitentiary (c1883-87). J. E. Windrow, "Collins D. Elliott and the Nashville Female Academy," *Tenn. Hist. Mag.*, Ser. 2, III (1935), 74-105; White, *Messages*, VII, 120, 199; Parole Bond, November 18, 1862, Johnson Papers, LC; see also Letter from Peter Zinn, November 18, 1862.

8. Possibly William (d. 1881) and George F. Elliott (1826-1896), the latter a prosperous Ohio farmer with $35,000 in real property on the eve of the war. Raising a company of the 69th Ohio Inf., now serving in Nashville, he was in October, 1862, promoted lieutenant colonel. A farmer and distiller after the war, he served in the state legislature (1884-85). Burt S. Bartlow, ed., *Centennial History of Butler County, Ohio* (n.p., 1905), 139, 159; 1860 Census, Ohio, Butler, St. Clair Township, 80; Jean B. Waggener to Johnson Project, August 31, 1977.

9. Appearing before the governor ten days later, they refused to take the oath and five—Howell, Sehon, Ford, Sawrie, and Baldwin—were dispatched to Acting Provost Marshal McClain and confined in the penitentiary until sent north. Nashville *Union*, June 29, 1862; see also Letter to Richard W. McClain, June 28, 1862.

From John Edwards[1]

Chariton Iowa June 20/62

Governor Johnson
Dear Sir

The recent joint Convention[2] held by the Republicans and Union Democracy of Indiana—Is a good Omen— It seperates the gold of the democratic party from the dross—and by nature of things will compell the Union Movement there to be conservative—and the further effect will be to annihilate the Bright[3] secesh wing of the party— From indications in all the North Western states, This will be the last time in my opinion the Democratic party—will attempt to go before the people at least under the Old name and Organization[.] If they had not been committed to a call for a convention in this state I believe at this time they would not call one[.] even now many of them are in favor when the

Convention meets to disband, they will have no earthly show at the election[.]

There is difficulty bewing in the republican party—which nothing but the continuane of the war prevents from coming to an issue—

That the rebellion has destroyed the political pwer of slavery to a great extent cannot be denied—and going on the assumption that the war closes, without Mr Lincolns Military necessity arrising—to abolish slavery than that the goverment should go down—(which I believe the necessity can never arrise) The South will have to modefy its views very much on the slavery question— Southern politiceans see this and the former appoligist for the institution are Squaring their actions accordingly[.]

It is thought Sumner Greely Giddings Wade & Co will bolt the Presidents policy— If so Lincoln will head the Consevative Movment[.] If Lincoln and the great body of the republicans should Succumb to the Ultras[4]—Then a new consevative organization made up of Democrats and republicans will be forced into existence— Politicians are very shy at the north[?] about committing themselves— The great phase connected with the Negro question is going to be—what is to be the disposition of the Negro. The Abolitionist will Contend to have them remain in the Country enjoying the same political priviledges with the White race— This proposition will be rejected by 2/3 of the Northern people—

When the excitement dies out—after the rebellion is crushed out— Extreme Men or Measures north or South cannot exist—provided a plan is fallen on which will unite the Consevative Men of all parties together— This can be done when the time arrives by calling a National Convention—on an entire new name and basis of action[.]

This is the last letter I shall address you on the subject; by the middle of July—I assume the Command of the 18th Regiment now Organizing in this state—and will soon be on my way to Dixie—to assist loyal Men there in upholding the Old Flag— With sentiments of kind regards— I am Your obdt servant—   John Edwards

ALS, DLC-JP.
1. John Edwards (1815-1894), Kentucky-born lawyer and Indiana legislator (1845-46, 1853), settled in Chariton, Iowa (1855), serving in the state constitutional convention, the legislature (1856-60), of which he was speaker (1859-60), and founding the Chariton *Patriot* (1857). During the war he was colonel, 18th Iowa Inf. (1862) and brigadier general of volunteers (1864). U. S. assessor of internal revenue at Fort Smith, Arkansas (1866-69) and congressman (1871-72), he spent his last years in Washington, D.C. *BDAC*, 849; Warner, *Generals in Blue*, 137-38.
2. This joint convention met at Indianapolis June 18, 1862, to decide unionist strategy for the October state election. Meeting separately in the morning, the two groups came together in an afternoon session, chaired by Gov. Oliver P. Morton, and agreed that the war should be vigorously pursued to maintain the Union, not to abolish slavery. John D. Barnhart, "The Impact of the Civil War on Indiana," *Indiana Magazine*

of History, LVII (1961), 198; William D. Foulke, *Life of Oliver P. Morton* (2 vols., Indianapolis, 1899), I, 205.

3. Jesse D. Bright.

4. The Radicals of the Republican party, made up originally of a small body of antislavery fanatics. Craigie and Hulbert, *Dictionary of American English*, IV, 2386.

From Samuel P. Tipton[1]

Trenton Tenn. June 20th 1862

Hon Andrew Johnson
Sir

I consider it my duty as an officer in the United States Volunteer Army sworn to support the laws and constitution of my Country and also as a former citizen of this State; to inform you how matters are conducted by a portion of this Army, and urgently call on you to exercise the power invested in yourself to put a stop to the theiving propensities of a portion of this command. I have more particular reference to some Kansas Troops, truthfully called "Kansas "Jayhawkers"[2] which you well know is the Military name for "Theif[.]" I have seen some of their wagons with negro women and children loaded on them.[3] the impression that one such Regt will give to our would be friends through this country will more than counteract the good effects of half a dozen good union Regts. I do not wish to lay all the blame at the door of these "Jayhawkers[.]" other of our troops are slightly innocculated with the same disease or distemper as you may call it. I am satisfied that the general sentiment of the people here is Union if they were assured of there rights and property being protected. as things are going here at present they have *no such* assurance and feel as though all the falsehoods which have been told them of our coming here to rob and devastate their property was coming true. therefore I beseech Your Excllency to make some enquiry in this matter and as far as your authority permits throw the shadow of your protecting wing over our now troubled and bewildered fellow citizens. I hold myself personally responsible for any statements I have made here. I do it from a sense of duty to myself and of respect to the *high and responsible* office which you hold[.]

I have the Honor to be Your Obt Servt
Samuel P. Tipton
Capt. Co. "E" 2nd Regt. Ill. Cav

ALS, DLC-JP.

1. See *Johnson Papers*, IV, 98n.

2. Originally applied to free-soil residents of Kansas who, during the prewar border conflict, raided across into Missouri combining pillage with guerrilla fighting, "Jayhawker" became the designation of the 7th Kans. Cav. Rgt. during the war. Having displayed a penchant for looting and destroying both unionist and secessionist property in Kansas, the 7th was transferred in May, 1862, to the Columbus, Kentucky, District of the Department of Tennessee and during June was active in West Tennessee where it maintained its unenviable reputation by indiscriminate depredations on Federal and Confederate sympathizers alike. *OED*, V, 561; *OR*, Ser. 1, VIII, 449, 507, 546-47;

XVII, Pt. II, 91-92; Richard S. Brownlee, *Gray Ghosts of the Confederacy: Guerrilla Warfare in the West, 1861-65* (Baton Rouge, 1958), 42-43; Stephen Z. Starr, *Jennison's Jayhawkers* (Baton Rouge, 1973), 166-69.

3. The 7th Kans. Inf. had already gained a reputation for "Negro stealing." Maj. Daniel R. Anthony wrote his sister in February, 1862: "In our march we free every slave, *every man* of all nations" and "hope to stir up an insurrection among the negroes." Almost immediately after the unit's arrival in Tennessee, Anthony issued an order (June 18) expressly prohibiting under pain of severe punishment the return of any fugitive slave. Because this injunction countermanded both the November orders of Halleck and those of district commander Isaac F. Quinby forbidding admission of slaves within Federal lines, Anthony was relieved from command. *Ibid.*, 174-75; Edgar Langsdorf and R. W. Richmond, eds., "Letters of Daniel R. Anthony, 1857-62," *Kansas Historical Quarterly*, XXIV (1958), 359, 458-63.

From Daniel C. Trewhitt and Others[1]

Head Quarters 25th Brigade
Army of the Ohio
Cumberland Gap June 20th 1862

Hon Andrew Johnson:

Dear Governor,

We have at last taken possession of Powells Valley, and Cumberland Gap, by way of Big Creek, and Rogers Gap. We are now at and occupying Cumberland Gap. The Rebels are Reported to be fleeing Southward. In performing this herculeanian task—for such it was— William Cook and Daniel M Ray,[2] the first Sutler, and the last Adjutant 3d Regt East Tennessee Vols.' proved themselves brave and valiant, and rendered important Service, and deserve high applause, and credit!

We now need Cavalry in East Tennessee.

Except Col Munday and his Small force, we have none! Cook and Ray desire authority to raise a Regiment of Cavalry, Cook Col: and Ray Lt Col.

They can raise the Regiment in a very short time, if the authority can be had!

Many men are now ready prepared, and waiting to join such Regiment! They will furnish their own horses, and want only arms, ammunition, and clothing furnished by the government! The authority being given and an assurance of arms, and the Regiment will at once be made! Gov we are now in East Tennessee, safe and secure and the Cavalry absolutely necessary to straighten things in this portion of the State: and feeling Satisfied no braver nor more worthy men could be Selected, we earnestly ask you to send to them Such authority, and power, as will Secure the end desired to be accomplished! We feel confident that these gentlemen are the men for the purpose!

Verry respectfully
Your obedient servts.
D. C. Trewhitt A. A. G.
25th Brigade Army of the Ohio

ALS, T-Mil. Gov's Papers, 1862-65.

1. The other signers were James G. Spears, Leonidas C. Houk, Robert Johnson, Charles L. Barton, Pleasant W. Logan, James O. Berry, John Hall, and James T. Shelley.

2. William R. Cook (b. *c*1830), a native Kentuckian, and Daniel M. Ray (b. *c*1829), North Carolina-born, became respectively lieutenant colonel and colonel of the 2nd Tenn. Cav., USA. Ray, one of the bridge burners from Sevier County, had attended the Union convention at Greeneville in June, 1861. Cook, of Nicholasville, Kentucky, was dismissed from service in late 1863 on Colonel Ray's charges of "gross neglect of duty and conduct prejudicial to good order and discipline," for supplying liquor to the regiment and for delay in following orders. Immediately restored to rolls and rank, however, Cook was wounded and captured at Okolona, Mississippi, February 22, 1864, but released in time to participate in the battle of Nashville. CSR, RG94, NA; *Tennesseans in the Civil War*, I, 321-22; *Tenn. Adj. Gen. Report* (1866), 57, 330.

From Henry W. Halleck

Corinth June, 22 [21] 1862

To Gov A Johnson

The enemy is driven out of all West Tennessee[.] East Tennessee soon will be clear of the Rebles— Obstraperous women in & about Nashville[1] you can easily Manage— The regeneration of the entire State is not far off— I shall call Genl Buells attention to your complaints of Capt Green the Provost Marshall & others[.][2] if he does not afford a remedy soon I will[.]

H W Halleck Maj Genl

Tel, DLC-JP; DNA-RG393, Dept. of the Missouri, Tels. Sent and Recd., H. W. Halleck (Apr. 15-July 16, 1862).

1. In sundry ways—making "mouths," pinching noses, flaunting skirts, and generally snubbing the occupying forces—the secesh ladies showed their distaste for the new regime. Louisville *Journal*, March 29, 1862.

2. Halleck wired Buell: "I hope you will inquire into this; as it is not the first time that such complaints have been made. None but undoubted Union men should be in office in Nashville." Halleck to Buell, June 21, 1862, Tels. Sent and Recd., Dept. of the Missouri, RG393, NA.

From Absalom H. Markland[1]

Post-office, Memphis Tenne.
June 21st 1862.

Gov A. Johnson,
Dr Sir,

Memphis is beginning to assume a healthy, loyal appearance— business is reviving and the people look more cheerful. Everything is encouraging to the lovers of law and order. That state of things for which you so boldly struggled for in the Senate twelve months ago, & to which your energies have since been directed in Nashville is fast breaking upon the citizens of Memphis. A little nerve and bone liniment[2] freely administered to some rampant individuals & West Tennessee is fully redeemed. There is a better feeling here to-day than there was in Nashville when I left that place.

Col Slack[3] who is in Command of the city knows how, and when, to turn the screws so as to make loyalty set well on the unruly. Maj Genl Lewis Wallace has a part of his division in the city.

Applications for the various Federal Offices are numerous— The Post-office is likely to be a bone of contention with men who have neither claim, nor capacity to preside over it. I am not prepared to make any recommendation from among the applicants I have seen in person[.] I shall await your arrival hoping that you will be here before a great while. You will be more kindly welcomed here than you were at Nashville. My kind regards to East, Browning & other friends.

I am Very Respectfully Your Obt Servt

A. H. Markland

Special Agt P. O. D.

ALS, DLC-JP.

1. Absalom H. Markland (1825-1888), Kentucky native and classmate of Ulysses S. Grant at Maysville Seminary, attended Augusta [Ky.] College. Moving to Washington, D.C., with Henry Clay in 1849, Markland worked as a clerk in the office of Indian affairs and the post office department. In private business by 1861, he was appointed to Grant's staff as colonel in charge of the mail, becoming known as "the postmaster general of the army." After the war he practiced law, then served as assistant postmaster general and special agent for Ohio, Indiana, and Kentucky (1869-73). *American Annual Cyclopaedia* (1888), 645; Simon, *Grant Papers*, IV, 204-5; "Affairs of Southern Railroads," *House Report* No. 34, 39 Cong., 2 Sess., 14.

2. Probably to be taken figuratively rather than literally, although some bone liniments of the time promised to cure everything from apoplexy to St. Vitus's dance, with vertigo, convulsions, and fits included, as well as "all nervous diseases." Robert F. Karolevitz, *Doctors of the Old West* (Seattle, 1967), 149.

3. James R. Slack.

To Edwin M. Stanton[1]

Nashville Tenn. June 21 1862.

Hon Edwin M Stanton

Secretary of War

There is great need of two (2) Cavalry Regts in East Tennessee[2] & I trust that it will be in your power to have them sent[.] The rebel Cavalry are committing the most atrocious outrages upon the people & there are no means to protect them[.] with two (2) good Cav. Regts immediately security & protection could be given to the people[.][3]

Andw. Johnson.

Governor Tennessee.

Tel, DNA-RG107, Tels. Recd., Sec. of War, Vol. 16 (June 17-20, 1862); DLC-E. M. Stanton Papers, Vol. 8.

1. An identical telegram went to Gen. Henry W. Halleck at Corinth. Johnson Papers, LC.

2. In addition to the preceding day's request from Trewhitt and others, Johnson had received a wire from George W. Morgan at Cumberland Gap to the effect that "the rebel

cavalry are committing atrocious outrages & I have not the means to protect the people. with one good Regt [of cavalry] much could be done and with two 2 I could give Immediate security to the people of this portion of the State[.]" It was this concern for his fellow East Tennesseans which spurred the governor to action. Morgan to Johnson, June 20, and Johnson to Morgan, June 21, 1862, Johnson Papers, LC.

3. Explaining that "the Govt has not a single regiment at its disposal that can be sent you," Stanton at once authorized the raising of two regiments for "three 3 years or during the war" with "a premium of two 2 dollars for each recruit accepted & one months pay in advance upon the company being mustered." Stanton to Johnson, June 21, 1862, Johnson Papers, LC.

From John W. Leftwich

June 22, 1862, Memphis; ALS, DLC-JP.

Emphasizing that "The ultimate success of our cause in Memphis will depend so much on the character of the appointments to fill our Ofices," recommends William Chase for the postmastership. Although "The conduct of the citizens of Memphis is much better than of those of Nashville," he urges the governor to visit the city: "your presence here a few days would certainly accomplish much good[.]"

From Marcellus Mundy

Head Quarters United States Forces,
Pulaski, Tennessee June 22, 1862.

Brig Gen A Johnson
Mil. Gov. of Tennessee
General

Our meeting yesterday[1] was all we could wish save your presence. The Country people for twenty miles around were here eager to learn and anxious for the adoption of some plan by which the war may be ended and their sons and friends called home. The resolutions, a copy of which I sent you[2] were adopted with great unanimity after the speeches of Messrs Cooper & Brown[3] both of whom struck the right line of argument with peculiar aptitude.—Necessity—being the text. And I am prepared to say to you without hesitation Giles County is right. Were an election ordered here now I don't believe ten votes would be cast in this County against reconstruction of the Union. Bitter experience has made this people wise. I had read their desires before I put the ball in motion, and was satisfied that all they needed was a bold start in the right direction— And experience has convinced me that I had read them rightly. Would to God the balance of your state was as near right as Giles County[.] After the speaking yesterday while dining at my quarters Major Jones[4] made a remark which has exercised me exceedingly, which was made in reply to this question I put to Gov. Brown. "What plan is being discussed at Nashville for getting your state back?" Gov Brown replied that he knew of none. Major Jones said I have understood that as

soon as East Tennessee is occupied by the federal forces Governor
Johnson proposes to recall Gov. Harris and the Legislature of the state
by Proclimation whereby any unconstitutional procedure in getting the
state right may be avoided."[5] Govnor your frequent indulgences make
me bold and I tell you such policy would in my humble opinion be
unwise and unfair. Unwise because both Govnor Harris and that Legislature who appropriated money to fight our government and furnished
soldiers for that purpose, thereby committed overt acts of treason against
the government which disqualifies them— Govenor Harris and that
Legislature while legitimately the body of Tennessee were the agents of
the so called confederate Government and enemies to the federal Government. And could those representatives elected under the auspices of
our enemies properly and legally do that which loyalty to the federal
Government requires? Besides it would be unfair because wrong has
been committed to which heavy penalties are affixed.   somebody must
be responsible for that wrong and somebody must pay the penalties[.]
Thirty thousand of your young men in obedience to that legislation and
the call of Gov. Harris took up arms to commit active treason against the
government we serve— Of that 30,000 but few had what the law terms
animus—because but few understood even the prejudice they were
called upon to battle for and none of them even knew a *reason* for
rebellion. Now these young men must bear the responsibilities and
burthen of treason or their masters must shoulder the responsibility,
whereby the law in clemency may excuse them. You will find my
resolutions shift all the responsibility upon the Legislature and Govnor
and propose the organization of a loyal and proper legislature whereby
your young men *by state authority* may be recalled. I have been compelled
to admit the doctrine of state sovereignty further than I believe it exists in
order to perfect this plan; but I have done so because I could see no other
way to excuse your young men who were cajoled bullied, divided and
driven into rebellion, and no other door whereby they can consistently
with their false tenets of honor reenter the sacred precents [precincts] of
Loyalty. I take it Govnor that there is a proper interregnum in your state.
The terms of your legitimate legislators have expired. And those elected
under the southern Confederate flag cannot hold office—therefore you
have no legislature and my plan would be (pardon the suggestion) to
immediately issue a proclimation fixing an early day say twenty days
hence for an election of legislators under the Constitution of Tennessee as
provided for vacancies— Then in your message to that legislature you
may properly suggest the rescinding of the acts severing your state from
the Union—and calling out troops as the first work and their resolution
calling for an election of Congressmen and Govnor would be the next
deed which you could there upon order by proclimation— And thus
your state might be placed right within sixty days and your sons and
friends relieved from prisons and exile: Then again too we might have

the happiness of seeing you in your more important post as Senator of the United States which you have so highly honored and which the general good of this great republic so much requires. Govnor I have written very hastily without time to correct the language which has but poorly conveyed my ideas— I hope however you will understand them and forgive my presumption as you know but one purpose guides me now which is a speedy and proper restoration of our government.

I have the Honor to be Your &

M Mundy Col. Com. Post

ALS, DLC-JP2.

1. A successful rally held in Pulaski on June 17, featuring Mundy and other speakers, prompted the calling of a "Great Union Meeting" for June 21 at which the citizens of Giles County would have an opportunity to hear Neill S. Brown and Governor Johnson. Nashville *Union*, June 20, 1862.

2. Not found.

3. Edmund Cooper and ex-governor Neill S. Brown.

4. Thomas M. Jones, former Pulaski mayor and recent member of the Confederate Provisional Congress.

5. Johnson never entertained such a scheme. See Telegram to Marcellus Mundy, June 23, 1862.

From Lewis Wallace

June 22, 1862, Memphis; ALS, DLC-JP.

Advises that he has delayed assuming command of Memphis because he "strongly hoped" that Johnson would be there "in person or by representative to take the Governorship." Reports that "Certain citizens, of influence in the rebellion, are beginning to negotiate for the privilege of a safe return to the city. All they seek is a pledge of safety from both the civil and military authorities." Cites R[obert] C. Brinkley, "a citizen of large property and influence socially and politically," who "wishes to be allowed to mind his own business," and to whom Wallace will give such guarantee if Johnson agrees.

To Robert Johnson

Nashville June 22nd 1862

Col R. Johnson

I have just received a dispatch from Secretary of War authorizing me to raise Cavalry regiments in Tennessee,[1] Consult Genl Morgan, if he is of the opinion that it would be good policy to convert your infantry regiment into Cavalry you will at once proceed to do so.[2] You will say to Genl Morgan that the Secy of War dispatches to me that there is no Cavalry at his disposal that can be sent for the immediate relief of East Tennessee. hence the importance of acting at once if you act at all. let me know the result of your Conference with Genl Morgan immediately—

Andrew Johnson

Tel draft, DLC-JP.
    1. See Telegram to Edwin M. Stanton, June 21, 1862, note 3.
    2. On June 26 Stanton authorized the conversion of Robert's 4th Tenn. from infantry to cavalry at Johnson's "discretion." RG107, Tels. Sent, Sec. of War, Vol. 11 (June 19-25, 1862).

From George W. Morgan

Cumberland Gap June. 23 1862

To His Excellency Andrew Johnson

I might as well be without eyes as without cavalry[.][1]   The enemy is said to have taken up a strong position in the clinch mountains in the direction of Morristown but not on the route I would advance if authorized to go forward but this place would be threatened by the enemies position were I to pursue another route[.]   one strong brigade with 6 heavy guns and five hundred 500 cavalry to act as scouts & foragers should be left here & I should be strengthened by two brigades of infantry one battery of artillery & two 2 regiments of cavalry[.]   with such a force I can sweep East Tenn of every rebel soldier[.]   my effective force is now about seven thousand five hundred 7500 men of all arms. The people flock in & implore protection[.]

George W. Morgan
Brig Gen Vols Comg

Tel, DLC-JP.
    1. Under the same date Morgan wired that he must have more cavalry to remain on the defensive as the secretary of war wished. Johnson Papers, LC.

From James S. Negley

Columbia Tenn June 23 1862

To Gov Andrew Johnson

I submit to you the absolute necessity of arresting & severely punishing a few of the active secessionists of this vicinity. Depredations are committed daily through their influence & the Union men kept in a state of terror[.]   simply arresting & administering the oath is not sufficient[.]   It only serves to cloak their movements. I have arrested Young S. Packard this morning as one of these men[.]   what shall I do with him[?]   He is one of the old C. S. A. speculators.[1] Your wishes relative to the man we arrested in East Tennessee was complied with[.][2]   The extent of contraband trade carried on by both Union men & rebels with Chattanooga rendered it necessary to make a few examples.

Jas S Negley Brig Genl

Tel, DLC-JP.
    1. Perhaps Young S. Pickard had participated in the illegal salt trade, funnelled through Columbia to the Confederate army at McMinnville during May. Futrell, Federal Trade, 67.
    2. Not found.

From B. O. Williams[1]

[Clarksville, Tenn 23 June, 1862]

To his Excellency Andr. Johnson
Governor of Tenessee

You must certainly be apprised of the existence of a company in this neighborhood which intends leaving in a week to join Morgan, guerrilla, but it is passing strange that you have not shown more disposition to quell these secret organizations. This one has been gotten up by one John Dortch[2] near Forts Station on the E & K. R. Road. he has over two hundred men and they are all leaving daily in squads.

It is impossible to detect them with an armed force for they are all sworn to secresy and will die rather than betray their leader[.]

I had a conversation to day with a young man who is in all their movements and if you approach right you can get into their plans, he remarked to me that he would have to be well paid before he would tell anything of it[.]

I will suggest the following plan which I hope will be of interest to you[.] Send some one out to see this young [man] with a written assurance that he will not be molested and induce him to come and see you and I am confident from his circumstances you can bribe him to reveal all their arrangements wherewith you will be enabled to bag the whole company[.]

They are all armed with colts navy pistols, these pistols were smuggled from Louisville by one Jame. H. Mallory[3] near Fort's Station and the mony was furnished by Dr J. T. Darden[4] near Port Royal and G. A. Washington[5] near Turnersville[.] I have gained this much but cannot get the important portion as all the members are cautious and swear they know nothing about it[.] Let the person who calls on this young man be dressed in citizen clothes to avoid detection or suspicion[.] I enclose his address on a card and request you to destroy my letter[.]

You must act fast in this as the company is leaving now in small numbers[.]

Respectfully   B. O. Williams

I have to write with a pencil as I am away from home[.]

ALS, DLC-JP.

1. Possibly B. Williams (b. *c*1822), a North Carolina-born Robertson County farmer with $250 personal property. 1860 Census, Tenn., Robertson, W. Div., 57.

2. John B. Dortch (b. *c*1830), Tennessee-born farmer with $76,000 in real and $23,300 in personal property, was captain, Co. E, 50th Tenn. Inf., CSA. Escaping capture at Donelson, he attached himself to the 23rd Tenn. Inf. at Shiloh, and later recruited and served as captain, 2nd Ky. Cav. Btn., which became part of Wheeler's corps. *Ibid.*, Montgomery, Clarksville, 51; *Tennesseans in the Civil War*, I, 285-86; II, 132; *OR*, Ser. 1, X, Pt. I, 590; XXXIX, Pt. II, 856.

3. James H. Mallory (*c*1830-*fl*1880), born in Tennessee, was postmaster at Fort's Station (1861-67) and later an auctioneer. Deane Porch, tr., *Robertson County, Tennessee, 1850 Census* (n. p., 1968), 95; 1880 Census, Tenn., Robertson, 17th Dist., 8; *U.S. Official Register* (1861-67), *passim*.

4. Jacob T. Darden (*c*1828-*fl*1880), native Tennessean and physician, possessed $18,000 real and $10,000 personal property. 1860 Census, Tenn., Montgomery, Clarksville, 51; (1880), 5th Dist., 24.

5. George A. Washington (1815-1892), a Robertson County native and owner of "Wessington," a large tobacco plantation four miles south of Cedar Hill, had $250,000 real and $279,000 personal property on the eve of the war. Vice president of the Louisville and Nashville Railroad and a director of the Nashville, Chattanooga, and St. Louis Railroad, he served as a Confederate presidential elector in 1861 and as a Robertson County representative (1873-75). *Ibid.* (1860), Robertson, W. Div., 107; Robison, *Preliminary Directory, Robertson*, 41.

From Samuel Williams[1]

Trenton June 23d 62

Hon. A. Johnson

Dear sir it has been some time since I have had an oportunity of writing you but I am inclined at the first oportunity to draft you a line[.]   shortly before the June election of 1861, I advised my friends to seek to oppose the seperation & let it go by default[.]   a Millitary camp had been ordered to our Town & it was certain that for the time at Least the state was overrun[.]   after the election I was inclined to resign but my friends objected because a verry radical officer would be put in my place greatly to the prejudice of conservative men[.]   I yelded to their wishes[.]   in this county the conservative men have a large majority[.] after the election of June 1861 the confederate government took controle of Tenn & I believed all residents in the state bound to yeld obedience to it while it held controle of the state[.]   they could do nothingless & live[.]   things passed on & we preserved more of our rights than any county that took a Stronger position doing the best we could & as we belive sustained by the laws of Nations in all we did taking no oaths of Allgiance to the Confederate government—   on the 17th the Federal Forces entered our Town[.]   they have been treated respectfully as they all admit[.]   I have gotten acquainted with all the officers who seem to [be] gentlemen but have excedingly wrong notions on the subject of slavery[.]   the jayhawkers have outraged the rights of our people beyond any thing that we had thought of[.]   in my circuit the courts have been Regularly held & the sivil government is Amply Able to sustain itself if there was no soldiers on either side within its bounds[.]   I merely give you an out line of the reasons upon which we have acted and belive we are entitled to have oppressive eliments removed from among us[.]   no officer here will say that they have received other than satisfactery respect in this community[.]

I shall be at Nashville as soon as the body of the soldiers leave us[.]   I am not enformed as to whither I am now considered in or out of office[.]   you will do me the kindness to enform me how that is[.] if I am to be superseeded I would prefer to resign as I dont want it understood that you have turned me out[.][2]   if that is the course to be taken immediately on hearing from you I will send you my resignation & I shall do this with the kindest feelings[.] I am verry Anxious to see you[.]

I remain your friend Truly

S. Williams

ALS, DLC-JP.

    1. For Williams, judge of the 15th judicial circuit, see *Johnson Papers*, III, 686*n*.

    2. While there is no record of Johnson's reply, Williams was evidently commissioned "Circuit Judge for 16th [*sic*] Judicial District" on December 6, 1862. Ex. Record Book (1862-63), Ser. 4C, Johnson Papers, LC.

To Oliver D. Greene

Nashville, June 23d. 1862

Capt. O. D. Greene,

Assistant Adjutant General,

Dr. Sir,

    I enclose herewith a note from the Telegraph Agent in which he communicates what is represented to be your reason for refusing to order the payment of the telegraph account which bears my endorsement of approval as Military Governor.

    If such is the case, it seems to me that you misapprehend the nature of the authority I assume to exercise, and I therefore most respectfully beg to call your attention to the enclosed copy of my Commission for information as to the authority—whether military or civil—under which I act.

    I will state that these dispatches were for the most part to and from the President, Sect'y of War, Generals Halleck, Buell, Morgan, &c, on business connected with the military service, and it seems to me that the payment of the account by Quartermaster-Capt Bingham[1] would be perfectly proper, and hope that you will order payment to be made in that manner.[2]

Very Respectfully, Your Obt. Svt.

Andrew Johnson, Military Governor.

L, DNA-RG393, Dept. of the Cumberland, Lets. Recd., 59-J-1862; DLC-JP.

    1. Judson D. Bingham (1831-1909), New York-born West Pointer (1854), participated in the suppression of John Brown's raid. Promoted to captain and assistant quartermaster (May, 1861), he was supervisor of the Nashville depot (1862-63), and chief quartermaster for the Army of the Tennessee, serving in the siege of Vicksburg and the march through Georgia. Brevetted brigadier in April, 1865, he became chief quartermaster for the Pacific and Missouri divisions and assistant quartermaster general before his retirement in 1895. *Appleton's Cyclopaedia*, I, 263-64; Heitman, *Register*, I, 218; *West Point Register* (1970), 247.

    2. The final sentence of the original draft, found in the Johnson Papers, reads, "I hope therefore you will be pleased to order the payment of the account." Receiving no

response, Johnson wrote Greene on July 1 asking him to "favor me with an early reply, advising me whether or not payment of accounts . . . on military business of the Military Governor, will be ordered through the Quarter Master at this place[.]" Johnson Papers, LC.

To Richard W. McClain[1]

Nashville, June 23d 1862

Lt. Col R. W. McClain,
Acting Provost Marshal,
Dr. Sir

I am in receipt of your reply to my enquiries of this date. The property occupied by Maj Thurneck's family[2] does not come within the scope of an order dated Nashville May 7th '62[3] purporting to be by authority of General Buell in regard to the occupancy of houses in this city by officers &c. It is not property occupied as "Quarters". Maj Thurneck is individually [responsi]ble as a citizen for everything pertaining to the premises, and no one has a right to interfere with his possession thereof unless it is necessary for Governmental purposes. I am not aware that this property is needed for Government use, and must therefore ask you to suspend the execution of the alleged order until General Buell can be consulted by despatch or otherwise. Maj Thurneck's wife, as I am advised is confined to her bed by sickness which is a further reason for the suspension of action in this matter especially so when it is not claimed that the property is for public use[.] I wish to make no question of authority with Capt. O. D. Greene or anyone else—and desire simply to call your attention to the reasons I give herein for the suspension of this order. For information as to the authority under which I act I ask your attention to the enclosed copy of my commission & copies of letter & order of Genl Buell[.]

Very Resp'y Your obt svt
Andrew Johnson Mil Governor

Tel draft, DLC-JP.

1. Richard W. McClain (c1823-1880), resident of Coshocton County, Ohio, and Mexican War veteran, served as captain, Co. D, 16th Ohio Inf., rising to colonel, 51st Ohio Inf., during the war. Wounded at Murfreesboro and captured at Chickamauga, he was held at Libby Prison until March, 1864. CSR, RG94, NA; Catherine McClain, widow's certificate, Pension File, RG15, NA.

2. Alexander S. Thurneck (c1826-1869), major, 10th Tenn. Inf., subsequently became a Nashville attorney, serving as justice of the peace (1869) and North German consular agent for Tennessee (1868-69). CSR, RG94, NA; *King's Nashville Directory* (1869), 220; Mt. Olivet Cemetery Records, Interment Book II (microfilm, Public Library of Nashville and Davidson County), 31.

3. "Officers performing Staff duties in the city, Surgeons in charge of Hospitals, and officers of the Provost Guard are alone allowed to live in quarters." Oliver D. Greene to Stanley Matthews, May 7, 1862, Nashville *Union*, June 20, 1862.

To Marcellus Mundy

June 23 [1862]

Col M: Mundy.
Pulaski, Tenn

I have just received your letter of yesterday. I was utterly astonished to find that anybody could for one moment have entertained the idea that I intended to recall Gov Harris & the late treasonable Legislature[.]

I have intended at a proper time to offer a reward for Gov Harris' apprehension & return to this state as a Traitor where he could be tried & convicted of treason[.]   Where Maj. Jones derived his information I am not prepared to say. I know it has never eminated from me.

It is my intention as soon as the rebel army is driven from the State & the people are in a condition to come to the ballotbox unrestrained to order an election for members of the Legislature under such restrictions as will secure without doubt members who are loyal & true to the Constitution & the Govt. I hope you will correct at once any such impression as that indicated in your letter in regard to Harris & the Legislature[.] I rejoice that your meeting was a success. Indications from various sections of the State are encouraging, and in a short time after the repulsion of the Rebel army Tennessee can & will be restored to her former relations to the Federal Govt.

I hope you will manage Maj. Jones' case according the dictates of your own good judgment[.]

Accept assurances of my esteem
Andrew Johnson

Tel draft, DLC-JP.

From William L. Pope[1]

Camp Morton Indiana
June 24th 1862

Hon. Andrew Johnson,
Dear Sir.

In the last few days, myself in conjunction with Several hundred of the Tennesseeans imprisoned here, have entered a written protest against being exchanged and returned to the Southern Army, declaring that we will never return to the Confederate Army unless forced to do so by the Federal authorities to be exchanged. I address you for the purpose of Soliciting your influence in our behalf; and, I trust we will not hope in vain, when we hope that you will use your influence with the Federal Authorities never to exchange those of us, who have handed in our protest to the Commander of this post, under any Circumstances whatever. The reasons for determining upon Such a Course by us are these: 1st If we desired to contend longer, we as Tennesseeans cannot fight for the independence of the Cotton States when Tennessee will never be a part of the Southern Confederacy: 2nd. We have found by talking with citizens and Soldiers and reading the different political papers here that a large portion of the masses North are Conservative and really never intended to interfere with our institutions as we were led honestly to believe[.] they, not intending to interfere with our institutions and we being Satisfied of that, there is no longer any Sense in our fighting; because, we Started out in this rebellion, believing, that the Conservative Sentiment North was powerless for good, and that mad fanaticism was the great ruling element here, which had gotten hold upon the government, and which would overthrow and destroy the "peculiar institution" which belonged to our State and the South; of Course then, being Satisfied that we were most egregiously mistaken in our former views, we cannot as honest and concientious men, fight against an intended wrong upon us which really does not nor never did exist only in the imagination of the misinformed and in the misconcieved ideas of a large portion of our Southern brethren. We believe it is our duty to return to our allegiance to the Federal government, and be Contented to go home, and remain peaceable citizens, and aid in restoring peace and quietude to our distracted State once more, and in removing, as far as we can, the false views of our fellow citizens we have left behind us. There isn't a Tennesseean who does not revere the old flag and the Constitution of our fathers, and it was a Source of mortification and regret when we believed they had been grossly perverted by evil and designing men: You may rest assured that it affords us great pleasure and gratification to know that we were so wide of the mark in our former views and notions of the intentions of our Northern brethren. Allow me again to ask your influence in our behalf, those of us at least, who have entered our protest with the authorities here against being exchanged; hoping that we may be allowed to return to our former allegiance, when it is our choice in preference to being sent South. I trust you will let us *here* from you immediately upon the Subject.

I Remain, Very Respectfully
Your humble Servant
William L. Pope

P. S. I am from Columbia and most of the Tennesseans who have entered there protest against being exchanged are from Middle Tennessee. W. L. P

ALS, DLC-JP.

1. William L. Pope (c1828-1863), Tennessee-born physician who served as a private, Co. A, 9th Tenn. Cav. Btn., CSA, was captured at Donelson, imprisoned, and exchanged. Again taken at Columbia on September 11, 1863, he was sent to Camp Chase, where two months later he was shot and killed by a guard. Porch, *1850 Census, Maury*, 244; CSR, RG109, NA.

To Lewis D. Campbell, Nashville

June 24, 1862, Nashville; L, CLU.

Introduces Peyton Randolph, one of whose slaves "has been seen in your camp, and, as he is a loyal man, I hope if such is the case, that the negro will be put outside of your lines."

Proclamation Re Edgefield and Kentucky Railroad[1]

June 24, 1862

State of Tennessee

To all who shall see these presents—Greeting—Whereas The Edgefield and Kentucky Rail Road Company has failed to deposite a sum requisite to pay the interest on the bonds issued to it and the Governor having been notified by the Comptroller as provided in Sec 1101 of the Code.

Now Therefore I Andrew Johnson Governor of the State of Tennessee by virtue of the power and authority in me vested do hereby appoint and commission E. M. Reynolds[2] of the county of Robertson state aforesaid, Receiver with full power [to] take possession of and comptol the road of said company and all its property and effects to manage the same and receive the rents issues and profits thereof as prescribed by law during the period that he shall hold said office. In testimony whereof I Andrew Johnson Governor of the State of Tennessee have hereunto set my hand and caused the Great seal of the state to be affixed, This 24th day of June 1862.

Andrew Johnson

DS, DLC-JP.

1. For Edgefield and Kentucky Railroad, see Letter from Gilbert C. Breed, April 12, 1862, note 4.

2. E. M. Reynolds (b. c1818), a native Kentuckian and prosperous Springfield, Tennessee, merchant before the war, was clerk of the chancery court (1844, 1851) and of the circuit court (1850) in Robertson County. He resigned from this assignment early in July. 1860 Census, Tenn., Robertson, W. Div., 114; *Goodspeed's Robertson*, 837, 841; Reynolds to Johnson, July 5, 1862, Johnson Papers, LC.

To Edwin M. Stanton

Nashville June 25 1862.

Hon Edwin M Stanton

I have just received despatch from Col Johnson[1] fourth Tenn Vols pressing the importance of that regt being at once converted into Cavalry. It is composed of men perfectly familiar with the region where cavalry is now needed. This change cannot be made I understand without order of secy of war[.]   Gen Morgan in command at Cumberland Gap states that the proposed change meets his intire views & that the regt will be changed at once if you so direct. I hope instructions will be at once given to furnish horses & equipments[.][2] Matters in Middle & West Tenn are working well[.] if we only had some impediments[3] that have been in the way since I reached here removed our success would be complete.

Yours Truly Andw. Johnson

Tel, RG107, Tels. Recd., Sec. of War, Vol. 16 (June 17-30, 1862).

1. Robert Johnson to Andrew Johnson, June 21, 1862, Johnson Papers, LC.

2. The following day the governor returned to the fray with this terse message: "I can have horses purchased at a fair price in this state and Kentucky. Send me the authority." Johnson to Stanton, June 26, 1862, Johnson Papers, LC.

3. An allusion to his conflict with representatives of the regular army in the Nashville vicinity.

From "a Union Man"[1]

[Nashville] June 26, 1862—

To Gov Johnson

State of things at the insane asylum

this time last summer I heard docter and Mrs Cheatham[2] and old man ready[3] say that King harris mist it by leting andy Johnson the treator go that he should be hung— now sir them very people are this very day I believe a stealing from the state[.] them have sent some three large chests to town one to cheathams wharehouse the other tow to Parrishes wharehouse[.][4] I am not certain what is in them but there are a grate many here that the[y] have just packed[.] I am told that tow contain ladys bolts of dry goods beding carpeting and so he has keep a bout, 3000. Pds. of rebel bacon that was stored here the time rebels run a way likewise 12 steers a large quantity of lard[.] you can find out if he has charged them to the state or not[.] he keeps 12 hors here[.] the most of them is blood stock[.] he raisd the most of them here[.] he did get 2 carag horses from his brother in the rebel army[.][5] he did keep until lately a seamstress with 4 children to sew for his lady and the ready famaly[.] bill cheatham the gambler is out here[.][6] he was the first in nashville to raise a company the[y] caul the cheathe rifeles[.] he stays out of the way here boarding at the docters No. 1 table[.] the famaly the[y] think the[y] are above all others[.] there is knothing is cared for here but the one table and the pachents can have knothing only the one thing all the time and I am told he dus not goe in to som of the wards in monnths[.] there is three cooking departments here one for the ladys the other for the gents the other for the superier negroes that cooks[.] the[y] can just dow as the[y] please] in tow of them[.] I have not seen in four years the steward[7] the docter or Mrs cheatham eather to order or see what the pachents got[.] the thrustees dus not know any thing about this[.] it is time that it was known to them and the public at large so as to make a change for the benefit of the poor inmates[.]   the steward keeps the books[.]   he is the man to keep until he lets the cat out of the bag[.]   the docter has been one of the fourth or fifth on the rebel list in the gazette and ever since he has devoted all his time to help it[.]

from a Union Man

ALS, DLC-JP.

1. Not identified.
2. William A. Cheatham (c1820-fl1890), a native of Middle Tennessee, studied medicine in Pennsylvania, began practice at Nashville in 1845, and was appointed superintendent of the insane asylum in 1852, a position he held until July, 1862. His wife, Mary E. Cheatham (c1827-1864), the oldest daughter of Charles and Martha Ready of Rutherford County, was sister-in-law to Gen. John H. Morgan. Letters between Mrs. Cheatham and her sister Martha Morgan were carried to Federal headquarters at Nashville by a double agent employed by General Rosecrans. For corresponding with the enemy and encouraging spying, the Cheathams were arrested in April, 1863, and ordered sent to prison at Alton, Illinois; but, through the efforts of Cheatham's brother Richard, former mayor of Nashville, they were released in June. 1860 Census, Tenn., Davidson, 5th Dist., 76; Wooldridge, *Nashville*, 530; Fitch, *Annals*, 564-73; Holland, *Morgan and His Raiders*, 203-5; Nashville *Dispatch*, May 17, June 20, 1863; *Nashville City Cemetery Index*, 15; Louisville *Journal*, April 17, 1863.
3. Charles Ready.
4. A reference to the storage facilities of M. A. Parrish and Company, a wholesale grocery and commission agency located at College and Merchant streets and headed by Micajah A. Parrish (c1826-fl1880), a Tennessee native. According to W. A. Cheatham, Parrish had been among those willing to extend credit to the asylum prior to his removal from the superintendancy. Porch, *1850 Census, Nashville*, 3; 1860 Census, Tenn., Davidson, Nashville, 6th Ward, 110; (1880), 42; *Nashville Bus. Dir.* (1860-61), 240; "Report of the Superintendent of the Tennessee Hospital for the Insane," *Tenn. House Journal*, 1865-66, App. 226.
5. Boyd M. Cheatham (c1839-1877), who had lived with his older brother while a student in 1860, was commissioned captain, Co. G, 10th Inf., CSA, in May, 1861, escaped capture at Donelson, and served in Mississippi and Georgia (1862-63). Settling in Springfield after the war, he became a merchant and was elected mayor and state representative (1871-73). 1860 Census, Tenn., Davidson, 5th Dist., 76; Robison, *Preliminary Directory, Robertson*, 6; McGavock, *Pen and Sword*, 668; CSR, RG109, NA.
6. W[illiam?] T. Cheatham (1837-1919), of Marshall County, commissioned in May, 1861, first lieutenant, "Cheatham's Rifles," resigned in July, but reappeared on the rolls in September, 1863. *Ibid.*; Sallie A. Cheatham, Confederate widow's pension application no. 10148, Tennessee State Library and Archives.
7. Thomas Farmer (b. c1802), native Tennessean, was the asylum steward (c1858-68). 1860 Census, Tenn., Davidson, 5th Dist., 76; *Tenn. House Journal*, 1857-58, App. 283; *ibid.*, 1869-70, App. 320.

From Edmund Cooper

June 27, 1862, Shelbyville; ALS, DLC-JP.

Forwards petitions from Asa L. Stamps and William S. Jett, unionists, asking that rebel property in the vicinity of Cornersville be confiscated and that the petitioners receive such property in reparation for cotton burned by the Confederates.

From Narcissa R. Hall[1]

[Readyville, Rutherford County]
June the 27th 1862

Mr Andrew Johnson. Govner of Tennessee

I have a request to make of you wicth I hope you may grant[.] The favour I have to ask is that you will let Alley Abernathy[2] come home on a parole of honor and stay 2 months as a prisoner at home,

he is my oldest child I hav a living[.] his brother got killed in blowing rock in a sistern two years ago. my husband died 15 months ago, the only son I have with me had his thigh broke, and his breast bone broke and twisted out of its natural place, and is injured inwardly so blood passes from him whenever he fatiuegs himselfe, he is disabled for life.

it was done by falling from a swing 2 years ago, I have three little girles to rase, if you would grant my requst it would confer a great favour on me, I will now state the character of Alley[.] He is a study kind hearted boy and if he has a enimy on earth I do not know it. Profeser Jarmon says he is the best boy that ever went to school to him in Murfreesboro[.][3] he is also a Christain, and you must remember that the privats did not cause the war, theay were forced to take up arms on one side or the other and theay made their choice to go with the south[.] As to Alley he said had rather be in his grave if it was the lords will than to go to war, but he said he would not go as a drafted man,

As to my own part I am not bitter at either party, as I think it a fulfillment of the bible. as the learned of all denominations admit that their is some important event to take place between this and 1866 the melenial year is to ursure [usher] in it is expected by a great maney. and if that be a correct opinion we all should be ready to appear before the juge to receive our final doom. that knows no change, here we hope for a change of our prisnors or pease, that theay may return to their homes. but one hope I have for my child if we meet hear on earth nomore that I will meet him around the throne of god whear no harm can reach him,

Mr Johnson you have power now but recollect the bible says whatsoever measure we meete out it will be measured back again, but I must stop for perhaps I have written more than you will read but remmember the feeling of a parent and grant my requst.

Please answer this, and I will ever be under many obligations to you, if you would let all of the boys come home on a parole of honor it is my opinon that theay, would return when called for, and I do not think it would be any injury to the north for theay are escaping, and coming home and as theay, cannot stay at home, theay are foced to go to the southern army, but if theay were permited to come home on a parole of honor theay would be glad to remain at home in a honorable way[.]   no more at present[.]

> yours with respet
> Narcissa R Hall

This letter I wish to be kept private[.]

The Prisoners that I wish released was taken at Donolson[.]   theay are at camp Butler near springfield Illinois[.]

ALS, DLC-JP.

1. Narcissa Wright Abernathy Hall (b. 1822), married Rutherford countian Charles C. Abernathy in 1839 and had three sons by him: Thompson (c1840-c1860), Albert (Alben) A., and Charles (b.c1844). By 1850 she had married farmer and miller G. B. Hall (c1820-1861) of the same county and had several more children. Porch, *1850 Census, Rutherford*, 203; WPA, Tenn., Rutherford County Marriage Records, 1838-1845, p.9; 1860 Census, Tenn., Rutherford, McCracken, 125.

2. Albert (or Alben) A. Abernathy (c1841-1863), Narcissa's second son and a private, Co. C, 18th Tenn. Inf., CSA, was captured at Donelson and imprisoned at Camp Butler. Exchanged with his regiment at Vicksburg in September, 1862, he was killed at Murfreesboro. *Ibid.*; CSR, RG109, NA.

3. George W. Jarman (b. c1826), native Alabamian and member of the original faculty of Union College founded at Murfreesboro in 1849, returned to teach there after the war. Porch, *1850 Census, Rutherford*, 368; *Goodspeed's Rutherford*, 836; Sims, *Rutherford County*, 152.

From Alexander P. Smith[1]

> Fayetteville June 27th 1862.

Gov. A. Johnson.

Dear Sir.

Below you have a copy of a portion of a letter recd by me from R Gilchrist[2] Policeman of Louisville Ky.

The Girl Tabby[3] mentioned in your letter (now in Jail in this place) is undoubtedly yours—   When you come be sure to get a requisition from the governor of your State for the return of Fisher, (the free Negro who enticed your girl to leave you,) to your State for trial for the act. We have evidence Sufficient to convict him of the Crime. Get the requisition as Soon as possible—

As it is uncertain when I Shall go for my girl, you are left to act in the case as you may deem right. I would be much pleased to have Fisher brought here for trial, but that is as you may decide to act. In a letter from the Jailor he stated that the demand for Fisher must be made in 60 days. He was arrested I think about the 20th of May. Will you let me know what you will do in the case shortly.

> With much respect A. P. Smith

address A. P. Smith Fayetteville

Care R. P. Shapard[4] Shelbyville

P. S.   If you decide to make a demand for Fisher, it will not do to send him here to be confined for the reason that the runaway negroes put in Jail here, are Set at liberty by the military authority of this place. On

Sunday last 9 were taken by armed men from our Jail and carried off with the army.

A. P. Smith

ALS, DLC-JP.

1. Alexander P. Smith (1796-1879), a Virginia-born Lincoln County farmer, had accumulated $6,000 in real estate and $7,000 in personal property. 1860 Census, Tenn., Lincoln, 8th Dist., 212; Tucker and Waller, *Lincoln County Bible Records*, II, 22-23.

2. Robert Gilchrist (c1826-fl1881), New York native and a moulder by trade, who recently became a member of the Louisville police department, was chief (1868-69) and later a tobacconist, inventor, and home hardware salesman. 1860 Census, Ky., Jefferson, Louisville, 8th Ward, 254; Louisville directories (1861-81), *passim*.

3. Tabby (b. c1830), a mulatto house slave held by Smith as guardian of the estate of Levi Cole (d. 1862) of Lincoln County, had obtained a pass to go north from Capt. William B. Curtis of Gen. John C. Turchin's staff. Disguised as a man she traveled in company with George Fisher and James Cromwell who also had passes representing each as free men of color who had been in the service of various officers of the 19th Ill. and were now returning to their homes. En route the train conductor suspecting that they might be runaway slaves, notified the Louisville police, and they were arrested at the depot, May 29. At the subsequent examination, Cromwell, testifying that Tabby was a slave and that Fisher had been a party to her escape, was released, while the latter was committed to jail "to await a requisition from the Governor of Tennessee." There was no question that the Illinois soldiers were accomplices, if not instigators, of this escape. Louisville *Journal*, June 7, 13, 1862; Nashville *Dispatch*, June 8, 1862; also Letter from Alexander P. Smith, August 18, 1862.

4. Robert P. Shapard (1805-1871), a native of North Carolina, was a commission merchant with $1,500 in real estate and $15,000 in personal property. 1860 Census, Tenn., Bedford, Shelbyville, 7th Dist., 6; Helen Crawford Marsh and Timothy R. Marsh, *Cemetery Records of Bedford County, Tennessee* (Shelbyville, 1976), 199.

To Don Carlos Buell

Nashville June 27th 1862

Maj Genl Buell
Florence
a short time since there was a battery fitted up at this place by an order from you obtained by Genl Dumont & myself[.] I have been advised this morning that Capt Green has ordered the battery to be disbanded[.] I desire to know whether this has been done by instructions from you[.][1]

Andrew Johnson

Tel, DNA-RG94, Gens. Papers, D. C. Buell.

1. Buell's chief of staff reassured Johnson that "The Genl has given no specific instructions about disbanding the Battery. Inquiry will be at once made into the matter and proper orders given." J. B. Fry to Johnson, June 29, 1862, Johnson Papers, LC.

From William B. Cassilly[1]

Franklin June 28/62

Gov Johnson
Dr Sir—
I find Williamson County to be the hottest bed of secessionism in the

state— untill yesterday—not a man in it had taken the oath— I have given notice that all persons holding office shall subscribe to it—and they are to decide at 4 P.M. to day— They have already asked to resign their offices to evade it—but I have declined to receive their resignatins— My reasons for this course is—that their is an understanding amongst all, not to take it—and so soon as I can force some few prominant ones into it—I think there will be no trouble—as I am sure there are hundred who want to take it—but fear to do so—as the balance threaten them— Judge Perkins,[2] judge of the County Court is the most prominant one here— he posatively declines, and I send him down to day—to the Comdg. Officer with the request that he be sent *south*—

My principle reason for writing you—is for information in reference to what course to pursue—for carring on the government of the county—

Judge Perkins having refused to take the oath there is no county court— no taxes have been ordered to be collected—and I may say there is no funds for any purpose in the hands of the treasurer—That for County purposes being less than 50 $—

The Poor Fund is exhausted—and many poor are in the County— The bridges want repairs—

I propose to levy a special tax[3] of Some 2 or 3000 $—to be collected from the most prominant and richest secesh farmers in the neigh-bourhood—this money to be placed in the hands of the County Treasure if he takes the oath—and if not to appoint one—From this fund, to support the poor & repair bridges and all other matters of actual necessity—under the proper officers if they take the oath—if not, to appoint— It being understood, that this is only a temporary meas-ure—to be abandoned when the proper wheels of government can be put in operation—

The office of the Planters Bk of Tennessee is open here— I propose to close it unless the cashier[4] takes the oath—

If these steps do not meet your approbation please advise me[.]

Resp Yours   Wm. B Cassilly
Lt Col 69th Ohio—

ALS, DLC-JP.

1. William B. Cassilly (*fl*1881), a partner in Bryson & Brother, "Manufact'rs and Wholesale Dealers in Domestic Wines and Liquors" of Cincinnati, was at this time lieutenant colonel and later colonel of the 69th Ohio Inf. Sick at the battle of Murfrees-boro, he partook of an alcoholic stimulant which rendered him "stupid" and, though wounded, was dismissed from the service. Following the war he served on the Cincinnati city council (1873-75) and achieved success in the insurance business. Cincinnati city directories (1861-81), *passim*; CSR, RG94, NA; *Official Army Register: Volunteers*, V, 161; *OR*, Ser. 1, XX, Pt. I, 421.

2. Philip G. S. Perkins.

3. There was precedent for such a tax, inasmuch as the Williamson County court in May, 1861, had levied a tax for the relief of soldiers' (CSA) families and had ordered County Judge Perkins to issue script to be sold to Planters' Bank for cash to be used in relief work. *Goodspeed's Williamson*, 798.

4. The cashier, possibly Thomas Parks (b. *c*1801), English-born holder of that office in 1850, "agreed to take it," according to Cassilly's marginal notation. 1850 Census, Tenn., Williamson, 9th Dist., 496.

From Robert B. C. Howell

January [June] 28, 1862

Gov. Johnson—Sir: Summoned before you I am requested to take the following oath:

I do solemnly swear that I will support, protect and defend the Constitution and government of the United States against all enemies, whether domestic or foreign, and that I will bear true faith, allegiance and loyalty to the same, any laws, ordinances, resolution or convention to the contrary notwithstanding; and, farther, that I do this with a full determination, pledge and purpose without any mental reservation or evasion whatsoever; and, further, that I will well and faithfully perform all the duties which may be required of me by law[.] So help me God.

Sworn to and subscribed before me.

I have ever scrupulously conformed myself to the government under which I have lived. I do this as a religious duty. I have never knowingly violated any law of the Federal government, of the state government, nor of the military government now established. I am informed that no violation of the law is charged against me. My purpose is to pursue the same course hereafter. I intend not to resist the "powers that be," but to comply with their requisition as far as they do not come in conflict with my duty to God. Respectfully I feel myself obliged to say that I cannot do it, and for several reasons, some of which I beg permission very briefly to state.

First—I cannot take this oath, because there are some parts of it which I do not understand. When I am requested to swear that I will "bear true faith, allegiance and loyalty to the Constitution and government of the United States, any law, ordinances, resolution or convention to the contrary notwithstanding," I am at a loss as to the meaning. What law, ordinances, resolution or convention is referred to, I know not. I cannot tell whether reference is had to some existing law, ordinance, resolution or convention which I am likely to suppose obligatory upon me, or to something of this kind which may hereafter be inaugurated. Nor do I know who is to be the judge, I myself, or some one else, whether such laws, ordinances, resolutions or conventions if there be any such, are or are not in conflict with the Constitution and government of the United States.

And further, when I am called upon to swear "that I will well and faithfully perform all the duties which may be required of me by law," I perceive no conditions nor limitations. What laws may be adopted by the United States and by the State of Tennessee, who knows? They may be laws in conflict with my duty to God; they may be laws in collision with the constitution; they may be laws in antagonism with other laws claiming my obedience. Such compliance with them is impossible, yet it is demanded of me to swear that "I will well and faithfully perform all the duties required of me by law," without condition and without limitations.

An oath so vague, indefinite and impracticable respectfully I must decline to take.

Second—I cannot take this oath, because once having sworn to support the Constitution of the United States, and having up to this hour faithfully complied with the obligation, and receiving now no office nor privilege of any kind under the government of the United States nor of the State of Tennessee, there is nothing known to me in the Federal Constitution, nor in the constitution of this state, nor in the laws made in the pursuance of either which requires me to repeat that oath. The demand that I shall do so under the circumstances in which I am placed implies that I am an offender against the Constitution or the laws, or both. That implication I respectfully decline to countenance by taking the oath.

Third—I cannot take this oath because, since the present government of the United States, and the Constitution of the United States, are in some respects at least confessedly in antagonism, to "support, protect and defend" both is clearly impossible.

To support, protect and defend the one is necessarily to oppose and resist the other. To keep this oath, therefore, (I speak for myself only) is impracticable. Perjury is inevitable. From taking it, therefore, I must be excusable.

Fourth—I cannot take this oath because it binds me to support and protect and defend the "government of the United States," by which doubtless is meant the government of United States as at present administered. Already the administration has done many things which I cannot support and defend, and which I cannot conscientiously swear that I will support and defend. What it may do hereafter, and what its successors may do, I cannot tell. This oath makes me swear without conditions and without limitations "that I will support, protect and defend the government of the United States."

To do this would be to "resign my right of thought" and so renounce my liberty as a free citizen of my country.

Fifth—Nor can I take this oath as a measure of expediency. By expediency I refer to the fact that since an oath taken under duress is not binding then on those who resort to it to save their families from suffering and themselves from punishment. I have a large, helpless and dependent family;[1] I am myself not indifferent to the ease and comforts of life, but I cannot avail myself of this plea for several reasons, one only of which need

William G. Brownlow

John Hunt Morgan

Don Carlos Buell

Elizabeth Harding
(Mrs. William G.)

Horace Maynard

R. B. C. Howell

Neill S. Brown

A garland of friends and foes.
Buell, Brownlow, and Maynard, *courtesy National Archives*; Brown and Howell,
courtesy Tennessee State Library and Archives; Harding, *courtesy Mrs. Jesse E.
Wills, Nashville*; Morgan, *courtesy Valentine Museum, Richmond, Virginia.*

be mentioned. This oath makes me swear that I take upon me those obligations "without any mental reservation or evasion whatever;" that is as I understand it, that I do not avail myself of this expedient, but take the obligation heartily and in good faith. In me, who cannot disregard its moral binding force, this would be perjury.

Sixth—I cannot take this oath because it would be a violation of my duty to God. My duty to God requires that I shall take no oath the entire import of which I do not fully understand, that I shall not swear unless there be good and sufficient reasons for it, that I swear to do contradictory things, that I shall not do impracticable things, and that if I do swear that I shall not swear falsely, but shall truly and fully perform my oath. To take this oath would therefore be to violate my duty to God.

Seventh—Without an oath I shall in future, as I have heretofore, perform as a religious duty every just obligation to the "powers that be," but this oath I cannot take. I cannot take it as a measure of expediency; I cannot take it at all. I must respectfully decline it and take the consequences.

January [sic] 26, 1862   R. B. C. Howell

Nashville *Banner*, October 1, 1892; Howell Memorial, First Baptist Church Records, Nashville, Tennessee (microfilm), Tennessee State Library and Archives.

1. Howell and his wife had six children still at home, four girls and two boys, ranging from a daughter of twenty-three to an eight-year-old son. 1860 Census, Tenn., Davidson, Nashville, 5th Ward, 148.

To Richard W. McClain

State of Tenn., Executive Depar't.
Nashville, June 28, 1862.

Lieut. Col. R. W. McClain, Acting Provost Marshal:

Sir: Reverend Doctors Howell, Ford, Sehon, Sawrie, and Baldwin,[1] are under arrest, and they are hereby placed in your custody.

Should they desire to give evidence of their loyalty by taking the oath of allegiance and giving their individual bonds in the sum of $5,000 each for the faithful observance thereof, they will be permitted to do so, and their release ordered accordingly.

If, however, it is their determination not to give such evidence of loyalty, they will be committed to prison, there to remain until arrangements are completed for their transportation South, beyond the Federal lines, there to be left, with the distinct understanding that if they recross or come again within said lines during the existing rebellion, they will be considered spies and dealt with accordingly.

Very respectfully, Andrew Johnson,
Military Governor.

Nashville *Union*, June 29, 1862; also in Rufus B. Spain, "R. B. C. Howell: Nashville Baptist Leader in the Civil War Period," *Tenn. Hist. Quar.*, XIV (1955), 336.

1. Absent from the city a week earlier when Johnson confronted the other ministers,

Samuel D. Baldwin had just returned "from the country." Baldwin (1818-1866), Ohio native, entered the ministry in Kentucky, moving to Tennessee in 1848 and serving in the early fifties as pastor of the First Methodist Church and as president of Soule College in Murfreesboro (1853-56). Minister of Nashville's McKendree Church (1861-66), he had two days earlier received notice to appear before the governor; sent to Camp Chase in July, he was paroled in October. Howell Memorial, First Baptist Church, Nashville, Tennessee, 1820-63 (microfilm), Tennessee State Library and Archives; Nashville *Dispatch*, October 9, 1866; Sims, *Rutherford County*, 128, 197; Baldwin to Johnson, June 26, 1862; Parole for Samuel D. Baldwin, October 8, 1862, Johnson Papers, LC.

To Richard W. McClain

Executive Department,
June 28, 1862

Lieut. Col. McClain, Acting Provost Marshal:

Sir: I have to request that you will issue stringent orders prohibiting all visitors to the Members of the Clergy this day sent as prisoners to the Penitentiary, except such as have special permission from [me] for that purpose; and I would add, this privilege should be granted only for good and sufficient reasons. I would suggest that no encouragement should be given to that secession spirit and feeling which are manifested in the numerous offerings of delicacies, &c., by sympathizing rebel friends.

These men were not sent to the Penitentiary there to be kept as objects of especial attention from traitors, nor to be lionized by a class of people, who, if properly dealt with, would be allowed the privilege of expressing their sympathy only within the same place of confinement.

They are there as enemies of our Government, and as such, are entitled to and should receive such consideration only as attaches to a person guilty of so infamous a crime.

Very respectfully,
Andrew Johnson,
Military Governor.

Nashville *Union*, June 29, 1862.

Dialogue with Chaplain Wharton[1]

June 28, 1862

Chap.—Governor, I am present at your requisition.

Gov.—I wish simply to say to you that the time has arrived when the Government must know its friends and put down its enemies. You are suspected of being hostile to the Government whose agent I am.

Chap.—Well, I regard myself as a loyal man, and expect to be obedient to the Government. I believe, that my very first temporal allegiance is due to Tennessee, and am ready to go whichever way she goes. But I am a citizen of a higher government than that.

Gov.—What government is that?

Chap.—*I am a citizen of Heaven!*

Gov.—There are men in Nashville professing that citizenship who are responsible for the blood of more of our countrymen, than the soldiers who have bayonets in their hands. You call yourself a citizen of Heaven. Just look at this document—(*handing him the following extract with the name of Wm. H. Wharton annexed to it.*)[2]

I have witnessed *with much satisfaction* the cheerful alacrity and diligence with which the prisoners (in the Penitentiary) have labored for the State in the last few months, in preparing the materials of war, to which they were stimulated by a *most commendable and patriotic ardor*; they have labored *faithfully* for their country, and *many* of them young men placed in confinement for minor offences, might be judiciously selected as objects of Executive clemency, who would endeavor to *atone for the misdeeds of the past by acts of bravery and heroism on the battle-field*.

COMMENDING WITH EARNESTNESS THE ABOVE SUGGESTION TO THE AUTHORITIES,

I remain, most respectfully,
Wm. H. Wharton,
Chaplain.

Is that your report sir, and your name? Do you call that the language of a "citizen of "Heaven," to advise the turning loose of felons from the cells where justice has placed them, that they may join in the work of killing loyal men and of destroying the best government in the world? I don't believe the Almighty approves of such teaching as that.

Chap.—Well, the first duty is to defend our State and I thought it was right to repel the North when she invaded us. Self-defence is the only fighting I approve of.

Gov.—Did not Tennessee invade Kentucky?[3] Did not South Carolina invade the property of the United States and fire on our fellow-citizens? You have learned your facts very incorrectly.

Chap.—(Looking terribly perplexed) I don't wish to argue the case with you, Governor. My mission is to preach Christ. I am no politician and submit to whatever government may get the power.

Gov.—But you could urge the release of felons to aid in murdering loyal men, Do you pretend that your gospel is confined to the limits of your Southern Confederacy? I always thought its precepts of love and charity were co-extensive with the world. You cannot justify your conduct before man or God.

Chap.—I had to go with my State and defend her. That is justifiable warfare.

Gov.—There are rules of warfare which christians and barbarians alike observe. You advised the turning loose of felons and placing arms in their hands. Did you get that from your Bible? Does it tell you that a man *may atone for a felony by committing treason*?

Chap.—As I said before, I cannot discuss politics—it is not my profession. Christ said to his apostles, "my Kingdom is not of this world."

Gov.—Yes, and I believe there was a Judas among his disciples. If he

were on earth again there are some of his professed teachers who would
sell him for less than thirty pieces of silver. They would betray him for
half the money.[4]

Nashville *Union*, June 29, 1862.
    1. Although he had not been among the clergymen appearing before Johnson ten
days earlier, penitentiary Chaplain William H. Wharton was on hand when five of the
original group refused to take the oath and were sent off to the penitentiary. Following
their removal, he was called into the governor's office where this "dialogue" occurred.
"Quite a portly and sedate looking gentleman," Wharton (1790-1871) was a native of
Albemarle County, Virginia, and a graduate of Jefferson Medical College at Philadelphia (1818). In 1843, after practicing at Tuscumbia, Alabama, he moved to Nashville
where he served the community as a Campbellite preacher, physician, and chaplain of
the penitentiary. It would appear that during the war he was both prisoner and chaplain!
In 1869 he ended formal practice and became the state librarian. Nashville *Union*, June
29, 1862, Porch, *1850 Census, Nashville*, 77; Clayton, *Davidson County*, 211, 285;
Frederick J. Dreyfus, "Life and Works of George Michael Wharton, M.D., (Pseudonym
'Stahl'), 1825-1853," *Tenn. Hist. Quar.*, VI (1947), 316-17, 325-26; Nashville *Union
and American*, May 9, 1871; Wharton to Johnson, July 27, 1864, Johnson Papers, LC.
    2. The Nashville *Union* of June 28, in printing this extract from Wharton's October,
1861, report as chaplain of the penitentiary, observed that it was probably written at the
dictation of Governor Harris, "who pardoned numbers of felons on condition they would
enlist in the rebel army."
    3. Johnson refers to Confederate occupation of Columbus, September 3, 1861, by
Tennessee troops under Gideon Pillow, thereby ending Kentucky's "neutrality"; a few
days later, on September 19, Zollicoffer's forces advanced into eastern Kentucky to
prevent strategic points from falling into Federal hands. Coulter, *Civil War in Kentucky*,
107-8, 110; Long, *Civil War Almanac*, 114-15, 119.
    4. "In consequence of bad health," Wharton was paroled for several days, only to be
sent subsequently to Louisville and then to Camp Chase, Ohio, where on October 23,
1862, he was paroled under bond for $5,000. Nashville *Union*, June 29, 1862; Johnson
to Wharton, October 9, 1862, Johnson Papers, LC.

From Marcellus Mundy

Head Quarters United States Forces
Pulaski Tennessee June 29 1862.

Brig Gen A. Johnson
Mil Governor of Tennessee
Nashville
General
    The following order I had executed and now report to you.

Pulaski Tennessee
Hd.Qrs. U.S. Forces June 25th 62

Special Orders No 6.
    Revt Wellburn Mooney, Booker Shapard Dr. Jas. A Sumpter, Dr. Charles C.
Abernathey and Robert Winstead,[1] Citizens of Giles County who have been
active participants in the rebellion as far as urging the enlistment of soldiers in the
rebel army and furnishing them with money, arms and outfits—who have
industriously circulated reports calculated to aggravate the already inflamed
minds of their Country men, keep alive false hopes and check returning loyalty,
and who sympathise with the rebellion to such an extent as to not only forget but
endanger if not destroy the interests of their own people—having been duly
notified on the 12th day of this month by the Commandant at this post, that the
United States could no longer brook treason in any shape under her flag—and

warned, that by ten o clock of this day they should determine whether they would
return to their allegiance to the Federal Government or travel into their prefered
Country and aid their friends who so much need them, having decided that their
conscientious scruples prevented them from taking the oath of allegiance. It is
ordered that Captain Twyman[2] with an escort of twenty mounted scouts conduct
them carefully and safely to our lines and deliver them under a flag of truce to any
officer of the rebel army that may be met with, together with a Copy of this order
and a request from the Commandant at this Post, that they be so disposed of as to
benefit their cause more by *deeds* then *words*—   They are allowed to carry with
them into the land of their choice their families and property and should they
return within our lines except as prisoners of war they will be dealt with as
spies—   This disposition has been made of the above named gentlemen because
the Commandant has *conscientious scruples* against taxing the Federal government for their support—

By order of M Mundy
Col. Com. Post.

I gave Major Jones[3] further time. He is allowed forty eight hours from
Monday June 30. to place himself beyond our lines. As the offense of
Major Jones is one of peculiar inquiry for Civil Courts I am little
disposed to let him take the oath which by fair inference may wipe out the
record against him. It will not do to leave him here free and untromeled
as justice must be equal handed. The execution of the above order has
had a salutary effect—   Many are coming forward voluntarily to take the
oath,   General I pray for the success of our cause & I am wearing out in
my efforts—   unless I can be relieved here soon and ordered to some
more congenial post, I shall be compelled to resign or go into the ground.

Very Respectfully Your Obt Sert
M Mundy Col. Com. Post

General—   My wife will arrive in Nashville by the Tuesday or Wednesday cars from Louisville en route to see me. Should there be difficulty in
her passing to this place, may I ask your kind intercession—

Respectfully M Mundy

ALS, DLC-JP.

    1. Welborn Mooney (c1830-fl1889),·Virginia-born Methodist minister who had
held pastorates in Grundy, Giles, and Maury counties, served as a missionary to the
Army of Tennessee and was a member of the Tennessee delegation to the 1866 Method-
ist conference in New Orleans. Booker Shapard (c1803-fl1870) was a native of North
Carolina and a Giles County merchant with property valued at $13,500 in 1860.
Possibly Robert Winstead (b. c1839), Williamson County native, whose father John
M., a magistrate, was in charge of that county's Confederate home guard. 1850 Census,
Tenn., Grundy, 1st Dist., 1; Fitzgerald, *John B. McFerrin*, 346; WPA, Tenn., Giles
County Marriage Records, II (1865-70), 11, 110; *Maury County Cousins*, I, 429;
*Minutes of the Annual Conferences of the Methodist Episcopal Church, South, for the Year
1889* (Nashville, 1890), 28; 1860 Census, Tenn., Giles, N. Subdiv., 180; (1870),
Pulaski, 18; Sistler, *1850 Tenn. Census*, VII, 103; *Goodspeed's Williamson*, 798, 1019.
    2. Henry G. Twyman was captain of an independent company of Kentucky scouts
which eventually became part of Co. G, 3rd Ky. Cav., USA. *OR*, Ser. 1, XVI, Pt. II, 8,
596; William F. Amann, ed., *Personnel of the Civil War* (2 vols., New York, 1961), II, 109.
    3. Because of Thomas Jones's prominence as former mayor and member of the
Confederate Provisional Congress, Mundy believed he should set an example by taking
the oath. Johnson's parole, conditioned on his taking the oath, was issued July 1; Jones
ultimately went South. Letter from Marcellus Mundy, June 15, 1862; Jones to

Johnson, July 29, 1862, Johnson Papers, LC (a copy of parole enclosed in latter); John Trotwood Moore and Austin P. Foster, *Tennessee: the Volunteer State, 1769-1923* (4 vols., Nashville, 1923), II, 163. See also Letter from Thomas M. Jones, June 14, 1862.

From Josephine T. Bryan[1]

June 30, 1862

Gov. Johnson
Sir

I enclose a list of the furniture taken from our residence by Capt. Green while we were at our plantation in Ala.

I am truly thankful to you for your many acts of kindness to me[.]

Very Respectfully
Josephine T Bryan

Nashville

The following is a list of furniture taken from our residence by Capt. O. D. Green U.S.A.

    2 Sofas
    2 Large Armed Chairs
    1 Do cushioned sleeping Do
    1 Marble top center table
    1 Marble cased clock
    2 Gilt china chamber setts
    2 Feather pillows-and
    The portrait of our son[.]

Josephine T Bryan

ALS, DLC-JP.
    1. Josephine T. Bryan (b. *c*1838) was the wife of W. P. Bryan (b. *c*1822), "Gentleman," who had $40,000 in real estate and $25,000 in personal property. 1860 Census, Tenn., Davidson, Nashville, 5th Ward, 155.

From George W. Childs[1]

Philadelphia June 30 1862

Gov. Andrew Johnson,
Dear Sir,

At the request of Dr. Brownlow I send you by this day's mail an autograph Copy of his work,[2] as a slight token of his appreciation of your stern and unswerving resistance to Rebel aggression.

He loses no opportunity to assert, both in public and private, that you are the right man in the right place. Next to the Salvation of his country; his highest ambition would be to see you President of the U. S.

I am now printing the 75th thousand of the Dr's. book, and the demand increases.

Very Respectfully Yours,

Geo. W. Childs

P.S. I would be glad to have your opinion of the work.[3]

G. W. C.

ALS, DLC-JP.

    1. George W. Childs (1829-1894), Baltimore-born publisher and philanthropist, became associated in 1849 with the Philadelphia bookselling business which came to be known as Childs and Peterson. After a year with J. B. Lippincott and Company, he began in 1861 to publish books connected with the war. Buying the Philadelphia *Public Ledger* in 1864, he built it to a daily circulation of 90,000 by 1876. *DAB*, IV, 70-71.

    2. W. G. Brownlow, *Sketches of the Rise, Progress, and Decline of Secession; with a Narrative of Personal Adventures among the Rebels.*

    3. Apparently Johnson did not honor the request.

From Richard W. McClain

Office Provost Marshal

Nashville Tenn June 30th,'/62

Governor Johnson

Sir,

    Your instructions pertaining to the Clergy of this place have been and will be to the letter carried into effect— Shall I permit any of the substantials (as delicacies are forbidden) being taken to said Clergy by their own Families no other persons being admited or shall I confine them to the usual Fare of the Prison[?][1]

I remain Your most obedient

R. W. McClain Lt. Col 51st Regt.

Acting Provost Marshal

ALS, DLC-JP.

    1. Johnson seems not to have sent a written reply.

From Edwin D. Morgan and Andrew G. Curtin[1]

New York June 30, 1862

To Andrew Johnson

Private & confidential[.]   in view of the present state of Military Movement & the depleted condition of our efficient forces in the field resulting from the usual & unavoidable cassualties of the service together with the large numbers of men required to garrison the numberous cities & Military positions that have been captured as well as to protect our avenues of supply in the enemys country it is proposed to address a memoral to president[2] today to be signed by all the Governors of the loyal states & some other officals of the country requesting him at once to call upon the several loyal states for such number of men as may be required to fill up all organizations in the field and such increased number of men to the army heretofore authorized as may in his judgement be necessary to speedily crush this rebellion & restore our gov.   the descisive moment to accomplish this end it is belived has arrived[.]   shall we add your name to the memorial[.]   answer immedeately[.][3]

E D Morgan   Gov of New York
A G Curtin   Gov of Penn

Tel, DLC-JP.

1. Edwin D. Morgan (1811-1883), a Massachusetts native who moved to New York City in 1836, was a city alderman (1849), state senator (1850-55), commissioner of immigration (1855-58), chairman of the Republican national committee (1856-64, 1872), governor (1859-62), major general of volunteers, serving as a commander of the Department of New York (1861-63), and U. S. senator (1863-69). *BDAC*, 1356. For Curtin, see *Johnson Papers*, IV, 510*n*.

2. The memorial, dated June 28 but not issued until the 30th, was actually in response to Lincoln's suggestion, brought by Seward to a conference of governors in New York City, that additional troops were desperately needed to maintain and advance the Union military effort. In what was apparently a private statement of his "view of the present condition of the War," the President explained, "I would publicly appeal to the country for this new force, were it not that I fear a general panic and stampede would follow." Ultimately sixteen governors, the remaining three—Massachusetts, Rhode Island, and Iowa—could not be reached in time, and the president of the military board of Kentucky signed. Basler, *Works of Lincoln*, V, 291-97.

3. Johnson cooperated with alacrity: "Your despatch has just been recieved[.] The objects therein indicated are more than approbated, & you can add my name without hesitancy." The following day, in a "Call for 300,000 Volunteers," Lincoln responded to the memorial, and a week later Johnson was asked to raise two regiments of volunteer infantry as part of Tennessee's quota. Johnson to Morgan and Curtin, June 30, 1862; C. P. Buckingham to Johnson, July 7, 1862, Johnson Papers, LC; Basler, *Works of Lincoln*, V, 296-97; Nashville *Union*, July 8, 1862.

To Lewis Wallace

Nashville June 30th [1862]

Major General Lewis Wallace, Memphis, Tenn

I thank you for your letter just received.[1] I will be in Memphis as soon as it is possible for me to leave here, which I think will be in a very few days. I will notify you when I leave.

You must permit me to thank you for your letter to Honorable Schuyler Colfax[2] last winter, suggesting an expedition into East Tennessee, which, if adopted, would have redeemed that people from oppression long before this. It was laid before Genl. McClellan & its adoption pressed— When they will be relieved—God only knows. I have almost despaired.

Accept assurances of my high esteem.
Andrew Johnson.

Tel draft, DLC-JP.

1. Letter from Lewis Wallace, June 22, 1862. Johnson was evidently unaware that the day after Wallace wrote, he was given two weeks' leave by General Grant, a directive soon modified by a formal command from Stanton instructing him to await further

orders at his Crawfordsville home. The Indianian was at this time in disfavor because his division had gotten lost during the first day's fighting at Shiloh; it was fall before he again held an active command. McKee, *"Ben-Hur" Wallace*, 52-53, 58.

2. Schuyler Colfax (1823-1885), New York native, became an Indiana Whig politician and newspaper publisher during the forties. With the advent of the Republican party, he moved onto the national scene as a member of the House of Representatives. (1855-69; speaker from 1863) and as vice president (1869-73). *DAB*, IV, 297-98; *BDAC*, 721. Although Wallace's letter has not been found, its purport has been cited in note 2, Letter to William H. Seward, January 2, 1862.

From William G. Brownlow

Washington, July 1st, 1862

Gov Johnson:

Gen. Campbell was confirmed on yesterday, as a Brigadier, and in a conversation with Lincoln to-day, between him, Maynard and myself, we learned that he would assign Campbell to such command as you might direct—at least I inferred this from the conversation. We think that you ought to ask that Campbell be appointed in lieu of the man you have, Dumont.[1]

Gen John B. Rogers, of Rock Island, came [with] in *one* of being made Federal Judge over Trigg,[2] but we have given Lincoln and Bates[3] a talk that has stopped the mater. You had better protest to Lincoln against Rogers' appointment to that office, and have Judge Catron[4] help you. I told Lincoln and Bates, that if they could not appoint a better *Lawyer* than Rogers, to leave the office vacant, for the next fifty years, as we did not wish to be made fun of by secesh.

Clemens[5] has been urging Rogers, and Rogers has been urging himself by every sort of means.

I write in haste, &C,
W. G. Brownlow

ALS, DLC-JP.
1. Ebenezer Dumont.
2. Connally F. Trigg.
3. Edward Bates, attorney general.
4. John Catron.
5. Andrew J. Clements had been seated as Tennessee congressman in January, 1862, despite the state's withdrawal from the Union.

From David H. Creekmore[1]

Huntsville Tenn July 1st 1862

Dear sir

the condition of our country is this we have no circuit court clerk no Judge but what few Justices of the peace but these [three?] but their commissions expired last spring. Sheriffs term of office expired Last spring[.]   no Election held[.]   our clerk[2] was a Rebel & has left[.]   our county people are some of them very recolass [reckless] & know chance to punish for crime & we want some information from you to know how to proceed to bring a bout a regulation for the benefit of our citizans & we do not know how to proceed[.] Collonel Wm Cliff[3] is in our Town recruiting the 7th Tenn Redgiment & all appears quiett. Governer I never did love to be troubblesome but you must try to excuse[.]

Your Obt Servt   D. H. Creekmore

Andrew Johnson
Gov. of Tenn

ALS, DLC-JP.
    1. David H. Creekmore (b. c1818), a Virginia-born farmer and boardinghouse operator with $750 real and $800 personal property, enlisted in October, 1861, in Co. G, 2nd Tenn. Inf., USA, at Camp Dick Robinson, was discharged for disabilities in December, and had only recently returned with his family from exile in Kentucky. See Letter from David H. Creekmore, March 7, 1862; Creekmore to Johnson, December 9, 1864, Johnson Papers, LC; CSR, RG94, NA; 1860 Census, Tenn., Scott, 2nd Dist., 80.
    2. The circuit court clerk (1860-70) was Tennessee-born J. N. Carlock (b. c1828), with $1,800 in real and $1,600 in personal property. Ibid., 76; Sanderson, County Scott, 246.
    3. For an endorsement of the need to get the Scott County courts organized and the machinery of law enforcement in operation, see William Clift to Johnson, July 1, 1862, Johnson Papers, LC.

From Jonathan D. Hale

Glasgow July 1st 1862

Honorable Andrew Johnson
Dear Sir

The Negrow man of mine Lavinder[1] which the Pirates stole last winter has escaped from them & is now with Col Woolfords[2] Regiment at Murphreesboro[.]   will you see that he has a Pass along the Railroad to Lebanon Ky via Louisville[?]   send him to the care of Genl. Boyle[.]   he will need about 5 days rations[.]

I am advised that I am entitled to some pay for aiding Fugatives from East Tennessee[.]   how can I get it[?] I have been compelled to remove my Family farther into Ky. they have to purchase all they use & I find hard work to keep them going & if I am entitled to anything it would be very acceptable just now[.]

Very Respectfuly
J D Hale

Please answer at Columbia Ky[.]

ALS, DLC-JP.
    1. Given Hale's slave holdings in 1860, the missing Lavinder was probably a twenty-year-old black. 1860 Census, Slave Schedules, Tenn., Fentress, Jamestown, 2.
    2. Frank L. Wolford.

From Alpheus Matson

July 1, 1862, Memphis; ALS, DLC-JP.

A "decided Union Man," intending to settle in Memphis, seeks appointment as postmaster; asserts that the number of unionists would be "verry considerably Augmented" if Johnson came for a visit.

From Horace Maynard

Washington, July 1, 1862

Dr. Sir,

The Senate yesterday confirmed the nomination of Gov. Campbell[1] as Brig. Genl.

Please write me what command you wish him assigned to. Would it not be well to place him in a charge of the stationary military force in Tennessee, something like the position Gen. Boyle occupies in Ky.[2] Between you & him (supposing always & only that you concur in your views, as I understand you do) the state could be restored to quiet & peace.

Humphrey's impeachment was quickly over. Gen. John B. Rodgers is applying for the place, with a pretty good prospect for getting it! Clements,[3] I believe, is the only Tennessean in favor of it. I wish you would write me what you wish to be done, that I may with some intelligence, aid in carrying out your policy.

I dislike to originate any measure here, without knowing that it will certainly harmonize with your system of operation[.]

I am vy Truly Yours
Horace Maynard

His Excy, Andrew Johnson—

ALS, DLC-JP.

1. Former Governor William B. Campbell. Failing in his efforts to obtain for Campbell a military command, Johnson in early August commissioned him to visit Tennessee prisoners in Federal custody to offer the oath of allegiance as the condition of their release. *OR*, Ser. 2, IV, 362; Johnson to Buell, July 26, 1862, Johnson Papers, LC.

2. Jeremiah T. Boyle was commander of the Kentucky military district.

3. Congressman Andrew J. Clements.

To Robert Johnson

Nashville, July 1st 1862

Col Robt. Johnson
Commanding 4th. Tenn Regt.
Cumberland Gap Tenn

I have received following despatch from Secty of War

You are authorized to purchase in Kentucky and Tennessee at fair prices sufficient to mount one Regiment of Cavalry[.] the purchases should be made through a Quarter Master and requisitions made upon the Quarter Master General approved by you[.] Report the prices paid[.]

signed Edwin M. Stanton[1]

Show this to General Morgan. I presume arrangements can be made to purchase horses there. Be careful to have no fraud committed on the Government in any purchases that you may be connected with. If horses cannot be procured in time why not take them from Secessionists and give them a certificate of the value which the Government may act upon hereafter. If horses can be raised by any authority you have there, it would be better to do so, and I can apply the horses authorized in this order of Secty of War to the Cavalry being raised here.

Let me hear from you in regard to this[.]

Andrew Johnson

Tel, DLC-JP.
1. The original of this June 27 telegram is in Johnson Papers, LC.

From A. Clark Denson[1]

Memphis July the 2nd 1862

To His Excellency
Gov Andy Johnson

My Dear Sir, pleas to allow me to address you as one of natures noblemen, whose name will stand as the most splendid beacon on the Latitudes of time, as the Immortal Hero. This Union it must and *it shall be preserved*. I was in Napoleon Arkansas siting between Maj A J. Donalson and Gen Yell[2] when we first saw the course you had taken. I declared unequivocally in the justice of your Pollicy.[3]   the two gentlemen both said that Andy Johnson was the smartest man in the united States, and would be the next president, and if the Rebellion was carried out, and a civil war broke out, that they were bound by interest to follow the fortunes of the South, but that the South must be overcome and the Rebellion would be the overthrow of Slavery on the american continent. I merely make these remarkes as a prelude to this correspondence. I have been one of the unfortunate union men during the rebellion[.]   I had but four thousand dollars worth of property and that was invested in lumber and Shingles lying in Arkans' River when Westmorland was by [*sic*] fired into by the insane mob at Napoleon.[4] I simply remarked the next day that it was the most perfidious and wanton outrage that the world had ever witnessed.   for this I was arrested and kept in custidy 15 days by the Vigilence Committee, and finnaly Escaped with my life but the loss of my Effects. I went to Mobile Holly Springs and several other places and was Harrassed assailed and run off from every place barely with my life.   finally I came to Memphis last January and remained here

untill releived by that glorious old flag and its supporters, but secession
and treason was rife as you are well aware,   it was truly dangerous for
many days to even speak union sentiments or to be seen speak to a United
States Soldier or officer[.]   but notwithstanding at the first oppertunity I
came out to the world and showed the ground I occupied. On the 19th
June a Leuitenant Harring[5] arive here and opened a recruiting office. I
immediately procured a commission as a recruiting officer and advertised
largely[6] and had numbers of hand bills printed and posted which was
torn down as fast as posted, and not withstending the order of General
Slack[7] and the vigilence of the whole police civil and milatary it was
impossible to keep the bills up. Hence I took my revolver by permission
and my Hand bills and book and walked every street in Memphis
recruiting having been assaild three times with sticks and brick bats. Yet
I have faild to shoot a Secesionist[.]   notwithstanding I have recruited
ninety one men and had them sworn into the State Service and yesterday
Sent 68 of[f] to Nashville by Leuitenant Harring and shall be able to soon
fill a company.   this communication is to ask you for Some place civil or
miletary by which I can earn a living for myself and family, and at the
same time help to protect this Goverment from all its enimies. I am not a
millatary man[.] Hence something like a quartermaster, commasay Custom House post office, or anything that I could serve my country usefully
in, I would gladly do. I send you the certificate of Capt Richard Lampe[8]
cooperating [corroborating] my statements. I am Sir a buisness-man,
and feel myself compitent to fill almost any place you might pleas to
bestow. Satisfactory refferences as to my Loyalty, capacity, and Honesty
can be given.

Hopeing to hear from you soon I have the Honor to remain your most
obediant and very humble Servant.

Respectfully &c

A. Clark Denson

ALS, DLC-JP.

1. Absalom Clark Denson (b. c1812), native of Morgan County, Georgia, and a
peripatetic carpenter with $10,000 in personal property, was currently located in
Shelby County after having lived in Loujsiana, Texas, and Arkansas. Although he
helped raise what became Co. A, 1st Tenn. Lgt. Arty. Btn., USA, and led it to Nashville,
he served neither with this organization nor with Co. C, 5th Tenn. Cav., of which he
became 2nd lieutenant in August, 1862, only to resign in November because of ill
health. CSR, RG94, NA; 1860 Census, Tenn., Shelby, 8th Ward, 138; Memphis *Union
Appeal*, July 2, 1862; Johnson to Denson, August 22, 1862, Johnson Papers, LC.

2. Andrew J. Donelson, Know-Nothing candidate for vice president in 1856, had
subsequently turned his attention to planting in Coahoma County, Mississippi. Although his brother Daniel S. was a Confederate brigadier, A. J., as late as July 24, 1862,
was "reported as a Union man, and yet we learn he has scruples about taking the oath of
allegiance." Charged with high treason in 1863, he was nonetheless permitted to return
to his plantation. James Yell (b. c1811), native Tennessean, lawyer, and resident of Pine
Bluff, Arkansas, served as major general of the Arkansas state forces only from May 23 to
July 15, 1861, when they were transferred to Confederate service. Memphis *Union
Appeal*, July 24, 1862; Nashville *Union*, November 27, 1863; see also *Johnson Papers*, I,
367n; 1860 Census, Ark., Jefferson, Pine Bluff, 14; Leo E. Huff, "The Military Board
in Confederate Arkansas," *Arkansas Historical Quarterly*, XXVI (1967), 76-79.

3. Probably a reference to Johnson's original opposition to secession, particularly in his December 18-19, 1860, and February 5-6, 1861, Senate speeches.

4. The *Westmoreland*, a 270-ton river steamer making its way from New Orleans to Cincinnati with passengers and unspecified cargo, was stopped and boarded at Napoleon, Arkansas, on April 26, 1861. When the captain refused a search and broke the mooring ropes to escape, armed citizens on shore fired into the boat, killing one passenger and wounding a fireman. The damaged ship managed to reach Memphis. This, and similar seizures during the last week in April, particularly of Cincinnati-owned vessels, were in retaliation for Federal confiscation at Cairo and Cincinnati of arms and munitions headed south. Memphis *Appeal*, April 27-May 5, 1861, *passim*; John Ferguson (Arkansas state historian) to Andrew Johnson Project, February 24, 1976.

5. Citing his authorization from Johnson to raise a light artillery company for service in Tennessee, a "1st Lt. C. P. Haring" advertised for recruits in the Memphis *Bulletin*, July 6, 1862.

6. Having opened his recruiting offices at once, Denson was in full swing by this time. One notice—headlined, "Wanted! 140 able-bodied men! for light artillery for the State of Tennessee . . . $100 Bounty! and 160 acres land when mustered out of service. By authority of Governor Andrew Johnson"—appealed to patriotism and concluded, "This Company will be stationed at Nashville, in comfortable quarters, and if we only remain in service six months our bounty and land will be promptly paid." Memphis *Union Appeal*, July 2, 1862; Memphis *Bulletin*, July 4-29, 1862, *passim*.

7. Although Col. James R. Slack served as the Union commander at Memphis only during June 14-24, he took significant steps to tighten Federal control. His Order No. 9 (June 24) warned that "unmitigated traitorous rascals" who conducted such billboard raids "upon detection, shall be arrested and most severely punished by the military authorities." The *Bulletin* praised Denson's "indomitable perseverance," observing that when his "hand bills were torn down faster than the posters could post them," he hand-carried them through the streets, and "With that prudence which is always the better part of valor, he bore those unmitigated outrages as long as they kept their hands off, and succeeded in filling up his company and sending it to Nashville." Ernest W. Hooper, Memphis, Tennessee: Federal Occupation and Reconstruction, 1862-1870 (Ph.D. dissertation, University of North Carolina, 1957), 12, 14; Memphis *Bulletin*, July 3-12 *passim*, July 22, 1862.

8. Richard Lampe, who acted as a Union recruiter in Memphis during June-August, 1862, and is variously referred to in the Memphis papers as "1st Lieutenant" and "Captain," 1st Tenn. Arty., apparently was never officially mustered into service. According to Lampe, Denson had "done every thing in his power for the Union cause in this city, even beeing constantly in danger of his life." Lampe to Johnson, July 3, 1862, Johnson Papers, LC; Memphis *Union Appeal*, August 10, 13, 14, 1862.

To Oliver D. Greene

Nashville, July 3d 1862

Capt O. D. Greene
Ass't Adj't Gen'l. Nashville, Tenn.
Sir:

I have to acknowledge the receipt of your communication of the 2nd ins't in reply to mine of same date.[1] I do not wish to be impertinent, but really it seems to me that if the view I take of this matter as set forth in my letter of the 28th ult'o was correctly understood, you would have no hesitancy in ordering the payment of those telegraph accounts in the manner already indicated. By referring to that letter you will find that I ask for the settlement of two accounts for the Quarter Master at this point on the ground that dispatches to & from me, as Brigadier General and Military Governor, on military business, should be paid for in the same manner as such accounts against other military officers here are adjusted. Entertaining this view, I would most respectfully ask that you will reconsidered your action in this matter & advise me of your determination in regard thereto.

> Very Respectfully Your Obt Sert.
> Andrew Johnson   Military Govr—

L draft, DLC-JP.

1. Under date of July 1, Johnson had called Greene's attention to a letter of June 23 concerning payment of his telegraph account and asking for action. The following day Greene explained his delay as arising from an effort "to find some authority or precedent which would enable me to conscientiously use the name of Comdg Genl for ordering the payment of the account." Finding none, he has referred the matter to General Buell. Johnson to Greene, July 1, 1862; Greene to Johnson, July 2, 1862, Johnson Papers, LC.

From Oliver D. Greene

> Head-Quarters District of the Ohio
> Nashville Tenn July 3d 1862

To His Excellency Governor Andrew Johnson
Nashville Tenn
Governor

I am in receipt of your communication of this date asking me to reconsider my action in regard to declining to order the Payment of the Telegraph account contracted by you in your capacity of Brig Genl & Military Governor of the state of Tennessee—

In reply I have to say that I would most cheerfully reconsider my views of the matter, and would be most glad of any suggestions which would enable me to think that in using Genl Buell's name to order the payment of the Account I should not be involving him in a pecuniary difficulty with the Treasury Dept on matters of form—

My own experience in having accounts stopped at the Treasury for not being on the proper Form or paid from the exact appropriation is such that I have deemed it best to refer the whole matter to Genl Buell for his personal consideration—

I doubt not Genl Buell will take the same view of the case you do yourself and by return mail I shall be directed to order the payment of the account—

> I am Sir With sentiments of the highest &c
> Your Most Obt Servt
> Oliver D. Greene Asst Adjt Genl

L, DLC-JP; DNA-RG393, Dept. of the Cumberland, Lets. Sent, Vol. 1 (Feb.-Dec., 1862).

From Robert Johnson

Cumberland Gap July 3 1862

To Gov A. Johnson

Kirk & Elkins[1] of Greenville arrived tonight[.] Mother's health improving[.] She is at Stovers[.] Pattersons family well[.][2] Bob Mick[3] has possession of our office books & Papers undisturbed. But few troops in upper East Tennessee on twenty Eighth 28 June when the above left[.] John Arnold,[4] at Greenville has raised one guerilla Company[.] Sam Davis[5] & Lewis Headrick[6] raising another company[.] Be on your gaurd about assassination[.] three 3 of Morgans men left Knoxville on Tuesday for that purpose[.]

Robt. Johnson Col 4th Tenn Regt

Tel, DLC-JP.

1. John L. Kirk (b. c1842), a shoemaker, and James H. Elkins (b. c1842), both began their service at this time as privates in the 1st Tenn. Cav., rising respectively to 1st lieutenant, 5th Tenn. Cav. and captain, 1st Tenn. Cav. CSR, RG94, NA; 1860 Census, Tenn., Greene, 10th Dist., 84.

2. Johnson's daughter Mary Stover and her children resided in Carter County; his daughter Martha, her husband David T. Patterson, and their children were in Greeneville.

3. Possibly Robert McKee (c1834-fl1880), a Greene County railroad postmaster and neighbor of Johnson who became a lawyer after the war. Ibid., 82; (1880), Greeneville, 7.

4. John Q. Arnold, twenty-year-old son of former congressman Thomas D. Arnold and earlier a captain of "The Greeneville Guards," Co. F, 29th Tenn., Inf., CSA, had just organized Co. B, one of four units of independent partisan rangers composing the 12th Tenn. Cav. Btn. being recruited in upper East Tennessee. Rising to the rank of major, he was wounded at Chickamauga and died in late March, 1865. Tennesseans in the Civil War, I, 33, 235; Reynolds, Greene County Cemeteries, 257; OR, Ser. 1, XXX, Pt. II, 529; see also Johnson Papers, IV, 190n.

5. Probably Samuel W. Davis (b. c1812), a prosperous Greene County farmer who owned ten slaves and had personal property of $12,000 and real estate of $20,000. In July, 1862, he, W. M. Fry, and John T. Reynolds were advertising for volunteers for the Confederate army in the Greeneville Tri-Weekly Banner. 1860 Census, Tenn., Greene, 22nd Dist., 38; ibid., Slave Schedule, Tenn., Greene, 2; Doughty, Greeneville, 215.

6. Lewis B. Headrick (1836-1899), Greeneville attorney and mayor (1861) who served as a private in the 64th N. C. Inf. and in Co. H, 5th (McKenzie's) Tenn. Cav., CSA (December, 1862-64), was elected to the Confederate state legislature (1864). After the war he was a merchant at Tunnel Hill, Georgia, before settling in Hamilton County (1874) where he practiced law, served briefly as county surveyor (1881-82, 1890) and state senator (May-December, 1882), in addition to being a partner in the Daisy Coal Company. CSR, RG109, NA; Robison, Preliminary Directory, Hamilton, 36-37; LeRoy P. Graf, ed., "The Greeneville Legal Association (1858)," ETHS Publications, No. 24 (1952), 157.

From Abraham Lincoln

[Washington, D. C.]
July 3, 1862.

Hon. Andrew Johnson.

My Dear Sir: You are aware we have called for a big levy of new troops. If we can get a fair share of them in Tennessee I shall value it more highly than a like number most anywhere else, because of the face of the thing, and because they will be at the very place that needs protection. Please do what you can, and do it quickly. Time is everything. A word on another subject. If we could, somehow, get a vote of the people of Tennessee and have it result properly it would be worth more to us than a battle gained. How long before we can get such a vote?

Yours truly,   A. Lincoln

Basler, *Works of Lincoln*, V, 302-3.

From William P. Mellen

Louisville July 3. 1862

Sir:

I find here several recommendations of your Nashville Committee[1] for parties to bring liquors to Nashville.

The order of Genl. Halleck is that "no intoxicating drinks be permitted to be brought into any post occupied by the United States forces"[2] In several interviews with him, I have called his attention to the fact that the Commandants of posts are constantly recommending parties to be permitted to bring liquors to their respective posts. He desires all such reported to him, and insists upon a rigid observance of the order. Hence the 7th rule of the regulation of the Treasury Department of 22nd April.[3]

I would suggest that all such recommendations of your Committee or "Board of Trade" be discontinued. Also that *all* trafic in it, *into*, or *out of* Nashville or other place within your control be strictly prohibited in future. Much bad whisky is *manufactured* in Tennessee and Southern Kentucky, and is out of reach of the Surveyors of Customs or other officers of the Treasury Department, and their disposition of this should be prevented as much as possible.

As a mere question of *commerce*, I have no right to discriminate between Whisky and any other merchandize, and it is only as a military measure that the effort is made to keep it out of military posts and insurrectionary districts.

I will add however, that in my judgment very many bad things are done by the use of intoxicating drinks. Men under its influence are excited to joining in marauding excursions against the persons and property of loyal men, who if they could be kept sober and in proper condition for reflection would conduct themselves more peacably & properly.

I shall be glad to hear from you on the subject at your earliest convenience. *Direct to me at Cincinnati.*

An afterthought occurs to me. Why would not an order from you as Military Governor of the State covering the question in its limitations, conditions and penalties, be judicious?[4]

I am very respectfully Your Obt Servt
Wm P. Mellen
Spl. Agent Treas. Dept.

His Excellency, Andrew Johnson
Military Governor of Tennessee

LB copy, DNA-RG366, Lets, Sent by Treasury Dept. Special Agent, William P. Mellen, Unnumbered Vol. (Sept. 3, 1861-Dec. 27, 1862).

1. Under the April 22 regulations of Secretary of the Treasury Chase, Johnson appointed a board of trade—A. V. S. Lindsley and E. H. East of Nashville and O. B. Blackman of Clarksville—to supervise the issuance of permits. Letter from Salmon P. Chase, April 4, 1862; Futrell, *Federal Trade*, 62-63; Nashville *Union*, May 6, 1862.

2. Not found.

3. The seventh among the eight "rules for commercial intercourse adapted to trade in the west," approved by the treasury department April 20, and published two days later, specified that "no permit shall be granted to ship intoxicating drinks, or anything else forbidden by the military authorities, into the territories occupied by the forces of the United States or heretofore under insurrectionary control, except upon the written permission of the commandant of the department in which such territory is embraced, or of some person duly authorized by him to grant such permission. This rule does not apply to ale, beer, and Catawba wine." *Senate Report* No. 108, pt. 3, 37 Cong., 3 Sess., 590.

4. Johnson never issued the suggested order.

From George W. Morgan

Cumberland Gap July 3 1862

To His Excellency Andrew Johnson

The following telegram has just been received from the Brigade Camp of Genl Carter. "A German is just in[.] says he left Knoxville yesterday morning[.] was directed by Union men to state that four 4 of Morgan's men left Knoxville on Tuesday to assassinate Gov Andy Johnson[.] wishes him to be put on his guard[.] not more than two hundred 200 troops at Knoxville[.] will send the German up in the morning[.]

Geo W Morgan

Tel, DLC-JP.

To Edwin M. Stanton

Nashville July 3 1862.

Hon Edwin M. Stanton

A battery is needed at this place[.] There is one here which can be fitted up with little trouble & expense. The horses & men are ready to turn into the service. The men are Tennesseeans. Am I authorized to call upon the Quarter Master and the Ordnance Officer[1] for the battery horses & Equipments & have it fitted up to be placed under my control?

And. Johnson

Tel, DNA-RG107, Tels. Recd., Sec. of War, Vol. 17 (July 1-14, 1862).
1. In the original draft the passage read "Ordnance officer *here* for the battery." Johnson Papers, LC.

Speech at Nashville[1]

July 4, 1862

He said it had been his fixed determination not to speak again in Nashville without preparation. He had spoken so often in this place that he feared his remarks would grow stale. (Shouts of "Go on! go on!") He came here to-night to listen to a distinguished gentleman who was prevented by sickness from attending, and with no expectation of speaking himself. But as no one else seemed to be willing to speak, he would contribute his mite to the entertainment and information, if possible, of this vast, orderly and intelligent audience. From the first of this wicked rebellion he had made up his mind as to his duty, and survive or perish, sink or swim, he was determined to fight it through to the end. He was a soldier for the war. He had been denounced, calumniated and traduced as a traitor for his devotion to his country, but challenged any one to point to an act where he had violated his duty or his oath of office. In fighting under the old flag, for the Government, he was but conforming to the principles he had avowed from his earliest manhood. He had always stood before the people as the advocate of popular government, against the government of property, as a democrat in the *true* and *primary* sense of that word. And to night he appeared to defend the great principles of civil and religious liberty. In our old contests, political parties contended whose policy was best adapted to promote the good and prosperity of the Government and of the Union, but now the great question was, shall this Government and this Union exist, or shall they perish? There were only two parties now, one composed of the friends, the other of the foes of the Union. And although demagogues attempted to raise the cry of Slavery and Abolition, the real question to be decided was, shall free government live on the Western Continet? Be assured that this is the question which underlies the rubbish and rant of corrupt and reckless office-hunters. Negroes! Slavery! Southern Rights! Coercion! What terrible bug-bears to frighten timid people and blind them to the real point at issue. He asked the vast multitude before him, What Southern right any one of them had lost in the Union? Did it ever rob or impoverish? Did it ever defraud or oppress you? Then if you have lost no right, why all these vast armies? Why these bayonets, and cannon, and fleets, and tented fields? Why all these newmade graves and oceans of blood? Why are hundreds of you coming to the Capitol, praying for the release of your deluded boys? He could tell why. It was because some corrupt and reckless politicians wanted place and power. *They were determined to ruin the country if they could not govern the whole of the Union—they were determined to govern a part.* He knew these Southern politicians, YANCEY, TOOMBS, DAVIS, WIGFALL, MASON, BENJAMIN and others well, for he had served with them for years in Congress. He was familiar with their views and feelings, and having watched their course closely, believed that he understood their motives clearly. He sat side by side with them, when they professed that they wanted a compromise with the North. But the journals of Congress proved that these traitors had an opportunity to get the Compromise they professed to desire, and yet they allowed it to be defeated when their vote would have obtained it. They talked hypocritically. *A settlement of difficulties was the very last thing that these rebel Senators wanted.* They sought continually how they might defeat a peaceable settlement of the questions in dispute. They took their seats in the Federal Congress for the purpose of breaking up the Union, and founding one which they could control. They succeeded, unhappily for the country, in plunging us into a bloody and cruel and unholy war. A war, and for what? Why this fearful sacrifice of life, this blight upon the happiness of a once happy people? People of Davidson county, what have you lost that you should go to war? I ask those thoughtless boys who have returned from the rebel army, the quickest way they could, how many negroes they had lost by the Abolitionists? You were induced, and cajoled by rich rebels, and threatened into the army to fight against your country, but when you returned didn't you find these aristocratic chivalry sitting snugly at home? The very men who were most clamorous for Southern rights were the very last to go into the army to fight for them, but they were busy in getting others to go. The chivalry champions of Southern rights indeed! Why they have robbed and plundered and devastated the South. They have made East Tennessee a desert because her people are loyal. I am a slave owner myself, not by inheritance, but by hard labour, and they not only robbed me of my negroes, but turned my wife and little boy into the streets, and converted my dwelling into a hospital and barracks. The Southern chivalry have been the greatest robbers and enemies of the rights of the people, that the country has ever seen. And if this war goes on through the folly and wickedness of Southern rebels, slavery is at an end, for it has no protection, and no guarantee outside of the Union. With the death of the Federal Union dies slavery. The Abolitionist and Secessionist on this point occupy the same stand; there is no difference between them. The Abolitionists, such as WENDELL PHILLIPS, GARRISON and others denounce President LINCOLN as worse than JEFF. DAVIS. From the hands of these incendiaries on both sides the people must rescue the Union. There is a great middle party between these two extremes who must maintain the government. The work must be done by the people. Don't wait for your leaders to guide you. I know the people of Nashville well and know the feeling which controls them, and I know the men who have been your leaders; for I have been with them for years as a member of the Legislature, as Governor of your State, and as a Senator in Congress. You have relied on these leaders as oracles whose bidding you must obey. You ask where are our leaders, the John Bells, Ewings, Neil Browns, and the *Union and American*? You seem to cease to act and speak for yourselves. Are you, intelligent freemen, dependent on the arm of a leader? Are you incapable of acting for yourselves? If so, then, you concede the very thing for which the tories of the South are contending, and admit that you are unfit for self-government. Cast off this unmanly and degrading feeling. This is the people's government; they received it as a legacy from Heaven, and they must defend and preserve it, if it is to be preserved at all. I am for this Government above all earthly possessions, and if it perish, I do not wish to survive it. I am for it, though slavery should be struck from existence and Africa be swept from the balance of the world. I believe indeed that the Union is the only protection of slavery—its sole guarantee; but if you persist in forcing the issue of slavery against the Government, I say in the face of Heaven, "Give me my Government, and let the negroes go!"

These traitors who are perpetually clamoring about Southern rights and slave property, as if there were no other rights or property in existence, manifest the utmost bitterness, bigotry, and narrow-minded sectionalism. They are perpetually calling out Slavery, Abolitionist, Yankee, and Lincolnite! How malicious and invidious are all these slang phrases. Are we not all Americans, descended of one blood, and composing one great family? I recognize no such miserably narrow and selfish feeling as that which refuses fellowship to the loyal and just of all sections of the Republic. I scorn the tramels and fetters of sectional bigotry. I claim this world as my home, and every honest man as my brother. I love my country, her Constitution, her laws, and her free institutions. I love her history and the memory of her glorious dead. I love the precepts and teachings of her illustrious founders. I love my State, and pray for her happiness and prosperity, which must be found in the laws and under the flag of the Union. Looking around me to-night, I say to the gallant and patriotic soldiers who bear this flag, "Welcome, welcome, thrice welcome, defenders of the Union!" On with your glorious work, and in the face of all opposition, even at the point of the sword and bayonet, and amid the roar and crash of battle let the Government of Washington be defended. We have heard these troops called Northern invaders and Hessians, but we have seen and compared the rebel and patriot armies. The first spread horror and desolation among us, the latter have been law-abiding and orderly, and have been a protection to the people.

This rebellion is animated and controlled by the worst spirit that ever filled the bosom of man. With singular audacity or ignorance, some persons pretended to compare the rebellion of 1861 with that of 1776. How preposterous and absurd! There is not the remotest analogy between them. They were, on the contrary, the very antipodes of each other. The old revolution was to establish and perpetuate freedom, but this one was to subvert and destroy it, and make us the vassals of France or Great Britain. The modern revolution would, if possible, reduce us to the very servitude from which the former delivered us. The spirit of rebellion was fiendish, proud, cruel and lawless. It was so from the day when the Devil raised the standard of revolt in heaven, and warred with Michael the Archangel, for the supremacy of the skies. We are told that the Devil was conquered, and chained in the infernal pit, but that he was to be let loose for a season. If ever the devil was let loose in the world, I believe that now is the time, and that he is actuating the Southern rebellion. Yet men who had aided this diabolical rebellion now pretended to talk of tyranny and oppression! How long has it been since you had your Minute Men, your Vigilance Committees and your Passport Committees? How long has it been since men were driven from their homes for the *crime* of loyalty? I was driven from my own home, and for what? What crime, what offence had I done? None, save my devotion to the Government, and my attachment to the Stars and Stripes. Yet men talk of oppression, and complained of the arrest of Ministers of the Gospel. Ministers of the Gospel indeed! Pardon the expression! Oh, it was a great outrage to arrest Parson Elliott, and Parson Howell, and Baldwin—Armageddon Baldwin![2] What claim had these traitors to indulgence? I do not profess to be a profound theologian; but I reverence the teachings of the Gospel, and I thought that the Gospel of Jesus arched the whole circuit of the skies, and rested on the ends of the Universe. Who are these reverend traitors that they should go unpunished for their crimes? I hold that this Government is of divine birth, that it is a gift of God himself, and that neither Parson Elliott, not Parson Sehon, nor Parson Howell, not Armageddon have a right to break it up. I punish these men, not because they are priests, but because they are traitors and enemies of society, law and order. They have pursued and corrupted boys and silly women, and inculcated rebellion, and now let them suffer the penalty. I received the other day a request to allow some ham, sweet pickle and other delicacies to be carried to these persons. I told the applicant to send his luxuries to me, and I would find persons a good deal more worthy to receive them than these rebels. I would give them to the suffering widows and orphans among us, whose husbands and fathers were deluded by these men into the Rebel army, and now fill a rebel's grave, or lie in prison. (Shouts of "Good! good! that's right!") If delicacies are to be distributed, I think that these innocent sufferers, the victims of these corrupt rebel priests, are a good deal more worthy objects of charity and compassion than the deceivers themselves. Why should they be feasted and lionized, and their wretched victims be left to perish? (A whistle in the rear of the crowd.) I hear a whistle. I believe it is GOLDSMITH who says in his Natural History,[3] that there are only two animals which hiss, the viper, by reason of his venom, and the goose, for its simplicity. I think the present instance is an exception, and that the whistler is a gosling. It is some foolish creature instigated by others who are too cowardly to show themselves. Let your masters show themselves and I will attend to them. But why should these parsons ask for sympathy? When did they ever express sympathy for the loyal men who lie in the jail of Tuscaloosa,[4] covered with filth and fed on tainted meat? Alas, to their agonizing cries no response is made but the clanking of their chains. These men who claim special regard, have stolen the livery of Heaven to serve the devil in, but I am determined they shall feel the power of the government which they have sought to destroy. Some professed to entertain a holy horror of coercion. Why, force and terror have coerced the South into her present position, and nothing but force and power will bring her back. You were coerced by the violence and force of Secession, and the spirit of Secession must be subdued and controlled by force. The strong arm of the Government must be bared and justice must do her work. We may as well understand the fact first as last, and go to work rationally. Without force and power to coerce we have no Government. How have matters gone on heretofore? Why when the Union army came here the first to run to it for protection and privileges were Secessionists, who got promises of protection, if they would remain neutral. On the other hand, the poor Union men were terrified with threats of vengeance if the rebel army should return. The Secessionist was protected by the Union army, and was equally confident of protection should the rebel army return, so he felt perfectly easy. The Union man dreaded utter ruin, should a reverse occur, and was filled with perpetual alarm. So, under this strange policy the rebel has *two* guarantees, and the Union man but *one*. It is time this was stopped. *The time has arrived, when treason must be made odious and traitors impoverished*. These men have used their property to destroy the government, and fill the land with bankruptcy and distress; they have given their wealth freely to aid rebellion and treason, and drench the land in fraternal blood, and crush out the last vestige of liberty, *and their property should be taken from them to defray the expenses of the war. They* are the guilty ones. *They* are the real criminals. The poor have been deluded and dragged into this war, while the authors and instigators who have kept up the war by their money and contributions, have skulked at home and demanded the protection of the Federal Government. And what was the motive of many of these men in Nashville for bringing on and aiding the rebellion? Why many of these elegant gentlemen rebelled *to get rid of paying their Northern debts*! If a miserable, crippled negro, worth five hundred dollars, was stolen, the government must be overthrown if the negro could not be recovered, but your polite, fastidious and chivalrous merchant, can go among what he calls "blue bellied Yankees," buy their goods on credit, and then, when pay-day comes, tell his creditors in the North: "Oh, I have seceded!" It is an outrageous crime to steal a negro, but it is gentlemanly financiering to defraud a Northern creditor of $50,000 or $100,000. Hundreds of instances could be related showing how far the rebellion was impelled and advanced by this swindling spirit. Yet these very men who had disgraced themselves by these frauds, would talk gravely about the sin of slave-stealing. Now take the value of all the negroes that have been stolen from the South, and then take the sum of all the Northern debts that have been repudiated by Southern men, and the latter will surpass the former at least ten to one. Who own many of your public buildings, railroad stocks, bank stocks and other property? Northern men. Yet you who clamor about your Southern rights can coolly defraud your Northern friends of millions of dollars. The rebels of Tennessee must be coerced. They coerced Tennessee, or tried to coerce her, out of the Union, and they must be coerced, into the performance of their duty. You talk of withholding your cotton and *starving* out the North. Just make the calculation which, will starve out the soonest—the North, with her breadstuffs and no cotton, or the South, with cotton and no breadstuffs!

Governor JOHNSON paid an elegant tribute to the loyalty and fidelity of the East Tennesseans, who, under the crushing weight of oppression, still remained faithful to the Union. The conduct of many of the rebel women, he remarked, was astonishing. How dare you breathe treason and insult the flag of your country? Hold up your hands in the light of Heaven—gaze steadfastly on them, and see if they are not red with blood! Yes, the blood of your own husbands, brothers and sons, whom your wretched infatuation drove to treason and a rebel's grave. Men who would have gladly staid at home, who felt no sympathy for the wicked cause, and who, but for your counsels, might to-night be with us in the enjoyment of life and health, have been sent by your pernicious influence to an untimely and ignominious grave. And yet, these women, as they pass loyal men on the streets, flout their dresses as though they were terrific comets and the world was to be dashed out of existence by a sweep of their trains! For a true woman he ever cherished an exalted reverence and admiration, but for those who unsexed themselves by a display of treason and ill breeding, he had none. This rebellion must be put down, treason be made odious, and traitors impoverished and punished. The strong arm of the Government must fall heavily and terribly on the heads of the men who have brought this war on the country. For one, I am resolved to stand by my Government, at whatever personal risk. I have enlisted for the war, and will not go back. I expect to receive in the future, as I have received already, much obloquy and abuse. I know that I am assailed with fiendish malignity. Even to-day, I received a dispatch from one high in authority, warning me that a band of assassins are on my track.[5] How or where they mean to strike, I know not. They are a craven, dastardly set, who cannot look you in the eye, and who do their work from behind your back, or in the dark, or by poison. Some wretch even now may be skulking in this crowd awaiting a chance to do the deed to which his master has bribed him. I defy all this venom and malignity. Suppose the assassin succeeds, what then? What have they obtained? What signifies one life when the life of the nation is at stake? Even from the blood of the patriot armies of patriots will arise, and the blood of the martyrs will become the seed of the church. In vain the threat of the assassin's dagger or the poisoned bowl, for patriots unintimidated will press forward to freedom and victory, or falling will be blessed by posterity. Awake to your duty Tennesseans! Come up to the glorious work of saving your country. Let us take a long pull, and a strong pull, and a pull altogether, and our country shall stand forth regenerated and redeemed, and peace and prosperity again shall bless our borders.[6]

Nashville *Union*, July 6, 1862.

1. During the evening of July 4 a crowd assembled on the steps and in the yard of the capitol. Following the reading of a letter from ex-governor Neill S. Brown explaining that he was sick and "unable to fill his appointment for the evening," Col. Lewis D. Campbell offered a few short remarks, at the conclusion of which Governor Johnson came forward and made "a most powerful and rousing speech." Nashville *Union*, July 5, 1862.

2. The best known of the Reverend Samuel D. Baldwin's works was entitled *Armageddon: or the Overthrow of Romanism and Monarchy* (1854).

3. Although Oliver Goldsmith, in his *History of the Earth and Animated Nature* (3 vols., London, 1828), III, 254-55, discusses the hissing of serpents, likening the sound to "the music of an English grove," he does not draw an analogy with geese.

4. To relieve the crowded prisons at Richmond, the Confederate government decided during the fall of 1861 to equip an abandoned paper mill at Tuscaloosa, Alabama. Although advised that it was unsuitable—the first story lacked a floor, one room was without sills, the grounds were low and damp, the walls full of holes, and no chimneys or cooking arrangements were present—the authorities sent prisoners from Richmond in November and the prison remained in use until the following fall. Many East Tennesseans had been incarcerated there. Hesseltine, *Civil War Prisons*, 62-63, 237; *OR*, Ser. 2, III, 751; James M. Page, *The True Story of Andersonville Prison: A Defense of Major Henry Wirz* (New York, 1908), 186; "List of Prisoners from East Tennessee . . . in Tuscaloosa," Nashville *Union*, June 6, 1862.

5. See Telegram from George W. Morgan, July 3, 1862.

6. In printing his report of the address, the editor, blaming the "very unfavorable circumstances" under which he was obliged to make his notes, apologized that "A great deal of its power, piquancy, and fire is wanting in our abstract, but we trust that we have still succeeded in preserving some of its striking points." Nashville *Union*, July 6, 1862.

From Schuyler Colfax

H.R. Wash, July 5, 1862

My dear Sir,

You have heard, of course, of the Union movement[1] in our State of Indiana. It promises to be a decided success[.] I fear your important duties at home will prevent you from redeeming your promise to assist us in the canvass[.] But we could not, of course, ask you to leave Tennessee.

You know that one of the difficulties in the way will be inducing those who have heretofore been Democrats to vote for Republicans. I expect to be again a candidate for Congress on the Union ticket. A few lines from you would be of great value in swelling my vote. But I do not ask it if you fear it would embarrass you.

The President has told me twice that, while he has had troublesome questions to settle from other Military Governors & officers, as in North Carolina, New Orleans[2] &c, "Andy Johnson" had never embarrassed him in the slightest degree. You enjoy his fullest confidence as you so richly deserve.

Wishing you the fullest success in your arduous & patriotic labors, & rejoicing that you have exhibited such firmness & decision in all your acts & speeches, I am as ever

Very truly yrs.
Schuyler Colfax

If you reply, address me at *South* Bend Inda.

ALS, DLC-JP.

1. An attempt to merge Republicans and Union Democrats into a political force, the Union movement was not the success in Indiana that Colfax predicted. Although some Democrats supported the war, they nevertheless opposed Lincoln's policies. The ten-thousand Republican majority of 1860 was replaced in 1862 by a comparable majority for the Democrats who not only captured the legislature but also increased from four to seven their congressional representation. Those Republicans who were elected received reduced majorities, a condition which Colfax was later to blame on the absence of the soldier vote. Winfred A. Harbison, "Lincoln and Indiana Republicans, 1861-62," *Indiana Magazine of History*, XXXIII (1937), 300-301, 302n.

2. Perhaps an allusion to Stanly's problems with Negroes in North Carolina, cited earlier, and to Benjamin F. Butler's difficulties with foreign consuls in New Orleans. Butler, whose administration in New Orleans was controversial from the beginning, embarrassed the Lincoln government with his June 10 order requiring the oath from foreign-born living in New Orleans, including consuls, suspected of aiding the Confederate cause. Searches of consulates and censorship of their mail, at a time when Lincoln was hoping to ward off recognition of the Confederacy, aggravated the situation. *OR*, Ser. 1, XV, 483-84; Ser. 3, II, 154-62, 172, 497, 515; Hans L. Trefousse, *Ben Butler: The South Called Him Beast!* (New York, 1957), 125-26.

To James W. Ripley, Washington, D.C.

July 5, 1862, Nashville, Tenn.; Tel, DNA-RG107, Tels. Recd., U. S. Mil. Tel.,
Vol. 14 (July 4-14, 1862); DLC-JP.

Authorized "to raise two regiments of cavalry for the purpose of exterminating
the guerrilla bands which infest this state," Johnson asks that the chief of
ordnance dispatch "one thousand carbines (Sharps or Merrills) one thousand
Colt's pistols and belts, and one thousand sets of horse equipments."

From James G. Benton[1]

Ordnance Office, War Department.
Washington July 6 1862

Governor Andrew Johnson
Nashville Tenn.
Sir

I have the honor to acknowledge the receipt of your Telegram of
to-day,[2] and to state, that the following stores have been ordered to be
forwarded to you, viz.

from the Washington Arsenal
500 Merrill's Carbines, with accoutrements
50,000 Cartridges for the Carbines
from New York, (By Capt. Crispin)[3]
1,000 Whitney's Navy pistols
from the Allegheny Arsenal
1000 sets of Horse equipments
1000 Infantry waist belts & plates
1000 Holsters & Cartridge pouches for the pistols
500 Cap pouches & picks

and from the New York Arsenal 50,000 Ball Cartridges, for the pistols[.]

The remaining 500 Carbines will be issued as soon as possible—

Respectfully Yr obd St.
J. G. Benton Capt. & Asst

Tel, DLC-JP.

1. James G. Benton (1820-1881), a New Hampshire native and West Point graduate (1842), began his career as an ordnance officer. An instructor at the academy
(1857-61) where he published a textbook, Benton was principal assistant to the chief of
ordnance (1861-63), commanded the Washington Arsenal (1863-66) and the National
Armory at Springfield, Massachusetts (1866-81), and designed and improved a number
of ordnance mechanisms. *DAB*, II, 208-9.

2. See Telegram to James W. Ripley [Benton's superior], July 5, 1862.

3. Silas Crispin (c1830-1889) of Pennsylvania, who graduated third in his class at
West Point (1850), was in charge of the New York ordnance agency during the war.
Promoted to major in 1867 and colonel in 1881, he was stationed at Benicia Arsenal,
California, at the time of his death. *Appleton's Cyclopaedia*, II, 9; *Official Army Register*
(1889), 45, 371; *OR*, Ser. 1, XXVII, Pt. II, 914; XLIII, Pt. II, 568.

To Abraham Lincoln

Confidential

Nashville July 6th 1862.

His Excellency Abm. Lincoln
Prest of U S

I see there is some contest in reference to the appointment of Judge for Tennessee. Rodgers is my personal friend but he will not do for Judge at this time. I hope he will not [be] put upon us—[1] If I were permitted I could name the man who is eminently qualified for the position & adapted to the Present Crisis & who would be acceptable to the Union men, throughout the State.[2]

Andrew Johnson

Tel, DLC-Lincoln Papers; DLC-JP; DNA-RG107, Tels. Recd., Sec. of War, Vol. 17 (July 1-17, 1862).

1. In a telegram to Horace Maynard on the same date, Johnson stressed the inappropriateness of naming John B. Rodgers, who "has not the first qualification for the appointment and especially so at this time," and urged the congressman to "see the President and make a correct statement of the facts—" Johnson to Maynard, July 6, 1862, Johnson Papers, LC.

2. Although there is no clear evidence, Johnson may have had in mind Connally F. Trigg who had been his agent to the northern prisons and who ultimately received the appointment.

From Asa Faulkner[1]

Murfreesboro Tenn July 8th 1862

Gov A. Johnson
Dear sir

I live as you doubtless remember near McMinnville and am one of the few Union man of the County of Warren, and now look for the time soon to arrive when that few will have to leave our homes and all that may be dear to us. the Southren Cavalry are now in the mountains of this and the adjoining Counties and are threatneng all the Union men. I learn that Gov Harris & the Hon A Ewing are at Beersheba Springs. which clearly indicate that the Southren Cavalry are near in force[.] I came here this day to ask Col Lester[2] for protection to our Cotton Factory at McMinnville as it is threatened by a Company of Cavalry that is now forming in the Countys of Coffee and Warren. Col Lester tells me that there will be a force at McMinnville soon. You will confer a very great favour on me and my partner by forwarding the force. this will be handed you by Mr Walling[3] who is a very much persecuted Union man, and any thing you could do for him will be a favour highly appreciated[.] I must again refer you to my friend John Lellyett Esqr for my standing, and hope it will not be long before I can visit you without the fear of being destroyed for it[.]

yours truly   Asa Faulkner

ALS, DLC-JP.

1. Asa Faulkner (1802-1886), a South Carolina native, machinist, pioneer cotton manufacturer, and Warren County farmer who possessed $2,000 in real and $22,000 in personal property on the eve of the war, served in the lower house (1865-66) and in the state senate (1869-71). He built his first cotton mill in 1846; his second, constructed in 1861 and destroyed by Federals in 1863, was rebuilt after the war. 1860 Census, Tenn., Warren, 174; Robison, *Preliminary Directory*, *Warren*, 14-15; Walter Womack, *McMinnville at a Milestone, 1810-1960* (McMinnville, 1960), 299-300.

2. Henry C. Lester, colonel of the 3rd Minn. Inf.

3. Not identified.

From Lewis D. Campbell

Head Quarters Provost Guard
Nashville July 9th 1862.

Governor

In reply to my enquiry of yesterday[1] you stated that the house formerly owned by Col. Heiman[2] of the rebel army, is occupied under your direction and authority as Military Governor of the State of Tennessee. I immediately communicated this fact to Capt. Green, who to-day peremptorily and piquantly orders me in the name of Major Gen Buell to vacate the premises.

You will please inform me whether I can have possession of the house or whether you as Military Governor intend to hold and occupy it[.]

Very truly Yours &c
Lewis D Campbell,
Col 69th O.V.I Provost Marshal,

His Excellency Andrew Johnson
Military Governor &c.

ALS, DLC-JP.

1. Campbell, directed by Oliver D. Greene, acting adjutant general, to vacate Colonel Heiman's property, had asked whether Johnson's power exercised as military governor in seizing the house took precedence over Greene's authority. Campbell to Johnson, July 8, 1862, Johnson Papers, LC.

2. Adolphus Heiman (1809-1862), Prussian-born stonecutter-turned-architect, who owned considerable real estate in and around Nashville, had been an officer in the Mexican War and served as colonel of the 10th Tenn. Inf., CSA, from 1861 until his death at Jackson, Mississippi, in November, 1862. John C. Frank, "Adolphus Heiman: Architect and Soldier," *Tenn. Hist. Quar.*, V (1946), 35-57.

To Lewis D. Campbell

Nashville, July 9th 1862

Col L. D. Campbell, Provost Marshal,
Nashville, Tenn.
Colonel:

In reply to yours of this date I have to state that it is my intention to continue to hold and occupy the premises referred to as Military Governor of the State of Tennessee for the use and benefit of the Government. I assume that I have full power to do this by virtue of my commission from the President any order issued by Captain Greene to the contrary notwithstanding. In addition to this I have special orders from the War Department to call on Major General Halleck for adequate force to execute my orders. I have likewise the authority of Major General Buell for saying to you that my *"requisitions made directly to the Provost Marshal shall be executed by him without further reference."*

Therefore I direct that the order issued by Captain Greene to you in reference to said premises be suspended, and I require that neither you as Provost Marshal nor any of your Command shall interfere with or molest the persons now in possession of the premises aforesaid, without my authority.

Very Respectfully Your Obt Sevt
Andrew Johnson   Military Governor.

L draft, DLC-JP.

From Edmund Cooper

Shelbyville Ten.
July 10th 1862.

His Excellency Andrew Johnson.
Dear Sir.

Pardon me for writing to you, at this time, as I hear you have been quite unwell—but the urgency of the business on hand, requires prompt, and vigorous action. The Guerilla's in this and the adjoining counties have become so bold, as to demand at our hands, the prompt enforcement of your proclamation in regard to them.[1]

On Tuesday morning about 10 oclock they attacked a train of cotton waggons nine miles beyond Fayetteville, and burned sixty five bales of cotton—and also took one mule the property of D. F. Jackson,[2] and two fine horses the property of Robert Sanders[3] both loyal men of my county. On Wednesday night they burned fifty bales of cotton, on waggons, three miles this side of Fayetteville—

On Tuesday night they took from G. W. Castleman[4] of my county two fine horses, because of his devotion to the Government of the United States—and a few nights before one from W. J. Shofner[5] for the same cause— These Gentlemen live in that part of the county next to Lynchburg—Lincoln cty[.] It is evident that since the fight at Richmond[6]—they have become emboldened—and are rapidly organizing their bands. On one night last week near Cornersville Giles cty—they burned a load of cotton for Wm Gosling[7] of my county—a true Union man.

Now, would it not be better for us all, that we should immediately, order "Military Commissions," under the petitions of A. L. Stamps & W. S. Jett,[8] forwarded to you some weeks ago—and let them *act*.

The *people* were alarmed when your proclamation was first issued, but as no *Action* has been had under it, they seem to have lost all *terror* about it[.] It must be *enforced* to have the desired effect—otherwise it will be considered a *dead letter*—

We have to strike hard, fast and rapid—and I feel the sooner the better. I however make these suggestions, confiding in your own judgment—with all the facts before you—

We are here with but a small force—but doing well.

Truly   Edmund Cooper

ALS, DLC-JP.

1. Johnson's May 9 proclamation which threatened reprisals for Confederate guerrilla activity.

2. Probably Daniel Jackson (b. *c*1837), a farmer who had $1,400 real and $3,750 personal property. 1860 Census, Tenn., Bedford, 10th Dist., 118; (1870), 24.

3. Not identified.

4. Probably George H. Castleman (b. *c*1820), a farmer whose real estate was worth $1,500 and personal property, $1,500. *Ibid*. (1860), 24th Dist., 156.

5. William J. Shofner (1819-1907) was a native Lincoln countian, who, following his marriage to Rhoda Boone (1828-1887), a distant relative of Daniel Boone, settled in 1849 on a 480-acre farm, and by 1860 had an estate of $13,000. *Ibid*., 25th Dist., 121; *Goodspeed's Bedford*, 1174; Frost, *The Frosts and Related Families*, 65.

6. The Seven Days' Campaign followed by the Federal retreat, June 25-July 1.

7. William Gosling (b. *c*1816), an English-born Bedford County "Factoryist," in 1860 had property worth $19,000. Gosling's home was used by Confederate Gen. Leonidas Polk as his headquarters. Gunter, Bedford County, 62; 1860 Census, Tenn., Bedford, Shelbyville, 60.

8. Asa L. Stamps (*c*1821-*fl*1880), a Virginian who became a Shelbyville merchant, had a combined estate of $15,000 in 1860. William S. Jett (b. *c*1815), a successful Shelbyville merchant in the 1840's and 50's, was a bank cashier in 1860 possessing a combined estate of $45,000. *Ibid*., 64, 66; (1880), 19; *Goodspeed's Bedford*, 874.

From *"Lizzie"*[1]

Clarksville, Tenn. July 10th, 1862.

To Honble. Andrew Johnson.

It would require a new language and faculty combined to express to you the morbid state of feeling the rampant and diabolical opposition now extant in this whirlpool of secessionism: no logic, however powerful, no admissions in their favor, however conciliatory in strength or purport; no evidences of marked benefits, which under the present rule is slowly, yet surely accruing to them serve to convince them of their madness, of their wild, fanatical error.

A poor widow with five children, was requested by a Federal Officer to make a Union Flag, which she did, and for which she received the compensation of three dollars; the ladies of this place called on her, *"en masse"*, and with bitter denunciations, told her, in the future there should be a total withdrawal of their favor and charitable aid, and herself and children left to endure the horrors of privation and want:

So soon as my arrival was made known, and my numerous friends of past years with all their happy reminescences gathered around me, the first query, was, "what are you"?—emphatically—strong as chains of triple steel,—*Union!*—to the heart, unto death! was, is, and ever shall be my reply!

Sorely have I been denounced, my kindest and most generous emotions outraged; the noblest sentiments of my patriotism reviled; and myself dubbed as a *"Lincoln Spy,"* and absolutely forbidden to breathe a single aspiration that has for its crowning joy the song of freedom:—with a stout heart and a brave courage I go on my way, one prayer in my soul, one solemn adjuration on my lips, *"Union forever, as it was, as it is,* "It must and shall be preserved"!—

Each day, I thank my God, that the assurance is given to me, through my unvarying belief in his immutable wisdom and beneficent goodness, that in our union is strength, and through that strength we shall be sustained. In this struggle, I read anew the crisis of our own life, and the strife before us in the page of history brings into clearer interpretation the conflict that we are always waging, more or less earnestly, with stubborn circumstances or unkind men. It is from this very fact, our whole life being such a struggle, that we are led to take so intense an interest in war, until, upon the issue of battles, we hang our hearts, as well as our fortunes.— How proud I am that mine is the privilege to vindicate the American name, and for all who bear the proud insignia of Americans, do I vindicate it; and truly do I believe that not far distant is the day when those who are now in arms against us will profess a pride in bequeathing to their children the one noble name which they are now doing so much and so vainly to disparage and destroy.

They defied me to walk under the Union Flag erected in this place; without defining precisely the governing power of that national spirit which possessed me, for it is felt more easily than defined, *I did walk under it*! and looking upon the dear old Stars and Stripes that had won so many successes over sedition, felt that thrill of my pulses which mount-. ing to my head, told me more in that brief moment what our nationality means than any disquisition, however learned, upon the value of the Union or the authority of the Constitution.

Oh! what a long while the taint of secession will rest upon every district that has been infected with the virus of treason, and that very fact should make us more eager to purify ourselves by removing every malignant character, and giving at all times, and under all circumstances, solid proofs of our loyalty.

Surely, there can be nothing but madness itself in this persistence to feed the sources of treason by depriving any section of the rights and duties of citizenship who wish to be loyal to the Government and why should we care how summarily all malignants are dealt with who may persist in embroiling the country in feuds, and the sooner the rope is about their necks the better for their neighbors and the whole world. Never before have I had so just an idea, of the spirit which has plunged the nation into so fearful a war; the earnest vindictiveness, the deep, calm bitterness of hate is to me a tragic revelation of the kind and extent of crime that the spirit of a society familiar with injustice promoted, and the qualities of character that it produces. There is but one other Union woman in this place beside myself so far as I can ascertain:—quite a feeling of joy seemed to animate the hearts of the poor Union Officers, stationed here; they gave me every expression of it; by calling on me and presenting me with a magnificent Bouquet, and giving me a fine serenade, playing all of our National airs, and overtures from our finest Opera's; Do not suppose my valued friend that I am forgetful of your past kindness to me, on my return through Nashville I shall fully reciprocate it.—

                                                                          Lizzie.

ALS, DLC-JP.
    1. Not identified.

From Josiah V. Meigs[1]

                                                        Washington D. C.
                                                        July 10, 1862.

Dear Governor.

Miss C. M. Melville now on a visit to New Ham[pshir]e with Miss Gay,[2] desires one of the 25 authorized clerkships; about to be appointed in the Pension Bureau[.][3]

You know the peculiar fitness, and the qualifications of Miss Melville, and I will not enumerate—

She would like to be employed at Washington because of her interest in the War, and more particularly because of the acquaintance she has made in her year of care and labor with the Sodiers in the Hospitals—

Mrs Secy Smith[4] is aware of Miss Melvilles value, and I hope, after receiving so much assistance from her, will advance her cause.

If any one has a claim upon Secy Smith for one of these offices, Miss Melville has— But Some one must urge the Case and I hope you will write a strong letter in her favor to Secy Smith, who has these offices to fill.

Ask for it as from Tennessee.

Father is well, and will pay us a visit soon— I am as well as I could expect after confinement each day—

With my regards to Secy. East I am as ever

Your young Friend   Joe V. Meigs.

ALS, DLC-JP.

1. Josiah V. Meigs (1840-1907), Nashville-born son of Return J. Meigs, was a clerk in the war department (1862-63) and captain, Bty. A, 2nd U. S. Cld. Lgt. Arty. (1864). After the war he lived primarily in Lowell, Massachusetts. *Hutchinson's Washington and Georgetown Directory* (1863), 146; CSR, RG94, NA; Pension File, RG15, NA.

2. Eliza Jane Gay (*c*1835-*fl*1880), Scottish-born companion of Catherine Melville, with whom she served as co-principal of the East Tennessee Female Institute, had also moved to Washington where she was a post office clerk after the war. 1860 Census, Tenn., Greene, 10th Dist., 87; Luttrell, "One Hundred Years of a Female Academy," 80; Washington city directories (1868-81), *passim*.

3. Miss Melville ultimately received an appointment paying $600 a year as one of the "Ladies Employed in the Quarter Master General's Office." *U. S. Official Register* (1863), 130.

4. Elizabeth B. Walton, the wife of Secretary of the Interior Caleb Smith, whom she had married in 1831. *DAB*, XVII, 245.

To Abraham Lincoln

Nashville Tenn. July 10. 1862.

His Excellency, A. Lincoln

Last night I received dispatches[1] from Genl Boyle Commanding in Kentucky stating that a raid by a cavalry force of 2000. has been made into Ky & asking me to send one or two Regts to his relief— This morning I have 3 more dispatches[2] from the same source asking that troops to be sent immediately as the raid is of magnitude[.] Capt O D Greene Asst Adjt Genl of Buell's staff who exercises command over the troops here so far as to order them wherever he wishes refuses to take notice of these dispatches & afford the necessary relief for Kentucky & Tennessee— This attack is aimed at the highway the Louisville & Nashville R. R. which should be protected by all means as necessary for the safety of this place and all middle Tennessee.

This Captain Green has not only refused to cooperate with me but has used his position as Ass't Adj't Gen'l in locating the troops here directly in opposition to my view & with great damage to the cause. right in the face of these important dispatches an order sending away nearly all the force from this place, is persisted in— I consider the policy which has been pursued by Buell's adj't Genl here in the absence of Buell as most decidedly detrimntal to the public interest— My opinion is that he is at this time in complicity with the traitors here & shall therefor have him arrested & sent beyond the Influence of rebels and traitors if he is not immediately removed.

Your letter of the third received— I thank you for it—

The number of troops suggested can and will be raised in Tennessee[.] as to an expression of public opinion as soon as the rebel army can be expelled from East Tennessee there can & will be an expression of public opinion that will surprise you but I am constrained to say one thing as I said to you repeatedly in the fall Genl Buell is not the man to redeem East Tennessee[.]

The troops to be raised and concentrated at this point must be placed under the command & control of some one familiar with & identified with Tennessee— And Govr Campbell will be a good selection.

Mr President since I reached this place there has been a struggle & a contest going on between the provost Marshall's Brigadier Generals & Staff officers of Genl Buell which has retarded the reaction & development of Union sentiment here—

All I ask is to be sustained by the President & I will sustain the President— Please send an answer immediately as it is highly important to properly dispose of the small force we have & that Capt Greene shall not be allowed to damage the cause we are laboring to maintain—[3]

With great respect
Andrew Johnson—

Tel, DLC-Lincoln Papers; DNA-RG107, Tels. Recd., Sec. of War, Vol. 17 (July 1-14, 1862).

1. See Johnson to Don Carlos Buell, July 10, 1862, Johnson Papers, LC, transmitting Boyle's July 9 telegram to Johnson.

2. Boyle's three telegrams of this date indicate that the enemy troops were moving toward Gallatin and that a regiment and some artillery would be sent to meet them. See Boyle to Johnson, July 10, 1862, Johnson Papers, LC.

3. Angered by the arrest and removal of Provost Marshal Lewis D. Campbell, Johnson later the same day reiterated his demand for Greene's transfer "to some post beyond the limits of this State" and for a presidential order reinstating Campbell. See Johnson's second telegram to Lincoln, July 10, 1862, Lincoln Papers, LC, and on the same subject, Johnson to Stanton and to Maynard, both July 10, Johnson Papers, LC.

From Alexander S. Ballard

Lebanon July 11th 62

Gov Johnson

Dear Sir

I have Reliable Information that a pass Issued by you to a Mrs Suttle[1] on the Recomendation of Gov Campbell was Intended to be used to the Detriment of the union cause[.] I therefore have Demanded & taken it from her[.] She has Just returned from Richmond and as I understand made an arrangement that the pass should be returned to Gen Foster[2] for the purpose of using in passing our lines[.] this She of course denes yet I deemed it prudent as an officer to take up the pass[.]

I have the Honor to bee   Your Obedient Servent
Major A. S. Ballard
Commanding Post at Lebanon

Enclosed find pass[.]

ALS, DLC-JP.

1. Margery Settle (1817-1891) was the widow of Leroy B. Settle (c1802-1861), a successful Virginia-born merchant whose property in 1860 was valued at $106,875. Two of their sons were in the Confederate army: Archibald G. (c1839-1864), the adjutant, Smith's 2nd Tenn. Cav., and Leroy B. (1841-1888), a private in Co. H, 7th Tenn. Inf., stationed in Virginia. Mrs. Settle, "a lady of worth and position and unquestioned integrity," and a son, probably Willis (1847-1891), were given a pass on June 10 "to visit Richmond for the purpose of seeing her two Sons and returning with them." 1860 Census, Tenn., Wilson, 10th Dist., 182; Acklen, *Tenn. Records*, I, 144, 292; Merritt, *Wilson County*, 229; *Tennesseans in the Civil War*, I, 189; II, 359; Military Pass to Mrs. Settle, June 10, 1862, Johnson Papers, LC.

2. Probably Robert C. (1818-1871), native Nashville lawyer and son of Ephraim H. Foster. Captain, Harrison Guards, 1st Tenn. Inf., in Mexico and afterwards attorney general of the judicial district of Maury, Marshall, Giles, and Hickman (until 1852), he possessed an estate worth $164,950 on the eve of the war. A state brigadier general during the summer of 1861, he resigned after Tennessee forces were turned over to the Confederacy. Still in Nashville just prior to its capture by Buell, he reportedly spent the "greater portion" of the war as a refugee in the South, though it is not clear when he departed. After the war he served as Nashville city recorder (1866-67) and as secretary of an insurance company. 1860 Census, Tenn., Davidson, Nashville, 5th Ward, 183; Nashville *Republican Banner*, December 29, 1871; Clayton, *Davidson County*, 181, 199, 394; White, *Messages*, V, 697; Nashville *Patriot*, September 18, 1861; Nashville *Union*, May 24, 1862; *King's Nashville City Directory* (1867), 146; (1868), 121.

From Abraham Lincoln

Washington, D.C. July 11th 1862

To Hon Andrew Johnson

My Dear Sir,

Yours of yesterday is received[.] Do you not my good friend percieve that what you ask is simply to put you in Command in the west. I do not suppose you desire this.

Rec'd July 11th 12.20 A.M. 1862

By Telegraph from Washington D.C. Jul 11th 1862

To Hon Andrew Johnson

My Dear Sir,

Yours of yesterday is received Do you not my good friend perceive that what you ask is simply to put you in Command in the west, I do not suppose you desire this, You only wish to Control in your own localities, but this you must know may derange all other parts

Can you not & will you not have a full Conference with Maj Genl H. W. Halleck Telegraph him & meet him at such place as he & you Can agree upon, I telegraph him to meet you & confer fully with you — 5015

A Lincoln, President

A rebuke from the President.
Courtesy Library of Congress.

You only wish to Control in your own localities, but this you must know may derange all other parts[.]

Can you not & *will* you not have a full Conference with Maj Gen'l H. W. Halleck[?]

Telegraph him & meet him at such place as he & you Can agree upon. I telegraph him to meet you & confer fully with you—[1]

A Lincoln, President

Tel, DLC-JP.

1. Having that very day appointed Halleck general-in-chief, the President directed the new appointee, before coming to Washington, to confer with the military governor—"a true, and a valuable man—indispensable to us in Tennessee"—who is "in trouble and great anxiety about a raid into Kentucky." Lincoln to Halleck, July 11, 1862, Basler, *Works of Lincoln*, V, 313.

From Michael L. Patterson

Cincinnati Ohio,
July 11th 1862.

Gov. Johnson

I arrived here from Cumberland Gap last evening. I left there on last Saturday evening, all was quiett when I left. Robert was well, and by your assistance, and the Consent of Gen. Morgan, had succeeded in turning his Infantry Regt. in a Cavalry Regt. and Robt was looking for his horses when I left. There was two young men came into camp a few days before I left, right from Greeneville, there names was Kirk—and Elkins.[1] They stated that all was tolerable quiett when they left. Mrs. Johnson was at Mrs. Stovers, and her health was improving— Charles was also in Carter County. Judge Patterson and family was well. Your dwelling house was standing there Unoccupied, John Arnold had Came home, and Raised and organised a Company of Guirrilliers—there at Greeneville— They was to be Mounted by taking horses wherever they Could find one that Suited them. Sam. Davis and Lewis Headrick was Raising another Company of the Same Kind.—

There is a good deal of clammer heard among the troops at Cumberland Gap, about going on, and the question is asked over and over again and again, why are we not allowed to go on to the Rail Road—and take possession of the Same. Why are we kept here? &c &c. Gov. there is a good deal of Complaint about the mail not being Brought up. Some times the Army gits there mail every other day—Some times once in 3 days & Some times not for a week. The mail Seems to lie over at the different post Offices between Lexington and the Gap, And if there was Some one to go along the line, and Stur up the Different Post masters also—the mail Carryer—then the mails would Come up—in Due time—

If agreeable, I would like to have the agency.[2] But if not then I am Content—And would suggest one other thing: that I am willing to undertake— I am impressed with the Idea that East Tennessee Should have a Battery. And I am willing to undertake Raising an Artillery Company of 150 men, for that, purpose and if there has not been any application for a permit to Raise such a Company then I would like to have the privelege of Doing it myself: And when raised, I do not want to Command the Company, But want you to select Some good Gunner to Command the Same.

What do. you think of the Idia— please let me hear from you immidiately— Direct to– Louisville Ky Care of the National Hotel as I will be there in a very few days.

Yours in Love
Mike L. Patterson

ALS, DLC-JP.
1. John L. Kirk and James H. Elkins.
2. Robert had earlier telegraphed asking his father to intercede with Postmaster Blair on Patterson's behalf. Robert Johnson to Johnson, July 2, 1862, Johnson Papers, LC.

To William B. Cassilly

Nashville, July 11th 1862

Lt. Col. Wm. B. Cassilly,
Provost Marshal, Nashville, Tenn.
Sir:

I have to inform you that as Military Governor of the State of Tennessee I have taken possession of and intend to hold and occupy, for the use and benefit of the Government of the United States, the premises formerly owned by Col Heiman of the Rebel Army. I assume that I have full power to do this by virtue of my commission from the President (a Copy of which is herewith enclosed) any order issued by Captain Greene, claiming to be by authority of General Buell, to the contrary notwithstanding. In addition to this I have special orders from the War Department to call on Major General Halleck for adequate force to execute my orders. I have likewise the authority of Maj General Buell for saying to you that my *"requisitions made directly to the Provost Marshal shall be executed by him without further reference"*. For your information I enclose herewith a copy of my commission. Therefore I direct by virtue of the authority in me vested that any order issued by Captain Greene in regard to the occupancy of said premises be suspended, and I require not only that neither you, as Provost Marshal, nor any of your command shall without my authority interfere with or molest the persons now in possession of the premises aforesaid, and I respectfully call upon you, as Provost Marshal, to place a sufficient guard over said premises to protect the same against all persons claiming to interfere with those now in possession as aforesaid—[1]

L draft, DLC-JP.
   1. Cassilly replied that, Johnson's commission from the war department notwithstanding, "I—am immediatly under the direction of the Commanding General of the
Department of the Ohio," and "have no option in the matter—and trust you will see the
propriety of referring the matter to him—" Cassilly to Johnson, July 11, 1862, Johnson
Papers, LC.

From Oliver D. Greene

                                              Head-Quarters District of the Ohio,
                                                      Nashville Tenn July 12th 1862
To His Excellency Gov Andrew Johnson
Nashville Tenn
Sir—
   I am directed to inform your Excellency that the matter of your
telegraphic accounts has been laid before the Genrl Comdg and received
his personal attention—
   I am directed to say that the Genl Comdg regrets that any doubt
should have existed in the mind of his Staff officer at Nashville as to the
propriety of ordering the payment of them from Quarter Master funds[.]
   If you will have the kindness to cause the accounts to be sent to me they
will be ordered paid[.]
                                       I am Sir Very Respectfully Yr obdt Servt
                                                      O. D. Greene A. A. G.

Tel, DLC-JP.

From Edwin M. Stanton

                                                      Washington July 12, 1862
To Gov. Andrew Johnson
The President authorizes you to appoint a provost Marshal to exercise
the Jurisdiction and authority of that office under you within the city of
Nashville[.] he has ordered Col Campbell to be released from arrest and
that Capt Greene turn over his command to the officer next in rank
without delay and leave the city of Nashville and report himself in person
to Gen Buell[.]   the President hopes this will be satisfactory to you and
that you will use efforts to prevent any disputes or collision of authority
between your subordinates and those of Gen Buell.
                                              Edwin M. Stanton, Sec War

Tel, DLC-JP; DNA-RG107, Tels. Sent, Sec. of War, Vol. 11 (June 19-July 23, 1862).

To Don Carlos Buell, Huntsville, Ala.

Nashville 12 July [1862]

Major Gen Buell

Some time since I gave authority to the family of A. S. Thurnick to occupy the house owned by Col. Heimer [Heiman] of the Rebel army.

Capt. Green of your staff issued an order to the Provost Marshal Col Mathews to put the family out. I notified Col. Matthews that the house was so occupied by my authority & Matthews took no further action. Col. Campbell of 69th Ohio was appointed provost Marshal & rec'd the same order but he refused to comply with it upon my notifying him that the premises were in my possession as Military Governor of Tennessee and that I had a right to hold the same. Col. Campbell was put under arrest by Capt. Greene & Lieut. Col of 69th made Provost Marshal.[1]

Capt. Green issues the same order to him & notwithstanding my earnest protestation against any interference in a matter belonging exclusively as I conceived to the Military Governor the order was executed. These orders purported to be by your command. I cannot believe it possible that such is the case. I desire to know from you if you gave orders to the Provost Marshal to take out of my possession property I took charge as Military Governor[?] If not I respectfully ask that the Provost Marshal be directed to put me in possession of said premises again. Please give an early reply.[2] I will add that these premises were not needed by Capt. Green for any public use.

Andrew Johnson
Military Governor

L, DNA-RG94, Gens. Papers, D. C. Buell; DNA-RG393, Dept. of the Ohio, Tels. Recd. (Jan.-Aug., 1862); DLC-JP.
    1. William B. Cassilly.
    2. Buell responded that he "gave no such order & the house shall be restored to you." Buell to Johnson, July 12, 1862, Johnson Papers, LC.

To Henry W. Halleck, Corinth, Miss.

Nashville July 13, 1862

To Maj Gen Halleck

Of Morgans expedition into Kentucky we learn the burning of Lebanon & robbing of bank there & that he is marching & near Lexington.[1] The people join him on the road. Stearns[2] with his division of the expedition attacked Murfreesboro Tenn this morning in force.

Latest reports considered rebel [reliable] are that 9th Mich regt stationed there is captured[3] & the 3d Minn reg't was still engaging the enemy there. Two regts were all the force at that place. It is reported that Stearns will reach here tonight or in the morning. I do not believe it[.] There is comparatively no force at this place at this time & no hope for reinforcements[.] in the event the attack is made we will give them as warm a reception as we know how & if forced to yield will leave them a site on which there can be [a city] erected at some future day.[4] I shall see you in person in a few days.[5] Genl Boyle telegraphed last night that the raid in Kentucky was of alarming magnitude[.][6]

Andrew Johnson

LB copy, DNA-RG94, Gens. Papers, H. W. Halleck, Tels. Recd. (Mar. 11-July 7, 1862); DLC-JP; *OR*, Ser. 1, XVI, Pt. II, 142.

1. Halleck had asked for news of Morgan's Kentucky raid. Halleck to Johnson, July 13, 1862, Lets. Sent and Recd., Dept. of the Missouri, RG393, NA.

2. James W. Starnes.

3. A Confederate attack at daybreak on the thirteenth surprised Federal units in Murfreesboro. By noon the 9th Mich. had capitulated, and at three in the afternoon Col. Henry C. Lester surrendered the 3rd Minn. without engaging the enemy. *OR*, Ser. 1, XVI, Pt. II, 792-809.

4. The bracketed words appear in Johnson's original draft.

5. This meeting never occurred.

6. Not found. In his reply Johnson briefly reported the capture of Murfreesboro and asked "Can not the Regt. at Bowling Green return here immediately." Johnson to Boyle, July 13, 1862, Johnson Papers, LC.

To John F. Miller[1]

[July 13? 1862]

Col J. F. Miller
Comdg U. S. Forces
Nashville Tenn

Colonel: quite a number of the loyal citizens of Nashville have come forward & volunteered to serve until the present emergency shall have passed over. The state of Tenn has no arms to furnish them. will you order the ordnance officer in this city to furnish the Mayor Mr Smith,[2] with one hundred stand of arms, complete with 40 rounds of amu for the purpose of enabling the loyal citizens to assist in the defence of Nashville in the apprehended attack—

Tel draft, DLC-JP.

1. John F. Miller (1831-1886), Indiana native and graduate of the New York State Law School (1852), had practiced in South Bend and California and been elected to the Indiana senate (1861). Becoming colonel of the 29th Ind. Inf. at the beginning of the war, he was appointed brigadier general in 1864 and as commander of the city and post of Nashville was brevetted major general in 1865 "for gallant and meritorious services." Subsequently he served as collector of the port of San Francisco (1865-69), three times as presidential elector, as delegate to the California constitutional convention (1878-79), and as U. S. senator (1881-86). Warner, *Generals in Blue*, 324-25; *BDAC*, 1331.

2. John Hugh Smith.

From William G. Brownlow

Philadelphia, July 14, 1862

Gov. Johnson:

We have bad news here, from Tennessee and Kentucky. The indications are, that the Rebels will have Tennessee and Kentucky. I told a crowd of gentlemen here, that if I were Gov. Johnson I would resign on the ground of not being backed up by the Government[.][1]

The Administration seems to look only to *Richmond*, and neglects every other point. I am out of patience, and feel like breaking out upon the Government. *You* are in great danger. And as to Union men, they cant avow Union sentiments when they see no prospect of being sustained.

Our boys will all be killed and captured, at Cumberland Ford:[2]

In haste   W. G. Brownlow

ALS, DLC-JP.

1. Contemporary newspapers do not provide specific evidence for this statement, which may be viewed as an emotional reaction arising from John Morgan's incursion into Kentucky and the attack on Murfreesboro by James W. Starnes. The government's "neglect of East Tennessee" and, by implication, neighboring and border areas, was an allegation voiced frequently during the war by Brownlow, Johnson, and others.

2. The Parson's fears, prompted by news of Morgan's July 9-17 raid, proved to be unfounded. George Morgan held the Gap until mid-September when he withdrew without serious losses.

To Don Carlos Buell, Huntsville, Ala.

Nashville July 14, 1862

To Maj Genl Buell

Murfreesboro taken[.][1] 9th & 3rd Minnesota regiments & battry Captured— 1000 Texan rangers reported at McMinnville[.] reliable reports are to the Effect that this Cavalry are followed by large Infantry force under Breckinridge[.][2] there is no doubt but that this Section is in great danger[.] A portion of the Enemy from Murfreesboro will bear toward Columbia & cut the Communication between you & this place—[3]

Andrew Johnson

Tel, DNA-RG94, Mil. Corres. of the Rebellion, Dept. of the Cumberland; DNA-RG393, Dept. of the Ohio, Tels. Recd. (Jan.-Aug., 1862); DLC-JP.

1. Earlier Johnson had relayed reports concerning conditions in the vicinity of Chattanooga. Johnson to Buell, July 14, in Buell to Halleck, July 14, 1862, *OR*, Ser. 1, XVI, Pt. II, 143.

2. This was a false rumor which the Confederates were circulating. Gen. John C. Breckinridge was at Vicksburg, Mississippi, and did not join the forces in Tennessee until October. Generals Bragg and Kirby Smith were planning an invasion of Kentucky, but there were no troop movements until July 23 when Bragg began transferring his

infantry by rail from Tupelo, Mississippi, to Chattanooga. McWhiney, *Braxton Bragg*, 267-71, 295; Jeremiah Boyle to E. M. Stanton, July 19, 1862, *OR*, Ser. 1, XVI, Pt. I, 747.

3. Buell wired "I am making the proper dispositions. What I apprehend is that our bridges will be destroyed at Franklin or Columbia[.] A very large infantry force from East Tennessee is not to be expected at Nashville." Buell to Johnson, July 14, 1862, Johnson Papers, LC.

Speech at Nashville[1]

July 14, 1862

He said this spontaneous outpouring of the loyal men of this city astonished him. Knowing the hope that existed on the one hand to capture the city, and the fear which had grown out of the long intimidation on the other hand, which had been exercised over all who dared to be for the Government of their fathers, he had not expected that such a meeting could be gotten up without a moment's warning. But the best time to show our manhood is in the face of the enemy, and when he is on us. If his shells were falling on the capitol, let us fall, if need be, amid its crumbling and smoking ruins. Could we labor in a nobler cause than in encircling our capitol with our bodies as a breastwork, and if fate decreed it, by sprinkling its ruins with our blood? I shall make no vanting professings on the present occupation, if my past life does not speak in my behalf I shall make no toast this evening; but I would be prouder to perish in this Capitol tonight to preserve the Government of our fathers, than to be the monarch who may rest his throne upon its ruins. Yes, in the language of PATRICK HENRY, "Give me liberty or give me death!" Have we not bowed to despotism long enough, and will you again cringe as suppliants before a relentless despotism? No, it is not in your hearts or natures to do so. In the face of the enemy, I say, let him come, and you with me, and I with you, will make a tremendous effect to save the Government of our fathers. I am proud to see this noble rally. I would not have thought that such a gathering could be had. It tells that the love of the Union, and liberty lies deep in the hearts of our people forever. Let us on to the noble work. In the words of the poet:

> Freedom's battle once begun,
> Transmitted down from sire to son
> Though baffled oft, is ever won.[2]

Though tyranny may riot for a season, it must ultimately go down, and freedom will reign in its stead. This is a preliminary meeting to rally loyal men to defend the city, their families and their homes. Could you engage in a nobler work? This foe is as much your enemy as Great Britain ever was, and it is your duty to meet him in his path. I would like to see all Union men enlisted—I mean all sincere, honest, true-hearted Union men—not these pseudo loyalists—these hermaphrodites—these counterfeit coins. We want the genuine, pure coin, with the clear ring, who love their country. I would not wonder if there were a few here now professing to be Union men who have come here as spies to report and betray us to the enemy—some craven-hearted thing who has shrunk from the dimensions of a man to those of a miserable informer, prying around and skulking in a corner. I believe I can detect a few such persons here now. I have seen them during the day prowling around the Capitol.

Now you spy—rebel spy!—you may be even now standing with your stilleto in your bosom, and longing to shed some honest man's blood, but you have not the courage to do it. This, however, is an episode. I wished to say that all who wish to enroll themselves as volunteers to defend the city and their families will please attend the meeting to-morrow. All loyal men, who will take the obligation, will be furnished with arms and ammunition. Take them, take them, in good earnest, and to work! The foe has his dagger and bayonet at your throats, and now make the issue with him. They come with the torch of destruction; let them make this issue if they dare! We will meet them just as they please, and trust to the God of justice and freedom. If the volunteers serve as much as a month, they shall be paid for their time, and, if absent from home, shall receive rations. There are mechanics here—and I have a right to speak of mechanics, for I have been one myself, and am prouder of it than I am of having been your United States Senator—who have probably as mechanics often do, become dependant as it were on some proud aristocrat for employment, and perhaps dread losing his patronage if they were to engage in this work which their consciences approve. Shame on such feelings—away with them! Stand up like men, and tell these would-be masters, that you are their equals. You can do as long without making shoes as they can without wearing them. You can do as long without making coats as they can without wearing them. The time has come when labor must be respected and dignified, and mechanics, and men who live by hard labor must assert and defend their rights. In referring to mechanical labor, I merely take these as one of the departments of industry, for the sake of illustration. When you band yourselves as manly and honest citizens you have power. Tell the rebels that you are determined to have free Government and you can have it. And if you have the power, and lack the courage to use it, you deserve to be slaves. It is yours to defend yourselves, and assert your manhood,

Who would be free themselves must strike the blow.[3]

and *now* is the time to strike it! I thank the men who inaugurated this meeting, and I trust and hope you will go on. And though some fled in dastardly precipitation to the bayonets of others for protection, flying from your Capitol, although your professed Governor and champion, I fly in the hour of danger to your Capitol, and with uplifted arm I swear that this arm shall strike for freedom until the last drop of life is poured out as a libation to liberty. In the words of another, let us burn every blade of grass, and perish, if need be in the last entrenchment of freedom![4]

Nashville *Union*, July 15, 1862.
 1. Rumors that Confederate cavalry were advancing on Nashville, which was poorly prepared for defense, caused considerable alarm. At the suggestion of private parties, the military band of the 69th Ohio marched through the streets gathering an impromptu parade of loyal citizens. A hastily called meeting assembled at the capitol to consider organizing a force for home defense and to hear several short addresses. Nashville *Union*, July 15, 1862; *American Annual Cyclopaedia* (1862), 598.
 2. An inaccurate rendering of "For Freedom's battle once begun, / Bequeathed by bleeding Sire to Son / Though baffled oft is ever won," from Lord Byron's *The Giaour*, ll. 123-26.
 3. Byron, *Childe Harold's Pilgrimage*, Canto II, st. 76.
 4. A paraphrase from Robert Emmet, Irish patriot. See *Johnson Papers*, IV, 45-46.

From Jeremiah T. Boyle

Louisville July 15, 1862

To Gov Johnson
I hope you will shell the city, & burn it to ashes before you surrender it[.] Notify the women & children to leave & be ready for it[.]
Morgans band are scattered over the state and gathering more recruits[.]   burned bridge over Railroad from Lexington to Cincinnati[.]

J T Boyle
Brig Genl Comdg

Tel, DLC-JP.

To Abraham Lincoln

Nashville Tenn July 15th 62

His Excellency A Lincoln—
 I have just received the following dispatch from Gen Halleck

 Gen Buell has sent large detachments against Morgan and Starns but he wants more cavalry which we have not got[.] Cannot Cavalry be raised in Tennessee for home purposes as was done in Missouri under the authority of the President[?]

signed H W. Halleck M G
Corinth 15th July

 Cannot I be authorized to do so?[1] The work will be commenced at once[.] Your other dispatches in regard to affairs here have been received. I thank you and the Secretary of War for them.[2]

Andrew Johnson

Tel, DNA-RG107, Tels. Recd., Sec. of War, Vol. 18 (July 15-Aug. 5, 1862).
 1. The following day Stanton, apparently in response to this query, authorized the governor "to raise any amount of Cavalry in your State that may be required for the Service." Edwin M. Stanton to Johnson, July 16, 1862, Tels. Sent, Sec. of War, Vol. 11 (June 19-23, 1862), RG107, NA.

2. This rather cryptic comment is the only response which Johnson seems to have made to the series of telegrams, especially Lincoln's of July 11, which so concisely reminded him of the logical end toward which his complaints against Oliver D. Greene were leading. It should be noted, however, that the governor ultimately was successful in getting Buell's aide out of Nashville.

To Henry W. Halleck

Nashville July 15.

Maj Genl Halleck
Corinth, Miss.

I have telegraphed the President for authority to raise the Cavalry as indicated by you. The Cavalry forces under Command of the rebel Forrest,[1] who captured two Regiments at Murfreesboro have fallen back in direction of McMinnville.

One Regiment I think could retake Murfreesboro tomorrow, sustained by some cavalry. The Capture of these Regiments is an extraordinary affair and has not been satisfactorily accounted for.

Andrew Johnson
Military Governor

Tel draft, DLC-JP.

1. Nathan Bedford Forrest (1821-1877), native Tennessean with no formal education, was a slave and real estate trader, wealthy planter, and sometime Memphis alderman. Enlisting as a private in June, 1861, he raised a regiment in October and served as its lieutenant colonel. Escaping with his command at Donelson, he rose to brigadier after capture of a Union garrison at Murfreesboro in July, 1862. His brilliant exploits from Shiloh to the end of the war brought him legendary fame. Subsequently he returned to farming, was identified with the Ku Klux Klan, and served as president of the Selma, Marion & Memphis Railroad. Warner, *Generals in Gray*, 92-93; *DAB*, VI, 532-33; see also Robert Selph Henry, *"First with the Most" Forrest* (New York, 1944).

To David Tod[1]

Nashville, July 16th, 1862

Gov Tod,
Columbus, Ohio

You will please [have] Rev Jesse R. Ferguson[2] arrested and held in custody until you hear further from me. He is a traitor and, as I am advised, has been preaching treason of the most odious character. You have been expecting, perhaps, to hear of the fall of Nashville. You need have no fears on that score. The policy has been bad in withdrawing almost the entire military force from this place, but we are determined to defend it to the last extremity. Tennessee must be redeemed. God willing, she shall be.

Andrew Johnson.

Tel draft, DLC-JP.

1. Two days earlier Tod had telegraphed: "The Rev Jesse B Ferguson Supposed to

be a refugee from your City is in this Vicinity[.]" Tod to Johnson, July 14, 1862, Johnson Papers, LC.

2. Jesse B. Ferguson (1819-1870), Philadelphia-born Christian minister, resided in Virginia and Ohio where he was associated with the *Heretic Detector*, a Christian periodical published in Middleburg, Ohio, before becoming pastor of Nashville's Church of Christ in 1847 and the following year co-editor of the *Christian Magazine*. Under his leadership the congregation grew and prospered, but by the mid-1850's a serious split led to his departure from Nashville to lecture and preach in Mississippi, Alabama, and Missouri, until the eve of the war when he returned to Nashville. F. Garvin Davenport, *Cultural Life in Nashville on the Eve of the Civil War* (Chapel Hill, 1941), 100-102, 107; *Nashville Bus. Dir.* (1860-61), 166.

From Eugene Lallemand[1]

[Nashville] July 17th [1862]

To the Honble Andrew Johnson.
Governor of The State of Tennessee.

Sir, Your Petitioner Eugene Lallemand would respectfully represent to your Excellency, that he happened to be at Murfreesborough in this State on Sunday morning the 13th day of July 1862, and present at the time when the Rebel troops under the command of Col Forrest, attacked the Federal troops, and engaged in battle with them; that your Petitioner had in a Livery Stable in said town a wagon loaded with Dry Goods and other articles of trade, and one mule. The Rebel troops went into said Livery Stable and seized and took away from him the said wagon & load of merchandize and mule, and carried them off. Since which time he has heard nothing from them, that the value of said property was between seven and eight hundred Dollars. This is all the property that your Petitioner owned in the world, and has been earned by his hard labour in an honest and legitimate way, and he therefore feels very keenly and sensibly the loss of it. Your Petitioner would therefore pray your Excellency, to grant him such relief in the premises, as may appear just and reasonable. And your Petitioner as in duty bound will ever pray &c.[2]

Eugene Lallemand

Pet, DLC-JP.

1. Eugene Lallemand (c1840-fl1880), native Frenchman, was a driver and candy maker after the war, employed in 1877 by Dugger & Lindsey, wholesale bakers and confectioners. 1880 Census, Tenn., Davidson, 21st Dist., 2; Nashville city directories (1866-79), *passim*.

2. As accompanying evidence, Davidson County acting justice of the peace, George M. Southgate, certified "that the Statements made . . . in the foregoing Petition so far as they come within his own knowledge are true and correct, and those derived from the information of others he believes to be true." Johnson Papers, LC.

To Benjamin F. Larned

Nashville 17th July

Pay Master Genl Larned
    I have rec"d the following dispatch—

Cumberland Gap July 11th

Hon Andrew Johnson—
    The 3d Regt. East Tenn. Vols. has 807 men, 4th, 539, 5th, 770, & 6th, 625.
These compose twenty fifth Brigade. Have been in service nearly 4 months. No
money or pay & paymaster Barber[1] says he has no authority to pay because Each
Regt has not it minimum number. The Colonels are authorized to appoint their
Officers[.] No Commissions except by way appointment have been forwarded.
It is respectfully requested that Maj. Barber be directed at once to pay off 25th
Brigade including all officers of Regt. and my staff. It is desired you telegraph
Secty of War. & have the matter settled by telegraph desired.

J. G. Spears

These men have suffered greatly & I hope they will be paid without
delay[.][2]

Andrew Johnson Mil. Gov.

Tel, DNA-RG107, Tels. Recd., U. S. Mil. Tel., Vol. 15 (July 14-23, 1862).
    1. Richard P. L. Baber (b. c1822), native Virginian and Columbus, Ohio, lawyer,
whose former partner was Supreme Court Justice Noah H. Swayne, served as paymaster
of volunteers from 1861 to 1865, being breveted lieutenant colonel in 1866. 1860
Census, Ohio, Franklin, Columbus, 3rd Ward, 259; *U. S. Official Register* (1863), 187;
Columbus City Directory (1856-57), 15, 191; (1860-62), 3; Appointment, Commission,
and Personal Branch, RG94, NA.
    2. Five days later Johnson wired again about the failure to pay these volunteers,
adding that the "1st Middle Tenn. Regiment have not received any pay since muster into
service now over four months." Johnson to Larned, [July] 22, 1862, Johnson Papers,
LC.

To Henry W. Halleck, St. Louis, Mo.[1]

Nashville [July] 20, [1862]

H W Halleck Maj Genl.
It will be impossible for me to meet you on your way to Washn.[2] I hope
that Ex Governor Wm. B Campbell recently appointed Brigadier General will be given a command in this section. We are taking steps to raise a
brigade of our own people as soon as possible. I think we will succeed.

Andw. Johnson

Tel, DNA-RG107, Tels. Recd., U. S. Mil. Tel., Vol. 15 (July 14-23, 1862).
    1. Halleck having left St. Louis by the 21st when the wire arrived, it was forwarded
to Washington.
    2. For more than a week, Lincoln had been trying to arrange a personal meeting
between Johnson and Halleck while the latter was en route to Washington to assume his
new post as general-in-chief. On the 16th Halleck had wired from Corinth: "I leave
tomorrow for St Louis where I will remain one day enroute to Washington[.] Can I see
you at St Louis Cincinnati or any other place on the road." Johnson Papers, LC.

To Rodney Mason

Nashville, July 20 1862

Col Mason
Commanding at Clarksville, Tenn

You will exercise your best judgement and arrest such persons as by their enmity to the Government are injurious to the cause and who should be put beyond the power of doing great harm— we have sent for another battery and will telegraph you tomorrow. They can be imprisoned there or sent here.

Andrew Johnson

Tel draft, DLC-JP.

To Rodney Mason

Nashville, July 21 1862

Col Mason
Comdg Post, Clarksville, Tenn.

I hope there is no truth in the report of the number of forces you refer to. The present disposition of the troops here & in Murfreesboro makes it impracticable to send you reinforcements at this moment. I will at once lay your despatch before Commandant of this Post.

There are rumors of an attack on Nashville to night or tomorrow morning. I do not believe it. There is no doubt of their being considerable force at Lebanon, Tenn menacing in this direction. My opinion is they will attack Gallatin first—only 15 miles off, with the view of cutting off the Rail Road. I hope this may all turn out rumor. Despatch me your latest intelligence.[1]

Andrew Johnson.

Tel draft, DLC-JP.
1. The following day Mason wired: "I have not been able to obtain more definite information but am rather confirmed in the opinion that there is a force there[.]   will try & ascertain today with certainty[.]" Johnson Papers, LC.

From George W. Morgan

Cumberland Gap July 22, 1862

To His Excellency Andrew Johnson
Mil Gov. of Tenn
Governor.

Lieut Craighill[1] Military Engineer has telegraphed to Genl. Totton[2] strongly reccommending that a Military road be Immediately constructed from Crab Orchard to this place and that the Quarter Master of this division be authorized to contract for making the same at a cost not to exceed one hundred & fifty thousand (150000) dollars. This work should be placed under the supervision of a U.S. Engineer[.] without such a Road it will be impossible to hold this position after the rainy weather sets in as the Country for one hundred 100 miles to the rear is now & The Country in front soon will be entirely Exhausted[.] permit me to suggest that you communicate directly with the President upon this important subject[.]

Geo. W. Morgan
Brig Genl Comg

Tel, DLC-JP.
1. William P. Craighill (1833-1909), Virginia native and West Point graduate (1853), held all ranks in the corps of engineers through brigadier general (1895). Assistant professor of engineering at the academy (1859-63), he served there during the war, at Washington as an assistant in the engineer department, and in the field where he was breveted lieutenant colonel for his services in the defense of Cumberland Gap (1865). *NCAB*, XII, 223; Powell, *Army List*, 261; *West Point Register* (1970), 246.
2. Joseph G. Totten, chief of the corps of engineers.

From Jeremiah T. Boyle

Louisville July 24 1862

To Andrew Johnson
Gov
Rebels take the oath before your provost marchal get passes return to Kentucky as spies & Engage in guerilla band[.] I protest against Ketucky being flooded with such scoundrels[.]   Can you not prevent it. Rebel women are allowed to come into the state the wives of rebel officers[.][1]

J T Boyle
Brig Genl Comdg

Tel, DLC-JP.
1. No evidence has been found that Johnson responded to this communication.

From Leonidas C. Houk

Clarksville July 24 1862

To Gov Johnson
The number of cavalry near here was exaggerated[.]   there are however some[.] how many I cannot learn[.] they are in uniform & well armed[.]   I sent to the Place where their Camp was said to be[.]   they were not there nor can I learn where their camp is— They represent themselves as belonging to Forrests command[.] there [are] a few Union men who have become alarmed & are leaving the country. I have

tried to reassure them— I have strengthened my camp & I have no
hesitancy in saying that to give other authority to raise cavalry would
greatly Embarras Cooks Reg't who are doing well & progressing
finely[.][1]

L C Houll [Houk]
Col 3rd E Tenn Vols

Tel, DLC-JP.
1. With authorization from Johnson, William R. Cook and Daniel M. Ray were
attempting to raise a regiment which became the 2nd Cav. Three days later Cook wired:
"We have one hundred and three 103 men and recruits are coming in rapidly." Johnson
to Houk, July 16; Cook to Johnson, July 25, 27, 1862, Johnson Papers, LC.

To Oliver P. Morton[1]

Nashville, July 24th, 1862

Private
Governor O. P. Morton
Indianapolis, Ind.
Some–time since about half a dozen rabid secession preachers of this City
were arrested by my direction and are now in prison here. I desire to send
some of them North and some South. Can you take charge of two of them
in some camp or Prison in Indiana[2] where political prisoners are now
held, and where they cannot exert an evil influence on others and at the
same time receive only such treatment as traitors deserve.

Very Truly Your friend   Andrew Johnson,
Military Governor.

Tel draft, DLC-JP.
1. Oliver P. Morton (1823-1877), who worked as a hatter in his youth, graduated
from Miami University, Ohio (1845), began to practice law two years later in Cen-
terville, Indiana, became a circuit judge in 1852, and was subsequently lieutenant
governor (1860), governor (1861-67), U. S. senator (1867-77), and member of the
commission which decided the disputed election of 1876. *DAB*, XIII, 262-64; *BDAC*,
1365.
2. The same day Johnson wrote a similar request to Governor David Tod of Ohio,
and three days later to Jeremiah Boyle, the commanding officer at Louisville. Johnson to
Tod, July 24; Johnson to Boyle, July 27, Johnson Papers, LC; see also Telegram to
Charles E. Hovey, July 26, 1862.

From Ulysses S. Grant

Corinth July 25 1862

To Brig Genl. A Johnson
Mr J. W. Tarkington[1] a Union man of Henderson Co reports that he has
now five 5 companies already organized & five 5 more partially that will
be filled soon[.] He wishes to be Commissioned as Col of the Regt. raised
in Henderson Haden Carroll & McNary counties & Filan Huritt[2] to be
Commissioned as Lt. Col[.][3] Huritt has been a refugee from his home &

has acted as guide & scout for the army until our forces rendered it safe for him to return[.]   this Regt if accepted will want arms orders of locating[.]   allow me to suggest Perryville until fully prepared to move[.]   Dispatches sent to me will reach Col Tarkington[.] Col Tarkington has been petitioned by the union men of his County to organize a Regiment[.]

U S Grant Maj Genl

Tel, DLC-JP.

1. J. W. Tarkington (b. *c*1807), a Tennessee-born Henderson County farmer, possessed $1,000 real and $2,500 personal property. Although Tarkington may have raised five companies, there is no evidence that he was ever in service. 1860 Census, Tenn., Henderson, 14th Dist., 214; E. Walker to Andrew Johnson, June 14, 1862, Johnson Papers, LC.

2. Fielding Hurst (1810-1881), McNairy County unionist and slaveholder, became colonel, 6th Tenn. Cav., USA, in August, 1862. During early 1864 the Confederates charged Hurst and his regiment with many depredations upon southern sympathizers in West Tennessee, such as extracting $5,139.25 from the citizens of Jackson and murdering several captured Confederates. After the war he was briefly in the state senate (1865), resigning to become judge of the 12th judicial circuit of Tennessee and Freedmen's Bureau assistant (1867-68). *Tennesseans in the Civil War*, I, 333-35; Robison, *Preliminary Directory, McNairy*, 27; Preliminary Inventory of the Records of the field offices of the Bureau of Refugees, Freedmen, and Abandoned Lands, Pt. III, 449, RG105, NA.

3. Three days earlier, Tarkington and Hurst, telegraphing from Savannah, the county seat of Hardin, had inquired about their commissions; "secessionists have taken two Union men thirty miles below here" and "citizens here are apprehensive of an attack on this place." Johnson Papers, LC.

To William A. Cheatham, Nashville

Nashville, July 25, 1862.

Dr. Wm. A. Cheatham, Superintendent
     of the Tennessee Hospital for the Insane:

Dear Sir—The multiplicity of my duties have compelled me to delay giving that attention to the Tennessee Hospital for the Insane, that its great importance demands. I hope, however, that no serious inconvenience has in consequence resulted to yourself. I am now happy to inform you that I am enabled to relieve you of your responsibility, and that you will pardon the delay.

It is with pleasure that I am enabled to inform you, that Dr. W. P. Jones has been appointed to succeed you as Superintendent of the Hospital. You will be kind enough to deliver into his possession, the Institution, together with all the property of every kind connected therewith, which properly belongs to the State.[1]

Respectfully,   Andrew Johnson,
Military Governor.

Tenn. House Journal, 1865-66, App. 226.

1. That Cheatham had other ideas about the disposition of the institution's property is seen in a request for instructions which Johnson received five days later. William B. Cassilly, acting provost marshal in Nashville, had seized "A very large quantity of boxes,

containing clothing—bedding and furniture from the State Lunatic Asylum" which had been sent into town during the previous two days and asked for "some directions as to what we shall do—" Cassilly to Johnson, July 30, 1862, Johnson Papers, LC.

To Abraham Lincoln

Nashville, July 26 [25] 1862.[1]

His Excy. A Lincoln.

In the exchange of prisoners reported soon to take place,[2] all Tennessee prisoners who are not willing to take the oath of allegiance and enter into bonds &C should be exchanged first. And if there should be any left I hope they will be at once released upon taking the oath &c, and permitted to return to their homes. I hope the Tennessee prisoners will be held up for the last, except those who are deserving of being sent back to the Rebel army. Let them go. The expense and burthen of this rebellion must be felt by Rebels. I wish the commanding General of this Department would issue an order[3] like that recently issued by Genl Pope,[4] which is universally approved by the Unionists of Tennessee.

We have all come to the conclusion here that treason must be made odious and traitors punished and impoverished. I am doing the best I can.[5]

Andw. Johnson
Military Govr

Tel, NHi; DNA-RG107, Tels. Recd., U. S. Mil. Tel., Vol. 16 (July 23-31, 1862).

1. The governor must have prepared this communication on the 25th, inasmuch as it was transmitted at 12:31 A.M. of the 26th.

2. The first formal cartel arranging for a general prisoner exchange was signed July 22 by Union Gen. John A. Dix and Confederate Gen. Daniel H. Hill. The agreement, following the *modus operandi* of individual exchange currently in use, mostly between field commanders, provided for exchange on the basis of equality in rank, "man for man, officer for officer," with a scale of equivalents where equal discharges were unavailable—for example, a colonel for fifteen privates. Paroled captives henceforth were to be held only ten days before release but were forbidden to rejoin ranks until a formal exchange had been worked out. Hesseltine, *Civil War Prisons*, 31-33; *OR*, Ser. 2, IV, 266-68.

3. In mid-July Maj. Gen. John Pope, commander of the Army of Virginia, issued several orders designed to make the Confederates feel more of the weight of the war. General Orders No. 5 announced that the army would, as far as practical, subsist upon the country in which it was operating and that vouchers would be given to contributors stating that they would be payable at the end of the war, upon testimony that such contributors had been loyal U. S. citizens since the date of the vouchers. General Orders No. 7 provided that wherever a railroad, wagon road, or telegraph was injured by guerrillas, the citizens living within five miles of the spot would be turned out in mass to repair the damage and pay in money or property the full amount of the pay and subsistence of the force necessary to coerce them to perform the work. Also, if a soldier was fired on from a house, the house would be razed to the ground and the inhabitants sent as prisoners to the headquarters of Pope's army. *OR*, Ser. 1, XII, Pt. II, 50-51.

4. John Pope (1822-1892), a Kentuckian and West Point graduate (1842), saw service in the Mexican War and spent most of the 1850's in the topographical engineers. Appointed brigadier general of volunteers in June, 1861, he made a name for himself in the western theatre, capturing Madrid and Island No. Ten and after promotion to major general commanding the left wing of Halleck's army in the advance upon Corinth. Given command of all the Federal forces in the east except those under General McClellan in

June, 1862, he tactlessly published a series of bombastic general orders which reflected unfavorably on his new command and earned him the hatred and contempt of the Confederates. After his sound defeat by Lee at Bull Run in August, he was transferred to the Department of the Northwest where he served with credit during the Sioux uprising in Minnesota. From then until his retirement in 1886, he held various departmental commands, the last being the Division of the Pacific. Warner, *Generals in Blue*, 376-77.

5. Lincoln's endorsement, dated July 26, reads "Respectfully submitted to the Sec. of War, with the request that he respond, particularly as to Gen. Pope's order."

To George W. Morgan

Nashville July 25th [1862]

Genl. Morgan, Commanding,
Cumberland Gap, Tenn.

We have nothing from Chattanooga of recent date of an interesting character.[1] You are aware that a portion of our troops are on Battle Creek near Jasper. The recent raid made by Forest upon Murfreesboro and threatened attack on Nashville has caused some delay in Genl. Buell's advance upon Chattanooga. Forrest at last account with his forces has retreated back towards the mountains. It has been stated that his advance was to be followed by a large Infantry force. I am satisfied from information of very late date that no Infantry force is marching from Chattanooga in this direction. Communication is open between here & Huntsville[.] I hope that ere long you will have it in your power to advance into East Tennessee with safety & success. I hope you will not hesitate to give Robert, my son, such advice & instruction as you may think would be of service to him. The time has come when the burden of this war must be put upon the rebels. They must be made to feel the weight of the rebellion & the power of the Government. Vigor and determination should be infused into every department of the Government[.][2]

Andrew Johnson Mil. Gov'r.

Tel draft, DLC-JP.

1. Johnson is replying to Morgan's inquiry for news from Chattanooga. See Morgan to Johnson, July 25, 1862, Johnson Papers, LC.

2. In response Morgan, while indicating his "pleasure to render any personal service" to Robert Johnson, informed the governor of his pending resignation, due to the illness of his wife, and asked Johnson "to press upon the President the Immediate construction of a military Road to Crab Orchard" so that Cumberland Gap may be held during the coming winter. *Ibid*.

To George W. Morgan

[July 25, 1862][1]

Brig Genl. Morgan
Commanding at Cumberland Gap, Tenn

I thank you for your despatch, and your offers of kindness towards Robert.

I cannot press the acceptance of your resignation by the War Department, but have urged the immediate construction of the road referred to by you,[2] so that you can the better maintain your present position & give more efficient aid to your column when advancing into E. T.

Quiet prevails here now. The blow struck the other day on Murfreesboro resulting in the capture of 2 Regt's was caused by inexcusable negligence and difference between Commanders[.][3] It had a bad influence on the public mind at the time but has subsided & things seem to be moving on well.

Andrew Johnson

Tel draft, DLC-JP.

1. Although this communication is dated July 1, internal evidence and adjacent telegrams leave no doubt that it should bear this assigned date.

2. See Telegram from George W. Morgan, July 22, 1862; Morgan to Johnson, July 25, 1862, Johnson Papers, LC.

3. Undoubtedly the post was embroiled in dissension before the town fell to Forrest on July 13. Two days earlier, when Col. William W. Duffield arrived, he found the officers "on ill terms with each other [resulting in] a great lack of discipline and a bitter feeling of jealousy between the regiments." Much of the blame was placed on Col. Henry C. Lester, 3rd Minn. Inf., temporary commander for two months prior to the surrender of Murfreesboro. "We are looked upon with envy and jealousy by the Col . . . of the Minnesota Regt.," wrote Lt. Col. John G. Parkhurst of the 9th Michigan on July 3. When Forrest attacked, Lester ignored Parkhurst's pleas for reinforcements, arrested as spies two of the latter's couriers, and finally surrendered without risking a major encounter; for this he was dismissed in December. Such tensions contributed immeasurably to a debacle in which between 1,100 and 1,200 enlisted men were captured and supplies valued at one million dollars were lost. Trenerry, "Lester's Surrender at Murfreesboro," 192, 195; *OR*, Ser. 1, XVI, Pt. I, 801, 805, 811.

From Richard M. Edwards

Cumberland Gap July 26th 1862

Gov Johnson:

For want of proper information men often commit blunders at least it has been so with me, as I shall proceed to explain. When I obtained the commission which you sent me to raise a Cavalry Regiment at Barboursville I wrote you to aid me to get authority from the Government to muster the men into service not thinking for a moment that your authority was sufficient.

From Barboursville I went to Williamsburg where Mr Browning's[1] letter reached me enclosing authority from the War Dept to raise a *Regiment* of *Infantry*—and in that I was directed to report to you at Nashville to be mustered into service. Believing that I could not subsist my men while organizing the Regt of cavalry under your authority I for the time gave up the idea of raising cavalry & wrote that I would report to you as directed by the War Dept. & content myself with a Regiment of Infantry.

I started back to the Gap to make arrangements to visit you accordingly & on getting up to Cumberland Ford I there learned that Spear's

Brigade was marching along between the mountains to a point some where down in Dixie and that a fine prospect was open for a fight[.]

I immediately started through the mountains after him & overtook his command about 2 O'clock the next morning & went the trip with him—got to see the Rebels run and came back with a whole skin.

On arriving at the Gap again I found that a certain Kentuckian by the name of Cooke & a Mr Ray[2] had obtained authority by Telegraph from you to raise a Regt of Cavalry and further learned that Gen Morgan would subsist & equip their men.[3]

I immediately went to the General & showed him my authority and asked him if he would subsist my men if I should raise a Regt under it. To which he replied that he should feel bound to furnish me every thing necessary to my full outfit with the exception of forage for my horses—& that I would have to forage for myself. I asked him if he would permit me to go in the *advance* for that purpose to which he replied "Yes sir as far as you please." This was all I wanted[.] I immediately set about making up my Cavalry Regiment, and am happy to state have fair prospects of success. By date of authority mine is the 1st Tenn Cavalry and I hope to give it as good a standing in the cavalry as Col Birds[4] has in the infantry line.

If Col Beard[5] is at Nashville I would be glad to have him here to take a position as field officer & Dr. Brown[6] must be my Surgeon.

You perhaps will see both & may communicate those facts. I wish Beard to select our horses, & desire him at once. My Head quarters will be for some time at the Gap.

Your friend as ever   R M Edwards

ALS, DLC-JP.

1. William A. Browning, Johnson's military secretary.

2. William R. Cook and Daniel M. Ray.

3. Morgan had telegraphed he was ready to issue rations upon receipt of Johnson's authority. Morgan to Johnson, July 22, 1862, Johnson Papers, LC.

4. Robert K. Byrd.

5. Stephen Beard (b. c1817), a prosperous Bradley County farmer, attended the Union convention at Knoxville in May, 1861, and sometime later was arrested by Confederate authorities. He was released and in 1864-65 served as major and lieutenant colonel, 5th Tenn. Mtd. Inf., USA. *OR*, Ser. 1, LII, Pt. I, 150; Hurlburt, *Bradley County*, 113-14; *Tennesseans in the Civil War*, I, 358.

6. John G. Brown (1820-1867), a Bradley County doctor who attended the East Tennessee Union Convention at Greeneville, was arrested in November, 1861, by Confederate authorities and imprisoned in Knoxville, Tuscaloosa, and Mobile, before being released in early 1862. He fled to Nashville and in August, 1863, became the surgeon of the 4th Tenn. Cav., USA. Hurlburt, *Bradley County*, 113-15, 117-18; *OR*, Ser. 1, LII, Pt. I, 168; *Tenn. Adj. Gen. Report* (1866), 389; John M. Wooten, *A History of Bradley County* (Cleveland, Tenn., 1949), 209.

From Asa C. Ketchum[1]

Memphis Tenn
July 26th 1862

Hon Andrew Johnson
Governor of Tenn
Dear Sir

I address you for the purpose of ascertaining if Something can be done for us at this place to remedy the difficulty we are placed in, by the leaving of Secesh officers. The Judge of the Common Law & Chancery Courts, The Sheriff of the County and other officers, have left, and no probability of their return. It is the intention of all that Sympathize with Rebellion to delay as far as possible the collection of debts or redress of wrongs, where the creditor or party aggreived is a Unionist; and I find in endeavoring to aid parties to obtain their rights great difficulty for the want of officers, to execute the law— I had thought I would not trouble you with a letter on the Subject as the Hon B. D. Nabors[2] had informed me that you was expected in Memphis Soon, when I could lay the Subject before you[.] We Shall all be highly gratified to See you and hear you again, (that is all Union people)

If anything can be done to fill vacancies in office it would facilitate Business much[.]

I am Sir very Respectfully
your most obedient Servant
A. C. Ketchum

ALS, DLC-JP.

1. Asa C. Ketchum (c1820-fl1869), a New York native who had migrated to Wisconsin, where he practiced law in Portage City and served in the legislature (1854) before moving to Memphis about 1860, was briefly captain, Co. B, 15th Tenn. Inf., CSA, before resigning in October, 1861. Unsuccessful in efforts to get a military commission from Johnson in the summer of 1862, he was appointed by the general commanding in Memphis to a three-man judicial commission to settle citizen claims (April, 1863) and·the following year served as colonel of a Memphis militia regiment. Returning to the practice of law, he sought as late as February, 1869, to realize the reward of public office from the hands of the man whose selection as vice president in 1864, according to Ketchum, owed so much to his efforts. CSR, RG109, NA; *Halpin's Memphis Directory* (1867-68), 155; George Gale to Johnson, December 19, 1862; Ketchum to Johnson, August 28, 1862, September 16, 1864, February 3, 1869, Johnson Papers, LC; Hooper, Memphis, 87. For reflections on Ketchum's integrity and veracity, see M[ilton] Barnes to Johnson, n.d. (enclosed in B. D. Nabers to Johnson, February 5, 1863), Johnson Papers, LC.

2. Appointed to the Memphis board of trade in June, 1862, to supervise shipments and issue permits until a surveyor was appointed, Benjamin D. Nabers resigned in November. Futrell, Federal Trade, 80, 99; see *Johnson Papers*, IV, 290n.

To Charles E. Hovey[1]

Nashville July 26th 1862

Genl. Hovey
Comd'g at Memphis, Tenn.

I have a number of rabid rebel preachers I desire to send south. Can I send them to your charge & have them turned loose beyond our southern lines with the distinct understanding that if they return or recross our lines during the existing rebellion they shall be treated as spies and punished accordingly. I hope to be in Memphis soon.

Andrew Johnson
Military Governor.

Tel draft, DLC-JP.

1. Charles E. Hovey (1827-1897), Vermont native and Dartmouth graduate (1852), was a high school principal in Framingham, Massachusetts (1852-54), and Peoria, Illinois (1854-56). Superintendent of Peoria public schools (1856-57), he also edited the *Illinois Teacher* (1856-58) and became first principal of the state normal university (1857-61). Colonel of the 33rd Ill. Inf. ("Normal Regiment"), he rose to brigadier (1862) and brevet major general (1865) of volunteers. Subsequently he practiced law in Washington, D. C. *DAB*, IX, 271-72.

To John A. McClernand[1]

Nashville, July 26th 1862

Maj: Genl. McClernand,
Jackson, Tenn.

We have been endeavoring to concentrate some forces here, raised in Tennessee, and are succeeding very well. If the Rebel Army was expelled from the State we could raise a large force in a short time.[2] Is there not some suitable and responsible man who resides in that vicinity who can and will undertake to raise a Regiment? If so he can be commissioned Colonel, then indicating other officers to aid him in the work. If Captain Parsons[3] has a full company & is willing to be mustered regularly into the service he can be commissioned and remain where he is until otherwise directed, and furnished with subsistence, equipments &c as soon as practicable.[4]

I hope you will give him all the instruction necessary to the regular organization of his Company.

I must even in a despatch tender assurances of my high esteem and great respect for you as a man and a soldier. I expect to be in Memphis soon.

Andrew Johnson. Mil: Gov'r.

Tel draft, DLC-JP.

1. John A. McClernand (1812-1900), born in Kentucky but reared in Illinois, was a lawyer, Democratic state legislator (1836, 1840, 1842-43), and U. S. representative (1843-51, 1858-61) prior to his appointment as brigadier general of volunteers in 1861.

Promoted to major general, he led the expedition which captured Arkansas Post (January, 1863), but after a disastrous assault on Vicksburg was relieved from command of the XIII Corps by General Grant for giving the press a congratulatory order "extolling his men as the heroes of the campaign." Restored to active command in 1864, he resigned in November and returned to Illinois, later serving as circuit judge (1870-73) and presiding over the 1876 Democratic national convention. Warner, *Generals in Blue*, 293-94; *BDAC*, 1285-86.

2. The day before McClernand had telegraphed, "Can't home guard be immediately organized & armed here[?] there is the greatest necessity for it." McClernand to Johnson, July 25, 1862, Johnson Papers, LC.

3. Pleasant K. Parsons (c1826-fl1870), Carroll County farmer, became captain, Co. E, 7th Tenn. Cav., USA, August 11, 1862. Captured at Union City in March, 1864, he escaped four days later but soon after was court martialed and held in arrest for over a year; apparently never sentenced, he was honorably discharged August 7, 1865. 1870 Census, Tenn., Carroll, 14th Dist., 5; CSR, RG94, NA; *OR*, Ser. 1, XXXII, Pt. I, 544.

4. Ten days prior to this communication, Parsons had wired Johnson reporting that he had assembled from Decatur County "a Cavalry Company of One hundred men (100) and Horses which I wish received into the State Service. We hold ourselves in readiness for marching orders to any point as soon as received." Parsons to Johnson, July 16, 1862, Johnson Papers, LC.

To William Nelson

Nashville, July 26th 1862

Maj: Genl. Nelson,
Murfreesboro, Tenn.

I have just been advised that Gen'l Morgan commanding at Cumberland Gap has resigned. If accepted by War Department, can't you take command of that expedition[1] and redeem East Tennessee, and end your military career with the expedition that you were first connected with, and which you should have commanded without interruption, and before this time the Southern Confederacy would have been segregated and its unity destroyed. This is to be the crowning achievement in this War.

Andrew Johnson. Mil: Gov'r

Tel, DLC-JP.

1. Embarked on a movement of his own to relieve lower East Tennessee, Nelson wrote that he could not "quit this theatre of action now" but that "so soon as circumstances will warrant my leaving here I will notify you." Nelson to Johnson, July 26, 1862, Johnson Papers, LC.

To Edwin M. Stanton

Nashville July 26, 1862

Hon Edwin M. Stanton
Sec of War

I have just learned from Gen Morgan, comd'g at Cumberland Gap that he has tendered his resignation. If it is accepted I hope that Genl Nelson or Thomas of Buell's army will be assigned the command at that place, they are familiar with the Country, the expedition from its commencement, the oppression of the people & their necessities. I would suggest also Ex. Gov. W. B. Campbell recently appointed Brig. Genl as being a suitable appointment for that command[.][1] large portion of the troops there are Tennesseeans. I hope the Secy of war will cause the Commanding General of this Dept to issue an order similar to that of Gen Pope in Virginia in regard to subsisting &c. on the Enemy. It is needed & will bring rebels to their senses. The rebels must be made so feel to the weight & ravages of the War they have brought upon the Country, treason must be made odious & traitors impoverished. We are raising forces here—infantry & Cavalry—and in obtaining horses & supplies the sec'y of War need not be surprised if we make rebels meet the demand. I must be permitted to take some latitude in this respect.

Genl Morgan is pressing with great force the construction of a road from Crab Orchard to Cumberland Gap[.] if the railroad[2] you intended to construct when I left Washn. had been then commenced it would have been now completed & the cost of construction saved in transportation & a connection with that portion of Tennessee formed which would have segregated & destroyed the unity of the contemplated Southern Confederacy.

Accept assurance of my confidence and esteem.

Andrew Johnson.

Tel, DNA-RG107, Tels. Recd., Sec. of War, Vol. 18 (July 15-Aug. 5, 1862); DLC-JP; Johnson-Bartlett Col.

1. Johnson made similar recommendations to General Buell. Johnson to Buell, July 26, 1862, Johnson Papers, LC.

2. In his first annual message to Congress in December, 1861, Lincoln recommended as a military measure the construction of a railroad from Kentucky to the loyal regions of East Tennessee and western North Carolina. The main route considered, from Danville to Knoxville, was to have been used as a supply line for the advancing army. But after Chattanooga and Knoxville fell into Union hands (1863), the road was no longer considered necessary. Basler, *Works of Lincoln*, V, 37; *Senate Misc. Doc.* No. 132, 38 Cong., 1 Sess.

To Jeremiah T. Boyle[1]

Nashville, July 28 1862

Genl Boyle,
Louisville, Ky.

I sent you three rebel clergymen by this morning's train. I will send three more by train to-morrow—and one, who altho' not a preacher is equally obnoxious.[2] I will only trouble you with them for a few days. I thank you most sincerely for your aid and assistance in this matter. I want them away from here, and in a few days will decide whether they shall go South or be confined elsewhere.

Andrew Johnson Mil. Gov'r.

Tel draft, DLC-JP.

1. The day before Johnson had inquired whether Boyle could "take charge of two or four rabid preachers for a few days, and have them confined seperately," to which Boyle

replied affirmatively. Johnson to Boyle and Boyle to Johnson, July 27, 1862, Johnson Papers, LC.

2. Probably Turner S. Foster (b. *c*1823), Nashville lawyer with property valued at $76,000, who had served as secretary of the Confederate passport office. Elected circuit court judge on May 22, proving that the population's sentiments were still strongly anti-Union, he was arrested by Johnson and sent to Louisville, apparently at the same time as Nashville ministers Reuben Ford, C. D. Elliott, and Samuel D. Baldwin. Suffering with rheumatism, Foster was paroled at Camp Chase in November on condition that he be exchanged for Edmund Cooper, Johnson's new secretarial appointee who had been captured by the Confederates. 1860 Census, Tenn., Davidson, Edgefield, 17; Maslowski, "*Treason Must Be Made Odious*," 161-62; Turner Foster Parole, November 3, 1862, Johnson Papers, LC; Nashville *Dispatch*, November 22, 1862. See also Turner S. Foster to Harriet Foster, August 31, 1862, Johnson Papers, LC.

To Charles T. Larned[1]

Nashville, July 28th 1862

Major C. T. Larned
Chief Paymaster Dist of the Ohio
Louisville, Ky.
The 1st Regiment Middle Tennessee Volunteers have received no pay for four or five months. On that account the officers and men are complaining. They need their pay badly. We are raising Infantry & Cavalry forces. The fact of the First Regiment having received no pay is operating against us[.] If there could be a Pay-Master sent here and pay off this Regiment it would do great good. I hope you will have this attended to immediately. When may we look for a Paymaster here for this purpose[.]

Andrew Johnson
Mil: Governor

Tel draft, DLC-JP.

1. Charles T. Larned (1836-1882), son of Paymaster General Benjamin F. Larned, was a Michigan native who later moved to Missouri. Attending West Point (1851-54), he served in the paymaster department from 1861 until his death at Eureka Springs, Arkansas. *U. S. Official Register* (1863), 151; Powell, *Army List*, 424; Appointment, Commission, and Personal Branch, RG94, NA.

To Rodney Mason

Nashville, July 28th 1862

Col Mason
Clarksville, Tenn.
We have no horses here,[1] and are trying to raise some, and if they cannot be had otherwise, we intend to press them into the service giving the secession owners a certificate of value to be paid at the conclusion of the rebellion if they are loyal. Cant you find forty horses somewhere in that vicinity on which you can mount your Infantry.

Will not some good men in your neighborhood undertake to raise a

Company of Cavalry and when raised they will be furnished with horses, arms, equipments &c.

Andrew Johnson Mil Gov'r

Tel draft, DLC-JP.

1. Mason had requested forty horses to mount some infantry in the absence of cavalry. Mason to Johnson, July 28, 1862, Johnson Papers, LC.

From Jeremiah T. Boyle

Louisville July 29, 1862

To Gov. Johnson

Second batch of prisoners here except Howell who is reported sick[.][1] will do your wishes as far as practicable[.] some of those who came up yesterday offered to bet the rebels would have Nashville in Ten (10) days[.]

J T. Boyle.
Brig Genl. Comdg

Tel, DLC-JP.

1. Rev. R. B. C. Howell was paroled on a day-to-day basis "in consequence of very severe indisposition," as there were no accommodations for ill prisoners at the penitentiary in Nashville. William B. Cassilly to Johnson, July 30, 1862, Johnson Papers, LC.

From Edwin D. Judd[1]

Pay Department
Louisville Ky 29. July 1862

to His Excellency Andrew Johnson
Military Governor State of Tenn
Dear Sir

Your letter of the 16th inst relating to the claims of Thomas Gardom[2] watchman of the Bank of Tenn. is received.

Major John Coon[3] who was the Paymaster in charge when the Bank was first occupied by our Department, states that he did not employ him, but allowed him to remain there at the request of his owner, and I think also at your own request. the Bank having contracted with his owner for his services for the whole year, the owner wished to fulfil her part of the contract. We had no use for him, inasmuch as a military guard were always on duty there. Under these circumstances we do not feel authorized to pay the acct. but we presume that General Buell's order would induce the Quartermaster to pay it. I return the papers[.][4]

I am Very Respy, Your Obdt Servt.

Edwin D. Judd
acting chief paymaster

Your telegraph just received. Maj. Larned[5] is absent, will send Paymaster as soon as we receive more money, but they send it very slowly.

L, DLC-JP.

1. Edwin D. Judd (c1834-1908), a Hartford, Connecticut, bank clerk appointed paymaster of volunteers in June, 1861, served in the Department of Kentucky and Tennessee, February-December, 1862. In 1865 he was breveted lieutenant colonel and two years later attained the permanent rank of major, retiring in 1879. Powell, *Army List*, 405; Appointment, Commission, and Personal Branch, RG94, NA.

2. Thomas Gardom (c1830-1870), Philadelphia-born Nashville plasterer, with $200 in personal property, sought payment of $122 for service as night watchman from April 23 to June 23. 1860 Census, Tenn., Davidson, Nashville, 6th Ward, 138; Nashville *Republican Banner*, January 29, 1870; voucher No. 22 for Thomas Gardom, July 15, 1862, Johnson Papers, LC.

3. John Coon (b. c1823), New York native and Cleveland, Ohio, lawyer in 1861 with the firm of Keith & Coon, served as paymaster of volunteers from June, 1861, to March, 1865. *U. S. Official Register* (1863), 187; *Cleveland City Directory* (1861), 61; Appointment, Commission, and Personal Branch, RG94, NA.

4. This description of the quartermaster corps' employment arrangements with Gardom implies that he was a slave. And so both Coon and Judd had thought. Some ten days later, evidently in response to a letter from Johnson challenging this assumption, Judd acknowledged his having been "led into error by the information given me by Maj. Coon," who had "thought the letter [inquiring about payment of Gardom's claim] referred to a slave who had been employed there." Meantime, Johnson had much earlier (July 15) approved the bill calling for Gardom's payment at the rate of $2.00 a night for sixty-one nights. Judd to Johnson, August 8; Charles T. Larned to Johnson, August 16; voucher No. 22 for Thomas Gardom, July 15, 1862, Johnson Papers, LC.

5. Charles T. Larned.

To William H. Sidell[1]

Nashville, July 29th 1862.

Maj. Sidell, A.A.A.G.

Sir:

The within letter of Lieut C. T. Wharton[2] addressed to you in regard to the removal of the ordnance stores to the Capitol Building which was referred to me by you for my opinion, is returned.

The propriety and expediency of depositing all the ordnance stores in the Capitol will be determined by the Military authority, being much more competent to do so than I am. The decision when made will be most cheerfully acquiesced in by me. I must be permitted to remark though that before they are removed the question should be carefully considered in view of the peculiar condition of this city & the surrounding circumstances[.] There is now being deposited a large quantity of equipments for Cavalry in the basement story and other stores will soon be here. In fine Ass't Adj't Sidell, and Gen'l Buell will do that which they deem best for the public interest and the military service, and it will be entirely satisfactory to me[.]

[Andrew Johnson]

L draft, DLC-JP.

1. William H. Sidell (1810-1873), New York native and West Point graduate (1829), resigned from the army in 1833 to work as an engineer. Commissioned major of the 15th U. S. Inf. in 1861, he was appointed assistant adjutant general of the Department of the Cumberland (1862), became acting provost marshal general for Kentucky, general superintendent of recruiting, chief mustering and disbursing officer at Louisville (1863), and ultimately brigadier-general (1865), retiring five years later because of disability. *DAB*, XVII, 151-52.

2. Clifton T. Wharton (*c*1836-1899), Chicago bookkeeper and 1st lieutenant, Co. A, 19th Ill. Inf., was detached as acting assistant adjutant general on General Buell's staff, March, 1862, two months later becoming the ordnance officer for the post of Nashville, where he served until his discharge in July, 1864. *Cooke's Chicago Directory* (1860-61), 379; *OR*, Ser. 1, XVI, Pt. II, 59; LII, Pt. I, 227; CSR, RG94, NA; Pension Records, RG15, NA.

From George W. Ashburn

Murfreesboro Tenn July 30/62

On monday the 12/Inst a man in confederate uniform accompanied by two citizens took & carried off my large gray horse, one that I paid in may last 300 dollar for & have refused 350. I, therefore, claim damages under your proclamation. The two citizens with the thief who pointed out my horse, were Frank. Baxter[1] an Overseer of Ed. Arnolds[2] living one mile from Town & Dr. Kings son[3] who lives with his Father on the same block of myself. Ed. Arnolds, in whose employment Baxter was, belongs to the confederate army & led in the fight at Murfreesboro & his residence is now a Hospital for the confederates who were wounded in the Murfreesboro fight. Frank Baxter has nothing & went off with the Guerillas[.]

Very Respectfully &C   G. W. Ashburn

To Andrew Johnson
Military Gov of Tenn.

ALS, DLC-JP.

1. Possibly Benjamin F. Baxter (b. *c*1841), son of overseer David Baxter. Enlisting at Murfreesboro in November, 1862, Baxter served as a corporal, Co. I, 45th Tenn. Inf., CSA, before he deserted in September, 1863, "with gun and accouterments." Deane Porch, *1850 Census, Rutherford County, Tennessee* (Nashville, 1967), 40; CSR, RG109, NA.

2. Edwin Arnold (*c*1818-1884), a native of Virginia, was a Murfreesboro farmer, mason, and contractor, with $12,500 in real and $15,350 in personal property. A 2nd lieutenant, Co. I, 45th Inf., he served as a guide for General Forrest and after the war was Rutherford County sheriff (1870-76). 1860 Census, Tenn., Rutherford, Bushnell's Creek, 136; *Goodspeed's Rutherford*, 818, 1021; Bromfield L. Ridley, *Battles and Sketches of the Army of Tennessee* (Mexico, Mo., 1906), 107; *Tennesseans in the Civil War*, II, 19.

3. John D. King (b. *c*1842), the son of Dr. J. D. King (b. *c*1816), was a private in Co. I, 1st (Maney's) Inf., CSA. 1860 Census, Tenn., Rutherford, Murfreesboro. 8; *Tennesseans in the Civil War*, II, 237.

From Robert Johnson

Hd. Qrs. Cumberland Ford July 30 1862

To Andrew Johnson Mil Gov

No information in regard to Horses & equpments[.] Have them forwarded immediately[.] Boys just in from Greenville[.] Mothers Health improving[.] rebels have our house for barracks. From your son.

Col Robt Johnson

Tel, DLC-JP.

To Rodney Mason

Nashville, July 30th 1862.

Col Mason,
Clarksville, Tenn.

If your officers have been despoiled of property by secessionists[1] of that vicinity, you are authorized to proceed under my proclamation of the 9th May,[2] and levy full and ample remuneration upon the property of the leading secessionists of the neighborhood.

You will be careful to guard against injury to union men, and confine the levy to well known and influential rebels.

Andrew Johnson
Military Governor.

Tel draft, DLC-JP.
1. Mason had telegraphed that in consequence of his men being robbed of property amounting to about four hundred dollars, he proposed to "levy at least five hundred dollars on the leading secesh" of Providence near where the robbery took place. Mason to Johnson, July 30, 1862, Johnson Papers, LC.
2. Proclamation Concerning Guerrilla Raids, May 9, 1862.

From George W. Lane[1]

Huntsville Ala—
July 31st 1862—

Hon Andy Johnson—
Dr Sir—

I wrote to you some days since, stating that the Atty Genl of the U. S. Mr Bates, had written to me,[2] that in the Spring of this year a Treasury warrant for over Twenty seven hundred dollars was forwarded to your care at Nashville, intended for my use.[3]

An opportunity now presents itself of sending this letter by a friend, who will hand it to you, and who will return to this place in a few days.

Should the warrant from Washington have reached you, you can send it to me by Mr Windham,[4] the bearer of this letter—Let me hear from you. All is pretty quiet here.

Wishing you personal safety and health, and peace to our common country—

I am Yrs Respectfully
Geo: W. Lane

ALS, DLC-JP.

1. George W. Lane (1806-1863), Georgia native and lawyer, moved to Alabama where he represented Limestone County in the legislature (1829, 1832) and was judge of the county court. Settling later in Madison County, he was a strong unionist during the secession crisis. Appointed U. S. district judge by Lincoln (1861), he held no sessions, even though northern Alabama was controlled by Union troops in the spring and summer of 1862. He died a refugee in Louisville. Faye Acton Axford, ed., *The Journals of Thomas Hubbard Hobbs* (University, Ala., 1976), 79; James P. Jones and William Warren Rogers, eds., "Montgomery as the Confederate Capital: View of a New Nation," *Alabama Historical Quarterly*, XXVI (1964), 74.

2. On May 28, 1862, Bates had written Johnson, enclosing a letter to Lane "because I do not know how to send it to him," and asking Johnson to "forward it as soon as it may be conveniently and safely done." On August 6, 1862, William J. Windham received the letter from Johnson with a government draft for $2,780.55 for Lane's salary. Edward Bates to Johnson, May 28; Receipt of William J. Windham, August 6, 1862, Johnson Papers, LC.

3. A week before Johnson had received a similar inquiry about an identical sum of money from Bates on its way to another Alabama unionist, Jeremiah Clemens. As the nearest officer responsible for civil government, Johnson was evidently used by the attorney general as an agent to transmit salaries to Union officeholders in the adjacent state. Clemens to Johnson, July 24, 1862, Johnson Papers, LC.

4. William J. Windham (c1829-fl1880), native Alabamian, was a steam sawmill proprietor after the war. 1860 Census, Ala., Madison, Huntsville, 22; (1880), 2nd Ward, 12.

From Addison S. Norton[1]

Office of the Provost Marshal.
Bolivar, Tenn., July 31st 1862.

His Excellency Andrew Johnson
Governor of Tennessee.
Sir,

A case has just come before me in which the Circuit Court of Hardeman County—issued an attachment & c. The Sherriff of this County[2] has taken the Oath of allegiance to the so called Confederate Government and has exercised his functions as Sherriff since that time. The other officers have failed to take the Oath prescribed— I set aside their action as illegal and treasonable, and remanded the property to its proper owner—

I desire to procure a copy of your proclamation refering to this matter, as well as any other rules which may have been prescribed by you.

I have the honor to be sir

Respectfully your obd't serv't
A. S. Norton
Maj U. S. Vol & Provost Marshal.

ALS, DLC-JP.

1. Addison S. Norton (c1821-1874), New York native and Peoria, Illinois, painter with $3,300 real and $1,500 personal property, was captain and colonel, 17th Ill. Inf. (1861-63) before resigning and reenlisting as major and aide-de-camp (July, 1863-October, 1865). 1860 Census, Ill., Peoria, Peoria City, 3rd Ward, 219; Heitman, *Register*, I, 751; *The History of Peoria County* (Chicago, 1880), 517.

2. The Hardeman County sheriff (1856-62) was J. W. Deming (c1824-fl1870), a North Carolina-born farmer. 1860 Census, Tenn., Hardeman, 14th Dist., 198; (1870), 11th Dist., 40; *Goodspeed's Hardeman*, 823.

From James S. Negley

August 1, 1862, Columbia; Tel, DLC-JP.

Has arrested A. O. P. Nicholson, Col. Joseph Branch, and Judge William P. Martin, "who avow their Treason & refuse to take the Oath"; has ordered them outside the Federal lines under heavy bonds. Does Johnson have further instructions?

From James S. Negley

Columbia Tenn August 1 1862

To Gov Andrew Johnson

There are a number of Country merchants turning their oath of Allegiance to profit by Bringing out goods & sending them to secessionists[.] in many cases have formed partners and One Rebel who has taken the Oath[.] the abuse of permission to pass goods has been so extensively abused that I deem it necessary to require every dealer to not only take the Oath but obligate himself not to sell [to] disloyal persons[.] Yours

Jas S Negley Brig Gen'l

Tel, DLC-JP.

From William S. Smith[1]

Hd. Qrs. Manchester Tenn
Aug 1st 1862

Gen. Andrew Johnson
Mil Gov. of Tennessee
Sir

By a recent order from the Hd. Qrs. of the Army of the Ohio, I have been placed in command of all the forces guarding the lines of R. Rds from Nashville to Decatur, Decatur to Stevenson and Stevenson to Nashville.

The troops under my command are necessarily scattered in small detachments and stationed at the vital points of the lines mentioned. They are thus exposed to destruction or capture by the guerrilla and marauding bands which infest the whole State of Tennessee. They are surrounded by enemies who in the garb of peaceable quiet citizens run off intelligence of our strength and positions, so much in detail and so accurate as to enable the rebels to kill or capture their pickets and to hurl overwhelming forces upon them—to carry them away as prisoners and destroy our railroads and thus threaten our whole army with starvation. This must so derange our plans as to prevent any successful warfare on our part and throwing us upon the country for support cause us to deprive the people of that which is absolutely necessary of their sustenance. Then again the presence of those hostile to our government throughout this State serves to keep those cowed and subdued who would otherwise declare in our favor and undertake the quieting of all local difficulties. The guerrillas threaten them and do actually drag them away from their homes or drive them into our camps for refuge. I have many of these refugees now in my camps and amongst them a poor old man by the name of Williams[2] eighty years of age and almost blind. Now Sir, how long shall this condition of things continue in the State of Tennessee? I but expressed the common feeling of the officers of our army when I wrote the Secry. of War a few days ago claiming a release from this service within one month unless a more decisive policy is adopted in the treatment of these mixed communities[.]

With enemies in our rear and in our very midst such success as we should achieve is utterly and entirely out of the question, and I am unwilling for one to put forth aimless, objectless effort.

1st. Let all disloyal persons be driven at once across the lines to the rebels where they belong.

2nd. Let the loyal patriotic citizens of the land be organized, armed and equipped for their own home defence and the protection of our lines of communication.

This much Your State owes to us who are here to aid you in the preservation of Your liberties. If the rebels will permit a portion of our army to remain behind their lines unmolested, we can do our country a hundred fold service. And it will take five hundred thousand men to guard our lines of communication alone in the territory occupied by us, unless forays and guerrilla warefare can be suppressed and prevented by some such stringent measures. There are many true men ready to take up arms and put down the infamous scoundrels who have inaugerrated a wholesale system of rapine and murder throughout nearly this while region of Country. Guerrilla bands are constantly organizing and stealing all the horses and provisions they can lay their hands on, and escaping with them to the enemy to swell his ranks and increase his resources.

In the name of our country humanity and God let us tolerate this condition of things no longer. Let home guards be organized everywhere and men drafted into service if necessary rather than endure anarchy any longer[.]

Very Respectfully Yr Most Obdt Svt.
Wm Sooy Smith Brig Gen

ALS, DLC-JP.

1. William S. Smith (1830-1916) of Ohio, a West Point graduate (1853), resigned his commission to work as a construction engineer on the Illinois Central Railroad. He served with Ohio volunteers from June, 1861, until, disabled by rheumatism, he resigned in 1864 and retired to his farm in Oak Park, Illinois. Resuming practice as a civil engineer in 1866, he constructed the first steel bridge to span the Missouri River and later engaged in building in Chicago. *DAB*, XVII, 367-68; Warner, *Generals in Blue*, 464.

2. Not identified.

To Benjamin F. Butler[1]

Nashville, Aug. 1st, 1862

Maj. Gen. B. F. Butler, Commanding at New Orleans

Dear Sir: Fully aware of the many and laborious duties which your position imposes upon you, I do not desire to increase them, but the criminal appropriation, by rebels, of all the resources of the Treasury of Tennessee compels me to make every effort in my power to furnish means for carrying on the civil and military powers of the state. My high regard for your patriotism and ability has induced me to refer to you for collection a list of Notes and Drafts, assets of the Bank of Tennessee, and, of course, the property of the state.

By application to Mr. Geo. A. French,[2] cashier of the Union Bank of New Orleans, you can in all probability obtain the Notes and Drafts mentioned in this list.

I shall by the same mail write to Mr. French to furnish you with all the assets of the Bank. If you can by any means collect these assets, you will confer a favor which will be gratefully received by the patriotic and loyal people of the state. I shall be happy to hear from you as soon as you have had an opportunity to take the subject into consideration.

I hope that success may continue to crown your patriotism, zeal, and ability in the great cause of our common country and constitutional liberty. With sentiments of the highest regard and esteem,

Your obedient Servant,
Andrew Johnson

Private and Official Correspondence of Gen. Benjamin F. Butler, During the Period of the Civil War (5 vols., Norwood, Mass., 1917), II, 139-40.

1. Benjamin F. Butler (1818-1893), New Hampshire native and lawyer who served in the Massachusetts house (1853) and senate (1859) as a Democrat, supported Jefferson Davis and later John C. Breckinridge for President in 1860, but by the Reconstruction period was a radical Republican. Appointed major-general of volunteers in May, 1861, he was the first to apply the term "contrabands-of-war" to slaves who fled into Union lines. As commander of occupied New Orleans from May until December, 1862, he governed effectively but undeniably lined his own pockets and those of his family and friends. After the war he was a Republican congressman (1867-75, 1877-79)—taking a prominent part in the impeachment of Johnson in 1868—Massachusetts governor (1882), and the Greenback presidential candidate (1884). Warner, *Generals in Blue*, 60-61; *BDAC*, 638.

2. George A. Freret (b. c1817), a Louisianian possessing property worth $22,000 was cashier of the Union Bank of Louisiana both before and after the war. 1860 Census, La., New Orleans, 6th Ward, 239; New Orleans city directories (1853-71), *passim*.

To Robert Johnson, Cumberland Ford, Ky.

Nashville August 1st 1862

Col Robt Johnson

I have made an effort through the Quarter Master at Louisville[1] to procure horses for your regiment— He informs me that it cannot be done by him for the present—[2] are there no horses suitable for cavalry service in all that region of country about you[?]   if we cant do any better horses must be pressed into the service[.] You will remember that I telegraphed you to consult Genl Morgan in reference to the equipments & horses & expected steps had been taken for their procurement[.][3] I will have equipments ordered at once if it has not been done by Genl Morgan[.][4] It will be an immense job to haul all the equipments & clothing for a thousand men & horses[.] If the men were mounted could they not travel to nearest point on railroad & receive equipments quicker safer & cheaper than to carry them in wagons all the way to Cumberland Gap[?]   this war must be put upon the enemy & if we take horses we will do it regularly giving them certificates of the value to be paid at close of rebellion if the party is loyal[.]

Andrew Johnson
Mil Gov of tenn

Tel, DLC-JP.

1. Thomas Swords (1806-1886), New York City native and West Point graduate (1829), served in the southern states and the frontier through the Mexican War. Assigned to the quartermaster department in 1846, he was promoted to assistant quartermaster general, August, 1861, and late the same year became chief quartermaster of the Department of the Cumberland, with headquarters at Louisville, in which capacity he continued until his retirement in 1869. *NCAB*, IV, 542; Powell, *Army List*, 619.

2. A sizeable segment of Johnson's correspondence during the preceding week, including telegrams to Lorenzo Thomas (July 27), James W. Ripley (July 28 and 30), Thomas Swords (July 30), and their replies, had been devoted to vain efforts to make horses available for his son's regiment. Two days before this wire, Swords had reported that Generals Buell and Boyle had contracted for all the horses on hand.

3. See Telegram to Robert Johnson, July 1, 1862.

4. The following day Morgan informed Robert that Buell had no orders to mount the regiment. Robert Johnson to Johnson, August 2, 1862, Johnson Papers, LC.

Authorization to Raise Troops[1]

[August 1, 1862]

Ordered that Brigadier General Andrew Johnson, Military and Civil Governor of Tennessee, be and he is hereby authorized to raise troops for the United States service to rendezvous at such place or places in Tennessee as may be designated by him or the Secretary of War, Infantry, Cavalry and Artillery, to be organized according to the rules and regulations of the service, the number to be ten Regiments of Infantry, ten of Cavalry, and ten Batteries of Artillery.

Governor Johnson will commission the officers, and when so commissioned they will be mustered into the service of the United States. The troops will be enlisted for the term of three years or during the war, and when organized are first to be employed in an expedition for the redemption of East Tennessee from rebel rule, unless such redemption shall have been sooner accomplished.

D, DLC-JP.

1. The governor first received word of this action in a wire dispatched at 10:30 A. M. Stanton to Johnson, August 1, 1862, Johnson Papers, LC.

Parole Oath and Bond of Josephus C. Guild

[August 1, 1862]

United States of America.

State of Michigan—Wayne County.

I, Joseph C. Guild of Tennessee, and of the County of Sumner, do solemnly swear that I will support, protect and defend the Constitution and Government of the United States against all enemies, whether domestic or foreign; that I will bear true faith, allegiance and loyalty to the Same, any ordinance, resolution or laws of any state, Convention or Legislature to the Contrary notwithstanding; and further, that I will well and faithfully perform all the duties which may be required of me by the laws of the United States; and I take this oath freely and voluntarily, without any mental reservation or evasion whatsoever.

Seal

Subscribed and sworn to in duplicate before me this   day of   A.D. 1862. By authority of Brigadier General Andrew Johnson Military Governor of Tennessee.

We, Joseph C. Guild, of Sumner County, State of Tennessee principal,

The man behind the barricades.
Courtesy Library of Congress.

and Balie Peyton & John S. Brien of Sumner & Davidson Counties respectively, State of Tennessee, Sureties, are held and firmly bound unto the United States of America in the penal sum of Ten Thousand Dollars, for the payment of which, well and truly to be made, we and each of us, jointly and severally bind ourselves, our heirs, executors and administrators, firmly by these presents.

Signed and sealed this Fist day of August 1862, at Nashville.
The Condition of this obligation is such that whereas, the above bounden Joseph C. Guild, has this day taken an oath of allegiance to the Constitution and Government of the United States;

Now, therefore, If he shall faithfully observe the same, and in all respects conduct himself as a faithful and loyal Citizen thereof, then these presents shall be void; otherwise to be and remain in full force.

Seal

Balie Peyton   Seal

John S. Brien   Seal

Copy, DNA-RG249, Lets. Recd. (1862-67).

From Jeremiah T. Boyle

Head-Quarters U. S. Forces in Kentucky,
Louisville, Aug 2d 1862

Gov Johnson
Nashville, Tenn
Dear Sir

Your preachers are a pestiferous set— I enclose letters or petitions with which they are bothering me—[1] I have some in Ind. Penitentiary and some in Mil Prison here— What shall I do with them—

There is much apprehension of a raid into our state— I have some fear of it myself— We will never succeed until we drive out or put to the sword every man or woman in the state, who are laboring to accomp. the destruction of the government— I feel incompetent for the position I am in— I shall signify this to the government & ask them to appoint a better man in my place— I think this important— I am sure I am not fit for it— Its duties are arduous and responsible, and demands ability far above mine— If you know a Suitable person I will ask his appointment—[2]

I am very resptly. & truly
Yr Friend & Obt Servt
J. T. Boyle

ALS, DLC-JP.

1. Boyle sent both a letter of August 1 from Revs. Samuel Baldwin and Reuben Ford, and an "accompanying letter which is without address," which Boyle was asked to consider and if he lacked the power "to act in the premises," to forward it to the

President. Johnson returned it in his indignant Letter to Jeremiah T. Boyle, August 4, 1862.

2. Boyle's assessment of his inadequacy would appear to have been accurate. Both his civilian policy, including harsh penalties for suspected disloyalty, assessments on the populace for guerrilla damages, and use of troops during elections, and his poor military decisions which nearly allowed Bragg to succeed in the invasion of 1862, were severely criticized by even zealous unionists. When finally transferred in January, 1864, and sent to Knoxville, he resigned from the service. Warner, *Generals in Blue*, 40.

From Rodney Mason

Clarksville August 2 1862

To Gov Johnson

Mr Lellyett[1] of Nashville overheard a conversation in which a man just from Columbia via Charlott stated that there were considerable forces between Columbia & Charlott. Colonel Johnson[2] from this city of one of the Tennessee Regiments passed through here this morning going towards Hopkinsville[.]   There are a good [number of] rebel soldiers in this part of the country Engaged in recruiting[.]   I hear of mounted men in different places dressed in federal uniform who dont belong here[.]   I doubt whether Blacks guilt can be Established by white witnesses[.][3] There are no magistrates here to examine the case[.]   I have him in jail[.]

R Mason   Comdg Post

Tel, DLC-JP.

1. John Lellyett.

2. Mason probably refers to Confederate Col. Adam R. Johnson, who a few days later (August 18) captured Mason's entire command. The Kentucky [not Tennessee]-born Johnson (1834-1922) settled in Burnet County, Texas, in 1854, working as a surveyor and overland mail driver. During the war he scouted for Forrest, operated out of Hopkinsville, Kentucky, a partisan ranger command within the Union lines, and was eventually promoted to brigadier in June, 1864. Two months later he was accidentally wounded and blinded by his own men. Returning to Texas, he founded the town of Marble Falls and was involved in a variety of business ventures. Webb, *Handbook of Texas*, I, 915; Warner, *Generals in Gray*, 156; William J. Davis, ed., *The Partisan Rangers of the Confederate States of America* (Louisville, 1904), 38, 112.

3. The previous day, Mason had reported that John G. Black (b. *c*1838), a Tennessee-born Montgomery County farmer with $5,000 in real and $3,500 in personal property, had shot his next door neighbor William Parry (*c*1808-1862), a Pennsylvania native with a combined estate valued at $48,700. This "cowardly assassination by shooting from the bushes," according to the post commander was in consequence of an old "fued . . . & had no relation to politics both being rebels . . . though Black's Father is a hot Unionist[.]" 1860 Census, Tenn., Montgomery, S. and W. of the Cumberland River, 44; Mason to Johnson, August 1, 1862, Johnson Papers, LC.

To Don Carlos Buell, Huntsville, Ala.

August 2, 1862, Nashville; DNA-RG393, Dept. of the Ohio, Tels. Recd. (Jan.-Aug., 1862).

Wants horses for Col. Stokes's cavalry of 122 men, some of whom are mounted already but all of whom "are Tennesseans & understand the Country and People where their immediate services are required to aid in recruiting and scattering Guerrilla Bands now forming. We have arms and all the equipments here ready—"

To Byrd Douglas[1]

Nashville, August 2d, 1862.

Byrd Douglas[2]
Davidson County Tenn
Sir:
Mr. Alexander Carter[3] has been authorized by me to call upon you for *five* horses, suitable for Cavalry to be employed in the service of the State of Tennessee and the Government of the United States, in putting down the existing rebellion.

It is hoped that you will have no hesitancy in complying with this Requisition for so patriotic a purpose and that too without delay.

The terms and conditions upon which the horses will be received in the service of the Government will be set forth in a Certificate of indebtedness, which will be given as evidence that the horses have been received by a properly authorized Agent of the Government.[4]

Respectfully, &c.   Andrew Johnson,
Military Governor.

Edward H East
Official:

PL, DLC-JP.

1. William Byrd Douglas (1815-1882), native Virginian orphaned at an early age, came to Greeneville with his brother Hu to live with an uncle and receive business training. Early friends of Johnson, they established themselves as merchants, moving to Fayetteville and by 1847 to Nashville where on the eve of the war they operated one of the largest wholesale firms in the South and were known as the "Cotton Kings of Nashville." So ardent a secessionist that before Tennessee seceded he offered South Carolina Governor Pickens his five sons and $5,000 in gold, Byrd Douglas later ordered cotton, stored in Montgomery and Memphis and worth four million, destroyed rather than have it fall into Federal hands. In April, 1862, a Boston correspondent of Stanton, calling Douglas "a great *rascal*" for aiding the rebellion early and "assisting the rebel Gov. Harris in taking Tennessee" out of the Union, urged that Johnson arrest him and confiscate his property "to help pay the cost of the war" and serve as "a simple act of justice." Douglas' property was seized and he himself imprisoned, but, because of his earlier friendship with Johnson, justice was tempered by mercy and his incarceration was brief. Biographical data from Mary Stahlman (Mrs. Byrd) Douglas, Nashville; George H. Armistead, Jr., ed., " 'He is a Great Rascal,' A Sketch of Byrd Douglas," *Tenn. Hist. Quar.*, XXVII (1968), 37-39.

2. The italicized portions of this letter were inserted in longhand on a printed form.

3. Alexander Carter (1807-1884), owner of a "tipling House" in Nashville, possessed $20,000 in real and $60,000 in personal property. 1860 Census, Tenn., Davidson, Nashville, 3rd Ward, 78; Mt. Olivet Cemetery Records, Interment Book, II, 146; Nashville *American*, September 9, 1884.

4. An endorsement followed: "Mr. Byrd Douglas has not the horses called for within, but I will say that he will furnish the money to buy such number of horses as may be required of him. Hu Douglas[.]"

From William C. Rutland[1]

Dover Tennessee Augt. 3, 1862

A Johnson Govr.

Your Excellency I would Moste Respectfully Represint to your Honor that this place Surinderd about the 15th of February last— Consequently there was no Election at the Regular March Ellection[.] Consequently Many of the County offices are Vacant Amongst that of Sheriff County Court— clerk all of the Constables the Magistrates of the County were Elected in 1860 for Six years and Sworn into office under the Constitution of the U. S. as well as the Constitution of the State of Tennessee[.] A B Ross's[2] Term as Circuit Court Clerk will Expire first March 1864— Since the Suspension of Civil law many Ignorant & Evil Minded persons thinking that there is no law to punish them for misconduct have been Marauding the Citizens Killing Stock Burning Houses and doing many other unlawfull things[.] by Restablishing the Supremacy of the Law those things will be Stoped[.] I would suggest that James Stanley Ralls[3] (former Deputy) be appointed Sheriff that Judson Horn Esq[4] be appointed County Court Clerk that Clerk Ross be ordered back to his office or Resign that George W. Brandon[5] Be appointed Clerk of the Chancery Court that Shff Ralls open and hold an Election for Constables in the different precincts in the County that the Chancelor and Circuit Judges be notified to Open and hold their Respective Courts at this place at the usual and Regular times[.] This is the wish of many Citizens that I have Consulted of all the Difrent Political feelings having had an opportunity for Consulting— My profession that of Medicine Calling me to Every Neighborhood in the County[.] Your prompt attention will give much Satisfaction to all Law abiding Citizens—[6]

Respectfully Yours Truly
Wm. C Rutland

Govr. A Johnson

ALS, DLC-JP.

1. William C. Rutland (b. c1815) was a Stewart County physician listed in 1850 with $8,000 worth of real estate. 1850 Census, Tenn., Stewart, 792; McClain, *Stewart County*, 45.

2. Ambrose B. Ross (b. c1825) was circuit court clerk (1856-70) and county court clerk (1870-82). *Ibid.*, 130; 1870 Census, Tenn., Stewart, 7th Dist., 8; *Goodspeed's Stewart*, 905.

3. James S. Ralls (b. c1816), a North Carolina native, was a farmer. 1860 Census, Tenn., Stewart, 2nd Dist., 19.

4. Judson Horn (b. c1817) was a Tennessee-born hotel keeper. *Ibid.*, Dover, 185.

5. George W. Brandon (c1822-fl1880), Tennessee native and grocery merchant with $1,400 worth of real estate and $2,000 of personal property, later became sheriff (1872-74). *Ibid.*, 4th Dist., 48; (1880), 5th Dist., 34; McClain, *Stewart County*, 130.

6. Several days later Rutland, upon "further Consultation with prominent Citizens," withdrew his nomination of Ralls, because he was and is "at present A Violent Ceces-

sioniss" and recommended George M. Stewart, "A Straight forward Union man," for
the office of sheriff. Rutland to Johnson, August 8, 1862, Johnson Papers, LC.

To James S. Negley

Nashville, Augt. 3 1862

Genl. Negley
Columbia, Tenn.

There are a large number of fine horses owned by secessionists of Maury
Co. Press them into the service, giving certificates of value to be paid by
the Govt. when the party proves that he is loyal and acknowledges
allegiance to the Govt. Put Infantry on these horses & give them the
best arms you have got.   Rout & drive the Guerrillas from the State or
put them to death.

How do Barker & Julian[1] come on in raising Cavalry forces.

Andrew Johnson   Mil: Gov'r.

Tel draft, DLC-JP.
  1. William W. Barker (b. 1839), a Pittsburgh produce and commission merchant,
enlisted in the 12th Pa. Vols. and transferred in September, 1862, to Co. B, 5th Tenn.
Cav. as 2nd lieutenant. In 1864 he became captain and commissary of subsistence.
Armine T. Julian (c1829-1863), Alabama native and Maury County blacksmith and
engineer, enlisted in July, 1862, in Columbia, and was commissioned lieutenant in
charge of recruiting for the 5th Tenn. Cav. Promoted to captain in November, he was
killed in action on a scouting expedition near Hillsboro the following March. 1860
Census, Tenn., Maury, 9th Dist., 72; CSR, RG94, NA; Garrett and Lightfoot, *Civil
War in Maury County*, 151; Fitch, *Annals*, 117.

To Peter H. Watson,[1] Washington, D.C.

Nashville Aug 3 1862

Hon P H Watson Asst Secy

In reply to your enquiry by telegraph[2] I have to state, first all Tennessee prisoners who are willing to take the oath of allegiance & enter into
bond for its faithful observance should be released upon parole subject to
notice[.] If they were released as suggested & permitted to return to
Tennessee it would exert a powerful influence upon the state at this
time[.] The oath when taken & the bond should be forwarded to the
Governor of Tennessee & filed in Secy's office— If the power was
conferred on me as indicated a short time since by the President the
power to prescribe the terms of release, I would at once appoint an agent
competent to exercise proper Judgement & send him to the various
prisons where Tennesseans are confined authorized to examine & release
all who would take the oath & give bond[.] All these who were not
willing to comply with foregoing conditions I would either exchange or
retain in prison[.] If this course was adopted I feel well assured that much
good would result from it[.] I repeat that I hope none of those Tennessee

prisoners will be exchanged & sent South who are willing to conform to the conditions herein set forth[.]

Andrew Johnson Milty Gov

Tel, DNA-RG107, Tels. Recd., Sec. of War, Vol. 18 (July 15-Aug. 5, 1862).

1. Peter H. Watson (c1820-1885), English-born Washington, D. C., patent lawyer who reportedly earned $50,000 a year before the war, was assistant secretary of war (1862-64). While generally in charge of quartermaster ordnance, he also supervised a large force of war department detectives and performed the duties of the secretary of war in Stanton's absence. In the postwar years, he settled in Ashtabula, Ohio, practicing law and engaging in railroad interests, serving as president of the Erie Railroad (1872-74). 1860 Census, District of Columbia, Washington, 2nd Ward, 58; Frank A. Flower, *Edwin McMasters Stanton* (Akron, Ohio, 1905), 127, 397; Thomas and Hyman, *Stanton*, 152, 153; New York *Times*, July 24, 1885.

2. Watson's inquiry was prompted by the concern of the "Custodian of the prisoners at Indianapolis" who wanted advice from the war department as to the course to follow with some "one thousand to twelve hundred prisoners" [at Camp Morton] who wished to take the oath of allegiance and be paroled rather than be exchanged. Watson to Johnson, August 2, 1862, Johnson Papers, LC.

From William H. Mills[1]

Murfreesboro Tenn Augt 4/62

His Excellency Gov A Johnson
Nashville Tenn.
Sir

I have been informed that you would make good all losses sustained at the Murfreesboro affair on the 13 July[.] Accordingly I append the following list of money & articles with their values estimated at their real worth

Money all greenback	210..00
Dress Coat & Pants	40..00
Sword & Sash (fine article) cost	90..00
Bed & cot	12..00
Trunk Shirts & other clothing	40..00
Saddle & Bridle	12..00
Mess chest & furniture	20..00
	424..00

I certify on honor that the above articles were all destroyed besides many others not mentioned & that the values assessed are the real worth according to the best of my judgment[.]

W H Mills Capt Co C
3d. Regt. Minn Vols.

P S I am a poor man & own no property at home[.] I hope you do me the favor of restoring what was lost under circumstances over which I had no control[.] Please answer immediately[.]

W H Mills

Address me at Murfreesboro[.]
Gov Johnson

ALS, DLC-JP.

1. William H. Mills (1826-1908), a Center County, Pennsylvania, native and Mexican War veteran, was captain, Co. C, 3rd Minn. Inf., when he was dismissed from the service December, 1862, "for recommending the surrender of his regiment while in face of the enemy at Murfreesboro, Tennessee." He died in Minneapolis, Minnesota. CSR, RG94, NA; Clara Mills, widow's certificate, Pension File, RG15, NA.

From Peter H. Watson

War Dept Washington
August 4 1862

To His Excley Gov of Tenn

You are authorized to examine the Tennessee prisoners at the several places at which they are confined & determine which of them shall be exchanged & which released & the terms upon which their release shall be granted[.]   for this purpose you are authorized to employ such agents as you may designate[.]   Capt Ekin[1] at Indpolis has been advised that this authority has been given to you.

P H Watson Asst Secy War

Tel, DLC-JP; DNA-RG107, Tels. Sent, Sec. of War, Vol. 12 (July 26-Aug. 18, 1862).

1. James A. Ekin (1819-1891), a shipbuilder of Pittsburgh, Pennsylvania, before the war, joined the 12th Pa. Inf. as first lieutenant and regimental quartermaster. Stationed in Indianapolis (1861-63) as assistant quartermaster, he later became chief quartermaster of the cavalry with a regular commission and remained in the service until retiring as quartermaster general in 1883. NCAB, V, 352.

To Jeremiah T. Boyle

Nashville, Augt. 4th, 1862.

Genl Boyle Louisville Ky

Dear Sir,

The signers of the Petition you enclose to me under date of Augt. [2][1] Rev Drs Baldwin & Ford state that I was asked what charges were preferred against them & that my reply was "none". This is absolutely false[.]   When they appeared before me, I stated to them in express and distinct terms that they were not arrested as preachers of Christ or as Ministers of the Gospel but that they were arrested for reasons of State for being unfriendly to the Govt., aiding and exercising all their influence in favor of the Rebellion, that they were unfriendly and inimical to the institutions of the Country and therefore being an agent of the Govt. felt it my duty to arrest and remove them from this community, thereby destroying their influence and give them an opportunity to go and live with the Rebels beyond our lines where all their sympathies were. But aside from this, their preaching in the pulpit was treasonable itself as understood here and asserted by concurring persons of undisputed character— These assumed Ministers of Christ have done more to poison & corrupt the female mind of this community than all others, in fact changing their entire character from that of women and ladies to fanatics and fiends. One of these very ministers in leaving here for Louisville told those who were collected to see him off "Don't forget your God, Jeff Davis and the Southern Confederacy." This is a specimen of the "blameless" course pursued by these traitors and hypocrites, who, in the language of Pollack, are wearing the livery of heaven to serve the devil in.[2]

If you think proper to send their petition to the President, you can do so and send this letter along with it. Please let them remain where they are for a few days and I will have them disposed of. I concur with you most fully in regard to expelling and putting to the Sword all traitors who continue to occupy a hostile attitude to the Govt. There must be a vigorous and efficient prosecution of this War. The burdens and penalties resulting from it must be made to rest upon rebels, and they to feel it. *Treason must be made odious, traitors punished* and *impoverished*." I hope you will abandon all idea of resigning. You have done all that could be done, and who could do more? The doubt you have of your own ability to discharge the arduous & varied duties which have been imposed upon you by your position, is the best proof of your fitness and qualification.

Very Respectfully, Your Obt. Servt.

Andrew Johnson Mil: Gov'r.

Copy, DLC-JP.

1. The August 1 letter and petition of Revs. Samuel Baldwin and Reuben Ford to Boyle had been sent to Johnson the following day. The governor hastened to reply in an August 3 telegram which he now amplified. Johnson to Boyle, August 3, Johnson Papers, LC; see also Telegram from Jeremiah T. Boyle, August 2, 1862.

2. Robert Pollok, *The Course of Time*, Bk. VIII, l. 615, in reference to the hypocrite: "He was a man/ Who stole the livery of the court of heaven;/ To serve the devil in." Burton Stevenson, comp., *Home Book of Quotations* (New York, 1964), 949.

From William S. Smith

August 5, 1862, Tullahoma; ALS, T-Mil. Gov's Papers, 1862-65.

Because Henry C. McQuiddy, Coffee County guide and "many others of similar feelings in this Neighborhood . . . are anxious to form a Company or Battallion to surpress the Guerilla Warfare that has been inaugerated in this region of Country," Brigadier General Smith requests that authority be granted McQuiddy to organize a unit, which would then guard communication lines after guerrillas are subdued.

From Nathaniel H. Allen[1]

Clarksville Tenn, Agst. 6th 1862

Govr. Johnson

D Sir

Having been retained by Capt. R. Black[2] as Councel for his son Jno.

Black now in the dungeon at Clarksville for (or rather charged with killing Parry)[.] at first publick opinion was greatly agst. Black & Rumor said the proof was sufficient to convict him, now I find there is no proof whatever of any white man or woman or any lawful proof agst. the young man now in jail.[3] His Father is as all Fathers would be under like circumstances greatly distressed, he wishes a spedy examination[.][4] please Exercise your kindness in behalf of suffering Humanity in awarding a spedy Examination, before some Magistrate appointed by your Excellency or some judge & we will gratefully remember your favour.

N. H. Allen

ALS, DLC-JP.

1. Nathaniel H. Allen (1793-1871) was a Clarksville lawyer who had been appointed by Governor Harris as special judge for the circuit court after William W. Pepper's death in February, 1861. About the same time he reportedly was for secession "unless all attempts at coercion were abandoned." Titus, *Picturesque Clarksville*, 21; Alley and Beach, *1850 Census, Montgomery*, 122; *Goodspeed's Montgomery*, 767, 789; Clarksville *Tobacco Leaf*, January 11, 1871.

2. Robert Black (b. *c*1790), a farmer and native Pennsylvanian. 1850 Census, Tenn., Montgomery, 440.

3. Col. Rodney Mason, the post commander at Clarksville, had earlier admitted that "no one saw the murderer at the time." Mason to Johnson, August 1, 1862, Johnson Papers, LC.

4. On the same day Black, Sr., went to Nashville for an audience with Johnson. See Mason to Johnson, August 6, 1862, *ibid.*

From S[amuel] H. Tarr

August 6, 1862[Nashville]; ALS, DLC-JP.

A young man originally from Massachusetts—"a true & Loyal citizen"—who lost "2 Horses & 1 wagon" valued at $500 to the secessionists, asks Johnson's aid in securing another horse from a Mr. Peacock, who "owes me $200 for which sum he pleged me his Horse for security."

From James S. Negley

Columbia Aug 7 1862

To Gov A Johnson

The party of guerillas between three and four hundred reported to you yesterday[1] at Kinderhook attacked the mail train this morning 12 miles South of Spring Hill at 9 am Having first placed a large number ties on the Road. Two hundred (200) balls were fired into the wood & iron work of the Locomotive[.] The brakesman was wounded with four balls[.] twelve passengers citizens & Soldiers were wounded[.] the Engine forced the obstructions of the Road & came to this place under high speed.

Jas S Negley Brig Genl

Tel, DLC-JP.
1. While no Negley communication of August 6 is extant, there is one dated August 4 in which he reported that "a force of over two hundred" was at Kinderhook. Johnson Papers, LC.

To George W. Morgan

Nashville, August 7, 1862

General Morgan,
Cumberland Gap, Tenn.
(*Private*)

Cant you send me the name of some other person who will answer your purpose as well as the name submitted.[1] There are strong reasons in my mind against commissioning him, but if there is no other person that will do, and you still desire it, your request will be complied with. I am glad to hear that Robert is doing well, and thank you for the attention you have given him.[2]

Andrew Johnson.

Tel draft, DLC-JP.
1. Morgan had recommended William Blount Carter for appointment as colonel "of one of your Regiments[.]   it is for an important service." Morgan to Johnson, August 6, 1862, Johnson Papers, LC.
2. Morgan had commented: "Robt is doing well[.] have had a long talk with him[.]"

Appointment of Prisoner of War Commissioners

State of Tennessee,
Executive Department.
Nashville, August 7th 1862.

To All Whom it May Concern:—

Having been authorized by the War Department under date of the 4th ins't "to examine the Tennessee prisoners at the several places at which they are confined, and determine which of them shall be exchanged and which released, and the terms upon which their release shall be granted; and having the further authority conferred to employ such Agents as I may designate for the purpose;–

Now therefore, I, Andrew Johnson, Governor of the State of Tennessee, by virtue of the power and authority in me vested as aforesaid, do hereby Commission Ex-Gov William B. Campbell of the County of Wilson, and Hon. Edmund Cooper of the County of Bedford and State of Tennessee, as Commissioners to visit the various prisons in which Tennessee Prisoners of War are confined, for the purpose of examining and prescribing the terms and conditions upon which they shall be exchanged or released, as hereinbefore indicated.

In testimony whereof, I, Andrew Johnson, Governor of the State of Tennessee, have hereunto set my hand, this the Seventh day of August A.D. 1862[.]

By the Governor:

Secretary of State.

D, DLC-JP.

From Christopher L. Johnson[1]

Camp Cumberland Gap, Tennessee
August 8th 1862

Gov. Johnson
Dear Sir:

About the first of July 1861 Dr. J. W. Thornburgh[2] of New Market East Tennessee enroled and organized a Company of Cavelry for the United States Service. The Co. was organized in Union County E. Tenn. and as the Rebelion got rather warm in the neighborhood Capt. Thornburgh called his Co. together and started to Barbourville Ky. to be mustered into the service and get arms for his Co. And on the 8th of August & at night the Company got together and started and traveled all night, getting near the Cumberland Mountain 19 miles from Cumberland Gap, and stoped and rested their horses & got a cup of coffee, and then resumed their journey. As the Company got to the top of the Cumberland Mountain at the Baptist Gap, The Rebels dashed in & cut off about half of the Co. driving them back into Tennessee, taking Capt. Thornburgh a prisoner & eight of his men. The men were turned loose at Knoxville after being held at this place for some time & Capt. Thornburgh was taken to the City of Nashville & held for a long time & finally discharged there.

About thirty of the Co. in Command of Lt. B. F. Skaggs[3] went on to Barbourville Ky. where they were mustered into the U. S. Service as a squad of Cavelry by Lt. S. P. Carter (now our Brig. General)[.] Soon after being mustered into Service, their co. was ordered to Camp Dick Robinson, and as the Tennesseans were not coming in very fast and as the co. could not be filled out in a reasonable time with Tennesseeans, the Company was then ordered to sell their horses, as best they could and attach themselves to the Infantry or else join a Regiment of Ky. Cavelry.

The Tennesseeans did not wish to join a Regt. of Ky. Cavelry & they joined the first E. Tennessee Infantry, with a promise from Lt. Carter (now Brig. Genl. Carter) that as soon as they came back into the State of Tennessee, (if there should be a call for Cavelry) they should be turned into the Cavelry service again.

Now that we have got back into the State again, we want to be ordered by the proper authority to return to the Cavelry service. Application has been made by the members of the Co. to Genl. Carter and he to Genl. Morgan to have the order issued, but as yet we have no answer.

Now we do not expect you have the power to make such order. But we ask you to aid with your influance, and have the Company revived and transfered or joined to the first East Tennessee Cavelry under Lt. Benjamin F. Skaggs as commander of the co. and authorize him to fill up the Co.

The members of the Co. belong to five of the Infantry companies in this Regt. and it would not interfere or weaken the Infantry as they could be filled with good men in their places in a few days.[4]

I am Truly &c one of the Company.

Christopher L. Johnson

P.S. The names of the men who belong to the co. will be given at any time when necessary or called upon to do so.

C. L. J.

ALS, DLC-JP.

1. Christopher L. Johnson (c1829-1864), a Union County cabinet maker who enlisted at Jacksboro, August 1, 1861, served in Co. B, 1st Tenn. Inf., USA, was captured in December, 1862, sent to Richmond, and exchanged at City Point, Virginia, in February, 1863. Later wounded, he died in a Marietta, Georgia, field hospital, August 21, 1864. 1860 Census, Tenn., Union, 6th Dist., 75; CSR, RG94, NA.

2. John W. Thornburgh (1828-1888), a New Market doctor and Mexican War veteran, was captured, imprisoned, and released as reported in this letter. Resuming his practice at home, he became assistant surgeon in the hospital at Knoxville when the Federals took over East Tennessee. In 1867 he was elected to represent Grainger County in the legislature and the following year served as surgeon-general of the Tennessee militia for a year. Temple, *East Tennessee*, 369; *Goodspeed's Jefferson*, 1190; WPA, Jefferson County, Tennessee, Tombstone Records (Nashville, 1938), 204.

3. Benjamin F. Skaggs (c1830-fl1890), a Union County carpenter, was a private, Co. B, 1st Tenn. Inf., USA (August 1, 1861, to September 17, 1864). 1860 Census, Tenn., Union, 4th Dist., 48; (1890) Special Census, Union Veterans and Widows, Tenn., Union, 14th and 4th Dists., 7; CSR, RG94, NA.

4. In June, 1863, Johnson's regiment was restored to horse as the 1st East Tenn. Mtd. Inf., but in spring of 1864 was fighting as regular infantry and so remained for the duration of the war. *Tennesseans in the Civil War*, I, 376-77.

To Don Carlos Buell, Huntsville, Ala.

August 8, 1862, Nashville; Tel, DNA-RG393, Dept. of the Ohio, Tels. Recd. (Jan.-Aug., 1862); DLC-JP; *OR*, Ser. 1, XVI, Pt. II, 286.

Johnson and Col. John F. Miller, convinced "that change and reformation of the Office of Provost Marshal [of Nashville] should be made & that without delay," because "of former abuses having transpired in that office" and others which "are now transpiring," recommend that Col. Alvan C. Gillem be appointed.

To James S. Negley

Nashville, Augt. 8th 1862.

Genl. Negley,
Columbia, Tenn.

In every instance, after exercising your best judgment, where secessionists have robbed and plundered Union men of their property, you will out of the property of secessionists compensate them to the full extent of the loss and damage sustained. In Making arrests you will make them to the extent that the public interests require— Let them be many or few. There is a man now in Columbia recently from South and intends returning— His name is Squire Guest.[1] He ought to be arrested if he can be identified.

What has become of Nicholson?[2] Did he express any desire to see me.

Andrew Johnson Mil: Gov'r.

Tel draft, DLC-JP.

1. Probably James L. Guest (1819-1886), mayor of Columbia with $9,000 real and $20,000 personal property, who served as private and 3rd lieutenant, Co. K, 48th (Voorhies') Tenn. Inf., CSA. After the war he was a local constable. 1860 Census, Tenn., Maury, 9th Dist., 19; (1870), Columbia, 3rd Ward, 9; Garrett, *Confederate Soldiers*, 144; CSR, RG109, NA.

2. A. O. P. Nicholson, sent South by Negley's order of July 29 and also required to post a $10,000 bond as security for his exile, refugeed at Florence, Alabama, probably with his wife's relatives, the Samuel Craigs. See *Johnson Papers*, I, 73*n*; Nashville *Union*, August 12, 1862; Nicholson to Lincoln, March 28, 1865, in Patricia P. Clark, A. O. P. Nicholson: Editor, Statesman, and Jurist (M. A. thesis, University of Tennessee, Knoxville, 1965), 133, 192.

From A. Clark Denson

Cairo Aug 9th 1862

To Gov Andrew Johnson

Genl Sherman[1] refused to give me an order for transportation from Memphis to Nashville or any other point[.] I have pressed the Steamer Lady Franklin[2] into Service in your name & am on my way to Louisville with one hundred & fifty 150 men. will arrive there monday noon. ask Col Gilson[3] to meet me at Louisville & assist me to get transportation to Nashville & make arrangements to settle with [t]his Steamer[.]

A. Clark Dennison
Capt. Co A. 2nd Tenn

Tel, DLC-JP.

1. Maj. Gen. William T. Sherman, commanding operations on the Mississippi.

2. Denson and his men who left Memphis on August 7 aboard the *Lady Franklin*, a steamboat making frequent runs between Memphis and Cincinnati and used during the war for hauling troops, arrived in Nashville on August 14, although rumor circulated

that Denson had been hanged on the banks of the Cumberland and his men captured en route. Memphis *Union Appeal*, July 15, 17, August 7, 20, 22, 1862.

3. Probably Col. Alvan C. Gillem, in whose regiment some of the men Denson raised were to serve.

From George W. Morgan

Cumberland Gap Aug. 9th 1862

To His Excellency Andw. Johnson
Governor.

it is now impossible to execute the design to aid which I asked the appointment of.[1] the enemy in force in our front on the fifth 5 & sixth 6 Inst. Decoursey[2] brigade with the fourteenth 14 Kentucky had a series of brilliant affairs with Stevensons[3] division in entire force. The enemy outnumbered Decoursey four 4 to one[.] the enemy lost two hundred & twenty five 225 in killed & wounded & Lt. Col Gordon of the Eleventh 11th Tenn was taken prisoner.[4] we captured two hundred wagon loads of forage twelve hundred 1200 pounds of tobacco & thirty 30 horses & mules[.] we lost three 3 killed fifteen 15 wounded & fifty 50 prisoners[.] two 2 companies of the sixteenth 16 Ohio were surrounded by two 2 rebel regts but two thirds of them cut their way through[.] John Morgan at the head of two thousand 2000 cavalry left Knoxville for Kingston about the second inst[.] it is rumored that Kentucky is to be invaded[.][5]

Geo. W. Morgan Brig Genl

Tel, DLC-JP; revised version, Nashville *Union*, August 12, 1862.

1. Three days earlier Morgan had requested William B. Carter's appointment as colonel "of one of your Regiments" for "an Important Service," after which Carter would resign. Morgan to Johnson, August 6, 1862, Johnson Papers, LC.

2. John F. DeCourcy.

3. Carter L. Stevenson (1817-1888), Virginia West Point graduate (1838) and Mexican War veteran, was dismissed from service, June 25, 1861, for expressing "treasonable designs against the Government of the United States." Entering the Confederate army as a major of the regular army and colonel of the 53rd Va. Inf., he was promoted brigadier in February and ordered to the west, where he served under Kirby Smith. In September, 1862, he forced Morgan's retreat from Cumberland Gap. Captured at Vicksburg, paroled and exchanged, he saw service with the Army of Tennessee until the end of the war. Returning to Virginia, he spent the rest of his life as a civil and mining engineer. Warner, *Generals in Gray*, 292-93.

4. George W. Gordon (1836-1911), a Giles County surveyor and lieutenant colonel, 11th Tenn. Inf., CSA, who preceded his regiment to the crest of a mountain to confer with the commander of another regiment, was captured and held prisoner ten days before being exchanged. Promoted to colonel in December, 1862, he was wounded and captured at Murfreesboro, exchanged, and returned to his regiment in May. Appointed brigadier in August, 1864, he was again wounded and captured at Franklin in November. After the war he studied law, practiced in Memphis, and in 1906 was elected to Congress, the last Confederate general to sit in that body. *Ibid.*, 109; Lindsley, *Military Annals*, 294-95.

5. The governor wired this information almost verbatim to General Boyle in Louisville. Johnson to Jeremiah Boyle, undated, Johnson Papers, LC.

To Lorenzo Thomas

Nashville Tenn Aug 9th 1862

Gen L. Thomas
Adj't Gen'l.

In compliance with authority & instructions from War Dept on 4th Inst. I have appointed Ex Gov. Campbell Commissioner to visit the various prisons Containing Tennessee prisoners & prescribe the terms & conditions of their release[.]¹ All prisoners not Officers who are willing to take the oath of allegiance & give bonds will be released upon Parole to report to the Governor of Tenn & all who refuse to do so will be retained in prison or Exchanged— Gov Campbell will communicate to the War Department what policy he adopts in regard to the release of these prisoners[.]² I trust in God that in making an Exchange of prisoners that the East Tennesseeans now confined in Southern Dungeons will not be overlooked. The eastern part of the state has been too long neglected & our people left to oppression. Let that portion of her people who are now in dungeons be set free at least while there is an opportunity to redeem them with Traitors & Rebels[.]

Andrew Johnson Mily Gov'r

Tel, DNA-RG107, Tels. Recd., Sec. of War, Vol. 19 (Aug. 6-14, 1862); DLC-E.M. Stanton Papers, Vol. 8, pp. 51917-18.

1. This telegram is in response to Thomas's query about disposal of Tennessee prisoners who are willing to take the oath: "Shall they be discharged where they now are . . . or be sent to Tennessee?" Thomas to Johnson, August 9, 1862, Johnson Papers, LC.

2. On this same date, the governor in another wire to the secretary praised Campbell's qualifications for his mission and commented: "He leaves here for Indianapolis to-morrow. If you have any instructions please communicate them." Johnson to Secretary of War, August 9, 1862, Tels. Recd., Vol. 19 (Aug. 6-14, 1862), RG107, NA.

From Robert B. Blackwell¹

Shelbyville Ten Aug 10th 1862

Gov Johnson
D Sir

I understan that it has been reported at Nashville that I was running salt through the lines or was aiding in doing so[.] I State that the charge is untrue, it is true, that I have bought salt at Nashville at three (3) different times, and taken it to Richmond Bedford County, wher I have a grocery store. I there sold it to citizens and I have also bought salt at Shelbyville, and taken it out to my house & sold it in the same way. I have not except in one instance (and then there was no provo Marshall here) taken any salt to Richmond with the permission of Military authorities at Shelbyville and the last time I took salt to Richmond I would have obtained the permission of the authorities if there had been a post here; my house is at Richmond 10 or 11 miles from Shelbyville where I am doing business openly & publicly. I have never sold salt to any one that I had any reason to suspect that was purchasing it to re-sell; nor have I sent any salt off from Richmond to be sold, or carried beyond the lines, but my sales were confined to citizens and not in large quantities. In fact when I commenced selling salt in that neighbourhood there was no salt in it and the farmers the very first oportunity they had supplied themselves, for the year which they were in the habit of done in peaceful times[.]   I am ready to make a showing at any time you or any officer may want to see it as I have done nothing that I believed I was not authorised to do and if it is not right for me to sell to Citizens I want to know it, as I do not intend to violate any rule knowingly. I have witten a much longer letter than I intended, but I dont like such charges to be made against me[.]

Yours &c   R B Blackwell

N.B   If it necessary I will come down & make a showing.

R B B

ALS, T-Mil. Gov's Papers, 1862-65.

1. Robert B. Blackwell (b. c1829), constable at Richmond, Bedford County, in 1860, became a notorious bushwhacker who in 1864 burned the Shelbyville depot containing arms and munitions of war, captured thirty-two home guards who were guarding it, and shot ten of them near Fayetteville, delivering the balance to Forrest. 1860 Census, Tenn., Bedford, W. Div., 19th Dist., 80; OR, Ser. 1, XXXIX, Pt. III, 238; Nashville Press, October 6, 1864.

From Don Carlos Buell

Huntsville 10th Aug 1862

To Gov Andrew Johnson

I need not tell you that the Collection of information in regard to the plans and movements of the Enemy is an object of the very highest importance. Your position and extensive acquaintance and influence with the people place it in your power to promote the object very greatly and I should be exceedingly obliged to you if you will do so. If you know anyone who could arrange a chain of Couriers and informants on the principal Roads through to East Tennessee the service would be particularly valuable at this time. The information could be communicated to Major Sidell or any officer whose Command would be affected by it or who could forward it. Persons performing such service will be liberally compensated. I hope I need not apologize for begging you to assist me in this important matter if it wont tax you too much.[1]

D. C. Buell Maj Genl

Tel (in cipher), DLC-JP; OR, Ser. 1, XVI, Pt. II, 296.

1. The governor agreed to "take steps at once to organize the force suggested,"

observing that "the great difficulty is in finding the proper persons[.]" He went on to report progress in the fortification of Nashville—"I believe it will exert a salutary influence." Johnson to Buell, August 11, 1862, Generals' Papers, D. C. Buell, RG94, NA.

From James S. Negley

Columbia Aug 10. 1862.

To Gov. Andrew Johnson

have arrested the writer of those letters.[1] Young Joseph Martin[2] son of widow Martin[.] any instructions relative to him. Nicholson did not speak of you but seemed under influence of his wife[3] who is like many other women here intense bitter & unbearable[.] have ordered one woman & her husband South[.] arrested Sid Fleming Fred Watkins Jas Webster Leon Frierson[4] & many other similar Traitors[.] required them to take the oath give bonds thru. To Ten Thousand (10 000) & pay a fine.

Jas. S Negley Brig Genl.

Tel, DLC-JP.
1. Not found, nor is their content known.
2. Joseph M. (b. 1845), the son of George W. (1808-1854) and Narcissa Pillow Martin (1811-1883), and the nephew of Gideon J. Pillow, served as a private, Co. G, 9th Tenn. Cav., CSA, until the latter half of 1863 when he "straggled" from his command and apparently quit the Confederate cause. Acklen, *Tenn. Records*, I, 275; Garrett, *Confederate Soldiers*, 236, 277; Garrett and Lightfoot, *Civil War in Maury County*, 16, 41.
3. Caroline O'Reilly (1811-1894), who married Nicholson in 1829. Garrett, *Maury County Historical Sketches*, 231.
4. James Sidney Fleming (1797-1886), a South Carolinian who became a Maury County farmer, had accumulated an estate worth $72,620. He served in the Maury County home guards, 13th Dist., CSA. Frederick H. Watkins (1816-1895), Virginia-born farmer with $101,250 real and $151,912 personal property, was a private in Co. F, 1st (also known as the 6th) Tenn. Cav., CSA. James H. Webster (b. c1808), native Georgian and well-to-do farmer ($37,500 real and $64,880 personal property), had two sons in Co. H, 1st Tenn. (Feild's) Inf. Leonidas Frierson (1827-1908), the son of Robert L. Frierson, a successful Maury County farmer, was listed as a teacher in 1850 and during the war was a member of the Maury County home guards, 13th Dist., CSA. During the late 1800's he lived in the Mount Pleasant community and served as chairman of the Maury County court for several years. *Ibid.*, 160, 209; Porch, *1850 Census, Maury County*, 66; 1860 Census, Tenn., Maury, 13th Dist., 267, 271; 14th Dist., 210; Garrett, *Confederate Soldiers*, 111, 119, 349, 353.

From James S. Negley

August 10, 1861 [1862], Columbia; Tel, DLC-JP.

Reports on guerrilla activity in vicinity: "about 30 attacked guards at Lynville wounding one man[.] they fired into the cars afterwards[.] Captured 7 men & 4 wagons near Reynolds—" Is planning expedition against Hickman County guerrillas. "The wealthy secessionists of this neighborhood are undoubtedly aiding & sympathizing with these guerrillas parties[.] many of their sons are with them[.]"

From William T. Sherman

Head Qrs. 5th Division
Memphis Tenn Aug 10. 1862

To his Excellency.
Gov Andrew Johnson. Nashville
Sir

Your esteemed favor of August 1[1] was handed me yesterday by Mr Smith[2] Cashier of the Memphis Branch of the Union Bank of Tennessee and I promptly gave him the desired permission to go to Grenada to look up the assets of his Bank. but I know full well that his visit will prove unsuccessful. No officer there would dare give up anything of use or value to them[.] I explained at length to Mr Smith my view of the duties & obligations of himself and associates in their present strait. The Bank has put in circulation notes to the extent of over a million of Dollars and are indebted to their Depositors for funds to a large amount[.]

These liabilities are of a high and honorable character. and the Bank must redeem them. As trustees of this Debt they will be held to a strict account. They must do all that is possible to secure the property and assets of their Bank and apply them honestly to the redemption of their Circulation & deposits.

It seems their Bullion or Coin and assets, notes made here & elsewhere, have been Carried away by force & fraud. They deny Complicity. They have not the power to retake their Coin which is therefore lost to them but they can secure the notes. These notes are made payable here and are secured by property in Tennessee. Although the mere pieces of paper are at Grenada the debts are here, andI must insist that the officers of the Bank give public notice that the notes *must be paid* here by the makers, or the securities will be proceeded against.

Again the assets were removed by force & fraud by Beauregard & others who have property here which is liable for their unlawful acts. Out of these the Branch Bank can & must recover the means to redeem their notes & pay back to their Depositors.

They should do so at once lest lockes be changed & men pay or pretend to pay their notes elsewhere.

The difficulty only is they fear the power of their Common Enemy and are trembling lest they commit themselves in case our enemy prevails. The Branch Bank here was vacant or not in use. Gen Grant ordered me to take possession of all vacant buildings and appropriate them to the use of the United States. I could have taken this Building but have foreborn until the Directors have time to assume their ground. They must be true to their trust, declare boldly & openly against the parties who robbed them and at once begin to realize on assets, which though seemingly removed are still here. Else I have no alternative but to Conclude that they are in Complicity with Our Enemies & treat them as such.

I know that you agree with me in this, that all men must now choose which king[.] This by play is more dangerous than open bold Rebellion. A large amount of the success of our Enemies has resulted from their boldness. They have no hair splitting. We too must imitate & surpass their game & compel all men & Corporations to at once espouse the Cause of their state & National Govts thereby securing full right to protection, or openly to rebel & forfeit their property & their lives. Please say as much to the Presdt of the Bank.[3]

I am with great respect,

W. T. Sherman Maj Genl.

ALS, DLC-JP.

1. Not found.

2. Frederick W. Smith (c1818-fl1870), a North Carolinian who had a long associa-tion with the Memphis branch of the Bank of Tennessee, first as teller (1846) and later as cashier (1855), had $175,000 in real and $6,000 in personal property on the eve of the war. 1860 Census, Tenn., Shelby, Memphis, 5th Ward, 97; (1870), 62; John M. Keating, *History of the City of Memphis* (3 Pts., Syracuse, 1888), I, 245; *Rainey's Memphis City Directory* (1855-56), 169.

3. Granville C. Torbett was elected president early in 1861. Nashville *Union and American*, February 15, 1872; see also *Johnson Papers*, I, 80n.

From Henry H. Haynes[1]

Nashville Augt 11.th 1862

Gov. Andrew Johnson.

Agreeable to your order[2] I send you the following list of Negroes in our sale yard;

Genl. W. G Harding owns,

	1 boy	Frank	18 year old	} Confined for crimes
"	"	Burwell	25 " "	
"	Girl	Margaret	21 " "	

Jno Harding

1 boy	Wilson	26 year old	
" "	Mac	24 " "	
" "	Elbert	24 " "	(one arm)
" "	Jim	25 " "	

James Lumsden
     1 boy Wilson 22 years old (Unsound)

Mrs. Virginia Quarls Wilson County
     1 boy Nelson 22 year old

Wm Shelton Rutherford County
     1 boy John 16 years old

Genl W W Woodfolk
     1 boy Jerry 28 year old Robbery[3]

Thos. McCall
    1 boy Henry 12 years old
Rev. Mr. Hunter   Edgfield
    1 boy Henry 34 years old (Worthless
Micheal Vaughn
    1 boy Manuel 38 years old (Nearly blind)
Richard Free Negro dangeriously ill)
Charles Hillman
    1 boy Andrew 40 year old (diseased)
Dr W A Cheatham
    1 boy Henry 26 years old (very sick)
Ben Litton
    1 boy Soloman 12 years old
Daniel Hillman Kentucky
    1 boy George 25 year old
Nathaniel Baxter
    1 boy Peter 21 years old
Thos. Chadwell
    1 boy Washington 36 years old
Felix Compton
    1 boy George 21 years old
Henry Compton
    1 boy Willis 20 years old
Morris & Stratton
    1 boy William 23 years old (ruptured badly)
David McGavock
    1 boy Sam 26 years old
    1 Woman Charlotte 25 years old
Lysander McGavocks Heirs
    1 boy Wilks 28 years old
Jno M Lea
    1 Girl Malinda, 18 years old
James Morton or Mr. Langley
    1 Girl Amy 18 years old
Russell Houston
    1 Girl Ellis 16 years old   sold and deliver[ed?][4]
Mrs. Amelia Tucker
    1 Girl Sallie 13 years old
A M Waddell
    1 Girl Mary 12 years old
Jno Turner, Sumner County
    1 Woman Ann 50 year old
Robt H McEwen
    1 Woman, Louisa 21 years old & child 14 months

The above comprises a full list of all the Negroes in our Sale House[.]

Respectfully yours,

H. H. Haynes.

P.S. The agent calling on me this Evening made the list for himself with his pencil and then requested me to sign it, which I did supposing that to be right[.][5]

H. H. Haynes

L, DLC-JP.

1. Henry H. Haynes (b. c1810), native of Virginia and in 1855 a Nashville clerk, five years later was a slave dealer with $12,000 in personal property, doing business at 16 Cedar Street. 1860 Census, Tenn., Davidson, Nashville, 4th Ward, 117; *Nashville Bus. Dir.* (1855-56), 55; (1860-61), 188.

2. Not found.

3. In another hand.

4. In another hand.

5. Reflecting the northern antecedents of the agent who drafted it, the original list, which Haynes signed, identified an adult male as a "man," rather than the "boy" of the slave dealer's revised version here printed. It is further interesting to note that Haynes, having hastily signed the agent's tabulation of twenty-two male slaves below a declaration "these are all the Negroes in my possession," had second thoughts, adding "Except/Boys small sizes 12 to 14 year old & 6 or 8 women 1 negro man in jail worthless[.]" All of the latter were subsequently included in the formal response to the governor. "Statement of H. H. Haynes negroes in his sale house," n.d., Johnson Papers, LC.

From John Q. Dodd[1]

Nashville Work House Aug. 12th 1862

To His Excellency Andrew Johnson

In compliance with your request I hand you the list of the negroes now in work House their names and Owners

    Saml Belonging to George Armstrong

    Dick Belonging to Saml Peat   Sickly

    Jack Belonging to Woods Bell & Co

    Robert Belonging to John S. Brien

    Henry Belonging to A Fall

    Calvin Belonging to E. A. Horne

    Charles Belonging to Mrs Beard   Murfreesboro

    Anderson Belonging to James Collier   Murfreesboro

    James Belonging to O. L. Shropshire   Louisville Ky

    Ned Belonging to Dr Patterson   County

    Frank Belonging to Gardner   City

The above negroes works out their board[.]

By order of Mayor

    Phil Belonging to Geo W Smith

    Claiborne Belonging to John Herriford

    Jack Belonging to Sam Watkins

Bill Belonging to Mathews hired By Douty   City
John Belonging to S. A. G. Noel   Texas
Henry Belonging to Alloway   Diseased
The Six mentioned above are here placed for safe keeping.
          Runaways Put in by Lyter at Govt. Stables[2]
One boy belonging to Dr Blythe Williamson   Cty
  "   "   "   " Geo Chrisman   "   "
  "   "   "   " Blythe Pratt   sent away

John Q Dodd

ALS, DLC-JP.
    1. John Q. Dodd (c1810-1872), native Virginian and Nashville stonemason living
on South Market Street, was a city councilman before being elected workhouse keeper
(April 26, 1862); after the war he became a steamboat captain. *Nashville Bus. Dir.*
(1855-56), 37; 1860 Census, Tenn., Davidson, Nashville, 7th Ward, 87; (1870), 63;
Nashville City Cemetery Index, 22; Nashville *Dispatch*, April 27, 1862.
    2. This phrase was added by another hand, as was "sent away" below.

From Charles Kahn, Jr.[1]

August 12, 1862

To His Excellency Andrew Johnson,
Governor of the State of Tennessee,
Respected Sir

Your Petitioner would respectfully represent to your Honor, that he is the Beef Contractor for the United States Government for the troops composing the Army of the Ohio, that in fulfillment of the terms and requirements of his said Contract, he sent one hundred and eleven head of Cattle shipped by Railroad from Reynolds's Station, to Huntsville Alabama as intended, but in driving them on the road between Elkton Tenn and Huntsville Alaa. the company driving the Cattle, were attacked by Guerillas, at a point seventeen miles this side of Huntsville on the same Road, and the whole party together with all the cattle were captured by the same company of Guerillas, all the men were released on their Parole, after a detention of two days, the cattle were carried away by the Guerilla's, the Parole is dated August 10th 1862 Lincoln County, Tennessee. The Company of Drivers were forced by the Confederate Guerilla's, to drive the said Cattle to a field in the possession of the Guerilla Party. In consequence of this capture of said Cattle from him your Petitioner has sustained a loss amounting to the sum of Five thousand Dollars or more.[2]

Your Petitioner would therefore humbly pray your Excellency, to grant to him such relief in the premises, as may seem to your Excellency just and reasonable.

And your Petitioner as in duty bound will ever pray &c
Nashville Tenn. August 12, 1862.   Chas. Kahn. Jr.

Subscribed and sworn to before me, this 12th day of August 1862
George M Southgate L.S. Justice of the Peace.

Pet, DLC-JP.

1. Charles Kahn, Jr. (1833-*fl*1893), Bavarian-born Cincinnati butcher, on June 23, 1862, contracted to supply General Buell's command with fresh beef at $6.49 per 100 pounds for three months, commencing July 1, which contract was later renewed. From 1863 to 1877 he was associated with the pork-packing firms of Richard Beresford and Kahn & Forbus, afterwards engaging in a variety of other business ventures. He served two terms (1868-72) as a Cincinnati councilman. *History of Cincinnati*, 873; Cincinnati city directories (1860-80), *passim*; Louisville *Journal*, October 10, 1862.

2. Attached were affidavits of the six drovers, with phrasing almost identical to that of the petition, attesting to the circumstances and value of the loss.

To John A. McClernand

Nashville, Augt. 12 1862

Maj. Genl. McClernand,
Jackson, Tenn.

I have commissioned Fielding Hurst Colonel of 1st West Tenn Cavalry—also a second Lieutenant who will act as mustering officer & Quarter Master.

I have been authorized by Sect'y of War to receive any amount of Infantry & Cavalry, necessary for service in Tennessee.

Col Hurst is authorized by me to draw subsistence clothing &c from any Quarter Master. I hope you will give Colonel Hurst all the aid and instruction you can in raising & organizing Cavalry Regt. and in obtaining subsistence & supplies. Col Hurst left this morning & will see you in few days. Horses are to be procured from the government if they can be had. If not, I shall authorize their being pressed into service, giving a certificate of value to be paid some time hereafter provided the party proves to have been loyal from the date thereof—

Will this accomplish the object you desire[?][1] If not, telegraph and what you desire shall be done.

You will please send General Dodd[2] at Trenton a copy hereof, as answer to one sent by him to me,[3] in regard to raising troops. your dispatch covers the subject of his dispatch.

Andrew Johnson, Mil Gov'r

Tel draft, DLC-JP.

1. Reporting that Judge Isaac R. Hawkins of Huntsville [Huntingdon] was raising a brigade and that if encouraged "the Loyal men of this part of the state will guard it against any bands that can be raised here," McClernand had asked the governor "to send an aid or appoint some man here to assist him." Obviously Hurst was to be such an "aid." McClernand to Johnson, August 12[9], 1862, Johnson Papers, LC.

2. Grenville M. Dodge (1831-1916), Massachusetts-born military and civil engineer, was engaged in railroad construction and surveying in Iowa, Illinois, and Nebraska during the decade preceding the war. Commissioned colonel, 4th Iowa Inf. in July, 1861, he served in Missouri and Arkansas; promoted to brigadier (March, 1862), he was currently in charge of rebuilding the Mobile and Ohio Railroad between Columbus, Kentucky, and Corinth, Mississippi. Subsequently he commanded a portion of the

XVI Corps in the Atlanta campaign and later was assigned to the Departments of Missouri and Kansas. Resigning in 1866, he served briefly in Congress (1867-69) and continued his involvment in the promotion and building of western railroads for more than forty years. Warner, *Generals in Blue*, 127-28; Stanley P. Hirshson, *Grenville M. Dodge* (Bloomington, Ind., 1967), 60, 62.

3. In response to Johnson's request conveyed through McClernand, Dodge had appointed Capt. J. Morris Young as mustering officer to function in the Trenton vicinity. His wire of the previous day had expressed doubt about "the legality of the muster unless it is sanctioned at Washington." G. M. Dodd [Dodge] to Johnson, August 11, 1862, Johnson Papers, LC.

From Valeria Hulbert[1]

Do the honour to read—& then *destroy*!

Memphis Aug 13 62

Gov Johnson
Sir.

More than a year since I wrote asking your influence in favor of my Brother[2] & your generous response—was—So much appreciated that I did not Venture to tell you how much, I thanked you— Now I write on a Subject which cannot be other than delicate—as it is in reference to my husbands interests—

Through the Kindness of yourself & other friends—Mr Hulbert—was continued in office under Mr Lincoln but was afterward removed by an *assumed* power,[3] which I will frankly tell you deprived him of the means of Supporting his family— but God is Just & Knowing this—& being So *forcibly* impressed Gov Johnson—by the *Singularly–Striking* Co-incidence which occured in our family on the eve of this unhappy Conflict—I have determined to State to your Excellency—Mr Hs posi-tion—& then leave it with your Sense of *Justice* to Say—if he Should not be reinstated? I am not Superstitious but I have ever tried to do unto others as I would have them [do] unto me—& my *faith* tells me that God will raise up for me in this hour *those* whom *He* hath given the power—to place my husband in a position which he So much deserves.— He has never taken any part in this terrible Rebellion[.] it is true he became a member of the Home Guard—for the *protection* of the City—to avoid— being *forced* in the Malitia— he ever discharged his duties faith-fully—& I do not think I am Saying too much—when I Say I do not think a more acceptable appointment could be made to the Loyal Citizens of Memphis— I presume—however—no appointment *will* be made— permanent—until the War is ended? but as I know—"delays are dangerous"—& that *your* Excellency—would have many applicants for your influence— I have determined to approach you—& ask you will do the Kindness *not to Commit* yourself— Mr H. thinks it unecessary to apply at present as he thinks no action will be taken for Sometime[.] he also feels that he was removed—& that he has now by taking the Oath—taken a prominent Stand for the Union & that he Should wait until he can ascertain his chance of Success— he would not be *disap-pointed* & I would not have him. but I am *irristably* impeled to write your Excellency—& may I not hope my request will meet your Kind Considerations?— Mr Hulbert is entirely out of employment—& there is nothing doing at the bar—& indeed he finds it very difficult to provide for us— I feel very much *troubled* Gov Johnson but as I Said—I am *Strangely* impressed—to beleive—that God hath *directed* me to you & I write with the Conviction that *He* will bless my efforts to Secure *through yourself* Some position, which will enable Mr H. to Sustain his family— On the *4th* March 60. just as Mr Lincoln was being inauge-rated President of the United States the birth of my little Boy was dispatched to Washington City. Mr H was there as you remember? on that day—4 weeks after & at *Same* hour *Same* day of week—& month the Sad death—by Suicide—of my Brother, Dick Collins—was dispatched to the *Same* City? These *two* Singularly Striking events occuring in the *Same* family—& at the beginning of this Great *National* trouble & *both* being dispatched to the *Same* City—I think—Gov Johnson will impress even your "Master Mind"—as being Certainly a *remarkable* Coinci-dence? & the fact too that I am (after So many *eventful* months here in the room where this brother Committed the Sad deed—*again* writting you!— God moves in a misterious "way"—& I have ever trusted Him—& I repeat I am very much troubled & I feel assured He is Guiding me— But for this unhappy Rebellion—we would have been prosper-ous & happy— God alone Can ever Know how *I* Struggled against it—but few Know it Sir—but I wrote thousands of lines against it— Do not think I mention this to influence you in Mr Hs favor— I tell you to prove to you—that I beleive God will bless me for it by raising up Friends—for us— He had blessed us with the best Government the World ever knew! & we Should have been grateful[.] Pardon me for thus taking your time!— I have heard Mr H. Speak of you So often I had forgotten you are a Stranger! In conclusion I must beg your Excel-lency will regard *all* I have written as *Sacred*! I know it is unusal for Ladies to take part in matters of this Kind but under the Circum-stances—I felt that I was prompted by an irristable power— it would place me in an unplesant position were it known— So do the Kindness Gov Johnson—not to mention it even there, in N. as it is my native place—or Franklin—

I have the pleasure of a visit from Gen Grant & family— he promised to See you when you visited Mem— Do the honour to answer me!— There is but one office profitable the P. Office— Doubtless you have already been applied to—but I hope I am in time to Secure your influence for Mr H!— if I Should—I will feel that I am indeed blessed & be assured you Could not give it to one *more desering* than Mr H—& to none who Could appreciate the Kindness more— if you have committed yourself will you not write to Mr L *at once* & ask to Suspend App. indeed

Gov Johnson—in the unsettled condition of Tenn—I presume you think it useless to make any appointments—but may I not hope you will *remember my* appeal?—& God will reward you if prayers will avail—for the prosperity of yourself & family! I have written *hurriedly*. please Excuse writting.

Respectfully,   Valeria Hulbert

ALS, DLC-JP.

1. Valeria Hulbert (b. *c*1827), native Tennessean and wife of Henry T. Hulbert, later (October, 1862) penned a letter of protest to General Sherman about expelling families from Memphis because of guerrilla ambushes upon U. S. boats. 1860 Census, Tenn., Shelby, Memphis, 8th Ward, 133; *OR*, Ser. 1, XVII, Pt. II, 860.

2. Richard W. Collins (*c*1837-1861), native Tennessean employed as a clerk in the pension office at Washington, only hours after arriving at his sister's residence in Memphis, shot himself "in the breast with a pistol," March 31, 1861. Earlier that month his sister had solicited Johnson's aid in retaining Collins' position. 1860 Census, Dist. of Columbia, Washington, 2nd Ward, 200; *U. S. Official Register* (1859), 96; Memphis *Appeal*, April 2, 1861; Mrs. Henry T. Hulbert to Johnson, March 18, 1861, Johnson Papers, LC.

3. During the late 1850's and early 1860's, Henry T. Hulbert was customs collector at Memphis. In 1862 he was a private in Co. E, 3rd Tenn. Inf. Btn. (Memphis Btn.), CSA, which was organized for local defense and special service in Memphis and disbanded upon the surrender of the city. *Memphis City Directory* (1859), 101; *U. S. Official Register* (1859), 75; *Tennesseans in the Civil War*, I, 165; II, 216. For Hulbert, see *Johnson Papers*, IV, 413n.

From James S. Negley

August 13 1862
H Quarters Columbia

To Gov Andrew Johnson.

receive the pleasing intelligence. that there is a sudden change in public sentiment relative to taking the oath resulting from our determination that no disloyal citizen shall receive any protection from the Govt. they are attempting to distroy. the refusal to take the oath is sufficient proof of the persons disloyalty and immediately subjects him to a proper punishment[.] numbers of prominant citizens formerly strong secessionists have appeared & voluntarily take the oath[.] those who are arrested show no determined opposition to taking it[.]

Jas. S Negley Brig Genl

Tel, DLC-JP.

To Montgomery C. Meigs, Washington, D.C.

Nashville August 13 1862

Genl Meigs

The Standard for Cavalry horses as I understand it is from fifteen to sixteen hands highs and that mares are excluded. We are in a great press for mounted men here & there are many horses here a shade below the standard that have as much endurance & action & will make better horses than those 16 hands high, also some mares not in foal which be equal if not superior to horses for the service. The Q.M. Genl is unwilling to depart from the standard laid down. I hope you will at once give us some little lattitude on this subject[.][1]

Andrew Johnson Mil. Gov

Tel, DNA-RG107, Tels. Recd., U. S. Mil. Tel., Vol. 18 (Aug. 10-15, 1862).

1. In his reply of the same date, the quartermaster general indicated that "The standard for cavalry horses was fixed as the result of experience," and advised that "it be not changed without absolute necessity." He went on to explain that his agents formerly took one-fifth in mares "but got so many in foal & diminished so much the brood stock a bad thing in time of war [that] lately they have been Entirely Excluded from the army & purchases[.]"

To J. Morris Young[1]

Nashville, Augt. 13th 1862

J Morice Young, Captain &c
Humboldt, Tenn.

Battalion or Regiment of Cavalry or any amount of Infantry that can be raised will be received.[2] You will please correspond with Genl. McClernand on this subject.[3] I regret to inform you that Morgan's Cavalry made attack on Gallatin yesterday, burning two or three bridges on Nashville & Louisville R.R. & some 30 cars, twenty with Govt. stores & 70 horses. He left in direction of Scottsville. Col Boone[4] & 2 companies were captured by him, & paroled[.] our forces reached there just as they were leaving, & had a little fight killing six of the enemy & wounding two, as far as ascertained.

Among killed is Captain Breckinridge[5] and one other Capt. We lost none.[6]

Andrew Johnson Mil Govr.

Tel draft, DLC-JP.

1. John Morris Young (1833-1906), Indiana native and a farmer who had lived in Iowa and Nebraska before the war, raised a company for the 1st Neb. Cav., which became Co. C, 5th Iowa Cav., and was later promoted to major on the staff of Gen. James H. Wilson. At this time he was the mustering officer at Humboldt. Later he lived in Missouri where he farmed, superintended a mining and smelting company, and practiced law. CSR, RG94, NA; Pension Records, RG15, NA; OR, Ser. 1, XLV, Pt. II, 189.

2. "Col Fielding Hurst has been authorized to provide subsistance" was deleted at this juncture. This telegram was prompted by Young's of the previous day reporting on the progress of his muster in Huntingdon and vicinity and asking instructions on the number of companies to be received from that neighborhood, whether they are all to be cavalry, what regimental or battalion numbers they are to have, etc., concluding: "appearances are Encouraging for recruiting in this portion of the State[.]" Young to Johnson, August 12, 1862, Johnson Papers, LC.

3. John A. McClernand was mustering units in the adjacent county. McClernand to Johnson, August 2; Johnson to McClernand, August 3, 1862, ibid.

4. William P. Boone (1813-1875) of the 28th Ky. Inf., USA, Louisville lawyer and legislator, had been captured with two hundred of his men the previous day. In June, 1864, he resigned and by 1865 had resumed law practice. CSR, RG94, NA; History of

the Ohio Falls Cities and Their Counties with Illustrations and Biographical Sketches (2 vols., Cleveland, 1882), I, 496c-e.

5. William C. P. Breckinridge, captain of the 2nd Ky. Cav., CSA, was erroneously reported as killed. *OR*, Ser. 1, XVI, Pt. I, 844; see also *Johnson Papers*, IV, 558n.

6. Johnson had received this information in a telegram from John F. Miller, August 13, 1862. Nashville *Union*, August 14, 1862.

From Jeptha Fowlkes

August 16, 1862, Memphis; ALS, DLC-JP.

Introduces F. S. Richards, a "*first class* man of business," who not only "can fully post you of men and matters at Memphis," but also explain "*my* views, which when fully understood by you, would I think be satisfactory to you." Complains about the military policy in that part of the state and the removal of Col. [Graham] Fitch, who "would soon have secured the people of this section." Urges Johnson to visit Memphis.

From Robert B. C. Howell

Military Prison, Nashville T.
August 16th 1862

His Excellency Andrew Johnson
Governor of Tennessee

Dear Sir— I had the honor of addressing to you a communication dated the 28th day of June Ultimo, in regard to the oath then proposed to me, which I entrusted to Mr. Fowler,[1] the Comptroller of State, and recieved his promise that he would place it in your hands. I presume you recieved it. In that letter I said—(I quote from memory, not having a copy before me) "I feel myself under obligation, as a religious duty, to conform myself strictly, to the government under which I live. This principle I am not conscious of ever having violated in any instance". In another part of the same letter I said:—"This principle I have ever observed conscienciously, and shall hereafter continue to observe it. An oath would not increase my sense of obligation to regard it, nor the absence of an oath diminish it."

I have waited now seven weeks, in hopes of a response from you. I have recieved none. I beg permission again to call your attention to that letter. I have fully carried out this principle here in prison. When first before you, I was assure by Mr. East, the Secretary of State upon your authority, that there was no charge against me, but that I must evince my loyalty by taking the prescribed oath. I declined to do so, and was sent here. Since I have been in this place, Mr. Fowler, the Comptroller has informed me that I am now charged with "general disloyalty," based upon the fact that I do not take the oath referred to. This charge I do not think can be sustained, since the man who conscienciously obeys "the powers that be," cannot be disloyal to any government.

May I not therefore hope that you will concur with me in opinion, and release me from the confinement in which I am at present held?[2]

I subscribe myself with high consideration,

Your obt. humble Servt.
R. B. C. Howell.

ALS, DLC-JP.

1. Joseph S. Fowler.

2. Stricken with a fever during the last days of July when Johnson was shipping the other jailed ministers to the North, Howell had stayed on in Nashville. His efforts to be released were successful, for two days later he was permitted to go home, there to remain under military surveillance. Within a few weeks he returned to his pastoral duties. Spain, "R. B. C. Howell," 337.

To George H. Thomas

Private   Nashville, Augt. 16th 1862

Maj Genl. Thomas,
Deckerds, Tenn

When I first heard that a portion of the forces under Hallecks command were to be sent in direction of East Tennessee I pressed with as much earnestness & force as I could that you should be placed in command of the expedition, and assigned some reasons for it. I presume that you have been placed in possession of the fact that I did so.

The redemption of East Tennessee seems almost to be as remote as it was when I was with you at Camp Dick Robinson. I have almost despaired of that people ever being releived from their oppression, unless the policy that has been pursued is abandoned at once. There must be more vigor & the enemy made to bear the expense and feel the pressure of war. Leniency is construed into timidity, compromising to concession, which inspires them with confidence & keeps alive the fell spirit of rebellion. I trust & hope that ere long you will be placed in command & successfully lead the column that will drive the Rebel hosts from my adopted home, and if not prevented by uncontrolable circumstances I would be with you[.][1]

Can you send me no word that will inspire hope. May God crown your efforts with success in this great work.

Andrew Johnson

Tel draft, DLC-JP; IHi.

1. Johnson's administrative burdens were particularly onerous during these weeks because of the continued threats to Nashville of the Confederate raiders Forrest and Morgan. Maslowski, *"Treason Must Be Made Odious,"* 72; Hall, *Military Governor,* 54-58, 62; *OR,* Ser. 1, XVI, Pt. I, 815-19, 843-57.

From George H. Thomas

Decherd Aug 16. 1862

To Gov Andrew Johnson

Gov. Your favor of this days date has just been handed me[.] I learn from it for the first time that you had urged me as the Commander of the Expedition to be sent into East Tennessee[.] although I am under obligations to you for your favorable opinion still I most earnestly hope that I may not be placed in the position for several reason[s.] one particular reason is that we have never yet had a commander of any Expedition who has been allowed to work out his own policy & it is utterly Impossible for the most able General in the world to conduct a campaign with success when his hands are tied as it were by the constant apprehension that his plans may be interfered with at any moment either by higher authority dirctely or through the influence of others who may have other plans and other motives of policy[.] I believe that the relief of East Tennessee has been Entrusted to an able commander[1] & that he will Eventually give it sure & permanent releif[.] our Enemies are at this time fully aware of the desperate condition of their affairs & the possession of both Tennessee & Kentucky is absolutely necessary to them or their cause is lost[.] They will therefore make every Effort to repossess themselves of Tennessee and wrest Kentucky from our hands but I am sure that I can confidentialy assure you & the Government that Genl Buells dispositions will Eventually force [free][2] all Tennessee & Go very far to crush the rebeleon entirely[.][3] if our Army will not permit itself to degrade [degenerate] into Idleness the rebelion will be crushed out in sixty 60 days for the confederacy cannot possible Subsist its army [troops] a great while longer. hoping this may afford you some assurance of our ultimate success,

I remain Yours Truly
Geo H Thomas

Tel, DLC-JP; CSmH-23392.

1. Don Carlos Buell.

2. The bracketed words here and subsequently are found in the Huntington Library manuscript of this communication, presumably the original draft (or a copy of it) from which the telegram, with its errors of transmission, was derived.

3. For Buell's plans and Thomas' deference to him, see *OR*, Ser. 1, XVI, Pt. II, 344 *et seq.*, 554-55.

From Daniel Smith[1]

Nashville Tenn
Aug. 17, 1862

To his Excellency Andrew Johnson Gov. &c

Your Petitioner Daniel Smith a citizen of DeKalb County Tenn. Begs leave to respectfully show your Excellency, that he is now confined in the state Penitentiary, under arrest by military authority. As to the charges against him he is not fully advised. He is informed however, that he is suspected of giving aid and comfort to the rebellion by going to Sparta resently and informing Gens. Forrest & Morgan of the Rebel Army or some one else of the *rebels*, that the Federals were at Liberty &c, and for attempting to shoot and molest Col Stokes Pickets. All of which he most positively denies. He was not at Sparta and neither saw or sent word to any of Morgans or Forrest Cavalry.

Your petitioner frankly admits that his feelings were formerly with the south and the rebellion; that he had two sons[2] with the confederate army and that his feelings were with them; so much so, that he admits as he supposes that he talked too much, and would be arrested for so doing. That when Gens Jackson[3] or Johnson[4] Cavalry were at Liberty, recently for fear of an arrest he took to the woods. After they left his little Village, he returned home, and while going to his neighbors house in company with a good union man when he fell in with Col Stokes pickets whom he did not know was in the County and was arrested[.]

Your Petitioner will here state; that he is willing to take the oath of allegiance and strictly adhere to and keep it. That he will give any bond in reson, that you may require. That he will further give his parole of honor to do all he can to get his sons out of the Rebel Army, and to do all that he can to stop and put down the rebellion. That he never was in heart opposed to the government of the United States but was led off and influenced by the natural love he had for his sons, he yealded his feelings for the desire of the success of his sons. That he has commited no crime, upon this he hopes to be brought out and examined by your excellency and if found worthy upon giving bond and taking the oath of allegiance to be discharged: For which as in duty bound he will ever pray &c.

Daniel Smith By his Counsel M. M. Brien

Pet, DLC-JP.

1. Daniel Smith (b. *c*1808), a DeKalb County slaveowner who lived near Liberty, had an estate worth $35,000 on the eve of the war. 1860 Census, Tenn., DeKalb, 2nd Dist., 28; Will T. Hale, *History of DeKalb County, Tennessee* (Nashville, 1915), 99, 218.

2. Probably Isaac N. (b. *c*1838) and possibly James H. (b. *c*1837) Smith, both of whom were privates in Co. B, 1st (Carter's) Tenn. Cav., CSA. Sistler, *1850 Tenn. Census*, VI, 90; 1860 Census, Tenn., DeKalb, 2nd Dist., 28; 10th Dist., 162; *Tennesseans in the Civil War*, II, 371.

3. James S. Jackson (1823-1862), Kentucky native who began law practice at Greenupsburg in 1845, became involved in a duel during cavalry service in the Mexican War, subsequently resigning to escape court martial. In 1859 he moved to Hopkinsville and the next year was elected to Congress as a unionist only to resign in December, 1861, to become colonel of the 3rd Ky. Cav., USA. Promoted to brigadier in July and soon after given charge of the cavalry of Gen. William Nelson's Army of Kentucky, he became commander of an infantry division of the Army of the Ohio on September 29 and nine days later was killed at Perryville. *NCAB*, V, 11; Warner, *Generals in Blue*, 247-48.

4. Richard W. Johnson (1827-1897), a Kentuckian, graduated from West Point (1849) and served on the western frontier prior to the war. Appointed lieutenant colonel, 3rd Ky. Cav., USA, in August, 1861, and brigadier general in October, he was

defeated and surrendered to Morgan near Gallatin on August 21, 1862. Following his exchange in December, he was given command of a division of the Army of the Cumberland, was badly wounded in May, 1864, and subsequently led a division under Gen. James H. Wilson in the Nashville campaign. After the war he taught military science at the universities of Missouri and Minnesota and published several military manuals and treatises. *Ibid.*, 253-54; *DAB*, X, 116.

From Charles T. Larned

Chief Paymaster's Office
Louisville, Ky. August 18th 1862.

Brig. Gen'l Andrew Johnson
Mil. Gov. State of Tenn, Nashville.
Sir—

I have to acknowledge the receipt of your telegraphic appeal for the payment of Tennessee Volunteers, & to express my sincere though unavailing regret that embarassment occasioned by the want of funds has prevented & may perhaps for some time still continue to prevent my affording any relief.

Weeks ago I had planned the entire payment to June 30th of Gen. Buell's corps. Assignments of all troops in Ky, Tenn., Northern Ala., & Mississippi, to the different paymasters available for the duty, were arranged *upon paper* as early as July 15th, since which date paymasters have been idle, awaiting orders. My estimates of funds required for paym'ts to June 30th were duly forwarded to Washington, & I have on file notifications from the 2d. Auditor that requisitions based thereon had been sent to the Treasury where they have been lying unmet for weeks. The small amount of funds which I was able to obtain on personal application at Washington, was at once absorbed by the payment in progress at Corinth. Not a single dollar has been received for the payment of any portion of Buells Army.

A communication from Col. Gillem[1] of the 1st Tenn. Vol's to Gen Buells Adj't Gen'l at Nashville, has been referred by the latter to me with a strong endorsement urging immediate payment— Had I money enough for the payment of a single reg't, Col. Gillem's command, under the peculiar circumstances which recommend it to special favor, should have the preference & be first paid.

This delay—which is wholly chargeable upon the inability of the Treasury Dep't to provide funds as fast as is required—is the more to be regretted because it promises to be indefinitely prolonged. The enclosed extract[2] from a late letter of the Acting Paym'r General[3] concerning the months "pay in advance," will sufficiently explain my embarrassment when I add that I am without money even for the payment of the new recruits—[4]

I am, General, Very Respectfully
Yr Obed't Servt   Chas. T. Larned
Chief Paym'r Dist of Ky—

LS, DLC-JP.

1. Alvan C. Gillem.

2. Headed "Copy of letter extract," the attached passage advised Larned that "The President has directed that advance pay to new troops now organizing shall be paid at once" and have preference over all other requisitions. "The Treasury Dep't is unable to meet all calls on it as fast as made, & under the order of the President the requisitions in your favor not yet cashed will be suspended till those for this advance pay are met." Cary H. Fry to C. T. Larned, August 12, 1862, Johnson Papers, LC.

3. Cary H. Fry (c1813-1873), Kentucky native and West Point graduate (1834), was major, 2nd Ky. Vols. during the Mexican War, and paymaster, with the rank of major, from 1853 through the Civil War. Upon the death of Benjamin F. Larned he served as acting paymaster general (July 15-December 10, 1862). Promoted to lieutenant colonel in July, 1866, he was, at the time of his death in San Francisco, chief paymaster of the Military Division of the Pacific. *U. S. Official Register* (1859), 112; Heitman, *Register*, I, 439; *OR*, Ser. 3, II, 957; New York *Times*, March 16, 1873; *West Point Register* (1970), 224.

4. The military governor was not to be silenced by a fulsome, even reasonable, explanation. Five days later, presumably after receiving this letter, Johnson returned to the fray seeking not only payment for the regiments at Cumberland Gap and vicinity, which "had recd. no pay since mustered into service," but also for the first Middle Tennessee Regiment at Nashville, likewise unpaid since mustering in four months earlier. Johnson to C. T. Larned, August 23, [1862], Tels. Recd., U. S. Mil. Tel., Vol. 20 (Aug. 21-26, 1862), RG107, NA.

From Henry R. Myer

August 18, 1862, Battle Creek; LS, DLC-JP.

Colonel of 9th East Tenn. Rgt. complains that "There seems to be quite a number of men who get authority to recruit men for those Middle Tenn regiments, merely to get passed over the Roads free; and who never think of recruiting, except when they want to go back to Nashville, and then they try to induce men that have been sworn into the service, to go with them, by making false promises to them &c."

From William H. Sidell

August 18, 1862, Nashville; ALS, DLC-JP.

Acting assistant adjutant general of the Department of the Cumberland declines to take responsibility of saying that arms in charge of the ordnance department will be safe in Nashville at a place other than the capitol.

From Alexander P. Smith

Fayetteville Ten. Augt. 18th 1862

Gov. A. Johnson.

Dear Sir.

Inclosed I send you a letter directed (to A. M. Beatie)[1] in reply to one written by me in his name, for the purpose of geting the bagage belonging to the two Girls, who made their escape from Beatie while in Nashville on his way home with them from the Jail in Louisville Ky where they had been confined about two months. From the facts in the

Case you will percieve that you have been grossly decieved.

One of the girls (Tabby) is under my control as guardian of an Idiot, the other is the property of C C McKenny[2] of this place—

My Girl was carried off by a free negro by the name of Fisher,[3] who was arrested and lodged in Jail at the time the girls were, and may be still there. The girls mistoled the fact when they told you they had no money, for Beatie sayd he paid over to Tabby between 24 & 34 $ in Louisville— So you see the object in geting a pass from you was to decieve the tavern Keeper, and by that means obtain their bagage; and not for the purpose of returning home, as they told the Inn Keeper[4] they had told you, was their wish—

I have no doubt they have been advised and assisted by the federal officer who escorted them to get their bagage.

If, you thing it not improper, I would ask of you the favor (if it will not be asking what I should not) to examine a little into the affair and, if my Girl can, by any means be restored to me I would be truly thankful. I would not, however, knowingly ask any thing of you that is improper, if I have done so, please excuse me and charge it to my ignorance. I am willing to pay a liberal reward for her arrest and confinement so that I get her. I would be highly pleased to hear any thing from you in relation to the matter. If you think proper to communicate any thing please direct to me at Fayetteville care of E. Cooper[5] Shelbyville—

The Girl I claim is very valable, a good house Servant and an excellent seamstress, and I should be extremely glad to regain possession of her. The negro Fisher who enticed her off, should be sent to the Penitentiary. The Jailor of Louisville Jail says there is sufficient testimony to convict him of having persuaded my girl to run off with him[.]   Be good enough to let me hear from you, if not inconsistant with propriety[.]

Yours with much respect
A. P. Smith

I refer you to Messrs H & B. Douglas[6] for the truthfulness of any statement I may make[.]

A. P. S.

ALS, DLC-JP.

1. Andrew M. Beatie (c1822-fl1880), native Tennessean and a railroad conductor with a personal estate of $800, became a farmer after the war. The letter referred to was written by the bookkeeper of the Sewanee House in Nashville with whom Beatie evidently had left the baggage of the two slave girls who had escaped from his custody on the way back from Louisville. 1860 Census, Tenn., Lincoln, 8th Dist., 214; (1880), 56; R. H. Patten to A. M. Beatie, August 12, 1862, Johnson Papers, LC.

2. Christopher C. McKinney (1828-fl1885), native Lincoln County lawyer, served in the 8th Tenn. Inf., CSA, first as adjutant and 1st lieutenant of Co. B, then as major and lieutenant colonel. 1860 Census, Tenn., Lincoln, 8th Dist., 210; Goodspeed's Lincoln, 776, 899; OR, Ser. 1, XLVII, Pt. III, 735.

3. George Fisher.

4. R. H. Patten (d. c1870), the bookkeeper, had been in Nashville since 1860. Nashville city directories (1860-70), passim.

5. Edmund Cooper.

6. Hu and Byrd Douglas, Nashville merchants. For Hu Douglas, see Johnson Papers, I, 21n.

To Lorenzo Thomas

Nashville Tenn Aug 18 1862

L Thomas

If the East Tenn. Union Citizens who expressed their sentiments fully & were regarded as violent in their opposition are held as prisoners of state. We have a corresponding number of Tennesseeans of the same character that can be exchanged for them if the exchange can be made. Please advise me & I will send list of names.

A. Johnson
Governor

Tel, DNA-RG107, Tels. Recd., U. S. Mil. Tel., Vol. 19 (Aug. 15-21, 1862).

From Lorenzo Thomas

Washgton Aug 18th 1862

To Gov Andrew Johnson

I presented the case of the Eastern Tenn Union citizens in confinement to Robt Ould[1] Esqr agent for the exchange of prisoners who informed me that the Union citizens were divided in three classes those of the third class being those who expressed their sentiments fully & were regarded as violent in their opposition & that this was the class in confinement & held as prisoners of state[.]   this exchange of prisoners of state is not held as obligatory[.]

L Thomas Adjt Genl

Tel, DLC-JP; Nashville *Union*, August 20, 1862.
    1. Robert Ould (1820-1881), Georgetown, D. C., native and graduate of William and Mary College (1842), became the District of Columbia prosecuting attorney during Buchanan's administration. Casting his lot with Virginia when the war began, he served first as assistant secretary of war and from 1862 until the close of hostilities as Confederate commissioner for the exchange of prisoners. Later he practiced law in Richmond, Virginia. *NCAB*, XIX, 275.

Circular Assessing Confederate Sympathizers[1]

State of Tennessee, Executive Department,
Nashville, August 18, 1862.

Sir:

There are many wives and helpless children in the City of Nashville, and County of Davidson, who have been reduced to poverty and wretchedness in consequence of their husbands and fathers having been forced into the armies of this unholy and nefarious rebellion. Their necessities have become so manifest, and their demands for the necessaries of life so

State of Tennessee.

EXECUTIVE DEPARTMENT.

Nashville, August 18th, 1862.

Sir:

There are many wives and helpless children in the City of Nashville, and County of Davidson, who have been reduced to poverty and wretchedness in consequence of their husbands and fathers having been forced into the Armies of this unholy and nefarious rebellion. Their necessities have become so manifest, and their demands for the necessaries of life so urgent, that the laws of justice and humanity would be violated unless something was done to relieve their suffering and destitute condition.

You are therefore requested to contribute the sum of .... Dollars, which you will pay over to James Whitworth, Esq., Judge of the County Court, to be by him distributed amongst these destitute families in such manner as may be prescribed.

Respectfully, &c.

ANDREW JOHNSON,
Military Governor.

ATTEST:

Secretary of State.

Retribution in the name of charity.
Courtesy Library of Congress.

urgent, that the laws of justice and humanity would be violated unless something was done to relieve their suffering and destitute condition.

You are therefore requested to contribute the sum of   dollars, which you will pay over within the next five days to James Whitworth,[2] Esq., Judge of the County Court, to be by him distributed amongst these destitute families in such manner as may be prescribed.

Respectfully, &c,

Andrew Johnson,

Military Governor.

Attest:

Edward H. East,

Secretary of State.

List of Persons Assessed.[3]

Bass, William	$150	Foster, Sr., Robt. C.	100
Beach [Beech], A. C.	100	Frazier, Henry	150
Beach, A. B.	150	Gardner & Co.,	300
Beach [Beech], L. F.	150	Hagan, William H.	100
Brown, Aris,	100	Hamilton, James M.	100
Carter, Daniel F.	150	Manlove, J. E.	100
Cheatham, Archie [Archer],	100	McGavock, Jacob	300
Cheatham, F. R.	100	McGavock, David H.	150
Cockrill, Mark R.	200	McGavock, Frank [Francis]	150
Cunningham, Enoch P.	50	Williams, John	100
Dortch, W. B.	150	Woodfolk, W. W.	150
Douglas, Byrd	500	Vanlier [Vanleer], A. W.	200
Duncan, Andrew J.	100	[R. S.] Hollins & Co.,	200
Ensley, Enoch,	150		

Nashville *Union*, August 20, 1862; broadside, NcD.

1. This document reflects the governor's well-known assumption that Tennesseans were fundamentally unionist and that many who wore the gray had been inveigled or even "forced" into the rebel army by affluent secessionists. Observing that "the sufferings of our poor people . . . are directly chargeable to the influence of such persons," the administration organ called the levy "just as well as philanthropic." Nashville *Union*, August 20, 1862.

2. James Whitworth (1816-*fl*1890), Sumner County native, was admitted to the bar in 1842 and practiced in Nashville, moving in 1853 to a farm near the city; by 1860 he had acquired property worth $77,500. Serving as Davidson County judge (1856-66), he returned to law practice after the war, subsequently becoming president of the Fourth National Bank of Nashville and one of the founders of the Tennessee Manufacturing Company. 1860 Census, Tenn., Davidson, 21st Dist., 105; Clayton, *Davidson County*, 428; Wooldridge, *Nashville*, 641-43.

3. The following list would appear to be merely the first contingent of those on whom a levy would be made. For a facsimile of the notice, directed to "Anthony W. Johnson, Davidson Co.," see White, *Messages*, V, opp. 376.

From John A. Rogers

Dresden Tenn Aug 20th 1862.

Gov. Andrew Johnson
Sir:

On the 14th day of May 1862 I was appointed Colonel by the President of the United States with authority to raise a Regiment of Infantry Volanteers in Tennessee[.] Immediately upon the reception of my commission I entered upon the duty assigned me and have now in Camp at Dresden Tennessee five full minimum companies and about four half companies[.] The Secretary of War directed me upon receipt of my Commission to report to you; and that you would detail an officer to Dresden to muster us into the service. I therefore write to you by Captain Arbuckle[1] hoping that you will detail an officer to muster us into the service. The officer I presume will be furnished with the necessary ammount of money to enable him to comply with a late act of Congress which entitles each soldier, upon being mustered into the service, to Twenty five Dollars out of one hundred dollars of there extra pay. When you detail an officer to muster us into the service I hope you will see that this provision which has been made for the benefit of the soldiers is strictly complied with, as many of our men have families that are in destitute circumstances and could be much relieved by a verry small sum of money,   I am now satisfied as to my success in raising the Regt.; at least it is beyond any doubt, and if we were permited to attach one or Two *Cavelry companies* to our Regiment we could as I think in a verry short time raise a *Brigade* in the western district. I have been requested by a large number of the citizens to call upon you for authority to raise Cavalry companies so that we might relieve the Union men who in many localities are oppressed by Guerilla Companies and deterred from entering the Volanteer service owing to there frequent attacks in the County— My own experience here Governor satisfies me that the *Rebels* in Tennessee can only be quelled by Tennesseans, and that the Cavelry from other states is almost inefectual for that purpose, for instance: a short time since I become convinced that it was necessary for the safety of our camp that some turbulent citizens in our adjoining County should be arrested; and ordered out some of our men for that purpose. In a verry short time they succeeded in arresting them all, When in other instances the Cavelry under similar circumstances were baffled by the Rebels for months,   The necessity for Tennessee Cavelry when considered is as I think very obvious, for the reason that they are acquainted with the country and people, and could obtain such information as would enable them to operate effecually when it could not be done by strangers,   Mr. Etheridge will also write with me to assure you of the necesity of raiseing

Cavelry Companies.[2] Any orders you wish executed please give me the information and they shall receive my prompt attention[.]   your friend

John A. Rogers, Col. Com.

7th Regt Tennessee Volanteers

P.S. Please let Capt Arbuckle have suficient Muster Rolls for 10 Companies; also paroles Also Regimental Documents[.]

Yours J. A. Rogers

ALS, DLC-JP.

1. Edward Arbuckle (c1821-fl1880), Kentucky-born Henry County physician, served as assistant surgeon in the 6th (1862-63) and 7th (1863-65) Tenn. Cav. Rgts., USA. 1860 Census, Tenn., Henry, 5th Dist., 65; (1880), 9th Dist., 218; CSR, RG94, NA.

2. Emerson Etheridge enclosed a note attesting to the soundness of Rogers' suggestion. Etheridge to Johnson, August 21, 1862, Johnson Papers, LC.

From Mark R. Cockrill[1]

Stock Place near Nashville August 21st—/62

Gov Johnson

Sir I have just rec'd notice to furnish five Cavalry horses[.]

You will please allow me to say that the southern Armey & Buels Armey in March when they left here *took* about 30 horses from my place all they thought suitable for Cavalry except one that I have for my own use when I am able to ride out.[2] I have a splendid old horse 18 or 19 years old[.] If you think he would be of any use I will immediatly send him in. Sir I hope you will leave me one horse for my own use[.]

Yours Respectfully Mark R Cockrill

ALS, DLC-JP.

1. Mark R. Cockrill (1788-1872), who began his adult life as a surveyor, became a leading Davidson County stock raiser with landholdings in both Tennessee and Mississippi. He owned some of the earliest merino sheep and shorthorn cattle in this country. Wooldridge, *Nashville*, 593-96.

2. A southern sympathizer, Cockrill's partisanship cost him dearly. The Federals took from his place on Charlotte Pike 20,000 bushels of corn, 26 horses, 60 head of Durham cattle, 220 sheep, 200 tons of hay, 2,000 bushels of oats, and 2,000 pounds of bacon. Four months later he was arrested "for using seditious language, and was required to give bonds in fifty thousand dollars." Crabb, "Twilight of the Nashville Gods," 300-301; Nashville *Dispatch*, December 31, 1862.

From R. J. Wood[1]

Nashville Aug 21st. 1862

Gov Johnson

Dear Sir

the Barrer has Come to me and gav me his name desiring to be pressed— he has worked three days and is well Satesfied. his Mistress Mrs Creaghead[2] is coming to you to day in order to try and get him

Back[.] you will pleas not to let him go for he is a good hand[.]

Yours Respectfouly.   R. J. Wood

In charge of Countrabands

ALS, DLC-JP2.

1. Not found.

2. Probably Mary H. Craighead (b. c1800) who had $25,000 in personal property including six slaves, although it might be her daughter-in-law, Ellen (b. c1833), wife of Capt. James B. Craighead, CSA, who had five adult males. 1860 Census, Davidson, Nashville, 3rd Ward, 91; 5th Ward, 158; *ibid.*, Slave Schedules, Wards 1-4, p. 13; 5th Ward, 11.

To Don Carlos Buell

Nashville, Augt. 22nd 1862.

Major General Buell:

Huntsville, Ala.

You have no doubt received before this news of capture of General Johnson[1] and most of his command near Gallatin yesterday. To day at Red River Bridge 100 more Federals were captured by the rebels & paroled. Reforms and changes are essentially necessary at this place. I believe it would be to the interest of the Country, and especially of the middle portion of the state for Ex-Governor Campbell to be placed in command here. I think he would be efficient, & would inspire more confidence on the part of the Union men, and dread with. . . .[2] I hope you will not think it out of place in me when I state that there must be more efficiency imparted to the Army in this part of Tennessee, or we are doomed to meet with reverses that will retard and protract the War if not in the end to result in the loss of Tennessee[.] The conduct of Col Mason 71st Ohio at Clarksville is not only humiliating but disgraceful in the extreme.[3] I am gratified to know that your order in reference to paroles was issued before his surrender, and trust we will have some examples now made.

Very Truly,   Andrew Johnson

Mil: Gov'r

Tel draft (in cipher), DLC-JP; *OR*, Ser. 1, XVI, Pt. II, 388.

1. Richard W. Johnson.

2. A page is missing.

3. The press was unusually severe in its denunciation of Col. Rodney Mason immediately after his surrender and demanded his court-martial, citing earlier acts of cowardice at Bull Run and Shiloh and representing that he yielded a very strong position with two cannon to an inferior force of guerrillas armed with shotguns. Mason in his official report mentioned his repeated requests for reinforcements—Governor Johnson was the recipient of at least one appeal for artillery—because it was known rebels were massing to attack him. When apprised of the strength of the Confederate force on the morning of the 18th, three-fourths of Mason's officers voted to surrender. With fewer than 175 men (the Confederates reportedly had 800), no artillery or hope of reinforcements, Mason yielded the camp at sundown without firing a shot. Nashville *Union*, August 22, 28, 1862; Nashville *Dispatch*, August 31, 1862; *OR*, Ser. 1, XVI, Pt. I, 863-67; Mason to Johnson, August 6, 1862, Johnson Papers, LC.

To William B. Campbell

Nashville, [cAug. 23 1862]

General Wm B Campbell,
Tennessee Commissioner
Indianapolis, Ind
Are you willing to take Command of this Post. I have dispatched and received answer from General Buell stating that he would appoint you Commandant you having a full understanding of all the conflicts that might occur between senior and junior officers, he stating that he would always avoid as far as possible throwing senior officer within your Command.[1] I hope you will answer at once.[2]

Andrew Johnson.

Tel draft, DLC-JP.
1. Johnson's wire fails to convey the grim, perhaps even threatening, message of Buell's reply. The commanding general, it is true, agreed to place Campbell in charge at Nashville but reminded Johnson that "it may happen that a senior [officer] would unavoidably fall there and if he were capable I could not keep the senior out of Command[.] I should like Gov Campbell to understand that matter rightly." Surely Johnson's mumbo jumbo about junior-senior officers carries no implication of Campbell's being removed. Buell to Johnson, August 22, 1862, Johnson Papers, LC.
2. Campbell's answer has not been found.

From Thomas H. Cox[1]

Nashville, Tenn Aug 24th 1862

To Gov Andrew Johnson
Sir I have the honour to report &c the following arrests made by the Nashville Union Guard from the 15th July to 24th Aug 1862[.]

July 22	J. W. Langley	(act Spy
" "	John. Morton	"
" "	—— Morton	"
" "	Thos. Roberts	"
" "	—— Grisholm	"
" "	James. Mason	"
" "	John Shneider	(Treas. Lang.
" 26	Turner. S. Foster	(Treason
Aug 2d	L. D. Berchtold	Spy
" "	S. Picard	"
" "	L. Ronenau	"
" "	F. Linkauf	"
" "	S. H. Solomon	"
" "	B. Kahn	"
" 3d	A. Richards	"
" "	B. Ropler	"
" 5th	John Samuels	(Treasonable Lang

```
 "   6th    J. Dolan                    "           "
Aug  6th    Ed. Strother              (Confd Army
 "  12th    J. D. Thomas             (Treasonable Lang
 "  15      J. W. Fuller             (Examined & Disch[arged]
 "          H. Spencer                 "           "
 "          G. Spencer                 "           "
 "  18      P. Haslem                (Confd Army
    24      J. Dillon                (Treasonable Language
```

Thos. H. Cox
Capt Nashville Union Guard

ALS, DLC-JP.

1. Possibly Thomas Cox (b. *c*1824), a North Carolina native elected captain of the Nashville guards in mid-July, 1862. Porch, *1850 Census, Davidson*, 268; Nashville *Union*, July 17, 1862.

From Thomas H. Cox

Nashville, Tenn. Aug 24th, 1862

To Gov Andrew Johnson

Sir I have the honour to report &c the following Arms & Goods Captured by the Nashville Union Guard From the 15th July to the 24th Aug 1862[.]

```
July 22d.  three Pistols, one Double Bbl shot gun   From Adam
                 Cole
 "   28    One Rifle and one Double Bbl shot gun " Mrs. Swan
 "   "     One Rifle one Double Bbl shot gun & one single Bbl
                 shot gun From Mr. Shwab
Aug 2d.    One  Pistol From F Linkauf
 "   3 ,   One  Pistol From B. Ropler
 "   8th. 11    Boxes Clothing (Confederate) From, Morris
                 Stratton & Co
 "   9th. 23    Boxes Shoes From R S Hollins & Co
 "  12th.       150 Coverlids, From Urban Ozanie
 "             2 Ambulance Carts from O'Kane
 "             One Box one Bale Clothing from Mr. Strong
 "  24     One  cooking stove⎫ Confederate
 "   "     2    tents         ⎭
```

There was a lot of salt seized but Capt McPheely[1] decided that it was Private Property and returned it to the Parties claiming it.

Your Obedn Servant   Thos. H. Cox
Capt Nashville Union Guard

ALS, DLC-JP.

1. Robert Macfeely (*c*1825-1901), native Pennsylvanian and West Point graduate (1850), was on frontier duty until 1860. Chief commissary of the Department of the Ohio (1861-62), commissary of subsistence at Nashville (1862), acting chief quarter-

master for Grant (1863), and chief commissary of subsistence for the Army of the Tennessee (1864), he remained in service, becoming brigadier general of subsistence (1875) before his retirement in 1890. Heitman, *Register*, I, 665; *West Point Register* (1970), 243; *OR*, Ser. 1, XVI, Pt. I, 333; XXXVIII, Pt. III, 47; LII, Pt. II, 193, 217.

From Alfred Eaton[1]

Lynchburg Tenn August 25th 1862

Hon. Andrew Johnson
Governor Nashville Tenn.
Dear Sir

About the first of this month I employed John Brown, James Landers and Harvey Gowan[2] to go to Bedford County to get two of my negro boys that had runaway and gone there a few days before. They succeeded in getting the negro boys and on their return to this place with the negros learned that a body of United States troops were coming up the road. They took a by path to avoid meeting them. They were captured in company with the negros in a few hundred yards of the public highway by Col. Steadmans[3] 14th Ohio Regiment on the 2nd Inst and carried to Winchester and sent thence to Nashville Ten and are now held in custody there.

John Brown has been in the Confederate Army but was discharged in regular form on account of physical disability. None of the above persons have ever been engaged in any species of unlawful warfare and are in no way connected with the Confederate Army or with those parties called Guerrillas or bush whackers.

The above is a true statement of the cause of their capture to the truth of which I hereby certify upon honor.

Very Respectfully Submitted
Alfred Eaton

ALS, DLC-JP.

1. Alfred Eaton (*c*1808-*fl*1880) was a South Carolina-born Lincoln County farmer. Porch, *1850 Census, Lincoln*, 185; 1880 Census, Tenn., Moore, Lynchburg, 1st Dist., 4.

2. James Sanders (b. *c*1832), Harvey Gowan (b. *c*1835), and probably John W. Brown (b. *c*1837), all Tennessee-born Lincoln County farmers. Brown served in Co. E, 1st Tenn. Inf., CSA, from April to December, 1861. *Ibid.* (1860), Lincoln, 18th Dist., 24; 1st Dist., 2; 2nd Dist., 98; CSR (Brown), RG107, NA.

3. James B. Steedman (1817-1883), native Pennsylvanian who moved to Ohio, did contract work on the Wabash and Erie Canal, served in the Ohio legislature (1843), spent a year in the California gold fields (1849-50), and became the U. S. public printer (1857). In April, 1861, he became colonel, 14th Ohio Inf., and served first in West Virginia and then in the Kentucky, Tennessee, Georgia region, advancing to major general in April, 1864. Military governor of Georgia after the war, he resigned in August, 1866, to become New Orleans collector of internal revenue. In later years he edited a paper in Toledo, served in the state senate (1879), and became chief of police of Toledo (May, 1883). Warner, *Generals in Blue*, 473-74.

From George W. Morgan

Cumberland Gap Aug 25 1862
To Gen Buell & Gov Johnson

Have just recd. a flag of truce from Maj Gen Kirby Smith dated on Yesterday at Barboursville & a note date at Rogers [Gap] today from Maj Gen McCowan[.][1] I send Col Garard[2] with four Hundred 400 mounted infantry & two Hundred Cavalry to join any force which may march to the relief of this place. I do so to save the forces from starvation & to send a gallant officer with a Brave little Band of veterans to lead all the new troops. If attacked I pledge myself & this command upon the security of this fortress. we won & do not intend to loose it[.][3]

Geo W Morgan
Brig General Cmg

Tel, DLC-JP.

1. John P. McCown (1815-1879), of Sevierville, a West Point graduate (1840) and veteran who served in the U. S. artillery until 1861, was colonel of the Tennessee Provisional Army's artillery corps, becoming a major general by March, 1862. Temporary commander of the Department of East Tennessee in late August, he was court-martialed by Bragg in February, 1863, for disobedience of orders, found guilty, and sentenced to be suspended from rank and pay for six months. After the war he taught school in Tennessee, later removing to a farm near Magnolia, Arkansas. Warner, *Generals in Gray*, 199-200; *OR*, Ser. 1, XVI, Pt. I, 2; Horn, *Army of Tennessee*, 158.

2. Theophilus T. Garrard with 7th Ky. Inf., USA.

3. The same day Morgan telegraphed Johnson, "The enemy . . . evinces no desire to attack us although his force is so greatly superior to ours in numbers. . . . prudence compels me to act mainly on the defensive. . . . the Enemy take advantage of our destitution in Cavalry & horse artillery to seize our wagons & fill them with salt. . . . fifteen hundred cavalry with four cannon could cut off their Salt Expedition." Morgan to Johnson, August 25, 1862, Johnson Papers, LC.

Certification of Loyalty

State of Tennessee
Executive Department
Nashville Augt. 25th 1862

The bearor of this Mr T. T. Burgess[1] of Cornersville Giles County Tenn is a Loyal Citizen and it is therefore hoped that all Federal troops passing in that Vicinity will avoid Committing depredations on his property and that he will be protected against the Same[.]

Andrew Johnson
Military Governor

D, NNC.

1. Thomas T. Burgess (b. *c*1817), a native of Maryland, was a Giles County merchant with an estate of $9,700. 1860 Census, Tenn., Giles, N. Subdiv., 163.

From Elizabeth M. Harding[1]

Belle Meade August 27th 1862.

Gov Johnson

Sir,

I have learned through the medium of Mr Hague,[2] that a boy named John Martin[3] was arrested by the Provost Marshal, under a charge of endeavoring to convey letters, or information to the Southern Army; that I also was suspected of sending or intending to send letters by him to the South, and had furnished him with a horse to go on. This suspicion, for I know it can be nothing else, calls upon me to state the facts, so far as they relate to my agency in giving a horse to young Martin. Under ordinary circumstances, I could have let my own innocense of wrong intention have been found out, by yourself through some other channel, but I cannot, after the apparent interest which you have manifested in me & mine, forbear an explanation which is due both to you & myself— Johnny Martin was an old race rider of Gen Hardings, of whom he thought a great deal; he is a South Carolinian by birth, & is an orphan. Gen H. finding him a good honest truthful boy, offered to send him to school & befriend him in every way in his power, & did send him to school for some time, & also told him when ever he was in need of assistance to call upon him & he would help him; this promise was known to me.— For some months past, I have seen but little of Johnny, but while in Nashville a few days ago, where I had gone to call upon yourself, he called at my Fathers door, & asked to see me: he then told me, he wished to go South, to his friends & relatives, and asked me to give him a wild thorough-bred young gelding, who was placed here to pasture, & had long since, in common phrase "eaten his head off"; the horse was so wild & unruly, & threw several of my negroes, & was finally turned loose in the parks as incorrigible & dangerous. This was known by John, & others, but he asked for him, as I thought, & still believe, to go to his home, (& he informed me that he intended to take the oath of allegience, & go openly & not clandestinely.) I gave him the horse & parted from him there, & I here affirm (more on his account than my own) that I neither sent letters or messages, or thought of doing so, nor do I believe he intended taking them for others. I do not believe that John would so deceive me, his friend, as to his objects in going South. I knew his occupation as a race rider, was entirely broken up, by the war, & sincerely believe him to have been in earnest, when he expressed his desire to go home—to his sisters & friends, & I do not believe that he ever intended to carry either letters, or information south; at all events, if such was his intention, he concealed his objects from me. God forbid that I should so unsex myself, as to be playing the spy, for either North, or

South. I have now, & have had, no other wish, & my prayer has ever been, that this bloody war, might come to an end, & Peace, blessed Peace, again be restored to our unhappy country.— I have some pride in showing to you, that while you were endeavoring to forward my wishes, I was not stabbing you secretly at the same time. But for the wish to exonerate myself to you, I would scorn to notice this blow dealt at me, by some secret foe of my husband; who has betrayed alike, an ignorance of my sex, & of my feelings.— To *you alone*, of all Federal officers, who hold in your hands, what is to me dearer than life,—& for the kindness you have expressed for me & mine, I owed this explanation, in order that your kindness to me, may be vindicated, to yourself.—

> very respectfully,
> Mrs Wm. G. Harding

ALS, DLC-JP.

1. Elizabeth M. Harding (c1819-1867), daughter of Randal McGavock of Williamson County, in 1840 became the second wife of William G. Harding and served as mistress of the huge plantation, Belle Meade, near Nashville. Planning to visit her husband, a prisoner at Fort Mackinac, Michigan, Mrs. Harding called upon Johnson in July and August to arrange the necessary permission and to obtain protection for Belle Meade in her absence. According to a relative who wrote Harding, "your plantation has suffered less than any other one in the country, owing perhaps to the interference in your behalf of Governor Johnson, who has exhibited (perhaps as far as he could consistently) a disposition to make the blow upon you as light as possible—for the present at least." Mrs. Harding did not go to Michigan; Harding was paroled in September and returned home. Gower, "Belle Meade," 208, 213-14; Ridley Wills, II, "Letters from Nashville, 1862, I: A Portrait of Belle Meade," *Tenn. Hist. Quar.*, XXXIII (1974), 80-81; 1860 Census, Tenn., Davidson, 11th Dist., 12.

2. William Hague (b. c1819), Pennsylvania-born stonecutter and Belle Meade's stock manager at this time, became the personal conveyor of Harding's parole to him at Mackinac. *Ibid;* Wills, "Portrait of Belle Meade," 72, 82.

3. "Little Johnny Martin," Harding's former jockey, who came as a "paroled prisoner" to borrow a horse from Mrs. Harding, saying that he had taken the oath and that he desired to go South to his sisters, is otherwise unidentified. McGavock Miller, "Letters from Nashville, 1862, II: 'Dear Master,' " *Tenn. Hist. Quar.*, XXXIII (1974), 91.

From *William H. Sidell*

> Head-Quarters District of the Ohio,
> 28th August 1862

His Excy. Andrew Johnson
Govr. of Tennessee
Governor

The essential part of Col Rogers[1] letter viz regarding the payment of the *bounty* advance of $25 cannot be for the reason that no money has been recieved for that purpose. Col Rogers should raise his regiment exclusively under your control and it was out of order for him to proceed so far as to raise five companies & parts of four others under other authority than yours. I give an extract from an order on that subject. This irregularity need not however interfere with the completion of the regiment & the mustering in only that the authority & the commissions of the officers should come from you[.]   As to mixing Cavalry with Infantry or other army it is wrong in principle & practice & contrary to all orders and is without law to authorize it. A Colonel or other officer of Infantry will adhere to his Infantry and if Cavalry be raised another officer may do it for instance a captain of a company or captains of two companies or more but under a separate officer from the Infantry and the two having nothing to do with each other[.]

Excuse haste rendered necessary by your call for immediate response to enable you to answer.

I am forever Yr Obt Servt   W H Sidell
Maj 15 US Infry AAAG

ALS, DLC-JP.

1. John A. Rogers was currently recruiting the 7th Tenn. Inf., USA.

From Parthenia P. Mayfield[1]

Nashville Aug 29 [1862]

Mr Johnson

Sir

It is something at a period so politically gloomy, almost chaotic, when the patient soul is agitated and sickened by bare audacious treason and yet more tortured by doubts, and surmises of secret connivance in public stations by apprehension of an infernal force in course of performance at the expense of the sustenance, the blood, and honour of a liberal, confiding and betrayed people, criminality, in comparison of which the bold, black, ugly rebellion assumed the proportions, and traits of beauty; it is something to be privilege to repose confidence in, at least, one entrusted with power.

This allusion to your character will not be misunderstood if I do not flatter myself too much in presuming that you retain any recollection of the kindred simplicity, and frankness of mine.[2]

In this same candid spirit I confess to addressing you with the desire of a favourable interference on your part in my behalf. My health is so greatly impaired that I find the duties of housekeeping too onerous for my present condition. Wishing to board, after making a journey, I would suggest the purchase of our dwelling by the United States for a post office. It would seem appropriate from the site, and immediate proximity to the government lot.[3] The house is conveniently arranged, and the rooms on the second and third floors would afford pleasant apartments for government officers.

If your occupations allow you a few moments to attend to this affair you will greatly oblige

Yours very respectfully
Parthenia P. Mayfield

ALS, DLC-JP.
    1. Parthenia P. Mayfield (b. *c*1820), Pennsylvania native, was the wife of George A. J. Mayfield (b. *c*1820), a Nashville physician who claimed $22,500 real and $2,500 personal property on the eve of the war. 1860 Census, Tenn., Davidson, 3rd Ward, 89.
    2. The Mayfields boarded at the St. Cloud Hotel in 1853 when Johnson lived there during his first term as governor. Thomas, *Old Days in Nashville*, 98, 99.
    3. The house stood at 49 Spring (later Church) Street; the post office in 1860 was located at the corner of Spring and Cherry. *Campbell's Nashville Directory* (1859), 104.

From William H. Sidell

Head-Quarters District of the Ohio,
Nashville 29th August 1862

His Excy. Andrew Johnson
Governor of Tennessee
Governor

I return respectfully your communication of the 27th inst[1] in regard to discharged teamsters with the endorsement in explanation of the officer who is responsible and to whom it was referred.

This officer, Captain Stevenson,[2] states that he establishes certain rules of which the men are advised on taking service which therefore form part of the contract, that nevertheless he suffers several violations of these rules to pass without inflicting the penalty until finally he finds it just and expedient to apply them and that unless he do so all discipline and system in his complicated office will be broken up.

It strikes me that the explanations are sufficient and that the men should be held amenable to the discipline he establishes without resort. His employees are very numerous, over a Thousand, and it is impossible to concieve that they can be held in order for any military purposes unless the chief be permitted to enforce the rules laid down when the engagement is made in a manner to ensure respect for his authority.

I am forever Respectfully Your Obt Servt
W H Sidell
Maj 15 US Infy AAAG

ALS, DLC-JP.
    1. On August 27 Johnson sent a note to Sidell with two U. S. teamsters, Pat Lynch and Peter Reilly, who had been discharged without receiving their pay. He asked Sidell to explain to these men their cases and suggested that since "complaints of this kind are very numerous . . . some system should be adopted that would give more satisfaction." Johnson Papers, LC.
    2. Richard Stevenson (d. 1862), a resident of Lawrenceburg, Indiana, was a captain, assistant quartermaster of volunteers from October, 1861, until his death from typhoid fever at Nashville, October 4, 1862. Heitman, *Register*, I, 924; Louisville *Journal*, October 11, 1862. See also Letter from Benjamin C. Truman, November 17, 1862, note 2.

From Don Carlos Buell

[Head Quarters, Decherd]
1862 Aug 30

Genl. Rousseau for Gov. Johnson Nashville[1]

I think it but proper and due that I should advise you of our situation with reference to the enemy in Tennessee and of the course I find it necessary to adopt.

You are aware that when this army was separated again from the force which operated against Corinth it was expected that it would attack Chattanooga and perhaps advance into East Tennessee— You cannot very well know all the circumstances which rendered that impossible and which now force us upon a defensive campaign. At first it was necessary to rebuild the bridges over a long line of railroad and in some cases it had to be repeated several times[.] so constant has been the interruption of our communication that it has been with the greatest difficulty the troops could be subsisted at all and even then some fifteen thousand men were required to occupy position and guard our communication which starting necessarily from Louisville extend in all over some four hundred miles of railroad[.] From this cause the force which I can bring to bear so far in advance of the source of supply is reduced to twenty five or thirty thousand men[.]   this force is not only very much less than that which is now crossing the mountains under Bragg but labors under all the difficulty and peril of operating virtually in an enemy's country surrounded with an immense force of irregular cavalry[.]   Bragg's force I apprehend does not amount to less than fifty thousand[.]

All the information I got represented it much greater[.]   it probably is between fifty and sixty thousand not including the force operating against Kentucky[.]   If it be forty thousand it is still too large under the circumstances to be engaged by twenty five or thirty thousand[.]

By falling back to Nashville my force will increase to forty thousand of the army of the Ohio proper and including troops that are coming from Corinth it will be about fifty thousand— these facts make it plain that I should fall back on Nashville and I am now preparing to do so. I have stated the reasons which lead to this necessity until it would be criminal to delay any longer, that we shall triumph in the struggle to preserve Tenn I do not for a moment doubt. It is necessary that this communication shall be strictly confidential and I request that you will destroy it to guard against the possibility of discovery[.][2]

Buell

a very fine day

Copy, DLC-JP; Tel, DNA-393, Dept. of the Ohio, Tels. Sent, Vol. 52 (Feb.-Aug., 1862); OR, Ser. 1, XVI, Pt. II, 451.

1. It is interesting to speculate why Buell employed this peculiar device for

communicating with Johnson. Clearly he wished Rousseau and the governor to be aware that both were privy to the contents of the wire; otherwise he could have sent identical dispatches directly to each. Was he trying to ensure an early conference by making Rousseau the bearer? If so, it is not certain that he succeeded, for the endorsement on the recipient's copy is equivocal on that point: "Genl. Rousseau arrived at Nashville from Huntsville August 27th 1862[.] On Thursday 28th August 1862 he assumed command of forces at Nashville and on Saturday following 30th August 1862 this paper was handed to me[.]"

2. Far from destroying this telegram, Johnson preserved it and had at least one copy made.

To Don Carlos Buell

Nashville, Augt. 31st 1862

Maj Genl. Buell,
Decherd, Tenn.

I have forwarded your dispatch[1] to Hon W. H. Polk & others.[2] The forces which have been estimated as coming through from Chattanooga & other points in the direction of Nashville will not exceed 25,000. My own opinion is that it is not half that number. I do not believe that Bragg's force at this time designs attacking Nashville unless induced to do so by a retreat of our forces. In expressing this opinion, of course I do so in absence of what information you may have. Fifty thousand troops can't be supplied or subsisted between McMinnville & Chattanooga or any other place from which they have marched.

Andrew Johnson.

Tel draft, DLC-JP; *OR*, Ser. 1, XVI, Pt. II, 461.

1. Buell had wired: "The withdrawal of the troops from Columbia could be delayed a day or so perhaps if very important. It could not be worked altogether." Buell to Johnson, and Johnson to William H. Polk and others, both August 31, 1862, Johnson Papers, LC.

2. At this point the following sentence had a line drawn through it. "I think it would be well for the forces to remain there, if not inconsistent with your general plan."

Appendix

The social organization of the Southern States has not favored the rise of the lowly born to favor and distinction. "good blood" is as much prized and honored in the older planting states and districts as in Great Britain or any other aristocratic country. Not many of their men of mark have lacked wealthy, or at least well placed, grandfathers. The few striking exceptions—Jackson, Clay, and perhaps one or two others—migrated in youth to a newly settled region, where their talent and energy readily over bore the yet vacant barriers of caste and exclusiveness. Sergeant A. Prentiss was a New Englander by birth and education, who took his place early in life at the bar of a young State and fairly conquered prejudice by the force of his genius and eloquence. Alexander H. Stephens was a foundling; but he was adopted as an infant into a family whose prestige he shared and whose means paid for his education and smoothed away the difficulties which thickly beset the path of the friendless and penniless. 'Sandhillers,' 'corn-crackers,' 'dirt-eaters,' and other terms far from complimentary, attest the estimation in which the low-born and untaught masses are held by the upper classes—planters, merchants, lawyers, &c.—whereof the contemptuous 'White trash' of the negroes is a faithful echo. The absence of common Schools and of any provision whatever for the education of the children of the poor, the prevalent, undisguised contempt for manual labor, necessarily affecting all who gain their living by it, and the limited diffusion of intellectual aliment through mails, books and periodicals, render the Slave States less favorable to the aspirations of humble men than in almost any country in Europe. He, therefore, who, in climbing over every impediment, raises himself from a childhood of ignorance, of obscurity and want, to a manhood of signal usefulness, power and distinction, honors himself any where; but nowhere more truly than in the American States now scourged and desolated by a wicked and parricidal rebellion.

ANDREW JOHNSON was born at Raleigh, North Carolina, on the 29th of December, 1808. His father died four years afterward, in consequence of injuries received in attempting to save a friend from drowning, leaving his wife and infant son in utter poverty. At ten years of age, that son, ignorant even of his letters, was apprenticed to a tailor, with whom he served seven years, never in his life attending school for even a day. But he early evinced a love of information and acquired the art of reading, being stimulated thereto by hearing a volume of the speeches of eminent British statesmen read in his master's shop by a neighbor who used to visit it for that purpose. There is a story current that he learned to read from his wife after their marriage, but it is not according to the fact. On the contrary, he was accustomed, while an apprentice, to devote his hours not required for labor, in learning to spell and read, mainly by himself, but aided at times by one of the journeymen who worked beside him. He was known as a good reader before he finished his apprenticeship and, at 17 years of age, went out into the wide world to seek his fortune.

His first stop was at Laurens Court House, South Carolina where he found employment and worked nearly two years at his trade; returning in 1826 to Raleigh, and being employed there as a journeyman from May till September, when he struck across the Alleghenies for Tennessee, taking his mother with him. He found employment as a journeyman at Greenville, in the Eastern division of the last-named State, tarried a year, married, while still a minor, and migrated westward; but found no place that seemed to want him, and returned to Greenville, which he has since made his home, and where he at once opened a shop on his own account. Now his wife's superior literary attainments were made conducive to his instruction; and he devoted his evening hours under her tuition to learning to write and cypher; and thus his technical education was completed.

The poor young tailor shared liberally in the general addiction of Americans of his class to politics, and was an ardent supporter of Gen. Jackson, then in his second canvass for the Presidency and on the eve of his first election. He was chosen an alderman of the little borough of Greenville—a post of small account and no emolument—in 1828, when he was still under age; reelected in 1829 and again in 1830; and then chosen Mayor, which position he filled for three years; in 1835 chosen to the Legislature of Tennessee, where he rendered himself unpopular by opposing a magnificent system of internal improvements and was beaten at the ensuing election; but at the next (1839) he was again a candidate and the great improvement scheme having meantime become unpopular in his County—he was again elected. In 1840, he was one of the democratic (Van Buren) Electors of President, and as such canvassed effectively a good portion of the State, but of course could not make head against the Harrison tornado of that stirring contest. The next year saw him transfer from the House to the State Senate, where he served a single term, and at its close he was chosen a Member of Congress, (House) and four times successively re-elected, closing his service in that body in 1853. He was thereupon made the democratic candidate for governor, meeting in the ensuing canvass the eloquent and popular Gustavus A. Henry, whom he beat by a small majority, though the State had cast its Electoral vote for Gen. Scott, the Whig candidate for President, in the election of the preceding year. In 1855, he was supported for reëlection, with Col. Meredith P. Gentry for his main competitor, and was again successful after an animated struggle.

When his second term as Governor expired, he had been chosen a Senator of the United States for the six years ensuing, ending in March, 1863. He is of course still a Senator, though now absent from his seat as provisional or military Governor of Tennessee, pending the reëstablishment of a loyal State Government by her people.

Mr. Johnson's career has, therefore, been eminently that of a politician, he having been in public life nearly all his adult years, and some fifteen times a candidate for office, only beaten once save as a Presidential Elector, when his defeat was in no sense personal.

In a republic, it is every citizen's duty to be in one sense a politician; but to make politics the business of a life is neither desirable nor wholesome. Such a life is necessarily belligerent, gladiatorial, one-sided; the mind is warped and poisoned by the seeming necessity of always eulogizing one set of men and measures and depreciating another. The lawyer's vocation is less perfective; for he who is engaged to-day in this cause, to-morrow in that, and next day in another, and thus compelled to-day to combat nearly the same positions that he supported yesterday, must learn at least that there are two sides to most questions, and that the wise man has a larger charity for opinion adverse to his own than the fool. But the pillar and champion of a party, especially if he may boast that he has kept straight on in the same identical rut through a career of thirty or forty years, may have served his country meantime but he can hardly have widened and clarified his own perceptions or sweetened his moral nature. He is far more likely to have confirmed if not aggravated whatever tendency he may have inherited to a stubborn dogmatism and a blind presumption that no good can come out of Nazareth. He may possibly have filled his pocket, and pampered his body, but he will almost certainly have starved his soul.

Yet the western game of politics is nobler and manlier than that which prevails at the East. In Tennessee, every candidate for Governor, for Congress, or other important post, must face the people and his competitor on the stump, and give reasons for the faith that is in him in a series of elaborate popular harangues, subject to the immediate observation and trenchant criticism of his vigilant antagonist. The confident misstatement which in the North will be emphasized with a round of applause and swallowed by the ill-informed or prejudiced men as gospel—no one being present and at liberty to correct it—will not answer in the West; nay, that hideous jumble of fact and fiction—of incidents imperfectly understood and unfairly presented—of history travestied and innocent acts perverted into misdemeanors by exaggeration, distortion and uncharitable presumption—which is the delight of a mob and the despair of an intelligent auditor—will rather damage the cause it was intended to advance, if, when subjected to the keen dissection of an able and thoroughly posted antagonist. There are hundreds in Tennessee today who cannot read a paragraph, yet who, having listened to elaborate speeches on the public questions of 1830 to 1850 by such men as Judge White, John Bell, Felix Grundy, James K. Polk, Andrew Johnson, Gentry, Henry, &c., understand those questions far better than does an average College graduate in the Eastern States. In fact, the stump speeches of Western politicians concerning the Banks, Tariffs, Internal Improvements, &c, have often been more elaborate, more thorough, more exhaustive, than would be patiently endured by an average New-York or New England audience, who fail to mark the decided degeneracy of our average political speeches since the days when Webster, Everett and Silas Wright were among our stump orators.

Up to the opening of the year 1861, Mr. Johnson was known to the country only as an active, efficient and successful politician of the democratic school. He had ably advocated the measures of his party, struggled for its ascendancy, and received a liberal share of its honors. On a single question only—that of the Freedom of the Public Lands—he had taken a course which brought him into collision with the great body of his brother Members of Congress from the Slave States, and his advocacy of the policy of allotting a quarter-section of the Public domain without charge to each citizen who may choose to settle upon and improve it did not cease, though it seemed less ardent, when nearly every other Southern man who had formerly commended it became its earnest opponents. He supported the famous Senate resolves of 1860, setting forth the rights and immunities of Slavery in the territories, which were drawn up with obvious intent to brand Senator Douglas with heresy and preclude his election to the Presidency, and he supported Mr. Breckinridge as the only true and orthodox democratic candidate for that post.

But Andrew Johnson had begun his arduous career as a laborer with his hands for a humble subsistence, and the hour of extreme trial found him faithful to the interests of Free Labor. The great conspiracy to divide and destroy the Union in the interest of Human Slavery was no sooner fully developed, at the session of 1860-61, than it found in him an open and unsparing antagonist. Though he supported every proposition looking to compromise and peace, he made the success of none of them a condition of his fidelity to the Union, but stood up for the integrity of the Nation and the vindication of the Federal authority under all circumstances and at all hazards. When no other Senator from the South, and hardly one of his party, openly affirmed the right and duty of [the nation] to act was stigmatized as "coercion," Mr. Johnson met the great and sudden peril in the true spirit of a Jackson, insisting that the Union must stand, whatever and whoever should be shattered and crushed through his own plotting and striving for its subversion: "No traitor has a right to own *any thing*"[2] were the emphatic words with which he silenced all cavils as to the right to confiscation of the property of rebels; and he has never hesitated to declare that those conspirators who so wantonly plunged this free and happy land into anarchy and blood, bringing desolation to his own among many thousands of homes, subjecting his family to outrage and insult, and filling that loyal portion of Tennessee with violence, terror and murder, were flagrant criminals, who have nobly merited condign and exemplary punishment[.]

Such is the man wisely chosen by the President to direct the efforts now in progress to disabuse Tennessee of the falsehoods, by which a very large proportion of her citizens have been alienated from the flag of their country, and made to sympathize with if not coöperate in the struggle to rend her into fragments and deprive her of her standing among the nations. His appointment cannot have been expected to disarm opposition—it will rather embitter and inflame it. He returns to his own State an open enemy to those who claim that they have wrested her from the Union under whose auspices she was called into being and in the shadow of which she has arisen to a high position among the sister commonwealths which are blended in the great American Republic. To disabuse the deceived and perverted—to protect the loyal and patriotic—to recall to their duty the misguided and erring—and to vanquish and scatter the malignantly, invincibly traitorous—such is the exalted mission of the man whom Tennessee has often delighted to honor, but who never before attempted to serve her so nobly and so perilously as now. That his struggle will be chequered with reverses and discouragements is probable; nor is his ultimate success so absolutely certain as to dispel anxiety and banish doubt; but, even though overborne and defeated, he will not fail. They who should by cooperation ensure his success may prove ineffective [or] recreant; but he, whether worsted or triumphant, will prove himself a gallant and fearless champion of Order and Liberty, Law and Right, and a worthy guardian of the momentous destinies which are involved in the preservation and perpetuity of the American Union.

*   *   *

Essay, DLC-Horace Greeley Papers, Scrapbook (Ac 4322).

1. This effort to introduce the recently designated military governor to a broader audience seems not to have appeared in print. The surviving draft, in Greeley's typically execrable script, is replete with printer's directions ("1 G," "Pica," and "Solid Brev"), bears the notation "Not for Tribune," but gives no clue to the intended channel of publication or to the specific date of composition; the endorsement, however, reads "Andrew Johnson by Horace Greeley 1862." Internal evidence suggests that it was written sometime during March, soon after Johnson left Washington for his home state.

2. Confirming evidence for this extreme statement has not been found. That Johnson hated secessionists is a truism; that he had expressed himself as willing to sweep aside their right to property remains thus far unsubstantiated. Yet Greeley was convinced that the senator had so expressed himself. In an address at the Smithsonian Institution on the evening of January 2, before an audience which included the President, members of the cabinet, and other dignitaries, the editor was quoted as attributing to Andy Johnson the opinion that "rebels had no right to own anything"—a sentiment which he declared to be "the enunciation of a patriot and the wisdom of a statesman." Chicago *Tribune*, January 4, 1862.

Index

Primary identification of a person is indicated by an italic *n* following the page reference. Identifications found in earlier volumes are shown by a parenthesized Roman numeral and page number immediately after the name. For abbreviations, *see* Editorial Method.

Abernathy, Albert A., 509, 510*n*
Abernathy, Charles, 510*n*
Abernathy, Charles C. (of Giles County), 414*n*, 423n, 519
Abernathy, Charles C. (of Rutherford County), 510n
Abernathy, Thompson, 510*n*
Abolition, abolitionists, 4; in Congress, 46; as disunionists, xxiv-xxv, 18, 229, 328; England as mother of, 90, 91n; support for, waning, 166-67; want South disfranchised, 347-48
Adair, H. H.: from, 201
Adams, Alexander H., 13n
Adams, George M. (IV, 556*n*), 297
Adams, Green (IV, 525*n*), 29, 31n, 89, 373
Adams, John (of Tenn.), 469, 472*n*
Adams, John Quincy: on expulsions from Senate, 118
Adams, William H., 213*n*; from, 212-13
Adams Express Company: restoration of service by, 251, 283; rifles shipped by, 362
Agriculture: in Confederate states, 386n
Akin, L. D., 354*n*
Alabama: East Tennesseans incarcerated in, 149, 237, 241n; guerrilla activity in, 610; secession of, 3, 21, 27n, 231, 240n; Union officeholders in, 582n
Allen, Nathaniel H., 597*n*; from, 596-97
Allman, Nathan T., 191*n*, 453; from, 190-91; paroled, 454n
Alloway, Mr.: slave of, 610
American Home Missionary Society, 111n
Amnesty: promised by Johnson, xliii, 211, 304n, 417; offered by Kirby Smith, 353n
Anderson, Joseph, 262, 263*n*
Anderson, Robert (IV, 113*n*), 8n, 232; from, 108-9
Anderson County: June 8, 1861, vote in, 27n
André, John, 125-26
Andrews, Christopher C., xli, 328n
Andrews, Mark L., 345*n*
"Andy Johnson Guard," 188, 301; *see also* Ohio infantry (69th)

Anthony, Daniel R., 493n
Apperson, Richard: from, 7
Appointments, presidential: confirmed, 109n, 332n, 336n, 403n, 407n; requests for (civil), 113, 314, 406-7, 469, 543 (military), 290, 301, 308-9, 441, 477; *see also* Patronage; Tenn. appointments
Arbuckle, Edward, 626, 627*n*
Arkansas: vigilance committees in, 527
Arms and munitions: Clarksville foundry for, 483n; confiscated from civilians, 630; lack of, 215; manufactured in Nashville, 265; purchased by Confederates in Nashville, 370; secreted by Confederates in Clarksville, 425; stored in capitol, 621; for Tenn. rgts., 68-69, 218, 362, 542; for Union home guards, 431, 557; *see also* Ordnance
Armstrong, Fearless A., 110*n*
Armstrong, George, 609
Armstrong, Landon, 479n
Armstrong, Pleasant M., 478, 479n
Armstrong, Thomas M., 479n
Army, Confederate: aid promised families of recruits in, 302n, 311; forced recruitment for, 242, 301, 303, 382, 450, 509, 625*n*; impoverished condition of, 460; Negroes in, 61; property in West Tenn. destroyed by, 462-63; refugees from, 442; release sought for draftees in, 274-75, 482-83; in Ky., 57, 104; supported by wealthy secessionists, 160, 240n, 397, 407, 457, 482-83, 517
Army, U. S.: aid for soldiers in, 112; bakeries of, xxvii, 189; misconduct of officers in, 98; Negroes in, 417n; quartermaster supplies in, 283, 297; relief for families of soldiers of, 310; sutlers regulated in, 102-3; 25th Bde., 353
Army of the Ohio: beef contract for, 610; in Ky., 48
Army of Tennessee, Provisional: on flight from Nashville, 168; Johnson's estimate of strength of, 638
Arnold, Benedict, 125-26
Arnold, Edwin, 580*n*
Arnold, John Q. (IV, 190*n*), 531, 553

Index

Primary identification of a person is indicated by an italic *n* following the page reference. Identifications found in earlier volumes are shown by a parenthesized Roman numeral and page number immediately after the name. For abbreviations, *see* Editorial Method.

Stratton, Thomas E., 280n; *see also* Morris & Stratton
Strickland, Jesse Hartley, 282*n*; from, 282
Stringham, Silas H., 79n
Strong, Mr., 630
Strother, Ed., 630
Sugar: confiscated in Memphis, 462
Summers, Thomas O., 316n, 320*n*
Sumner, Charles, xxvii, 46, 239*n*, 491; Johnson attacks, 229; plans to disfranchise southerners, 347–48
Sumpter, James A., 414*n*, 423n, 519
Sutlers, 46n; regulation of, 101–3
Swan, Mrs., 630
Swan, William G. (II, 214*n*), 161n
Sweden's Cove: skirmish at, 469, 472n
Swisher, A. P., 362, 363*n*
Swisher, Harvey H., 363*n*
Swisher, Sinar Boyd (Mrs. Henry), 363
Swords, Thomas, 586*n*

Tabby (slave), 510, 511*n*, 622
Talbott, Jeremiah J., 419, 420*n*
Tammany Hall: Johnson invited to speak at, 46
Tarkington, J. W., 567, 568*n*
Tarr, Samuel H.: from, 597
Tarrant, Henry C.: from, 93
Taxes: to finance war, 221n–22n; levied for aid to soldiers' families, 302n; proposed as war levy on Confederates, 160, 512
Telegraph: payment controversy over use of, 529–30, 555
Temple, Oliver P. (IV, 195*n*), 27n; on Johnson, xxxiv
Ten Eyck, John C., 125, 131, 134*n*, 184n
Tennessee: elections in (Feb. 9, 1861), 26n (June 8, 1861), 21, 27n, 59n, 383, 386*n*; enters military agreement with the Confederacy, 207, 261; estate laws in, 363; Harris government moved to Memphis, xxvi, 210, 240, 384, 386n; home guard in, 181, 181n–82n; immigration to, urged, 193; Johnson on oppression in, 122–23, 123–25; Johnson on restoration of, 210–11, 220, 384, 442, 469, 504; Johnson on secession of, 20–22, 26n, 27n, 206, 209–10, 382, 383; as livestock supplier, 386n; militia drafts in (May 6, 1861), 12n, 497, (Nov. 19, 1861), 57, 59n, 61, 65–66, 67n, 68, 303; partisan politics in, 379–80; provisional government established in, xxxi; reconstruction proposals for, 206–8, 497; state bonds of, 367, 368n; trade restored in, 163, 267n, 280; Union sentiment in, misrepresented,

Tennessee (*cont.*)
376; unionists as a majority in, 344; unionist property confiscated in, 153; *see also* East Tennessee; Middle Tennessee; West Tennessee; specific counties
appointments: district attorneys, 185, 332n; Federal judges, 403, 524, 543n; Johnson responsible for, 206, 211, 278n, 329; marshals, 185, 349; military, 108, 171n, 277, 282, 283, 337, 406, 464, 465n, 478n, 524; postmasters and mail agents, 168, 344, 365, 406–7, 526, 613; recommendations for, 185, 419; to West Point, 195
artillery, U. S., 534
cavalry, U. S.: (1st), 281, 571–72; horses for, 590; recruiting for, 626–27, 635; (2nd), 567n; (6th), 567, 568n
infantry, Confederate: dissatisfaction among, 390–91, 391n–92n; at prisoner of war camps, 242, 250, 252, 318n, 358n; (23rd), 351, 352n
infantry, U. S.: at battle of Mill Springs, 111; call for additional rgts., 523n, 532; command problems in, 140, 270, 271n; fund to equip, 297–98; Johnson and control of, 332; Nashville Union Guard, 629, 630; organized, 86, 146, 277, 296, 297, 326–27; pay of, 564, 577, 620, 621n, 626, 634; recruiting of, 31, 104, 146–47, 215, 281, 297, 364n, 532, 567–68, 574, 626, 634–35; with Gen. Morgan, 326, 355; (1st), 48, 84, 171n, 197, 215, 600n; (2nd), 48, 86, 140, 171n, 197, 215, 270, 271n; (3rd), 146, 297, 564; (4th), 278n, 281, 296, 297, 397n, 498, 499n, 506, 527, 564; (5th), 297, 564; (6th), 564; (7th), 416n, 525, 626, 634–35; (10th), 391n, 577, 620
legislature: adopts Declaration of Independence, 21, 27n, 206, 207; authorizes use of Negro troops, 61n; moves to Memphis, 240n; Johnson's plans for election to, 504
militia: drafts (May 6, 1861), 12n, 497 (Nov. 19, 1861), 57, 59n, 61, 65–66, 67n, 68, 303
Tennessee Baptist, 305
Tennessee Code: on mining corporations, 177n
Tennessee Hospital for the Insane: change of superintendents, 568; conditions at, 507
Tennessee Regiments (U. S.) Officers: from, 170–71
Texas: secession of, 117
Textbooks: copied by southern press, 319, 320n

The Papers of Andrew Johnson

Monticello, the type chosen for this series, is a Linotype design based on the first successful American face, which was cut by Archibald Binney at Philadelphia in 1796. The clean legibility of Monticello, especially in the smaller sizes, suits it admirably for a series in which documentation is extensive.

Volume 5 of *The Papers of Andrew Johnson* was composed by Williams of Chattanooga, Tennessee, and printed offset by McNaughton & Gunn of Ann Arbor, Michigan, and bound by John H. Dekker & Sons of Grand Rapids, Michigan. The text paper is Olde Style Wove, which adheres to the specifications of the National Historical Publications and Records Commission, and was manufactured by the S. D. Warren Company, Boston, Massachusetts. The Holliston Mills, Inc., Hyannis, Massachusetts, manufactured the binding cloth. The book was designed by Hugh Bailey and Helen Orton.

THE UNIVERSITY OF TENNESSEE PRESS